Readings in Rhetorical Criticism

Fourth Edition

Readings in
Rhetorical Criticism

Edited by
Carl R. Burgchardt, Colorado State University

STRATA PUBLISHING, INC.
State College, Pennsylvania

Published by:
Strata Publishing, Inc.
P.O. 1303
State College, PA 16804
USA
telephone: 1-814-234-8545
fax: 1-814-238-7222
web site: http://www.stratapub.com

Text and cover design by WhiteOak Creative, Inc.

Cover image and background image on pages iii, 1, 147, 199, 237, 289, 347, 395, 443, 497,
561, and 633: Abstruse Grunge © iStockphoto.com/4x6

Library of Congress Cataloging-in-Publication Data

Readings in rhetorical criticism / edited by Carl R. Burgchardt.--4th ed.
    p. cm.
  Includes bibliographical references and index.
  ISBN-13: 978-1-891136-23-8 (alk. paper)
  ISBN-10: 1-891136-23-2 (alk. paper)
  1.   Rhetorical criticism. I. Burgchardt, Carl R.

PN4061.R43 2010
808'.009--dc22

                                2009054260

ISBN-10: 1-891136-23-2

ISBN-13: 978-1-891136-23-8

CREDITS AND ACKNOWLEDGMENTS

Herbert A. Wichelns, "The Literary Criticism of Oratory." Reprinted from A. M. Drummond, ed., *Studies in Rhetoric and Public Speaking in Honor of James Albert Winans* (NY: The Century Co., 1925).

Ernest J. Wrage, "Public Address: A Study in Social and Intellectual History." *Quarterly Journal of Speech*, 33 (1947), 451–457. Copyright by the National Communication Association. Reproduced by permission of the publisher.

Wayland Maxfield Parrish, "The Study of Speeches." Reprinted from Wayland Maxfield Parrish and Marie Hochmuth Nichols (eds.), *American Speeches* (NY: Longmans, Green & Co., Inc., 1954)

Lloyd F. Bitzer, "The Rhetorical Situation." *Philosophy and Rhetoric*, vol. 1, no. 1, 1–14. Copyright 1968 by The Pennsylvania State University. Reproduced by permission of The Pennsylvania State University Press.

Edwin Black, "Excerpts from *Rhetorical Criticism: A Study in Method*." Black, Edwin. RHETORICAL CRITICISM. © 1978. Reprinted by the Board of Regents of the University of Wisconsin system. Reprinted by permission of the University of Wisconsin Press.

Edwin Black, "The Second Persona." *Quarterly Journal of Speech*, 56 (1970), 109–119. Copyright by the National Communication Association. Reproduced by permission of the publisher.

Philip Wander, "The Ideological Turn in Modern Criticism." *Central States Speech Journal*, 34 (1983), 1–18. Reprinted by permission of the Central States Communication Association.

Raymie E. McKerrow, "Critical Rhetoric: Theory and Praxis." *Communication Monographs*, 56 (1989), 91–111. Copyright by the National Communication Association. Reproduced by permission of the publisher.

Carole Blair, Marsha S. Jeppeson, and Enrico Pucci, Jr., "Public Memorializing in Postmodernity: The Vietnam Veterans Memorial as Prototype." *Quarterly Journal of Speech*, 77 (1991), 289–308. Copyright by the National Communication Association. Reproduced by permission of the publisher.

Forbes Hill, "Conventional Wisdom—Traditional Form—The President's Message of November 3, 1969." *Quarterly Journal of Speech*, 58 (1972), 373–386. Copyright by the National Communication Association. Reproduced by permission of the publisher.

Michael C. Leff and Gerald P. Mohrmann, "Lincoln at Cooper Union: A Rhetorical Analysis of the Text." *Quarterly Journal of Speech*, 60 (1974), 346–358. Copyright by the National Communication Association. Reproduced by permission of the publisher.

Stephen Howard Browne, "'The Circle of Our Felicities': Thomas Jefferson's First Inaugural Address and the Rhetoric of Nationhood." This work originally appeared in *Rhetoric & Public Affairs*, vol. 5, no. 3, 2002, published by Michigan State University Press.

Michael Leff, "Dimensions of Temporality in Lincoln's Second Inaugural." *Communication Reports*, 1 (1988), 26–31. Reprinted by permission of the Western States Communication Association.

Stephen E. Lucas, "The Stylistic Artistry of the Declaration of Independence." Reprinted from *Prologue: Quarterly of the National Archives*, 22 (Spring 1990), 25–43. Copyright © Stephen E. Lucas. Reprinted by permission of the author and the National Archives.

Edwin Black, "Gettysburg and Silence." *Quarterly Journal of Speech*, 80 (1994), 21–36. Copyright by the National Communication Association. Reproduced by permission of the National Communication Association.

Kenneth Burke, "The Rhetoric of Hitler's 'Battle,'" from Kenneth Burke, *The Philosophy of Literary Form: Studies in Symbolic Action*, 3rd edition, revised. University of California Press, pages 191–220. Copyright © 1973 The Regents of the University of California. Reprinted by permission of the publisher.

Mari Boor Tonn, Valerie A. Endress, and John N. Diamond, "Hunting and Heritage on Trial: A Dramatistic Debate over Tragedy, Tradition, and Territory." *Quarterly Journal of Speech*, 79 (1993), 165–181. Copyright by the National Communication Association. Reproduced by permission of the National Communication Association.

Brian L. Ott and Eric Aoki, "The Politics of Negotiating Public Tragedy: Media Framing of the Matthew Shepherd Murder." This work originally appeared in *Rhetoric & Public Affairs*, vol. 5, no. 3, 2002, published by Michigan State University Press.

Walter R. Fisher, "Narration as a Human Communication Paradigm: The Case of Public Moral Argument." *Communication Monographs*, 51 (1984), 1–22. Copyright by the National Communication Association. Reproduced by permission of the publisher.

William F. Lewis, "Telling America's Story: Narrative Form and the Reagan Presidency." *Quarterly Journal of Speech*, 73 (1987), 267–279. Copyright by the National Communication Association. Reproduced by permission of the publisher.

Herbert W. Simons, "From Post-9/11 Melodrama to Quagmire in Iraq: A Rhetorical History." This work originally appeared in *Rhetoric & Public Affairs*, vol. 10, no. 2, 2007, published by Michigan State University Press.

to Edwin Black

CONTENTS

V
Narrative Criticism

VI
Metaphoric Criticism

VII
Social Movement Criticism

VIII
Genre Criticism

IX
Ideographic Criticism

X
Gender Criticism

XI
Critical Rhetoric

PREFACE

The fourth edition of this anthology, like the previous editions, presents major classical and contemporary approaches to rhetorical criticism and illustrates them for undergraduate and graduate students. When I first began work on *Readings in Rhetorical Criticism,* conversations with colleagues around the country led me to realize that many of us assign the same basic readings and address similar topics. Teachers who used previous editions confirmed my judgment that the book includes many of the most important and commonly assigned essays in the discipline.

Readers and reviewers have endorsed the design of the book and generously suggested several ways it could represent the current, dynamic state of rhetorical criticism more fully, while at the same time illuminating traditional scholarship and the evolution of the field. Their perceptive comments guided my efforts to make the fourth edition more useful for those who teach—and learn about—rhetorical criticism. While retaining the basic structure and approach of previous editions, I have reorganized the book to some extent and replaced some of the earlier selections with essays that reflect more recent scholarship, seem more accessible to students, or represent an approach more clearly.

In this edition, as in previous editions, I have endeavored to (1) conform to a focused concept of rhetorical criticism; (2) offer a survey of pathbreaking essays that are frequently cited in the literature; (3) provide access to some classic essays that are out of print or difficult to obtain; (4) introduce students to contemporary critical practice; and (5) present the major critical methods, approaches, and philosophies in an evenhanded way. The essays included in the chapters and listed in the "Additional Readings" section in the back of the book reflect the major historical and contemporary controversies concerning rhetorical criticism.

To include everything that merits anthologizing would have been impossible. Instead, I selected essays that could provide a starting point for discussion and be supplemented in a variety of ways. I chose some essays because they are famous, some because they illustrate a concept particularly well, and some because they explore promising new directions. I preferred to use primary sources rather than secondary interpretations of major critical concepts. Finally, I attempted to find pieces that refer to and challenge one another.

Most of the essays analyze traditional objects of criticism: speeches, essays, pamphlets, editorials, and so forth. In order to represent recent approaches more fully, however, I have also included some works that criticize nontraditional objects, such as media coverage, architecture, postcards, photographs, television, and common cultural practices.

Each chapter begins with a headnote that describes the selections briefly and explains how they are related to each other. The headnotes provide background information and alert the student to important issues in the essays; however, I have neither systematically outlined the readings nor attempted to describe all the salient points. I have attempted to prepare students to read productively, without interfering with their processes of discovery.

ORGANIZATION OF THE BOOK

The first chapter in the book presents nine views of the purposes of rhetorical criticism. These essays, taken together, form the conceptual foundation for the remaining chapters, which often refer back to one or more of these trailblazing articles.

The chapters that follow define and illustrate many of the most popular and enduring approaches to rhetorical criticism. Generally, each chapter presents an essay that proposes a particular approach or method, followed by one or more essays that apply and illustrate the theory.

The "Additional Readings" section, structured to correspond to the chapter organization, provides supplemental resources for students who are grappling with methodological concepts or seeking scholarly models. This carefully selected bibliography contains a variety of authors, subjects, and methodological choices that reflect the breadth and depth of rhetorical criticism.

The anthology can be assigned from the first page to the last, but is also flexible to alternative arrangements. Each chapter is designed to be a free-standing unit; there is no assumption that students have read the chapters in order. For example, although Chapter 1 is meant to stand as an internally cohesive unit, some instructors may prefer to combine specific readings from this chapter with later chapters in the book. Herbert A. Wichelns's "The Literary Criticism of Oratory" could productively be assigned with Chapter 2, "Neo-Classical Criticism." Raymie E. McKerrow's "Critical Rhetoric: Theory and Praxis" complements Chapter 11, "Critical Rhetoric."

Some instructors may prefer to group essays that analyze the same or similar critical objects from different perspectives. For example, Lincoln's rhetoric is critiqued in Chapters 2 and 3, from neo-classical and close textual analysis approaches. Essays that rhetorically analyze the media coverage of events include those by Tonn, Endress, and Diamond and by Ott and Aoki in Chapter 4, "Dramatism," as well as Dow's and Sloop's essays in Chapter 10, "Gender Criticism." The Palczewski essay and the Lucaites and Condit essay in Chapter 9, "Ideographic Criticism," as well as Campbell's and Dow's essays in Chapter 10, "Gender Criticism," analyze social movement discourse and could profitably be read in conjunction with Chapter 7, "Social Movement Criticism." The "Additional Readings" list more essays that use different methods to analyze similar critical objects.

Since the publication of the third edition of this anthology, the "critical rhetoric" approach, often designated as "critical/cultural studies," has become pervasive in the field of rhetorical criticism. Indeed, in the last few years, nearly every new piece of rhetorical criticism reflects, to some extent, the perspectives and politics of critical rhetoric. Teachers who wish to accentuate this transformation may combine Chapter 11, "Critical Rhetoric," with the essays by McKerrow (Chapter 1, "Purposes of Rhetorical Criticism"), Ott and Aoki (Chapter 4, "Dramatism"), Butterworth (Chapter 6, "Metaphoric Criticism"), Zaeske (Chapter 7, "Social Movement Criticism"), Morris (Chapter 10, "Gender Criticism"), and Sloop (also in Chapter 10).

As editor, I attempted to reproduce the original essays faithfully. Optical scanning technology and computer conversion tools, in conjunction with some excellent proofreaders, were enormously helpful in accomplishing this goal. I corrected only minor typographical errors. Occasionally, I inserted "[sic]" to indicate unorthodox or archaic phrasing in the original publication. (When "[sic]" appears in roman type, the original publication included it.) For the sake of consistency, I converted all footnotes to endnotes.

FEATURES OF THE NEW EDITION

In revising this volume, I tried to update the readings, refine my classification of critical approaches, and, in general, create a more interesting, accessible, and relevant book for scholars, students, and teachers, while maintaining the basic structure, selection criteria, and approach of the previous editions.

First, in response to insightful comments from colleagues, I reframed (and sometimes moved) chapters to illustrate more fully the dynamic nature of rhetorical criticism, as well as its continuities. For example, I have retitled Chapter 2 as "Neo-Classical Criticism," because some readers found the previous label, "traditional criticism," to be ambiguous. The chapter on close textual analysis, previously Chapter 10, is now Chapter 3. This placement, I believe, more clearly reveals the roots of close textual analysis in the neo-classical approach. In order to represent current issues and directions, the chapter on "Feminist Criticism" has been renamed "Gender Criticism"; it has also been significantly reorganized and broadened in scope. For similar reasons, the last chapter has been restructured and is now called "Critical Rhetoric." In making these changes, I strove to maintain a productive balance between historically important articles and works that reflect vibrant new directions in scholarship.

Second, whenever possible, I have introduced more recent illustrations of contemporary critical practices. Five chapters include at least one new essay. Most of the new selections were first published after 2005.

Third, I aimed to maintain the wide-ranging subject matter and critical variety of previous editions. New essays use cutting edge (as well as more established) methods and perspectives to explore historical and contemporary subjects, such as Abraham Lincoln's oratory, rhetorical controversies surrounding the war in Iraq, pictorial representations of the woman suffrage movement in the United States, the struggle to define what it means to be a feminist, and the gendered world of race car driving.

Fourth, in the chapter introductions, I have tried to emphasize, once again, that the critical approaches represented in the book do not constitute mutually exclusive categories. Several selections reflect more than one critical perspective and could legitimately appear in more than one chapter. I have tried to structure the material in a way that invites students and teachers to discover multiple connections between the readings.

Finally, the bibliography for the fourth edition has been expanded and updated to reflect current issues and scholarship.

ACKNOWLEDGMENTS

Most books require the help of many people to reach completion. This is particularly true in the case of a large anthology such as *Readings in Rhetorical Criticism*. Throughout the project, I relied on the good will, generosity, dedication, and hard work of numerous individuals.

I wish to recognize the encouragement and sound advice of everyone who helped me with the first three editions. The valuable contributions of these individuals carried forward into the fourth edition: Heather Aldridge, Augustana College; John Arthos, Denison University; Jacinta M. Behne, Colorado State University; William L. Benoit, University of Missouri; Dale A. Bertelsen, Bloomsburg University; Barbara Biesecker, University of Georgia; Lloyd F. Bitzer, University of Wisconsin–Madison; Edwin Black, University of Wisconsin–Madison; Barry Brummett, University of Texas at Austin; Thomas R. Burkholder, University of Nevada Las Vegas; Karlyn Kohrs Campbell, University of Minnesota; A. Cheree Carlson, Arizona State University; J. Robert Cox, University of North Carolina at Chapel Hill; Adrienne Hacker Daniels, University of St. Thomas; James Darsey, Georgia State University; Ray D. Dearin, Iowa State University; Janis L. Edwards, University of Alabama; Keith Erickson, University of Southern Mississippi; Susan E. Fillippeli,

Auburn University; Trischa Goodnow, Oregon State University; Richard B. Gregg, Pennsylvania State University; Charles Griffin, Kansas State University; Cindy L. Griffin, Colorado State University; Bruce Gronbeck, University of Iowa; Dan Hahn, New York University; Jeffrey Hobbs, Abilene Christian University; Carol Jablonski, University of South Florida; Richard L. Johannesen, Northern Illinois University; Peter Kane, State University of New York, College at Brockport; David J. Kavalec, Colorado State University; Amos Kiewe, Syracuse University; Janis King, Southwest Missouri State University; Brenda K. Kuseski, Colorado State University; Randall A. Lake, University of Southern California; Ed Lamoureux, Bradley University; Michael C. Leff, University of Memphis; Camille K. Lewis, Bob Jones University; David A. Ling, Central Michigan University; Bruce Loebs, Idaho State University; John Louis Lucaites, Indiana University; Stephen E. Lucas, University of Wisconsin–Madison; Daniel R. Lutz, Colorado State University; John J. Makay, Bowling Green State University; Susan Mackey-Kallis, Villanova University; Roseann M. Mandziuk, Southwest Texas State University; Suzanne McCorkle, Boise State University; Martin J. Medhurst, Baylor University; Charles E. Morris III, Boston College; Star A. Muir, George Mason University; Teresa Nance, Villanova University; Janice Norton, Arizona State University; Barbara O'Connor, California State University, Sacramento; Lester C. Olson, University of Pittsburgh; Tracey M. Owens, University of Wyoming; John Pauley, Saint Mary's College; Anne Pym, California State University, East Bay; Angela G. Ray, Northwestern University; Tom Roach, Purdue University Calumet; Edward A. Schiappa, University of Minnesota; Mike Schliessman, South Dakota State University; Enid M. I. Sefcovic, Florida Atlantic University; Kara Shultz, Bloomsburg University; David Thomas, University of Richmond; Laurie Thurneck, Saint Mary's College; Pamela J. Tosch, Colorado State University; Rebecca M. Townsend, University of Massachusetts; Paul Turpin, University of the Pacific; Karen Whedbee, Northern Illinois University; Joe Wilferth, State University of West Georgia; and Susan Zaeske, University of Wisconsin–Madison.

For the fourth edition, I gratefully acknowledge the insightful and supportive advice of the following people who served as reviewers or responded to our survey of adopters: Benjamin Bates, Ohio University; Bill Benoit, University of Missouri; Thomas W. Benson, Pennsylvania State University; Jason Edward Black, University of Alabama; Jim Cherney, Miami University; Dana L. Cloud, University of Texas at Austin; James Darsey, Georgia State University; Greg Dickinson, Colorado State University; Catherine A. Dobris, Indiana University–Purdue University Indianapolis; Janis Edwards, University of Alabama; Jean Goodwin, Iowa State University; Sara Hayden, University of Montana; Davis Houck, Florida State University; Michael Leff, University of Memphis; John Llewellyn, Wake Forest University; Susan Mackey-Kallis, Villanova University; Steve Martin, Ripon College; Kelly McDonald, Arizona State University; Martin Medhurst, Baylor University; Catherine H. Palczewski, University of Northern Iowa; Robert Patterson, University of Virginia; Larry Prelli, University of New Hampshire; Anne Pym, California State University, East Bay; Angela G. Ray, Northwestern University; Jody Roy, Ripon College; Mari Boor Tonn, University of Maryland; Jacob Thompson, University of Northern Iowa; Ron Von Burg, Christopher Newport University; and David Zarefsky, Northwestern University.

Special thanks go to Susan Zaeske, University of Wisconsin–Madison; Bonnie Dow, Vanderbilt University; and Dana Cloud, University of Texas at Austin, who offered valuable advice concerning difficult questions of organization and naming.

I am grateful to all of the graduate students at Colorado State University who read and discussed my book during seminars. Their questions and comments helped hone my thinking about rhetorical criticism. Three students in particular made specific suggestions that were incorporated in the fourth edition: Laura Crum, Stephanie Whalls, and Elise Clement. I am also grateful to my "official" proof-readers from Colorado State University: Beth Meyers-Bass, Hollie Petit, Elizabeth Sink, Hannah Werntz, and Amanda Vilim Wright.

For the fourth time, Kathleen M. Domenig, editor and publisher of Strata, exceeded all my expectations. I am grateful for her attention to detail, dedication to quality, patience, tact, knowledge, encouragement, and friendship. She is simply the best.

I wish to acknowledge the crucial contributions of my family, which I relied upon for emotional sustenance. I appreciate deeply the patience and understanding shown by my wife, Jill C. Burgchardt, and my daughters: Jane E. Burgchardt and Lucy A. Burgchardt. As always, I thank my mother, Elva L. Burgchardt, for providing love and support from the beginning. She is a model of courage, intelligence, and devotion.

Finally, I want to recognize the profound contributions of the late Edwin Black to this book and my life. It has been over three decades since I sat enthralled in one of Professor Black's seminars at the University of Wisconsin–Madison, but I remember vividly the intellectual discoveries I made there. His teaching opened my eyes to the possibilities of rhetorical criticism and the larger world of humane scholarship. I dedicate this volume to his memory.

Chapter 1

Purposes of Rhetorical Criticism

What is rhetorical criticism, and what are its legitimate purposes? This chapter presents some of the most important answers to these questions, beginning with Herbert A. Wichelns's famous definition of the activity and tracing its development through contemporary practice.

Wichelns's 1925 essay, "The Literary Criticism of Oratory," explains how to evaluate public speeches methodically. Further, it provides a rationale for speech communication as a separate discipline, distinguishable from English. Wichelns argues that there are important differences between literary and rhetorical criticism: Literary criticism is concerned with evaluating the wisdom, beauty, and truth contained in the great works of fiction, while rhetorical criticism is devoted to assessing the persuasive effect of situated oratory. Rhetorical criticism, according to Wichelns, focuses on discovering and appreciating how speakers adapt their ideas to particular audiences.

Ernest J. Wrage's 1947 article, "Public Address: A Study in Social and Intellectual History," broadens Wichelns's conception by claiming rhetorical criticism can make important contributions to social and intellectual history. Wrage notes that ideas are produced by particular historical contexts, are linked to change, and have social consequences. Thus, ideas should not be viewed primarily as disengaged concepts for scholars to ponder and appreciate in a vacuum. Wrage also claims ideas are expressed in many different forms—not just in the major philosophical, literary, or historical works. Specifically, the ideas, values, and beliefs of a culture are expressed in speeches. As a consequence, Wrage maintains, rhetorical critics can make valuable contributions to intellectual and social history because they are trained to understand the nuances of meaning that come from analyzing discourse in its historical context. Finally, Wrage advocates shifting rhetorical criticism from the "speaker centered" model of traditional critics to an "idea centered" basis. While the traditional critic attempts to understand how an individual speaker persuades an audience, Wrage urges the study of persuasion on a cultural level.

"The Study of Speeches," published by Wayland Maxfield Parrish in 1954, also disagrees with the traditional prescription that a speech should be judged according to its actual effect on an immediate audience. Instead, Parrish argues that critics should evaluate the quality of a speech. According to Parrish, the effect of a speech is difficult to assess, but the quality of a speech can be determined separately from its actual impact on an audience. Parrish advocates relying upon the judgment of qualified critics, rather than trying to compute audience reactions, and outlines the necessary education and qualifications of a competent judge.

Lloyd F. Bitzer's 1968 essay, "The Rhetorical Situation," provides another perspective on the purpose of rhetorical criticism. While Bitzer's article is primarily concerned with rhetorical theory, it has important implications for criticism. Bitzer focuses on the situation that calls rhetorical discourse into being, maintaining that an act is rhetorical because it responds to a situation of a certain kind. This "rhetorical situation" provides the basis for persuasive interaction. Instead of concentrating on the personality, motives, and background of the speaker, as traditional critics do, Bitzer implies the critic should objectively judge whether a speaker's response to a rhetorical situation is "fitting." Bitzer's analysis suggests a critic should not evaluate the quality of a speech in itself, but judge whether it is appropriate for a particular "exigence."

Edwin Black's 1965 book, *Rhetorical Criticism: A Study in Method*, critiques traditional criticism as it had been commonly practiced for the preceding forty years. Black maintains that a particular type of traditional criticism (which he calls "neo-Aristotelian") is formulaic, unimaginative, and unnecessarily restrictive. Further, Black contends, the neo-Aristotelian critic must defer to the goals of the rhetor without evaluating them. He demonstrates the inherent limitations of the neo-Aristotelian approach through a case study of John Jay Chapman's "Coatesville Address." Black argues that a strict neo-Aristotelian critic would have to conclude that Chapman's eloquent speech is defective because it did not make an immediate impact. In other words, Black claims that because the standard topics of neo-Aristotelian criticism are inadequate to analyze the text, neo-Aristotelianism is an unsatisfactory critical method.

Edwin Black's 1970 essay "The Second Persona" builds upon his 1965 book by arguing that rhetoric should be morally judged. The key to Black's approach is the idea that "language has a symptomatic function." In other words, the critic can evaluate the "saliently human dimensions" of discourse without judging the actual life of a rhetor. Black's theory of a "second persona" is a radical challenge to the basic procedures of traditional criticism. Rather than considering whether discourse is well adapted for a particular, situated audience, Black analyzes rhetorical texts to discover what audience is implied by the discourse. The ideology of this implied audience will be manifested in language. This discursive representation can then be judged morally. Black illustrates his approach by evaluating the rhetoric of the John Birch Society.

Philip Wander's "The Ideological Turn in Modern Criticism," published in 1983, asserts that rhetorical analysis should introduce political ideology as a standard for judgment. Wander reviews the role of ideology in the critical literature, beginning with Wichelns, moving through Kenneth Burke, culminating in the sharp debate over Richard Nixon's rhetoric, and concluding with a discussion of Martin Heidegger. Wander argues that critics should go beyond assessing the efficacy of political discourse; that instead, they should openly challenge rhetorical purposes if they are corrupt. In light of real crises in the world, such as famine, war, racism, oppression, and environmental destruction, he maintains, critics should take an activist role through the analysis of public discourse.

Raymie E. McKerrow's 1989 essay, "Critical Rhetoric: Theory and Praxis," advocates postmodern philosophy. According to McKerrow, a "critical rhetoric" focuses especially on how public communication fosters "domination" and "freedom" in an uncertain world. In McKerrow's view, rhetorical discourse is primarily concerned with maintaining or challenging power, and the critic's role is to reveal how discourse oppresses and silences. Further, the critic should seek discursive avenues for bringing about changes in power relationships. McKerrow outlines the principles that would support such a critical practice. He concludes that criticism should be directed away from universal concepts of reason and instead focus on rhetoric as relativistic. Finally, he regards the act of criticism as "performance."

Carole Blair, Marsha S. Jeppeson, and Enrico Pucci, Jr., in their 1991 essay, "Public Memorializing in Postmodernity: The Vietnam Veterans Memorial as

Prototype," discuss postmodern concepts and describe how they can be applied to rhetorical criticism. According to the authors, postmodern theory challenges traditional assumptions about what constitutes a "text," whether the creator of a work can make authoritative claims about what it means, and whether interpretation of rhetorical objects can be free from politics. The authors argue that the Vietnam Veterans Memorial is a "postmodern commemorative text" that should be understood as "multivocal rhetoric" with a strong political character.

THE LITERARY CRITICISM OF ORATORY

HERBERT A. WICHELNS

I

Samuel Johnson once projected a history of criticism "as it relates to judging of authors." Had the great eighteenth-century critic ever carried out his intention, he would have included some interesting comments on the orators and their judges. Histories of criticism, in whole or in part, we now have, and histories of orators. But that section of the history of criticism which deals with judging of orators is still unwritten. Yet the problem is an interesting one, and one which involves some important conceptions. Oratory—the waning influence of which is often discussed in current periodicals—has definitely lost the established place in literature that it once had. Demosthenes and Cicero, Bossuet and Burke, all hold their places in literary histories. But Webster inspires more than one modern critic to ponder the question whether oratory is literature; and if we may judge by the emphasis of literary historians generally, both in England and in America, oratory is either an outcast or a poor relation. What are the reasons for this change? It is a question not easily answered. Involved in it is some shift in the conception of oratory or of literature, or of both; nor can these conceptions have changed except in response to the life of which oratory, as well as literature, is part.

This essay, it should be said, is merely an attempt to spy out the land, to see what some critics have said of some orators, to discover what their mode of criticism has been. The discussion is limited in the main to Burke and a few nineteenth-century figures—Webster, Lincoln, Gladstone, Bright, Cobden—and to the verdicts on these found in the surveys of literary history, in critical essays, in histories of oratory, and in biographies.

Of course, we are not here concerned with the disparagement of oratory. With that, John Morley once dealt in a phrase: "Yet, after all, to disparage eloquence is to depreciate mankind."[1] Nor is the praise of eloquence of moment here. What interests us is the method of the critic: his standards, his categories of judgment, what he regards as important. These will show, not so much what he thinks of a great and ancient literary type, as how he thinks in dealing with that type. The chief aim is to know how critics have spoken of orators.

We have not much serious criticism of oratory. The reasons are patent. Oratory is intimately associated with statecraft; it is bound up with the things of the moment; its occasion, its terms, its background, can often be understood only by the careful student of history. Again, the publication of orations as pamphlets leaves us free to regard any speech merely as an essay, as a literary effort deposited at the shrine of the muses in hope of being blessed with immortality. This view is encouraged by the difficulty of reconstructing the conditions under which the speech was delivered; by the doubt, often, whether the printed text of the speech represents what was actually said, or what the orator elaborated afterwards. Burke's corrections are said to have been the despair of his printers.[2] Some of Chatham's speeches, by a paradox of fate, have been reported to us by Samuel Johnson, whose style is as remote as possible from that of the Great Commoner, and who wrote without even having heard the speeches pronounced.[3] Only in comparatively recent times has parliamentary reporting pretended to give full records of what was actually said; and even now speeches are published for literary or political purposes which justify the corrector's pencil in changes both great and small. Under such conditions the historical study of speech making is far from easy.

Yet the conditions of democracy necessitate both the making of speeches and the study of the art. It is true that other ways of influencing opinion have long been practiced, that oratory is no longer the chief means of communicating ideas to the masses. And the change is emphasized by the fact that the newer methods are now beginning to be investigated, sometimes from the point of view of the political student, sometimes from that of the "publicity expert." But, human nature being what it is, there is no likelihood that face to face persuasion will cease to be a principal mode of exerting influence, whether in courts, in senate-houses, or on the platform. It follows that the critical study of oratorical method is the study, not of a mode outworn, but of a permanent and important human activity.

Upon the great figures of the past who have used the art of public address, countless judgments have been given. These judgments have varied with the bias and preoccupation of the critics, who have been historians, biographers, or literary men, and have written accordingly. The context in which we find criticism of speeches, we must, for the purposes of this essay at least, both note and set aside. For though the aim of the critic conditions his approach to our more limited problem—the method of dealing with oratory—still we find that an historian may view an orator in the same light as does a biographer or an essayist. The literary form in which criticism of oratory is set does not afford classification of the critics.

"There are," says a critic of literary critics, "three definite points, on one of which, or all of which, criticism must base itself. There is the date, and the author, and the work."[4] The points on which writers base their judgments of orators do afford a classification. The man, his work, his times, are the necessary common topics of criticism; no one of them can be wholly disregarded by any critic. But mere difference in emphasis on one or another of them is important enough to suggest a rough grouping. The writers with whom this essay deals give but a subordinate position to the date; they are interested chiefly in the man or in his works. Accordingly, we have as the first type of criticism that which is predominantly personal or biographical, is occupied with the character and the mind of the orator, goes behind the work to the man. The second type attempts to hold the scales even between the biographical and the literary interest. The third is occupied with the work and tends to ignore the man. These three classes, then, seem to represent the practice of modern writers in dealing with orators. Each merits a more detailed examination.

II

We may begin with that type of critic whose interest is in personality, who seeks the man behind the work. Critics of this type furnish forth the appreciative essays and the occasional addresses on the orators. They are as the sands of the sea. Lord Rosebery's two speeches on Burke, Whitelaw Reid's on Lincoln and on Burke, may stand as examples of the character sketch.[5] The second part of Birrell's essay on Burke will serve for the mental character sketch (the first half of the essay is biographical); other examples are Sir Walter Raleigh's essay on Burke and that by Robert Lynd.[6] All these emphasize the concrete nature of Burke's thought, the realism of his imagination, his peculiar combination of breadth of vision with intensity; they pass to the guiding principles of his thought: his hatred of abstraction, his love of order and of settled ways. But they do not occupy themselves with Burke as a speaker, nor even with him as a writer; their first and their last concern is with the man rather than with his works; and their method is to fuse into a single impression whatever of knowledge or opinion they may have of the orator's life and works. These critics, in dealing with the public speaker, think of him as something other than a speaker. Since this type of writing makes but an indirect contribution to our judgment of the orator, there is no need of a more extended account of the method, except as we find it combined with a discussion of the orator's works.

III

Embedded in biographies and histories of literature, we find another type of criticism, that which combines the sketch of the mind and character with some discussion of style. Of the general interest of such essays there can be no doubt. Nine-tenths of so-called literary criticism deals with the lives and personalities of authors, and for the obvious reason, that everyone is interested in them, whereas few will follow a technical study, however broadly based. At its best, the type of study that starts with the orator's mind and character is justified by the fact that nothing can better illuminate his work as a persuader of men. But when not at its best, the description of a man's general cast of mind stands utterly unrelated to his art: the critic fails to fuse his comment on the individual with his comment on the artist; and as a result we get some statements about the man, and some statements about the orator, but neither casts light on the other. Almost any of the literary histories will supply examples of the gulf that may yawn between a stylistic study and a study of personality.

The best example of the successful combination of the two strains is Grierson's essay on Burke in the *Cambridge History of English Literature*. In this, Burke's style, though in largest outline only, is seen to emerge from the essential nature of the man. Yet of this essay, too, it must be said that the analysis of the orator is incomplete, being overshadowed by the treatment of Burke as a writer, though, as we shall see, the passages on style have the rare virtue of keeping to the high road of criticism. The majority of critics who use the mixed method, however, do not make their study of personality fruitful for a study of style, do not separate literary style from oratorical style even to the extent that Grierson does, and do conceive of literary style as a matter of details. In fact, most of the critics of this group tend to supply a discussion of style by jotting down what has occurred to them about the author's management of words; and in the main, they notice the lesser strokes of literary art, but not its broader aspects. They have an eye for tactics, but not for strategy. This is the more strange, as these same writers habitually take large views of the orator himself, considered as a personality, and because they often remark the speaker's great themes and his leading ideas. The management of ideas— what the Romans called invention and disposition—the critics do not observe; their practice is the *salto mortale* from the largest to the smallest considerations. And it needs no mention that a critic who does not observe the management of ideas even from the point of view of structure and arrangement can have nothing to say of the adaptation of ideas to the orator's audience.

It is thus with Professor McLaughlin in his chapter in the *Cambridge History of American Literature* on Clay and Calhoun and some lesser lights. The pages are covered with such expression as diffuse, florid, diction restrained and strong, neatly phrased, power of attack, invective, gracious persuasiveness. Of the structure of the speeches by which Clay and Calhoun exercised their influence—nothing. The drive of ideas is not represented. The background of habitual feeling which the orators at times appealed to and at times modified, is hinted at in a passage about Clay's awakening the spirit of nationalism, and in another passage contrasting the full-blooded oratory of Benton with the more polished speech of Quincy and Everett; but these are the merest hints. In the main, style for McLaughlin is neither the expression of personality nor the order and movement given to thought, but a thing of shreds and patches. It is thus, too, with Morley's pages on Burke's style in his life of the orator, and with Lodge's treatment of Webster in his life of the great American. A rather better analysis, though on the same plane of detail, may be used as an example. Oliver Elton says of Burke:

> He embodies, more powerfully than any one, the mental tendencies and changes that are seen gathering force through the eighteenth century. A volume of positive knowledge, critically sifted and ascertained; a constructive vision of the past and its institutions; the imagination, under this guidance, everywhere at play; all these elements unite in Burke. His main field is political philosophy. . . . His favorite form is oratory, uttered or written. His medium is prose, and the work of his later years, alone, outweighs all contemporary prose in power. . . . His whole body of production has the unity of some large cathedral, whose successive accretions reveal the natural growth of a single mind, without any change or essential break. . . .
>
> Already [in the *Thoughts* and in the *Observations*] the characteristics of Burke's thought and style appear, as well as his profound conversance with constitutional history, finance, and affairs. There is a constant reference to general principles, as in the famous defence of Party. The maxims that come into play go far beyond the occasion. There is a perpetual ground-swell of passion, embanked and held in check, but ever breaking out into sombre irony and sometimes into figure; but metaphors and other tropes are not yet very frequent. . . .
>
> In the art of unfolding and amplifying, Burke is the rival of the ancients. . . .
>
> In the speech on Conciliation the [oft-repeated] key-word is peace. . . . This iteration makes us see the stubborn faces on the opposite benches. There is contempt in it; their ears must be dinned, they must remember the word peace through the long intricate survey that is to follow. . . .
>
> Often he has a turn that would have aroused the fervor of the great appreciator known to us by the name of Longinus. In his speech on Economical Reform (1780) Burke risks an appeal, in the face of the Commons, to the example of the enemy. He has described . . . the reforms of the French revenue. He says: "The French have imitated us; let us, through them, imitate ourselves, ourselves in our better and happier days." A speaker who was

willing to offend for the sake of startling, and to defeat his purpose, would simply have said, "The French have imitated us; let us imitate them." Burke comes to the verge of this imprudence, but he sees the outcry on the lips of the adversary, and silences them by the word *ourselves;* and then, seizing the moment of bewilderment, repeats it and explains it by the noble past; he does not say when those days were; the days of Elizabeth or of Cromwell? Let the House choose! This is true oratory, honest diplomacy.[7]

Here, in some twenty pages, we have but two hints that Burke had to put his ideas in a form adapted to his audience; only the reiterated *peace* in all Burke's writings reminds the critic of Burke's hearers; only one stroke of tact draws his attention. Most of his account is devoted to Burke's style in the limited use of the term: to his power of amplification—his conduct of the paragraph, his use of clauses now long, now short—to his figures, comparisons, and metaphors, to his management of the sentence pattern, and to his rhythms. For Professor Elton, evidently, Burke was a man, and a mind, and an artist in prose; but he was not an orator. Interest in the minutiae of style has kept Elton from bringing his view of Burke the man to bear on his view of Burke's writings. The fusing point evidently is in the strategic purpose of the works, in their function as speeches. By holding steadily to the conception of Burke as a public man, one could make the analysis of mind and the analysis of art more illuminating for each other than Elton does.

It cannot be said that in all respects Stephenson's chapter on Lincoln in the *Cambridge History of American Literature* is more successful than Elton's treatment of Burke; but it is a better interweaving of the biographical and the literary strands of interest. Stephenson's study of the personality of Lincoln is directly and persistently used in the study of Lincoln's style:

> Is it fanciful to find a connection between the way in which his mysticism develops—its atmospheric, non-dogmatic pervasiveness—and the way in which his style develops? Certainly the literary part of him works into all the portions of his utterance with the gradualness of daylight through a shadowy wood. . . . And it is to be noted that the literary quality . . . is of the whole, not of the detail. It does not appear as a gift of phrases. Rather it is the slow unfolding of those two original characteristics, taste and rhythm. What is growing is the degree of both things. The man is becoming deeper, and as he does so he imposes himself, in this atmospheric way, more steadily on his language.[8]

The psychology of mystical experience may appear a poor support for the study of style. It is but one factor of many, and Stephenson may justly be reproached for leaning too heavily upon it. Compared to Grierson's subtler analysis of Burke's mind and art, the essay of Stephenson seems forced and one-sided. Yet he illuminates his subject more than many of the writers so far mentioned, because he begins with vigorous effort to bring his knowledge of the man to bear upon his interpretation of the work. But though we find in Stephenson's pages a suggestive study of Lincoln as literary man, we find no special regard for Lincoln as orator. The qualities of style that Stephenson mentions are the qualities of prose generally:

> At last he has his second manner, a manner quite his own. It is not his final manner, the one that was to give him his assured place in literature. However, in a wonderful blend of simplicity, directness, candor, joined with a clearness

beyond praise, and a delightful cadence, it has outstripped every other politician of the hour. And back of its words, subtly affecting its phrases, . . . is that brooding sadness which was to be with him to the end.[9]

The final manner, it appears, is a sublimation of the qualities of the earlier, which was "keen, powerful, full of character, melodious, impressive";[10] and it is a sublimation which has the power to awaken the imagination by its flexibility, directness, pregnancy, wealth.

In this we have nothing new, unless it be the choice of stylistic categories that emphasize the larger pattern of ideas rather than the minute pattern of grammatical units, such as we have found in Elton and to some extent shall find in Saintsbury; it must be granted, too, that Stephenson has dispensed with detail and gained his larger view at the cost of no little vagueness. "Two things," says Stephenson of the Lincoln of 1849–1858, "grew upon him. The first was his understanding of men, the generality of men. . . . The other thing that grew upon him was his power to reach and influence them through words."[11] We have here the text for any study of Lincoln as orator; but the study itself this critic does not give us.

Elton's characterization of Burke's style stands out from the usual run of superficial comment by the closeness of its analysis and its regard for the architectonic element. Stephenson's characterization of Lincoln's style is distinguished by a vigorous if forced effort to unite the study of the man and of the work. With both we may contrast a better essay, by a critic of greater insight. Grierson says of Burke:

> What Burke has of the deeper spirit of that movement [the romantic revival] is seen not so much in the poetic imagery of his finest prose as in the philosophical imagination which informs his conception of the state, in virtue of which he transcends the rationalism of the century. . . . This temper of Burke's mind is reflected in his prose. . . . To the direct, conversational prose of Dryden and Swift, changed social circumstances and the influence of Johnson had given a more oratorical cast, more dignity and weight, but, also, more of heaviness and conventional elegance. From the latter faults, Burke is saved by his passionate temperament, his ardent imagination, and the fact that he was a speaker conscious always of his audience. . . . [Burke] could delight, astound, and convince an audience. He did not easily conciliate and win them over. He lacked the first essential and index of the conciliatory speaker, *lenitas vocis;* his voice was harsh and unmusical, his gesture ungainly. . . . And, even in the text of his speeches there is a strain of irony and scorn which is not well fitted to conciliate. . . . We have evidence that he could do both things on which Cicero lays stress—move his audience to tears and delight them by his wit. . . . Yet, neither pathos nor humor is Burke's *forte.* . . . Burke's unique power as an orator lies in the peculiar interpenetration of thought and passion. Like the poet and the prophet, he thinks most profoundly when he thinks most passionately. When he is not deeply moved, his oratory verges toward the turgid; when he indulges feeling for his own sake, as in parts of *Letters on a Regicide Peace,* it becomes hysterical. But, in his greatest speeches and pamphlets, the passion of Burke's mind shows itself in the luminous thoughts which it emits, in the imagery which at once moves *and* teaches, throwing a flood of light not only on the point in question, but on the whole neighboring sphere of man's moral and political nature.[12]

The most notable feature of these passages is not their recognition that Burke was a speaker, but their recognition that his being a speaker conditioned his style, and that he is to be judged in part at least as one who attempted to influence men by the spoken word. Grierson, like Elton, attends to the element of structure and has something to say of the nature of Burke's prose; but, unlike Elton, he distinguishes this from the description of Burke's oratory—although without maintaining the distinction: he illustrates Burke's peculiar oratorical power from a pamphlet as readily as from a speech. His categories seem less mechanical than those of Elton, who is more concerned with the development of the paragraph than with the general cast of Burke's style; nor is his judgment warped, as is Stephenson's, by having a theory to market. Each has suffered from the necessity of compression. Yet, all told, Grierson realizes better than the others that Burke's task was not merely to express his thoughts and his feelings in distinguished prose, but to communicate his thoughts and his feelings effectively. It is hardly true, however, that Grierson has in mind the actual audience of Burke; the audience of Grierson's vision seems to be universalized, to consist of the judicious listeners or readers of any age. Those judicious listeners have no practical interest in the situation; they have only a philosophical and aesthetic interest.

Of Taine in his description of Burke it cannot be said that he descends to the minutiae of style. He deals with his author's character and ideas, as do all the critics of this group, but his comments on style are simply a single impression, vivid and picturesque:

> Burke had one of those fertile and precise imaginations which believe that finished knowledge is an inner view, which never quits a subject without having clothed it in its colors and forms. . . . To all these powers of mind, which constitute a man of system, he added all those energies of heart which constitute an enthusiast. . . . He brought to politics a horror of crime, a vivacity and sincerity of conscience, a sensibility, which seem suitable only to a young man.
>
> . . . The vast amount of his works rolls impetuously in a current of eloquence. Sometimes a spoken or written discourse needs a whole volume to unfold the train of his multiplied proofs and courageous anger. It is either the exposé of a ministry, or the whole history of British India, or the complete theory of revolutions . . . which comes down like a vast overflowing stream. . . . Doubtless there is foam on its eddies, mud in its bed; thousands of strange creatures sport wildly on its surface: he does not select, he lavishes. . . . Nothing strikes him as in excess. . . . He continues half a barbarian, battening in exaggeration and violence; but his fire is so sustained, his conviction so strong, his emotion so warm and abundant, that we suffer him to go on, forget our repugnance, see in his irregularities and his trespasses only the outpourings of a great heart and a deep mind, too open and too full.[13]

This is brilliant writing, unencumbered by the subaltern's interest in tactics, but it is strategy as described by a war-correspondent, not by a general. We get from it little light on how Burke solved the problem that confronts every orator: so to present ideas as to bring them into the consciousness of his hearers.

Where the critic divides his interest between the man and the work, without allowing either interest to predominate, he is often compelled to consider the work *in toto,* and we get only observations so generalized as not to include consideration of the form of the work. The speech is not thought of as essentially a means of influence; it is regarded as a specimen of prose, or as an example of philosophic thought. The date, the historical interest, the orator's own intention, are often lost from view; and criticism suffers in consequence.

IV

We have seen that the critic who is occupied chiefly with the orator as a man can contribute, although indirectly, to the study of the orator as such, and that the critic who divides his attention between the man and the work must effect a fusion of the two interests if he is to help materially in the understanding of the orator. We come now to critics more distinctly literary in aim. Within this group several classes may be discriminated: the first comprises the judicial critics; the second includes the interpretative critics who take the point of view of literary style generally, regarding the speech as an essay, or as a specimen of prose; the third and last group is composed of the writers who tend to regard the speech as a special literary form.

The type of criticism that attempts a judicial evaluation of the literary merits of the work—of the orator's "literary remains"—tends to center the inquiry on the question: Is this literature? The futility of the question appears equally in the affirmative and in the negative replies to it. The fault is less with the query, however, than with the hastiness of the answers generally given. For the most part, the critics who raise this problem are not disposed really to consider it: they formulate no conception either of literature or of oratory; they will not consider their own literary standards critically and comprehensively. In short, the question is employed as a way to dispose briefly of the subject of a lecture or of a short essay in a survey of a national literature.

Thus Phelps, in his treatment of Webster and Lincoln in *Some Makers of American Literature,*[14] tells us that they have a place in literature by virtue of their style, gives us some excerpts from Lincoln and some comments on Webster's politics, but offers no reasoned criticism. St. Peter swings wide the gates of the literary heaven, but does not explain his action. We may suspect that the solemn award of a "place in literature" sometimes conceals the absence of any real principle of judgment.

Professor Trent is less easily satisfied that Webster deserves a "place in literature." He grants Webster's power to stimulate patriotism, his sonorous dignity and massiveness, his clearness and strength of style, his powers of dramatic description. But he finds only occasional splendor of imagination, discovers no soaring quality of intelligence, and is not dazzled by his philosophy or his grasp of history. Mr. Trent would like more vivacity and humor and color in Webster's style.[15] This mode of deciding Webster's place in or out of literature is important to us only as it reveals the critic's method of judging. Trent looks for clearness and strength, imagination, philosophic grasp, vivacity, humor, color in style. This is excellent so far as it goes, but goes no further than to suggest some qualities which are to be sought in any and all works of literary art: in dramas, in essays, in lyric poems, as well as in speeches.

Let us take a third judge. Gosse will not allow Burke to be a complete master of English prose: "Notwithstanding all its magnificence, it appears to me that the prose of Burke lacks the variety, the delicacy, the modulated music of the very finest writers."[16] Gosse adds that Burke lacks flexibility, humor, and pathos. As critical method, this is one with that of Trent.

Gosse, with his question about mastery of prose, does not directly ask, "Is this literature?" Henry Cabot Lodge does, and his treatment of Webster (in the *Cambridge History of American Literature*) is curious. Lodge is concerned to show that Webster belongs to literature, and to explain the quality in his work that gives him a place among the best makers of literature. The test applied is permanence: Is Webster still read? The answer is, yes, for he is part of every schoolboy's education, and is the most quoted author in Congress. The sight of a literary critic resigning the judicial bench to the schoolmaster and the Congressman is an enjoyable one; as enjoyable as Mr. H. L. Mencken's reaction to it would be; but one could wish for grounds more relative than this. Mr. Lodge goes on to account for Webster's permanence: it lies in his power to impart to rhetoric the literary touch. The distinction between rhetoric and literature is not explained, but apparently the matter lies thus: rhetorical verse may be poetry; Byron is an example. Rhetorical prose is not literature until there is added the literary touch. We get a clue as to how the literary touch may be added: put in something imaginative, something that strikes the hearer at once. The example chosen by Lodge is a passage from Webster in which the imaginative or literary touch is given by the single word "mildew."[17] This method of criticism, too, we may reduce to that of Trent, with the exception that only one quality—imagination—is requisite for admission to the literary Valhalla.

Whether the critic's standard be imagination, or this together with other qualities such as intelligence, vivacity, humor, or whether it be merely "style," undefined and unexplained, the point of view is always that of the printed page. The oration is lost from view, and becomes an exercise in prose, musical, colorful, varied, and delicate, but, so far as the critic is concerned, formless and purposeless. Distinctions of literary type or kind are erased; the architectonic element is neglected; and the speech is regarded as a musical meditation might be regarded: as a kind of harmonious musing that drifts pleasantly along, with little of inner form and nothing of objective purpose. This, it should be recognized, is not the result of judicial criticism so much as the result of the attempt to decide too hastily whether a given work is to be admitted into the canon of literature.

V

It is, perhaps, natural for the historian of literature to reduce all literary production to one standard, and thus to discuss only the common elements in all prose. One can understand also that the biographer, when in the course of his task he must turn literary critic, finds himself often inadequately equipped and his judgment of little value, except on the scale of literature generally rather than of oratory or of any given type. More is to be expected, however, of those who set up as literary critics in the first instance: those who deal directly with Webster's style, or with Lincoln as man of letters. We shall find such critics as Whipple, Hazlitt, and Saintsbury devoting themselves to the description of literary style in the orators whom they discuss. Like the summary judicial critics we have mentioned, their center of interest is the work; but they are less hurried than Gosse and Lodge and Phelps and Trent; and their aim is not judgment so much as understanding. Yet their interpretations, in the main, take the point of view of the printed page, of the prose essay. Only to a slight degree is there a shift to another point of view, that of the orator in relation to the audience on whom he exerts his influence; the immediate public begins to loom a little larger; the essential nature of the oration as a type begins to be suggested.

Saintsbury has a procedure which much resembles that of Elton, though we must note the fact that the former omits consideration of Burke as a personality and centers attention on his work. We saw that Elton, in his passages on Burke's style, attends both to the larger elements of structure and to such relatively minute points as the management of the sentence and the clause. In Saintsbury the range of considerations is the same. At times, indeed, the juxtaposition of large and small ideas is ludicrous, as when one sentence ends by awarding to Burke literary immortality, and the next describes the sentences of an early work as "short and crisp, arranged with succinct antithetic parallels, which seldom exceed a single pair of clauses."[18] The award of immortality is not, it should be said, based entirely on the shortness of Burke's sentences in his earliest works. Indeed much of Saintsbury's comment is of decided interest:

> The style of Burke is necessarily to be considered throughout as conditioned by oratory. . . . In other words, he was first of all a rhetorician, and probably the greatest that modern times have ever produced. But his rhetoric always inclined much more to the written than to the spoken form, with results annoying perhaps to him at the time, but even to him satisfactory afterwards, and an inestimable gain to the world. . . .
>
> The most important of these properties of Burke's style, in so far as it is possible to enumerate them here, are as follows. First of all, and most distinctive, so much so as to have escaped no competent critic, is a very curious and, until his example made it imitable, nearly unique faculty of building up an argument or a picture by a succession of complementary strokes, not added at haphazard but growing out of and onto one another. No one has ever been such a master of the best and grandest kind of the figure called . . . Amplification, and this . . . is the direct implement by which he achieves his greatest effects.
>
> . . . The piece [*Present Discontents*] may be said to consist of a certain number of specially labored paragraphs in which the arguments or pictures just spoken of are put as forcibly as the author can put them, and as a rule in a succession of shortish sentences, built up and glued together with the strength and flexibility of a newly fashioned fishing-rod. In the intervals the texts thus given are turned about, commented on, justified, or discussed in detail, in a rhetoric for the most part, though not always, rather less serried, less evidently burnished, and in less full dress. And this general arrangement proceeds through the rest of his works.[19]

After a number of comments on Burke's skill in handling various kinds of ornament, such as humor, epigram, simile, Saintsbury returns to the idea that Burke's special and definite weapon was "imaginative argument, and the marshalling of vast masses of complicated detail into properly rhetorical battalions or (to alter the image) mosaic pictures of enduring beauty."[20] Saintsbury's attitude toward the communicative, impulsive nature of the orator's task is indicated in a passage on the well-known description of Windsor Castle. This description the critic terms "at once . . . a perfect harmonic chord, a complete visual picture, and a forcible argument."[21] It is significant that he adds, "The minor rhetoric, the suasive purpose [presumably the argumentative intent] must be kept in view; if it be left out the thing loses"; and holds Burke "far below Browne, who had no needs of purpose."[22] It is less important that a critic think well of the suasive purpose than that he reckon with it, and of Saintsbury at least it must be said that he recognizes it, although grudgingly; but it cannot be said that Saintsbury has a clear conception of rhetoric as the art of communication: sometimes it means the art of prose, sometimes that of suasion.

Hazlitt's method of dealing with Burke resembles Taine's as Saintsbury's resembles that of Elton. In Hazlitt we have a critic who deals with style in the large; details of rhythm, of sentence pattern, of imagery, are ignored. His principal criticism of Burke as orator is contained in the well-known contrast with Chatham, really a contrast of mind and temperament in relation to oratorical style. He follows this with some excellent comment on Burke's prose style; nothing more is said of his oratory; only in a few passages do we get a flash of light on the relation of Burke to his audience, as in the remark about his eagerness to impress his reader, and in the description of his conversational quality. It is notable too that Hazlitt finds those works which never had the form of speeches the most significant and most typical of Burke's style.

> Burke was so far from being a gaudy or flowery writer, that he was one of the severest writers we have. His words are the most like things; his style is the most strictly limited to the subject. He unites every extreme and every variety of composition; the lowest and the meanest words and descriptions with the highest. . . . He had no other object but to produce the strongest impression on his reader, by giving the truest, the most characteristic, the fullest, and most forcible description of things, trusting to the power of his own mind to mold them into grace and beauty. . . . Burke most frequently produced an effect by the remoteness and novelty of his combinations, by the force of contrast, by the striking manner in which the most opposite and unpromising materials were harmoniously blended together; not by laying his hands on all the fine things he could think of, but by bringing together those things which he knew would blaze out into glorious light by their collision.[23]

Twelve years after writing the essay from which we have quoted, Hazlitt had occasion to revise his estimate of Burke as a statesman; but his sketch of Burke's style is essentially unaltered.[24] In Hazlitt we find a sense of style as an instrument of communication; that sense is no stronger in dealing with Burke's speeches than in dealing with his pamphlets, but it gives to Hazlitt's criticisms a reality not often found. What is lacking is a clear sense of Burke's communicative impulse, of his persuasive purpose, as operating in a concrete situation. Hazlitt does not suggest the background of Burke's speeches, ignores the events that called them forth. He views his subject, in a sense, as Grierson does: as speaking to the judicious but disinterested hearer of any age other than Burke's own. But the problem of the speaker, as well as of the pamphleteer, is to interest men here and now; the understanding of that problem requires, on the part of the critic, a strong historical sense for the ideas and attitudes of the people (not merely of their leaders), and a full knowledge of the public opinion of the times in which the orator spoke. This we do not find in Hazlitt.

Two recent writers on Lincoln commit the opposite error: they devote themselves so completely to description of the situation in which Lincoln wrote as to leave no room for criticism. L. E. Robinson's *Lincoln as Man of Letters*[25] is a biography rewritten around Lincoln's writings. It is nothing more. Instead of giving us a criticism, Professor Robinson has furnished us with some of the materials of the critic; his own judgments are too largely laudatory to cast much light. The book, therefore, is not all that its title implies. A single chapter of accurate summary and evaluation would do much to increase our understanding of Lincoln as man of letters, even though it said nothing of Lincoln as speaker. A chapter or two on Lincoln's work in various kinds—letters, state papers, speeches—would help us to a finer discrimination than Professor Robinson's book offers. Again, the proper estimate of style in any satisfactory sense requires us to do more than to weigh the soundness of an author's thought and to notice the isolated beauties of his expression. Something should be said of structure, something of adaptation to the immediate audience, whose convictions and habits of thought, whose literary usages, and whose general cultural background all condition the work both of writer and speaker. Mr. Robinson has given us the political situation as a problem in controlling political forces, with little regard to the force even of public opinion, and with almost none to the cultural background. Lincoln's works, therefore, emerge as items in a political sequence, but not as resultants of the life of his time.

Some of the deficiencies of Robinson's volume are supplied by Dodge's essay, *Lincoln as Master of Words*.[26] Dodge considers, more definitely than Robinson, the types in which Lincoln worked: he separates messages from campaign speeches, letters from occasional addresses. He has an eye on Lincoln's relation to his audience, but this manifests itself chiefly in an account of the immediate reception of a work. Reports of newspaper comments on the speeches may be a notable addition to Lincolniana; supported by more political information and more insight than Mr. Dodge's short book reveals, they might become an aid to the critical evaluation of the speeches. But in themselves they are neither a criticism nor an interpretation of Lincoln's mastery of words.

Robinson and Dodge, then, stand at opposite poles to Saintsbury and Hazlitt. The date is put in opposition to the work as a center of critical interest. If the two writers on Lincoln lack a full perception of their author's background, they do not lack a sense of its importance. If the critics of Burke do not produce a complete and rounded criticism, neither do they lose themselves in preparatory studies. Each method is incomplete; each should supplement the other.

We turn now to a critic who neglects the contribution of history to the study of oratory, but who has two compensating merits: the merit of recognizing the types in which his subject worked, and the merit of remembering that an orator has as his audience, not posterity, but certain classes of his own contemporaries. Whipple's essay on Webster is open to attack from various directions: it is padded, it "dates," it is overlaudatory, it is overpatriotic, it lacks distinction of style. But there is wheat in the chaff. Scattered through the customary discussion of Webster's choice of words, his power of epithet, his compactness of statement, his images, the development of his style, are definite suggestions of a new point of view. It is the point of view of the actual audience. To Whipple, at times at least, Webster was not a writer, but a speaker; the critic tries to imagine the man, and also his hearers; he thinks of the speech as a communication to a certain body of auditors. A phrase often betrays a mental attitude; Whipple alone of the critics we have mentioned would have written of "the eloquence, the moral power, he infused into his reasoning, so as to make the dullest citation of legal authority *tell* on the minds he addressed."[27] Nor would any other writer of this group have attempted to distinguish the types of audience Webster met. That Whipple's effort is a rambling and incoherent one, is not here in point. Nor is it pertinent that the critic goes completely astray in explaining why Webster's speeches have the nature of "organic formations, or at least of skilful engineering or architectural constructions"; though to say that the art of giving objective reality to a speech consists only of "a happy collocation and combination of words"[28] is certainly as far as possible from explaining Webster's sense of structure. What is significant in Whipple's essay is the occasional indication of a point of view that includes the audience. Such an indication is the passage in which the critic explains the source of Webster's influence:

> What gave Webster his immense influence over the opinions of the people of New England, was first, his power of so "putting things" that everybody could understand his statements; secondly, his power of so framing his arguments that all the steps, from one point to another, in a logical series, could be clearly apprehended by every intelligent farmer or mechanic who had a thoughtful interest in the affairs of the country; and thirdly, his power of inflaming the sentiment of patriotism in all honest and well-intentioned men by overwhelming appeals to that sentiment, so that after convincing their understandings, he clinched the matter by sweeping away their wills. Perhaps to these sources of influence may be added . . . a genuine respect for the intellect, as well as for the manhood, of average men.[29]

In various ways the descriptive critics recognize the orator's function. In some, that recognition takes the form of a regard to the background of the speeches; in others, it takes the form of a regard to the effectiveness of the work, though that effectiveness is often construed as for the reader rather than for the listener. The "minor rhetoric, the suasive purpose" is beginning to be felt, though not always recognized and never fully taken into account.

VI

The distinction involved in the presence of a persuasive purpose is clearly recognized by some of those who have written on oratory, and by some biographers and historians. The writers now to be mentioned are aware, more keenly than any of those we have so far met, of the speech as a literary form—or if not as a literary form, then as a form of power; they tend accordingly to deal with the orator's work as limited by the conditions of the platform and the occasion, and to summon history to the aid of criticism.

The method of approach of the critics of oratory as oratory is well put by Lord Curzon at the beginning of his essay, *Modern Parliamentary Eloquence*:

> In dealing with the Parliamentary speakers of our time I shall, accordingly, confine myself to those whom I have myself heard, or for whom I can quote the testimony of others who heard them; and I shall not regard them as prose writers or literary men, still less as purveyors of instruction to their own or to future generations, but as men who produced, by the exercise of certain talents of speech, a definite impression upon contemporary audiences, and whose reputation for eloquence must be judged by that test, and that test alone.[30]

The last phrase, "that test alone," would be scanned; the judgment of orators is not solely to be determined by the impression of contemporary audiences. For the present it will be enough to note the topics touched in Curzon's anecdotes and reminiscences—his lecture is far from a systematic or searching inquiry into the subject, and is of interest rather for its method of approach than for any considered study of an orator or of a period. We value him for his promises rather than for his performance. Curzon deals with the relative rank of speakers, with the comparative value of various speeches by a single man, with the orator's appearance and demeanor, with his mode of preparation and of delivery, with his mastery of epigram or image. Skill in seizing upon the dominant characteristics of each of his subjects saves the author from the worst triviality of reminiscence. Throughout, the point of view is that of the man experienced in public life discussing the eloquence of other public men, most of whom he had known and actually heard. That this is not the point of view of criticism in any strict sense, is of course true; but the *naïveté* and directness of this observer correct forcibly some of the extravagances we have been examining.

The lecture on Chatham as an orator by H. M. Butler exemplifies a very different method arising from a different subject and purpose. The lecturer is thinking, he tells us, "of Oratory partly as an art, partly as a branch of literature, partly as a power of making history."[31] His method is first to touch lightly upon Chatham's early training and upon his mode of preparing and delivering his speeches; next, to present some of the general judgments upon the Great Commoner, whether of contemporaries or of later historians; then to re-create a few of the most important speeches, partly by picturing the historical setting, partly by quotation, partly by the comments of contemporary writers. The purpose of the essay is "to reawaken, however faintly, some echoes of the kingly voice of a genuine Patriot, of whom his country is still justly proud."[32] The patriotic purpose we may ignore, but the wish to reconstruct the *mise en scène* of Chatham's speeches, to put the modern Oxford audience at the point of view of those who listened to the voice of Pitt, saw the flash of his eye and felt the force of his noble bearing, this is a purpose different from that of the critics whom we have examined. It may be objected that Butler's lecture has the defects of its method: the amenities observed by a Cambridge don delivering a formal lecture at Oxford keeps us from getting on with the subject; the brevity of the discourse prevents anything like a full treatment; the aim, revivification of the past, must be very broadly interpreted if it is to be really critical. Let us admit these things; it still is true that in a few pages the essential features of Pitt's eloquence are brought vividly before us, and that this is accomplished by thinking of the speech as originally delivered to its first audience rather than as read by the modern reader.

The same sense of the speaker in his relation to his audience appears in Lecky's account of Burke. This account, too, is marked by the use of contemporary witnesses, and of comparisons with Burke's great rivals. But let Lecky's method speak in part for itself:

> He spoke too often, too vehemently, and much too long; and his eloquence, though in the highest degree intellectual, powerful, various, and original, was not well adapted to a popular audience. He had little or nothing of that fire and majesty of declamation with which Chatham thrilled his hearers, and often almost overawed opposition; and as a parliamentary debater he was far inferior to Charles Fox. . . . Burke was not inferior to Fox in readiness, and in the power of clear and cogent reasoning. His wit, though not of the highest order, was only equalled by that of Townshend, Sheridan, and perhaps North, and it rarely failed in its effect upon the House. He far surpassed every other speaker in the copiousness and correctness of his diction, in the range of knowledge he brought to bear on every subject of debate, in the

richness and variety of his imagination, in the gorgeous beauty of his descriptive passages, in the depth of the philosophical reflections and the felicity of the personal sketches which he delighted in scattering over his speeches. But these gifts were frequently marred by a strange want of judgment, measure, and self-control. His speeches were full of episodes and digressions, of excessive ornamentation and illustration, of dissertations on general principles of politics, which were invaluable in themselves, but very unpalatable to a tired or excited House waiting eagerly for a division.[33]

These sentences suggest, and the pages from which they are excerpted show, that historical imagination has led Lecky to regard Burke as primarily a speaker, both limited and formed by the conditions of his platform; and they exemplify, too, a happier use of stylistic categories than do the essays of Curzon and Butler. The requirements of the historian's art have fused the character sketch and the literary criticism; the fusing agent has been the conception of Burke as a public man, and of his work as public address. Both Lecky's biographical interpretation and his literary criticism are less subtle than that of Grierson; but Lecky is more definitely guided in his treatment of Burke by the conception of oratory as a special form of the literature of power and as a form molded always by the pressure of the time.

The merits of Lecky are contained, in ampler form, in Morley's biography of Gladstone. The long and varied career of the great parliamentarian makes a general summary and final judgment difficult and perhaps inadvisable; Morley does not attempt them. But his running account of Gladstone as orator, if assembled from his thousand pages, is an admirable example of what can be done by one who has the point of view of the public man, sympathy with his subject, and understanding of the speaker's art. Morley gives us much contemporary reporting: the descriptions and judgments of journalists at various stages in Gladstone's career, the impression made by the speeches upon delivery, comparison with other speakers of the time. Here history is contemporary: the biographer was himself the witness of much that he describes, and has the experienced parliamentarian's flair for the scene and the situation. Gladstone's temperament and physical equipment for the platform, his training in the art of speaking, the nature of his chief appeals, the factor of character and personality, these are some of the topics repeatedly touched. There is added a sense for the permanent results of Gladstone's speaking: not the votes in the House merely, but the changed state of public opinion brought about by the speeches.

Mr. Gladstone conquered the House, because he was saturated with a subject and its arguments; because he could state and enforce his case; because he plainly believed every word he said, and earnestly wished to press the same belief into the minds of his hearers; finally because he was from the first an eager and a powerful athlete. . . . Yet with this inborn readiness for combat, nobody was less addicted to aggression or provocation.

In finance, the most important of all the many fields of his activity, Mr. Gladstone had the signal distinction of creating the public opinion by which he worked, and warming the climate in which his projects throve. . . . Nobody denies that he was often declamatory and discursive, that he often overargued and overrefined, [but] he nowhere exerted greater influence than in that department of affairs where words out of relation to fact are most surely exposed. If he often carried the proper rhetorical arts of amplification and development to excess, yet the basis of fact was both sound and clear. . . . Just as Macaulay made thousands read history, who before had turned from it as dry and repulsive, so Mr. Gladstone made thousands eager to follow the public balance-sheet, and the whole nation became his audience. . . .

[In the Midlothian campaign] it was the orator of concrete detail, of inductive instances, of energetic and immediate object; the orator confidently and by sure touch startling into watchfulness the whole spirit of civil duty in man; elastic and supple, pressing fact and figure with a fervid insistence that was known from his career and character to be neither forced nor feigned, but to be himself. In a word, it was a man—a man impressing himself upon the kindled throngs by the breadth of his survey of great affairs of life and nations, by the depth of his vision, by the power of his stroke.[34]

Objections may be made to Morley's method, chiefly on the ground of omissions. Though much is done to re-create the scene, though ample use is made of the date and the man, there is little formal analysis of the work. It is as if one had come from the House of Commons after the wealth of argument; not as if one came from a calm study of the speeches; not even as if one had corrected personal impressions by such a study. Of the structure of the speeches, little is said; but a few orations are quoted; the details of style, one feels, although noticed at too great length by some critics, might well receive a modicum of attention here.

Although these deficiencies of Morley's treatment are not supplied by Bryce in his short and popular sketch of Gladstone, there is a summary which well supplements the running account offered by Morley. It has the merit of dealing explicitly with the orator as orator, and it offers more analysis and an adequate judgment by a qualified critic.

Twenty years hence Mr. Gladstone's [speeches] will not be read, except of course by historians. They are too long, too diffuse, too minute in their handling of details, too elaborately qualified in their enunciation of general principles. They contain few epigrams and few . . . weighty thoughts put into telling phrases. . . . The style, in short, is not sufficiently rich or finished to give a perpetual interest to matters whose practical importance has vanished. . . .

If, on the other hand, Mr. Gladstone be judged by the impression he made on his own time, his place will be high in the front rank. . . . His oratory had many conspicuous merits. There was a lively imagination, which enabled him to relieve even dull matter by pleasing figures, together with a large command of quotations and illustrations. . . . There was admirable lucidity and accuracy in exposition. There was great skill in the disposition and marshalling of his arguments, and finally . . . there was a wonderful variety and grace of appropriate gesture. But above and beyond everything else which enthralled the listener, there were four qualities, two specially conspicuous in the substance of his eloquence—inventiveness and elevation; two not less remarkable in his manner—force in the delivery, expressive modulation in the voice.[35]

One is tempted to say that Morley has provided the historical setting, Bryce the critical verdict. The statement would be only partially true, for Morley does much more than set the scene. He enacts the drama; and thus he conveys his judgment—not, it is true, in the form of a critical estimate, but in the course of his narrative. The difference between these two excellent accounts is a difference in emphasis. The one lays stress on the setting; the other takes it for granted. The one tries to suggest his judgment by description; the other employs the formal categories of criticism.

Less full and rounded than either of these descriptions of an orator's style is Trevelyan's estimate of Bright. Yet in a few pages the biographer has indicated clearly the two distinguishing features of Bright's eloquence—the moral weight he carried with his audience, the persuasiveness of his visible earnestness and of his reputation for integrity, and his "sense for the value of words and for the rhythm of words and sentences";[36] has drawn a contrast between Bright and Gladstone; and has added a description of Bright's mode of work, together with some comments on the permanence of the speeches and various examples of details of his style. Only the mass and weight of that style are not represented.

If we leave the biographers and return to those who, like Curzon and Butler, have written directly upon eloquence, we find little of importance. Of the two general histories of oratory that we have in English, Hardwicke's[37] is so ill organized and so ill written as to be negligible; that by Sears[38] may deserve mention. It is uneven and inaccurate. It is rather a popular handbook which strings together the great names than a history: the author does not seriously consider the evolution of oratory. His sketches are of unequal merit; some give way to the interest in mere anecdote; some yield too large a place to biographical detail; others are given over to moralizing. Sears touches most of the topics of rhetorical criticism without making the point of view of public address dominant; his work is too episodic for that. And any given criticism shows marked defects in execution. It would not be fair to compare Sears's show-piece, his chapter on Webster, with Morley or Bryce on Gladstone; but compare it with Trevelyan's few pages on Bright. With far greater economy, Trevelyan tells us more of Bright as a speaker than Sears can of Webster. The *History of Oratory* gives us little more than hints and suggestions of a good method.

With a single exception, the collections of eloquence have no critical significance. The exception is *Select British Eloquence*,[39] edited by Chauncey A. Goodrich, who prefaced the works of each of his orators with a sketch partly biographical and partly critical. The criticisms of Goodrich, like those of Sears, are of unequal value; some are slight, yet none descends to mere anecdote, and at his best, as in the characterizations of the eloquence of Chatham, Fox, and Burke, Goodrich reveals a more powerful grasp and a more comprehensive view of his problem than does Sears, as well as a more consistent view of his subject as a speaker. Sears at times takes the point of view of the printed page; Goodrich consistently thinks of the speeches he discusses as intended for oral delivery.

Goodrich's topics of criticism are: the orator's training, mode of work, personal (physical) qualifications, character as known to his audience, range of powers, dominant traits as a speaker. He deals too, of course, with those topics to which certain of the critics we have noticed confine themselves: illustration, ornament, gift of phrase, diction, wit, imagination, arrangement. But these he does not over-emphasize, nor view as independent of their effect upon an audience. Thus he can say of Chatham's sentence structure: "The sentences are not rounded or balanced periods, but are made up of short clauses, which flash themselves upon the mind with all the vividness of distinct ideas, and yet are closely connected together as tending to the same point, and uniting to form larger masses of thought."[40] Perhaps the best brief indication of Goodrich's quality is his statement of Fox's "leading peculiarities."[41] According to Goodrich, Fox had a luminous simplicity, which combined unity of impression with irregular arrangement; he took everything in the concrete; he struck instantly at the heart of his subject, going to the issue at once; he did not amplify, he repeated; he rarely employed a pre-conceived order of argument; reasoning was his *forte*, but it was the reasoning of the debater; he abounded in *hits*—abrupt and startling turns of thought—and in side-blows delivered in passing; he was often dramatic; he had astonishing skill in turning the course of debate to his own advantage. Here is the point of view of public address, expressed as clearly as in Morley or in Curzon, though in a different idiom, and without the biographer's ful[l]ness of treatment.

But probably the best single specimen of the kind of criticism now under discussion is Morley's chapter on Cobden as an agitator. This is as admirable a summary sketch as the same writer's account of Gladstone is a detailed historical picture. Bryce's brief essay on Gladstone is inferior to it both in the range of its technical criticisms and in the extent to which the critic realizes the situation in which his subject was an actor. In a few pages Morley has drawn the physical characteristics of his subject, his bent of mind, temperament, idiosyncrasies; has compared and contrasted Cobden with his great associate, Bright; has given us contemporary judgments; has sketched out the dominant quality of his style, its variety and range; has noted Cobden's attitude to his hearers, his view of human nature; and has dealt with the impression given by Cobden's printed speeches and the total impression of his personality on the platform. The method, the angle of approach, the categories of description or of criticism, are the same as those employed in the great life of Gladstone; but we find them here condensed into twenty pages. It will be worth while to present the most interesting parts of Morley's criticism, if only for comparison with some of the passages already given:

> I have asked many scores of those who knew him, Conservatives as well as Liberals, what this secret [of his oratorical success] was, and in no single case did my interlocutor fail to begin, and in nearly every case he ended as he had begun, with the word *persuasiveness*. Cobden made his way to men's hearts by the union which they saw in him of simplicity, earnestness, and conviction, with a singular facility of exposition. This facility consisted in a remarkable power of apt and homely illustration, and a curious ingenuity in framing the argument that happened to be wanted. Besides his skill in thus hitting on the right argument, Cobden had the oratorical art of presenting it in the way that made its admission to the understanding of a listener easy and undenied. He always seemed to have made exactly the right degree of allowance for the difficulty with which men follow a speech, as compared with the ease of following the same argument on a printed page. . . .
>
> Though he abounded in matter, Cobden can hardly be described as copious. He is neat and pointed, nor is his argument ever left unclinched; but he permits himself no large excursions. What he was thinking of was the matter immediately in hand, the audience before his eyes, the point that would tell best then and there, and would be most likely to remain in men's recollections. . . . What is remarkable is, that while he kept close to the matter and substance of his case, and resorted comparatively little to sarcasm, humor, invective, pathos, or the other elements that are catalogued in manuals of rhetoric, yet no speaker was ever further removed from prosiness, or came into more real and sympathetic contact with his audience. . . .
>
> After all, it is not tropes and perorations that make the popular speaker; it is the whole impression of his personality. We who only read them can discern certain admirable qualities in Cobden's speeches; aptness in choosing topics, lucidity in presenting them, buoyant confidence in pressing them home. But

those who listened to them felt much more than all this. They were delighted by mingled vivacity and ease, by directness, by spontaneousness and reality, by the charm . . . of personal friendliness and undisguised cordiality.[42]

These passages are written in the spirit of the critic of public speaking. They have the point of view that is but faintly suggested in Elton and Grierson, that Saintsbury recognizes but does not use, and Hazlitt uses but does not recognize, and that Whipple, however irregularly, both understands and employs. But such critics as Curzon and Butler, Sears and Goodrich, Trevelyan and Bryce, think differently of their problem; they take the point of view of public address consistently and without question. Morley's superiority is not in conception, but in execution. In all the writers of this group, whether historians, biographers, or professed students of oratory, there is a consciousness that oratory is partly an art, partly a power of making history, and occasionally a branch of literature. Style is less considered for its own sake than for its effect in a given situation. The question of literary immortality is regarded as beside the mark, or else, as in Bryce, as a separate question requiring separate consideration. There are, of course, differences of emphasis. Some of the biographers may be thought to deal too lightly with style. Sears perhaps thinks too little of the time, of the drama of the situation, and too much of style. But we have arrived at a different attitude towards the orator; his function is recognized for what it is: the art of influencing men in some concrete situation. Neither the personal nor the literary evaluation is the primary object. The critic speaks of the orator as a public man whose function it is to exert influence by speech.

VII

Any attempt to sum up the results of this casual survey of what some writers have said of some public speakers must deal with the differences between literary criticism as represented by Gosse and Trent, by Elton and Grierson, and rhetorical criticism as represented by Curzon, Morley, Bryce, and Trevelyan. The literary critics seem at first to have no common point of view and no agreement as to the categories of judgment or description. But by reading between their lines and searching for the main endeavor of these critics, one can discover at least a unity of purpose. Different in method as are Gosse, Elton, Saintsbury, Whipple, Hazlitt, the ends they have in view are not different.

  Coupled with almost every description of the excellences of prose and with every attempt to describe the man in connection with his work, is the same effort as we find clearly and even arbitrarily expressed by those whom we have termed judicial critics. All the literary critics unite in the attempt to interpret the permanent value that they find in the work under consideration. That permanent value is not precisely indicated by the term beauty, but the two strands of aesthetic excellence and permanence are clearly found, not only in the avowed judicial criticism but in those writers who emphasize description rather than judgment. Thus Grierson says of Burke:

His preoccupation at every juncture with the fundamental issues of wise government, and the splendor of the eloquence in which he set forth these principles, an eloquence in which the wisdom of his thought and the felicity of his language and imagery seem inseparable from one another . . . have made his speeches and pamphlets a source of perennial freshness and interest.[43]

Perhaps a critic of temper different from Grierson's—Saintsbury, for example—would turn from the wisdom of Burke's thought to the felicity of his language and imagery. But always there is implicit in the critic's mind the absolute standard of a timeless world: the wisdom of Burke's thought (found in the principles to which his mind always gravitates rather than in his decisions on points of policy) and the felicity of his language are not considered as of an age, but for all time. Whether the critic considers the technical excellence merely, or both technique and substance, his preoccupation is with that which age cannot wither nor custom stale. (From this point of view, the distinction between the speech and the pamphlet is of no moment, and Elton wisely speaks of Burke's favorite form as "oratory, uttered or written";[44] for a speech cannot be the subject of a permanent evaluation unless it is preserved in print.)

This is the implied attitude of all the literary critics. On this common ground their differences disappear or become merely differences of method or of competence. They are all, in various ways, interpreters of the permanent and universal values they find in the works of which they treat. Nor can there be any quarrel with this attitude—unless all standards be swept away. The impressionist and the historian of the evolution of literature as a self-contained activity may deny the utility or the possibility of a truly judicial criticism. But the human mind insists upon judgment *sub specie æternitatis*. The motive often appears as a merely practical one: the reader wishes to be apprised of the best that has been said and thought in all ages; he is less concerned with the descent of literary species or with the critic's adventures among masterpieces than with the perennial freshness and interest those masterpieces may hold for him. There is, of course, much more than a practical motive to justify the interest in permanent values; but this is not the place to raise a moot question of general critical theory. We wished only to note the common ground of literary criticism in its preoccupation with the thought and the eloquence which is permanent.

If now we turn to rhetorical criticism as we found it exemplified in the preceding section, we find that its point of view is patently single. It is not concerned with permanence, nor yet with beauty. It is concerned with effect. It regards a speech as a communication to a specific audience, and holds its business to be the analysis and appreciation of the orator's method of imparting his ideas to his hearers.

Rhetoric, however, is a word that requires explanation; its use in connection with criticism is neither general nor consistent. The merely deprecatory sense in which it is often applied to bombast or false ornament need not delay us. The limited meaning which confines the term to the devices of a correct and even of an elegant prose style—in the sense of manner of writing and speaking—may also be eliminated, as likewise the broad interpretation which makes rhetoric inclusive of all style whether in prose or in poetry. There remain some definitions which have greater promise. We may mention first that of Aristotle: "the faculty of observing in any given case the available means of persuasion";[45] this readily turns into the art of persuasion, as the editors of the *New English Dictionary* recognize when they define rhetoric as "the art of using language so as to persuade or influence others." The gloss on "persuade" afforded by the additional term "influence" is worthy of note. Jebb achieves the same result by defining rhetoric as "the art of using language in such a way as to produce a desired impression upon the hearer or reader."[46] There is yet a fourth definition, one which serves to illuminate the others as well as to emphasize their essential agreement: "taken broadly [rhetoric is] the science and art of communication in language";[47] the framers of this definition add that to throw the emphasis on communication is to emphasize prose, poetry being regarded as more distinctly expressive than communicative. A German writer has made a similar distinction between poetic as the art of poetry and rhetoric as the art of prose, but rather on the basis that prose is of the intellect, poetry of the imagination.[48] Wackernagel's basis for the distinction will hardly stand in face of the attitude of modern psychology to the "faculties"; yet the distinction itself is suggestive, and it does not contravene the more significant opposition of expression and communication. That opposition has been well stated, though with some exaggeration, by Professor Hudson:

> The writer in pure literature has his eye on his subject; his subject has filled his mind and engaged his interest, and he must tell about it; his task is expression; his form and style are organic with his subject. The writer of rhetorical discourse has his eye upon the audience and occasion; his task is persuasion; his form and style are organic with the occasion.[49]

The element of the author's personality should not be lost from sight in the case of the writer of pure literature; nor may the critic think of the audience and the occasion as alone conditioning the work of the composer of rhetorical discourse, unless indeed he include in the occasion both the personality of the speaker and the subject. The distinction is better put by Professor Baldwin:

> Rhetoric meant to the ancient world the art of instructing and moving men in their affairs; poetic the art of sharpening and expanding their vision. . . . The one is the composition of ideas; the other, composition of images. In the one field life is discussed; in the other it is presented. The type of the one is a public address, moving us to assent and action; the type of the other is a play, showing us [an] action moving to an end of character. The one argues and urges; the other represents. Though both appeal to imagination, the method of rhetoric is logical; the method of poetic, as well as its detail, is imaginative.[50]

It is noteworthy that in this passage there is nothing to oppose poetry, in its common acceptation of verse, to prose. Indeed, in discussing the four forms of discourse usually treated in textbooks, Baldwin explicitly classes exposition and argument under rhetoric, leaving narrative and description to the other field. But rhetoric has been applied to the art of prose by some who include under the term even non-metrical works of fiction. This is the attitude of Wackernagel, already mentioned, and of Saintsbury, who observes that Aristotle's *Rhetoric* holds, "if not intentionally, yet actually, something of the same position towards Prose as that which the *Poetics* holds towards verse."[51] In Saintsbury's view, the *Rhetoric* achieves this position in virtue of its third book, that on style and arrangement: the first two books contain "a great deal of matter which has either the faintest connection with literary criticism or else no connection with it at all."[52] Saintsbury finds it objectionable in Aristotle that to him, "prose as prose is merely and avowedly a secondary consideration: it is always in the main, and sometimes wholly, a mere necessary instrument of divers practical purposes,"[53] and that "he does not *wish* to consider a piece of prose as a work of art destined, first of all, if not finally, to fulfil its own laws on the one hand, and to give pleasure on the other."[54] The distinction between verse and prose has often troubled the waters of criticism. The explanation is probably that the outer form of a work is more easily understood and more constantly present to the mind than is the real form. Yet it is strange that those who find the distinction between verse and prose important should parallel this with a distinction between imagination and intellect, as if a novel had more affinities with a speech than with an epic. It is strange, too, that Saintsbury's own phrase about the right way to consider a "piece of prose"—as a work of art destined "to fulfil its own laws"—did not suggest to him the fundamental importance of a distinction between what he terms the minor or suasive rhetoric on the one hand, and on the other poetic, whether or not in verse. For poetry always is free to fulfil its own law, but the writer of rhetorical discourse is, in a sense, perpetually in bondage to the occasion and the audience; and in that fact we find the line of cleavage between rhetoric and poetic.

The distinction between rhetoric as theory of public address and poetic as theory of pure literature, says Professor Baldwin, "seems not to have controlled any consecutive movement of modern criticism."[55] That it has not controlled the procedure of critics in dealing with orators is indicated in the foregoing pages; yet we have found, too, many suggestions of a better method, and some few critical performances against which the only charge is overcondensation.

Rhetorical criticism is necessarily analytical. The scheme of a rhetorical study includes the element of the speaker's personality as a conditioning factor; it includes also the public character of the man—not what he was, but what he was thought to be. It requires a description of the speaker's audience, and of the leading ideas with which he plied his hearers—his topics, the motives to which he appealed, the nature of the proofs he offered. These will reveal his own judgment of human nature in his audiences, and also his judgment on the questions which he discussed. Attention must be paid, too, to the relation of the surviving texts to what was actually uttered: in case the nature of the changes is known, there may be occasion to consider adaptation to two audiences—that which heard and that which read. Nor can rhetorical criticism omit the speaker's mode of arrangement and his mode of expression, nor his habit of preparation and his manner of delivery from the platform; though the last two are perhaps less significant. "Style"—in the sense which corresponds to diction and sentence movement—must receive attention, but only as one among various means that secure for the speaker ready access to the minds of his auditors. Finally, the effect of the discourse on its immediate hearers is not to be ignored, neither in the testimony of witnesses, nor in the record of events. And throughout such a study one must conceive of the public man as influencing the men of his own times by the power of his discourse.

VIII

What is the relation of rhetorical criticism, so understood, to literary criticism? The latter is at once broader and more limited than rhetorical criticism. It is broader because of its concern with permanent values: because it takes no account of special purpose nor of immediate effect; because it views a literary work as the voice of a human spirit addressing itself to men of all ages and times; because the critic speaks as the spectator of all time and all existence. But this universalizing of attitude brings its own limits with it: the influence of the period is necessarily relegated to the background; interpretation in the light of the writer's intention and of his situation may be ignored or slighted; and the speaker who directed his words to a definite and limited group of hearers may be made to address a universal audience. The result can only be confusion. In short, the point of view of literary criticism is proper only to its own objects, the permanent works. Upon such as are found to lie without the pale, the verdict of literary criticism is of negative value merely, and its interpretation is false and misleading because it proceeds upon a wrong assumption. If Henry Clay and Charles Fox are to be dealt with at all, it must not be on the assumption that their works, in respect of wisdom and eloquence, are or ought to be sources of perennial freshness and interest. Morley has put the matter well:

> The statesman who makes or dominates a crisis, who has to rouse and mold the mind of senate or nation, has something else to think about than the production of literary masterpieces. The great political speech, which for that matter is a sort of drama, is not made by passages for elegant extract or anthologies, but by personality, movement, climax, spectacle, and the action of the time.[56]

But we cannot always divorce rhetorical criticism from literary. In the case of Fox or Clay or Cobden, as opposed to Fielding or Addison or De Quincy, it is proper to do so; the fact that language is a common medium to the writer of rhetorical discourse and to the writer in pure literature will give to the critics of each a common vocabulary of stylistic terms, but not a common standard. In the case of Burke the relation of the two points of view is more complex. Burke belongs to literature; but in all his important works he was a practitioner of public address written or uttered. Since his approach to *belles-lettres* was through rhetoric, it follows that rhetorical criticism is at least a preliminary to literary criticism, for it will erect the factual basis for the understanding of the works: will not merely explain allusions and establish dates, but recall the setting, reconstruct the author's own intention, and analyze his method. But the rhetorical inquiry is more than a mere preliminary; it permeates and governs all subsequent interpretation and criticism. For the statesman in letters is a statesman still: compare Burke to Charles Lamb, or even to Montaigne, and it is clear that the public man is in a sense inseparable from his audience. A statesman's wisdom and eloquence are not to be read without some share of his own sense of the body politic, and of the body politic not merely as a construct of thought, but as a living human society. A speech, like a satire, like a comedy of manners, grows directly out of a social situation; it is a man's response to a condition in human affairs. However broadly typical the situation may be when its essential elements are laid bare, it never appears without its coverings. On no plane of thought—philosophical, literary, political—is Burke to be understood without reference to the great events in America, India, France, which evoked his eloquence; nor is he to be understood without reference to the state of English society. (It is this last that is lacking in Grierson's essay: the page of comment on Burke's qualities in actual debate wants its supplement in some account of the House of Commons and the national life it represented. Perhaps the latter is the more needful to a full understanding of the abiding excellence in Burke's pages.) Something of the spirit of Morley's chapter on Cobden, and more of the spirit of the social historian (which Morley has in other parts of the biography) is necessary to the literary critic in dealing with the statesman who is also a man of letters.

In the case of Burke, then, one of the functions of rhetorical criticism is as a preliminary, but an essential and governing preliminary, to the literary criticism which occupies itself with the permanent values of wisdom and of eloquence, of thought and of beauty, that are found in the works of the orator.

Rhetorical criticism may also be regarded as an end in itself. Even Burke may be studied from that point of view alone. Fox and Cobden and the majority of public speakers are not to be regarded from any other. No one will offer Cobden's works a place in pure literature. Yet the method of the great agitator has a place in the history of his times. That place is not in the history of *belles-lettres;* nor is it in the literary history which is a "survey of the life of a people as expressed in their writings." The idea of "writings" is a merely mechanical one; it does not really provide a point of view or a method; it is a book-maker's cloak for many and diverse points of view. Such a compilation as the *Cambridge History of American Literature,* for example, in spite of the excellence of single essays, may not unjustly be characterized as an uneven commentary on the literary life of the country and as a still more uneven commentary on its social and political life. It may be questioned whether the scant treatment of public men in such a compilation throws light either on the creators of pure literature, or on the makers of rhetorical discourse, or on the life of the times.

Rhetorical criticism lies at the boundary of politics (in the broadest sense) and literature; its atmosphere is that of the public life,[57] its tools are those of literature, its concern is with the ideas of the people as influenced by their leaders. The effective wielder of public discourse, like the military man, belongs to social and political history because he is one of its makers. Like the soldier, he has an art of his own which is the source of his power; but the soldier's art is distinct from the life which his conquests affect. The rhetorician's art represents a natural and normal process within that life. It includes the work of the speaker, of the pamphleteer, of the writer of editorials, and of the sermon maker. It is to be thought of as the art of popularization. Its practitioners are the Huxleys, not the Darwins, of science; the Jeffersons, not the Lockes and the Rousseaus, of politics.

Of late years the art of popularization has received a degree of attention: propaganda and publicity have been words much used; the influence of the press has been discussed; there have been some studies of public opinion. Professor Robinson's *Humanizing of Knowledge*[58] is a cogent statement of the need for popularization by the instructed element in the state, and of the need for a technique in doing so. But the book indicates, too, how little is known of the methods its author so earnestly desires to see put to use. Yet ever since Homer's day men have woven the web of words and counsel in the face of all. And ever since Aristotle's day there has been a mode of analysis of public address. Perhaps the preoccupation of literary criticism with "style" rather than with composition in the large has diverted interest from the more significant problem. Perhaps the conventional categories of historical thought have helped to obscure the problem: the history of thought, for example, is generally interpreted as the history of invention and discovery, both physical and intellectual. Yet the history of the thought of the people is at least as potent a factor in the progress of the race. True, the popular thought may often represent a resisting force, and we need not marvel that the many movements of a poet's mind more readily capture the critic's attention than the few and uncertain movements of that Leviathan, the public mind. Nor is it surprising that the historians tend to be occupied with the acts and the motives of leaders. But those historians who find the spirit of an age in the total mass of its literary productions, as well as all who would tame Leviathan to the end that he shall not threaten civilization, must examine more thoroughly than they as yet have done the interactions of the inventive genius, the popularizing talent, and the public mind.

NOTES

[1]*Life of William Ewart Gladstone,* New York, 1903, II, 593.

[2]*Select Works,* ed. E. J. Payne, Oxford, 1892, I, xxxviii.

[3]Basil Williams, *Life of William Pitt,* New York, 1913, II, 335–337.

[4]D. Nichol Smith, *Functions of Criticism,* Oxford, 1909, p. 15.

[5]See Rosebery, *Appreciations and Addresses,* London, 1899, and Whitelaw Reid, *American and English Studies,* New York, 1913, II.

[6]See Augustine Birrell, *Obiter Dicta,* New York, 1887, II; Walter Raleigh, *Some Authors,* Oxford, 1923; Robert Lynd, *Books and Authors,* London, 1922.

[7]Oliver Elton, *Survey of English Literature, 1780–1830,* I, 234–53.

[8]*Cambridge History of American Literature,* New York, 1921, III, 374–5.

[9]*Cambridge History of American Literature,* III, 378.

[10]*Ibid.,* pp. 381–2.

[11]*Ibid.,* p. 377.

[12]*Cambridge History of English Literature,* New York, 1914, XI, 30–5.

[13]H. A. Taine, *History of English Literature,* tr. H. Van Laun, London, 1878, II, 81–3.

[14]Boston, 1923.

[15]W. P. Trent, *History of American Literature, 1607–1865,* New York, 1917, pp. 576–7.

[16]Edmund Gosse, *History of Eighteenth Century English Literature, 1660–1780,* 1889, pp. 365–6.

[17]*Cambridge History of American Literature,* New York, 1918, II, 101.

[18]G. E. B. Saintsbury, *Short History of English Literature,* New York, 1915, p. 630.

[19]*Ibid.,* pp. 629–30.

[20]*Ibid.,* p. 631.

[21]*Ibid.*

[22]*Ibid.*

[23]*Sketches and Essays,* ed. W. C. Hazlitt, London, 1872, II, 420–1.

[24]*Political Essays with Sketches of Public Characters,* London, 1819, pp. 264–79.

[25]New York, 1923.

[26]New York, 1924.

[27]E. P. Whipple, "Daniel Webster as a Master of English Style," in *American Literature,* Boston, 1887, p. 157.

[28]*Ibid.,* p. 208.

[29]*Ibid.,* p. 144.

[30]London, 1914, p. 7.

[31]*Lord Chatham as an Orator,* Oxford, 1912, p. 5.

[32]*Ibid.,* pp. 39–40.

[33]W. E. H. Lecky, *History of England in the Eighteenth Century,* New York, 1888, III, 203–4.

[34]*Life of William Ewart Gladstone,* I, 193–4; II, 54–5, 593.

[35]*Gladstone, His Characteristics as Man and Statesman,* New York, 1898, pp. 41–4.

[36]G. M. Trevelyan, *Life of John Bright,* Boston, 1913, p. 384.

[37]Henry Hardwicke, *History of Oratory and Orators,* New York, 1896.

[38]Lorenzo Sears, *History of Oratory,* Chicago, 1896.

[39]New York, 1852.

[40]P. 75.

[41]P. 461.

[42]*Life of Richard Cobden,* Boston, 1881, pp. 130–2.

[43]*Cambridge History of English Literature,* New York, 1914, XI, 8.

[44]Oliver Elton, *Survey of English Literature, 1780–1830,* 1912, I, 234.

[45]*Rhetoric,* ii, 2, tr. W. Rhys Roberts in *The Works of Aristotle,* XI, Oxford, 1924.

[46]Article "Rhetoric" in the *Encyclopædia Britannica,* 9th and 11th editions.

[47]J. L. Gerig and F. N. Scott, article "Rhetoric" in the *New International Encyclopædia.*

[48]K. H. W. Wackernagel, *Poetik, Rhetorik, and Stilistik,* ed. L. Sieber, Halle, 1873, p. 11.

[49]H. H. Hudson, "The Field of Rhetoric," *Quarterly Journal of Speech Education,* IX (1923), 177. See also the same writer's "Rhetoric and Poetry," *ibid.,* X (1924), 143ff.

[50]C. S. Baldwin, *Ancient Rhetoric and Poetic,* New York, 1924, p. 134.

[51]G. E. B. Saintsbury, *History of Criticism and Literary Taste in Europe,* New York, 1900, I, 39.

[52]*Ibid.,* p. 42.

[53]*History of Criticism and Literary Taste in Europe,* p. 48.

[54]*Ibid.,* p. 52.

[55]*Op. Cit.,* p. 4.

[56]*Life of William Ewart Gladstone,* II, 589–90.

[57]For a popular but suggestive presentation of the background of rhetorical discourse, see J. A. Spender, *The Public Life,* New York, 1925.

[58]New York, 1923.

PUBLIC ADDRESS: A STUDY
IN SOCIAL AND INTELLECTUAL HISTORY

ERNEST J. WRAGE

In the title of a book, *Ideas Are Weapons,* Max Lerner gives to ideas a twentieth century connotation, for in this century all of the resources of man have twice comprised actual or potential materiel of warfare. The merit of the title lies in the emphasis it places upon function, although one must read beyond it to grasp the diversity of function which ideas perform. Man's capacities for thought somewhat resemble modern industrial plants which are capable of converting raw materials into either soap or bullets, of refining sugar into nutritive food or into alcohol for the manufacture of explosives. Similarly, from the biochemical processes of individual minds responding to environment may emerge ideas which serve to promote social conflict, while there are yet others, fortunately, which contribute to resolution of differences. Man's intellectual activities may result in ideas which clarify his relationships with his fellow men and to the cosmos, or in ideas which close minds against further exploration in favor of blind conformity to tradition and authority. It is axiomatic that the extant records of man's responses to the social and physical world as expressed in formulations of thought provide one approach to a study of the history of his culture. Whether we seek explanations for an overt act of human behavior in the genesis and moral compulsion of an idea, or whether we accept the view that men seek out ideas which promote their interests and justify their activities, the illuminating fact is that in either case the study of ideas provides an index to the history of man's values and goals, his hopes and fears, his aspirations and negations, to what he considers expedient or inapplicable.

The word *ideas,* therefore, is not restricted here to a description of the great and noble thoughts uttered by accredited spokesmen for the edification of old and young. It is employed in a more inclusive sense and refers widely to formulations of thought as the product and expression of social incentives, which give rise and importance now to one idea, then to another. They are viewed as the product of social environment, as arising from many levels of life, and as possessing social utility. Ideas are not here treated as entities which enjoy an independent existence and which serve as objects of contemplation by the self-avowed or occasional ascetic. While the history of ideas is undeniably concerned with major works in systematized thought, and with the influence of thinker upon thinker, exclusive devotion to monumental works is hopelessly inadequate as a way of discovering and assessing those ideas which find expression in the market place. Subtle intellectual fare may be very well for stomachs accustomed to large helpings of ideational substances rich in concentration; but there also is nutritional value in the aphoristic crumbs which fall into stomachs unaccustomed and unconditioned to large helpings of such fare, and the life sustained by the crumbs is not without historical interest. The force of Emerson's ideas upon the popular mind of his time, and even later, derives less from his intricate elaborations upon man and the cosmos than from his dicta on self-reliance. Moreover, ideas arise at many levels of human life and find expression in and attain force through casual opinion as well as learned discourse; and while the life span of many popularly-held ideas is admittedly short, often these "out-of-the-way" ideas thrive and emerge at higher levels of development. This extension in the conception of the history of ideas which includes more than monumental distillations of thought in philosophy, religion, literature, and science may be offensive to those of fastidious intellectual tastes, but there is increasing awareness that adequate social and intellectual history cannot be written without accounting for popular opinions, beliefs, constellations of attitudes, and the like.

I

Ideas attain history in process, which includes transmission. The reach of an idea, its viability within a setting of time and place, and its modifications are expressed in a vast quantity of documentary sources. Man's conscious declarations of thought are embodied in a mosaic of documents, in constitutions and laws, literature and song, scientific treatises and folklore, in lectures, sermons, and speeches. Of these, not the least either in quantity or value, as Curti points out, are the lectures, sermons, and speeches:

> Historians of ideas in America have too largely based their conclusions on the study of formal treatises. But formal treatises do not tell the whole story. In fact, they sometimes give a quite false impression, for such writings are only a fraction of the records of intellectual history. For every person who laboriously wrote a systematic treatise, dozens touched the subject in a more or less casual fashion. Sometimes the fugitive essays of relatively obscure writers influenced the systematizers and formal writers quite as much as the works of better-known men. The influence of a thinker does not pass from one major writer to another without frequently being transformed or dissipated, or compressed in the hands of a whole series of people who responded to the thinker and his ideas. It is reasonably certain, moreover, that in the America of the early nineteenth century ephemeral writings, widely scattered as they were in pamphlets, tracts, and essays, reached a much wider audience and are often more reliable evidence of the climate of opinion than the more familiar works to which historians of ideas have naturally turned. The student of the vitality and modification of ideas may well direct his attention, then, toward out-of-the-way sermons, academic addresses, Fourth of July oration and casual guides and essays.[1]

As a parenthetical comment, one recent study which makes extensive use of fugitive literature, particularly speeches, is Merle Curti's *The Roots Of American Loyalty*, published in 1946. But in the main, the rich vein of literature in speaking has hardly been tapped for this purpose except by the occasional prospector.

Curti's observations have germinal significance for the student of public address. They suggest an approach which is interesting for its freshness and fruitful in intellectual promise. If American life, to adopt his point of reference, is viewed through ideas historically viable, then ideas are to be studied as a body of intricate tissues, of differentiated yet related thought. While the establishment of macroscopic relationships provides the ultimate reasons for tracing out an American intellectual pattern, explorations of the parts is a necessary preliminary to this achievement. As an enterprise in scholarship, then, the first operation is one of collecting and classifying data within limited areas amenable to description and analysis. This accomplished, generalizations from the data become at once permissible and desirable, and provide a basis from which further exploration may be conducted.

It is at once apparent that the delineation of an American intellectual tradition calls for division of labor. It is not only the magnitude in task but diversity in data and in media of expression which invites specialization and varied technical skills in scholarship. There are, after all, appreciable and striking differences between the materials of hymnology and constitutional law. While students of philosophy, history, and literature are traditionally accredited as the official custodians and interpreters of intellectual history, it is the thesis of this paper that students of public address may contribute in substantial ways to the history of ideas. They possess credentials worthy of acknowledgment and interest in a type of materials germane to the object.

It has been amply treated and clearly said by others that the rhetoric of public address does not exist for its own sake, that its value is instrumental, and that its meaning apart from an application to something is sterile. An endorsement of this doctrine leads us to an immediate recognition that the basic ingredient of a speech is its content. The transmission of this content is its legitimate function. It is a vehicle for the conveyance of ideas. It is a mode of communication by means of which something of the thought of the speaker is incorporated and expressed in language in ways which make for ready comprehension and acceptance by one or more audiences. It is for the very reason that public speeches and lectures are prepared with a listening audience in mind that they serve so admirably in a study of social thought. The full import of this point is disclosed by some comparisons.

When reporting the results of work to members of his guild, the physical scientist may confine himself to an exclusive concern with data, intricate operations, and complex thought. In preparation and presentation neither detail nor comprehensiveness needs to be sacrificed, for his discourse is not prepared with an eye to the limiting factors present in the differentiated audience. As distinguished from this highly specialized form of reporting, a public speech is a more distinctly popular medium which is useful for explaining the essence of an idea, for explaining the applicability of a particular, for establishing impressions and evoking attitudes, for direction in the more or less common affairs of men. Because speeches are instruments of utility designed in the main for the popular mind, conversely and in significant ways they bear the impress of the popular mind. It is because they are pitched to levels of information, to take account of prevalent beliefs, and to mirror tone and temper of audiences that they serve as useful indices to the popular mind.

This interaction between the individual mind of the speaker and the collective mind of the audience has long been appreciated, but for the most part this interaction has been considered in terms of its relationship to the speaker's techniques. What has happened to the ideas themselves under the impact of this interaction remains a field which is relatively unexplored in any systematic sense by students of public address. The techniques of the speakers are often highly individualized and perish with their bones; their ideas live after them. From the study of speeches may be gained additional knowledge about the growth of ideas, their currency and vitality, their modifications under the impress of social requirements, and their eclipse by other ideas with different values. Such a study of speeches belongs to what Max Lerner calls the "naturalistic approach" to the history of ideas, one which includes "not only the conditions of the creation of ideas but also the conditions of their reception, not only the impulsions behind the ideas, but also the uses to which they are put, not only the thinkers but also the popularizers, the propagandists, the opinion skill-groups, the final audience that believes or disbelieves and acts accordingly."[2]

Is not such scholarship properly confined to the professional historian? The question is dated and should be so treated. Squabbles over contested rights are hang-overs from an age of academic primogeniture. A study is to be judged by its merits, not by the writer's union card. But a more convincing argument for participation in scholarship of the history of ideas by students of public address is made apparent when we take another step in our thinking. The very nature and character of ideas in transmission is dependent upon configurations of language. The interpretation of a speech calls for complete understanding of what goes into a speech, the purpose of the speech and the interplay of factors which comprise the public speaking situation, of nuances of meaning which emerge only from the reading of a speech in the light of its setting. At this juncture a special kind of skill becomes useful, for the problem now relates directly to the craftsmanship of the rhetorician. The student who is sensitized to rhetoric, who is schooled in its principles and techniques, brings an interest, insight, discernment, and essential skill which are assets for scholarship in the history of ideas, as that history is portrayed in public speeches.

II

The prevailing approach to the history and criticism of public address appears to consist of a study of individual speakers for their influence upon history. If one may judge from studies available through publication, they fall short of that ambitious goal for reasons which are painfully apparent to anyone who has attempted to assess influence in history. Nevertheless, they do provide a defensible pattern in research which has yielded highly interesting data about prominent speakers, their speechmaking and speaking careers. Reference is made to this standard approach to public address simply as a means of establishing and clarifying some distinctions between it and the proposed method of study which concentrates upon the ideas in speeches. The differences are those of focus, of knowledge to be gained, and of procedure to be followed in investigation. While one approach is "speaker centered," the other is "idea centered." One focuses mainly upon the speaker and the speaking activity, the other upon the speech and its content. One seeks to explain factors which contributed to personal persuasion; the other yields knowledge of more general interest in terms of man's cultural strivings and heritage.

In point of procedure it should be at once apparent that there are differences involved in a study which centers, let us say, upon Henry Clay as an orator and in a study which centers upon the ideas embodied in his speeches on the American System. To pursue the example, a study of the ideas in Clay's speeches is not committed to searching out the sources of his personal power with an audience, but is concerned with the doctrine of a self-contained economy as portrayed in his speeches in the perspective of that doctrine's history, from Hamilton to Matthew Carey's *Olive Branch,* to the congenial, nascent nationalism of Clay and contemporary speakers. Inasmuch as the American System is compounded of political and economic ideas, competence in handling the data of history is necessary; but it is also to be remembered that inasmuch as the ideas are projected through speeches, they are also the province of the rhetorician; that inasmuch as they are employed in speeches with the object of reaching and affecting a wide audience, the ideas are framed in a context of rhetorical necessities and possibilities. To adopt the rhetorical perspective is actually to approximate more closely a genuinely historical point of view when analyzing and interpreting speeches as documents of ideas in social history.

The possibilities for analysis in the rhetoric of ideas is illustrated in Roy P. Basler's essay on "Lincoln's Development As A Writer." The title of the essay should properly have included "And Speaker," for much of the brilliance of Basler's commentary arises from the treatment he gives the speeches.[3] Basler sets forth the basic ideas which are the essence of Lincoln's philosophy and links them to the dominant intellectual currents of Lincoln's age. He analyzes the rhetoric of Lincoln, not because he is interested in rhetoric *per se,* but because Lincoln's ideas were framed by his rhetoric, which, in turn, was profoundly affected by the exigencies present in the totality of social factors bearing upon the speaking situation. From an analysis of his rhetoric in this relationship, it is possible to come into a closer under-standing of Lincoln's thought patterns and of the ideas he sought to lodge in the minds of his audiences. For instance, Basler recounts how the theme in the "House Divided" speech was carried through many stages of inference, that it underwent many modifications in order to achieve the nuances and implications which Lincoln desired. Basler concludes that "It would be difficult to find in all history a precise instance in which rhetoric played a more important role in human destiny than it did in Lincoln's speeches of 1858."[4] He speaks, of course, of the instrumental role of rhetoric as it served to crystallize the meanings which Lincoln sought to convey. Through a masterful analysis of the rhetoric in the Gettysburg Address, Basler presents the underlying pattern of Lincoln's thought, as is suggested by a short excerpt from his treatment:

> Lincoln's problem at Gettysburg was to do two things: to commemo-rate the past and to prophesy for the future. To do these things he took the theme dearest to his audience, honor for the heroic dead sons and fathers, and combined it with the theme nearest to his own heart, the preservation of democracy. Out of this double theme grew his poetic metaphor of birth, death, and spiritual rebirth, of the life of man and the life of the nation. To it he brought the fervor of devoutly religious belief. Democracy was to Lincoln a religion, and he wanted it to be in a real sense the religion of his audience. Thus he combined an elegiac theme with a patriotic theme, skillfully blending the hope of eternal life with the hope of eternal democracy.[5]

A speech is an agency of its time, one whose surviving record provides a repository of themes and their elaborations from which we may gain insight into the life of an era as well as into the mind of a man. From the study of speeches given by many men, then, it is possible to observe the reflections of prevailing social ideas and attitudes. Just as the speeches of Schwab and Barton, of Coolidge and Dawes (accompanied by the latter's broom-sweeping histrionics) portray the ethos of business and a negative view toward government intervention in social affairs, so do the speeches of Roosevelt and other New Dealers mark the break from the attitudes and conceptions which dominated the twenties. Both schools of thought express the social and economic values of the times. Both mirror the dominant moods of their respective audiences. The very structure, idiom, and tone of the speeches, moreover, play their parts in the delineation of those ideas. For example, the full import of Roosevelt's First Inaugural Address is not perceived without reference to the many nuances and imperatives of his rhetoric. It is in the metaphor of war and the image of the religious crusade, as well as in argument and statements of intention, that the speech articulates the inchoate feelings of the people on government's social responsibility. Similarly, from a wide investigation of sermons, lectures, and speeches related to issues, movements, and periods, might we not extend and refine our knowledge of social ideas portrayed in history? Such an attempt would constitute a kind of anthropological approach to a segment of cultural history.

III

Let the final argument be a practical one. Specifically, what applications may be made of this approach to public address in a university classroom? Experience has made it apparent to the writer that a course consisting only of successive case histories of individual speakers and speech-making leaves much to be desired. It certainly is open to question if an accidental chronology or arbitrary selection of orators provides a satisfactory focus and basic framework to warrant the label, "history of public address," or if it provides adequate intellectual and educational outcomes for the time expended. Interesting in its way as may be the study for its own sake of the personality, platform virtuosity, and career of an individual speaker, a mere progression of such more or less independent treatments is likely to be without secure linkage to historical processes. It is likely to result in an assortment of isolated, episodical, or even esoteric information which can make little claim to the advancement of the student's general culture.

There is more than a suggestion of antiquarianism in the whole business. We need, therefore, to provide a more solid intellectual residual. This may be realized when the focus of a course consists in the ideas communicated, in the ascertainable sources of those ideas, the historical vitality and force of the ideas, and of demonstrable refractions, modifications, or substitutions. As an adjunct to the materials of such a course, the study of the speaking careers and skills of individual speakers makes a valuable contribution. Such studies have supplementary value; but even more important is the study of the speeches themselves against a backdrop of history. Naturally, the exclusive study of speeches would result in historical distortion unless related to a larger framework of life and thought, to allied and competing ideas in the intellectual market place.

Seen against a broad and organized body of materials in intellectual and social history, the study of speeches both gives and takes on meaning in ways which contribute substantially to educational experience. Especially helpful as leads in providing background are such familiar works as Vernon L. Parrington, *Main Currents in American Thought*; Merle Curti, *The Growth of American Thought*; and Ralph H. Gabriel, *The Course of American Democratic Thought*, to mention but a few. Such literature supplies references and guidance to the main lines of thought which underlie movements and problems in American life; it brings into view not only tributaries which fed the main streams, but also rivulets of ideas which had a kind of independent existence. Speeches may be studied in relation to these movements. For example, intellectual turmoil and diluvial expression were provoked by the slavery controversy. Antislavery appeals, historians tell us, were couched in the language of personal liberty and Christian humanitarianism. Proslavery speakers, forced to compete upon an equally elevated plane, advanced arguments which derived from similar or equivalent ethical bases but which were interpreted in ways congenial to Southern institutional life and practice. True, the rhetoric of ideas fails to account for all the forces at work; yet a wide reading in sermons, lectures, and speeches does bring one into a deeper understanding of the basic ideational themes, variations upon the themes, and the dissonance which were a part of the controversy and contributed to ultimate settlement. When seen against a contextual backdrop, speeches become at once a means of illustrating and testing, of verifying or revising generalizations offered by other workers in social and intellectual history.

There is an implied recognition in what has been said, of a deficiency in the scholarship of public address. There is need for an organized body of literature which places speeches and speaking in proper relationship to the history of ideas. Quite apart from reasons of classroom utility, research in the ideas communicated through speeches needs doing as a means of contributing to knowledge and understanding generally. Adequate social and intellectual history cannot be written without reference to public speaking as it contributed to the ideas injected into public consciousness. But if research is to move forward, perhaps the time has arrived to explore in our individual and joint capacities the rationale, procedures, and materials by which it may be carried on. To this end, a symposium of papers which deals with these problems would help to clarify and stimulate research in public address in its relation to social and intellectual history.

NOTES

[1]Merle Curti, "The Great Mr. Locke: America's Philosopher, 1783–1861," *The Huntington Library Bulletin*, April, 1937, pp. 108–109.

[2]Max Lerner, *Ideas Are Weapons* (1940), p. 6.

[3]Roy P. Basler, *Abraham Lincoln; His Speeches and Writings* (Cleveland and New York, 1946), pp. 1–49.

[4]*Ibid.*, p. 28.

[5]*Ibid.*, p. 42.

THE STUDY OF SPEECHES

WAYLAND MAXFIELD PARRISH

Why do we study the speeches of the past?

What values do we seek in exhuming the long-silent utterances of dead orators on issues that are equally dead? Questions of burning interest in the time of Webster or of Lincoln have long since lost their heat, and an attempt to rekindle their embers may seem impertinent now when the whole world trembles before the problems of controlling atomic energy and containing communist Russia. And in any age what can be learned from orators that could not be better learned from the study of state papers, government reports, editorials, and scholarly essays in politics, economics, and philosophy?

When Socrates once referred to himself as "a pining man who was frantic to hear speeches," he defined a human trait which, in greater or lesser degree, is present in all of us. If, as Emerson said, "every man is an orator, how long soever he may have been a mute," perhaps we study speeches to find vicarious expression of our own unuttered eloquence. And both the lover of speeches for their own sake and the frustrated orator may find in their study something of "practical" value, for it is true of our age as it was of Aristotle's that "all men attempt to discuss statements and to maintain them, to defend themselves and to attack others,"[1] and whether we do this in formal addresses or in informal discussions we may expect to learn from a study of the notable addresses of the past some lessons that we can apply to the preparation of our own speeches, for though the subjects of controversy that concern us may be quite different from those that exercised the talents of earlier speakers, yet the *methods* of discussion and argument remain very much the same from age to age.

If we have progressed far enough in our study of rhetoric to have developed a coherent theory of speech construction we may wish to test it by applying it to the recorded speeches of the past. And if we do not have a method of our own and wish to develop one, it is surely the part of wisdom to observe carefully and analytically the practices of earlier speakers instead of depending entirely upon our own fumbling trials and errors. Any sound theory of speechmaking must be derived from observation of the practices of the best speakers. In this book are recorded some of the best efforts of some of the best speakers in American history. They can be studied with profit by any aspiring rhetorician.

This suggests another reason for the study of public addresses that applies especially to more mature students of rhetoric. It is not always wise to accept uncritically the precepts of some standard textbook, whether by Aristotle, Cicero, or a modern writer, and assume its soundness and validity. The careful student will wish to compare these theories with the actual practice of masters of public address. If our textbook says, for instance, that a speaker should begin by conciliating his audience, let us examine the beginnings of a dozen or two representative addresses to see whether the theorist is supported by practice. And when Aristotle says we may argue that what is rare is a greater good than what is plentiful we may well examine a number of speeches to discover whether such an argument has actually been used.

The student who is interested in history will not lack a motive for the study of public address. He cannot be indifferent to the utterances of important men on important questions of the period he is studying. He will study speeches for the light they throw on contemporary events, and he will study events for the light they throw upon speeches. And he may discover that speeches have often been instrumental in shaping the course of history, in defining and strengthening a people's ideals, and in determining its culture.

Taking a deeper and more philosophical view, we may say that the study of speeches is worth while because all of man's activities are of interest to us and we assume that "in some sense human experience is worth while."[2] The Greeks believed that one of man's greatest pleasures lay in learning new things. Such a doctrine can hardly be questioned when we contemplate the insatiable modern drive for learning and discovery. In the physical sciences it has led to the quest for the innermost secrets of the atom, and in the philological sciences to the attempt to relearn all that was once known. To recover the great speeches of the past, to reconstruct the circumstances under which they were given, to discover the motives that prompted the orator to speak and the motives that prompted the audience to respond—these may surely be counted among interesting and worthy studies.

In recovering or in exploring the great thought currents of earlier times the speech may or may not be a more useful instrument than other writings, in prose or verse, but it is from its very nature likely to be more interesting and more vital. And this leads us to a consideration of the nature of public address.

WHAT IS A SPEECH?

Typically, a speech is an utterance meant to be heard and intended to exert an influence of some kind on those who hear it. Typically, also the kind of influence intended may be described as persuasion. The hearer is to be moved to action or argued into the acceptance of some belief. The aim of the speaker is, in the words of William Caxton "to cause another man . . . to believe or to do that thing which thou wouldst have him for to do."[3]

Such a purpose is plainly enough discerned in Webster's Reply to Hayne or in Patrick Henry's plea for war against England. But in some presidential addresses, public lectures, and eulogies it is not so clear. In such addresses the speaker's aim may incline toward pure exposition or pure self-expression, and certainly these are legitimate aims in public address. But even so, a persuasive purpose is pretty sure to be present, for the expositor wishes to have his ideas approved and accepted, and even the plowboy who declaims his own sentiments or another's while following the furrows may have an imaginary audience in his eye. A very popular and successful modern preacher once confessed that the chief appeal of the ministry for him was in its opportunity for self-expression, but it is not on record that he ever delivered his sermons in an empty church. The orator may say, and may believe, that he is merely giving vent to his inmost convictions, and this would seem to be true of some orations and parts of orations. "I know not what course others may take, but as for me—" cried Patrick Henry. Just so, many artists assert that their work is purely personal and deny that they have any intention to communicate with others. But Professor I. A. Richards contends that the artist's "conscious neglect of communication does not in the least diminish the importance of the communicative aspect. . . . Denial that he is at all influenced in his work by a desire to affect other people, is no evidence that communication is not actually his principal object."[4] Just so, a speech may have a persuasive efficacy even though the speaker denies any intention to persuade.

It should be noted, however, that lectures or addresses that are designed solely to give the hearer information or instruction,[5] to furnish him with facts, must, from their very lack of urgency, fall short of the highest eloquence. It is the essential nature of oratory that it be moving, that it be persuasive. All of the notable speeches in American history have, directly or indirectly, this persuasive purpose. All of those included in this volume have it.

It should be noted also that typically, but not always, a speech is designed to meet a specific situation, to affect a given audience, as when a United States Senator argues for the passage of a bill, or a prosecutor pleads before a jury for the conviction of a culprit. It follows, as we shall find later, that there can be no adequate judgment of the effectiveness of an address unless we understand fully the situation which it was designed to meet.

Many speeches, however, do not have such an immediate specific purpose or a sharply defined audience. A public lecture may be intended for repeated delivery to many audiences, and a president's address, though delivered before an immediate audience, may be intended for the whole nation or for the whole world. And such speeches may not be directed to any specific occasion but may aim generally at winning good will, creating confidence, allaying fears, strengthening loyalties and beliefs, warning of impending dangers, preparing the public mind for measures to come, or building a more tolerant or favorable attitude toward some person or proposal or institution. But whether the audience is specific or general, present or remote, a speech is likely to have more urgency, more directness of address, and more simplicity in vocabulary, style, and structure than compositions intended to be read in private.

Keeping in mind the exceptions and reservations and modifications discussed above, we may say, then, that a speech is a spoken discourse intended to work some kind of persuasive effect upon a given audience.

THE NATURE OF CRITICISM

"Let us say that the task of literary criticism is to put the reader in possession of the work of art," says Cleanth Brooks.[6] He continues, "Is this a mere reading of the work or is it a judgment of it? Frankly, I do not see how the two activities can be separated. . . . The attempt to drive a wedge between close reading of the text and evaluation of the work seems to me confused and confusing." Let us say the same of rhetorical criticism. We are concerned with the interpretation of speeches, with analysis of their content, structure, and method; and we are concerned at the same time with judgment or evaluation of their excellences and defects.

It will be apparent from the definition above that putting a reader in possession of a speech involves more than analysis of its content and form. Since the purpose of a speech is to work persuasion upon an audience, we cannot properly explain or evaluate it until we have learned a great deal about the occasion which called it forth, the speaker's relation to the occasion, the resources available to him, and the climate of opinion and current of events amidst which he operated. Particularly do we need to know the nature of the audience for whom the speech was intended so that we may understand why certain things were said and certain others omitted, and so that we may judge whether the speaker has wisely and skillfully adapted his ideas and methods to those for whom they are intended. It will help also to know something of the speaker's character, education, and experience, for these are important conditioners of what he says. And when we have formed an impression of the speech we may wish to test its validity by examining whatever evidence is available concerning its actual effect upon those who heard or read it.

If we study, for example, the First Inaugural Address of Franklin D. Roosevelt, how are we to understand and evaluate such phrases as "the only thing we have to fear is fear itself," "the money changers have fled from their high seats in the temple of our civilization," "a stricken nation in the midst of a stricken world"? We will have to make a careful examination of contemporary events and conditions as we find them recorded in newspapers, magazines, surveys, and histories of the period. Through similar sources we will need to examine the life and character of the speaker to discover why this kind of man was likely to say the kind of thing he did say. We will wish to know what advisers he consulted while preparing the address and how their advice influenced him. The composition of the immediate audience scattered over the Capitol Plaza is not of great importance, for the speech was addressed not to them primarily but to the nation at large, indeed to the whole world. Analysis of such an audience is a formidable task, but the critic must learn what he can of the fears and hopes of the people of the world at that time.

It is obvious that an attempt to discover and to analyze *all* the factors in the historical situation, in the consciousness of the audience, and in the baffling personality of the speaker on this occasion would require a lifetime of study and could never be complete. The critic must be selective. He must distinguish what is relevant to his purpose from what is merely interesting, and he must be limited by the prescribed scope of his study.

It is all the more important that he should not get lost in such studies, since they are, strictly speaking, extraneous to rhetoric. They are useful only insofar as they help in the rhetorical analysis of the speech itself. Properly speaking, they are excursions into the fields of history, sociology, or biography which furnish a background against which the speech itself may be studied.

It is even more important that the critic should not be diverted into an attempt to assess the *result* of a speech except as its effect may help us to judge the quality of the speech itself. Rhetoric, strictly speaking, is not concerned with the *effect* of a speech, but with its *quality,* and its quality can be determined quite apart from its effect. This is apparent when we consider that a properly qualified rhetorician should be able to analyze and to judge a written speech before it is delivered, and so before it can have had any effect. So also he should be able to criticize it after it is delivered without paying any attention to its effect.

It cannot be too often repeated that the effect of a speech *may* bear little relation to its intrinsic worth. A speaker's success in achieving a desired response from his audience is not necessarily proof that he has spoken well, or his failure, that he has spoken ill. His objective may have been too easy, or his audience may have responded as he wished despite the fact that they were actually repelled by his plea. Or, on the other hand, their votes may have been bought up in advance, or they may have had a stubborn prejudice against him or his proposal that nothing could dispel. Many of the great speeches of history have been made in lost causes. Some have been called forth by the speaker's very consciousness that his case was hopeless. Under such circumstances an orator may speak merely to put his views on record, or he may speak in defiant challenge to an opposition which he knows is invincible. Witness John Brown's moving defense when about to receive a sentence of death. One may say in such cases that the orator is speaking to posterity, or to the larger audience who will read his plea, and often that is true. But who can assess the effect of a speech on posterity? Who can determine today the effect of Woodrow Wilson's pleas for the League of Nations? How can one determine the actual influence of Lincoln's plea for malice toward none and charity for all? Indeed how can we be sure that a speech that "gets the votes" or "wins a verdict" is really the cause of the alleged results? The real reasons for a man's vote may lie hidden in his own mind. In most cases, all we know is that a plea was made, and the vote was so and so. The relation between the two is seldom discoverable.

Let us not be too confident, then, that we are measuring the effect of a speech. And in any case the totting up of such responses as are discernible is a task for a historian, a clerk, or a comptometer, not for a rhetorician. If the results of a speech are measurable, it is the job of the rhetorician to analyze the *causes* of its alleged success or failure as these are discoverable in the speech itself.

THE CRITIC'S QUALIFICATIONS

It is true that anyone can pronounce judgment on speeches, and most everyone does, but only a judgment that comes from a qualified critic is worthy of respect. One of the first qualifications we look for in seeking a competent critic is a judicious temperament. Many of us are prone to make decisions before we have examined all the factors involved in a situation and weighed each in its relation to others. In judging speeches we must not hastily jump to conclusions merely because we have found something that pleases or displeases us. We must school ourselves to examine patiently all the factors relevant to a sound judgment and not to depend upon whim, prejudice, or individual preference. It is not opinion we seek, but truth.

But how can one speak of truth in a field so incapable of scientific certitude as rhetoric? We have no calipers or test tubes or mathematical formulas to help us. How can one be sure of the quality of a speech, or of its value? Sir William Osler's advice to young doctors is pertinent here. "At the outset," he said, "do not be worried about this big question—Truth. It is a very simple matter if each one of you starts with the desire to get as much as possible. No human being is constituted to know the truth, and nothing but the truth; and even the best of men must be content with fragments, with partial glimpses, never the full fruition. In this unsatisfied quest the attitude of mind, the desire, the thirst . . . the fervent longing, are the be-all and the end-all. . . . The truth is the best you can get with your best endeavor, *the best that the best men accept*—with this you must learn to be satisfied, retaining at the same time with due humility an earnest desire for an ever larger portion."[7]

Besides a thirst for truth and a judicious temperament in dealing with it, the critic of rhetoric must have special education for his task. He must have, first, a wide general education in history, politics, literature, and all the liberal studies. The speeches he studies may range through all the fields of human knowledge, they may be rich in allusions to persons and events, and the critic must be able to follow all the workings of the orator's mind. If he comes across such phrases as "a house divided against itself," "a consummation devoutly to be wished," or "be in earnest, don't equivocate, don't excuse, don't retreat a single inch," he should be able to identify and explain them. In one paragraph of a speech by George William Curtis there are references to James Otis, Wendell Phillips, Quincy, John Quincy Adams, Whittier, Wrongfully, Lowell, Emerson, Parker, Beecher, Jonathan Mayhew, Roger Williams, and William Ellery Channing, and an understanding of the paragraph requires some familiarity with their lives and achievements. In such cases one must, of course, consult encyclopedias, biographical dictionaries, histories, and so on, but with the understanding that they do not take the place of a well-furnished mind.

Second, the critic must know speeches. He must have read and heard and studied many of them if he is to know the nature of the genus, speech. Only from familiarity with a large number of representative specimens will he know what he should look for in a given speech and what its distinctive qualities and merits are. To understand or to evaluate a particular thing—a horse, a motor car, a drama, a painting—one must be familiar with many specimens of that thing. It is only thus that standards of judgment are formed. Until the student acquires such a background in public address, he is not qualified to interpret or judge speeches. One of the purposes of this book is to make available some materials for that background.

Men have been studying speeches for as long as speeches have been made, and through the ages many treatises have been written to define the principles of speech-making and to reduce them to a system. The third qualification of the modern critic is familiarity with these treatises on rhetoric. Where so many competent guides have mapped out the ground, it is folly for anyone to stumble alone over such difficult and treacherous terrain, especially so since among these writers on rhetoric are some of the most eminent minds in the history of the race. With the best of these works the modern critic of public address should become thoroughly familiar. The fact that some of them were written centuries ago does not measurably diminish their value for the criticism of speeches in the middle of the nineteenth century. Rhetoric deals in the main with man's motives and desires and, whether we like it or not, basic human nature has not changed essentially in two thousand years. The way to a man's heart in ancient Athens is still the way to a man's heart today. Styles and modes of speaking may change in different ages, but wherever the fundamental purpose of speaking is to influence human conduct its essence will remain the same.

So much has been written on rhetoric that its study might absorb a whole lifetime, but for most purposes such thorough study is not needed. It is enough if one knows the best of the treatises on the subject. It is not by swallowing whole libraries, but by repeatedly and intently contemplating a few very great works, that the mind is best disciplined. And as Lane Cooper has said, "The best-read man is the one who has oftenest read the best things."[8]

There is little disagreement among modern scholars on which are the best works on rhetoric, at least until we come to modern writings. The following list contains most, if not all, of the older works that modern scholars consider most worthy of study. They should be available in any good college library.

STANDARD WORKS ON RHETORIC

Plato: *Phaedrus* and *Gorgias*

Aristotle: *Rhetoric*

Cicero: *De Oratore*

Quintilian: *Institutio Oratoria*

Longinus (?): *On the Sublime*

Francis Bacon: *The Advancement of Learning, Chapter III*

George Campbell: *The Philosophy of Rhetoric*

Hugh Blair: *Lectures on Rhetoric and Belles Lettres*

Richard Whately: *Elements of Rhetoric*

These will serve as a base from which to examine the flood of modern studies, criticisms, and textbooks on public speaking which issue yearly from the press. A very useful summation of rhetorical theories with many suggestions of lines of study will be found in *Speech Criticism: The Development of Standards for Rhetorical Appraisal* by Lester Thonssen and A. Craig Baird.[9] Many model studies of orators may be found in *A History and Criticism of American Public Address,* sponsored by The National Association of Teachers of Speech and edited by W. N. Brigance.[10]

A word of caution may be needed against using any one of the works listed above as a sole guide in the criticism of an address. To derive all one's criteria from Whately, for instance, or even from so comprehensive a treatise as Aristotle's, is pretty sure to result in a criticism that is only partial, with neglect of some important matters and too much attention to others. So far as is possible one should be guided by all of "the best" theories of appraisal, difficult as this makes the task. Jacques Barzun has well said, "The critic's role is . . . to see, hear, and talk about everything in the light of *some imaginary standard set by the books with the toughest lives.*"[11] Some suggestions for forming this imaginary standard will be found in the section that follows.

THE BASIS OF CRITICISM

There is general agreement among scholars that of all the books that have been written on rhetoric the one with the toughest life is Aristotle's *Rhetoric*. It has profoundly influenced nearly all subsequent writers, and its present liveliness is attested by the fact that it is available today in more English translations than probably any other ancient work. We shall lean heavily upon it in forming our "imaginary standard" of criticism.

Aristotle defined rhetoric as "the faculty of observing in any given case the available means of persuasion." Note first in this definition that rhetoric is a *faculty*. That is, it is not a definite technique with fixed rules of procedure, but merely the ability to find the elements of persuasion in a given speech. Note also that the rhetorician is not to limit his attention to the means of persuasion actually used, but is to consider all the means *available* to the speaker whether he used them or not. He should discover what the speaker *might* have said, what the situation called for, what resources were accessible to him. This, of course, points toward a careful analysis of the situation that called forth the address, the environment in which it was made, the problem that it was intended to solve. It suggests also that the critic's concern is not with the literal result of the speech, but with the speaker's use of a correct method; not with the speech's effect, but with its effectiveness. Persuasive always means persuasive to someone—a judge in a case at law, a prospective voter in an election, a listener in a popular audience. But the judge or listener as Aristotle conceives him is always a *qualified* judge—a person of good education, sound sense, and judicious temper. This is the kind of audience we must assume in assessing the effectiveness of a speech, for it is the kind of audience aimed at in the best efforts of all our orators. We admire Burke's great addresses, not because they were well adapted to the boozy country squires who sometimes sat in Parliament, but because they were designed for a better audience. In speech-making, as in life, not failure, but low aim, is crime. And so in criticism we interpret and evaluate a speech in terms of its effect upon an audience of qualified listeners.

THE MEANS OF PERSUASION

With rhetorical criticism thus defined we proceed to consider some of the most important means by which a speech works persuasion in those who hear and judge it.

One of the most important elements in persuasiveness is the impression made by the speaker's character and personality. Much of this impression is made, of course, by his appearance, voice, manner, and delivery, and cannot be recovered from study of the printed speech. Many indications of his trustworthiness *can*, however, be found in the printed text. We can learn whether he possesses those personal qualities that Aristotle thought most persuasive—virtue, intelligence, and good will. When Theodore Roosevelt said, "There should be relentless exposure of and attack upon every evil man, whether politician or business man," and when Franklin D. Roosevelt said, "Happiness lies not in the mere possession of money; it lies in the joy of achievement, in the thrill of creative effort," they were revealing a moral bent that should have stimulated their hearers to greater confidence in their integrity. Most speeches are full of such indicators of the speaker's trustworthiness, and the critic must note them and assess their value. He may note such things as whether the speaker establishes his own authority with the audience, whether he has a sympathetic understanding of their way of life, their thoughts, and their problems, whether he impresses them as being well informed on his subject, whether he is given to dogmatism, exaggeration, and overstatement, whether he has a sense of humor, whether he seems sincere, friendly, fair-minded, modest, self-respecting, respectful, courteous, and tactful.[12] The presence or absence of one or more of these qualities may dispose the hearers so favorably or so unfavorably toward the speaker that they pay little attention to what he says.

This, however, is not always true, and the second element of effectiveness we must consider is the *content* of the speech. The essential question to ask here is: Did the speaker choose the right things to say? It is desirable to separate *what* was said from *how* it was said—often a difficult task—and this may best be done by making a summary or précis of the speaker's thought which avoids the wording of the original. We must consider whether he seems to be acquainted with all the pertinent facts bearing on his subject and whether he uses those that are most significant or persuasive. We must determine also whether they really are facts, or only guesses, opinions, or hearsay, whether he has drawn valid inferences from them, and whether he has combined them into a coherent logical structure that will satisfy the understanding and win conviction.

It is helpful to separate the structure of the speech from the structure of the reasoning that supports it, and to outline both. Rarely will they coincide, for rarely do experienced speakers put their thoughts into the mechanical form favored by schoolboy debaters: "I will prove so and so, and my reasons are, first, second, third, etc." A chronological outline will reveal the order of the speaker's thoughts; a logical outline will reveal the structure and validity of his thinking. The main proposition (or propositions) may nowhere be specifically stated, but it should be ferreted out by the critic and clearly formulated, and the supporting arguments should be marshaled under it to form a logical brief. He should ask: Just what is this speaker trying to prove, and what does he adduce to support his thesis? By this means he will best discover the essential substance of the speech—or its lack of substance.

The critic should assess also the depth and weight of the ideas presented. A great speech cannot consist of mere eloquent nothings. It must deal with great issues, not with trivial ephemera. And the critic must consider whether the orator is actuated by lofty ideals of justice, honor, liberty, and the like, or whether he is concerned with such local and temporary matters as balancing this year's budget or getting a subsidy for farmers. It is true that persuasion may be as skillful in small matters as in great, but we cannot divorce the value of a speech from the value of the ideas with which it deals.

When the plan and structure of a speech are clearly perceived, the critic may note whether there is any persuasive effect in the *order* in which ideas are presented. In the given situation is there any advantage in presenting this idea first and that one second? The notion is as old as Plato that a speech should have a beginning, a middle, and an end, and the disposition of materials, *dispositio,* was a main consideration of Roman rhetoricians. In most speeches the threefold division—introduction, discussion, conclusion—is easily discernible. And in general it will be found that the introduction is designed to win an intelligent, sympathetic, and attentive hearing, and the conclusion to sum up what has been said and to make a final appeal. These are their time-honored functions. But what the critic should note is not merely whether the speech follows this classical pattern, but whether it proceeds step by step in conformity with the need, the mood, and the expectation of the audience. The hearers may require an analysis of a problem before they will attend to its solution. They may want certain objections answered before they will listen to a proposal. Or they may entertain certain doubts or suspicions that the speaker will have to remove before he can get a fair hearing. The situation may be such that he will need to establish a common ground of interest, of feeling, or of belief with his audience before he presents his proposal. And it may be that the presentation of an unpopular theme calls for a strategy whereby the hearers are led to agree with the speaker on several non-controversial matters so that they will continue to agree when a less acceptable matter is presented. That is, the critic must look not only to the *chronological* order of materials and their logical structure, but also to the *psychological* order of presentation if one exists.

Another means of persuasion, and perhaps the most important of all, is by appeal to certain *motives* to which an audience can be expected to respond. The most persuasive speaker is he who most effectively directs his appeal to the basic interests, desires, wants, instincts, and emotions of his hearers. A complete catalogue of such motives has never been made, but the critic may get most help in this matter from Aristotle's discussion of the "Constituents of Happiness" and "Goods," and his analysis of the emotions.[13] He will be helped also, by the analyses of audiences by the Reverend George Campbell[14] and James A. Winans.[15]

Sometimes the "motivation" of a speech will be immediately clear. Patrick Henry's "Liberty or Death," for instance, is obviously an appeal to our love of liberty, though it contains many other appeals also. Curtis's "Public Duty of Educated Men" appeals, of course, to the sense of duty of the young graduates to whom it was addressed. But often the motive to which the orator appeals is hidden or obscure. It may nowhere be mentioned, and the emotions he seeks to arouse may not be named. One of the most rewarding tasks of the critic is to search them out and to determine from a study of them what kind of audience the orator presumes himself to be addressing. Does he assume that his hearers will respond to such motives as group loyalty, honor, courage, fair play, altruism, or does he appeal only to self-interest and personal security? Does he assume that they are progressive and forward-looking, or that they are timid, conservative, and fearful of anything new? Does he rely on challenges to reason than on appeals to emotion? Does he attempt to arouse fear, anger, hatred, jealousy, or confidence, temperance, and love? And so on.

When the nature of the appeal is understood one must consider the manner in which it is presented. A speaker may scold an audience for its failure in duty, or he may ridicule its negligence, or try to shame it into action. He may present an unpopular proposal with challenging bluntness, or skillfully identify it with accepted beliefs and habitual conduct. He may rely upon effective repetition to drum in an idea and get it accepted. He may arouse emotion by effective play upon the imagination. By moving examples and illustrations he may fix responsibility upon his hearers and compel them to face the truth. And he may win them to a favorable response, as Franklin D. Roosevelt so often did, by a serene and cheerful confidence that they *will* respond favorably. All such methods of presenting a proposal the critic will note and assess.

STYLE

Another important means of persuasion lies in the speaker's *style*. It is style, the choice and arrangement of words, that determines in the main the value of a speech as enduring literature. And it is style that more than any other factor gives a speaker the uniqueness by which he is distinguished from other speakers. Here the authenticity of the text of the speech becomes especially important, though the critic may be more interested in what the speaker *meant* to say than in what he *did* say. But he will want to know whether the words he is studying are the speaker's own or contributed by some adviser or ghost writer.

It has been a truism since Aristotle that the first virtue of style is to be clear. But clarity is a relative matter, and the critic must ask always: Clear to whom? The brilliant academic addresses of Curtis and Phillips with their wealth of allusions to literature and history make difficult reading today. Were they clear to the erudite audiences before whom they were spoken? In its effect on its audience a speech must, of course, be *immediately* clear since, once uttered, it cannot be called back for a rehearing (unless it was recorded). In its vocabulary, its allusions, its illustrations, and its sentence structure it must be suited to the intelligence of those for whom it is intended. These are the principal considerations in criticizing the clarity of a speech.

Because audiences may be dull, indifferent, and subject to many distractions, we expect a speech to have a vividness and vivacity that will win and hold attention. This is the quality that Aristotle well described as "setting a thing before the eyes." Such an effect may be obtained by concrete wording, effective descriptions, flights of imagination and fancy, the use of metaphors, examples, illustrations, analogies, by vivid narratives and dramatic dialogues and rhetorical questions. Such devices may be used in connection with parallelism of phrase and antithesis. Vivacity is obtained also by conciseness of statement, economy of style, brevity of utterance, though in this respect audiences and periods vary in their taste. Apparently the audiences of Webster's day tolerated an elaborateness of amplification that may impress us as mere flatulence and bombast. In this, as in other matters, the critic must consider the peculiar nature of the audience addressed. Finally, the vividness of a speech will depend largely upon whether the various oratorical elements are presented with appropriate variety, for any device if endlessly repeated loses its power to hold attention.

A third characteristic of a good style is its appropriateness. It should be suited to the speaker, to the audience, and to the occasion. Factors to be considered are vocabulary, the nature of the materials—facts, arguments, illustrations, and the like—the mood and temper of the speaker and of the audience, the gravity of the subject, the nature of the occasion, and so on. Here again, the validity of the criticism will depend upon how effectively the occasion has been analyzed.

Another quality to be considered is the orality or "speak-ability" of the style. There should be indications that it was meant to be spoken to an audience rather than read silently and privately by an individual reader. The factors that distinguish an oral from a written style have never been definitely set forth, but the critic will look for such things as directness of address, as revealed by personal pronouns and questions; simplicity of sentence structure; heat and vitality of expression demanded by the need for holding the attention of an audience; and a choice of words and phrases that allow for ease, smoothness, and force of utterance.[16]

In studying style one should look also for those occasional passages of sustained nobility and beauty which sometimes lift oratory into the realm of poetry. The ideas and sentiments that inspired them may no longer be meaningful, but still they live and move us by their intrinsic aptness and beauty. Sometimes, as occasionally with Ingersoll, they seem to be merely "purple patches" sewed onto the fabric of the discourse to attract attention, but often they are developed authentically from the orator's feeling and imagination. A thorough study of oratory cannot fail to take account of them.

There are other aspects of style, but those we have just discussed are perhaps the most important. For additional criteria and suggestions we recommend especially the works cited above by Aristotle, Campbell, and Blair.

CONCLUSION

These, then, are the principal means of persuasion that the critic of speeches will consider—character, content, logic, arrangement, motivation, and style. He will be interested also in the speaker's delivery and will learn what he can about it from available reports of the speech, but the text itself will seldom offer any suggestions about how the address was spoken. Students of classical rhetoric will note that this classification cuts across the Aristotelian three-fold division into ethical, pathetic, and logical proofs, and the five-fold Roman division of speech preparation into invention, disposition, style, delivery, and memorization. However, it will be found that all of these are accounted for, except the last.

We have been concerned chiefly with the analysis of single speeches, but it should be obvious that such analyses will prepare the student for other critical adventures. He may wish to attempt a comparative study of two or more orators, noting whether they appeal to the same or different motives, whether they arrange their materials in similar ways, how obtrusively each speaker's ego appears, how they compare in the use of illustrations and examples, how they differ or resemble each other in imagery, in vitality, in sentence form, in vocabulary, or in style. From such studies the critic will prepare himself for a sound judgment of what is unique and distinctive about a given orator. He may concern himself with the varying styles and methods that seemed to prevail in different periods of history. Or he may become interested in discovering certain recurring themes in oratory and changes in attitude toward them—such themes as liberty, democracy, human welfare, the function of government, the concept of honor, the hope of peace, the function of leadership.

These and many other lines of study may prove to be interesting and rewarding. The avenues of research are so various, and the possibility of getting lost in a blind alley is so great that we feel impelled to warn that a rhetorical criticism is likely to be the less valuable the farther it strays from the central core of our discipline, which is the determination of whether the speaker has discovered and employed in the given case the available means of persuasion.

NOTES

[1] *Rhetoric,* I, i.
[2] David Daiches, *A Study of Literature* (Ithaca, N.Y.: Cornell University Press, 1948), p. 228.
[3] *Myrrour & Dyscrypcyon of the Worlde,* 1481.
[4] See his chapter on Communication and the Artist in *Principles of Literary Criticism* (New York: Harcourt Brace & Co., 1952).

[5]W. M. Parrish, *Speaking in Public* (New York: Charles Scribner's Sons, 1947), pp. 308–16.

[6]Foreword to R. W. Stallman, *Critiques and Essays in Criticism,* 1920–1948 (New York: The Ronald Press Co., 1949), p. xx.

[7]*Aequanimitas* (3rd ed.; Philadelphia: The Blakiston Co., 1932), pp. 397–98.

[8]*Two Views of Education* (New Haven: Yale University Press, 1922), p. 118.

[9]New York: The Ronald Press Co., 1948.

[10]New York: McGraw-Hill Book Co., 1943.

[11]*Harper's Magazine* (July, 1949), p. 105. (Italics ours.)

[12]See the chapter, "The Speaker Himself," in James A. Winans, *Speech-Making* (New York: D. Appleton-Century Co., 1938).

[13]*Rhetoric,* I, v, vi, vii; II, iix–ii.

[14]*Philosophy and Rhetoric* (New York: Funk and Wagnalls Co., 1911), Book I, Chap. VII.

[15]*Op. cit.,* Chap. XV.

[16]J. M. Clapp, "Oratorical Style and Structure," in S. B. Harding, *Select Orations Illustrating American Political History* (New York: The Macmillan Co., 1909).

THE RHETORICAL SITUATION

LLOYD F. BITZER

If someone says, That is a dangerous situation, his words suggest the presence of events, persons, or objects which threaten him, someone else, or something of value. If someone remarks, I find myself in an embarrassing situation, again the statement implies certain situational characteristics. If someone remarks that he found himself in an ethical situation, we understand that he probably either contemplated or made some choice of action from a sense of duty or obligation or with a view to the Good. In other words, there are circumstances of this or that kind of structure which are recognized as ethical, dangerous, or embarrassing. What characteristics, then, are implied when one refers to "the rhetorical situation"— the context in which speakers or writers create rhetorical discourse? Perhaps this question is puzzling because "situation" is not a standard term in the vocabulary of rhetorical theory. "Audience" is standard; so also are "speaker," "subject," "occasion," and "speech." If I were to ask, "What is a rhetorical audience?" or "What is a rhetorical subject?"—the reader would catch the meaning of my question.

When I ask, What is a rhetorical situation?, I want to know the nature of those contexts in which speakers or writers create rhetorical discourse: How should they be described? What are their characteristics? Why and how do they result in the creation of rhetoric? By analogy, a theorist of science might well ask, What are the characteristics of situations which inspire scientific thought? A philosopher might ask, What is the nature of the situation in which a philosopher "does philosophy"? And a theorist of poetry might ask, How shall we describe the context in which poetry comes into existence?

The presence of rhetorical discourse obviously indicates the presence of a rhetorical situation. The Declaration of Independence, Lincoln's Gettysburg Address, Churchill's Address on Dunkirk, John F. Kennedy's Inaugural Address—each is a clear instance of rhetoric and each indicates the presence of a situation. While the existence of a rhetorical address is a reliable sign of the existence of situation, it does not follow that a situation exists only when the discourse exists. Each reader probably can recall a specific time and place when there was opportunity to speak on some urgent matter, and after the opportunity was gone he created in private thought the speech he should have uttered earlier in the situation. It is clear that situations are not always accompanied by discourse. Nor should we assume that a rhetorical address gives existence to the situation; on the contrary, it is the situation which calls the discourse into existence. Clement Attlee once said that Winston Churchill went around looking for "finest hours." The point to observe is that Churchill found them—the crisis situations—and spoke in response to them.

No major theorist has treated rhetorical situation thoroughly as a distinct subject in rhetorical theory; many ignore it. Those rhetoricians who discuss situation do so indirectly—as does Aristotle, for example who is led to consider situation when he treats types of discourse. None, to my knowledge, has asked the nature of rhetorical situation. Instead rhetoricians have asked: What is the process by which the orator creates and presents discourse? What is the nature of rhetorical discourse? What sorts of interaction occur between speaker, audience, subject, and occasion? Typically the questions which trigger theories of rhetoric focus upon the orator's method or upon the discourse itself, rather than upon the situation which invites the orator's application of his method and the creation of discourse. Thus rhetoricians distinguish among and characterize the types of speeches (forensic, deliberative, epideictic); they treat issues, types of proof, lines of argument, strategies of ethical and emotional persuasion, the parts of a discourse and the functions of these parts, qualities of styles, figures of speech. They cover approximately the same materials, the formal aspects of rhetorical method and discourse, whether focusing upon method, product or process; while conceptions of situation are implicit in some theories of rhetoric, none explicitly treat the formal aspects of situation.

I hope that enough has been said to show that the question—What is a rhetorical situation?—is not an idle one. I propose in what follows to set forth part of a theory of situation. This essay, therefore, should be understood as an attempt to revive the notion of rhetorical situation, to provide at least the outline of an adequate conception of it, and to establish it as a controlling and fundamental concern of rhetorical theory.

I

It seems clear that rhetoric is situational. In saying this, I do not mean merely that understanding a speech hinges upon understanding the context of meaning in which the speech is located. Virtually no utterance is fully intelligible unless meaning-context and utterance are understood; this is true of rhetorical and non-rhetorical discourse. Meaning-context is a general condition of human communication and is not synonymous with rhetorical situation. Nor do I mean merely that rhetoric occurs in a setting which involves interaction of speaker, audience, subject, and communicative purpose. This is too general since many types of utterances—philosophical, scientific, poetic, and rhetorical—occur in such settings. Nor would I equate rhetorical situation with persuasive situation, which exists whenever an audience can be changed in belief or action by means of speech. Every audience at any moment is capable of being changed in some way by speech; persuasive situation is altogether general.

Finally, I do not mean that a rhetorical discourse must be embedded in historic context in the sense that a living tree must be rooted in soil. A tree does not obtain its character-as-tree from the soil, but rhetorical discourse, I shall argue, does obtain its character-as-rhetorical from the situation which generates it. Rhetorical works belong to the class of things which obtain their character from the circumstances of the historic context in which they occur. A rhetorical work is analogous to a moral action rather than to a tree. An act is moral because it is an act performed in a situation of a certain kind; similarly, a work is rhetorical because it is a response to a situation of a certain kind.

In order to clarify rhetoric-as-essentially-related-to-situation, we should acknowledge a viewpoint that is commonplace but fundamental: a work of rhetoric is pragmatic; it comes into existence for the sake of something beyond itself; it functions ultimately to produce action or change in the world; it performs some task. In short, rhetoric is a mode of altering reality, not by the direct application of energy to objects, but by the creation of discourse which changes reality through the mediation of thought and action. The rhetor alters reality by bringing into existence a discourse of such a character that the audience, in thought and action, is so engaged that it becomes mediator of change. In this sense rhetoric is always persuasive.

To say that rhetorical discourse comes into being in order to effect change is altogether general. We need to understand that a particular discourse comes into existence because of some specific condition or situation which invites utterance. Bronislaw Malinowski refers to just this sort of situation in his discussion of primitive language, which he finds to be essentially pragmatic and "embedded in situation." He describes a party of fishermen in the Trobriand Islands whose functional speech occurs in a "context of situation."

> The canoes glide slowly and noiselessly, punted by men especially good at this task and always used for it. Other experts who know the bottom of the lagoon . . . are on the look-out for fish. . . . Customary signs, or sounds or words are uttered. Sometimes a sentence full of technical references to the channels or patches on the lagoon has to be spoken; sometimes . . . a conventional cry is uttered. . . . Again, a word of command is passed here and there, a technical expression or explanation which serves to harmonize their behavior towards other men. . . . An animated scene, full of movement, follows, and now that the fish are in their power the fishermen speak loudly and give vent to their feelings. Short, telling exclamations fly about, which might be rendered by such words as: "Pull in," "Let go," "Shift further," "Lift the net."

In this whole scene, "each utterance is essentially bound up with the context of situation and with the aim of the pursuit. . . . The structure of all this linguistic material is inextricably mixed up with, and dependent upon, the course of the activity in which the utterances are embedded." Later the observer remarks: "In its primitive uses, language functions as a link in concerted human activity, as a piece of human behavior. It is a mode of action and not an instrument of reflection."[1]

These statements about primitive language and the "context of situation" provide for us a preliminary model of rhetorical situation. Let us regard rhetorical situation as a natural context of persons, events, objects, relations, and an exigence which strongly invites utterance; this invited utterance participates naturally in the situation, is in many instances necessary to the completion of situational activity, and by means of its participation with situation obtains its meaning and its rhetorical character. In Malinowski's example, the situation is the fishing expedition—consisting of objects, persons, events, and relations—and the ruling exigence, the success of the hunt. The situation dictates the sorts of observations to be made; it dictates the significant physical and verbal responses; and, we must admit, it constrains the words which are uttered in the same sense that it constrains the physical acts of paddling the canoes and throwing the nets. The verbal responses to the demands imposed by this situation are clearly as functional and necessary as the physical responses.

Traditional theories of rhetoric have dealt, of course, not with the sorts of primitive utterances described by Malinowski—"stop here," "throw the nets," "move closer"—but with larger units of speech which come more readily under the guidance of artistic principle and method. The difference between oratory and primitive utterance, however, is not a difference in function; the clear instances of rhetorical discourse and the fishermen's utterances are similarly functional and similarly situational. Observing both the traditions of the expedition and the facts before him, the leader of the fishermen finds himself *obliged* to speak at a given moment—to command, to supply information, to praise or blame—to respond appropriately to the situation. Clear instances of artistic rhetoric exhibit the same character: Cicero's speeches against Cataline were called forth by a specific union of persons, events, objects, and relations, and by an exigence which amounted to an imperative stimulus; the speeches in the Senate rotunda three days after the assassination of the President of the United States were actually required by the situation. So controlling is situation that we should consider it the very ground of rhetorical activity, whether that activity is primitive and productive of a simple utterance or artistic and productive of the Gettysburg Address.

Hence, to say that rhetoric is situational means: (1) rhetorical discourse comes into existence as a response to situation, in the same sense that an answer comes into existence in response to a question, or a solution in response to a problem; (2) a speech is given *rhetorical* significance by the situation, just as a unit of discourse is given significance *as* answer or *as* solution by the question or problem; (3) a rhetorical situation must exist as a necessary condition of rhetorical discourse, just as a question must exist as a necessary condition of an answer; (4) many questions go unanswered and many problems remain unsolved; similarly, many rhetorical situations mature and decay without giving birth to rhetorical utterance; (5) a situation is rhetorical insofar as it needs and invites discourse capable of participating with situation and thereby altering its reality; (6) discourse is rhetorical insofar as it functions (or seeks to function) as a fitting response to a situation which needs and invites it. (7) Finally, the situation controls the rhetorical response in the same sense that the question controls the answer and the problem controls the solution. Not the rhetor and not persuasive intent, but the situation is the source and ground of rhetorical activity—and, I should add, of rhetorical criticism.

II

Let us now amplify the nature of situation by providing a formal definition and examining constituents. Rhetorical situation may be defined as a complex of persons, events, objects, and relations presenting an actual or potential exigence which can be completely or partially removed if discourse, introduced into the situation, can so constrain human decision or action as to bring about the significant modification of the exigence. Prior to the creation and presentation of discourse, there are three constituents of any rhetorical situation: the first is the *exigence;* the second and third are elements of the complex, namely the *audience* to be constrained in decision and action, and the *constraints* which influence the rhetor and can be brought to bear upon the audience.

Any *exigence* is an imperfection marked by urgency; it is a defect, an obstacle, something waiting to be done, a thing which is other than it should be. In almost any sort of context, there will be numerous exigences, but not all are elements of a rhetorical situation—not all are rhetorical exigences. An exigence which cannot be modified is not rhetorical; thus, whatever comes about of necessity and cannot be changed—death, winter, and some natural disasters, for instance—are exigences to be sure, but they are not rhetorical. Further, an exigence which can be modified only by means other than discourse is not rhetorical; thus, an exigence is not rhetorical when its modification requires merely one's own action or the application of a tool, but neither requires nor invites the assistance of discourse. An exigence is rhetorical when it is capable of positive modification and when positive modification requires discourse or can be assisted by discourse. For example, suppose that a man's acts are injurious to others and that the quality of his acts can be changed only if discourse is addressed to him; the exigence—his injurious acts—is then unmistakably rhetorical. The pollution of our air is also a rhetorical exigence because its positive modification—reduction of pollution—strongly invites the assistance of discourse producing public awareness, indignation, and action of the right kind. Frequently rhetors encounter exigences which defy easy classification because of the absence of information enabling precise analysis and certain judgment—they may or may not be rhetorical. An attorney whose client has been convicted may strongly believe that a higher court would reject his appeal to have the verdict overturned, but because the matter is uncertain—because the exigence *might* be rhetorical—he elects to appeal. In this and similar instances of indeterminate exigences the rhetor's decision to speak is based mainly upon the urgency of the exigence and the probability that the exigence is rhetorical.

In any rhetorical situation there will be at least one controlling exigence which functions as the organizing principle: it specifies the audience to be addressed and the change to be effected. The exigence may or may not be perceived clearly by the rhetor or other persons in the situation; it may be strong or weak depending upon the clarity of their perception and the degree of their interest in it; it may be real or unreal depending on the facts of the case; it may be important or trivial, it may be such that discourse can completely remove it, or it may persist in spite of repeated modifications; it may be completely familiar—one of a type of exigences occurring frequently in our experience—or it may be totally new, unique. When it is perceived and when it is strong and important, then it constrains the thought and action of the perceiver who may respond rhetorically if he is in a position to do so.

The second constituent is the *audience.* Since rhetorical discourse produces change by influencing the decision and action of persons who function as mediators of change, it follows that rhetoric always requires an audience—even in those cases when a person engages himself or ideal mind as audience. It is clear also that a rhetorical audience must be distinguished from a body of mere hearers or readers: properly speaking, a rhetorical audience consists only of those persons who are capable of being influenced by discourse and of being mediators of change.

Neither scientific nor poetic discourse requires an audience in the same sense. Indeed, neither requires an audience in order to produce its end; the scientist can produce a discourse expressive or generative of knowledge without engaging another mind, and the poet's creative purpose is accomplished when the work is composed. It is true, of course, that scientists and poets present their works to audiences, but their audiences are not necessarily rhetorical. The scientific audience consists of persons capable of receiving knowledge, and the poetic audience, of persons capable of participating in aesthetic experiences induced by the poetry. But the rhetorical audience must be capable of serving as mediator of the change which the discourse functions to produce.

Besides exigence and audience, every rhetorical situation contains a set of *constraints* made up of persons, events, objects, and relations which are parts of the situation because they have the power to constrain decision and action needed to modify the exigence. Standard sources of constraint include beliefs, attitudes, documents, facts, traditions, images, interests, motives and the like; and when the orator enters the situation, his discourse not only harnesses constraints given by situation but provides additional important constraints—for example his personal character, his logical proofs, and his style. There are two main classes of con[s]traints: (1) those originated or managed by the rhetor and his method (Aristotle called these "artistic proofs"), and (2) those other constraints, in the situation, which may be operative (Aristotle's "inartistic proofs"). Both classes must be divided so as to separate those constraints that are proper from those that are improper.

These three constituents—exigence, audience, constraints—comprise everything relevant in a rhetorical situation. When the orator, invited by situation, enters it and creates and presents discourse, then both he and his speech are additional constituents.

III

I have broadly sketched a conception of rhetorical situation and discussed constituents. The following are general characteristics or features.

1. Rhetorical discourse is called into existence by situation; the situation which the rhetor perceives amounts to an invitation to create and present discourse. The clearest instances of rhetorical speaking and writing are strongly invited—often required. The situation generated by the assassination of President Kennedy was so highly structured and compelling that one could predict with near certainty the types and themes of forthcoming discourse. With the first reports of the assassination, there immediately developed a most urgent need for information; in response, reporters created hundreds of messages. Later as the situation altered, other exigences arose: the fantastic events in Dallas had to be explained; it was necessary to eulogize the dead President; the public needed to be assured that the transfer of government to new hands would be orderly. These messages were not idle performances. The historic situation was so compelling and clear that the responses were created almost out of necessity. The responses—news reports, explanations, eulogies—participated with the situation and positively modified the several exigences. Surely the power of situation is evident when one can predict that such discourse will be uttered. How else explain the phenomenon? One cannot say that the situation is the function of the speaker's intention, for in this case the speakers' intentions were determined by the situation. One cannot say that the rhetorical transaction is simply a response of the speaker to the demands or expectations of an audience, for the expectations of the audience were themselves keyed to a

tragic historic fact. Also, we must recognize that there came into existence countless eulogies to John F. Kennedy that never reached a public; they were filed, entered in diaries, or created in thought.

In contrast, imagine a person spending his time writing eulogies of men and women who never existed: his speeches meet no rhetorical situations; they are summoned into existence not by real events, but by his own imagination. They may exhibit formal features which we consider rhetorical—such as ethical and emotional appeals, and stylistic patterns; conceivably one of these fictive eulogies is even persuasive to someone; yet all remain unrhetorical unless, through the oddest of circumstances, one of them by chance should fit a situation. Neither the presence of formal features in the discourse nor persuasive effect in a reader or hearer can be regarded as reliable marks of rhetorical discourse: A speech will be rhetorical when it is a response to the kind of situation which is rhetorical.

2. Although rhetorical situation invites response, it obviously does not invite just any response. Thus the second characteristic of rhetorical situation is that it invites a *fitting* response, a response that fits the situation. Lincoln's Gettysburg Address was a most fitting response to the relevant features of the historic context which invited its existence and gave it rhetorical significance. Imagine for a moment the Gettysburg Address entirely separated from its situation and existing for us independent of any rhetorical context: as a discourse which does not "fit" any rhetorical situation, it becomes either poetry or declamation without rhetorical significance. In reality, however, the address continues to have profound rhetorical value precisely because some features of the Gettysburg situation persist; and the Gettysburg Address continues to participate with situation and to alter it.

Consider another instance. During one week of the 1964 presidential campaign, three events of national and international significance all but obscured the campaign: K[h]rushchev was suddenly deposed, China exploded an atomic bomb, and in England the Conservative Party was defeated by Labour. Any student of rhetoric could have given odds that President Johnson, in a major address, would speak to the significance of these events, and he did; his response to the situation generated by the events was fitting. Suppose that the President had treated not these events and their significance but the national budget, or imagine that he had reminisced about his childhood on a Texas farm. The critic of rhetoric would have said rightly, "He missed the mark; his speech did not fit; he did not speak to the pressing issues—the rhetorical situation shaped by the three crucial events of the week demanded a response, and he failed to provide the proper one."

3. If it makes sense to say that situation invites a "fitting" response, then situation must somehow prescribe the response which fits. To say that a rhetorical response fits a situation is to say that it meets the requirements established by the situation. A situation which is strong and clear dictates the purpose, theme, matter, and style of the response. Normally, the inauguration of a President of the United States demands an address which speaks to the nation's purposes, the central national and international problems, the unity of contesting parties; it demands speech style marked by dignity. What is evidenced on this occasion is the power of situation to constrain a fitting response. One might say metaphorically that every situation prescribes its fitting response; the rhetor may or may not read the prescription accurately.

4. The exigence and the complex of persons, objects, events and relations which generate rhetorical discourse are located in reality, are objective and publicly observable historic facts in the world we experience, are therefore available for scrutiny

by an observer or critic who attends to them. To say the situation is objective, publicly observable, and historic means that it is real or genuine—that our critical examination will certify its existence. Real situations are to be distinguished from sophistic ones in which, for example, a contrived exigence is asserted to be real; from spurious situations in which the existence or alleged existence of constituents is the result of error or ignorance; and from fantasy in which exigence, audience, and constraints may all be the imaginary objects of a mind at play.

The rhetorical situation as real is to be distinguished also from a fictive rhetorical situation. The speech of a character in a novel or play may be clearly required by a fictive rhetorical situation—a situation established by the story itself; but the speech is not genuinely rhetorical, even though, considered in itself, it looks exactly like a courtroom address or a senate speech. It is realistic, made so by fictive context. But the situation is not real, not grounded in history; neither the fictive situation nor the discourse generated by it is rhetorical. We should note, however, that the fictive rhetorical discourse within a play or novel may become genuinely rhetorical outside fictive context—if there is a real situation for which the discourse is a rhetorical response. Also, of course, the play or novel itself may be understood as a rhetorical response having poetic form.

5. Rhetorical situations exhibit structures which are simple or complex, and more or less organized. A situation's structure is simple when there are relatively few elements which must be made to interact; the fishing expedition is a case in point—there is a clear and easy relationship among utterances, the audiences, constraints, and exigence. Franklin D. Roosevelt's brief Declaration of War speech is another example: the message exists as a response to one clear exigence easily perceived by one major audience, and the one overpowering constraint is the necessity of war. On the other hand, the structure of a situation is complex when many elements must be made to interact: practically any presidential political campaign provides numerous complex rhetorical situations.

A situation, whether simple or complex, will be highly structured or loosely structured. It is highly structured when all of its elements are located and readied for the task to be performed. Malinowski's example, the fishing expedition, is a situation which is relatively simple and highly structured; everything is ordered to the task to be performed. The usual courtroom case is a good example of situation which is complex and highly structured. The jury is not a random and scattered audience but a selected and concentrated one; it knows its relation to judge, law, defendant, counsels; it is instructed in what to observe and what to disregard. The judge is located and prepared; he knows exactly his relation to jury, law, counsels, defendant. The counsels know the ultimate object of their case; they know what they must prove; they know the audience and can easily reach it. This situation will be even more highly structured if the issue of the case is sharp, the evidence decisive, and the law clear. On the other hand, consider a complex but loosely structured situation, William Lloyd Garrison preaching abolition from town to town. He is actually looking for an audience and for constraints; even when he finds an audience, he does not know that it is a genuinely rhetorical audience—one able to be the mediator of change. Or consider the plight of many contemporary civil rights advocates who, failing to locate compelling constraints and rhetorical audiences, abandon rhetorical discourse in favor of physical action.

Situations may become weakened in structure due to complexity or disconnectedness. A list of causes includes these: (a) a single situation may involve numerous exigences; (b) exigences in the same situation may be incompatible; (c) two or more simultaneous rhetorical situations may compete for our attention, as in some parliamentary debates; (d) at a given moment, persons comprising the audience of situation A may also be the audience of situations B, C, and D; (e) the rhetorical audience may be scattered, uneducated regarding its duties and powers, or it may dissipate; (f) constraints may be limited in number and force, and they may be incompatible. This is enough to suggest the sorts of things which weaken the structure of situations.

6. Finally, rhetorical situations come into existence, then either mature or decay or mature and persist—conceivably some persist indefinitely. In any case, situations grow and come to maturity; they evolve to just the time when a rhetorical discourse would be most fitting. In Malinowski's example, there comes a time in the situation when the leader of the fisherman should say, "Throw the nets." In the situation generated by the assassination of the President, there was a time for giving descriptive accounts of the scene in Dallas, later a time for giving eulogies. In a political campaign, there is a time for generating an issue and a time for answering a charge. Every rhetorical situation in principle evolves to a propitious moment for the fitting rhetorical response. After this moment, most situations decay; we all have the experience of creating a rhetorical response when it is too late to make it public.

Some situations, on the other hand, persist; this is why it is possible to have a body of truly *rhetorical* literature. The Gettysburg Address, Burke's Speech to the Electors of Bristol, Socrates' Apology—these are more than historical documents, more than specimens for stylistic or logical analysis. They exist as rhetorical responses *for us* precisely because they speak to situations which persist—which are in some measure universal.

Due to either the nature of things or convention, or both, some situations recur. The courtroom is the locus for several kinds of situations generating the speech of accusation, the speech of defense, the charge to the jury. From day to day, year to year, comparable situations occur, prompting comparable responses; hence rhetorical forms are born and a special vocabulary, grammar, and style are established. This is true also of the situation which invites the inaugural address of a President. The situation recurs and, because we experience situations and the rhetorical responses to them, a form of discourse is not only established but comes to have a power of its own—the tradition itself tends to function as a constraint upon any new response in the form.

IV

In the best of all possible worlds, there would be communication perhaps, but no rhetoric—since exigences would not arise. In our real world, however, rhetorical exigences abound; the world really invites change—change conceived and effected by human agents who quite properly address a mediating audience. The practical justification of rhetoric is analogous to that of scientific inquiry: the world presents objects to be known, puzzles to be resolved, complexities to be understood—hence the practical need for scientific inquiry and discourse; similarly, the world presents imperfections to be modified by means of discourse—hence the practical need for rhetorical investigation and discourse. As a discipline, scientific method is justified philosophically insofar as it provides principles, concepts, and procedures by which we come to know reality; similarly, rhetoric as a discipline is justified philosophically insofar as it provides principles, concepts, and procedures by which we effect valuable changes in reality. Thus rhetoric is distinguished from the mere craft of persuasion which, although it is a legitimate object of scientific investigation, lacks philosophical warrant as a practical discipline.

NOTES

[1] "The Problem of Meaning in Primitive Languages," sections III and IV. This essay appears as a supplement in Ogden and Richards' *The Meaning of Meaning*.

EXCERPTS FROM
Rhetorical Criticism: A Study in Method
EDWIN BLACK

THE NEO-ARISTOTELIAN STUDY

By far the dominant mode of rhetorical criticism of the present century in the United States has been neo-Aristotelianism. Of the forty essays on individual speakers included in the three volumes of *A History and Criticism of American Public Address,* fifteen of the studies employ techniques of criticism derived from Aristotle's *Rhetoric.*[27] The proportion of neo-Aristotelian essays becomes even more striking when we note that of the twenty-five essays that remain unaccounted for, some employ only one or two of Aristotle's canons to serve for the entire critical apparatus,[28] some are biographical essays which make little attempt at critical interpretation or appraisal,[29] and some are appreciations, eulogies, or of dubious character.[30] Only eight of the essays attempt an examination and appraisal of rhetorical discourses by the employment of techniques which are singular or which represent unconventional interpretations or applications of traditional rhetoric.[31] It is further noteworthy that the editor of the first two volumes of these studies takes Aristotelian rhetoric as his point of departure in commenting upon the essays,[32] and that the editor of the third volume recommends the Aristotelian definition of rhetoric in her introductory essay,[33] and borrows several of the Aristotelian categories in the critical system she delineates.[34]

Hitchcock's essay on Jonathan Edwards will serve as a clear example of neo-Aristotelian criticism.[35] After arguing that Edwards' rhetorical biography has been neglected and is a needful study, Hitchcock has brief sections on the ethos of colonial Northampton and on Edwards' training and intellectual development. Then there follows the main critical section of the essay. In this critique Hitchcock first enumerates the "doctrines which Edwards preached."[36] He finds eight of them, and is able to convey each of the eight in a single sentence. Hitchcock then proceeds to his topics of criticism. First is organization: "Jonathan Edwards's sermons are highly organized . . . Each is divided broadly into four large sections; the thesis is carefully stated; the discussion is developed in three or four main points; these main points are arranged according to a definite system (the order is usually logical or topical); and each tends to establish the principal thesis; the transitions from one idea to another are smoothly and easily made; frequent summaries occur."[37]

Under the heading "Organization" Hitchcock goes on to discuss the character of Edwards' introductions and conclusions, after having made some additional observations on Edwards' general practices in arranging discourse.

"Types of Proof" is the next topic. "Edwards's argumentative method" is divided into inductive and deductive methods.[38] We are told that "categorical, hypothetical, and disjunctive enthymemes appear in every sermon,"[39] that "argument from authority greatly predominates,"[40] and that "argument by explanation also becomes an important instrument of proof."[41]

Next Hitchcock examines the "emotional approach": "While Edwards uses a great many pathetic arguments, these appeals are, in general, subordinated to the logical elements."[42] "The principal appeals are to fear, shame, desire for happiness, security, and pride. Gratitude, common sense, emulation, greed, and courage receive less emphasis. In appealing to fear, Edwards frequently refers to hell."[43]

"Ethical proof" is examined: "Edwards . . . presented a strong ethical argument. His life was exemplary; he followed a strict moral code; his friends and neighbors thought well of him."[44]

Then style:

> Edwards wrote his sermons in a precise, plain, exact style. Nothing of fine writing or of excessive display creeps into his text. Nor are there classical allusions or other learned references. The language is the language of the audience; it is constantly toned down to the listeners' level. The analogies and comparisons are of an everyday type, apt and exact, yet often the commonest form. The quotations are Biblical and are cited with a matter-of-factness that appealed to the most unlearned listener. Even Edwards's own language has a Biblical flavor. His style can best be described as common and precise, patterned after that of the Scriptures.[45]

After further considerations of "style," Hitchcock concludes with a short section on "methods of preparation and delivery" and one on "effect." In the latter section, Hitchcock is concerned with the effects of Edwards' sermons on his immediate audience.

Enough of Hitchcock's essay has been quoted to disclose his particular merits and defects as a critic. What is important here is the general method of criticism being employed, irrespective of the skill of its particular applications. The general method is what has been designated *neo-Aristotelianism,* and Hitchcock's essay is an especially clear example of it because of the literalness with which the method is applied in this essay and the clarity with which its canons of criticism are invoked.

The primary and identifying ideas of neo-Aristotelianism that we can find recurring in the critical essays of this school are the classification of rhetorical discourses into forensic, deliberative, and epideictic; the classification of "proofs" or "means of persuasion" into logical, pathetic, and ethical; the assessment of discourse in the categories of invention, arrangement, delivery, and style; and the evaluation of rhetorical discourse in terms of its effects on its immediate audience. Each of these ideas is prominent in the Hitchcock essay except for the first. In the case of the tripartite typology of rhetorical discourses, Hitchcock was dealing with a genre—the sermon—that is post-Aristotelian and, consequently, is not easily reconciled with the traditional typology; but even in dealing with this special genre, Hitchcock scrupulously adheres to the conventions of neo-Aristotelianism.

The practice of neo-Aristotelian criticism has received formal statement in an essay first published in 1925. Wichelns' program for rhetorical criticism appeared in a significant paragraph.

> Rhetorical criticism is necessarily analytic. The scheme of a rhetorical study includes the element of the speaker's personality as a conditioning factor; it includes also the public character of the man—not what he was, but what he

was thought to be. It requires a description of the speaker's audience, and of the leading ideas with which he plied his hearers—his topics, the motives to which he appealed, the nature of the proofs he offered. These will reveal his own judgment of human nature in his audiences, and also his judgment on the questions which he discussed. Attention must be paid, too, to the relation of the surviving texts to what was actually uttered: in case the nature of the changes is known, there may be occasion to consider adaptation to two audiences—that which heard and that which read. Nor can rhetorical criticism omit the speaker's mode of arrangement and his mode of expression, nor his habit of preparation and his manner of delivery from the platform; though the last two are perhaps less significant. "Style"—in the sense which corresponds to diction and sentence movement—must receive attention, but only as one among various means that secure for the speaker ready access to the minds of his auditors. Finally, the effect of the discourse on its immediate hearers is not to be ignored, either in the testimony of witnesses, nor in the record of events. And throughout such a study one must conceive of the public man as influencing the men of his own times by the power of his discourse.[46]

Bryant's judgment—that this essay "set the pattern and determined the direction of rhetorical criticism for more than a quarter of a century and has had a greater and more continuous influence upon the development of the scholarship of rhetoric and public address than any other single work published in this century"[47]— suggests that one of the main sources of neo-Aristotelianism may lie in the influence of Wichelns' program of 1925. The elements of analysis recommended in the quoted paragraph could be a compendium of the topics of Aristotle or Cicero: ". . . the public character of the man . . . his topics, the motives to which he appealed, the nature of the proofs he offered . . . the speaker's mode of arrangement and his mode of expression . . . his manner of delivery from the platform . . . diction and sentence movement . . . the effect of the discourse on its immediate hearers."

The uses to which Aristotle can be interpreted as having put these topics is not the present issue. What is pertinent in clarifying neo-Aristotelianism is the fact that these are subjects for discussion in the neo-Aristotelian essay, just as they were subjects for discussion in the *Rhetoric*. Even in its most faithful executions, neo-Aristotelian criticism cannot be certain of serving the purposes of Aristotle's *Rhetoric*. Aristotle has left us with no substantial body of criticism, and we can only conjecture the extent to which, had Aristotle left any, his critical writing would adhere to the principles of the *Rhetoric* or would strictly subordinate rhetorical criticism to logical analysis and political commentary. There may be little that the neo-Aristotelians have in common with Aristotle besides some recurrent topics of discussion and a vaguely derivative view of rhetorical discourse; but even so, these topics and this view may serve to define neo-Aristotelianism.

The view itself must be found behind neo-Aristotelian critiques rather than explicitly stated in them. It is a view which the neo-Aristotelian essays share. The first element of this view is the comprehension of the rhetorical discourse as tactically designed to achieve certain results with a specific audience on a specific occasion. Of the fifteen neo-Aristotelian essays in *A History and Criticism of American Public Address*, only two undertake an appraisal of rhetorical discourse in terms other than its effect on an immediate audience.[48] There is little disposition among neo-Aristotelian critics to comprehend the discourse in a larger context, to see it, as for example the movement study would, as part of a historical process of argument. To the neo-Aristotelian, the discourse is discrete and its relevant effects are immediate.[49]

Another element of the view of rhetorical discourse sustained in neo-Aristotelianism is the close relationship between rhetoric and logic. Perhaps the most striking result of this relationship is the tendency of neo-Aristotelian critics to concentrate on discourses that approach logical demonstration and to eschew the explication of discourses that do not have a demonstrative form. All the subjects of neo-Aristotelian essays in *A History and Criticism of American Public Address* are orators in the genteel tradition. Most of them are of the nineteenth century. The few orators treated in these volumes whose discourses are ill-suited to logical analysis—Patrick Henry, Dwight L. Moody, perhaps William Jennings Bryan—are not subjected to neo-Aristotelian criticism.

Following also from the close relationship between rhetoric and logic, which seems to characterize neo-Aristotelianism, is the tendency to assume the rationality of audiences. The very terms argument and proof are borrowed from logic and are repeatedly employed by neo-Aristotelian critics. Audiences are conceived of as responsive to arguments and proofs; and even "emotional appeals," which appears to be the rubric for persuasive discourse not susceptible to logical explanation, are often conceived of as a type of proof.

In charting the pattern of influence that flows through the rhetorical transaction, the neo-Aristotelian critic typically sees only one direction of movement: the background, training, interests, and aims of the rhetor influence his discourse, which in turn influences the audience. The neo-Aristotelians ignore the impact of the discourse on rhetorical conventions, its capacity for disposing an audience to expect certain ways of arguing and certain kinds of justifications in later discourses that they encounter, even on different subjects. Similarly, the neo-Aristotelian critics do not account for the influence of the discourse on its author: the future commitments it makes for him, rhetorically and ideologically; the choices it closes to him, rhetorically and ideologically; the public image it portrays to which he must adjust.

. . . .

[Editor's note: The preceding excerpt is from Chapter 2, in which Black also discusses two other critical approaches. In Chapter 3 Black analyzes neo-Aristotelian criticism in more detail and concludes that this method fulfills the "historical" function of general criticism, but is severely limited in the "re-creative" and "judicial" functions. Specifically, Black claims, neo-Aristotelian criticism excludes the subjective reactions of the critic and accepts the purposes of the rhetor without question. In this chapter, Black also presents the following case study to illustrate the shortcomings of neo-Aristotelianism.]

A single example can illustrate the point. The "Coatesville Address" by John Jay Chapman, delivered in 1912, is a discourse neo-Aristotelian criticism would be hard pressed to fathom.[62] On August 14, 1911[,] Chapman read in New York City newspapers an account of a particularly brutal lynching of a Negro in Coatesville, Pennsylvania. Although he was not personally associated in any way with the persons or place involved in the atrocity, Chapman brooded on the event.

As the first anniversary of the lynching approached, Chapman announced to his family that he was going to Coatesville to hold a prayer meeting and to deliver a speech commemorating the terrible occasion. In Coatesville Chapman encountered a population suspicious of his motives and growing increasingly sensitive to the approaching anniversary. After frustrating attempts to find a hall in Coatesville suitable for his meeting, Chapman finally succeeded in renting an empty store. He placed advertisements in the local paper, and held his prayer meeting on Sunday, August 18, 1912. The speech was his sermon. He delivered it to an audience of three persons: a lady friend who had accompanied him to Coatesville, an elderly Negro woman, and an unidentified man, believed to be a local spy.[63]

We are met to commemorate the anniversary of one of the most dreadful crimes in history—not for the purpose of condemning it, but to repent for our share in it. We do not start any agitation with regard to that particular crime. I understand that an attempt to prosecute the chief criminals has been made, and has entirely failed; because the whole community, and in a sense our whole people, are really involved in the guilt. The failure of the prosecution in this case, in all such cases, is only a proof of the magnitude of the guilt, and of the awful fact that everyone shares in it.

I will tell you why I am here; I will tell you what happened to me. When I read in the newspapers of August 14, a year ago, about the burning alive of a human being, and of how a few desperate, fiend-minded men had been permitted to torture a man chained to an iron bedstead, burning alive, thrust back by pitchforks when he struggled out of it, while around about stood hundreds of well-dressed American citizens, both from the vicinity and from afar, coming on foot and in wagons, assembling on telephone call, as if by magic, silent, whether from terror or indifference, fascinated and impotent, hundreds of persons watching this awful sight and making no attempt to stay the wickedness, and no one man among them all who was inspired to risk his life in an attempt to stop it, no one man to name the name of Christ, of humanity, of government! As I read the newspaper accounts of the scene enacted here in Coatesville a year ago, I seemed to get a glimpse into the unconscious soul of this country. I saw a seldom revealed picture of the American heart and of the American nature. I seemed to be looking into the heart of the criminal—a cold thing, an awful thing.

I said to myself, "I shall forget this, we shall all forget it; but it will be there. What I have seen is not an illusion. It is the truth. I have seen death in the heart of this people." For to look at the agony of a fellow-being and remain aloof means death in the heart of the onlooker. Religious fanaticism has sometimes lifted men to the frenzy of such cruelty, political passion has sometimes done it, personal hatred might do it, the excitement of the amphitheater in the degenerate days of Roman luxury could do it. But here an audience chosen by chance in America has stood spellbound through an improvised *auto-da-fé*, irregular, illegal, having no religious significance, not sanctioned by custom, having no immediate provocation, the audience standing by merely in cold dislike.

I saw during one moment something beyond all argument in the depth of its significance. You might call it the paralysis of the nerves about the heart in a people habitually and unconsciously given over to selfish aims, an ignorant people who knew not what spectacle they were providing, or what part they were playing in a judgment-play which history was exhibiting on that day.

No theories about the race problem, no statistics, legislation, or mere educational endeavor, can quite meet the lack which that day revealed in the American people. For what we saw was death. The people stood like blighted things, like ghosts about Acheron, waiting for someone or something to determine their destiny for them.

Whatever life itself is, that thing must be replenished in us. The opposite of hate is love, the opposite of cold is heat; what we need is the love of God and reverence for human nature. For one moment I knew that I had seen our true need; and I was afraid that I should forget it and that I should start schemes of education, when the need was deeper than education. And I became filled with one idea, that I must not forget what I had seen, and that I must do something to remember it. And I am here today chiefly that I may remember that vision. It seems fitting to come to this town where the crime occurred and hold a prayer-meeting, so that our hearts may be turned to God through whom mercy may flow into us.

Let me say something more about the whole matter. The subject we are dealing with is not local. The act, to be sure, took place at Coatesville and everyone looked to Coatesville to follow it up. Some months ago I asked a friend who lives not far from here something about this case, and about the expected prosecutions, and he replied to me: "It wasn't in my county," and that made me wonder whose county it was in. And it seemed to be in my county. I live on the Hudson River; but I knew that this great wickedness that happened in Coatesville is not the wickedness of Coatesville nor of today. It is the wickedness of all America and of three hundred years—the wickedness of the slave trade. All of us are tinctured by it. No special place, no special persons, are to blame. A nation cannot practice a course of inhuman crime for three hundred years and then suddenly throw off the effects of it. Less than fifty years ago domestic slavery was abolished among us; and in one way and another the marks of that vice are in our faces. There is no country in Europe where the Coatesville tragedy or anything remotely like it could have been enacted, probably no country in the world.

On the day of the calamity, those people in the automobiles came by the hundred and watched the torture, and passers-by came in a great multitude and watched it—and did nothing. On the next morning the newspapers spread the news and spread the paralysis until the whole country seemed to be helplessly watching this awful murder, as awful as anything ever done on the earth; and the whole of our people seemed to be looking on helplessly, not able to respond, not knowing what to do next. That spectacle has been in my mind.

The trouble has come down to us out of the past. The only reason slavery is wrong is that it is cruel and makes men cruel and leaves them cruel. Someone may say that you and I cannot repent because we did not do the act. But we are involved in it. We are still looking on. Do you not see that this whole event is merely the last parable, the most vivid, the most terrible illustration that ever was given by man or imagined by a Jewish prophet, of the relation between good and evil in this world, and of the relation of men to one another?

This whole matter has been an historic episode; but it is a part, not only of our national history, but of the personal history of each one of us. With the great disease (slavery) came the climax (the war), and after the climax gradually began the cure, and in the process of cure comes now the knowledge of what the evil was. I say that our need is new life, and that books and resolutions will not save us, but only such disposition in our hearts and souls as will enable the new life, love, force, hope, virtue, which surround us always, to enter into us.

This is the discovery that each man must make for himself—the discovery that what he really stands in need of he cannot get for himself, but must wait till God gives it to him. I have felt the impulse to come here today to testify to this truth.

The occasion is not small; the occasion looks back on three centuries and embraces a hemisphere. Yet the occasion is small compared with the truth it leads us to. For this truth touches all ages and affects every soul in the world.

The verdict of neo-Aristotelianism on this speech would have to be negative. It did not fetch results. We do not know whether its hearers were impressed by the speech, but even if they were, their number was too small to matter. Further, the speech does not appear in anthologies of great orations, nor did it receive notice or acclaim after its delivery. But for a recent revival of interest in Chapman's work, it might have remained obscure indefinitely.[64] By any feasible standard of immediate effect, the speech would have to be put down as a failure.

Even the application of the Aristotelian canons cannot save the speech. In structure, the speech does sustain a mood, but there is no unfolding of a strict form. The fourth through the seventh paragraphs could be rearranged in any other order than the order in which they actually occur, and the effect would be the same. The logical supports for arguments are non-existent, as are arguments themselves, in the logical sense. The main thesis, if it can be said to have one—that deliverance from Evil, of which the Coatesville atrocity was an example, can come only from God—is submitted *ex cathedra,* without a shred of proof. The emotional appeals of the speech cannot be accurately described as anger, love, fear, shame, pity, benevolence, indignation, envy, or their opposites. The ethos of the speaker, insofar as the people of Coatesville were concerned, probably consisted of the image of a fanatical crank. Chapman's solitary gesture to his immediate audience—that of seeing the crime as American rather than Coatesvillian—would hardly have been considered comforting to a group who considered themselves Americans as well as Coatesvillians. The style of the speech has the merit of vividness in its description of the lynching, but so did the newspaper accounts of the crime.

One could extend indefinitely the list of formal defects: the introduction that does not placate; the presentation of ideas embarrassing to the audience on a ceremonial occasion; the absence of a specific program or policy; the contravention of patriotic sentiments in discussing America and her people. But why go on? The speech had virtually no immediate audience anyhow, and why bother with a soliloquy that was overheard by three people? And yet, as Edmund Wilson has commented, the speech is "strange and moving."[65]

Moving it is, moving enough so that the bare calculation of its immediate effects is insufficient to account for it, moving enough so that the contemporary reader cannot feel its power as having been spent on that audience of three. The speech is not a cold marble monument. It lives. But to see its life, we must find its proper context.

The context of the Coatesville Address is not the vacant grocery store in 1912. Rather, the discourse must be understood as joining the dialogue participated in by Jefferson, Tocqueville, Lincoln, Melville, Henry Adams, Samuel Clemens, Santayana, and Faulkner—a dialogue on the moral dimension of the American experience. The Coatesville Address is a particularly interesting statement in the dialogue because it is one of the very few of this century that is not cast in the form of fiction.

The context of the Coatesville Address is less a specific place than a culture, but culture in the sense that Lionel Trilling designated: "A culture is not a flow, nor even a confluence; the form of its existence is struggle, or at least debate—it is nothing if not a dialectic."[66] It is a context whose place must be measured by a continent and whose time must be reckoned in centuries. Its direct audience has been and is all of those who are interested in a meaningful interpretation of the history and moral status of this country, and indirectly its audience is all of those who are influenced by the direct audience. This dialogue has not ended, but still continues, and insofar as the model of the United States is increasingly influential in other parts of the world, the potential audience to this dialogue grows larger.

Our warrant for taking the context of the Coatesville Address so broadly is suggested by Chapman himself. The first two paragraphs insistently demand that his auditors focus, not on Coatesville, but on the country. His very first idea is that "our whole people are involved in the guilt." From there he talks of "American citizens . . . of the American heart and of the American nature." Later he makes it explicit: ". . . this great wickedness that happened in Coatesville is not the wickedness of Coatesville nor of today. It is the wickedness of all America and of three hundred years . . ."

So much for context. Next we must consider what the speech actually says. It is, most obviously, an interpretation of an event. The event, of course, is the lynching of the preceding year. Reduced to its manifest essentials, the event is the killing of a Negro by a group of whites. That would be the simplest way of describing it; but hardly anyone then, and hardly anyone now, could perceive the event so simply. Our perceptions of the event will be colored by our moral dispositions. Hence, there would conceivably be those who would perceive the event as a righteous act of vengeful justice; there would be those who would perceive it is a hideous expression of mob violence; there would be those who would perceive it, clinically, as the concrete illustration of an abstract sociopathic idea; there would be those who would refuse to perceive the event at all, who would dismiss it and put it out of mind.

This range of reactions does not exhaust the possibilities. Indeed, the possibilities are, in a sense, inexhaustible, for we must always allow the possibility of someone's perceiving the event with a singular collocation of responses drawn from his personal history; but these are the most conspicuous reactions, and, because they are most conspicuous, they would also probably be the most popular ones. Of these four reactions, we can infer that Chapman regarded the first and last of them as wrong, and the second and third of them as requiring emendation. The function of his speech was to provide this emendation—to shape the appropriate reaction to the event.

We must look to the speech for verification of this inference. Chapman makes no allowance for the defensibility of the first response, which would constitute approval of the event. He does not assume—he probably could not conceive of—an auditor to his speech regarding the event as a righteous act. His description of

the killers—"desperate, fiend-minded men"—and his description of the event—
"burning alive of a human being . . . wickedness . . . the heart of the criminal"—
presuppose disapproval of the event. He who would applaud the event is not a part
of Chapman's audience, by Chapman's own choice.

The fourth of our responses—indifference to the event—is explicitly repudiated
by Chapman: ". . . it seemed to be in my county. . . . It is the wickedness
of all America . . . All of us are tinctured by it . . . it is a part, not only of our
national history, but of the personal history of each one of us." Chapman recognizes
the possibility of an initial reaction of indifference (for example, his friend who
said, "It wasn't in my county"), but Chapman's argument on the national guilt
for the event renders passive indifference impossible. One who, having read his
speech, would remain detached from the event would have to deny his responsibility for the killing, and by the very act of denial he would enter into a relationship with the event. His reaction could not longer be passively indifferent because
his act of denial would itself betoken a connection with the event. Admittedly, it
would be a negative connection—the denial of a connection—but not even this
denial could be made without a focus on the relationship between the auditor and
the event. Chapman's speech forces the auditor to perceive the event and to
examine his own relationship to it; hence, the speech undermines the possibility of
passive indifference.

Of the second and third responses—the outraged response and the clinical
response—Chapman's speech combines and emends the two. We can infer that
neither of these responses is singly acceptable to Chapman. Outrage is unacceptable
because it represents an excess of moral zeal; didacticism is unacceptable because
it represents a deficiency of moral zeal. Chapman's effort is to combine the two
in such a way that the event is perceived with moral color but at the same time
perceived with perspective. We are here confronting a fine and delicate balance
requiring patient exposition.

Let us look more closely at the outraged response. Let us, in fact, consider what
would constitute a case of ideal outrage. Would it not be the case of one who would
seize his own pitchfork and push the killers into the fire? Is not punishment the
characteristic satisfaction of outrage? And further, to be truly satisfying, does not
this punishment have, in some way, to fit the crime—that is, to be as severe in its
way as the crime was? The practical expression of outrage is the invocation of the
Mosaic Law. We need look no further than Coatesville to see the relationship illustrated, for the man who was lynched was suspected of murder. His own murder by
the lynch mob was no more than an equivalent act, and it does not strain our credu-
lity to imagine the Coatesville mob claiming the sanction of justice in the midst
of their sanguinary business. Thus, the outraged response to the Coatesville affair
would be merely a perpetuation of the response that led to the affair in the first
place. Outrage, with its concomitant thirst for revenge, would be morally indistinguishable from the crime itself.

And what of the alternative reaction—the clinical perception of the event as
a concrete illustration of an abstract idea? Here we see another extreme, for this
perception of the event, though it would promote the composure of poised tran-
quility, would approach indifference in its moral concern. The clinical attitude has
no moral counterpart; it paralyzes action. If vengeance is the practical expression of
outrage, then acquiescence is the practical expression of didacticism. And we must

further consider that the very sensibility required by didacticism can be destroyed by it, "for to look at the agony of a fellow-being and remain aloof means death in the heart of the onlooker."

Chapman thus shapes a perception of the lynching that moderates outrage with detachment, moderates it, in fact, so extensively that it is substantively transformed and becomes a reaction for which we have no precise word in English. We do not need a word so long as we have Chapman's speech, for it enables us to experience the reaction. We are his audience.

Chapman would have us perceive the event as a scene in a morality play. The play itself is the history of this country, seen as the death-through-sin and the potential rebirth-through-purification of a whole people. The issues of crime and punishment, of blame and defense, would not shape the auditor's response, just as they do not shape it in a tragic drama. The lynching is seen as a ritual murder, and the appropriate response to it is a religious experience. We are able, through this response, to view the lynching unequivocally as a crime, and yet we do not hate the criminals, for we feel ourselves to be responsible. The net practical effect of the speech on the thoroughly attentive auditor is to make him incapable of lynching— incapable because, instead of being aware of a specific and singular case, he has become aware of the moral nature of lynching. He has, in sum, not simply a moral reaction, but a moral insight.

And how are we to appraise the speech? First, we must reiterate that the speech still lives. That is, it addresses itself to the contemporary auditor. Its point of view is not transitory; it is not a product of the historical moment; it is not a collection of rhetorical tactics. The speech is built upon settled conclusions regarding the nature of men and their world, the history and destiny of a country, and it is this solid foundation that makes for its persistent viability. The speech is a symptom of an intricately moral interpretation of American history. It is the token of a complex of judgments, attitudes, and discriminations so manifested that the auditor is passed beyond the surface of the discourse and confronts its resonant implications. The passage of time, therefore, can only enable the audiences to this speech to appre- hend its ramifications, to discern the range of its applicability, to explicate its complexities and absorb its overtones.

There is also a historical accident—or perhaps it is a historical inevitability—that will work to guarantee its continued life. That is the loss of innocence in America. Chapman's audience is primarily his countrymen, and this audience has grown better able to understand the Coatesville Address since 1912. We have endured two world wars, we have destroyed cities, we have felt the temptations of empire, and we have seen the fall of the god Progress. We are not the innocent children of 1912, and though we may not be wiser than our grandfathers, we are certainly less confi- dent of our rectitude. Hence, it may be that Chapman's Coatesville Address is only just now finding its understanding audience, and it may be that that audience will grow larger and more attentive with every passing day. We can surmise a future for this speech: a future of influence in shaping our perception, not just of a crime committed in 1911, but of the sort of crime for which this century has had a special proclivity.

Moreover, our generation seems to have an appetite for guilt, one that the Coatesville address tends to gratify. The causes of this appetite are obscure, but whatever the reason for it, it is there—so that we are greedy for the books of our alien critics and savor every flagellation, and we brood and debate upon where we went wrong as a nation and what we should do to set things right again. Insofar as the Coatesville Address treats of national guilt, that speech should increasingly find its audience.

And yet another attainment: the speech preserves a morally significant event; it makes it permanent in history—timeless. By shaping a perception, instead of merely re-creating an incident as a newsreel camera might, the speech makes available to the future the experience of a sensitive mind in converse with an objective occurrence that has struck that mind as morally critical. It is through the speech that we know the moral crisis, and by the speech that we are persuaded of it. This, again, is because the speech shapes a perception; it does not neutrally record. In functioning in this way, in conveying an experience that is unique for almost all its auditors and thus opening to them a new possibility for subsequent experience and creating in them a new potentiality for perceiving subsequent events, the speech shares, in its more modest way, a quality of the supreme works of our literature.

Our appraisal of the Coatesville Address must be high. The most convincing gesture of evidence for this appraisal would be to point to the speech. But beyond the speech, confirming our approval, is its capacity for continuing to live as an influence, and for illuminating many of those aspects of our national experience with which we are most concerned.

Finally, there is the strongest confirmation of all: the vision of the fullest rhetorical potentialities of the speech. Insofar as we can imagine an auditor who yields himself completely to its influence, we can see one who would be delivered from the conflict of niggling ideologies. He would be moral without being righteous, passionate without being violent. He would be a reformer of the spirit, whose domain of responsibility would extend to all men everywhere.

It is a tragic irony that the life of John Jay Chapman illustrated the very *harmatia* that he saw most clearly at Coatesville. Four years after the speech was given, Chapman's son was killed in the First World War, and Chapman gave rabid expression to his agony in anti-German pamphlets. Afterwards he slipped into parochialism: Boston and the affairs of Harvard were the center of his universe; anti-Semitism and anti-Catholicism poured out of him, and Chapman, half mad, sank into death, hating. It is Chapman at Coatesville who gives us the measure of his own tragedy, a tragedy wherein the anti-ideologue falls victim to ideology; the man who would transcend hate dies a hater.

We can even see in Chapman's later surrender to vindictiveness how triumphant was his sublimation of it at Coatesville. The tendency toward it was already a strong force in him—other aspects of his life bear this out—and it held for him a terrible attraction, so that the seed of his insight and the seed of his destruction were the same seed. Yet, for a few minutes at least, in a vacant grocery store in an obscure Pennsylvania town, the diverse convictions of John Jay Chapman came together in such a way as to open to him the darker recesses of our society; and his response to that disclosure, as well as the particular convergence of his values that made it possible, are imperishably preserved in his speech.

It will suffice for the present to observe that a system of rhetorical criticism that can give no satisfactory accounting of an excellent work—as neo-Aristotelianism can give no accounting of the Coatesville Address—is seriously compromised as a critical system. And the critic who is obliged by the nature of his theories to yield to the judgment of those who may be less qualified than he to judge little qualifies as a critic so long as he suffers those theories to guide him.

NOTES

[Editor's note: Notes 27–49 appear in Chapter 2, "The Practice of Rhetorical Criticism." Note 27 refers to the following citation: William Norwood Brigance, ed., vols. I & II (New York, 1943); and Marie Kathryn Hochmuth, ed., vol. III, A History and Criticism of American Public Address (New York, 1955).]

---

[27]Brigance and Hochmuth, *op. cit.* The neo-Aristotelian essays are Orville Hitchcock, "Jonathan Edwards," I, pp. 213–237; Roy C. McCall, "Theodore Parker," I, pp. 238–264; Wayland Maxfield Parrish and Alfred Dwight Huston, "Robert G. Ingersoll," I, pp. 363–386; Karl R. Wallace, "Booker T. Washington," I, pp. 407–433; John W. Black, "Rufus Choate," I, pp. 434–458; Charles A. Fritz, "Edwin A. Alderman," II, pp. 540–556; Walter B. Emery, "Samuel Gompers," II, pp. 557–579; Ernest J. Wrage, "Henry Clay," II, pp. 603–638; Herbert L. Curry, "John C. Calhoun," II, pp. 639–664; R. Elaine Pagel and Carl Dallinger, "Charles Sumner," II, pp. 751–775; Carroll P. Lahman, "Robert M. LaFollete," II, pp. 942–967; Dayton David McKean, "Woodrow Wilson," II, pp. 968–992; Bower Aly, "Alexander Hamilton," III, pp. 24–51; Richard Murphy, "Theodore Roosevelt," III, pp. 313–364; Earnest Brandenburg and Waldo W. Braden, "Franklin Delano Roosevelt," III, pp. 458–530.

[28]*Ibid.*, Lester Thonssen, "William M. Evarts," I, pp. 483–500; Louis M. Eich, "Charles W. Eliot," II, pp. 526–539; Forest L. Whan, "Stephen A. Douglas," II, pp. 777–827; Mildred Freburg Berry, "Abraham Lincoln: His Development in the Skills of the Platform," II, pp. 828–858; Robert D. Clark, "Harry Emerson Fosdick," III, pp. 411–457.

[29]*Ibid.*, Willard Hayes Yeager, "Wendell Phillips," I, pp. 329–362; Marvin G. Bauer, "Henry W. Grady," I, pp. 387–406; Louis A. Mallory, "Patrick Henry," II, pp. 580–602; Earl W. Wiley, "Abraham Lincoln: His Emergence as the Voice of the People," II, pp. 859–877; Henry G. Roberts, "James G. Blaine," II, pp. 878–890; Dallas C. Dickey and Donald C. Streeter, "Lucius Q. C. Lamar," III, pp. 175–221.

[30]*Ibid.*, Lionel Crocker, "Henry Ward Beecher," I, pp. 265–293; Rexford S. Mitchell, "William L. Yancy," II, pp. 734–750; Myron G. Phillips, "William Jennings Bryan," II, pp. 891–918; Herold Truslow Ross, "Albert J. Beveridge," II, pp. 919–941; Doris Yoakam Twichell, "Susan B. Anthony," III, pp. 97–132; Robert B. Huber, "Dwight L. Moody," III, pp. 222–261.

[31]*Ibid.*, Marie Hochmuth and Norman Mattis, "Phillips Brooks," I, pp. 294–328; William Norwood Brigance, "Jeremiah S. Black," I, pp. 459–482; Herbert A. Wichelns, "Ralph Waldo Emerson," II, pp. 501–525; Wilbur Samuel Howell and Hoyt Hopewell Hudson, "Daniel Webster," II, pp. 665–733; Norman W. Mattis, "Thomas Hart Benton," III, pp. 52–96; Carroll C. Arnold, "George William Curtis," III, pp. 133–174; Martin Maloney, "Clarence Darrow," III, pp. 262–312; A. E. Whitehead, "William E. Borah," III, pp. 365–410.

[32]*Ibid.*, William Norwood Brigance, "Preface," I, p. x.

[33]*Ibid.*, Marie Kathryn Hochmuth, "The Criticism of Rhetoric," III, pp. 4 and 8.

[34]*Ibid.*, passim.

[35]*Ibid.*, I, pp. 213–237.

[36]*Ibid.*, I, p. 220.

[37]*Ibid.*, I, p. 222.

[38]*Ibid.*, I, p. 223.

[39]*Ibid.*, I, p. 224.

[40]*Ibid.*

[41]*Ibid.*, I, p. 225.

[42]*Ibid.*, I, p. 227.

[43]*Ibid.*, I, p. 227.

[44]*Ibid.*, I, p. 230.

[45]*Ibid.*

[46]Herbert A. Wichelns, "The Literary Criticism of Oratory," *The Rhetorical Idiom. Essays in Rhetoric, Oratory, Language, and Drama,* ed. Donald C. Bryant (Ithaca, N.Y., 1958), pp. 38–39.

[47]Donald C. Bryant, ed., *The Rhetorical Idiom. Essays in Rhetoric, Oratory, Language, and Drama* (Ithaca, N.Y., 1958), p. 5.

[48]The two exceptions are Bower Aly, "Alexander Hamilton," III, pp. 24–51; and Richard Murphy, "Theodore Roosevelt," II, pp. 313–364. Aly attempts to determine Hamilton's "place in the history of oratory" (pp. 49–50); Murphy attempts an assessment of Roosevelt's permanent value as an orator as well as his effectiveness (pp. 359–360).

[49]In this connection, it is instructive to note the series of experimental studies conducted by Hovland and his associates at Yale University: Carl I. Hovland, Irving L. Janis, and Harold H. Kelley, *Communication and Persuasion* (New Haven, 1953); Carl I. Hovland (ed.), *The Order of Presentation in Persuasion* (New Haven, 1957); Carl I. Hovland and Irving L. Janis (ed.), *Personality and Persuasibility* (New Haven, 1959). Insofar as the social scientists focus on discourses rather than on audience reactions to them, they display the same interest as neo-Aristotelian critics in the discreteness of the discourse, and in its immediate effects. Cf. *Communication and Persuasion,* pp. 56–130; and all of *The Order of Presentation in Persuasion.* Moreover, they have the same tendency as neo-Aristotelian critics to fragment the discourse and to investigate its constituents as independent variables. The approach of the Hovland group, of course, is necessitated by the technical demands of the experimental method rather than by a commitment to a critical system; however, the approaches to the rhetorical discourse are sufficiently similar so that the data unearthed by the Yale investigators could, with a minimum of mediation, directly inform neo-Aristotelianism.

The Yale studies of audiences, *Communication and Persuasion,* pp. 134–265, and all of *Personality and Persuasibility,* are in a different category. Enlisting the resources of psychology for the measurement of personality, learning, and intelligence, and relating these factors to persuasibility, these investigations have relevance to any conceivable system of rhetorical criticism and, indeed, are in the area in which rhetorical criticism must rely heavily on the findings of the social sciences.

. . . .

[Editor's note: Notes 62–66 appear in Chapter 3, "Rhetoric and General Criticism."]

[62]This speech has been reprinted in *American Issues,* ed. Edwin Black and Harry P. Kerr (New York, 1961), pp. 111–114.

[63]Mark A. DeWolf Howe, *John Jay Chapman and His Letters* (Boston 1937), p. 219.

[64]The speech is given a paragraph's attention by Edmund Wilson in *The Triple Thinkers* (New York, 1948), p. 159. It is reported on but not reprinted in full in Howe's biography, *op. cit.,* pp. 473–475. I can find no other commentary on the speech.

[65]*Ibid.*

[66]Lionel Trilling, "Reality in America," *Literary Opinion in America,* ed. Morton Dauwen Zabel, 3rd ed., rev. (New York and Evanston, Ill. 1962), p. 40.

THE SECOND PERSONA

EDWIN BLACK

The moral evaluation of rhetorical discourse is a subject that receives and merits attention. It is not necessary to dwell on why rhetorical critics tend to evade moral judgments in their criticism, or on why the whole subject has the forbiddingly suspicious quality of a half-hidden scandal. Suffice it to note that the motives for doubting the enterprise are not frivolous ones. Most of us understand that the moral judgment of a text is a portentous act in the process of criticism, and that the terminal character of such a judgment works to close critical discussion rather than open or encourage it.

Moral judgments, however balanced, however elaborately qualified, are none-theless categorical. Once rendered, they shape decisively one's relationship to the object judged. They compel, as forcefully as the mind can be compelled, a manner of apprehending an object. Moral judgments coerce one's perceptions of things. It is perhaps for these reasons that critics are on the whole diffident about pronouncing moral appraisals of the discourses they criticize. They prefer keeping their options open; they prefer allowing free play to their own perceptual instruments; they prefer investigating to issuing dicta. These are preferences that strongly commend them-selves, for they are no less than the scruples of liberal scholarship.

Nevertheless there is something acutely unsatisfying about criticism that stops short of appraisal. It is not so much that we crave magistracy as that we require order, and the judicial phase of criticism is a way of bringing order to our history.

History is a long, long time. Its raw material is an awesome garbage heap of facts, and even the man who aspires to be nothing more than a simple chronicler still must make decisions about perspective. It is through moral judgments that we sort out our past, that we coax the networks and the continuities out of what has come before, that we disclose the precursive patterns that may in turn present them-selves to us as potentialities, and thus extend our very freedom. Even so limited a quest as conceiving a history of public address requires the sort of ordering and apportioning that must inevitably be infected with moral values. The hand that would shape a "usable past" can grasp only fragments of the world, and the prin-ciples by which it makes its selections are bound to have moral significance.

The technical difficulty of making moral judgments of rhetorical discourses is that we are accustomed to thinking of discourses as objects, and we are not equipped to render moral judgments of objects. Ever since Prometheus taught us hubris, we in the West have regarded objects as our own instruments, latent or actual, and we have insisted that an instrument is a perfectly neutral thing, that it is solely the use to which the instrument is put that can enlist our moral interest. And it was, of course, the ubiquitous Aristotle who firmly placed rhetoric into the instrumental category.[1] Thanks in part to that influence, we are to this day disposed to regard discourses as objects, and to evaluate them, if at all, according to what is done with them. If the demagogue inflames his audience to rancor, or the prophet exalts their consciousness, in either case we allow ourselves a judgment, but the judgment is of consequences, real or supposed. We do not appraise the discourse in itself except in a technical or prudential way. Our moral judgments are reserved for men and their deeds, and appropriately the literature of moral philosophy is bent toward those subjects. My purpose here is by no means to challenge this arrangement. Instead,

I propose exploring the hypothesis that if students of communication could more proficiently explicate the saliently human dimensions of a discourse—if we could, in a sense, discover for a complex linguistic formulation a corresponding form of character—we should then be able to subsume that discourse under a moral order and thus satisfy our obligation to history.

This aspiration may seem excessively grand until we remember that we have been at least playing about its fringes for a long time in criticism. The persistent and recurrently fashionable interest among rhetorical and literary critics in the relationship between a text and its author is a specific expression of the sort of general interest embodied in the hypothesis. Despite our disputes over whether the Intentional Fallacy is really a fallacy, despite our perplexities over the uses of psychoanalysis in criticism and the evidentiary problems they present, despite even the difficulties posed the critic by the phenomenon of ghost writing, where the very identity of the author may be elusive, we still are inclined to recognize, as our predecessors have for many centuries, that language has a symptomatic function. Discourses contain tokens of their authors. Discourses are, directly or in a transmuted form, the external signs of internal states. In short, we accept it as true that a discourse implies an author, and we mean by that more than the tautology that an act entails an agent. We mean, more specifically, that certain features of a linguistic act entail certain characteristics of the language user.

The classic formulation of this position is, of course, in the *Rhetoric* and the *Poetics*. There we find the claim developed that a speech or set of speeches, constituting either the literal discourse of a public man or the lines associated with a role in a play, reveal two dimensions of character: the moral and the intellectual. It is common knowledge that the discussion of moral character—ethos—in the *Rhetoric* is for many reasons an intriguing account, that the discussion of intellectual character—dianoia—which appears mainly in the *Poetics* is cryptic and evidently incomplete in the form in which we have it, and that there are ample textual hints that we are to take ethos and dianoia as distinguishable but complementary constituents of the same thing. They are aspects of the psyche. In a play their tokens suggest to the audience the psyche of a character. In a speech they suggest the speaker.

It is also common knowledge that today we are not inclined to talk about the discursive symptoms of character in quite the way men did in Aristotle's time. We are more skeptical about the veracity of the representation; we are more conscious that there may be a disparity between the man and his image; we have, in a sense, less trust. Wayne Booth, among others, has illuminated the distinction between the real author of a work and the author implied by the work, noting that there may be few similarities between the two, and this distinction better comports than does the classical account with our modern sense of how discourses work.[2] We have learned to keep continuously before us the possibility, and in some cases the probability, that the author implied by the discourse is an artificial creation: a persona, but not necessarily a person. A fine illustration of this kind of sensibility appears in a report on the 1968 Republican convention by Gore Vidal:

> Ronald Reagan is a well-preserved not young man. Close-to, the painted face is webbed with delicate lines while the dyed hair, eyebrows, and the eyelashes contrast oddly with the sagging muscle beneath the as yet unlifted chin, soft earnest of wattle soon-to-be. The effect, in repose, suggests the work of a skillful embalmer. Animated, the face is quite attractive and at a distance

youthful, particularly engaging is the crooked smile full of large porcelain-capped teeth. The eyes are the only interesting feature: small, narrow, apparently dark, they glitter in the hot light. . . .[3]

Note that last twist of the knife: the eyes are *apparently* dark." Not even the windows of the soul can quite be trusted, thanks to optometry.

The Vidal description is more nearly a kind of journalism than a kind of criticism, but its thrust is clearly illustrative of the distinction we have become accustomed to making—the distinction between the man and the image, between reality and illusion. And we have to acknowledge that in an age when seventy percent of the population of this country lives in a preprocessed environment, when our main connection with a larger world consists of shadows on a pane of glass, when our politics seems at times a public nightmare privately dreamed, we have, to say the least, some adjustments to make in the ancient doctrine of ethical proof. But however revised, we know that the concept amounts to something, that the implied author of a discourse is a persona that figures importantly in rhetorical transactions.

What equally well solicits our attention is that there is a second persona also implied by a discourse, and that persona is its implied auditor. This notion is not a novel one, but its uses to criticism deserve more attention.

In the classical theories of rhetoric the implied auditor—this second persona—is but cursorily treated. We are told that he is sometimes sitting in judgment of the past, sometimes of the present, and sometimes of the future, depending on whether the discourse is forensic, epideictic, or deliberative.[4] We are informed too that a discourse may imply an elderly auditor or a youthful one.[5] More recently we have learned that the second persona may be favorably or unfavorably disposed toward the thesis of the discourse, or he may have a neutral attitude toward it.[6]

These typologies have been presented as a way of classifying real audiences. They are what has been yielded when theorists focused on the relationship between a discourse and some specific group responding to it. And we, of course, convert these typologies to another use when we think of them as applying to implied auditors. That application does not focus on a relationship between a discourse and an actual auditor. It focuses instead on the discourse alone, and extracts from it the audience it implies. The commonest manifestation of this orientation is that we adopt when we examine a discourse and say of it, for example, "This is designed for a hostile audience." We would be claiming nothing about those who attended the discourse. Indeed, perhaps our statement concerns a closet speech, known to no one except ourselves as critics and its author. But we are able nonetheless to observe the sort of audience that would be appropriate to it. We would have derived from the discourse a hypothetical construct that is the implied auditor.

One more observation must be made about these traditional audience typologies before we leave them. It is that one must be struck by their poverty. No doubt they are leads into sometimes useful observations, but even after one has noted of a discourse that it implies an auditor who is old, uncommitted, and sitting in judgment of the past, one has left to say—well, everything.

Especially must we note what is important in characterizing personae. It is not age or temperament or even discrete attitude. It is ideology—ideology in the sense that Marx used the term: the network of interconnected convictions that functions in a man epistemically and that shapes his identity by determining how he views the world.

Quite clearly we have had raging in the West at least since the Reformation a febrile combat of ideologies, each tending to generate its own idiom of discourse, each tending to have decisive effects on the psychological character of its adherents. While in ages past men living in the tribal warmth of the *polis* had the essential nature of the world determined for them in their communal heritage of mytho-poesis, and they were able then to assess the probity of utterance by reference to its mimetic relationship to the stable reality that undergirded their consciousness, there is now but the rending of change and the clamor of competing fictions. The elegant trope of Heraclitus has become the delirium of politics. Thus is philosophy democratized.

It is this perspective on ideology that may inform our attention to the auditor implied by the discourse. It seems a useful methodological assumption to hold that rhetorical discourses, either singly or cumulatively in a persuasive movement, will imply an auditor, and that in most cases the implication will be sufficiently sugges-tive as to enable the critic to link this implied auditor to an ideology. The best evidence in the discourse for this implication will be the substantive claims that are made, but the most likely evidence available will be in the form of stylistic tokens. For example, if the thesis of a discourse is that the communists have infiltrated the Supreme Court and the universities, its ideological bent would be obvious. However[,] even if a discourse made neutral and in[n]ocuous claims, but contained the term "bleeding hearts" to refer to proponents of welfare legislation, one would be justified in suspecting that a general attitude—more, a whole set of general atti-tudes were being summoned, for the term is only used tendentiously and it can no more blend with a noncommittal context than a spirochete can be domesticated.

The expectation that a verbal token of ideology can be taken as implying an auditor who shares that ideology is something more than a hypothesis about a relationship. It rather should be viewed as expressing a vector of influence. These sometimes modest tokens indeed tend to fulfill themselves in that way. Actual audi-tors look to the discourse they are attending for cues that tell them how they are to view the world, even beyond the expressed concerns, the overt propositional sense, of the discourse. Let the rhetor, for example, who is talking about school integra-tion use a pejorative term to refer to black people, and the auditor is confronted with more than a decision about school integration. He is confronted with a plexus of attitudes that may not at all be discussed in the discourse or even implied in any way other than the use of the single term. The discourse will exert on him the pull of an ideology. It will move, unless he rejects it, to structure his experience on many subjects besides school integration. And more, if the auditor himself begins using the pejorative term, it will be a fallible sign that he has adopted not just a position on school integration, but an ideology.

Each one of us, after all, defines himself by what he believes and does. Few of us are born to grow into an identity that was incipiently structured before our births. That was, centuries ago, the way with men, but it certainly is not with us. The quest for identity is the modern pilgrimage. And we look to one another for hints as to whom we should become. Perhaps these reflections do not apply to everyone, but they do apply to the persuasible, and that makes them germane to rhetoric.

The critic can see in the auditor implied by a discourse a model of what the rhetor would have his real auditor become. What the critic can find projected by the discourse is the image of a man, and though that man may never find actual embodiment, it is still a man that the image is of. This condition makes moral judgment possible, and it is at this point in the process of criticism that it can illuminatingly be rendered. We know how to make appraisals of men. We know how to evaluate potentialities of character. We are compelled to do so for ourselves constantly. And this sort of judgment, when fully ramified, constitutes a definitive act of judicial criticism.

A PARADIGM

Since a scruple of rationality mandates that claims be warranted, and since the most convincing sanction of a critical position is its efficacy, we turn now to a test. That test will be an essay in the original sense of the word: a trial, an attempt, an exploration. The subject of the essay is a small but recurrent characteristic of discourses associated with the Radical Right in contemporary American politics. That characteristic is the metaphor, "the cancer of communism."

The phrase, "the cancer of communism," is a familiar one. Indeed, it may be so familiar as to approach the condition of a dead metaphor, a cliche. What is less familiar is that this metaphor seems to have become the exclusive property of spokesmen for the Radical Right. Although speakers and writers who clearly are unsympathetic to the Right do sometimes use "cancer" as the vehicle of metaphors, the whole communism-as-cancer metaphor simply is not present in "liberal" or Leftist discourses.[7] Yet it seems to crop up constantly among Rightists—Rightists who sometimes have little else in common besides a political position and the metaphor itself. Perhaps the best source of illustration of the metaphor is the Holy Writ of the John Birch Society, *The Blue Book* by Robert Welch. More than most of his compatriots, Welch really relishes the metaphor. He does not simply sprinkle his pages with it, as for example does Billy James Hargis. Welch amplifies the figure; he expands it; he returns to it again and again. For example: ". . . every thinking and informed man senses that, even as cunning, as ruthless, and as determined as are the activists whom we call Communists with a capital 'C', the conspiracy could never have reached its present extensiveness, and the gangsters at the head of it could never have reached their present power, unless there were tremendous weaknesses to make the advance of such a disease so rapid and its ravages so disastrous."[8] And again: "An individual human being may die of any number of causes. But if he escapes the fortuitous diseases, does not meet with any fatal accident, does not starve to death, does not have his heart give out, but lives in normal health to his three score years and ten and then keeps on living—if he escapes or survives everything else and keeps on doing so, he will eventually succumb to the degenerative disease of cancer. For death must come, and cancer is merely death coming by stages, instead of all at once. And exactly the same thing seems to be true of those organic aggregations of human beings, which we called cultures or civilizations."[9] And again: ". . . collectivism destroys the value to the organism of the individual cells—that is, the individual human beings—without replacing them with new ones with new strength. The Roman Empire of the West, for instance, started dying from the cancer of collectivism from the time Diocletian imposed on it his New Deal."[10] And again: "Until now, there is a tremendous question whether, even if we did not have the Communist conspirators deliberately helping to spread the virus for their own purposes, we could recover from just the natural demagogue-fed spread of that virus when it is already so far advanced."[11] And again: "We have got to stop the Communists, for many reasons. One reason is to keep them from agitating our cancerous tissues, reimplanting the virus, and working to spread it, so that we never have a chance of recovery."[12] And finally: "Push the Communists back, get out of the bed of a Europe that is dying with this cancer of collectivism, and breathe our own healthy air of opportunity, enterprise, and freedom; then the cancer we already have, even though it is of considerable growth can be cut out."[13]

There are other examples to be taken from Welch's book, but we have a sample sufficient for our biopsy. Welch, of course, is an extreme case even for the Radical Right. He cultivates the metaphor with the fixity of a true connoisseur. But though the metaphor is not present in the discourses of all Rightists, it seems almost never to appear in the discourses of non-Rightists. It is the idiomatic token of an ideology, the fallible sign of a frame of reference, and it is what we essay to explore.

This metaphor is not the only idiomatic token of American right[-]wing ideology. There is, to name another, the inventory of perished civilizations that crops up in discourses that are right of center. It is a topos that goes a long way back into our history, and that has evidently been associated with a Rightist orientation for more than a century. Perry Miller, writing of the political conservatism of nineteenth-century revivalism, notes of a sermon delivered in 1841 that it "called the roll . . . of the great kingdoms which had perished—Chaldea, Egypt, Greece, Rome—but gave America the chance, unique in history, of escaping the treadmill to oblivion if it would only adhere to the conserving Christianity. In the same year, George Cheever, yielding himself to what had in literature and painting become . . . a strangely popular theme in the midst of American progress, told how he had stood beneath the walls of the Colosseum, of the Parthenon, of Karnak, and 'read the proofs of God's veracity in the vestiges at once of such stupendous glory and such a stupendous overthrow.'"[14] Miller goes on to observe, "William Williams delivered in 1843 a discourse entitled 'The Conservative Principle,' and Charles White one in 1852 more specifically named 'The Conservative Element in Christianity.' These are merely examples of hundreds in the same vein all calling attention to how previous empires had perished because they had relied entirely upon the intellect, upon 'Political Economy,' and upon 'false liberalism.'"[15]

That topos is with us yet, and it is almost as much a recurrent feature of Rightist discourse as the communism-as-cancer figure. Both the topos and the metaphor are examples of an idiomatic token of ideology.

Regarding the communism-as-cancer metaphor, it could make considerable difference to critical analysis whether a preoccupation with or morbid fear of cancer had any psychopathological significance, whether such a fear had been identified by psychiatrists as a symptom of sufficient frequency as to have been systematically investigated and associated with any particular psychological condition. If that were the case—if psychiatry had a "line" of any kind on this symptom—such clinical information could be applicable in some way to those people who are affected by the communism-as-cancer metaphor. Moreover, if an obsessive fear of cancer were the symptom of an acknowledged and recognizable psychological condition, the tendency of Rightist discourse to cultivate this fear may work to induce in its auditors some form of that psychological condition. Such would be the enticing prospects of a marriage between science and criticism, but unfortunately both psychiatry and clinical psychology are frigid inamoratas, for the literature of neither recognizes such a symptom. It remains, then, for the critic alone to make what sense he can of the metaphor:

1) Cancer is a kind of horrible pregnancy. It is not an invasion of the body by alien organisms, which is itself a metaphor of war, and therefore suitable to the purposes of the Radical Right. Nor is it the malfunction of one of the body's organs—a mechanical metaphor. The actual affliction may, of course, be related to either or both of these; that is, some kinds of cancer may in fact be produced by a virus (invasion), or they may be the result of the body's failure to produce

cancer-rejecting chemicals (malfunction), but these are only the hypotheses of some medical researchers, and not associated with the popular conception of cancer. Cancer is conceived as a growth of some group of the body's own cells. The cancer is a part of oneself, a sinister and homicidal extension of one's own body. And one's attitude toward one's body is bound up with one's attitude toward cancer; more so than in the case of invasions or malfunctions, for neither of these is an extension of oneself. It is a living and unconscious malignancy that the body itself has created, in indifference to, even defiance of, the conscious will. And because one's attitude toward one's body is bound up with one's attitude toward cancer, we may suspect that a metaphor that employed cancer as its vehicle would have a particular resonance for an auditor who was ambivalent about his own body. We may suspect, in fact, that the metaphor would strike a special fire with a congeries of more generally puritanical attitudes.

2) In the popular imagination, cancer is thought to be incurable. Now this is a curious aspect of the metaphor. If the metaphor serves to convey the gravity, agony, and malignancy of communism, why would it not convey also its inexorability, and thus promote in the auditor a terror that robs him of the will to resist? That consequence would seem to be contrary to the Rightist's objectives. Why, then, is the metaphor not excessive?

Some auditors possibly are affected by the metaphor or understand it in this way—that is, as a metaphor conveying not just the horror of communism but also the inevitability of its triumph. Hence, Rightists seem less inhibited by the fear of nuclear war than others. Perhaps there is associated with this metaphor not a different estimate of the probable effects of nuclear war, but rather a conviction that the body-politic is already doomed, so that its preservation—the preservation of an organism already ravaged and fast expiring—is not really important.

We must understand the *Weltansicht* with which the metaphor is associated. The world is not a place where one lives in an enclave of political well-being with a relatively remote enemy approaching. No, the enemy is here and his conquests surround one. To the Rightist, communism is not just in Russia or China or North Vietnam. It is also in the local newspaper; it is in the magazines on the newsstand; it is in television and the movies; it has permeated the government at all levels; it may even be in the house next door. We understand well enough that when the Rightist speaks of communism he refers to virtually all social welfare and civil rights legislation. What we understand less well is that when he refers to America, he refers to a polity already in the advanced stages of an inexorable disease whose suppurating sores are everywhere manifest and whose voice is a death rattle.

And what organs of this afflicted body need be spared amputation? The country is deathly ill. Its policies are cowardly; its spokesmen are treasonous; its cities are anarchical; its discipline is flaccid; its poor are arrogant; its rich are greedy; its courts are unjust; its universities are mendacious. True there is a chance of salvation—of cure, but the chance is a slight one, and every moment diminishes it. The patient is *in extremis*. It is in this light that risks must be calculated, and in this light the prospect of nuclear war becomes thinkable. Why not chance it, after all? What alternative is there? The patient is dying; is it not time for the ultimate surgery? What is there to lose? In such a context, an unalarmed attitude toward the use of atomic weapons is not just reasonable; it is obvious.

3) The metaphor seems related to an organismic view of the state. The polity is a living creature, susceptible to disease; a creature with a will, with a consciousness of itself, with a metabolism and a personality, with a life. The polity is a great

beast: a beast that first must be cured, and then must be tamed. The question arises, what is the nature of other organisms if the state itself is one? What is the individual if he is a cell in the body-politic? Contrary to what one might expect, we know that the Rightist places great emphasis on individualism, at least verbally. Recall, for example, Goldwater's often used phrase, "the whole man," from the 1964 campaign.[16] It is true, the Rightist is suspicious of beards, of unconventional dress, of colorful styles of living. He has antipathy for deviance from a fairly narrow norm of art, politics, sex, or religion, so that his endorsement of individualism has about it the aura of a self-indulgent hypocrisy. Nonetheless, there is something of great value to him that he calls individualism, and if we would understand him, we must understand what he means by individualism. He probably acts consistent with his own use of the term.

It appears that when the Rightist refers to individualism, he is referring to the acquisition and possession of property. Individualism is the right to get and to spend without interference, and this is an important right because a man asserts himself in his possessions. What he owns is what he has to say. So conceived, individualism is perfectly compatible with an organismic conception of the polity. And moreover, the polity's own hideous possession—its tumor—is an expression of its corruption.

4) At first glance the metaphor seems to place communism in the category of natural phenomena. If one does not create a cancer, then one cannot be responsible for it, and if communism is a kind of cancer, then it would seem that one cannot develop a moral attitude toward its agents. This would constitute a difficulty with the metaphor only if people behaved rationally. Fortunately for the metaphor—and unfortunately for us—there is a demonstrable pervasive and utterly irrational attitude toward cancer that saves the metaphor from difficulty. Morton Bard, a psychologist who investigated the psychological reactions of a hundred patients at Memorial Sloan-Kettering Cancer Center, found that forty-eight of them spontaneously expressed beliefs about the cause of their illness that assigned culpability either to themselves or to others or to some supernatural agent.[17] His study suggests, in other words, that an extraordinarily high proportion of people who have cancer—or for our purposes it may be better to say *who become convinced* that they have cancer—are disposed to blame the cancer on a morally responsible agent. Surely it is no great leap from this study to the suspicion that an auditor who is responsive to the metaphor would likely be just the sort of person who would seek culpability. The link between responsiveness to the metaphor and the disposition to seek culpability lies, perhaps, in religious fundamentalism. Various studies indicate that the members of Radical Right organizations tend also to be affiliated with fundamentalist religious sects.[18] Surely it is possible that a life-time of reverent attention to sermons that seek a purpose behind the universe can end by developing a telic cast of mind, can end by inducing some people to seek purpose and plan behind everything, so that they must explain political misfortunes and illnesses alike by hypothesizing conspiracies.

5) Cancer is probably the most terrifying affliction that is popularly known. So terrible is it, in fact, that medical authorities have reported difficulty in inducing people to submit to physical examinations designed to detect cancer. For many, it seems, cancer has become unthinkable—so horrifying to contemplate that one cannot even admit the possibility of having it. The concept of cancer is intimately connected with the concept of death itself. Thus, to equate communism with cancer is to take an ultimately implacable position. One would not quit the struggle against

death except in two circumstances: either one acknowledged its futility and surrendered in despair, or one transmuted the death-concept into a life-concept through an act of religious faith.

Given the equation, communism = cancer = death, we may expect that those enamored of the metaphor would, in the face of really proximate "communism," tend either to despairing acts of suicide or to the fervent embrace of communism as an avenue to grace. The former, suicidal tendency is already discernible in some Rightist political programs, for example, the casual attitude toward nuclear warfare that has already been remarked in another connection. If it were possible for a communist agency to increase its pressure on the United States, we could expect to see the latter tendency increasing, with some of our most impassioned Rightists moving with equal passion to the Left. John Burnham, Elizabeth Bentley, Whitaker Chambers, and others famous from the decade of the fifties for having abandoned the Communist Party have already traveled that road in the opposite direction. The path clearly is there to be trod.

6) Finally, we may note the impressive measure of guilt that seems to be associated with the metaphor. The organism of which one is a cell is afflicted with a culpable illness. Can the whole be infected and the part entirely well?

As the Archbishop in the second part of *Henry IV* says in the midst of political upheaval:

> . . . we are all diseas'd;
> And with our surfeiting and wanton hours
> Have brought ourselves into a burning fever
> And we must bleed for it . . .

The guilt is there. Coherence demands it, and the discourse confirms it. It finds expression in all the classic patterns: the zealous righteousness, the suspiciousness, the morbidity, the feverish expiations. The condition suits the metaphor; the metaphor, the condition.[19]

What moral judgment may we make of this metaphor and of discourse that importantly contains it? The judgment seems superfluous, not because it is elusive, but because it is so clearly implied. The form of consciousness to which the metaphor is attached is not one that commends itself. It is not one that a reasonable man would freely choose, and he would not choose it because it does not compensate him with either prudential efficacy or spiritual solace for the anguished exactions it demands.

In discourse of the Radical Right, as in all rhetorical discourse, we can find enticements not simply to believe something, but to *be* something. We are solicited by the discourse to fulfill its brandishments with our very selves. And it is this dimension of rhetorical discourse that leads us finally to moral judgment, and in this specific case, to adverse judgment.

If our exploration has revealed anything, it is how exceedingly well the metaphor of communism-as-cancer fits the Rightist ideology. The two are not merely compatible; they are complementary at every curve and angle. They serve one another at a variety of levels; they meet in a seamless jointure. This relationship, if it holds for all or even many such stylistic tokens, suggests that the association between an idiom and an ideology is much more than a matter of arbitrary convention or inexplicable accident. It suggests that there are strong and multifarious links between a style and an outlook, and that the critic may, with legitimate confidence, move from the manifest evidence of style to the human personality that this evidence projects as a beckoning archetype.

NOTES

[1]Aristotle, *Rhetoric,* 1355a–b.

[2]Wayne C. Booth, *The Rhetoric of Fiction* (Chicago, 1961), esp. Part II, "The Author's Voice in Fiction."

[3]"The Late Show," *The New York Review of Books,* XI (September 12, 1968), 5.

[4]Aristotle, Book I, Ch. 3.

[5]Aristotle, Book II, Chs. 12–13.

[6]See for example Irving L. Janis, Carl I. Hovland, *et al., Personality and Persuasibility* (New Haven, 1959), esp. pp. 29–54.

[7]Norman Mailer, for example, has lately been making "cancer" and ["]malignancy" the vehicles of frequent metaphors, but the tenor of these metaphors, usually implied, seems to be something like "the dehumanization that results from technological society." It clearly is not "communism," although Soviet society is not exempt from Mailer's condemnations. One can also find occasional references to the "cancer of racism" among left-of-center spokesmen, but these references seem to be no more than occasional. Where, as in Mailer, cancer is a frequently recurring metaphorical vehicle, the analysis that follows may, with appropriate substitution of tenors, be applied. In Mailer's case, at least, it works.

[8]Robert Welch, *The Blue Book of the John Birch Society* (Belmont, Mass., 1961), p. 41.

[9]*Ibid.,* p. 45.

[10]*Ibid.,* p. 46.

[11]*Ibid.,* pp. 53–54.

[12]*Ibid.,* p. 55.

[13]*Ibid.*

[14]*The Life of the Mind in America* (New York, 1965), pp. 70–71.

[15]*Ibid.,* p. 71.

[16]For example, roughly the last third of Goldwater's speech accepting the Republican nomination in 1964 was a panegyric to individuality and nonconformity.

[17]"The Price of Survival for Cancer Victims," *Trans-action,* III (March/April 1966), 11.

[18]See, for example *The Radical Right,* ed. Daniel Bell (Garden City, N. Y., 1964), esp. Seymour Martin Lipset, "Three Decades of the Radical Right: Coughlinites, McCarthyites, and Birchers (1962)," pp. 373–446.

[19]Some illuminating comments on the component of guilt in Rightist style and ideology can be found in Richard Hofstadter, "The Paranoid Style in American Politics," *The Paranoid Style in American Politics and Other Essays* (New York, 1967), esp. pp. 30–32.

THE IDEOLOGICAL TURN IN MODERN CRITICISM

PHILIP WANDER

[Rhetoric and ideology limit choices and guide the decisions of men.] For men are influenced in their use of the powers they possess by the rhetoric they feel they must employ and by the ideological coin in which they transact affairs with one another. The leaders as well as the led, even the hired mythmakers and hack apologists, are influenced by their own rhetoric of justification and by the ideological consolidation that prevails.

C. Wright Mills[1]

Ideology does not represent another tec[h]nique, a new approach to criticism embedded in some mysterious European intellectual tradition. First introduced by French revolutionaries, "ideology" referred to the critical study of ideas.

Napoleon, annoyed by attacks on his policies and the myths used to justify them, contrasted ideology with knowledge of the heart and the lessons of history. Ideologues, in his view, were mere intellectuals, impractical thinkers with subversive impulses. Marx appropriated the term and used it to mean the ruling ideas of the ruling class. He stressed the connection between established economic interests and the spiritual formulations in law, religion, and philosophy growing out of them and working in their favor. In the twentieth century, critical theorists, those associated with the Frankfurt school of sociology, noting that even "Marxism" can be exploited in defense of an established order, used the term to designate the lack of totality or completeness in any attempt to generalize. Ideology, in this view, encompasses not only the partiality or "party" interest in any formulation but also the connection between what is embraced or concealed and the interests served by a particular formulation.[2]

While one may intone a phrase like "ideological view" with a solemn and mysterious look, it represents little more than robust common sense—scepticism not as a way of life, but as a leavening making its way among high sounding ideals, innocence, and hype. No credo, however lyrical, authentically expressed, or truly believed, should escape cross-examination. This sounds fair enough, especially when applied to other people's rhetoric, but it can be disconcerting when taken seriously. In an academic context, for example, an ideological critique would bore in, at some point, on the connection between what scholars in a given field call "knowledge," even "scientific" knowledge, and professional interest. It would confront ideals professed with what they obscure in either theory or practice in light of the possibilities for real or "emancipatory" change.[3]

It is in this light that I would like to reconsider the work of Herbert Wichelns and Kenneth Burke; reexamine a dispute which took place during the war in Vietnam over the nature of criticism; and respond to an effort, grounded in the work of Martin Heidegger, to free criticism once and for all from ideological concerns. Out of all this, I hope, we will get some glimmerings about method and purpose in criticism.

AN IDEOLOGICAL VIEW: WICHELNS AND BURKE

The partiality of a world view, body of belief, or universe of discourse may reveal itself only after painstaking analysis; or it may be affirmed openly. In the case of Herbert Wichelns' 1925 essay, "The Literary Criticism of Oratory,"[4] the implications for academic politics were subtle—there was at the time no "field" as we think of it—while political commitments in the public space were spelled out. The title of the essay, in a university system dominated by departments of English and favoring the study of literature, performed a delicate maneuver. It not only claimed a new body of discourse (oratory) for literary criticism, but it also established for the student of speeches a new type of criticism, coordinate with literary criticism, for which the generic label of "public address" was appropriate.[5] In this way, Wichelns legitimized the study of speeches and, in his defense of the importance of oratory in American and English history, the teaching of public speaking, both its production and its interpretation, to college students. Barely a generation after the last great wave of immigration in this country, this group included students from non-English speaking families who would benefit from learning about America's political traditions as well as students who would, as leaders in society, have to cope with this politically disturbing population.

Wichelns was writing only five years after the Palmer raids, when politically suspect immigrants (anarchists and communists) were being rounded up, over six thousand deported without trial, and tens of thousands more set to be arrested;[6] he was commending the educational importance of studying the classics of American and English oratory—the works of Webster, Lincoln, Gladstone, Bright, Cobden, and Burke. There is no need, I think, to place a sinister interpretation on these facts. We know that Cornell's faculty during this period considered topics such as political speaking in Scandinavian countries, French and American eulogies, Negro eloquence, agitation, as well as patriotic oratory.[7] Regardless of his intent, however, Wichelns' arguments for taking public speaking out of the streets and studying it in the classroom, for treating it less as an expression of protest and more an exercise in conforming to Aristotelian standards, for teaching it in ways that inspired a more responsible citizenry, and for securing it in an Anglo-Saxon tradition were not irrelevant in the creation of courses in and departments of public speaking in this country.

The political significance of what Wichelns left out, the concept of the "public space" within which he worked, namely two-party politics and party leaders, became mirrored in neo-Aristotelian tradition. Between 1922 and 1944, the major figures studied were Edmund Burke, Robert Ingersoll, Franklin Roosevelt, Woodrow Wilson, Daniel Webster, William Jennings Bryan, Henry Ward Beecher, Wendell Phillips, and Edgar Borah. Only Ingersoll, Beecher, and Phillips broke through the monopoly of officialdom.[8] That this tradition tended to exclude women, Indians, "Negro" speakers, and labor leaders was noted by a panel of historians who, in 1945, reviewed A History and Criticism of American Public Address.[9]

But if Wichelns' neo-Aristotelianism tended to narrow the public space, to celebrate the "instructed element in the state," it was unambiguous about the importance of politics in the study of public address. "Rhetorical criticism," wrote Wichelns, "lies at the boundary of politics (in the broadest sense) and literature; its atmosphere is that of public life . . ." (p. 215). His dual interest—breaking through the limits of "literature" as the proper object of academic study on the one hand, and coping with the turmoil in public life on the other—appears in the final paragraph:

> We need not marvel that the many movements of the poet's mind more readily capture the critic's attention than the few and uncertain movements of that Leviathan, the public mind. Nor is it surprising that the historians tend to be occupied with the acts and the motives of leaders.

Distinguishing the study of oratory from work performed by literary critics and historians, Wichelns concluded with a comment on the political utility of rhetorical criticism:

> But those historians who find the spirit of an age in the total mass of its literary productions, as well as all who would tame Leviathan to the end that he shall not threaten civilization, must examine more thoroughly than they as yet have done the interactions of the inventive genius, the popularizing talent, and the public mind. [p. 216]

The cultural and political cast of Wichelns' essay, its function in an academic world dominated by English, History, and the Classics (we should not overlook his grounding the study of oratory in Aristotle's Rhetoric and thus its relevance to classical studies), does not, I think, detract from the brilliance of his strategy nor its value in legitimizing "speech" as a field of study. It deepens our understanding of the historical context or rhetorical situation prompting the essay. It also enables us to appreciate the ideological significance of events outside the university involving non-English speaking peoples whose place in American society was being challenged by established authority and whose labor was being exploited in existing economic and political arrangements.

This is not to say that Anglo-American studies, classical research, or rhetorical criticism is inherently apologetic of a social, political, or economic status quo—only that a full understanding of a text cannot be achieved without situating it in an historical context, a point emphasized in Wichelns' essay; and further that this "context" is both highly selective and complex, and not something dictated by the speaker or the "nature" of the event.[10] Our analysis included references to a university setting, with its various fields and jurisdictional disputes, along with a sociopolitical context outside that setting drawing in actions taken by government officials, decisions handed down by the judiciary, and the agitation of labor organizers and political radicals. Such inclusiveness coupled with an expanded sense of where critical choices are made gives to an ideologically informed investigation a claim to being more integrative, more aware of and concerned about the making of history, than do traditional approaches to criticism.[11]

But again, Wichelns' essay is instructive. It cannot easily be caged. It roams over several fields of study and out, beyond the academic compound, into the world of affairs. Whatever his limitations, Wichelns invites, through his sources of inspiration and his theoretical formulation, an encounter with history and the human struggle which has been virtually abandoned in the practice of criticism.[12] A more catholic and, I think, surer grip on ideological analysis understands that it does not force a doctrinaire rejection of Idealism in favor of Materialism or the dismissal of Aristotle in favor of Marx or Habermas. What such a critique draws out is the emancipatory moment in whatever tradition, event, or text that is of concern. It is in the emancipatory moment in "The Literary Criticism of Oratory" where we discover that the world view articulated by Wichelns, though politically conservative, preserves an interest in human action, arguments over public policy, [and] problems of audience adaptation. With its respect for an art bounded on one side by ethical and on the other by political issues, it could accommodate an approach to criticism bent on "unmasking" rhetoric in light of the way it functioned in an historical context and which expanded the traditional definition of rhetoric to include literature and philosophy. This, too was the tack taken by another venerated figure in the field, Kenneth Burke.

Burke was not exactly of the field. In the 1930's and 40's, he made his living as a professional writer, and was less interested in the academic implications of his world than in its contribution to the political, cultural, and intellectual struggles of the period. During the 1930's, Burke considered himself a Marxist and was strongly sympathetic to the Communist party.[13] Unlike Philip Wheelwright who, during this period, urged radical intellectuals to translate the vulgar and sectarian statements of the party into persuasive and sophisticated ideology,[14] Burke thought that "fostering intellectual distrust" in established parties would hasten the victory of socialism.[15] In a paper delivered at the first Congress of American Writers, Burke argued that an effective use of propaganda was as important as the workers seizing control of the means of production. For Burke, the significance of rhetoric, folklore, and myth lay in their potential for securing an intuitive sense of community among all Americans. They offered a strategy for satisfying collectivist dreams of the 1930's superior to the concepts of planning and socialism. Unmasking, debunking, and spelling out incipient programs for action in literary, philosophical, and political texts, Burke pursued a Marxist, even at times a Marxist-Leninist, critique, though his commitment to the independence of the intellectual cut him off from vanguardism and the imperatives of party discipline.[16]

In the academic world, however, the fact that Burke oriented his project around "rhetoric" and traced its origins back to Aristotle, and had, by the 1950's, begun to detach himself from radical politics to meditate on literary texts made him an acceptable candidate for canonization in the field—even by those for whom efforts to deal with sociopolitical issues reached beyond the pale of legitimate scholarship.[17] With the intrusion of McCarthyism into the universities in the early 1950's and with it a flagging sense of what merit, tenure, and trustees could or would secure, Burke's strategies for obscuring political motivation in interpreting texts through methodological analysis and a vocabulary too improvised and elaborate for forthright reactionaries to penetrate had to be an inspiration for the intellectual underground of the period.[18] His comedic frame and delight in drama erected a bridge between factions in departments housing both speech and drama; his project for studying human behavior, albeit dramatistically,[19] provided some solace for emergent behaviorists, while his strictures on the dangers of science as an agency perverted by a perverted political structure[20] gave aid and comfort to non-behaviorists in the struggle over the distribution of status, wealth, and power in departments of speech all over the country.

Burke's appeal transcended departmental struggles and national politics in the 1950's. "Dramatistic" perspectives and "Burkean" criticism began to appear in various disciplines. That Burke was legitimized in scholarship in political science, English, and sociology made him all the more attractive to a field sensitive about its credentials and whose application for membership in the American Council of Learned Societies had been, was about to be, or had been again turned down. As one who was commended in disciplines with higher status and advocating rhetorical studies as uniquely insightful into, among other things, the symbolic uses of politics, the rhetoric of fiction, and symbolic interaction within a social context, Burke appeared a commanding figure. And he also, through the breadth of his work and its application in several areas, encouraged a more comprehensive view of scholarly activity.[21]

In the field of speech, however, Burkeanism rarely carried with it the emancipatory sociopolitical critique that made it an intellectual force in the social sciences. Among speech and rhetorical critics, Burkeanism, refracted through a pentagonal prism, became an alternative to the prevailing but intellectually embarrassing schematic known as "neo-Aristotelianism" which, as Black made clear in the early 1960's, was little more than a set of categories lifted, with slight emendation, out of Wichelns' early essay.[22]

IDEOLOGICAL CONFLICT:
POLITICS AND PROFESSIONALISM

Just as the political impulse underlying Wichelns' project, his concern about taming the "Leviathan" of public opinion and the influence of demagogues, was abandoned or formally suppressed in neo-Aristotelian criticism, so the political commitments underlying Burke's project in the 1930's and 40's—his attack on capitalism, authoritarianism, bureaucratization, and victimage—got lost in "Burkeanism." That this loss of sociopolitical concerns was no accident, but a reflection of "Weaveresque" politics of a field filled with former ministers, incipient lawyers, and, more important, a guild mentality developed during the 1950's to ward off conflicts with forces outside the university, became apparent during the late 1960's and 70's. Civil Rights, Black Power, Anti-War, the Feminist revolt—all these began to enter into the scholarship of the period. As this scholarship probed the divisions in the larger society, it encountered similar divisions in the academic provinces, though expressed in more elaborate, less intelligible, forms.

During the war in Vietnam, for example, critics debated the propriety of addressing the content of public argument. There were those who embraced partisan politics, and there were those who denounced the tyranny of relevance. In retrospect, both sides proceeded in ignorance of a tradition including Burke and Wichelns that, if it could not moderate the quarrel, might have taken it beyond disputes over scholarly decorum. The way in which the dispute was conducted, however, reveals a great deal about the tensions existing between professional interest and ethical, moral, and political commitment.

There were two essays dealing with the conflict and published during this period which deserve special attention: one by Forbes Hill, which included a critique of a speech by then-President Richard Nixon; and the other by Lawrence Rosenfield, which sought to orient criticism around the insights of Martin Heidegger.

Let us begin with Hill. In his essay, "Conventional Wisdom—Traditional Form: The President's Message of November 3, 1969,"[23] Hill tried to resurrect neo-Aristotelian criticism. He argued that the inventory given in the *Rhetoric* (he dissociated himself from Wichelns' revisionism) limits criticism to specifying the relationship between the premises of prediction and value held by the target audience and the verbal framework likely to elicit a favorable response.

Beyond the advantage of analytic clarity, the rules being laid out in a particular text, such criticism had, in Hill's view, the added advantage of preventing the critic from making judgments outside the success or failure of a particular framework in meeting audience expectations. Neo-Aristotelianism prevented the critic from estimating the truth of a speaker's statements and the adequacy of the values the speaker assumes or recommends. Even if one were inclined to take on this burden, the result would not be "rhetorical criticism" (pp. 385–6). On this basis, Hill dismissed the efforts of would-be rhetorical critics (Newman, Stelzner, and Campbell) to come to grips with President Nixon's "Vietnamization speech."

Those whose work had been singled out were invited to respond in the same issue of the *Quarterly Journal of Speech*. Karlyn Campbell was the only one who replied; her response was followed by a rejoinder by Hill.[24] Campbell moved immediately to attack "monolithic" Aristotelianism, offering in its place a "pluralistic" approach. But she went further and, in an attempt to legitimize her work as "rhetorical criticism" under the terms Hill set down, cited Lane Cooper's translation to prove the point. She also questioned Hill's notion of objectivity, noting a "conservative" bias in his criticism. This opening enabled Hill, in a rejoinder, to accomplish three things: (1) display his professional credentials—he attacked Cooper's notoriously loose translation of the *Rhetoric*; (2) present his political credentials—he had, he said, canvassed for George McGovern, establishing himself as a starry-eyed radic-lib, but one who exercised restraint in his professional capacity; and most significantly (3) avoid responding to what I believe to be more pertinent questions, such as why ignoring the murder of men, women, and children following from actions justified in public address should count as a triumph of scholarly restraint.

A number of theoretical problems with Hill's approach also remained unexplored. I wish here to distinguish between the perspective he commends—that of a classically trained specialist in public relations ("public relations machinery," "target audience," "secondary audience," etc.)—and what he conceals by equating the activity fostered by this role with criticism. There is no way, except through the *Rhetoric,* to stand outside the world view of the speaker. No matter what actions are advocated, the critic, following Hill, is limited to assessing the degree to which the speech conforms to the *Rhetoric* in eliciting the psychological response desired from its "target audience." What this leads to in theory and, on reading the Nixon analysis, in practice is little more than recapitulation: The "content" of the speech is summarized, synopsized, its assumptions spelled out, its world view abstracted and handed over virtually intact in the act of displaying its formal characteristics.

Hill found this a strength in "neo-Aristotelianism." It imposed limitations that made "true significance" possible. Even then he had to go beyond Aristotle to seal off substantive questions:

> If the critic questions the President's choice of policy and premises, he is forced to examine systematically all the political factors involved in this choice. [p. 385]

What a challenge this would be in the real world of politics where, as Weber reminds us, bureaucracies strive to maintain secrecy in order to ward off criticism.[25] If those in power manage to seal off information about the political factors involved in the decision-making process, criticism, following Hill, comes to a stop. Neither insight into the reality of what is being recommended, nor a history of duplicity or evidence of limited information on the part of the speaker, nor identification with the victim justifies critique in the absence of knowledge of how the speaker arrived at his or her decision. The "magnitude of the question" and a speaker-centered analysis combine, in Hill's formulation, to justify extraordinary restraint when it comes to presidential rhetoric.

The problem with this view revealed itself during the course of Vietnam. If criticism takes what the President says as a given, if it does not envision the possibility of a rejoinder, then the critic, save for a few marginal notes on structure and technical proficiency, takes the position of many reporters in Vietnam who relied on official handouts. If one cannot get beyond the net of words or the "text," if in the course of Vietnam one did not come to the realization that "light" casualties lay just as still as "heavy" casualties, then it all threatens to become too complex, too confusing for those who are not privy to information available to officials. Thus even though, as Hill pointed out, Nixon was advocating continuation of the war, there was no sense in Hill's analysis of the reality that is war and was Vietnam, that in back of every column of print and every word there was, as Michael Herr wrote at the time, a "dripping, laughing death-face." But it was there:

> It hid there in newspapers and magazines and held to your television screens for hours after the set was turned off for the night, an after image that simply wanted to tell you at last what somehow had not been told.[26]

Hill's formulation makes a virtue out of omitting such realities, makes it an imperative for "neo-Aristotelian" critics to avoid such issues, unless of course the speaker happens to raise them.

This does not mean that neo-Aristotelian analysis lacks all validity, and in fact Hill's discussion of Nixon's speech, as far as it went, was actually quite good.

He unpacked values and predictions that were unclear; identified primary and secondary audiences through the text; led us beyond blind opposition to appreciate the subtlety with which Nixon sought to attract and persuade his constituency. It was his insensitivity to ideological issues—evident both in his equation of "well known" with an objective analysis of the "situation" and his use of popular terms like "fanatical opponents" to characterize Nixon's opposition—which led him to believe that neo-Aristotelianism offered a refuge from conflict. Note here the theoretical problem: The issue is not which side Hill was on, but that his view of criticism automatically links the critic and his or her reader with the "speaker," setting aside any response critical of the speaker's world view—the content, substance, or actions implied.

At issue is nothing less than the nature and purpose of criticism. But there is no need to become melodramatic about it. We can clarify the issue by asking ourselves what in everyday language we would call the person Hill calls a critic. What would we call one who examines or rewrites drafts of official statements so that their impact on specific audiences can be ascertained or improved; for whom policy, audience, and situation are a given and the overriding question is how to assess the effectiveness of the speech? Not, I suggest, a critic. We would be more inclined to call him or her a "public relations consultant." Consultancy was not Hill's regulative context, however, and speech writers and consultants were not his target audience. His primary audience was composed of speech teachers, and his purpose was to persuade them—critics, editors, and readers of scholarly journals in the field—to avoid sociopolitical controversy by working within a professional context.

It is this context which explains why Hill could set aside the reality of war and justify it through an appeal to a great book. Put more precisely: This is why Aristotle's *Rhetoric* could be called upon to authorize a disengagement from concerns about values, predictions, and human suffering attending the way those in power act and/or justify their actions. In any but an academic context suffused with the spirit of professionalism, this would, I suspect, be thought more than a little eccentric.

Fidelity to the text, whether an ancient philosophical treatise or a presidential address, can lead to important discoveries about internal structure, the audience it would create or persuade, the kind of appeals it makes. With a holy text, the object is to pierce through to deeper truths; with official documents, one stays within the text only at the risk of obscuring alternative views of the world. If the criticism of public address should reach into ethical and political matters, instead of treating this act as a professional scandal or a threat to the discrete categories we are, in an increasingly departmentalized universe, inclined to use in setting out fields of learning, we might accept it as the price we pay for dealing with issues that do not fall neatly within what Theodore Adorno has called our "pedantically drawn, inflatedly defended trenches."[27] More positively stated, we could embrace this as the broader range of intellectual concerns the critical tradition brings to the study of rhetoric.[28]

Criticism, T. S. Eliot once remarked, is not much more than a Sunday park of contending and contentious orators. But instead of a lively and potentially illuminating exchange, what Eliot, whose democratic sympathies never fully matured, heard was a number of people making a livelihood out of the violence and extremity of their opposition to other critics. He wanted to expel the lot.[29] What may appear quaint in disputes over literary matters—removing those who set their talents against a preferred cultural tradition—takes on a different hue in politics. In a struggle for power, real interests exist, life and death decisions are made, and there are those who believe that reasoned and vigorous debate is an important means for clarifying the issues and directing the struggle.

There are others who believe that such struggles can be and ought to be transcended. In 1974, two years after American troops had been withdrawn from Vietnam, Lawrence Rosenfield took issue with those who would treat socio-political issues.[30] His project was to show how criticism could rise above dualities embedded in sociopolitical conflict through spontaneous pleasure, a cosmic principle of loving care for the world as one finds it. Rosenfield's essay was framed as a response to a work by Steven Jenkins and myself.[31] Two things should, I think, be borne in mind: (1) Rosenfield's essay appeared after the crisis and the need for immediate action had died down, while the Wander-Jenkins essay appeared during and was designed in response to an existing crisis; (2) Rosenfield points to a valid moment in the critical act and in life itself, so special a moment that it is sad to think that there could be a time when one would have to be reminded of it.

The central and defining feature of criticism to Rosenfield is the epiphanic moment when the critic releases himself,

> . . . letting the phenomena 'speak to him' through their luminosity . . . only one who Wills not to Will, who so releases himself from sheer calculative investigation as to allow himself to be touched by reality, only he can escape the paradoxes that object isolation forces on him. [p. 492]

This experience is at once expansive, penetrating, and transparent. The critic is impelled, as if lacking choice in the matter, to enhance pleasure at the coming-forth of *aletheia* by sharing it with the community at large; the critic's remarks are a rejoicing, a representation of the moment of insight. There is no debate over what occurred, no need for deliberation. It is nothing less than "reality's revelation," and thus the critic's only obligation is not to "forget his gift, not to lose it by letting it out of sight and mind" (p. 495).

Given Rosenfield's rejection of dualistic thinking, we might assume that his project would involve reconciling political struggle with appreciative criticism. In his formulation, however, they are philosophically and psychologically incompatible. Concern about politics and the deliberation of public issues reflect a pedestrian mind; in contrast, writing in the epideictic mode and celebrating things as they are evidence cosmic consciousness. He resolves the conflict by abandoning one side of the duality. Thus, while opening up a vast spiritual continent for the critic to explore, he radically constricts the range of criticism and the choices open to the critic in other domains.

He argues against the inclusion of social and political issues because they generally lead to bad criticism by uninformed critics; rejects the notion that the critic should take any responsibility for choosing the critical object, as the phenomena speak to a critic through their luminosity; denies that, having heard the phenomena, the critic has any decisions to make about what has been heard. The attitude to be assumed by the critic is stipulated. It will not include indignation or outrage. Regardless of what the critic is evaluating, the attitude will be one of "spontaneous pleasure." Similarly the tone is pre-given; not one of rejection or denunciation, it will be one of "appreciation." There is no choice about how the critic's remarks are to be cast. Criticism will avoid the deliberative and the forensic in favor of the epideictic or eulogistic mode. Finally, he specifies the audience for criticism—not the self; not one's peers; but a Universal Audience or "Being."

The tension Rosenfield develops in his essay lies in the expanse of "cosmic consciousness" on one hand and the constriction of criticism on the other. In an attempt to render this constriction as other than arbitrary, willful, or the product of oracular first principles, Rosenfield grounds his efforts in the work of Martin Heidegger. Thus in order to understand the strengths and weaknesses of "Being" as a way of orienting the practice of criticism, we should I think turn to the work of Heidegger, in particular to the moment of "Being" and its appearance in history.

BEYOND IDEOLOGY:
HISTORY, CRITICISM, AND MARTIN HEIDEGGER

Being and Time was published in 1929. It addressed a generation in whose eyes could be seen the shrieking iron and flame, in whose inward shudder was rooted the blood red poppies of Flanders' fields. The trenches had stretched across Europe and in between was a vast wasteland littered with rotting corpses. This was a world where roses bloomed whose petals ran, and gooseberries (e[u]phemism for coils of barbed wire) grew year round.[32] In *Being and Time,* notes George Steiner, metaphors of forest and land predominate. He subsumes them under the phrase "agrarian romanticism."[33] With the bias of a textual critic working in an idealist tradition, he does not probe the ethos of the Front Generation. For them the romance was informed by the torn and blackened fields of France, the mud at the Somme which interred tens of thousands, the spikes that once were trees, and afterward in Germany, because of a food blockade lasting into 1919, starvation and the impetus it gave for a return to the soil.

Moving into an historical context, stylistic devices take on the fragrances and hues which make them work in the lives of real people. Thus we struggle to appreciate what grounding one's being in the earth meant on the moment of utterance, meant in the lives of those who, having known hunger, understood why a fallen horse could be stripped of its flesh on the street. In 1936, nine years after the publication of *Being and Time,* Heidegger lectured in Frankfurt on the origins of the work of art. Meditating on Van Gogh's painting of a peasant woman working in a field, he reflected:

> In the stiffly rugged heaviness of the shoes there is the accumulated tenacity of her slow trudge through the far-spreading and ever-uniform furrows the field swept by a raw wind. On the leath[er] lie the dampness and richness of the soil . . . In the shoes vibrates the silent call of the earth, its quiet gift of the ripening grain and its unexplained self-refusal in the fallow desolation of the wintery field.

There is a spaciousness in Heidegger's rhetoric belying the immediacy and power of its associations for an audience which had known the terrible destruction of war and the threat of starvation. He continues:

> This equipment is pervaded by uncomplaining worry as to the certainty of bread, the wordlessness of joy of having once more withstood want, the trembling before the impending childbed and shivering at the surrounding menace of death.[34]

In this way, Heidegger spoke, in the period after the Great War, not only of hope and the care necessary to sustain it, but also of the primacy of the earth in the human world and the need to till the land that babies might not die in their mother's arms.

Astonishment is the response of innocence. It is a childlike embrace of the world, open to the mystery, to the feeling of the sun's warmth, the fullness of Being in a peasant's shoes. In the illumination and comfort of Being, one transcends a world that is no more and never again will be. Buildings in rubble, land destroyed, a generation crushed and disillusioned—it was in this context that Carl Jung, in 1928, spoke of the spiritual crisis of "modern" man who has come "to the very edge of the world, leaving behind him all that has been discarded and outgrown, and acknowledging that he stands before the Nothing out of which All may grow."[35] In the face of Nothing, of dread, anxiety, guilt, and horror, Heidegger spoke of a return to the promise of a new and more fundamental order in true Being.

In a moment of social chaos, political uncertainty, and near-fatal psychological shock, Heidegger celebrated the dance of creation, the ecstasy of primeval possibility, the lyrical song of authentic speech. He welcomed the loss of a grasping, imperial, aggrandizing self who looked upon things as its personal and only domain. When things are no more, when Nothing presents itself, appropriating and exploiting the world makes no sense, and may be seen as the mechanism through which things that count—food, a homestead, communion with others—are destroyed. Anaximander's transformation of Being into things out there begins the march toward a world in which knowledge is equated with what Man knows about things that interest him; and thus to the oblivion of Being, the source of all things—things that are and all things that are not—the source of knowledge, the light within which the first things disclose themselves to a child and disclosed themselves to the early Greek philosophers, the question "What is being?" was a vital inquiry.

But the moment for entertaining the fullness of Being passes; must pass if one is to return to the everyday world; and must pass as the moment for being-open to all possibilities must pass, if one is to regain possession of one's self. To be self-possessed is to be able to sort through the gifts of Being and decide what is worth building on and what is not. Being, in the ripeness of imagination, does not order the world. Being embraces chaos as well as cosmos. Under its spell, one leaves off writing poetry—the transcription of authentic speech—to move about in the world of affairs as though in a daze. Being soars through language, fusing it with force primeval; but however entrancing, Being does not *clear* the fire trails, does not *plant* the seed, does not *build* the temple. It may be said to disclose their possibility, to fill one with wonder or lead one to take care in his or her project. But wonder and care do not chop wood, guide the hoe, or place the stone. The figure who performs this work is a concrete living, breathing person.[36]

The point is crucial. While a philosopher may be charmed by people working in the field, learn to value their activity, and dwell on the relationship between hoeing and the harvest, nonetheless taking a hoe in hand, striking the soil, and drawing it toward oneself from dawn to dusk is sweaty, blistering, and numbingly repetitive activity. A child playing in the fields does not hoe. Hoeing is not playing. It is labor. In the world of affairs, the politics of land distribution, city construction, and the effort to marshall the forces of a nation involve choices to be made between competing alternatives. The alternatives in German political life in the 1920's were real, disturbing, and in the early 1930's underwent a radical transformation. In the struggle for power, there is, Plato argues, no place for poets. The manifold Truth of poetry cannot provide the hard clarity necessary to overcome real obstacles. The illuminating ambiguities of authentic speech in the face of despair give way to the coercive simplicities of direct speech in efforts to mobilize.

And so Heidegger, the master of astonishment, as Steiner calls him, encountered a second crisis, one quite different from the first. The child, amazed at the fullness of Being, hears the voice of its Father, hears talk about his Father's land, the soil required to make things grow, the blood and sweat required for planting and harvesting, and the glories of a life dedicated to the Fatherland. Death, revealing itself as the most proper, nonrelational, insurmountable possibility, holds no fear. The child knows death in the family, has a presentiment of mortality. Being rose above the carnage of the Great War and above the bloody skirmishes taking place on the streets of Berlin in the 1920's and 30's. Astonished at the sense of well-being that springs from one who knows, who is completely, unambiguously, ineluctably sure of himself, the child hears the voice of its Father. Masculine, resolute and unafraid, Adolf Hitler to many Germans in the 1930's became the voice of the Nation. This voice spoke of a new Germany founded on its true origins in the Soil and the Blood of the German people.

Nothing, in this moment, could have been more astonishing. History was abandoned; morality became opaque; and Art relinquished the ordinary and withdrew into itself. For Heidegger it did so triumphantly:

> To submit to this displacement means to transform our accustomed ties to world and to earth and henceforth to restrain all usual doing and prizing, knowing and looking, in order to stay within the truth that is happening in the work.[37]

Two years after Hitler had established absolute dictatorship, "total democracy" through the people's will to have dictatorship by acclamation, or so went the argument of the famous jurist Carl Schmitt,[38] Heidegger, who by then had left the Party, could treat works of art originating in the speech of the people as somehow immune from censorship.[39] The "people" were now unified. The political struggle was over. All could be contained in language wherein the "living word fights the battle and puts up for decision what is holy and what unholy, what great and what small, what brave and what cowardly, what lofty and what flight [sic], what master and what slave."[40] Still ecstatic, cut loose from everyday life in which decisions were being made about who was and who was not to be included in the "people" and what works of art could and could not be communicated, Heidegger walked along the woodpaths, rejoiced in an occasional clearing, and mediated on certain poems as signposts toward Being.

In an attitude of utter receptivity, he had heard the voice of authority and called it authentic speech; walked about the Fatherland and felt the Earth; heard a call for purification and thought it good. On November 11, 1933, in an address at the election meeting of German Scholars in Leipzig, Heidegger declared:

> We have completely broken with the idealization of a landless and powerless thinking. We see the end of all philosophy which could serve it. We are certain of this: that clear toughness and security about the plain question of the nature of being are returning to us. . . . The Führer has awakened this resolve in the whole people and has fused it into a single resolution.[41]

A few days earlier, addressing German students, Heidegger characterized the National Socialist "revolution" as a new school for the German spirit:

> Doctrine and 'ideas' shall no longer govern your existence. The Führer himself, and only he, is the current and future reality in Germany, and his word is your law.[42]

Being became personified.

The moment for astonishment may be enveloped by history. In the midst of social and political struggles choices have to be made. But for one seeking communion with Being, for whom death is the orienting reality of existence, ordinary people may become a distraction. Being there, their cries and whispers fall on deaf ears.[43] One strains to hear not the chatter of *das Man,* but the clear and resolute voice of pure Being. Slowly, imperceptibly, the "Nation," the "Race," the "leader" entered into the outer recesses of Being, a being longed for, a being at the end of a quest, a being through whom the unutterable loneliness of intense thought could be brought into the light of day.

Does this mean that Heidegger's early commitment to the Nazi cause sprang from basic tendencies in his thought? One gets the impression on reading philosophers that his was a regrettable lapse. David Farrell Krell, in his introduction to Heidegger's works, attributes it to physical and psychological causes. Weariness and demoralization plagued postwar Germany, leading many German academics to support the National Socialist's call for German "resurgence."[44] A critique less interested in or transfixed by moral summation than in the partiality of ideas would look to what is and what is not said in the context of socio-political struggle. Heideggerian reality, brought to earth in the 1930's, participated in the struggle for power, so that what in retrospect, isolated and completely detached, sounds like prayer was freighted with ideological significance at the time.

The question, then, is not whether there were basic tendencies in Heidegger's thought which enlisted his sympathies and led him to join the National Socialist movement, but about the resonance between Heidegger's thought and Nazi ideology. This is not the same as asking whether or not Heidegger influenced or followed the Party line. Only peripherally is this line of analysis interested in actual Party membership. The relationship of Nietzsche's work to Nazi ideology does not depend on membership, conscious intent, and it need not culminate in moral judgement. The question has to do with the appeal of groups struggling for power at a particular time and place, the rhetorical strategies employed, and the connections between them and a given work or author.

In the case of *Being and Time,* George Steiner offers a brief and suggestive analysis of its affinities for National Socialism:

> [Both] stress the concreteness of man's function in the world, the primordial sanctity of hand and body. Both exalt the mystical kinship between the laborer and his tools in an existential innocence which must be cleansed of the pretensions and illusions of abstract intellect. With this emphasis goes a closely related stress on rootedness, on the intimacies of blood and remembrance that an authentic human being cultivates his native ground.

Steiner continues, using rhetoric to exploit the tension between philosophy and history:

> Heidegger's rhetoric of 'at-homeness,' of the organic continuum which knits the living to the ancestral dead buried close by, fits effortlessly into the Nazi cult of 'blood and soil.' Concomitantly, the Hitlerite denunciations of 'rootless cosmopolitans,' the urban riffraff, and unhoused intelligentsia that live parasitically on the modish surface of society, chime in readily with the Heideggerian critique of 'theyness,' of technological modernity, of the busy restlessness of the inauthentic.

The stress on authority and death also forms a link:

> Heideggerian 'resoluteness' (*Entschlossenheit*) has more than a hint of the mystique of commitment of self-sacrificial and self-projective élan preached by the Führer and his 'hard-clear' acolytes. Both enact that heightening of personal fate into national and ethnic vocation which is analyzed in *Sein und Zeit*. In both there is, logically and essentially, an exaltation of death as life's purposed summit and fulfillment.[45]

The adequacy or extent of this fit I leave to those more versed in Heidegger and Nazi ideology.[46] The type of analysis is, I think, suggestive. Notice it is not argued that Heidegger's text was caused by or designed with Party interests in mind. The argument is that they are comparable or analogous in various and significant ways: they "stress," "emphasized," "chime," and "enact." The analogue, however, does not lie exclusively in textual similarities. It is also a matter of historical context. Situating Heidegger's "philosophy" in and among competing world views—the universalizing efforts of political parties in this instance, we gain a sense of the ideological implications of Being. Being in the moment becomes Being-in-History.[47]

When morality attaches itself to words, it is all a matter of appearances. The reality of human effort and human suffering lie beyond the power of words to capture or evoke; yet it is here that one can gain some clarity on the question of right and wrong. This is why criticism bound by the "text" or the work of "art" runs so thin in a confrontation with human struggle; and why a statement conceived during moments of crisis, perhaps even confused about the nature of the crisis, may be found to be compelling in a different time. The anti-technological romanticism, reverence for the earth, concern about human relations and the destruction of human potential, and mystical vision of potentiality in the Heideggerian critique re-emerged in the United States during the 1960's in the work of one of his most famous students, Herbert Marcuse.[48] One-dimensionality results from a flight from other than officially sanctioned modes of thought, a flight encouraged by an entertainment industry which in place of *Dasein* celebrates the consumption of commercial products. Marcuse, driven to despair not only by the triumph of authoritarian bureaucracy and the destruction of the individual in Germany during the 1930's, but also by what he perceived to be similar tendencies in the United States in the 1960's, was compelled to discover in Nothing—the Negation of what is—real alternatives.

IDEOLOGY CRITIQUE AND THE MATTER OF SURVIVAL

What Marcuse and another former student, Jean-Paul Sartre, add to a Heideggerian critique is both profound and liable to be ignored in the abstractions ordinarily used to talk about such things. They bring to it larger and more generous sympathies: a more cosmopolitan view of the world; a moral sensibility firmly rooted in humanity; and an emphasis on the centrality of choice in moments of crisis. Situated in the midst of social and political struggle and what these struggles mean to real people, Being may become an academic or quasi-theological entity. An absolute refusal to examine Being-in-History or, stated in the positive, an unflinching commitment to Being-Beyond-History does, I think, make it easier to lose sight of the connections among nation, race, humanity, and authority. There is no lack of historical evidence to support the thesis that white, patriotic, academic males are liable to confuse being with Being and, further, to assume that commitment to other than what is constitutes an ominous flight from Truth or Objectivity. The crises we face now and in whatever definition of the future we might like to entertain seem almost insurmountable. War, famine, accidental destruction by our own technology, ruin of our environment—the problems are global. With vast expenditures on war in this country, estimates ranging up to $1.6 trillion over the next few years, a program in place to develop new and more powerful nuclear weapons (adding to the over thirty thousand warheads we already possess), and the invocation once again of a "Communist menace" to justify it all, we struggle to realize in ourselves the possibilities for a universal public and to develop a language appropriate to such a conception. War is real. It is of this world. It is the ground on which, the flux of everyday life, may cease for all people for all time.[49]

But war, as C. Wright Mills argued nearly a quarter of a century ago, is not inevitable. This he wrote in the face of two World Wars and in the midst of the Cold War:

> [I]t is, immediately, the result of nationalist definitions of world reality, of dogmatic reliance upon military endeavor as the major or even the only means of solving the explosive social problems of this epoch of despair and terror. And because this is now so, to cultivate moral sensibility and to make it knowledgeable is the strategic talk of those intellectuals who would be at peace.

There is no question but that such a critical strategy involves political activity, the promise of partiality that party politics entails. There are alternatives to public debate, to involving masses of people in an effort to stay the conflagration, but they have been tried in this century and have been found wanting. Thus Mills went on to say that intellectuals "*should* debate short-run and immediate policies, but, even more, they should confront the whole attitude toward war, they should teach new views of it, and on this basis they should criticize current policies and decisions."[50] It is in this context, a real crisis involving actual alternatives, that a reconsideration of the purposes of criticism and the study of rhetoric take on meaning.

In the effort to make or, in the atomic age, to insure the possibility that history will be made, there are a few saints. Saints do not struggle. They have no purpose other than being purified and purged of self-interest. The spiritual as distinct from the social-moral life is sufficient unto itself and needs no goal or purpose by which to shape the means of the present moment; this moment is ever-present and doing is in No-mind or in Being. In this formulation, truth is torn between that which is present in the contemplation of the sacred, and that which is produced through human action. Yet I think that this is a false duality. It is rooted in notions of specialized activity and, given the split between church and street, in speech and prayer, poetry and deliberation, spacial and verbal decorum. In heaven there is no need for such distinctions, and even during periods of crisis there are different moments. Opening oneself up to or being astonished by unforeseen possibilities when all seems lost is no more and no less important than being able to choose from among and act on a given alternative in resolving the crisis.

Criticism takes an ideological turn when it recognizes the existence of powerful vested interests benefiting from and consistently urging policies and technology that threaten life on this planet, when it realizes that we search for alternatives. The situation is being constructed; it will not be averted either by ignoring it or placing it beyond our province. An ideological turn in modern criticism reflects the existence of crisis, acknowledges the influence of established interests and the reality of alternative worldviews, and commends rhetorical analyses not only of the actions implied but also of the interests represented. More than "informed talk about matters of importance,"[51] criticism carries us to the point of recognizing good reasons and engaging in right action. What an ideological view does is to situate "good" and "right" in an historical context, the efforts of real people to create a better world.

NOTES

[1]C. Wright Mills, *The Marxists* (New York: Dell Publishing Co., Inc. 1962), p. 27.

[2]See J. Gould, "Ideology," *A Dictionary of the Social Sciences,* ed. Julius Gould and William L. Kolb (New York: The Free Press, 1962), pp. 315–317; George Lichtheim, *The Concept of Ideology* (New York: Random House, 1967), pp. 3–47; Alvin W. Gouldner, *The Dialectic of Ideology and Technology: The Origins, Grammar, and Future of Ideology* (New York: The Seabury Press, 1976); Douglas Kellner, "Ideology, Marxism, and Advanced Capitalism," *Socialist Review,* 8 (1978), 37–66. An interest in ideology is beginning to appear in rhetorical studies. See Thomas B. Farrell, "Knowledge, Consensus, and Rhetorical Theory," *Quarterly Journal of Speech,* 62 (1976), 1–14; William R. Brown, "Ideology as Communication Process," *Quarterly Journal of Speech,* 64 (1978), 123–40; Michael Calvin McGee, "'Not Men, But Measures': The Origins and Import of an Ideological Principle," *Quarterly Journal of Speech,* 64 (1978), 141–54; and his "The 'Ideograph': A Link Between Rhetoric and Ideology," *Quarterly Journal of Speech,* 66 (1980), 1–16.

[3]The locution "emancipatory" is associated with the work of Jürgen Habermas. Originating in the Greek usage of critical judgment—a crisis involving a dispute over right which moves toward a decision, the term enabled Habermas to explore the tendency of reason in our scientific civilization to stifle the spontaneity of hope, the act of taking a position, the experience of relevance or indifference, the response to suffering and oppression, the desire for adult autonomy, all moments of enlightened volition (*Theory and Practice,* trans. John Viertel [Boston: Beacon Press, 1973], pp. 262–263).

[4]Herbert August Wichelns, "The Literary Criticism of Oratory," *Studies in Rhetoric and Public Speaking in Honor of James Albert Winans* (1925; rpt. New York: Russell & Russell, Inc., 1962), pp. 181–216. Further references to Wichelns are made within the text.

[5]See Donald C. Bryant, "Rhetorical Dimensions in Criticism," *Rhetorical Dimensions in Criticism* (Baton Rouge: La. State Univ. Press, 1973), pp. 27–28; and Walter R. Fisher, "Genre: Concepts and Applications in Rhetorical Criticism," *Western Journal of Speech Communication,* 44 (Fall 1980), 288–299. Fisher links Wichelns and Burke with other members of the field (i.e. Baird, Wrage, and Black).

[6]Stanley Cobden, "A Study in Nativism: The American Red Scare of 1919–20," *Political Science Quarterly,* 79 (1964), 52–75.

[7]The faculty at Cornell drew up a list of 129 topics for study in 1923; see *Quarterly Journal of Speech,* 9 (1923), 147–153.

[8]Charles J. Stewart, "Historical Survey: Rhetorical Criticism in Twentieth Century America," *Explorations in Rhetorical Criticism,* ed. G. P. Mohrmann et al. (University Park, Pa.: The Penn. State Univ. Press, 1973), pp. 6–7.

[9]Stewart, p. 13.

[10]An "historical context" is not a text, but it is inaccessible to us except in textual form. Ideological analysis, writes Fredric Jameson, involves a rewriting of the literary text so that it may be grasped as the rewriting of a prior ideological or historical "subtext," "provided it is understood that the later—what we used to call the 'context'—must always be (re)-constructed after the fact, for purposes of analysis" (Fredric Jameson, "The Symbolic Inference; or, Kenneth Burke and Ideological Analysis," *Critical Inquiry,* 5 [1978], 511).

[11]Traditional theory and criticism may be understood as a tendency towards a purely mathematical system of symbols, a retreat from experiential objects, verification and classification by means of categories which are as neutral as possible. It contrasts with the transformative, experientially inclusive, intellectually integrative (crossing all specialized "fields" of study and linking theory and practice) activity of Critical Theory. See Max Horkheimer, "Traditional and Critical Theory," *Critical Theory; Selected Essays,* trans. Matthew J. O'Connell (New York: The Seabury Press, 1972), pp. 188–243.

[12]See Stephen E. Lucas, "The Schism in Rhetorical Scholarship," *Quarterly Journal of Speech,* 67 (1981), 1–20. Lucas' notion of history, as events past, is informed by his under[s]tanding of rhetoric as functional in a real context. Fredric Jameson takes a critical view of rhetoric and its relation to history in his essay, "History and Criticism," *Weapons of Criticism: Marxism in America and the Literary Tradition,* ed. Norman Rudich (Palo Alto, Ca.: Ramparts Press, 1976), pp. 31–50.

[13]See Richard Pells, *Radical Visions and American Dreams: Culture and Social Thought in the Depression Years* (New York: Harper & Row, 1973) p. 190.

[14]James Burnham and Philip Wheelwright, "Thirteen Propositions," *Symposium,* 4 (1933), 409–19; James Burnham and Philip Wheelwright, "Comment," *Symposium,* 4 (1933), 409–19.

[15]Kenneth Burke, "Boring from Within," *New Republic,* 65 (1931), 329.

[16]Pells, p. 323. For Burke's views, see his "Revolutionary Symbolism in America," *American Writer's Congress,* ed. Henry Hart (New York, 1935), pp. 87–90; and "Twelve Propositions by Kenneth Burke on the Relation Between Economics and Psychology," *Science and Society,* 2 (1938), 242–249.

[17]Neither Marie Hochmuth (Nichols) nor Virginia Holland mention Burke's historical project in their essays introducing him to the field of rhetorical studies. See Marie Hochmuth, "Kenneth Burke and the 'New Rhetoric,'" *Quarterly Journal of Speech,* 38 (1952), 133–144; Virginia Holland, "Rhetorical Criticism: A Burkeian Method," *Quarterly Journal of Speech,* 39 (1953), 444–450. On Burke's gradual detachment from history in favor of the "text," see Fredric R. Jameson, "The Symbolic Inference: or, Kenneth Burke and Ideological Analysis," pp. 507–523.

The exchange between Burke and Jameson highlights the issue. Burke ("Critical Response: Methodological Repression and/or Strategies of Containment," *Critical Inquiry,* 5 [1978], 401–416) cites a number of passages to prove his interest in ideology, suggests Jameson might have objected to his "brand of ideology" which he characterizes as "ironic wavering," and concludes that his method ("logology") must "confront history, first of all, not in propagandist terms of class struggle, but in terms of the question, 'What is to be the typically symbol-using animal?'" (p. 416).

Jameson ("Critical Response: Ideology and Symbolic Action," *Critical Inquiry,* 5 [1978], 417–422), noting that Burke documents the Marxian strain in his own work, summarizes the dispute: "Burke's too immediate celebration of the free creativity of human language (in its broadest symbol making sense) overlaps the whole dimension of our (nonnatural) determination by transindividual forces" (p. 422). Symptomatic of Burke's "wavering" and the restricted concerns of academic criticism is Robert Heath's essay, "Kenneth Burke on Form," *Quarterly Journal of Speech,* 65 (1979), 392–404; while arguing that form and substance are inseparable, Heath does not make any connection among form, content, and history. And Michael Feehan's "Kenneth Burke's Discovery of Dramatism" (pp. 405–411 in the same issue) explores Burke's debate with an orthodox Marxist but draws back from Burke's own political commitments to explore the origins of his "methodology" for the study of human relations.

[18]Even during Burke's revolutionary period, he counselled writers to avoid potentially alienating terms like "proletarian" in favor of the more acceptable and inclusive "people." The writer, he advised, should "propagandize his cause by surrounding it with as full a cultural texture as he can manage, thus thinking of propaganda not as an over-simplified, literal, explicit writing of lawyer's briefs, but as a process of broadly and generally associating his political alignment with cultural awareness at large" ("Revolutionary Symbolism," p. 93). The extent to which a "cultural texture" could mask if not entirely obscure political concerns in Burke's work reveals itself in the contrast between his essay on "Revolutionary Symbolism," published in 1935, and his essay, "Fact, Inference, and Proof in the Analysis of Literary Symbolism," *Symbols and Values: An Initial Study,* ed. Lyman Bryson (New York: Harper and Brothers, 1954), pp. 283–306.

[19]Kenneth Burke, "On Considering Human Behavior Dramatistically," *Permanence and Change: An Anatomy of Purpose* (Los Altos, Ca.: Hermes Publication, 1954), pp. 274–294.

[20]Kenneth Burke, *A Rhetoric of Motives* (1950; rpt. Berkeley, Ca.: Univ. of Calif. Press, 1969), pp. 28–30.

[21]The breadth of Burke's influence—political science, sociology, criminology, psychology, mass communication, anthropology, psychiatry, literary criticism—has been documented in Bruce E. Gronbeck, "Dramaturgical Theory and Criticism: The State of the Art (or Science?)," *Western Journal of Speech Communication,* 44 (Fall 1980), 315–330.

[22]See Edwin Black, *Rhetorical Criticism: A Study in Method* (New York: The Macmillan Company, 1965), pp. 31–35. Black's app[r]oach was not to offer another set of content categories—Burkean or otherwise—in place of neo-Aristotelian. He moved away from "method" to focus on actual criticism, a shift spelled out in his "Author's Foreword" in the reprint of his book (Madison: University of Wisconsin Press, 1978), pp. ix–xv. The shifting of "standards of rigor from the method of investigation to the person of the investigator" is critiqued by Michael Leff, "Interpretation and the Art of the Rhetorical Critic," *Western Journal of Speech Communication,* 44 (Fall 1980), 337–349. See also in the same issue Black's essay, "A Note on Theory and Practice in Rhetorical Criticism," pp. 331–336.

[23]Forbes I. Hill, "Conventional Wisdom—Traditional Form: The President's Message of November 3, 1969," *Quarterly Journal of Speech,* 58 (1972), 373–386. Further citations are offered in the text.

[24]Karlyn Kohrs Campbell, "'Conventional Wisdom—Traditional Form' A Rejoinder," pp. 451–454; and Forbes I. Hill, "Reply to Professor Campbell," pp. 454–460.

[25]*The Essays of Max Weber,* ed. Hans Geron and C. Wright Mills (New York: Oxford Univ. Press, 1970), p. 233. On the manipulation of information over Vietnam, see Paul Joseph, "The Politics of 'Good' and 'Bad' Information: The National Security Bureaucracy and the Vietnam War," *Politics and Society,* (1977), 105–126.

[26]Michael Herr, *Dispatches* (1968; rpt. New York: Avon Books, 1978), p. 233.

[27]Theodore Adorno, *Negative Dialectics,* trans. E. B. Ashton (New York: The Seabury Press, 1973), p. 75.

[28]Within the rhetorical tradition is a powerful critical strain. Rhetorical speech, writes Grassi, "is 'dialogue,' that is[,] that which breaks out with vehemence in the urgency of the particular human situation and 'here' and 'now' begins to form a specifically human order in the confrontation with other human beings" (*Rhetor[i]c as Philosophy: The Humanist Tradition* [University Park: The Pennsylvania Press, 1980], p. 113). The Italian humanist tradition emphasizes the "Public role of the rhetorician [and] militates against

philosophical or religious withdrawal and helps make possible a methodic 'saving of the phenomena' and thus a saving of history" (Nancy Struever, *The Language of History in the Renaissance: Rhetoric and Historical Consciousness in Florentine Humanism* [Princeton: Princeton Univ. Press, 1970], p. 39). For a link between rhetorical and critical theory, see Antonio Grassi, "Marxism, Humanism and the Problem of Imagination in Vico's Works," *G. B. Vico's Science of Humanity*, ed. G. Tagliacozzo and D. Verene (Baltimore: Johns Hopkins Univ. Press, 1976), pp. 275–294.

[29]T. S. Eliot, "Criticism (1928)," *Selected Prose*, ed. John Hayward (Harmondsworth, Middlesex: Penguin Books, 1953), p. 18.

[30]Lawrence W. Rosenfield, "The Experience of Criticism," *Quarterly Journal of Speech*, 69 (1974), 489–496. Further citations are included in the text.

[31]Philip Wander and Steven Jenkins, "Rhetoric, Society, and the Critical Response," *Quarterly Journal of Speech*, 58 (1972), 441–450.

[32]See Paul Fussel's brilliant book, *The Great War and Modern Memory* (New York: Oxford Unive[r]sity Press, 1979), "Arcadian Resources," pp. 231–269.

[33]George Steiner, *Martin Heidegger* (New York: Penguin Books, 1980), pp. 148–149.

[34]Martin Heidegger, "The Origin of the Work of Art," *Martin Heidegger; Basic Writings*, ed. David Krell (New York: Harper & Row, 1977), p. 163. The lecture on which this essay is based was originally delivered in 1936.

[35]Carl Jung, "The Spiritual Problem of Modern Man (1928)," *The Portable Jung*, ed. Joseph Campbell (New York: The Viking Press, 1971), p. 458. Jung based his analysis on the "intimate psychic life of many hundreds of educated persons, both sick and healthy, coming from every quarter of the civilized, white world" (p. 461).

[36]See Grassi, *Rhetoric As Philosophy*, p. 6.

[37]Heidegger, "The Origin," p. 83.

[38]Kurt Sontheimer, "Anti-Democratic Thought in the Weimar Republic," *The Path to Dictatorship 1918–1933*, trans. John Conway. ed. Fritz Stern (Garden City, N.Y.: Anchor Books, 1966), p. 44.

[39]"As soon as Hitler came to power in 1933, his thirty-six-year-old Minister of Popular Enlightenment and Propaganda, Joseph Goebbels, began steps to bring all media under his control. On political or racial grounds, countless workers were driven from their jobs. . . . By October 1933 anyone with editorial duties had to be licensed by Goebbels. Proclaiming that censorship would be positive, not merely negative, he gradually took charge of all aspects of production, distribution, and exhibition" (Erik Barnouw, *Documentary: A History of the Non-Fiction Film* [New York: Oxford, 1979], p. 100).

[40]Heidegger, p. 170.

[41]*German Existentialism*, trans. D. D. Runes (New York Philosophical Library, 1965), pp. 31–2.

[42]*German Existentialism*, p. 28.

[43]See Stephen Eric Broner, "Martin Heidegger: The Consequences of Political Mystification," *Salmagundi* (1977), 153–175.

[44]David Farrell Krell, "General Introduction: 'The Question of Being,'" *Martin Heidegger: Basic Writings*, pp. 27–28.

[45]Steiner, p. 119.

[46]For a more extensive biographical, verbal, and syntactical fit, see Henry Patcher, "Heidegger and Hitler: The Incompatibility of *Geist* and Politics," *Boston University Journal*, 24 (1976), 47–55.

[47]Being-in-History is not Being. We can, writes Heidegger, note historically the abundance of transformations of presencing ("Being"), but "Being does not have a history in the way in which a city or a people have their history. What is history-like in the history of Being is obviously determined by the way in which Being takes place and by this alone" (*On Time and Being*, trans. Joan Stambaugh [New York: Harper & Row, 1972], pp. 7–8).

Grounding "Being" in history and seeing it in relation to particular situations and audiences as a rhetorical appeal recognizes, as Perelman and Olbrechts-Tyteca observe, that each culture has "its own conception of the universal audience." The study of these variations—*hen, logos,* the All, along with Being—teaches us what human beings, at different times in history, have regarded as *real, true,* and *objectively valid.* (*The New Rhetoric: A Treatise on Argumentation,* trans. John Wilkinson and Purcell Weaver [1958, trans. Notre Dame: Univ. of Notre Dame Press, 1969], p. 33.)

[48]Herbert Marcuse, *One-Dimensional Man* (Boston: Beacon Press, 1964).

[49]Heidegger's perplexing ability to subordinate real crises to the interests of his conception of Being reveals itself in an address given on October 30, 1955. Both the Soviet Union and the United States had recently exploded hydrogen bombs. Man finds himself in a perilous situation, declares Heidegger: "Why? Just because a third world war might break out unexpectedly and bring about the complete annihilation of humanity and the destruction of the earth? No. In this dawning atomic age a far greater danger threatens— precisely when the danger of a third world war been removed. . . . the issue is the saving of man's essential nature . . . keeping meditative thinking alive" (*Discourse on Thinking,* trans. J. M. Anderson and E. Hans Freund [New York: Harper and Row, 1966], p. 56).

[50]C. Wright Mills, *The Causes of World War Three* (New York: Simon [&] Schuster, 1958), p. 129.

[51]Wander and Jenkins, p. 450.

CRITICAL RHETORIC: THEORY AND PRAXIS

RAYMIE E. McKERROW

Since the time of Plato's attack marginalizing rhetoric by placing it at the service of truth, theorists have assumed a burden of explaining why rhetoric is "*not* an inferior art" (Hariman, 1986, p. 47). Attempts to rescue rhetoric from its subservient role have often been dependent on universal standards of reason as a means of responding to Plato's critique. While rehabilitating rhetoric in some degree, the efforts nonetheless continue to place it on the periphery, at the service of other, more fundamental standards. Habermas's (1984, 1987) "ideal speech situation," Perelman's (1969) "universal audience," and Toulmin's (1972) "impartial standpoint of rationality" all privilege reason above all else as the avenue to emancipation. In so doing, they preserve for rhetoric a subordinate role in the service of reason. If we are to escape from the trivializing influence of universalist approaches, the task is not to rehabilitate rhetoric, but to announce it in terms of a critical practice.

In response to this challenge, this essay articulates the concept of a *critical rhetoric*—a perspective on rhetoric that explores, in theoretical and practical terms, the implications of a theory that is divorced from the constraints of a Platonic conception. As theory, a critical rhetoric examines the dimensions of domination and freedom as these are exercised in a relativized world. Thus, the first part of this essay focuses on what I am terming a "critique of domination" and a "critique of freedom." The critique of domination has an emancipatory purpose—a telos toward which it aims in the process of demystifying the conditions of domination. The critique of freedom, premised on Michel Foucault's treatment of power relations, has as its telos the prospect of permanent criticism—a self-reflexive critique that turns back on itself even as it promotes a realignment in the forces of power that construct social relations. In practice, a critical rhetoric seeks to unmask or demystify the discourse of power. The aim is to understand the integration of power/ knowledge in society—what possibilities for change the integration invites or inhibits and what intervention strategies might be considered appropriate to effect social change. The second part of the essay delineates the *principles* underlying a critical practice. While the principles are not an exhaustive account, they constitute the core ideas of an *orientation* to critique. As will be argued, the principles also recast the nature of rhetoric from one grounded on Platonic, universalist conceptions of reason to one that recaptures the sense of rhetoric as contingent, of knowledge as doxastic, and of critique as a performance. In so doing, a critical rhetoric reclaims the status (Hariman, 1986) of centrality in the analysis of a discourse of power.

Before considering the twin critiques of domination and freedom, the generic features of a "critical rhetoric" need to be set forth. These features name the enterprise and determine its overall telos. First, a critical rhetoric shares the same "critical spirit" that is held in common among the divergent perspectives of Horkheimer, Adorno, Habermas and Foucault. Second, what Slack and Allor (1983) identify as the "effectivity of communication in the exercise of social power" (p. 215) refers to the manner in which discourse insinuates itself in the fabric of social power, and thereby "effects" the status of knowledge among the members of the social group. As Mosco (1983) suggests, "critical research makes explicit the dense web connecting seemingly unrelated forces in society" (p. 239). By doing so, a critical rhetoric serves a demystifying function (West, 1988, p. 18) by demonstrating the silent and often non-deliberate ways in which rhetoric conceals as much as it reveals through its relationship with power/knowledge. As Marx (1843) put it, a critique serves as "the self-clarification of the struggles and wishes of the age" (cited in Fraser, 1985, p. 97). Third, "a critical social theory frames its research program and its conceptual framework with an eye to the aims and activities of those oppositional social movements with which it has a partisan though not uncritical identification" (Fraser, 1985, p. 97). Critique is not detached and impersonal; it has as its object something which it is "against."[1] Finally, a critical practice must have consequences. In Misgeld's (1985) view, "the ultimate test for the validity of a critical theory of society consists in the possibility of the incorporation of its insights into practically consequential interpretations of social situations" (p. 55). Whether the critique establishes a social judgment about "what to do" as a result of the analysis, it must nonetheless serve to identify the possibilities of future action available to the participants.

A THEORETICAL RATIONALE FOR A CRITICAL RHETORIC

A critical rhetoric encompasses at least two complementary perspectives. The critiques of domination and freedom may not embrace all of those possible, but they allow us to establish the general thrust of critical rhetoric's analysis of discourse. A specific critique may focus on one or the other, or may select elements of both in exploring rhetoric's central role in the creation of social practices. Following the "theoretical rationale," the essay considers the principles that govern analysis within or across these perspectives.

The Critique of Domination: The Discourse of Power

The focus of a critique of domination is on the discourse of power which creates and sustains the social practices which control the dominated. It is, more particularly, a critique of ideologies, perceived as rhetorical creations. The interrelationships between these key concepts deserves closer examination.

Domination, Power and Ideology

A traditional critique of ideology has been in terms of the domination thesis. Giddens (1979) provides a theoretical rationale for viewing power in terms of the dominant or ruling class. He distinguishes between "ideology *as referring to discourse* on the one hand, and ideology *as referring to the involvement of beliefs within 'modes of lived existence'*" (p. 183) and goes on to insist "*that the chief usefulness of the concept of ideology concerns the critique of domination*" (p. 188). This does not mean that the emphasis on discourse itself has been reduced or rejected. Instead, the emphasis has shifted from the question "is this discourse true or false?" to "how the discourse is *mobilized to legitimate the sectional interests of hegemonic groups*" (p. 187). The critique is directed to an analysis of discourse as it contributes to the interests of the ruling class, and as it empowers the ruled to present their interests in a forceful and compelling manner.

Domination occurs through "the construction and maintenance of a particular order of discourse . . . [and] the deployment of non-discursive affirmations and sanctions" (Therborn, 1980, p. 82). The ruling class is affirmed by recourse to *rituals* wherein its power is expressed; its role as ruler is sanctioned, in a negative sense, by the ultimate act of *excommunicating* those who fail to participate in or accede to the rituals. The social structures of discourse, taking their cue from Michel Foucault's "orders of discourse," begin with "*restrictions* on who may speak, how much may be said, what may be talked about, and on what occasion" (Therborn, 1980, p. 83). These restrictions are more than socially derived regulators of discourse; they are institutionalized rules accepted and used by the dominant class to control the discursive actions of the dominated. The ruling class does not need to resort to overt censorship of opposing ideas, as these rules effectively contain inflammatory rhetoric within socially approved bounds—bounds accepted by the people who form the community. As Hall (1988) notes:

> Ruling or dominant conceptions of the world do not directly prescribe the mental content of the illusions that supposedly fill the heads of the dominated classes. But the circle of dominant ideas *does* accumulate the symbolic power to map or classify the world for others; its classifications do acquire not only the constraining power of dominance over other modes of thought but also the inertial authority of habit and instinct. It becomes the horizon of the taken-for-granted: what the world is and how it works, for all practical purposes. (p. 44)

Within the world of the "taken-for-granted," discourse is further *shielded* by accepting only certain individuals as the authorities who can speak. The Moral Majority, for example, would typify this order of discourse by limiting the "word" to the Bible and its author, God. Their discourse is further shielded by allowing repetition by God's servants on earth, only so long as their pronouncements conform to the valid meaning of the original text. Governmental "gag orders" perform the same function, only in this case the intent is to protect interests by limiting the privilege of speech to those whose words can be counted on to be supportive of the establishment. Finally, the structuring of the discursive order involves the *delimited appropriation of discourse*, whereby its reception is restrictively situated. This is not a new category, as research on genre has already established the nature and form of "delimited" address in particular contexts (see Simons & Aghazarian, 1986).

Those who are dominated also participate in the social structure and are affected by—and affect—the orders of discourse by which their actions are moderated.

Bisseret (1979) suggests that "the more the speaker is subjected to power, the more he [she] situates himself [herself] conceptually in reference to the very place where power is concretely exercised" (p. 64). A person cannot escape from the influence of dominant actors, even though the discourse of the latter involves no overt attempt to censor or to entrap the dominated. One can participate in the "dialectic of control" (Giddens, 1979, p. 149) and thereby affect the discourse of power by which individual choice is governed. Nevertheless, the impetus to so function, and the possibility of change, is muted by the fact that the subject already is interpellated with the dominant ideology. Actions oriented toward change will tend to be conducive to power maintenance rather than to its removal.

The locus of the "dialectic of control" can be found in discourse which articulates between class and people. The dominant and the dominated both have recourse to a rhetoric which addresses the people in terms of the classes to which they belong. Domination requires a subject—and the manner of articulation will determine the mode of discourse required to address either "class" or "people." There is no necessary connection between a given ideology and a given class, either ruling or subordinate, at any moment in history (Therborn, 1980, p. 54). As Hall (1988) notes, "ideologies may not be affixed, as organic entities, to their appropriate classes, but this does not mean that the production and transformation of ideology in society could proceed free of or outside the structuring lines of force of power and class" (p. 45). An emphasis on class does not mean that the "people" either cease to exist or fail to be of major theoretical import in the analysis of power relationships. Laclau (1977) differentiates class struggles (dominated by the relations of production) and struggles between a people and the ruling elite (when antagonism cannot be traced clearly to relations of production alone). In the latter sense,

> [T]he "people" or "popular sectors" are not, as some conceptions suppose, rhetorical abstractions or a liberal or idealist conception smuggled into Marxist discourse. The "people" form an objective determination of the system which is different from class determination; the people are one of the poles or the dominant contradiction in a social formation, that is, a contradiction whose intelligibility depends on the ensemble of political and ideological relations of domination and not just the relations of production. If class contradiction is the dominant contradiction at the abstract level of the mode of production, the people-power bloc contradiction is dominant at the level of the social formation. (pp. 107–08)

The *people,* as is clear from the above, have no clear class content. As subjects, they are very much involved in the struggle for hegemony: "The very articulation of the subject's diverse positions is the result of a struggle for hegemony. . . . Hegemony is the very process of constructing politically the masses' subjectivity and *not* the practice of a pre-constituted subject" (Laclau, 1983, p. 118). What is important here is the interaction between class and people in the articulation of a "position" as subject: To win adherence to a class position, the themes are expressed in terms of the rhetoric of the "people." To maintain power, the ruling class also must address themes in terms of a "people." Where, in Therborn's formulation, the nexus of struggle is between differentiated ideological themes or terms, here the nexus is between the ruling elite's and the class's demarcation of the people. The ideological discourse that expresses the will of the people at the same time it constitutes the people as a rhetorical force (Charland, 1987) will reflect a broader interpretation of the "interests" of both dominant and dominated. The creation of a sense of ideological unity derives from the constitution of a discourse of the people; the discourse of the people overrides that of the class in establishing an overall ideological structure. In Laclau's formulation, *"classes cannot assert their hegemony without articulating the people in their discourse"* (1977, p. 196). Additionally, the ruling class cannot maintain its hegemony without clearly articulating its motives for support in terms of the people.

The "people" are both real and fictive. They exist as an "objective determination" (Laclau, 1977, p. 165); one can define their presence in economic and social terms. An agent can construct a definition of "people" to whom discourse is addressed. They are fictive because they exist only inside the symbolic world in which they are called into being (McGee, 1975). They are constituted in the "field of the symbolic" (Laclau & Mouffe, 1985, p. 97) and have no meaning outside of this context. As Charland (1987) notes in his case study of the constitutive nature of rhetoric, the *peuple québécois* "do not exist in nature, but only within a discursively constituted history" (p. 137). They are called into being by discourse (McGee, 1980), and from that moment forward, are "real" to those whose lives their discourse affects—the boundaries of their membership can have "real" economic indexes and socio-political connections.

Critical Practice

A critique of domination can proceed from Therborn's (1980) classification of ideology types, keeping in mind that these are "class-specific *core themes* of discourses that vary enormously in concrete form and degree of elaboration" (p. 79). Therborn isolates "ego" ideologies as those core themes identifying "who we are"; these exist in conjunction with "alter" ideologies that define what we are not. In the 1950s "patriot" was a key term of the ego-ideology, while "communist" was a key term of the corresponding "opposing" ideology. Within contemporary feminism, a core egocentric theme might be "cooperation" with "competition" serving as the "alter" term. In the case of class formations, the conflict between ego and alter ideologies serves as the battleground. Both are inscribed in the social practices of the society and both serve as the impetus for maintenance and change: "From the standpoint of the constitution of class-struggle subjects, the crucial aspect of the alter-ideology is, in the case of exploiting classes, the rationale for their domination of other classes; in the case of exploited classes, it is the basis for their resistance to the exploiters" (Therborn, 1980, p. 61). In pre–civil war [*sic*] days, to property owners, the perception of slaves as "property" served as a reason to keep them under control. To the slaves, the same perception served as the impetus for revolt. In this sense, it is not so much how I see myself as how I see the Other—my appropriation of an alter-ideology for the Other defines the locus of our struggle. The "ego-alter" distinction, as with others Therborn delineates, serve [*sic*] as potential *topoi* for the unraveling of universes of discourse, as well as for locating the nexus of struggle.

A second key element in the unraveling of the discourse of power within this context is to recognize that the issue is not one of simple oppositions. If it were, societal members would be in a relatively "fixed" state, they would "relate to a given regime in a conscious, homogeneous . . . and consistent manner" (Therborn, 1980, p. 102). If this were the case, one would assume the following:

> *Either* a regime has legitimacy *or* it does not; people obey *either* because of normative consent *or* because of physical coercion; *either* the dominated class or classes have a conception of revolutionary change *or* they accept the status

quo or are content with piecemeal reforms; people act *either* on the basis of true knowledge *or* on the basis of false ideas. (Therborn, 1980, p. 102)

The world of the social is not this simple. There are a variety of positions which the dominated and dominant alike can take at any given moment. Hegemony, as Laclau and Mouffe (1985) note, is "not a determinable location within the topography of the social" (p. 139). The analysis of the discourse of power thus must begin with the assumption that any articulatory practice may emerge as relevant or consequential—nothing can be "taken-for-granted" with respect to the impact of any particular discursive practice.

Finally, a critical practice must recognize that the critique of domination alone is not an exhaustive account of the potential discourses of power which govern social practices. This is not to deny the importance of a focus on domination, as there is a compelling sense in which power is negative or repressive in delimiting the potential of the human subject. It is easy to accept the force of the dominant thesis—if you were a Black American in the 1840's, or even in the 1940's, if you are a contemporary feminist, the power of the ruling group may indeed be (if not only appear to be) repressive. The discourse which flows from or expresses power functions to keep people "in their place" as that status is defined and determined by the interest of the dominant class in maintaining its social role. Nevertheless, a focus on the hierarchy of dominant/dominated may deflect attention from the existence of multiple classes, groups, or even individuals with varying degrees of power over others. For this reason, there is a need to examine the critique of power relations across a broader social spectrum.

The Critique of Freedom and the Discourse of Power

Michel Foucault, whose works concern the pervasive effects of power in daily life, articulates a broader conception of power by challenging the power-repression formula endemic to the domination thesis. In the process, he articulates a specialized form of critique that is amenable to the needs of a critical rhetoric. In his terms, "the work of profound transformation can only be done in an atmosphere which is free and always agitated by permanent criticism" (Foucault, 1982, p. 34). The search is not towards a freedom *for* something predetermined. As noted at the outset of this essay, the telos that marks the project is one of never-ending skepticism, hence permanent criticism. Results are never satisfying as the new social relations which emerge from a reaction to a critique are themselves simply new forms of power and hence subject to renewed skepticism. His is not the skepticism of Descarte[s] or Hume. Attempts at transformation do not end in futility. As Rajchman (1985) observes, "Sextus Empiricus is Foucault's precursor. Foucault's philosophy does not aim for sure truths, but for the freedom of withholding judgment on philosophical dogmas" (p. 2). Skepticism is a healthy response to a society which takes universalist dogma and the "truths" it yields for granted: "to question the self-evidence of a form of experience, knowledge, or power, is to free it for our purposes, to open new possibilities for thought and action" (Rajchman, 1985, p. 4).

This approach to questions of social relations yields, for Foucault, a non-traditional historical analysis. Reacting against the "totalizing" emphasis of traditional intellectual history, Foucault is decidedly "anti-Whig" (Kent, 1986). By seeking differences rather than similarities, Foucault's analysis of history focuses on discontinuities in an attempt to discover why certain social relations occurred and not others. History teaches us that there are no certainties, there are no universalizing truths against which we can measure our progress toward some ultimate destiny (Clark & McKerrow, 1987). In consequence, the most we can do is to ever guard against "taken for granteds" that endanger our freedom—our chance to consider new possibilities for action.

Concomitantly, Foucault is not seeking a particular normative structure—critique is not about the business of moving us toward perfection (it is not transcendental in the Neo-Kantian, Habermasian sense), nor is it avowedly anarchistic (Fields [1988, p. 143] overstates the case). Rather, it is simply non-privileging with respect to the options its analysis raises for consideration. On demonstrating the manner in which our social relations constrain us, often in ways that are virtually invisible, which occur at such a deep and remote level in our past as to be anonymous, the possibility of revolt is opened. Anarchism is freedom without a point, and once realized is content to defend its privileged position. Foucault's project privileges nothing, hence contains no such contentment.[2]

The Pervasiveness of Power

As noted earlier, the analysis of power relations need not focus solely on the question of the legitimacy of the state. As Foucault (1980a) notes, "one impoverishes power if one poses it solely in terms of legislation and constitution, in terms solely of the state and the state apparatus" (p. 158). Foucault's analysis of power, in terms of relations that are existent throughout the "social body" (1980a, p. 119), is a radical critique that eschews both analyses of state and economic power, and politically-oriented analyses that have as their motive the "demystification of ideologically distorted belief systems" (Fraser, 1981, p. 272).[3] Instead, the focus is on power as it is manifest across a variety of social practices. His contrast between two historically grounded conceptions of power offers a beginning point for our examination: "the contract-oppression schema, which is the juridical one, and the domination-repression or war-repression schema for which the pertinent opposition is not between the legitimate and illegitimate, as in the first schema, but between struggle and submission" (1980a, p. 92). Within these two versions, it is clear that the discourse of power will be qualitatively different. That is, discourse which upholds a juridical theme of power will speak in terms of rights, obligations, and of the possibility of exchanging power through the legal mediation of conflicting interests. In essence, it is a Western, democratic conception of power that is rational and orderly, and whose discursive themes are deeply imbedded in the historical consciousness of the participants. Contemporary criticism of political rhetoric "buys in" to this perception of power as a model which grounds evaluative claims.

The discourse emanating from what Foucault terms "Nietzsche's hypothesis," on the other hand, will draw on the themes of the opposition of forces in conflict, struggle, and ultimately, war. The theme of oppression in the juridical perspective will occur when rights are over-extended, contracts are broken, or obligations are left unfulfilled. In the case of power as "the hostile engagement of forces," the discursive theme of repression will occur both as a justification for a resort to force and as an account of the "political consequences of war" (1980a, p. 91). One could argue that critical assessments of Western "war rhetoric" are implicitly trapped by the established vision of the dominant group. They are not, as Wander (1983) would argue, essays which take an "ideological turn," as this "reflects the existence of crisis, acknowledges the influence of established interests and the reality of alternative world-views, and commends rhetorical analyses not only of the actions implied but also of the interests represented" (p. 18).

Over against these orientations toward power, Foucault presents a third perspective in his attempt to relate the "mechanisms [of power] to two points of reference, two limits; on the one hand, to the rules of right that provide a formal delimitation of power; on the other, to the effects of truth that this power produces and transmits, and which in their turn reproduce this power. Hence, we have a triangle: power, right, truth" (1980a, pp. 92–93). Of importance for our purpose is the role of discourse in this interactive network: "There are manifold relations of power which permeate, characterize and constitute the social body, and these relations of power cannot themselves be established, consolidated nor implemented without the production, accumulation, circulation and functioning of a discourse" (1980a, p. 93). The discourse identified herein brings power into existence in social relations and gives expression to the ideology that the exercise of power in that relation represents. The sense of "power" brought into being through discourse is not conceived as a stable, continuous force:

> Discourses are not once and for all subservient to power or raised up against it, any more than silences are. We must make allowance for the concept's complex and unstable process whereby discourse can be both an instrument and an effect of power, but also a hindrance, a stumbling block, a point of resistance and a starting point for an opposing strategy. Discourse transmits and produces power; it reinforces it, but also undermines and exposes it, renders it fragile and makes it possible to thwart it. (1980b, pp. 100–101)

Discourse is the tactical dimension of the operation of power in its manifold relations at all levels of society, within and between its institutions, groups and individuals. The task of a critical rhetoric is to undermine and expose the discourse of power in order to thwart its effects in a social relation (the task is not so dissimilar from Burke's [1961] own attempt in *Attitudes Toward History*).

In this context, an examination of the power of the state would take on a special cast: "The power of the state would be an *effet d'ensemble,* the result of an attempt to immobilize, to encode, to make permanent, and to serialize or realign or homogenize innumerable local (and necessarily unstable) confrontations. The state gives an immobilizing intelligibility to the scattered, wildly productive effects of these power generating confrontations" (Bersani, 1977, p. 3). Outside the state, the localization of power lies within an unstable and shifting environment of social relations: "There is no single underlying principle fixing—and hence constituting—the whole field of differences" between and among the social practices that could be energized by a discourse of power (Laclau & Mouffe, 1985, p. 110). Foucault's object in analyzing this dimension of power, in his *History of Sexuality,* for example, is "to define the regime of power-knowledge-pleasure that sustains the discourse on human sexuality in our part of the world" (1980b, p. 11). In this context, the analysis of power in terms of a juridical model, or in terms of a "war" model[,] would be too far from the mark to be helpful. As Fraser (1981) notes, "if power is instantiated in mundane social practices and relations, then efforts to dismantle or transform the regime must address those practices and relations" (p. 280). The critic must attend to the "microphysics of power" in order to understand what *sustains* social practices. Power, thus conceived, is not repressive, but productive—it is an active potentially positive force which creates social relations and sustains them through the appropriation of a discourse that "models" the relations through its expression.

Underlying Foucault's approach is the belief that power, exercised in terms of law and sovereign right, transforms, or in Therborn's terms, naturalizes the social relation: it becomes the norm, and discourse related to its maintenance is "normal." Challenges are therefore abnormal and irrational by definition. This stigma attached to the agents of change is present even though they might work within the confines of the "order of power." Consider, for example, Edelman's (1988) observation that "the language of the helping professions functions as a form of political action" (p. 107) within the established social structure. Challenges to the social relations normalized within the "helping professions" would be met, by those still adhering to the established order, with arguments that assert naivete or irrationality on the part of the "naysayers." Power, in this context, is *not a possession or a content*—it is instead an integral part of social relations. The discourse of power creates and perpetuates the relations, and gives form to the ideology which it projects. Ideology, regardless of its expression, begins with these social relations as integral to its creation, continuance, and change. A thorough-going Foucauldian critique, however, would go beyond Edelman's (1988) analysis, conducted primarily at the level of "agents of change." Power is expressed anonymously, in nondeliberate ways, at a "deep structure" level and may have its origins in the remoteness of our past (carried forward through a particularizing discursive formation).

To be an agent for change requires, from a Foucauldian perspective, an understanding of the reasons for the current social relations of power—and those reasons do not necessarily have to presuppose an earlier production via a named agent. The "denial" of an agent as productive of contingently derived social practices does not rule out the present role of persons as active participants in "revolt" against the present dangers. Otherwise, there is no point to positing the possibilities of freedom—and a Sartrean angst is preordained as the condition of passive acceptance of one's fate.

Power and Truth in the Critique of Freedom

Foucault's analysis of the relationship between power and truth raises the question of the role of discourse as an agent of truth. The rejection of transcendental or universalist standards against which rhetoric is evaluated, as suggested in the beginning of this essay, raises a question: "Have we abandoned the Platonic quest and embraced sophism?" The answer is "yes." The orientation is shifted from an expression of "truth" as the opposite of "false consciousness" (and away from the naive notion that laying bare the latter would inevitably move people toward revolution on the basis of a revealed truth). Engels stated the case for a view of ideology predicated on "false consciousness": "Ideology is a process accomplished by the so-called thinker consciously, it is true, but with a false consciousness. The real forces impelling him remain unknown to him" (1893, p. 459, cited in Therborn, 1980, p. 4). This assumes, however, that (1) all ideology is necessarily false and (2) that "only scientific knowledge is 'true' or 'real' knowledge" (Therborn, 1980, p. 8). In contemporary accounts of culture, this perception has been discredited (Hall, 1988; but see Markovic, 1983). There is an advantage to dispensing with a perception of truth that is hidden behind a "cloud of unknowing" (Hall, 1988, p. 44): If ideology is not equated with false consciousness, it "is no longer treated as untextual, homogeneous, cultural mush—as a synonym for ideas in general, distorted ideas in general, Weltanschauung, ethos, spirit of the times, and so forth" (Mullins, 1979, p. 153). To consider ideology in terms of truth and falsity is to focus attention on its character and to typify it as product rather than as process.

Nevertheless, a consideration of "truth" is an appropriate focus of a critical rhetoric. In Foucault's (1980a) words: "The problem does not consist in drawing the line between that in a discourse which falls under the category of scientificity or truth, and that which comes under some other category, but in seeing historically how effects of truth are produced within discourses which in themselves are neither true nor false" (p. 118). By focusing on the "effects of truth," as expressed in a social relation typified by power, one approximates an Isocratean sense of "community knowledge":

> The important thing here, I believe, is that truth isn't outside power, or lacking in power: Contrary to a myth whose history and functions repay further study, truth isn't the reward of free spirits, the child of protracted solitude, nor the privilege of those who have succeeded in liberating themselves. Truth is a thing of this world: It is produced by virtue of multiple forms of constraint. And it induces regular effects of power. Each society has its regime of truth, its "general politics" of truth: that is, the types of discourse which it accepts and makes function as true; the mechanisms and instances which enable one to distinguish true and false statements, the means by which each is sanctioned; the techniques and procedures accorded value in the acquisition of truth; the status of those who are charged with saying what counts as true. (Foucault, 1980a, p. 131)

The analysis of the discourse of power focuses on the "normalization" of language intended to maintain the status quo. By producing a description of "what is," unfettered by predetermined notions of what "should be," the critic is in a position to posit the possibilities of freedom. Recharacterization of the images changes the power relations and recreates a new "normal" order. In this interaction, "truth" is that which is supplanted by a newly articulated version that is accepted as a basis for the revised social relation. Once instantiated anew in social relations, the critique continues.

THE PRINCIPLES OF PRAXIS

> Discourse lives, as it were, beyond itself, in a living impulse . . . toward the object; if we detach ourselves completely from this impulse all we have left is the naked corpse of the word, from which we can learn nothing at all about the social situation or the fate of a given word in life. (Bakhtin, 1981, p. 292)

Bakhtin's observation about the relation between selves and words is an appropriate grounding for the discussion of the "principles of praxis." This section of the essay does not seek to establish the *methodology* (in the narrow sense of formula or prescription) appropriate to a critical rhetoric. Rather, it seeks to outline the "orientation" (invoked in Burke's sense) that a critic takes toward the object of study. The "object" of a critical rhetoric, however, requires reconsideration prior to a discussion of the principles of a critical practice.

Critical Practice as Invention

Public address, as traditionally conceived, is *agent-centered*. Even the study of social movements has been dominated by this perspective. Given public address's "quasi-theological" (to borrow Cawelti's [1985] term) nature, there is the danger that the inclusion of a "critical rhetoric" perspective would merely perpetuate the traditional model of criticism. The acceptance of a critical rhetoric is premised on the reversal of the phrase "public address"—we need to reconceptualize the endeavor to focus attention on *that symbolism which addresses publics*. The term "address" conjures up the image of a preconceived message, with a beginning, middle, and an end—a ratiocinative discourse which can be located in space and time as an isolated event, or can be placed in a "rhetorical situation" out of which it grew and to which it responds. More often than not, the products of discourse are mediated—are no longer the simple property of a speaker-audience relation. In the context of such mediated communication, Becker (1971) noted the *fragmented* nature of most of the messages impinging on any one consumer. More recently, McGee (1987) has exhorted critics to attend to "formations of texts" in their original fragmented form. What he calls for is the role of a critic as "inventor"—interpreting for the consumer the meaning of fragments collected as *text* or *address*. To approach mediated communication as rhetorical is to see it in its fragmented, unconnected, even contradictory or momentarily oppositional mode of presentation. The task is to construct addresses out of the fabric of mediated experience prior to passing judgment on what those addresses might tell us about our social world. The process one employs is thus geared to uncovering the "dense web" (Mosco, 1983, p. 239), not by means of a simple speaker-audience interaction, but also by means of a "pulling together" of disparate scraps of discourse which, when constructed as an argument, serve to illuminate otherwise hidden or taken for granted social practices.

The reversal of "public address" to "discourse which addresses publics" places the critic in the role of "inventor." As such, s/he is more than an observer of the social scene. And s/he will have as the *text* more than traditional "speaker-audience" scenarios in engaging in a critique. The movement toward communication as "mediated," including the analysis of popular culture, is one way to recover what Turner (1986) refers to as "missed opportunities" in the practice of criticism. If the reversal is not in place, there is the danger that a "public address" vision of popular culture would be constrained to think in terms of "agent" rather than symbol as the focus of attention. There also is the danger that such extension of traditional forms of analysis would simply perpetuate modernist cliches in constructing, through the myopic lenses of a predefined vision of the media as a "cultural wasteland," elitist standards of excellence. "Facts of Life" may never aspire to inclusion in the "canons of oratorical excellence," but it may have more influence on a teenager's conception of social reality than all the great speeches by long-dead great speakers. To ignore "symbols which address publics" in all their manifest forms has, as its ultimate consequence, the perpetuation of sterile forms of criticism.

Principles of a Critical Practice

In the discussion which follows, the principles of a critical praxis, and the alterations in rhetoric's nature they imply, encompass both the critique of domination and of freedom. Neither critique, although it may be carried out alone, is ultimately "complete" without attention to the other. It *is* the case that state power exists, is repressive, and is accessible to critique. It is *equally* the case that power is not only repressive but potentially productive, that its effects are pervasive throughout the social world, and that these effects are accessible to analysis. While a critical practice need not focus on both, the overall analysis of the impact of the discourse of power requires, at a minimum, attention to each dimension. A thorough-going critical rhetoric, therefore, is one whose principles provide an orientation common to both perspectives on *ideologiekritik*. More precisely, then, an *ideologiekritik* is "the production of knowledge to the ends of power and, maybe, of social change" (Lentricchia, 1983, p. 11). Whether cast as a critique of domination or of freedom, the initial task of a critical rhetoric is one of re-creation—constructing an argument that identifies the integration of power and knowledge and delineates the role of power/knowledge in structuring social practices. Reconceptualizing address as textual fragments, and assuming the orientation of a critical rhetoric, brings a critic to the discourse of power with a blank slate if there are no additional principles underwriting the perspective. While not pretending to catalog an exhaustive list, the following "principles" serve to describe, without limiting, the orientation suggested by a critical rhetoric.

Principle #1. "*Ideologiekritik* is in fact not a method, but a *practice*" (McGee, 1984, p. 49).

McGee (1984, 1987) is correct in chastising critics for paying too much attention to methodological concerns. If reading Burke prompts any lesson it is that creative insights are constrained by the systematicity of method. This lesson was lost on legions of academics who, by imposing a system on an unmethodological critic, created their own fiction and termed it a method.[4] Considered as practice, understanding and evaluation are one: "Understanding is impossible without evaluation. Understanding cannot be separated from evaluation: they are simultaneous and constitute a unified integral act. . . . In the act of understanding [unless one is a dogmatist and therefore impervious to change] a struggle occurs that results in mutual change and enrichment" (Bakhtin, 1986, p. 142). In this context, "description" implies evaluation by the very fact of choice with respect to what is described, as well as what is not. Burke's (1966, p. 45) dictum that a selection of reality is also a deflection and a rejection applies to the act of criticism as well as to other symbolic acts that are taken as the object of a critical perspective. This does not mean a critic functions as an anarchist. Rather, it means one operates from a "perspective" (McGee, 1984, p. 47) or an "orientation": embracing a set of principles does not commit one to prescriptivism any more than it renders the critical act directionless. An orientation is the least restrictive stage from which the critical act might be launched; it maximizes the possibilities of what will "count" as evidence for critical judgment, and allows for creativity in the assessment of the "effects of truth" upon social practices.

Principle #2. The discourse of power is material.

An ideology exists, in a material sense, in and through the language which constitutes it (McGee, 1982). As Therborn (1980) notes, "ideology operates as discourse. . . . [It] is the medium through which men make their history as conscious actors" (pp. 15, 3). Participants are not passive bystanders, simply absorbing the ideology and having no power to alter its force or its character. Ideology is a property of the social world, but agents have the capacity to interact in that world to modify the discourse (see Mumby, 1987). They do not come to the particular ideology as a *tabula rasa:* They come to a system of discourse with an ideological grid already in place and participate in terms of that grid's determinative nature. This is the implication of Burke's (1966) "terministic screens" as mechanisms which control how alternate discourses are heard. As Althusser (1971) has noted, "ideology has always-already interpellated individuals as subjects" (p. 164). This focuses our attention on the social dimension or consciousness of the collectivity that utilizes or adheres to a particular discourse. As Charland (1987) has illustrated, a traditional speaker-audience model presumes that an audience is already constituted as subject, and employs discourse in a manner to sustain present relations of domination. He succeeds in carrying the "constitution of a subject" a step backward to its initiation in a discourse—as the audience is called into being as a *peuple québécois* (p. 134). In either case, the rhetor is capable of participating in a "dialectic of control" to shape the on-going nature of the social relation being sustained or entered into. In fact, to the extent that a person fails to enter into a dialectical relation with the ideology, that individual ceases to function as an *agent* in the social system (see Giddens, 1979, p. 149).

The materiality of discourse focuses attention on the sense of "praxis" utilized in a critical rhetoric. Aristotle's vision of praxis identified it with the goals of *phronesis* or practical wisdom (the "doing of fine and noble deeds" [Benhabib, 1986, p. 157] in the service of virtue). A critical rhetoric no longer looks at praxis in its ethical dimension, tying it to an ideal life-style. Rather, a critical rhetoric links praxis, both as object of study and as style, to "a mode of *transformative activity*" (Benhabib, 1986, p. 67) in which the social relations in which people participate are perceived as "real" to them even though they exist only as fictions in a rhetorically constituted universe of discourse. What is differentiated for the purposes of critical practice is not a rejection of ethical values, but a reordering of the perspective to one in which *transformation* (or at minimum, the delineation of the possibilities for transformation) is seen as the ultimate aim. Even theorizing, in this sense, is critical practice, as it lays out the preconditions for transformation within a set of social relations. The product of a critique may be seen in the Aristotelian sense of a "noble deed," but that is not its *raison d'etre*.

What is constituted as "real" is not only so structured through discursive practices. What is perceived as real to the populace, in economic, social, and political terms also is created in non-discursive ways. Following Laclau and Mouffe (1985) the practice of a critical rhetoric

> rejects the distinction between discursive and non-discursive practices. It affirms: (a) that every object is constituted as an object of discourse insofar as no object is given outside every discursive condition of emergence; and (b) that any distinction between what are usually called linguistic and behavioural aspects of a social practice is either an incorrect distinction or ought to find its place as a differentiation within the social production of meaning which is structured under the form of discursive totalities. (p. 107)

This is not to diminish the importance of non-discursive practices, but rather to acknowledge that the discussion of such practices takes place in terms of discursive practices. The analysis of social praxis must, if it is to accomplish its transformative goal, deal in concrete terms with those relations which are "real"—which do in fact constrain discourse, and do so in ways that are seldom seen without such analysis.

Principle #3. Rhetoric constitutes *doxastic* rather than *epistemic* knowledge.

A critical rhetoric must be grounded on a reconstitution of the concept of *doxa* (Hariman, 1986). Plato's impact on the status of rhetoric needs little elaboration— the attempts to rehabilitate rhetoric, to save it from its own "shame" are many and varied (Hariman, 1986; Nelson & Megill, 1986). In essence, that is what the "epistemic"[5] movement attempts, regardless of its claim to establish rhetoric's role in the constitution of subjects. By subsuming the constitution of subjects under the rubric of *episteme,* theorists do no more than attempt to rescue rhetoric from the oblivion to which Plato consigned it. Considerations of rhetoric as epistemic are inextricably linked to a neo-Kantian definition of what constitutes knowledge, as that will always be seen in terms of independent, universal standards of judgment

(whether invoked by Perelman, Toulmin, or Habermas). In the process, the rehabilitation remains subservient to a Platonic, neo-Kantian perception of rhetoric's
"true" role in society. A more positive approach is to reassert the value of rhetoric's
province—*doxa*—and thereby resituate theory and practice in a context far more
amenable to its continuance.

Nelson and Megill (1986), writing on the nature of the "rhetoric of inquiry,"
observe the history of "certitude" under which rhetoric has served:

> Plato denigrated opinion and rhetoric so as to celebrate truth and order at a
> time of Greek conflict and Athenian decline. Similarly, Aristotle subordinated
> mythos to logos and rhetoric to dialectic. In an era when radical disagree-
> ments racked the peace of Europe, Descartes wrote off rhetoric in favor of
> mathematical reason and Hobbes enslaved language to the sovereign. Later,
> Kant sought perpetual peace through pure and practical reason. Craving
> certainty as a path to peace and order in our own troubled times, many of
> us may be tempted by similar visions. But after more than three centuries of
> such abstract utopias, not to mention the programs for their enforcement, we
> have every reason to resist their temptation and revise their anti-rhetorical
> premises. (p. 23)

As they demonstrate, there is a wealth of philosophical support for the rejection of such anti-rhetorics. Their own limitation, notwithstanding brief references
to the social and political facets of inquiry, is that the rhetoric of inquiry ends
in description.[6] In this sense, the rhetoric of inquiry, as is the case with the
Habermasian project, remains locked into a mode of reason (even when viewed as
rhetorical [Brown, 1987]) that aims for universalizing the standards of judgment—
in this case, across the academy. A critical rhetoric ends in transformation of the
conditions of domination or in the possibility of revolt as the consequence of a
critique of freedom. Thus, even though the rhetoric of inquiry is premised on
a positive reassertion of rhetoric's role in society, its rationale (wedded to rhetoric
as epistemic) does not go far enough to embrace the practice of a critical rhetoric.

Hariman (1986) offers a reconceptualization of *doxa* that removes it from an
opposition to *episteme*. *Doxa*, as he notes, includes not only the traditional characteristic of "opinion" but also "reputation" or "regard" and functions as much
by concealment as by revelation: "*Doxa* is created by acts of concealment, and
so a complete conceptualization of *doxa* must include the idea that regard is in
part achieved by the concealment of rank. This interpretation repositions *doxa*: it
is no longer contrasted with *episteme*, but rather with *alethia*, truth (literally
'unhiddenness'). . . . This dynamic of concealment and unconcealment [truth]—
of authorizing and marginalizing—is the means by which we determine what we
believe, what we know, and what we believe to be true" (pp. 49–50). Doxastic
knowledge functions as the grounding of a critical rhetoric.[7] Rather than focusing
on questions of "truth" or "falsity," a view of rhetoric as doxastic allows the focus
to shift to how the symbols come to possess power—what they "do" in society as
contrasted to what they "are."

The sense of *doxa* as concealment is implied in Bourdieu's (1977, 1979) notion of
doxa as the realm of the "undiscussed." Bourdieu (1977, 1979, 1980) employs metaphors of capitalism in his examination of the relationships between authority to speak
and the appropriation of symbols—those in authority simply have more "capital"
at their disposal, as well as enjoy control of the means of distribution of symbols.
They have, as a result, the interest of conserving or preserving the "state of *doxa*

in which the established structure is not questioned" (Thompson, 1984, p. 49). Bringing the "undiscussed" or concealed to the forefront is an act of heterodoxical rhetoric, met, naturally enough, by an orthodox rhetoric of defense of the status quo. Central to this discussion of *doxa,* as in the case of Hariman's analysis, is the recognition of its contingent nature, as well as its implicit sense of having an inscribed status (estimate of worth) by having been appropriated as the symbolic capital of the dominant group. Those with less capital are accordingly "marginalized" until or unless their heterodoxical rhetoric can successfully supplant that of the ruling elite.

Principle #4. Naming is the central symbolic act of a *nominalist* rhetoric.

The power of language to constitute subjects implicit in "naming as an interpretive act" (in Burke's [1941, pp. 5–71] sense; see Blankenship, 1976, p. 236) suggests that it is a justifiable principle to incorporate in a critical perspective. The principle encompasses all that has been said in criticism under the rubric of "rhetorical visions," "ideographs," and "condensation symbols." As a specific example, though it is not discussed in any of these terms, consider Hall's (1985) own treatment of his personal experience as a "coloured" person in Jamaica and then as a person from Jamaica. As the contexts shift, so too do the meanings inherent in social practices legitimated by reactions to a label. The subject is "fractured" into a multiplicity of selves as the perception/label shifts. Bakhtin's (1986) observation that "nothing is absolutely dead: every meaning will have its homecoming festival" (p. 170) applies: A return to Jamaica brings with it all of the old associations that one has grown away from in another cultural milieu. In the recent Iran-Contra hearings, McFarlane legitimated a foreign country's contribution to the contras, at a time when solicitation was expressly forbidden by Congress, as "not a solicitation per se." One can't put too fine an edge on the power or process of naming, when potentially illegal actions are justified by linguistic sleights of hand.

What is left out of the above analysis is perhaps the most crucial aspect of the process of naming. Consonant with recapturing a sense of rhetoric as doxastic rather than epistemic, a reinterpretation of rhetoric as nominalist fits well with the contingent nature of the social reality in which humans are both subject and subjected (Therborn, 1980). Rajchman (1985) observes of Foucault that "his histories are *themselves* nominalist histories. They are not histories of things, but of the terms, categories, and techniques through which certain things become at certain times the focus of a whole configuration of discussion and procedure" (p. 51). For a critical rhetoric, the significance is the parallel sense in which rhetoric itself adopts a nominalist stance. Foucault's nominalist history is directed against the totalizing and deterministic effects of an intellectual (Whiggish) history which sacrifices difference in the search for similarity. In similar fashion, a nominalist rhetoric is directed against the universalizing tendencies of a Habermasian communicative ethics or a Perelmanesque philosophical rhetoric (see Benhabib, 1986; McKerrow, 1986).

The implications of a nominalist rhetoric are evidenced in a comparison of different forms of hermeneutic analysis:

Hermeneutic realism, for example, assumes a stability of meaning before any rhetorical acts take place. Meaning is determinate, objective, and eternally fixed because of constraints in the text itself that are independent of historically situated critical debate. In a strangely similar way, hermeneutic idealism also assumes a stability of meaning outside situated practices. Meaning is determinate, intersubjective, and temporarily fixed because of constraints provided by the communal convention in readers' and critics' minds. (Mailloux, 1985, p. 630)

Rhetorical hermeneutics, on the other hand, tries to correct the error of "presupposing the possibility of meaning outside specific historical contexts of rhetorical practices" (Mailloux, 1985, p. 630). A nominalist rhetoric shares, with Mailloux's formulation of a rhetorical hermeneutics, a sense that terms are contingently based—the reasons for their emergence are not premised on fixed, determinative models of inquiry.

Principle #5. Influence is not *causality.*

This simple claim has profound implications for understanding the assumptive framework underlying the analysis of the discourse of power. As Condit (1987) argues, "to say that something 'influences' a process, or has 'force,' eschews the determinism latent in the term 'cause.' An influence or force may be overridden or supplemented by other forces. It may even require the active participation of other forces (e.g., 'human choice') to become actualized" (p. 2). Thus, given the contingency with which rhetoric historically concerns itself, to say that a symbol has influence is to claim that it impacts on others (one might term this a soft cause if one wished to retain the term).

Presence of a symbol is not actuality, but at least is potentiality. The potential for images of crime to influence the social reality of the elderly is present through the depiction of such symbolic acts on nightly crime drama. As empirical studies have shown, such acts do in fact influence the elderly's perception of the amount of actual crime in their own social community.

The claim separates a critical rhetoric from the structural causality inherent in an Althusserian critique of culture, as well as from other "pure" Marxist reductionisms of the determinist stripe. Seen in this context, the notion of "influence" rejects the twin claims that nothing is connected to anything else (culturalism) and that everything is determined by something (structuralism) (see Hall, 1985). Hall's own cultural perspective is far more amenable to this principle, as it allows for contingency in the convergence of events that would determine social practices, or social change. Noting that there is no "necessary correspondence" between an ideological expression and one's social class does not invalidate the possibility of social change. From a rhetorical perspective, what it implies is that the impetus for change has not yet been articulated—the necessary symbolic act bridging the ideology and the social position has not yet been created. This doesn't imply that it won't or can't be formulated. The following statement from Hall (1985) identifies the role of rhetoric, without so naming it: "The aim of a theoretically-informed political practice must surely be to bring about or construct the articulation between social and economic forces and those forms of politics and ideology which might lead them in practice to intervene in history in a progressive way—an articulation which has to be *constructed* through practice precisely because it is not guaranteed by how those forces are constituted in the first place" (p. 95).

If there is a lack of correspondence between an ideology and a class position, symbols must be invented in such a way as to accommodate the "difference" that exists. In the various analyses of Hart's debacle, there is ample suggestion of the variance between cultural mores and the position of the candidate. Hart's "affair," or more recently, the travails of Jimmy Swaggart, are not morality plays. They are, much more fundamentally, failures to bridge the gap between a lived practice and a non-corresponding ideology. As Abravanel (1983) points out, the contradiction is between a moral sense of "what should be done" and "what is being done" (p 280). The contradiction is mediated, both in the life of the individual and within the public realm, by recourse to suitable myths that gloss the incompatibilities, and thereby provide a rationalization for action. The task of a critical rhetoric is to call attention to the myth, and the manner in which it mediates between contradictory impulses to action.

Principle #6. Absence is as important as *presence* in understanding and evaluating symbolic action.

Hall's experience is again helpful; as he writes, "positively marked terms 'signify' because of their position in relation to what is absent, unmarked, the unspoken, the unsayable. Meaning is relational within an ideological system of presences and absences" (1985, p 109). Terms are not "unconnected"; in the formation of a text, out of fragments of what is said, the resulting "picture" needs to be checked against "what is absent" as well as what is present Wander's analysis of media also supports the influence of the "not said," particularly as it reinforces that which is said (1981). To the extent that the following is an accurate statement about what appears on television, the negation also may be considered an accurate reflection of reality:

> Most characters on prime time conform to conventional standards of beauty—they tend to be white or near white, fine-featured, young, well proportioned, and of average height.
> NEGATION: Few characters appear on prime time who are fat. Not many have scars, limps, or protruding lips. Few adult characters are under five feet or over six feet, four inches tall. Not many characters appear to be over 65. When physically "deviant" characters do appear, they tend not to be cast as intelligent, strong, or virtuous. (pp. 518–19)

As the culture changes, and the "said" shifts in identifiable patterns, the negation can be revised.

The Iran-Contra hearings provide a very different exemplar: over and over, the concern was with what was left out, the "unsaid" in a situation. McFarlane may have said that such and such knowledge is "not known concretely" but did not say that such knowledge is known in some degree. Answers to specific questions may only be partial statements, accurate insofar as they are expressed, but certainly not the answers that would be given if other questions were asked. Inferences based on such answers more often than not play directly into the hands of those in control of both knowledge and the power that it provides.

Principle #7. Fragments contain the potential for *polysemic* rather than *monosemic* interpretation.

This probably shouldn't need saying. Nevertheless, given the dominance of a modernist critique which, as a particularizing example, sees mediated communication as a corruptive influence, as promoting the declining standards of the culture, such a claim deserves renewed attention. First, to use Cawelti's (1985) term, the early "quasi-theological" cast of much media criticism is on the wane. As Grossberg (1984) and Becker (1986) suggest in their respective surveys of media criticism, there is a much stronger influence from ideological, social/cultural perspectives currently in vogue. Even so, as Fiske (1986) notes, ideological criticism has been myopic in its vision of television as a monosemic text, underwriting the dominant cultural forces at work in society. An underlying weakness of a critique which sees the viewer as ultimately passive and unable to participate in social change limits ideological criticism to that "of increasing the viewer's ability to resist the imposition of cultural meanings that may not fit one's own social identity, and in so doing to resist the homogenization of culture" (p. 399). While this has value, it is, in the main, a negative one. A polysemic critique is one which uncovers a subordinate or secondary reading which contains the seeds of subversion or rejection of authority, at the same time that the primary reading appears to confirm the power of the dominant cultural norms. As Fiske (1986) says, "different socially located viewers will activate" the meaning of a text differently. Those who come to the experience from the domain of power may see only legitimization, while those subjected to power can "take the signifying practices and products of the dominant" and "use them for different social purposes" (p. 406).

Principle #8. Criticism is a *performance.*

This is the thrust of McGee's (1987) analysis of the critique of culture. In the sense of a critical rhetoric, it places the focus on the activity as a statement; the critic as inventor becomes arguer or advocate for an interpretation of the collected fragments. Is this to say anything more than Brockriede (1974), who long ago acknowledged that criticism is an argumentative activity? If I understand McGee's point, the emphasis goes beyond the simple assertion that any interpretation must give reasons. In McGee's (1987) words, "rhetoricians are performers" (p. 8). The act of performing, within the context of our expertise as critics/readers of the social condition, moves the focus from criticism as method to critique as practice.

This principle also encompasses the recent advocacy of an "ideological turn" in criticism. Wander (1983) argues that "criticism takes an ideological turn when it recognizes the existence of powerful vested interests benefiting from and consistently urging politics and technology that threatens life on this planet" (p. 18). As written, however, the frame of reference for the insertion of ideological intent is unnecessarily confined to a narrow range of human experience. The function of an ideologiekritik is to counter the excesses of a society's own enabling actions, its "repressive tolerance" in Marcuse's terms, that underwrites the continuation of social practices that ultimately are harmful to the community (see McGee, 1984). Thus, the sense of that which is harmful may be much broader than Wander implies.

To escape the implication that what Wander desires is for academics to take to the streets as practicing revolutionaries (and that may, in fact, be what he desires) there is an important caveat. The practice of a critical rhetoric can take refuge in Foucault's (1980a) defense of his own writing as that of a *specific intellectual* (p. 126). To borrow Lentricchia's (1983) statement of the practice, a specific intellectual is "one whose radical work of transformation, whose fight against repression is carried on at the specific institutional site where he [she] finds himself [herself] and on the terms of his [her] own expertise, on the terms inherent to his [her] own functioning as an intellectual" (pp. 6–7). This also gives meaning to theorizing as a critical practice—as a performance of a rhetor advocating a critique as a sensible reading of the discourse of power.

SUMMARY: THEORY, PRAXIS AND THE FUTURE

I have, in this essay, taken Jensen's (1987) observation, "communication media engage audiences in the construction of cultural forms" (p. 24) as a given. My purpose has been to suggest a theoretical rationale and a set of principles for the critique of domination and of freedom. As such, this essay serves as a "synthetic statement" of both forms of critique. There are many other forms of criticism, and of critiques; the conception of a critical rhetoric need not displace all other rhetorics. What it must do, however, is provide an avenue—an orientation—toward a postmodern conception of the relationship between discourse and power. In so doing, it announces a critical practice that stands on its own, without reliance on universal standards of reason. Instead, a critical rhetoric celebrates its reliance on contingency, on doxa as the basis for knowledge, on nominalism as the ground of language meaning as doxastic, and critique viewed as a performance. Rhetoric, in the context of these principles, emerges with *status* (Hariman, 1986) in the analysis of a discourse of power.

What then of the "future" of a critical rhetoric? If I have been marginally successful in setting forth the "image" of a critical rhetoric as theory and praxis, I rest my case on Blankenship and Muir's (1987) observation that such an image contains "both the vision of the future and the [instrument] for realizing it" (p. 6).

NOTES

[1] As may be obvious, this is a more violent wrenching of traditional modes of rhetorical criticism than some may tolerate (e.g., Campbell, 1983; Hill, 1983).

[2] It is in this sense that his project is anti-humanist (see Blair & Cooper [1987] and Fisher [1985] to the contrary). By privileging no one subject or topic, Foucault is not anti-human, but anti-humanist in the sense that he does not place humans at the center or core of our philosophical tradition. He places nothing, and especially not transcendental reason, at the center, so to claim an "anti-humanism" stance is simply to affirm that "human choice and freedom" (Blair & Cooper, 1987, p. 167) will not be constrained by an a priori privilege.

[3] In the process, Foucault suspends traditional rationalistic orientations toward truth and falsity (a tradition Marxist analysis of false consciousness embraces, though for different effects), and "brackets" questions of epistemic and normative justifications of social practices (Fraser, 1981, pp. 273–75). The suspension of criteria of justification is consonant with the absence of privilege alluded to earlier.

[4] There is a similar danger in perceiving Foucault's "perspective" as a "method" (Blair & Cooper, 1987, p. 161). As Shiner (1982) argues, "If one persists in seeing Foucault as a methodologist, the phrase 'genealogy of power' which from 1972 replaces 'archaeology of knowledge' will be even more grossly misinterpreted. . . . His method is an anti-method in the sense that it seeks to free us from the illusion that an apolitical method is possible" (p. 386). There is not an apparent contradiction between a political project (any analysis of the relations of knowledge and power is inherently political) and the absence of privilege, even of a method of analysis. To privilege any one method, including genealogy or its precursor, archaeology, is to preordain the conclusion and hence restrict freedom. What Blair and Cooper (1987) see as a method is in actuality a parody—what a method might be if one were to consciously adopt it—that Foucault has no intention of following slavishly (Clark & McKerrow, 1987).

[5] For representative essays, see Scott (1967, 1976), Farrell (1976, 1978), Leff (1978), Cherwitz & Hikins (1986).

[6] For representative essays, see Simons (1985), McGee (1980, 1987), Lyne (1985), Nelson & Megill (1986), Nelson, Megill, & McCloskey (1987), Hariman (1986).

[7] The orientation to knowledge grounds the critique of domination's focus on what is concealed as well as revealed in the discourse of power (thereby conferring status on the elite and marginalizing the dominated). Foucault's concern with understanding how certain "mentalities" came into being at a particular time also resonates well with this reconceptualized sense of doxa—certain discursive formations are granted status within

social relations while others are marginalized. The aim of a Foucauldian critique is, in these terms, to set forth the conditions by which the nature of what is taken to be doxastic knowledge at any given time can be recast.

REFERENCES

Abravanel, H. (1983). Mediatory myths in the service of organizational ideology. In L. R. Pony, P. J. Frost, G. Morgan, & T. C. Dandridge (Eds.). *Organizational symbolism* (pp. 273–293). Greenwich, CT: JAI Press.

Althusser, L. (1971). *Lenin and philosophy, and other essays.* (B. Brewster, Trans.). London: NLB.

Bakhtin, M. M. (1981). *The dialogic imagination.* M. Holquist (Ed.). (C. Emerson & M. Holquist, Trans.). Austin: University of Texas Press.

Bakhtin, M. M. (1986). *Speech genres and other late essays.* C. Emerson & M. Holquist (Eds.), (V. McGee, Trans.). Austin: University of Texas Press.

Becker, S. (1971). Rhetorical studies for the contemporary world. In E. Black & L. Bitzer (Eds.), *The prospect of rhetoric* (pp. 21–43). NJ: Prentice-Hall.

Becker, S. (1986, November). *Rhetoric, media and culture or the rhetorical turn in media studies.* Paper presented at the annual meeting of the Speech Communication Association, Chicago.

Benhabib, S. (1986). *Critique, norm, and utopia: A study of the foundations of critical theory.* New York: Columbia University Press.

Bersani, L. (1977). The subject of power. *Diacritics, 7,* 3.

Bisseret, N. (1979). *Education, class language and ideology.* London: Routledge & Kegan Paul.

Blair, C., & Cooper, M. (1987). The humanist turn in Foucault's rhetoric of inquiry. *Quarterly Journal of Speech, 73,* 151–71.

Blankenship, J. (1976). The search for the 1972 Democratic nomination: A metaphorical perspective. In J. Blankenship & H. G. Stelzner (Eds.). *Rhetoric and communication: Studies in the University of Illinois tradition* (pp. 236–260). Urbana, IL: University of Illinois Press.

Blankenship, J., & Muir, J. K. (1987). On imaging the future: The secular search for 'piety.' *Communication Quarterly, 35,* 1–12.

Bourdieu, P. (1977). *Outline of a theory of practice.* (R. Nice, Trans.). Cambridge: Cambridge University Press.

Bourdieu, P. (1979). Symbolic power. *Critique of Anthropology, 4,* 77–85 (R. Nice, Trans.).

Bourdieu, P. (1980). The production of belief: Contribution to an economy of symbolic goods. *Media, Culture, & Society, 2,* 261–293. (R. Nice, Trans.).

Brockriede, W. (1974). Rhetorical criticism as argument. *Quarterly Journal of Speech, 60,* 165–174.

Brown, R. H. (1987). *Society as text: Essays on rhetoric, reason and reality.* Chicago: University of Chicago Press.

Burke, K. (1941). *The philosophy of literary form.* Baton Rouge, LA: Louisiana State University Press.

Burke, K. (1961). *Attitudes toward history.* Boston: Beacon Press.

Burke, K. (1966). *Language as symbolic action.* Berkeley, CA: University of California Press.

Campbell, K. K. (1983). Response to Forbes Hill. *Central States Speech Journal, 34,* 126–127.

Cawelti, J. G. (1985). With the benefit of hindsight: Popular cultural criticism. *Critical Studies in Mass Communication, 2,* 363–379.

Charland, M. (1987). Constitutive rhetoric: The case of the Peuple Québécois. *Quarterly Journal of Speech, 73,* 133–150.

Cherwitz, R. A., & Hikins, J. (1986) *Communication and knowledge: An investigation in rhetorical knowledge.* Columbia, SC: University of South Carolina Press.

Clark, E. C., & McKerrow, R. E. (1987). The historiographical dilemma in Myrdal's American creed: Rhetoric's role in rescuing a historical moment. *Quarterly Journal of Speech, 73,* 303–316.

Condit, C. (1987). Democracy and civil rights: The universalizing influence of public argumentation. *Communication Monographs, 54,* 1–18.

Edelman, M. (1988). *Constructing the political spectacle.* Chicago, IL: University of Chicago Press.

Engels, F. (14 July, 1893). Engels to Mehring. In *K. Marx & F. Engels, Selected Correspondence: 1846–1895,* Vol. 29. (pp. 511–512). (D. Torr, Trans.). New York: International Publishers, 1942.

Farrell, T. B. (1976). Knowledge, consensus, and rhetorical theory. *Quarterly Journal of Speech, 62,* 258–266.

Farrell, T. B. (1978). Social knowledge II. *Quarterly Journal of Speech, 64,* 329–334.

Fields, A. B. (1988). In defense of political economy and systemic analysis: A critique of prevailing theoretical approaches to the new social movements. In C. Nelson & L. Grossberg (Eds.), *Marxism and the interpretation of culture* (pp. 141–156). Urbana, IL: University of Illinois Press.

Fisher, W. (1985). The narrative paradigm: An elaboration. *Communication Monographs, 52,* 347–367.

Fiske, J. (1986). Television: Polysemy and popularity. *Critical Studies in Mass Communication, 3,* 391–408.

Foucault, M. (1980a). *Power/knowledge.* C. Gordon (Ed.). (C. Gordon, L. Marshall, J. Mephau, K. Soper, Trans.). New York: Pantheon Books.

Foucault, M. (1980b). *The history of sexuality,* Vol. 1. (R. Hurley, Trans.). New York: Vintage Books.

Foucault, M. (1982). Is it really important to think? An interview. *Philosophical and Social Criticism, 9,* 29–40. (T. Keenan, Trans.).

Fraser, N. (1981). Foucault on modern power: Empirical insights and normative confusions. *Praxis International, 1,* 272–287.

Fraser, N. (1985). What's critical about critical theory? The case of Habermas and gender. *New German Critique, 35,* 97–131.

Giddens, A. (1979). *Central problems in social theory.* Berkeley, CA: University of California Press.

Giddens, A. (1984). *The constitution of society: Outline of a theory of structuration.* Cambridge: Polity Press.

Grossberg, L. (1984). Strategies of Marxist cultural interpretation. *Critical Studies in Mass Communication, 1,* 391–421.

Habermas, J. (1984). *The theory of communicative action: Reason and rationalization of society* (Vol. 1) (Trans. T. McCarthy). Boston: Beacon Press.

Habermas, J. (1987). *The philosophical discourses of modernity.* (Trans. F. Lawrence). Cambridge: MIT Press.

Hall, S. (1985). Signification, representation, ideology: Althusser and the post-structuralist debates. *Critical Studies In Mass Communication, 2,* 91–114.

Hall, S. (1988). The toad in the garden: Thatcherism among the theorists. In C. Nelson & L. Grossberg (Eds.). *Marxism and the interpretation of culture* (pp. 35–57). Urbana, IL. University of Illinois Press.

Hariman, R. (1986). Status, marginality and rhetorical theory. *Quarterly Journal of Speech, 72,* 38–54.

Hill, F. (1983). A turn against ideology: Reply to Professor Wander. *Central States Speech Journal, 34,* 121–126.

Hiley, D. (1984). Foucault and the analysis of power. *Praxis International, 4,* 192–207.

Jensen, K. B. (1987). Qualitative audience research: Toward an integrative approach to reception. *Critical Studies in Mass Communication, 4,* 21–36.

Kent, C. A. (1986). Michel Foucault: Doing history or undoing it? *Canadian Journal of History, 21,* 371–396.

Laclau, E. (1977). *Politics and ideology in Marxist theory*. London: NLB.

Laclau, E. (1980). Populist rupture and discourse. *Screen Education, 34,* 87–93. (J. Grealy, Trans.).

Laclau, E. (1983). 'Socialism,' the 'people,' 'democracy': The transformation of hegemonic logic. *Social Text, 7,* 115–119.

Laclau, E., & Mouffe, C. (1985). *Hegemony and socialist strategy: Towards a radical democratic politics* (W. Moore & P. Cammack, Trans.). London: Verso.

Leff, M. (1978). In search of Ariadne's thread: A review of the recent literature on rhetorical theory. *Central States Speech Journal, 29,* 73–91.

Lentricchia, F. (1983). *Criticism and social change*. University of Chicago Press.

Lyne, J. (1985). Rhetorics of inquiry. *Quarterly Journal of Speech, 71,* 65–73.

Mailloux, S. (1985). Rhetorical hermeneutics. *Critical Inquiry, 11,* 620–641.

Markovic, M. (1983). The idea of critique in social theory. *Praxis International, 3,* 108–120.

McGee, M. C. (1975). In search of the 'people': A rhetorical alternative. *Quarterly Journal of Speech, 61,* 235–249.

McGee, M. C. (1980). The 'ideograph': A link between rhetoric and ideology. *Quarterly Journal of Speech, 66,* 1–16.

McGee, M. C. (1982). A materialist's conception of rhetoric. In R. E. McKerrow (Ed.). *Explorations in rhetoric* (pp. 23–48). Glenview, IL: Scott-Foresman.

McGee, M. C. (1984). Another philippic: Notes on the ideological turn in criticism. *Central States Speech Journal, 35,* 43–50.

McGee, M. C. (1987, April). Public address and culture studies. Paper presented at the annual meeting of the Central States Speech Association, St. Louis.

McKerrow, R. E. (1986). Pragmatic justification and Perelman's philosophical rhetoric. In J. Golden & J. J. Pilotta (Eds.). *Practical reasoning in human affairs: Studies in honor of Chaim Perelman* (pp. 207–225). Dordrecht, The Netherlands: D. Reidel.

Misgeld, D. (1985). Critical hermeneutics versus Neoparsonianism? *New German Critique, 35,* 55–82.

Mosco, V. (1983). Critical research and the role of labor. *Journal of Communication, 33,* 248.

Mullins, W. A. (1979). Truth and ideology: Reflections on Mannheim's paradox. *History and Theory, 18,* 141–154.

Mumby, D. K. (1987). The political function of narrative in organizations. *Communication Monographs, 54,* 113–127.

Nelson, J. S., & Megill, A. (1986). Rhetoric of inquiry: Prospects and projects. *Quarterly Journal of Speech, 72,* 20–37.

Nelson, J. S., Megill, A., & McCloskey, D. N. (1987). (Eds.). *The rhetoric of the human sciences*. Madison: University of Wisconsin Press.

Perelman, C., & Olbrechts-Tyteca, L. (1969). *The new rhetoric: A treatise on argumentation*. (J. Wilkinson & P. Weaver, Trans.). Notre Dame: University of Notre Dame Press.

Rajchman, J. (1985). *Michel Foucault: The freedom of philosophy*. New York: Columbia University Press.

Ross, S. D. (1985). Foucault's radical politics. *Praxis International, 5,* 131–144.

Scott, R. L. (1967). On viewing rhetoric as epistemic. *Central States Speech Journal, 18,* 9–17.

Scott, R. L. (1976). On viewing rhetoric as epistemic: Ten years later. *Central States Speech Journal, 27,* 258–266.

Shiner, L. (1982). Reading Foucault: Anti-method and the genealogy of power/knowledge. *History and Theory, 21,* 382–398.

Simons, H. (1985). Chronicle and critique of a conference. *Quarterly Journal of Speech, 71,* 52–64.

Simons, H., & Aghazarian, A. A. (Eds.). (1986). *Form, genre, and the study of political discourse*. Columbia, SC: University of South Carolina Press.

Slack, J. D., & Allor, M. (1983). The political and epistemological constituents of critical communication research. *Journal of Communication, 33,* 208–218.

Therborn, G. (1980). *The ideology of power and the power of ideology.* London: NLB.

Thompson, J. B. (1984). *Studies in the theory of ideology.* Berkeley, CA: University of California Press.

Toulmin, S. (1972). *Human understanding.* Princeton, NJ: Princeton University Press.

Turner, K. (1986, April). *Rhetoric of, by, and for the media: Public address studies in an age of mass communication.* Paper presented at the annual meeting of the Central States Speech Association, Cincinnati.

Wander, P. (1981). Cultural criticism. In D. Nimmo & K. Sanders (Eds.). *Handbook of political communication* (pp. 497–528). Beverly Hills, CA: Sage.

Wander, P. (1983). The ideological turn in modern criticism. *Central States Speech Journal, 34,* 1–18.

West, C. (1988). Marxist theory and the specificity of Afro-American oppression. In C. Nelson & L. Grossberg (Eds.), *Marxism and the interpretation of culture* (pp. 17–29). Urbana, IL: University of Illinois Press.

PUBLIC MEMORIALIZING IN POSTMODERNITY: THE VIETNAM VETERANS MEMORIAL AS PROTOTYPE

CAROLE BLAIR, MARSHA S. JEPPESON, AND ENRICO PUCCI, JR.

Public commemorative monuments are rhetorical products of some significance. They select from history those events, individuals, places, and ideas that will be sacralized by a culture or a polity.[1] Barry Schwartz distinguishes between chronicling and commemorating, arguing that "Commemoration lifts from an ordinary historical sequence those extraordinary events which embody our deepest and most fundamental values" (377). Though the epideictic function of public commemorative monuments may be their most obvious rhetorical feature, these monuments also display tendencies toward the political or deliberative. Conflicts over whom or what to memorialize and in what ways have occurred frequently, and these conflicts often are registers of present and future political concern.[2] Moreover, commemorative monuments "instruct" their visitors about what is to be valued in the future as well as in the past. As Griswold notes, "The word 'monument' derives from the Latin *monere,* which means not just 'to remind' but also 'to admonish,' 'warn,' 'advise,' 'instruct'" (691).[3]

The 1980s gave us a particularly striking and evocative, if unusual, commemorative monument—the Vietnam Veterans Memorial in Washington, D.C. The critical commentary it has engendered as well as its extraordinary rhetorical power have rendered the Memorial an artifact of considerable significance.[4] Lang calls the Vietnam Veterans Memorial "the most emotional ground in the nation's capital" (68). Fish describes some of the reactions: "People have cried at the wall, prayed there, screamed in anger and in pain, found friends and comforted strangers. And always they touch it" (25). Members of the design jury commented that, "There's no escape from its power," and described it as "totally eloquent" (Scruggs and Swerdlow 63). The design jury's report concluded that, "The designer has created an eloquent place where the simple meeting of earth, sky, and remembered names contain messages for all who know this place" (qtd. in Ashabranner 38).[5] Howard K. Smith remarked that the Memorial's "final result has the quality of magic" (qtd. in Scruggs and Swerdlow xiv).

The rhetorical power of the Memorial is multiplied by its reach. It has enormous drawing power, and it is "reproduced" and "replicated" in popular culture products, thus expanding the range of possible impact. The Vietnam Veterans Memorial is the most visited memorial site in Washington, D.C., attracting between 12,000 and 15,000 visitors per day (deBlaye 263). It has been reproduced on postcards, t-shirts, buttons, brochures, posters, and books. Moreover, it was "the first national war monument introduced to the public through television" (Haines 7).

But this monument's capacity to attract and to move its visitors does not exhaust its rhetorical significance. Nor does its extended appeal through media and popular culture reproduction. We will argue here that the Vietnam Veterans Memorial is an instance of an emergent discourse within the cultural rhetoric of public commemorative monuments. Specifically we will claim that it is a prototype of postmodern memorializing, perhaps among the first of its kind, but certainly one of the most visible.

Our principal aim is not to advance a generic typology of postmodern architecture or even of postmodern commemorative monuments. The potential of such a project would be limited by the fact that we deal centrally with only one case. Furthermore, any encounter with postmodern discourses problematizes the very notion of a genre.[6] Rather, by contextualizing the Vietnam Veterans Memorial within the conflicts between modernists and postmodernists over the "built environment," we hope to contribute sensibly to the critical conversation about how the Memorial "works" rhetorically, as well as about a postmodern criticism in rhetoric.[7] Specifically, we will argue that a reading of the Vietnam Veterans Memorial as a postmodern commemorative text contributes to our understanding of it as a multivocal rhetoric, highlights and helps to account for differences among other critical accounts of the Memorial, firmly establishes the political character of the Memorial's rhetoric, and helps to explain its peculiar power to evoke response. Moreover, such a consideration suggests that the Vietnam Veterans Memorial has established at least tentatively the conditions for a postmodern monumentality.

We will begin with a general discussion of the differences between the discourses of modernist and postmodern architecture, as a context for understanding the rhetoric of what we call postmodern memorializing. Following that, we will describe how the Vietnam Veterans Memorial appropriates the rhetoric of postmodern architecture for its unique acts of memorializing.[8] We will conclude with a discussion of the rhetorical, cultural, and political significance of this emergent postmodern discourse of memorializing.

THE CONTESTATION OF METANARRATIVES: MODERNIST AND POSTMODERN ARCHITECTURE

Postmodernism is a many-faceted "ism," whether it is articulated with literature, criticism, feminist theory, the graphic and performing arts, popular culture production, or architecture. But perhaps the most encompassing and intuitively appealing description of postmodernism is Lyotard's; he designates the postmodern as "incredulity towards metanarratives" (*Postmodern Condition* xxiv). While Lyotard's definition is by his own admission extremely simplified, it does serve an orienting function in the midst (not necessarily the center) of the strategic dislocations and disjunctions that constitute the postmodern. Lyotard's concern is with the displacement of legitimating discourses (metanarratives) to which other discourses are submitted for judgment.[9] These metanarratives are problematized by postmodernism for various reasons, but one principal concern stands out, at least for Lyotard. Because of their status as legitimating discourses, metanarratives rigidify forms and patterns of thought, and they "terrorize" the non-normalized:

> By terror I mean the efficiency gained by eliminating, or threatening to elimi-nate, a player from the language game one shares with him. He is silenced or consents, not because he has been refuted, but because his ability to partici-pate has been threatened (there are many ways to prevent someone from playing) (*Postmodern Condition* 63–4).

The postmodern constitutes a refutation or dislocation of the legitimating capacity of these metanarratives. The central mission of postmodernism, if there is one, appears to be to reveal the non-necessity of what appears to be necessary.[10]

The postmodern, thus, seeks a disruption of the "normalized." This stance is exemplified perhaps more clearly in architecture than in other arts, for the modernist movement in architecture was explicitly and thoroughly committed to a metanarrative of social transformation through progress, in the form of techno-logical innovation, universal rationality, and corporate power.[11]

MODERN ARCHITECTURE

McLeod describes the principle of the modern movement in architecture as a "messianic faith in the new" (19). Progress was the driving objective, and it entailed a deliberate break with history, as Fisher, et al. suggest:

> For one of the fundamentals of Modernist thinking has been . . . to see the architecture of the past not as a source but as an enemy of the new. Modernity in the twentieth century had no intention of compounding the supposed error made in the nineteenth, that of using historical architectural styles as models for all architectural thought. Modernism represented a rejection of history (8).

The architecture of modernism was to be "purged of every intentional historic or symbolic contamination" (Portoghesi 4), because of its commitment to the new and for fear that historical reference or mannerism might interfere with the efficiency and functioning of a structure (Broadbent 120). The goal was, according to Jencks, to design "neutral buildings which have a 'zero degree' of historical association" (*Language* 20).

Rather than constituting an art form, modernist architecture was to signify the twentieth century's achievements and dominance of technological innovation, ratio-nality, and corporate power. The beauty of architecture would lie not in its form or style but in its function (Connor 67). Technological progress would constitute the aesthetic and provide the solution to social ills (McLeod 19). Modern architecture would insure a rational society by ordering the physical space of the social world in such a way as to invite (or demand) a functionalism and efficiency modeled on the factory (Connor 76; Jencks, *Language* 31). As Moriarty describes it, "Ostensibly freed of history, the Modernist celebration of the future could be characterized by a faith in social and aesthetic progress . . . the Modernist program of the Bauhaus, Mies and Gropius, C.I.A.M. and Corbusier [*sic*] mapped a utopian vision onto a rational program for a rational society" (2).[12]

With the rationalization of the social world as their goal, modernist architects sought a perfect, universal style of simplicity. As Hattenhauer suggests, "Modernists believed that they were beyond cultural relativity. They believed that their structures would mirror natural laws, not block them with cultural conventions" (75). Hence the frequent designation of modernist architecture as "the International Style." Because their forms were supposedly timeless and universal, they transcended national and historical boundaries. In fact, the notion of a "style" is not quite accurate to describe modernist architecture, for as Portoghesi points out, "a style by its very nature can be substituted by another which follows. Instead it [modernism] was seen as something beyond style, the definitive fulfillment of a program which cannot change . . ." (4).[13] Modernist architecture's prototype was "the box," typically massive and frequently calling attention to itself only by its size and display of its own structural elements such as pipes and girders; these typically were its only ornaments (Jencks, *Language* 13; Connor 77).

The "purity," "essence," and "unity" attempted by the modernists has been criticized roundly; their structures are frequently characterized as "desolate," anonymous, and "mute" (Fisher et al. 7; McLeod 34).[14] Modernism's economies of scale have led to its description as "cheapskate." Modernist architects' seeming inattention to "context," or the urban fabric in which their buildings are situated, has driven critics to suggest, as Jencks does, that such construction is "dropped unceremoniously, like an urban bomb" (*Language* 125–6). Moreover, the status of the architect as an artist ultimately conflicted with the modernist ideal of simplicity and efficiency as art. Holenstein suggests that the modernist architect needed to be an expert in organizational efficiency rather than an artist. Connor elaborates the conflict, arguing that the impersonality of the modernist program was a fundamental contradiction of the idea of architecture as an art with "heroic individual vision and expression—architecture as the 'pure creation of the mind' as Le Corbusier put it" (73).[15]

Nor have critics been alone in commenting on modernism's shortcomings. McLeod points to the "popular dissatisfaction with corporate skyscrapers and public housing projects" that argued for architects "to recognize emotional and social needs" of their clientele (29).

POSTMODERN REACTIONS

Both the ideology and the "style" of modernism have been placed at issue by postmodern architecture. Although there are numerous brands of postmodern architecture, particular features arise frequently enough so that they might be considered characteristic. Most generally, the postmodern architectural project must be seen as political, as a deliberate dissolution of the utopian metanarrative of modernism and frequently of metanarrativity in general.[16] Postmodern architecture symbolically undercuts modernism's progressivist faith in the new and its valorization of rationality, technology, and corporatism, all of which objectify and dehumanize the social sphere and the individuals who inhabit it. Moreover, postmodern architecture formally and symbolically questions the value of metanarrativity at large. Its refusal of a single, signature style and its reliance on multiple, sometimes conflicting, genres defy reference to singular standards of judgment. In so doing, it removes the legitimating grounds for the valorization or normalization of any particular architectural rhetoric.

Postmodernists, furthermore, insist upon restoring architecture's "voice." Jencks describes architecture as "a form of social discourse," offering choices among alternatives, and being able to either acknowledge or disguise its "partisan nature" (*Architecture Today* 15). Postmodern architects are quite explicitly interested in their art as a rhetoric, as a partisan and meaningful language.[17] They are particularly concerned with restoring to architecture what it lost in modernist manifestation—all aspects of its language save the syntactic. Modernist architecture's signs were almost purely self-referential and limited by a closed system of "legitimate" signifiers. Modernism jettisoned the symbolic and rhetorical dimensions of its language, as Connor acknowledges in describing a modernist building, as "pure sign, which does not refer to anything outside itself . . ." (70). Modernism, according to Hattenhauer, attempted to "exclude all semantic content, all connotation" (76).

By contrast, Stern argues that:

> Traditional post-modernism recognizes both the discursive and expressive meaning of formal language. It recognizes the language of form as communicating sign as well as infra-referential symbol: that is to say, it deals with both physical and associational experience, with the world of art as act of "presentation" and "representation" ("Doubles" 86).

Postmodern architecture restores the symbolic dimension to architecture, and its proponents recognize, as well, the actional and political character of architectural language. Jencks suggests that, "architecture really is a verb, an *action*" (*Language* 104), that the presence of a structure is itself a message. Portoghesi argues that the postmodernist reaction "restores 'the word' to architecture, through the reappropriation of metaphor and symbol and the capacity of shape itself to evoke not just abstract ideas, but also forms which accord with the taste and sensibility of the people" (29). Jencks goes so far as to suggest that, "the term 'Post-Modern' has to be . . . used more precisely to cover, in general, only those designers who are aware of architecture as a *language* . . ." (*Language* 6).[18] The "language" of postmodern architecture is disruptive; it displaces the tendencies of its modernist counterpart by: 1) a refusal of unities or universals, 2) attention to and use of context, and 3) an interrogative, critical stance.

McLeod describes postmodern architecture as a *refusal of universal models* and as a corresponding embrace of pluralistic objectives (19). The rejection of universals and espousal of pluralism are formulated in a number of ways in architectural structures, perhaps the most common of which is a melding of incompatible symbols, forms, styles, and textures within a particular structure. This strategy, frequently referred to as the characteristic postmodern "pastiche," "collage," or "eclecticism," results in a symbolic fragmentation of unity (Connor 72; Foster 127; Harvey 82). Connor describes this as a "movement from univalence to 'multivalence'" (72), an active cultivation of the "symbolic contamination" that modernism sought to eliminate (Portoghesi 4).

Another important gesture in postmodernism's espousal of pluralism is its integration of the historical. "Where modernist architecture seemed to celebrate its absolute break with the past in its rigorous purging of all archaism," Connor explains, "postmodernism shows a new willingness to retrieve and engage with historical styles and techniques" (74). Postmodern architecture "cites" or "quotes" historical motifs as part of its eclectic and pluralistic rhetoric.

Postmodern architecture frequently incorporates regional characteristics and ornament as well as historical forms to achieve this pluralism. The vernacularization of architecture involves the use of particular materials, forms, and styles found in the locale of a building as a counter to the culturally sterile modernist concrete box design. Occasionally, "regionalisms" are imported, that is[,] borrowed from one locale for integration in another.[19] Ornament also is some times incorporated, almost gratuitously, for interest or to reassert the symbolic and aesthetic functions of architecture (Jencks, *Language* 142).

While these strategies of eclecticism, historicism, regionalism, and ornament are clearly disruptive of modernist purity, modernist statements are not wholly eliminated from postmodern architecture. Modernist themes are freely incorporated as parts or aspects of a structure. Fisher, et al. suggest that, "A major part of this rediscovered architectural language consists in playing off the contrasts between a modern form . . . and a historical reference" (8). Jencks concurs, arguing that postmodernism "includes" modernist style "as a potential approach." He points to the work of Venturi, Stern, and Moore, whom he describes as "hard-core" postmodernists and whose work quotes modernist design (*Language* 7). Portoghesi describes one purpose of this "citation" of modernism, in his description of the New York Five:[20] "Forms which had symbolized a hope to change the world are used to demonstrate the fact that it cannot change . . ." (88). Not all citations of modernism are so strongly anti-utopian; some are simply ironic or humorous elements that distance the postmodern structure from its thoroughly modernist predecessor.

By juxtaposing historical, vernacular, ornamental, and even modernist themes, postmodern architecture eschews the simplicity, symmetry, and unity of modernism as well as the possibility of a governing or legitimating universal. Equally important, postmodern architecture *interacts with its contexts* in a definitive manner. Connor explains:

> [T]he language of architecture, as well as depending upon internal relationships of difference, is itself part of a much larger field of intersecting language and communication structures. . . . Where, for Le Corbusier, an architectural construction was to be seen in the rigorously reduced terms of its own lines, surfaces, and masses, for Jencks these abstractions are always placed in signifying contexts. What is more, the codes which are used to understand or interpret the abstract forms of architecture are not fixed or unchanging, since they always derive from and reflect the multiple contexts in which any world of architecture is experienced and 'read' (72).

He continues, suggesting that, "for many champions of postmodernism, architecture always consists precisely in the relationships to what is not itself" (72–3). These relationships drawn in postmodernism emphasize the character of a structure with regard to its surroundings as well as its "personability."

In contrast to Jencks' description of modernist building as the dropping of an urban bomb, postmodern architecture takes into account its natural and built environment; it is "carefully set in its context" (*Language* 126). He characterizes one development as "sympathetic" to its natural setting (*Language* 126). Stern emphasizes the importance of contextualization within the built environment as well:

> Buildings which relate to surrounding buildings have more power than those which don't relate to them (what was once called "common courtesy" could also be called "contextual integration"). . . . Architecture is "story telling" or a communicative art. . . . [S]ingle buildings—no matter how distant from other pieces of architecture—are part of a cultural and physical context and

we, as architects, are compelled to recognize these connections in our theories and in the combination of forms which we establish in that which we too casually call 'design' (qtd. by Portoghesi 88).

Stern's concern is an important one, for he suggests that buildings collaborate in a sense to produce their "story"; a structure articulates with its cultural and physical contexts in communicating.[21]

Postmodern architects also differ from their modernist counterparts in their concern for the physical and psychological comfort of people who use or inhabit their buildings. Rather than attempting to adapt people to buildings as modernists tended to do, postmodernists make efforts to adapt buildings to people. The goal is to make buildings appealing to the senses, directing a "constant attention to tight space, to touchable close-grained details [that] adds up to a consistent bodily experience" (Jencks, *Language* 117).[22] Some postmodernists even have turned toward a populist, anti-*avant-garde* collaborative design program with clients or communities. Instead of imposing design solutions on their clients, clients or users "co-author" structures. The result, says Jencks, are buildings that "show a complexity and richness of meaning, a delicate pluralism, that usually takes years to achieve" (*Language* 105–6).

In addition to its refusal of universals and its contextual gestures toward its surroundings and users, postmodern architecture is characterized by an *interrogative, critical stance*. As Jencks points out, "Not only does [architecture] express the values (and land values) of a society, but also its ideologies, hopes, fears, religion, social structure, and metaphysics. It may represent these facts and ideas or betray them . . ." (*Architecture Today* 178). Portoghesi puts the case somewhat differently, in his suggestion that the rhetorical tendency displayed by postmodern architecture "allows architecture to criticize and dissent as well as accept . . ." (29). This critical function provides commentary not merely on technical architectural concerns but on larger social issues as well. Postmodernism's critical position is rarely assertive; it seeks to "raise, if not answer," questions (Jencks, *Language* 138). Nonetheless, as Connor argues, "postmodern architectural theory gives its object, the postmodern building itself, the status of a kind of theory, or critical reflection on itself . . ." and on its physical and cultural environment (78).

IMPLICATIONS FOR CRITICISM

The character of postmodern architecture suggests particular critical assumptions. Providing more than a litany of characteristics to identify, this characterization of postmodern architecture implies elements of an appropriate critical stance. As Connor puts it, postmodern architecture allows "into its own form something of the multiplicity of ways of reading it, or, in a sense, reading itself in advance" (72). Perhaps most obviously, the postmodernists' effort to reincorporate symbolic and advocative meaning in their structures suggests the legitimacy in general of rhetorical readings of these structures. However, the manner of such a reading is circumscribed by the peculiarities of postmodern architecture. Postmodernism's refusal of unities invites multivalent readings. The goal is not to locate *the* message but the multiple, frequently conflicting, messages. To attempt a unified, centered reading, thus, is to miss the point.

Postmodern architecture's contextualism—its sensitivity to its environment and users—also invites a particular critical focus. Foster correctly recognizes the importance of approaching postmodern architecture as a "text" rather than as a "work" (129).

This distinction was formulated most clearly by Barthes, who suggested that, "the work is a fragment of substance, occupying a . . . space . . ." ("From Work" 156). "[T]he work can be seen" and is tangible ("From Work" 157). By contrast, the text "can cut across the work, several works" ("From Work" 157). It is a "multi-dimensional space in which a variety of writings . . . blend and clash. The text is a tissue of quotations drawn from innumerable centres of culture" ("Death" 146). The appropriate model for modernist structures is the "work," for this type of architecture seeks a unity of its own without reference to elements outside itself. By contrast, postmodern architecture draws from outside the structure itself to form the character of the structure. Postmodern architecture is composed of its building in relationship to what the building is not, its "outside" or its "other." The "text," because it problematizes the boundaries of "inside" and "outside," or "work" and "context," is a more appropriate model for understanding postmodern architecture. The "other," what might be understood as the physical or cultural context of a building in the "work" model, becomes an integral and inseparable part of the architectural "text."[23] The postmodern structure's "references" to its surroundings and its "citation" of regional and historical motifs are inscribed in that structure. Thus, the critic must take account of a structure's relation to the physical environment, cultural situation, and use, for all of these are as much a part of the "text" as the building itself.[24]

"Authorship" also is problematized in "reading" postmodern architecture. That is so not only because some postmodern structures are "authored" or designed by collectives, but also because the "text" model implies a displacement of authorship. In the case of a collectively-designed building or development, "authorship" as a unifying principle or as an interpretive precept fails. No unity arises from collective design; in fact, plurality is cultivated. And authorial intent is of negligible value in interpreting a "design" that may incorporate as many intentions as there are collaborative designers.

The authorship principle is displaced, though, even in critical engagement with non-collaborative projects. To consider architecture as "text" is to recognize that no single individual "creates" that text, for it is a reiteration and weaving together of multiple quotations, forms, and gestures, many of which exist apart from the intervention of an "author" or architect. Thus, while architects can and certainly do voice their intentions, the critic must consider their statements as merely part of the architectural text, not as an interpretive foundation upon which to build a reading.

The interrogative, critical posture of postmodern architecture suggests that the critic be particularly attentive to the political character of an architectural text. Postmodern architecture is an attempt to "speak" not only to architects about technical architectural matters, but also to viewers and users of buildings about substantive socio-cultural matters. It questions and critiques ideas as well as architectural forms. To assume that postmodern structures are composed solely of building techniques or that they are merely reflections of a culture, therefore, would be inappropriate. They frequently question and critique the norms and values of a culture.

The strategic difficulty of a postmodern text imposes an additional requirement on the "reader" or critic. Although describing the reading of postmodern writings and not of architecture, Bannet's discussion is useful. She suggests that such difficult writings:

> are designed to . . . make the reader look *at* them and to work at them, actively involving him in their construction or recreation. As Barthes points

out, the difficulty and indeterminacy of such texts prevents the reader from consuming them at a gulp and throwing them away. The reader cannot simply glance through [such] a . . . text, extract a discursive message and shelve the book. He must come back to the text again and again; he must brood on it; he must relate to it as a puzzle or a game, in which he participates by deciphering the allusions, by reconstructing the relations between parts, by seeking the significations which govern the form (8–9).

Postmodern architectural structures invite the same kind of care and thoughtfulness in reading that a postmodern thinker's writings do. They are "difficult," strewn with allusions, frequently lacking in a structural or conceptual unity, and cryptic in the extreme. Their rhetoric requires more than a glance; it demands engagement.

The critical posture of postmodern architecture raises a final concern peculiar to analyzing public commemorative monuments. It places at issue the conditions of possibility for a postmodern "monumentality," a problem that has plagued architects of both modern and postmodern ilk.[25] Given modernism's insistence on pure rationality and functionalism and on the purgation of history and symbolism, monumentality was rendered virtually inconceivable. As Collins and Collins argue, "The 'international' modern movement made such a point of breaking with history, with historic styles and tradition, that the achievement of monumentality as it had been previously thought of was at first not even considered worthwhile" (15). They conclude that, "the quality of being monumental . . . was considered by the modernists to be rather evil . . ." (19). Even those who considered monumentality to be important "never seemed to know or to agree generally about just what it was and how best to achieve it and still be 'modern'" (Collins and Collins 26).[26]

That exemplars of modernist commemorative monuments are difficult to find reinforces the problematic nature of these questions. Eero Saarinen's "Gateway Arch"—the Jefferson National Expansion Memorial—in St. Louis certainly is the best example of a modernist "non-utilitarian" monument, but there are few others that are notable.[27] The most purely modernist commemorative tendency was that of naming bridges, freeways, and turnpike service areas after prominent individuals.[28] This practice reflects modernism's concern for rationality and functionalism. But, it hardly provides a postmodern architect with stylistic or formal architectural properties to incorporate or to dislodge. Thus, without a clear[-]cut modernist formula for public commemoration, how is a recognizably postmodern commemoration possible?

Public commemorative monuments "sacralize" individuals, places, and ideas, as we have pointed out. Thus, monumentality appears to be beyond the grasp of modernist architecture. For much the same reason, though, the question must be put of postmodern architecture. How, given its presuppositions, is a postmodern monumentality possible? Decisions about whom or what to memorialize appear to require recourse to some principle of who or what is *worthy* of public commemoration. They seem to demand a reliance, in fact, upon a metanarrative. James Ackerman points out the problem: ". . . the whole question of monumentality is the wrong question for now, another holdover from the past we've lost. How can a society like our own, which has no dreams, no confidences, and no faith, deal with monuments or monumentality?" ("Forum" 38).[29] If the postmodern is definitionally "incredulity toward metanarratives," how can a postmodern architectural statement assume or sanction a metanarrative? This problem raises the question again of how public commemoration is possible within the terms and conditions of postmodernism. This concern is vital, but it cannot be resolved in the absence of specific cases. Thus, we turn to an examination of the Vietnam Veterans Memorial for a determination.

ANALYSIS OF THE VIETNAM VETERANS MEMORIAL

The Vietnam Veterans Memorial consists of three structures: the well-known, black, V-shaped wall, a flagpole, and a statue of three American soldiers. The wall, the original and unanimous choice of the design selection committee, was supplemented later by the flagpole and statue in a compromise. The wall is heavily reliant upon modernist gestures.[30] Its sheer, unadorned surfaces and apparent formal symmetry bespeak a unity of design that seems to deny a link with postmodern architecture.[31] However, other features of the wall, and of the Memorial taken as a whole, justify and even invite such a characterization. A reading of the Memorial as postmodern accommodates and accounts for diverse, sometimes contradictory readings, and it adds to the critical conversation, especially in helping to identify and explain the Memorial's *political* rhetoric. It also helps to account for the Memorial's rhetorical power and its instigation of a new monumentality.

We will describe first the ways in which critical assumptions about textuality and authorship come into play in accounting for the Memorial's rhetoric. Second, we will discuss peculiarly postmodern characteristics of the Memorial that lend support to other critical readings and also help to account for differences in those readings. Third, we will argue, contrary to most critics, that the Vietnam Veterans Memorial assumes a provocative political stance. Fourth, we will describe how the postmodern textual "difficulty" enhances the Memorial's capacity to evoke response. Finally, we will suggest how the Vietnam Veterans Memorial negotiates the problem of postmodern monumentality, essentially relegitimizing monumental architecture in postmodernity.

The critical assumptions implied by the character of postmodern architecture are particularly appropriate to a reading of the Vietnam Veterans Memorial. To approach the monument as an inclusive text is to recognize its peculiar character as two monuments contained in one. Although some critics may choose to treat the Lin wall and the flag and Hart statues as two separate monuments (Morris), or to consider only the wall (Foss), the fact remains that the Memorial is constituted by both. To treat them as separable is to neglect the Memorial's character as culturally constituted and to overlook its nature as itself a political compromise. The antithetical designs of the wall and the statue undercut any possibility of bringing a single warrant to bear for interpretation, and they foreclose a unitary standard of judgment. Their status as parts of the Vietnam Veterans Memorial suggests that multivalent readings are not just possible but that they are necessary. Moreover, they invite a textual reading that places no demands on the unity or consistency of the rhetorical object.

That conclusion is reinforced by the Memorial's character as a site for supplemental rhetorical activity. Items that visitors leave at the Memorial relieve its starkness and alter its symbolic field. These artifacts are collected each day and housed elsewhere, to be replaced with others left by subsequent visitors. The text of the Memorial changes materially over time. Each addition alters the text, for it focuses on a different individual, a different aspect of the war, or a different meaning a visitor has attached to his/her experience of the Memorial. The wall, thus, serves as a repository of more than its own story; it admits within its text the multiple decorations, stories, interpretations, elaborations, and arguments that visitors leave at the site.[32] These supplements question the "completeness" or unity of the Memorial as a work and suggest that it be approached as a text.

Also inviting textual consideration is the wall's mirror-like granite surface, which "quotes" whomever and whatever is within its reflective range. Mirrored consistently in the wall's surface are the Lincoln Memorial and Washington Monument. But the visitors and activities in which they engage (mourning, reuniting, comforting) are also cited in the reflective surface, contributing to what Haines calls the Memorial's "shifting symbolic ground, a fluctuating, constantly renegotiated field" (9).[33]

There can be little doubt that the wall is the focal point of the Memorial. It is more interesting, more unusual, and more inviting than the statue. It has received far more public comment. And even the figures in the statue refer to the wall—their gaze is directed toward it. Nevertheless, it is important to consider the Vietnam Veterans Memorial as it has been socially named and politically constituted—as a monument composed of two principal parts. If we consider the wall as the locus of the rhetorical text, supplemented by the addition of statuary, mementos, and visitors, we will be in a better position to understand the rhetorical stance of the Memorial.[34]

To consider the Vietnam Veterans Memorial as a text is necessarily to problematize its authorship. The Memorial is technically a collectively-designed monument, even though the wall and the statue were not the result of a cooperative effort. Even the design of the wall itself, though, must be considered a product of more than one individual's creativity. The criteria for design selection, set by the Vietnam Veterans Memorial Fund, constrained significantly the possibilities for the monument and, in fact, specifically *required* what has become one of the wall's most noteworthy features—the list of names of the dead and missing.[35] Thus, the Vietnam Veterans Memorial Fund must be considered partially responsible for the wall's design; the motivations of more than one individual resulted in the monument's particular character. And, as we will discuss further on, the compromise that led to the supplement of the wall by the statue and flag also was the outcome of a collective effort. Whatever the intent of the Vietnam Veterans Memorial Fund in establishing its criteria, and whatever Maya Lin's and Frederick Hart's design intentions, the compromise that incorporated them all in the Memorial also removed any special interpretive authority from these "authors." Hart's and Lin's designs, when juxtaposed, alter one another's rhetoric substantially, thus restricting the designers' ability as authors to interpret or account for their own work.

To consider the Vietnam Veterans Memorial as a text and to deauthorize its authors is also necessarily to expect multiple, possibly strongly divergent, readings. Starting with the wall as the locus of the Memorial's text, three peculiarly postmodern accents—its displaced symmetry, "regional" citations, and contextualism— begin to explain the Memorial's rhetorical character and also help to account for conflicting claims advanced by other critics.

Although the structural profile of the wall is symmetrical, the sequence of names listed on its surfaces undermines the symmetry. The list of names is chronologically ordered by date of death, but the list begins at the vertex of the angle formed by the two walls, proceeds to the right and begins again on the left wall, ending at the vertex. In order to read the names sequentially one must necessarily divert attention from the wall in the midst of his/her reading, walk the length of the wall, and begin reading again. To accept the symmetry of the wall's structure is to break the sequence; to follow the sequence is necessarily to counter the symmetry.

These agonistic elements of symmetry and sequence help to explain how some critics can arrive at the conclusion that the wall provides a sense of closure while others claim that it denies this sense.[36] To focus on one element or the other, structural symmetry or "narrative" sequence, is to allow for a sense of closure. The symmetrical structure has borders; it designates completion of itself and of the war. It is uninterrupted and whole, perfectly balanced, and finished. The sequence of names, though broken, leads to a sense of closure by bringing "the names of those killed at the beginning and at the end of the war . . . together" (Carlson and Hocking 205). However, the structural symmetry and the sequence of names that can individually produce a sense of closure countermand one another. Thus, to read the symmetry or the sequence may be to experience a feeling of closure, but to read both together is to be denied that sense.[37]

The wall's regional and contextual motifs also lend credence to a postmodern reading and help to account for some critical disagreements. The wall's formalist character is dispersed in two particular regional, in this case local, designations.[38] First, its polished granite surfaces with inscribed names is reminiscent of a gravestone, a resemblance heightened by the flowers, flags, and other items left by visitors at the Memorial (Griswold 706–7).[39] Second, its collection of names is no different, except in magnitude, from many smaller memorials commemorating sacrifices of locals in a war or in several wars. As Haines suggests, the wall recapitulates these "familiar 'roles of honor' [sic] erected on courthouse squares following other wars" (4). The wall, thus, presents itself as a local memorial, but one of enormous proportion and sited on "national" territory.[40]

The familiar, local sense of the wall is supplemented by its accommodation of the physical environment and its visitors. The wall is unobtrusive, invisible in fact from the north, for it is built into a rise in the earth. It does not dominate the landscape but respects it. Too, it is accessible to visitors. Unlike many statuary monuments, it is not raised on a base, forcing visitors to gaze always upward. Neither its height nor an official rule prohibits physical contact with the wall. It is, unlike many other monuments, accessible to touch. As Griswold observes of the Memorial, "When people find . . . the name they've been looking for, they touch, even caress it, remembering. One sees this ritual repeated over and over" (709). Many visitors also take with them a rubbing of the name, a special token that the wall gives to them as a remembrance.

These imported localisms and accommodations to the physical and peopled environment not only reflect characteristics of a postmodern architectural rhetoric, they also help to account for critics' antithetical views regarding the degree of comfort one feels at the Memorial. The wall has been described by some as promoting a sense of serenity, security, and comfort (Foss 333; Haines 7), while for others like Griswold, it "is not a comforting memorial" (709). Again, conflicting claims are legitimized by the symbolic gestures of the Memorial. If one reads local sites like cemeteries and courthouse squares in the wall, the very familiarity of these citations may provide security or comfort. So too might the "shelter" of the hill into which the wall is built, or the "personability" of the wall.[41] However, if one reads the strong reference to death and the magnitude of that reference, the effect is anything but comforting.

Consideration of other postmodern characteristics of the Vietnam Veterans Memorial, particularly its departure from generic norms, articulation with its built environment, its encoding of its own history, its symbolic collage of names, and its actional character, point to the Memorial's function as itself critical and decidedly political. Critics frequently have claimed that the wall or the Memorial makes no political statement.[42] Some ground this claim in the criterial [sic] stipulation for the design competition, that the chosen design for the monument would make no political statement (Ehrenhaus, "Silence" 49). Others base their claim on Maya Lin's early insistence that the wall made no political statement (Foss 334).[43] Some argue that the wall maintains an apolitical character through a studied ambiguity (Foss 334; Haines 6), or by refusing to answer questions that it raises (Carlson and Hocking 206; Griswold 711). We will maintain, to the contrary, that the wall itself bears a strongly political statement and that statement is reinforced by the wall's relationship to other monuments within its proximity and to its "other side"—the Hart statue and flag.[44] We will suggest that the interrogative features of the wall, which have been interpreted as politically ambiguous, do not serve as a means to eschew political statement. Rather these features constitute the political message; questioning is the point, and that point is a thoroughly political one.

The departure of the Vietnam Veterans Memorial's wall from the generic norms of commemorative public monuments has been noted frequently by critics. Foss' description makes the case most emphatically:

> That this memorial is a far cry from the customary warrior's monument is immediately evident. . . . We have, then, in the Vietnam Veterans Memorial, violation of the conventional form of war memorial. . . . Lacking the clear, patriotic sense that emerges from most war memorials, visitors to the Vietnam Veterans Memorial are able to bring new kinds of expectations to the work (332–3).[45]

The sense of generic violation is intensified by the Memorial's placement in West Potomac Park. The principal monuments there—the Lincoln Memorial, the Washington Monument, and the Jefferson Memorial—provide a sharp contrast to the Vietnam Veterans Memorial. They are stately and white. They impose upon the landscape and draw attention to themselves by means of their size and emulation of ancient architectural forms. The wall is dwarfed in stature by these monuments, it is black rather than white, and it eschews the *gravitas* of neo-classical construction. In fact, the geometry of the wall reinforces the contrast; its two walls "point" directly to the Washington Monument and the Lincoln Memorial. Moreover, because the wall is built into the ground, it is invisible from the north side (interestingly the direction of the White House).

That the violation of norms and the placement of the wall *can* be read as political is undeniable. The objections that were raised in 1981 were based on those characteristics. Ehrenhaus summarizes:

> For James Watt, former Secretary of the Interior, and a delegation of 27 Republican Congressmen, the design "makes a political statement of shame and dishonor, rather than an expression of national pride." . . . Tom Carhart, a West Point graduate and Vietnam Veteran, is a vocal opponent of the Memorial's design because it violates traditional form. He refers to it as a "black trench" that is "anti-heroic." Its black walls are "the universal color of sorrow and dishonor," and he asks, "Why can't we have something white and traditional and above ground?" ("Silence" 50).[46]

While others claimed in response that the wall's design was apolitical, the wall's contrast with its built environment and its fracturing of generic norms remained unaddressed. The wall is relatively small in stature; it is the color of sorrow, if not shame; and it offers no vainglorious narrative of the virtues and values preserved by the U.S. involvement in the war. Although we do not share the views of Carhart or Watt that the wall resembles a trench, or that it is a symbol of shame or dishonor for veterans, we do concur that it takes a political stance. It does so by virtue of these departures from the norm and the contextual emphasis of those departures.

The generic violations and the contextual emphasis of those violations is not merely incidental to a reading of the wall; these features are vital components of the Memorial's text. A departure from generic norms in rhetoric typically signals either a peculiarity of situation calling for alterations of type and/or the inadequacy of a generic norm to appropriately respond to a situation.[47] Simply put, generic violations typically are not gratuitous. The generic violations in the case of the wall certainly are not; they mark a dissatisfaction with the capacity of the "normal," monumental discourse to adequately commemorate Vietnam veterans. Given the public response to the Vietnam war itself, that should not be surprising. Public commemorative monuments are usually heavily reliant upon a socially shared sense that those who perished did so for the greater good or for a cause worth pursuing. But this extremely unpopular, by many accounts immoral, war provides nothing like a consensual warrant to authorize valorization of the war dead. That such a premise is clearly lacking, and that that lack *demands* a departure from generic conventions, itself is a political statement. To honor the veterans of the Vietnam war, something besides the derived value or political merit of the war itself is necessary as a premise.

Ironically, the compromise that added the flag and Hart statue intensified the wall's already political character. Represented in the Memorial are two radically different historical accounts of the Vietnam war itself. The wall inscribes names in the order of death, providing a sequential account of U.S. involvement in the war. The temporal sequence is registered and divided by years and by each loss of life. The historical narrative is a chronicle of death. The statue of the three soldiers symbolizes a hypothetical inflection point in time, capturing a "close-up" image of what one scene in Vietnam might have looked like. Rather than representing history as a sequence, the statue encapsulates it synecdochically in its representation of all Vietnam veterans by three particular soldiers. This moment of life contrasts sharply with the wall's narrative of death. The structures taken together inscribe a history, forming a space of cooperative conflict and commenting on each other's statement about the war. Their presence together on the memorial site, in fact, serves as a historical marker for both the contestation of an appropriate commemorative rhetoric for Vietnam veterans (itself a political dispute),[48] and for the historical domestic conflict over the war and its conduct.

The Memorial is a testimony to the conflict that led to the compromise of its own character; it is a historical recapitulation of the battle over the appropriate rhetoric of commemoration. The construction of the wall was given final approval only after a compromise was struck to include the flag and the Hart statue along with the wall. The "nasty fight" leading to the compromise began after Maya Lin's design for the wall had been chosen from among 1421 proposals in the spring of 1981 (Hess 125). Lin's design also had been approved by all requisite authorities— the National Capital Planning Commission, the Commission of Fine Arts, and the Department of the Interior. However, as a response to objections raised by some veterans, congresspersons, and H. Ross Perot, then Interior Secretary Watt "placed a stop order on the Memorial's construction permit" (Gans 325).[49] The stop order was lifted only after the compromise was struck to add the statue and flag.

The three structures are not only symbolic of the conflict over appropriate commemoration; they constitute the actual historical residue of that conflict. Together they mark a historical battle over "what can be said" about the war, a battle that proved too contentious to be resolved in consensus; only a compromise that allowed both voices to be heard allowed the Memorial's construction to proceed.

It is difficult to maintain that this battle and its results are apolitical. At issue in the conflict and in its resulting compromise was what rhetoric about the Vietnam war would be sanctioned by being given public voice. The conflict over appropriate commemoration resulted in a compromise, but it certainly did not resolve the issue. The Memorial represents the conflict itself, and like the conflict, culminates in the two sides being endlessly articulated rather than transcended. The presence together of the wall and the statue allows them to "question" one another's legitimacy indefinitely.

But the tension between the compromise structures does more than comment on the socio-political problem of public commemoration; it designates the domestic conflict over the war itself. As members of the Commission of Fine Arts observed, the battle over appropriate commemoration penetrated to a battle over the appropriateness of the war. The wall does not portray the Vietnam conflict as an event worthy of admiration or its veterans as heroic. The flag and statue add precisely those dimensions of meaning to the memorial site. The inscription at the base of the flag pole "affirms the principles of freedom for which [the Vietnam veterans] fought." And the statue, as Morris notes, depicts the soldiers as heroic:

> Neither speaking of death nor even inviting us to contemplate death, this second memorial encourages only heroism and the silence of heroes. Weary though they may be, these heroes are alive. And that is how we are to remember them: alive and heroic (215).

While the wall chronicles U.S. involvement in the war according to a sequence of death, the statue designates a hypothetical moment of the war by reference to life and courage.

The two views represented by these structures are not compatible, but the compromise renders the site as a trace of the conflict over the war. As Maya Lin suggested, "in a funny sense the compromise . . . brings the memorial closer to the truth. What is memorialized is that people still cannot resolve the war . . ." (qtd. by Gans 328). Even the placement of the structures in relation to one another reinforces her conclusion. Although the soldiers in Hart's statue appear to be gazing at the wall, nothing else connects the wall and the statue. To contemplate one, a visitor must turn his/her back on the other.

The Memorial's political statements in no way detract from its capacity to commemorate Vietnam veterans. If architecture is a verb, as Jencks has suggested, its power as such is nowhere better demonstrated than in the Vietnam Veterans Memorial. Its presence alone acknowledges the veterans, provides them a "space" that recognizes them as a group, and thus renegotiates their status in the culture.[50] The Memorial's existence is one of many cultural signs that the country has recovered from its "trance of collective amnesia" concerning the war (Butterfield 26).[51]

Furthermore, the Memorial emphasizes perhaps more clearly than any monument that has preceded it the worth of the individual. The wall refuses to cede representation of all the war's veterans into a singular, iconic representation. In addition, it makes no attempt to prize the worth of the collective above the value of individual life. The wall is a unity in that it serves as a monument to Vietnam veterans as a unified group, but it also commemorates each of the dead and missing as an individual by its "collaging" of names. Each of the names references a unique individual. Each name insists upon consideration beyond its presence in the midst of the others, for each refers to much more than the collective of which it is a part. Each individual named on the wall had as *one* role in life to be a soldier in Vietnam. But many other aspects of his/her life also are referenced by his/her name; they become a part of the memorial as well, diversifying the apparent unity of the wall's signification. The structural integrity of the wall unifies as a collective those who died or were listed as missing in Vietnam, but the unity disintegrates in the face of the symbolic potency of each name. The wall's inscribed dialectic between individual and collective does not culminate in synthesis; it preserves reference to the veterans as individuals *and* as a group. The Memorial provides a space of recognition and acknowledges Vietnam veterans both as a group and as individuals. In so doing, it allows for legitimate commemoration even in the absence of an expressed valorization of the war effort or outcome.

As a result of the Vietnam Veterans Memorial's conflicting messages, visitors could leave the site with their views fundamentally unaffected, having been reaffirmed in "whatever individual expectations and perspective [they] wish to bring to the memorial . . ." (Foss 334). More likely, though, visitors to the Memorial leave with more than they brought with them, as a result of the Memorial's difficulty as a text. The complexity and agonistic character of the Memorial's rhetoric invite active engagement by the visitor. It seems unlikely that anyone could be unaffected by the opposed views and difficult issues posed by the Memorial. Its rhetoric virtually demands that one either resolve the issues in a tentative or qualified fashion, or that he/she leave with critical and gnawing questions still to consider. In either case, the questions and qualifications *constitute* a major component of the message. Regardless of the stance one may take regarding the Vietnam war or the most appropriate way of commemorating its veterans, the Memorial invites doubt and critical differentiation of issues. Someone who believes that U.S. commitment to the war was justified still sees, like other visitors, the chronicle of death that resulted from that stance. He/she is invited to weigh the cause against the cost. One convinced that the U.S. involvement was wrong or foolish still witnesses each name and the tragedy it represents. He/she is invited to honor the dead, if not the "cause" for which they died. In sum, the Vietnam Veterans Memorial provokes engagement; it is not easily consumed or immediately intelligible. Its rhetoric does not sanction a touristic, consumptive response; it invites an engaged and thoughtful reading.

Also related to the absence of an explicit warrant for valorization in the Memorial is the final question to be addressed here: how a postmodern monumentality is possible. It is important to examine what the Vietnam Veterans Memorial can tell us about what the conditions are of a postmodern monumentality, *how* it is possible given the situational and theoretical problems confronting it. Two conditions for a postmodern monumentality are suggested by the Vietnam Veterans Memorial. It suggests, first, that postmodern monuments eschew metanarrative sanction. Second, while not necessarily foregrounding an explicit confrontation with modernism, the Vietnam Veterans Memorial suggests that the postmodern monument must at least differentiate itself substantially from modernist attempts at memorializing.

It is difficult to imagine a language—of architecture or of any other kind—that can completely divest itself of recourse to the legitimating capacity of metanarrative.[52]

That the Vietnam Veterans Memorial approaches that state, however, is almost undeniable. A single "story" about the war or its veterans cannot "contain," account for, or legitimate the rhetorics of both the Hart statue and the Lin wall.[53] Nor can any account of the war encompass, much less do justice to, the individual lives represented by the inscriptions on the wall. If the Memorial does not eschew metanarrative altogether, it certainly does challenge us to find an *adequate* discourse that would authorize and hold together its multiple and disjunctive "stories."

This kind of challenge may prove to be a necessary characteristic of postmodern monumentality. Rather than telling *the* story, it tells multiple stories. Any one of the stories—of victimization, of a just cause for the war, of individual sacrifice—warrants commemoration of the dead. But the stories conflict, refusing easy containment within a single account. Because of the difficulty of the text, then, the monument becomes a site not only of commemoration but also of questioning, perhaps even of incredulity. The problem of contemporary monumentality, long wrestled with by architects and other artists, is transformed from a specialists' debate to a cultural problem; it is not solved but rearticulated. The monument itself declares the postmodern "problem"—the lack of a metadiscourse that legitimates or sanctions another discourse. Such a declaration may prove to be the only possibility for a postmodern monumentality.

Since the modern tendency was to commemorate primarily by naming functional structures, it provides few gestural or thematic architectural signs that can be called into question directly by a postmodern monumentality. However, the existence of the Vietnam Veterans Memorial is already a reaction to such rational functionalism. By its having been conceived and built at all, it abrogates this modernist tendency; it plainly differs in character from the turnpike service area, with the memorial swimming pool, or the memorial student union. It reinvokes the *primary* goal of monumentality: to commemorate. It leaves the functionalism of modernism aside, essentially changing the subject. It does not comment on modernist functional memorials; it simply questions them by being and by differing.

The rare modernist "intentional" monument receives essentially the same kind of treatment. It receives no explicit commentary, but its mode of discourse is essentially renounced. A brief encounter with the Jefferson National Expansion Memorial establishes a clear case of contrast with the Vietnam Veterans Memorial. Saarinen's graceful Arch is a study in size, engineering, and technological achievement. While it has come to represent a "gateway to the West," such rhetorical implications were incidental to the design. According to Temko, Saarinen's goal was "to create a monument not only to the Virginian and the nation, but also to the modern age" (18). Temko explains further that, for Saarinen, the "spirit" of the monument was to be its "mechanical" character. It was to be absolutely permanent and comparable as a work to the Washington Monument. Hence its stainless steel frame and enormous height. "[I]ts scale," reports Temko, "is that of the civilized future" (19). Even the shape of the monument was rationalistic:

> Although the first Jefferson Memorial design of 1948 was of partly subjective inspiration, it was also a stroke of rational structural functionalism: a catenary arch which, geometrically, was as predictable as a circle. The steel-plate shell of the G.M. dome and the concrete shell of the M.I.T. auditorium are governed by the same geometric purism, and thus absolutely subject to the laws of what Nervi calls "Building Science" (Temko 42).[54]

The "remarkable engineering feat" of the monument is commented upon at least as much as the pioneering effort that it commemorates (Bricker, et al. 261). The "don't miss" at the Museum of Westward Expansion (under the Arch), according to one tourist guide, is the documentary, *Monument to the Dream* (Charters 421). This half-hour chronicle is not about westward expansion but the building of the Arch. The Arch and everything associated with it refers primarily to the structure itself, its engineering and its magnificent (modern) accomplishment. Its commemoration, except of itself, however, is strained. As Gass puts it, the Arch is "simple, direct, and grand enough to wrench a WOW! from a clod," but it is also "a logarithm," "a speechless overhang" (140). He continues:

> Beneath the Arch—this quintessentially American symbol of Finnish design . . . —lies history, dead as we desire it to be; so dead indeed that the museum buried there has nothing much to display, and concentrates instead on exhibiting the techniques of exhibition: on layouts, labels, lighting, models and montages . . . everything absolutely up to date. History is as dead as God, but there is no history (Gass 142).

The monument is an outstanding example of the modernist rational program. It only nominally refers to anything outside itself. It is a feat of modern technology and a defeat of history. It is a "pure" form, remarkable not because of what it represents or says but because it "stands without inner frame support" (Bricker 261).

The Vietnam Veterans Memorial obviously eschews this brand of monumentalizing. It does not represent a great engineering achievement, nor is its construction its message. It references stories from and about the war, and it acknowledges and refers to elements of its historical landscape. It does not command respect for its syntactical elements of size, shape, or structural integrity, but for its symbolic gestures outside itself. The Vietnam Veterans Memorial refuses the modernist program, at least as it is exemplified in Saarinen's prototype and in the "functionalist" memorial. In so doing, it suggests the second possible condition of postmodern monumentality, an abrogation of modernist formulae for commemoration.

CONCLUSION

In addition to arguing for a type of reading of the Vietnam Veterans Memorial that emphasizes its postmodern rhetorical features, this discussion also highlights concern for the rhetoric of public commemorative monuments at large. Furthermore, it brings to the surface a number of assumptive issues that rhetorical critics must address.

That the Vietnam Veterans Memorial incorporates the characteristic features of postmodern architecture itself is significant. The wall *looks* more like a modernist structure than a postmodern one, but any reading that embraces more than its symmetrical silhouette will acknowledge its departure from modernist style and dogma.[55] And, any reading that takes account of both the wall and the statue must dismiss the possibility of reading the Memorial as a modernist "work."

The significance of classification, though, is less important in its own right than its implications for the posture assumed by the critic in reading the monument. Because of its complexity, the Vietnam Veterans Memorial lends itself to a "textual" reading. Because of its multiple "authorship," it reads well in the absence of an "authorized" interpretive grounding from the planners and architects. Its multiplicity argues for numerous readings, but it demands no agreement among them.

The Vietnam Veterans Memorial reflects what is frequently called the "both-and" of postmodern architectural practice, in contrast to the modernist "either-or." In other words, it is inclusive; it does not suggest one reading or the other, but embraces even contradictory interpretations. The Memorial both comforts and refuses to comfort. It both provides closure and denies it. It does not offer a unitary message but multiple and conflicting ones. Its "syntactical" elements (for example, color, size, shape, geometry, placement, material, and inscriptions) do not speak with one voice. These, and the more complex symbolic gestures of symmetry, sequence, regionalism, contextualism, contrast, and reference, speak agonistically. They do not add up to a correct or synthetic interpretation. They offer diverse messages, sanctioning the legitimacy of "both-and."

Though the wall appears at first to be a simple and easily readable structure, it is remarkably complex, even when considered apart from the statue and flag. Its structure and shape give it a unity and self-containedness that are undermined by the presence of thousands of names, the order of the names, the reflective capacity of the polished granite surface, and the mirroring of and gesturing toward other structures. Those already complex features of the wall are complicated further by consideration of the wall together with its counterpart statue and flag; to examine both as parts of the Memorial is to render any unifying reading virtually impossible.

The dual and dialectical expressions of the two "parts" of the Memorial add difficulty to any reading. Most important, they intensify the sense that the Memorial speaks politically. The two components oppose one another in what they say about the war. The opposition defies synthesis. The structures stand as durable, visible representatives of opposing stances, "arguing" their cases against each other without mediation. They *constitute* the outcome of political compromise. Moreover, they vouchsafe the cultural legitimacy of two opposed points of view about the Vietnam war and commemoration of its veterans. The Memorial stands as a commemoration of veterans of the war, *and* as a monument to political struggle.

Since the Vietnam Veterans Memorial was approved and built, numerous "intentional" monuments have been proposed, and some of these have been constructed. As Haines suggests, "Construction of The Wall seems to have started a trend" (18n). Monuments have been proposed to honor Korean war veterans, as well as protesters of the Vietnam war (Haines 18n). Maya Lin was commissioned to design the Civil Rights Memorial in Montgomery, Alabama, which was dedicated in November 1989. A monument to the students killed at Kent State in 1970 also has been built. The NAMES Project International AIDS Memorial Quilt was displayed for the first time in 1987 and continues its memorializing journey throughout the world.[56]

That the Vietnam Veterans Memorial may have begun a new trend in monument building is itself an important contribution, especially in response to modernism's inclination toward "functionalist" memorials. Equally important, however, is the degree to which these new monuments respond to the demands of a postmodern condition. Such an extended subject is well beyond the scope of this paper, but it is worth noting that two of these newer monuments clearly appropriate elements of the Vietnam Veterans Memorial's rhetoric. Fox recognizes the "same combinations" of elements in the Civil Rights Memorial and in the Vietnam Veterans Memorial. And, the AIDS Quilt follows the Vietnam Veterans Memorial in its emphasis on naming the dead. Only additional critical study can bear out the degree and character of influence exerted by the Vietnam Veterans Memorial. But these similarities do suggest that the Memorial may have altered the public commemorative norm for the foreseeable future.

In addition to the concerns raised here about the rhetoric of the Vietnam Veterans Memorial and of public commemorative monuments, several issues more generally pertinent to rhetorical criticism emerge in this analysis. Traditional views of textuality, authorship, and the politics of discourse are all raised as problems.

First is the question of textuality. The frontiers of a discourse are, by some accounts, *never* certain (Foucault, *Archaeology* 23–5). That is, since any discourse is "caught up in a system of references to other books, other texts, other sentences," its boundaries are not certain nor easily identifiable (Foucault, *Archaeology* 23). To assume that a speech or a book or an architectural structure is a "unit," complete unto itself, is to assume and to make a crucial, critical *choice;* it is not to recognize an absolute fact. Put another way, a discourse, at least by Foucault's way of thinking, is not an entity given in reality. Its character is a premise of critical argument.

Even if one can assume, in some cases (for example, that of a modernist building), the unity of a work as pregiven in its material form, postmodern discourses seek to problematize that unity. Thus, the distinction between treating rhetoric as a work and as a text becomes tremendously important, if not in the case of all discourse, then at least in the case of postmodern discourses. Postmodern rhetoric recommends a critical practice that considers pregiven material unity irrelevant. To treat a postmodern discourse as a complete or unified structure is to utterly miss the point. The goal of a textual reading is to grasp the multiplicity of any discourse; to constrict or expand the scope of a text is to yield very different readings.

When the material unity of a work is suspended in favor of considering a text, authorship becomes a tertiary consideration. The "fragments" that are treated as part of a text have various sources; they compose a unity drawn by a critic rather than by an author (McGee). Thus, the authority of the speaker, writer, or architect to interpret his/her own *work* is displaced by the critic's reading of a multiple text. The critic takes on the task of defining the range of inclusiveness of his/her object of study. The critic's intervention begins with the construction of the text, not with the selection of a work.

Finally, this discussion questions the wisdom of treating any discourse as if it were apolitical. Jencks' claim, that architecture is a verb, provides the key. If we expand his claim to read, "rhetoric is really a verb or an action," the case becomes clearer. To the extent that a discourse is an action, it impinges upon the meaning, truth, value, status, and range of action of other discourses (Foucault, "Subject and Power" 219–21). It exerts force, in other words, within its field of action. The choice to consider politics as a *type* of rhetoric rather than as an aspect of all rhetoric is called seriously into question.

These concerns reinforce similar views expressed by post-structuralist thinkers. Lyotard, Barthes, Foucault, and others, have argued for reconsideration of some of the most taken-for-granted critical assumptions. The assumptions that the "text" is not at issue, that authorship offers unifying and interpretive grounding, and that the political is simply another genre of rhetoric, are raised as questions; their status as assumptions is displaced. But, if these thinkers' arguments are not convincing to rhetorical critics, certainly the character of postmodern discourses must be. These rhetorical events themselves invite reconsideration of the assumptions critics typically make. To accept these traditional assumptions (that the work is a given, that authorship constitutes interpretive authority, and that a genre matrix contains politics within a single category of discourse) is to refuse important elements of critical practice. These assumptions remove the critic's tasks of *forming* a text, of becoming the authorizing voice, and of understanding rhetoric as praxis. In challenging these assumptions, the critic becomes an interventionist rather than a deferential, if expert, spectator.

NOTES

[1]See Barthes, who argues that, "human space in general (and not only urban space) has always been a signifying space" ("Semiology" 191), and that contact with the majority of monuments is an encounter with the "historical Sacred" ("Eiffel Tower" 241). Also see Curtis, who suggests that, "Monumentality seems to be related to intensity of expression, elemental formal power, dignity, and gravity: In a phrase, it is a matter of lasting presence" (65).

[2]Schwartz notes, for example, the conflict over whom to memorialize iconically in the Capitol building in Washington, D.C. These conflicts during the antebellum period account for the early lack of commemoration of anyone or anything save the "founders" and founding events of the country. Antebellum leaders were unable to come to agreement on legitimate figures for commemoration, and their inability to do so was related to the larger political tensions between North and South. Similarly, Gregory and Lewis remark on the difficulty of establishing agreement on a monument commemorating the students killed at Kent State in May 1970 and upon the ways in which the meaning of the Statue of Liberty was placed at issue. Morris discusses the conflicts over cemetery design and about the difficulty involved in appropriately memorializing George Washington in the nation's capital.

[3]For more on the derivation and symbolic range of the term "monument," see Choay. Morris argues that, "public memorials 'speak' publicly by attempting to shape and possess the affective norms of the present and the future by first shaping and possessing the past. . . . Literal constructions of social reality, memorials 'speak' through cultural form, and their 'speaking' is a signification of the culture(s) to which they belong" (202). Morris suggests not only that public memorials have epideictic and deliberative functions, but also that they provide a rich interpretive source for understanding the cultures that produce them.

[4]The Vietnam Veterans Memorial has been the subject of several critical discussions in rhetoric and communication studies. See: Carlson and Hocking; Ehrenhaus, "Silence"; Ehrenhaus, "Vietnam Veteran Memorial"; Foss; Haines; and Morris. Essays also displaying a particular sensitivity to the rhetorical potential of the Vietnam Veterans Memorial include Gans; and Griswold. Also see Jensen, who argues that both the Vietnam Veterans Memorial and the AIDS Quilt provide opportunity for "creative adjustment" to complex, tragic realities.

[5]The design jury was a group of eight internationally recognized artists and designers elected by the Vietnam Veterans Memorial Fund (VVMF). It was chaired by Grady Clay, editor of *Landscape Architecture.*

[6]See, for example, Hutcheon on the boundary disputes in postmodernism. Also see Rosemarin.

[7]While we intend to demonstrate how the monument reflects the postmodern profile, our primary concern is with how it "speaks" by assuming that profile. Our primary goal is to afford some insight about the unique rhetorical statements of the Vietnam Veterans Memorial. We are not as concerned with whether there is a group of monuments in the world that we could dub as "postmodern monuments" as we are with understanding this one.

Our stance is much like that advocated in Rosemarin's treatment of genre. She argues that genres should be seen as premises of critical practices, not as hypotheses about "reality," and that the value of a generic premise is predicated upon its ability to illuminate a literary (or rhetorical) act.

Interest in a postmodern critical stance in rhetoric has emerged recently with such statements as those by Hart 386–98; and Brock, Scott, and Chesebro 427–500.

[8]What we see as a postmodern commemorative monument does not, and probably cannot, align precisely with postmodern architecture, even in the case of the Vietnam Veterans Memorial. Commemorative monuments present a problematic case for both modernist and postmodern architecture, as we will discuss further on. Thus, our characterization of the Vietnam Veterans Memorial will not fit precisely the characteristics of postmodern architecture considered generally. Since our goal is not to establish the verifiable or falsifiable legitimacy in "reality" of the genre of postmodern memorializing but to comment on the Vietnam Veterans Memorial, we do not see this as a particular problem.

[9]He expands upon this concern in *The Differend*.

[10]Foucault described the work of the intellectual "to describe that-which-is by making it appear as something that might not be, or that might not be as it is . . . [H]istory serves to show how that-which-is has not always been; i.e., that the things which seem most evident to us are always formed in the confluence of encounters and chances, during the course of a precarious and fragile history. . . . It means that they reside on a base of human practice and human history; and that since these things have been made, they can be unmade as long as we know how it was that they were made" ("Critical Theory" 36–7). Speaking of Foucault's histories, Flynn describes them as leaving us "with a heightened sense of the contingency of our most prized necessities . . ." (116).

[11]Postmodernism does not oppose all modern architecture. It places itself in opposition to the modernist (International Style) movement in particular. See Stern 75–77, for the distinction. Also see the editor's headnote to Serenyi 181.

[12]"Mies" refers to Mies van der Rohe. C.I.A.M. was the Congrès Internationaux de l'Architecture Moderne. For further discussion of the ideological character of the modernist movement, see Holenstein.

[13]Collins and Collins compare it to Esperanto and to Richards and Ogden's Basic English project (15). Also see Holenstein 52–4; and Wingler 195.

[14]Professional criticism of modernist architecture has been widespread. Among its most well-known criticisms are the following: Blaxe; Jacobs; Venturi; Venturi, Brown, and Izenour; and Wolfe. Prince Charles' recent assault on the architecture of Great Britain is exemplary of the popular distaste for the International Style.

[15]Connor's reference is to Le Corbusier, *Towards a New Architecture* 218.

[16]The one exception seems to be postmodern "classicism," which remains closer to a norm than do other "brands" of postmodern architecture. For a description of postmodern classicism, see Jencks. *Architecture Today* 292–311.

[17]For examples of others (in addition to architects) who treat architecture as a rhetoric, see: Altman; Eco; Hattenhauer; Mechling and Mechling; Medhurst and Benson 387–8; and Stuart. Medhurst and Benson, in their introduction to a section on "Rhetoric of Architecture," suggest that architects "take on the role of cultural rhetoricians. Often expressing the views and values of the society from which they come—occasionally reacting against these traditional views" (387).

[18]Some acknowledge that modernist architecture also was rhetorical, but inadvertently so. See, for example, Jencks, *Language* 50. He seems to imply that architecture cannot not communicate.

[19]For a discussion of "critical regionalism" in architecture, see Frampton.

[20]The "New York Five" are Peter Eisenmann, Michael Craves, John Hejduk, Charles Gwathmey, and Richard Meier.

[21]Also see Venturi, Brown and Izenour.

[22]Also see Connor 75; and Frampton.

[23]For further useful discussion of the distinction between work and text, see LaCapra; and McGee.

[24]This sets our view of a "text" in opposition to that of the so called "textual critics." See, for example, Leff; and the essays in Leff and Kauffeld.

[25]The entirety of Volume 4 (1984) of the *Harvard Architectural Review* is devoted to the issue of monumentality in the urban environment. Monumentality was the concern of a special issue of *Oppositions* also in the Fall 1982 (Volume 25). The essays in these two journals point to the continuing and serious concern registered about the problem.

[26]They do suggest, however, that modernism found its particular brand of monumentalism but only later in the movement.

[27]A non-utilitarian monument is one that serves no purpose except for commemoration. See Barber; Riegl 21–2; and Forster 2. Giurgola ("Forum" 39) makes a similar distinction, suggesting the possibility of building a monument or "simply using monumentality only in an architectural sense."

[28]Collins and Collins also note that useable structures, like hospitals, schools, and homes, were sometimes considered monumental (28). They suggest further that the Tennessee Valley Authority development was seen as a prototype of modernist monumentality (31). Mayo too notes this "new tradition of commemoration" that grew in importance after World War II; he links it specifically with modernism as well (202–3).

[29]In fact, the editor's introduction to the forum transcript of the Harvard conference suggests that, "The most formidable challenge . . . remained unanswered throughout the day: that our society is too diverse for any symbolic expression in architecture to convey or embody a collective ideal" ("Forum" 37).

[30]Several critics, in fact, have described it as a modern or modernist design, among them: Ehrenhaus, "Silence"; Hess; and Hubbard. Our view is more consistent with Griswold's argument in response to Hubbard, that the Vietnam Veterans Memorial is "erroneously assimilate[d] to modernist architecture whose purpose is not to be *about* anything in the world so much as to *be* a thing in the world." Griswold attributes Hubbard's mistake to a "failure to consider the complex symbolism of the Vietnam Veterans Memorial" (719).

[31]Griswold, despite his rejection of Hubbard's classification of the wall as modernist, still claims that the wall is symmetrical and that there is no tension in its design (20).

[32]For an extensive analysis of a selection of these artifacts, see Carlson and Hocking; also see Ehrenhaus, "Silence" 54.

[33]The use of mirroring surfaces is itself a symptom of the postmodern turn in architecture. Agrest suggests that in her observation that, "The meaning of an architecture of mirrors today is more a symptom of a moment of transition and adjustment than an established condition in and of itself" (120). Her discussion also indicates how mirroring serves to reinforce the need for a "textual" reading. She argues that a mirror "*dematerializes* the building, producing other images instead" (119). She continues: "The architecture of object by the use of mirrors paradoxically negates its own objecthood. This is clear particularly if one considers the architecture in context. The presence of the object is subdued by the fact that it attempts to absorb its context; it is object and context at the same time. Permeated by the qualities of its context, the building seems to replace, literally, its style and materials with an illusory image" (129).

[34]This case for changing the boundaries of the rhetorical object for analysis is consistent with McGee's notion that "text construction is now something done more by the consumers than by the producers of discourse" (288).

[35]Actually, the original idea for the inclusion of all the names was Jan Scruggs'. It was later incorporated as a criterion for the design jury by the Vietnam Veterans Memorial Fund. See Fish 1.

  The other criteria specified a "reflective and contemplative" design that would "harmonize with its surroundings, especially the neighboring national memorial" and that made "no political statement about the war" ("Vietnam Veterans Memorial").

The Vietnam Veterans Memorial Fund was a non-profit organization that ultimately raised $9 million and secured the parkland site for the Memorial. Site selection was accomplished with the aid of Senators Domenici and Mathias. See Fish 2; and Lang 69. Public Law 96-297 provided the site.

[36]See Carlson and Hocking 205; Ehrenhaus, "Vietnam Veterans Memorial" 64; and Griswold 708.

[37]This is nowhere close to Ehrenhaus' reasoning for his claim that the wall "prevents" closure ("Vietnam Veterans Memorial" 64). However, it provides specific textual evidence for his claim.

[38]Although regionalism and localism are not precisely the same, their effect—structural features that are recognizable and familiar because of their "normal" locale—is similar.

[39]Morris discusses the site's similarity to a "romanticist" style of cemetery design.

[40]Two other national monuments bear this "local" characteristic—the U.S.S. Arizona Memorial in Pearl Harbor and the First Division Monument in Washington, D.C. The U.S.S. Arizona Memorial displays a white tablet listing the names of the 1177 crewmen who died on the ship. The base of the First Division Memorial is inscribed with the names of 5,599 men of that division who were killed in World War I. The names of the 4,365 First Division soldiers killed in World War II were added later. See Murfin 106; and Goode 133.

[41]Gans provides another possibility in her anthropomorphic reading (323). She sees the wall as representing a person with arms reaching out in an embrace. Anthropomorphism is a favorite token of some postmodern architects. See Jencks, *Architecture Today* 313.

[42]Rather than assuming a rather disingen[u]ous stance on the part of these critics, one that would have them suggesting that an apolitical rhetoric is even conceivable, we assume that they mean specifically that the wall makes no political statement about the Vietnam war. Some make that qualification explicitly; others do not. It is our assumption that no rhetoric is able to eschew politics. This is a position consistent with most postmodern critics, but it is most clearly articulated by Lyotard. He argues that, politics "is not a genre, it is the multiplicity of genres. . . . It is, if you will, the state of language" (*The Differend* 138). But, by arguing that the Memorial makes a political statement, we are not merely begging the semantic question of "politics." We will suggest that the Memorial makes a political statement about the war specifically and about commemorative rhetoric generally.

[43]That Maya Lin is hardly a credible source on this issue is not typically considered. For her to claim that her design *did* make a political statement would have been to acknowledge that selection criteria were violated.

[44]No doubt the differences between our view and that of other critics are due in part to divergent critical assumptions. Most of the critics considered here discuss only the wall, and they treat it as a work rather than as the locus of a text. Moreover, some are reliant on the "authors'" statements as interpretive grounding.

[45]Also see Carlson and Hocking 204; Ehrenhaus, "Silence" 48; Ehrenhaus, "Vietnam Veterans Memorial" 54–5; Griswold; and Hess.

It should be noted that, if one considers the whole Memorial, violations of convention are intensified. It is extremely unusual, perhaps unprecedented, for two monuments commemorating the same "event" in different ways to be located on one site.

[46]Ehrenhaus' references are to "Watt Raises Obstacles"; and Carhart.

[47]These are merely differences of emphasis. Both derive from the notion of a "fit" between a situation and the rhetoric that responds to it.

[48]As Morris points out, the Vietnam Veterans Memorial engaged a "cultural conflict over the correct form and function of memorializing" (199).

[49]Perot, a Texas millionaire, had provided seed money for the design competition.

[50]Fox notes the "important statement" made by the "very existence" of a memorial in another case—Montgomery, Alabama's Civil Rights Memorial.

[51]Haines remarks on the virtual flood of other cultural products about the Vietnam war: "the struggle over the war's meaning now approaches the size of a major communications industry, including films, recorded music, novels, memoirs, biographies, histories, oral histories, television dramas and documentaries, plays and symposia" (3).

[52]By using the term "meta*narrative*" throughout, and by suggesting that such discourses are difficult to escape, we do not mean to imply that a narrative is a privileged *state* or characteristic of all discourse. Nor does Lyotard. He is very clear about his designation of narrative as a genre of discourse in *The Differend*.

[53]Any attempt to contain one or the other or to hold them to the standards of the other would be to commit "terror" in Lyotard's sense, or to victimize the "phrase regimen" of one or the other. The two components of the Memorial constitute a "differend," in Lyotard's terms, "a case of conflict, between (at least) two parties, that cannot be equitably re[s]olved for lack of a rule of judgment applicable to both arguments" (*The Differend* xi).

[54]"Nervi" refers to Pier Luigi Nervi, a modern rationalist architect.

[55]Actually, even a clearly modernist monument (like the Gateway Arch) does not look very much like a modernist building. The simple reason is that monuments frequently do not look like buildings. To argue that the Vietnam Veterans Memorial, or any other monument, is "modernist," therefore, one would have to consider more than its resemblance to typical modernist buildings.

[56]Although it is not an architectural monument, it is an important successor of the Vietnam Veteran's Memorial.

WORKS CITED

Agrest, Diana. "Architecture of Mirror/Mirror of Architecture." *Oppositions* 26 (Spring 1984): 119–33.

Altman, Charles F. "The Medieval Marquee: Church Portal Sculpture as Publicity." *Journal of Popular Culture* 14 (1980): 37–46. Rpt. in Medhurst and Benson. 389–99.

Ashabranner, Brent. *Always to Remember: The Story of the Vietnam Veteran's Memorial.* New York: Dodd, Mead, 1988.

Bannet, Eve Tavor. *Structuralism and the Logic of Dissent: Barthes, Derrida, Foucault, Lacan.* Urbana: U of Illinois P, 1989.

Barber, Bernard. "Place, Symbol, and Utilitarian Function in War Memorials." *Social Forces* 28 (October 1949): 64–8.

Barthes, Roland. "The Death of the Author." *Image, Music, Text.* Trans. Stephen Heath. New York: Hill and Wang, 1977. 142–8.

Barthes, Roland. "The Eiffel Tower." *A Barthes Reader.* Ed. Susan Sontag. New York: Hill and Wang, 1982. 236–50.

Barthes, Roland. "From Work to Text." *Image, Music, Text.* Trans. Stephen Heath. New York: Hill and Wang, 1977, 155–64.

Barthes, Roland. "Semiology and Urbanism." *The Semiotic Challenge.* Trans. Richard Howard. New York: Hill and Wang, 1988, 191–201.

Blake, Peter. *Form Follows fiasco: Why Modern Architecture Hasn't Worked.* Boston: Little, Brown, 1977.

Bricker, Charles C., et al. *America's Historic Places: An Illustrated Guide to Our Country's Past.* Ed. Richard L. Scheffel. Pleasantville, NY: Reader's Digest, 1988.

Broadbent, Geoffrey. "The Deep Structures of Architecture." *Signs, Symbols and Architecture.* Ed. Geoffrey Broadbent, Richard Bunt, and Charles Jencks. New York: John Wiley and Sons, 1980. 119–68.

Brock, Bernard L., Robert L. Scott, and James W. Chesebro, eds. *Methods of Rhetorical Criticism: A Twentieth-Century Perspective.* 3d ed. Detroit: Wayne State UP, 1989.

Butterfield, Fox. "The New Vietnam Scholarship." *New York Times Magazine* 13 February 1983. 26–32.

Carhart, Tom. "Insulting Vietnam Vets." *New York Times.* 24 October 1981. 23.

Carlson, A. Cheree, and John E. Hocking. "Strategies of Redemption at the Vietnam Veterans Memorial." *Western Journal of Speech Communication* 52 (1988): 203–15.

Charters, Mallay B. *Let's Go: The Budget Guide to the USA, 1990.* New York: St. Martin's, 1990.

Choay, François. "Alberti: The Invention of Monumentality and Memory." *Harvard Architectural Review* 4 (1984): 99–105.

Collins, Christiane C., and George R. Collins. "Monumentality: A Critical Matter in Modern Architecture." *Harvard Architectural Review* 4 (1984): 15–35.

Connor, Steven. *Postmodern Culture: An Introduction to Theories of the Contemporary.* Oxford: Basil Blackwell, 1989.

Crook, J. Mordaunt. *The Dilemma of Style: Architectural Ideas From the Picturesque to the Postmodern.* London: John Murray, 1987.

Curtis, William J. R. "Modern Architecture, Monumentality and the Meaning of Institutions: Reflections on Authenticity." *Harvard Architectural Review* 4 (1984): 65–85.

deBlaye, Edouard. *Dollarwise USA, 1989–1990.* Ed. Susan Poole. Trans. Maxwell R. D. Vos. New York: Simon and Schuster, 1989.

Eco, Umberto. "Function and Sign: The Semiotics of Architecture." *Signs, Symbols and Architecture.* Ed. Geoffrey Broadbent, Richard Bunt, and Charles Jencks. New York: John Wiley and Sons, 1980. 11–69.

Ehrenhaus, Peter. "Silence and Symbolic Expression." *Communication Monographs* 55 (1988): 41–57.

Ehrenhaus, Peter. "The Vietnam Veterans Memorial: An Invitation to Argument." *Journal of the American Forensic Association* 25 (1988): 54–64.

Fish, Lydia. *The Last Firebase: A Guide to the Vietnam Veterans Memorial.* Shippen[s]burg, PA: White Mane, 1987.

Fisher, Volker, Andrea Gleiniger-Neumann, Heinrich Klotz, and Hans-Peter Schwartz. *Postmodern Visions: Drawings, Paintings, and Models by Contemporary Architects.* Ed. Heinrich Klotz. Trans. Yehuda Shapiro. New York: Abbeville, 1985.

Flynn, Thomas. "Foucault as Parrhesiast: His Last Course at the Collège de France (1984)." *The Final Foucault.* Ed. James Bernauer and David Rasmussen. Cambridge, MA: MIT Press, 1988. 102–18.

Forster, Kurt W. "Monument/Memory and the Mortality of Architecture." *Oppositions* 25 (Fall 1982): 2–19.

"Forum Transcript: Monumentality and the city, December 12, 1981." Conference held at Harvard Graduate School of Design. *Harvard Architectural Review* 4 (1984): 37–51.

Foss, Sonja K. "Ambiguity as Persuasion: The Vietnam Veterans Memorial." *Communication Quarterly* 34 (1986): 326–40.

Foster, Hal. *Recodings: Art, Spectacle, Cultural Politics.* Seattle: Bay Press, 1985.

Foucault, Michel. *The Archaeology of Knowledge and The Discourse on Language.* Trans. A. M. Sheridan Smith. New York: Harper, 1972.

Foucault, Michel. "Critical Theory/Intellectual History." Trans. Jeremy Harding. *Michel Foucault: Politics, Philosophy, Culture: Interviews and Other Writings, 1977–1984.* Ed. Lawrence D. Kritzman. New York: Routledge, 1988. 17–46.

Foucault, Michel. "The Subject and Power." Afterword to Hubert L. Dreyfus and Paul Rabinow. *Michel Foucault: Beyond Structuralism and Hermeneutics.* 2d ed. Chicago: U of Chicago P, 1983. 208–26.

Fox, Catherine. "No Catharsis in Civil Rights Memorial." *Los Angeles Daily Journal* 10 November 1989. II:1.

Frampton, Kenneth. "Towards a Critical Regionalism: Six Points for an Architecture of Resistance." *The Anti-Aesthetic: Essays on Postmodern Culture.* Ed. Hal Foster. Port Townsend, WA: Bay Press, 1983: 16–30.

Gandelsonas, Mario. "On Reading Architecture." *Progressive Architecture* 53 (March 1972): 68–88.

Gans, Adrienne. "The War and Peace of the Vietnam Memorials." *American Imago* 44 (1987): 315–29.

Gass, William H. "Monumentality/Mentality." *Oppositions* 25 (Fall 1982): 21–51.

Goode, James M. *The Outdoor Sculpture of Washington, D.C.: A Comprehensive Historical Guide.* Washington, D.C.: Smithsonian Institution Press, 1974.

Gregory, Stanford W., Jr., and Jerry M. Lewis. "Symbols of Collective Memory: The Social Process of Memorializing May 4, 1970, at Kent State University." *Symbolic Interaction* 11 (1988): 213–33.

Griswold, Charles L. "The Vietnam Veterans Memorial and the Washington Mall: Philosophical Thoughts on Political Iconography." *Critical Inquiry* 12 (1986): 688–719.

Guillerme, Jacque. "The Idea of Architectural Language: A Critical Inquiry." *Oppositions* 10 (Fall 1977): 21–26.

Haines, Harry W. "'What Kind of War?': An Analysis of the Vietnam Veterans Memorial." *Critical Studies in Mass Communication* 3 (1986): 1–20.

Hart, Roderick P. *Modern Rhetorical Criticism.* Glenview, IL: Scott, Foresman, 1989.

Harvey, David. *The Condition of Postmodernity: An Enquiry into the Origins of Cultural Change.* Oxford: Basil Blackwell, 1989.

Hattenhauer, Darryl. "The Rhetoric of Architecture: A Semiotic Approach." *Communication Quarterly* 32 (1984): 71–7.

Hess, Elizabeth. "A Tale of Two Memorials." *Art in America* 71 (1983): 121–6.

Holenstein, Elmar. "Exursus: Monofunctionalism in Architecture between the Wars (Le Corbusier and the Bauhaus)." Trans. Diane Nelson. *Oppositions* 24 (Spring 1981): 49–61.

Hutcheon, Linda. *A Poetics of Postmodernism: History, Theory, Fiction.* New York: Routledge, 1988.

Jacobs, Jane. *The Death and Life of Great American Cities.* New York: Random House, 1961.

Jameson, Fredric. "Architecture and the Critique of Ideology." *The Ideologies of Theory: Essays 1971–1986. Volume 2: The Syntax of History.* Minneapolis: U of Minnesota P, 1988. 35–60.

Jencks, Charles. *Architecture Today.* London: Academy Editions, 1988.

Jencks, Charles. *The Language of Post-Modern Architecture.* Rev. enlarged ed. London: Academy Editions, 1981.

Jencks, Charles. "Rhetoric and Architecture." *Architectural Association Quarterly* 4 (1972): 4–17.

Jensen, Marvin D. "Making Contact: The Vietnam Veterans Memorial and The NAMES Project Quilt." Paper presented at the Speech Communication Association Convention. New Orleans, LA, November 1988.

LaCapra, Dominic. *Rethinking Intellectual History: Texts, Contexts, Language.* Ithaca: Cornell UP, 1983.

Lang, John S. "A Memorial Wall That Healed Our Wounds." *U.S. News and World Report.* 21 November 1983. 68–70.

Le Corbusier, Henri. *Towards a New Architecture.* Trans. Frederick Etchells. London: John Rodker, 1927.

Leff, Michael. "Textual Criticism: The Legacy of G. P. Mohrmann." *QJS* 72 (1986): 377–89.

Leff, Michael C., and Fred J. Kauffeld, eds. *Texts in Context: Critical Dialogues on Significant Episodes in American Political Rhetoric.* Davis, CA: Hermagoras Press, 1989.

Lyotard, Jean-François. *The Differend: Phrases in Dispute.* Trans. Georges Van Den Abbeele. Minneapolis: U of Minnesota P, 1988.

Lyotard, Jean-François. *The Postmodern Condition: A Report on Knowledge.* Trans. Geoff Bennington and Brian Massumi. Minneapolis: U of Minnesota P, 1984.

Mayo, James M. *War Memorials as Political Landscape: The American Experience and Beyond.* New York: Praeger, 1988.

McGee, Michael Calvin. "Text, Context, and the Fragmentation of Contemporary Culture." *Western Journal of Speech Communication* 54 (1990): 274–89.

McLeod, Mary. "Architecture." *The Postmodern Moment: A Handbook of Contemporary Innovation in the Arts*. Ed. Stanley Trachtenberg. Westport, CT: Greenwood, 1985. 19–52.

Mechling, Elizabeth Walker, and Jay Mechling. "The Sale of Two Cities: A Semiotic Comparison of Disneyland with Marriott's Great America." *Journal of Popular Culture* 37 (1973): 253–63. Rpt. in Medhurst and Benson. 400–13.

Medhurst, Martin J., and Thomas W. Benson, eds. *Rhetorical Dimensions in Media: A Critical Casebook*. Dubuque, IA: Kendall/Hunt, 1984.

Moriarty, Marilyn F. "Perspectives on Postmodern Architecture." *In Conference Schedule and Supplement for Postmodernism and Beyond: Architecture as the Critical Art of Contemporary Culture*. University of California, Irvine. October 26–28, 1989. 1–3.

Morris, Richard. "The Vietnam Veterans Memorial and the Myth of Superiority." In *Cultural Legacies of Vietnam: Uses of the Past in the Present*. Ed. Richard Morris and Peter Ehrenhaus. Norwood, NJ: Ablex, 1990. 199–222.

Murfin, James. *The National Park of America*. New York: Multimedia, 1989.

Portoghesi, Paolo. *After Modern Architecture*. Trans. Meg Shore. New York: Rizzoli, 1980.

Riegl, Alois. "The Modern Cult of Monuments: Its Character and Its Origin" [1903]. Trans. Kurt W. Forsler and Diane Ghirardo. *Oppositions* 25 (Fall 1982): 21–51.

Rosemarin, Adena. *The Power of Genre*. Minneapolis: U of Minnesota P, 1985.

Schwartz, Barry. "The Social Context of Commemoration: A Study in Collective Memory." *Social Forces* 61 (1982): 374–402.

Scruggs, Jan C., and Joel L. Swerdlow. *To Heal a Nation: The Vietnam Veterans Memorial*. New York: Harper, 1985.

Serenyi, Peter. "Mies' New National Gallery: An Essay on Architectural Content." *Harvard Architectural Review* 1 (1980): 181–9.

Stern, Robert. "The Doubles of Post-modern." *Harvard Architectural Review* 1 (1980): 75–87.

Stuart, Charlotte L. "Architecture in Nazi Germany: A Rhetorical Perspective." *Western Speech* 37 (1973): 253–63.

Temko, Allan. *Eero Saarinen*. New York: George Braziller, 1962.

Venturi, Robert. *Complexity and Contradiction in Architecture* (New York: Museum of Modern Art and Graham Foundation, 1966).

Venturi, Robert, Denise Scott Brown, and Steven Izenour. *Learning from Las Vegas*. Cambridge: MIT Press, 1972.

"Vietnam Veterans Memorial." U.S. National Park Service pamphlet. 1984.

"Watt Raises Obstacles on Vietnam Memorial." *New York Times* 13 January 1982. A12.

Wingler, Hans W. *The Bauhaus*. Cambridge, MA: MIT Press, 1969.

Wolfe, Tom. *From Bauhaus to Our House*. New York: Farrar, Straus and Giroux, 1981.

Chapter II

Neo-Classical Criticism

The traditional, neo-classical method is founded on Herbert A. Wichelns's 1925 essay, "The Literary Criticism of Oratory."[1] According to Wichelns, rhetorical criticism should systematically analyze a speaker's audience, perceived character, major themes, emotional appeals, arguments, arrangement of ideas, style, and delivery. In short, it should address the major topics of classical rhetorical theory. Evaluation of these factors enables the critic to understand the effect of discourse on its immediate hearers. The proper object of criticism, according to Wichelns, is the persuasive speech, and the ultimate goal is the "appreciation of the orator's method of imparting his ideas to his hearers."

Neo-classical criticism has a long and controversial history. From 1925 to the 1960s, this method dominated speech criticism. In 1965, however, Edwin Black (among others) led a movement to break away from the constraints of the "neo-Aristotelian" approach: a particularly formulaic, unimaginative type of traditional criticism.[2] In subsequent decades, neo-classical criticism fell from favor, and strikingly different concepts of rhetorical criticism proliferated; however, many critics continued to address the central questions of traditional neo-classical criticism, whether they acknowledged it or not.[3] In 1988 Stephen E. Lucas identified a "renaissance" of traditional analysis.[4] Although neo-classical criticism is no longer the dominant paradigm, many critics continue to use Wichelns's approach, with modifications to avoid pitfalls of earlier work. The readings in this chapter highlight three milestones in the evolution of neo-classical criticism.

Forbes Hill's 1972 publication, "Conventional Wisdom—Traditional Form—The President's Message of November 3, 1969," questions the appropriateness of ideological critiques of Richard Nixon's wartime rhetoric. Hill suggests rhetorical criticism should not be concerned with judging the political wisdom or truthfulness of a speaker's discourse. He claims Aristotelian theory is the best method for understanding the effectiveness of Richard Nixon's oratory about the Vietnam war. Hill also argues, however, that true Aristotelian analysis does not hinge on assessing the actual effect of a speech on a target audience. Instead, he maintains, the goal of such criticism should be to ascertain whether the rhetor made strategically sound decisions in light of the audience and historical context. According to Hill, Aristotle's *Rhetoric* provides a "comprehensive inventory" that the critic uses to evaluate a speaker's choices. Hill vigorously defends traditional neo-classical criticism and provides an insightful analysis of one of Nixon's most famous speeches.

Michael C. Leff and Gerald P. Mohrmann's 1974 essay "Lincoln at Cooper Union: A Rhetorical Analysis of the Text" attempts to draw from classical rhetorical theory to analyze a speech, while correcting some of the weaknesses that Edwin Black pointed out in "neo-Aristotelian" criticism. Mohrmann and Leff evaluate many of the same factors that Wichelns recommends, but broaden the analysis to consider Lincoln's discourse as part of a genre (type) of political discourse.[5]

Stephen Howard Browne's 2002 article "'The Circle of Our Felicities': Thomas Jefferson's First Inaugural Address and the Rhetoric of Nationhood" demonstrates how a critic can attend to classical topics of criticism without being locked into a rigid formula. Browne situates Jefferson's speech in its historical context, examines its immediate effects and enduring influence, and explains how the speech "functions rhetorically." Integrating elements of close textual analysis and genre criticism, Browne concludes that Jefferson's inaugural "constitutes its own theory of rhetoric."[6]

NOTES

[1] "The Literary Criticism of Oratory" is reprinted in Chapter 1 of this book.

[2] For Black's position, see the selections from *Rhetorical Criticism: A Study in Method,* reprinted in Chapter 1 of this book.

[3] See G. P. Mohrmann's "Elegy in a Critical Grave-Yard," *Western Journal of Speech Communication* 44 (1980): 269.

[4] Stephen E. Lucas, "The Renaissance of American Public Address: Text and Context in Rhetorical Criticism," *Quarterly Journal of Speech* 74 (1988): 241–60.

[5] Mohrmann and Leff meld Wichelns' approach with genre criticism, which is discussed in Chapter 8 of this anthology.

[6] Close textual analysis is the subject of Chapter 3. Genre criticism is discussed in Chapter 8.

CONVENTIONAL WISDOM—TRADITIONAL FORM— THE PRESIDENT'S MESSAGE OF NOVEMBER 3, 1969

FORBES HILL

More than one critique of President Nixon's address to the nation on November 3, 1969 has appeared,[1] which is not remarkable, since it was the most obvious feature of the public relations machine that appears to have dammed back the flood of sentiment for quick withdrawal of American forces from Southeast Asia. To be sure, the dike built by this machine hardly endured forever, but some time was gained— an important achievement. It seems natural, then, that we should want to examine this obvious feature from more than one angle.

Preceding critiques have looked at Nixon's message from notably non-traditional perspectives. Stelzner magnified it in the lens of archetypal criticism, which reveals a non-literary version of the quest story archetype, but he concluded that the President's is an incomplete telling of the story that does not adequately interact with the listeners' subjective experiences. Newman condemned the message as "shoddy rhetoric" because its tough stance and false dilemmas are directed to white, urban, uptight voters. Campbell condemned it on the basis of intrinsic criticism because though its stated purposes are to tell the truth, increase credibility, promote unity, and affirm moral responsibility, its rhetoric conceals truth, decreases credibility, promotes division, and dodges moral responsibility. Then, stepping outside the intrinsic framework, she makes her most significant criticism: the message perpetuates myths about American values instead of scrutinizing the real values of America.

I propose to juxtapose these examinations with a strict neo-Aristotelian analysis. If it differs slightly from analyses that follow Wichelns[2] and Hochmuth-Nichols,[3] that is because it attempts a critique that re-interprets neo-Aristotelianism slightly—a critique guided by the spirit and usually the letter of the Aristotelian text as I understand it. What the neo-Aristotelian method can and should do will be demonstrated, I hope, by this juxtaposition.

Neo-Aristotelian criticism compares the means of persuasion used by a speaker with a comprehensive inventory given in Aristotle's *Rhetoric*. Its end is to discover whether the speaker makes the best choices from the inventory to get a favorable decision from a specified group of auditors in a specific situation. It does not, of course, aim to discover whether or not the speaker actually gets his favorable decision; decisions in practice are often upset by chance factors.[4] First the neo-Aristotelian critic must outline the situation, then specify the group of auditors and define the kind of decision they are to make. Finally he must reveal the choice and disposition of three intertwined persuasive factors—logical, psychological, and characterological—and evaluate this choice and disposition against the standard of the *Rhetoric*.

THE SITUATION

The state of affairs for the Nixon Administration in the fall of 1969 is well known. The United States had been fighting a stalemated war for several years. The cost in lives and money was immense. The goal of the war was not clear; presumably the United States wanted South Viet Nam as a stable non-Communist buffer state between Communist areas and the rest of Southeast Asia. To the extent that this goal was understood, it seemed as far from being realized in 1969 as it had been in 1964. In the meantime, a large and vocal movement had grown up, particularly among the young, of people who held that there should have been no intervention in Viet Nam in the first place and that it would never be possible to realize any conceivable goal of intervention. The movement was especially dangerous to the Administration because it numbered among its supporters many of the elements of the population who were most interested in foreign policy and best informed about it. There were variations of position within the peace movement, but on one point all its members were agreed: the United States should commit itself immediately to withdraw its forces from Viet Nam.

The policy of the Nixon Administration, like that of the Johnson Administration before it, was limited war to gain a position of strength from which to negotiate. By fall 1969 the Administration was willing to make any concessions that did not jeopardize a fifty-fifty chance of achieving the goal, but it was not willing to make concessions that amounted to sure abandonment of the goal. A premature withdrawal amounted to public abandonment and was to be avoided at all costs. When the major organizations of the peace movement announced the first Moratorium Day for October 15 and organized school and work stoppages, demonstrations, and a great "March on Washington" to dramatize the demand for immediate withdrawal from Viet Nam, the Administration launched a counterattack. The President announced that he would make a major address on Viet Nam November 3. This announcement seems to have moderated the force of the October moratorium, but plans were soon laid for a second moratorium on November 15. Nixon's counterattack aimed at rallying the mass of the people to disregard the vocal minority and oppose immediate withdrawal; it aimed to get support for a modified version of the old strategy: limited war followed by negotiated peace. The address was broadcast the evening of November 3 over the national radio and television networks.

THE AUDITORS AND THE KIND OF DECISION

An American President having a monopoly of the media at prime time potentially reaches an audience of upwards of a hundred million adults of heterogeneous backgrounds and opinions. Obviously it is impossible to design a message to move every segment of this audience, let alone the international audience. The speaker must choose his targets. An examination of the texts shows us which groups were eliminated as targets, which were made secondary targets, and which were primary. The speaker did not address himself to certain fanatical opponents of the war: the ones who hoped that the Viet Cong would gain a signal victory over the Americans and their South Vietnamese allies, or those who denied that Communist advances were threats to non-Communist countries, or those against any war for any reason. These were the groups the President sought to isolate and stigmatize. On the other hand, there was a large group of Americans who would be willing to give their all to fight any kind of Communist expansion anywhere at any time. These people also were not a target group: their support could be counted on in any case.

The speaker did show himself aware that the Viet Cong and other Communist decision-makers were listening in. He represented himself to them as willing and anxious to negotiate and warned them that escalation of the war would be followed by effective retaliation. The Communists constituted a secondary target audience, but the analysis that follows will make plain that the message was not primarily intended for them.

The primary target was those Americans not driven by a clearly defined ideological commitment to oppose or support the war at any cost. Resentment of the sacrifice in money and lives, bewilderment at the stalemate, longing for some movement in a clearly marked direction—these were the principal aspects of their state of mind assumed by Nixon. He solicited them saying "tonight—to you, the great silent majority of my fellow Americans—I ask for your support."[5]

His address asks the target group of auditors to make a decision to support a policy to be continued in the future. In traditional terms, then, it is primarily a deliberative speech. Those who receive the message are decision-makers, and they are concerned with the past only as it serves as analogy to future decisions. The subjects treated are usual ones for deliberation: war and peace.[6]

DISPOSITION AND SYNOPSIS

The address begins with an enthymeme that attacks the credibility gap.[7] Those who decide on war and peace must know the truth about these policies, and the conclusion is implied that the President is going to tell the truth. The rest of the *proem* is taken up by a series of questions constructing a formal partition of the subjects to be covered. The partition stops short of revealing the nature of the modification in policy that constitutes the Nixon plan. The message fits almost perfectly into the Aristotelian pattern of *proem*, narrative, proofs both constructive and refutative, and epilogue. Just as *proem* has served as a general heading for a synoptic statement of what was done in the first few sentences, so the other four parts will serve us as analytical headings for a synopsis of the rest.

The narrative commences with Nixon's statement of the situation as he saw it on taking office. He could have ordered immediate withdrawal of American forces, but he decided to fulfill "a greater obligation . . . to think of the effect" of his decision "on the next generation, and on the future of peace and freedom in America, and in the world." Applicable here is the precept: the better the moral end that the speaker can in his narrative be seen consciously choosing, the better the *ethos* he reveals.[8] An end can hardly be better than "the future of peace and freedom in America, and in the world." The narrative goes on to explain why and how the United States became involved in Viet Nam in the first place. This explanation masquerades as a simple chronological statement—"Fifteen years ago . . ." but thinly disguised in the chronology lie two propositions: first, that the leaders of America were right in intervening on behalf of the government of South Viet Nam; second, that the great mistake in their conduct of the war was over-reliance on American combat forces. Some doubt has been cast on the wisdom of Nixon's choice among the means of persuasion here. The history, writes one critic, "is a surprising candidate for priority in any discussion today. . . . The President's chief foreign policy advisors, his allies on Capitol Hill, and the memorandum he got from the Cabinet bureaucracy all urged him to skip discussions of the causes and manner of our involvement. Yet history comes out with top billing."[9] This criticism fails to conceive the rhetorical function of the narrative: in the two propositions the whole content of the proofs that follow is foreshadowed, and foreshadowed in the guise of a non-controversial statement about the historical facts. Among traditional orators this use of the narrative to foreshadow proofs is common, but it has seldom been handled with more artistry than here.

Constructive proofs are not opened with an analytical partition but with a general question: what is the best way to end the war? The answer is structured as a long argument from logical division: there are four plans to end American involvement; three should be rejected so that the listener is left with no alternative within the structure but to accept the fourth.[10] The four plans are: immediate withdrawal, the consequences of which are shown at some length to be bad; negotiated settlement, shown to be impossible in the near future because the enemy will not negotiate in earnest; shifting the burden of the war to the Vietnamese with American withdrawal on a fixed timetable, also argued to have bad consequences; and shifting the burden of the war to the Vietnamese with American withdrawal on a flexible schedule, said to have good consequences, since it will eventually bring "the complete withdrawal of all United States *combat ground* forces," whether earnest negotiations become possible or not. Constructive proofs close with one last evil consequence of immediate withdrawal: that it would lead eventually to Americans' loss of confidence in themselves and divisive recrimination that "would scar our spirit as a people."

As refutative proof is introduced, opponents of the Administration are characterized by a demonstrator carrying a sign, "Lose in Viet Nam"; they are an irrational minority who want to decide policy in the streets, as opposed to the elected officials—Congress and the President—who will decide policy by Constitutional and orderly means. This attack on his presumed opponents leads to a passage which reassures the majority of young people that the President really wants peace as much as they do. Reassuring ends with the statement of Nixon's personal belief that his plan will succeed; this statement may be taken as transitional to the epilogue.

The epilogue reiterates the bad consequences of immediate withdrawal—loss of confidence and loss of other nations to totalitarianism—it exhorts the silent majority to support the plan, predicting its success; it evokes the memory of Woodrow Wilson; then it closes with the President's pledge to meet his responsibilities to lead the nation with strength and wisdom. Recapitulation, building of *ethos*, and reinforcing the right climate of feeling—these are what a traditional rhetorician would advise that the epilogue do,[11] and these are what Nixon's epilogue does.

Indeed, this was our jumping-off place for the synopsis of the message: it falls into the traditional paradigm; each frame of the paradigm contains the lines of argument conventional for that frame. The two unconventional elements in the paradigm—the unusual placement of the last evil consequence of immediate withdrawal and the use of the frame by logical division for the constructive proofs—are there for good rhetorical reasons. That last consequence, loss of confidence and divisive recrimination, serves to lead into the refutation which opens with the demonstrator and his sign. It is as if the demonstrator were being made an example in advance of just this evil consequence. The auditor is brought into precisely the right set for a refutation section that does not so much argue with opponents as it pushes them into an isolated, unpopular position.

Because of the residues-like structure, the message creates the illusion of proving that Vietnamization and flexible withdrawal constitute the best policy. By process of elimination it is the only policy available, and even a somewhat skeptical listener is less likely to question the only policy available. Approaching the proposal with skepticism dulled, he perhaps does not so much miss a development of the plan. In particular, he might not ask the crucial question: does the plan actually provide for complete American withdrawal? The answer to this question is contained in the single phrase, "complete withdrawal of all United States *combat ground* forces." It is fairly clear, in retrospect, that this phrase concealed the intention to keep in Viet Nam for several years a large contingent of air and support forces. Nixon treats the difference between plan three, Vietnamization and withdrawal on a fixed schedule, and plan four, Vietnamization and withdrawal on a flexible schedule, as a matter of whether or not the schedule is announced in advance. But the crucial difference is really that plan three was understood by its advocates as a plan for quick, complete withdrawal; plan four was a plan for partial withdrawal. The strategic reason for not announcing a fixed schedule was that the announcement would give away this fact. The residues structure concealed the lack of development of the plan; the lack of development of the plan suppressed the critical fact that Nixon did not propose complete withdrawal. Although Nixon's message shows traditionally conventional structure, these variations from the traditional show a remarkable ability at designing the best adaptations to the specific rhetorical situation.

LOGICAL AND PSYCHOLOGICAL PERSUASIVE FACTORS

Central to an Aristotelian assessment of the means of persuasion is an account of two interdependent factors: (1) the choice of major premises on which enthymemes[12] that form "the body of the proof" are based, and (2) the means whereby auditors are brought into states of feeling favorable to accepting these premises and the conclusions following from them. Premises important here are of two kinds: predictions and values. Both kinds[,] as they relate to good and evil consequences of the four plans to end American involvement, will be assessed. The first enthymeme involving prediction is that immediate withdrawal followed by a Communist takeover would lead to murder and imprisonment of innocent civilians. This conclusion follows from the general predictive rule: the future will resemble the past.[13] Since the Communists murdered and imprisoned opponents on taking over North Viet Nam in 1954 and murdered opponents in the city of Hue in 1968, they will do the same when they take over South Viet Nam. Implied also is an enthymeme based on the value premise that security of life and freedom from bondage are primary goods for men;[14] a Communist takeover would destroy life and freedom and therefore destroy primary goods for men.

Presumably no one would try to refute this complex of enthymemes by saying that life and freedom are not primary goods, though he might argue from more and less;[15] more life is lost by continuing the war than would be lost by a Communist takeover, or American–South Vietnamese political structures allow for even less political freedom than the Communist alternatives. Nixon buries these questions far enough beneath the surface of the message that probably auditors in the target group are not encouraged to raise them. One could also attack the predictive premise: after all, the future is not always the past writ over again. But this kind of refutation is merely irritating; we know that the premise is not universally true, yet everyone finds it necessary to operate in ordinary life as if it were. People on the left of the target group, of course, reject the evidence—North Viet Nam and Hue.

A related prediction is that immediate withdrawal would result in a collapse of confidence in American leadership. It rests on the premise that allies only have confidence in those who both have power and will act in their support.[16] If the United States shows it lacks power and will in Viet Nam, there will be a collapse of confidence, which entails further consequences: it would "promote recklessness" on the part of enemies everywhere else the country has commitments, i.e., as a general premise, when one party to a power struggle loses the confidence of its allies, its enemies grow bolder.[17] The conclusion is bolstered by citations from former presidents Eisenhower, Johnson, and Kennedy: the statement of the "liberal saint," Kennedy, is featured.

It is difficult to attack the related premises of these tandem arguments. They rest on what experience from the sandbox up shows to be probable. The target group consists of people with the usual American upbringing and experience. Someone will question the premises only if he questions the world-view out of which they develop. That view structures the world into Communist powers—actual or potential enemies—and non-Communist powers—allies. America is the leader of the allies, referred to elsewhere as the forces of "peace and freedom" opposed by "the forces of totalitarianism." Because of its association with freedom, American leadership is indisputably good, and whatever weakens confidence in it helps the enemies. Only a few people on the far left would categorically reject this structure.

The foregoing premises and the world view fundamental to them are even more likely to be accepted if the auditors are in a state of fear. Fear may be defined as distress caused by a vision of impending evil of the destructive or painful kind.[18] This message promotes a state of fear by the nature of the evil consequences developed— murder and imprisonment of innocents, collapse of leadership in the free world, and reckless aggressiveness of implacable enemies. America is the proto[t]ype of a nation that is fearful; her enemies are watching their opportunities all over the globe, from Berlin to the Middle East, yes even in the Western Hemisphere itself. The enemies are cruel and opposed to American ideals. They are strong on the battlefield and intransigent in negotiations. Conditions are such that America's allies may lose confidence in her and leave her to fight these enemies alone. But these circumstances are not too much amplified: only enough to create a state of feeling favorable to rejecting immediate withdrawal, not so much as to create the disposition for escalation.

Nixon claims to have tried hard to make a negotiated settlement, but he could not make one because the Communists refused to compromise. The evidence that they would not compromise is developed at length: public initiatives through the peace conference in Paris are cited, terms for participation of the Communist forces in internationally supervised elections offered, and promises made to negotiate on any of these terms. Then there were private initiatives through the Soviet Union and directly by letter to the leaders of North Viet Nam, as well as private efforts by the United States ambassador to the Paris talks. These efforts brought only demands for the equivalent of unconditional surrender. The citation of evidence is impressive and destroys the credibility of the position that negotiations can bring a quick end to the war.

Nixon does not explicitly predict that the plan for negotiated settlement will not work ever; on the contrary, he says that he will keep trying. But if the auditor believes the evidence, he finds it difficult to avoid making his own enthymeme with the conclusion that negotiated settlement will never work; the major premise is the same old rule, the future will be like the past. Nixon gives another reason, too: it will not work while the opposite side "is convinced that all it has to do is to wait for our next concession, and our next concession after that one, until it gets everything it wants." The major premise—no power convinced that victory is probable by forcing repeated concessions will ever compromise—constitutes a commonplace of bargaining for virtually everyone.

Peace is seen in these arguments as almost an unqualified good. Although compromise through bargaining is the fastest way to peace, the other side must make concessions to assure compromise. Reasons for continuing the war, such as an ideological commitment, are evil. There is no glory in war and prolonging it is not justified by political gains made but only by a commitment to higher values like saving lives and preserving freedom. Prolonging the war is also justified as avoiding future wars by not losing Southeast Asia altogether and not promoting the spirit of recklessness in the enemies. "I want," states Nixon, "to end it [the war] in a way which will increase the chance that their [the soldiers'] younger brothers and their sons will not have to fight in some future Vietnam. . . ."

A listener is prone to reject the likelihood of a negotiated peace if he is angry with his opponents. Anger is a painful desire for revenge and arises from an evident, unjustified slight to a person or his friends.[19] People visualizing revenge ordinarily refuse compromise except as a temporary tactic. Nixon presents the American people as having been slighted: they value peace, and their leaders have with humility taken every peace initiative possible: public, private, and secret. The Communist powers wish to gain politically from the war; they have rebuffed with spite all initiatives and frustrated our good intentions by demanding the equivalent of unconditional surrender. Frustration is, of course, a necessary condition of anger.[20] Again, Nixon does not go too far—not far enough to create a psychological climate out of which a demand for escalation would grow.

Nixon announces that his plan for Vietnamization and American withdrawal on a flexible timetable is in effect already. Its consequences: American men coming home, South Vietnamese forces gaining in strength, enemy infiltration measurably reduced, and United States casualties also reduced. He predicts: policies that have had such consequences in the past will have them in the future, i.e., the future will be like the past. Again, the undisputed value that saving lives is good is assumed. But in this case the argument, while resting on an acceptable premise, was, at the time of this speech, somewhat more doubtful of acceptance by the target group.

The evidence constitutes the problem: obviously the sample of the past since the policy of Vietnamization commenced was so short that no one could really judge the alleged consequences to be correlated with the change in policy, let alone caused by it. There is, then, little reason why that audience should have believed the minor premise—that the consequences of Vietnamization were good.

A temporizing and moderate policy is best presented to auditors who while temporarily fearful are basically confident. Nothing saps the will to accept such a proposal as does the opposite state, basically fearful and only temporarily confident. Confidence is the other side of the coin from fear: it is pleasure because destructive and painful evils seem far away and sources of aid near at hand.[21] The sources of aid here are the forces of the Republic of South Viet Nam. They have continued to gain in strength and as a result have been able to take over combat responsibilities from American forces. In contrast, danger from the enemy is receding—"enemy infiltration . . . over the last three months is less than 20 per cent of what it was over the same period last year." Nixon assures his auditors that he has confidence the plan will succeed. America is the "strongest and richest nation in the world"; it can afford the level of aid that needs to be continued in Viet Nam. It will show the moral stamina to meet the challenge of free world leadership.

For some time rumors about gradual American withdrawal from Viet Nam had been discounted by the peace movement. The only acceptable proof of American intentions would be a timetable showing withdrawal to be accomplished soon. Thus the third plan: withdrawal on a fixed timetable. Nixon predicts that announcing of a timetable would remove the incentive to negotiate and reduce flexibility of response. The general premise behind the first is a commonplace of bargaining: negotiations never take place without a *quid pro quo;* a promise to remove American forces by a certain date gives away the *quid pro quo.* For most Americans, who are used to getting things by bargaining, this premise is unquestionable. Only those few who think that the country can gain no vestige of the objective of the war are willing to throw away the incentive. The premise behind the notion of flexibility—that any workable plan is adaptable to changes in the situation—is a commonplace of legislation and not likely to be questioned by anyone. Nixon adds to this generally acceptable premise a specific incentive. Since withdrawal will occur more rapidly if enemy military activity decreases and the South Vietnamese forces become stronger, there is a possibility that forces can be withdrawn even sooner than would be predicted by a timetable. This specific incentive is illusory, since it is obvious that one can always withdraw sooner than the timetable says, even if he has one; it is hard to see how a timetable actually reduces flexibility. Everyone makes timetables, of course, and having to re-make them when conditions change is a familiar experience. But the average man who works from nine to five probably thinks that the government should be different: when it announces a timetable it must stick to it; otherwise nothing is secure. This argument may seem weak to the critic, but it is probably well directed to the target group. The real reason for not announcing a timetable has already been noted.[22]

One final prediction is founded on the preceding predictions—whenever a policy leads to such evil consequences as movement of Southeast Asia into alliance with the enemy and a new recklessness on the part of enemies everywhere, it will eventually result in remorse and divisive recrimination which will, in turn, result in a loss of self-confidence. Guiltlessness and internal unity, the opposites of remorse and recrimination, are here assumed as secondary goods leading to self-confidence, a primary good. The enthymeme predicting loss of self-confidence consequent on immediate withdrawal is summary in position: it seems to tie together all previous arguments. It comes right after a particularly effective effort at *ethos* building—the series of statements developed in parallel construction about not having chosen the easy way (immediate withdrawal) but the right way. However, it rests on the assumption that the long[-]term mood of confidence in the country depends on the future of Southeast Asia and the recklessness of our enemies. Since these two factors are only an aspect of a larger picture in which many other events play their parts, it is surely not true that they alone will produce a loss of confidence. The enthymeme based on this assumption, placed where it is, however, does not invite questioning by the target group. Doubtful though it may look under searching scrutiny, it has an important function for the structure of psychological proof in this message. It reinforces the vague image of the danger of facing a stronger enemy in a weakened condition: America itself would be less united, less confident, and less able to fight in the future if this consequence of immediate withdrawal were realized.

Other things being equal, the more commonplace and universally accepted the premises of prediction in a deliberative speech, the more effective the speech. This is especially true if they are set in a frame that prepares the auditor psychologically for their acceptance. There is almost no doubt that given the policy of the Nixon Administration—Vietnamization and partial withdrawal on a flexible schedule not announced in advance—the message shows a potentially effective choice of premises. In some cases it is almost the only possible choice. Likewise the value structure of the message is wisely chosen from materials familiar to any observer of the American scene: it could be duplicated in hundreds of other messages from recent American history.

Several additional value assumptions are equally commonplace. Betraying allies and letting down friends is assumed to be an evil, and its opposite, loyalty to friends and allies[,] the virtue of a great nation. This premise equates personal loyalty, like that a man feels for his friend, with what the people of the whole nation should feel for an allied nation. Many people think this way about international relations, and the good citizens of the target group can be presumed to be among them.

Policies endorsed by the people they are supposed to help are said to be better policies than those not endorsed by them. This statement undoubtedly makes a good political rule if one expects participation in the execution of policy of those to be helped. Policies that result from the operation of representative government are good, whereas those made on the streets are bad. This value is, of course, an essential of republican government: only the most radical, even of those outside the target group, would question it. Finally, Nixon assumes that the right thing is usually the opposite of the easy thing, and, of course, *he* chooses to do the right thing. Such a value premise does not occur in rhetorics by Aristotle or even George Campbell; it is probably a peculiar product of Protestant-American-on-the-frontier thinking. Its drawing power for twentieth-century urban youngsters is negligible, but the bulk of the target group probably is made up of suburbanites in the 30–50 category who still have some affinity for this kind of thinking.

Some shift from the traditional values of American culture can be seen in the tone of Nixon's dealing with the war: the lack of indication that it is glorious, the muted appeal to patriotism (only one brief reference to the first defeat in America's history), the lack of complete victory as a goal. But nowhere else does the culture of the post-atomic age show through; by and large the speech would have been applauded if delivered in the nineteenth century. That there has been a radical revolution of values among the young does not affect the message, and one might predict that Nixon is right in deciding that the revolution in values has not yet significantly infected the target group.

CHARACTEROLOGICAL AND STYLISTIC FACTORS

Nixon's choice of value premises is, of course, closely related to his *ethos* as conveyed by the speech. He promises to tell the truth before he asks the American people to support a policy which involves the overriding issues of war and peace—phraseology that echoes previous Nixonian messages. He refrains from harsh criticism of the previous administration; he is more interested in the future America than in political gains; such an avowal of disinterestedness is the commonest topic for self-character building.

Nixon is against political murders and imprisonments and active pushing initiatives for peace. He is flexible and compromising, unlike the negotiators for the enemy. He chooses the right way and not the easy way. He is the champion of policy made by constitutional processes; his opponents conduct unruly demonstrations in the streets. But he has healthy respect for the idealism and commitment of the young; he pledges himself in the tradition of Woodrow Wilson to win a peace that will avoid future wars. He has the courage to make a tasteful appeal to patriotism even when it's unpopular. Such is the character portrait drawn for us by Richard Nixon: restrained not hawkish, hardworking and active, flexible, yet firm where he needs to be. He seems an American style democrat, a moral but also a practical and sensitive man. The message is crowded with these overt clues from which we infer the good *ethos* of political figures in situations like this. Any more intensive development of the means of persuasion derived from the character of the speaker would surely have been counter-productive.

The language of Nixon's message helps to reinforce his *ethos*. His tone is unbrokenly serious. The first two-thirds of the message is in a self-consciously plain style—the effort is clearly made to give the impression of bluntness and forthrightness. This bluntness of tone correlates with the style of deliberative argumentation:[23] few epideictic elements are present in the first part of the speech. Everything seems to be adjusted to making the structure of residues exceedingly clear.

About two-thirds of the way through, the message shifts to a more impassioned tone. The alternative plans are collapsed into two, thus polarizing the situation: either immediate withdrawal or Nixon's plan for Vietnamization and unscheduled withdrawal. From here on parallel repetitions are persistent, and they serve no obvious logical function, but rather function to deepen the serious tone. There is, in short, an attempt to rise to a peroration of real eloquence. The qualities aimed at in the last third of the message seem to be gravity and impressiveness more than clarity and forthrightness. The effort seems to tax the speechwriter's literary skill to the limit, and the only new phrases he comes up with are the "silent majority" and the description of the energies of the young as "too often directed to bitter hatred against those they think are responsible for the war." All else is a moderately skillful pastiche of familiar phrases.

GENERAL ASSESSMENT

A summary answer can now be given to the question, how well did Nixon and his advisors choose among the available means of persuasion for this situation? The message was designed for those not ideologically overcommitted either to victory over Communism or to peace in any case while frustrated by the prolonged war. It operates from the most universally accepted premises of value and prediction; it buries deep in its texture most premises not likely to be immediately accepted. Enough of the means for bringing auditors into states of fear, anger, and confidence are used to create a psychological climate unfavorable to immediate withdrawal and favorable to Vietnamization. The goals—life, political freedom, peace, and self-confidence—are those shared by nearly all Americans, and connections of policies to them are tactfully handled for the target group. The structure is largely according to tradition: it can best be seen as falling into the four parts, and the right elements are contained in each of the parts. Two minor variations from the traditional are artfully designed to realize evident psychological ends. Conventional wisdom and conventional value judgments come dressed in conventional structure. The style of the narrative and proofs reflects adequately Nixon's reliance on clearly developed arguments from accepted premises; the style of the latter part of the message shows a moderately successful attempt at grandeur. In choice and arrangement of the means of persuasion for this situation this message is by and large a considerable success.

Neo-Aristotelian criticism tells a great deal about Nixon's message. It reveals the speech writer as a superior technician. It permits us to predict that given this target group the message should be successful in leading to a decision to support the Administration's policies. It brings into sharp focus the speechwriter's greatest technical successes: the choice of the right premises to make a version of the domino theory plausible for these auditors and the creation of a controlled atmosphere of fear in which the theory is more likely to be accepted. Likewise, the choice of the right means of making success for peace negotiations seems impossible and the building of a controlled state of anger in which a pessimistic estimate of the chances for success seems plausible. Also the finely crafted structure that conceals exactly what needs to be concealed while revealing the favored plan in a context most favorable to its being chosen.

What neo-Aristotelianism does not attempt to account for are some basic and long-run questions. For instance, it does not assess the wisdom of the speaker's choice of target audience as does Newman, who wanted the President to alleviate the fears of the doves. All critics observe that Nixon excludes the radical opponent of the war from his audience. Not only is this opponent excluded by his choice of policy but even by the choice of premises from which he argues: premises such as that the Government of South Viet Nam is freer than that of North Viet Nam, or that the right course is the opposite of the easy one. Radical opponents of the war were mostly young—often college students. The obvious cliché, "they are the political leadership of tomorrow," should have applied. Was it in the long run a wise choice to exclude them from the target? An important question, but a neo-Aristotelian approach does not warrant us to ask it. There is a gain, though, from this limitation. If the critic questions the President's choice of policy and premises, he is forced to examine systematically all the political factors involved in this choice. Neither Newman nor Campbell do this in the objective and systematic fashion required by the magnitude of the subject. Indeed, would they not be better off with a kind of criticism that does not require them to do it?

Nor does the neo-Aristotelian approach predict whether a policy will remain rhetorically viable. If the critic assumes as given the Nixon Administration's choice of policy from among the options available, he will no doubt judge this choice of value and predictive premises likely to effect the decision wanted. To put it another way, Nixon's policy was *then* most defensible by arguing from the kinds of premises Nixon used. It seems less defensible at this writing, and in time may come to seem indefensible even to people like those in the target group. Why the same arguments for the same policy should be predictably less effective to people so little removed in time is a special case of the question, why do some policies remain rhetorically viable for decades while others do not. This question might in part be answered by pointing, as was done before, to the maturing of the students into political leadership. But however the question might be answered, neo-Aristotelianism does not encourage us to ask it. As Black truly said, the neo-Aristotelian comprehends "the rhetorical discourse as tactically designed to achieve certain results with a specific audience on a specific occasion[,]"[24] in this case that audience Nixon aimed at on the night of November 3, 1969.

Finally, neo-Aristotelian criticism does not warrant us to estimate the truth of Nixon's statements or the reality of the values he assumes as aspects of American life. When Nixon finds the origin of the war in a North Vietnamese "campaign to impose a Communist government on South Vietnam by instigating and supporting a revolution," Campbell takes him to task for not telling the truth. This criticism raises a serious question: are we sure that Nixon is not telling the truth? We know, of course, that Nixon oversimplifies a complex series of events—any speaker in his situation necessarily does that. But will the scholar of tomorrow with the perspective of history judge his account totally false? Campbell endorses the view that basically this is a civil war resulting from the failure of the Diem government backed by the United States to hold elections under the Geneva Agreements of 1954. But her view and Nixon's are not mutually exclusive: it seems evident to me that both the United States and the Communist powers involved themselves from the first to the extent they thought necessary to force an outcome in their favor in Viet Nam. If a scientific historian of the future had to pick one view of the conflict or the other, he would probably pick Nixon's because it more clearly recognizes the power politics behind the struggle. But I am not really intending to press the point that Campbell commits herself to a wrong view, or even a superficially partial one. The point is that she espouses here a theory of criticism that requires her to commit herself at all. If anyone writing in a scholarly journal seeks to assess the truth of Nixon's statements, he must be willing to assume the burden of proving them evidently false. This cannot be done by appealing to the wisdom of the liberal intellectuals of today.[25] If the essential task were accomplished, would the result be called a *rhetorical* critique? By Aristotle's standards it would not, and for my part I think we will write more significant criticism if we follow Aristotle in this case. To generalize, I submit that the limitations of neo-Aristotelian criticism are like the metrical conventions of the poet—limitations that make true significance possible.

NOTES

[1]Robert P. Newman, "Under the Veneer: Nixon's Vietnam Speech of November 3, 1969," *QJS*, 56 (Apr. 1970), 168–178; Hermann G. Stelzner, "The Quest Story and Nixon's November 3, 1969 Address," *QJS*, 57 (Apr. 1971), 163–172; Karlyn Kohrs Campbell, "An Exercise in the Rhetoric of Mythical America," in *Critiques of Contemporary Rhetoric* (Belmont, Calif.: Wadsworth, 1972), pp. 50–58.

[2]Herbert A. Wichelns, "The Literary Criticism of Oratory," in Donald C. Bryant, ed., *The Rhetorical Idiom: Essays in Rhetoric, Oratory, Language, and Drama* (1925; rpt. Ithaca: Cornell Univ. Press, 1958), pp. 5–42.

[3]Marie Hochmuth [Nichols], "The Criticism of Rhetoric," in *A History and Criticism of American Public Address* (New York: Longmans, Green, 1955) III, 1–23.

[4]Aristotle, *Rhetoric* I. 1. 1355b 10–14. "To persuade is not the function of rhetoric but to investigate the persuasive factors inherent in the particular case. It is just the same as in all other arts; for example, it is not the function of medicine to bring health, rather to bring the patient as near to health as is possible in his case. Indeed, there are some patients who cannot be changed to healthfulness; nevertheless, they can be given the right therapy." (Translation mine.) I understand the medical analogy to mean that even if auditors chance to be proof against any of the means of persuasion, the persuader has functioned adequately as a rhetorician if he has investigated these means so that he has in effect "given the right therapy."

[5]Text as printed in *Vital Speeches*, 36 (15 Nov. 1969), 69.

[6]Aristotle *Rhetoric* I. 4. 1359b 33–1360a 5.

[7]Aristotle *Rhetoric* III. 14. 1415a 29–33. Here Nixon functions like a defendant in a forensic speech. "When defending he will first deal with any prejudicial insinuation against him . . . it is necessary that the defendant when he steps forward first reduce the obstacles, so he must immediately dissolve prejudice."

[8]See Aristotle *Rhetoric* III. 16. 1417a 16–36.

[9]Newman, p. 173.

[10]See Aristotle *Rhetoric* II. 23. 1398a 30–31. This basic structure is called method of residues in most modern argumentation textbooks.

[11]Aristotle *Rhetoric* III. 19. 1419b 10–1420a 8.

[12]For the purpose of this paper the term enthymeme is taken to mean any deductive argument. Aristotle gives a more technical definition of enthymeme that fits into the total design of his organon; in my opinion it is not useful for neo-Aristotelian criticism.

[13]Remarkably enough Aristotle does not state this general rule, though it clearly underlies his treatment of the historical example, *Rhetoric* II. 20.

[14]See Aristotle *Rhetoric* I. 6. 1362b 26–27 for life as a good; I. 8. 1366a for freedom as the object of choice for the citizens of a democracy.

[15]The subject of *Rhetoric* I. 7. Chaim Perelman and L. Olbrechts-Tyteca, commenting on this chapter, indicate that there is usually a consensus on such statements as 'life is good'; the dispute is over whether life is a greater good than honor in this particular situation. See *The New Rhetoric: A Treatise on Argumentation*, trans. John Wilkinson and Purcell Weaver (Notre Dame, Ind.: Univ. of Notre Dame Press, 1969), pp. 81–82.

[16]See Aristotle *Rhetoric* II. 19. 1393a 1–3.

[17]This principle follows from *Rhetoric* II. 5. 1383a 24–25.

[18]Aristotle *Rhetoric* II. 5. 1382a 21–22. Aristotle treated the *pathe* as states of feeling that a man enters into because he draws certain inferences from the situation around him: he sees, for example, that he is the type of man who experiences pity when faced with this type of victim in these circumstances. The means of getting a man to draw inferences are themselves logical proofs; hence *pathos* does not work apart from the logical proofs in a message but through them. See Aristotle *Rhetoric* II. 1. 1378a 19–28 and my explication in James J. Murphy, ed. *A Synoptic History of Classical Rhetoric* (New York: Random House, 1972).

[19]Aristotle *Rhetoric* II. 2. 1378a 30–32.

[20]Aristotle *Rhetoric* II. 2. 1379a 10–18.

[21]Aristotle *Rhetoric* II. 5. 1383a 16–19.

[22]Since he gave this speech Nixon has made a general timetable for American withdrawal, thus, presumably, showing that he was not utterly convinced by his own argument. But he has never quite fixed a date for complete withdrawal of all American support forces from Viet Nam; he has been consistent in maintaining that withdrawal as a bargaining point for negotiation with the Viet Cong and North Vietnamese.

[23]See Aristotle *Rhetoric* III. 12. 1414a 8–19.

[24]Edwin B. Black, *Rhetorical Criticism: A Study in Method* (New York: Macmillan, 1965), p. 33.

[25]Richard H. Kendall, writing a reply to Newman, "The Forum," *QJS*, 56 (Dec. 1970), 432, makes this same point particularly in connection with Newman's implication that ex-President Johnson was a fraud. "If so, let us have some evidence of his fraudulent actions. If there is no evidence, or if there is evidence, but an essay on the rhetoric of President Nixon does not provide proper scope for a presentation of such evidence, then it seems to me inclusion of such a charge (or judgment) may fall into the category of gratuitous." Newman in rejoinder asks, "Should such summary judgments be left out of an article in a scholarly journal because space prohibits extensively supporting them? Omission might contribute to a sterile academic purity, but it would improve neither cogency nor understanding." I would certainly answer Newman's rhetorical question, yes, and I would go on to judge that view of criticism which encourages such summary judgments not to be a useful one.

LINCOLN AT COOPER UNION: A RHETORICAL ANALYSIS OF THE TEXT

MICHAEL C. LEFF AND GERALD P. MOHRMANN

When Abraham Lincoln spoke at the Cooper Union on the evening of February 27, 1860, his audience responded enthusiastically, and the speech has continued to elicit praise throughout the intervening years. Biographers, historians, and literary scholars agree that it was "one of his most significant speeches,"[1] one that illustrated "his abilities as a reasoner,"[2] and one to which posterity has ascribed his "subsequent nomination and election to the presidency."[3] Ironically, however, this model of "logical analysis and construction"[4] has failed to generate a critical response in kind. Most of what has been written treats of the background, and, too often, the man as myth has intruded; caught up in the drama of the performance, writers find no bit of information too trivial to report, whether it be the price of tickets or the fit of Lincoln's new shoes.[5] Such details can deepen our appreciation of the event, but they do not illuminate the speech as a speech.

Unhappily, little light is shed by those who do comment on the speech text. Nicolay and Hay assert, for example, that Lincoln's conclusions "were irresistibly convincing,"[6] but their sole piece of supporting evidence is a four-hundred[-]word excerpt. And if they happen to be "firmly in the hero-worshipping tradition,"[7] those of sterner stuff fare no better. Basler makes the curious claim that the rhetorical "high-water mark" occurs toward the end of the first section;[8] Nevins mistakenly argues that the speech "fell into two halves";[9] reputable scholars equate summary and quotation with explication;[10] and it is generally accepted that Lincoln demonstrated a conciliatory attitude toward the South.[11]

Certainly all is not dross in previous studies, but wherever one turns in the literature, no satisfying account of the speech is to be found.[12] We are convinced that a systematic rhetorical analysis can help rectify the situation and what follows is our attempt to accomplish such an analysis. In that attempt, we center on the text of the speech, but our purpose demands some preliminary remarks about the rhetorical context.

Although it was not until after the speech that Lincoln frankly admitted his presidential aspirations, saying, "The taste *is* in my mouth a little,"[13] he had been savoring the possibility for months. The preceding November, he had written that the next canvas would find him laboring "faithfully in the ranks" unless "the judgment of the party shall assign me a different position,"[14] but even as he wrote, Lincoln was grasping for a different assignment, "busy using the knife on his rivals . . . and doing all he could to enhance his reputation as an outstanding Republican leader."[15] Small wonder that he decided early to "make a political speech of it" in New York.[16] Here was the opportunity to make himself more available to Republicans in the East. The appearance alone would make for greater recognition, but political availability required more; Lincoln had to be an acceptable Republican, and he had to be an attractive alternative to the Democratic candidate.

William A. Seward and Stephen A. Douglas were the presumptive nominees, and they, patently, were Lincoln's antagonists. Moreover, their views on slavery created an intertwining threat that menaced his conception of the party and his personal ambitions. When Seward spoke about a "higher law" and an "irrepressible conflict," he strained Lincoln's sense of moral and political conservatism; these pronouncements smacked too much of radicalism.[17] Douglas, meanwhile, exacerbated the situation with his doctrine of popular sovereignty. Lincoln feared that this siren song would cause wholesale apostasy in Republican ranks, an eventuality all the more likely if the party nominee was tinctured with radicalism. He knew, however, that a middle ground existed, and he long had occupied it with his insistence that slavery should be protected but not extended. Consequently, when Lincoln addressed the Eastern Republicans, both principle and expediency permitted, even dictated, that he speak for party and for self and that he maintain party and self in a position between those taken by Seward and Douglas.

That he took such a course is revealed by an examination of the speech text, but all the external evidence shows a man running hard, if humbly, for political office, and while Lincoln spoke for his party, he spoke first for his own nomination. In fact, the Cooper Union Address is best characterized as a campaign oration, a speech designed to win nomination for the speaker. This identification of genre is basic to our analysis, and the nature of the genre is suggested by Rosenthal's distinction between nonpersonal and personal persuasion;[18] in the former, the speaker attempts to influence audience attitudes about a particular issue, and ethos is important insofar as it lends credence to the substance of the argument. In the latter the process is reversed. The focal point is the speaker, and the message becomes a vehicle for enhancing ethos. Campaign orations, on this basis, tend to be examples of personal persuasion, for while "the ostensible purpose of a given speech may be to gain acceptance of a particular policy, . . . the actual purpose is to gain votes for the candidate."[19] In other words, the ultimate goal of the campaign orator is to promote himself as a candidate. Both policies and character are in question, but the treatment of issues is subsidiary to the purpose of creating a general identification between the speaker and the audience. The objective, then, in a campaign oration is ingratiation.

With genre and purpose in mind, we can approach the speech through familiar topics. Addressing himself first to the people of New York, then to the South and finally to the Republican Party, Lincoln divides his speech into three sections, and this pattern of organization invites seriatim analysis of the major dispositional units. Furthermore, argument and style immediately loom as important elements, since they disclose essential characteristics in and significant interrelationships among the main units of the discourse. Consequently, our critique will follow Lincoln's pattern of organization and will have special reference to matters of argument and style. This approach, however, is not without its hazards. The convenience of tracing the natural sequence of the argument may foster fragmentary analysis and obscure the dominant rhetorical motive. Yet to be mindful of the genre is to find a corrective.

The central concern is ingratiation, and recognition of this purpose unifies the elements of analysis by giving them a more precise focus; awareness of the ultimate goal becomes shuttle to the threads of structure, argument, and style.

In the address, Lincoln deals exclusively with slavery, and although this inflam[m]atory issue might seem a shaky bridge to ingratiation, the choice is a fitting response to the rhetorical problem. What better point of departure than the paramount issue of the day, the issue with which he was most closely identified, and the issue that had spawned the Republican Party?[20] And Lincoln starts with the very motivation that had driven men to Ripon only a few years before, the question of slavery in the territories. Capitalizing on these initial associations, he counters the emotionalism inherent in the topic by assuming a severely rational posture and enunciating a moderate but firm set of principles. The approach distinguishes him from his chief rivals and solicits an intensified association from Eastern Republicans. These objectives govern the matter and manner of the opening argument, and this argument lays a foundation for subsequent developments in the speech. In the opening section and throughout, Lincoln associates himself and Republicans with the founding fathers and Constitutional principle, and he dissociates rival candidates and factions from those fathers and that principle.

Acknowledging his "fellow citizens of New York," Lincoln begins by adopting a "text for this discourse."[21] The text is a statement in which Stephen A. Douglas had asserted, "Our fathers, when they framed the government under which we live, understood this question just as well and even better than we do now." Defining terms in catechistic sequence, Lincoln maintains that "the frame of government under which we live" consists of the Constitution and the "twelve subsequently framed amendments" and that "our fathers" are "the 'thirty-nine' who signed the original instrument." He then asks, what is the question "those fathers understood 'just as well and even better, than we do now'?" The answer "is this: Does the proper division of local from Federal authority, or anything else in the Constitution, forbid our Federal Government to control as to slavery in our Federal Territories?" The question joins the issue because it is a matter upon which "Senator Douglas holds the affirmative, and the Republicans the negative."

That Douglas should play the foil is most fitting. National newspaper coverage of the 1858 senatorial campaign had linked the two men together, and the debates were to be published in March.[22] Moreover, Lincoln had continued the argument during 1859, worrying whether the Republican Party would "maintain it's [sic] identity, or be broken up to form the tail of Douglas' new kite."[23] Nevertheless, Lincoln knew that Douglas was vulnerable. The Freeport Doctrine had convinced many in the North that the man was only too "willing to subordinate moral considerations to political expediency."[24] Douglas, then, was an established rival, one whom Lincoln perceived as a threat to party unity, and one whose strategic position was open to attack from principle.

On a tactical level, the "text" quoted from Douglas affords Lincoln an ideal starting point. The allusion to the fathers is a symbolic reference with the potential for universal respect, and Douglas' implicit attack upon the principles that had generated the Republican Party creates an antithesis binding speaker and audience together in opposition to a common enemy. This antithesis is a channel for ingratiation; Lincoln makes Republicanism the voice of rational analysis, and the precise terms of Douglas' assertion form the premises of logical inquiry. Moving into the inquiry, Lincoln pursues a vigorous *ad hominem* attack.[25] He accepts Douglas' logic and then turns it against him.

The argument of the first section develops out of a single hypothetical proposition: if the better understanding evinced by our fathers shows that they believed nothing forbade federal control of slavery in the territories, then such regulatory power is inherent in the governmental frame. Lincoln affirms the antecedent with an elaborate chain of inductive evidence. Instances in the induction consist of actions by the fathers before and after they signed the Constitution because the question "seems not to have been directly before the convention."[26] From the Northwest Ordinance of 1784 to the Missouri Compromise of 1820, Lincoln enumerates seven statutes regulating slavery in the territories, and he accounts for votes by twenty-three of the fathers.[27] Twenty-one voted in favor of such regulation. Since these men were bound by "official responsibility and their corporal oaths" to uphold the Constitution, the implication of their affirmative votes is beyond question. To conclude that the twenty-one would have condoned federal regulation if they thought it unconstitutional would be to accuse these fathers of "gross political impropriety and willful perjury," and "as actions speak louder than words, so actions under such responsibility speak still louder."

Emphasizing deeds and "adhering rigidly to the text," Lincoln cannot offer in evidence "whatever understanding may have been manifested by any person" other than the thirty-nine, nor can he cite the sixteen who left no voting records. But the latter include the likes of Franklin, Hamilton, and Morris, and he believes that this group "would probably have acted just as the twenty-three did." In any event, "a clear majority of the whole" understood that nothing "forbade the Federal Government to control slavery in the Federal Territories," and with the remaining fathers probably agreeing, there can be little doubt about "the understanding of our fathers who framed the original Constitution; and the text affirms that they understood the question 'better than we.'"

Lincoln now uses this understanding to discredit arguments based on the fifth and tenth amendments; he says it is "a little presumptuous" to suggest that the fathers embraced one principle when writing the Constitution and another when writing the amendments. And does not this suggestion "become impudently absurd when coupled with the other affirmation, from the same mouth, that those who did the two things alleged to be inconsistent, understood whether they really were inconsistent better than we—better than he who affirms that they are inconsistent?" The touch of sarcasm reveals a more aggressive attitude, but it is justified by the inductive process; Douglas' own criterion forces the conclusion that he does not comprehend the understanding of the fathers. Lincoln will become even more combative before he brings the first section to a close, but some comments on style are merited, and they will lead us into his conclusion.

The style of this section is entirely consistent with Lincoln's severely rational approach. The audience probably did not expect the "rhetorical fireworks of a Western stump-speaker,"[28] but Lincoln is most circumspect. There are none of the "many excuses" that made him a Uriah Heep to some of his opponents,[29] and he avoids all display, indulging neither in anecdotes nor figurative language. The syntax is complex at times, but the complexity is that of legal rather than literary prose, as is evidenced in the following sentence: "It, therefore, would be unsafe to set down even the two who voted against the prohibition as having done so because, in their understanding, any proper division of local from Federal authority, or anything in the Constitution, forbade the Federal Government to control as to slavery in Federal territory."

The preceding quotation, with its echo of the text, points to a noteworthy stylistic element: repetition. Lincoln includes fifteen extended citations of the issue and an equal number from the "text," repetitions that accentuate the single line of argument. He adds to the emphasis by stressing certain key words and phrases. For example, there are over thirty uses of the root "understand," usually in the participial "understanding," and Lincoln alludes to the "fathers" more than thirty-five times. None of these repetitions is blatant or forced because he weaves them into the fabric of the inductive process. Furthermore, the repetitions concomitantly reinforce and control the emotional association with the fathers and their under-standing of the Constitution. This point is crucial to an appreciation of Lincoln's rhetorical method. Both the direction of the argument and the symbols expressing it are fiercely emotional; yet, all is enmeshed in an incisive logical and linguistic structure, and while the tone remains rationalistic and legalistic, it also creates a subtle emotive nexus between the Republican audience and the founding fathers.

As noted above, style and argument shift in the concluding paragraphs, after Lincoln already has established his logical credentials. The argument becomes bolder, and the style alters appropriately. When developing the induction, Lincoln refers to the framers of the Constitution as the "thirty-nine," but they become "our fathers" again in the conclusion of the long first section of the speech. And there periods become more polished and sophisticated:

> If any man at this day sincerely believes that a proper division of local from Federal authority, or any part of the Constitution, forbids the Federal Government to control as to slavery in the Federal Territories, he is right to say so, and to enforce his position by all truthful evidence and fair argument which he can. But he has no right to mislead others, who have less access to history, and less leisure to study it, into the false belief that 'our fathers who framed the government under which we live' were of the same opinion—thus substituting falsehood and deception for truthful evidence and fair argument.

This passage completes the negative phase of Lincoln's argumentation. Both matter and manner drive a rational wedge between the speaker and his rivals. Clearly, Lincoln suggests that Douglas may be guilty of deliberate "falsehood and deception," and just as clearly, his own position represents "truthful evidence and fair argument." Lincoln, one of those with "access to history" and some "leisure to study it," attempts to set the record straight. Another direct slash at Douglas, the very source of the text and issue. At the same time, Lincoln indirectly differentiates himself from Seward and his radical posture. Lincoln's position is more to the right, closer to the demands of objective inquiry, closer also to the demands of political availability, and it is important to remark that he achieves this dissociation without recourse to divisive rhetoric. The foray against the man and his position is patent, but it is completely inferential.

Although less obtrusive than the refutation, an equally important constructive movement exists within this part of the oration. Not only does Lincoln distinguish himself from his opponents, he nurtures Republican unity because he makes himself and party the vessels for transmitting the faith of the fathers. Avoiding self-references, he presents himself as the voice of Republicanism, and he caps this appeal with words both to and from the party:

> But enough! Let all who believe that 'our fathers who framed the govern-ment under which we live understood this question just as well, and even better, than we do now,' speak as they spoke, and act as they acted upon it. This is all Republicans ask—all Republicans desire—in relation to slavery. As those fathers marked it, so let it be again marked, as an evil not to be

extended, but to be tolerated and protected only because of and so far as its actual presence among us makes that toleration and protection a necessity. Let all the guarantees those fathers gave it be not grudgingly, but fully and fairly, maintained. For this Republicans contend, and with this, so far as I know or believe, they will be content.

At this point in the speech, Lincoln has associated himself and his audience with the spirit, the principles and the actions of the founding fathers, and in doing so, he has taken the first steps toward ingratiation.

Comprising nearly half the speech, this initial section is so clearly logical that it regularly is cited as a demonstration of Lincoln's powers as a reasoner, but to say no more is to grossly underestimate his achievement. The next section, too, is remarkable for its logical development, and all that follows in the speech is anticipated and controlled by the attack upon Douglas. Failure to appreciate this unity has confounded commentators, and their confusion is strikingly illustrated in the generally accepted conclusion that Lincoln follows his attack with remarks "conciliatory toward the South."[30]

The second section does begin with an ostensible change in audience: "And now, if they would listen,—as I suppose they will not,—I would address a few words to the Southern people." But we learn more about the beholders than the object when we are told that the next twenty-six paragraphs are filled with "words of kindly admonition and protest,"[31] words of "sweet reasonableness to allay Southern fears."[32] Presuming that he will not be heard, Lincoln notes that "our party gets no votes" in the South, and he flatly asserts later that "the Southern people will not so much as listen to us." These are not idle reservations. They represent the realistic assessment of an astute politician who knows that the coming election will be won or lost in the North; it is hardly plausible that this man would detract from his ultimate purpose by directing nearly forty per cent of his speech to an unavailable audience.

In truth, the audience does not change. Lincoln merely casts the second section of the speech in the form of a *prosopopoeia,* a figure he had rehearsed five months earlier in Cincinnati.[33] The device suits his purposes admirably. It enables him to create a mock debate between Republicans and the South, a debate in which he becomes spokesman for the party. In this role, Lincoln can strengthen the identification between himself and the available Republican audience. He is careful to extend the refutation of Douglas into the second section and thus carry over the lines of association and disassociation begun earlier in the discourse. If Lincoln leaves Douglas with little ground on which to stand, he performs the same argumentative service for the South, and the debate he manufactures is far from being conciliatory.

The *prosopopoeia* develops into another *ad hominem* argument. This time, however, the presentation is complicated by the need to deal with the collective contentions of a collective opposition. To provide control, Lincoln again begins by stressing reason, saying to the South, "I consider that in the general qualities of reason and justice you are not inferior to any other people." Yet, in the specific case, rational discourse is stymied because the Southerners never refer to Republicans except "to denounce us as reptiles, or, at the best, as no better than outlaws." Such responses are unjust to both sides. The proper course would be to "bring forward your charges and specifications, and then be patient long enough to hear us deny or justify." Obviously, the South is unwilling and unable to follow this procedure, and becoming persona for both Republicanism and reason, Lincoln reconstructs the charges and specifications; these include sectionalism, radicalism, agitation of the slavery question, and slave insurrections.

The putative debate begins: "You say we are sectional. We deny it. That makes an issue; and the burden of proof is upon you." The crux of the matter is whether Republicans repel the South with "some wrong principle." Republican principle, however, is based in the beliefs and actions of the fathers, and Lincoln challenges the South to respond to this fact. "Do you accept the challenge? No! Then you really believe that the principle which 'our fathers who framed the government under which we live' thought so clearly right as to adopt it, and indorse it again and again, upon their official oaths, is in fact so clearly wrong as to demand your condemnation without a moment's consideration." Closing and reinforcing this line of reasoning Lincoln refers to the pre-eminent father: "Some of you delight to flaunt in our faces the warning . . . given by Washington in his Farewell Address," but if he were to speak for himself "would he cast the blame of that sectionalism upon us, who sustain his policy, or upon you, who repudiate it? We respect that warning of Washington, and we commend it to you, together with his example pointing to the right application of it."[34] Thus, the South claims to be the injured party, but analysis of the charge proves that the wounds are self-inflicted.

Lincoln uses the same refutational method for each of the other issues; first defining the charge with a series of rhetorical questions, he then turns the argument against the adversary. The South proclaims itself the bastion of conservatism and denounces Republican radicalism, but "what is conservatism? Is it not adherence to the old and tried, against the new and untried? We stick to, contend for, the identical old policy . . . which was adopted by 'our fathers who framed the government under which we live'; while you with one accord reject, and scout, and spit upon that old policy, and insist upon substituting something new." The South alleges that Republicans have made the slavery issue more prominent. True, the issue is more prominent, but this situation arose because the South "discarded the old policy of the fathers." Finally, Southerners complain that Republicans foment insurrection among the slaves, but they can adduce no evidence to support this allegation, cannot "implicate a single Republican" and ignore that "Republican doctrines and declarations are accompanied with a continual protest against any interference whatever" with the institution in the slave states. Indeed, were it not for the loud and misleading protestations of Southern politicians, the slaves would hardly know that the Republican Party existed. Worse yet, the South refuses to acknowledge a simple truth contained in Republican doctrine, a truth articulated "many years ago" when Jefferson indicated that the cause of slave insurrections was slavery itself. Like Jefferson, Republicans would not interfere with slavery where it exists, but Republicans do insist, as the fathers did, that the federal government "has the power of restraining the extension of the institution—the power to insure that a slave insurrection shall never occur on any American soil which is now free."

Finishing his treatment of specific charges, Lincoln builds to a more forceful and aggressive tone, just as he did at the end of the first section. His arrangement of responses to Southern allegations is itself climatic, the issue of insurrections being both last and most critical. Always volatile, this issue had become extremely explosive in the wake of the Harper's Ferry raid and the trial of John Brown, and Lincoln understandably chooses this matter as the instrument for his most extensive defense of party and principle. He is not content, however, to assume a merely defensive posture; the entire pattern of his argumentation reveals a movement from reply to attack that gathers momentum as the discourse proceeds. Thus, having disposed of the insurrection controversy, Lincoln assails the very character of the Southern position, and he concludes this section with an examination of threats emanating from the South.

The South hopes to "break up the Republican organization." That failing, "you will break up the Union rather than submit to a denial of your constitutional rights." This is a course of "rule or ruin"; the union will be destroyed unless people are permitted to take slaves into the federal territories. But no such right exists in the Constitution, and Southern threats are fruitless. Neither the Constitution nor the Republican Party are so malleable as to bend at the touch of Southern fancy. Not even the Dred Scott decision offers a refuge. That verdict was made "in a divided court, by a bare majority of the judges, and they not quite agreeing with one another in the reasons for making it." The decision rests upon "the opinion that 'the right of property in a slave is distinctly and expressly affirmed in the Constitution,'" but careful analysis shows that this right is not even implied. Surely it is reasonable to expect the Court to retract "the mistaken statement" when apprised of its error. Furthermore, the verdict runs contrary to the judgment of the fathers, those who decided the same question long ago "without division among themselves when making the decision," without division "about the meaning of it after it was made," and without "basing it upon any mistaken statement of facts." Having thus contrasted the babel of the Court with the unity of the fathers and their lineal descendants, Lincoln builds to a striking analogy:

> Under these circumstances, do you really feel yourselves justified to break up this government unless such a court decision as yours is shall be at once submitted to as a conclusive and final rule of political action? But you will not abide the election of a Republican president! In that supposed event, you say, you will destroy the Union; and then, you say, the crime of having destroyed it will be upon us! That is cool. A highwayman holds a pistol to my ear, and mutters through his teeth, 'Stand and deliver, or I shall kill you, and then you will be a murderer!'

Adding that the highwayman's threat can "scarcely be distinguished in principle" from "the threat of destruction to the Union," Lincoln completes his *ad hominem* assault against the Southern position, and the *prosopopoeia* ends.

The parallels and interrelationships between the first and the second sections of the speech are evident. Some shifts in invention and style between the two sections are occasioned by the change of antagonist, but it is more significant that Lincoln elects to argue against adversaries in both and that he uses the same fundamental argument to dispatch them all. In both sections, he strives to become spokesman for the party by demonstrating that he is a man of reason and that this characteristic melds himself and party with the principles of the founding fathers. In addition, the same characteristic distinguishes him from other candidates. Finally, each section is based on a severely rational framework and builds to a terminal climax that unifies and heightens logical and emotional dimensions.

Merging style and argument within and between parts of the discourse, Lincoln unquestionably remains in touch with his immediate audience, and he unquestionably has his eye on ingratiation. In the first movement, he separates himself and party from Douglas and Seward; in the second, he favorably contrasts the position of the party with that of its most vociferous opponent.[35] But one further step remains. To this juncture, the identification of speaker, party, and principle has been closely tied to a series of negative definitions. A positive gesture seems necessary, and in the final section of the speech, Lincoln fuses his audience together through more directly constructive appeals.

He begins by saying he will address "a few words now to Republicans," and though he puts aside both text and issue, his remarks evolve naturally from what has proceeded. Once more reason is the point of departure. Having, in the high-wayman metaphor, implied a contrast between cool reason and hot passion, Lincoln urges Republicans to "do nothing through passion and ill-temper" that might cause discord within the nation, and, as he draws out the ultimate implications of the Southern position, antithesis becomes the dominant mode of argument and style. The section centers on a contrast between the Republicans and the South (between "we" and "they"); it extends and amplifies the distinction between word and deed that is present throughout the speech; and the argument is couched in and reinforced by antithetical syntax.

Recognizing Southern intransigence, Lincoln still wants his party to "calmly consider their demands" and reach conclusions based on all "they say and do." Pursuing the inquiry, he asks, "Will they be satisfied if the Territories be uncondi-tionally surrendered to them? We know they will not." And "will it satisfy them if, in the future, we have nothing to do with invasions and insurrections? We know it will not." It will not because past abstention has not exempted "us from the charge and the denunciation." To satisfy them, "we must not only leave them alone, but we must somehow convince them that we do let them alone." Experience shows that this is no easy task because Republican policy and actions have been misconstrued consistently. The only recourse seems to be "this and only this: cease to call slavery wrong, and join them in calling it right. And this must be done thoroughly—done in acts as well as words. Silence will not be tolerated—we must place ourselves avowedly with them." Republicans must suppress all "declarations that slavery is wrong," must return "fugitive slaves with greedy pleasure," and must pull down all free state constitutions "before they will cease to believe that all their troubles proceed from us."

Most Southerners, Lincoln admits, would not put the argument in this extreme form. Most would simply claim that they want to be left alone, but "we do let them alone." Consequently, it is apparent that "they will continue to accuse us of doing, until we cease saying." Given the nature of their arguments and the character of their actions, the Southerners cannot stop short of the demand that all Republicans desist from speaking and acting out of conviction. Those who hold that "slavery is morally right and socially elevating" must necessarily call for its recognition "as a legal right and a social blessing." Stripped of its veneer and examined in the cold light of reason, the Southern position reveals the disagreement governing the entire conflict; it also underscores the principle from which Republicans cannot retreat. Lincoln expresses both points in a final antithesis that reduces the issue of slavery to a matter of right and wrong, to a matter of moral conviction:

> Their thinking it right and our thinking it wrong is the precise fact upon which depends the whole controversy. Thinking it right, as they do, they are not to blame for desiring its full recognition as being right; but thinking it wrong, as we do, can we yield to them? Can we cast our votes with their view, and against our own? In view of our moral, social, and political responsibili-ties, can we do this?

Providing no answers because they are only too obvious, Lincoln moves on to merge self and party with the fathers, and Washington is the exemplar.

Style changes appropriately as Lincoln makes his final call for unity. Antithetical elements appear in the penultimate paragraph, but the opposed clauses are subordinated within the long, periodic flow of the final sentence, a flow that builds emotionally to a union with Washington's words and deeds. Lincoln repeats that slavery can be left alone where it exists, but he insists that there can be no temporizing when it comes to the extension of slavery:

> If our sense of duty forbids this, then let us stand by our duty fearlessly and effectively. Let us be diverted by none of those sophistical contrivances wherewith we are so industriously plied, and belabored—contrivances such as groping for some middle ground between the right and the wrong: vain as the search for a man who should be neither a living man nor a dead man; such as a policy of 'don't care' on a question about which all true men do care; such as Union appeals beseeching true Union men to yield to Disunionists, reversing the divine rule, and calling, not the sinners, but the righteous to repentance: such as invocations to Washington, imploring men to unsay what Washington said and undo what Washington did.
>
> Neither let us be slandered from our duty by false accusations against us, nor frightened from it by menaces of destruction to the government, nor of dungeons to ourselves. Let us have faith that right makes might, and in that faith let us to the end dare to do our duty as we understand it.

This short third section, constituting less than fifteen per cent of the text, is a fitting climax to Lincoln's efforts. Rational principle develops into moral conviction, and the resulting emotional intensity emerges from and synthesizes all that has gone before. Yet the intensity is controlled. Speaker and audience are resolute and principled, but at the same time, they are poised and logical. Others may indulge in "false accusations" and "menaces of destruction," but Lincoln and Republicans will have faith in right and in their understanding.

With this closing suggestion of antithetical behavior, Lincoln harks back to all he has said, and with it, he completes his exercise in ingratiation. Douglas is a pitiful example of one who argues misguided principle in maladroit fashion, and Seward's notion of an irrepressible conflict is at odds with the true spirit of the Republican Party, a party whose words and deeds follow from what the framers of the government said and did. Neither opponent measures up to the new and higher self-conception that the speaker has created for his audience. Furthermore, Lincoln has, by this very performance, demonstrated that he is the one who will best represent party and principle. Starting with reason and principle, he has shunted aside opposition, differentiated between Republicans and the South, and pushed on to unite the party in the faith that will "let us to the end dare to do our duty as we understand it."

The very wording of the concluding paragraphs reflects the organic quality of Lincoln's quest for unity. "Understand" echoes the "text"; Washington is a synecdochic reminder of the fathers; and the antithetical language recalls dissociations that are fundamental. In examining the discourse, we have attempted to explicate this internal coherence by tracing the sequence of arguments and images as they appear in the text, by dealing with the speech on its own terms. We are satisfied that the analysis has produced a reading that is more accurate than those previously available, a reading that goes farther toward explaining why the Cooper Union Address was one of Lincoln's most significant speeches.

Our interpretation is at odds, of course, with the conventional wisdom concerning his attitude toward the South. Where others have found him conciliatory, we argue that his position on slavery was calculated to win the nomination, not to propitiate an unavailable audience. That he had made "many similar declarations, and had never recanted any of them"[36] unquestionably contributed to the triumph of availability that was to be his, but his position ultimately pointed to an ideological conflict between North and South. Some Southerners took solace from Lincoln's assurances that slavery would be left alone where it existed, but extremists perceived him as the personification of Black Republicanism, even as the source of the irrepressible conflict doctrine.[37] The latter perceptions were distorted. So are ours, if we blink the realities of political rhetoric, and whatever else the speech might have been, it was certainly an oration designed to meet the immediate problems of a political campaign.

This perspective emphasizes that alternatives sometimes really do exclude and that rhetoric may nurture exclusion. Such a perspective may be uncomfortable for those who want to cast Lincoln as the Great Conciliator, but we are convinced that an accurate reading of the Cooper Union Address demands a frank recognition of the immediate rhetorical motives. Despite the mythology, the man was human, perhaps gloriously so, and it does him no disservice to accept this speech as evidence of his political skill, as evidence that "he was an astute and dextrous operator of the political machine."[38] Nor does this acceptance detract from the speech as literature and as logical exposition. The political artistry and the rhetorical artistry are functions of each other, and an appreciation of this coalescence can only enhance our understanding of the Cooper Union Address. And viewing the speech as a whole, we are quite content to close with a slightly altered evaluation from another context: "The speech is—to put it as crudely as possible—an immortal masterpiece."[39]

NOTES

[1]J. G. Randall, *Lincoln the President* (New York: Dodd, Mead, 1945), I, 135.

[2]Howard Mumford Jones and Ernest E. Leisy, eds., *Major American Writers* (New York: Harcourt, Brace, 1945), p. 681.

[3]Benjamin Barondess, *Three Lincoln Masterpieces* (Charleston: Education Foundation of West Virginia, 1954), p. 3.

[4]R. Franklin Smith, "A Night at Cooper Union," *Central States Speech Journal* 13 (Autumn 1962), 272.

[5]The most influential account of this sort is Carl Sandburg, *The Prairie Years* (New York: Harcourt, Brace, 1927), II, 200–216, but the most complete is Andrew A. Freeman, *Abraham Lincoln Goes to New York* (New York: Coward-McCann, 1960).

[6]John G. Nicolay and John Hay, *Abraham Lincoln: A History* (New York: Century, 1917), II, 219–220.

[7]Richard Hofstadter, *The American Political Tradition* (New York: Alfred A. Knopf, 1948), p. 364.

[8]*Abraham Lincoln: His Speeches and Writings,* ed. Roy P. Basler (Cleveland: World, 1946), p. 32.

[9]Allan Nevins, *The Emergence of Lincoln* (New York: Charles Scribner's Sons, 1950), II, 186.

[10]Randall, pp. 136–137; Basler, pp. 32–33; Nevins, pp. 186–187; Reinhard H. Luthin, *The Real Abraham Lincoln* (Englewood Cliffs, New Jersey: Prentice-Hall, 1960), p. 210.

[11]Randall, p. 136; Barondess, p. 18; Nicolay and Hay, p. 220, Nevins, p. 186; Luthin, pp. 243–244.

[12]Freeman treats of the text briefly, pp. 84–88, and although Barondess ranges from preparation to audience reaction, pp. 3–30, Hofstadter's observation applies, n. 7 above. Earl W. Wiley discusses the address in *Four Speeches by Lincoln* (Columbus: Ohio State

Univ. Press, 1927), pp. 15–27, but he limits analysis to the first section of the speech, a limitation also applied in his "Abraham Lincoln: His Emergence as the Voice of the People," in *A History and Criticism of American Public Address,* ed. William N. Brigance (New York: McGraw-Hill, 1943), II, 859–877. In the same volume, the speech is the basis for comments on delivery in Mildred Freburg Berry, "Abraham Lincoln: His Development in the Skills of the Platform," pp. 828–858.

[13]Letter to Lyman Trumbull, April 29, 1860, *The Collected Works of Abraham Lincoln,* ed. Roy P. Basler (New Brunswick. New Jersey: Rutgers Univ. Press, 1955), IV, 45.

[14]Letter to William E. Frazer, November 1, 1859, *Collected Works,* III, 491.

[15]Richard N. Current, *The Lincoln Nobody Knows* (New York: McGraw-Hill, 1958), p. 199. For an indication of Lincoln's activities see *Collected Works,* III, 384–521.

[16]Letter to James A. Briggs, *Collected Works,* III, 494.

[17]See Letter to Salmon P. Chase, June 9, 1859, *Collected Works,* III, 384; Letter to Nathan Sargent, June 23, 1859, *Collected Works,* III, 387–388; Letter to Richard M. Corwine, April 6, 1860, *Collected Works,* IV, 36.

[18]Paul I. Rosenthal, "The Concept of Ethos and the Structure of Persuasion," *Speech Monographs* 33 (June 1966), 114–126.

[19]Rosenthal, p. 120.

[20]In 1854, "northern whigs persuaded that their old party was moribund, Democrats weary of planting dominance, and free-soilers eager to exclude slavery from the territories began to draw together to resist the advance of the planting power"; Charles A. Beard and Mary R. Beard, *The Rise of American Civilization* (New York: Macmillan, 1937), II, 22. Cf. Don E. Fehrenbacher, "Lincoln and the Formation of the Republican Party," in *Prelude to Greatness* (Stanford: Stanford Univ. Press, 1962), pp. 19–47.

[21]We follow the text in *Complete Works,* ed. John G. Nicolay and John Hay (New York: Francis D. Tandy, 1905), V, 293–328; we include no footnotes because aside from unimportant exceptions, citations are sequential. This text is more conservative in typography than that edited and published as a campaign document by Charles C. Nott and Cephas Brainerd. The latter appears in *Collected Works,* III, 522–550; 1860, p. 1. Substantive variations in extant see also the *New York Times,* February 28, texts are minuscule, and this consistency deserves comment. Lincoln ignored suggested alterations in the original (Sandburg, II, 210 and 215–216); he proofread the newspaper copy (Freeman, pp. 92–93); pamphlet copies were available by the first of April (*Collected Works,* IV, 38–39); and Lincoln adamantly resisted editorial changes by Nott (*Collected Works,* IV, 58–59). This evidence emphasizes the care with which he constructed the speech, but it also suggests that he anticipated a wider audience from the outset. Publication practices and his own experience told Lincoln that he would reach many who would not hear him speak.

[22]General interest in the debates is underlined by the favorable editorial notice appearing in the Brooklyn *Daily Times,* August 26, 1858, an editorial written by one Walt Whitman; Walt Whitman, *I Sit and Look Out,* ed. Emory Holloway and Vernolian Schwartz (New York: Columbia Univ. Press, 1932), p. 96. For letters referring to publication of the debates, see *Collected Works,* III, 341, 343, 372–374, 515, and 516.

[23]Letter to Lyman Trumbull, Dec. 11, 1858, *Collected Works,* III, 345.

[24]Harry J. Carman and Harold C. Syrett, *A History of the American People* (New York: Alfred A. Knopf, 1952), I, 588. Cf. Fehrenbacher, "The Famous 'Freeport Question,'" in *Prelude to Greatness,* pp. 121–142.

[25]Logicians often define *ad hominem* as a fallacy resulting from an attack upon the character of a man rather than the quality of argument. In this essay, however, we use the term as Schopenhauer does in distinguishing between *ad hominem* and *ad rem* as the two basic modes of refutation. He differentiates in this manner: "We may show either that the proposition is not in accordance with the nature of things, i.e., with absolute, objective truth [*ad rem*]; or that it is inconsistent with other statements or admissions of our opponent, i.e., with truth as it appears to him [*ad hominem*]"; Arthur Schopenhauer, "The Art of Controversy," in *The Will to Live: Selected Writings of Arthur*

Schopenhauer, zed. Richard Taylor (New York: Anchor Books, 1962), p. 341. See Henry W. Johnstone, Jr., "Philosophy and *Argumentum ad Hominem,*" *Journal of Philosophy* 49 (July 1952), 489–498.

[26]Lincoln undoubtedly knew that James Wilson, Patrick Henry and Edmund Randolph had discussed the topic (See *Collected Works,* III, 526–527, n. 9.), but he is accurate in asserting that the subject did not come "directly" before the convention.

[27]Washington's vote was his signature, as President, on the Act of 1789 which enforced the Ordinance of 1787.

[28]Nicolay and Hay, *Abraham Lincoln,* II, 220.

[29]See Hofstadter, p. 94; *Collected Works,* III, 396.

[30]Randall, I, 136.

[31]Nicolay and Hay, *Abraham Lincoln,* II, 220.

[32]Nevins, II, 186.

[33]*Collected Works,* III, 438–454. Speaking at Cincinnati, September 17, 1859, Lincoln directs so much of his speech across the river "to the Kentuckians" (p. 440) that one listener complained aloud, "Speak to Ohio men, and not to Kentuckians!" (p. 445). Interestingly, Nevins appreciates the *prosopopoeia* in this speech, noting that Lincoln was "ostensibly speaking to Kentuckians," II, 56.

[34]The varied interpretations of Washington's warning and their longevity are illustrated in debates, early in 1850, over the purchase of the Farewell Address manuscript for the Library of Congress. Much of the debate is reproduced in William Dawson Johnston, *History of the Library of Congress* (Washington: Government Printing Office, 1904), I, 326–340.

[35]The second movement continues the implicit attack upon Seward, and all texts indicate a mimicking of Douglas' "gur-reat pur-rinciple." Buchanan also is a victim here, for he had championed popular sovereignty in his "Third Annual Message," December 19, 1859; *The Works of James Buchanan,* ed. John Bassett More (1908–1911; rpt. New York: Antiquarian Press Ltd., 1960), X, 342. Lincoln's efforts were not lost on a *New York Evening Post* reporter who wrote that "the speaker places the Republican party on the very ground occupied by the framers of our constitution and the fathers of our Republic" and that "in this great controversy the Republicans are the real conservative party." His report is reprinted in the *Chicago Tribune,* 1 Mar. 1860, p. 1.

[36]Abraham Lincoln, "First Inaugural Address," in *Collected Works,* IV, 263.

[37]Michael Davis, *The Image of Lincoln in the South* (Knoxville: Univ. of Tennessee, 1971), pp. 7–40, traces Southern views from nomination through inauguration. See *Southern Editorials on Secession,* ed. Dwight L. Dumond (1931; rpt. Gloucester, Mass.: Peter-Smith, 1964), pp. 103–105, 112–115, 159–162, *et passim.*

[38]David Donald, *Lincoln Reconsidered* (New York: Alfred A. Knopf, 1956), p. 65.

[39]The original is Randall Jarrell's comment on a poem, Robert Frost's "Provide[,] provide," in *Poetry and the Age* (New York: Vintage-Knopf, 1953), p. 41.

"THE CIRCLE OF OUR FELICITIES": THOMAS JEFFERSON'S FIRST INAUGURAL ADDRESS AND THE RHETORIC OF NATIONHOOD

STEPHEN HOWARD BROWNE

Late in the morning of March 4, 1801, the tall, fair, and conspicuously informal Virginian walked several hundred yards from his lodgings to mount the steps of the unfinished Capitol. Accompanied by a small but impressive parade of militia officers, Thomas Jefferson made his way to the Senate chamber dressed, as Henry Adams recounted, as "a plain citizen, without any distinctive badge of office." The president-elect was received by approximately a thousand supporters, congressmen, and the curious, most of whom had no chance of actually hearing the soft-spoken leader of the Republican Party. Greeting him too were Aaron Burr, who had been sworn in as vice president earlier that morning, and John Marshall, the dour Chief Justice whose task this day was to administer to his relative the oath of office. It was a trio gathered out of obligation alone, and now, as Adams put it, "the assembled senators looked up at three men who profoundly disliked and distrusted each other."[1]

The words Jefferson spoke that day may have done little to dispel personal resentments, but when he finished the nation knew itself to have witnessed a masterpiece. At 1,716 words, 41 sentences, and 7 paragraphs the address did not take long to deliver; indeed no student of Jefferson's rhetorical art would have expected otherwise. In its "language, its perspicuity, its arrangement, its felicity of thought and expression," wrote one observer, the inaugural address was "a model of eloquence," a virtuoso performance by "one of the best writers which our country had produced." The principles Jefferson enshrined that day, reported the *Independent Chronicle*, were "compressed within such precise limits, as to enforce them on the memory, and expressed with such classical elegance, as to charm the scholar with their rhetorical brilliancy." News of the address soon traveled to distant ports, where French supporters in particular welcomed its universal message of conciliation, peace, and republican virtue. "Your message," Pierre Samuel DuPont Nemour declared to Jefferson, "like all your thoughts and writings, is full of wisdom, judgment, and illumination, and contains a divine moral." Jefferson himself, characteristically modest, hoped that the address "will present the leading objects to be conciliation and adherence to sound principle." History records the speaker to have succeeded.[2]

Widely celebrated in its own time, the first inaugural address continues to command the regard of Americans from across the political spectrum. And for much the same reason: it took as its task the subordination of local and temporary interests to the general and abiding principles of republican government. In 1837, George Tucker observed the distinctive manner in which Jefferson's boldness was tempered by that quality of refined understatement we have come to attach to most of his writings. "Though couched in language of humility, and breathing the spirit of benevolence and liberality," Tucker wrote, the address nevertheless "asserts all the cardinal principles of the republican faith, but in such general terms as not to alarm the fears or irritate the prejudices of his opponents." More than half a century after its delivery, Henry Randall found the circulation of its maxims in the press and popular letters to be "astonishing, and perhaps unequaled in the instance of any similar production."[3]

By the twentieth century, far removed from the bitter party struggles and uncertainties from which it emerged and to which it immediately spoke, the address was fully enshrined into the canonical literature of American nationhood. To the populist Tom Watson, Jefferson's speech "will always be to good government what the Sermon on the Mount is to religion," and Woodrow Wilson noted that nothing "could exceed the fine tact and gentleness with which Mr. Jefferson gave tone of order and patriotic purpose in his inaugural address to the new way of government his followers expected of him." Fawn Brodie judged the address to be "one of the great seminal papers in American political history," indeed of "almost Biblical impact." Jefferson's masterpiece stands today, in the word of the distinguished Jefferson scholar Peter Onuf, as "one of the great texts in the American libertarian tradition, a blast against 'political intolerance and persecution.'"[4]

The significance, stature, and abiding appeal of Jefferson's inaugural address are now universally acknowledged; how curious, then, that it has yet to receive sustained and systematic analysis. This essay seeks to initiate that process. I argue in the following that the first inaugural address is understood best as a conspicuous display of its author's style and thought; it is in this sense a statement about what oratory ought to look and sound like to a nation of republicans. A speech about politics, it offers as well a politics of speech; it is a rhetorical expression of the republican creed, and the republican expression of a rhetorical creed. The first inaugural address thus constitutes its own theory of rhetoric; it is an exemplification of republican virtue, the conception, design, and delivery of which was meant to instantiate Jefferson's vision of a new moral and political order.

So much is not to suggest, of course, that the first inaugural address, for all its singularity, was *sui generis*. It is to suggest that we might well look elsewhere than to conventional rhetoric manuals alone as a means of giving it context and location within the cultural moment in which it was delivered. This context is appropriately the oratorical milieu of late eighteenth-century America, the robust and energetic environment of public speech, debate, sermonizing, and pamphleteering that helped define the political life of the early republic. Here we will find our ingress, our route toward a fuller explication of the inaugural text. Such an approach grants us a degree of intimacy and association that theoretical abstractions cannot; it gives us access to voices and personalities, lived experiences and popular sentiments that go far toward helping us understand the immediate and enduring circumstances of the address. In the following, some of the more significant features of this oratorical culture are briefly discussed as a way of framing the more detailed work of the subsequent textual analysis.

RHETORICAL CONTEXTS

History reveals to us time and again how interlocked are the fortunes of democracy and the arts of persuasion. From antiquity to the present, the health of one remains in no small measure a function of the other: as the polity goes, so goes rhetoric. Americans of the eighteenth and nineteenth centuries knew as much, indeed reflected a good deal on this persistent but quite fragile relationship. "The experience of the world has shown pretty conclusively," observed the *North American Review,* "that eloquence and political liberty go hand in hand, flourish under similar favoring influences, and, dying together, are buried in the same grave." Looking back over the nation's first century of existence, the writer confidently surmised that both liberty and eloquence were given new life, meaning, and energy in republican America, with all its "links of electric sympathy between the patriot speaker and the tumultuous assemblages of free and sovereign citizens, gathered to consider questions of moment to the public weal, or to celebrate, with the pomp of solemn processions, religious rites, and commemorative orations, the illustrious achievements of the mighty dead, to call up the famous days which have been turning points in the history of national greatness." Pride so confident may be appreciated ironically for having been expressed a decade before the Civil War. But it may just as well remind us that the symbiosis thought to animate the political and the rhetorical was never taken for granted, indeed was revisited most frequently at moments of greatest uncertainty.[5]

To grasp the achievement of Jefferson's first inaugural address is to acknowledge what the "experience of the world" confirms, that eloquence and liberty either flourish together or, "dying together, are buried in the same grave." The proximity of this relationship suggests that what is observed of one term ought to be observed of the other, as in fact we must in reference to Jefferson's address. That is to say, the qualities attributable to political life in the 1790s and in the first years of the new century find their unmistakable analogue in the rhetorical practices through which that life was mediated. The instability, the heat, the apparently boundless energies, the push and pull of tradition and novelty, the dialectics of expansion and retraction—all characteristic, too, of the rhetorical dynamics shaping and given shape by political developments. As a preliminary for our reading of the inaugural address, this interplay of the political and the rhetorical is best comprehended as a description of public life generally, where rapid transformation in the social, economic, and cultural factors making up that life set the stage for Jefferson's "revolution." Historians continue to debate the precise sources, meaning, and consequences of the period, but all agree that the "first generation of Americans," as Joyce Appleby subtitles a recent work, effected powerful new realities on the shared lives of citizens throughout the republic.[6]

Two such realities are especially pertinent here. First, the unprecedented expansion of the spaces of political action drastically transformed the opportunities for those already or newly enfranchised to let their voices be heard. "The frothy political discourses," Appleby writes, "the marketing of printed material, and the enlarged circle of readers worked together to make publicity the shaping force in the public realm." Second, and by direct implication, this unleashing of popular power became at once the source and object of public opinion formation. Citizens and their leaders knew themselves to be in a different world than that which obtained before the Revolution; certain continuities were still evident, of course, but the sheer fact of a new and formidable type—the American citizen—asserted itself with unmistakable force. Political activity, as a result, and the rhetorical labor required to organize this new creature "public opinion," changed for good (or ill, depending on how one viewed the prospects of a government of, by, and for the people). "The Revolution," Gordon Wood explains, "rapidly expanded this 'public' and democratized its opinion. Every conceivable form of printed matter[:] books, pamphlets, handbills, posters, broadsides, and especially newspapers multiplied and were now written and read by many more ordinary people than ever before in history."[7]

A new nation, a literate and politically engaged public, a president whose very identity announced the triumph of republican values upon and for which independence was fought and gained: here was a combination of novelties bound to enthrall or terrify. But of course no generation is ever born entirely anew, no revolution so complete as to wipe out all precedent. And this is true no less for the rhetorical culture of the new republic than for its attendant political life. Just as certain principles and practices of the latter continued to make themselves felt under the new order, so the former continued to shape the nation's discursive habits. Jefferson's inaugural, like his politics, was at once forward looking and indebted to certain rhetorical traditions, and by looking at those traditions, we can situate it where it rightfully belongs at the cusp, between the eighteenth and nineteenth centuries, between the old and new. To this end, the following briefly examines three conventions of public discourse—religious, civic, and political—that in general ways shaped the address, its reception, and its legacy.

Religious Contexts

Any attempt to situate Jefferson's address in relation to the religious culture of his time may well strike us as misguided from the outset. Readers familiar with his reputation as an inveterate enemy of sectarianism, his work on behalf of religious freedom, and his notorious indifference to institutionalized Christianity are apt to dismiss, indeed ignore, Jefferson's debt to the rhetorical conventions shaping the religious life of the new republic. At the personal level, to be sure, we must be very careful in attributing to his thought anything like a coherent or neatly packaged set of religious convictions; at a minimum, Jefferson must be recognized as being deeply skeptical about the probity of organized Christianity, and there can be no gainsaying his fierce resistance to those who would return his new country back into the hands of a discredited religious elite. Jefferson the man was in fact much concerned about matters of faith and divinity; Jefferson the politician was adamant not to have his or anyone else's religious convictions intrude into the affairs of state.[8]

On what basis, then, can it be said that his inaugural address owed its character, its rhetorical power, in some measure to the religious culture of the period? The answer must be pitched at a rather broad level, and no effort will be made here to link specific words with specific doctrine; that is not how this speech—nor any inaugural address for that matter—functions rhetorically. Jefferson rather sought to give his words their most general application and their broadest possible scope; in this, he fully appreciated the fact that Americans were a people deeply, in some ways definitively, religious. Again, such recognition presumed no uniformity of faith. Indeed it was precisely the fact that Americans were so diverse, sometimes at odds, sometimes losing and then regaining perspective that Jefferson appealed not to their differences but to what it was they held in common when it came to religious sentiment. In view of this challenge, Jefferson sought to effect in the first inaugural address what he previously had sought when composing the Declaration of Independence: "Not to find out new principles, or new arguments, never before thought of, not merely to say things which had never been said before; but to place before mankind the common sense of the subject, in terms so plain and firm as to command their assent. . . . Neither aiming at originality of principle or sentiment, nor yet copied from any particular and previous writing, it was intended to be an expression of the American mind, and to give to that expression the proper tone and spirit called for by the occasion." When it came to the religious dimensions of "the American mind" Jefferson had before him a set of perfectly familiar and still-powerful thematics from which to draw. Among those figuring most prominently in the inaugural address are three propositions embraced by nearly all citizens: that Americans were a chosen people; that by virtue of that fact the nation was set on a path toward ever greater progress; and that to keep on this path Americans must undertake rituals of rededication and renewal.[9]

Whatever their creed, wherever they practiced it and whenever they reflected on it, Americans had remained convinced that they were singular. Divine Providence had ordained that this people, for all their faults, were possessed of a special mission and qualities of mind, body, and spirit alone up to the task of making the new world truly a New World. Almost two centuries before, John Winthrop had invoked on board the *Arabella* Matthew's faith "that we shall be as a city upon a hill" and warned too that the "eyes of all people are upon us." That conviction, that insistence for better or worse never failed to shape the colonists' sense of themselves and their role in the world. A nation now, Americans continued to thank God, in the words of Israel Evans, "by whose providential goodness and power the lines are fallen unto us in pleasant places; yea, we have a godly heritage. Here harvests grow for the free and cheerful husbandman: here, neither awed by lordly and rapacious injustice, nor dejected by beholding idleness high fed and fattened on the labors of other men, they reap and enjoy the pleasing fruits of their honest industry." Thus when Jefferson spoke during his inaugural of "the world's best hope," of "the strongest Government on earth," of "possessing a chosen country, with room enough for our descendants to the thousandth and thousandth generation," he spoke in a language of abiding and peculiar power. Federalists and republicans, Puritan and deist, rich and poor, Yankee and Cavalier: all could see an image of themselves written into this twice-told tale of America as a chosen people.[10]

A chosen people, Jefferson and his audience knew, was an active people. Fleeing persecution and finding freedom, the early colonists had only begun to realize the full responsibility and the full prospect before them. Because they were select, they were bound in covenant, and that covenant bound all Americans to the cultivation and increase of the bounty God had bestowed. The rewards, as Samuel Danforth reminded his congregants, were as great as the labor required to summon them forth: "Attend we our Errand," Danforth promised, "upon which Christ sent us into the Wilderness, and he will provide Bread for us." At the dawn of a new century it seemed to many Americans that providence had more than made good on that promise; progress was evident everywhere, and was this not proof positive that the new nation had in fact secured the full blessings of liberty? "We possess an extensive, noble country," declared Samuel Miller in a sermon of 1793. "Fertility and beauty vie with each other, in favor of our ease, accommodation, and delight. Every avenue to national importance, and the felicity of individuals, is opened wide. Let it then, in addition to all these advantages, and to complete its glory, let it be Immanuel's land. This will render you at once the pattern," Miller told his listeners, "and the wonder of the world." Jefferson no less than the Presbyterian minister was enthralled by what he saw before him, "A rising nation, spread over a wide and fruitful land, traversing all the seas with the rich productions of their industry . . . advancing rapidly to destinies beyond the reach of mortal eye." All this, Jefferson and his audience knew, was the just reward due a people chosen by a "Providence, which by all its dispensations proves that it delights in the happiness of man here and his greater happiness hereafter." Surely even the most inveterate critic of Jefferson's religious views would be hard put to deny his or her own place in such a scheme of things.[11]

Jefferson was known in his own time as he is in ours as the consummate optimist. This quality, so apparent throughout his writings, in no small degree accounts for his popularity then and his enduring appeal ever since. Indeed it has been transcribed onto the American spirit itself, as if in Jefferson's unfailing hopes for republican government we might find the self-flattering reflection of our own boundless faith in American destiny. But faith, religious, political, or otherwise, requires labor. This much Jefferson understood keenly. The inaugural address was in fact part of this labor, a work designed to shore up confidence, assuage anxieties, keep his audience on that path pointing so auspiciously to the future. Recalling again that this was but the fourth such inaugural address of the new nation, we can appreciate the imperative under which this task was undertaken: When the object of faith is so new, so alone in the world, what rituals of rededication are necessary to remind this people of their special role and retain their confidence in the rewards that surely lie ahead? For all its novelty, Jefferson's address was recognizable as a ritualized performance crafted specifically to strengthen collective resolve; it accordingly participated in a venerable tradition of religious discourse focused on just this challenge. Again, this is not to imply that Jefferson was self-consciously patterning his language on such discourse or on any special strain within it. It is to alert us to the common and nearly universal function of rhetoric to rededicate common values and mutual commitment to each other's fortunes.

Jefferson's audience that day was heir to a longstanding, diverse, and still-resonant tradition of such rituals, ranging from fast day and artillery sermons to prayers of thanksgiving. The key to these rituals was their capacity to bind together again a people at peril, to forge again a commanding rationale for standing together with faces turned courageously toward the future. Thus Jonathan Mayhew steadied his audience during the Stamp Act crisis by insisting that it was "most prudent, most christian, to bury in oblivion what is past; to begin our civil, political life anew as it were, from this joyful and glorious area of restored and confirmed liberty; to be at union among ourselves; to abstain from all party names and national reflections, respecting any of our fellow subjects, and to exert ourselves, in our several stations, to promote the common good, by 'love serving one another.'" These and countless sermons throughout the founding era attest to a telling combination of optimism and anxiety about the American errand; rhetorically, they functioned to restore a faith already strong but always exposed to doubt; to reunite a people destined to move forward but given to laxity and bouts of disorientation; to remind citizens, as did David Tappan in his 1792 election sermon, to be "just and kind to one another, united and jealously attached to the great interests of America, and of the whole human fraternity. Then we shall hold out an inviting example to all the world," Tappan said, "of the propitious operation of a free government; we shall encourage and accelerate the progress of reason, and of liberty, through the globe." Like Tappan, Mayhew, and many other leaders before him, Jefferson availed himself in 1801 of a rich storehouse of experiences and symbols from the American religious tradition. From that tradition, he found one way, at least, to "look with encouragement for that guidance and support which may enable us to steer with safety the vessel in which we are all embarked amidst the conflicting elements of a troubled world."[12]

Civic Commemoration

As broad and deep as such religious tradition was in the early republic, it was but a part of a more general and complex rhetorical culture. Closely related to it was an equally vibrant set of conventions associated with rituals of civic commemoration. Americans then as now were tireless workers of public memory, bent, it often seems, on fixing every glance toward the future from coordinates set by the past. The many occasions and motives through which such celebrations were mediated meant that the arts of civic commemoration could not be limited to a specific genre or rhetorical type; not oratory alone but any number of symbolic practices were set in motion to assist in bringing history into the national present. Songs, poetry, monuments, essays, painting, and public speech all helped to turn the past into a spectacle for the education, entertainment, and aspirations of the new republic. Taken together, all these forms represented a loose but powerful chain with which Americans bound themselves locally and nationally as citizens of one country. The productions flowing from these occasions may strike us now as mere ephemera, but it is a mistake to discount their centrality to the labor of citizenship. They are, as David Waldstreicher has argued, definitively "nationalist practices, every bit as much as the processions they announced, punctuated, and described. They did more than spread nationalism," Waldstreicher notes, "they constituted a national popular political culture."[13]

The first inaugural address, singularly eloquent, so distinctively Jefferson, would seem far distant from the messier world of parades, toasts, and popular oratory. In many ways it is, of course, but in another sense Jefferson's masterpiece cannot be fully understood independent of such ritualized rehearsals of nationhood. It was in no small part an artifact of a robust public culture; as a rhetorical performance, it thus relied for its intended effect on the habits and expectations of that culture. Whether or not they discerned in Jefferson's language the full range of its meaning, the people who heard or read the speech were well-positioned to recognize it for what it was and what it hoped to accomplish. What they perceived must have been reassuringly familiar: an event at once dignified but not excessively so; local in its delivery and source but reaching out to the nation as a whole; about political life but not overtly partisan. These were indeed the markers of many other such performances: the ubiquitous Fourth of July oration, the annual celebrations of Washington's birthday, commencement day addresses. This was, certainly, an exemplary instance of civic commemoration, but it held in common with all such rituals the purpose of rallying citizens to the banner of republican government by appealing to a shared past, a collective identity, and a future befitting a free and united future. The first inaugural address was of a piece, a particularly striking instance of a process described by James Farrell as a national effort to "express the praise and admiration of celebrants for the noble deeds of American revolutionaries, to craft a useful history and consign those narratives to the public memory, to suggest a dominant national identity proud of its past and confident of its future, and to hold up models of civic virtue and patriotism to be emulated by future political and military leaders."[14]

If Jefferson's oration is to be regarded in part as participating in this more general context of civic commemoration, we need now to consider more specifically how these rituals took on their rhetorical force. If, that is to say, these rituals worked by staging the drama of nationhood, with what materials was that spectacle composed? How and to what effect was it so framed as to present in the most compelling terms possible the story of America and its victorious republican revolution? Three broad and clearly interdependent characteristics suggest themselves as answers to that question. At the local level, these rituals were presented as a kind of political theater, the chief function of which was to give to the occasion its maximum visual, auditory, and affective power; at the national level, this appeal was expanded and applied through developing technologies of print and reportage; and at the level of historical transformation, the rituals of nationhood extended their reach across generations to insure the survival of a citizenry up to the task of self-government.

By way of perspective on just how theatrical politics could be in the early republic, we might recall the events surrounding the nation's first inaugural ceremonies. In April of 1789, George Washington was accompanied from Philadelphia to New York by a seemingly endless series of parades, orations, and pageantry. At one point, Charles Wilson Peel's daughter Angelica (in white robes) managed with the help of a special contraption to lower onto the new president's head a laurel crown as he passed onto a bridge into Philadelphia. Young Angelica's was but one of thousands of such gestures that swept Washington to his appointed speech in New York's Federal Hall. Nearing Trenton, he was greeted by girls (also in white) tossing flowers before him and singing "Virgins fair, and Matrons grave,/Those thy conquering arms did save/Build for these triumphal bowers/Strew, ye fair, his way with flowers/Strew your Hero's way with flowers."[15]

True, spectacle at this level could be appropriate to Washington alone, and Jefferson, it is safe to say, neither warranted nor expected any girls to gild his path with rose petals. In the event, his inauguration ceremonies were conspicuously simple; so much so, in fact, that his critics accused him of debasing the office. But the key word here is conspicuous, for Jefferson knew as well as anyone that the inauguration of power was above all a symbolic act, the meaning and force of which depended on what people actually saw, heard, and experienced. His own inauguration and the speech attending were artfully rendered scenes in the drama that was republicanism. They were accordingly designed to impart the spectacle of dignity without monarchical trappings, to embody and enact that special virtue Americans claimed as their own.

Not everyone, of course, was fortunate enough to bear direct witness to such scenes. That all could learn of them from a distance was the result of a rapidly developing print culture that included newspapers, broadsides, pamphlets, and periodicals. Consequently, readers from Maine to Georgia and virtually everywhere in between learned of the day's events when, as Philadelphia's *Aurora* reported, "there appeared to be a calm and exquisite diffusion of delight[;] the cessation of party animosity was for a time complete, and from the tears which bedewed many manly cheeks, and union of opinion in applause, there appeared to be a total, and prospect of a perpetual annihilation of party passions." That much was optimistic, to be sure. Party passions erupted soon thereafter, and readers could gauge their own sentiments by tracking debates and commentary in newspapers throughout the states. "In Virginia," wrote one skeptic in the Charleston *Gazette,* "we are not so sanguine as you are, and we read the inaugural speech, without finding any thing in it to cherish the hopes of the friends of regular government, good order, and peace."[16]

The partisan energies driving the press at the time meant that whatever pretensions to being above party Jefferson may have had were quickly deflated. But the more general and relevant fact is that the press played a key role in sustaining the drama of politics and hence the life of the new nation. Put another way, print culture and reportage assisted directly in the process whereby a people distant to each other come to recognize themselves as fellow citizens; in the words of Benedict Anderson, they "gradually become aware of the hundreds of thousands, even millions, of people in their particular language-field, and at the same time that only those hundreds of thousands, or millions, so belonged. These fellow-readers, to whom they were connected through print, formed, in their secular, particular, visible invisibility, the embryo of the nationally imagined community."[17]

Both in the immediate experience of witnessing civic ceremony and in reading about it, Americans were fast moving from Anderson's embryonic stage toward greater levels of maturation. This was so in part because they were not *merely* witnessing such rituals of national affirmation as presidential inaugurations: they were actively participating in that very process. To do so, to be aware of national as well as local events, to read, perhaps even write an ode to virtue, to strew flowers or to attend a Fourth of July celebration was to act as a citizen of the republic. But the instantiation of republican virtue through these rituals required more even than attending or reading about them; it obliged all citizens to pass on their legacy of freedom to future generations. So obviously the beneficiaries of the struggle for republican government, Americans shouldered the responsibility to insure against its demise by keeping its promises ever alive in the hearts and minds of those about to receive its blessings. Whether they participated in person or at a distance, celebrants were expected to somehow disseminate the experience of citizenship. This they did by establishing recurrent and regular celebrations of nationhood (eventually including Jefferson's own March 4 address). It is central to our understanding of Jefferson's inaugural address, and of the rhetorical culture to which it spoke, that we see it in its ritualized aspect. A great deal of the rhetorical power of ritual is precisely its reproducibility; it can be observed time and again; it endures across state lines and partisan difference; it persists through generations to bind citizens together in history as well as place.

In a nation so young as Jefferson's, threatened within by party strife and without by foreign wars and intrigue, it would be nearly impossible to overstate the significance of these functions. Like the many other forms of civic ceremony to which it was related, the inaugural address as such provided a certain ballast against the waves of social change and political strife. It is crucial to recognize, moreover, that the stability purchased through ritual did not come at the cost of eliminating dissent; ballast only works when countered by competing forces. In this context we may observe that Jefferson's inaugural address works not in the absence of conflict but by virtue of it; that is in part its brilliance, as clear and compelling an example as could be got of Waldstreicher's keen insight: the remarkable thing about Jeffersonian Americans was that they fashioned such rituals "in order to have their partisanship with their nationalism, their *communitas* with their campaigning: to be local citizens and national subjects."[18]

Political Debate

The rhetorical culture of the new nation was textured in decisive and discernible ways by these traditions of religious and civic discourse. Jefferson's inaugural address, while not wholly explicable with reference to them, is not wholly explicable unless we take these conventions into account. Similarly, a third broad context bears directly on our understanding of the address, its sources, character, and legacy. For nearly half a century, public life in America had been defined and transformed by political disputation—unabashed, sometimes shrill, often eloquent—but resolutely polemical efforts to forge the national ethos. Much of this work, as we have seen, took its inspiration from certain religious and civic influences, and no effort will be made here to select out political debate as a separate rhetorical genre. At the same time, there is reason to acknowledge the role of an overtly political tradition of public "discussion"—the gloves-off, hard-hitting give-and-take of debate that made no attempt to mask its ambitions under the guise of religious or civic ritual. For evidence of this tradition we need not seek far: the rhetoric of nationhood is always a noisy affair, and as Bernard Bailyn dryly reminds us, reticence was not a problem for most Americans. Before the war, colonial leaders "wrote easily and amply, and turned out in the space of scarcely a decade and a half and from a small number of presses a rich literature of theory, argument, opinion, and polemic. Every medium of expression was put to use." If that was the case before independence, it was even more so afterward, and Jefferson figures very much as a leading voice in this already crowded and vocal life of the new republic.[19]

But how? If the inaugural address is to be situated within this tradition, in what ways specifically does it work its political ends? The question is more complex than it may appear at first glance, if only because Jefferson's own posture in the political wrangling of his time proved so paradoxical. The first inaugural was at one level an intensely partisan document, evidence if any were needed that its author was a political animal of the most primal type. And, too, Jefferson had played a leading role at the avant-garde of radical politics for a quarter-century of American life; surely no further evidence need be summoned to establish his credentials as a disputant of the first order. At the same time, his inaugural address is notable as much for what it appears not to be as for what it actually is: a highly political expression of values that claim no partisan allegiances. Here we arrive at the nub of Jefferson's complex stance toward the rhetorical culture of which he was both a product and an enemy. Joseph Ellis's pointed comment captures nicely the point: "One of the reasons he [Jefferson] was so notoriously ineffective in debate was that argument itself offended him. The voices he heard inside himself were all harmonious and agreeable, reliable expressions of the providentially aligned universal laws that governed the world as he knew it, so that argument struck him as dissonant noise that defied the natural order of things."[20]

The quality of mind to which Ellis refers may be directly mapped onto the rhetorical quality of the inaugural address. It is, paradoxically, a performance born of political debate but designed to transcend it; fashioned by one of history's great polemicists, who at the same time was deeply distrustful of conflict. We should not be surprised, then, to see in its language the imprint of two tendencies, mutually at odds but coexisting by virtue of the rhetorical artistry it commands. We shall address these features in greater detail below, but here, where we seek a general sense of how the inaugural may be placed in the context of eighteenth-century political debate, it will be worth noting several key markers. On the one hand, the speech works thematically by taking into itself many, perhaps most, of the commonplaces associated with revolutionary, constitutional, and early republican rhetoric. A quick list makes the point:

A rising nation spread over a wide and fruitful land

engaged in commerce with nations who feel power and forget right

advancing rapidly to destinies beyond the reach of mortal eye

all will, of course, arrange themselves under the will of the law

and unite in common efforts for the common good

the will of the majority is in all cases to prevail

that will to be rightful must be reasonable

the minority possess their equal rights

This government, the world's best hope

the strongest government on earth

possessing a chosen country

a wise and frugal Government

shall not take from the mouth of labor the bread it has earned

Equal and exact justice to all men

freedom of religion

freedom of the press

freedom of person

peace, liberty, and safety

What true republican could but applaud such principles? They are among those for which the revolution was fought and secured; to believe in them was to be an American. That these transcendent values were now in fact commonplaces was the result of a rhetorical process, a culture of debate and dissent that propelled thirteen colonies into nationhood. And here we gain our clue to the rhetorical ingenuity of Jefferson's address, for in appealing to that to which all would agree, the speaker appealed to that which was now beyond debate and dissent, to the "creed of our political faith." Jefferson sought accordingly to speak to a citizenry for whom these verities were no longer at issue, no longer subject to dispute. His was an argument that presumed argument no longer necessary.

Finally, the status of Jefferson's speech as an *inaugural* address is an obvious but important clue to its meaning, shape, and delivery. To speak of such address as constituting a genre is perhaps overly generous: only three presidential inaugurations, after all, had been accompanied by the ritual of speech we have come to take for granted. As Stephen Lucas has pointed out, however, certain rhetorical antecedents can be traced to explain the distinctive form and content marking the inaugural address generally. Chief among these, Lucas notes, was the rhetoric of office taking evident in British and colonial tradition. Under these circumstances, "the new office-holder typically acknowledged the person or persons responsible for granting the office, noted the magnitude and/or importance of the duties attached to that office, expressed humility about his capacity to carry out those duties, and pledged his utmost effort to meet his responsibilities ably and honorably." More specifically, Lucas locates the template for early presidential inaugural addresses in the office-taking rituals associated with the arrival of new governors to the Virginia Council and House of Burgesses. In these cases, Lucas writes, the governor "announced the general principles that would guide his administration, mentioned one or two issues of pressing importance, praised the legislature for its knowledge, virtue, and loyalty, and urged that it avoid faction and promote the public weal in every respect." Jefferson's address unmistakably bears these antecedent imprints, and in recalling them we take one step further toward a full appreciation for how he realized the potential inherent to the form.[21]

Taken together, these religious, civic, and political traditions of rhetorical discourse shaped Jefferson's first inaugural address in complex but recognizable ways. They remind us, too, that we have in that text evidence of an original mind and extraordinary stylist, even as that mind and that style is put to the task of rehearsing cultural truisms. To give singular expression to common values: that was Jefferson's rare gift. As we move closer to a more detailed examination of the text, it will prove useful to briefly recall how that gift was itself shaped and developed through the author's personal engagement in his nation's founding. Turning to several of his most notable rhetorical performances previous to the inaugural address, we shall be in a better position to discern in it that distinctive quality here referred to as the Jeffersonian style.

BETWEEN TEXT AND CONTEXT: A NOTE ON JEFFERSONIAN STYLE

In the spring of 1781 the Marquis de Chastellux journeyed from his encampment in Williamsburg up to the more serene environs of Monticello. After a few days with the newly retired (as governor of Virginia) Jefferson, the marquis could only marvel at the range and depth of his new friend's learning: "Sometimes natural philosophy, at others politicks or the arts were the topics of our conversation, for no object had escaped Mr. Jefferson," Chastellux later recalled, "and it seemed as if from his youth he had placed his mind, as he has done his house, on an elevated situation, from which he might contemplate the universe." That the mind and the house bore an analogous relationship to each other would in time become a frequent means to describe the peculiar style of Jefferson's thinking, where form and content combined to create a singular and lasting image of the man. It was a trait destined to command the admiration of his supporters and the scorn of his critics, but everyone who reflected on the matter recognized that in Jefferson the manner and the matter were one. As a recent scholar has put the case, Jefferson's "immense intellectual influence came through the cultivation of affinities within the American Enlightenment of the eighteenth century and the creation of symbols and images—Monticello comes to mind—that would reflect a secular, classical humanism in American thought."[22]

Among American presidents Lincoln alone rivals Jefferson as a prose stylist. But where Lincoln's formidable powers were trained almost exclusively on a single subject and to a single end, Jefferson's were applied over more than three decades of public life to an unmatched variety of problems and topics. From political tract to scientific treatise, from constitutions and charters, from correspondence to the inaugural address, he sought always to give to his ideas what John Adams memorably described as a "peculiar felicity of expression." Nearing our examination of the first inaugural address, accordingly, it will be worth our time to briefly dwell on the rhetorical quality that so distinguishes Jefferson's major writings. By way of a general strategy, we may recall the view advanced above that Jefferson offers in the address a stylized rendering of its own subject matter, a rhetorical instantiation of republican virtue, in short, a fusion of idiom and ideology. Students of Jefferson seldom fail to note how conspicuous was this feature: "Having something to say," Carl Becker noted, "he says it, with as much art as may be, yet not solely for the art's sake, aiming rather at the ease, the simplicity, and the genial urbanity of cultivated conversation. The grace and felicity of his style have a distinctively personal flavor, something Jeffersonian in the implication of the idea, or in the beat and measure of his words."[23]

But what, more specifically, is this Jeffersonian "something"? Becker was an especially astute critic of Jefferson's rhetorical style, but like many others he turns in the end to vague or metaphorical descriptors to grasp the seemingly ineffable. Thus one reviewer notes in 1830 that the "style and character of Mr. Jefferson's writings resemble . . . those well drawn portraits, which regard and follow us with their eyes in whatever direction we move," while another assured readers of the *North American Review* that Jefferson was one of those rare geniuses who, "by combining literary and active pursuits, and exhibiting in both a first-rate talent, furnish in their works the most complete reflection that can possibly be given, of the finished man." Others have shown themselves less enthralled by Jefferson's characteristic style, especially as it worked to elevate his words above the mundane but pressing realities of political life. Joseph Ellis, perhaps the sharpest observer of Jefferson on this score, locates the Jeffersonian ethos within a larger and more complex matrix of executive, diplomatic, domestic, and republican styles evident throughout his public life. "The common ingredient in all these contexts," argues Ellis, "was Jefferson's urge to cloak his exercise of power from others and from himself."[24]

The point is at once simple and brilliant, for what Ellis discerns comes very close to identifying the persuasive achievement of the first inaugural address. As we have noted above, the speech functions on a number of levels as a partisan tract and as a political treatise, without announcing itself as either. The third level at which we are treating the address, as a rhetorical performance, allows us to see how such a cloaking operation takes place. That is to say, its rhetorical artistry consists in giving to republican principles their maximum aesthetic appeal; the result is a stylistically flawless rendering of arguments that from another perspective might well appear uncertain, exposed, or inconsistent. The inaugural address in this sense stands in an iconic relationship to the ideological energies swirling about and giving rise to it; put another way, the speech composes itself seamlessly as an unanswerable proclamation that this is what republicanism—true republicanism, American republicanism—looks and sounds like. The rough edges of politics are thereby filed smooth, power is honed and buffed to an exquisite finish, and argument, in the end, is burnished to the point where it disappears all together.

It is worth reminding ourselves in this context that the inaugural address was the first major statement by Jefferson on political affairs that was not overtly oppositional (although, as we have seen, it was certainly partisan). *The Summary View*, the Declaration, the Kentucky Resolutions all were played out in the crucible of intense political strife; now, in 1801, the speaker in effect proclaims the end of politics thus conceived and thus practiced. From here on out, politics was to be seen and heard on a different and truer register, played on a key set by the triumph of republican government and the new American nation. Jefferson aimed to place his country, like his mind and house, on what Chastellux rightly called an "elevated situation," an exalted and perfectly figured space where the prospects of nationhood could be glimpsed with breathtaking clarity. The first inaugural address allows us such a glimpse. Turning to it now, we will examine how it shapes our own view by strategically constructing a particular image of the speaker; by exemplifying norms of propriety; and by embodying in its very language the virtues of republican simplicity.

A Republican Ethos

Neither critic nor champion could in 1801 dispute the republicanism of Thomas Jefferson. He brought with him to the podium a reputation for faith in its promises and commitment to its defense that few could match and none could supercede. At the same time, he must have known that reputation alone was insufficient to the task at hand; under the circumstances, Jefferson needed through the act of speech to craft and set on display his distinctive vision not only of what the nation had meant, but what it was to mean in the coming time. This much was to be demonstrated rather than assumed, created in and through the inaugural address as living testimony to the ideals he embraced. At stake in this process was the character of the speaker himself, and character, as Aristotle reminded readers of his *Rhetoric,* was "the controlling factor in persuasion." Here was no small challenge, if only because the inaugural ceremonies demanded of Jefferson talents for self-expression nearly unprecedented in his public life. The speaker had spent a good deal of his career in one role of opposition or another; he was by experience a writer of critical tracts, of declarations and resolutions against constituted authority. Jefferson now occupied the highest office in the land. How then to authorize *that* authority?[25]

Any response to the question would need to take into account a rhetorical problem intrinsic to republicanism itself. Jefferson's position demanded that he at once embody the principles of republican government, to give them eloquent voice and presence in speech, but not so much as to eclipse by his person the democratic and equalitarian ideals upon which it was based and for which his office was but a conduit. Here was the very nub of all republican leadership. The problem was not Jefferson's alone, but his response to it represents one of the crowning rhetorical achievements of his life and that of his nation.

It is a matter of self and subject, and to better get at the means through which he negotiates this delicate balance, we need first to ask who Jefferson is in the speech. What work is this rhetorically crafted person, this Jefferson-in-the-text, made to perform? How does the image of the speaker, simultaneously projected from and supervising the meaning in the text, organize and promote its values? One strategy for addressing the question is to note the presence of first person pronouns in the speech—the Jeffersonian "I"—and to observe how such usage assists in forging the message as a whole. It is a modest measure, to be sure, but an efficient and telling one, and it will reveal to us at least one means through which Jefferson orchestrates a finely tuned movement between one sense of authority (understood as a necessary attribute of leadership) and another (understood as the province and privilege of republicanism alone). Here the Jeffersonian style, so attuned to the equipoise of opposites, may be seen at in its most rhetorical aspect.

The first person pronoun is used on 21 occasions in the inaugural address. Of these, nearly half—nine—appear in the first of its six paragraphs alone. At first glance, this repetition might seem to violate the rhetorical convention of the *ingratio,* or the opening moments of a speech devoted to the effacement of the speaker in view of the greater needs of the moment and audience. On closer inspection, however, we see that in fact Jefferson stages these self-references in a highly strategic manner, at once drawing attention to his own role in bringing the day's events into being and establishing a becoming relationship to the complex of forces within which they are situated. This strategy is made especially evident when we note the verbs accompanying such usage: "I avail myself," "I approach it with those anxious and awful presentiments," "I contemplate these transcendent objects," "I shrink from the contemplation," "I shall find resources of wisdom," "I look with encouragement." Thus Jefferson's well-known modesty is at once underscored and put to work not by coyly removing himself from the scene (his predecessor John Adams did not refer to himself until the fifth paragraph of his inaugural address), but by conspicuously subordinating himself to his audience, the nation, his office, and the Constitution. Like all good republicans, Jefferson understood that virtue was an essentially dramatic quality and that it, too, needed a stage upon which it was to effect its ends.

Given the uncertainty and tensions of which this speech was an artifact, Jefferson's opening lines could not have been better conceived. Having triumphed over an "Anglican monarchical, and aristocratic party," having defeated the Anglo-leaning Adams and vanquished the aristocratic Hamilton, Jefferson needed now to occupy not a ground vacated by them but an entirely new, an entirely republican terrain. This he does in the inaugural address's brief introduction by subtly drawing attention to his presence in the near background of the drama; thus asserting by subordination, Jefferson in effect exemplifies the republican commitment to both the popular will and limited executive authority.[26]

The republican ethos made to superintend the work of paragraph one accordingly sets the terms for what follows. Here, in the long and complex second phase of the speech, Jefferson establishes an authorial perspective so poised as to reconcile and ultimately transcend the conflicts shaping—and misshaping—late eighteenth-century political culture. The authority to which Jefferson now lays claim and the credibility it confers has been secured by divesting himself of any desire for personal aggrandizement or self-interest. The stance is at once elevated and open, and from it the speaker can be seen seeing beyond the particulars of the moment, past the transient and surface elements to the heights and frontiers of the authentic nation. This act of conspicuous discernment is in turn made to illustrate precisely that quality of judgment necessary to republican leadership. It is altogether appropriate, then, that here Jefferson should exercise that judgment by asserting more positively his own active voice. Here the refrain involves not shrinking or contemplation or despair, but declarations of fact and faith: "I know, indeed, that some honest men fear that a republican government cannot be strong," "I believe this, on the contrary, the strongest Government on earth," "I believe it the only one where every man, at the call of the law, would fly to the standard of the law." By unavoidable implication, Jefferson's authority thus voiced is predicated on his capacity to command a perspective when others have been blinded by the winds of conflict; he must therefore reveal the delusion of others, correct their errors, remind them of the republican way.

Although clearly different in tone and function from the speech's opening lines, the second paragraph stands not in contrast but as an extension. If there is transformation here, it takes place by shifting to a different plane of symbolic action; that is, having expressed his reliance on the people for whatever authority he may exercise, Jefferson now assumes and applies that authority to realign a nation momentarily disordered by a malevolent few. They had done their work, but now, as Jefferson had noted to Joseph Priestly shortly after the speech, the "order and good sense displayed in this recovery from delusion, and in the momentous crisis which lately arose, really bespeak a strength of character in our nation which augurs well for the duration of our Republic." It is in part the task of this second paragraph to fuse the nation's "strength of character" to his own; hence Jefferson symbolically invites all true republicans onto the platform to see what he sees and to embrace each other in republican concord.[27]

In his politics as in his art, Jefferson reached for symmetry when he could find it. And when he did, he put that aesthetic principle to rhetorical ends, made it work in his writings and speeches to effect by words what he would create politically. Again, this constitutive interplay between idiom and ideology obliges us to look beyond broad thematic categories and attend, as we have, to textual particulars. With respect to the functions performed by the Jeffersonian "I," we can see in the speech's closing passages both this symmetry achieved formally and the rhetorical purposes to which that form is suited. The concluding two paragraphs recall the tone registered at the beginning and help close, so to speak, the circle of the text's felicity. Some of this, of course, is owing to convention, prudence and assurances of good will being the better part of rhetorical wisdom. But we will have missed the more interesting entailments of this return by leaving it at that. As we saw in paragraphs one and two, we find here a similar effort to negotiate the speaker's self into an optimal relationship with those sources of power from which he must derive his own authority. Having introduced and ingratiated that self early in the speech, and having asserted it in an image of enlightened reason in the middle, Jefferson now eases toward his exit by stepping backward while facing stage front:

"I repair, then, fellow-citizens, to the post you have assigned me"

"I have learnt to expect that it will rarely fall to the lot of imperfect man to retire from this station with the reputation and the favor which bring him into it"

"I ask so much confidence only as may give firmness and effect to the legal administration of your affairs"

"I shall often go wrong through defect of judgment"

Here is modesty befitting a republican leader. But lest we lose sight of Jefferson's own ends, we need note too how careful he is not to let these constructions devolve into courtly obsequies. In truth there is nothing passive or even very deferential in these final lines, and we need not look far to see how the Jeffersonian "I" hints at a very near political future. Immediately after the steps taken above, that is, Jefferson takes several forward again by reminding his audience that those who would judge him critically may be viewed as "those whose positions will not command a view of the whole ground." Even as he takes his leave, then, Jefferson reinvokes the assertive phase in the body of the address and, promising never to err intentionally, begs his nation's "support against the errors of others, who may condemn what they would not if seen in all its parts." It is Jefferson and his followers, by fairly obvious juxtaposition, who in fact command such a view and see all the parts together, that are in no small measure what Jefferson took to be the essence of enlightened republican leadership. The final brief paragraph captures just this synthesis of personal authority and popular warrant so basic to Jefferson's unflagging optimism, and gives us reason to see why, in his words, "I advance with obedience to the work, ready to retire from it whenever you become sensible how much better choice it is in your power to make." That is old-fashioned political power wrapped in the plain but spotless glove of the republican style.

Republicanism was for Jefferson a revolutionary idea because it radically displaced power from its historical claimants and replaced it with popular sovereignty. That revolution—and truly it was—dramatically exposed the question of leadership divested of its monarchical trappings, parliamentary corruptions, and courtly intrigues. The question for the generation following independence was, What kind of authority, what kind of voice was appropriate to the task of leading a new nation "to destinies beyond the reach of mortal eye"? The answer, Jefferson understood, rested in the same place as the question—in the concept of republicanism itself, where the character of leadership was shaped always by the will of the people *and* a firm commitment to keep that people on its appointed errand. Thus the rhetorical power of the republican ethos but also its complexity: in Jefferson's address, it is a composite image of a leader whose authority comes from being authorized, an individual of unmistakable distinction who is also the symbolic embodiment of a revolutionary people and creed. And that, as Jefferson understood with equal force, requires style.

Republican Propriety

To lead as a republican, Jefferson demonstrated, was to exercise judgment of a kind and to give that judgment expression of a kind. It is this capacity for stylized discernment that accordingly distinguishes the first inaugural address, for in it can be seen the symbolic display of what a republican president ought to think and how he ought to say what he thinks. If a particular vision may be said to animate Jefferson's thought of a free people unfettered by artifice and arbitrary power and if that thought were appropriately communicated with becoming simplicity, then we may ask where these two values intersect with greatest effect. Lest we err by separating the content and form of Jefferson's rhetorical art, we need to press on those dimensions of the text that seem to conjoin these two functions, and it is here, at the nodal point of his performance, that we discover where republican judgment (as manifested in the Jeffersonian ethos) and republican simplicity meet in the principle of *propriety*.

Surely no other statesman of his time was more attuned to questions of proportion than Thomas Jefferson. One need only survey at a glance the range of his activities to be struck by this lifelong preoccupation with measure, balance, decorum, fitness. Whether he was charting out a curriculum for aspirants to the bar, plotting revolution, practicing his violin, designing Monticello, making nails, reflecting on prosody, drafting constitutions, or planning administrative policy, Jefferson was consumed by the problem of what goes appropriately with what. This is above all a style of thought as much as it is thinking about style, and here we find a key for reading the inaugural address as a rhetorical performance. That it shaped his politics is evident throughout the several phases of his public life, especially as he considered what kinds of responses were appropriate to the assertion of power. Prior to the ascent of his party to the executive office, Jefferson's writings on this score were primarily negative. Thus he sought to explain in the Declaration the conditions under which it was fitting for a people, "disposed to suffer, while evils are sufferable," to declare themselves free and independent. So with Shay's rebels he urged leaders "not to be too severe upon their errors, but reclaim them by enlightening them," and that to "punish these errors too severely would be to suppress the only safeguard of the public liberty." Public condemnation of the democratic-republican societies Jefferson called an "extraordinary act of boldness," and the Alien and Sedition Acts "altogether void, and of no force."[28]

In each of these crises, government had been revealed as transgressing what was known to be the proper balance between instituted power and a republican citizenry. Because power, rightful power, could only rest with the people, any attempt to obviate it was on its face suspect, no more clearly than when governments sought to squelch the popular uprising inevitable in a republican country. This was why, as Jefferson famously wrote to Abigail Adams, "I like a little rebellion now and then, it is like a storm in the Atmosphere," and why "this truth should render honest republican governors so mild in their punishment of rebellions, as not to discourage them too much." Governments failing to react mildly lacked that sense of proportion, that principle of propriety, so essential to the faith. At best they assented to the tenets of republicanism, but did not understand what forms of action such conviction entailed. To grasp that distinction was, by contrast, to grasp both essence and practice; it meant that the assertion of principle necessarily implied a course of behavior through which that principle was to be realized to full advantage. Here then is the crux of propriety as a marker of political style: the capacity to arrange all factors in a situation so as to create and sustain the conditions for principled action. It is characterized specifically by a dialectic of assertion and restraint, of saying what must be said but no more and no less.[29]

Jefferson's inaugural address allows us to see this sense of propriety at work in less abstract terms. There he undertakes in two phases to provide a model of reasoning proportionate to the circumstances at hand: in the first, he explicitly indicates which modes of action are attendant to the principles declared; in the second, he defers to the wisdom of the people by conspicuously leaving such prescriptions unstated. But whether stated or implied, the direction of Jefferson's argument remains the same: in all cases of uncertainty, novelty, or crisis, the appropriate response for a republican people is to return to the essential principles of the American experiment. His speech operates accordingly to state those essential principles with the authority granted his person and office, to do so with the utmost simplicity, and to remind his auditors of how they are to compose themselves in view of those principles.

Propriety, like simplicity, is a virtue requiring no little art. It is, for one thing, called for precisely when exigencies are most unsettling and disorganized. Rhetorically speaking, propriety is made more complex because it seems to work best when noticed least. Thus Aristotle observes that when propriety is at stake, the "author should compose without being noticed and should seem to speak not artificially but naturally," for "if one composes well, there will be an unfamiliar quality and it escapes notice and will be clear." This, we may suppose, serves better than most to explain Jefferson's "peculiar felicity of expression." In the specific context of his inaugural address, it characterizes an unfolding process through which principles and the actions they entail are organized with such elegant clarity as to elide their artful management. Bending to the prose more closely, however, we may see that art as clearly as the politics it promotes. In the first phase of this process, Jefferson establishes a recurrent pattern of signification, initially by pointing to a state of instability, then to a principle essential to republican government, and finally to modes of action appropriate to the realization of that principle. The effect, again, is to set on display an example of propriety as both a political and rhetorical virtue.[30]

What, in short, is the proper or fitting response to "the contest of opinion" through which Americans had recently passed? True, so bumptious had been that experience that "strangers" became alarmed and doubted the prospects of republicanism altogether. To this question Jefferson posits the answer by reference to the Constitution and the principle of rule by law. Consequently, he confidently predicts, all will now "arrange themselves" under that rule, will "unite in common efforts for the common good," and "bear in mind" the balance between majority will and minority rights essential to republican government. A similar ordering is evident in Jefferson's portrayal of the international and domestic upheavals shaping the recent decade, when "religious intolerance," "bitter and bloody persecutions," "the throes and convulsions of the ancient world," "the agonizing spasms of infuriated man," and the "agitation of the billows" threatened domestic concord. In the face of these formidable elements, Jefferson again summons the principle of republican government, "the world's best hope." And, again, he underscores what kind of action is fitting to those living within its auspices: they will "fly to the standard of the law," they will "meet invasions of the public" as their own concerns, they will trust themselves with government by themselves. It is, moreover, perfectly consistent with Jefferson's republican propriety that he not elaborate upon nor vilify those who would resist the tide of such government: hence the much-observed tone of conciliation and temperance that shades the address. To do otherwise would on its own terms violate the standards of restraint appropriate to the assertion of republican principle.

Knowing what *not* to say is as key to the exercise of republican propriety as what *must* be said. This much we have seen in the breach with regard to Federalist reactions of the past decade. But the rule suggests something more than tactical prudence, a desire to seem "mild" by contrast to the excesses of one's opponents. Some of this is at work, of course, but the more general assumption has to do with the nature of republican thought itself. In Jefferson's view, at least, the people were naturally inclined to act for the good of themselves and their fellow-citizens; in order to activate this civic virtue, they needed only to see the principle to act on its behalf. In other words, there was no need for dwelling upon differences because the audience was presumptively agreed upon the constants of their collective identity. Indeed, the sheer act of not saying something, of relying upon the implied, the axiomatic, and the silently acknowledged underscores the common sense of the matter being expressed. Having recalled and reorganized the complex of persons, events, and values to their rightful and fitting relationship, Jefferson can now proceed in the address in the most efficient, the most appropriate manner, that is, by simply stating the principles sure to guide his government. In this way, he signals to his audience a complete trust in their capacity to grasp the essence of his (hence their own) thought and to arrange themselves accordingly. Paragraphs three and four thus represent a virtual compendium of republican principles, compressed, as Jefferson says, "within the narrowest compass they will bear." Within such narrow compass no qualifications, "limitations," or hedging are granted because the source, direction, and authority of these principles are already acknowledged by all true republicans. In this case, at least, ideology is made to rest easily within an idiom ideally suited to the needs of the speaker, the audience, and the occasion. Like vessels journeying to sacred shores, each element in Jefferson's universe is bound by common laws, each distinctive in its own right, equidistant to the other, and moving in paths brightened by enlightened humanity. From this perspective, that is fitting which conduces to the forward motion of the republican "Argosie"; that which intervenes or retards this motion could only be the grossest violation of nature and of nature's God.

Republicanism and the Virtues of Simplicity

On the eve of revolution Thomas Paine promised readers of his wildly popular pamphlet "nothing more than simple facts, plain arguments, and common sense." The author delivered on that promise to unprecedented effect, and in the process helped enshrine a key principle of republican letters: "the more simple anything is," Paine averred, "the less liable it is to be disordered." Unlike the tortured and artificially complex style typical of aristocratic prose, republican writing was henceforth to express itself in language that was clear, natural, and unadorned by the linguistic pretensions of his British opponents. How one argued, with what style and tone, was thus not incidental but essential to the politics being argued. As John Quincy Adams later explained, "Our institutions . . . are republican," then "Persuasion, or the influence of reason and feeling, is the great if not the only instrument, whose operation can affect the acts of all our corporate bodies." And if the art of persuasion was to prove up to such a task, it must therefore give to republican government its optimal mode of expression, must express itself in a style that was, as Paine wrote, "simple," "plain," and "common."[31]

No other figure in the early republic better exemplified this style, at once a political and rhetorical virtue, than Thomas Jefferson. His prose was widely acknowledged, as we have seen, for its "felicity of expression," not alone in the Declaration but in the *Summary View,* the *Notes on the State of Virginia,* even in the more strident Kentucky Resolutions. Like comedy, however, simplicity of style is a deceptively difficult achievement, the effect of great discipline and even greater art. He who would seek it, Cicero noted in *De oratore,* "must clothe his thoughts in such a manner as to comprise them in a flow of numbers, at once confined to measure, yet free from restraint; for, after restricting it to proper modulation and structure, he gives it an ease and freedom by a variety in the flow, so that the words are neither bound by strict laws, as those of verse, nor yet have such a degree of liberty as to wander without control." Jefferson, who knew his Cicero well, would have found on his shelves other volumes stressing much the same point; thus Hugh Blair's standard *Lectures on Rhetoric and Belles Lettres* insisted that perspicuity "is the fundamental quality of style, a quality so essential in every kind of writing, that for the want of it, nothing can atone. Without this," Blair concluded, "the richest ornaments of style only glimmer through the dark; and puzzle, instead of pleasing the reader."[32]

The form and content of the first inaugural address cannot, therefore, be put asunder; to grasp its politics is to grasp the style with which it is given expression. There are a variety of ways in which this interplay may be observed, but perhaps one approach will suffice in making the point. As a model of republican simplicity, the speech displays three prominent metaphors; while unobtrusive, these tropes shape and direct the ideological force of the message in important ways. In the image of the *vessel,* the *circle,* and the *road,* Jefferson renders his ideas to striking effect; he thus gives us reason to briefly identify and trace out the entailments of each as evidence of the speaker's rhetorical art.

Several days after delivering his inaugural address, Jefferson assured John Dickinson that "the storm though which we have passed, has been tremendous indeed. The tough sides of our Argosie have been thoroughly tried. Her strength has stood the waves into which she was steered, with a view to sink her." Optimistic as always, Jefferson nevertheless was certain that now "We shall put her on her republican tack, and she will now show by the beauty of her motion the skill of her builders."[33]

The vessel of state was of course a prominent image in eighteenth-century letters, and Jefferson was fond of it, capturing as it did so well the otherwise complex associations of adventure and uncertainty that was the republican experiment. It was altogether appropriate, therefore, that he should employ the metaphor early in the inaugural address:

> To you, then, gentlemen, who are charged with the sovereign functions of legislation, and to those associated with you, I look with encouragement for that guidance and support which may enable us to steer with safety the vessel in which we are all embarked amidst the conflicting elements of a troubled world.

Jefferson, who had little experience with nautical life beyond transport across the Atlantic, nevertheless grasped fully the range and resonance of the image. Here, as below with reference to federal government as "the sheet anchor of our peace at home and safety abroad," the speaker captures in very few words a rich array of meanings. Chief among these is the relationship struck between peril and collective effort; that is, we see in these lines on the one hand the sense of danger and conflict confronting the ship of state, and on the other the prospects for safe passage should captain and crew work harmoniously together. All the opportunities, the riches and success of republican government, Jefferson implies, lay just ahead on the nation's rapidly approaching horizon; without a shared sense of purpose and mutual aid, however, that future must remain clouded and ominous. Given the tempests of the past decade, this image, so simple and yet so resonant, is ideally suited to the speaker's rhetorical purposes.

In the vessel Jefferson found a figure of speech denoting containment as well as expanse, community as well as direction and progress. In the image of the circle, he discovers a means to give this set of dynamics a more abstract but equally forceful expression. Jefferson was, as Ellis has abundantly demonstrated, possessed of a mind given to abstractions of all kinds and not always to happy effect. Certainly he tended to lift from the disorder and debris of experience structures of meaning that could comprehend ever-higher orders of significance; to his critics, this was evidence of a visionary and impractical cast of mind; to his supporters, it was the very stuff of genius. In any case, the figure of the circle gave to Jefferson an equally simple but powerful means to say a great deal in few words:

> what more is necessary to make us a happy and a prosperous people? Still one thing more, fellow-citizens; a wise and frugal Government, which shall restrain men from injuring one another, shall leave them otherwise free to regulate their own pursuits of industry and improvement, and shall not take from the mouth of labor the bread it has earned. This is the sum of good government, and this is necessary to close the circle of our felicities.

As with the vessel metaphor, in the circle we find a wealth of entailments that belies the simplicity of the figure itself. In general we may note that it is at once abstract but universally recognizable; visual but not beholden to contingent experience; at once an ideal form and a concrete image. More specifically, we see how it functions in the passage above to shape complex matter into elegant form. Its usage here serves, like that of the vessel, a double function: it imposes a symmetrical order onto the flux of experience, *and* it does so without appearing to restrain the expansive energies that constitute the life of the nation.

It is worth noting in this regard that the paragraph closed by the "circle of our felicities" is devoted to an aggregation of claims and principles conspicuous for their expansive and transformative tendencies. Jefferson thus closes that circle not as a way of circumscribing his "empire of liberty," but by identifying the form of government necessary for its extension. Hence republicanism gets envisioned as an expanding circle, perfectly ordered, self-evident in its truth, clearly demarcated from what it is not but infinitely capable of containing that which belongs rightfully to it. And it is, of course, an image of politics that will motivate some of the best and worst ambitions of America for centuries to come; for the moment, however, it was to prove as useful, as stylistically and ideologically fitting an image, as might be imagined.

The nautical and geometric tropes at work in this speech give to its message both shape and direction. As a result, they dramatize in their very efficiency of statement what Jefferson envisions of republican government: principles activated by common purpose and formed by historical experience and future aspirations. In their different significations, the vessel and the circle represent variations on this theme of the republican mission. That mission, at once backward- and forward-looking, is further emplotted into the speech through the metaphor of the journey. Again, this is scarcely unique to Jefferson; in fact it is perhaps the single most enduring figure in American rhetorical culture. From the days of the Puritans until this day, the concept of America's errand undergirds virtually every major social, religious, and political transformation to which this nation has been subject. Jefferson's appeal to it would then have been wholly recognizable to his audience, and he could trust his readers and listeners to take from his words precisely what he meant:

> These principles form the bright constellation which has gone before us and guided our steps through an age of revolution and reformation. The wisdom of our sages and blood of our heroes have been devoted to their attainment. They should be the creed of our political faith, the text of civic instruction, the touchstone by which to try the services of those we trust; and should we wander from them in moments of error or of alarm, let us hasten to retrace our steps and to regain the road which alone leads to peace, liberty, and safety.

Here as in the previous two instances, the image of the path or road works on several levels to secure the speaker's intentions. We note, for example, how it reproduces on land what Jefferson earlier alluded to in terms of the sea: that all are gathered as on a journey; that while hazardous, hope is to be found in the wisdom of the people and the principles to which all pay obeisance; and that, ultimately, it is a journey toward a greater world. It is especially important in this context to appreciate Jefferson's stress on what was required to keep Americans on this road or, having fallen off it, what was to return them again.

The principles enunciated in paragraphs two and three are to be read as a "bright constellation," a "creed of our political faith," a "text of civic instruction," a "touchstone." In short, the prospects of republican government are enlightened as the people are enlightened, taught, that is, to see in the rule of law and the values upon which they rest a template for civic action. A secular analogue to the Mosaic tradition, this image of a people guided by the laws to their destined fulfillment takes on poignant dimensions: who more than Americans have been so confident that their journey could in fact be realized? And who among Americans was at once more certain, more anxious, that the new nation "regain the road which alone leads to peace, liberty, and safety" than Thomas Jefferson?

CONCLUSION

To interpret the inaugural address as a rhetorical performance is to seek after its craft, the tactical and artistic management of language to secure the conviction of its auditors. It is not for that reason to isolate the text from its other tasks; Jefferson can be read with equal profit as giving expression to partisan principles and to a certain conception of nationhood. The rhetorical work of the text is to consolidate and give force to those principles, even as it exemplifies them through the strategic choice of words, images, and appeals. I have sought in this essay to demonstrate the nuances of Jefferson's art of effective expression; to that end, we have examined the text with reference to the traditions of which he availed himself, including sermons, civic commemorations, and political debate. The task has been made more challenging by acknowledging that Jefferson's own relation to the rhetorical arts generally was complex, specifically that he cannot be considered in any normal sense an orator as such. But we have seen that this need not limit access to the ambitions at work behind the speech nor its exquisite rendering of principle. If anything, close attention to the internal and external energies circulating through can only confirm the judgment of posterity that here we have an unmistakable masterpiece.

Jefferson's rhetorical art has not always and everywhere been met with unalloyed enthusiasm. Critics in his own time took him to task for stylistic pretension and partisan stealth, for speaking in airy abstractions and self-serving platitudes. Charles Francis Adams later could charge that Jefferson "has left hanging over a part of his public life a vapor of duplicity, or, to say the least, of indirection, the presence of which is generally felt more than it is seen." More damningly, the redoubtable Carl Becker granted Jefferson's "felicity of expression," but noted too that such felicity "gives one at times a certain feeling of insecurity, as of resting one's weight on something fragile. Jefferson's placidity," Becker concluded, "the complacent optimism of his sentiments and ideas, carry him at times perilously near the fatuous. One would like more evidence that the iron had some time or other entered his soul, more evidence of having profoundly reflected on the enigma of existence, of having more deeply felt its tragic import, of having won his convictions and his optimisms and his felicities at the expense of some travail of the spirit." Becker's insight is keen: in his rhetorical craft as in his thought, Jefferson could appear almost too eloquent, as if in the finely crafted sentiment he could make the world over again, in his image, to his own satisfaction, heedless of others.[34]

Perhaps. Without dismissing such suspicions, it may be worth reflecting as well on what it is that animates not only the performance but our abiding interest in it. To ask that question is to ask after the man himself and, ultimately, the cultural forces that sustain the speech on the winds of history. That much is beyond the scope of this essay, but we have at least the beginnings of an answer here. The "faculty of observing in any given case the available means of persuasion" to which Aristotle alluded was Jefferson's own. With it, he discerned like no one else what was lasting in the American soul; here was the source and object of his words, and with them he eloquently summoned his fellow republicans to a better version of themselves.

NOTES

[1]Henry Adams, *History of the United States of America,* 2 vols. (New York: Charles Scribner's Sons, 1889), 1:196.

[2]As based on the text in *Thomas Jefferson: Writings,* ed. Merrill Peterson (New York: Library of America, 1984), 492–96. For purposes of convenience, all further citations of the inaugural address are to this edition; *Independent Chronicle,* March 3, 1801, 2; Du Pont de Nemours to Thomas Jefferson, in *Correspondence Between Thomas Jefferson and Pierre Samuel Du Pont Nemours, 1798–1817,* ed. Dumas Malone, trans. Linwood Lehman (Boston and New York: Mifflin Co., 1930), 30; Thomas Jefferson to James Monroe, quoted in George Tucker, *The Life of Thomas Jefferson* (Philadelphia: Carey, Lea, and Blanchard, 1837), 1:xi.

[3]Tucker, *The Life of Thomas Jefferson,* 2:85; Henry Randall, *The Life of Thomas Jefferson* (New York: Derby and Jackson, 1858), 633.

[4]Tom Watson, *The Life and Times of Thomas Jefferson* (New York: D. Appleton and Co., 1903), 398; Woodrow Wilson, quoted in "Jefferson-Wilson: A Record and a Forecast," *North American Review* 197 (1913): 291; Fawn M. Brodie, *Thomas Jefferson: An Intimate History* (New York: W. W. Norton, 1974), 336; Peter S. Onuf, *Jefferson's Empire: The Language of American Nationhood* (Charlottesville: University Press of Virginia, 2000), 106.

[5]*North American Review* 45 (1850): 445.

[6]Joyce Oldham Appleby, *Inheriting the Revolution: The First Generation of Americans* (Cambridge: Harvard University Press, 2000).

[7]Appleby, *First Generation,* 36; Gordon Wood, *The Radicalism of the American Revolution* (New York: Alfred Knopf, 1992), 363.

[8]For a succinct account of Jefferson's religious thought, see especially Paul Conkin, "The Religious Pilgrimage of Thomas Jefferson," in *Jeffersonian Legacies,* ed. Peter Onuf (Charlottesville: University Press of Virginia, 1993), 19–49.

[9]Thomas Jefferson to Henry Lee, May 8, 1825, in Peterson, *Writings,* 1501.

[10]John Winthrop, "A Model of Christian Charity," in *American Rhetorical Discourse,* ed. Ronald F. Reid (Prospect Heights, Ill.: Waveland Press, 1988), 34; Israel Evans, "A Sermon, Delivered at Concord," in *Political Sermons of the Founding Era, 1730–1805,* ed. Ellis Sandoz (Indianapolis: Liberty Press, 1991), 1077; on the theme of America as a chosen people, see especially Sacvan Bercovitch, *Rites of Assent: Transformations in the Symbolic Construction of America* (New York: Routledge, 1993).

[11]Samuel Danforth, "Errand into the Wilderness,["] in Reid, *American Rhetorical Discourse,* 51; Samuel Miller, "A Sermon, Preached in New-York," in Sandoz, *Political Sermons,* 1166.

[12]Jonathan Mayhew, "The Snare Broken," in Sandoz, *Political Sermons,* 262; David Tappan, "A Sermon Preached Before His excellency John Hancock, Esq.," in Sandoz, *Political Sermons,* 1126.

[13]David Waldstreicher, *'In the Midst of Perpetual Fetes': The Making of American Nationalism, 1776–1820* (Chapel Hill: University of North Carolina Press, 1997), 12.

[14]James M. Farrell, book review, *Rhetoric & Public Affairs* 2 (1999): 148.

[15]Kenneth Silverman, *A Cultural History of the American Revolution* (New York, Crowell, 1976), 605.

[16]*Aurora,* March 18, 1801, 2; quoted in *Connecticut Courant,* June 22, 1801, 1.

[17]Benedict Anderson, *Imagined Communities: Reflections on the Origin and Spread of Nationalism* (New York: Verso, 1993), 44.

[18]Waldstreicher, *Perpetual Fetes,* chaps. 3–4.

[19]Bernard Bailyn, *The Ideological Origins of the American Revolution* (Cambridge: Harvard University Press, 1974), 1.

[20]Joseph Ellis, *Founding Brothers: The Revolutionary Generation* (New York: Alfred Knopf, 2000), 68.

[21]Stephen E. Lucas, "Genre Criticism and Historical Context: The Case of George Washington's First Inaugural Address," *Southern Speech Communication Journal* 51 (1986): 363, 368.

[22]Quoted in Dumas Malone, *Jefferson the Virginian* (Boston: Little, Brown, and Co., 1948), 391; Wood, "Trials and Tribulations of Thomas Jefferson," in Onuf, *Legacies,* 401.

[23]John Adams, in Charles Francis Adams, *Works of John Adams* (Boston: Little, Brown, and Co., 1856), 2:514; Carl Becker, *The Declaration of Independence: A Study in the History of Political Ideas* (New York: Vintage Books, 1942), 196.

[24]*North American Review* 31 (1830): 34; Joseph Ellis, *American Sphinx: The Character of Thomas Jefferson* (New York: Vintage, 1998), 225.

[25]George A. Kennedy, *Aristotle on Rhetoric: A Theory of Civic Discourse* (New York: Oxford University Press, 1991), 38.

[26]Thomas Jefferson to Philip Mazzei, April 24, 1796, in Peterson, *Writings,* 1036.

[27]Thomas Jefferson to Joseph Priestly, March 21, 1801, in Peterson, *Writings,* 1086.

[28]Thomas Jefferson, Declaration of Independence, in Peterson, *Writings,* 19; Jefferson to Edward Carrington, January 16, 1787, in Peterson, *Writings,* 880; Jefferson to James Madison, December 28, 1794, in Peterson, *Writings,* 1015; Jefferson, Draft of Kentucky Resolutions, in Peterson, *Writings,* 451.

[29]Thomas Jefferson to Abigail Adams, February 22, 1787, in Peterson, *Writings,* 890.

[30]Kennedy, *Aristotle on Rhetoric*, 222.

[31]Thomas Paine, "Common Sense," in Reid, *American Rhetorical Discourse*, 121; John Quincy Adams, *Lectures on Rhetoric and Oratory* (Delmar: Scholars' Facsimile's and Reprints, 1997), 10.

[32]Cicero, *De Oratore*, in *Readings in Classical Rhetoric*, ed. Thomas W. Benson and Michael Prosser (Davis, Calif.: Hermagoras Press, 1987), 224, 243; Blair, quoted in James L. Golden and Edward P. J. Corbett, *The Rhetoric of Blair, Campbell, and Whately* (New York: Holt, Rinehart, and Winston, 1968), 67.

[33]Thomas Jefferson to John Dickinson, March 6, 1801, in Peterson, *Writings*, 1084.

[34]Charles Francis Adams, *Works of John Adams*, 616; Becker, *Declaration of Independence*, 218–19.

Chapter III

Close Textual Analysis

Close textual analysis studies the relationship between the inner workings of public discourse and its historical context in order to discover what makes a particular text function persuasively. To some extent, close textual analysis, or "close reading," is a reaction to the highly theoretical approaches to rhetorical criticism that proliferated in the 1970s. Opposing this trend, scholars such as Michael Leff and G. P. Mohrmann argue that rhetorical criticism should focus more on the "actual conduct of discourse," rather than "the generation of abstract methods."[1] In practical terms, close textual analysis aims to reveal and explicate the precise, often hidden, mechanisms that give a particular text artistic unity and rhetorical effect.

Michael Leff analyzes the central importance of time as a rhetorical element in "Dimensions of Temporality in Lincoln's Second Inaugural," published in 1988. Leff notes that many of Lincoln's most important speeches follow a clear chronological pattern. He argues that time is not merely a standard organizational device, but essential to the internal dynamics of the speech. In the Second Inaugural, Lincoln shifts from a "perspective grounded in secular time to one grounded in sacred time." The merging of the secular and sacred is accomplished through the "timing in the text itself." In other words, the internal sequence of the speech prepares the listener for the thematic transition.

Stephen E. Lucas takes another perspective on close textual analysis in his 1990 essay "The Stylistic Artistry of the Declaration of Independence." Lucas seeks to illustrate the ingenuity of the Declaration by "probing the discourse microscopically— at the level of the sentence, phrase, word, and syllable." His approach reveals the Declaration both as a literary masterpiece and as pragmatic communication designed to justify the move for independence. Lucas claims the Declaration is comprised of five major propositions that interlock and culminate in the conclusion that independence is justified. Moreover, he argues, the Declaration "sustains an almost perfect synthesis of style, form, and content." All the factors work together flawlessly to "contribute to its rhetorical power."

Edwin Black's 1994 article "Gettysburg and Silence" illustrates another approach to close textual analysis. Black argues that Abraham Lincoln's "Gettysburg Address" should be understood as "prismatic." In other words, the elements of Lincoln's speech "reflect back and forth on one another" in such a manner that the text can be appreciated both for its indivisibility and for its many-sidedness. Using the metaphor of the prism, Black endeavors to examine the facets of the speech one at a time. In order to understand how Lincoln's famous address functions persuasively, Black maintains, the critic must study the "details."

NOTES

[1] Michael Leff, "Textual Criticism: The Legacy of G. P. Mohrmann," *Quarterly Journal of Speech*, 72 (1986), 377–389.

DIMENSIONS OF TEMPORALITY
IN LINCOLN'S SECOND INAUGURAL

MICHAEL LEFF

Many of Lincoln's best remembered orations, including the House Divided Speech, the Cooper Union Address, and the Gettysburg Address, exhibit a clear pattern of temporal organization. The introductory remarks establish an orientation divided into past, present, and future, and then the three tenses reappear in the body of the speech, each marking out one of its major divisions. Close reading demonstrates that this progression is more than a device for separating the gross structural units of these discourses. Temporal movement, in fact, seems essential to their rhetorical economy; it frames the action of the various argumentative and stylistic elements, blends them into a unified field of textual action, and projects this field onto the public events that form the subject of the discourse (Leff and Mohrmann, 1974; Leff, 1983; Thurow, 1976, pp. 70–86; Warnick, 1987, pp. 236–239).

Nowhere is this pattern more evident or developed with greater skill than in the Second Inaugural. Yet, the temporal inflections that guide the text are not generally acknowledged in the existing critical literature. The reason, I believe, is that, despite its status as a masterpiece of eloquence, the speech has not often been studied as an artistic whole. Instead the critical focus has centered either on the historical context or on isolated sections that illustrate Lincoln's character or his excellence as a stylist.

Two recent studies attempt to remedy this defect. In a master's thesis devoted entirely to the text, Amy Slagell (1986) presents a careful and expert analysis of its rhetorical structure. And in his book, *Abraham Lincoln and American Political Religion*, Glen E. Thurow (1976) explicates Lincoln's political philosophy through a systematic reading of a number of his orations, including the Second Inaugural (pp. 88–108). Both studies demonstrate that the arrangement of temporal units directs the symbolic movement of the text and that no adequate interpretation can disregard this chronological pattern. My own analysis relies heavily on these earlier works, but I wish to extend and complicate their findings in two respects: first, I will argue that the speech builds to a creative equivocation in the middle of the third paragraph, an equivocation that blends the historical present into a conception of a sacred present; second, I hope to show that this conflation is central to the form of the speech and serves as the vehicle for sustaining its major themes. To establish these claims, I must review the text in the order of its presentation.

The opening paragraph contains no striking ideas or stylistic flourishes; in fact, it has a somewhat awkward appearance. Yet, it seems carefully constructed to achieve Lincoln's purposes and to establish the framework and tone for the speech as a whole. Most obviously, Lincoln introduces the temporal markers that define his perspective. The first sentence contrasts the present occasion with his previous inaugural. The second sentence refers to the past, the third and fourth to the present, and the final sentence looks fo[r]ward to the future. The same pattern resurfaces in the body of the address: the second paragraph and the first seven sentences of the third deal with the past; the remainder of that paragraph deals with the present, and the concluding paragraph offers advice for future conduct. (See Thurow, pp. 91–92, for a generally similar but more detailed account of the structure of the opening paragraph.)

On a more subtle level, the paragraph establishes a relentless tone of passivity and self-effacement. The first person pronoun occurs only twice (and never again appears anywhere in the speech). And the whole is constructed in what Slagell (p. 11) aptly calls the impersonal passive. The first sentence, for example, reads: "At this second appearing to take the oath of the presidential office, there is less occasion for an extended address than there was at the first" (Basler, 1953, p. 332; all quotations from the speech refer to this edition). The wording here contrasts sharply with the more personal and direct language of the First Inaugural. And, of course, Lincoln could have made his point more simply by recasting the sentence in a form such as this: On this occasion, I have less need to make an extended address than I did four years ago. But to speak in this way would suggest an orator striving to take command of the situation. Instead, Lincoln creates the impression that the occasion commands him, that it renders him captive and passive. This passive tone recurs throughout the speech.

The second paragraph refers to the past, as Lincoln recounts the circumstances surrounding his earlier inaugural and the outbreak of the war. The prose now changes markedly; it becomes subject to the nuances of artistic control and glides forward through elegantly balanced clauses. Apparently, the orator has gained command of his material, but he has done so only to articulate the passive frame through which he would have us view the historic drama. His point achieves sublime expression as the paragraph rolls to its conclusion: "Both parties deprecated war, but one of them would make war rather than let the nation survive; and the other would accept war rather than let it perish. And the war came." The cadence of this passage instantiates its message. The final clause seems to follow of necessity from what precedes it, even as the war was an inevitable event, manifesting itself regardless of the intentions of the parties involved.

The third paragraph lingers in the past, as Lincoln considers the causes and consequences of the war. Once again events have outrun conscious intentions: "Neither party expected for the war, the magnitude, or the duration, which it has already attained. Neither anticipated that the cause of the conflict might cease with, or even before, the conflict itself should cease. Each looked for an easier triumph, and a result less astounding." With these words, Lincoln completes his history of frustrated political and military efforts. The constraints are everywhere and apply to everyone. Just as Lincoln himself stands passive in the face of the occasion, so also the North and South were made to accept a war they sought to avoid and to suffer consequences they did not anticipate.

It is at this point, in the midst of the third paragraph, that Lincoln changes his temporal orientation. The shift occurs abruptly, and to appreciate it, we must return to the lines quoted immediately above and then attend to the next sentence in the text: "Neither [party] *anticipated* that the cause of the war might cease with, or even before, the conflict should cease. Each *looked* for an easier triumph, and a result less astounding. Both *read* the same Bible, and *pray* to the same God; and each *invokes* His aid against the other" (my emphasis). The italicized verbs indicate how Lincoln suddenly shifts from the past to the present tense, and without benefit of any perceptible transition, Lincoln moves from historic to present considerations. Equally important, Lincoln's perspective begins to change from the secular to the sacred. Up to this moment, the speaker has remained strictly within the confines of secular events, but from this first reference to the Bible through the end of the speech, he becomes sermonic; virtually every sentence quotes, paraphrases, or alludes to a passage in scripture.

Lincoln begins this section mindful of the divisions existing in the current historical situation. He stresses the competitive solicitation of divine aid by the warring parties, and in the ensuing sentence, he verges toward a partisan judgment: "It may seem strange that any men should dare to ask a just God's assistance in wringing their bread from the sweat of other men's faces." The sentence paraphrases Genesis 3:19, where God, casting Adam from Eden, declares that "In the sweat of thy face shalt thou eat bread. . . ." Thus, the South seems the culpable party, for it has sinned by resisting the curse God placed upon all mankind. And at this stage, we might anticipate a call for retribution. But Lincoln quickly arrests the partisan direction of his argument. Paraphrasing Mathew [sic] 7:1, he says "let us judge not that we be not judged."

The reference to Mathew draws the text deeply within a religious context. Lincoln has stepped well outside the immediate historical situation, has departed from the political frame which previously governed his remarks. Yet, in an important sense, the text retains a certain logical and emotional consistency. The speaker has prepared us for this transformation. In the previous section, he had argued that the war followed a course of its own; it resisted the plans and purposes of those caught up in its sweep. This understanding of the past almost mandates a present attitude directed toward the supernatural. What men cannot control, they cannot fully comprehend, and the meaning of the war, therefore, must be gauged against something that transcends the tangible interests of the two sides. The prayers of neither, Lincoln observes, have "been fully answered. The Almighty [has] his own purposes."

The war, then, represents a divine intervention in human history. It is evidence of a mystery that recurrently plays its way through human affairs. And as the orator considers this mystery, his prose remains fixed within the sacred order, his perspective located in a time beyond the flow of historic events. Quoting Mathew 8:7, Lincoln argues that slavery was an offence which came in the providence of God and continued through His appointed time. And in language that recalls the passion of Christ, Lincoln characterizes the war as a "mighty scourge," an instrument of atonement applied equally to North and South. Thus, the nation has endured redemptive suffering as it has lived through the drama of sin and mortification. It has shared the offence and the punishment meted out in God's time; all have participated in this mysterious relationship between man and God, which renders men responsible for their acts but unable to control their results. The war, then, offers no occasion for human judgment which would encourage one party to inflict further retribution on the other; it is itself a judgment from a higher source, and a redemptive vehicle that, like Christ's passion, purifies and opens the path to unity through spiritual rebirth. The whole process transcends the narrow limits of human understanding, and in the end, we can only accept the fact that, "as was said three thousand years ago, so still it must be said, 'the judgments of the Lord are true and righteous altogether.'"

In sum, Lincoln has shifted both from political to religious themes and from a perspective grounded in secular time to one grounded in sacred time. The thematic shift is obvious and relatively easy to explain. Given the magnitude of the events and Lincoln's immediate political goals, reference to divine purposes seems a logical, if not necessary, strategy. Moreover, as Ernest Bormann (1977) has demonstrated, a religious justification for secular disaster was a standard item in the repertoire of American political orators.

The temporal shift is much more subtle and demands special attention. In order to appreciate its significance, we must first consider the characteristic differences between secular and sacred time. As Eliade (1959) explains the matter, secular time proceeds in a single direction; it is homogeneous, continuous, and irreversible. Sacred time, on the other hand, calls us to a moment of origins; it is a "primordial mythical time made present," and this presence effects an immediate and total unification of the field of experience (pp. 68–69). It manifests itself recurrently as an interruption in our normal sense of temporality, and thus sacred time is cyclical and discontinuous; it is something always there that we occasionally recover.

It follows that our sense of present time is potentially ambiguous. On the secular level, it is an irreversible moment, of somewhat arbitrary duration, that divides past from future. On the sacred level, however, the present becomes recoverable as a return to origins, as an eternal now, a still moment when primal truths emerge in a chang[e]less pattern. It is possible, in fact normal, to overcome this ambiguity by dividing the two into wholly separate categories. Thus, the sacred, because it has no progressivity, becomes atemporal, and it can serve as a fixed standard for judging the flux of local circumstance. Nevertheless, the experience of the sacred seems explicable only in terms of our experience of something that occurs in normal time—the attention to what is now before us as opposed to what has happened before or will happen later. Perhaps for just this reason, we define the sacred in terms of that which occurs now, in terms of a radically present experience. Consequently, both semantically and conceptually, it is possible to weaken the conventional dichotomy between the temporal and atemporal and to effect at least a partial conflation between the historical present and the present-ness of sacred insight.

This creative equivocation is, I believe, the mainspring of the "Second Inaugural." Lincoln's purpose in the speech is to develop a frame of passive acceptance, a perspective capable of accounting for the horrors of the war and of justifying a conciliatory post-war policy. These purposes almost demand a tra[n]scendental strategy, but they do not permit a simple rejection of worldly affairs. A mere imposition of the sacred on the secular would not suffice to encompass the situation. Thus, Lincoln does not juxtapose these contexts, but makes the sacred appear to evolve from the secular, preserving their distinction while leaving them in a state of organic connection. In fact, the whole economy of the speech seems designed to achieve this elision of temporal perspectives. The studiously awkward language of the opening section suggests a present occasion that commands rather than challenges the resources of the speaker. The narration of past events discloses a force at work that confounds human intentions and passes beyond political understanding. Then, in the crucial third paragraph, the past glides into the present as though through its own momentum, and in the historical present, we see the impact of a past that we cannot comprehend on its own terms—a nation divided into two rival factions suffering blindly and issuing unanswered prayers. We are thus forced to contemplate a presence that exceeds our normal temporal experience. Repeatively and progressively, the text coaxes historical time to a point where it rises outside its own horizons. It imparts a character and movement to secular events that render them comprehensible only by reference to an enlarged and passive vision of divine purposes. The frame of acceptance, then, appears less a construction of the speaker than a residue of history; it is an atemporal insight forced upon us by an historical understanding of the limits of human history.

To put this point somewhat differently, Lincoln seems to merge secular time into sacred time through the use of still another dimension of temporality—the timing in the text itself. The text, that is, gathers its ideas, images, and rhythms in a sequence that prepares the auditor to regard the connection between the secular and the sacred as an inevitable process. The two temporal frames remain distinct; yet they seem to inform one another and to co-operate in imparting meaning to events. The mediation between these frames is effected by the rhetorical action of the text itself, which embodies the connection and, in doing so, induces us to accept its plausibility as an explanation of the moral significance of political events.

In the final paragraph, Lincoln turns to the future as he urges his listeners to "strive on to finish the work we are in." The temporal order, then, is moved forward, but in a way that blurs different temporal perspectives. Lincoln does not enumerate specific policies; instead he recommends the elemental virtues of Christianity—the avoidance of malice, the exercise of charity, the binding of wounds, the protection of the unfortunate, and the search for a just and lasting peace (For the scriptural echoes in this passage, see Slagell, pp. 51–54). Clearly, this is a future informed by the orator's vision of the eternal present. The tone of meditation, of spiritual reverie, continues, and Lincoln's language has not fully re-entered the directional flow of secular time. Yet, in the immediate political context, this paragraph indirectly but powerfully articulates a policy; it justifies a course of conciliation and repudiates the more vindicative and partisan stance adopted by many in Lincoln's own party. Thus, the speech ends with a secular prayer that blends the sacred frame of acceptance into the fabric of local political action.

Lincoln did not live to implement his policy; his successor was impeached for attempting to do so, and in the course of time, policy came to be formulated under the sign of the scape-goat rather than the cross. Whatever the turn of events, however, the Second Inaugural retains the power of its mode of articulation. The speech is a verbal act that embodies the limitations of human action. In the perfection of its utterance, it yields to the imperfections of the human condition, and by yielding, transcends them. Lincoln well understood the limits of any single voice in influencing the course of political history. That understanding permeates the speech, drives its symbolic action forward, and leads its author to a mood of reverie from which he only partially returns.

REFERENCES

Basler, R., ed. (1953). *The collected works of Abraham Lincoln.* Vol. 8. New Brunswick: Rutgers University Press.

Bormann, E. (1977). Fetching good out of evil: A rhetorical use of calamity. *Quarterly Journal of Speech.* 63. 130–139.

Eliade, M. (1959). *The sacred and the profane: The Nature of Religion.* New York: Harcourt, Brace, Jovanovich.

Leff, M. & Mohrmann, G. P. (1974). Lincoln at Cooper Union: A rhetorical analysis of the text. *Quarterly Journal of Speech.* 60. 346–358.

Leff, M. (1983). Rhetorical timing in Lincoln's House Divided speech. Van Zelst Lecture in Communication. Evanston: Northwestern University.

Slagell, A. (1986). *A textual analysis of Abraham Lincoln's Second Inaugural Address.* M.A. Thesis: University of Wisconsin–Madison.

Thurow, G. (1976). *Abraham Lincoln and American political religion.* Albany: State University of New York Press.

Warnick, B. (1987). A Ricoeurian approach to rhetorical criticism. *Western Journal of Speech Communication.* 51. 227–244.

THE STYLISTIC ARTISTRY
OF THE DECLARATION OF INDEPENDENCE

STEPHEN E. LUCAS

The Declaration of Independence is perhaps the most masterfully written state paper of Western civilization. As Moses Coit Tyler noted almost a century ago, no assessment of it can be complete without taking into account its extraordinary merits as a work of political prose style. Although many scholars have recognized those merits, there are surprisingly few sustained studies of the stylistic artistry of the Declaration.[1] This essay seeks to illuminate that artistry by probing the discourse microscopically—at the level of the sentence, phrase, word, and syllable. By approaching the Declaration in this way, we can shed light both on its literary qualities and on its rhetorical power as a work designed to convince a "candid world" that the American colonies were justified in seeking to establish themselves as an independent nation.[2]

The text of the Declaration can be divided into five sections—the introduction, the preamble, the indictment of George III, the denunciation of the British people, and the conclusion. Because space does not permit us to explicate each section in full detail, we shall select features from each that illustrate the stylistic artistry of the Declaration as a whole.[3]

The introduction consists of the first paragraph—a single, lengthy, periodic sentence:

> When in the course of human events, it becomes necessary for one people to dissolve the political bands which have connected them with another, and to assume among the powers of the earth, the separate and equal station to which the Laws of Nature and of Nature's God entitle them, a decent respect to the opinions of mankind requires that they should declare the causes which impel them to the separation.[4]

Taken out of context, this sentence is so general it could be used as the introduction to a declaration by any "oppressed" people. Seen within its original context, however, it is a model of subtlety, nuance, and implication that works on several levels of meaning and allusion to orient readers toward a favorable view of America and to prepare them for the rest of the Declaration. From its magisterial opening phrase, which sets the American Revolution within the whole "course of human events," to its assertion that "the Laws of Nature and of Nature's God" entitle America to a "separate and equal station among the powers of the earth," to its quest for sanction from "the opinions of mankind," the introduction elevates the quarrel with England from a petty political dispute to a major event in the grand sweep of history. It dignifies the Revolution as a contest of principle and implies that the American cause has a special claim to moral legitimacy—all without mentioning England or America by name.

Rather than defining the Declaration's task as one of persuasion, which would doubtless raise the defenses of readers as well as imply that there was more than one publicly credible view of the British-American conflict, the introduction identifies the purpose of the Declaration as simply to "declare"—to announce publicly in explicit terms—the "causes" impelling America to leave the British empire. This gives the Declaration, at the outset, an aura of philosophical (in the eighteenth-century sense of the term) objectivity that it will seek to maintain throughout. Rather than presenting one side in a public controversy on which good and decent people could differ, the Declaration purports to do no more than a natural philosopher would do in reporting the causes of any physical event. The issue, it implies, is not one of interpretation but of observation.

The most important word in the introduction is "necessary," which in the eighteenth century carried strongly deterministic overtones. To say an act was necessary implied that it was impelled by fate or determined by the operation of inextricable natural laws and was beyond the control of human agents. Thus Chambers's *Cyclopedia* defined "necessary" as "that which cannot but be, or cannot be otherwise." "The common notion of necessity and impossibility," Jonathan Edwards wrote in *Freedom of the Will,* "implies something that frustrates endeavor or desire. . . . That is necessary in the original and proper sense of the word, which is, or will be, notwithstanding all supposable opposition." Characterizing the Revolution as necessary suggested that it resulted from constraints that operated with lawlike force throughout the material universe and within the sphere of human action. The Revolution was not merely preferable, defensible, or justifiable. It was as inescapable, as inevitable, as unavoidable within the course of human events as the motions of the tides or the changing of the seasons within the course of natural events.[5]

Investing the Revolution with connotations of necessity was particularly important because, according to the law of nations, recourse to war was lawful only when it became "necessary"—only when amicable negotiation had failed and all other alternatives for settling the differences between two states had been exhausted. Nor was the burden of necessity limited to monarchs and established nations. At the start of the English Civil War in 1642, Parliament defended its recourse to military action against Charles I in a lengthy declaration demonstrating the "Necessity to take up Arms." Following this tradition, in July 1775 the Continental Congress issued its own Declaration Setting Forth the Causes and Necessity of Their Taking Up Arms. When, a year later, Congress decided the colonies could no longer retain their liberty within the British empire, it adhered to long-established rhetorical convention by describing independence as a matter of absolute and inescapable necessity.[6] Indeed, the notion of necessity was so important that in addition to appearing in the introduction of the Declaration, it was invoked twice more at crucial junctures in the rest of the text and appeared frequently in other congressional papers after July 4, 1776.[7]

Labeling the Americans "one people" and the British "another" was also laden with implication and performed several important strategic functions within the Declaration. First, because two alien peoples cannot be made one, it reinforced the notion that breaking the "political bands" with England was a necessary step in the course of human events. America and England were already separated by the more basic fact that they had become two different peoples. The gulf between them was much more than political; it was intellectual, social, moral, cultural and, according to the principles of nature, could no more be repaired, as Thomas Paine said, than one could "restore to us the time that is past" or "give to prostitution its former innocence." To try to perpetuate a purely political connection would be "forced and unnatural," "repugnant to reason, to the universal order of things."[8]

Second, once it is granted that Americans and Englishmen are two distinct peoples, the conflict between them is less likely to be seen as a civil war. The Continental Congress knew America could not withstand Britain's military might without foreign assistance. But they also knew America could not receive assistance as long as the colonies were fighting a civil war as part of the British empire. To help the colonies would constitute interference in Great Britain's internal affairs. As Samuel Adams explained, "no foreign Power can consistently yield Comfort to Rebels, or enter into any kind of Treaty with these Colonies till they declare themselves free and independent." The crucial factor in opening the way for foreign aid was the act of declaring independence. But by defining America and England as two separate peoples, the Declaration reinforced the perception that the conflict was not a civil war, thereby, as Congress noted in its debates on independence, making it more "consistent with European delicacy for European powers to treat with us, or even to receive an Ambassador."[9]

Third, defining the Americans as a separate people in the introduction eased the task of invoking the right of revolution in the preamble. That right, according to eighteenth-century revolutionary principles, could be invoked only in the most dire of circumstances when "resistance was absolutely necessary in order to preserve the nation from slavery, misery, and ruin"—and then only by "the Body of the People." If America and Great Britain were seen as one people, Congress could not justify revolution against the British government for the simple reason that the body of the people (of which the Americans would be only one part) did not support the American cause. For America to move against the government in such circumstances would not be a justifiable act of resistance but "a sort of Sedition, Tumult, and War . . . aiming only at the satisfaction of private Lust, without regard to the public Good." By defining the Americans as a separate people, Congress could more readily satisfy the requirement for invoking the right of revolution that "the whole Body of Subjects" rise up against the government "to rescue themselves from the most violent and illegal oppressions."[10]

Like the introduction, the next section of the Declaration—usually referred to as the preamble—is universal in tone and scope. It contains no explicit reference to the British-American conflict, but outlines a general philosophy of government that makes revolution justifiable, even meritorious:

> We hold these truths to be self-evident, that all men are created equal, that they are endowed by their Creator with certain unalienable Rights, that among these are Life, Liberty and the pursuit of Happiness. That to secure these rights, Governments are instituted among Men, deriving their just powers from the consent of the governed. That whenever any Form of Government becomes destructive of these ends, it is the Right of the People to alter or to abolish it, and to institute new Government, laying its foundation on such principles and organizing its powers in such form, as to them shall seem most likely to effect their Safety and Happiness. Prudence, indeed, will dictate that Governments long established should not be changed for light and transient causes; and accordingly all experience hath shown that mankind are more disposed to suffer, while evils are sufferable, than to right themselves by abolishing the forms to which they are accustomed. But when a long train of abuses and usurpations, pursuing invariably the same Object evinces a design to reduce them under absolute Despotism, it is their right, it is their duty, to throw off such Government, and to provide new Guards for their future security.

Like the rest of the Declaration, the preamble is "brief, free of verbiage, a model of clear, concise, simple statement."[11] It capsulizes in five sentences—202 words— what it took John Locke thousands of words to explain in his *Second Treatise of Government*. Each word is chosen and placed to achieve maximum impact. Each clause is indispensable to the progression of thought. Each sentence is carefully constructed internally and in relation to what precedes and follows. In its ability to compress complex ideas into a brief, clear statement, the preamble is a paradigm of eighteenth-century Enlightenment prose style, in which purity, simplicity, directness, precision, and, above all, perspicuity were the highest rhetorical and literary virtues. One word follows another with complete inevitability of sound and meaning. Not one word can be moved or replaced without disrupting the balance and harmony of the entire preamble.

The stately and dignified tone of the preamble—like that of the introduction—comes partly from what the eighteenth century called Style Periodique, in which, as Hugh Blair explained in his *Lectures on Rhetoric and Belles Lettres,* "the sentences are composed of several members linked together, and hanging upon one another, so that the sense of the whole is not brought out till the close." This, Blair said, "is the most pompous, musical, and oratorical manner of composing" and "gives an air of gravity and dignity to composition." The gravity and dignity of the preamble were reinforced by its conformance with the rhetorical precept that "when we aim at dignity or elevation, the sound [of each sentence] should be made to grow to the last; the longest members of the period, and the fullest and most sonorous words, should be reserved to the conclusion." None of the sentences of the preamble end on a single-syllable word; only one, the second (and least euphonious), ends on a two-syllable word. Of the other four, one ends with a four-syllable word ("security"), while three end with three-syllable words. Moreover, in each of the three-syllable words the closing syllable is at least a medium-length four-letter syllable, which helps bring the sentences to "a full and harmonious close."[12]

It is unlikely that any of this was accidental. Thoroughly versed in classical oratory and rhetorical theory as well as in the belletristic treatises of his own time, Thomas Jefferson, draftsman of the Declaration, was a diligent student of rhythm, accent, timing, and cadence in discourse. This can be seen most clearly in his "Thoughts on English Prosody," a remarkable twenty-eight-page unpublished essay written in Paris during the fall of 1786. Prompted by a discussion on language with the Marquis de Chastellux at Monticello four years earlier, it was a careful inquiry designed "to find out the real circumstance which gives harmony to English prose and laws to those who make it." Using roughly the same system of diacritical notation he had employed in 1776 in his reading draft of the Declaration, Jefferson systematically analyzed the patterns of accentuation in a wide range of English writers, including Milton, Pope, Shakespeare, Addison, Gray, and Garth. Although "Thoughts on English Prosody" deals with poetry, it displays Jefferson's keen sense of the interplay between sound and sense in language. There can be little doubt that, like many accomplished writers, he consciously composed for the ear as well as for the eye—a trait that is nowhere better illustrated than in the eloquent cadences of the preamble in the Declaration of Independence.[13]

The preamble also has a powerful sense of structural unity. This is achieved partly by the latent chronological progression of thought, in which the reader is moved from the creation of mankind, to the institution of government, to the throwing off of government when it fails to protect the people's unalienable rights, to the creation of new government that will better secure the people's safety and happiness. This dramatic scenario, with its first act implicitly set in the Garden of Eden (where man was "created equal"), may, for some readers, have contained mythic overtones of humanity's fall from divine grace. At the very least, it gives an almost archetypal quality to the ideas of the preamble and continues the notion, broached in the introduction, that the American Revolution is a major development in "the course of human events."

Because of their concern with the philosophy of the Declaration, many modern scholars have dealt with the opening sentence of the preamble out of context, as if Jefferson and the Continental Congress intended it to stand alone. Seen in context, however, it is part of a series of five propositions that build upon one another through the first three sentences of the preamble to establish the right of revolution against tyrannical authority:

Proposition 1:   All men are created equal.

Proposition 2:   They [all men, from proposition 1] are endowed by their creator with certain unalienable rights.

Proposition 3:   Among these [man's unalienable rights, from proposition 2] are life, liberty, and the pursuit of happiness.

Proposition 4:   To secure these rights [man's unalienable rights, from propositions 2 and 3] governments are instituted among men.

Proposition 5:   Whenever any form of government becomes destructive of these ends [securing man's unalienable rights, from propositions 2–4], it is the right of the people to alter or to abolish it.

When we look at all five propositions, we see they are meant to be read together and have been meticulously written to achieve a specific rhetorical purpose. The first three lead into the fourth, which in turn leads into the fifth. And it is the fifth, proclaiming the right of revolution when a government becomes destructive of the people's unalienable rights, that is most crucial in the overall argument of the Declaration. The first four propositions are merely preliminary steps designed to give philosophical grounding to the fifth.

At first glance, these propositions appear to comprise what was known in the eighteenth century as a *sorites*—"a Way of Argument in which a great Number of Propositions are so linked together, that the Predicate of one becomes continually the Subject of the next following, until at last a Conclusion is formed by bringing together the Subject of the First Proposition and the Predicate of the last." In his *Elements of Logick*, William Duncan provided the following example of a sorites:

God is omnipotent.
An omnipotent Being can do every thing possible.
He that can do every thing possible, can do whatever involves not a Contradiction.
Therefore God can do whatever involves not a Contradiction.[14]

Although the section of the preamble we have been considering is not a sorites (because it does not bring together the subject of the first proposition and the predicate of the last), its propositions are written in such a way as to take on the appearance of a logical demonstration. They are so tightly interwoven linguistically that they seem to make up a sequence in which the final proposition—asserting the right of revolution—is logically derived from the first four propositions. This is accomplished partly by the mimicry of the form of a sorites and partly by the sheer number of propositions, the accumulation of which is reinforced by the slow, deliberate pace of the text and by the use of "that" to introduce each proposition. There is also a step-like progression from proposition to proposition, a progression that is accentuated by the skillful use of demonstrative pronouns to make each succeeding proposition appear to be an inevitable consequence of the preceding proposition.

Although the preamble is the best known part of the Declaration today, it attracted considerably less attention in its own time. For most eighteenth-century readers, it was an unobjectionable statement of commonplace political principles. As Jefferson explained years later, the purpose of the Declaration was "not to find out new principles, or new arguments, never before thought of . . . but to place before mankind the common sense of the subject, in terms so plain and firm as to command their assent, and to justify ourselves in the independent stand we are compelled to take."[15]

Far from being a weakness of the preamble, the lack of new ideas was perhaps its greatest strength. If one overlooks the introductory first paragraph, the Declaration as a whole is structured along the lines of a deductive argument that can easily be put in syllogistic form:

Major premise: When Government deliberately seeks to reduce the people under absolute despotism, the people have a right, indeed a duty, to alter or abolish that form of government and to create new guards for their future security.

Minor premise: The government of Great Britain has deliberately sought to reduce the American people under absolute despotism.

Conclusion: Therefore the American people have a right, indeed a duty, to abolish their present form of government and to create new guards for their future security.

As the major premise in this argument, the preamble allowed Jefferson and the Congress to reason from self-evident principles of government accepted by almost all eighteenth-century readers of the Declaration.[16]

The key premise, however, was the minor premise. Since virtually everyone agreed the people had a right to overthrow a tyrannical ruler when all other remedies had failed, the crucial question in July 1776 was whether the necessary conditions for revolution existed in the colonies. Congress answered this question with a sustained attack on George III, an attack that makes up almost exactly two-thirds of the text.

The indictment of George III begins with a transitional sentence immediately following the preamble:

Such has been the patient sufferance of these Colonies; and such is now the necessity which constrains them to alter their former Systems of Government.

Now, 273 words into the Declaration, appears the first explicit reference to the British-American conflict. The parallel structure of the sentence reinforces the parallel movement of ideas from the preamble to the indictment of the king, while the next sentence states that indictment with the force of a legal accusation:

The history of the present King of Great Britain is a history of repeated injuries and usurpations, all having in direct object the establishment of an absolute Tyranny over these states.

Unlike the preamble, however, which most eighteenth-century readers could readily accept as self-evident, the indictment of the king required proof. In keeping with the rhetorical conventions Englishmen had followed for centuries when dethroning a "tyrannical" monarch, the Declaration contains a bill of particulars documenting the king's "repeated injuries and usurpations" of the Americans' rights and liberties. The bill of particulars lists twenty-eight specific grievances and is introduced with the shortest sentence of the Declaration:

To prove this [the king's tyranny], let Facts be submitted to a candid world.

This sentence is so innocuous one can easily overlook its artistry and importance. The opening phrase—"To prove this"—indicates the "facts" to follow will indeed prove that George III is a tyrant. But prove to whom? To a "candid world"—that is, to readers who are free from bias or malice, who are fair, impartial, and just. The implication is that any such reader will see the "facts" as demonstrating beyond doubt that the king has sought to establish an absolute tyranny in America. If a reader is not convinced, it is not because the "facts" are untrue or are insufficient to prove the king's villainy; it is because the reader is not "candid."

The pivotal word in the sentence, though, is "facts." As a term in eighteenth-century jurisprudence (Jefferson, like many of his colleagues in Congress, was a lawyer), it meant the circumstances and incidents of a legal case, looked at apart from their legal meaning. This usage fits with the Declaration's similarity to a legal declaration, the plaintiff's written statement of charges showing a "plain and certain" indictment against a defendant. If the Declaration were considered as analogous to a legal declaration or a bill of impeachment, the issue of dispute would not be the status of the law (the right of revolution as expressed in the preamble) but the facts of the specific case at hand (the king's actions to erect a "tyranny" in America).[17]

In ordinary usage "fact" had by 1776 taken on its current meaning of something that had actually occurred, a truth known by observation, reality rather than supposition or speculation.[18] By characterizing the colonists' grievances against George III as "facts," the Declaration implies that they are unmediated representations of empirical reality rather than interpretations of reality. They are the objective constraints that make the Revolution "necessary." This is reinforced by the passive voice in "let Facts be submitted to a candid world." Who is submitting the facts? No one. They have not been gathered, structured, rendered, or in any way contaminated by human agents—least of all by the Continental Congress. They are just being "submitted," direct from experience without the corrupting intervention of any observer or interpreter.

But "fact" had yet another connotation in the eighteenth century. The word derived from the Latin *facere*, to do. Its earliest meaning in English was "a thing done or performed"—an action or deed. In the sixteenth and seventeenth centuries it was used most frequently to denote an evil deed or a crime, a usage still in evidence at the time of the Revolution. In 1769, for example, Blackstone, in his *Commentaries on the Laws of England,* noted that "accessories after the fact" were "allowed the benefit of clergy in all cases." *The Annual Register* for 1772 wrote of a thief who was committed to prison for the "fact" of horse stealing. There is no way to know whether Jefferson and the Congress had this sense of "fact" in mind when they adopted the Declaration. Yet regardless of their intentions, for some eighteenth-century readers "facts" may have had a powerful double-edged meaning when applied to George III's actions toward America.[19]

Although one English critic assailed the Declaration for its "studied confusion in the arrangement" of the grievances against George III, they are not listed in random order but fall into four distinct groups.[20] The first group, consisting of charges 1–12, refers to such abuses of the king's executive power as suspending colonial laws, dissolving colonial legislatures, obstructing the administration of justice, and maintaining a standing army during peacetime. The second group, consisting of charges 13–22, attacks the king for combining with "others" (Parliament) to subject America to a variety of unconstitutional measures, including taxing the colonists without consent, cutting off their trade with the rest of the world, curtailing their right to trial by jury, and altering their charters.

The third set of charges, numbers 23–27, assails the king's violence and cruelty in waging war against his American subjects. They burden him with a litany of venal deeds that is worth quoting in full:

> He has abdicated Government here, by declaring us out of his Protection and waging War against us.
>
> He has plundered our seas, ravaged our Coasts, burnt our towns, and destroyed the Lives of our people.
>
> He is at this time transporting large Armies of foreign Mercenaries to complete the works of death, desolation and tyranny, already begun with circumstances of Cruelty and perfidy scarcely paralleled in the most barbarous ages, and totally unworthy the Head of a civilized nation.
>
> He has constrained our fellow Citizens taken Captive on the high Seas to bear Arms against their Country, to become the executioners of their friends and Brethren, or to fall themselves by their Hands.
>
> He has excited domestic insurrections amongst us, and has endeavored to bring on the inhabitants of our frontiers, the merciless Indian Savages, whose known rule of warfare, is an undistinguished destruction of all ages, sexes and conditions.

The war grievances are followed by the final charge against the king—that the colonists' "repeated Petitions" for redress of their grievances have produced only "repeated injury."

The presentation of what Samuel Adams called George III's "Catalogue of Crimes" is among the Declaration's most skillful features. First, the grievances could have been arranged chronologically, as Congress had done in all but one of its former state papers. Instead they are arranged topically and are listed seriatim, in sixteen successive sentences beginning "He has" or, in the case of one grievance, "He is." Throughout this section of the Declaration, form and content reinforce one another to magnify the perfidy of the king. The steady, laborious piling up of "facts" without comment takes on the character of a legal indictment, while the repetition of "He has" slows the movement of the text, draws attention to the accumulation of grievances, and accentuates George III's role as the prime conspirator against American liberty.[21]

Second, as Thomas Hutchinson complained, the charges were "most wickedly presented to cast reproach upon the King." Consider, for example, grievance 10: "He has erected a multitude of New Offices, and sent hither swarms of Officers to harass our people, and eat out their substance." The language is Biblical and conjures up Old Testament images of "swarms" of flies and locusts covering the face of the earth, "so that the land was darkened," and devouring all they found until "there remained not any green thing in the trees, or in the herbs of the field" (Exodus 10:14–15). It also recalls the denunciation, in Psalms 53:4, of "the workers of iniquity . . . who eat up my people as they eat bread," and the prophecy of Deuteronomy 28:51 that an enemy nation "shall eat the fruit of thy cattle, and the fruit of thy land until thou be destroyed: which also shall not leave thee either corn, wine, or oil, or the increase of thy kine, or flocks of thy sheep, until he have destroyed thee." For some readers the religious connotations may have been enhanced by "substance," which was used in theological discourse to signify "the Essence or Substance of the Godhead" and to describe the Holy Eucharist, in which Christ had "coupled the substance of his flesh and the substance of bread together, so we should receive both."[22]

From the revolutionaries' view, however, the primary advantage of the wording of charge 10 was probably its purposeful ambiguity. The "multitude of New Offices" referred to the customs posts that had been created in the 1760s to control colonial smuggling. The "swarms of Officers" that were purportedly eating out the substance of the colonies' three million people numbered about fifty in the entire continent. But Congress could hardly assail George III as a tyrant for appointing a few dozen men to enforce the laws against smuggling, so it clothed the charge in vague, evocative imagery that gave significance and emotional resonance to what otherwise might have seemed a rather paltry grievance.[23]

Third, although scholars often downplay the war grievances as "the weakest part of the Declaration," they were vital to its rhetorical strategy. They came last partly because they were the most recent of George III's "abuses and usurpations," but also because they constituted the ultimate proof of his plan to reduce the colonies under "absolute despotism." Whereas the first twenty-two grievances describe the king's acts with such temperate verbs as "refused," "called together," "dissolved," "endeavored," "made," "erected," "kept," and "affected," the war grievances use emotionally charged verbs such as "plundered," "ravaged," "burnt," and "destroyed." With the exception of grievance 10, there is nothing in the earlier charges to compare with the evocative accusation that George III was spreading "death, desolation and tyranny . . . with circumstances of Cruelty and perfidy scarcely paralleled in the most barbarous ages," or with the characterization of "the merciless Indian Savages, whose known mode of warfare is an undistinguished destruction of all ages, sexes and conditions." Coming on the heels of the previous twenty-two charges, the war grievances make George III out as little better than the notorious Richard III, who had forfeited his crown in 1485 for "unnatural, mischievous, and great Perjuries, Treasons, Homicides and Murders, in shedding of Infants' blood, with many other Wrongs, odious Offences, and abominations against God and Man."[24]

To some extent, of course, the emotional intensity of the war grievances was a natural outgrowth of their subject. It is hard to write about warfare without using strong language. Moreover, as Jefferson explained a decade later in his famous "Head and Heart" letter to Maria Cosway, for many of the revolutionaries independence was, at bottom, an emotional—or sentimental—issue. But the emotional pitch of the war grievances was also part of a rhetorical strategy designed to solidify support for independence in those parts of America that had yet to suffer the physical and economic hardships of war. As late as May 1776 John Adams lamented that while independence had strong support in New England and the South, it was less secure in the middle colonies, which "have never tasted the bitter Cup; they have never Smarted—and are therefore a little cooler." As Thomas Paine recognized, "the evil" of British domination was not yet "sufficiently brought to their doors to make them feel the precariousness with which all American property is possessed." Paine sought to bring the evil home to readers of *Common Sense* by inducing them to identify with the "horror" inflicted on other Americans by the British forces "that hath carried fire and sword" into the land. In similar fashion, the Declaration of Independence used images of terror to magnify the wickedness of George III, to arouse "the passions and feelings" of readers, and to awaken "from fatal and unmanly slumbers" those Americans who had yet to be directly touched by the ravages of war.[25]

Fourth, all of the charges against George III contain a substantial amount of strategic ambiguity. While they have a certain specificity in that they refer to actual historical events, they do not identify names, dates, or places. This magnified the seriousness of the grievances by making it seem as if each charge referred not to a particular piece of legislation or to an isolated act in a single colony, but to a violation of the constitution that had been repeated on many occasions throughout America.

The ambiguity of the grievances also made them more difficult to refute. In order to build a convincing case against the grievances, defenders of the king had to clarify each charge and what specific act or events it referred to, and then explain why the charge was not true. Thus it took John Lind, who composed the most sustained British response to the Declaration, 110 pages to answer the charges set forth by the Continental Congress in fewer than two dozen sentences. Although Lind deftly exposed many of the charges to be flimsy at best, his detailed and complex rebuttal did not stand a chance against the Declaration as a propaganda document. Nor has Lind's work fared much better since 1776. While the Declaration continues to command an international audience and has created a[n] indelible popular image of George III as a tyrant, Lind's tract remains a piece of arcana, buried in the dustheap of history.[26]

In addition to petitioning Parliament and George III, Whig leaders had also worked hard to cultivate friends of the American cause in England. But the British people had proved no more receptive to the Whigs than had the government, and so the Declaration follows the attack on George III by noting that the colonies had also appealed in vain to the people of Great Britain:

> Nor have we been wanting in attentions to our British brethren. We have warned them from time to time of attempts by their legislature to extend an unwarrantable jurisdiction over us. We have reminded them of the circumstances of our emigration and settlement here. We have appealed to their native justice and magnanimity, and we have conjured them by the ties of our common kindred to disavow these usurpations, which, would inevitably interrupt our connections and correspondence. They too have been deaf to the voice of justice and of consanguinity. We must, therefore, acquiesce in the necessity, which denounces our Separation, and hold them, as we hold the rest of mankind, Enemies in War, in Peace Friends.

This is one of the most artfully written sections of the Declaration. The first sentence, beginning "Nor . . . ," shifts attention quickly and cleanly away from George III to the colonists' "British brethren." The "have we" of the first sentence is neatly reversed in the "We have" at the start of the second. Sentences two through four, containing four successive clauses beginning "We Have . . . ," give a pronounced sense of momentum to the paragraph while underlining the colonists' active efforts to reach the British people. The repetition of "We have" here also parallels the repetition of "He has" in the grievances against George III.

The fifth sentence—"They too have been deaf to the voice of justice and of consanguinity"—contains one of the few metaphors in the Declaration and acquires added force by its simplicity and brevity, which contrast with the greater length and complexity of the preceding sentence. The final sentence unifies the paragraph by returning to the pattern of beginning with "We," and its intricate periodic structure plays off the simple structure of the fifth sentence so as to strengthen the cadence of the entire paragraph. The closing words—"Enemies in War, in Peace Friends"— employ chiasmus, a favorite rhetorical device of eighteenth-century writers. How effective the device is in this case can be gauged by rearranging the final words to read, "Enemies in War, Friends in Peace," which weakens both the force and harmony of the Declaration's phrasing.

It is worth noting, as well, that this is the only part of the Declaration to employ much alliteration: "*B*ritish *b*rethren," "*t*ime *to t*ime," "*c*ommon *k*indred," "*w*hich *w*ould," "*c*onnections and *c*orrespondence." The euphony gained by these phrases is fortified by the heavy repetition of medial and terminal consonants in adjoining words: ["]bee*n* wa*n*ting i*n* atte*n*tio*n*s *to*," "the*m* fro*m* ti*m*e to ti*m*e," "*to* their na*t*ive jus*t*ice," "di*s*avow the*s*e u*s*urpation*s*," "ha*v*e been dea*f* to the *v*oice o*f*." Finally, this paragraph, like the rest of the Declaration, contains a high proportion of one- and two-syllable words (82 percent). Of those words, an overwhelming number (eighty-one of ninety-six) contain only one syllable. The rest of the paragraph contains nine three-syllable words, eight four-syllable words, and four five-syllable words. This felicitous blend of a large number of very short words with a few very long ones is reminiscent of Lincoln's Gettysburg Address and contributes greatly to the harmony, cadence, and eloquence of the Declaration, much as it contributes to the same features in Lincoln's immortal speech.

The British brethren section essentially finished the case for independence. Congress had set forth the conditions that justified revolution and had shown, as best it could, that those conditions existed in Great Britain's thirteen North American colonies. All that remained was for Congress to conclude the Declaration:

> We, therefore, the Representatives of the United States of America, in General Congress, Assembled, appealing to the Supreme Judge of the world for the rectitude of our intentions, do, in the Name, and by Authority of the good People of these Colonies, solemnly publish and declare, That these United Colonies are, and of Right ought to be Free and Independent States; that they are Absolved from all Allegiance to the British Crown and that all political connection between them and the State of Great Britain, is and ought to be totally dissolved; and that as Free and Independent States, they have full Power to levy War, conclude Peace, contract Alliances, establish Commerce and to do all other Acts and Things which Independent States may of right do. And for the support of this Declaration, with a firm reliance on the Protection of divine Providence, we mutually pledge to each other our Lives, our Fortunes, and our sacred Honor.

This final section of the Declaration is highly formulaic and has attracted attention primarily because of its closing sentence. Carl Becker deemed this sentence "perfection itself":

> It is true (assuming that men value life more than property, which is doubtful) that the statement violates the rhetorical rule of climax; but it was a sure sense that made Jefferson place "lives" first and "fortunes" second. How much weaker if he had written "our fortunes, our lives, and our sacred honor"! Or suppose him to have used the word "property" instead of "fortunes"! Or suppose him to have omitted "sacred"! Consider the effect of omitting any of the words, such as the last two "ours"—"our lives, fortunes, and sacred honor." No, the sentence can hardly be improved.[27]

Becker is correct in his judgment about the wording and rhythm of the sentence, but he errs in attributing high marks to Jefferson for his "sure sense" in placing "lives" before "fortunes." "Lives and fortunes" was one of the most hackneyed phrases of eighteenth-century Anglo-American political discourse. Colonial writers had used it with numbing regularity throughout the dispute with England (along with other stock phrases such as "liberties and estates" and "life, liberty, and property"). Its appearance in the Declaration can hardly be taken as a measure of Jefferson's felicity of expression.

What marks Jefferson's "happy talent for composition" in this case is the coupling of "our sacred Honor" with "our Lives" and "our Fortunes" to create the eloquent trilogy that closes the Declaration. The concept of honor (and its cognates fame and glory) exerted a powerful hold on the eighteenth-century mind. Writers of all kinds—philosophers, preachers, politicians, playwrights, poets—repeatedly speculated about the sources of honor and how to achieve it. Virtually every educated man in England or America was schooled in the classical maxim, "What is left when honor is lost?" Or as Joseph Addison wrote in his *Cato,* whose sentiments were widely admired throughout the eighteenth century on both sides of the Atlantic: "Better to die ten thousand deaths/Than wound my honour." The cult of honor was so strong that in English judicial proceedings a peer of the realm did not answer to bills in chancery or give a verdict "upon oath, like an ordinary juryman, but upon his honor."[28]

By pledging "our sacred Honor" in support of the Declaration, Congress made a particularly solemn vow. The pledge also carried a latent message that the revolutionaries, contrary to the claims of their detractors, were men of honor whose motives and actions could not only withstand the closest scrutiny by contemporary persons of quality and merit but would also deserve the approbation of posterity. If the Revolution succeeded, its leaders stood to achieve lasting honor as what Francis Bacon called "*Liberatores* or *Salvatores*"—men who "compound the long Miseries of Civil Wars, or deliver their Countries from Servitude of Strangers or Tyrants." Historical examples included Augustus Caesar, Henry VII of England, and Henry IV of France. On Bacon's five-point scale of supreme honor, such heroes ranked below only "*Conditores Imperiorum,* Founders of States and Commonwealths," such as Romulus, Caesar, and Ottoman, and "Lawgivers" such as Solon, Lycurgus, and Justinian, "also called Second Founders, or *Perpetui Principes,* because they Govern by their Ordinances after they are gone." Seen in this way, "our sacred Honor" lifts the motives of Congress above the more immediate concerns of "our Lives" and "our Fortunes" and places the revolutionaries in the footsteps of history's most honorable figures. As a result it also unifies the whole text by subtly playing out the notion that the Revolution is a major turn in the broad "course of human events."[29]

At the same time, the final sentence completes a crucial metamorphosis in the text. Although the Declaration begins in an impersonal, even philosophical voice, it gradually becomes a kind of drama, with its tensions expressed more and more in personal terms. This transformation begins with the appearance of the villain, "the present King of Great Britain," who dominates the stage through the first nine grievances, all of which note what "He has" done without identifying the victim of his evil deeds. Beginning with grievance 10, the king is joined on stage by the American colonists, who are identified as the victim by some form of first person plural reference: The king has sent "swarms of officers to harass *our* people," has quartered "armed troops among *us*," has imposed "taxes on *us* without *our* consent," "has taken away *our* charters, abolished *our* most valuable laws," and altered "the Forms of *our* Governments." He has "plundered *our* seas, ravaged *our* coasts, burnt *our* towns, . . . destroyed the lives of *our* people," and "excited domestic insurrections amongst *us*." The word "our" is used twenty-six times from its first appearance in grievance 10 through the last sentence of the Declaration, while "us" occurs eleven times from its first appearance in grievance 11 through the rest of the grievances.[30]

Throughout the grievances, action is instigated by the king, as the colonists passively accept blow after blow without wavering in their loyalty. His villainy complete, George III leaves the stage and it is occupied next by the colonists and their "British brethren." The heavy use of personal pronouns continues, but by now the colonists have become the instigators of action as they actively seek redress of their grievances. This is marked by a shift in idiom from "He has" to "We have": "*We* have petitioned for redress . . . ," "*We* have reminded *them* . . . ," "*We* have appealed to *their* . . . ," and "*We* have conjured *them*." But "*they* have been deaf" to all pleas, so "*We* must . . . hold *them*" as enemies. By the conclusion, only the colonists remain on stage to pronounce their dramatic closing lines: "*We* . . . solemnly publish and declare . . ." And to support this declaration, "*we* mutually pledge to each other *our* Lives, *our* Fortunes and *our* sacred Honor."

The persistent use of "he" and "them," "us" and "our," "we" and "they" personalizes the British-American conflict and transfigures it from a complex struggle of multifarious origins and diverse motives to a simple moral drama in which a patiently suffering people courageously defend their liberty against a cruel and vicious tyrant. It also reduces the psychic distance between the reader and the text and coaxes the reader into seeing the dispute with Great Britain through the eyes of the revolutionaries. As the drama of the Declaration unfolds, the reader is increasingly solicited to identify with Congress and "the good People of these Colonies," to share their sense of victimage, to participate vicariously in their struggle, and ultimately to act with them in their heroic quest for freedom.

In this respect, as in others, the Declaration is a work of consummate artistry. From its eloquent introduction to its aphoristic maxims of government, to its relentless accumulation of charges against George III, to its elegiac denunciation of the British people, to its heroic closing sentence, it sustains an almost perfect synthesis of style, form, and content. Its solemn and dignified tone, its graceful and unhurried cadence, its symmetry, energy, and confidence, its combination of logical structure and dramatic appeal, its adroit use of nuance and implication—all contribute to its rhetorical power. And all help to explain why the Declaration remains one of the handful of American political documents that, in addition to meeting the immediate needs of the moment, continues to enjoy a lustrous literary reputation.

NOTES

[1] Moses Coit Tyler, *The Literary History of the American Revolution* (1897), vol. 1, p. 520. The best known study of the style of the Declaration is Carl Becker's "The Literary Qualities of the Declaration," in his *The Declaration of Independence: A Study in the History of Political Ideas* (1922), pp. 194–223. Useful also are Robert Ginsberg, "The Declaration as Rhetoric," in Robert Ginsberg, ed., *A Casebook on the Declaration of Independence* (1967), pp. 219–244; Edwin Gittleman, "Jefferson's 'Slave Narrative': The Declaration of Independence as a Literary Text," *Early American Literature* 8 (1974): 239–256; and James Boyd White, *When Words Lose Their Meaning: Constitutions and Reconstitutions of Language, Character, and Community* (1984), 231–240. Although most books on the Declaration contain a chapter on the "style" of the document, those chapters are typically historical accounts of the evolution of the text from its drafting by Thomas Jefferson through its approval by the Continental Congress or philosophical speculations about the meaning of its famous passages.

[2] As Garry Wills demonstrates in *Inventing America: Jefferson's Declaration of Independence* (1978), there are two Declarations of Independence—the version drafted by Thomas Jefferson and that revised and adopted on July 4, 1776, by the Continental Congress sitting as a committee of the whole. Altogether Congress deleted 630 words from Jefferson's draft and added 146, producing a final text of 1,322 words (excluding the title). Although Jefferson complained that Congress "mangled" his manuscript and altered it "much for the worse," the judgment of posterity, stated well by Becker, is that "Congress left the Declaration better than it found it" (*Declaration of Independence*, p. 209). In any event, for better or worse, it was Congress's text that presented America's case to the world, and it is that text with which we are concerned in this essay.

[3] Nothing in this essay should be interpreted to mean that a firm line can be drawn between style and substance in the Declaration or in any other work of political or literary discourse. As Peter Gay has noted, style is "form and content woven into the texture of every art and craft. . . . Apart from a few mechanical tricks of rhetoric, manner is indissolubly linked to matter; style shapes and is in turn shaped by, substance" (*Style in History* [1974], p. 3).

[4] All quotations from the Declaration follow the text as presented in Julian P. Boyd et al., eds., *The Papers of Thomas Jefferson* (1950–), vol. 1, pp. 429–432.

[5] Ephraim Chambers, *Cyclopedia: Or, An Universal Dictionary of Arts and Sciences* (1728), vol. 2, p. 621; Jonathan Edwards, *Freedom of the Will*, ed. Paul Ramsey (1957), p. 149.

[6] *Declaration of the Lords and Commons to Justify Their Taking Up Arms*, August 1642, in John Rushworth, ed., *Historical Collections of Private Passages of State, Weighty Matters in Law, Remarkable Proceedings in Five Parliaments* (1680–1722), vol. 4, pp. 761–768; Declaration of the Continental Congress Setting Forth the Causes and Necessity of Their Taking Up Arms, July 1775, in James H. Hutson, ed., *A Decent Respect to the Opinions of Mankind: Congressional State Papers, 1774–1776* (1975), pp. 89–98. The importance of necessity as a justification for war among nations is evident in the many declarations of war issued by European monarchs throughout the seventeenth and eighteenth centuries and is discussed in Tavers Twiss, *The Law of Nations Considered as Independent Political Communities* (1863), pp. 54–55.

[7] The first additional invocation of the doctrine of necessity in the Declaration comes immediately after the preamble, when Congress states, "Such has been the patient

sufferance of these Colonies; and such is now the necessity which constrains them to alter their former systems of Government." The second is at the end of the penultimate section, in which Congress ends its denunciation of the British people by announcing, "We must, therefore, acquiesce in the necessity, which denounces our Separation, and hold them, as we hold the rest of mankind, Enemies in War, in Peace Friends."

[8][Thomas Paine], *Common Sense: Addressed to the Inhabitants of America . . .* (1776), pp. 41, 43.

[9]Samuel Adams to Joseph Hawley, Apr. 15, 1776, *Letters of Delegates to Congress, 1774–1789*, ed. Paul H. Smith (1976–), vol. 3, p. 528; Thomas Jefferson, Notes of Proceedings in the Continental Congress, *Jefferson Papers* 1:312.

[10]Jonathan Mayhew, *A Discourse Concerning Unlimited Submission and Nonresistance to the Higher Powers . . .* (1750), p. 45; [John, Lord Somers], *The Judgment of Whole Kingdoms and Nations, Concerning the Rights, Power and Prerogative of Kings, and the Rights, Privileges and Properties of the People* (1710), par. 186; Algernon Sidney, *Discourses Concerning Government* (1693), p. 181; John Hoadly, ed., *The Works of Benjamin Hoadly* (1773), vol. 2, p. 36; "Pacificus," *Pennsylvania Gazette,* Sept. 14, 1774.

[11]Becker, *Declaration of Independence,* p. 201.

[12]Hugh Blair, *Lectures on Rhetoric and Belles Lettres* (1783), vol. 1, pp. 206–207, 259.

[13]"Thoughts on English Prosody" was enclosed in an undated letter of ca. October 1786 to the Marquis de Chastellux. The letter is printed in *Jefferson Papers* 10: 498; the draft of Jefferson's essay, which has not been printed, is with the letter to Chastellux in the Thomas Jefferson Papers, Library of Congress, Washington, DC. Julian P. Boyd, "The Declaration of Independence: The Mystery of the Lost Original," *Pennsylvania Magazine of History and Biography* 100 (1976): 455–462, discusses "Thoughts on English Prosody" and its relation to Jefferson's reading text of the Declaration. Given the changes made by Congress in some sections of the Declaration, it should be noted that the style of the preamble is distinctly Jeffersonian and was approved by Congress with only two minor changes in wording from Jefferson's fair copy as reported by the Committee of Five.

[14]William Duncan, *The Elements of Logick* (1748), p. 242. See also Isaac Watts, *Logick: or, The Right Use of Reason in the Enquiry After Truth,* 8th ed. (1745), p. 304; [Henry Aldrich], *A Compendium of Logic,* 3d ed. (1790), p. 23.

[15]Jefferson to Henry Lee, May 5, 1825, *The Writings of Thomas Jefferson,* ed. Paul Leicester Ford (1892–1899), vol. 10, p. 343.

[16]Wilbur Samuel Howell, "The Declaration of Independence and Eighteenth-Century Logic" *William and Mary Quarterly,* 3d Ser. 18 (1961): 463–484 claims Jefferson consciously structured the Declaration as a syllogism with a self-evident major premise to fit the standards for scientific proof advanced in William Duncan's *Elements of Logick,* a leading logical treatise of the eighteenth century. As I argue in a forthcoming essay, however, there is no hard evidence to connect Duncan's book with the Declaration. Jefferson may have read *Elements of Logick* while he was a student at the College of William and Mary, but we are not certain that he did. He owned a copy of it, but we cannot establish whether the edition he owned was purchased before or after 1776. We cannot even say with complete confidence that Jefferson inserted the words "self-evident" in the Declaration; if he did, it was only as an afterthought in the process of polishing his original draft. Moreover, upon close examination it becomes clear that the Declaration does not fit the method of scientific reasoning recommended in Duncan's *Logick.* Its "self-evident" truths are not self-evident in the rigorous technical sense used by Duncan; it does not provide the definitions of terms that Duncan regards as the crucial first step in syllogistic demonstration; and it does not follow Duncan's injunction that both the minor premise and the major premise must be self-evident if a conclusion is to be demonstrated in a single act of reasoning. The syllogism had been part of the intellectual baggage of Western civilization for two thousand years, and the notion of

self-evident truth was central to eighteenth-century philosophy. Jefferson could readily have used both without turning to Duncan's *Logick* for instruction.

[17] "Declaration" in John Cowell, *Nomothetes. The Interpreter, Concerning the Genuine Signification of Such Obscure Words and Terms Used Either in the Common or Statute Laws of This Realm* . . . (1684). For the requirements of legal declarations in various kinds of civil suits during the eighteenth century, see William Selwyn, *An Abridgement of the Law of Nisi Prius,* 4th ed. (1817).

[18] "Fact" in Samuel Johnson, *A Dictionary of the English Language: In Which the Words are Deduced from Their Origins and Illustrated in Their Different Significations by Examples from the Best Writers* (1755).

[19] *Oxford English Dictionary* (1933), vol. 4, pp. 11–12; Sir William Blackstone, *Commentaries on the Laws of England* (1771), vol. 4 p. 39; *The Annual Register, Or a View of the History, Politics, and Literature for the Year 1772* (1773), p. 57.

[20] John Lind, *Answer to the Declaration of the American Congress* . . . , 5th ed. (1776), p. 123. Because the grievances are not numbered in the Declaration, there has been disagreement over how many there are and how they should be numbered. I have followed Sidney George Fisher, "The Twenty-Eight Charges against the King in the Declaration of Independence," *Pennsylvania Magazine of History and Biography* 31 (1907): 257–303. An alternative numbering system is used by Wills, *Inventing America,* pp. 68–75.

[21] Samuel Adams to John Pitts, ca. July 9, 1776, *Letters of Delegates* 4:417. The sole congressional paper before the Declaration of Independence to list grievances topically was the 1774 Bill of Rights (Hutson, *Decent Respect* pp. 49–57).

[22] [Thomas Hutchinson], *Strictures upon the Declaration of the Congress at Philadelphia* . . . (1776), p. 16; Ralph Cudworth, *The True Intellectual System of the Universe* (1678) p. 601; Richard Hooker, *Of the Laws of Ecclesiasticall Politie* (1594–1596), vol. 5, sec. 67, p. 178.

[23] Between 1764 and 1766 England added twenty-five comptrollers, four surveyors general, and one plantation clerk to its customs service in America. It added seventeen more officials in 1767 with the creation of a Board of Customs Commissioners to reside in Boston. These appointments may also have generated a mild ripple effect, resulting in the hiring of a few lesser employees to help with office chores and customs searches, but there is no way to know, since the records are now lost. See Thomas C. Barrow, *Trade and Empire: The British Customs Service in Colonial America, 1660–1775* (1967), pp. 186–187, 220–221.

[24] Howard Mumford Jones, "The Declaration of Independence: A Critique," in *The Declaration of Independence: Two Essays* (1976), p. 7; sentence against Richard III in *Rotuli Parliamentorum; ut et petitiones placita in Parliamento* (1783–1832), vol. 6, p. 276.

[25] Thomas Jefferson to Maria Cosway, Oct. 12, 1786, *Jefferson Papers* 10:451; John Adams to Benjamin Hichborn, May 29, 1776, *Letters of Delegates* 4:96; Paine, *Common Sense,* pp. 40–42.

[26] See note 20 for bibliographic information on Lind's pamphlet.

[27] Becker, *Declaration of Independence,* p. 197.

[28] For the importance of fame and honor to the revolutionaries, see Douglass Adair, "Fame and the Founding Fathers," in *Fame and the Founding Fathers,* ed. Trevor Colbourn (1974), pp. 3–26; Garry Wills, *Cincinnatus: George Washington and the Enlightenment* (1984), pp. 109–148; Bruce Miroff, "John Adams: Merit, Fame, and Political Leadership," *Journal of Politics* 48 (1986): 116–132. The quotation about Jefferson's "happy talent for composition" is from John Adams to Timothy Pickering, Aug. 6, 1822, *The Works of John Adams,* ed. Charles Francis Adams (1850), vol. 2, p. 511. The statement about peers of the realm is from Blackstone, *Commentaries,* 1: 402.

[29] Francis Bacon, *The Essayes or Counsels, Civill and Morall* . . . (1625), pp. 313–314. See Adair, "Fame and the Founding Fathers," pp. 114–115, for the importance of Bacon's essay on honor among the revolutionaries.

[30] Cf. Ginsberg, "The Declaration as Rhetoric," p. 228.

GETTYSBURG AND SILENCE

EDWIN BLACK

1   *Four score and seven years ago our fathers brought forth on*
2   *this continent, a new nation, conceived in Liberty, and dedicated*
3   *to the proposition that all men are created equal.*
4   *Now we are engaged in a great civil war, testing whether that*
5   *nation or any nation so conceived and so dedicated, can long*
6   *endure. We are met on a great battle-field of that war. We have*
7   *come to dedicate a portion of that field, as a final resting place*
8   *for those who here gave their lives that that nation might live.*
9   *It is altogether fitting and proper that we should do this.*
10   *But, in a larger sense, we can not dedicate—we can not*
11 *consecrate—we can not hallow—this ground. The brave men, living*
12 *and dead, who struggled here, have consecrated it, far above our*
13 *poor power to add or detract. The world will little note, nor long*
14 *remember what we say here, but it can never forget what they did*
15 *here. It is for us the living, rather, to be dedicated here to the*
16 *unfinished work which they who fought here have thus far so nobly*
17 *advanced. It is rather for us to be here dedicated to the great*
18 *task remaining before us—that from these honored dead we take*
19 *increased devotion to that cause for which they gave the last full*
20 *measure of devotion—that we here highly resolve that these dead*
21 *shall not have died in vain—that this nation, under God, shall*
22 *have a new birth of freedom—and that government of the people, by*
23 *the people, for the people, shall not perish from the earth.*[1]

There is no more celebrated example of eloquence than the Gettysburg Address. From its first utterance to the latest moment, Lincoln's speech has generated intense responses. Initially they were responses, often partisan, of appreciation and deprecation; more recently they have been the responses of reverence that an acknowledged masterpiece receives. The historical importance of the Address is beyond doubting. Its eminence has been extravagantly affirmed, as much by the passion of its detractors as by the veneration of its admirers. The effects attributed to it are prodigious, ranging from the subversion of republican government[2] to the reconstitution of American political culture.[3]

Our era does not baffle itself about the quality of the Gettysburg Address. Its reputation has triumphed over hostility, parody, obscurity, and obsolescence.[4] The speech is fixed now in the history of a people. It is a testament of national identity.

The Gettysburg Address has been, from its genesis, an aesthetic object. Its career has recapitulated that of many another exalted work of art, a career that begins, invisibly, as an amorphy of inchoate ideas within the mind of an author. Those mental fragments, combined and recombined under the impulse of aspiration, are subjected to an impenetrable process of discrimination and refinement by the author, who finally forms them into an autonomous creation. That product somehow takes hold; it endures; it survives controversy and the vicissitudes of fashion; in time it achieves, as the Gettysburg Address has, an iconic status: the artifact has transcended the condition of being evaluated by having become an exemplary definition of value itself. Its entry into that pantheon is signalled when it begins to elicit a set of critical questions reserved only for paradigmatic works: questions no longer about how it should be judged; but rather, questions about how it has shaped the culture to which it has become sacred, what the sources are of its influence, what the secrets are of its enchantments. The masterpiece becomes to the critic what the mountain is to the climber.

Its reputation now established as a touchstone of public discourse, the Gettysburg Address is a subject that tests criticism more than it is tested by criticism. If the Gettysburg Address were a simple composition, it would long ago have depleted its own interpretive possibilities.[5] But the Address can probably not be exhausted by any single examination, and certainly not by any monistic one. Despite the inescapable temporality of its medium, it eludes even line-by-line or word-by-word analysis. The speech is at once too compressed and too intricate. It is so brief that its first portentous words are still held in the mind even as its last syllables are being comprehended. And yet, each element of the Address is so tightly implicated in other elements that its cumulative effect is but one of its multifarious effects. Its duration is an infrangible unity.

The Address is prismatic. Its aspects reflect back and forth on one another in such radiant multiplicity that, diamond-like, its fires are somehow both protean and integral. The complexity of the Address, which has been requisite to its ascendance, enables it to give back a singular answer to each critic who brings to it the question, how does it work? One mark of a masterpiece may be its critical inexhaustibility: its capacity to accommodate the diverse partialities of its observers, and yet to abide in its integrity. And the uniquely prismatic character of the Gettysburg Address brings it to reflect, with uncommon brilliance, any light that is thrown on it, however dim.

How does one examine a prism? By looking at it through one facet after another, in no particular order. That will be the method here. It is a method without system and therefore scarcely a method at all, at least not a predetermined one. But sometimes—maybe even all the time—a subject deserves to supersede a method, and to receive its own forms of disclosure.

How does the Gettysburg Address function rhetorically? The answer is in the details.

AUDIENCES

The first paragraph of the Gettysburg Address seems addressed to the ages. Lincoln does not imply a particular audience. He speaks the voice of omniscience, articulating a historical narrative with incontestable certitude. The first paragraph is a description of national genesis. It is a purposeful creation, an initiating fusion of origin and essence: the generation not only of an entity, but also of a mission. That account of genesis and meaning stipulates the frame of the speech. Anyone who would deny, doubt, or qualify the narrative is implicitly excluded from Lincoln's audience. By announcing a major premise, the form of the first sentence signals that a deductive procedure has been started, and that the procedure will be accordingly self-contained. The choice left the auditor is single: to be or not to be an auditor to this speech.

The narrative of national creation is austere, its only concession to embellishment being the natal metaphor, but even that metaphor is so fundamental that the metaphor itself is almost dead. The moribundity of the metaphor prevents its being experienced as an embellishment; its inconspicuousness as a stylistic decoration is compatible with the spartan character of the first paragraph. That quality of barrenness in the style of the first paragraph is characteristic of the enunciation of first principles. ("In the beginning God created the heavens and the earth.") No gratuities must be attached to an account that mandates unqualified commitment. The articulation of an absolute belief requires the exactitude of purity. The first paragraph's narrative is advanced as absolute truth, and so it has no specifiable audience. It constitutes the initial statement of the facts of the case, the undisputed and undisputable ground for any judgment that may be issued by the rhetor or formed by an auditor.

The second paragraph subsumes the war, the battlefield, and the ceremony to the synoptic historical narrative. The civil war is linked to the nation's beginning by being a test of its founding principle (4–6). And the ceremony is linked to the civil war by its location and its purpose (6–9). In anticipation of the Address's later reinterpretation of the occasion's purpose, the paragraph ends with an assurance that its conventionally understood rationale is an appropriate product of historical circumstance: "It is altogether fitting and proper that we should do this."

"But" (10) begins a decisive shift in perspective. The "larger sense" (10) that will now inform the discourse is a sense no longer merely of appropriateness, but, more encompassing, of moral adequacy. "But" also crystallizes a shift of the object of the Address to the audience at Gettysburg. The immediate audience had been discussed (6–9) only in its relation to the larger historical account. Beginning with "but," its capacities and obligations occupy the speech. The focus remains arrested on the cemetery at Gettysburg for awhile, reinforced by six references to "here"— six references in five lines (12, 14, 15, 16, 17).

The word "here" tolls like a bell through that period of fixation on the present moment. It appears a total of eight times in the speech. Two functions, at least, can be attributed to the repetition of "here," in addition to the enhancement of the rhythmic solemnity of the Address. One is the pointing these repetitions do of the occasion: their constituting a recurrent anchor for one moiety of a bipolar orientation in which the implicit "there," which contrasts with "here," is the future. During the section of the speech when the audience's attention is fastened to the occasion, "here" serves to remind them not only of that occasion, but also of how bounded the occasion is, and of the co-existence with the "here" of a "there": a different and less bounded time and place. "Here" is a particular location amidst infinity. "Here" is a particular moment during eternity. The other function of the repetition of "here"—a subtler function—relates to the pun on "hear," a recurrent command issued to the audience to attend. Faintly, allophonically, Lincoln directs his audience to listen.

The first-person plural references during the middle of the speech (6–14) all have the audience at Gettysburg at their center. With the instruction to "us the living" (15), however, the synecdochal character of the first-person plural begins reemerging to a point of unmistakable clarity (21) that "we" stand in deputy to the whole nation and act on its behalf. The audience, then, transcribes a movement through the speech from unspecified universal (1–3) to national (4) to local (6–14), back to national again.

THE MOVEMENT OF THE ADDRESS

A consideration of the implied audience brought us to observe that the word "But" in line 10 confirms a shift of perspective from the historical to the moral, and of object from a general to a more specific audience. This shift constitutes a hesitation: an arrest of time and place in the middle of the speech, a riveting on the present. The speech is so compressed that even that fixation passes too quickly to effect any sense of intellectual paralysis. The arrest is, rather, a short-lived entrancement, an instant in which the options are inventoried for the future of a moment whose past has been ascertained. What has led us to this moment is the subject of the speech from its beginning to "But."

"But" begins a process of rejection. The first two paragraphs of the Address constitute a historical setting of the occasion, and a normal extrapolation from the pronouncements of those paragraphs would lead toward performative utterance. Our past has led us to the point of declaring this burial ground sacred; but yet, we demur. Why? Because we have neither the right nor the duty. A moral intervention prevents the fulfillment of conventional form; a customary itinerary has been deflected. Our right has been superseded by those who have died. Our duty lies elsewhere: it is to take up the task left unfinished by the dead. The speech links us to the dead by virtue of the common task, and by the bond of our obligation to complete what they have left incomplete.

If we think of the movement of the Address in terms of what Berenson has called "respirational values," we can appreciate that the speech is temporarily arrested at the point of maximum contraction.[6] The narrowing of location from continent (2) to nation (2) to battle-field (6) to portion of that field (7) to resting place (7) finally pivots with "But" even to a rejection of our capacity to affect "this ground" (11). Then, in line 15, a movement recommences, and an expansion continues to the end.

The second "rather" (17) is the second pivot of the speech. It decisively turns from the focus on the present and commences the movement into the future. The first "rather" (15) prepares for that pivot by shifting the subject from the dead to the living. It signals a throwing off of the immobility that restrains the middle of the speech; it is a bestirring, a resumption. With the second "rather," the movement recommences, with its temporal and spatial directions clearly manifested.

The "new birth of freedom" (22) echoes "our forefathers brought forth" (1). An implicit contrast sponsored by the speech is not just between living and dying; it is also between birthing and dying: a subtle distinction, perhaps, but crucial to the character of the Gettysburg Address. That latter contrast enables Lincoln to subordinate the living (13–14, 15–18) to the task of political renascence (22).

The "brave men" (11) who "gave the last full measure of devotion" (19–20) have died, but in the end, it is a form of government that "shall not perish from the earth." They "gave their lives that that nation may live" (8). There are two forms of life, then: the life of the nation, which must endure, and the lives of the fallen soldiers, who died in order that the nation may continue living.

GEOGRAPHICAL REFERENCES

The references to place have the same pattern of progressive confinement followed by progressive enlargement as does the implied audience. First, continent (2), followed quickly by nation (2). Nation is reiterated twice more (5). Then, a process of narrowing proceeds: battle-field (6), then portion of that field (7), then resting place (7). There follows a reference to nation (8), but nation there is not place; it is organism ("that that nation might live"). "This ground" (11) is a slight loosening of the geographical constriction, preliminary to an expansionary movement, which goes to "world" (13)—but not altogether a place either, since it has memory.

Then "nation" (21), but having a birth, and so still an organism. And finally, the location of all knowable places: "the earth" (23). The designations of place, then, first proceed from "continent" to diminishing measures of location, to the nadir, "resting place." Then the direction of movement is reversed, and it proceeds toward increasingly enlarged measures, to the apogee, "the earth." The movement of spatial allusions is one of contraction followed by expansion.

The geographical references juxtapose animate with inanimate associations. The movement begins with an inanimate "continent," but moves quickly to the animate "nation," iterated three times. Then, inanimate references, three again, to battle-field, portion of field, and final resting place.

All five allusions to "nation" (2, 5, 8, 21) in the speech are in the same form, so that "nation," while animate, is stable. But the inanimate geographical references continuously alter in focus. The variety of allusions to the site—"battle-field," "portion of that field," "resting place," and "here" eight times—are variations in perspective, while the perspective on "the nation" is held constant. Moreover, the allusions to the site are uniformly inanimate—they allude simply to a place, but a place whose consecration is the issue presented by the speech. However, the references to other places—"nation" five times, and "the world" used synecdochically—are all animate, excepting only the ambiguous final reference to "the earth."

The speech presents two implicit and repeatedly reinforced geographical contrasts. One is the contrast between the site at Gettysburg, which is a consecrated place where lives were given, and "the nation," which has been endowed with life from the first sentence. The second is between "the nation," which is treated as a fixed conception in the speech, and all the other geographical references, which vary in size, location and function. Here we have one of the many ironies of the Address. While we would ordinarily associate stability—the cessation of change—with entropy and death, Lincoln sustains constancy in his animate conception of "the nation," and diversifies his other geographical references, which are inanimate. A consequence is that "nation," which is ostensibly a geographical term employed along with other geographical terms, is singularly endowed with the values of duration and viability.

Finally, the earth. The cemetery at Gettysburg is a place where the earth receives the dead. Lincoln's immediate audience would have had an active awareness of that fact, and even their successors are reminded by the speech of its setting (4–8). The earth, then, and all of its synecdochal variants—field, resting place, ground—is a continuously active referent in the web of meaning. And at the very end of the Address, where Lincoln specifies the earth as the place where the principle of the living nation will continue its life, he abruptly—with his last word—inverts a signification that preceded the speech in the minds of the auditors, and that the speech had been careful to maintain. In an instant, the resting place of the dead becomes the habitation of a vital principle, renascent and imperishable. The unity of the dead with the living is consummated in Lincoln's last word, the common home of all.

STRUCTURE

The structural elegance of the discourse can be rendered statistically. The speech consists of 367 syllables. Its first pivot occurs at syllable 146; its second pivot at syllable 263. One-third through the syllables is at 122; two-thirds through at 244. The speech consists of 272 words. The first pivot is at word 103; the second pivot at word 193. One-third through the words is at 91; two-thirds at 182.

The two major pivots in the speech are spaced with amazing precision. If the first word of the speech is given a value of 1, and the last word a value of 100, the first pivot occurs at word 37.8 (syllable 39.7); the second pivot at word 70.9 (syllable 71.6). If 33.3 and 66.6 represent a mathematical perfection of placement in each of the two cases, it is clear that Lincoln came remarkably close to such precision, considering that this was a speech and not a mathematical exercise. He is only twelve words off mathematical perfection in the first pivot and nine words off it in the second.

If the speech is divided into twenty-three lines (as it is on my computer): nine lines constitute the statement of facts; then five lines constitute the pause; then nine lines constitute the resolution. The mathematical proportioning of the speech is so close to perfect that it seems almost formulary, yet it is inconceivable that it actually was. The two sections of movement are equal in length; the middle section of arrest is virtually half the length of either of the sections of the movement.

In visual terms, the speech is shaped like an hourglass. Temporally, it is past, present, then future. Its visceral effects are contraction, strain, and then release. Respirationally, it is an exhalation, then a pause, then an inhalation.

The structure of the Gettysburg Address imposes a corresponding form on the experience of its auditor. That experience is composed of initial tension, followed by tightening, followed by progressive exhilaration. The opening sentence concentrates the attention of the auditor and contributes to the auditor's tension. In its effect, that sentence disciplines the auditor's response. The first sentence is a command to be reverential, a command yielded by the archaic solemnity of the sentence and by the august historical perspective that it announces. The command is reinforced by the inherent gravity of the occasion and by the high office of the speaker. The tension is sustained through the narrative that brings the historical account to the moment of the ceremony (4–8).

There is a brief, soothing reassurance (9), a promise that the contained energy of reverence will be discharged in an appropriate ceremony. But then, at that acme of expectation and vulnerability, the auditor's strain is suddenly intensified by the ostensible denial that the ceremony itself could be efficacious (10–15). It is a repudiation that dislocates the reverence that had been initially sponsored by the speech. And that concussion of form is followed by yet another reversal: At the most potentially explosive point in the stressing of the auditor, a controlled release of the auditor's tension begins (15). The medium of that release is the prescription for the continuing task of self-dedication by which the audience can be constructively absorbed and into which its reverence can be invested (15–23).

In lines 10–20, we have a series of contrasts, first between us and "the brave men, living and dead, who struggled here," and then, via the reference to "us the living" (15), between us and the dead: We cannot consecrate; they have consecrated. We say here; they did here. We have unfinished work; they nobly advanced work. We take devotion; they gave devotion. In each of these contrasts, we are passive and receptive; they who struggled are active and productive. Throughout these contrasts, our passivity is inferior to their activity. But at last we are given an activity (15–23) which can assuage the appetite that the contrasts have aroused: an appetite for moral equilibrium. This treatment of contrasts too is a pattern of strain followed by release.

There is not an instant in the course of the speech when the experience of the audience is not subjected to its controlling configuration of tension and resolution. We are coiled by the Address, and then sprung. The structure of the Gettysburg Address is an organization of the auditor's energy.

THE SCOPE OF THE ADDRESS

The Address has an oracular quality. The voice that speaks is not, at first hearing, an individual voice: it betrays no particular perspective. The speech abounds in first-person references, but none is singular.[7] The fifteen first-person, plural references are concessions to the ceremony that has prompted the Address.

The speech sustains distance from the dedicatory event; it hovers above the event, commenting on it in relation to history. Beginning with the founding of the Republic, the focus goes first to the war, then to the battle-field, then to the resting place, finally to the ceremony of dedication. However, after pronouncing approbation of the ceremony (9), the speech denies its efficacy (10–11), and proceeds to subordinate it to larger and longer-lived concerns. The treatment of the event too, then, follows the movement of the whole discourse. The view of the ceremony is initially expansive, then narrowing to the moment, then increasingly encompassing again until it reaches the limit of mortal experience.

The speech concludes with human concerns situated within their widest possible latitude and their longest possible duration: their scope is all of the world, and all of human history. Whatever is beyond that conclusion is beyond the human scale. Beyond it is the infinite: the venue of the supernal and the unknowable.

Lincoln's discourse propels us in the direction of metaphysical transcendence, but it stops at the boundary. It expands to subsume all of life, but it ceases at the point where life ceases, where death and infinity begin. Immediately beyond the scope of the discourse is ineffable mystery. The Gettysburg Address speaks words to the world of words, and it echoes silence before the vast silence that begins where speaking ends.

The speech is not just a vindication of the Civil War, or a poem to democracy, or a meditation on the legacies of the dead and the obligations of the living. It is also a map and a chronicle: it locates a burial ground in relation to all of space, and it fixes that moment of location in relation to all of time.

The ceremony at Gettysburg had begun with a prayer by the Reverend Doctor T. H. Stockton which was three and a half times the length of Lincoln's speech. With amplitude and confidence, the Reverend Doctor Stockton expatiated on the relations between the casualties of battle and the divinity. But Lincoln, in his turn, does not presume to pronounce on the fate of the dead. He does not presume, even from his exalted office, to issue the consolation of spiritual immortality. There is no mitigation of bereavement, no anodyne, no euphemism, no benign illusion. He approaches the subject of the dead by approaching the realm of the dead, but approaching only, never pretending to intrude. He talks of the bequests of the dead, of their memorials, but not of their souls. He carries discourse and any claims to knowledge to the border of extinction and eternity, to the outermost boundary of life and of time, but there he stops, and if that journey is to be continued, it must be in the imaginations of his auditors, for whom he has supplied a momentum and a trajectory.

What is extraordinary about that momentum and trajectory is not the transcendent conception toward which they propel the auditor, because that conception is really quite orthodox. It is the Great Chain of Being: the majestic cosmology of medieval Christendom that links time with timelessness, the past with the future, history with destiny, life with death and both with immortality. That cosmology is not affirmed in Lincoln's speech, but neither is it to the slightest degree contravened. It is suggested by the biblical echoes that resound in the account of the nation's genesis: "Four score and seven," and fathering a nation, and "brought forth."[8]

The distinction between dying, which may allow living on in another realm, and perishing from the earth, which implies anonymity and a complete cessation of existence, is also a reverberation of the King James Bible.[9]

The cosmology is an element of context—one with which Lincoln could be confident that his contemporary audiences would tacitly endow his speech. Lincoln knew his immediate audience's general view of life and death, and he made his speech wholly compatible with that general view without committing himself to it. Lincoln's tact confined him to exercising a solely secular authority.

The cosmological implications of the Gettysburg Address are probably more disengaged in us than in Lincoln's contemporaries. The idea of a Great Chain of Being is more faded in our time, a less active component of our convictions. We have, however, a perspective that is more than compensatory. It is augmented by the stronger sense of national identity that the Civil War made possible, and by our knowledge of Lincoln's martyrdom, which lends the Address a poignancy that was unavailable to Lincoln's contemporaries. In the end, then, we may infer that our responses are not quite equivalent in character to those of the immediate audience, but our responses may well be at least equivalent in intensity.

CYCLES AND ARCHETYPES

At the beginning, the nation is brought forth, and at the end, the nation has a new birth of freedom. The issue, finally, is not the life and death of the fallen, but the life and death and resurrection of the nation. One cycle embedded in the speech is, of course, the life-cycle of birth and death. The speech touches only the terminal poles of the cycle. No reference to growth or maturation appears in the speech, so that no intermediate historical interpretation is offered except of the war itself, an interpretation so purified of immediate reference and so frugal of emotionality as to seem epiphanic (4–6).

Another cycle, more subtly present, is decay and regeneration: the cycle in which organisms decompose into fertile organic matter and become nutriment for other organisms. The speech hints at that relation between the dead soldiers and the nation (8). It can do no more than hint; obviously, an overt equation between the honored dead and compost would be an offensive and unfeeling reduction. But an audience close to natural processes and seasons, as Lincoln's predominantly rural contemporaries were, would be sensitive to that hint, and would take it without flinching. Their piety and grief would inhibit their making any indelicate extension of the figure within their own imaginations. The hint, of course, is purely figural. Lincoln implies, alludes to a metaphor without explicitly declaring it. The allusion is a parsimonious reminder of a natural process; only its context works to provoke its being associated, by analogy, with obituary or patriotic motifs. The compression is striking: the containment within a very few words of a complex network of meaning.

CEREMONIAL SPEECH

Speaking has a variety of conventional functions. The most ordinary consist of conveying information—information about the world, or about oneself, or about one's judgments of the world. Another, less frequent but still familiar[,] function of speaking is to settle a perdurable aura around an event—to commemorate it, or to celebrate it, or to endow it with significance. This function brings speech close to magic, not in the sense that words alone are expected to alter physical reality, but rather in the sense that words are expected to be constitutive, performative. The speech is to be itself a presence that is functionally indistinguishable from the event to which it alludes. The words that are spoken at ceremonial transitions work to fix and consign an event, to articulate a common interpretation of it, so to fashion a public memory of it that it can hardly thereafter be remembered in any other way. This sort of speech conveys information in the strict sense in which anything called speech must convey information, but the information conveyed about the subject of ceremony is not new because the nature of that information is consensual, and the consensus has already been achieved prior to its expression. The conventional ceremonial speech aspires, at minimum, to declare that consensus, to dress an occasion in a socially necessary integument of words and, by remarking it, to mark it as remarkable. This sort of perlocution occurs in recognition of the fact that although there are times when silence is tributary, there are also times when silence is contemptuous, when words must be spoken. Moments of beginning and of ending require speech as a rhetorical ordination.

THE DEDICATORY FUNCTION

The contrast between the living and the dead that pervades the Gettysburg Address is played against the subject of consecration, which is the ostensible task of the ceremony containing the speech and the ostensible issue of the speech itself. Lincoln says, in effect, that the living cannot consecrate the graveyard; the dead already have. So, the task of the living is some other: it is to continue the work that the dead had begun. By linking the social task of the living and the dead, the speech resists a bifurcation between life and death, positing in its place a relationship of continuity. That continuity, in turn, reduces the distinction between honoring and being honored, replacing it with a relationship of common work—"unfinished work" (16)—and creating an equality between the living and the dead instead of the hierarchy that had prompted the ceremony. Honoring and being honored also participate in an active-passive diremption which is foregone in favor of a common, if temporally distinguishable, activity of consecration. The deadness of the dead is thus not contemplated. Rather, their deaths are interpreted to have been an action rather than a condition as the dead are shifted from being objects of reverence to being prefiguring participants in a common quest. And that flattening of the relationship comports with the historical perspective that the speech sponsors, because while the living and the dead live and died as individuals, it is the life of the nation that is paramount in this speech. The conception of individuality is subdued in the Gettysburg Address: its only subjects are aggregations. Its author has even effaced himself.

The dead were brave men; the living is the nation. Lincoln flirts with paradox in rendering the dead, who no longer have identity, as a plurality of individuals, but rendering the living as a composite. However, the paradox enables Lincoln's auditors to experience bereavement and yet simultaneously to dissolve their egos into a collective resolution. That elusive combination would enable the audience's mourning to attain an impersonality and still to ache.

There is a pun on "dedicated." The dedication of the cemetery is transformed into the dedication of the audience. The synonyms of "dedication" can be divided into three groups of terms: First, "allegiance, commitment, devotion, loyalty"; second, "consecration, designation"; third, "ordination, address, inscription, message." Lincoln begins with a focus on the middle terms—consecration and designation—both in relation to the official establishment of a cemetery. But in turning the subject of the dedication from the cemetery to the audience, the sense of the term shifts to the first four meanings: allegiance, commitment, devotion, and loyalty, especially the middle two of these four. And, of course, the last three senses—address, inscription, and message—are implicit in Lincoln's very act of speaking.

Lincoln rings the complete round of resonances of the term "dedication." We cannot, he is saying, dedicate this cemetery because the dead have already done that. We should, therefore, dedicate ourselves. The implicit premise is that something must be dedicated—that, having come together for a dedication, the collection of people at Gettysburg are obliged to accomplish that task. The task that he proffers, however, is not capable of accomplishment at the ceremony itself. Lincoln poses a task that must occupy the audience beyond the ceremony. The speech, therefore, refuses to permit the ceremony to be a consummation, refuses to make it whole and complete. The speech rejects the ceremony as a vehicle of fulfillment. It does so by beginning its focus on the "consecration" sense of dedication, transforming it to the "commitment" sense and, in the process, shifting its subject, and it ends by rendering the dedicatory ceremony itself into the "message" sense.

The inconclusiveness of the ceremony—Lincoln's refusal to allow it to consummate the mourning of the dead—is entailed by the first sentence of the speech (2–3). The first reference to a dedication appears there. The subject of that dedication is, of course, the country, but its object is the statement of a cynosure, a proposition that can be taken only as teleological, the enunciation not of a fulfillment, but of a quest.

CONTEXT

We are taught to think of discourses dialectically. We understand them in contexts: denying, qualifying, echoing, contesting other discourses. Discourses are participatory, and we comprehend them through their genealogy and genus. Edward Everett's oration at Gettysburg echoes Daniel Webster's epideictic mode; its set-piece on the battle aspires to Livy, with brushstrokes of Periclean melancholy. Everett's speech is in a grand ceremonial tradition, and it is through that tradition that we apprehend it. Its relationship to a family of other discourses is apparent, and even predictable.

Lincoln's Gettysburg Address is unique in that instead of springing from a chorus of discourses that comprise its context, it grows from silence. The Address imposes its own order without reference to any other text.[10] It achieves whatever tension it requires not by its collision with alternatives, nor by its juxtaposition with precedents, but by its deliberate opposition to the occasion that prompted it. Instead of rejecting an implicit contradiction of itself, the Address rejects its own ostensible purpose. In so detaching itself from its own grounding, the speech gains a functional autonomy. It makes itself incommensurable. Its sole alternative is not a contravening utterance, but a mortuary quietude.

There is a recording of a 1944 performance by Wilhelm Furtwängler of the Freischütz overture. The opening chord of the overture—a long bass crescendo—seems to swell up out of nothing. It begins so quietly that one's first hearing is not of a chord beginning to be played, but of an already playing chord slowly developing into audibility. And part of the effect that Furtwängler creates in his miraculous performance is a consciousness of the void that has preceded the music. It is as if silence itself had found a voice. The Gettysburg Address constructs a similar effect in its course. Unlike the subtle efflorescence with which Furtwängler performs Weber's chord, the Address begins with a magisterial pronouncement on history; but it then proceeds so to disengage itself from other utterance that it ends finally as an articulation within nonbeing. It does not grow from a void; rather, it grows a void around itself. The speech presents itself *sui generis*.

There is one other analogy to be drawn between the Furtwängler performance and the Gettysburg Address. The way in which Furtwängler has his orchestra voice the first chord anticipates his interpretation of the whole composition. His entire performance is a playing out of the urgency and mystery that are coiled in that opening chord. The whole is implicit in its genesis. Similarly, the Gettysburg Address is an exfoliation of its first sentence. The threads of Lincoln's tapestry are all plaited into that initial statement: the themes of religiosity, of historic continuity, of birth, of temporal movement, of the organic nation, of location, of dedication, and of unfulfilled aspiration. The whole of the discourse is a weaving of those threads.

NEGATIVITY

The negativity of the Address is striking: We can*not* dedicate this cemetery. We resolve that the dead shall *not* have died in vain, that people's government shall *not* perish. All are negatives. How curious that a speech should so powerfully survive, should so capture the popular imagination, should be marked as the greatest effusion of eloquence in the history of the country, and yet it is not cast affirmatively; rather, it denies, it disclaims, it negates.

Along with the sure sense of what he knows and does not know, Lincoln also sustains in the speech a sense of the limits of language. The deeds of the soldiers are far more important than the speeches of the dedicators (10–15); the will and intention of people is superior to what is said (15–18). The speech evokes a sense of human effort transcending verbal expression, a sense of life and history eluding utterance. This aspect of the speech can be equated with mysticism: with the conviction that there are realities beyond the powers of articulation, ineffable forces that shape our lives.

Without any overt allusion to a religious idea, without any invocation of the deity, Lincoln still manages to give his remarks a religious aura. The initial source of that aura is the biblical idiom of the first sentence, but its continuing source is the reflexive undercurrent in the Address: its contemplation of how unimportant and transitory speaking itself is (10–14), and of the fact that there are things not entailing speech—sentiments, intentions, resolutions, collective actions, values, ideals—that are important and enduring (15–23). The first half of that message by itself— that the occasion is a fugitive moment—would be a message of humbling disenchantment; but the second half of the message—that some noble deeds and some dispositions of consciousness are beyond language—redeems the moment by embedding utterance within a nimbus of silence.

The negativity of the Address is also an expression of its profound conservatism. The first sentence having announced the historical founding of a destiny, the speech serves the perpetuation of that original purpose. It refuses digressions. Like Lincoln's presentation of the government's role in the Civil War itself, the Address is concerned, most notably in its first and last sentences, with the conservation of a political idea and with the republic that instantiates it. Therefore, the Address would deny their alternatives. Grammatically, the concluding lines (22–23) are negative, but they negate an extinction, and so situate themselves as a nay-saying that affirms.

The end of the Address is a resolution (20) that the establishment described in the first sentence will not be terminated: "we here highly resolve." There is more than a single sense in which one may "highly resolve" something. One sense has to do with "resolve" in its sense of "making independently visible." In that meaning, a high resolution may refer, for example, to a photograph that clarifies different colors and volumes. Insofar as that sense of "highly resolve" is among its over-tones, the phrase inclines the auditor to understand resolving "that these dead shall not have died in vain" to constitute a clarity of disclosure—a resolution that we not only undertake but also one that we behold with a new precision—a statement of the essence not only of the speech up to that point, but also of its occasion and, beyond them both, of its living subject, the nation. The second sense—obviously closer to the center of Lincoln's intention—is a use of the term "highly" to suggest loftiness, intensity, solemnity, nobility. Such attributes of our "resolve" elevate the dignity of the promise that the deaths will be purposeful. And there is a reason, even beyond the intrinsic sobriety of the task, to make such a resolve most solemn.

In calling for the resolve that the dead shall not have died in vain, Lincoln is summoning his audience to perform an act of redemption: a redemption of the dead. To suggest that it is for us to redeem the dead could easily be construed as a sacrilege. The redemption of the dead, after all, would be regarded by Lincoln's contemporaries as a divine prerogative. Lincoln is advancing a secular version of redemption in the only way in which he tactfully can, and that is by the indirection of a negative construction. For him to have put the idea in a positive mode would have been too stark a revelation of his work to sanctify the nation and its defining principles.

Suppose the speech were not rewritten, but simply rearranged so that it ended with an affirmative statement. Suppose that, by more clearly echoing the beginning of the speech at its end, the rearrangement transmuted the Address into "that most pervasive of all rhetorical figures in ancient literature and even in modern, the ring-composition."[11] Suppose the last few lines went:

> . . . that from these honored dead we take increased devotion to that cause for which they gave the last full measure of devotion—that we here highly resolve that these dead shall not have died in vain—that government of the people, by the people, for the people, shall not perish from the earth—and that this nation, under God, shall have a new birth of freedom.

No reader of this rearrangement who has had a lifetime's memory of the Gettysburg Address can quite renounce the influence of the original. Yet, even after the most earnest deference to the probability of prejudice, the suspicion persists that the rhythm of the conclusion is debased by the rearrangement. The revision is too brusque. It is a terminus, but it is no longer a coda. It has gained positive declaration at the cost of majesty. The original ending has a tetrad of phrases, each composed of a tetrad of beats—"of the people, by the people, for the people, shall not perish"—followed by a single, emphatic, unaccented triad: "from the earth." The rhythmic indeterminacy of the rearranged ending must compare unfavorably to this solemn cadence, which measures out the final lines (20–23) with a gravity corresponding to their determinacy of purpose.

THE USES OF IRONY

The Gettysburg Address is a sacramental act. Its procedure is to abjure its own efficacy. It is through the process of that abjuration that it achieves its character.

The speech affirms by negating; it makes itself into an eloquent confession of inarticulateness; it gains celebrity by seeking obscurity; it commemorates the dead by obligating the living; it masters an occasion by retreating from it, and culminates a dedication by protracting it.

The speech abounds in ironies, in transformative disruptions of convention. And that condition of multifaceted reversal is itself a composite irony because its source is the head of a government who is resisting a rebellion. In rotating a meaning into its opposite, an irony is a miniature verbal revolution, and so it is supremely ironic to use irony in resistance to a revolution.[12] Lincoln at Gettysburg pre-empted the essential tool of his adversaries, whose most penetrating minds were less penetrating than his, and whose most agile wits were, compared to his wit, cumbrous.

DIANOIA AND ETHOS

It is only after one has recovered from the spell of the speech, and comes to realize that it is, after all, the product of a mind, that the character of that mind can be considered. On its most superficial level, the speech is asymptomatic. It is inexpressive. It displays nothing of the speaker except his mighty powers of comprehension, but even that display seems inadvert. That is, the speech proposes no more of the mind behind it than any speech—even the most spontaneous imaginable—necessarily proposes. The plays of Shakespeare reveal little of the attitudes of Shakespeare; but they reveal abundantly that the magnitude of his mind was beyond measure. By contrast, the Gettysburg Address does reveal some of the attitudes of Lincoln simply because, unlike the multifarious voices of a Shakespearian drama, its voice is the distinctive voice of its author, but the design of the Address distances the personality of Lincoln. The subordination of the occasion to historic considerations perforce subordinates also the orator—subordinates him to the point of invisibility. Lincoln does not intrude into the Gettysburg Address. He is not a reference in the speech, not literally, not even by specific implication. What presence he has in the speech is solely the product of linguistic necessity. He is present only to the extent that a speech requires a speaker.

The Gettysburg Address initiated a process of deliberate self-effacement that Lincoln conducted until his death. It was a process that reached its public culmination in the Second Inaugural Address.

Here is the beginning of the Second Inaugural Address. Forget for a moment Lincoln's reputation as an orator. Attend instead to the tortured construction of the language:

> At this second appearing to take the oath of the Presidential office there is less occasion for an extended address than there was at the first. Then a statement somewhat in detail of a course to be pursued seemed fitting and proper. Now, at the expiration of four years, during which public declarations have been constantly called forth on every point and phase of the great contest which still absorbs the attention and engrosses the energies of the nation, little that is new could be presented. . . . On the occasion corresponding to this four years ago all thoughts were anxiously directed to an impending civil war. . . . While the inaugural address was being delivered from this place, devoted altogether to *saving* the Union without war, insurgent agents were in the city seeking to *destroy* it without war . . .

Lincoln was a masterly stylist; yet, these are curiously strained sentences, their contortion exacerbated by their presence in a speech with some of the most magnificent passages in the history of the language. Those beginning sentences are bent and twisted to avoid self reference. During an inauguration—an occasion when, of all occasions, attention would be invited to the person who is the subject of the ceremony—Lincoln labors to escape being present in his speech.

The Second Inaugural Address has only two uses of the first-person singular, both in the same sentence: "The progress of our arms, upon which all else chiefly depends, is as well known to the public as to myself, and it is, I trust, reasonably satisfactory and encouraging to all." The context of "myself" is a disclaimer of special knowledge, and the context of "I trust" is, in effect, a disclaimer of superior knowledge. "I trust" also retards and enhances the rhythm of the sentence. None of these functions exalt the speaker. The implicit disclaimers, in fact, signal his humility. In this speech, as in the precursive Gettysburg Address, Lincoln had so refined his vision of his role and had so purified his expression of that vision, that he had all but extinguished his own authorial presence.

The rigor of Lincoln's self-discipline is given salience by its contrast to Everett's expansive speech. Everett reconstructed the battles of Gettysburg and, beyond them, a sufficient sampling of the history of warfare to subsume them to a heroic perspective. It was a virtuoso performance, inhibited by neither timidity nor reticence. The echoes of Everett's ambitious narrative had not wholly faded when the laconic Lincoln spoke what he knew.

The Gettysburg Address is, finally and inevitably, a projection of Lincoln himself, of his discretion, of his modesty on an occasion which invited him to don the mantle of the prophet, of his meticulous measure of how far he ought to go, of the assurance of his self-knowledge: his impeccable discernment of his own competence, his flawless sense of its depth and its limits. As an actor in history and a force in the world, Lincoln does not hesitate to comprehend history and the world. But he never presumes to cast his mind beyond human dimensions. He does not recite divine intentions; he does not issue cosmic judgments. He knows, to the bottom, what he knows. Of the rest, he is silent.

NOTES

[1]Numbers in parentheses throughout this essay refer to lines in this text of the Gettysburg Address.

[2]Edgar Lee Masters, *Lincoln, The Man* (New York: Dodd-Mead, 1931) esp. 478–498. Masters argues, in this angry biography, that Lincoln hypnotized the country, to its ruin.

[3]Garry Wills, *Lincoln at Gettysburg: The Words that Remade America* (New York: Simon & Schuster, 1992) 145–147.

[4]Early reception of the Gettysburg Address is surveyed by William E. Barton, *Lincoln at Gettysburg: What He Intended to Say; What He Said; What He was Reported to Have Said; What He Wished He had Said* (New York: Peter Smith, 1950) 89–92 and 114–123. Other initial responses to the Gettysburg Address, pro and con, have been collected by Svend Petersen, *The Gettysburg Addresses: The Story of Two Orations* (New York: Frederick Ungar Publishing Co., 1963) 53–64. Petersen has also collected parodies of the Address, pp. 65–94. They are uniformly dreary.

[5]Garry Wills's admirable *Lincoln at Gettysburg* is the most recent and arguably the most accomplished effort to scale the summit of the Address. Wills has anchored virtually every word of the Gettysburg Address to its historical antecedents in a meticulous documentation of its sources, its context, and its effects. Yet, not even Wills's excellent book has said all that there is to say about the construction and dynamics of the text. Nor, indeed, does it claim to.

[6]Bernard Berenson, *Aesthetics and History,* (Garden City, N.Y.: Doubleday & Co., 1954) 92: ". . . respirational values . . . refer to our feelings of liberation, of freedom from heaviness, and to the illusion of soaring into harmonious relations with sky and horizon."

[7]Barton observed the absence from the Address of the first-person singular in *Lincoln at Gettysburg,* 149. In comparing Lincoln's selfless performance with later speeches given at Gettysburg by Woodrow Wilson and Theodore Roosevelt, Barton is surprised to find that Roosevelt was, like Lincoln, "wholly impersonal." Wilson, however, referred to himself more than once a minute. See Barton 149–151.

[8]It is reasonable to suspect that the namesake of Abraham was especially attentive to those passages in the King James Bible that discussed Abraham. For example, Genesis 16:16 reports: "And Abram was fourscore and six years old, when Hagar bare Ishmail to Abram." In Genesis 17:5 God issues a directive: "Neither shall thy name any more be called Abram, but thy name shall be Abraham; for a father of many nations have I made thee." For "brought forth," see Genesis 1:20 and 1:24.

[9]See, for example, Job 18:17: "His remembrance shall perish from the earth, and he shall have no name in the street." And Job 34:14–15: "If he set his heart upon man if he gather unto himself his spirit and his breath; All flesh shall perish together, and man shall turn again unto dust." Also John 3:16: "For God so loved the world, that he gave his only begotten Son, that whosoever believeth in him should not perish, but have everlasting life."

[10]There are textual antecedents for the Address, but the Address contains no references to them. Lincoln had long been contending that slavery could not be contained, that ultimately it would have either to be universal or wholly abolished. See, for example, his "House Divided" Speech to the Republican State Convention, Springfield, Illinois, 16 June 1858, esp.: "I believe this government cannot endure, permanently half *slave* and half *free.*"

Lincoln had also advanced juridical arguments on the indivisibility of the nation, most notably in his First Inaugural Address, 4 March 1861, esp.: "I hold that, in contemplation of universal law and of the Constitution, the Union of these States is perpetual."

In his Message to Congress of 4 July 1861 Lincoln argued that the attack on Fort Sumter presented issues of principle that transcended even the nation:

It presents to the whole family of man, the question, whether a constitutional republic, or a democracy—a government of the people, by the same people—can, or cannot, maintain its territorial integrity, against its own domestic foes. It presents the question, whether discontented individuals, too few in numbers to control administration, according to organic law, in any case, can always, upon the pretences made in this case, or on any other pretences, or arbitrarily, without any pretence, break up their Government, and thus practically put an end to free government upon the earth.

Lincoln already had the germs of his conclusion ("government of the people, by the same people" and "an end to free government upon the earth") over two years before the Address.

[11]Roger A. Hornsby, "The Relevance of Ancient Literature: Recapitulation and Comment," *Papers in Rhetoric and Poetic,* ed. Donald C. Bryant (Iowa City, University of Iowa Press: 1965) 95.

[12]There was in Lincoln's day, as there is now, a common distinction between the terms "rebellion" and "revolution." *Webster's Third New International Dictionary* quotes *Instructions for Government of U.S. Armies:* "The term 'rebellion' is applied to an insurrection of large extent, and is usually a war between the legitimate government of a country and portions or provinces of the same who seek to throw off their allegiance to it

and set up a government of their own." The same source defines "revolution" as "a fundamental change in political organization or in a government or constitution."

Lincoln merged the two conceptions in the final section of the Gettysburg Address. He made the effect of the rebellion to be revolutionary. Its success, he was saying, would extinguish the form of government entailed in the genesis of the nation, a claim he had warranted in earlier discourses. See, for example, the Message to Congress of 4 July 1861.

Chapter IV

Dramatistic Criticism

Dramatism is Kenneth Burke's critical system for analyzing human symbolic interaction. While traditional criticism seeks to understand how persuasive techniques function to bring about specific results, dramatism is more concerned with philosophical, psychological, and sociological questions: What does rhetoric reveal about human motivation, action, and linguistic reality? This chapter will focus on several of the most significant aspects of dramatism, including Burke's emphasis on psychoanalysis, his use of criticism to bring about social change, the pentad, and his concept of tragic and comic frames.[1]

Burke explains that his method is called "dramatism" because it derives from the "analysis of drama."[2] The most concrete and describable feature of dramatism is the pentad. According to Burke, the five key elements of drama are "act," "agent," "scene," "agency," and "purpose." These components will be manifested in rhetoric and can be used to reveal the possible motives of speakers.[3]

A crucial part of Burke's perspective is that he regards language as fundamentally a "mode of action."[4] In other words, to use language is to act, as well as to convey content. Moreover, for Burke, language *is* reality; it is not a symbol for reality. Thus, language reflects as well as influences a rhetor's attitudes, values, and world view. Given this notion, dramatism allows a critic to analyze the reality experienced by different rhetors.

Kenneth Burke's 1941 essay "The Rhetoric of Hitler's 'Battle'" illustrates critical emphases on psychoanalysis and social action. Burke's exegesis of *Mein Kampf* is drawn loosely from Freudian psychology. According to Burke, Hitler used sexual symbolism to portray the Jew as a seducer of German people, making the Jew a "scapegoat," a kind of "medicine" for the sick Aryan middle class. Burke argues that the power of Hitler's rhetoric came from a "bad filling of a good need"—the need for a "universal" explanation. Burke concludes by urging the United States to make Hitlerism its enemy by turning Nazi doctrine into a national scapegoat. He claims the job of the critic is to expose Hitler's distortions and prevent a "similar swindle" in America.

Mari Boor Tonn, Valerie A. Endress, and John N. Diamond use the pentad to analyze the controversy surrounding an accidental shooting in "Hunting and Heritage on Trial in Maine: A Dramatistic Debate over Tragedy, Tradition, and Territory" (1993). The authors focus on Burke's concept of motivation and argue that the entire situation surrounding Karen Wood's death can best be interpreted from a dramatistic perspective. Tonn, Endress, and Diamond discover that "scene" is the dominant pentadic element in the discourse surrounding the controversy in Maine. Moreover, the authors find, the collision between pro- and anti-hunting factions illustrates the centrality of "turf." Their dramatistic analysis explains how the shooting victim, Karen Wood, was rhetorically transformed into a "victimizer," while the hunter, Donald Rogerson, was absolved of responsibility for the killing.

Brian L. Ott and Eric Aoki illustrate the critical value of Burke's theory of "terministic screens" in their 2002 essay "The Politics of Negotiating Public

Tragedy: Media Framing of the Matthew Shepard Murder." Drawing upon Burke's view of language as "equipment for living," the authors evaluate the ways that the news media "framed" the Matthew Shepard story and "named" the gay male body. Ott and Aoki attempt to "identify the underlying symbolic process and to analyze how it functions to construct and position citizens relative to the political process, and how it assists them in confronting and resolving public trauma." The authors argue that the news media adopted a "tragic frame" for the Shepard story. This allowed the public to expunge feelings of guilt through "victimage" and "scapegoating." One consequence of the tragic frame is that it "brings about symbolic resolution without turning the event into a lesson for those involved." An alternative perspective for the news media would have been to adopt a "comic frame," which might have resulted in greater social awareness and responsibility.

NOTES

[1] For general introductions to Burke's methods and theories, see Virginia Holland, "Rhetorical Criticism: A Burkeian Method," *Quarterly Journal of Speech* 39 (1953): 444–50; L. Virginia Holland, "Kenneth Burke's Dramatistic Approach in Speech Criticism," *Quarterly Journal of Speech* 41 (1955): 352–58; Marie Hochmuth, "Kenneth Burke and the 'New Rhetoric,'" *Quarterly Journal of Speech* 38 (1952): 133–44; Bernard L. Brock, "Rhetorical Criticism: A Burkeian Approach Revisited," in *Methods of Rhetorical Criticism*, 3rd ed., rev., ed. Bernard L. Brock, Robert L. Scott, and James W. Chesebro (Detroit, Mich.: Wayne State University Press, 1989), 183–95; Sonja K. Foss, Karen A. Foss, and Robert Trapp, *Contemporary Perspectives on Rhetoric*, 2nd ed. (Prospect Heights, IL: Waveland, 1991), 169–207.

[2] Kenneth Burke, *A Grammar of Motives* (1945; reprint, Berkeley: University of California Press, 1969), xxii.

[3] Burke, *A Grammar of Motives*, xv.

[4] Burke, *A Grammar of Motives*, xxii.

THE RHETORIC OF HITLER'S "BATTLE"

KENNETH BURKE

The appearance of *Mein Kampf* in unexpurgated translation has called forth far too many vandalistic comments. There are other ways of burning books than on the pyre—and the favorite method of the hasty reviewer is to deprive himself and his readers by inattention. I maintain that it is thoroughly vandalistic for the reviewer to content himself with the mere inflicting of a few symbolic wounds upon this book and its author, of an intensity varying with the resources of the reviewer and the time at his disposal. Hitler's "Battle" is exasperating, even nauseating; yet the fact remains: If the reviewer but knocks off a few adverse attitudinizings and calls it a day, with a guaranty in advance that his article will have a favorable reception among the decent members of our population, he is contributing more to our gratification than to our enlightenment.

Here is the testament of a man who swung a great people into his wake. Let us watch it carefully; and let us watch it, not merely to discover some grounds for prophesying what political move is to follow Munich, and what move to follow that move, etc.; let us try also to discover what kind of "medicine" this medicine-man has concocted, that we may know, with greater accuracy, exactly what to guard against, if we are to forestall the concocting of similar medicine in America.

Already, in many quarters of our country, we are "beyond" the stage where we are being saved from Nazism by our *virtues*. And fascist integration is being staved off, rather, by the *conflicts among our vices*. Our vices cannot get together in a grand united front of prejudices; and the result of this frustration, if or until they succeed in surmounting it, speaks, as the Bible might say, "in the name of" democracy. Hitler found a panacea, a "cure for what ails you," a "snakeoil," that made such sinister unifying possible within his own nation. And he was helpful enough to put his cards face up on the table, that we might examine his hands. Let us, then, for God's sake, examine them. This book is the well of Nazi magic; crude magic, but effective. A people trained in pragmatism should want to inspect this magic.

1

Every movement that would recruit its followers from among many discordant and divergent bands, must have some spot towards which all roads lead. Each man may get there in his own way, but it must be the one unifying center of reference for all. Hitler considered this matter carefully, and decided that this center must be not merely a centralizing hub of *ideas*, but a mecca geographically located, towards which all eyes could turn at the appointed hours of prayer (or, in this case, the appointed hours of prayer-in-reverse, the hours of vituperation). So he selected Munich as the *materialization* of his unifying panacea. As he puts it:

> The geo-political importance of a center of a movement cannot be overrated. Only the presence of such a center and of a place, bathed in the magic of a Mecca or a Rome, can at length give a movement that force which is rooted in the inner unity and in the recognition of a hand that represents this unity.

If a movement must have its Rome, it must also have its devil. For as Russell pointed out years ago, an important ingredient of unity in the Middle Ages (an ingredient that long did its unifying work despite the many factors driving towards disunity) was the symbol of a *common enemy*, the Prince of Evil himself. Men who can unite on nothing else can unite on the basis of a foe shared by all. Hitler himself states the case very succinctly:

> As a whole, and at all times, the efficiency of the truly national leader consists primarily in preventing the division of the attention of a people, and always in concentrating it on a single enemy. The more uniformly the fighting will of a people is put into action, the greater will be the magnetic force of the movement and the more powerful the impetus of the blow. It is part of the genius of a great leader to make adversaries of different fields appear as always belonging to one category only, because to weak and unstable characters the knowledge that there are various enemies will lead only too easily to incipient doubts as to their own cause.
>
> As soon as the wavering masses find themselves confronted with too many enemies, objectivity at once steps in, and the question is raised whether actually all the others are wrong and their own nation or their own movement alone is right.
>
> Also with this comes the first paralysis of their own strength. Therefore, a number of essentially different enemies must always be regarded as one in such a way that in the opinion of the mass of one's own adherents the war is

being waged against one enemy alone. This strengthens the belief in one's own cause and increases one's bitterness against the attacker.

As everyone knows, this policy was exemplified in his selection of an "international" devil, the "international Jew" (the Prince was international, universal, "catholic"). This *materialization* of a religious pattern is, I think, one terrifically effective weapon of propaganda in a period where religion has been progressively weakened by many centuries of capitalist materialism. You need but go back to the sermonizing of centuries to be reminded that religion had a powerful enemy long before organized atheism came upon the scene. Religion is based upon the "prosperity of poverty," upon the use of ways for converting our sufferings and handicaps into a good—but capitalism is based upon the prosperity of acquisitions, the only scheme of value, in fact, by which its proliferating store of gadgets could be sold, assuming for the moment that capitalism had not got so drastically in its own way that it can't sell its gadgets even after it has trained people to feel that human dignity, the "higher standard of living," could be attained only by their vast private accumulation.

So, we have, as unifying step No. 1, the international devil materialized, in the visible, point-to-able form of people with a certain kind of "blood," a burlesque of contemporary neo-positivism's ideal of meaning, which insists upon a *material* reference.

Once Hitler has thus essentialized his enemy, all "proof" henceforth is automatic. If you point out the enormous amount of evidence to show that the Jewish worker is at odds with the "international Jew stock exchange capitalist," Hitler replies with one hundred per cent regularity: That is one more indication of the cunning with which the "Jewish plot" is being engineered. Or would you point to "Aryans" who do the same as his conspiratorial Jews? Very well; that is proof that the "Aryan" has been "seduced" by the Jew.

The sexual symbolism that runs through Hitler's book, lying in wait to draw upon the responses of contemporary sexual values, is easily characterized: Germany in dispersion is the "dehorned Siegfried." The masses are "feminine." As such, they desire to be led by a dominating male. This male, as orator, woos them—and, when he has won them, he commands them. The rival male, the villainous Jew, would on the contrary "seduce" them. If he succeeds, he poisons their blood by intermingling with them. Whereupon, by purely associative connections of ideas, we are moved into attacks upon syphilis, prostitution, incest, and other similar misfortunes, which are introduced as a kind of "musical" argument when he is on the subject of "blood-poisoning" by inter-marriage or, in its "spiritual" equivalent, by the infection of "Jewish" ideas, such as democracy.[1]

The "medicinal" appeal of the Jew as scapegoat operates from another angle. The middle class contains, within the mind of each member, a duality: its members simultaneously have a cult of money and a detestation of this cult. When capitalism is going well, this conflict is left more or less in abeyance. But when capitalism is balked, it comes to the fore. Hence, there is "medicine" for the "Aryan" members of the middle class in the projective device of the scapegoat, whereby the "bad" features can be allocated to the "devil," and one can "respect himself" by a distinction between "good" capitalism and "bad" capitalism, with those of a different lodge being the vessels of the "bad" capitalism. It is doubtless the "relief" of this solution that spared Hitler the necessity of explaining just how the "Jewish plot" was to work out. Nowhere does this book, which is so full of war plans, make the slightest attempt to explain the steps whereby the triumph of "Jewish Bolshevism," which destroys *all* finance, will be the triumph of "*Jewish*" finance. Hitler well knows the point at which his "elucidations" should rely upon the lurid alone.

The question arises, in those trying to gauge Hitler: Was his selection of the Jew, as his unifying devil-function, a purely calculating act? Despite the quotation I have already given, I believe that it was *not*. The vigor with which he utilized it, I think, derives from a much more complex state of affairs. It seems that, when Hitler went to Vienna, in a state close to total poverty, he genuinely suffered. He lived among the impoverished; and he describes his misery at the spectacle. He was *sensitive* to it; and his way of manifesting this sensitiveness impresses me that he is, at this point, wholly genuine, as with his wincing at broken family relationships caused by alcoholism, which he in turn relates to impoverishment. During this time he began his attempts at political theorizing; and his disturbance was considerably increased by the skill with which Marxists tied him into knots. One passage in particular gives you reason, reading between the lines, to believe that the dialecticians of the class struggle, in their skill at blasting his muddled speculations, put him into a state of uncertainty that was finally "solved" by rage:

> The more I argued with them, the more I got to know their dialectics. First, they counted on the ignorance of their adversary; then, when there was no way out, they themselves pretended stupidity. If all this was of no avail, they refused to understand or they changed the subject when driven into a corner; they brought up truisms, but they immediately transferred their acceptance to quite different subjects, and, if attacked again, they gave way and pretended to know nothing exactly. Wherever one attacked one of these prophets, one's hands seized slimy jelly; it slipped through one's fingers only to collect again in the next moment. If one smote one of them so thoroughly that, with the bystanders watching, he could but agree, and if one thus thought he had advanced at least one step, one was greatly astonished the following day. The Jew did not in the least remember the day before, he continued to talk in the same old strain as if nothing had happened, and if indignantly confronted, he pretended to be astonished and could not remember anything except that his assertions had already been proved true the day before.
>
> Often I was stunned.
>
> One did not know what to admire more: their glibness of tongue or their skill in lying.
>
> I gradually began to hate them.

At this point, I think, he is tracing the *spontaneous* rise of his anti-Semitism. He tells how, once he had discovered the "cause" of misery about him, he could *confront it*. Where he had had to avert his eyes, he could now *positively welcome* the scene. Here his drastic structure of *acceptance* was being formed. He tells of the "internal happiness" that descended upon him.

> This was the time in which the greatest change I was ever to experience took place in me.
>
> From a feeble cosmopolite I turned into a fanatical anti-Semite,

and thence we move, by one of those associational tricks which he brings forth at all strategic moments, into a vision of the end of the world—out of which in turn he emerges with his slogan: "I am acting in the sense of the Almighty Creator: *By warding off Jews I am fighting for the Lord's work*" (italics his).

He talks of this transition as a period of "double life," a struggle of "reason" and "reality" against his "heart."[2] It was as "bitter" as it was "blissful." And finally, it was "reason" that won! Which prompts us to note that those who attack Hitlerism as a cult of the irrational should emend their statements to this extent: irrational it is, but it is carried on under the *slogan* of "Reason." Similarly, his cult of war is developed "in the name of" humility, love, and peace. Judged on a quantitative basis, Hitler's book certainly falls under the classification of hate. Its venom is everywhere, its charity is sparse. But the rationalized family tree for this hate situates it in "Aryan love." Some deep-probing German poets, whose work adumbrated the Nazi movement, did gravitate towards thinking *in the name of* war, irrationality, and hate. But Hitler was not among them. After all, when it is so easy to draw a doctrine of war out of a doctrine of peace, why should the astute politician do otherwise, particularly when Hitler has slung together his doctrines, without the slightest effort at logical symmetry? Furthermore, Church thinking always got to its wars in Hitler's "sounder" manner; and the patterns of Hitler's thought are a bastardized or caricatured version of religious thought.

I spoke of Hitler's fury at the dialectics of those who opposed him when his structure was in the stage of scaffolding. From this we may move to another tremendously important aspect of his theory: his attack upon the *parliamentary*. For it is again, I submit, an important aspect of his medicine, in its function as medicine for him personally and as medicine for those who were later to identify themselves with him.

There is a "problem" in the parliament—and nowhere was this problem more acutely in evidence than in the pre-war Vienna that was to serve as Hitler's political schooling. For the parliament, at its best, is a "babel" of voices. There is the wrangle of men representing interests lying awkwardly on the bias across one another, sometimes opposing, sometimes vaguely divergent. Morton Prince's psychiatric study of "Miss Beauchamp," the case of a woman split into several sub-personalities at odds with one another, variously combining under hypnosis, and frequently in turmoil, is the allegory of a democracy fallen upon evil days. The parliament of the Habsburg Empire just prior to its collapse was an especially drastic instance of such disruption, such vocal diaspora, with movements that would reduce one to a disintegrated mass of fragments if he attempted to encompass the totality of its discordancies. So Hitler, suffering under the alienation of poverty and confusion, yearning for some integrative core, came to take this parliament as the basic symbol of all that he would move away from. He damned the tottering Habsburg Empire as a "State of Nationalities." The many conflicting voices of the spokesmen of the many political blocs arose from the fact that various separationist movements of a nationalistic sort had arisen within a Catholic imperial structure formed prior to the nationalistic emphasis and slowly breaking apart under the development. So, you had this Babel of voices; and, by the method of associative mergers, *using ideas as imagery,* it became tied up, in the Hitler rhetoric, with "Babylon," Vienna as the city of poverty, prostitution, immorality, coalitions, half-measures, incest, democracy (i.e., majority rule leading to "lack of personal responsibility"), death, internationalism, seduction, and anything else of thumbs-down sort the sociative enterprise cared to add on this side of the balance.

Hitler's way of treating the parliamentary babel, I am sorry to say, was at one important point not much different from that of the customary editorial in our own newspapers. Every conflict among the parliamentary spokesmen represents a corresponding conflict among the material interests of the groups for whom they are speaking. But Hitler did not discuss the babel from this angle. He discussed it on a purely *symptomatic* basis. The strategy of our orthodox press, in thus ridiculing the cacophonous verbal output of Congress, is obvious: by centering attack upon the *symptoms* of business conflict, as they reveal themselves on the dial of political wrangling, and leaving the underlying cause, the business conflicts themselves, out of the case, they can gratify the very public they would otherwise alienate: namely, the businessmen who are the activating members of their reading public. Hitler, however, went them one better. For not only did he stress the purely *symptomatic* attack here. He proceeded to search for the "cause." And this "cause," of course, he derived from his medicine, his racial theory by which he could give a noneconomic interpretation of a phenomenon economically engendered.

Here again is where Hitler's corrupt use of religious patterns comes to the fore. Church thought, being primarily concerned with matters of the "personality," with problems of moral betterment, naturally, and I think rightly, stresses as a necessary feature, the act of will upon the part of the individual. Hence its resistance to a purely "environmental" account of human ills. Hence its emphasis upon the "person." Hence its proneness to seek a noneconomic explanation of economic phenomena. Hitler's proposal of a noneconomic "cause" for the disturbances thus had much to recommend it from this angle. And, as a matter of fact, it was Lueger's Christian-Social Party in Vienna that taught Hitler the tactics of tying up a program of social betterment with an anti-Semitic "unifier." The two parties that he carefully studied at that time were this Catholic faction and Schoenerer's Pan-German group. And his analysis of their attainments and shortcomings, from the standpoint of demagogic efficacy, is an extremely astute piece of work, revealing how carefully this man used the current situation in Vienna as an experimental laboratory for the maturing of his plans.

His unification device, we may summarize, had the following important features:

(1) Inborn dignity. In both religious and humanistic patterns of thought, a "natural born" dignity of man is stressed. And this categorical dignity is considered to be an attribute of *all* men, if they will but avail themselves of it, by right thinking and right living. But Hitler gives this ennobling attitude an ominous twist by his theories of race and nation, whereby the "Aryan" is elevated above all others by the innate endowment of his blood, while other "races," in particular Jews and Negroes, are innately inferior. This sinister secularized revision of Christian theology thus puts the sense of dignity upon a fighting basis, requiring the conquest of "inferior races." After the defeat of Germany in the World War, there were especially strong emotional needs that this compensatory doctrine of an *inborn* superiority could gratify.

(2) *Projection* device. The "curative" process that comes with the ability to hand over one's ills to a scapegoat, thereby getting purification by dissociation. This was especially medicinal, since the sense of frustration leads to a self-questioning. Hence if one can hand over his infirmities to a vessel, or "cause," outside the self, one can battle an external enemy instead of battling an enemy within. And the greater one's internal inadequacies, the greater amount of evils one can load upon the back of "the enemy." This device is furthermore given a semblance of reason because the individual properly realizes that he is not alone responsible for his condition. There *are* inimical factors in the scene itself. And he wants to have them "placed," preferably in a way that would require a minimum change in the ways of thinking to which he had been accustomed. This was especially appealing to the middle class,

who were encouraged to feel that they could conduct their businesses without any basic change whatever, once the businessmen of a different "race" were eliminated.

(3) Symbolic rebirth. Another aspect of the two features already noted. The projective device of the scapegoat, coupled with the Hitlerite doctrine of inborn racial superiority, provides its followers with a "positive" view of life. They can again get the feel of *moving forward,* towards a *goal* (a promissory feature of which Hitler makes much). In Hitler, as the group's prophet, such rebirth involved a symbolic change of lineage. Here, above all, we see Hitler giving a malign twist to a benign aspect of Christian thought. For whereas the Pope, in the familistic pattern of thought basic to the Church, stated that the Hebrew prophets were the *spiritual ancestors* of Christianity, Hitler uses this same mode of thinking in reverse. He renounces this "ancestry" in a "materialistic" way by voting himself and the members of his lodge a different "blood stream" from that of the Jews.

(4) Commercial use. Hitler obviously here had something to sell—and it was but a question of time until he sold it (i.e., got financial backers for his movement). For it provided a *noneconomic interpretation of economic ills.* As such, it served with maximum efficiency in deflecting the attention from the economic factors involved in modern conflict; hence by attacking "Jew finance" instead of *finance,* it could stimulate an enthusiastic movement that left "Aryan" finance in control.

Never once, throughout his book, does Hitler deviate from the above formula. Invariably, he ends his diatribes against contemporary economic ills by a shift into an insistence that we must get to the "true" cause, which is centered in "race." The "Aryan" is "constructive"; the Jew is "destructive"; and the "Aryan," to continue his *construction,* must *destroy* the Jewish *destruction.* The Aryan, as the vessel of *love,* must *hate* the Jewish *hate.*

Perhaps the most enterprising use of his method is in his chapter, "The Causes of the Collapse," where he refuses to consider Germany's plight as in any basic way connected with the consequences of war. Economic factors, he insists, are "only of second or even third importance," but "political, ethical-moral, as well as factors of blood and race, are of the first importance." His rhetorical steps are especially interesting here, in that he begins by seeming to flout the national susceptibilities: "The military defeat of the German people is not an undeserved catastrophe, but rather a deserved punishment by eternal retribution." He then proceeds to present the military collapse as but a "consequence of moral poisoning, visible to all, the consequence of a decrease in the instinct of self-preservation . . . which had already begun to undermine the foundations of the People and the Reich many years before." This moral decay derived from "a sin against the blood and the degradation of the race," so its innerness was an outerness after all: the Jew, who thereupon gets saddled with a vast amalgamation of evils, among them being capitalism, democracy, pacifism, journalism, poor housing, modernism, big cities, loss of religion, half measures, ill health, and weakness of the monarch.

2

Hitler had here another important psychological ingredient to play upon. If a State is in economic collapse (and his theories, tentatively taking shape in the pre-war Vienna, were but developed with greater efficiency in post-war Munich), you cannot possibly derive dignity from economic stability. Dignity must come first— and if you possess it, implement it, from it may follow its economic counterpart. There is much justice to this line of reasoning, so far as it goes. A people in collapse, suffering under economic frustration and the defeat of nationalistic aspirations, with the very midrib of their integrative efforts (the army) in a state of dispersion, have little other than some "spiritual" basis to which they could refer their nationalistic dignity. Hence, the categorical dignity of superior race was a perfect recipe for the situation. It was "spiritual" in so far as it was "above" crude economic "interests," but it was "materialized" at the psychologically "right" spot in that "the enemy" was something you could *see*.

Furthermore, you had the desire for unity, such as a discussion of class conflict, on the basis of conflicting interests, could not satisfy. The yearning for unity is so great that people are always willing to meet you halfway if you will give it to them by fiat, by flat statement, regardless of the facts. Hence, Hitler consistently refused to consider internal political conflict on the basis of conflicting interests. Here again, he could draw upon a religious pattern, by insisting upon a *personal* statement of the relation between classes, the relation between leaders and followers, each group in its way fulfilling the same commonalty of interests, as the soldiers and captains of an army share a common interest in victory. People so dislike the idea of internal division that, where there is a real internal division, their dislike can easily be turned against the man or group who would so much as *name* it, let alone proposing to act upon it. Their natural and justified resentment against internal division itself, is turned against the diagnostician who states it as a *fact*. This diagnostician, it is felt, is the *cause* of the disunity he named.

Cutting in from another angle, therefore, we note how two sets of equations were built up, with Hitler combining or coalescing *ideas* the way a poet combines or coalesces *images*. On the one side, were the ideas, or images, of disunity, centering in the parliamentary wrangle of the Habsburg "State of Nationalities." This was offered as the antithesis of German nationality, which was presented in the curative imagery of unity, focused upon the glories of the Prussian Reich, with its mecca now moved to "folkish" Vienna. For though Hitler at first attacked the many "folkish" movements, with their hankerings after a kind of Wagnerian mythology of Germanic origins, he subsequently took "folkish" as a basic word by which to conjure. It was, after all, another noneconomic basis of reference. At first we find him objecting to "those who drift about with the word 'folkish' on their caps," and asserting that "such a Babel of opinions cannot serve as the basis of a political fighting movement." But later he seems to have realized, as he well should, that its vagueness was a major point in its favor. So it was incorporated into the grand coalition of his relational imagery, or imagistic ideation; and Chapter XI ends with the vision of "a State which represents not a mechanism of economic considerations and interests, alien to the people, but a folkish organism."

So, as against the disunity equations, already listed briefly in our discussion of his attacks upon the parliamentary, we get a contrary purifying set; the wrangle of the parliamentary is to be stilled by the giving of *one* voice to the whole people, this to be the "inner voice" of Hitler, made uniform throughout the German boundaries, as leader and people were completely identified with each other. In sum: Hitler's inner voice, equals leader-people identification, equals unity, equals Reich, equals the mecca of Munich, equals plow, equals sword, equals work, equals war, equals army as midrib, equals responsibility (the personal responsibility of the absolute ruler), equals sacrifice, equals the theory of "German democracy" (the free popular choice of the leader, who then accepts the responsibility, and demands absolute obedience in exchange for his sacrifice), equals love (with the masses as feminine), equals idealism, equals obedience to nature, equals race, nation.[3]

And, of course, the two keystones of these opposite equations were Aryan "heroism" and "sacrifice" vs. Jewish "cunning" and "arrogance." Here again we get an astounding caricature of religious thought. For Hitler presents the concept of "Aryan" superiority, of all ways, in terms of "Aryan humility." This "humility" is extracted by a very delicate process that requires, I am afraid, considerable "good will" on the part of the reader who would follow it:

The Church, we may recall, had proclaimed an integral relationship between Divine Law and Natural Law. Natural Law was the expression of the Will of God. Thus, in the Middle Ages, it was a result of natural law, working through tradition, that some people were serfs and other people nobles. And every good member of the Church was "obedient" to this law. Everybody resigned himself to it. Hence, the serf resigned himself to his poverty, and the noble resigned himself to his riches. The monarch resigned himself to his position as representative of the people. And at times the Churchmen resigned themselves to the need of trying to represent the people instead. And the pattern was made symmetrical by the consideration that each traditional "right" had its corresponding "obligations." Similarly, the Aryan doctrine is a doctrine of resignation, hence of humility. It is in accordance with the laws of nature that the "Aryan blood" is superior to all other bloods. Also, the "law of the survival of the fittest" is God's law, working through natural law. Hence, if the Aryan blood has been vested with the awful responsibility of its inborn superiority, the bearers of this "culture-creating" blood must resign themselves to struggle in behalf of its triumph. Otherwise, the laws of God have been disobeyed, with human decadence as a result. We must fight, he says, in order to "deserve to be alive." The Aryan "obeys" nature. It is only "Jewish arrogance" that thinks of "conquering" nature by democratic ideals of equality.

This picture has some nice distinctions worth following. The major virtue of the Aryan race was its instinct for self-preservation (in obedience to natural law). But the major vice of the Jew was his instinct for self-preservation; for, if he did not have this instinct to a maximum degree, he would not be the "perfect" enemy—that is, he wouldn't be strong enough to account for the ubiquitousness and omnipotence of his conspiracy in destroying the world to become its master.

How, then, are we to distinguish between the benign instinct of self-preservation at the roots of Aryanism, and the malign instinct of self-preservation at the roots of Semitism? We shall distinguish thus: The Aryan self-preservation is based upon *sacrifice*, the sacrifice of the individual to the group, hence, militarism, army discipline, and one big company union. But Jewish self-preservation is based upon individualism, which attains its cunning ends by the exploitation of peace. How, then, can such arrant individualists concoct the world-wide plot? By the help of their "herd instinct." By their sheer "herd instinct" individualists can band together for a common end. They have no real solidarity, but unite opportunistically to seduce the Aryan. Still, that brings up another technical problem. For we have been hearing much about the importance of the *person*. We have been told how, by "law of the survival of the fittest," there is a sifting of people on the basis of their individual capacities. We even have a special chapter of pure Aryanism: "The Strong Man is Mightiest Alone." Hence, another distinction is necessary: The Jew represents individualism; the Aryan represents "super-individualism."

I had thought, when coming upon the "Strong Man is Mightiest Alone" chapter, that I was going to find Hitler at his weakest. Instead, I found him at his strongest. (I am not referring to *quality*, but to *demagogic effectiveness*.) For the chapter is not at all, as you might infer from the title, done in a "rise of Adolph Hitler" manner.

Instead, it deals with the Nazis' gradual absorption of the many disrelated "folkish" groups. And it is managed throughout by means of a spontaneous identification between leader and people. Hence, the Strong Man's "aloneness" is presented as a *public* attribute, in terms of tactics for the struggle against the *Party's* dismemberment under the pressure of rival saviors. There is no explicit talk of Hitler at all. And it is simply *taken for granted* that *his* leadership is the norm, and all other leaderships the abnorm. There is no "philosophy of the superman," in Nietzschean cast. Instead, Hitler's blandishments so integrate leader and people, commingling them so inextricably, that the politician does not even present himself as candidate. Somehow, the battle is over already, the decision has been made. "German democracy" has chosen. And the deployments of politics are, you might say, the chartings of Hitler's private mind translated into the vocabulary of nationalistic events. He says *what he thought* in terms of *what parties did.*

Here, I think, we see the distinguishing quality of Hitler's method as an instrument of persuasion, with reference to the question whether Hitler is sincere or deliberate, whether his vision of the omnipotent conspirator has the drastic honesty of paranoia or the sheer shrewdness of a demagogue trained in *Realpolitik* of the Machiavellian sort.[4] Must we choose? Or may we not, rather, replace the "either-or" with a "both-and"? Have we not by now offered grounds enough for our contention that Hitler's sinister powers of persuasion derive from the fact that he spontaneously evolved his "cure-all" in response to inner necessities?

3

So much, then, was "spontaneous." It was further channelized into the anti-Semitic pattern by the incentives he derived from the Catholic Christian-Social Party in Vienna itself. Add, now, the step into *criticism*. Not criticism in the "parliamentary" sense of doubt, of hearkening to the opposition and attempting to mature a policy in the light of counter-policies; but the "unified" kind of criticism that simply seeks for conscious ways of making one's position more "efficient," more thoroughly itself. This is the kind of criticism at which Hitler was an adept. As a result, he could *spontaneously* turn to a scapegoat mechanism, and he could, by conscious planning, perfect the symmetry of the solution towards which he had spontaneously turned.

This is the meaning of Hitler's diatribes against "objectivity." "Objectivity" is interference-criticism. What Hitler wanted was the kind of criticism that would be a pure and simple coefficient of power, enabling him to go most effectively in the direction he had chosen. And the "inner voice" of which he speaks would henceforth dictate to him the greatest amount of realism, as regards the tactics of efficiency. For instance, having decided that the masses required certainty, and simple certainty, quite as he did himself, he later worked out a 25-point program as the platform of his National Socialist German Workers Party and he resolutely refused to change one single item in this program, even for purposes of "improvement." He felt that the *fixity* of the platform was more important for propagandistic purposes than any revision of his slogans could be, even though the revisions in themselves had much to be said in their favor. The astounding thing is that, although such an attitude gave good cause to doubt the Hitlerite promises, he could explicitly explain his tactics in his book and still employ them without loss of effectiveness.[5]

Hitler also tells of his technique in speaking, once the Nazi party had become effectively organized, and had its army of guards, or bouncers, to maltreat hecklers and throw them from the hall. He would, he recounts, fill his speech with *provocative* remarks, whereat his bouncers would promptly swoop down in flying formation, with swinging fists, upon anyone whom these provocative remarks provoked to answer. The efficiency of Hitlerism is the efficiency of the one voice, implemented throughout a total organization. The trinity of government which he finally offers is: *popularity* of the leader, *force* to back the popularity, and popularity and force maintained together long enough to become backed by a *tradition*. Is such thinking spontaneous or deliberate—or is it not rather both?[6]

Freud has given us a succinct paragraph that bears upon the spontaneous aspect of Hitler's persecution mania. (A persecution mania, I should add, different from the pure product in that it was constructed of *public* materials; all the ingredients Hitler stirred into his brew were already rife, with spokesmen and bands of followers, before Hitler "took them over." Both the pre-war and post-war periods were dotted with saviors, of nationalistic and "folkish" cast. This proliferation was analogous to the swarm of barter schemes and currency-tinkering that burst loose upon the United States after the crash of 1929. Also, the commercial availability of Hitler's politics was, in a low sense of the term, a *public* qualification, removing it from the realm of "pure" paranoia where the sufferer develops a wholly *private* structure of interpretations.)

I cite from *Totem and Taboo:*

> Another trait in the attitude of primitive races towards their rulers recalls a mechanism which is universally present in mental disturbances, and is openly revealed in the so-called delusions of persecution. Here the importance of a particular person is extraordinarily heightened and his omnipotence is raised to the improbable in order to make it easier to attribute to him responsibility for everything painful which happens to the patient. Savages really do not act differently towards rulers when they ascribe to them power over rain and shine, wind and weather, and then dethrone them or kill them because nature has disappointed their expectation of a good hunt or a ripe harvest. The prototype which the paranoiac reconstructs in his persecution mania is found in the relation of the child to its father. Such omnipotence is regularly attributed to the father in the imagination of the son, and distrust of the father has been shown to be intimately connected with the heightened esteem for him. When a paranoiac names a person of his acquaintance as his "persecutor," he thereby elevates him to the paternal succession and brings him under conditions which enable him to make him responsible for all the misfortune which he experiences.

I have already proposed my modifications of this account when discussing the symbolic change of lineage connected with Hitler's project of a "new way of life." Hitler is symbolically changing from the "spiritual ancestry" of the Hebrew prophets to the "superior" ancestry of "Aryanism," and has given his story a kind of bastardized modernization, along the lines of naturalistic, materialistic "science," by his fiction of the special "blood-stream." He is voting himself a new identity (something contrary to the wrangles of the Habsburg Babylon, a soothing national unity); whereupon the vessels of the old identity become a "bad" father, i.e., the persecutor. It is not hard to see how, as his enmity becomes implemented by the backing of an organization, the rôle of "persecutor" is transformed into the rôle of persecuted, as he sets out with his like-minded band to "destroy the destroyer."

Were Hitler simply a poet, he might have written a work with an anti-Semitic turn, and let it go at that. But Hitler, who began as a student of painting, and later shifted to architecture, himself treats his political activities as an extension of his artistic ambitions. He remained, in his own eyes, an "architect," building a "folkish" State that was to match, in political materials, the "folkish" architecture of Munich.

We might consider the matter this way (still trying, that is, to make precise the relationship between the drastically sincere and the deliberately scheming): Do we not know of many authors who seem, as they turn from the rôle of citizen to the rôle of spokesman, to leave one room and enter another? Or who has not, on occasion, talked with a man in private conversation, and then been almost startled at the transformation this man undergoes when addressing a public audience? And I know persons today, who shift between the writing of items in the class of academic, philosophic speculation to items of political pamphleteering, and whose entire style and method changes [sic] with this change of rôle. In their academic manner, they are cautious, painstaking, eager to present all significant aspects of the case they are considering; but when they turn to political pamphleteering, they hammer forth with vituperation, they systematically misrepresent the position of their opponent, they go into a kind of political trance, in which, during its throes, they throb like a locomotive; and behold, a moment later, the mediumistic state is abandoned, and they are the most moderate of men.

Now, one will find few pages in Hitler that one could call "moderate." But there are many pages in which he gauges resistances and opportunities with the "rationality" of a skilled advertising man planning a new sales campaign. Politics, he says, must be sold like soap—and soap is not sold in a trance. But he did have the experience of his trance, in the "exaltation" of his anti-Semitism. And later, as he became a successful orator (he insists that revolutions are made solely by the power of the spoken word), he had this "poetic" rôle to draw upon, plus the great relief it provided as a way of slipping from the burden of logical analysis into the pure "spirituality" of vituperative prophecy. What more natural, therefore, than that a man so insistent upon unification would integrate this mood with less ecstatic moments, particularly when he had found the followers and the backers that put a price, both spiritual and material, upon such unification?

Once this happy "unity" is under way, one has a "logic" for the development of a method. One knows when to "spiritualize" a material issue, and when to "materialize" a spiritual one. Thus, when it is a matter of materialistic interests that cause a conflict between employer and employee, Hitler here disdainfully shifts to a high moral plane. He is "above" such low concerns. Everything becomes a matter of "sacrifices" and "personality." It becomes crass to treat employers and employees as different *classes* with a corresponding difference in the classification of their interests. Instead, relations between employer and employee must be on the "personal" basis of leader and follower and "whatever may have a divisive effect in national life should be given a unifying effect through the army." When talking of national rivalries, however, he makes a very shrewd materialistic gauging of Britain and France with relation to Germany. France, he says, desires the "Balkanization of Germany" (i.e., its breakup into separationist movements—the "disunity" theme again) in order to maintain commercial hegemony on the continent. But Britain desires the "Balkanization of *Europe*," hence would favor a fairly strong and unified Germany, to use as a counter-weight against French hegemony. *German* nationality, however, is unified by the *spiritual* quality of Aryanism (that would produce the national organization via the Party) while this in turn is *materialized* in the myth of the blood-stream.

What are we to learn from Hitler's book? For one thing, I believe that he has shown, to a very disturbing degree, the power of endless repetition. Every circular advertising a Nazi meeting had, at the bottom, two slogans: "Jews not admitted" and "War victims free." And the substance of Nazi propaganda was built about these two "complementary" themes. He describes the power of spectacle; insists that mass meetings are a fundamental way of giving the individual the sense of being protectively surrounded by a movement, the sense of "community." He also drops one wise hint that I wish the American authorities would take in treating Nazi gatherings. He says that the presence of a special Nazi guard, in Nazi uniforms, was of great importance in building up, among the followers, a tendency to place the center of authority in the Nazi party. I believe that we should take him at his word here, but use the advice in reverse, by insisting that, where Nazi meetings are to be permitted, they be policed by the authorities alone, and that uniformed Nazi guards to enforce the law be prohibited.

And is it possible that an equally important feature of appeal was not so much in the repetitiousness per se, but in the fact that, by means of it, Hitler provided a "world view" for people who had previously seen the world but piecemeal? Did not much of his lure derive, once more, from the *bad* filling of a *good* need? Are not those who insist upon a purely *planless* working of the market asking people to accept far too slovenly a scheme of human purpose, a slovenly scheme that can be accepted so long as it operates with a fair degree of satisfaction, but becomes abhorrent to the victims of its disarray? Are they not then psychologically ready for a rationale, *any* rationale, if it but offer them some specious "universal" explanation? Hence, I doubt whether the appeal was in the sloganizing element alone (particularly as even slogans can only be hammered home, in speech after speech, and two or three hours at a stretch, by endless variations on the themes). And Hitler himself somewhat justifies my interpretation by laying so much stress upon the *half-measures* of the middle-class politicians, and the contrasting *certainty* of his own methods. He was not offering people a *rival* world view; rather, he was offering a world view to people who had no other to pit against it.

As for the basic Nazi trick: the "curative" unification by a fictitious devil-function, gradually made convincing by the sloganizing repetitiousness of standard advertising technique—the opposition must be as unwearying in the attack upon it. It may well be that people, in their human frailty, require an enemy as well as a goal. Very well: Hitlerism itself has provided us with such an enemy—and the clear example of its operation is guaranty that we have, in Hitler and all he stands for, no purely fictitious "devil-function" made to look like a world menace by rhetorical blandishments, but a reality whose ominousness is clarified by the record of its conduct to date. In selecting his brand of doctrine as our "scapegoat," and in tracking down its equivalent in America, we shall be at the very center of accuracy. The Nazis themselves have made the task of clarification easier. Add to them Japan and Italy, and you have *case histories* of fascism for those who might find it more difficult to approach an understanding of its imperialistic drives by a vigorously economic explanation.

But above all, I believe, we must make it apparent that Hitler appeals by relying upon a bastardization of fundamentally religious patterns of thought. In this, if properly presented, there is no slight to religion. There is nothing in religion proper that requires a fascist state. There is much in religion, when misused, that does lead to a fascist state. There is a Latin proverb, *Corruptio optimi pessima,* "the corruption of the best is the worst." And it is the corruptors of religion who are a major menace to the world today, in giving the profound patterns of religious thought a crude and sinister distortion.

Our job, then, our anti-Hitler Battle, is to find all available ways of making the Hitlerite distortions of religion apparent, in order that politicians of his kind in America be unable to perform a similar swindle. The desire for unity is genuine and admirable. The desire for national unity, in the present state of the world, is genuine and admirable. But this unity, if attained on a deceptive basis, by emotional trickeries that shift our criticism from the accurate locus of our trouble, is no unity at all. For, even if we are among those who happen to be "Aryans," we solve no problems even for ourselves by such solutions, since the factors pressing towards calamity remain. Thus, in Germany, after all the upheaval, we see nothing beyond a drive for ever more and more upheaval, precisely because the "new way of life" was no new way, but the dismally oldest way of sheer deception—hence, after all the "change," the factors driving towards unrest are left intact, and even strengthened. True, the Germans had the resentment of a lost war to increase their susceptibility to Hitler's rhetoric. But in a wider sense, it has repeatedly been observed, the whole world lost the war—and the accumulating ills of the capitalist order were but accelerated in their movements towards confusion. Hence, here too there are the resentments that go with frustration of men's ability to work and earn. At that point a certain kind of industrial or financial monopolist may, annoyed by the contrary voices of our parliament, wish for the momentary peace of one voice, amplified by social organizations, with all the others not merely quieted but given the quietus. So he might, under Nazi promptings, be tempted to back a group of gangsters who, on becoming the political rulers of the state, would protect him against the necessary demands of the workers. His gangsters, then, would be his insurance against his workers. But who would be his insurance against his gangsters?

NOTES

[1]Hitler also strongly insists upon the total identification between leader and people. Thus, in wooing the people, he would in a roundabout way be wooing himself. The thought might suggest how the Führer, dominating the feminine masses by his diction, would have an incentive to remain unmarried.

[2]Other aspects of the career symbolism: Hitler's book begins: "Today I consider it my good fortune that Fate designated Braunau on the Inn as the place of my birth. For this small town is situated on the border between those two German States, the reunion of which seems, at least to us of the younger generation, a task to be furthered with every means our lives long," an indication of his "transitional" mind, what Wordsworth might have called the "borderer." He neglects to give the date of his birth, 1889, which is supplied by the editors. Again there is a certain "correctness" here, as Hitler was not "born" until many years later—but he does give the exact date of his war wounds, which were indeed formative. During his early years in Vienna and Munich, he foregoes protest, on the grounds that he is "nameless." And when his party is finally organized and effective, he stresses the fact that his "nameless" period is over (i.e., he has shaped himself an identity). When reading in an earlier passage of his book some generalizations to the effect that one should not crystallize his political views until he is thirty, I made a note: "See what Hitler does at thirty." I felt sure that, though such generalizations may be dubious as applied to people as a whole, they must, given the Hitler type of mind (with his complete identification between himself and his followers), be valid statements about himself. One *should* do what he *did.* The hunch was verified: about the age of thirty

Hitler, in a group of seven, began working with the party that was to conquer Germany. I trace these steps particularly because I believe that the orator who has a strong sense of his own "rebirth" has this to draw upon when persuading his audiences that he is offering them the way to a "new life." However, I see no categorical objection to this attitude; its menace derives solely from the values in which it is exemplified. They may be wholesome or unwholesome. If they are unwholesome, but backed by conviction, the basic sincerity of the conviction acts as a sound virtue to reinforce a vice—and this combination is the most disastrous one that a people can encounter in a demagogue.

[3]One could carry out the equations further, on both the disunity and unity side. In the aesthetic field, for instance, we have expressionism on the thumbs-down side, as against aesthetic hygiene on the thumbs-up side. This again is a particularly ironic moment in Hitler's strategy. For the expressionist movement was unquestionably a symptom of unhealthiness. It reflected the increasing alienation that went with the movement towards world war and the disorganization after the world war. It was "lost," vague in identity, a drastically accurate reflection of the response to material confusion, a pathetic attempt by sincere artists to make their wretchedness bearable at least to the extent that comes of giving it expression. And it attained its height during the period of wild inflation, when the capitalist world, which bases its morality of work and savings upon the soundness of its money structure, had this last prop of stability removed. The anguish, in short, reflected precisely the kind of disruption that made people *ripe* for a Hitler. It was the antecedent in a phrase of which Hitlerism was the consequent. But by thundering against this *symptom* he could gain persuasiveness, though attacking the very *foreshadowing of himself.*

[4]I should not want to use the word "Machiavellian," however, without offering a kind of apology to Machiavelli. It seems to me that Machiavelli's *Prince* has more to be said in extenuation than is usually said of it. Machiavelli's strategy, as I see it, was something like this: He accepted the values of the Renaissance rule as a *fact.* That is: whether you like these values or not, they were there and operating, and it was useless to try persuading the ambitious ruler to adopt other values, such as those of the Church. These men believed in the cult of material power, and they had the power to implement their beliefs. With so much as "the given," could anything in the way of benefits for the people be salvaged? Machiavelli evolved a typical "Machiavellian" argument in favor of popular benefits, on the basis of the prince's own scheme of values. That is: the ruler, to attain the maximum strength, requires the backing of the populace. That this backing be as effective as possible, the populace should be made as strong as possible. And that the populace be as strong as possible, they should be well treated. Their gratitude would further repay itself in the form of increased loyalty.

It was Machiavelli's hope that, for this roundabout project, he would be rewarded with a well-paying office in the prince's administrative bureaucracy.

[5]On this point Hitler reasons as follows: "Here, too, one can learn from the Catholic Church. Although its structure of doctrines in many instances collides, quite unnecessarily, with exact science and research, yet it is unwilling to sacrifice even one little syllable of its dogmas. It has rightly recognized that its resistibility does not lie in a more or less great adjustment to the scientific results of the moment, which in reality are always changing, but rather in a strict adherence to dogmas, once laid down, which alone give the entire structure the character of creed. Today, therefore, the Catholic Church stands firmer than ever. One can prophesy that in the same measure in which the appearances flee, the Church itself, as the resting pole in the flight of appearances, will gain more and more blind adherence."

[6]Hitler also paid great attention to the conditions under which political oratory is most effective. He sums up thus:

"All these cases involve encroachments upon man's freedom of will. This applies, of course, most of all to meetings to which people with a contrary orientation of will are coming, and who now have to be won for new intentions. It seems that in the morning and even during the day men's power revolts with highest energy against an attempt at being forced under another's will and another's opinion. In the evening, however they submit more easily to the dominating force of a stronger will. For truly every such meeting presents a wrestling match between two opposed forces. The superior oratorical talent of a domineering apostolic nature will now succeed more easily in winning for the new will people who themselves have in turn experienced a weakening of their force of resistance in the most natural way, than people who still have full command of the energies of their minds and their will power.

"The same purpose serves also the artificially created and yet mysterious dusk of the Catholic churches, the burning candles, incense, censers, etc."

HUNTING AND HERITAGE ON TRIAL: A DRAMATISTIC DEBATE OVER TRAGEDY, TRADITION, AND TERRITORY

MARI BOOR TONN, VALERIE A. ENDRESS, AND JOHN N. DIAMOND

On November 15, 1988, Donald Rogerson was deer hunting with a companion in a wooded area near Hermon, Maine. Shouldering a .30-06 rifle with a four-power scope, the veteran hunter and native Mainer was searching for a buck, the only prey his "bucks only" license allowed him to bag. Nearby in a residential development area lived Karen Wood, who recently had moved from Iowa with her husband and twin nine-month-old daughters. Rogerson, who later alleged he had seen a buck deer, fired. Then in the belief he had spotted two white "flags" of deer tails, he immediately fired again. Moments later, the hunter found Karen Wood lying in her wooded yard 134 feet from her backdoor. There she died within minutes from a single rifle slug to her chest. On the ground near Wood's body lay two buff-colored mittens (Warner, "Hunter Charged" 2; Clark 96–97; Kunstler 59).[1]

The shock over the killing was soon matched by the intense controversy the incident evoked. Immediately, the local newspaper editorialized the killing as a "double tragedy," headlined Rogerson's standing as a Bangor Boy Scout leader, and focused on his own and his family's personal anguish ("A Double Tragedy" 8). In response, angry readers acidulously reminded the editors that Wood was the victim—not the hunter who had slain her on her own property. A venomous volley ensued as another group of citizens rushed to Rogerson's defense and accused Wood of carelessly causing her own death. During hunting season, they argued, citizens were responsible for protecting themselves against the danger hunters present.

The debate escalated with a grand jury's failure to indict Rogerson. The furor grew more intense after three unsettling revelations nearly a full year after the incident: First, released evidence countered long-standing claims that Rogerson had been hunting legally; a neighboring residence was 286 feet from the spot where the hunter claimed he had fired, 14 feet under Maine's legal limit. Second, released investigators' reports revealed that no evidence of deer—tracks, blood, or droppings—had been found in the immediate vicinity of the shooting, despite Rogerson's alleged sighting (Warner, "Details Released" 1). Third, a reporter discovered that a juror was the nephew of Rogerson's defense attorney as well as an acquaintance of the accused hunter ("Lone Woman"; "Hunter Indicted" 1). This semblance of impropriety led to the convening of a new grand jury, which issued an indictment. Consequently, nearly two years after the incident, Donald Rogerson was tried for manslaughter in the shooting death of Karen Wood. And in October of 1990, the hunter was acquitted of all charges (Goodman 53). Although the verdict brought long-awaited legal resolution, the decision stoked rather than stemmed the conflict. Citizens in the embattled state remained polarized on exactly which of the principal characters was at fault.

Neither the jury's verdict nor the rationale of those citizens who blamed Wood can be illuminated by a sifting and resifting of the physical evidence. "[T]he subject of motivation," Kenneth Burke argues, "is a philosophic one, not ultimately to be solved in terms of empirical science" (*Grammar* xxiii). In this essay, we illuminate the events that occurred in Maine in the wake of Karen Wood's death by applying Burke's dramatistic theory of motivation. We argue that the tragedy itself and its divisive aftermath can be understood only in terms of a symbolic drama, one rooted in evolving traditions and communities and motivated by a desire by many to stem the tide of social change.

A DRAMATISTIC PERSPECTIVE

In his pentadic framework, Burke concedes that "act" is always the central term but explains that act may be substantially reinterpreted by featuring other terms either singly or, more commonly, by emphasizing a dominant term in a pentadic ratio (*Grammar* xv–xxii, 3–20). Arguments dominated by "scene," Burke claims, reflect a perspective that is committed to viewing the world as relatively permanent and deterministic. Persons functioning within the scene are regarded as seriously constrained by scenic elements. Immutable factors in the natural or social landscape limit their ability to act on their own volition: free will is supplanted largely by fate, thereby reducing action to motion (*Grammar* 127–170). Not uncommonly, rhetors may feature scene to absolve themselves from errors in personal judgment or public policy. David Ling (83), for example, contends that Edward Kennedy's Chappaquiddick apologia featured scene as controlling, a design intended to reduce his action into motion and thereby exonerate him from blame in the drowning of Mary Jo Kopechne. More recently, David Birdsell posits that Ronald Reagan rooted his account of the deaths of American marines in Lebanon in a malignant scene so as to protect American integrity from the "ignominy of a one-on-one defeat" by a more powerful agent (270).

By contrast, arguments that feature "agent" reveal a perspective that views agents as rational and reality as constructed or caused by human choices (Burke, *Grammar* 171). The term "agent," Burke adds, embraces not only all words general or specific for person, individual, hero, villain, but also words for the motivational properties of agents such as "drives," "instincts," or "states of mind." Moreover, agent may be applied to collectives such as nation, church, race, or cultural movements (*Grammar* 20).

But when members of specific communities express a scenic perspective, the ambiguity and flexibility of the pentadic terms (Burke, *Grammar* xviii–xxiii) come to the fore, particularly when communities interact or collide. Distinctions between "agent" and "scene" may become blurred in the concept of a community or social identity, which often includes both personal qualities and literal place.[2] Individuals who comprise a peculiar community may explain their own behavior as motion because it is controlled by communal traditions or "laws," norms that they as "agents" nonetheless have devised. Conversely, the behavior of those individuals in conflict with a community is often construed as action—the conscious or willful violation of rules and physical boundaries. These latter persons retain their status as "agents" who must make choices in interacting with the competing community around them, a scene to which they are alien. Exemplifying this phenomenon most clearly are rationalizations offered in skirmishes involving territory or "turf"; indeed, the terms themselves suggest a scenic worldview. Placing blame on the victim is a familiar defense for acts of violence against community trespassers. In the common refrain that victims deserved their punishment because they entered hostile or alien territory, accountability lies only with the individuals outside of the community; members of the community remain blameless because they are merely responding to *external* conditions. In this sense, Burke's notion of humans as "tribal" is perhaps the clearest. Competing communities or "tribes," if one will, react to each other and behave in a way to maintain their community, their "scene" as "impenetrable, eternally existent" (Burke, *Grammar* 131). Communal integrity, then, becomes analogous to survival in the material world: action is reduced to spontaneous reflexes to outside threats. In so doing, the agent-oriented rational "instincts" or "drives" of individuals within the dominant group are transformed into "instincts" or "drives" that are deterministic animal behaviors rather than rational and ethical human choices.[3]

COLLISION OF COMMUNITIES IN MAINE

All debates over territory or "turf" inescapably turn on Burke's concept of hierarchy, those elements that constitute a social order and imbue certain individuals with power in relationship to others (*Language* 15–20). The heated debate over culpability in the shooting death of Karen Wood was, in essence, a "representative anecdote" for a struggle over territory in both literal and figurative senses. Native Mainers have a tradition of grappling uncomfortably with their sense of place in the social pecking order of their state. A result of Maine's economic dependency upon tourists and wealthy "summer people" is resentment towards those "outsiders" whom many Mainers are compelled to serve for their livelihoods. Moreover, over the decades, many native Mainers have relocated further inland as choice coastal property is bought up by moneyed individuals from outside the state. Not uncommonly, the onus for accelerating property taxes that forced many Mainers to relinquish family beachfront lands or small family-owned businesses is placed on the wealthy buyers rather than on those enterprising natives who began the trend by selling. Recently, even inland property has been steadily settled by transplants lured from urban areas by Maine's breathtaking beauty, sense of safety and calm, opportunity for adventure, and open spaces that promise coveted privacy. Accompanying these people whom Mainers typically refer to as "from away" are habits and values that sometimes influence and occasionally conflict with local traditions. Inherent in Maine tradition, for example, is the notion of property as endemic. To many citizens, community or native ownership of wilderness and beaches is equal to or supersedes an individual's legal title, a view that many newcomers find bewildering and intrusive.

Perhaps the most salient symbol of this collision over territory is the state's escalating tension over hunting. The sport many Maine hunters regard as their birthright has faced increasing restrictions and criticism: residential development continues to encroach upon wilderness; safety and licensing regulations have proliferated; residents and corporations steadily have limited hunting access to privately owned land; and hunting opponents have become more numerous and vocal. Some

Maine citizens frame these developments as the handiwork of "outsiders," rather than "natives" who understand and revere the Maine "way of life."[4] Protecting the territorial privilege of hunters is, to some natives, the last cultural bastion in a state where privilege increasingly translates into money, class, and real estate holdings.[5]

Against this complex backdrop, nearly all interested parties agreed that the intense conflict over Karen Wood's killing transcended the guilt or innocence of a single man. A representative view from one camp pointed to the "urgent need to update some of our hunting laws" so that landowners' rights do not "take a back seat" (Demos 19). Others concurred that a changing social milieu was indeed at the heart of the tragedy. But this camp argued that "the most important" issue was not the death of Karen Wood but instead "the influx of large numbers of people who do not share and do not understand the traditional views and values of native Mainers" (Leavitt 11). To persons like Bangor sports columnist, Theodore Leavitt, "the heritage of Maine people" was at stake. He voiced the concerns of others who emphasized the need to "fight the anti-hunting, anti-gun hysteria this tragedy has brought about in order to retain our identity as a state." One angry hunter summarized the focus of the conflict more succinctly. "Donnie's not on trial," he said. "Hunting's on trial—hunting and guns. The damage has already been done" (Kloehn, "Hunters Keep" 1).

The death of Karen Wood, indeed, had tainted the sport more seriously than had all previous Maine hunting fatalities combined. With the shot that felled a young mother on her own residential property, sacred local order clashed violently with a more potent global order, one that places the enduring reverence for human life and the sanctity of one's home above the ephemeral pleasure of sport. "Karen Wood went out in her own backyard with the belief that this is America where each citizen is supposed to be secure in their own home and on their own land," wrote one Bangorite (Fisher 11). Beyond this transgression, the killing of a non-hunter and recent transplant confounded the part of Maine tradition which holds that in "insider-outsider" interactions, natives are typically victims of exploitation and aggression by "people from away."[6] To expunge the symbolic stain of Wood's death from the sport of hunting and the way of life it represented demanded a corresponding symbolic cleansing ritual to purify this autumn ritual and to restore community order.

SYMBOLIC REDEMPTION

The motivation for symbolic redemptive acts, Burke argues, is identification with the sin, so Maine hunters, in particular, felt the burden of Wood's killing. As one voiced in the local paper, "It made us feel guilty as hunters in general" (Kloehn, "A Controversial Tragedy" S1). Although many hunters shared a sense of complicity in Wood's death, they chose divergent paths to absolution, paths whereby the role of operative agent in the scene and, therefore, the corresponding negligent act, was assigned to different principal characters. In both cases, act, agent, and scene are inextricably linked. Birdsell argues that reconciling the dialectical incompatibility of "scene" and "act" can occur only via a third pentadic term, a coordinating term (271–73). In responses from both camps in the controversy, "agent" emerges as the third pentadic term—the coordinating term—between "scene" and "act."

Mortification

Some Maine hunters elected to purify themselves and their sport by admitting Rogerson's sin, a process Burke terms "mortification" or self-sacrifice (*Religion* 190–93, 206–207). Central to the rite of confession is recognition of the choice to act, which presumes an agent is moral and accountable, therefore capable of "sin." In the symbolic mortification ritual, Rogerson's *act* is negligent when viewed through a scene-agent-act relationship in which *Rogerson* as rational agent both dominates and coordinates scene and act. Rogerson, rather than Wood, failed to account for the physical scene. "A hunter who does not take the time to positively identify his or her target is a dangerous, inept idiot" (Edwards), said one hunter, a view echoed by many. To some, symbolic contrition demanded decisive, penitent acts of their own. A few vowed "never to hunt again," and one declared, "I don't plan to ever pay $16 for a hunting license again. My defense, if caught hunting without a license, will be that I have strong moral objections to holding a license that would allow me to shoot a human" (Merrill 15).

Victimization

Yet Rogerson as sinner was an agonizing fit for others in the state who strongly identified with the native Mainer, veteran hunter and Boy Scout leader. "I realized that I could have been standing in his boots when that fatal shot was fired," wrote Tom Hennessey, local sportswriter for the *Bangor Daily News* ("A Hunting Tragedy" 10). Exempting Rogerson from blame, however, left only Karen Wood, the victim, to provide some citizens with what Burke calls "catharsis by scapegoat," a symbolic process in which guilt is transferred to vessels "outside" (*Religion* 191).

To society at large, the personable, devoted young mother seems an unlikely candidate for villainy. Yet, we shall argue that she was, for many Mainers, what Burke would term "the 'perfect' enemy" (*Language* 18; *Permanence* 292–294; *Philosophy* 209). A non-hunting woman "from away," the wife of a Ph.D., and someone who lived in a residential area carved out of wilderness, Karen Wood could be molded to incarnate the forces that threatened a local order. Still to others who blamed Wood for her own death, the photos of the smiling, attractive young mother embracing her infants in their recently completed dream home may have been haunting for reasons beyond collective guilt and social resentment.

Through an examination of the symbolic implications present in both the physical and metaphysical scene of the Wood tragedy, we argue that those who lived dangerously near hunting territory also identified with the sin, but from the vantage point of Wood, the sinned against. For these persons, the tragic end to what seemed a storybook existence begged for a more comforting explanation other than a hunter's blatant negligence.[7] Again, Wood was the "perfect" scapegoat: the troubling similarities these residents shared with her were offset reassuringly by important differences. Unlike themselves, Wood was an "outsider," unversed in the local hunting culture and the accompanying behavioral expectations that they believed would guarantee their physical safety.

For many Mainers—hunters and non-hunters alike—only through a "symbolic killing" could the disturbing aspects of Karen Wood's actual death be rectified. Consequently, some who had never fired a gun joined forces with many hunters apparently for their own psychological protection. If Karen Wood had somehow caused her own death, hunting, hunters, and non-hunters all became "safer." Moreover, exonerating the native Mainer and indicting the newcomer would maintain a tradition that accrues natives power through victim status, a phenomenon some scholars argue is common to socially and/or economically oppressed groups.[8] Eschewing responsibility, Burke claims, typically means transferring responsibility on another. "Victimization," he says, "enables persons to 'project' upon the enemy any troublesome traits of our own that we would negate" (*Language* 18–19). For some Maine citizens, the "troublesome traits" that needed transferring to Wood included collective guilt over her death as well as a sense of social insecurity and physical vulnerability.

THE SYMBOLIC KILLING OF KAREN WOOD

Without question, Rogerson fired the fatal shot. Yet, as our analysis will demonstrate, his apologists symbolically transformed the act and reversed the roles of agent through two kinds of scenic perspectives: the first highlighted, omitted, and embellished the physical scene; the second interpreted the events through a metaphysical scenic perspective of symbolic territory. Defenders of Rogerson and accusers of Wood reversed the roles of operative agent and victim by featuring scene in the relationship of scene, agent, and act. Although scene becomes the featured term, the scene functions to *define* the agents and, in turn, the act. As Burke (*Religion* 176) and later Birdsell (276) suggest, the terms are interrelated and their boundaries permeable; altering one enables the altering of others. Hence, Rogerson as hunter becomes absolved because of the controlling nature of the malignant scene, a scene recast in such a way to make his behavior explicable. Conversely, Wood assumes the role of agent because her behavior was not consistent with the constructed scene—the symbolic territory of hunters in which Rogerson was merely an element. Consequently, rather than victim, Wood is portrayed as trespasser, a portrait that renders her action negligent and transforms Rogerson into a victim of her carelessness.

THE PHYSICAL SCENE

For over a year after the shooting, local media stressed that Donald Rogerson was an accomplished hunter who had been hunting legally. He had been dressed in regulation fluorescent orange and had been hunting in daylight in an area that was not posted against hunting (Warner, "Rogerson Pleads"). However, because he did not hold a doe permit, he was obligated to identify his target as a deer with antlers— a buck—in order to avoid costly fines (Kunstler 59). Yet Rogerson admitted he had fired at "flags," the flashes of white undertails for either does or bucks. Despite this admission, coupled with later revelations that he had fired illegally close to residences, his sympathizers argued that his action was mitigated by elements of the physical scene, which they recast in significant ways.

Absolving Rogerson

Because one aspect of Rogerson's hierarchial "sin" was violating the sanctity of another's home, his defenders reduced the conception of "home" in dramatic ways. In so doing, they reconstituted the location of the killing so as to absolve Rogerson of guilt. Repeatedly, the *Bangor Daily News* (Warner, "Rogerson Indicted"; Weber 1) reported that the shooting had occurred in "*woods near* her home" or "*wooded property behind* her house" rather than in Wood's "backyard" (emphasis added). The territorial distinctions implicit within the substitution were significant to restoring a psychological sense of territorial order.

Local editorial policy points to the importance of the physical scene in influencing public perception. Following Rogerson's indictment, V. Paul Reynolds, the *News*'s managing editor and self-described "devout deer hunter," issued a memo to reporters and editors assigned to the story and to the Maine bureau of the Associated Press. Reynolds wrote: "To me, and I think to the average reader, the term backyard confers an image of a person on his lawn or within eyeshot of his house." He added

> There is 20 feet of grass between Wood's house and the woods. Wood was 134 feet (45 yards) from her house, or 114 feet (38 yards) into a wooded area when she was shot. In short, Wood—no matter how many times repeated by media coverage—was not in her "backyard" at the time of the shooting. (Diamond, "Where Karen Wood" 15–16)

Although Reynolds concedes he had not personally visited the shooting scene, he, nonetheless, defended his newsroom ban on the term "backyard." The editor contended that the word "backyard" gave the impression "she was shot in her chaise lounge. She wasn't" (Diamond, "Where Karen Wood" 15). During the trial, the paper's reporters "thought it best to explain" to those with the impression that Wood "was standing on her patio" that she had, in fact, "walked *away from her house* and into a thinly *wooded area* bordering denser woods" (Weber 1, emphasis added).

Placing Wood near *dense* woods, rather than in the clearing of her yard, also made more plausible Rogerson's defense that he had become disoriented about his location, a factor the jury cited in their decision to acquit (Kloehn, "Jurors Believed" 1). As Burke (*Grammar* 142) explains, contemplation historically is considered within the realm of action and, hence, the moral. Although Rogerson's admitted confusion made his decision to fire even more imprudent, a jury member found testimony of another hunter who had been hunting nearby "particularly telling." Earlier in the day of the killing, the witness had told Rogerson that becoming turned around in the area was easy to do (Kloehn, "Jurors Believed" 1). Furthermore, despite the clearness of the afternoon (which Rogerson himself alluded to several times during his arrest), a local columnist emphasized "what the diffuse lights and shadows of woodlands do to dark clothing regardless of the time of day" (Hennessey, "A Hunting Tragedy" 10). With Rogerson devoid of consciousness— "in the dark" figuratively and almost literally—his apologists exonerated him of negligence because no real choice had taken place. Consequently, such descriptions of the physical scene absolved the hunter of moral responsibility.

Moreover, a picture of the immediate scene as malignant and controlling is augmented by early new stories quoting Rogerson's friends who "described the defendant in glowing terms and said the incident was uncharacteristic of him" (Warner, "Hunter Charged" I). As Birdsell, too, argues, a focus on scene can point to "forces operating upon the agent to make it not-the-agent, to make it different" (276). Highlighting Rogerson's ordinary kinds of behavior suggests that extraordinary circumstances must have accounted for his clouded judgment, circumstances most easily ascribed to scene.

Once Rogerson was firmly situated in "the woods," his own hunting territory, his defenders then embroidered elements of that scene to make his behavior consistent with it. The fact that no evidence of deer had been found in the immediate area of the shooting was summarily dismissed. The defense attorney argued that the team of game wardens possibly had obscured the evidence during their search (Warner,

"Prosecution Rests" 1; Kloehn, "Jury Finds" 1). The jury concurred (Kloehn, "Jurors Believed" 3). "The deer being there was a big factor," one juror explained. "We all believed he saw a deer. We felt the state didn't prove otherwise" (Kloehn, "Jurors Believed" 3; Goodman 35). Accepting only the word of the same man who admitted to shooting a woman he "saw" as "two deer," the jury viewed Rogerson's behavior as reasonable, rather than reckless. Because Rogerson identified the buck deer, they claimed, the second shot at the "two white flags" followed logically. "In that sequence, it seems to make sense," one juror argued (Kloehn, "Jurors Believed" 1).

Rogerson's absolution was eased by a symbolic transformation of the literal scene: A backyard clearing sparsely dotted with tree stumps and saplings (Hope 96) was transformed into dense woods; afternoon sunshine was transformed into diffused and shadowy light; and unsubstantiated testimony regarding the presence of deer was transformed into reality.

Implicating Wood

Manipulating the physical scene merely to absolve Rogerson, however, was insufficient for accomplishing the victimization ritual. By definition, victimization requires an agent. Thus, aspects of the literal scene had to be selected, emphasized, and interpreted in a way to *reverse* the victim roles of the principal characters. Transferring culpability from Rogerson to Wood required that her presence in the physical scene be both participative and contaminating.[9] Once in "the woods," she no longer was allowed to behave as one may at home but was governed by rules regulating hunters in *their* territory. Although Maine law requires only hunters to wear blaze orange, Wood was indicted repeatedly for not wearing the brightly colored clothing. "I can't help believing," said local sports columnist Hennessey, ["]that if she had been wearing one piece of orange clothing she'd be alive today," a view repeatedly expressed by others. "Just think how different the Karen Wood story might have ended," wrote one hunter, "if she had grabbed an orange hat instead of a pair of white mittens" (Smith 11).

Moreover, whereas Rogerson's disorientation apparently imbued him with innocence, Wood was not allowed the luxury of being confused or even unaware. To many, Wood's mere presence outside during hunting season was sufficient indication that she was *not* innocent of the danger surrounding her. Neighbors reported hearing only the two rapidly successive shots, one of which killed Wood, and Rogerson admitted to firing only twice. Nonetheless, speculation circulated that Wood had heard shots close by and had ventured outside to warn the hunters away from her home (Weber 1). Although admittedly uncertain about why she was "in the woods," investigators noted that her apparel—a jacket and gloves in mid-November—suggested that her behavior was "not spontaneous" (Warner, "Hunter Charged" 2). *Possible* reasons for Wood's presence outside were elevated by some to unqualified fact. A case in point was one woman's detailed and dramatic scenario, which she supplied to the local paper:

> Please look at the *facts*. This woman *knew* there were hunters out there. In *fact, she was going out to tell them* they were too close to her house yet she went out in dark clothes with white mittens instead of putting on something orange. She was not just in her "backyard," she was walking through *a wooded area* and *evidently she was fairly quiet doing it* when she should have been yelling something like "excuse me!" (Jackson 17, emphasis added)

Likewise, a local columnist argued that the main issue in the shooting was lack of good judgment. Yet, he too focused his criticism only on Wood. "Mrs. Wood was concerned with hunters near her house and justifiably so [as] some people will risk shooting anywhere, but did she really use common sense going in to the woods dressed as she was?" (Leavitt 11) In these arguments, important inventions helped shift the focus from Rogerson's failure to identify his prey to Wood's failure to clarify she was *not* prey. Hence, the moral act of contemplation, therefore accountability, for responding to the literal scene was exclusively Wood's.

Perhaps most significantly, Wood was depicted as having *tempted* Rogerson, in effect, having disguised herself as compelling prey. Based only on Rogerson's account that Wood had "put her hands over her head" ("Rogerson Interview" 1), critics of Wood flatly argued that she "stupidly" "presented herself as a target" (Clark 142). "She made a mistake!" trumpeted a local media commentator, "she never should have had on white gloves *to wave*" (Kunstler 60, emphasis added). To one sports columnist, Wood's inviting appearance extended even to her "dark hair" (Hennessey, "A Hunting Tragedy"). In these accounts of the literal scene, Rogerson was reduced from a moral, thinking agent to an organism who merely responded to external stimuli much as animals, for example, salivate in the presence of food. Rogerson became a hunter in the more global and primitive sense of the word; his behavior, rather than rational, was a reflex reaction. As Burke notes, "'Action' is to 'motion,' as 'mind' is to 'brain'" (*Religion* 39). Rogerson's capacity to think, therefore to "act," was restricted by a scene which stimulated the appetite, what Burke terms the "carnal" rather than spiritual will (*Religion* 110). As a result, the logical inconsistencies of Rogerson's account remained untested and unresolved. For example, his failure to identify Wood as a person rather than a deer belied his claim that he had seen her exhibiting the specific behaviors he described (putting her hands over her head), a glaring contradiction that neither his supporters nor the local media addressed. Nor did they explore his failure to recall why the mittens were found beside Wood's body rather than on her hands.[10] Most important in the accounts was the depiction of hierarchical claims of nature: Rogerson was responding to his nature as a hunter, whereas Wood was tempting nature.[11] She, rather than he, had violated order.

Through a careful construction of the physical scene, a more potent metaphysical scene was allowed to emerge, one that was crucial to completing the restoration of local order. These responses that focused on Maine traditions and heritage specifically supported and expounded upon a *metaphysical* scene in which *symbolic* territory was controlling. Expanding the parameters for hunting "territory" to include symbolic dimensions was necessary for neutralizing Rogerson's hierarchical transgressions. For many citizens, the figurative corollary to the "wooded area" in Maine was the proverbial Garden of Eden: a calculating Eve had seductively fooled an unsuspecting, even confused, Adam and paid the price in pain for her sin. Like the symbolic Eve who introduced suffering into paradise through contact with evil outside of it, Wood, in effect, personified a threat to a perfect community order, a threat that must be destroyed before it becomes destroying.

THE METAPHYSICAL SCENE

Community Perspective

Central to explaining why the physical scene rendered Rogerson *less* accountable and Wood *more* accountable is the notion of "turf," which is based on community hierarchy and is constituted by factors other than actual ownership of property. Rogerson's act and the physical scene itself became forcefully transfigured through *symbolic* territory, which always combines both physical *and* metaphysical elements.

To many Maine citizens, "Maine is a hunting state," which they interpret to mean that *all* Maine land reverts to hunters during the month of November. The right to live safely and freely, even on one's own property, is superseded by territorial claims of hunters accrued them through the community traditions. A trio wrote to the local paper that homeowners can "walk on [their] land the other 11 months of the year" (Irving et al. 11), a view that Rogerson himself advanced. "Sometimes we have to take measures that do infringe on other people's rights," he said. "Maybe in the month of November, is it such an infringement upon your freedom to put away that white coat, or a tan coat maybe with a fur collar or something?" (Warner, "Rogerson Reflects" 7) Likewise, in his regular sports column, Hennessey argued that persons moving into rural areas must acclimate themselves to the "rights of hunters" and "must accept the fact that during the month of November they should not walk woods roads, work in woodlots or fields, or allow children to play in areas bordering woods without wearing at least one piece of blaze-orange clothing" ("A Hunting Tragedy").[12] In these representative arguments, autonomy and literal ownership of property was supplanted by symbolic territorial rights which were defined and protected by the dominant members of the specific community. As Burke explains, "*Actual control* of a property differs from *nominal ownership* of it. . . . Where the *control* resides, there resides the *function* of ownership, whatever the *fictions* of ownership may be" (*Rhetoric* 33).

As a hunter and a native Mainer, Rogerson himself helped comprise the Maine hunting culture. Consequently, rather than an agent, he was viewed merely as an element in the cultural scene itself, an image that insulated him from blame and one that his defenders promoted with scenic metaphors borrowed from nature. One sports columnist obliquely compared the shooting to a "limb falling out of a tree" (Kunstler 60). Even more telling was one observation that blaming the hunter for shooting Wood during hunting season was analogous to going skating on thin ice and blaming the ice after falling through (classroom discussion 12 Apr. 1989). Via these metaphors, Rogerson becomes merely part of the natural landscape—a thing rather than a rational being—and his behavior is reduced to unavoidable, choice-less motion. In the latter case, only Wood remained an agent, a skater choosing to interact with the ice—Rogerson.

Similarly, other analogies used to explain the event also focused on scene but alluded specifically to heritage and traditions in a way that placed fault exclusively on the victim, who was portrayed as a trespasser of literal and symbolic territory. In these comments, "turf" constituted literal place (the physical scene) and also metaphysical factors such as nativity and/or residence and time. "I say when in Rome do as the Romans do," said one hunter. "The common knowledge around here is that you don't go into the woods during the fall without putting orange on" ("Hunting State"). Likewise, Rogerson's hunting companion compared Wood's "irresponsible" actions to those of a native Mainer who recklessly risks safety by walking in New York's Central Park at 3 a.m. (Bishop). Again, in these arguments, individuals who comprised the specific community (natives or residents) merely are scenic elements rather than agents. Conversely, individuals interacting with the dominant group retain their status as active participants. Scene functions to define the agents and their corresponding behavior: "Action" is assigned only to the *alien*—the agent who is set against the scene; "motion" is reserved for the natives, those submerged within the scene. Hence, by viewing the events of the shooting through a lens in which turf is comprised of factors such as nativity and time as well as literal place, Rogerson could be exonerated of his territorial transgression because he had committed none. Rather, the territorial violation was the "outsider" Wood's alone. "I don't think that man is guilty," an excused prospective juror argued. "That woman. It was hunting season" (Warner, "State vs. Rogerson" 3).

Rogerson's own statements reflected a scenic view of his role in the tragedy. Repeatedly, he depicted himself as a being acted upon rather than as an actor. He was, he argued time and again, "a victim of circumstances" (Warner, "Rogerson Reflects" 7). Shortly after the verdict, he responded to his detractors: "If I had [had] a clue that this could happen to me, I never would have hunted in the first place" (Warner, "Rogerson Reflects" 7). Because he believed he had committed no act, much less a "sin," Rogerson neither admitted guilt nor labored under it. "I say I was not neglectful. If I was negligent, I wouldn't be able to sleep nights" (Weber 1).

Rogerson's deterministic philosophy is vividly revealed in this contention that God had a reason for thrusting him into Maine's most notorious hunting fatality, a symbolic role he did not relish but to which he was resigned (Warner, "Rogerson Reflects" 7). Rogerson continued his transformation from agent into an agency for God's purpose by speculating on Divine intent: his plight, he concluded, could let other hunters see that "it" could happen to them as well (Warner, "Rogerson Reflects" 7).

Besides absolving Rogerson from sin, the suggestion that God had choreographed the hunter's behavior reflects an underlying premise that the shooting and its aftermath was and is rooted in a metaphysical conflict between the forces of good and evil. As an agency for God's will, Rogerson's personal anguish and that of his family was magnified because it was predicated on his persecution, not on his behavior.[13] In this sense, the hunter transcended his status as hapless victim in order to assume a role of martyr in the secular crusade to preserve the state's way of life against sinister agents bent on destroying it. "The incident is a new political cudgel in the hands of anti-hunting activists," opined the *Bangor Daily News,* adding that "hunters do not have to be reminded that they are in the minority" ("A Double Tragedy" 8). Roger Viafiades, Rogerson's defense attorney, described his client as "a victim of merciless publicity that has made him a target for anti-gun and anti-hunting forces" (Harkavy 5). Some even borrowed religious terms, such as references to crucifixion, to describe Rogerson's torture (Kloehn, "A Controversial Tragedy" S1) and ascribed it to "the will of the non-hunters and do-gooders and also the flatlanders" (Weymouth 17).

Many arguments were framed in an "us versus them" struggle. "They," the outsiders, were charged with culpability for hunting accidents by virtue of their contaminating presence on lands that were once wilderness. "I think *they* have hurt [Donald Rogerson] long enough," one citizen claimed. "A few years ago *we* never heard about hunting accidents. Doesn't that tell *us* something? *Out-of-state people* buy land and build right in deer yards. I would hope the state of Maine and its people would think of *our own* and less about out-of-state money" (Dowling 17, emphasis added). The most malevolent outsider role was delegated to Kevin Wood, Karen Wood's widower. "I hope Kevin Wood gets some counseling before his hate he apparently harbors for Maine and its citizens destroys his twins' other parent," wrote one woman to the local paper (Diamond, "Lessons Learned" 17). Just as Rogerson symbolically embodied the heritage of Mainers and the suffering they endured in trying to preserve it, Kevin Wood represented perhaps the greatest evil of all: the "system" that threatened the sacred local order. Rogerson's hunting companion angrily argued that the turmoil over Rogerson and hunting continues "because Kevin Wood has refused to let it die" (Kukka 21), presumably because he sought redress through the courts. Said one woman, "I wonder if Karen Wood would have wanted her husband to pursue this man with such a vengeance. . . . This is just another example of our sick justice system . . ." (McKinnon 15). Like a modern-day Job, Rogerson refused to falter under suffering he painted as undeserving and "system"-based. After the verdict, Rogerson himself declared that "I've had public ridicule." But then Rogerson added that if he and his family would have let the event change their lives dramatically then they would have been "giving in to the system or to society" (Warner, "Rogerson Reflects" 7). The result is that he, in essence, transformed his refusal to admit responsibility for his action into a moral act of stoicism.

Despite Rogerson's adamancy that he refused to "blame" Karen Wood or "say anything negative about the Wood family," he intimated in the same breath that she had erred rather than he. Although he claimed that "she was just as much a victim of circumstances as I was," he added that the time had arrived to require "anybody that is in legal hunting territory to wear blaze orange. . . . If there's any one signal in the woods, any signal that's going to trigger [that] something isn't right or where it's supposed to be, blaze orange is that signal" (Warner, "Rogerson Reflects" 7). Again, a scenic recasting was significant to transferring culpability and assigning moral action. He clearly and erroneously suggested that he had been hunting "in legal territory," while Wood was where she was not "supposed to be," "in the woods." Through these invented qualifiers, his claim that he did not blame her became transformed into a moral act of forgiveness. He assigned positive moral action to himself and negative moral action to Wood.

With the Woods, out-of-state people, non-hunters, and the pervasive and evil "system" as guilty perpetrators and Rogerson as victim, the second important aspect of the local cultural order was restored: natives were again the victims and outsiders the victimizers. The symbolic redemption cycle was complete.

Yet, although the battle may have been won for Rogerson and his champions, the war was far from over. The accounts of the cultural conflict continued. As with earlier versions, these later responses to a changing culture echoed themes of the Jeremiad: a Puritanical sermon that detailed a community's failure to live up to communal norms, the catastrophes that resulted, and the utopian vision if individuals repented and reformed (Johannesen 158).[14] A local sports columnist detailed the "great days," those Edenic times before "outsiders" polluted paradise. "'No Hunting' and 'No Trespassing' signs were scarcer than fireflies in February," he wrote. "Hunters, non-hunters, farmers, and landowners got along fine." But with the "Marketing of Maine," he recalled, "waves of anti-hunting sentiment began rising across the state," causing "ripples of bitterness and resentment" between the "opposing cultures of natives and newcomers." Many of those transplants, he argued, "intended to recreate what they left behind," which "included banning hunting." A return to the communal traditions could only be realized, he concluded, if hunters and other concerned citizens became "as vocal and active as those who have taken it upon themselves to put an end to the time-honored Maine traditions of hunting, trapping, fishing, etc." (Hennessey, "Words" 15).

Universal Perspective

Although this essay has focused on local tradition and nativity as elements of hierarchy, claims of territorial ownership are almost always informed by other dimensions of status besides residence/nativity or local customs. For example, holding the *female* Wood accountable for the tragedy that befell her was easier to do because of

a universal propensity to blame women for acts of violence visited upon them, especially when women unwisely venture into dangerous areas or male "turf" without
legitimating accompaniment. Ironically, Wood's gender, which made the death of a
young mother so intensely tragic and threatening, is also that which made it simpler
for many people to explain. As woman, Wood embodied the complex incongruous
relationship of "goodness" and "badness" universally assigned to females. In Wood,
the virgin-whore dichotomy took the form of mother-temptress. Manipulation of the
physical scene was useful in subordinating Wood as "mother" and calling forth the
darker side of Wood as calculating "temptress." The domestic sphere of babies,
home, and backyard was replaced by the public and profane dense and shadowy
woods, the symbolic territory of the hunter, the male.

Although recasting a scene is clearly useful in absolving one agent and indicting
another, doing so may not be essential if power differentials inhere in the principal
characters.[15] Historically, women as well as other groups lower on the social strata
have been defined in terms of "their place," which refers both to how they are
allowed to act and where they are allowed to go. In fact, for women, "action"
has traditionally been interpreted through "scene." In the nineteenth century,
for example, women speaking in public was sometimes acceptable if the audiences were women, but the same "act" was considered indecent if the audiences
were "promiscuous" or mixed (Welter; Cott; Kraditor). In our more enlightened
age, the identical physical scene may still render certain kinds of agents more
accountable for their behavior and others less so. The mix of men, women and
alcohol at social gatherings, for example, is too frequently invoked to excuse males
of violent behavior against female victims charged with inviting the attack by
virtue of their joining in the scene, as two recent cases in Maine attest.[16] In fact,
echoing disturbingly in the accusations lodged against Wood are arguments that
justify sexual assaults on women who enter sinister territory alone, wear seductive
clothing, and/or fail to clarify to their assailant that a violent act is undesired. In
the case of Karen Wood, the danger of "a wooded area" "during hunting season"
is exacerbated by her provocative mittens and her failure to utter a resounding
symbolic "no" to her shooting by wearing uninviting clothing: blaze orange. As
Rogerson himself argued, "White brings to mind the *possibility* of a deer. Orange
is a danger signal. It's that . . . black and white" (Warner, "Rogerson Reflects" 7,
emphasis added). Indeed, the belief that the victim "asked for" her own death
becomes *literally* interpreted in an observer's comment that Wood was "stupid" for
running into the woods, and in his words, waving her white-mittened hands, and
yelling "shoot me, shoot me!" (classroom discussion 12 Apr. 1989). Although many
defenders of Rogerson adamantly dismissed the sexual assault analogy, some outside
of the local media noted the similarities. "Blaming the victim, in this case a woman,"
wrote one reporter, "is an ugly tactic usually reserved for victims of rape. Rarely
are hunters who are accidentally shot by a companion blamed for their own misfortune" (Kukka 21). Of the three Maine hunting fatalities of the previous season in
which male humans were mistaken for animals, two resulted in convictions and jail
terms, one of which involved a non-hunter victim (Clark 138; Kunstler 118).[17]

Although blaming Karen Wood for her own death is inarguably disturbing, this
situation is not an anomaly. Bewilderment over the debate and the hunter's acquittal
fades into recognition when Bensonhurst is substituted for Bangor or the hunter
and non-hunter, native and non-native division is replaced by white and African-
American, Gentile or Jew, Catholic and Protestant, African-American and Asian,
male or female, or have and have-nots. Humans, Burke argues, are inherently tribal,

which means that individuals protect their own kind, their own community, society, or culture, against that which is alien. The social scene defines the agent, which in turn defines the act.

CONCLUSION

This case study supports earlier studies (Ling; Birdsell) that argue a scenic perspective can transform an agent's actions into motion, thereby providing absolution. By extending our analysis beyond the use of a single text, we have once again confirmed the value of this scenic interpretation. At the same time, this analysis suggests that a scenic perspective can accomplish the reverse—transforming motion into action—depending upon the qualities associated with or inherent in the "agent," the coordinating term here between "scene" and "act." Hierarchical status of an agent within a specific social scene may be central to determining when a scenic perspective can be employed to assign "sin" as well as to remove it. When the identical physical scene engenders polar interpretations of an "act," only the coordinating term of "agent" and its accompanying power within a particular social order can account for the variation. In short, the agent's *relationship* to the scene may determine whether scene may be used successfully as alibi. Rogerson is defined by his intimate connection to the community in which he operates. He is at once controlled by scene and submerged in it. At most, he becomes an agency for a purpose orchestrated by a higher power, a means to clarify to natives the destructive forces at work in their state. Conversely, Wood is defined as an "outsider" by her inability to share in a culture in which nativity and commitment to hunting tradition were membership requirements. A physical scene constructed and interpreted through a metaphysical scene defined by community norms, traditions, and native membership does not allow the outsider Wood to participate in it other than as a contaminating force. Because she was set *against* scene, she was not allowed, as alien, to be controlled and therefore absolved by it.

Given a quite different social backdrop and/or differing social status, Wood may have been the "insider" and Rogerson the "alien," yielding a different interpretation of act based upon the literal scene. But in Maine, traditions inherent in the scene helped define the roles of victim (Rogerson) and victimizer (Wood) even *before* the act occurred. As a result, the physical scene was less important than the metaphysical scene, allowing elements of the former to be embellished or ignored.[18] In this sense, the acquittal had less to do with literal scene or act than with community norms and traditions, which defined "agent" and thereby assigned guilt. The casting of the literal scene merely augmented this *a priori* conception of agent.

NOTES

[1]We use "buff" rather than the commonly reported "white" based on one author's eyewitness examination of the mittens. Additionally, a local reporter described the critical evidence as it was introduced in the trial: "large, cream-colored, knit mittens, with palms made of dirty, buff-colored suede." The reporter added, "From the time of the shooting, Rogerson has suggested that the two flags he thought he saw—the white tails and rumps of deer—might actually have been those mittens. In the brightly lit courtroom, however, it was difficult to see the resemblance" (Kloehn, "Mittens" 3; see also Warner, "Rogerson's Companion" 3; Kloehn, "Defense Grills" 1).

[2]Burke concedes the dual *identifying* nature of "property." On the one hand, he argues, property is clearly materialistic or scenic. But Burke adds that "in the surrounding of himself with properties that . . . establish his identity, man is ethical. 'Avarice' is but the scenic word for 'property' translated into terms of agent's attitude, or incipient act" (*Rhetoric* 23–24).

[3]Burke, in fact, compares a materialistic focus to the animal conditioning or instinct of a dog responding to a food signal (*Rhetoric* 24).

[4]For these Mainers, the concept of "nativity" is akin to a unification device Burke calls "inborn dignity," the purported natural-born superiority inherent in races, genders, or aristocracies (*Philosophy* 202).

[5]Much of the media coverage of the Karen Wood killing noted the attitudes of native Mainers toward non-natives, and many on both sides of the debate cited class conflict and residential development issues as contributing factors to it. To supplement the citations included in the text, which clearly reveal this attitude, we offer two additional examples. A couple wrote to the *Bangor Daily News* on December 15, 1988: "Are 'Maine natives' becoming a minority in our own state? We think so. We understand Maine is growing, but why can't Maine people afford to buy here? . . . We've read letters that indicate certain 'transplants' don't like the laws here . . . . If you don't like hunting, fishing, or trapping, and think 'blue laws' are stupid, what are you doing here? . . . Don't change our heritage, change yours!" (Shortt 15) In a July 1985 article appearing in *Downeast* magazine, James P. Brown underscores the importance of the relationship between Maine tradition and property rights through an examination of a legal conflict over beach property. According to Paul Stern of the Maine Attorney General's office, the central focus of this intrastate battle involved a clash between owners who wanted to restrict access to their property and those who claimed that Colonial law and practice have established a "right" to access that is "part of the heritage of the people of Maine" (82–83).

[6]Pure identification, Burke argues, does not result in strife. But because differences always exist in property issues, they nearly always lead to division and dispute. "When two men collaborate in an enterprise to which they contribute different kinds of services and from which they derive different amounts and kinds of profit, who is to say, once and for all, just where 'cooperation' ends and one partner's 'exploitation' of the other begins? The wavering line between the two cannot be 'scientifically' identified; rival rhetoricians can draw it at different places, and their persuasiveness varies with the resources each has at his command" (*Rhetoric* 25).

[7]This view has been expressed by psychologists in the area watching the case. Dr. Tim Rogers claimed, "No one wants to believe that a thing like that can happen to a woman who had everything going her way. I mean, if something like that can happen to someone with so much on the ball, what about the rest of us? It means that *anything* can happen. So we want her to be responsible so we can feel safe" (Clark 143). Dr. John Lorenz, a psychologist who lives within a mile of the shooting scene, reiterated Rogers's analysis (personal communication 15 Dec. 1990).

[8]Sociologist Shelby Steele, for example, contends that "the dynamic on the part of blacks is a clinging, at all costs and beyond reason, to a victim-focused identity" even when evidence to the contrary is compelling in specific cases. Steele argues that "innocence" is achieved "via victimization," the latter of which "transfers into power." Groups locked into victim status as a source of power are "reluctant to give it up," he claims, even though it "inadvertently means not taking responsibility" (Roberts).

[9]The concept that Burke variously terms "contamination," "poisoning" and "pollution" appears in numerous works. A vivid example of the pollution-scapegoating-redemption cycle is contained in Burke's "The Rhetoric of Hitler's 'Battle'" (*Philosophy* 191–220). This concept also appears throughout Burke's *The Rhetoric of Religion*. See Rueckert (279–282) for a more general interpretation of the concept.

[10]We found only one media story that mentioned Rogerson's inability to explain why the mittens were found beside Wood's body. The *Maine Times* of 10 Nov. 1989, addresses the concerns of John Giroux, a member of HAD ENOUGH (Homocides and Accidental Deaths: End Numbers of Growing Homocides [*sic*]). Giroux argues that if Wood had been carrying the mittens, they would have been flung away under the impact of the bullet. And if they were in her pockets, they cast doubt on Rogerson's story and open questions as to who put them beside her body and why. No other paper noted the inconsistency, and media accounts did not indicate that it entered into the trial debate.

[11]Burke notes that Natural Law historically was one expression of the Will of God (his capitalization), and that a natural order dictated superiority of one group over another. In his analysis of *Mein Kampf* Burke argues that Hitler depicts Aryans as obeying nature while Jews demonstrate their "arrogance" by trying to conquer nature through democratic ideals of equality (*Philosophy* 208–209).

[12]Such arguments reflect the contention that natural order does not recognize democratic ideals of equality as discussed in footnote 11.

[13]For a discussion of persecution paranoia, see *Philosophy* 213–214.

[14]Similarities between the Jeremiad and Burke's sin-guilt-purification-redemption cycle are evident in "The Rhetoric of Hitler's Battle" in which Burke argues that, above all, observers must recognize Hitler's "bastardization of fundamentally religious patterns of thought" (219).

[15]Race and gender are more pronounced examples of what Burke terms "inborn dignity" described in footnote 4.

[16]A few weeks after the Rogerson verdict, a Maine prosecuting attorney refused to press charges against four Navy men who had allegedly gang raped a Bowdoinham teenager, all of whom had been drinking. That the sexual assault had occurred was unquestioned, but the district attorney declined to press charges using the rationale that "Saying 'no' is not enough. There has to be some sort of force or threat of force . . ." (English 15). More recently, a University of Maine student was acquitted of a sexual assault that occurred at a function involving alcohol. Again, the assault itself was undisputed. The defense attorney argued, however, that the use of alcohol impaired his client's judgment as well as suggested the victim's complicity (Ordway). Such a defense is not peculiar to Maine, however.

[17]The Karen Wood killing was a unique hunting fatality in Maine, not in that she was a non-hunter, non-native, but because she was those things and female as well. We contend that, as a result, the legal road to justice itself was unique. A Bangor attorney commented following the first grand jury's failure to issue an indictment: "I've been around here since '72, and I've never known of a hunter death when there hasn't been an indictment" (Kunstler 119). The other recent hunting fatalities in Maine all involved male victims, only some of whom were hunters.

[18]The utility of emphasizing a physical scene in certain contexts and a metaphysical scene in others is suggested by Burke: "One knows when to 'spiritualize' a material issue and when to 'materialize' a spiritual one["] (*Philosophy* 216).

WORKS CITED

Birdsell, David S. "Ronald Reagan on Lebanon and Grenada: Flexibility and Interpretation in the Application of Kenneth Burke's Pentad." *Quarterly Journal of Speech* 73 (1987): 267–279.

Bishop, Tammy. "Hunters Have No Room for Error." Letter. *Bangor Daily News* 15 Oct. 1990: 15.

Brown, James P. "The Battle of Moody Beach: Property Owners Gird for a Landmark Showdown over Ownership of a Congested Strip of Maine's Scarce Sand Beach." *Downeast* July 1985: 62–63.

Burke, Kenneth. *A Grammar of Motives.* 1945. Berkeley: U of California Publisher, 1969.

———. *Language as Symbolic Action: Essays on Life, Literature, and Method.* Berkeley: U of California Publisher, 1966.

———. *Permanence and Change.* 1935. Los Altos, CA: Hermes, 1954.

———. *The Philosophy of Literary Form.* 1941. Berkeley: U of California Publisher, 1973.

———. *A Rhetoric of Motives.* 1950. Berkeley: U of California Publisher, 1969.

———. *The Rhetoric of Religion.* 1961. Berkeley: U of California Publisher, 1970.

Clark, Edie. "The Killing of Karen Wood." *Yankee Magazine* Nov. 1989: 95–99, 138–45.

Cott, Nancy. *The Bonds of Womanhood: "Woman's Sphere" in New England, 1780–1835.* New Haven: Yale UP, 1977.

Demos, Pat. "Hunting Regulations." Letter. *Bangor Daily News* 23 Nov. 1988: 19.

Diamond, Audrey E. "Lessons Learned from Wood Tragedy." Letter. *Bangor Daily News* 24 Oct. 1990: 17.

Diamond, John N. "Where Karen Wood was Killed: A Death, a Deerhunter, and a Definition." *Columbia Journalism Review* Nov.–Dec. 1990: 14–16.

"A Double Tragedy." Editorial. *Bangor Daily News* 19 Nov. 1988: 8.

Dowling, Marie. "Who Needs Out-of-State Money?" Letter. *Bangor Daily News* 24 Oct. 1990: 17.

Edwards, Jonathan M. "Rifle Shooter is Non-hunter." Letter. *Bangor Daily News* 24 Oct. 1990: 17.

English, Bella. "For a Little Lift, Look Around." *Boston Globe* 19 Nov. 1990: 15.

Fisher, Isabelle. "Serious Consideration." Letter. *Bangor Daily News* 1 Dec. 1988: 11.

Goodman, Denise. "Hunter Cleared of '88 Killing." *Boston Globe* 18 Oct. 1990: 35+.

Harkavy, Jerry. "Single Hunting Death Sparks Statewide Storm of Controversy." *Bangor Daily News* 26 Dec. 1989: 1+.

Hennessey, Tom. "Words to the Wise: Keep an Eye on Antihunting Groups." *Bangor Daily News* 19–20 Jan. 1991: 15.

———. "A Hunting Tragedy Seen from a Hunter's Perspective." *Bangor Daily News* 30 Nov. 1988: 10.

Hope, Jack. "'My Wife Shouldn't Have Died.'" *Good Housekeeping* Oct. 1989: 92–97.

"Hunter Indicted in Death of Woman." *Portland Press Herald* 9 Dec 1989: 1+.

"Hunting State Takes a Look Within." *New York Times* 22 Oct. 1990, late ed.: A12.

Irving, David Jr., Gregory James, and Jody Lozier. "Maine is a Hunting State." Letter. *Bangor Daily News* 24–25 Nov. 1990: 11.

Jackson, Tammy. "Be Seen in the Woods." Letter. *Bangor Daily News* 15 Dec. 1988: 17.

Johannesen, Richard L. "The Jeremiad and Jenkin Lloyd Jones." *Communication Monographs* 52 (1985): 156–172.

"Karen Wood Case: A Year Later, Questions Persist." *Maine Times* 10 Nov. 1989: 3.

Kloehn, Steve. "A Controversial Tragedy: Emotions Still Simmering Over Shooting Death of Karen Wood." *Bangor Daily News* 6–7 Oct. 1990: S1.

———. "Defense Grills Wardens in Hunter's Trial." *Bangor Daily News* 13–14 Oct. 1990: 1+.

———. "Hunters Keep a Low Profile at Court House." *Bangor Daily News* 16 Oct. 1990: 1.

———. "Jurors Believed Rogerson Saw Deer." *Bangor Daily News* 19 Oct. 1990: 1+.

———. "Jury Finds Rogerson Not Guilty of Manslaughter." *Bangor Daily News* 18 Oct. 1990: 1+.

———. "Mittens, Rifle Entered into Evidence." *Bangor Daily News* 13–14 Oct. 1990: 3.

Kraditor, Aileen S. *The Ideas of the Woman Suffrage Movement 1989–1920.* 1965. New York: Anchor, 1971.

Kukka, Christine. "Rogerson Not Guilty: Juror's Decision in Karen Wood Case Seems to Blame the Victim for Hunting Season Shooting." *Maine Times* 19 Oct. 1990: 20–21.

Kunstler, James H. "Killing in Maine." *New York Times Magazine,* 9 Oct. 1989: 58–60, 119.

Leavitt, Theodore. "Safer Hunting: Common Sense, Good Judgment, Caution." *Bangor Daily News* 1 Dec. 1988: 11.

Ling, David. "A Pentadic Analysis of Senator Edward Kennedy's Address to the People of Massachusetts, July 25, 1969." *Central States Speech Journal* 21 (1970): 81–86.

"Lone Woman Stages Protest Against Hunter's Killing of Wood." *Portland Press Herald* 16 Nov. 1989: 40.

Lorenz, John. Personal interview. 15 Dec. 1990.

McKinnon, Carolyn. "Would Karen Wood Have Wanted This?" Letter *Bangor Daily News* 15 Oct. 1991: 15.

Merrill, Ray. "Seeing a Buck in his Sights." Letter. *Bangor Daily News* 10 Dec. 1988: 15.

Ordway, Renee. "U-Maine Student Cleared of Sex Assault Charge." *Bangor Daily News* 13 Dec. 1990: 1.

Roberts, Sam. "For Some Blacks, Justice is Not Blind to Color." *New York Times* 9 Sept. 1990: E5.

Rueckert, William H. *Kenneth Burke and the Drama of Human Relations.* 1963. Berkeley: U of California Publisher, 1982.

Shortt, Terry, and Debby Shortt. "Don't Change Maine Heritage." Letter. *Bangor Daily News* 15 Dec. 1988: 15.

Smith, Alan. "Caution in the Woods." Letter. *Bangor Daily News* 1 Dec. 1988: 11.

Warner, Margaret. "Details Released in Wood Shooting." *Bangor Daily News* 23–24 Sept. 1989: 1+.

———. "Hunter Charged in Death is Scoutmaster." *Bangor Daily News* 17 Nov. 1988: 1.

———. "Prosecution Rests Case in Rogerson Trial." *Bangor Daily News* 16 Oct. 1990: 1+.

———. "Rogerson Indicted in Wood Death." *Bangor Daily News* 10 Dec. 1989: 1+.

———. "Rogerson Pleads Innocent in Shooting." *Bangor Daily News* 12 Dec. 1989: 5.

———. "Rogerson Reflects on Wood Death." *Bangor Daily News* 25 Oct. 1990: 7.

———. "Rogerson's Companion Tells Jury Treadwell Acres Teeming with Deer." *Bangor Daily News* 13–14 Oct. 1990: 3.

———. "State vs. Rogerson: Jury Selection Gets Underway in Bangor." *Bangor Daily News* 10 Oct. 1990: 1+.

Weber, Tom. "Shooting Tragedy Stirs Debate in Homes, Hunting Camps." *Bangor Daily News* 26 Nov. 1988: 1.

Welter, Barbara. "The Cult of True Womanhood: 1820–1860." *American Quarterly* 18 (1966): 151–174.

Weymouth, David. "Welcome News from the Courtroom." Letter. *Bangor Daily News* 24 Oct. 1990: 17.

THE POLITICS OF NEGOTIATING PUBLIC TRAGEDY: MEDIA FRAMING OF THE MATTHEW SHEPARD MURDER

BRIAN L. OTT AND ERIC AOKI

Even before Matt died, he underwent a strange, American transubstantiation, seized, filtered, and fixed as an icon by the national news media dedicated to swift and consumable tragedy and by a national politics convulsed by gay rights.

—Beth Loffreda, **Losing Matt Shepard**[1]

In the blustery evening hours of Tuesday, October 6, 1998, Aaron McKinney and Russell Henderson lured 21-year-old Matthew Shepard from the Fireside Bar in Laramie, Wyoming, to a desolate field on the edge of town. There the two high school dropouts bound the frail, youthful Shepard to a split-rail fence, viciously bludgeoned him 18 times with the butt of a .357 magnum, stole his shoes and wallet, and left him to die in the darkness and near-freezing temperatures. It was not until the evening of the next day that Aaron Kreifel[s], a passing mountain biker, discovered Shepard—his face so horribly disfigured that Kreifel[s] told police he thought at first it was a scarecrow. The only portions of his face not covered in blood were those that had been streaked clean by his tears. Unconscious, hypothermic, and suffering from severe brain trauma, Shepard was astonishingly still alive. He was rushed to Poudre Valley Hospital in Fort Collins, Colorado, where he would die five days later without ever having regained consciousness. McKinney and Henderson had been apprehended prior to his death, and as the gruesome details of that night began to unfold, it became clear that Matthew Shepard was brutally murdered for being gay. In the weeks that followed, Shepard became a symbol of the deep prejudice, hatred, and violence directed at homosexuals. Indeed, news of the event spawned vigils across the country and a nationwide debate about hate-crimes legislation. Shortly more than a year later, Henderson pled guilty and McKinney was convicted of murder. Both men are currently serving life sentences in the Wyoming State Penitentiary.

The basic contours of this story remain vividly etched in our memories—memories that have permanently altered our personal and public lives. Perhaps this event so profoundly affected both of us because, as educators in Colorado, we were less than five miles from the hospital where Matthew Shepard clung to life for five days in October 1998. Perhaps the memory still burns brightly for us because several students at our university mocked the event with a scarecrow and anti-gay epithets on a homecoming float even as Shepard lay comatose in the hospital across town. Perhaps the memory serves as a survival instinct, reminding us that being "out" in the community drastically alters the relation of our bodies to the landscape, and that cultural politics, discourse, and violence are intricately intertwined. Or perhaps, just perhaps, we fear the consequences of forgetting. We cling to the memory of Matthew Shepard because we sense that the nation has already forgotten, or worse, reconciled these events.[2] How has an event that sparked so much interest, concern, and public discussion seeped from the collective consciousness of a nation and its citizenry? Why is hate-crimes legislation no longer a "hot" political issue? The answers to these questions we believe reside, at least in large part, in the manner in which the news media told this story.

We also believe that the underlying form of the Matthew Shepard story may have resonance with the news media's framing of other public traumas, from the shootings at Columbine High School to the terrorist attacks in New York and Washington, D.C., on September 11, 2001. Our aim in this essay, then, is to identify the underlying symbolic process and to analyze how it functions to construct and position citizens relative to the political process, and how it assists them in confronting and resolving public trauma. With regard to the Matthew Shepard murder, we contend that the news media's tragic framing of that event works rhetorically and ideologically to relieve the public of its social complicity and culpability; to reaffirm a dominant set of discourses that socially stigmatizes gay, lesbian, bisexual, and transgendered (GLBT) persons; and to hamper efforts to create and enact a progressive GLBT social policy. To advance this argument, we begin by examining the literature on media framing.

SYMBOLIC ACTION, FRAME ANALYSIS, AND THE NEWS MEDIA

In *The Philosophy of Literary Form*, Kenneth Burke argues that art forms function as equipments for living, by which he means that discursive forms such as comedy, tragedy, satire, and epic furnish individuals and collectives with the symbolic resources and strategies for addressing and resolving the given historical and personal problems they face.[3] When there is a traumatic event such as the Matthew Shepard murder, then, discourse—and especially the public discourse of the news media—aids people in "coming to terms" with the event. For Burke, different discursive forms equip persons to confront and resolve problems in different ways. "[E]ach of the great poetic forms," he contends, "stresses its own peculiar way of building the mental equipment (meanings, attitudes, character) by which one handles the significant factors of his time."[4] That different discursive forms offer different mental equipments is significant because it frames what constitutes acceptable political and social action. Identifying prevailing discursive forms is a never-ending critical task, as symbolic forming is linked to the environment in which it occurs and new discursive forms are continually emerging. In Burke's words, "the conventional forms demanded by one age are as resolutely shunned by another."[5] Thus, to understand how the public made sense of and responded to the Shepard murder, one must attend to the underlying symbolic form of the discourse surrounding it.

One approach to analyzing discursive forms and the attendant attitudes (incipient actions) they foster toward a situation is by examining what Burke has called "terministic screens"[6] and media critics—drawing on a sociological perspective—have called "frame analysis."[7] Frame analysis looks to see how a situation or event is named/defined, and how that naming shapes public opinion. It accomplishes this analysis by highlighting the inherent biases in all storytelling, namely *selectivity* (what is included and excluded in the story?), *partiality* (what is emphasized and downplayed in the story?), and *structure* (how does the story formally play out?). One example of framing in the news media is the distinction between "episodic" stories and "thematic" stories. "The episodic frame," according to Shanto Iyengar and Adam Simon, "depicts public issues in terms of concrete instances or public events . . . [and] makes for 'good pictures.' The thematic news frame, by contrast, places public issues in some general or abstract context . . . [and] takes the form of a 'takeout' or 'backgrounder' report directed at general outcomes."[8] Though few news reports are exclusively episodic or thematic, the dominance of episodic frames in the news has been established in multiple studies.[9] How a story is framed in the news affects both how the public assigns responsibility for a traumatic event and "how people following the debate think about policy options and preferred outcomes."[10] To appreciate fully the political and ideological implications of framing, however, the critic must do more than simply classify a news story as episodic or thematic.

The subtle ebb and flow of symbolic forms is crucial to how they interpellate subjects and do the work of ideology. To get after these subtleties, we undertook a detailed frame analysis of the news coverage of the Matthew Shepard murder in the *Washington Post,* the *New York Times*, and the *Los Angeles Times*—three "large, nationally influential newspapers."[11] Since we were curious about how this story has been framed over time, we examined the news coverage from October 10, 1998 (when the story was first reported nationally), to December 2001 (roughly two years after McKinney was convicted). This approach generated a sample containing 71 news articles. Wanting to see if the coverage varied in publications with notably different politics, we also analyzed the news coverage in *Time* magazine and *The Advocate* over the same period. These magazines allowed us to compare and contrast the coverage of the event in a mainstream weekly with the coverage in an alternative news source specifically committed to issues affecting the GLBT community. Based on an analysis of these five news outlets, we identified four phases in the print media's framing of the Matthew Shepard story: naming the event, making a political symbol, expunging the evil within, and restoring the social order. In the following section, we describe each of these phases and the symbolic processes they entail.

THE MATTHEW SHEPARD STORY

All stories have *form,* which is to say they are temporally structured—creating and fulfilling appetites as they unfold.[12] As C. Allen Carter notes:

> When the narrative strategy is working as intended, the culmination of each episode sets the stage for the next . . . The story relieves its audience of the burden of having to 'choose between' different phases of its unfolding and, simply by taking them through one phase, prepares them for the next. Each successive step of the plot leads into the next, whether or not it leads its audience astray.[13]

Naming the Event

Given the formal characteristics of narrative, how a story begins is crucial to how a story develops. In this section, we examine how the Matthew Shepard story is framed in initial news reports and analyze how that framing functions rhetorically. To fully appreciate *how* this story begins, however, we must first look at *when* it begins. The *Washington Post, New York Times,* and *Los Angeles Times* did not run feature articles on Matthew Shepard until October 10, 1998, three days after he was discovered. The reason for the media's delay in treating the story as a national news item likely has to do with how the news is *made.* An event is selected to become a major news story based on its potential for drama. As W. Lance Bennett notes, "It is no secret that reporters and editors search for events with dramatic properties and then emphasize those properties in their reporting."[14] Prior to October 8, little was known about the details of the attack outside the Albany County sheriff's department. During a local press conference on that day, Sheriff Gary Puls told reporters that, "[Matthew] may have been beaten because he was gay . . . [and that he] was found by a mountain biker, tied to a fence like a scarecrow."[15] Local reporters covering the story immediately seized on the anti-gay aspect of the crime and the crucifix symbolism of the scarecrow image—two dramatic elements that quickly drew the attention of the national press.[16]

Matthew Shepard was officially "good melodrama" and the reports in the mainstream media that followed focused almost exclusively on two elements, the deplorable motives of Henderson and McKinney and the gruesome character of the scene. Indeed, these aspects of the story are evident in the initial headlines from all three papers we analyzed: "Gay Man Beaten and Left For Dead; 2 Are Charged,"[17] "Gay Student Brutally Beaten; 4 Arrested,"[18] and "Gay Man Near Death After Beating, Burning; Three Held in Wyoming Attack Near Campus; Hate Crimes Suspected."[19] The qualifier "gay" that begins each headline constructs the victim's sexuality as the focal point of the story, despite Laramie Police Commander O'Dalley's public claim at the time that "robbery was the chief motive."[20]

The news media's devotion to drama virtually insured that sensationalistic descriptions of Matthew Shepard's body would lead every story. In its first feature article, the *Washington Post* emphasized the savage and dehumanizing aspects of the crime, reporting that "Matthew Shepard, slight of stature, gentle of demeanor . . . was tied to a fence like a dead coyote . . . [with] his head badly battered and burn marks on his body."[21] Likewise, the *New York Times* began, "At first, the passing bicyclist thought the crumpled form lashed to a ranch fence was a scarecrow. But when he stopped, he found the burned, battered and nearly life-less body of Matthew Shepard, an openly gay college student."[22] The "scarecrow" image was also referenced in the *Los Angeles Times,* which began, "A gay University of Wyoming student was brutally beaten, burned and left tied to a wooden fence like a scarecrow, with grave injuries including a smashed skull."[23] The graphic and gruesome images of violence visited upon Shepard's body were shocking and trau-matic, and they begged the question, "How could something like this happen?" As unthinkable and unimaginable as the act seemed, the basic outline of the story already portrayed an answer—hatred fueled by homophobia. The naming of the attack as a "vicious . . . anti-gay hate crime"[24] would prove pivotal in the heated political discussion to ensue.

Key details, terms, and structures were already setting the stage for how the story *must* unfold. For instance, the near exclusive focus in early press reports on the brutality done to Matthew Shepard's body functioned in two interrelated ways. First, it personalized the event, making Shepard the *center* of the story. This was not, and never would become, a story about hate crimes in which Matthew Shepard was simply an example. It was a story about Shepard, in which hate was the motive for violence. One consequence of personalized news, according to Bennett, "[is that it] gives preference to the individual actors and human-interest angles in events while downplaying institutional and political considerations that establish the social context for those events."[25] In the Matthew Shepard story, hatred and homophobia—as we will demonstrate shortly—would come to be framed primarily as character flaws of the chief antagonists, rather than as wide-scale social prejudices that routinely result in violence toward gays and lesbians. Second, the repeated emphasis on the hideousness of the crime in both its barbarity and motivation profoundly disrupted the moral and social order. The images and descriptions were not only traumatic, they were traumatizing; they functioned to unsettle and even undermine the public's faith in basic civility and humanity. So great was the disruption to the social order that even at this early stage it fostered a desire for resolution.[26] For this story, for Matthew Shepard's story, to end (as all news stories must), *responsibility* had to be assigned and order had to be restored. Since this story centered on Shepard, responsibility had a face, or rather two faces, Russell Henderson and Aaron McKinney. But before they would come into focus, Shepard would be transformed into a national political symbol.

Making a Political Symbol

Even before his death, Shepard had become "a national symbol for the campaign against hate crimes and anti-gay violence."[27] A website created by Poudre Valley Hospital to provide updates on his condition "drew over 815,000 hits from around the world."[28] On Saturday, October 10, students, faculty, and community members from Laramie gathered for the University of Wyoming's homecoming parade, where "amid the usual hoopla . . . hundreds of people donned yellow arm bands and marched in tribute to Shepard and the belief that intolerance has no place in the Equality State."[29] Throughout the weekend, candlelight vigils for Shepard would be held across the country, with a Los Angeles memorial attracting an estimated 5,000 concerned citizens. Then, in the early morning hours of Monday, October 12, 1998, one day after National Coming Out Day, Matthew Shepard passed away with his parents at his be[d]side.

With the news of Shepard's death, a nation already stricken with grief was plunged even deeper into emotional turmoil. As Reverend Anne Kitch asked in her homily at Shepard's funeral, "How can we not let our hearts be deeply, deeply troubled? How can we not be immersed in despair, how can we not cry out against this? This is not the way it is supposed to be. A son has died, a brother has been lost, a child has been broken, torn, abandoned."[30] The Matthew Shepard story had struck a chord. It had "electrified gay America,"[31] and it had done much more. As *Post* reporters Justin Gillis and Patrice Gaines noted:

> For the first time, in cities across the United States and Canada, straight people . . . marched by the thousands to protest anti-gay violence. More than 60 marches and vigils have taken place since his death, and others are scheduled for today. People rallied in New York, Atlanta and Miami—and in West Lafayette, Ind., Fort Collins, Colo., and Corner Brook, Newfoundland. Under an indigo sky, on the steps of the Capitol, a crowd of several thousand gathered last week to hold candles aloft, celebrate Shepard's life and demand that Congress pass legislation to battle hate crimes. "Now!" they cried.[32]

Among the thousands at the candlelight vigil on the Capitol steps in Washington were actresses Ellen DeGeneres and Kristen Johnson, and numerous congressional representatives, who not only condemned the beating death of Shepard but also urged immediate passage of a federal hate crimes bill.[33] Earlier in the week, President Clinton had also pushed "Congress to pass the Hate Crimes Prevention Act . . . [which] would broaden the definition of hate crimes to include assaults on gays as well as women and the disabled."[34] As *The Advocate* would report a year later, there was little doubt that "Matthew Shepard's murder turned equal rights and protections for gays and lesbians into topics of nationwide debate."[35]

But how had Shepard been transformed into a martyr—"the most recognizable symbol of antigay violence in America"[36]—and what did that transformation mean for the political debate taking place? The previous year had seen "at least 27 gay people murdered in apparent hate crimes. . . . And the murders are only the extreme end of the spectrum of anti-gay attacks. A coalition that monitors anti-gay violence and harassment documented 2,445 episodes last year in American cities."[37] Though the motive for Shepard's murder was hardly an isolated incident, two aspects of this story made it unique and especially well suited for seizing the public's imagination. The first factor, of course, was the figure at its center. As Brian Levin, director of the Center on Hate and Extremism at Richard Stockton College in Pomona, New Jersey, told the *Washington Post,* "You can't get a more sympathetic person to face such a brutal attack than Matt Shepard. He looked like an all-American nice kid next door who'd look after your grandmother if you went out of town. He looked like a sweet kid and he was."[38] Shepard was "white and middle-class," "barely on the threshold of adulthood," and "frail [in] appearance."[39] Because of his slight stature, a mere 5'2", and "cherubic face" even those uncomfortable with homosexuality saw him as an *innocent* (that is, sexually nonthreatening) victim. The public identified with Shepard, viewing him as friend and son.

The second factor that contributed to the emerging mythology was the dramatic structure of the narrative. Jack Levin, professor of sociology and criminology at Northeastern University, speculates that, "If Matthew had died instantly of a gunshot wound to the head, his death may not have gotten as much publicity."[40] That Shepard lay comatose in a hospital for several days while people around the country prayed and stood vigil for him functioned to heighten the public's investment in the story. Moreover, it was during those days of vigil that the "heinous" and "morose" details of the crime were repeated over and over again in the news media. The juxtaposition of Shepard's ability to evoke identification with the crime's incomprehensibility shattered society's "'veneer of congeniality,' and prompted a collective self-examination."[41] In other words, the public's inability to quickly and easily reconcile Matthew Shepard's innocence (unlike most gay men, he didn't have this coming to him) with his "lynching" was a significant source of shame for the country and created wide-scale public guilt. As Steve Lopez wrote in *Time* magazine, "Shepard has ignited a national town hall meeting on the enduring hatred that *shames* this country" (emphasis added).[42] But guilt demands redemption, for as Burke reminds, "who would not be cleansed!" and redemption needs a redeemer, "which is to say, a Victim!"[43] Though guilt can be resolved symbolically in a variety of ways, ranging from transcendence to mortification, the tragic framing of the Matthew Shepard story foretold that purification would be achieved through victimage and the scapegoat process.

Expunging the Evil Within

In *A Grammar of Motives,* Burke contends that, "Criminals either actual or imaginary may . . . serve as [curative] scapegoats in a society that 'purifies itself' by 'moral indignation' in condemning them."[44] This is not to suggest, however, that those seeking to "ritualistically cleanse themselves" of guilt can simply blame a chosen party. The "scapegoat mechanism" is a complex process that entails three distinctive stages: "(1) an original state of merger, in that the iniquities are shared by both the iniquitous and their chosen vessel; (2) a principle of division, in that elements shared in common are being ritualistically alienated; (3) a new principle of merger, this time in the unification of those whose purified identity is defined in dialectical opposition to the sacrificial offering."[45] For a "sacrificial vessel" to perform the role of "vicarious atonement," it must be, *at first,* "profoundly consubstantial with . . . those who would be cured by attacking it."[46] It must represent *their* iniquities, because symbolic forms that manage guilt can only be "successful if the audience is guilty of the sins portrayed in the discourse."[47] Though the very earliest news reports about the hatred and violence directed at Shepard had identified Aaron McKinney and Russell Henderson as the main perpetrators, those same news reports cast the two as representative of both their local and national communities.

As McKinney and Henderson were being arraigned, a significant amount of discourse was being generated about the state of Wyoming and the "cowboy culture" that had nurtured them.[48] It was widely reported, for instance, that Wyoming was one of only nine U.S. states to "have no hate-crime laws."[49] Another report noted that, "Although Wyoming often bills itself as the 'equality state,' the state Legislature has repeatedly voted down hate crime legislation"; the article subsequently quotes Marv Johnson, executive director of the Wyoming chapter of the American Civil Liberties Union, as saying, "Wyoming is not really gay friendly. . . . The best way to characterize that is by a comment a legislator made a few years back, when he likened homosexuals to gay bulls as worthless and should be sent to the packing plant [sic]."[50] Similarly, Susanna Goodin, the University of Wyoming's Ethics Center director, told the *Washington Post,* "the beating [would] . . . prompt Wyoming *residents* to ponder the price of intolerance and indifference" (emphasis added).[51] In routinely referencing the "homophobia in the Wyoming legislature"[52] and noting that, in light of the attack, Laramie, Wyoming, "wrestled with *its* attitudes toward gay men" (emphasis added),[53] the news media initially framed the community's attitudes as consistent with the perpetrators' attitudes. In fact, when jury selection began for the trial of Henderson in March 1999, his defense attorney, Wyatt Skaggs, was rather reflective about this association and told potential jurors, "[The media] . . . has literally injected into our community a feeling of guilt. The press wants us to think that we are somehow responsible for what went on October 6. Are any of you here going to judge this case because you feel guilty and want to make a statement to the nation?"[54]

Nor was Wyoming alone in being identified with the perpetrators' attitudes and motives. As Lopez observed in *Time* magazine, "The cowboy state has its rednecks and yahoos, for sure, but there are no more bigots per capita in Wyoming than in New York, Florida or California."[55] In the first few days after the attack, the public was forced, if only temporarily, to confess the prevalence of homophobic attitudes around the country. First was the incident involving the scarecrow on a homecoming float at Colorado State University, which was reportedly painted with anti-gay epithets.[56] "While the papers were reluctant to report the full range of insults," Loffreda notes, "I heard that the signs read 'I'm Gay' and 'Up My Ass.'"[57] This incident prompted a number of reports about the prevalence of homophobic attitudes in schools around the country.[58] Additionally, there were widely circulated news stories about the protestors at Shepard's funeral. Shortly before he was eulogized, Tom Kenworthy writes, "a dozen anti-gay protestors from Texas and Kansas staged a demonstration across from St. Mark's, carrying signs saying 'No Fags in Heaven' and 'No Tears for Queers.' . . . [including] a young girl carrying a sign that read 'Fag=Anal Sex.'"[59] In light of these stories, it was hardly surprising that a *Time*/CNN poll found that "68 percent [of respondents] said attacks like the one against Shepard could happen in *their* community" (emphasis added).[60] For a few weeks following the attack, the message in the media was that McKinney and Henderson shared much in common with the country. But all of that was about to change.

"At one moment the chosen [party] is *a part of* the clan, being one of their number," explains Carter; "a moment later it symbolizes something *apart from* them, being the curse they wish to lift from themselves."[61] Division or the "casting out" of the vessel of unwanted evils is accomplished through vilification and through a redrawing of boundaries that excludes the scapegoat. Slowly, almost unnoticeably, discourse in the news media was shifting from the country's homophobia to that of the perpetrators, where it was being recoded as a character flaw rather than a widescale institutional prejudice. In a statement demarcating the new communal boundaries, Wyoming governor Jim Geringer told the *Washington Post,* "Wyoming people are discouraged that all of us could be unfairly stereotyped by the actions of two very sick and twisted people."[62] Accounts were also now suggesting that the two perpetrators were *uniquely* ignorant. *Time* magazine noted that the two men were "high school dropouts," adding that, "In addition to being an unspeakably gruesome crime, it was a profoundly dumb one."[63] After all, McKinney and Henderson had drawn undue attention to themselves by getting into a fistfight with two other men after beating Shepard. Reports such as this one functioned not only to cast the men as especially dull-witted, but also to highlight a *pattern* of violence and criminality—one that would be further reinforced in subsequent reports about their previous run-ins with the law, including convictions for felony burglary and drunk driving. Additionally, there was the matter of deception, premeditation, and merciless cruelty. The news media were now reporting that, according to law enforcement, the two men had pretended to be gay to lure Shepard out of the bar and into their pickup truck, and that they had continued to beat him as he begged for his life.[64]

As time passed, Shepard's attackers became ever more alienated from the public. They were uneducated, drug addicted, career criminals, who had maliciously sought out their victim because he was gay, and they now "found themselves called 'subhuman' and 'monsters.'"[65] In an uncharacteristic moment of reflective journalism, a *Los Angeles Times* staff writer comments on Henderson and McKinney's vilification:

> In the six months since Shepard's gruesome death, the protagonists have become dehumanized . . . transmuted by the American compulsion for fashioning moral lessons out of tragedy. This morality play staged in a Western prairie town has demanded simplistic roles: Shepard, the earnest college student who was targeted because he was gay and gave his life to advance a social cause. Henderson and McKinney, the high school dropouts accused of beating Shepard to death, have been cast as remorseless killers.[66]

The symbolic distance between the public and McKinney and Henderson grew even wider during McKinney's trial in October 1999, where gruesome new details from the night of the beating were revealed. The news media seized on one detail in particular, in which McKinney stopped beating Shepard to ask if he could read the license plate on his truck. When Shepard replied, "yes" and recited the plate's numbers, McKinney resumed the attack despite Shepard's repeated pleas for mercy. The story embodied the view that McKinney was not quite human, and prosecuting attorney Cal Rerucha retold it in his closing arguments, calling McKinney a "savage and a 'wolf' who preyed on the lamb-like Shepard."[67] As if to further distinguish McKinney from the public, following his conviction the news media widely reported that various national, leading gay rights groups had, along with the Shepard family, publicly condemned the death penalty in this case. As Matthew Shepard's father, Dennis Shepard, would tell the court in a written statement following the trial, "this is a time to begin the healing process. To show mercy to someone who refused to show any mercy."[68] Mr. Shepard's statement captured the essence of how the media was naming the difference between the public and the perpetrators, one human and the other not quite.

Restoring the Social Order

With the surrogate of evil driven from the community, all that remains for creating symbolic closure is the punishment of evil and the reaffirmation of the social and moral order. "Tragedy," explains Barry Brummett, "subjects the erring [figure] to trial, finds him or her to be criminal, and demands condemnation and penance."[69] In March 1999, Russell Henderson pled guilty, leaving only McKinney to stand trial. The significance of the trial to the outcome of the story was evident before it even began. "The trial will," wrote Kenworthy in the *Washington Post*, "*close* the book on an ugly crime that grabbed the nation by the shoulders and forced it to confront the price of hate and intolerance—and then served as a rallying point . . . for gay rights" (emphasis added).[70] During the case, McKinney's lawyers attempted to advance a "gay panic defense," which claimed the victim's sexual advances triggered panic and led to the beating. But Judge Barton Voigt ruled it "inadmissible . . . based on Wyoming law," and on November 3, 1999—shortly more than a year after Matthew Shepard's death—Aaron McKinney was convicted of murder and sentenced to two consecutive life terms with no chance of parole. "The trial," observed Phil Curtis in *The Advocate*, "delivered an emotionally satisfying vindication for Shepard's death and brought *closure* to the Shepard family and *to the public*, who had followed the grim case for the past year" (emphasis added).[71] As odd, perhaps even unbelievable, as it seems, the verdict did deliver both symbolic satisfaction and closure for some. Explains Robert Heath, "As a dynamic progression of an idea, each work [that is, story] leads toward some resolution. If it is achieved, reader and author experience a release, the sheer pleasure of having gone through the process."[72] To the extent that the story began with the brutal beating of Matthew Shepard, the conviction and punishment of *his* assailants signals its close.

But the conviction of McKinney had an additional and important side effect. In performing a cathartic function for the public (that is, purging them of their guilt through victimage) and bringing closure to the story, it also brought a sense of resolution to the debate about gay rights and hate-crimes legislation that Shepard's death had initiated. Since these issues had been framed *in relation to* the story about Matthew Shepard's murder, the story's conclusion functioned to bring closure to them as well. The national public debate over hate crimes and gay politics dissipated almost as quickly as it had emerged. Two weeks following Shepard's death in October 1998, a *Time*/CNN poll asked respondents, "Federal law mandates increased penalties for people who commit hate crimes against racial minorities. Do you favor or oppose the same treatment for people who commit hate crimes against homosexuals?"[73] At that time, 76 percent of the public favored hate-crimes legislation that protected homosexuals and 19 percent opposed it.[74] In the months following his death, legislation to increase the penalty for hate crimes against gays and lesbians was introduced in 26 states. By the time these bills came up for vote, however, the Matthew Shepard story was winding toward narrative conclusion, and only one state, Missouri, passed new legislation.[75] Perhaps even more telling, *The Advocate* reports that, "After McKinney's conviction Judy and Dennis Shepard . . . traveled to Washington, D.C., to lobby for federal hate-crimes legislation. Their effort failed. A hate-crimes measure was removed from a budget bill in congressional committee just weeks after the trial."[76] In fostering symbolic resolution through narrative closure, the news media's coverage of the story re-imposed order and eliminated the self-reflective space that might serve as the basis for social and political change.

FRAMING AND REFRAMING

Having described the news media's framing of the Matthew Shepard story and having analyzed how those frames functioned rhetorically to absolve the public of its guilt associated with the motives of the murder, we will now take a step back and pose the question, "What difference do the frames make for the larger world?"[77] That is, how does the news media's framing of that event also function ideologically? How does it invite the public to view the world, social relations, and GLBT identities? How does it affirm, challenge, and negotiate centers, margins, and relationships of power? To get after these questions, we propose to look at the way in which the story works to naturalize particular sets of social relations at both the level of language (microscopic) and the level of symbolic form (macroscopic).[78] With regard to the linguistic level, we are specifically interested in the consequences of the media's "naming" of the victim's body and the perpetrators' motives.

Prejudice and discrimination against GLBT persons have historically been connected to the stigmatization of the body as *different* or *abnormal*.[79] In fact, Erving Goffman notes that, "The Greeks, who were apparently strong on visual aids, originated the term stigma to refer to bodily signs designed to expose something unusual and bad about the moral status of the signifier."[80] The homosexual body has traditionally been stigmatized or marked as abnormal in a wide variety of ways; it has variously been coded as dirty and unclean, effeminate and queer, and threatening and predatory to suit the needs of those in power.[81] One way the bodies of gay men have been stigmatized as threatening and predatory, for instance, is "with the allegation that they are disproportionately responsible for child sexual abuse."[82] The obvious ridiculousness of this claim has not stopped the media from perpetuating it, and a 1998 study of *Newsweek* found that 60 percent of stories about child molestation involved homosexuals.[83] This pattern of naming in the media raises an important question about the Matthew Shepard story: "Would Shepard have received the attention he did had his body not so easily been coded as *unthreatening?*"

Though there is no way to answer this question with certainty, one thing that is clear is that Shepard's body *was* coded as unthreatening and *his* story captured national headlines. Writing in *The Progressive,* JoAnn Wypijewski speculated that one reason people uncomfortable with homosexuality may have sympathized with this case is because for them, "Shepard is the perfect queer: young, pretty, and dead."[84] Indeed, it is difficult not to wonder how this story might have been told differently, if at all, had the victim been a minority, especially when the murder of Fred Martinez, a 16-year-old transgendered Navajo in Colorado hardly raised an eyebrow,[85] as did the murder of Arthur Warren, a gay black man, in rural West Virginia,[86] and the murder of five black gay men in Washington "by someone authorities believe to be an antigay serial killer."[87] The media's double standard here would seem to suggest that an anti-gay murder is tragic so long as the victim is not too gay, which is to say, too different. The issue of Shepard's small, non-threatening stature raises still more questions about the intersection of stigmatization and the gay male body.

In McKinney's trial, the defense attempted to shift responsibility for the beating back to the victim by claiming that Shepard's homosexuality had evoked fear and panic. Though Judge Voight ruled this line of argument and testimony "inadmissible," he cautiously reminded the media that his ruling was "not intended to send a social or political commentary, [and rather] was based on Wyoming law."[88] In other anti-gay hate crimes where the victim was not as outwardly *innocent* (that is, frail, youthful, white, middle-class) as Matthew Shepard, the "gay panic" defense has been allowed.[89] The use of such a defense is not all that surprising, however, when one considers its ideological consistency with the term used to name the *motive* in such cases, "homophobia." According to Byrne Fone, "The term 'homophobia' is now popularly construed to mean fear and dislike of homosexuality and of those who practice it" or an "extreme rage and fear reaction to homosexuals."[90] Both definitions "place the onus on the oppressed rather than on the agents of oppression,"[91] effectively revictimizing the victim by making the oppressed the source, the instigator, of fear and disruption. The popularity of the term "homophobia" to describe anti-gay attitudes is just one example of how public discourse regarding GLBT persons continues to construct homosexuality as abnormal (in this case, "fear-producing"). In the Matt Shepard story, homosexuality was further marked as different and hence deviant by the media's consistent and ubiquitous references to Shepard's "gay" sexuality. There were no headlines that reported, "Man Killed by Straight Attackers," and no articles that named Henderson or McKinney's sexuality. In treating heterosexuality as invisible, the media both privilege it as the norm and as *normal.* At the level of language, then, the media's telling of the Matthew Shepard story functions to reproduce a hegemonic set of sociocultural categories in which homosexuality is marginal and Other. Until the unspoken assumptions that frame the dominant discourses about GLBT persons are questioned and interrogated, hatred and the violence it begets are likely to remain prominent features of our cultural landscape.

Like the linguistic particularities, we believe that the underlying symbolic form of the story matters ideologically, and so we turn now to the "big picture," to, as Burke explains, the various typical ways that the most basic of attitudes (that is, yes, no, maybe) are "grandly symbolized."[92] Symbolic forms can be, according to Burke, loosely grouped into "frames of acceptance" and "frames of rejection" based on the general orientation they adopt in "the face of anguish, injustice, disease, and death."[93] Literary forms such as epic, tragedy, and comedy are frames of acceptance because they equip persons to "come to terms" with an event and their place in the world. Precisely *how* they "come to terms" varies according to the symbolic form (that is, epic, tragedy, comedy, and so forth) at work, and influences, in turn, where they and the world can go with those terms. In shaping attitudes, symbolic forms serve as a basis for programmatic action. Our analysis of the Matthew Shepard story suggests that it was framed primarily in tragic terms, in which the public, through the scapegoat mechanism, cleansed itself of the guilt associated with prejudice, hatred, violence, and their intersection. The shortcoming of tragic framing is that it brings about symbolic resolution without turning the event into a lesson for those involved. By projecting its iniquity upon McKinney and Henderson and attacking them, the public achieves resolution *in this instance,* but does not substantively alter its character as to insure that future instances are less likely. On the contrary, this mode aggressively perpetuates the status quo, cloaking but not erasing the public's homophobia (and we do mean the politically loaded term "homophobia") so that it can return another day.

So what are the alternatives? The media could adopt frames of rejection such as those found in the literary forms of elegy, satire, burlesque, and the grotesque.[94] The difficulty here is that "frames stressing the ingredient of *rejection* tend to lack the well-rounded quality of a *complete* here-and-now philosophy. They make for fanaticism, the singling-out of one factor above others in the charting of human relationships."[95] By "coming to terms" with an event primarily by saying "no," frames of rejection are unable to equip individuals and groups to take programmatic action. A discourse that is wholly debunking is, at least in isolation, ill suited for bringing about social change.[96]

A second and preferable alternative, according to Burke, is adopting a "comic frame," which is "neither wholly euphemistic [as is tragedy], nor wholly debunking."[97] As numerous scholars have noted, the comic frame is not about seeing humor in everything;[98] it is about maximum consciousness—"self-awareness and social responsibility at the same time."[99] The comic frame is one of "ambivalence," a flexible, adaptive, charitable frame that enables "people to be *observers of themselves, while acting.*"[100] In shifting the emphasis "from crime to stupidity," Brummett maintains that the comic frame provides motives that "teach the fool—and vicariously the audience—about error so that it may be *corrected* rather than *punished*" (emphasis added).[101] "The progress of humane enlightenment," explains Burke, "can go no further than in picturing people not as *vicious*, but as *mistaken*."[102] When social injustices such as the anti-gay beating of Matthew Shepard are framed in tragic terms, naming McKinney and Henderson as vicious, the public finds expiation externally in the punishment of those identified as responsible. Framed in comic terms, however, one can identify with the mistaken, become a student of her/himself, "'transcend' himself by noting his own foibles," and learn from the experience.[103] The comic frame "promotes integrative, socializing knowledge"[104] by emphasizing *humility* (the recognition that we are all sometimes wrong) over *humiliation* (the desire to victimize others).

CRITICAL REFLECTIONS

A frame analysis of the print media's coverage of the Matthew Shepard murder reinforces a number of previous findings about how the news is made. The manner in which this story, for instance, gained national prominence testifies to the link between the dramatic qualities of an event and its perceived newsworthiness.[105] Since drama increases ratings and "[n]ews content is influenced by the fact that . . . media corporations have a profit orientation,"[106] news outlets both seek out stories with dramatic properties and emphasize those properties in their reporting. The profit-driven focus on a story's dramatic elements accounts, at least partially, for the striking consistency among news reports in the Matthew Shepard case. All three of the national newspapers we analyzed named the event as a vicious anti-gay hate crime, constructed Shepard as a political symbol of gay rights, and transferred the public's guilt onto McKinney and Henderson. Even *Time* and *The Advocate,* publications with varied political perspectives, framed the story in comparable ways. Though *The Advocate* offered more extensive coverage, particularly with regard to Matthew Shepard and his family, the basic contours of the story remained the same. Consistency among news reports is also a product of traditional journalistic routines and practices. Both the *New York Times* and the *Washington Post* assigned a primary reporter to the story, while the *Los Angeles Times* pulled the vast majority of its stories from the Associated Press. The homogeneity of the reports, then, reflects fewer voices gathering data from the same experts and highlighting the same dramatic properties.[107]

In addition to these broad findings, our analysis points to some specific conclusions about how the news media report on public traumas and the attendant social consequences of such reporting. The news media's fascination with personalities and drama over institutional and social problems contributes to the "tragic framing" of public disasters and events. Since tragic frames ultimately alleviate the social guilt associated with a disaster through victimage, they tend to bring both closure *and* resolution to the larger social issues they raise. As such, tragic frames do not serve the public well as a basis for social and political action. Though media research on agenda setting has clearly established that the news media influence which political issues are on the public's mind,[108] few studies have looked at how changes in the public agenda may be linked to the piggybacking of social issues onto specific dramatic stories. Future research on agenda setting should attend carefully to the connection between symbolic forms such as the tragic frame and shifts in the public agenda. Our analysis of news coverage of the Matthew Shepard murder found that hate-crimes legislation and gay rights were central public concerns until Shepard's story came to a close. In light of this finding, it would be worth examining how declining coverage of the Columbine shootings may have contributed similarly to the dissipation of national public discourse on youth violence. The implications of our analysis extend beyond the matter of the media's role in establishing a public agenda. Since "frames are fundamental aspects of human consciousness and shape our attitudes toward the world and each other,"[109] media frames function ideologically. In Matthew Shepard's case, we believe that news media reproduced a discursive system of prejudice that contributed to Shepard's death. We can, however, learn from this event and the media's coverage of it. To introduce this essay, we attempted to provide an outline of the Matthew Shepard story that accurately captured the news media's tragic framing of that event. To conclude, we return to that story and adopt an alternative, more comic frame.

Despite commitments to both diversity and equality, the nation continued its painful struggle with tolerance today, as Laramie, Wyoming, became the most recent in a long list of U.S. towns and cities to witness, experience, and participate in violence motivated by culturally constructed notions of difference. In an all-too-familiar scene, two young men, Aaron McKinney and Russell Henderson, foolishly allowed their actions to be guided by social ignorance. Goaded, like a vast majority of people, by a deep desire to feel accepted and acceptable, Aaron and Russell assaulted Matthew Shepard, a University of Wyoming student, for what they perceived to be an intolerable difference, homosexuality. The assault, which resulted in Matthew's death, highlights a pattern of behavior in which individuals seek communal identification and the comfort and security that accompanies it through the expulsion of difference. Such an impulse is, of course, profoundly misguided as it reduces community to sameness, while ignoring the fact that difference is always a matter of perspective and depends upon who is naming it. Aaron and Russell's actions serve as a powerful reminder that if we truly hope to build healthy and humane communities, then we must aim to bridge the very differences we create. When we cast out others, the attitude is one of superiority and humiliation, and the act is one of violence. For us to curb violence like that seen most recently in Wyoming, we must all begin to erase the "battle lines" that are drawn again and again when we exalt ourselves over others.

NOTES

[1]Beth Loffreda, *Losing Matt Shepard: Life and Politics in the Aftermath of Anti-Gay Murder* (New York: Columbia University Press, 2000), x.

[2]We are using "memory" in a somewhat more general sense than rhetorical and media scholars who study "public memory." Our concern is not with how the news media construct invitations to a shared sense of the past or with the politics of commemoration, but with how the "life" of a political issue—its birth, growth, and death—is related to its framing in the news media. For an overview of the literature on public memory in rhetorical studies, see Stephen H. Browne, "Reading, Rhetoric, and the Texture of Public Memory," *Quarterly Journal of Speech* 81 (1995): 237–65. For variations on this theme, see also Carole Blair, Marsha S. Jeppeson, and Enrico Pucci, Jr., "Public Memorializing in Postmodernity: The Vietnam Veterans Memorial as Prototype," *Quarterly Journal of Speech* 77 (1991): 263–88; John Bodnar, *Remaking America: Public Memory, Commemoration, and Patriotism in the Twentieth Century* (Princeton, N.J.: Princeton University Press, 1992); James E. Young, *The Texture of Memory: Holocaust Memorials and Meaning* (New Haven: Yale University Press, 1993). For an overview of the literature on public memory in media studies, see Barbie Zelizer, "Reading the Past Against the Grain: The Shape of Memory Studies," *Critical Studies in Mass Communication* 12 (1995): 214–39. For variations on this theme, see also Martin J. Medhurst, "The Rhetorical Structure of Oliver Stone's *JFK*," *Critical Studies in Mass Communication* 10 (1993): 128–43; Thomas W. Benson, "Thinking through Film: Hollywood Remembers the Blacklist," in *Rhetoric and*

Community: Studies in Unity and Fragmentation, ed. J. Michael Hogan (Columbia: University of South Carolina Press, 1988), 217–55.

[3]Kenneth Burke, *The Philosophy of Literary Form: Studies in Symbolic Action* (Louisiana State University Press, 1941), 302–4.

[4]Kenneth Burke, *Attitudes Toward History*, 3d ed. (Berkeley: University of California Press, 1984), 34.

[5]Kenneth Burke, *Counter-Statement*, 2d ed. (Los Altos, Calif.: Hermes Publications, 1953), 139.

[6]Kenneth Burke, *Language as Symbolic Action: Essays on Life, Literature, and Method* (Berkeley: University of California Press, 1968), 44–45.

[7]In media studies, "frames analysis" derives from the work of Erving Goffman, *Frame Analysis: An Essay on the Organization of Experience* (Cambridge: Harvard University Press, 1974). See W. Lance Bennett, *News: The Politics of Illusion*, 2d ed. (New York: Longman, 1988); W. Lance Bennett, "The News about Foreign Policy," in *Taken by Storm: The Media, Public Opinion, and U.S. Foreign Policy in the Gulf War*, ed. W. Lance Bennett and David L. Paletz (Chicago: University of Chicago Press, 1994), 12–40; Todd Gitlin, "The Whole World is Watching," in *Transmission: Toward a Post-Television Culture*, 2d ed., ed. Peter d'Agostine and David Tafler (Thousand Oaks, Calif.: Sage Publications, 1995), 91–103; Shanto Iyengar, *Is Anyone Responsible? How Television Frames Political Issues* (Chicago: University of Chicago Press, 1991); and Shanto Iyengar and Adam Simon, "News Coverage of the Gulf Crisis and Public Opinion: A Study of Agenda-Setting, Priming, and Framing," in *Taken by Storm*, 167–85.

[8]Iyengar and Simon, "News Coverage," 171.

[9]Iyengar, *Is Anyone Responsible?*, 14.

[10]Bennett, "News about Foreign Policy," 31.

[11]Everette Dennis et al., *Covering the Presidential Primaries* (New York: The Freedom Forum Media Studies Center, 1992), 59.

[12]Burke, *Counter-Statement*, 31, 124.

[13]C. Allen Carter, *Kenneth Burke and the Scapegoat Process* (Norman: University of Oklahoma Press, 1996), 40.

[14]Bennett, *News*, 35.

[15]Quoted in Loffreda, *Losing Matt Shepard*, 5.

[16]Though the "scarecrow" image would appear in news reports repeatedly and even in poetry long after the event, "Matt hadn't actually been tied like a scarecrow; when he was approached first by the mountain biker, Aaron Kreifels, and then by Reggie Fluty, the sheriff's deputy who answered Kreifels's emergency call, Matt lay on his back, head propped against the fence, legs outstretched. His hands were lashed behind him and tied barely four inches off the ground to a fencepost" (Loffreda, *Losing Matt Shepard*, 5).

[17]James Brooke, "Gay Man Beaten and Left For Dead; 2 Are Charged," *New York Times*, October 10, 1998, sec. A09.

[18]"Gay Student Brutally Beaten; 4 Arrested," *Los Angeles Times*, October 10, 1998, 16.

[19]Tom Kenworthy, "Gay Man Near Death after Beating, Burning; Three Held in Wyoming Attack Near Campus; Hate Crimes Suspected," *Washington Post*, October 10, 1998, sec. A01.

[20]"Gay Student Brutally Beaten," 16.

[21]Kenworthy, "Gay Man Near Death," sec. A01.

[22]Brooke, "Gay Man Beaten," sec. A09.

[23]"Gay Student Brutally Beaten," 16.

[24]Tom Kenworthy, "In Wyoming, Homecoming Infused with Hard Lesson on Intolerance," *Washington Post*, October 11, 1998, sec. A02.

[25]Bennett, *News*, 26.

[26]As Wyoming governor Jim Geringer told the *Washington Post* shortly after Shepard's death, "[we all] feel a sense of tragedy and disbelief that a human life could be taken in such a brutal way. We must now find closure." (Tom Kenworthy, "Gay Wyoming Student Succumbs to Injuries," *Washington Post*, October 13, 1998, sec. A07).

[27]Tom Kenworthy, "Hundreds Gather to Remember Slain Man as 'Light to the World'; Anti-Gay Forces Incite Shouting Match at Wyoming Funeral," *Washington Post,* October 17, 1998, sec. A03.

[28]Loffreda, *Losing Matt Shepard,* 13.

[29]Kenworthy, "In Wyoming," sec. A02.

[30]Kenworthy, "Hundreds Gather," sec. A03.

[31]Justin Gillis and Patrice Gaines, "Pattern of Hate Emerges on a Fence in Laramie; Gay Victims' Killers Say They Saw an Easy Crime Target," *Washington Post,* October 18, 1998, sec. A01.

[32]Gillis and Gaines, "Pattern of Hate," sec. A01.

[33]Allan Lengel, "Thousands Mourn Student's Death; Beating in Wyoming Sparks New Push for Hate-Crimes Laws," *Washington Post,* October 15, 1998, sec. A07.

[34]Richard Lacayo, "The New Gay Struggle," *Time,* October 26, 1998, 34. President Clinton continued to use the Matthew Shepard murder as a rallying cry for the passage of a federal hate-crimes bill over the course of the next year. See "Clinton Urges Expanding Federal Hate Crimes Law," *Los Angeles Times,* April 7, 1999, home edition, 4; "White House to Host Meeting on Tougher U.S. Hate Crime Law," *Los Angeles Times,* July 10, 1999, valley edition, 13B; Charles Babington, "Clinton Urges Congress to Toughen Laws on Hate Crimes, Guns," *Washington Post,* October 16, 1999, sec. A11.

[35]Lisa Neff, "The Best Defense: Activists Plan Demonstrations in 50 States to Fight for Basic Human Rights," *The Advocate,* March 16, 1999, 40. Shepard's centrality to the national debate surrounding gay rights and hate-crimes legislation is evident in press reports from the time of his death until the conviction of McKinney. "Shepard's brutal murder put a spotlight on hate crimes" ("Nation in Brief/Wyoming," *Los Angeles Times,* May 22, 1999, home edition, 12). "The crime galvanized the gay and lesbian community and became a rallying point in the push for hate crime laws" (John L. Mitchell, "Vigil Marks Anniversary of Slaying of Gay Student," *Los Angeles Times,* October 13, 1999, home edition, 3). "The death of Shepard focused public attention on violence against homosexuals and stimulated at-times feverish debate about hate crimes legislation" (Julie Cart, "Defense Says Homosexual Advance Triggered Slaying," *Los Angeles Times,* October 26, 1999, home edition, 20). "[Matt Shepard's] death galvanized those seeking to expand the nation's hate-crime laws" ("Attack on Gay Was Planned, Witness Says," *Los Angeles Times,* October 29, 1999, valley edition, 23A). "The death of the college student [Matt Shepard] ignited national debate over hate crimes and violence against homosexuals" (Julie Cart, "Man Guilty in Shepard Slaying, Could Get Death," *Los Angeles Times,* November 4, 1999, home edition, 37). "The brutal murder of the wholesome-looking Shepard struck a chord across America. It spurred calls for the enactment of hate crime legislation" (Julie Cart, "Killer of Gay Student Is Spared Death Penalty," *Los Angeles Times,* November 5, 1999, home edition, 1). "The murder [of Matt Shepard] last October gained nationwide publicity and spurred calls by gay and lesbian activists for enactment of tough anti-hate crime legislation nationally" (Tom Kenworthy, "2nd Man is Convicted of Killing Gay Student," *Washington Post,* November 4, 1999, sec. A1). "The case [of Matt Shepard] became a rallying cry for states and the Federal Government to pass and expand hate-crime measures" (Michael Janofsky, "A Defense to Avoid Execution," *New York Times,* October 26, 1999, sec. A18). See also Carl Ingram, "California and the West," *Los Angeles Times,* October 3, 1999, home edition, 24; "Families of Hate Crime Victims Unite at Rally," *Los Angeles Times,* October 10, 1999, home edition, 12; Tom Kenworthy, "'Gay Panic' Defense Stirs Wyo. Trial," *Washington Post,* October 26, 1999, sec. A2; Tom Kenworthy, "Wyo. Jury to Weigh Motives in Gay Killing," *Washington Post,* November 3, 1999, sec. A3; Bill Carter, "Shepard's Parents," *New York Times,* February 3, 1999, sec. E7.

[36]Bruce Shenitz, "Laramie's Legacy," *Out,* October 2001, 76, 110.

[37]Gillis and Gaines, "Pattern of Hate," sec. A01; A second article reported that "in 1996, 21 men and women were killed in the United States because of their sexual orientation, according to the Southern Poverty Law Center, an Alabama group that tracks violence against minorities. According to the Federal Bureau of Investigation, sexual orientation

was a factor in 11.6 percent of the 8,759 hate crimes recorded in 1996." (James Brooke, "Gay Man Dies from Attack, Fanning Outrage and Debate," *New York Times,* October 13, 1998, sec. A17). Sexual orientation ranks third behind race and religion as the motive for (reported) hate crimes. See "2000 FBI Hate Crime Statistics," *Human Rights Campaign,* retrieved April 20, 2002, from <http://www.hrc.org/issues/hate_crimes/background/stats/ stats2000.asp>.

[38]Gillis and Gaines, "Pattern of Hate," sec. A01.

[39]Shenitz, "Laramie's Legacy," 76, 110.

[40]Quoted in Shenitz, "Laramie's Legacy," 77.

[41]Kenworthy, "In Wyoming," sec. A02.

[42]Steve Lopez, "To Be Young and Gay in Wyoming," *Time,* October 26, 1998, 38.

[43]Kenneth Burke, *The Rhetoric of Religion: Studies in Logology* (Boston: Beacon Press, 1961), 5.

[44]Kenneth Burke, *A Grammar of Motives* (New York: Prentice Hall, 1945), 406.

[45]Burke, *A Grammar of Motives,* 406.

[46]Burke, *A Grammar of Motives,* 406.

[47]Barry Brummett, "Burkean Comedy and Tragedy, Illustrated in Reactions to the Arrest of John Delorean," *Central States Speech Journal* 35 (1984): 218.

[48]Lopez, "To Be Young," 38.

[49]Brooke, "Gay Man Dies," sec. A17. See also "2 Suspects in Gay's Killing to Face Death," *Los Angeles Times,* December 29, 1998, home edition, 14; "Death Penalty Asked in Gay Man's Murder," *Washington Post,* December 29, 1998; sec. A6; "Wyo. Governor Backs Bill on Hate Crimes," *Washington Post,* January 19, 1999, sec. A9.

[50]Brooke, "Gay Man Beaten," sec. A09.

[51]Kenworthy, "In Wyoming," sec. A02.

[52]Lopez, "To Be Young," 39.

[53]James Brooke, "After Beating of Gay Man, Town Looks at Its Attitudes," *New York Times,* October 12, 1998, sec. A12.

[54]"Jury Selection Starts in Wyoming Hate-Crime Trial," *Washington Post,* March 25, 1999, sec. A15. "Laramie, Wyo.—This small city on the high plains of southeast Wyoming has looked upon itself as a peaceful, law-abiding community ever since 1868. . . . Those images became blurred last fall with the brutal beating death of Matthew Shepard, a gay university student: To the outside world, Laramie suddenly became the place where a vicious hate crime took place, where below the patina of tolerance lurked a deep streak of cowboy intolerance" (Tom Kenworthy, "After Slaying, Community Takes a Punishing Look at Itself," *Washington Post,* April 5, 1999, sec. A3). See also James Brooke, "Wyoming City Braces for Gay Murder Trial," *New York Times,* April 4, 1999, sec. 14.

[55]Lopez, "To Be Young," 38.

[56]In one of our classrooms, a year after the murder, a student connected to individuals held accountable for the dehumanizing event in the Colorado State University parade would confirm, under the promise of anonymity, the use of the anti-gay epithets "I'm Gay" and "Up My Ass."

[57]Loffreda, *Losing Matt Shepard,* 10.

[58]James Brooke, "Homophobia Often Found in Schools, Data Show," *New York Times,* October 14, 1998, sec. A19.

[59]Kenworthy, "Hundreds Gather," sec. A03.

[60]Gillis and Gaines, "Pattern of Hate," sec. A01.

[61]Carter, *Kenneth Burke,* 18.

[62]The Wyoming governor went on to say, "[We] feel a sense of tragedy and disbelief that a human life could be taken in such a way. We must now find closure" (Kenworthy, "Gay Wyoming Student Succumbs," sec. A07).

[63]Lopez, "To Be Young," 39.

[64]"Brutal Beating of Gay Student is Condemned," *Los Angeles Times,* October 11, 1998, 16. News reports repeatedly emphasized that Matt Shepard was deceived into going with his attackers—that Henderson and McKinney "posed as homosexuals and

lured Shepard from the bar" (Tom Kenworthy, "'I'm Going to Grant You Life,'" *Washington Post*, February 5, 1999, sec. A2). See also Julie Cart, "Gay's Slaying Spawns Morality Play," *Los Angeles Times*, March 24, 1999, home edition, 11; Julie Cart, "Plea Averts 1st Trial in Slaying of Gay Student," *Los Angeles Times*, April 6, 1999, home edition, 1; "Attack on Gay," 23A; Tom Kenworthy, "Gay Student's Attacker Pleads Guilty, Gets Two Life Terms," *Washington Post*, April 6, 1999, sec. A2; "Wyoming Judge Bars 'Gay Panic' Defense," *Washington Post*, November 2, 1999, sec. A7; Kenworthy, "2nd Man Is Convicted," sec. A1; James Brooke, "Gay Murder Trial Ends with Guilty Plea," *New York Times*, April 6, 1999, sec. A20.

[65]Chris Bull, "A Matter of Life and Death," *The Advocate*, March 16, 1999, 38.

[66]Cart, "Gay's Slaying Spawns," 11.

[67]Kenworthy, "'Gay Panic' Defense," sec. A2; Cart, "Man Guilty," 37.

[68]Phil Curtis, "Hate Crimes: More than a Verdict," *The Advocate*, January 18, 2000, 36. See also Cart, "Killer of Gay Student," 1; Michael Janofsky, "Parents of Gay Obtain Mercy for His Killer," *New York Times*, November 5, 1999, sec. A1.

[69]Brummett, "Burkean Comedy," 219.

[70]Tom Kenworthy, "Slain Gay Man's Mother Tries to Show Hate's 'Real' Cost," *Washington Post*, October 10, 1999, sec. A2.

[71]Curtis, "Hate Crimes," 34–35. The notion that McKinney's conviction signaled the end for more than just the trial was evident in other news reports as well. "For the citizens of Wyoming, who often felt that their state's Western philosophies were on trial, the end of the yearlong ordeal was welcome" (Cart, "Killer of Gay Student," 1). "The verdict, which came after 10 hours of deliberations over two days, brought a swift end to a case that has been watched closely because of the brutality of the crime and the sexual orientation of the victim" (Michael Janofsky, "Man is Convicted of Killing of Gay Student," *New York Times*, November 4, 1999, sec. A14).

[72]Robert L. Heath, *Realism and Relativism: A Perspective on Kenneth Burke* (Macon, Ga.: Mercer University Press, 1986), 246.

[73]In Lopez, "To Be Young," 38.

[74]What is significant about this poll is not the distribution, which was likely a product of how the questions were asked, but that the poll was published in a news report at all. The inclusion of the poll contributes to the perception that this issue is significant. After McKinney's conviction, polls like this one disappeared from the public eye.

[75]Curtis, "Hate Crimes," 38. Since January 2000, four states have passed hate-crimes legislation, including Texas, which approved a hate-crimes bill in 2001. A similar bill, however, was suppressed two years earlier in Texas because it specifically included protection for gays. See Ross E. Milloy, "Texas Senate Passes Hate Crimes Bill that Bush's Allies Killed," *New York Times*, May 8, 2001, sec. A16. The five states, as of April 16, 2002, that still have no hate-crimes laws are Arkansas, Indiana, New Mexico, South Carolina, and Wyoming. Of the 45 states with hate-crimes laws, 18 states have laws that do not explicitly include sexual orientation. See "Does Your State's Hate Crimes Law Include Sexual Orientation and Gender Identity?" *Human Rights Campaign*, retrieved April 16, 2002, from <http://www.hrc.org/ issues/hate_crimes/background/statelaws.asp>.

[76]Curtis, "Hate Crimes," 38.

[77]Gitlin, "The Whole World," 96.

[78]We are suggesting that there are multiple layers of framing. A picture frame, for instance, shapes how viewers perceive a picture, but so too does the picture's presence in a larger structure such as the frame of a building. Indeed, individuals respond very differently to pictures hanging in a private home than to those hanging in a museum.

[79]See George Chauncey, *Gay New York: Gender, Urban Culture, and the Making of the Gay Male World, 1890–1940* (New York: Basic Books, 1994), 13.

[80]Erving Goffman, *Stigma: Notes on the Management of Spoiled Identity* (Englewood Cliffs, N.J.: Prentice-Hall, 1963), 1.

[81]Byrne Fone, *Homophobia: A History* (New York: Picador USA, 2000), 5.

[82]Gerhard Falk, *Stigma: How We Treat Outsiders* (New York: Prometheus Books, 2001), 74.

[83]See Falk, *Stigma,* 73–74.

[84]Quoted in Shenitz, "Laramie's Legacy," 110.

[85]See Shenitz, "Laramie's Legacy," 111.

[86]Tracey A. Reeves, "A Town Searches its Soul: After Gay Black Man is Slain, W.VA. Residents Ask Why," *Washington Post,* July 20, 2000, sec. A01.

[87]Fone, *Homophobia,* 413.

[88]Curtis, "Hate Crimes," 35.

[89]One of many cases where the "gay panic defense" was allowed is that of Michael Auker, who was stomped and beaten by Todd Clinger, 18, and Troy Clinger, 20, in Pennsylvania. "After rendering Auker unconscious, the two allegedly transported him to his home where he was found comatose two days later" (Barbara Dozetos, "Brothers Claim 'Gay Panic' after Beating that Left Man in Coma," *The Gay.com Network,* retrieved December 13, 2001, from <http://content.gay.com/channels/news/heads/ 010328_penn_gaypanic.html>). We found this example especially intriguing because of how closely the crime mirrored the Matthew Shepard beating.

[90]Fone, *Homophobia,* 5.

[91]Warren J. Blumenfeld, introduction to *Homophobia: How We All Pay the Price,* ed. Warren J. Blumenfeld (Boston: Beacon Press, 1992), 15.

[92]Burke, *Attitudes,* introduction.

[93]Burke, *Attitudes,* 3.

[94]"'Rejection' is a by-product of 'acceptance' . . . It is the heretical aspect of an orthodoxy—and as such, it has much in common with the 'frame of acceptance' that it rejects" (Burke, *Attitudes,* 21). Burke also posits, "Could we not say that *all* symbolic structures are designed to produce such 'acceptance' in one form or another?" (emphasis added, *Attitudes,* 19–20).

[95]Burke, *Attitudes,* 28–29.

[96]Burke, *Attitudes,* 92; see also William H. Rueckert, *Encounters with Kenneth Burke* (Urbana: University of Illinois Press, 1994), 118.

[97]Burke, *Attitudes,* 166.

[98]Stanley Edgar Hyman, "Kenneth Burke and the Criticism of Symbolic Action," in *Landmark Essays on Kenneth Burke,* ed. Barry Brummett (Davis, Calif.: Hermagoras Press, 1993), 29; Timothy N. Thompson and Anthony J. Palmeri, "Attitudes toward Counternature (with Notes on Nurturing a Poetic Psychosis)," in *Extensions of the Burkean System,* ed. James W. Chesebro (Tuscaloosa: University of Alabama Press, 1993), 276.

[99]Rueckert, *Encounters,* 121.

[100]Burke, *Attitudes,* 171.

[101]Brummett, "Burkean Comedy," 219.

[102]Burke, *Attitudes,* 41.

[103]Burke, *Attitudes,* 171.

[104]Rueckert, *Encounters,* 117–18.

[105]For extended discussion, see Bennett, *News;* Herbert J. Gans, *Deciding What's News: A Study of CBS Evening News, NBC Nightly News, Newsweek and Time* (New York: Pantheon, 1979).

[106]David Croteau and William Hoynes, *Media/Society: Industries, Images, and Audiences,* 2d ed. (Thousand Oaks, Calif.: Pine Forge Press, 2000), 241.

[107]Gans, *Deciding What's News,* 138–42.

[108]See Croteau and Hoynes, *Media/Society,* 239–41.

[109]Mark Lawrence McPhail, "Coherence as Representative Anecdote in the Rhetorics of Kenneth Burke and Ernesto Grassi," in *Kenneth Burke and Contemporary European Thought: Rhetoric in Transition,* ed. Bernard L. Brock (Tuscaloosa: University of Alabama Press), 85.

Chapter V

Narrative Criticism

Walter R. Fisher's 1984 essay "Narration as Human Communication Paradigm: The Case of Public Moral Argument" introduces narrative criticism, an approach related to the broad tradition of dramatism. Narration has been well understood as a rhetorical technique since ancient times, as neo-classical criticism recognizes.[1] Fisher, however, goes beyond the suggestion that narrative is a discrete persuasive technique. He claims stories are fundamental to communication because they provide structure for our experience as humans and because they influence people to live in communities that share common explanations and understandings. The narrative impulse is part of our being, and narratives are meaningful for everyone, across culture, time, and place. Fisher suggests narratives are moral constructs that are inherently egalitarian because everyone has the ability "to be rational in the narrative paradigm." Finally, he proposes a critical framework for assessing narratives based on the concepts of "probability" and "fidelity."

As Fisher explained in a later (1989) essay, however, his construct concerns more than the "depiction, anecdote, and characterization" of specific stories. Indeed, he maintained that "the narrative paradigm is a philosophical statement that is meant to offer an approach to interpretation and assessment of human communication—assuming that all forms of human communication can be seen fundamentally as stories, as interpretations of aspects of the world occurring in time and shaped by history, culture, and character."[2]

William F. Lewis's 1987 essay, "Telling America's Story: Narrative Form and the Reagan Presidency," applies Fisher's concepts. Lewis argues that narratives are central to understanding the workings of Ronald Reagan's presidential discourse. In fact, Lewis claims, the narrative nature of Reagan's discourse helps account for his success: "his story gave a clear, powerful, reassuring, and self-justifying meaning to America's public life." However, Lewis criticizes Reagan's reliance on a dominant narrative and suggests some potential problems that can be created by such a practice. Further, Lewis questions whether the narrative paradigm is necessarily morally superior to the rational world paradigm.

Herbert W. Simons's 2007 essay "From Post-9/11 Melodrama to Quagmire in Iraq: A Rhetorical History" analyzes former President George W. Bush's rhetoric from a narrative perspective. According to Simons, in the period immediately after the September 11, 2001, attacks on the World Trade Center and the Pentagon, President Bush told a powerful, melodramatic story, featuring an "us versus them" attitude and "two-dimensional characters" that justified the president's response to terrorism and eventually led to the Iraq war. In this story, Simons claims, "Victims, villains, and heroes are joined together in a sanitized narrative, shorn of moral complexity" that fit the president's image as a sheriff in a Hollywood western. According to the author, the use of rhetorical melodrama was effective in the short term and helps explain why Congress and the press went along with Bush's policies. However, Simons concludes, the "threads" of Bush's story "wore thin" because the narrative pattern no longer fit "real-world constraints."

NOTES

[1]See Carroll C. Arnold, "George William Curtis," in *A History and Criticism of American Public Address,* vol. 3, ed. Marie Hochmuth (New York: Longmans, Green, 1955), 158.

[2]Walter R. Fisher, "Clarifying the Narrative Paradigm," *Communication Monographs* 56 (1989): 55, 57

NARRATION AS A HUMAN COMMUNICATION PARADIGM: THE CASE OF PUBLIC MORAL ARGUMENT

WALTER R. FISHER

The corrective of the scientific rationalization would seem necessarily to be a rationale of art—not, however, a performer's art, not a specialist's art for some to produce and many to observe, but an art in its widest aspects, an art of living.

Kenneth Burke

When I wrote "Toward a Logic of Good Reasons" (Fisher, 1978), I was unaware that I was moving toward an alternative paradigm for human communication. Indications of it are to be found in the assumption that *"Humans as rhetorical beings are as much valuing as they are reasoning animals"* (p. 376) and in the conception of good reasons as *"those elements that provide warrants for accepting or adhering to the advice fostered by any form of communication that can be considered rhetorical"* (p. 378). While the assumption does not seriously disturb the view of rhetoric as practical reasoning, the conception implies a stance that goes beyond this theory. The logic of good reasons maintains that reasoning need not be bound to argumentative prose or be expressed in clear-cut inferential or implicative structures: Reasoning may be discovered in all sorts of symbolic action—nondiscursive as well as discursive.

That this is the case was demonstrated in an exploration of argument in *Death of a Salesman* and *The Great Gatsby* (Fisher & Filloy, 1982). The authors concluded that these works provide good reasons to distrust the materialist myth of the American Dream (Fisher, 1973, p. 161), for what it requires to live by it and for what it does not necessarily deliver even if one lives by it "successfully." This finding confirms Gerald Graff's thesis that a theory or practice of literature that denies reference to the world, that denies that literature has cognitive as well as aesthetic significance, is a *Literature Against Itself* (Graff, 1979). In other words, "some dramatic and literary works do, in fact, argue" (Fisher & Filloy, 1982, p. 343).

The paradigm I was moving toward did not become entirely clear until I examined the current nuclear controversy, where the traditional view of rationality did not serve well, and I read Alasdair MacIntyre's *After Virtue: A Study in Moral Theory* (1981). What impressed me most about the book was the observation that "man is in his actions and practice, as well as in his fictions, essentially a story-telling animal" (p. 201). Given this view, "enacted dramatic narrative" (p. 200) is the "basic and essential genre for the characterization of human actions" (p. 194). These ideas are the foundation of the paradigm I am proposing—the narrative paradigm. Thus, when I use the term "narration," I do not mean a fictive composition whose propositions may be true or false and have no necessary relationship to the message of that composition. By "narration," I refer to a theory of symbolic actions—words and/or deeds—that have sequence and meaning for those who live, create, or interpret them. The narrative perspective, therefore, has relevance to real as well as fictive worlds, to stories of living and to stories of the imagination.

The narrative paradigm, then, can be considered a dialectical synthesis of two traditional strands in the history of rhetoric: the argumentative, persuasive theme and the literary, aesthetic theme. As will be seen, the narrative paradigm insists that human communication should be viewed as historical as well as situational, as stories competing with other stories constituted by good reasons, as being rational when they satisfy the demands of narrative probability and narrative fidelity, and as inevitably moral inducements. The narrative paradigm challenges the notions that human communication—if it is to be considered rhetorical—must be an argumentative form, that reason is to be attributed only to discourse marked by clearly identifiable modes of inference and/or implication, and that the norms for evaluation of rhetorical communication must be rational standards taken essentially from informal or formal logic. The narrative paradigm does not deny reason and rationality; it reconstitutes them, making them amenable to all forms of human communication.

Before going further, I should clarify the sense in which I use the term "paradigm." By paradigm, I refer to a representation designed to formalize the structure of a component of experience and to direct understanding and inquiry into the nature and functions of that experience—in this instance, the experience of human communication. Masterman designates this form of paradigm "metaphysical" or as a "metaparadigm" (1970, p. 65; see also Kuhn, 1974). Since the narrative paradigm does not entail a particular method of investigation, I have not used a designation that might be suggested: "narratism." The narrative perspective, however, does have a critical connection with "dramatism," which will be discussed later.

Consistent with Wayne Brockriede's concept of perspectivism (1982), I shall not maintain that the narrative paradigm is the only legitimate, useful way to appreciate human communication or that it will necessarily supplant the traditional rational paradigm of human decision-making and action. As already indicated, I will propose the narrative paradigm as an alternative view. I do not even claim that it is entirely "new." W. Lance Bennett has published a book with Martha S. Feldman, *Reconstructing Reality in the Courtroom* (1981), and two essays that directly bear on the present enterprise, one concerning political communication (Bennett, 1975) and one on legal communication (Bennett, 1978; see also, Farrell, 1983; Gallie, 1964; Hawes, 1978; Mink, 1978; Schrag, 1984; Scott, 1978; Simons, 1978). Except for these studies, I know of no other attempt to suggest narration as a paradigm. There is, of course, a tradition in rhetorical theory and pedagogy that focuses on narration as an element in discourse and as a genre in and of itself (e.g., Ochs & Burritt, 1973). In addition, there is an increasing number of investigations involving storytelling (e.g., Kirkwood, 1983). Here again, narration is conceived as a mode, not a paradigm, of communication.

The context for what is to follow would not be complete without recognition of the work done by theologians and those interested in religious discourse. The most recent works in this tradition include Goldberg (1982) and Hauerwas (1981). It is worth pausing with these studies as they foreshadow several of the themes to be developed later. Goldberg claims that:

> a theologian, regardless of the propositional statements he or she may have to make about a community's convictions, must consciously strive to keep those statements in intimate contact with the narratives which give rise to those convictions, within which they gain their sense and meaning, and *from which they have been abstracted.* (p. 35)

The same can be said for those who would understand ordinary experience. The ground for determining meaning, validity, reason, rationality, and truth must be a narrative context: history, culture, biography, and character. Goldberg also argues:

> Neither "the facts" nor our "experience" come to us in discrete and discon- nected packets which simply await the appropriate moral principle to be applied. Rather, they stand in need of some narrative which can bind the facts of our experience together into a coherent pattern and it is thus in virtue of that narrative that our abstracted rules, principles, and notions gain their full intelligibility. (p. 242)

Again, the statement is relevant to more than the moral life; it is germane to social and political life as well. He observes, as I would, that "what counts as meeting the various conditions of justification will vary from story to story. . . ." (p. 246). I will suggest a foundation for such justifications in the discussion of narrative rationality. With some modifications, I would endorse two of Hauerwas' (1981) 10 theses. First, he claims that "The social significance of the Gospel requires recognition of the narrative structure of Christian convictions for the life of the church" (p. 9). I would say: The meaning and significance of life in all of its social dimensions require the recognition of its narrative structure. Second, Hauerwas asserts that "Every social ethic involves a narrative, whether it is conceived with the formulation of basic principles of social organization and/or concrete alternatives" (p. 9; see also Alter, 1981; Scult, 1983). The only change that I would make here is to delete the word "social." Any ethic, whether social, political, legal or otherwise, involves narrative.

Finally, mention should be made of the work on narration by such scholars as Derrida (1980), Kermode (1980), and Ricoeur (1980). Especially relevant to this project are essays by White (1980; see also, White, 1978), Turner (1980), and Danto (1982; see also Nelson, 1980; Todorov, 1977).

PURPOSE

If I can establish that narration deserves to be accepted as a paradigm, it will vie with the reigning paradigm, which I will refer to as the rational world paradigm. In truth, however, the narrative paradigm, like other paradigms in the human sciences, does not so much deny what has gone before as it subsumes it.

The rational world paradigm will be seen as one way to tell the story of how persons reason together in certain settings. For now, it is enough that the narrative paradigm be contemplated as worthy of co-existing with the rational world paradigm.

I shall begin by characterizing and contrasting the two paradigms. I shall then examine the controversy over nuclear warfare, a public moral argument, noting particular problems with the rational world paradigm and indicating how the narrative paradigm provides a way of possibly resolving them. Following this discussion, I shall reconsider the narrative paradigm and conclude with several implications for further inquiry. Needless to say, this essay does not constitute a finished statement. It offers a conceptual frame which, I am fully aware, requires much greater development for it to be considered compelling. At this point, as I have suggested, it is sufficient that it receive serious attention. From such attention, a fuller, more persuasive statement should emerge.

THE RATIONAL WORLD PARADIGM

This paradigm is very familiar, having been in existence since Aristotle's *Organon* became foundational to Western thought. Regardless of its historic forms, the rational world paradigm presupposes that: (1) humans are essentially rational beings; (2) the paradigmatic mode of human decision-making and communication is argument—clear-cut inferential (implicative) structures; (3) the conduct of argument is ruled by the dictates of situations—legal, scientific, legislative, public, and so on; (4) rationality is determined by subject matter knowledge, argumentative ability, and skill in employing the rules of advocacy in given fields; and (5) the world is a set of logical puzzles which can be resolved through appropriate analysis and application of reason conceived as an argumentative construct. In short, argument as product and process is *the* means of being human, the agency of all that humans can know and realize in achieving their *telos*. The philosophical ground of the rational world paradigm is epistemology. Its linguistic materials are self-evident propositions, demonstrations, and proofs, the verbal expressions of certain and probable knowing.

The actualization of the rational world paradigm, it should be noted, depends on a form of society that permits, if not requires, participation of qualified persons in public decision-making. It further demands a citizenry that shares a common language, general adherence to the values of the state, information relevant to the questions that confront the community to be arbitrated by argument, and an understanding of argumentative issues and the various forms of reasoning and their appropriate assessment. In other words, there must exist something that can be called public or social knowledge and there must be a "public" for argument to be the kind of force envisioned for it (Bitzer, 1978; Farrell, 1976). Because the rational world paradigm has these requirements and because *being rational* (being competent in argument) *must be learned,* an historic mission of education in the West has been to generate a consciousness of national community and to instruct citizens in at least the rudiments of logic and rhetoric (Hollis, 1977, pp. 165–166; Toulmin, 1970, p. 4).

Needless to say, the rational world paradigm, which is by and large a heritage of the classical period, has not been untouched by "modernism." The impact of modernism has been recounted and reacted to by many writers (Barrett, 1979; Booth, 1974; Gadamer, 1981, 1982; Lonergan, 1958; MacIntyre, 1981; Rorty, 1979; Schrag, 1980; Sennett, 1978; Toulmin, 1972, 1982; Voegelin, 1952, 1975). The line of thought that has done most to subvert the rational world paradigm is, along with existentialism, naturalism. One of its schools starts with physics and mathematics and makes the logical structure of scientific knowledge fundamental;

the other school, involving biology, psychology, and the social sciences, adapts this structure and conception of knowledge to the human sciences. According to John Herman Randall, Jr.:

> The major practical issue still left between the two types of naturalism concerns the treatment of values. The philosophies starting from physics tend to exclude questions of value from the field of science and the scope of scientific method. They either leave them to traditional non-scientific treatment, handing them over, with Russell, to the poet and mystic; or else with the logical empiricists they dismiss the whole matter as "meaningless," maintaining with Ayer that any judgment of value is an expression of mere personal feeling. The philosophies of human experience—all the heirs of Hegel, from dialectical materialism to Dewey—subject them to the same scientific methods of criticism and testing as other beliefs; and thus offer the hope of using all we have learned of scientific procedure to erect at last a science of values comparable to the science that was the glory of Greek thought. (1976, p. 651)

It is clear: With the first type of naturalism, there can be neither public or social knowledge nor rational public or social argument, for both are permeated by values. As Habermas notes, "the relationship of theory to practice can now only assert itself as the purposive rational application of techniques assured by empirical science" (Habermas, 1967, p. 254; Heidegger, 1972, pp. 58–59).

With the second type of naturalism, one can hope with Randall that it produces the work he sees possible in it. But the fact is that no science of values has appeared or seems likely to do so; further, Dewey (1927) himself noted the eclipse of the "public" and doubted its reemergence. His hope was the development of "communities." Interestingly, 55 years later, MacIntyre concludes *After Virtue* with the observation: "What matters at this state is the construction of local forms of community within which civility and the intellectual and moral life can be sustained" (1981, p. 245).

The effects of naturalism have been to restrict the rational world paradigm to specialized studies and to relegate everyday argument to an irrational exercise. The reaction to this state of affairs has been an historic effort to recover the rational world paradigm for human decision-making and communication by: (1) reconstituting the conception of knowledge (e.g. Bitzer, 1978; Farrell, 1976; Habermas, 1973; Lyne, 1982; McGee & Martin, 1983; Polanyi, 1958; Ziman, 1968); (2) reconceptualizing the public—in terms of rational enterprises, fields, and/or communities (e.g., McKerrow, 1980a, b; Toulmin, 1958, 1972; Toulmin, Rieke & Janik, 1979; Willard, 1982; see also the first 19 essays in Ziegelmueller & Rhodes, 1981); (3) formulating a logic appropriate for practical reasoning (e.g., Fisher, 1978; Perelman & Olbrechts-Tyteca, 1969; Toulmin, 1958; Wenzel, 1977); and (4) reconceiving the conceptions of validity, reason, and rationality (e.g., Apel, 1979; Ehninger, 1968; Farrell, 1977; Fisher, 1980; Gottlieb, 1968; Johnstone, 1978; McKerrow, 1977, 1982). Many of the studies cited here intimate, if not specifically state, proposals for reconstructing the concept of argument itself. Writers explicitly working on this task include Brockriede (1975, 1977), Burleson (1981), Jacobs and Jackson (1981), McKerrow (1981), O'Keefe (1977, 1982), Wenzel (1980), and Willard (1978).

The motive underlying these various studies, and the movement of which they are an energizing force, is, as I have suggested, to repair the rational world paradigm so that it once again will serve everyday argument. One may well applaud the motive and the movement and yet ask two questions: (1) Has the reformation been successful? (2) Is there a more beneficial way to conceive and to articulate the structures of everyday argument? It is too early to answer the first question with finality but one cannot deny that much useful work has been done, especially in establishing at least the semblance of rationality for fields of argument. I shall maintain, however, that similar progress has not been made in the arena where argument is most general and is most obviously concerned with values, public moral argument, as the examination of the nuclear controversy will show later.

This failure suggests to me that the problem in restoring rationality to everyday argument may be the assumption that the reaffirmation of the rational world paradigm is the only solution. The position I am taking is that another paradigm, the narrative paradigm, may offer a better solution, one that will provide substance not only for public moral argument, but also all other forms of argument, for human communication in general. My answer to the second question, then, is: "Yes, I think so." Adoption of the narrative paradigm, I hasten to repeat, does not mean rejection of all the good work that has been done; it means a rethinking of it and investigating new moves that can be made to enrich our understanding of communicative interaction. Representative of the good work that has already been done on public argument are essays by Cox (1981), Goodnight (1980), Hynes, Jr. (1980), Lucaites (1981), Pryor (1981), Sillars and Ganer (1982), and Zarefsky (1981).

THE NARRATIVE PARADIGM

Many different root metaphors have been put forth to represent the essential nature of human beings: *homo faber, homo economous, homo politicus, homo sociologicus,* "psychological man," "ecclesiastical man," *homo sapiens,* and, of course, "rational man." I now propose *homo narrans* to be added to the list.

Preliminary to an attempt to delineate the presuppositions that structure the narrative paradigm, I should indicate how the *homo narrans* metaphor relates to those that have preceded it. First, each of the root metaphors may be held to be the master metaphor, thereby standing as the ground, while the others are manifest as figures. In the terminology of the narrative perspective, the master metaphor sets the plot of human experience and the others the subplots. When any of the other metaphors are asserted as the master metaphor, narration is as it is considered now: a type of human interaction—an activity, an art, a genre, or mode of expression.

Second, when narration is taken as the master metaphor, it subsumes the others. The other metaphors are then considered conceptions that inform various ways of *recounting* or *accounting for* human choice and action. Recounting takes the forms of history, biography, or autobiography. Accounting for takes the forms of theoretical explanation or argument. Recounting and accounting for can be also expressed in poetic forms: drama, poetry, novel, and so on. Recounting and accounting for are, in addition, the bases for all advisory discourse. Regardless of the form they may assume, recounting and accounting for are stories we tell ourselves and each other to establish a meaningful life-world. The character of narrator(s), the conflicts, the resolutions, and the style will vary, but each mode of recounting and accounting for is but a way of relating a "truth" about the human condition.

Third, the *homo narrans* metaphor is an incorporation and extension of Burke's definition of "man" as the "symbol-using (symbol-making, symbol-misusing) animal" (Burke, 1968, p. 16; Cassirer, 1944, p. 26; see also Langer, 1953, pp. 264ff.). The idea of human beings as storytellers indicates the generic form of all symbol composition; it holds that symbols are created and communicated ultimately as stories meant to give order to human experience and to induce others to dwell in them to establish ways of living in common, in communities in which there is sanction for the story that constitutes one's life. And one's life is, as suggested by Burke, a story that participates in the stories of those who have lived, who live now, and who will live in the future. He asks: "Where does drama get its materials?" I would modify the question to read: "Where do our narratives get their materials?" And, I would accept his answer:

> From the "unending conversation" that is going on in history when we are born. Imagine that you enter a parlor. You come late. When you arrive, others have long preceded you, and they are engaged in a heated discussion, a discussion too heated for them to pause and tell you exactly what it is about. In fact, the discussion had already begun long before any of them got there, so that no one present is qualified to trace for you all the steps that had gone before. You listen for awhile, until you decide that you have caught the tenor of the argument; then you put in your oar. Someone answers; you answer him; another comes to your defense; another aligns himself against you, to either the embarrassment or gratification of your opponent, depending upon the quality of your ally's assistance. However, the discussion is interminable. The hour grows late, you must depart. And you do depart, with the discussion still vigorously in process. (Burke, 1957, pp. 94–97; for a discussion of the nature of conversation as narration, see MacIntyre, 1981; Campbell & Stewart, 1981).

As Heidegger observes, "We are a conversation . . . conversation and its unity support our existence" (Heidegger, 1949, p. 278; Gadamer, 1982, pp. 330ff.; Rorty, 1979, pp. 31ff.).

To clarify further the narrative paradigm, I should specify how it is related to Bormann's (1972) concepts of "fantasy themes" and "rhetorical visions," and to the Frentz and Farrell (1976) language action paradigm. Fantasy, Bormann holds, is a technical term, meaning "the creative and imaginative interpretation of events that fulfills a psychological or rhetorical need" (1983, p. 434). Fantasy themes arise "in group interaction out of a recollection of something that happened to the group in the *past* or a dream of what a group might do in the *future*" (1972, p. 397). When woven together, they become composite dramas, which Bormann calls "rhetorical visions" (1972, p. 398). From the narrative view, each of these concepts translates into dramatic stories constituting the fabric of social reality for those who compose them. They are, thus, "rhetorical fictions," constructions of fact and faith having persuasive force, rather than fantasies (Fisher, 1980b). Nevertheless, without getting into the problem of how group-generated stories become public stories, I would note that Bormann (1973) and others have demonstrated that "rhetorical visions" do exist (e.g., Bantz, 1975; Kidd, 1975; Rarick, Duncan, Lee & Porter, 1977). I take this demonstration as partial evidence for the validity of the narrative paradigm. (For further empirical evidence, see Bennett, 1978; Campbell, 1984.)

With minor adaptation, I find no incompatibility between the narrative paradigm and the language action paradigm. Indeed, language action is meaningful only in terms of narrative form (Ricoeur, 1976). What Frentz and Farrell (1976) designate as "form of life" and "encounters"—implicit matters of knowledge, aesthetic expectations, institutional constraints, and propriety rules—can be considered the forces that determine the structure of narratives in given interpersonal environments. What they call an "episode," a "rule-conforming sequence of symbolic acts generated by two or more actors who are collectively oriented toward emergent goals," can be thought of as the process by which one or more authors generate a short story or chapter—deciding on plot, the nature of characters, resolutions, and their meaning and import for them and others (p. 336).

I do not want to leave the impression that the narrative paradigm merely accommodates the constructs of Bormann, Frentz and Farrell. Their work enriches the narrative paradigm. I shall rely specifically on the language action paradigm in what follows.

The presuppositions that structure the narrative paradigm are: (1) humans are essentially storytellers; (2) the paradigmatic mode of human decision-making and communication is "good reasons" which vary in form among communication situations, genres, and media; (3) the production and practice of good reasons is ruled by matters of history, biography, culture, and character along with the kinds of forces identified in the Frentz and Farrell language action paradigm; (4) rationality is determined by the nature of persons as narrative beings—their inherent awareness of *narrative probability*, what constitutes a coherent story, and their constant habit of testing *narrative fidelity*, whether the stories they experience ring true with the stories they know to be true in their lives (narrative probability and narrative fidelity, it will be noted, are analogous to the concepts of dramatic probability and verisimilitude; as MacIntyre (1981, p. 200) observes, "The difference between imaginary characters and real ones is not in the narrative form of what they do; it is in the degree of their authorship of that form and of their own deeds"); and (5) the world is a set of stories which must be chosen among to live the good life in a process of continual recreation. In short, good reasons are the stuff of stories, the means by which humans realize their nature as reasoning-valuing animals. The philosophical ground of the narrative paradigm is ontology. The materials of the narrative paradigm are symbols, signs of consubstantiation, and good reasons, the communicative expressions of social reality.

The actualization of the narrative paradigm does not require a given form of society. Where the rational world paradigm is an ever-present part of our consciousness because we have been educated into it, the narrative impulse is part of our very being because we acquire narrativity in the natural process of socialization (Goody & Watt, 1962–1963; Krashen, 1982). That narrative, whether written or oral, is a feature of human nature and that it crosses time and culture is attested by historian White: "Far from being one code among many that a culture may utilize for endowing experience with meaning, narrative is a metacode, a human universal on the basis of which trans-cultural messages about the shared reality can be transmitted . . . the absence of narrative capacity or a refusal of narrative indicates an absence or refusal of meaning itself" (1980, p. 6); by anthropologist Turner: "if we regard narrative ethically, as the supreme instrument for building 'values' and 'goals,' in Dilthey's sense of these terms, which motivate human conduct into situational structures of 'meaning,' then we must concede it to be a universal cultural activity embedded in the very center of the social drama, itself another cross-cultural and transtemporal unit in social process" (1980, p. 167); and by linguist-folklorist Dell Hymes: "the narrative use of language is not a property of subordinate cultures, whether folk, or working class, or the like, but a universal function" (1980, p. 132; see also Barthes, 1977; Ong, 1982).

Gregory Bateson goes so far as to claim that "If I am at all fundamentally right in what I am saying, then *thinking in terms of stories* must be shared by all mind or minds, whether ours or those of redwood forests and sea anemones" (1979, p. 14).

And Burke observes that "We assume a time when our primal ancestors became able to go from SENSATIONS to WORDS. (When they could duplicate the experience of tasting an orange by saying 'the taste of an orange,' that was WHEN STORY CAME INTO THE WORLD)" (1983, p. 1).

In theme, if not in every detail, narrative, then, is meaningful for persons in particular and in general, across communities as well as cultures, across time and place. Narratives enable us to understand the actions of others "because we all live out narratives in our lives and because we understand our own lives in terms of narratives" (MacIntyre, 1981, p. 197).

Rationality from this perspective involves, as I have proposed, the principles of narrative probability and narrative fidelity. These principles contrast with but do not contradict the constituents of rationality I have outlined earlier (Fisher, 1978, 1980). They are, in fact, subsumed by the narrative paradigm. The earlier notion was attuned to the rational world paradigm and essentially held that rationality was a matter of argumentative competence: knowledge of issues, modes of reasoning, appropriate tests, and rules of advocacy in given fields. As such, rationality was something to be learned, depended on deliberation, and required a high degree of self-consciousness. Narrative rationality does not make these demands. It is a capacity we all share. It depends on our minds being as Booth (1974, pp. 114–137) represents them in *Modern Dogma and the Rhetoric of Assent*, a key point of which is: "Not only do human beings successfully infer other beings' states of mind from symbolic clues; we know that they characteristically, in all societies, build each other's minds. This is obvious knowledge—all the more genuine for being obvious" (p. 114). The operative principle of narrative rationality is identification rather than deliberation (Burke, 1955, pp. 20–46).

Narrative rationality differs from traditional rationality in another significant way. Narrative rationality is not an account of the "laws of thought" and it is not normative in the sense that one must reason according to prescribed rules of calculation or inference making. Traditional rationality posits the way people think when they reason truly or with certainty. MacIntyre notes, "To call an argument fallacious is always at once to describe and to evaluate it" (1978, p. 258). It is, therefore, a normative construct. Narrative rationality is, on the other hand, descriptive, as it offers an account, an understanding, of any instance of human choice and action, including science (Gadamer, 1982; Heidegger, 1972; Holton, 1973; Ramsey, 1969). At the same time, it is a basis for critique, because it implies a praxis, an ideal democratic society (McGee, Scult & Kientz, 1983). Traditional rationality implies some sort of hierarchical system, a community in which some persons are qualified to judge and to lead and some other persons are to follow.

For the sake of clarity, I should note that, while the narrative paradigm provides a radical democratic ground for social-political critique, it does not deny the legitimacy (the inevitability) of hierarchy. History records no community, uncivilized or civilized, without key story-makers/story-tellers, whether sanctioned by God, a "gift," heritage, power, intelligence, or election. It insists, however, that the "people" do judge the stories that are told for and about them and that they have a rational capacity to make such judgments. It holds, along with Aristotle (1954, bk. 1, ch. 1, 1355a20) that the "people" have a natural tendency to prefer the true and the just. Neither does the narrative paradigm deny that the "people" can be wrong. But, then so can elites, especially when a decision is social or political. And neither does the theory deny the existence and desirability of genius in individuals or the "people" to formulate and to adopt new stories that better account for their lives or the mystery of life itself. The sort of hierarchy condemned by the narrative praxis is the sort that is marked by the will to power, the kind of system in which elites struggle to dominate and to use the people for their own ends or that makes the people blind subjects of technology.

Narrative rationality, then, is inimical to elitist politics, whether fascist, communist, or even democratic—if traditional rationality is the prevailing societal view. And this seems to be the case with American democracy, as subsequent examination of the nuclear controversy will show. The prevalent position is that voters are rational if they know enough about public issues, are cognizant of argumentative procedures, forms, and functions, and weigh carefully all the arguments they hear and read in a systematic, deliberative process. Contrary to this notion is that of V. O. Key, Jr. In a classic study of presidential voting between 1936 and 1960, he concluded that "voters are not fools," which is what they must be considered if measured by traditional rationality. His data led him to conclude that the American electorate is not "straitjacketed by social determinants or moved by subconscious urges triggered by devilishly skillful propagandists." They are moved by their perceptions and appraisals of "central and relevant questions of public policy, of governmental performance, and of executive personality" (1966, pp. 7–8). These perceptions and appraisals of political discourse and action become stories, narratives that must stand the tests of probability and fidelity. And these stories are no less valuable than the stories constructed by persons who are rational in the traditional way. There is no evidence to support the claim that "experts" know better than anyone else who should be elected president.

Obviously, as I will note later, some stories are better than others, more coherent, more "true" to the way people and the world are—in fact and in value. In other words, some stor[i]es are better in satisfying the criteria of the logic of good reasons, which is attentive to reason and values. Persons may even choose not to participate in the making of public narratives (vote) if they feel that they are meaningless spectators rather than co-authors. But, all persons have the capacity to be rational in the narrative paradigm. And, by and large, persons are that—at least in the fashioning of their daily lives. Persons do not have the capacity to be equally rational in the rational world paradigm. Because persons have the capacity of narrative rationality, it is reasonable to have juries of lay persons and popular elections, as Bennett (1978; Bennett & Feldman, 1981) has well demonstrated. I want to stress, however, that narrative rationality does not negate traditional rationality. It holds that traditional rationality is only relevant in specialized fields and even in those arenas narrative rationality is meaningful and useful.

Certain other features of the narrative paradigm should be noted before moving to the case of public moral argument. First, the paradigm is a ground for resolving the dualisms of modernism: fact-value, intellect-imagination, reason-emotion, and so on. Stories are the enactment of the whole mind in concert with itself. Second, narratives are moral constructs. As White asserts: "Where, in any account of reality, narrativity is present, we can be sure that morality or a moral impulse is present too" (1980 p. 26; Benjamin, 1969). Third, the narrative paradigm is consonant with the notion of reason proposed by Schrag: "Reason, as the performance of vision and insight commemoration and foresight, occasions the recognition of a process of meaning formation that gathers within it the logic of technical reason and the *logos* of myth" (1980, p. 126). The appropriateness and validity of this view of reason for the narrative paradigm is supported by Angel Medina (1979). In a statement that reiterates several of the points I have made, he writes:

> it is necessary to define our reason primarily as biographical, that is, above all narrative and then symbolic. Human reason is narrative because it extends from its inception and in every one of its acts toward the foreshadowing of its total course. It is symbolic in that the major aim in the formation of this totality is its own self-presentation within the dialogue of consciousness. The meaning of my whole life is communicative; it emerges, as such, for the benefit of another consciousness when I attempt to present myself totally to it. Reciprocally, the meaning of another life becomes a totality only when received fully within my life (p. 30).

And, fourth, as I will attempt to show, the narrative paradigm offers ways of resolving the problems of public moral argument.

THE CASE: PUBLIC MORAL ARGUMENT

It should be apparent by now that I think that MacIntyre's (1981) *After Virtue* is a remarkable work. Equally remarkable, in its own way, is Jonathan Schell's (1982) *The Fate of the Earth*. Schell's book is exemplary of contemporary moral argument intended to persuade a general audience, the "public." His concluding argument is:

> Either we will sink into the final coma and end it all or, as I trust and believe, we will awaken to the truth of our peril, a truth as great as life itself, and, like a person who has swallowed a lethal poison but shakes off his stupor at the last moment and vomits the poison up, we will break through the layers of denials, put aside our faint-hearted excuses, and rise up to cleanse the earth of nuclear weapons. (p. 231)

The validity of Schell's argument is not the question here. Our concern is its reception, which reveals the limits, perhaps the impossibility, of persuasive moral argument in our time, given the rational world paradigm.

Critical response to *The Fate of the Earth* is of two sorts. The first is celebratory. Reviewers in this group are obviously in sympathy with the book's moral thrust, its depiction of the results of nuclear war and its call for action—for life instead of death—but not with every detail of its argument. Although reviewers in this group include distinguished figures from a variety of professions: journalists Walter Cronkite, James Reston, and James Kilpatrick; historians Harrison Salisbury, John Hersey, and Henry Steele Commager; and politicians Barry Commoner, W. Averell Harriman, and Walter Mondale; none is a current member of the federal administration or the defense establishment. Each of them bears witness to an attitude—opposition to nuclear annihilation—but none testifies to the technical merits of Schell's representation of "deterrence theory," his inferences about its meaning in regard to strategy and tactics, or his conclusions about national sovereignty. They, like Schell, are not "experts" in the field in which the argument is made. They, like Schell, are active in the realm of rhetorical knowledge, in the sphere of social-political policy and behavior (Bitzer, 1978; Farrell, 1976).

Reviewers in the second group, on the other hand, are purveyors of ideological, bureaucratic, or technical arguments. Such arguments may overlap, be used by the same arguer, but each is distinguished by a particular privileged position: political "truth," administrative sanction, or subject matter expertise. The thrust of the ideological argument is that one violates ultimate "facts," is fundamentally wrongheaded; the bureaucratic argument stresses feasibility in regard to administrative approval; and the technical argument alleges ignorance of the "facts," that opponents are "unrealistic," meaning they do not have a firm grasp on reality. These are, of course, the lines of refutation or subversion. Their opposites would be constructive arguments of affirmation or reaffirmation.

The subversive pattern of ideological, bureaucratic, and technical arguments is evident in the following attacks on Schell's reasoning. McCracken (1982) labels Schell an "alarmist" and concludes: "The danger is that Mr. Schell's followers may triumph and bring about a freeze that by making present inequities permanent will prove destabilizing in the short run and in the long run productive of both redness and deadness" (p. 905). Focusing on the linch-pin arguments of *The Fate of the Earth* (Schell's interpretation of deterrence theory and his suggested solution of abolishing national sovereignty), Hausknecht (1982) first cites Alexander Haig and then observes that "It is not hard to imagine Ronald Reagan saying, 'Okay, so it may be the end of the species, but we can't let the bastards get away with it.'" In regard to Schell's solution, he concludes that "Successful political action demands significant but realizable goals" (p. 284). The same charge is leveled by Pierre (1982), who approves the moral force of Schell's position but then charges "Schell provides no realistic alternative to our nuclear policy based on the concept of deterrence. His argument—that knowledge that nuclear weapons can extinguish mankind must be the new deterrent in a disarmed world—is very weak" (p. 1188).

The strategy of these reviews is clear: reaffirmation of the moral concern, subversion of the reasoning. The tactics are also obvious: juxtapose Schell's reasoning with what is right-headed, what is approved by the administration, or what is "realistic." Insofar as there is merit in these "arguments," it lies not in the way they foreclose dialogue but in their narrative probability and narrative fidelity. Yet, this is not their intended appeal or effect. The effects are to discredit Schell as an arguer and to dismiss his argument as unfounded. Public moral argument is thus overwhelmed by privileged argument. Put another way, it is submerged by ideological and bureaucratic arguments that insist on rival moralities and technical argument which denudes it of morality altogether, making the dispute one for "experts" alone to consider (see Farrell & Goodnight, 1981).

The question that arises at this point is: What happens when "experts" argue about moral issues in public? Before considering this question, however, it is essential to sketch the general characteristics of "public moral argument."

Public moral argument is to be distinguished from reasoned discourse in interpersonal interactions and arguments occurring in specialized communities, such as theological disputes, academic debates, and arguments before the Supreme Court. The features differentiating *public* moral argument from such encounters are: (1) It is publicized, made available for consumption and persuasion of the polity at large; and (2) it is aimed at what Aristotle called "untrained thinkers," or, to be effective, it should be (1954, bk. 1, ch. 2, 1357a10). Most important *public* moral argument is a form of controversy that inherently crosses fields. It is not contained in the way that legal, scientific, or theological arguments are by subject matter, particular conceptions of argumentative competence, and well recognized rules of advocacy. Because this is so and because its realm is public-social knowledge, *public* moral argument naturally invites participation by field experts and is dominated by the rational superiority of their arguments. *Public* moral argument, which is oriented toward what ought to be, is undermined by the "truth" that prevails at the moment. The presence of "experts" in *public* moral arguments makes it difficult, if not impossible, for the public of "untrained thinkers" to win an argument or even judge them well—given, again, the rational world paradigm.

Public *moral* argument is moral in the sense that it is founded on ultimate questions—of life and death, of how persons should be defined and treated, of preferred patterns of living. Gusfield (1976) designates such questions as "status issues." Their resolution, he writes, indicates "the group, culture, or style of life to which the government and society are publicly committed" (p. 173). In addition to nuclear warfare, desegregation would be included in the category as well as abortion and school prayer.

Public moral *argument* refers to clearcut inferential structures, in the rational world paradigm, and to "good reasons," in the narrative paradigm. Public moral *argument* may also refer to public controversies—disputes and debates—about moral issues. The nuclear warfare controversy is an obvious case in point, but so are the others mentioned above. One could add disputes over pornography, ERA, and crime and punishment. This characterization of public moral *argument* is attentive to argument as product and as process (Wenzel, 1980).

The problem posed by the presence of experts in public moral argument is illustrated by the dispute between Hans Bethe and Edward Teller over the 1982 nuclear freeze proposition in California. Their positions were published in the *Los Angeles Times* (1982, October 17, Part IV, pp. 1–2), so they were public. They obviously concerned a moral issue and they were reasoned statements. Both persons are credible. Which one is to be believed and followed? Who in the general public could contend with them? Teller answers the second question in unequivocal terms: "The American public is ignorant, even of the general ideas on which they [nuclear weapons] are based" (p. 2). Here is revealed the fate of non-experts who would argue about nuclear warfare. Only experts can argue with experts and their arguments—while public—cannot be rationally questioned. As Perelman (1979) notes, rationality in and of itself forecloses discussion and debate. In the audience of experts, the public is left with no compelling reason, from the perspective of the rational world paradigm, to believe one over the other. One is not a judge but a spectator who must choose between actors. From the narrative paradigm view, the experts are storytellers and the audience is not a group of observers but are active participants in the meaning-formation of the stories.

It may be asked at this point: How is it that freeze referendums were approved in eight out of nine states and in 28 cities and counties in 1982? One answer is "fear," the "most intelligent feeling of our time" (Wieseltier, 1983, p. 7). Another answer is "distrust," distrust of those responsible for the development, deployment, and use of nuclear weapons. This answer is, I believe, more accurate. It does not deny the existence of fear. It insists on the "rationality" of those who voted for and against the referendum. Those who opposed the referendum did so because of a basic distrust of Soviet leaders and a fundamental trust of our own. What I am saying is that there are good reasons for trust and distrust, that the response of voters was rational, given the narrative paradigm. The good reasons that are expressed in public moral argument relate to issues not accounted for in the rational world paradigm. These issues include the motivations and values of the characters involved in the ongoing narrative of nuclear warfare, the way in which they conceive and behave in respect to the conflict, and the narrative probability and narrative fidelity of the particular stories they tell, which may well take the form of "reasoned argument." Experts and lay persons meet on common ground, given the narrative paradigm. As Toulmin observes, "a scientist off duty is as much an 'ordinary' man as a tinker or a bus-conductor off duty" (1982, p. 81).

From the narrative perspective, the proper role of the expert in public moral argument is that of a counselor, which is, as Benjamin (1969) notes, the true function of the storyteller. His or her contribution to public dialogue is to impart knowledge, like a teacher, or wisdom, like a sage. It is not to pronounce a story that ends all storytelling. The expert assumes the role of public counselor whenever she or he crosses the boundary of technical knowledge into the territory of life as it ought to be lived. Once this invasion is made, the public, which then includes the expert, has its own criteria for determining whose story is most coherent and reliable as a guide to belief and action. The expert, in other words, then becomes subject to the demands of narrative rationality. Technical communities have their own conceptions and criteria for judging the rationality of communication. But, as Holton (1973) has demonstrated, the work even of scientists is inspired by stories; hence, their discourse can be interpreted usefully from the narrative perspective. Holton writes tellingly of the "nascent moment" in science, the impulse to do science in a particular or in a new way, and how science is informed by "themes"—thematic concepts, methods, and hypotheses inherited from Parmenides, Heraclitus, Pythagoras, Thales, and others (pp. 28–29; see also Ong, 1982, p. 140).

Viewed from the perspective of the rational world paradigm, Schell's case, his argument and its reception, evokes despair. If one looks to MacIntyre's *After Virtue* for relief, one will be disappointed and disheartened further, for he provides the historical and philosophical reasons for the fate of *The Fate of the Earth* and similar such arguments. His own argument is that "we still, in spite of the efforts of three centuries of moral philosophy and one of sociology, lack any coherent rationally defensible statement of a liberal individualist point of view" (1981, p. 241). He offers some hope with the idea that "the Aristotelian tradition can be restated in a way that restores intelligibility and rationality to our moral and social attitudes and commitments." He observes, however, "the new dark ages" are "already upon us." The "barbarians are not waiting beyond the frontiers; they have already been governing us for quite some time. And it is our lack of consciousness of this that constitutes part of our predicament. We are waiting not for Godot, but for another—doubtless very different—St. Benedict" (p. 245).

The reasons for this state of affairs are: (1) The rejection of a teleological view of human nature and the classical conception of reason as embodied in Aristotelian logic and rhetoric; (2) the separation of morality from theological, legal, and aesthetic concerns; and (3) the evolution of the individualistic sense of self and the rise of emotivism. The consequence of these movements is a situation in which ethical arguments in public are rendered ineffectual because of "conceptual incommensurability."

A case in point is protest—where advocates of reform argue from a position of "rights" and those who oppose them reason from the stance of "utility." MacIntyre observes:

> the facts of incommensurability ensure that protestors can never win an *argument*; the indignant self-righteousness of protestors arises because the facts of incommensurability ensure equally that the protestors can never lose an argument either. Hence, the *utterance* of protest is characteristically

addressed to those who already *share* the protestors' premises. . . . This is not to say that protest cannot be effective; it is to say that protest cannot be *rationally* effective. (p. 69)

Thus, when arguers appealing to justice and equality contend with adversaries who base their case on success, survival, and liberty, they talk past each other.

From the perspective of the narrative paradigm, the dynamic of this situation is that rival stories are being told. Any story, any form of rhetorical communication, not only says something about the world, it also implies an audience, persons who conceive of themselves in very specific ways. If a story denies a person's self-conception, it does not matter what it says about the world. In the instance of protest, the rival factions' stories deny each other in respect to self-conceptions and the world. The only way to bridge this gap, if it can be bridged through discourse, is by telling stories that do not negate the self-conceptions people hold of themselves.

It may be germane to note at this point that narrative as *a mode of discourse* is more universal and probably more efficacious than argument for nontechnical forms of communication (Fisher, 1982, p. 304). There are several reasons why this should be true. First, narration comes closer to capturing the experience of the world, simultaneously appealing to the various senses, to reason and emotion, to intellect and imagination, and to fact and value. It does not presume intellectual contact only. Second, one does not have to be taught narrative probability and narrative fidelity; one culturally acquires them through a universal faculty and experience. Obviously, one can, through education, become sophisticated in one's understanding and application of these principles. But, as Gadamer observes, "I am convinced of the fact that there are no people who do not 'think' sometime and somewhere. That means there is no one who does not form general views about life and death, about freedom and living together, about the good and about happiness" (1981, p. 58; see also Ogden, 1977, p. 114; Lonergan, 1958, xiv–xv, xxii–xxx). In other words, people are reflective and from such reflection they make the stories of their lives and have the basis for judging narratives for and about them. On the other hand, appreciation of argument requires not only reflection, but also specialized knowledge of issues, reasoning, rules of rationality, and so on. Third, narration works by suggestion and identification; argument operates by inferential moves and deliberation. Both forms however, are modes of expressing good reasons—given the narrative paradigm—so the differences between them are structural rather than substantive.

SUMMARY AND CONCLUSIONS

This essay began as a study of public moral argument—the nuclear controversy. It was undertaken with the rational world paradigm well in mind. The results of my analysis were disturbing not only in what I found to be the inevitable subversion of *The Fate of the Earth* and similar such arguments, but also in that the rational world paradigm was at least partly responsible for that fate. Then came MacIntyre's (1981) *After Virtue*. Reflection set in and the narrative paradigm came out of it.

I was concerned with the concept of technical reason and the way it rendered the public unreasonable; with the idea of rationality being a matter of argumentative competence in specialized fields, leaving the public and its discourse irrational; with the apparent impossibility of bridging the gaps between experts and the public and between segments of the public; and with the necessity to learn what was supposed to be of the essence of persons—rationality—so that one class of citizens can always be superior to another.

Although I do not mean to maintain that the narrative paradigm resolves these problems out of existence, I do think that it provides a basis for reconsideration of them. Before that, I am aware, the narrative paradigm itself needs further scrutiny. I know that I do not need to tell critics how to do their work—the examination of my representation of the rational world paradigm, the presuppositions of the narrative paradigm and its relationship to other constructs, my concept of public moral argument, and the analysis of the specific case. I welcome the "stories" the critics will tell.

In closing, I should like to make two additional comments. First, I think that the concepts of public and social knowledge should be reconceived in light of the narrative paradigm. The effect would be to give shape to these ideas as identifiable entities in the discourse of the citizenry, to give public knowledge a form of being. To consider that public-social knowledge is to be found in the stories that we tell one another would enable us to observe not only our differences, but also our commonalities, and in such observation we might be able to reform the notion of the "public."

Second, and closely related to the discovery of our communal identity, is the matter of what makes one story better than another. Two features come to mind: formal and substantive. Formal features are attributes of narrative probability: the consistency of characters and actions, the accommodation of auditors, and so on. In epistemological terms, the question would be whether a narrative satisfied the demands of a coherence theory of truth. The most compelling, persuasive stories are mythic in form (Campbell, 1973; Cassirer, 1944, 1979, p. 246; Eliade, 1963). Substantive features relate to narrative fidelity. Bormann has proposed two concepts pertinent to the problem of narrative fidelity: "corroboration" (1978) and "social convergence" (1983, p. 436). These concepts concern how people come to adhere to particular stories. They do not solve the problem of narrative fidelity because both suggest that narratives are valid by virtue of consensus and provide no criteria by which one can establish that one narrative is more sound than another. While there is work to be done on the problem, I think the logic of good reasons is the most viable scheme presently available by which narratives can be tested. Its application requires an examination of reasoning and "inspection of facts, values, self, and society" (Fisher, 1978, p. 382). In epistemological terms, narrative fidelity is a matter of truth according to the doctrine of correspondence. Though the most engaging stories are mythic, the most helpful and uplifting stories are moral. As John Gardner wrote, "Moral action is action that affirms life" (1978, p. 23).

One may get the impression that the conception of rationality I have presented leads to a denial of logic. It does, but only as logic is conceived so that persons are considered irrational beings. With Heidegger (1973, p. 170), I would assert that "To think counter to logic does not mean to stick up for the illogical, but only means to think the *logos*, and its essence as it appeared in the early days of thought; i.e. to make an effort first of all to prepare such an act of reflecting (*Nachdenka*)." In an earlier essay, I attempted to make such an effort by showing the relationship of the logic of good reasons to Aristotle's concept of "practical wisdom" (Fisher, 1980, pp. 127–128).

Application of narrative rationality to specific stories may further clarify its nature and value. From the perspective of narrative rationality, Hitler's *Mein Kampf* must be judged a bad story. Although it has formal coherence in its structure, as McGuire (1977) demonstrated, it denies the identity of significant persons and demeans others. It also lacks fidelity to the truths humanity shares in regard to reason, justice, veracity, and peaceful ways to resolve social-political differences. On the other hand, one may cite the cosmological myths of Lao-tse, Buddha, Zoroaster, Christ, and Mohammed which satisfy both narrative probability and narrative fidelity for those cultures for whom they were intended—and many others across time and place. Far from denying the humanity of persons, they elevate it to the profoundest moral and metaphysical level the world has known. One could also cite such works as the *Iliad, The Odyssey,* the tragedies of Aeschylus, Sophocles, Euripides, Virgil's *Aeneid,* Dante's *Commedia,* the plays of Shakespeare, and the novels of Tolstoy, Melville, Thomas Mann, and James Joyce. One could point to the lives of Jesus, Socrates, Lincoln, and Gandhi. Regarding political discourse, one could mention many of the speeches and writings of Adlai Stevenson and Winston Churchill. While these classic manifestations of religious, social, cultural, and political life have been celebrated by persons committed to traditional rationality, it has been because they have not restricted themselves to "logic" but have recognized and responded to the values fostered by them, by their reaffirmation of the human spirit as the transcendent ground of existence.

For a more detailed illustration of how narrative probability and fidelity can be usefully applied, I offer this brief analysis of *The Epic of Gilgamesh,* "the finest surviving epic poem from any period until the appearance of Homer's *Iliad:* and it is immeasurably older" (Sandars, 1982, p. 7). It is, in fact, 1500 years older.

The story, in sum, is as follows: Gilgamesh, the King of Urak, two-thirds god and one-third man, is possessed of a perfect body, unbounded courage, and extraordinary strength. He is a hero, a tragic hero, the "first tragic hero of whom anything is known" (Sandars, 1982, p. 7). His youth is spent in pursuit of fame as the means of immortality.

He is restless, with no one to match his appetites and physical feats. His people ask the gods to create a companion for him, which they do in Enkidu. Enkidu is Gilgamesh's counterpart in strength, energy, and exuberance for life. After a wrestling match, they become inseparable, brothers in every way but birth. Gilgamesh learns what it means to love.

Because Enkidu begins to lose his physical prowess—he had been an inhabitant of the wilds and ran with animals—Gilgamesh proposes that they pursue and slay Huwawa, a terrible monster. At first, Enkidu is reluctant but is chided into joining the quest. The monster is met, subdued, and, because of an insult, is slain by Enkidu.

When they return to Urak, the goddess, Ishtar, proposes to Gilgamesh. He not only refuses her, but he and Enkidu heap scorn upon her. She goes to her father, Anu, and asks him to have the bull of heaven kill Gilgamesh. But Gilgamesh and Enkidu kill the bull instead. It appears at this point that the "brothers" cannot be defeated by man, monsters, or the gods.

It turns out, however, that in killing Huwawa, Gilgamesh and Enkidu incurred the wrath of Enlil, guardian of the forest in which the monster lived. Enlil demands the death of Gilgamesh, but the sun god intervenes and Enkidu is doomed and dies.

With Enkidu's death, the world of Gilgamesh is shattered. He has not only lost his loving companion, he must now directly confront the fact of death. Up to this point he has lived as a willful child, acting as though the meaning of life is a matter of dominating it.

At first, Gilgamesh refuses to accept Enkidu's death as real. He becomes obsessed with death and starts a quest to learn the secret of immortality. His journey is tortured and long. He finally arrives, after incredible hardships, at the island of

Utanapishtim and asks him how one gains eternal life. Utanapishtim suggests that he try not to sleep for six days and seven nights. But he soon falls asleep, for seven days, a form of living death. He is awakened and realizes there is no escape from death. He resigns himself to his fate, the fate of all humankind, and returns home. On his return he learns to value the wall he has built around the city: immortality is, he apparently concludes, to be found in the monuments that one leaves behind.

The story provides good reasons to accept not only this truth, but others as well: Life is fullest when one loves and is loved; death is real; and maturity is achieved by accepting the reality of death. We learn these truths by dwelling in the characters in the story, by observing the outcomes of the several conflicts that arise throughout it, by seeing the unity of characters and their actions, and by comparing the truths to the truths we know to be true from our own lives. In other words, the story exhibits narrative probability and fidelity across time and culture (Jacobsen, 1976).

Finally, I do not mean to maintain that "knowledge of agents" is superior to "knowledge of objects." With Toulmin, I would hold that "A decent respect for each kind of knowledge is surely compatible with conceding the legitimate claims of the other" (1982, p. 244). With knowledge of agents, we can hope to find that which is *reliable or trustworthy;* with knowledge of objects, we can hope to discover that which has the quality of *veracity.* The world requires both kinds of knowledge.

Karl Wallace was right: "One could do worse than characterize rhetoric as the art of finding and effectively presenting good reasons" (1963, p. 248). MacIntyre is also right:

> The unity of human life is the unity of a narrative quest. Quests sometimes fail, are frustrated, abandoned or dissipated into distractions; and human lives may in all these ways also fail. But the criteria for success or failure in a human life as a whole are the criteria of success or failure in a narrated or to-be-narrated quest. (1981, p. 203)

And that quest is "for the good life" for all persons.

REFERENCES

Alter, R. (1981). *The art of biblical narrative.* New York: Basic Books.

Apel, K. O. (1979). Types of rationality today: The continuum of reason between science and ethics. In T. F. Geraets (Ed.), *Rationality to-day* (pp. 309–339). Ottawa: University of Ottawa Press.

Aristotle (1954). *Rhetoric* (W. R. Roberts, Trans). New York: The Modern Library Press.

Baier, A. (1983). Secular faith. In S. Hauerwas & A. MacIntyre (Eds.), *Revisions: Changing perspectives on moral philosophy* (pp. 203–221). Notre Dame: University of Notre Dame Press.

Bantz, C. R. (1975). Television news: Reality and research. *Western Journal of Speech Communication, 39,* 123–130.

Barrett, W. (1979). *The illusion of technique: A search for meaning in a technological civilization.* Garden City, NY: Anchor Press/Doubleday.

Barthes, R. (1977). Introduction to the structural analysis of narratives. In S. Heath (Ed.), *Image-music-text* (pp. 79–124) New York: Hill and Wang.

Bateson, G. (1979). *Mind and nature: A necessary unity.* Toronto: Bantam Books.

Benjamin, W. (1969). The storyteller. In H. Arendt (Ed.), *Illuminations* (pp. 83–109). New York: Schocken Books.

Bennett, L. W. (1975). Political scenarios and the nature of politics. *Philosophy and Rhetoric, 8,* 23–42.

Bennett, L. W. (1978). Story telling and criminal trials: A model of social judgment. *The Quarterly Journal of Speech, 64,* 1–22.

Bennett, L. W., & Feldman, M. S. (1981). *Reconstructing reality in the courtroom: Justice and judgment in American culture.* New Brunswick, NJ: Rutgers University Press.

Bitzer, L. F. (1978). Rhetoric and public knowledge. In D. Burks (Ed.), *Rhetoric, philosophy, and literature: An exploration* (pp. 67–93). West Lafayette, IN: Purdue University Press.

Brockriede, W. (1975). Where is argument? *Journal of the American Forensics Association, 11,* 179–182.

Brockriede, W. (1977). Characteristics of arguments and arguing. *Journal of the American Forensics Association, 13,* 129–132.

Brockriede, W. (1982). Arguing about human understanding. *Communication Monographs, 49,* 137–147.

Bormann, E. G. (1972). Fantasy and rhetorical vision: The rhetorical criticism of social reality. *The Quarterly Journal of Speech, 59,* 143–159. [*Editor's note: This citation should be The Quarterly Journal of Speech, 58, 396–407.*]

Bormann, E. G. (1973). The Eagleton affair: A fantasy theme analysis. *The Quarterly Journal of Speech, 59,* 143–159.

Bormann, E. G. (1978). The tentative and the certain in rhetoric: The role of corroboration on the rigidity or flexibility of rhetorical visions. Paper presented at the annual meeting of the Central States Speech Association, Minneapolis.

Bormann, E. G. (1983). Fantasy theme analysis. In J. L. Golden, G. F. Berquist & W. E. Coleman (Eds.), *The rhetoric of Western thought* (3rd ed., pp. 433–449). Dubuque, IA: Kendall/Hunt Publishing.

Booth, W. C. (1974). *Modern dogma and the rhetoric of assent.* Notre Dame: University of Notre Dame Press.

Burleson, B. R. (1981). Characteristics of argument. In G. Ziegelmueller & J. Rhodes (Eds.), *Dimensions of argument: Proceedings of the second conference on argumentation* (pp. 955–979). Annandale, VA: Speech Communication Association.

Burke, K. (1955). *A rhetoric of motives.* New York: George Braziller.

Burke, K. (1957). *The philosophy of literary form* (rev. ed.). New York: Vintage Books.

Burke, K. (1968). Definition of man. In K. Burke, *Language as symbolic action: Essays on life, literature, and method* (pp. 3–24). Berkeley, CA: University of California Press.

Burke, K. (1983). Lecture outline. Logology: An overall view. Personal correspondence.

Campbell, J. (1973). *Myths to live by.* New York: Bantam Books.

Campbell, J. A. (1984). On the rhetoric of history: Epochal disclosure and discovery of the universal audience. Unpublished paper, University of Washington, Department of Speech Communication.

Campbell, J. A., & Stewart, J. R. (1981). Rhetoric, philosophy, and conversation. Paper presented at the annual meeting of the Western Speech Communication Association, San Jose.

Cassirer, E. (1944). *An essay on man: An introduction to a philosophy of human culture.* New Haven, CT: Yale University Press.

Cassirer, E. (1979). The technique of our modern political myths. In D. P. Verene (Ed.), *Symbol, myth, and culture: Essays and lectures of Ernst Cassirer* (pp. 242–267). New Haven, CT: Yale University Press.

Cox, J. R. (1981). Investigating policy argument as a field. In G. Ziegelmueller & J. Rhodes (Eds.), *Dimensions of argument: Proceedings of the second conference on argumentation* (pp. 126–142). Annandale, VA: Speech Communication Association.

Danto, A. C. (1982). Narration and knowledge. *Philosophy and Literature, 6,* 17–32.

Derrida, J. (1980). The law of genre. *Critical Inquiry, 7,* 55–81.

Dewey, J. (1927). *The public and its problems.* Chicago Swallow Press.

Dijk, T. A. (1976). Philosophy of action and theory of narrative. *Poetics, 5,* 287–388.

Ehninger, D. (1968). Validity as moral obligation. *Southern Speech Journal, 33,* 215–222.

Eliade, M. (1963). *Myth and reality.* New York: Harper Colophon Books.

Farrell, T. B. (1976). Knowledge, consensus, and rhetorical theory. *The Quarterly Journal of Speech, 62,* 1–14.

Farrell, T. B. (1977). Validity and rationality: The rhetorical constituents of argumentative form. *Journal of the American Forensics Association, 13,* 142–149.

Farrell, T. B. (1983). The tradition of rhetoric and the philosophy of communication. *Communication, 7,* 151–180.

Farrell, T. B., & Goodnight, G. T. (1981). Accidental rhetoric: The root metaphor of Three Mile Island. *Communication Monographs, 48,* 271–300.

Fisher, W. R. (1973). Reaffirmation and subversion of the American Dream. *The Quarterly Journal of Speech, 9,* 160–169.

Fisher, W. R. (1978). Toward a logic of good reasons. *The Quarterly Journal of Speech, 64,* 376–384.

Fisher, W. R. (1980). Rationality and the logic of good reason. *Philosophy and Rhetoric, 13,* 121–130.

Fisher, W. R. (1982). Romantic democracy, Ronald Reagan, and presidential heroes. *Western Journal of Speech Communication, 46,* 299–310.

Fisher, W. R., & Burns, R. D. (1964). *Armament and disarmament: The continuing dispute.* Belmont, CA: Wadsworth Publishing.

Fisher, W. R., & Filloy, R. A. (1982). Argument in drama and literature: An exploration. In J. R. Cox & C. A. Willard (Eds.), *Advances in argumentation theory and research* (pp. 343–362). Carbondale, IL: Southern Illinois University Press.

Frentz, T. S., & Farrell, T. B. (1976). Language-action: A paradigm for communication. *The Quarterly Journal of Speech, 62,* 333–349.

Gadamer, H. G. (1980). *Dialogue and dialectic: Eight hermeneutical essays on Plato* (P. Christopher Smith, Trans.). New Haven, CT: Yale University Press.

Gadamer, H. G. (1981). *Reason in the age of science.* Cambridge: MIT Press.

Gadamer, H. G. (1982). *Truth and method.* New York: The Crossword Publishing Company.

Gallie, W. B. (1964). *Philosophy and historical understanding.* New York: Schocken Books.

Gardner, J. (1978). *On moral fiction.* New York: Basic Books.

Goldberg, M. (1982). *Theology and narrative.* Nashville, TN: The Parthenon Press.

Goodnight, G. T. (1980). The liberal and the conservative presumptions: On political philosophy and the foundation of public argument. In J. Rhodes & S. Newell (Eds.), *Proceedings of the summer conference on argumentation* (pp. 304 337). Falls Church, VA: Speech Communication Association.

Goody, J., & Watt, I. (1962–1963). The consequences of literacy. *Comparative Studies in Society and History, 5,* 304–326, 332–345.

Gottlieb, G. (1968). *The logic of choice: an investigation of the concepts of rule and rationality.* New York: Macmillan.

Graff, G. (1979). *Literature against itself: Literacy ideas in society.* Chicago: University of Chicago Press.

Gusfield, J. R. (1976). *Symbolic crusade: Status politics and the American temperance movement.* Urbana, IL: University of Illinois Press.

Habermas, J. (1967). *Theory and practice: The history of a concept.* Notre Dame: University of Notre Dame Press.

Habermas, J. (1973). *Knowledge and social interests.* Boston: Beacon Press.

Hauerwas, S. (1981). *A community of character: Toward a constructive Christian ethic.* Notre Dame: University of Notre Dame Press.

Hausknecht, M. (1982). Waiting for the end? Prospects for nuclear destruction. *Dissent, 29,* 282–284.

Hawes, L. C. (1978). The reflexivity of communication research. *Western Journal of Speech Communication, 42,* 12–20.

Heidegger, M. (1949). *Existence and being.* Chicago: Henry Regnery.

Heidegger, M. (1972). *On time and being.* (J. Stanbaugh, Trans.). New York: Harper and Row.

Heidegger, M. (1973). Letter on humanism. In R. Zaner & D. Ihde (Eds.), *Phenomenology and existentialism* (pp. 147–181). New York: Capricorn Books, G. P. Putnam's Sons.

Hollis, M. (1977). *Models of man: Philosophical thoughts on social action.* Cambridge: Cambridge University Press.

Holton, G. (1973). *Thematic origins of modern science.* Cambridge, MA: Harvard University Press.

Hymes, D. (1980). A narrative view of the world. In D. Hymes, *Language in education: Ethnolinguistic essays.* (pp. 129–138). Washington D.C.: Center for Applied Linguistics.

Hynes, T. J. Jr. (1980). Liberal and conservative presumptions in public argument: A critique. In J. Rhodes & S. Newell (Eds.), *Proceedings of the summer conference on argumentation* (pp. 338–347). Falls Church, VA: Speech Communication Association.

Jacobs, S., & Jackson, S. (1981). Argument as a natural category: The routine grounds for arguing in conversation. *Western Journal of Speech Communication, 45,* 118–132.

Jacobsen, T. (1976). *The treasures of darkness: A history of Mesopotamian religion.* New Haven, CT: Yale University Press.

Johnstone, H. W., Jr. (1978). *Validity and rhetoric in philosophical argument.* University Park, PA: Dialogue Press of Man and World.

Kermode, F. (1980). Secrets and narrative sequence. *Critical Inquiry, 7,* 83–101.

Key, V. O. (1966). *The responsible electorate: Rationality in presidential voting, 1936–1960.* New York: Vintage Books.

Kidd, V. (1975). Happily ever after and other relationship styles: Advice on interpersonal relations in popular magazines, 1951–1973. *The Quarterly Journal of Speech, 61,* 31–39.

Kirkwood, W. G. (1983). Storytelling and self-confrontation: Parables and communication strategies. *The Quarterly Journal of Speech, 69,* 58–74.

Krashen, S. D. (1982). *Principles and practice in second language acquisition.* Oxford: Pergamon Press.

Kuhn, T. S. (1974). Second thoughts on paradigms. In F. Suppe (Ed.), *The structure of scientific theories* (pp. 459–482). Urbana, IL: University of Illinois Press.

Langer, S. K. (1953). *Feeling and form: A theory of art.* New York: Charles Scribner's Sons.

Lonergan, B. J. F., SJ. (1958). *Insight: A study of human understanding.* New York: Harper and Row.

Lucaites, J. L. (1981). Rhetoric and the problem of legitimacy. In G. Ziegelmueller & J. Rhodes (Eds.), *Dimensions of argument: Proceedings of the second conference on argumentation.* Annandale, VA: Speech Communication Association.

Lyne, J. (1982). Discourse, knowledge, and social process: Some changing equations. *The Quarterly Journal of Speech, 68,* 201–214.

Masterman, M. (1970). The nature of a paradigm. In I. Lakatos & A. Musgrave (Eds.), *Criticism and the growth of knowledge.* (pp. 59–89). London: Cambridge University Press.

McCracken, S. (1982, July 23). The peace of the grave. *National Review,* pp. 904–905.

McGee, M. C., & Martin, M. A. (1983). Public knowledge and ideological argumentation. *Communication Monographs, 50,* 47–65.

McGee, M. C., Scult, A., & Kuntz, K. (1983). Genesis 1–3 as sacred text: An inquiry into the relationship of rhetoric and power. Unpublished paper, The University of Iowa, Department of Communication.

McGuire, M. (1977). Mythic rhetoric in *Mein Kampf:* A structural critique. *The Quarterly Journal of Speech, 68,* 1–13.

MacIntyre, A. (1978). Rationality and the explanation of action. In A. MacIntyre, *Against the self-images of the age: Essays on ideology and philosophy* (pp. 244–259). Notre Dame: University of Notre Dame Press.

MacIntyre, A. (1981). *After virtue: A study in moral theory.* Notre Dame: University of Notre Dame Press.

McKerrow, R. E. (1977). Rhetorical validity: An analysis of three perspectives on the justification of rhetorical argument. *Journal of the American Forensics Association, 13,* 133–141.

McKerrow, R. E. (1980a). Argument communities: A quest for distinctions. In J. Rhodes & S. Newell (Eds.), *Proceedings of the summer conference on argumentation* (pp. 214–227). Falls Church, VA: Speech Communication Association.

McKerrow, R. E. (1980b). On fields and rational enterprises: A reply to Willard. In J. Rhodes & S. Newell (Eds.), *Proceedings of the summer conference on argumentation* (pp. 401–411). Falls Church, VA: Speech Communication Association.

McKerrow, R. E. (1981). Senses of argument: Uses and limitations of the concept. In G. Ziegelmueller & J. Rhodes (Eds.), *Dimensions of argument: Proceedings of the second conference on argumentation* (pp. 980–986). Annandale, VA: Speech Communication Association.

McKerrow, R. E. (1982). Rationality and reasonableness in a theory of argument. In J. R. Cox & C. A. Willard (Eds.), *Advances in argumentation theory and research* (pp. 105–122). Carbondale, IL: Southern Illinois University Press.

Medina, A. (1979). *Reflection, time, and the novel: Toward a communicative theory of literature.* London: Routledge and Kegan Paul.

Mink, L. O. (1978). Narrative form as a cognitive instrument. In R. H. Canary (Ed.), *The writing of history* (pp. 129–149). Madison, WI: University of Wisconsin Press.

Nelson, J. S. (1980). Tropal history and the social sciences: Reflections on Struever's remarks. *History and Theory,* Beiheft 19, 80–101.

Ochs, D. J., & Burritt, R. J. (1973). Perceptual theory: Narrative suasion of Lysias. In C. J. Stewart, D. J. Ochs & G. P. Mohrmann (Eds.), *Explorations in rhetorical criticism* (pp. 51–74). University Park, PA: The Pennsylvania State University Press.

Ogden, S. M. (1977). Myth and truth. In S. M. Ogden, *The reality of God* (pp. 99–129). San Francisco: Harper and Row.

O'Keefe, D. J. (1977). Two concepts of argument. *Journal of the American Forensics Association, 13,* 121–128.

O'Keefe, D. J. (1982). The concepts of argument and arguing. In J. R. Cox & C. A. Willard (Eds.), *Advances in argumentation theory and research* (pp. 3–23). Carbondale, IL: Southern Illinois University Press.

Ong, W. (1982). *Orality and literacy: The technologizing of the word.* London: Methuen & Co.

Perelman, C., & Olbrechts-Tyteca, L. (1969). *The new rhetoric: A treatise on argument.* (J. Wilkinson & P. Weaver, Trans.). Notre Dame: University of Notre Dame Press.

Perelman, C. (1979). The rational and the reasonable. In C. Perelman, *The new rhetoric and the humanities: Essays on rhetoric and its applications* (pp. 117–123). Boston: D. Reidel.

Pierre, A. J. (1982). [Review of *The fate of the earth*]. *Foreign Affairs, 60,* 1188.

Polanyi, M. (1958). *Personal knowledge: Towards a postcritical philosophy.* Chicago: University of Chicago Press.

Pryor, B. (1981). Saving the public through rational discourse. In G. Ziegelmueller & J. Rhodes (Eds.), *Dimensions of argument: Proceedings of the second conference on argumentation* (pp. 848–864). Annandale, VA: Speech Communication Association.

Ramsey, I. T. (1969). Religion and science: A philosopher's approach. In D. M. High (Ed). *New essays on religious language* (pp. 36–53). New York: Oxford University Press.

Randall, J. H. Jr. (1976). *The making of the modern mind.* New York: Columbia University Press.

Rarick, D. L., Duncan, M. B., & Porter, L. W. (1977). The Carter persona: An empirical analysis of the rhetorical visions of campaign '76. *The Quarterly Journal of Speech, 63,* 258–273.

Ricoeur, P. (1976). *Interpretation theory: Discourse and the surplus of meaning.* Fort Worth, TX: The Texas Christian University Press.

Ricoeur, P. (1980). Narrative time. *Critical Inquiry, 7,* 169–190.

Rorty, R. (1979). *Philosophy and the mirror of nature.* Princeton, NJ: Princeton University Press.

Sandars, N. K. (1982). *The epic of Gilgamesh.* New York: Penguin Books.

Schell, J. (1982). *The fate of the earth.* New York: Avon Books.

Schrag, C. O. (1980). *Radical reflection and the origins of the human sciences.* West Lafayette, IN: Purdue University Press.

Schrag, C. O. (1984). Rhetoric, hermeneutics, and communication. Unpublished manuscript, Purdue University, Department of Philosophy.

Scott, R. L. (1978). Evidence in communication: We are such stuff. *Western Journal of Speech Communication, 42,* 29–36.

Scult, A. (1983). The rhetorical character of the Old Testament and its interpretation. Paper presented at the meeting of the International Society for the History of Rhetoric, Florence, Italy.

Sennett, R. (1978). *The fall of public man: On the social psychology of capitalism.* New York: Vintage Books.

Sillars, M. O., & Ganer, P. (1982). Values and beliefs: A systematic basis for argumentation. In J. R. Cox & C. A. Willard (Eds.), *Advances in argumentation theory and research* (pp. 184–201). Carbondale, IL: Southern Illinois University Press.

Simons, H. C. (1978). In praise of muddleheaded anecdotalism. *Western Journal of Speech Communication, 42,* 21–28.

Todorov, T. (1977). *The poetics of prose* (R. Howard, Trans.). Ithaca, NY: Cornell University Press.

Toulmin, S. E. (1958). *The uses of argument.* Cambridge: Cambridge University Press.

Toulmin, S. E. (1970). Reason and causes. In R. Borger & F. Cioffi (Eds.), *Explanation in the behavioral sciences* (pp. 1–41). Cambridge: Cambridge University Press.

Toulmin, S. E. (1972). *Human understanding.* Princeton, NJ: Princeton University Press.

Toulmin, S. E. (1982). *The return to cosmology: Postmodern science and the theology of nature.* Berkeley CA: The University of California Press.

Toulmin, S. E., Rieke, R., & Janik, A. (1979). *Introduction to reasoning.* New York: Macmillan.

Turner, V. (1980). Social dramas and stories about them. *Critical Inquiry, 7,* 141–168.

Voegelin, E. (1952). *The new science of politics.* Chicago: University of Chicago Press.

Voegelin, E. (1975). *From enlightenment to revolution.* Durham, NC: Duke University Press.

Wallace, K. (1963). The substance of rhetoric: Good reasons. *The Quarterly Journal of Speech, 49,* 239–249.

Wenzel, J. W. (1977). Toward a rationale for value-centered argument. *Journal of the American Forensics Association, 13,* 150–158.

Wenzel, J. W. (1980). Perspectives on argument. In J. Rhodes & S. Newell (Eds.), *Proceedings of the summer conference on argumentation* (pp. 112–133). Falls Church, VA: Speech Communication Association.

White, H. (1978). *Metahistory; tropics of history.* Baltimore, MD: Johns Hopkins University.

White, H. (1980). The value of narrativity in the representation of reality. *Critical Inquiry, 7,* 5–27.

Wieseltier, L. (1983, January 10 and 17). The great nuclear debate. *The New Republic,* 7–38.

Willard, C. A. (1978). A reformulation of the concept of argument: The constructivist/interactionist foundations of a sociology of argument. *Journal of the American Forensics Association, 14,* 121–140.

Willard, C. A. (1982) Argument fields. In J. R. Cox & C. A. Willard (Eds.), *Advances in argumentation theory and research* (pp. 24–77) Carbondale, IL: Southern Illinois University Press.

Zarefsky, D. (1981). Reasonableness in public policy: Fields as institutions. In
    G. Ziegelmueller & J. Rhodes (Eds.), *Dimensions of argument: Proceedings of the second
    conference on argumentation* (pp. 88–100). Annandale, VA: Speech Communication
    Association.
Ziegelmueller, G., & Rhodes, J. *Dimensions of argument: Proceedings of the second
    conference on argumentation.* Annandale, VA: Speech Communication Association.
Ziman, J. (1968). *Public knowledge.* London: Cambridge University Press.

TELLING AMERICA'S STORY:
NARRATIVE FORM
AND THE REAGAN PRESIDENCY

WILLIAM F. LEWIS

By 1980, America had lost its sense of direction. Economic troubles, a series of foreign policy failures, and corruption in its government had created a national malaise. Then Ronald Reagan came onto the scene with a vision of America that reinvigorated the nation. His great skills as a communicator and his commitment to fundamental ideals were just what the nation needed. We were once again proud to be Americans.

This familiar and well accepted story follows the pattern of many political success stories in which the hero rescues the country from a time of great trouble. This story is special, however, in that Reagan is said to have accomplished the feat through the power of his speaking and, eventually, to have been brought down when that power failed him. After more than five years in office, Reagan was still referred to as "the Western world's most gifted communicator."[1]

Objection to Ronald Reagan did not originate with the discovery of the Iran arms deal, however. Despite Reagan's consistent popularity and continuing praise for his speaking,[2] there has been a substantial segment of a critical public who not only remained unpersuaded by the President, but were offended by his persuasive manner. What is seen by his supporters as clear direction has been attacked by opponents as "ideology without ideas."[3] While it has been noted often that Reagan has provided a renewed sense of confidence and security in the country, expressions of fear about his ineptitude or his willingness to risk war have been frequent. Despite his continuing high levels of approval, a whole genre of literature against Reagan has developed.[4] What makes these books a genre is not just that they share a common opposition to Reagan and his policies, but also that they share a common approach to their criticisms. Reagan is accused repeatedly of being unrealistic, simplistic, and misinformed. Ronald Dallek, for example, claims that Reagan's anti-Communist foreign policy is "a simplistic and ineffective way to meet a complex problem."[5] He explains Reagan's repeated policy mistakes as a manifestation of his psychological make-up and concludes that his ideology and policy-making are "nonrational."[6] The sense of these criticisms is epitomized in the mocking tone of a *New Republic* editorial that, in the course of bemoaning Reagan's historical ignorance, comments that: "Ronald Reagan has never let the facts get in the way of a good story."[7]

Similar themes recur frequently in the scholarly evaluation of Reagan's rhetoric. His effectiveness is widely recognized, but while Reagan is praised by some for his strategic prowess and for his ability to inspire the American public,[8] others find his success problematic. How, it is asked, can he be so popular when he is uninformed, irrational, and inconsistent?[9] The dominant explanation has been that Reagan manipulates his language, his strategy, or his style to make himself and his policies appear to be attractive.[10] While the power of rhetoric to affect appearances has been demonstrated amply, this insight provides only a partial explanation for the nature of Reagan's rhetoric and the response to it. It does not account satisfactorily for the differences in perception and judgment among Reagan's various audiences, for the difference between support for Reagan and support for his policies, or for the fact that journalistic and scholarly analysis debunking his competence and sincerity was largely irrelevant through most of his presidency.

The purpose of this essay is to account for the distinctive reputation, style, and effect of Ronald Reagan's discourse by providing a consistent and sufficiently comprehensive explanation for the contradictory perceptions of his speaking and for the related paradoxes of this "Great Communicator's" presidency. To construct this account in terms of his discourse requires an explicit awareness of the distinction between a "rational" and a narrative perspective.[11] Narrative theory can provide a powerful account of political discourse, and it is essential for explaining Ronald Reagan's rhetoric, for it is the predominance of the narrative form in Reagan's rhetoric that has established the climate of interpretation within which he is seen and judged.

The frequency of Reagan's story-telling has been widely noted[12] and some perceptive commentaries have demonstrated his consistency with dominant American myths,[13] but what remains to be emphasized is that story-telling is fundamental to the relationship between Reagan and his audience. Stories are not just a rhetorical device that Reagan uses to embellish his ideas; Reagan's message is a story. Reagan uses story-telling to direct his policies, ground his explanations, and inspire his audiences, and the dominance of narrative helps to account for the variety of reactions to his rhetoric.

There is general agreement about the course of the Reagan presidency—the story of his ascendency has now become the story of his rise and fall—but explanations differ. Those who have criticized Reagan using the standards of technical reasoning and policy-making are likely to contend that his rhetoric is simplistic, untrue, or irrational and to lament the lack of public response to his patent deficiencies.[14] They are likely to explain Reagan's successes as being the result of rhetorical manipulation and to explain the Iran/*contra* crisis as being the inevitable result of his continuing lack of realism.[15] Those who listen to Ronald Reagan as a story-teller are likely to emphasize Reagan's character and to praise him for providing vision, reassurance, and inspiration to the American public.[16] They are likely to see Reagan as having struck a responsive chord and to explain the Iranian crisis as a weakening of Reagan's previously strong grasp on public leadership.[17] Reactions diverge because listeners perceive Reagan and his speeches differently, and because they apply different standards of judgment to what they perceive.

This essay will (1) explicate the varieties of narrative form active in Reagan's discourse to help explain his presidency and the reactions to it; and (2) discuss some of the moral and epistemic consequences of Reagan's use of narrative, and of the narrative form itself.

NARRATIVE FORM IN REAGAN'S RHETORIC

Reagan tells two kinds of stories that differ in scale and purpose, but that work together to establish the dominance of narrative form in the creation and in the interpretation of his rhetoric. *Anecdotes* define the character of an issue at the same time that they illustrate, reinforce, and make his policies and ideas more vivid. *Myth* structures his message.

Anecdotes are the quick stories, jokes, or incidents that are the verbal counterpart of the visual image. The anecdote is intended to spark interest, and its meaning is established in reference to some larger frame of understanding that is either specified within a discourse or assumed in an audience. In this way, the story of Albert Einstein's difficulty in understanding the 1040 form[18] defines a relationship to the tax code—given a belief that complexity is likely to be the reflection of excessive bureaucracy and that government ought to be accessible to all citizens without requiring special expertise. Similarly, Reagan's story of the Supreme Court decision that, he says, prevented New York children from praying in their cafeteria[19] defines a relationship to the issue of school prayer—given a belief that religious belief is a necessary part of moral order and that people ought to be able to act in private without governmental restriction. In both these instances, a simple story carries a clear message to those whose experience leads them to accept the story as either true or as true-to-life and whose values lead them to accept the moral. As one would expect, Reagan uses anecdotes more often when speaking to audiences that are expected to be uniformly Republican or conservative.

Myth informs all of Reagan's rhetoric. In the broad sense in which it is used here, myth refers to "any anonymously composed story telling of origins and destinies: the explanations a society offers its young of why the world is and why we do as we do, its pedagogic images of the nature and destiny of man."[20] Reagan's myth applies not to the origin of the world, but to the origin of America; not to the destiny of humanity, but to the destiny of Americans. It is a simple and familiar story that is widely taught and widely believed. It is not exactly a true story in the sense that academic historians would want their descriptions and explanations to be true, but it is not exactly fiction either. As Jerome Bruner wrote of myth in general, "its power is that it lives on the feather line between fantasy and reality. It must be neither too good nor too bad to be true, nor must it be too true."[21] Myth provides a sense of importance and direction and it provides a communal focus for individual identity.

AMERICA IN THE STORY

Reagan never tells the whole of his American story at any one time, but the myth that emerges in his speeches is familiar and easily stated:

> America is a chosen nation, grounded in its families and neighborhoods, and driven inevitably forward by its heroic working people toward a world of freedom and economic progress unless blocked by moral or military weakness.

Reagan portrays American history as a continuing struggle for progress against great obstacles imposed by economic adversity, barbaric enemies, or Big Government. It is a story with great heroes—Washington, Jefferson, Lincoln,

Roosevelt—with great villains—the monarchs of pre-Revolutionary Europe, the Depression, the Communists, the Democrats—and with a great theme—the rise of freedom and economic progress. It is a story that is sanctified by God[22] and validated by the American experience.[23] All the themes of Reagan's rhetoric are contained in the mythic history—America's greatness, its commitment to freedom, the heroism of the American people, the moral imperative of work, the priority of economic advancement, the domestic evil of taxes and government regulation, and the necessity of maintaining military strength. The story fulfills all the requirements of myth—it is widely believed, generally unquestioned, and clearly pedagogical. And Reagan tells the story extremely well. His message is always clear, his examples are chosen well, and his consistent tone of buoyant optimism and unyielding faith in progress complements the picture of continuing success that is proclaimed in the myth. Finally, it provides a focus for identification by his audience. Reagan repeatedly tells his audiences that if they choose to participate in the story, they will become a part of America's greatness.

Reagan's version of the course and direction of American history pervades all of his rhetoric, but he tells his story most clearly on those occasions when he intends to be most inspirational. The character of the myth and the moral implications that he draws from it can be seen clearly in Reagan's Second Inaugural Address.[24]

The key to understanding the Second Inaugural is to see it as a story. Like all of Reagan's rhetoric, the logic of the speech is a narrative logic that emphasizes the connection between character and action, not a rational logic that emphasizes the connections between problems and solutions. In this speech, Reagan establishes the identity of America and the American people, that identity establishes the direction for America's story, and the direction implies the actions that should be taken. By making intelligible the *public* identity of the audience members (as American), the narrative makes those who accept this identity accountable to a system of values and virtues that are used as standards against which to judge policies.

The center of the speech is itself a story. Reagan describes "two of our Founding Fathers, a Boston lawyer named Adams and a Virginia planter named Jefferson." Though they had been "bitter political rivals," Reagan told of how "age had softened their anger" as they exchanged letters and finally came together to the extent that "in 1826, the 50th anniversary of the Declaration of Independence, they both died. They died on the same day, within a few hours of each other. And that day was the Fourth of July." The cosmic harmony of this story is perfectly in keeping with the mythic frame of the speech, and the "important lesson" that Reagan draws from the story is perfectly in keeping with the dominant theme. Reagan concludes his story with a quotation from one of Jefferson's letters to Adams recalling their mutual struggle "for what is most valuable to man, his right of self government." In this story America represents a single message for all time and for all people. History has been transformed into a lesson that transcends the contingencies of circumstance.

For Reagan, America's meaning is to be found as much in the future as it has been in the past. Seeking to perfect the ultimate American goal of individual freedom, he says, will guarantee peace and prosperity: "There are no limits to growth and human progress, when men and women are free to follow their dreams"; "Every victory for human freedom will be a victory for world peace." Progress toward freedom is tied directly to economic progress by linking unrestrained individual action to economic productivity: "At the heart of our efforts is one idea vindicated by 25 straight months of economic growth: freedom and incentives unleash the drive and entrepreneurial genius that are the core of human progress." The powerfully future-oriented, forward-looking perspective is summed up in his conclusion: America is "one people, under God, dedicated to the dream of freedom he has placed in the human heart, called upon now to pass that dream on to a waiting and a hopeful world."

The only impediments to the fulfillment of this dream that Reagan identifies are those that America imposes on itself.[25] For a time, said Reagan, "we failed the system." We suffered through times of economic and social stress because "we yielded authority to the national government that properly belonged to the states or to local governments or to the people themselves." These were temporary difficulties, however. By renewing our faith in freedom "we are creating a nation once again vibrant, robust, and alive." The other great risk that Reagan identifies is military weakness. "History has shown," he states, "that peace does not come, nor will our freedom be preserved, by good will alone."

Reagan's Second Inaugural is based upon a story of America's origins and its quest for freedom. In it, Reagan shows the dire consequences of being distracted from the quest and the rewards and potential glory of regaining faith and direction. He defines the values that are needed (unity, freedom, strength) and he outlines the future and calls upon Americans to dedicate themselves to living this story.

The Audience in the Story

In the same way in which Reagan's stories give meaning to America, they define what it means to be an American. The narrative form offers a special kind of identification to Reagan's audience because each auditor is encouraged to see himself or herself as a central actor in America's quest for freedom. To accept Reagan's story is not just to understand the course of an American history that is enacted in other places by other people, it is to know that the direction and outcome of the story depend upon you. Proper action makes the audience member into a hero; inaction or improper action makes the listener responsible for America's decline. The narrative logic that defines the nature of heroism in Reagan's rhetoric was the central theme of his First Inaugural Address.[26]

America is defined as the greatest country in the world. It "guarantees individual liberty to a greater degree than any other," it is the "last and greatest bastion of freedom," and, consequently, it has "the world's strongest economy." To be heroes, the audience members must act in ways that will contribute to America's goals. The narrative defines their virtues—determination, courage, strength, faith, hope, work, compassion—and Reagan identifies their character.

In his most explicit and extensive consideration of heroism, Reagan makes it clear that America's real heroes are its ordinary people—the factory workers and the farmers, those who market goods and those who consume them, those who produce ("entrepreneurs" are given special mention here as elsewhere), and those who give to others.[27]

The idea of the American hero is epitomized in the story of Martin Treptow, "a young man . . . who left his job in a small town barbershop in 1917" to serve in WWI. "We're told," said Reagan, "that on his body was found a diary" in which he had written: "America must win this war. Therefore I will work, I will save, I will sacrifice, I will endure, I will fight cheerfully and do my utmost, as if the issue of the whole struggle depended on me alone." The character of the individual and the values that he holds are defined by their contribution to America's struggle. If the audience accepts Reagan's description of the nature of that continuing struggle, then they will be encouraged to accept the same kind of values, actions, and commitments that Treptow accepted in his struggle. In this case, Reagan's use of anecdote defines the character that best fits his story of America. World War I is taken to exemplify America's struggle for freedom against hostile forces; Treptow exemplifies the common man; the dedication of the soldier exemplifies the dedication to country and the fighting spirit that are necessary to prevail in the struggle; and the diary entry exemplifies the commitment to act upon these principles (work, save, sacrifice, endure) and the attitude that is appropriate to the fight ("cheerfully"). Significantly, the story is presented as true, but the primary sense of its accuracy is that it represents a larger truth. "We're told" is a weak claim to factuality, but the application of the story in a Presidential Inaugural is a strong claim to moral legitimacy.

Reagan's definition of American heroism is primarily, but not exclusively, economic. The key to heroism is effective action in the ongoing struggle to achieve freedom and prosperity. Reagan encourages identification on the ground of a general commitment to the America of his story and discourages distinctions based on differences in politics or interests.[28] The stories he tells as President feature the audience members as Americans rather than as members of different political parties, and *Time* magazine supports the sharing of this perception when it cites as typical the comment by "a retired brewery worker from San Antonio" that: "He really isn't like a Republican. He's more like an American, which is what we really need."[29]

Reagan in the Story

Some of Reagan's critics have attempted to portray him as a dangerous man, seeing him either as a demagogue[30] or a warmonger.[31] Other critics have marveled at his ability to retain his role as a critic of government even after he became its symbolic head and have worried about his detachment from the policies of his own administration[32] or about his lack of accountability.[33] Such criticisms, however, fail to take account of the nature of the public perception that is encouraged by the narrative form.

To understand the response to Reagan it is necessary to see and understand Reagan-in-the-story, not Reagan-the-policy-maker or even Reagan-the-speaker. Since the story is the dominant mode through which the political situation is interpreted, Reagan will not be perceived or judged as a politician or a policymaker or an ideologue unless that is the role that is defined for Reagan as part of the story. In the story that emerges through his speeches, however, Reagan plays two roles that have succeeded in encompassing the perspective of his critics. As a character in the story, Reagan is a mythic hero. He embodies the role of the compassionate, committed political outsider; he is the active force that has arrived to help right the prevailing wrongs and to get things moving again. As the narrator of the story, Reagan is portrayed as simply presenting the nature of the situation. There is no artifice and no threat in this style of realistic narration; Reagan-as-narrator just presents things as they are.

Reagan's character has been a dominant focus among those who attempt to explain the impact of his rhetoric. One explanation for Reagan's success is that he has "character"—that is, he projects an image of "manly effectiveness."[34] Reagan is said to be "the political embodiment of the heroic westerner,"[35] both in his appearance ("tall, lank, rugged"[36]) and in his character traits ("honesty and sincerity, innocence, optimism, and certainty"[37]). He is compared with other Presidential heroes such as Thomas Jefferson, Theodore Roosevelt, and Franklin Roosevelt, whose virtues were those of the visionary and the man of action.[38] In this respect, he is said to contrast with the "softer" Democratic candidates who have opposed him. Reagan has been able to establish the perception of his competence through "tough talk, vigorous promises, and his emphasis on immediate solutions."[39] Reagan's opponents are said to have been pushed by the contrast into appearing "impractical, ineffectual, and effete."[40] Such descriptions reveal Reagan's success in establishing himself as a variation on a dominant type of American mythic hero—strong, aggressive, distant, in control, and in Reagan's case, able to see the situation clearly and to explain it to a confused public.[41]

The most familiar form of attack on Reagan's character attempts to reveal a true Reagan behind a constructed mask. "Character" becomes a criticism of Reagan when he is accused of playing a role as he did during his movie career. The criticism appears in a number of related forms—he is said to be a "performer," a "host," an "image," to be playing a "game of cultural make-believe," or to be "using" his role to manipulate the public and to more effectively pursue his political or ideological or personal goals.[42] This use of "character" as artifice will succeed as a criticism only if Reagan is perceived as constructing a fictional persona. It cannot succeed if his persona is seen as matching or expressing his "real" character. The criticism of Reagan as an artificial creation, however, neglects his role as narrator of the story. Reagan's story, and his role in the story, are presented as a realistic and sensible portrayal of the normal and ordinary course of events. The combination of Reagan's calm demeanor,[43] his frequent reference to familiar situations to explain complex or threatening events,[44] and his reliance on American commonplaces[45] combine to create an air of reassuring certainty that has suggested to some commentators that Reagan would be more aptly compared with Harding or Eisenhower than with Theodore or Franklin Roosevelt.[46]

If criticisms of Reagan's character are not adjusted to fit the story, they are likely either to be dismissed or to be reinterpreted—sometimes with unexpected results. The charge that to elect Reagan was to risk war, for example, was unsuccessful for Carter in the 1980 presidential election and for Gerald Ford in the 1976 California primary because these attempts at criticism were perfectly consistent with the strong character that Reagan had established in his story and with the story's assumption that strength is a necessary precondition of peace. From the point of view of the story, Reagan's emphasis on increases in weapons, his assertion of the need to stand up to the Soviets, and his willingness to risk war in pursuit of the higher goals of freedom and democracy reinforced his repeated declaration that "peace is the highest aspiration of the American people," and that he, personally, wanted nothing so much as a peaceful world.[47] The result was that, in both of these elections, the charges made against Reagan did more harm to the accuser than to Reagan. In 1976, Ford's ads were even used by the Reagan campaign.[48] Similarly, Reagan can continue to use "government" as a character in his stories and to oppose himself and his audience to the Federal government after being President for more than one full term because Reagan's role in the narrative situation is to give meaning to the country and its government; he and his vision may inspire and shape policy, but he is not held responsible because designing the particulars of policy will not be seen as his role from within this perspective.

The dominance of the story is also revealed by those occasions in which Reagan's character has been called into question. In the first debate with Walter Mondale during the 1984 presidential campaign, his advisors attempted to prepare him with sufficient information and detail, but this tactic was unsuccessful because it did not accord with the character of Reagan in his own story. In the second debate, his advisors resolved to "let Reagan be Reagan."[49] The failure of this attempt to alter Reagan's "character" to meet the demands of his critics and the success of his return to his "normal" style in the second debate confirms the acceptance of Reagan's story and of his role in it. In the Iran/*contra* affair, Reagan's apparent willingness to deal with an archetypal enemy and to compromise his previously firm stance against terrorism seemed completely inconsistent with the character he had established. There seemed to be only two "rational" explanations (from the point of view of the story): either that Reagan was not responsible for the actions or that his character had changed. Hence, one response to the crisis has been to question Reagan's control over his subordinates and another has been to inquire into his mental and physical health. Neither of these explanations, however, is consistent with the story's image of presidential leadership. The story can encompass Reagan's critics, but it is vulnerable to his own inconsistencies.

Reagan's story encourages his audience to see America as a chosen nation leading the world to freedom and economic progress, to see Reagan as a friendly well-motivated leader and as a narrator of the American story, and to see themselves as heroes in the unfolding drama of American greatness. In Reagan's rhetoric, the nature of the world, his policies, his values, his character, and the character of his audience are defined together by the story that he tells. The consequences of this reliance on narrative form need to be considered carefully.

CONSEQUENCES OF REAGAN'S USE OF NARRATIVE FORM

In a 1984 review essay on "Narrative Theory and Communication Research," Robert L. Scott observed that despite the suggestive correspondences between narrative forms and rhetorical functions, "no rhetorical critic . . . has pressed along the lines suggested thus far by narrative theorists."[50] At the same time, Walter Fisher proposed a theory of human communication based on narrative. Fisher argued that traditional investigation of communication was regulated by the "rational world paradigm," which presumed that rational communicators managed a world that "is a set of logical puzzles which can be resolved through appropriate analysis and application of reason conceived as an argumentative construct."[51] Fisher found this approach to be more incomplete than wrong. Specifically, he objected to its inability to grasp the manner in which symbolization is a universal though non-rational characteristic of human nature, and to its imposition of ideological restrictions upon the process of moral choice. In contrast, Fisher offered the "narrative paradigm," which presumes that humans are essentially story-tellers who act on the basis of good reasons derived from their experience in a world that is "a set of stories which must be chosen among to live the good life in a process of continual recreation."[52]

The distinction between narrative and "rational" forms of consciousness is well grounded in the literature of narrative theory. Drawing from the texts of history, literature, and anthropology, these theorists have shown that narrative is a distinctive and distinctively important means of giving meaning to events. The important question for political discourse parallels Hayden White's inquiry into historical narrative: "With *what kind of meaning* does storying endow" political events?[53] The answers provided by narrative theorists suggest that narrative is a fundamental form of human understanding that directs perception, judgment, and knowledge. Narrative form shapes ontology by making meaningfulness a product of consistent relationships between situations, subjects, and events and by making truth a property that refers primarily to narratives and only secondarily to propositions; narrative form shapes morality by placing characters and events within a context where moral judgment is a necessary part of making sense of the action; and narrative form shapes epistemology by suggesting that all important events are open to common sense understanding.

These characteristics of narrative suggest an explanation for the apparent incongruity of a President with high levels of personal support despite opposition to his policies, and it explains the particular way in which support and opposition to Reagan has been expressed—*Reagan's exclusive and explicit reliance on a single story has dominated the realm of political judgment*. The story is the primary basis for defining the situation, morality is the primary basis for justifying public policy, and common sense is the primary basis for analyzing political issues.

Narrative Truth

Reagan's stories are sometimes presented as fictional, sometimes as fact. In either case, their appropriateness to political discourse depends upon their consistency with the historical world of the audience. If the story is not true, it must be true-to-life; if it did not actually happen, it must be evident that it could have happened or that, given the way things are, it should have happened. When narrative dominates, epistemological standards move away from empiricism. History is more likely to be seen as a literary artifact, fiction is more likely to be seen as a mimetic representation of reality, and the two forms "cross" in the historicity of the narrative form.[54] Understanding this shift in perspective is essential to understanding Reagan's rhetoric and the reactions to it.

As Bennett and Feldman found in their examination of story-telling in jury trials, "judgments based on story construction are, in many important respects, unverifiable in terms of the reality of the situation that the story represents."[55] The story becomes increasingly dominant as the empirically defined context for the story becomes increasingly distant from confirmation by either experience or consensus. Bennett and Feldman identify two situations in which "structural characteristics of stories become more central to judgment": (1) if "facts or documentary evidence are absent," or (2) if "a collection of facts or evidence is subject to competing interpretations."[56] Both of these conditions are typically present in major political disputes.

Even the most obviously fantastic stories make a claim to truth for the order that they impose on a chaotic world. To support the claim that fairy tales give meaning to a child's life, for example, Bruno Bettelheim quotes the German poet Schiller as saying that, "deeper meaning resides in the fairy tales told to me in my childhood than in the truth that is taught by life."[57] Events become meaningful in stories and meaning depends upon the significance of the events within the context of the story. As a consequence, the perception of truth depends upon the story as a whole rather than upon the accuracy of its individual statements. Louis O. Mink argues that a historical narrative "claims truth not merely for each of its individual statements taken distributively, but for the complex form of the narrative itself."[58] The "complex form" of a narrative makes isolated events and individual statements meaningful. Mink concludes that "the significance of past occurrences is understandable only as they are locatable in the ensemble of interrelationships that can be grasped only in the construction of narrative form."[59]

The variety of technical terms developed here all lead to a single basic conclusion: somehow we must recognize that stories admit to a dual evaluation.

Alasdair MacIntyre studies moral discourse in terms of *verisimilitude* and *dramatic probability*.[60] Fisher uses *narrative fidelity* and *narrative probability* to express a parallel distinction.[61] In other words, each theorist sees narrative credibility (and narrative power) as having both substantive and formal properties.

An examination of the reaction to Reagan's dominant narrative suggests that the two properties are interdependent, and recognizing the reflexive quality of his narrative suggests an explanation for the difference in claims about the truth of his rhetoric: the kind of "narrative probability" established in Reagan's explicitly narrative and mythic rhetoric has affected judgments of "narrative fidelity." Because his story is so dominant, so explicit, and so consistent, political claims are likely to be measured against the standard of Reagan's mythic American history rather than against other possible standards such as technical competence or ideological dogma. In this way, the story's dominance has diminished the significance of claims about Reagan's factual inaccuracies. For example, in the 1984 campaign Reagan claimed that the tax proposal being advanced by the Democrats would be equivalent to adding $1800 to the tax bill of every American household.[62] The figure was questioned widely, but the charge of inaccuracy never affected Reagan's credibility or popularity. The meaning of the general story was more important than the particular figure. If Reagan's estimate erred by 10% or by 100% that would not affect the meaning of his story—that the Democrats were, once again, offering a "massive tax and spending scheme" that threatened American economic progress—so the error could be dismissed as trivial.

In addition, relying on the internal relationships established in stories to determine the truth discourages direct denial or refutation and encourages the audience to discover their own place in the story. One reason for the lack of success of many of Reagan's critics has been their tendency to attempt to refute Reagan's assertions.[63] Those most successful in confronting Reagan, such as Mario Cuomo, have been those few politicians who offer alternative stories. The argument must be adjusted to the narrative paradigm—for example, by making the "city on a hill" a "tale of two cities"—or it is likely to be seen as trivial or irrelevant.

The stories that have caused the most trouble for Reagan are those which are least in accord with the generally accepted understanding. In a speech to the VFW during the 1980 campaign, for example, Reagan referred to the Vietnam War as "a noble cause." Despite the approval of the immediate audience, the story complicated his national campaign because of its inconsistency with the general understanding of Vietnam as an unjust war in which America played an ignoble role.[64] Similarly, Reagan's difficulties with the Bitburg ceremony stemmed from his account contradicting the received understanding of America waging war to destroy the evils of Nazi conquest. Neither of these cases resulted in lasting damage to Reagan's popularity or credibility, however, because he was able to show that his actions were consistent with his story of America.[65] The distinctiveness of the Iran/*contra* affair is that Reagan's actions have been interpreted as being inconsistent with Reagan's own story. Trading arms for hostages was not seen as consistent with standing up to terrorism; providing arms to Iran was not seen as consistent with strong opposition to America's enemies. Because it was perceived as being inconsistent with the established story of the Reagan presidency, the effects of the Iranian arms deal have been general and severe.[66] Even a story that is powerfully resistant to outside criticism cannot survive inconsistency with itself.

Reagan's stories are not completely self-contained—if they could not be interpreted as representing real events in the real world they would be vulnerable to charges that they are merely fantasies conjured up by the conservative imagination[67]—but this is a special kind of reality. The basis for accepting the referential value of Reagan's stories is not empirical justification, but consistency with the moral standards and common sense of his audience.

Moral Argument

Narrative form shapes interpretation by emphasizing the moral dimension of understanding. As Hayden White says of historical narrative, "story forms not only permit us to judge the moral significance of human projects, they also provide the means by which to judge them, even while we pretend to be merely describing them."[68] White takes the "moral impulse" to be a defining characteristic of narrativity,[69] Fisher uses *moral* argument to distinguish that form of public argument most suited to narrative,[70] and Alasdair MacIntyre makes the connection between narrative, personal identity, intelligibility, and accountability fundamental to his attempt to rescue ethical judgment from what he sees as the sterile standards of enlightenment thinkers.[71] The nature of the narrative form is said to be moral because stories make events intelligible by imposing a temporal order that leads to some end that defines the moral frame of the story and because the nature of the characters and events in the story will be defined with reference to that purpose.

Ronald Beiner explains and exemplifies the moral impulse of narrative in political discourse. "In attempting to define a conception of the human good," he writes, *"we tell a story."*[72] Not all stories work equally well, but rich and penetrating stories are what we look for in the work of political theorists and in the statements of politicians. The quality of the story will make it more or less effective in disclosing some truth about the human condition. And different stories will suggest different truths, not all of which will be consistent with each other. "For instance," Beiner continues, "if we wish to expound the necessary place of political freedom in a meaningfully human life, we may wish to tell a story about how the union organizers of Solidarity in Poland, against all odds, forced a remote party machine to listen to the voice of the Polish people."[73] Or we may recall the heroic acts and noble sentiments of the American Revolution as conservative spokesmen like Reagan often do. Or we may reverse the focus and tell of the horrors of repression and segregation in South Africa. The significant point here is that whatever story is told will provide a moral direction and that this is especially true for narratives that are presented as historical fact.

The heavily moral orientation of Reagan's rhetoric helps to account both for the character of his rhetoric and for the character of the response to it. Reagan characteristically justifies his policies by citing their goals, while critics of his policies characteristically cite problems of conception or implementation. Reagan's moral focus has worked well because the shift of emphasis to ends rather than means pre-empts arguments about practicality and because it provides Reagan with a ready response by transforming opposition to policy into opposition to principle. The difficulties of reaching the goal are not ignored, but in this idealistic framework they take on the status of technicalities—potentially bothersome, but not really fundamental to judging policies or people.

The focus on goals has also led to two sorts of criticisms. Reagan is accused of overlooking the impact that means can have on ends,[74] and of assuming that stating the goal is equivalent to its achievement.[75] These tendencies can be seen clearly in the justification and defense that Reagan provides for his policies.

Reagan's justification for the Strategic Defense Initiative in the 1985 State of the Union Address provides a good example of the ways in which a moral emphasis can influence public argument. There is, said Reagan, "a better way of eliminating the threat of nuclear war" than deterrence:

> It is a Strategic Defense Initiative aimed at finding a non-nuclear defense against ballistic missiles. It is the most hopeful possibility of the nuclear age. But it is not well understood.
>
> Some say it will bring war to the heavens—but its purpose is to deter war, in the heavens and on earth. Some say the research would be expensive. Perhaps, but it could save millions of lives, indeed humanity itself. Some say if we build such a system, the Soviets will build a defense system of their own. They already have strategic defenses that surpass ours; a civil defense system, where we have almost none; and a research program covering roughly the same areas of technology we're exploring. And finally, some say the research will take a long time. The answer to that is: "Let's get started."[76]

The pattern of response is revealing. While the objections cited by Reagan are primarily pragmatic (expense, Soviet response, time), Reagan's justifications are made in terms of the goals of the program. Reagan does not deny that this program might "bring war to the heavens," he cites the goal of the program as sufficient justification; he does not deny its expense, he invokes the goal of saving lives. The relationship between means and ends is skewed to an exclusive focus on goals as a means of judgment. If the move from practicality to principle is accepted, it makes the policy immune from most objections. From this point of view, the only reasonable explanation for opposition is the one that Reagan cites, the policy must not be "well understood."[77]

The same combination of an exclusive focus upon ends defined within a particular historical narrative has resulted in charges that Reagan "has been pushing his civil-rights policies with a campaign of 'astonishing misrepresentation.'"[78] Reagan's response to such criticisms is that they are the result of "misperceptions" and "misunderstandings."[79] While his critics cite his factual errors and what they see as inconsistencies between his statements and the actions of his administration, Reagan relies on the story of his life and his story of America to counter the accusations. When questioned about his negative image among black leaders, for example, Reagan responded with a reference to his character (that is to the character of Reagan-in-the-story): "it's very disturbing to me, because anyone who knows my life story knows that long before there was a thing called the civil-rights movement, I was busy on that side."[80] In his Second Inaugural, he again used reference to the past to make racial equality a part of America's story: "As an older American, I remember a time when people of different race, creed, or ethnic origin in our land found hatred and prejudice installed in social custom and, yes, in law. There is no story more heartening in our history than the progress that we've made toward the 'brotherhood of man' that God intended for us." From the narrative point of view, it is sufficient to have the appropriate character, and to believe in the appropriate goals. The proper results are the consequence of the story's progression.

Common Sense

Narrative truth assumes a type of knowledge that differs from the knowledge produced within and sanctioned by rational argument. Both Mink and White claim that narrative is the basic medium of common sense.[81] MacIntyre and Fisher identify narrative with the received wisdom of the community and contrast that to the "elitist" and "technical" knowledge of the academic and political establishment.[82] Since narrative makes sense of experience, the sense that is made will be grounded in the presuppositions of those who accept the narrative, and those presuppositions are common sense. Persuasive narratives, then, both express and assume a knowledge that is shared by the community.

The emphasis on common sense is significant for, as Clifford Geertz in anthropology and Alasdair MacIntyre in philosophy have shown, "common sense" is a culturally defined set of rules and expectations.[83] Just as reliance on a common morality de-emphasizes practical and technical concerns, reliance on a common understanding de-emphasizes objections based on claims to special knowledge or expertise. Common sense is so obvious to those who accept it that disagreement with its implications will often seem irrelevant, impractical, or unintelligible. Hayden White notes approvingly that "one of its virtues is the conviction that informs it; agreement with its dicta is the very mark of goodwill."[84] In this way, common sense insulates its claims from alternative conceptions; it consists of an unreflective, self-evidently "true" set of beliefs that are used to make sense out of situations and events. Common sense establishes a transparent realism—a common sense statement is what everyone knows; a common sense judgment is what any sensible person would do.

Reagan's reliance upon common sense as a standard for understanding and judgment has been noted both by commentators and by Reagan himself,[85] and the consequences of the emphasis on common sense on his expression and his analysis are evident in the style, the logic, and the attitude of his rhetoric. In brief, the common sense grounding that is an element of Reagan's dominant narrative suggests a pattern of understanding that parallels Geertz's informal categorization of the "stylistic features, marks of attitude" of common sense.[86] Reagan's rhetoric employs a simple, familiar, and personal style; a logic grounded in practical analogy; and an attitude that offers a singular perspective, unquestioned assumptions, and definitive portrayals.

Reagan's style encourages the perception that political problems are accessible to solution by the common action of ordinary people. Since common sense is "thin," political understanding requires no mysterious or arcane perceptiveness; things are as they appear.[87] The simplicity of apparently complex issues has been a continuing theme in Reagan's rhetoric. In the so-called Reaganomics speech, he declined to present "a jumble of charts, figures, and economic jargon"; his Strategic Defense Initiative was "not about spending arithmetic"; his proposal for Tax Reform was "a simple, straightforward message"; on Nicaragua, "the question the Congress of the United States will now answer is a simple one"; and on arms control, "the answer, my friends, is simple."[88]

One consequence of Reagan's simple style of common sense rhetoric is that he has been subject to charges of being simplistic throughout his political career. In a revealing response to that claim in his Inaugural Address as governor of California, Reagan said: "For many years, you and I have been shushed like children and told there are no simple answers to complex problems that are beyond our comprehension. Well, the truth is there *are* simple answers—just not easy ones."[89] Much of Reagan's relationship to his audience is contained in this "common sense" observation. The reference to "you and I" places Reagan and the audience together against the unspecified forces that oppose the participation of the people in political decision-making and the reference to "simple answers" opens up the political process. Character and style combine to reinforce the presumption that will and courage, not intelligence or expertise, are required to solve difficult political problems.

Aristotle noted that comparison with the familiar allows us to understand the unfamiliar[90] and the assumptions of common sense move that observation farther: unfamiliar events and complex situations are seen to be "really" like the simple and familiar understandings and beliefs of the group.[91] Reagan often uses a "common sense" logic of practical analogies to explain and justify his policy choices. In his Acceptance Address at the 1980 Republican Convention, for example, Reagan said: "I believe it is clear our federal government is overgrown and overweight. Indeed, it is time for our government to go on a diet."[92] And in his first speech on "Reaganomics," he met his opposition with common sense: "There were always those who told us that taxes couldn't be cut until spending was reduced. Well, you know, we can lecture our children against extravagance until we run out of voice and breath. Or we can cure their extravagance by simply reducing their allowance."[93] In Reagan's 1986 address on Nicaragua, the Nicaraguan government is referred to as "a second Cuba, a second Libya," while the *contras* are said to be "freedom fighters" who are "like the French Resistance that fought the Nazis."[94] By using the daily dilemmas of diets and allowances and the widely accepted evils of the Nazis and Cuba as parallels to current American policy-making, Reagan suggests that what might have been seen as complex and distant problems are amenable to simple and familiar (if not always pleasant) solutions. As he concluded later in the "Reaganomics" speech, "All it takes is a little common sense and recognition of our own ability."[95]

Since common sense is assumed to be "natural," the correctness and universality of the perceptions and judgments that Reagan propounds is also assumed.[96] His is not a carefully weighed reflection involving doubts and reservations; Reagan presents the picture clearly and incontestably and the actions follow naturally from his descriptions. In his Address to the Nation on Defense and National Security (the so-called "Star Wars" speech), for example, Reagan began by stating that further defense cuts "cannot be made" and that there is "no logical way" to reduce the defense budget without reducing security. In his description of Soviet power he stated that "the . . . militarization of Grenada . . . can only be seen as a power projection into that region" and that "the Soviet Union is acquiring what can only be considered an offensive military force." The appropriate actions are just as clear: "it was obvious that we had to begin a major modernization program," "we must continue to restore our military strength"; and with regard to his proposal: "Are we not capable of demonstrating our peaceful intentions by applying all our abilities and our ingenuity to achieving a truly lasting stability? I think we are. Indeed we must."[97]

This sense of unquestioned truth explains why the observations of theorists about common sense in general apply so smoothly to Reagan's rhetoric—a "maddening air of simple wisdom" exercises Reagan's critics and "comfortable certainties" reassure his supporters.[98] Since common sense justification relies on doing what any sensible person would do based on what everyone knows to be true, a narrative frame may encourage those within it to see intelligence in practical terms and to emphasize sensibility over intellectual analysis. The differing perspectives help to explain why his supporters can recognize that Reagan is "no rocket scientist" and still respect his intelligence,[99] at the same time that his opponents lament what seems to them to be his obvious intellectual weakness. Technical accomplishment has its place in a common sense perspective—expertise is useful, even essential, in making applications and in completing the details of policy—but one need not be a nuclear engineer or a tax accountant to know that nuclear strength ensures peace or that simplicity brings fairness."[100]

Consequences for Policy: Incommensurable Frames

Fisher's description of the rational and narrative paradigms neatly summarizes major difference in perspective. From the point of view of the rational world paradigm, a story should be substantively true so that it can be used as evidence by example or analogy, or it should be vivid enough to illustrate the problem or its possible solution. In either case, stories are not considered likely to be able to carry the knowledge one needs to analyze and solve a problem. From the point of view of the narrative paradigm, a story should be a good story judged by internal aesthetic criteria and by external criteria of "fit" with the audience's experience and morality. In any case, it is likely to best express what one really needs to know to get by in the world. The two perspectives clash over standards for evidence and the appropriate basis for judgment.

The rhetorical critic should consider that any discourse can be described differently according to these competing though not contradictory accounts. Furthermore, the critic should consider that different auditors may respond differently to the same message because they are applying these different standards of apprehension.

The incommensurability of these two frames of reference is illustrated neatly in Walter Mondale's attack on Reagan's fiscal policy in the 1984 presidential campaign. In his acceptance address at the Democratic Convention, Mondale called for "a new realism." He challenged Reagan to "put his plan on the table next to mine" and then to "debate it on national television before the American people," and he contrasted Reagan's approach with "the truth" five times including his memorable promise to raise taxes: "Let's tell the truth. . . . Mr. Reagan will raise taxes, and so will I. He won't tell you. I just did."[101] Calls for realism, debate, and truth are fundamental to rational analysis, but they take on a different meaning from within the narrative paradigm.

In the Second Inaugural and in the related speeches that followed,[102] Reagan offered two directions for reducing budget deficits. First, "a dynamic economy, with more citizens working and paying taxes," and second, an amendment that would "make it unconstitutional for the federal government to spend more than the federal government takes in." Both these strategies are grounded in the *telos* of Reagan's narrative. Working individuals tend naturally toward economic success unless blocked by barriers constructed by government. The federal government, on the other hand, will tend naturally toward expansion and will increase taxes and spending unless blocked by a permanent control that is beyond its power to change.[103] From the point of view of the rational paradigm, tax increases are the logical solution because adding revenue would correct the imbalance between income and expenditure. From the point of view of Reagan's story, tax increases are illogical because they would frustrate the individual initiative that is the basis for economic growth and they are immoral because they would violate the natural order by restraining individuals to benefit government. From the rational point of view, a Balanced Budget Amendment is irrelevant because it addresses a principle without dealing with the underlying problem. From the point of view of Reagan's narrative, the amendment is logical because the federal government will never act contrary to its natural character without some outside restraint and it is moral because it is directed toward the quest for individual freedom.

The dispute over tax policy reveals different structures of perception that lead to different policy conclusions. The distinctive character of these differences is that they are defined by Reagan's reliance on narrative form. It is not just the nature of the particular story, but the reliance on story-telling that defines the relationship of those who accept Reagan's rhetoric to a complex of significant issues. A narrative perspective uses consistency with the story as the primary measure of truth, emphasizes moral standards for judgment, and features common sense as the basis for making political decisions.

CONCLUSIONS

When Reagan is seen as a story-teller and his message is seen as a story, it becomes evident why he was so successful in "re-invigorating" the country—his story gave a clear, powerful, reassuring, and self-justifying meaning to America's public life. And it is evident why Reagan's personal popularity consistently exceeds support for his policies—to accept the story is to see Reagan both as a hero exemplifying the virtues of manly efficacy and as a realistic narrator telling things as they are; it makes sense to rely on Reagan-in-the-story. The reason that charges against Reagan's lack of compassion or his militarism have been ineffectual is that the nature of social justice and peace, and the appropriate means for their achievement, are defined from within his story. The reason that repeated charges of ignorance and factual error have not affected either Reagan's popularity or his credibility is that truth is judged in the context of the story and the story is judged for its fit with popular morality and common sense. In short, Reagan demonstrates the enormous appeal of a narrative form handled with artistry by a major public figure.

Reagan also demonstrates how limiting reliance on a single, unquestioned narrative structure can be when applied to the range of national and international concerns that comprise American political discourse. The effectiveness of Reagan's transcendent narrative depends upon establishing the story as the primary context for understanding people and events. Such a self-contained communication form is effective because it is clear, complete, and (therefore) reassuring. In addition to its evident effectiveness, however, such a narrative is also fragile and dangerous.

A dominant narrative structure is fragile because the requirement of internal consistency is permanent, while the ability of people responding to events to maintain that consistency is inevitably partial and temporary. The fragility of Reagan's story became evident in the public response to the Iran/*contra* affair. Since Reagan's character and his actions were perceived as a part of his story and were judged on the basis of their consistency with that story, his credibility was intact as long as he remained consistent. Perceived inconsistency with the standards that he had established, however, was devastating and the effects were immediate and (apparently) lasting.[104]

Reagan's dominant narrative is dangerous because its assertion of permanence assumes both insularity from material conditions and isolation from social commentary. His mythic rhetoric appeals to a tradition of belief and action that lends credence to the virtues and actions that are justified by his historical sense, but the justification is limited by Reagan's limited notion of history. An essential part of Alasdair MacIntyre's consideration of the ethical role of narrative thinking is that "a living tradition . . . is an historically extended, socially embodied argument, and an argument precisely in part about the goods which constitute that tradition."[105] When Reagan treats American history as a clearly defined set of actions with a clear and constant set of lessons to be applied to present action and future policy direction, he isolates his vision from historical reinterpretation and from current controversy. Reagan's consistency provides his audiences with a clear, simple, and familiar framework within which to encompass complex or unfamiliar problems. Yielding to this enticing vision can be dangerous, however, because the assumption of the story's truth hides its contingent nature and its implicit ideology. Adherence to a single story with a single point of view can make good judgment more difficult by reinforcing the legitimacy of a single set of social stereotypes and by promoting an exclusively American point of view on international problems.[106]

A related danger concerns the role of the public in Reagan's version of America's story. Relying on the (presumably) established moral code and the (presumably) accepted common sense of the American people to establish the legitimacy of the story implicitly denies the legitimacy of either change or challenge with the result that the story's participants are driven to a posture of passive acceptance.[107] Ironically, Reagan's story of an actively heroic American public forces those who accept it into the position of being listeners rather than creators. At most, the individual becomes a participant in a pre-established historical frame.

The application of narrative theory to Reagan's rhetoric also raises some broader questions regarding narrative and political judgment. Fisher's assertion of the moral superiority of the narrative paradigm[108] is not confirmed. Reagan's story-telling does emphasize moral argument and it does act as an explicit counter to technical elitism, but, as just noted, it may also damage public morality. This examination of Reagan's rhetoric suggests that Fisher's reliance on the Aristotelian dictum that "the 'people' have a natural tendency to prefer the true and the just"[109] may be a mystification that requires a more careful examination of the ways in which stories are accepted or rejected. Reagan has shown that powerful appeals can be made to popular belief and popular morality through the narrative form, but the acceptance of his story and the durability of his popularity also seem to show that there is a preference for clarity over complexity, for consistency over aberration, for positive direction over acceptance of limitations, and for self-justification by the derogation of one's enemies. Goods internal to the story need to be consistent with the moral judgment of the audience, and truths that are accepted within the story need to be consistent with the common sense of the audience, but it is not clear from examining this case in which narrative form is dominant that narrative is likely to provide a morality or truth that is superior to other forms of discourse or to combinations of other forms.

There are other disturbing problems as well. Despite identifying two "paradigms," Fisher assumes that rational and narrative modes of thinking are fundamentally compatible.[110] He argues that considerations of narrative fidelity can subsume the skills and requirements of logic. But this examination of Reagan's rhetoric and the responses to it suggests that the narrative and the rational perspectives can be distinctive and incommensurable. One need not claim that narrative is irrational to distinguish its characteristic form of rationality from that of the "rational world" paradigm. Having made the distinction between these two modes of thought clear, it becomes difficult to accept Fisher's conclusion that narrative offers a superior and fully encompassing alternative.[111]

Americans have listened to Ronald Reagan as President for almost a decade, usually with admiration, but often without agreement. Some have heard poor arguments and marveled at his ability to delude audiences; others have heard good stories and dismissed his errors as trivial. And while the Iran/*contra* crisis has diminished the credibility of Reagan's presidency, it has not altered the forms of understanding through which he is heard. Until the differences in judgment are identified as differences in perspective, there will be little ground for common discussion and little motivation for self-analysis.

NOTES

[1]Mary McGrory, ". . . and growls from the training camp," *Des Moines Register,* 6 September 1985, 12A. Paul Erickson begins his book on Reagan with the judgment that, "Ronald Reagan is by far the most persuasive speaker of our time." *Reagan Speaks* (New York: New York University Press, 1985), 1.

[2]"More Popular Than Ever," *Time,* 12 August 1985, 17.

[3]Sidney Blumenthal, "The Reagan Millennium," *New Republic,* 19 November 1984, 12.

[4]The books cover a range of policies and perspectives, some are explicitly political and were designed to influence election campaigns: Edmund G. Brown, *Reagan and Reality* (New York: Praeger, 1970); Brown and Bill Brown, *Reagan: the Political Chameleon* (New York: Praeger, 1976); Mark Green and Gail MacColl, *There He Goes Again: Ronald Reagan's Reign of Error* (New York: Pantheon Books, 1983). Others respond to specific issues: Robert Scheer, *With Enough Shovels: Reagan, Bush, and Nuclear War* (New York: Random House, 1982); Strobe Talbott, *Deadly Gambits: The Reagan Administration and the Stalemate in Nuclear Arms* (New York: Knopf, 1984); Fred Ackerman, *Reaganomics: Rhetoric vs. Reality* (Boston: South End Press, 1982); Joan Claybrook, *Retreat From Safety: Reagan's Attack on America's Health* (New York: Pantheon, 1984). Others attempt more thorough or scholarly appraisals of Reagan's statements and policies: Ronald Dallek, *Reagan: The Politics of Symbolism* (Cambridge: Harvard University Press, 1984); Ronnie Dugger, *On Reagan: The Man and his Presidency* (New York: McGraw-Hill, 1983).

[5]Dallek, 178.

[6]Dallek, viii.

[7]"Innocence Abroad," *The New Republic,* 3 June 1985, 7.

[8]Martin Medhurst, "Postponing the Social Agenda: Reagan's Strategy and Tactics," *Western Journal of Speech Communication* 48 (1984): 262–76; Henry Z. Scheele, "Ronald Reagan's 1980 Acceptance Address: A Focus on American Values," *Western Journal of Speech Communication* 48 (1984): 51–61; Bert E. Bradley, "Jefferson and Reagan: The Rhetoric of Two Inaugurals," *Southern Speech Communication Journal* 48 (1983): 119–36; Walter Fisher, "Romantic Democracy, Ronald Reagan, and Presidential Heroes," *Western Journal of Speech Communication* 46 (1982): 299–310.

[9]Richard L. Johannesen, "An Ethical Assessment of the Reagan Rhetoric, 1981–82," *Political Communication Yearbook 1984,* eds[.] Keith R. Sanders, Lynda Lee Kaid, and Dan Nimmo (Carbondale: Southern Illinois University Press, 1985), 226–41; C. Thomas Preston, Jr., "Reagan's 'New Beginning': Is it the 'New Deal' of the Eighties?" *Southern Speech Communication Journal* 49 (1984): 198–211; Gregg Phifer, "Two Inaugurals: A Second Look," *Southern Speech Communication Journal* 48 (1983): 378–85.

[10]David Zarefsky, Carol Miller-Tutzauer, and Frank E. Tutzauer, "Reagan's Safety Net for the Truly Needy: The Rhetorical Uses of Definition," *Central States Speech Journal* 35 (1984): 113–19; Richard E. Crable and Steven L. Vibbert, "Argumentative Stance and Political Faith Healing: 'The Dream Will Come True,[']" *Quarterly Journal of Speech* 69 (1983): 290–301. In his explanation of Reagan's approach to Soviet-American relations Robert L. Ivie found that "a flawed policy is being perceived as successful because of how it is symbolized." "Speaking 'Common Sense' About the Soviet Threat: Reagan's Rhetorical Stance," *Western Journal of Speech Communication* 48 (1984): 40. Sarah Russell Hankins concluded that "the presidential choice in 1980 was an attempt to align

the human with the illusion of the heroic." "Archetypal Alloy: Reagan's Rhetorical Image," *Central States Speech Journal* 34 (1983): 34. Similarly, Martha Anna Martin wrote that "the cumulative language, if not the reality, suggested that Carter was an 'unfit' leader." "Ideologues, Ideographs, and 'The Best Men': From Carter to Reagan," *Southern Speech Communication Journal* 49 (1983): 19. Gary C. Woodward makes a parallel claim about Reagan's populist appeal: "Populism has taken on a cosmetic and ironic purpose . . . pretending to serve the 'public interest', but serving what may be very private interests indeed." "Reagan as Roosevelt: The Elasticity of Pseudo-Populist Appeals," *Central States Speech Journal* 34 (1983): 57–8.

[11]Walter R. Fisher, "Narration as a Human Communication Paradigm: The Case of Public Moral Argument," *Communication Monographs* 51 (1984): 1–22.

[12]See Erickson, esp. chapter 3, "Analogies, Allegories, and Homilies," 32–50; David Stockman, *The Triumph of Politics* (New York: Harper & Row, 1986), 90.

[13]Martin Medhurst demonstrates the way in which Reagan employs the theme of America as a nation that was set apart, by God. As he notes, "the theme of a people set apart is . . . a standard topos of civil-religious discourse in America." Medhurst, 270. Both Erickson and Johannesen suggest that Reagan's rhetoric uses the form of the jeremiad and the substance of American civil religion. *Reagan Speaks,* 86–93; Richard Johannesen, "Ronald Reagan's Economic Jeremiad," *Central States Speech Journal,* forthcoming. Janice Hocker Rushing argues that "the mythic milieu of the ['Star Wars'] speech is the transformation of the Old West into the New Frontier." "Ronald Reagan's 'Star Wars' Address: Mythic Containment of Technical Reasoning," *Quarterly Journal of Speech* 72 (1986): 417. Perhaps the most notable development of this idea is Gary Wills, *Reagan's America* (New York: Doubleday, 1987).

[14]For example, in commenting on Reagan's arms negotiations in Iceland, Anthony Lewis wrote: "Ronald Reagan has never been more breathtaking as a politician than in the weeks since Reykjavik. He has pictured failure as success, black as white, incompetence as standing up to the Russians. And according to the polls, Americans love the performance." Quoted in Thomas Griffith, "Being Too Easy on Reagan," *Time,* 17 November 1986, 88.

[15]This has been evident particularly in the response of the press. A *Time* magazine editorial, for example, offered the following explanation: "A frustrated Washington press corps had felt itself ignored by a public that did not want to hear criticism of a popular President. But the sudden and steep decline in Reagan's popularity suggests that all along the public had recognized, in a man it admired, how casually he minded the store, and how willfully he could deny facts or distort them." Thomas Griffith, "Watergate: A Poor Parallel," *Time,* 29 December 1986, 57.

[16]As even the *Washington Post* conceded, "this president has given tens of millions of people in this country a feeling that safe, stable times are returned and that fundamental values they hold dear are back in vogue and unashamedly so" (January 22, 1985).

[17]Since the narrative logic of Reagan's story makes his actions in the arms deal difficult to explain, the dominant response has been to remove Reagan from the story either by suggesting that he had no control over the actions of his subordinates or by suggesting that Reagan himself had changed and questioning his mental or physical health.

[18]In his campaign speeches, Reagan told the story as a humorous example. In Milwaukee, for example, he said, "Our pledge is for tax simplification, to make the system more fair, to make it easier to understand. Do you know that Einstein has admitted he cannot understand the Form 1040? [*laughter*]." *Weekly Compilation of Presidential Documents* (hereafter, *WCPD*), 8 October 1985, 1381. In his speech to the nation he told the story in slightly different form: "We call it America's tax plan because it will reduce tax burdens on the working people of this country, close loopholes that benefit a privileged few, simplify a code so complex even Albert Einstein reportedly needed help on his 1040 Form, and lead us into a future of greater growth and opportunity for all." "Tax Reform," 28 May 1985, *WCPD*, 704.

[19]"A Debate on Religious Freedom," *Harper's*, October 1984, 15, 18.

[20]Rene Wellek and Austin Warren, *Theory of Literature* (New York: Harcourt, Brace, & World, 1956), 119.

[21]"Myth and Identity," in *Myth and Mythology*[,] ed. Gilbert Murray (1959; rpt. Boston: Beacon, 1968), 279.

[22]Reagan frequently refers to America as a nation "chosen by God." In the 1987 State of the Union Address, for example, Reagan said that "our nation could not have been conceived without divine help" and that "The United States Constitution . . . grew out of the most fundamental inspiration of our existence: that we are here to serve Him by living free." "The State of the Union," *WCPD*, 27 January 1987, 63, 64.

[23]In the 1985 State of the Union Address, for example, Reagan supports his confidence in American abilities by saying, "Two hundred years of American history should have taught us that nothing is impossible." "The State of the Union," *WCPD*, 6 February 1985, 146. Reagan's conception of the American experience closely parallels the "American monomyth" that Robert Jewett and John Shelton Lawrence have found pervading the productions of popular culture. *The American Monomyth* (Garden City, NY: Anchor Press/Doubleday, 1977), xx.

[24]All quotations from Reagan's Second Inaugural Address are from the "50th American Presidential Inaugural," *WCPD*, 21 January 1985, 67–70.

[25]In the 1985 State of the Union Address, Reagan said, "There are no constraints on the human mind, no walls around the human spirit, no barriers to our progress except those we ourselves erect." "The State of the Union," 141.

[26]All quotations are from "Inaugural Address," *Public Papers of the Presidents: Ronald Reagan*, 1981, (Washington, D.C.: GPO, 1982), 1–4.

[27]Reagan's language features particular actions and concrete situations that will be familiar to all Americans and that encourage most to see themselves in his description: "Those who say that we're in a time when there are no heroes, they just don't know where to look. You can see heroes every day going in and out of factory gates. Others, a handful in number, produce enough food to feed all of us and then the world beyond. You meet heroes across a counter, and they're on both sides of that counter. There are entrepreneurs with faith in themselves and faith in an idea who create new jobs, new wealth and opportunity. They're individuals and families whose taxes support the government and whose voluntary gifts support church, charity, culture, art, and education. Their patriotism is quiet, but deep. Their values sustain our national life." "Inaugural Address," 2.

[28]Unity of interests and goals is a major and continuing theme in Reagan's rhetoric. In welcoming the debate on tax reform, for example, he also stated that "it should not be a partisan debate for the authors of tax reform come from both parties, and all of us want greater fairness, incentives, and simplicity in taxation." "Tax Reform," *WCPD*, 28 May 1985, 707. In urging support for the contras in Nicaragua he quoted "Senator Scoop Jackson" as saying: "On matters of national security, the best politics is no politics." "Nicaragua," *WCPD*, 16 March 1986, 374. The quotation was also used in the 1986 State of the Union Address, *WCPD*, 4 February 1986, 139.

[29]"Every Region, Every Age Group, Almost Every Voting Bloc," *Time*, 19 November 1984, 45.

[30]For example, Edmund G. Brown classes Reagan's speeches with "the unreasoned attacks of simplistic self-servers who pander [to] the lowest urges that plague our troubled people," in Brown and Bill Brown, *Reagan: The Political Chameleon*, 8.

[31]Dugger, for example, charges that, "[Reagan] has long been allied with the most bellicose elements in the American military establishment; now he is using the power and glory the White House gives him to bring about . . . a mortally dangerous shift in U.S. nuclear strategy." *On Reagan*, xiv.

[32]Stanley Hoffman, "Semidetached Politics," *New York Review of Books*, 8 November 1984, 34–6.

[33]Reporters have repeatedly expressed their frustration with Reagan's "Teflon Presidency." For example, Tom Wicker, "A smile, a quip and no mud on his shoes . . ." *Kansas City Times,* 31 May 1984, A-18; Sidney Blumenthal, "Reagan the Unassailable," *New Republic,* 12 September 1983, 11–16.

[34]Martin, 21. She uses the phrase in a comparison of Reagan with Theodore Roosevelt.

[35]Hankins, 41.

[36]Fisher, "Romantic Democracy," 302.

[37]Fisher, "Romantic Democracy," 302.

[38]See, Bradley, "Jefferson and Reagan: The Rhetoric of Two Inaugurals"; Martin, 18–23; Woodward, 44–58.

[39]Martin, 22. Fisher reached an almost identical conclusion about Reagan's "manly" character: "Reagan's tough stands on America's military posture and his decisive views on domestic problems gave substance to the perception." "Romantic Democracy," 302.

[40]Martin, 15.

[41]This role matches the recurring character of the American hero in popular culture identified by Jewett and Lawrence in *The American Monomyth,* xx, 195–6.

[42]Christopher J. Matthews, "Your Host Ronald Reagan," *New Republic,* 26 March 1984, 15–18. Robert J. Kaiser, "Your Host of Hosts," *New York Review of Books,* 28 June 1984, 38–41. Hankins, 42: Reagan is "one step removed . . . we are content to have him play the part." Martin, 24: "Ironically, the media age had no Teddy Roosevelt to offer. Instead, the 1980's offered an actor whose identification was with pseudo-heroism as filtered through film of his ranch, his horses, possibly even his ability as a 'nice' guy to defeat the guy in the black hat (the Ayatollah and the Communists), Hollywood version."

[43]Illustrated most vividly in his reaction to the assassination attempt. Reactions of critics and admirers converge in an appreciation of Reagan's response after being shot. Fisher, "Romantic Democracy," 307–8; Kaiser, 39.

[44]For examples see below in the discussion of common sense.

[45]See Ivie for a discussion of Reagan's appeal to American "common sense" about the Soviet Union. Scheele documents Reagan's reliance on American values.

[46]Kaiser, 41. French sociologist Michael Crozier believes that Reagan's "soothing style" is a perfect fit for the country's "craving for normalcy." *The Trouble with America* (Berkeley: University of California Press, 1984), 57–60.

[47]"Inaugural Address," 20 January 1981, 3. For examples of Reagan's emphasis on the value of "peace" in his Acceptance Address at the 1980 Republican Convention, see Scheele, 56.

[48]Lou Cannon, Reagan (New York: G. P. Putnam's Sons, 1982) 281–2; Jack W. Germond and Jules Witcover, *Blue Smoke and Mirrors* (New York: Viking Press, 1981), 243, 224–5.

[49]See Rushing, n. 62.

[50]Robert L. Scott, "Narrative Theory and Communication Research," *Quarterly Journal of Speech* 70 (1984): 200.

[51]Fisher, "Narration," 4.

[52]Fisher, "Narration," 8.

[53]"The Narrativization Of Real Events," *On Narrative,* ed. W. J. T. Mitchell (Chicago: University of Chicago Press, 1981), 251.

[54]Paul Ricoeur, "The Narrative Function," *Hermeneutics and the Human Sciences,* ed. and trans. by John B. Thompson (Cambridge: Cambridge University Press, 1981), 289–96.

[55]W. Lance Bennett and Martha S. Feldman, *Reconstructing Reality in the Courtroom* (New Brunswick: Rutgers University Press, 1981), 33.

[56]Bennett and Feldman, 89.

[57]*The Uses of Enchantment* (New York: Vintage Books, 1976), 5.

[58]"Narrative Form as a Cognitive Instrument," in the *Writing of History*[,] ed. by R. H. Canary and Henry Kozicki (Madison: University of Wisconsin Press, 1978), 144.

[59]Mink, 148.

[60]Alasdair MacIntyre, *After Virtue,* 2nd ed. (Notre Dame: University of Notre Dame Press, 1981), 200.

[61]Fisher, 8.

[62]Reagan made the claim repeatedly in his campaign speeches, often adapting the particulars to the place where he was speaking. In one week, for example, he gave the Democrat's version of Vince Lombardi's famous statement about winning to an audience in Milwaukee ("They're saying, 'Tax increases aren't ever[y]thing. They're the only thing.'") and he re-defined "shrimp" for an audience in Gulfport, Mississippi ("To you, it's a livelihood; to them, it's your paycheck after they get their hands on it."). *WCPD,* 8 October 1984, 1380, 1405.

[63]Sidney Blumenthal suggests that attempts by the press to refute Reagan's errors have been largely ineffectual because Reagan's world view is based on a "unifying vision" which facts "can never fatally undermine." "Reagan the Unassailable," 14.

[64]Cannon, *Reagan,* 271–2.

[65]William Safire's assessment of Reagan's speeches at Bitburg and Bergen-Belsen demonstrates how the message of Reagan's general story was able to dominate doubts about the propriety of his particular actions: "In driving home the lessons of history, his incredible series of blunders turned out to be a blessing. . . . [H]e drew the central lesson clearly: 'that freedom must always be stronger than totalitarianism, that good must always be stronger than evil.'" "I am a Jew . . ." in *Bitburg in Moral and Political Perspective,* ed. Geoffrey H. Hartman (Bloomington: Indiana University Press, 1986), 212–13.

[66]*Time* emphasized the damage to Reagan's credibility: "it seems almost certain that whatever comes out of the many investigations now in progress, Reagan will emerge as a diminished President, his aura of invincibility shattered, his fabled luck vanished, his every policy regarded with new suspicion." "Who Was Betrayed," *Time,* 8 December 1986, 19.

[67]Significantly, exactly these charges were made against Reagan. See, for example, Benjamin Barber, "Celluloid Vistas: What the President's Dreams are Made Of," *Harper's,* July 1985, 74–5; Sidney Blumenthal, "The Reagan Millennium." *New Republic,* 19 November 1984, 12–14; Green and MacColl, 8–15.

[68]"The Narrativization of Real Events," 253.

[69]"Where, in any account of reality, narrative is present, we can be sure that morality or a moral impulse is present too." "The Value of Narrativity in the Representation of Reality," in Mitchell, 22. (Quoted approvingly by Fisher, "Narration," 10.)

[70]Fisher, "Narration," 12.

[71]*After Virtue,* chapter 15, "The Virtues, the Unity of a Human Life and the Concept of a Tradition," esp., 218.

[72]*Political Judgment* (Chicago: University of Chicago Press, 1983), 126.

[73]Beiner, 126.

[74]Jonathon Jacky, "The 'Star Wars' Defense Won't Compute," *Atlantic,* June 1985, 18–30.

[75]John Kessel notes that Reagan's aides are sensitive to these problems because his "optimism . . . often leads Reagan to overlook difficulties that bar the path to achievement." "The Structures of the Reagan White House," *American Journal of Political Science* 28 (1984): 233.

[76]"The State of the Union," 6 February 1985, 145.

[77]Reagan has used a similar strategy in dealing with the opposition to other issues as well. Theodore Windt and Kathleen Farrell, for example, came to the following conclusion about Reagan's support for his 1981 tax cut: "If the rhetoric took hold in the public consciousness, then anyone opposing him would be perceived as being unfair or as one willing to perpetuate waste and fraud to save some special interest program." "Presidential Rhetoric and Presidential Power: The Reagan Initiatives," *Essays in Presidential Rhetoric* (Dubuque, IA: Kendall/Hunt, 1983), 316.

[78]James Nathan Miller, "Ronald Reagan and the Techniques of Deception," *Atlantic,* February 1984, 64.

[79]Miller, 62.

[80]Quoted in Miller, 68.

[81]Mink emphasizes the cognitive element of the common understanding. White adds that the meaning of historical narrative also presumes a common base of moral legitimacy. "The Narrativization of Real Events" in Mitchell, 253.

[82]MacIntyre, "Epistemological Crises, Dramatic Narrative and the Philosophy of Science," *Monist* 60 (1977): 453–73; Fisher, 9–10.

[83]Clifford Geertz, "Common Sense as a Cultural System" in *Local Knowledge* (New York: Basic Books, 1983): 73–93; and MacIntyre, "Epistemological Crises," 453–54.

[84]"The Narrativization of Real Events" in Mitchell, 254.

[85]Ivie, "Speaking Common Sense"; Reagan's reliance on common sense has also been noted outside of the United States. In a conversation about Reagan between François Mitterand and Marguerite Duras, Mitterand says "He is a man of common sense" (10), and Duras says later "He governs less with his intellect than with common sense" (12). In "Mitterand and Duras on Reagan's America[,]" *Harper's*, August 1986, 10–14.

[86]Geertz identifies five "quasi-qualities" of common sense: naturalness, practicalness, thinness, immethodicalness, and accessibleness. "Common Sense as a Cultural System," 84–92.

[87]Some critics have taken this implication of his style to be a quality of Reagan's rhetoric. Edward Chester observed that, "when one encounters an address by Ronald Reagan, the appearance coincides with the reality." "Shadow or Substance?: Critiquing Reagan's Inaugural Address," in *Essays in Presidential Rhetoric*, 303.

[88]"Address to the Nation on the Economy," 5 February 1981, Public Papers, 79; "Address to the Nation on Defense and National Security," *WCPD*, 23 March 1983, 437; "Tax Reform," 705; "Meeting with Soviet General Secretary Gorbachev in Reykjavik, Iceland," *WCPD*, 13 October 1986, 1377.

[89]Inaugural Message, Governor of California, January 5, 1967. Quoted in "Reagan" by Lou Cannon, *The Pursuit of the Presidency*, 1980, ed. Richard Harwood (New York: Berkeley Books, 1980), 253.

[90]*Rhetoric*, 1410b.

[91]For example, Reagan concluded a major address on Soviet-American relations with a story that began as follows: "Just suppose with me for a minute that an Ivan and an Anya could find themselves, oh, say, in a waiting room or sharing shelter from the rain or a storm with a Jim and Sally." "Soviet-American Relations," *WCPD*, 16 January 1984, 44–5. International relations between two superpowers are represented by (reduced to?) the familiar circumstances of a chance meeting between two couples and we discover (as common sense always confirms) that people are pretty much the same everywhere.

[92]"Acceptance Speech by Governor Ronald Reagan, Republican National Convention, Detroit, Michigan, July 17, 1980," in *The Pursuit of the Presidency*, 1980, 419–20.

[93]"Address to the Nation on the Economy," 5 February 1981, 81.

[94]"Nicaragua," *WCPD*, 16 March 1986, 371, 373.

[95]"Address to the Nation on the Economy," 83.

[96]This assumption is so clear that the beliefs often need not even be stated. As Richard Allen, Reagan's former national security advisor, wrote: "Ronald Reagan may no longer say that communists lie and cheat, but he believes that they do—and so does the rest of informed mankind." Quoted in "Damage-Control Diplomacy," *Newsweek*, 7 February 1983, 27.

[97]*WCPD*, 23 March 1983, 437, 438, 440, 442.

[98]Geertz, 85; Mink, 129.

[99]Cannon, "Reagan," *Pursuit*, 270. "Reagan consistently has confounded those who have underestimated him. There is a kind of small-town common sense about him that serves him well and shows in moments when it is least expected" (270).

[100]In the 1980 campaign, Carter's "intelligence" was subordinated to Reagan's "good sense." The fact that he knew more than Reagan became a liability when the perception

grew that "his particular brand of 'intelligence' was more suitable to the world of academic test-taking than to the pragmatic world of presidential decision-making." Martin, 15.

[101]"Mondale Accepts Presidential Nomination," *Congressional Quarterly,* 21 July 1984, 12–14.

[102]"Fiscal Year 1986 Budget," *WCPD,* 2 February 1985, 117–8; "Overhauling the Tax System," *WCPD,* 28 May 1985, 703–707; "The State of the Union," *WCPD,* 4 February 1986, 136–7; "The State of the Union," 1987.

[103]". . . we must take further steps to permanently control government's power to tax and spend. We must act now to protect future generations from government's desire to spend its citizens' money and tax them into servitude when the bills come due." "50th Presidential Inaugural," 21 January 1985, 68. The natural tendency of government expansion is a continuing theme in Reagan's rhetoric. See, for example, his "Address to the Nation on the Economy" delivered in his first year as President: ". . . government—any government—has a built-in tendency to grow." 5 February 1981, *Public Papers,* 80.

[104]Just one month after the initial revelations, *Time* reported: "A *New York Times*/CBS poll last week showed the President's approval rating plunging 21 points in the past four weeks, from 67% to 46%. That is the most dramatic one-month drop since presidential opinion polls began 50 years ago. The survey found that 53% of the voters think Reagan knew money from the Iranian arms sale was going to help the *contras,* even though the President insists that he did not." "Under Heavy Fire," *Time,* 15 December 1986, 21–22. A *Newsweek* report on Reagan's 1987 State of the Union speech, for example, offered the following general (and typical) assessment of the effect of the Iran/*contra* affair on public perception: "It didn't add up to a sudden crisis, but somehow he seemed on the edge of irrelevance." "Going Nowhere Fast," *Newsweek,* 9 February 1987, 24. See, James Reston, "Reagan administration already being spoken of in the past tense," *Des Moines Register,* 24 February 1987, 6A.

[105]*After Virtue,* 222.

[106]Stanley Hoffman, for example, worries that national pride may be manifest in "self-righteousness and a sense of moral superiority" and that Reagan's rhetoric may have encouraged "a desire not to be bothered or battered by data." "Semidetached Politics," 36. Similarly, George Ball has expressed concerns about the lack of consideration of the effects of "Star Wars" program in other parts of the world. "The War for Star Wars," *New York Review of Books,* 11 April 1985, 41.

[107]Janet Rushing found a similar result in her examination of Reagan's "Star Wars" address: "Reagan's 'Star Wars' address cuts off its auditors as effectively and completely as if it were couched in the most convoluted esoterica." Rushing, 428. Our explanations differ, however. While she attributes the audience's acquiescence to the important role of "technoscience" in that issue, this analysis suggests that the passivity of Reagan's auditors is a concomitant of his narrative form and is not a reaction to technical discourse or limited to technical issues.

[108]See Fisher's discussion of the responses to Jonathan Schell's *The Fate of the Earth,* "Narration," 11–15.

[109]Fisher, "Narration," 9.

[110]The assumption is expressed repeatedly in Fisher's first article on the narrative paradigm: "The narrative paradigm does not deny reason and rationality; it reconstitutes them, making them amenable to all forms of human communication" (2); "In truth, . . . the narrative paradigm . . . does not so much deny what has gone before as it subsumes it" (3); "when narration is taken as the master metaphor, it subsumes the others" (6); "Both forms . . . are modes for expressing good reasons—given the narrative paradigm—so the differences between them are structural rather than substantive" (15).

[111]Fisher's assertion of the universality of the narrative paradigm is clearest in "The Narrative Paradigm: An Elaboration," *Communication Monographs* 52 (1985): 347–67.

Fisher's reading of the contemporary social scientific and humanistic literature confirms his opening observation that "there is no genre, including technical communication, that is not an episode in the story of life (a part of the 'conversation') and is not itself constituted by *logos* and *mythos.* . . . Put another way: Technical discourse is imbued with myth and metaphor, and aesthetic discourse has cognitive capacity and import" (347). All of the theorists and philosophers that he considers are found to be helpful (in greater or lesser measure) in confirming Fisher's thesis. The extent to which important differences in background, perspective, and assumptions are glossed, however, suggests that Fisher may be demonstrating how these approaches can be viewed from within the narrative perspective rather than establishing the dominance or universality of this "metaparadigm" (347).

FROM POST-9/11 MELODRAMA
TO QUAGMIRE IN IRAQ: A RHETORICAL HISTORY

HERBERT W. SIMONS

For most Americans the 9/11 bombings were a tragedy; for neoconservatives bent on invading Iraq they were also an opportunity, providing what David Zarefsky calls a *kairotic* moment. The administration's rhetoric fueled and channeled the fury already aroused by the attacks themselves. As both Robert L. Ivie and Carol Winkler maintain in this issue, the president's hype was not unlike the rhetoric of past presidents responding to past crises. President Bush was right when he said that 9/11 was a turning point in American history. Given that history, given the shock and severity of the attacks, given America's distinctive position as the world's sole surviving superpower, given the political advantages to the president of meeting fire with rhetorical fire, the administration's vitriolic response was surely understandable. We may ultimately conclude that it was also regrettable.

As Sue Lockett John and colleagues and Ivie observe, the president's post-9/11 rhetoric provided the basic melodramatic binaries in terms of which the "war on terror" was launched and then morphed into the war in Iraq. Its short-term effectiveness conferred enormous power upon the president, which he has been able to use not just to persuade, but also to intimidate, coerce, and control. Periodic reminders of 9/11 have served as well to trump concerns about usurpations of power by the Bush administration and to override criticisms even by appointed commissions and counterterrorism experts. In the weeks and months following 9/11, Americans were particularly vulnerable to projections of future threats from Middle East pariahs, however ill-founded and unsubstantiated the claims.

From the outset, it seemed, consideration of invading Iraq occasioned more debate than usual. This debate, said George Packer, was because it was a war of choice, without any visible evidence of an imminent threat to America or the United Kingdom from Iraq.[1] In addition to the war of words, verbal battles have also been fought over words about words—disputes over whose words were "mere rhetoric" and whose were credible, over who said what when and with what ulterior motives, over what should have been said but wasn't, and over meanings of politically sensitive words like *democracy, patriotism, terrorism,* and *torture.*[2] Along with the words and words about words have been the stark and unforgettable television images of violence, themselves powerful influences but also fought over rhetorically as evidence for this or that claim about the war.[3]

Rhetorical analysis serves importantly as a vehicle for understanding rhetorical choices and the strategic considerations giving rise to them. It helps explain why, for example, in the immediate wake of the 9/11 bombings, the administration chose to evade the hard questions of motivation for the attacks and to respond instead with a sanitized, melodramatic framing of the crisis, coupled with the launch of a vaguely defined, seemingly unlimited "war on terror." It also helps to explain why the press, the Democrats, and the Republicans in Congress deferred to the administration, adding their own exaggerations, evasions, and outright distortions to those of the administration in the aftermath of 9/11, and how the rhetoric of antiterrorism led from the Trade Towers and the Pentagon to the bombings of Baghdad. The still-troubled occupation of Iraq provides further evidence that what worked rhetorically in the short run has been a source of subsequent difficulties.

The case for invading Iraq had been made ever since the Gulf War ended in 1991 with Saddam Hussein still in power,[4] but it took a giant leap forward ten years later with the 9/11 attacks. Active discussion took place shortly after the attacks in Secretary of Defense Donald Rumsfeld's war council about using the terrorism in building a case for removing Saddam Hussein's regime from power.[5] A major television speech by the president to the Congress on September 20, 2001, was a step in that direction.[6] There he framed the 9/11 attacks as an assault on America's sacred virtues of freedom and democracy and launched his "war on terror." In the wake of 9/11, the news media spoke as one in their condemnation of the attacks and in support of the president, helping send his approval ratings from below 50 percent before 9/11 to nearly 90 percent, a record high, after September 20.[7]

The 9/11 attacks and the melodramatic crisis rhetoric that followed in their wake made the invasion of Iraq politically feasible. No sooner had the president completed his televised "Address to the Congress" on 9/20 than the pundits joined as one in concluding that the president had demonstrated extraordinary leadership ability.[8] Threat-induced crisis rhetoric routinely has that effect. Says Denise M. Bostdorff, who has studied the genre, it has enabled American presidents to show leadership, grab headlines, exhibit toughness, and demand unity. It also gains them policy support on unrelated issues, increases their party's electoral power, accrues symbolic reserves, and helps them weather untidy endings.[9] Crisis rhetoric, says Elisabeth Anker, is often melodramatic, presenting conflict in the simplistic terms of pure good versus pure evil.[10] The events of 9/11 in particular seemed to cry out for a hyperbolic, decontextualized account of what had occurred, akin to cowboy westerns and children's fables.

The two-dimensional characters of fictional melodrama and the use of exaggeration and polarization for dramatic effect find their way into political crisis rhetoric by way of a valorized "us" and a dehumanized or demonized "them."[11] Victims, villains, and heroes are joined together in a sanitized narrative, shorn of moral complexity. "We" have an urgent mission to perform. We must act, not just out of fear but from a clear sense of moral purpose. Good must triumph, and good will triumph, but victory will not be easy. The enemy is wily, clever, and will stop at nothing. It has already threatened (or victimized) us. By some accounts, this danger may justify borrowing a page from their book while exempting ourselves from moral standards that we impose upon others.[12] After all, God is on our side, Satan (or his equivalent) on theirs.[13] These narrative components may be crosscultural and transhistorical; they are by no means confined to contemporary American militarists. Yet the themes run deep in the American psyche,[14] and are daily reinforced in American popular culture.[15] They also fit well with President Bush's persona as religious warrior, a Texas-styled sheriff in a Hollywood western who has been called upon by God to make the world a better place.[16] While the president's rhetorical response to 9/11 on September 20, 2001, was uniquely adapted to his ends, audiences, and circumstances, his speechwriters were able to craft much of the address before policy was set, merely by adhering to scriptlike, scripturelike melodramatic formulas.[17]

True to form, the Bush narrative presented a stripped-down account of how the 9/11 attacks came to be that left no room for moral ambiguity, or for criticism. Bush constructed America as a nation unified by an attack on nothing less than its sacred virtues of freedom and democracy, said Anker, a country whose victimage therefore entitled it to "enact heroic retribution on the evil forces that caused its injury."[18]

With polar oppositions such as these, the administration rallied the American people and reassured them, while also serving notice to the rest of the world of America's unmistakable resolve. Doing anything less at the time might well have seemed heretical. And from the Bush administration's perspective, its melodramatic rhetoric also had the virtue of cowing potential critics while equipping its legions of supporters and spokespersons with a simple, easily repeatable message. Introducing complexity was discouraged. Merely inviting discussion of why American foreign policies were widely disliked in the Arab and Muslim worlds became "playing their game." Yet these same polarities would ultimately be undermined by stubborn realities on the ground in Iraq and by inconsistencies between Bush administration rhetoric and its practices elsewhere in the world.

THE RUN-UP TO INVASION

Building on its melodramatic construction of the threat confronting the United States, the Bush administration launched its open-ended, vaguely stated "war on terror." A chief virtue of its vagaries was its rhetorical adaptability. The antiterror campaign began with assaults on the Taliban and al Qaeda in Afghanistan coupled with swift passage of legislation designed to fortify the military and to increase national security. At this time it was difficult if not impossible to challenge even such draconian measures as unlimited prison detentions of enemy suspects without court hearings. Periodic reminders of 9/11 served to trump concerns about usurpations of power by the Bush administration and to override criticisms even by appointed commissions and counterterrorism experts. The 9/11 attacks and the crisis rhetoric that followed in their wake enabled the administration to gain control over the terms and limits of permissible debate.

Much of the rest of this story is well known, but new light can be shed by retelling it from a rhetorical perspective.[19] Emboldened by his success, the president chose in January 2002 to extend the reach of his rhetoric to what he called, in his State of the Union message, the "Axis of Evil." Iraq was earmarked as a possible target of U.S. military might, along with Iran and North Korea. Months after 9/11 Americans remained highly vulnerable to insinuations of possible connections between Saddam Hussein and Osama bin Laden. For millions of Americans innuendo sufficed as a substitute for proof.

By August 2002 a full-scale campaign to win support for invading Iraq and deposing Saddam Hussein's Baathist regime had begun. It comported with the long-standing ambitions of a group of influential neoconservatives as part of a larger plan to exert America's will in the Middle East. The Bush administration chose its public rationales for invasion carefully. In a major speech by the president on October 7, Saddam was said to possess weapons of mass destruction (WMD) and the means to deploy them. It was also suggested that he had secret links to al Qaeda, and may have had something to do with the 9/11 attacks. Later these allegations were to be severely undermined, but not before the Republicans scored heavily in the November 2002 midterm elections. The Bush administration clung stubbornly to these rationales in the face of troubling counterindicators, even to the point of incurring the wrath of traditional allies when, in March 2003, it declared its intention to intervene militarily in Iraq in the absence of a UN Security Council mandate.

Thus did the administration's post-9/11 crisis rhetoric morph into its case for war with Iraq. In subsequent speeches Bush would continue to capitalize on the appeal of his antiterrorist rhetoric, finding new enemies and new rationales for aggressive action.[20] Iraq was now but a "battle" in the larger war on terrorism. A flow of resistance fighters into Iraq to lend assistance to its homegrown insurgents lent self-fulfilling evidence that the American-led effort to "liberate" Iraq was truly critical to the larger antiterrorist struggle.

One indication of the president's increased power was the willingness of the mainstream news media to put aside doubts and help make the administration's case for war. This compliance continued through to the "liberation" of Iraq in May 2003. A tragic consequence of that complicity was America's failure to prepare adequately for the occupation of Iraq. Another was the failure of editorialists, commentators, columnists, and the like to weigh in candidly on possible motives for the U.S.-led intervention or on its long-term consequences. Once the war commenced, Fox News demonstrated beyond doubt to rivals like CNN and MSNBC the pulling power of unabashed jingoism.[21]

INVASION AND BEYOND

U.S. troops went into Baghdad expecting to be greeted as liberators.[22] They soon learned that they were unwelcome occupiers. Yet the administration's "war on terror" has displayed great resilience, the Bush administration demonstrating great skill at fending off criticism while repeatedly invoking 9/11 as an emblematic reminder of the need for steadfast vigilance. A stunning example of that resilience was the Bush administration's ability to survive high-level exposures of pre-9/11 ineptness at preventing the 9/11 attacks. Yet another indicator of resilience was the administration's ability to roll with the punches over 9/11-related news from elsewhere in the world, including, for example, the mysterious disappearance from Tora Bora in Afghanistan of Osama bin Laden, and his subsequent appearances on Arab TV. Still another example has been the occupation, at human and economic costs to Americans and Iraqis alike, reminiscent of Vietnam. Despite these problems the Bush administration managed in fall 2004 to maintain public support for "staying the course" in Iraq and to triumph over the Democrats in the 2004 elections.

Gradually, however, the narrative began to unravel. And while not all of the problems can be laid at the feet of rhetoric, it appears that the Bush administration increasingly fell victim to its own desperate efforts to prop up the case for war, offering, for example, overly optimistic projections for success in Iraq based on spurious statistics, denying high-level authorization for the use of torture while at the same time calling for exemptions to the Geneva Convention's strictures against torture, and efforts to discredit former acting ambassador to Iraq, Joseph Wilson, who had been a vociferous critic of some of the administration's earlier intelligence claims.

Increasingly over time the threads in the narrative linking the war on terror to the war in Iraq wore thin. What did Iraq have to do with the bombings of the Trade Towers and the Pentagon, asked Security Council members even before the invasion? Why not go after corrupt and autocratic Saudi Arabia, from which not just the hijackers had come but also the insane form of jihad that Saudi extremists had helped export to the rest of the Muslim world? Why, asked the Spanish after Madrid was terrorized by an al Qaeda–type attack, must we keep troops in Iraq in order to prevent further such attacks on our territory? By remaining in Iraq, aren't we creating more terrorists than we are killing or imprisoning?

Troublesome questions such as these continued to plague the Bush administration. They included questions of mission in Iraq, of who our friends and enemies were, of why the Sunni Arab world continued to support the Iraqi resistance, and of whether, by turning political power over to the Iraqi Shiites, the United States was playing into the hands of Islamic extremists, including its long-standing enemies in Iran.

Once having invaded and occupied, it was of course impolitic simply to turn back, or to confess wrongdoing. The decision to invade and the decisions made in the course of the occupation created other rhetorical dilemmas, not least tensions between the need to appear consistent and the need for flexibility, the need to appear credible and the need to dissemble. Dilemmas such as these bedevil political leaders. Routinely advised to stay on message, they are also criticized for sticking with failed messages. Damned if they seem evasive, they are ridiculed if their self-disclosures become self-damning. Honesty and openness are regarded as qualifications for office by a trusting public, but political leaders are often obliged to cover over narrow self-interest with the fig leaf of morality and the aura of sincerity.

Neither is it always possible to satisfy competing interests simultaneously, or to reconcile conflicting interests. Consider the paradoxes, for example, of "liberating" Iraq by way of a "shock and awe" aerial bombardment, and of ordering its people to become "free" by way of an America-imposed electoral process. Imposing one's will on a people while also trying to win their hearts and minds has been a perennial problem ever since the United States invaded and occupied Iraq.

One year after President Bush's reelection, polls indicated that Americans had become disenchanted with the war—no longer willing to reward its congressional supporters and punish its critics as they did in the 2002 elections; no longer eager to cheer on the president, as they did when he stood aboard the carrier *U.S.S. Abraham Lincoln* to proclaim "Mission accomplished" in Iraq; not sure whether to place much stock in the transfer of political power under way in Iraq; not certain, even, whether American troops should remain in Iraq, with whatever consequences that might entail.

As this is written it is too early to know whether the present instability in Iraq will persist and even get worse. However there is little doubt but that the Bush administration was unprepared for the aftermath of the Iraq invasion, including the strength of the Sunni Arab resistance and the developing civil war. The United States continued to be incapable of reconciling its ongoing mythic crisis narrative with real-world constraints. Outside the United States its sanitized version of "why they hate us" was generally not believed. Nor was the president credible when he declared (repeatedly) that our aim in Iraq was to stop "terror" in its tracks—before it could return to the United States. Not until after the 2004 elections did the president acknowledge that the Iraq insurgency was mostly homegrown. As the United States attempted to reach out to Arabs and Muslims by way of "public diplomacy" campaigns in the Middle East and declarations of intent to bring peace, freedom, and democracy to that troubled region, its efforts fell afoul of its continuing alliances with Arab dictatorships, its tilt toward Israel in the Israeli-Palestinian conflict, and its own record of human rights violations in Iraq and Afghanistan, including killings of innocents, illegal detentions of Muslim suspects, and widespread prison abuses.

This is not to say that the Democrats were in a better position to fix in Iraq what the Bush administration had broken. President Bush's electoral success in 2004 was as much a function of Democrats' failures, due in large measure to their rhetorical dilemmas. Critics of the war were in the unenviable position of appearing to welcome bad news from Iraq—either that or to mute their opposition by focusing on means rather than ends. The nomination of John Kerry over Howard Dean was regarded initially as an opportunity for the Democrats to adopt a centrist stance on the war, and even to "out-hawk" the Bush administration on a number of issues, such as the alleged failure of the Defense Department to supply U.S. troops with sufficient armor to conduct its rightful mission. But the Republicans managed to reframe that attempted centrism as flip-flopping. In general, the Republicans proved themselves masterful at rendering as treasonable, or at least unpatriotic, any criticisms that cut to the heart of their own overblown rhetoric.

But beating back the Democrats in 2004 proved a lot easier than overcoming the wrath of ordinary Americans, increasing numbers of whom were expressing disillusionment with the war in Iraq and demanding a pullout or significant cutbacks of American troops. From time to time since the occupation began, news of hopeful developments—the transfer of political power to Iraqis, signs of economic redevelopment in Iraq, and the planned replacement of American troops by Iraqi soldiers and police—had seemed to give renewed meaning to the invasion. But the president's options became increasingly limited.

LESSONS LEARNED

Looking back on the praise bestowed upon President Bush for his melodramatic framing of the threat to America made manifest on 9/11, it seems that the conventional standards for judging crisis rhetoric of this kind need rethinking. Opinion polls at the time confirmed expert judgments that his speech of September 20, 2001, had been highly effective on its target audiences. But findings such as these provide scant indication of the long-term consequences of an important speech. What works in the short run often fails over the long term. What meets immediate expectations often fails to take into account what in retrospect were the needs of the moment. What persuades targeted audiences may have deleterious effects on unintended audiences, including potential recruits for the Jihadists' cause.[23] What led journalists and politicians at the time to pronounce unequivocally favorable judgments may have concealed privately held doubts and suspicions. And too, there is the danger that those who crafted or delivered the important speech may get carried away by their own rhetoric.

We should be wary, then, of crisis rhetoric constructed on simplistic melodramatic binaries. We should be wary too of cultural predispositions toward assuming our inherent moral superiority. To the extent that these assumptions are fed by the news and entertainment media, or by our schools and places of worship, they too need critical scrutiny. This is not to say that moral outrage is never justified or that the world's sole remaining superpower can dispense altogether with its outrage melodramatically in response to attacks like those on 9/11. But that rhetoric needs to make room for alternatives between war and capitulation. In retrospect, President Bush's post-9/11 rhetoric served his own good (for a while) but not the nation's good. Realism dictated a more modulated response to the attacks, if not in their immediate wake, then shortly thereafter.

As the Bush administration floundered in Iraq, a turn away from melodramatic binaries seemed all the more urgent. The condition known as quagmire, or situational entrapment, is marked by dilemmas of a sort that seem at once unendurable and unsolvable. A striking example as of this writing: the presence of U.S. troops in Iraq appeared essential for purposes of preventing civil war but served also to fuel the Iraq insurgency and the larger Jihadist movement. What to do?

I do not pretend to know how quagmire can be avoided, but it does seem, as of this writing, that the time for melodrama is long past. A cooler rhetoric is surely needed, whether by the Bush administration or one that succeeds it. Such a rhetoric must exhibit greater respect for differences, greater openness to compromise and inclusion in the evolving political process, and a greater willingness to address fundamental problems that virtually guarantee continued strife. These problems include U.S. support for repressive regimes in the Middle East and elsewhere in the world that make a mockery of its self-declared commitments to freedom and democracy.

It is possible too that sheer exhaustion with continuous armed struggle will drive the opposing factions in Iraq toward a U.S.-brokered peace agreement, one that includes plans for redevelopment of infrastructure and equitable redistribution of resources. It is even conceivable that the Bush administration, or one of its successors, will come to appreciate the value of America's "soft power," its powers of attraction and alliance-building, as opposed to its current inclination to bully others by use of punitive "hard power."[24] When that happens we may discover that those whom we count as our worst enemies will prefer to talk with us rather than terrorize us. Rhetoric, said Kenneth Burke, is an advantage-seeking activity, but we should not forget that the benefits it reaps for us need not disadvantage others; the benefits may instead be mutually advantageous.[25]

More realistically, it appears that we and our enemies will be locked into conflicts that are mutually destructive for some time to come. Rhetoric will have had a role to play in that outcome as well.

NOTES

[1]See George Packer, *The Assassin's Gate: America in Iraq* (New York: Farrar, Strauss and Giroux, 2005).

[2]See for example Daniel Okrent, "The War of the Words: A Dispatch from the Front Lines," *New York Times*, March 6, 2005, 12.

[3]Robert L. Ivie, *Democracy and the War on Terror* (Tuscaloosa: University of Alabama Press, 2005).

[4]For an excellent account of how 9/11 played to the interests of neocons and of others in and close to the Bush administration who had long campaigned for forceful removal of Saddam Hussein and his Baathist regime, see Packer, *The Assassin's Gate*, chaps. 1–4. See also James Mann, *Rise of the Vulcans: The History of Bush's War Cabinet*

(New York: Viking Books, 2004). On the horrors perpetrated by Saddam Hussein and his regime, see Con Coughlin, *Saddam: His Rise and Fall* (New York: Harper, 2004).

[5]See Packer, *The Assassin's Gate,* 40–41. According to Packer, history began anew for George W. Bush on 9/11, and made him newly receptive to a national security staff already predisposed toward regime change in Iraq. Apparently it was an easy sell.

[6]See http://www.cnn.com/2001/US/09/20/gen.bush.transcript/.

[7]Following the 9/11 attacks, President Bush enjoyed the highest presidential approval ratings in recorded history, upwards of 90 percent. See Stephen F. Frantzich, "September 11th and the Bush Presidency: Rally-Round-the-Rubble," *White House Studies* (Spring 2004): 1–3.

[8]Media reactions were overwhelmingly positive. See Packer, *The Assassin's Gate,* chap. 2.

[9]Denise M. Bostdorff, *The Presidency and the Rhetoric of Foreign Crisis* (Columbia: University of South Carolina Press, 1994).

[10]See Elisabeth Anker, "Villains, Victims, and Heroes: Melodrama, Media, and September 11th," *Journal of Communication* 55 (2005): 22–37; Elisabeth Anker, "From Politics to Evil: Melodrama and State Politics," *eScholarship Repository* (Berkeley: Institute of Government Studies, 2005) at http://repositories.cdlib.org/igs/WP2005–1. That which is subsumed by Anker under the heading of melodramatic discourse or melodramatic narrative finds expression by other names: e.g., agonistic rhetoric, binary discourse, political fundamentalism, prophetic dualism, crisis rhetoric, or simply domestic war propaganda. See for example David Domke, *God Willing: Political Fundamentalism in the White House* (London: Pluto Press, 2004). On binary discourse, see Kevin Coe, David Domke, Erica S. Graham, Sue Lockett John, and Victor W. Pickard, "No Shades of Gray: The Binary Discourse of George W. Bush and an Echoing Press," *Journal of Communication* 54 (2004): 234–52. See Bostdorff, *The Presidency and the Rhetoric of Foreign Crisis,* on crisis rhetoric. On prophetic dualism, see Philip Wander, "The Rhetoric of American Foreign Policy," *Quarterly Journal of Speech* 70 (1984): 339–61. On domestic propaganda and agonistic discourse, see James J. Kimble, "'Whither Propaganda?' Agonism and the 'Engineering of Dissent,'" *Quarterly Journal of Speech* 91 (2005): 201–18.

[11]See Anker, "From Politics to Evil"; Domke, *God Willing;* Kimble, "'Whither Propaganda?'"

[12]Chris Hedges, *War Is a Force That Gives Us Meaning* (New York: Anchor Books, 2003).

[13]On American exceptionalism, see Dan Nimmo and James E. Combs, *Subliminal Politics: Myths and Mythmakers in America* (Englewood Cliffs, NJ: Prentice Hall, 1980). See also Denise M. Bostdorff, "George W. Bush's Post–September 11 Rhetoric of Covenant Renewal: Upholding the Faith of the Greatest Generation," *Quarterly Journal of Speech* 89 (2003): 293–319.

[14]See, for example, Andrew J. Bacevich, *The New American Militarism: How Americans Are Seduced by War* (New York: Oxford University Press, 2005); Kimble, "'Whither Propaganda?'"; and Bostdorff, "George W. Bush's Post–September 11 Rhetoric."

[15]Several essays in Lee Artz and Yahya R. Kamilipour's *Bring 'Em On: Media and Politics in the Iraq War* (Lanham, MD: Rowman and Littlefield, 2005) speak to this point. See especially Tanja Thomas and Fabian Virchow's "Banal Militarism and the Culture of War." See also Michael Billig's *Banal Nationalism* (London: Sage, 1995) for its astute analysis of how nationalism insinuates itself into British and American culture in subtle, barely noticeable ways.

[16]Gone from modern-day political melodramas are the grandiose gestures and stirring music that marked old-fashioned morality plays, but they have been more than adequately replaced by television's capacity to bring heart-rending documentary footage and diatribe directly into the home.

[17]See, for example, D. T. Max's excellent account of the crafting of the September 20 address: "The Making of the Speech," *New York Times Magazine,* October 7, 2001.

[18]Anker, "From Politics to Evil," 4.

[19]Of particular interest to me as a rhetorician were the Bush administration's uses of deception short of outright lying in making the case for war; also its ability to "pre-persuade," as Pratkanis and Aronson put it, by their influence and/or control of the terms and conditions of debate. This included, for example, gaining widespread acceptance of the assumption that skeptics and naysayers had the burden of proof in showing that Saddam *didn't* possess hidden weapons of mass destruction. See A. Pratkanis and E. Aronson, *Age of Propaganda* (New York: Freeman, 2000). In this special issue see especially the essays by Jamieson and Zarefsky.

[20]Mark Danner, *The Secret Way to War: The Downing Street Memo and the Iraq War's Buried History* (New York: New York Review of Books, 2006).

[21]See for example Sheldon Rampton and John Stauber, *The Best War Ever: Lies, Damned Lies, and the Mess in Iraq* (New York: Tarcher/Penguin, 2006).

[22]But see Sheldon Rampton and John Stauber's *Weapons of Mass Deception* (New York: Tarcher/Penguin, 2003) on Iraqi perceptions of the American-assisted toppling of Saddam's statue.

[23]See Danner, *The Secret Way to War*; also Daniel Benjamin and Steven Simon, *The Next Attack: The Failure of the War on Terror and a Strategy for Getting It Right* (New York: New York Times Books, 2005).

[24]See Joseph Nye's *Soft Power: The Means to Success in World Politics* (New York: Public Affairs, 2004).

[25]Kenneth Burke, *A Grammar of Motives* (Berkeley: University of California Press, 1969).

Chapter VI

Metaphoric Criticism

Metaphoric criticism is not a unified method; rather, it is a perspective that places metaphors at the heart of rhetorical action. Neo-classical criticism analyzes metaphors as part of the classical canon of style. The metaphoric critic, however, believes metaphors are more than superficial ornamentation: they are the means by which arguments are expressed. Moreover, metaphors may provide insight into a speaker's motives or an audience's social reality. A central metaphor may be the controlling persuasive element in a particular text. The metaphoric critic focuses on describing, evaluating, and understanding such metaphors as vital rhetorical phenomena. The articles in this chapter illustrate some of the diverse approaches a metaphoric critic might employ.

Michael Osborn's 1967 essay, "Archetypal Metaphor in Rhetoric: The Light-Dark Family," focuses on familiar metaphors that recur across time and in different cultures. These metaphors are grounded in human experience, embody motives, and often occur at crucial junctures in a speech. Osborn argues that a speaker's use of an archetypal metaphor has a high probability of affecting audience members. In this essay, Osborn explores the persuasive potentialities of the light-dark metaphor.

Robert L. Ivie's 1987 essay "Metaphor and the Rhetorical Invention of Cold War 'Idealists'" demonstrates the centrality of metaphors to the rhetoric of three Cold War opponents: Henry Wallace, J. William Fulbright, and Helen Caldicott. According to Ivie, each rhetor used different metaphoric clusters to oppose the prevailing view that the Soviet Union was a savage enemy. Analyzing the controlling metaphors of these speakers provides insights into their failures. Ivie suggests that different metaphors might have resulted in a different persuasive outcome for the Cold War era. In addition, this essay explains how a critic might isolate and analyze key metaphors from a movement or historical period.

Michael L. Butterworth's 2007 essay "The Politics of the Pitch: Claiming and Contesting Democracy through the Iraqi National Soccer Team" focuses on the "reciprocal metaphors of sport and war." In the author's analysis, "George W. Bush turned to international soccer to construct a metaphor of democratic triumph in the midst of his 'war on terrorism'" by presenting the Iraqi national soccer team as "a metaphorical embodiment of the war in Iraq" during the 2004 presidential election campaign. When the team did well at the Olympics, the war seemed justified, initially, as a "mission of liberation." However, many Iraqi team members resented the U.S. occupation of their homeland and the president's attempted symbolism. Butterworth considers the schism between the ideals of democracy and its actual practice, and concludes that Bush's rhetorical efforts failed to foster democracy in either Iraq or the United States.

ARCHETYPAL METAPHOR IN RHETORIC: THE LIGHT-DARK FAMILY

MICHAEL OSBORN

This study probes the possibilities of one form of "new criticism" occasionally mentioned by critics of rhetorical criticism—the idea that a fresh and sensitive look at the figurative language of a speech, focusing especially upon its metaphors, might yield a critical product rich and useful as some similar ventures in literary criticism.[1] For example, one could study the speeches of a man, or speeches of a certain type, or the public address of different ages, in order to determine preferred patterns of imagery or to trace the evolution of a particular image. One could even consider questions such as whether the quantity of imagery varies according to rhythms such as crisis and calm or development and deterioration within a culture.[2]

From this plenitude the present study selects for more extensive consideration what an earlier article has termed "archetypal metaphor."[3] Investigation indicates that the archetypal metaphor of rhetorical discourse has certain characterizing features.[4]

First, archetypal metaphors are especially popular in rhetorical discourse. Within the almost limitless range of possibility for figurative association, such metaphors will be selected more frequently than non-archetypal approximations. For example, when speakers wish to place figurative value judgments upon subjects, they will more often prefer a light or darkness association over an association with Cadillac or Edsel, ivy or poison ivy, touchdown or fumble, etc.

Second, this popularity appears immune to changes wrought by time, so that the pattern of preferential selection recurs without remarkable change from one generation to another. A similar immunity belongs to archetypal metaphor considered cross-culturally, for such preferential behavior appears unaffected by cultural variation.[5] Thus, when Dante conceives of God as a light blindingly bright, and of Hades as a place of gloomy darkness, or when Demosthenes speaks of troubled Athens as launched upon a stormy sea, the meaning comes to us clearly across the barriers raised by time and cultural change.

Third, archetypal metaphors are grounded in prominent features of experience, in objects, actions, or conditions which are inescapably salient in human consciousness. For example, death and sex are promontories in the geography of experience.

Fourth, the appeal of the archetypal metaphor is contingent upon its embodiment of basic human motivations. Vertical scale images, which project desirable objects above the listener and undesirable objects below, often seem to express symbolically man's quest for power. Such basic motivations appear to cluster naturally about prominent features of experience and to find in them symbolic expression. Thus, when a rhetorical subject is related to an archetypal metaphor, a kind of double-association occurs. The subject is associated with a prominent feature of experience, which has already become associated with basic human motivations.

This peculiar double-association may well explain a fifth characteristic, the persuasive potency of archetypal metaphors. Because of a certain universality of appeal provided by their attachment to basic, commonly shared motives, the speaker can expect such metaphors to touch the greater part of his audience. Arising from fundamental interests of men, they in turn activate basic motivational energies within [an] audience, and if successful turn such energies into a powerful current running in favor of the speaker's recommendations. Certain archetypal combinations such as the disease-remedy metaphors are quite obvious in this respect. They provide a figurative form of the threat-reassurance cycle discussed by Hovland *et al.*[6] Images of disease arouse strong feelings of fear; images of remedy focus that emotional energy towards the acceptance of some reassuring recommendation.

Finally, as the result of the foregoing considerations, archetypal metaphors are characterized by their prominence in rhetoric, their tendency to occupy important positions within speeches, and their especial significance within the most significant speeches of a society. One can expect to find such images developed at the most critical junctures in a speech: establishing a mood and a perspective in the introduction, reinforcing a critical argument in the body, and synthesizing the meaning and force of a speech at its conclusion.[7] And because of their persuasive power, their potential for cross-cultural communication, and their time-proofing, one can expect the perceptive rhetorician to choose them when he wishes to effect crucial changes in societal attitude, to speak to audiences beyond his own people, or to be remembered for a speech beyond his lifetime.

This paper focuses particularly on four sources of archetypal metaphor—light and darkness, the sun, heat and cold, and the cycle of the seasons—related by their affinity in nature and by their sharing of a basic motivational grounding. The paper's organizing metaphor is of a solar system: it is most illuminating to think of these sources as a kind of spatial family in which light and darkness occupies the center, and the sun, heat and cold, and seasonal cycle sources range out from it in that order of proximity.

Light and darkness is the sun of its own archetypal system, in which the sun itself has only planetary significance. The reason for placing light and darkness at the center is that its motivational basis is shared in varying degrees by the other archetypes to be considered here. The nature of these motives and the rationale for their attachment to light and darkness are immediately apparent.

Light (and the day) relates to the fundamental struggle for survival and development. Light is a condition for sight, the most essential of man's sensory attachments to the world about him. With light and sight one is informed of his environment, can escape its dangers, can take advantage of its rewards, and can even exert some influence over its nature.[8] Light also means the warmth and engendering power of the sun, which enable both directly and indirectly man's physical development.

In utter contrast is darkness (and the night), bringing fear of the unknown, discouraging sight, making one ignorant of his environment—vulnerable to its dangers and blind to its rewards. One is reduced to a helpless state, no longer able to control the world about him. Finally, darkness is cold, suggesting stagnation and thoughts of the grave.

What happens, therefore, when a speaker uses light and dark metaphors? Because of their strong positive and negative associations with survival and developmental motives, such metaphors express intense value judgments and may thus be expected to elicit significant value responses from an audience. When light and dark images are used together in a speech, they indicate and perpetuate the simplistic, two-valued, black-white attitudes which rhetoricians and their audiences seem so often to prefer. Thus, the present situation is darker than midnight, but the speaker's solutions will bring the dawn.

Light-dark metaphor combinations carry still another important implication which students of rhetoric appear to have neglected. There are occasions when speakers find it expedient to express an attitude of *inevitability* or *determinism* about the state of present affairs or the shape of the future. Change not simply *should have* occurred or *should* occur, but *had to* or *will* occur.

The deterministic attitude usually has more strategic value in speeches concerning the future. The speaker may wish to build a bandwagon effect: "you had better come join us: the future is going to happen just as we predict." In moments of public crisis and despondency, the speaker may wish to reassure his audience: "there's no reason to lose heart: good times are just ahead." Statements such as the latter will have not simply a public reassurance value, but also a personal rhetorical value: public declarations of confidence in a future desired by his audience will enhance the speaker's *ethos,* suggesting him as "a man of faith."

The combination of light-dark metaphors is ideally suited to symbolize such confidence and optimism, because light and dark are more than sharply contrasting environmental qualities. They are rooted in a fixed chronological process, the movement of day into night and night into day. Therefore, symbolic conceptions of the past as dark and present as light or the present as dark and the future as light always carry with them a latent element of determinism, which the speaker can bring forth according to his purpose.

Most often, it appears, this sense of historical determinism in rhetoric is tempered by conditions, and therefore can not often be equated with philosophical determinism. The latter eliminates the significance of all contingencies, and, in works such as Hegel's *Reason in History,* sees historical process as one ceaseless, remorseless flow toward a fixed end or "Absolute." Rhetorical determinism, while it also eliminates or ignores the myriad accidents and contingencies of life, nevertheless stops this reductive process one step short of philosophical determinism. It usually offers a conception of two patterned alternatives potential in historical process, depending upon a choice specified in the speech. One of those fundamental, possibly unconscious strategies of rhetoric, it therefore simplifies complex situations and facilitates choice, at the same time lending a certain dramatic significance to the rhetorical situation. If an auditor feels he is playing an important role in an elemental conflict, his gratitude for this feeling of personal significance may well predispose him in favor of the speaker's position.

The choice situation which a speaker thrusts upon his audience always concerns the acquisition of an attitude or the adoption of a solution; these forms of choice become conditions when a speech is imbued with rhetorical determinism. The speaker will say: "the present flowed from the past *because* you adopted (or did not adopt) my solutions or *because* you possessed (or did not possess) certain qualities. The future I envision will flow from the present *if* you adopt my solution or *if* you possess certain qualities." While both conditions may be present in a speech, the solutional condition is suited more to deliberative speeches, the qualitative condition more to ceremonial or inspirational speeches.

Whatever the conditions, patterns of light-dark metaphors can serve to suggest (where the determinism is left implicit) or to reinforce (where the determinism becomes explicit) the impression that some particular series of events had to or will occur. The metaphoric combination creates and strengthens this feeling by associating possibly controversial assertions concerning the inevitability of a particular process with a general, unquestionably determined cycle of nature. One could, therefore, simply classify this important work of light-dark metaphor combinations as argument by analogy. The classification, however, seems somewhat bald, especially when qualitative conditions are the hinge upon which rhetorical determinism turns. With such conditions, the symbolic combination emerges as an analogical form significant enough to be individuated as *argument by archetype.*

To discover the reason for this special significance, one must examine more carefully the effectiveness of qualitative conditions. This effectiveness depends upon audience acceptance of a basic ethical premise, which indeed animates a good part of the public discourse of Western nations and even provides much of the rationale for the significant occurrence of such discourse in the first place. This usually invisible axiom may be reconstructed in the following form: *material conditions follow from moral causes.* If a man or state qualifies by having certain specified virtues, the present condition of well-being is explained, or a radiant future is assured. Corresponding qualities of evil in a man or state have led or will lead to correspondingly opposite material conditions.[9] The Western quality of this submerged premise becomes apparent when one considers that the tracing of material conditions to moral causes tends to enhance the stature and responsibility of individual man within the historical process. The world is made to turn upon the struggle between good and evil within the human soul, giving a grand historical significance to intensely personal crises. An Eastern or Marxist point of view might well reverse the terms of the cause-effect relationship and, accordingly, diminish the stature of the individual.

An assertion that some series of events has been or will be determined, according to the presence of certain moral qualities, may depend therefore upon dual sources of support. First, the assertion rests upon a faith in moral causation and is the conclusion of a submerged enthymematic structure. Second, the assertion may call also upon an association with the fact of an unquestionably determined archetypal process. But the two forms of support do not operate independently. The faith itself is confirmed by an association with the fact of archetypal process, which constantly suggests to the impressionable mind of man that evil darkness contains the promise of light, good light the potential for darkness, in unending succession. Therefore, vivid symbolic representations of light and darkness may often perform a subtle but fundamental probative function in a speech, well deserving individuation in such cases as *argument by archetype.*

Among rhetoricians, ancient and modern, none has been more aware of the potential power of light and dark metaphors than Sir Winston Churchill. Indeed, Churchill in his war speeches shows a remarkably consistent preference for archetypal images in general. This favoritism may be a symptom of a more general truth, that in moments of great crisis, when society is in upheaval and fashionable contemporary forms of symbolic cultural identity are swept away, the speaker must turn to the bedrock of symbolism, the archetype, which represents the unchanging essence of human identity. Audiences also are unusually susceptible in such moments to archetypal images, for it is comforting to return with a speaker to the ancient archetypal verities, to the cycle of light and darkness, to the cycle of life and death and birth again, to the mountains and rivers and seas, and find them all unchanged, all still appealing symbolically to the human heart and thus reassuring one that man himself, despite all the surface turbulence, remains after all man.

One example among Churchill's many finely wrought images illustrates clearly most of the characteristics discussed in the preceding section:

> If we stand up to him [Hitler], all Europe may be free and the life of the world may move forward into broad, sunlit uplands. But if we fail, then the

whole world, including the United States, including all that we have known and cared for, will sink into the abyss of a new Dark Age made more sinister, and perhaps more protracted, by the lights of perverted science.[10]

One first observes a fusion here between the archetypes of light and darkness and the vertical scale, a frequent combination because of the natural association of light with the above and darkness with the below. The opposing value judgments are intense, the presence of rhetorical determinism unmistakable. The situation has been simplified until there are two—and only two—alternatives, one of which must become the pattern for the future. The conditional factor is qualitative, whether the British people choose to remain steadfast in the face of danger. Their moral choice will determine the future material condition. Churchill utilizes symbolism to strengthen their commitment to this virtue, first by conceptualizing a reward, the "sunlit uplands," second by specifying even more vividly a punishment, "the abyss of a new Dark Age." By an intense initial contrast of light and dark images, Churchill reawakens the figurative tension of what could be—out of context—a threadbare metaphoric phrase, "the lights of perverted science." This reinvigorated metaphor provides a grotesque, unnatural association of light with evil, reinforcing the power of the threat. Thus the example is an impressive, apparently intuitive display of potentialities discussed previously.

Churchill's purpose with this image was exhortation. When he intends comfort and reassurance, certain variations occur in the image patterns:

> Good night, then: sleep to gather strength for the morning. For the morning will come. Brightly will it shine on the brave and true, kindly upon all who suffer for the cause, glorious upon the tombs of heroes. Thus will shine the dawn.[11]

This example forms much of the conclusion of his address "To the French People." He is speaking to a defeated people: because they are already in "the new Dark Age," he does not mention light and dark alternatives, and the sense of conflict and contrast has faded. There is only one pattern now for the future, the reassuring movement from darkness into light. The speaker sees this movement as so inexorable, so inevitable, that he does not even mention conditions. They are present only implicitly: the moral qualities of endurance, courage, and loyalty to the "cause" even to the point of suffering and death. To strengthen his assertion that the future is favorably determined, Churchill relies upon—and at the same time reinforces— his *ethos* as "a man of faith." But is such confidence actually more confidence than it is prayer, an effort to invoke the predicted future by a kind of public incantation? Whatever it is, the immediate effect of consolation and encouragement is compromised only if his auditors can sense uncertainty behind the brave words.

The nature of the figuration, as well as the patterns of figurative development, appear to have changed. The first example, consonant with its vigorous, exhortative temper, thrusts its changes of meaning directly upon the audience. "Sunlit uplands," "abyss," "Dark Age," are obviously metaphors from the first crack of the language. They force their auditors immediately into the experience of resolution.[12] But this second example illustrates a somewhat slower—perhaps more soothing—tempo of meaning change. Churchill's speech was delivered during the evening, and he has obviously taken advantage of the circumstance.[13] "Good night . . . sleep to gather strength for the morning" could be taken quite literally. But from that moment the metaphoric intent begins to reveal itself, so that the movement into figurative meaning develops gradually throughout the example. One can not escape a certain physical similarity with the coming of dawn itself: a subtle onomatopoeic quality pervades the whole.

The sun is implicit in all light-dark images, and in the planetary system around light and darkness it is especially close to the center. But it does have special functions as an archetypal source. While light-dark images serve generally as value judgments upon the actions and conditions of men, the sun can symbolize more aptly human character. Most often it serves a eulogistic purpose, suggesting qualities of goodness which belong to a man. Thus sun images are at once less dynamic and more personal than metaphors of light and darkness.

An especially artful example occurs in Edmund Burke's "On American Taxation," in which the image first apotheosizes Lord Chatham, then comments less favorably by the subtlest form of ironic contrast upon the character of Charles Townsend:

> For even then, sir, even before this splendid orb was entirely set, and while the western horizon was in a blaze with his descending glory, on the opposite quarter of the heavens arose another luminary, and for his hour, became lord of the ascendant.
>   This light, too, is passed and set forever.[14]

The example indicates still another implication of sun imagery. While light and darkness are grounded in a chronological sequence, there are also subordinate cycles in the various phases of the night and day. The night phases are not archetypally significant, but different moments of the day are charged with such significance. The dawn-twilight cycle emerges especially as a symbol for human life from birth to death, indicating that the birth-death cycle, itself an archetypal source, may require metaphoric illumination when it becomes the subject for discourse. MacArthur's sentimentalized self-portrait in his "Address to Congress" further exemplifies this usage. In both his introduction and conclusion, he sees himself "in the fading twilight of life." By positioning the images in these critical places, he reveals that his primary purpose in the speech is to focus sympathetically upon himself. To enhance further the symbolic appeal, MacArthur uses images contrast, referring in the body of the speech to "the dawn of opportunity" in Asia.[15]

Sun metaphors may serve also to distinguish between qualities of light. Natural, sun-produced light is preferred over man-made light, permitting metaphoric value contrasts within the symbolic scope of light itself. Such contrasts occur infrequently, and are of a finer, more subtle sort than the obvious figurative oppositions of light and darkness. Edmund Burke provides an example in "Previous to the Bristol Election," which contrasts rather obscurely the light of open day with candlelight:

> The part I have acted has been in open day; and to hold out to a conduct, which stands in that clear and steady light for all its good and all its evil, to hold out to that conduct the paltry winking tapers of excuses and promises, I never will do it. They may obscure it with their smoke, but they never can illumine sunshine by such a flame as theirs.[16]

Burke illustrates also a final potential of sun metaphors based upon the eclipse phenomenon. Eclipse has an obvious, trite connection with "bad luck," "misfortune," but in the hands of a master rhetorician it may acquire fresh, more interesting associations. Implicit in it is the suggestion that darkness may be momentary, that a period of misfortune in national life may be only transitory, and that the nation will emerge again quickly into its former brightness. Generally some modicum of sunlight remains to reassure and sustain the observer. Thus there may be an occasional rhetorical advantage in suggesting that a nation is in the darkness of eclipse, rather than in the darkness of night. Burke's example illustrates this potential only in a partial sense:

> Tarnished as the glory of this nation is, and as far as it has waded into the shades of an eclipse, some beams of its former illumination still play upon its surface, and what is done in England is still looked to as argument, and as example.[17]

Somewhat farther distant from the center of the light-dark system is the contrast of heat and cold, represented most vividly and frequently in fire imagery. Fire partakes not only of the central light-dark motivational basis but also that of the sun to which it is contiguous. It has an extensive range of possible metabolic associations, as Philip Wheelwright's discussion indicates.[18]

Wheelwright notes that the warmth of fire associates it with bodily comfort, with the growth of the body and its food, and with the preparation of food. Its tendency to shoot upward relates it to the motivational basis of vertical-scale imagery: that which reaches above can symbolize the difficult effort by man to improve upon his condition, to aspire to "higher" ideals and attainments. Because fire is the most active, most rapidly changing of nature's elements, it can represent youth and regeneration. On the other hand, in its sun embodiment it can symbolize the permanence of nature, an association which gives meaning to the home's hearth-fire and to the church's altar-fire. Because fire burns and disintegrates substance, it can be viewed either as a destructive or as a purifying force: symbolically it can be either infernal or purgatorial. Because of its spontaneous generation and rapid reproduction, fire can represent also the birth of an idea and how it proliferates in the mind. Furthermore, just as a torch spreads flame from one place to another, an idea can leap from one mind to another.

With respect to the relationship between fire and light, Wheelwright claims an inseparable connection, such that fire suggests light, light fire to the mind of the recipient:

> Modern household appliances have so successfully enabled us to separate light and heat, that we are prone to forget how naturally in ancient times the two phenomena went together. . . . Even on a cold winter's day the sun could be felt in one's marrow. Consequently, in those contexts where light served as a symbol of intellectual clarity it tended to carry certain metaphoric connotations of fire as well. . . . As fire, glowing with light, warms the body, so intellectual light not only instructs but also stimulates the mind and spirit.[19]

His suggestion, however, that the modern mind may no longer be as susceptible to the ancient association of fire and light is not supported by a prominent example from the rhetoric of John Kennedy:

> Let the word go forth from this time and place . . . that the torch has been passed to a new generation of Americans. . . . The energy, the faith and the devotion which we bring to this endeavor will light our country and all who serve it—and the glow from that fire can truly light the world.[20]

The example confirms Wheelwright's notion that fire has a natural association with youth and regeneration.

While fire represents here dedication, a constructive impulse, Churchill provides an example which symbolizes destruction—and perhaps purification.

> What he [Hitler] has done is to kindle a fire in British hearts, here and all over the world, which will glow long after all traces of the conflagration he has caused in London have been removed. He has lighted a fire which will burn with a steady and consuming flame until the last vestiges of Nazi tyranny have been burnt out of Europe, and until the Old World—and the New—can join hands to rebuild the temples of man's freedom and man's honor, upon foundations which will not soon or easily be overthrown.[21]

One notes again Churchill's tendency to build figurative, enlarged meanings out of literal conditions. The "conflagration" in London caused by Nazi bombings extends figuratively to the anger felt in "British hearts," and extends again to represent the nature of future retaliation. In such cases Churchill does not introduce *items for association* out of context, which is the usual practice in metaphor,[22] so much as he uses a previous subject as an *item for association* with subjects which follow. This practice provides a certain artistic cohesiveness in his image patterns.

One notes also the coupling of fire, symbolic destruction, with the activity of building, symbolic construction. This archetypal combination suggests that an especially arresting metaphor, because of the adventure of creating and resolving it, can establish an appetite for imagery in both speaker and audience which makes further vivid figuration appropriate and perhaps even mandatory.[23] The destruction-construction effects suggest also that, as with disease-recovery metaphors, some balancing function, partly aesthetic and partly reassuring, is served by the second member of the metaphoric combination.

The cycle of the seasons, most distant from the center in the light-dark system, impinges upon the motivational bases of all which precede it in proximity to that source. The variations in light and darkness from one season to another, the different qualities of sunlight, the extreme variations in heat and cold, all give seasonal contrasts a complex and powerful potential for symbolizing value judgments rising from hope and despair, fruition and decay. Furthermore, the inescapable rhythm of seasonal succession provides another potential symbol for all stipulations of a determined present or an assured future. For these reasons the cycle of the seasons is immensely significant in poetry and fictional prose; Shakespeare, for example, made superb use of the source.[24] Therefore, it is surprising and somewhat perplexing that this basic environmental archetype is virtually ignored by rhetoricians.[25]

Understanding this strange neglect, which one must assume points to some special inadequacy or inappropriateness of the seasonal cycle for rhetorical purposes, requires a consideration of the nature of the source and a comparison with similar, more popular archetypes. Seasonal images are unpopular in rhetoric because of the subject matter with which the rhetorician typically deals and because of the usual nature of his audience. The succession of the seasons is a slow, deliberate process. It is suited more for long-range representation of the process of change and of the general condition of men within that process. It fits more the poet's or philosopher's elevated perspective upon time and the gradually evolving nature of man's destiny. But the subject matter of rhetoric is most often dynamic, immediate, and concrete. It has to do with specific problems and specific solutions. Some innate inappropriateness appears, therefore, between the subject matter of rhetoric and the symbolizing potential of seasonal contrasts.

A further reason for the unpopularity of the source lies in the psychology of audience and in the interaction between rhetorical subject matter and that audience. The succession of phases in light and darkness is immediate and vividly obvious: to promise light after darkness implies that a solution will come quickly, an attractive assurance for popular audiences who are impatient of long term effects or whose needs are felt concretely and acutely. The succession of the seasons, on the other hand, implies a slower and more deliberate process, not especially gratifying for such audiences. Moreover, while the succession of phases in light and darkness is rapid and spectacular, the prolonged process of seasonal change lacks dramatic impact for people who are not attuned aesthetically to long-range contrasts and subtle changes.

Thus the cycle of the seasons is an aristocratic source, which provides specialized symbols for subjects at higher levels of abstraction for the consideration of sophisticated audiences. One must conclude that the seasonal archetype provides a dimension of potential power and appeal from which the rhetorician, by the nature and circumstances of his art, is usually excluded.

The examination of one family of archetypal sources does not yield a complete, precise set of questions which the critic can use to exhaust the implications of any given rhetorical image. However, these explorations do suggest an initial pattern of inquiry.

Concerning metaphoric *invention,* what characterizes a speaker's selection of *items for association?* Does he have favorite metaphors for favorite subjects, and among these metaphors is there any kind of harmonizing relationship which would indicate an underlying unity of imaginative outlook on public questions? Does the speaker vary the tempo of meaning change in different situations, and if so for what purpose and to what effect?

With respect to *organization,* how significant is the position of an image within a speech? If its major appearance is in the introduction, does the metaphor echo and reverberate through the remainder of the speech in minor variations? Or if especially arresting, does it appear to create an eidetic disposition within speaker and audience, causing a chain-reaction of imagery to extend throughout the speech? If its major statement is in the conclusion, is the image prepared for by minor variations which condition the audience? If any of these phenomena occur, has one in effect an organization of images which runs parallel with the organization of topics? Does this image order dominate the substantive order, or is it subservient to that order? Do such patterns repeat themselves among the various speeches of a man, and if so, what can one infer that would individuate the speaker's rhetorical artistry?

Concerning *ethical proof* implications, does the intensive use of light-dark contrasts project the speaker as one who has little difficulty in making clear, decisive choices between good and evil? Does the speaker suggest himself as a man of faith or conviction by his symbolic representations of the past-present, present-future relationships? If he does communicate some sense of rhetorical determinism, does he attach conditions, and if so, what is their nature?

The *motive* basis of archetypal metaphor suggests other questions. Among the range of motivational attachments which surround an archetype, what particular motive does a specific image emphasize? Does this implicit motive stimulation reinforce, or run counter to, the system of motivational appeals made explicit within the speech? From the same subject comes a somewhat more general question with important implications for the rhetorical theorist. Might one construct inductively from the study of archetypes a system of motives particularly relevant to rhetorical discourse, rather than adopting by authoritative warrant some general list of "impelling motives"?

At least one important question may be asked relating to the *logical proof* function. Does an image embody some tacit enthymematic structure and function as a demonstration within itself, or does it serve more to dramatize, illustrate, and reinforce a logical structure made explicit elsewhere in the speech?

Two final possibilities and questions, directed as much to the theorist as to the critic, merit discussion. The first concerns the long-pursued relationships between rhetoric and poetic. Published research for some time now has been seeking general distinctions between the two arts, and while often suggestive seems, perhaps fortunately, not to have produced final answers. The discussion of seasonal images here supports the possibility that a more microscopic venture, concerned with tracing fine distinctions according to the imagery appropriate to each art form, might advance this inquiry.[26]

The second question concerns the relationships between archetypal and non-archetypal metaphor. At what moments might the non-archetype be preferable to its archetypal counterpart? That there are such moments is suggested by Laura Crowell's analysis of Franklin Roosevelt's 1936 presidential campaign address at Pittsburgh.[27] The critic finds a sustained baseball image and explains that the speech was given at Forbes Field. Thus the same kind of special circumstance which enhanced Churchill's images of dawn and fire made in this case a non-archetypal figure more appropriate.

A more significant possibility is raised by a different interpretation of the evidence presented in Wilcomb E. Washburn's excellent survey of early American political symbolism.[28] In the perspective here Washburn's evidence suggests that archetypal images may be especially crucial not only when a society is in upheaval, but also in its formative stages before it has achieved a certain national identity. Such images, which appeal to *all* men, must bear the burden of figurative persuasion before the emergence of images which appeal to *these* men. Thus, in the popular demonstrations of 1788 which urged the adoption of the federal constitution, structural and ship-of-state images were emphasized. But by 1840 a set of indigenous symbols— "log cabin," "hard cider," and the "plough"—had emerged to dominate the political imagery of the day. Such images are creatures of the moment, but they are more timely even as they are more evanescent. They may permit a more precise focusing upon whatever values and motives are salient in society at a given time.

NOTES

[1]See for example: Martin Maloney, "Some New Directions in Rhetorical Criticism," *Central States Speech Journal*, IV (March 1953), 1–5, and Robert D. Clark, "Lessons from the Literary Critics," *Western Speech*, XXI (Spring 1957), 83–89. Various approaches in literary criticism are illustrated by: Richard Harter Fogle, *Hawthorne's Fiction: The Light and the Dark* (Norman, 1964); Caroline F. E. Spurgeon, *Shakespeare's Imagery and What It Tells Us* (Cambridge, 1935); and Stephen Ullmann, *The Image in the Modern French Novel* (Cambridge, 1960).

[2]Some work in these directions has already been accomplished, as occasional references to published research here will indicate. Among unpublished research, William Martin Reynolds provides a study of societal symbols and metaphors in his "Deliberative Speaking in Ante-Bellum South Carolina: The Idiom of a Culture," unpubl. Ph.D. diss. (University of Florida, 1960). Reynolds argues that when invention becomes exhausted during the course of a protracted argument, rhetorical energies may

then be concentrated upon the development of stylistic devices in order to dramatize and reinforce entrenched argumentative positions.

Examination of the annual listings in *Speech Monographs* indicates that a movement towards image study developed at the masters thesis level in the early 1930's. This movement, which withered as quickly as it appeared, produced two works which deserve more than the usual oblivion reserved for masters theses. Junella Teeter's "A Study of the Homely Figures of Speech Used by Abraham Lincoln in his Speeches" (Northwestern, 1931) shows appreciation in the manner suggested by Clark of the functional, "communicative" aspects of imagery. Melba Hurd's "Edmund Burke's Imaginative Consistency in the Use of Comparative Figures of Speech" (University of Minnesota, 1931) is a highly competent study of the kind projected by Maloney.

[3]Michael M. Osborn and Douglas Ehninger, "The Metaphor in Public Address," *Speech Monographs*, XXIX (August 1962), 223–234.

[4]The usefulness of the term, "archetype," may be impaired somewhat by ambiguity, for writers in various fields have extended it to suit their purposes. The word may refer to myth and symbol, or to a certain "depth" responsiveness to great literature, or to ancient themes reverberated in literature, or even to structural phenomena of the brain that have developed as a kind of "race consciousness" to certain forms of recurrent experience. See for example: Philip Wheelwright, *The Burning Fountain: A Study in the Language of Symbolism* (Bloomington, 1954), pp. 86–93, 123–154, and *Metaphor and Reality* (Bloomington, 1962), pp. 111–128; Northrop Frye, "The Archetypes of Literature," in *Myth and Method: Modern Theories of Fiction*, ed. James E. Miller, Jr. (Lincoln, 1960), pp. 144–162; and Maud Bodkin, *Archetypal Patterns in Poetry: Psychological Studies of Imagination* (London, 1934). Despite such variation, the term carries the idea of basic, unchanging patterns of experience. The use here is consonant with that theme.

[5]A general concept of cultural similarity in the use of metaphor gathers some empirical support from Solomon E. Asch, "The Metaphor: A Psychological Inquiry," *Person Perception and Interpersonal Behavior*, ed. Renato Taguiri and Luigi Petrullo (Stanford, 1958), pp. 86–94.

[6]Carl I. Hovland, Irving L. Janis, and Harold H. Kelley, *Communication and Persuasion: Psychological Studies of Opinion Change* (New Haven, 1953) pp. 59–96.

[7]Concluding sex and death metaphors are investigated in John Waite Bowers and Michael M. Osborn, "Attitudinal Effects of Selected Types of Concluding Metaphors in Persuasive Speeches," *Speech Monographs*, XXXIII (June 1966), 147–155.

[8]This conception of man in the presence or absence of light is influenced somewhat by the account of essential aspects of behavior offered by Charles Morris, *Signs, Language, and Behavior* (New York, 1946), p. 95.

[9]Kenneth Burke discloses an excellent example of the past-present relationship regarded as dependent upon moral qualities in his analysis of Hitler's rhetoric, *The Philosophy of Symbolic Form* (Baton Rouge, 1941), pp. 204–205. One infers from Burke's analysis that Hitler fused his views of the past and present, present and future into a panoramic interpretation and prediction of German history. To blame the present ills of Germany upon past moral degeneracy (sin) was to promise the future well-being of Germany when moral health should be restored (redemption).

[10]"Their Finest Hour," *Blood, Sweat, and Tears*, ed. Randolph S. Churchill (New York, 1941), p. 314.

[11]"To the French People," *Blood, Sweat, and Tears*, p. 403. See other prominent examples in "Be Ye Men of Valor" and "The War of the Unknown Soldiers."

[12]Osborn and Ehninger, pp. 226–231, offer a model which describes how the mind reacts when it encounters a metaphoric stimulus. Resolution is a critical phase within the reaction process.

[13]A similar exploitation for figurative purposes of a physical circumstance in the speech situation occurs in William Pitt's "On the Abolition of the Slave Trade," *Select British Eloquence*, ed. Chauncey A. Goodrich (New York, 1963), pp. 579–592. The conclusion

of Pitt's speech, which develops a striking dawn image, happened just as dawn was lighting the windows of Parliament. See Philip Henry Stanhope, *Life of the Right Honourable William Pitt* (London, 1861), II, 145–146; Lord Roseberry, *Pitt* (London, 1898), p. 98; and J. Holland Rose, *William Pitt and National Revival* (London, 1911), p. 470.

[14]Goodrich, p. 259.

[15]*The Speaker's Resource Book,* eds. Carroll C. Arnold, Douglas Ehninger, and John C. Gerber (Chicago, 1966), pp. 279–284.

[16]Goodrich, p. 293.

[17]*Ibid.,* p. 305.

[18]*The Burning Fountain,* pp. 303–306; and *Metaphor & Reality,* pp. 118–120.

[19]*Metaphor & Reality,* p. 118.

[20]Arnold, Ehninger, and Gerber, pp. 226–227.

[21]"Every Man to His Post," *Blood, Sweat, and Tears,* p. 369.

[22]See Osborn and Ehninger, p. 227.

[23]The concept of form as "appetite" is developed in Kenneth Burke's *Counterstatement* (New York, 1931). See especially the discussion in Chapter VII. The appetitive aspect of metaphor-sequence mentioned here seems related to Burke's "qualitative" and "repetitive" forms.

[24]His use of seasonal imagery in drama is catalogued extensively by Spurgeon, *Shakespeare's Imagery.*

[25]The few examples encountered illustrate the concept discussed herein of an abstract subject matter and, significantly, occur in ceremonial speeches of a mixed rhetorical/poetic genre. See Franklin Roosevelt, "First Inaugural," *American Speeches,* eds. Wayland Maxfield Parrish and Marie Hochmuth Nichols (New York, 1954), p. 502; and George Canning, "On the Fall of Bonaparte," Goodrich, p. 863.

[26]See also Osborn and Ehninger, pp. 233–234; and Michael Osborn, "The Function and Significance of Metaphor in Rhetorical Discourse," unpubl. Ph.D. diss. (University of Florida, 1963), pp. 274–299.

[27]"Franklin D. Roosevelt's Audience Persuasion in the 1936 Campaign," *Speech Monographs,* XVII (March 1950), 48–64.

[28]"Great Autumnal Madness: Political Symbolism in Mid-Nineteenth-Century America," *QJS,* XLIX (December 1963), 417–431.

METAPHOR AND THE RHETORICAL INVENTION OF COLD WAR "IDEALISTS"

ROBERT L. IVIE

Since the beginning of the Cold War, those who have spoken out against Soviet-American confrontation have appealed foremost to the fear of nuclear holocaust, replete with visions of civilization destroyed. Their principal argument has been that the two sides must learn to cooperate in the abolition of nuclear weapons or risk extinction of the species (e.g., Schell, 1982, 1984). E. P. Thompson's metaphor of "exterminism" (1982, pp. 41–79) captured for many the essence of the survival motive on which contemporary peace advocates have heavily relied. Yet, fear of total annihilation has failed so far to produce public pressure sufficient even to slow the arms race, let alone reverse it.

Assessing their losses (or at least their lack of satisfactory progress), proponents of nuclear disarmament have acknowledged that support for the movement has been undercut by the prevailing image of the Soviet threat. Thus, Ground Zero

(1983) attempted to "educate" the public on such matters with the publication of *What About the Russians—and Nuclear War?* As Molander and Molander write in their forward [*sic*] to the book:

> "What about the Russians?" has long been a stock response to the notion that the United States set limits on its nuclear weapons program. Whether the proposals be for unilateral action or for bilateral action . . . the question is the same. . . . The policies of the Soviet Union, whether we like them or not, are fundamental when we think about American security. For too long, those who have proposed curtailment of the U.S. weapons buildup by arms negotiations or other means have given too little thought to that basic question in the minds of so many Americans: "What about the Russians?" (p. xi)

Just as Ground Zero's book, written "to provide the public with strictly nonpartisan, nonadvocacy educational materials" (p. xii), was designed to correct false images of the Soviet adversary and thereby establish a political atmosphere more conducive to arms negotiations, many other voices have been raised to protest historic Cold War antagonisms and challenge visions, in George Kennan's words, "of the totally inhuman and totally malevolent adversary." According to Kennan, those in government who hold such an "unreal" view of the Soviets have been largely responsible for undermining progress toward better relations between the two great rivals (1982, pp. 33, 57, 65).

Henry Wallace, J. William Fulbright, and Helen Caldicott must be counted, at various stages of the Cold War, among the most vociferous critics of the persistent enemy-image. They, among others, have attempted mightily to dispel the myth of Soviet savagery that goaded the nation into supporting Harry Truman's "get tough" policy, Lyndon Johnson's "Americanization" of the Vietnam war, and Ronald Reagan's program of "peace through strength." Yet today the essential problem remains: Americans are forced to choose between radically opposing and potentially disastrous views of the Russians. One view, advocated by "realists," threatens them with extermination should the arms race touch off a nuclear war. The other view, advanced by "idealists," threatens them with loss of national power and personal freedom should the Russians take advantage of a disarmed America. As Lifton and Falk (1982, p. 208) have observed:

> The vector of nuclear intentions is, of course, the Soviet Union. More and more Americans grasp the tragic flaws bound up with nuclearism and yet they support the nuclearist path as the lesser of evils. Pushed, the majority of Americans would rather take their chances with nuclear war than expose the country, or even its world position, to Soviet aggression. A rigidifying either/ or mentality that can only envisage pacifism as an alternative to nuclearism confines choice and creates a national and species destiny.

Thus, the advocates of superpower accommodation have achieved little more than a negative critique of the implacable-foe image, leaving those they have convinced with only a pacifist's alternative.

My goal in this paper is to identify sources of rhetorical invention that have undermined efforts so far to transcend the choice between chauvinism and pacifism. By examining the structure of metaphor, primarily in the rhetoric of Wallace, Fulbright, and Caldicott, I intend to show the roots of their collective failure. On a more hopeful note, I believe the analysis also reveals a recurring opportunity for rhetorical transcendence created, ironically enough, by the confrontation of "realists" and "idealists." In order to reveal the sources both of failure and opportunity, I turn next to a brief discussion of my method of analysis.

IDENTIFYING KEY METAPHORS

I begin with the premise that metaphor is at the base of rhetorical invention. Elaborating a primary image into a well formed argument produces a motive, or interpretation of reality, with which the intended audience is invited to identify. The form of the argument actualizes and literalizes the potential of the incipient figure (Ivie, 1982, pp. 240–241; Leff, 1983, pp. 219, 222–223). In the most important uses of metaphor, as a source of rhetorical invention, a term (or "vehicle") from one domain of meaning acts upon a subject (or "tenor") from another domain. Their "co-presence" routinely yields a meaning "which is not attainable without the interaction," and in certain cases the tenor becomes so closely identified with its vehicle that it "is imagined 'to be that very thing which it only resembles'" (Richards, 1965, pp. 100–101). In such instances, the vehicle and its "system of associated commonplaces" organize our view of the tenor much like a filter determines which particles will be selected out and a mold defines a final shape (Black, 1981, pp. 73–75). This kind of metaphor serves as a nomenclature that "necessarily directs the attention into some channels rather than others" and thus establishes what Kenneth Burke has called a "terministic incentive" (1968, p. 45).

Given the assumption that metaphors are routinely elaborated into motivating perspectives, it stands to reason that vestiges of these generating images will regularly appear in speeches (or texts) as the speaker's favorite vehicles. As Lakoff and Johnson (1981, p. 290) say, "Since metaphorical expressions in our language are tied to metaphorical concepts in a systematic way, we can use metaphorical linguistic expressions to study the nature of metaphorical concepts and to gain an understanding of the metaphorical nature of our activities." The pattern of vehicles revealed in a corpus of discourse, then, leads directly back to master metaphors, which more often than not are the essential terms of the speaker's "terministic screen" (Burke, 1965, p. 95; Burke, 1968, p. 46; Lakoff & Johnson, 1981, p. 312). Speaking of one thing in terms of another is the norm rather than the exception in rhetorical discourse. For, as Richards has written, "metaphor is omnipresent in speech"; our "pretence to do without metaphor is never more than a bluff waiting to be called" (1965, pp. 92–93).

The value of locating underlying metaphors is in revealing their limits or untapped potential as sources of invention, something that is far more difficult to accomplish when a generating term is allowed to operate without being explicitly acknowledged as such. Speakers lose sight of alternatives when they become accustomed to routine extensions of images no longer serving their original purposes. Stripping away the outer layers of literalized metaphors exposes them to closer scrutiny and possible reconstruction (Turba[y]ne, 1970).

Five basic steps provide a rudimentary procedure for identifying key metaphors. First, familiarizing oneself with the speaker's text and context is essential to interpreting any particular selection of his or her discourse. Critics achieve this objective in various ways, but whatever their preferred method, they attempt to create a sense of the complete experience before attending to its particulars. They gather information from sources contemporaneous with the speaking event—reviewing a broad sample of speeches, counter-speeches, audience reactions, etc.—and supplement their primary materials by consulting relevant scholarship—e.g., histories, theories, and previous works of criticism.

Second, representative texts are selected for a series of close readings undertaken to identify and mark vehicles employed by the speaker. Typically, each reading yields previously overlooked vehicles as the critic becomes more sensitized to figurative terms disguised initially by their seemingly literal usage. Marked vehicles are then filed along with their immediate contexts, amounting usually to a paragraph or less for every occurrence of a vehicle (or for every concurrence of two or more vehicles). Anyone working with word processing equipment may find it convenient to mark each vehicle in bold letters while keying paragraphs for entry into the document file designated for the particular speech or text being analyzed. Whatever storage system is utilized, however, the result is to reduce the original text to an abridged version that comprises only marked vehicles and their immediate contexts.

The third step is to arrange the complete set of marked vehicles into subgroups by clustering those with similar "entailments." Each cluster, it can be tentatively assumed, represents one of the "metaphorical concepts" featured in the speaker's discourse, and the clusters together indicate the speaker's "system of metaphorical concepts" (Lakoff & Johnson, 1981, pp. 289–292).

Fourth, a separate file of vehicles and their immediate contexts is compiled for each cluster of terms, i.e., one file for every metaphorical concept. The most extreme procedure is to search the abridged text until all occurrences of the vehicles in a given cluster have been identified and placed in a single file. Word processing equipment makes the task relatively easy by the use of word-search commands and block-and-file operations. These "concept" files, however they are compiled, display the speaker's various applications of vehicles within a given cluster, as well as concurrences with vehicles from other clusters.

Finally, the "concept" files compiled in step four are analyzed one-by-one for patterns of usage within and between clusters, thereby revealing the speaker's system of metaphorical concepts. Attention is focused on prevailing patterns, assuming that the critic may have inaccurately assigned a few of the vehicles in each cluster and that the speaker may have drawn upon certain vehicles in isolated instances to meet special purposes. With this fifth step completed, the critic is in a position to assess both the limits and untapped potential of the metaphorical system guiding the speaker's rhetorical invention.

The matter of immediate interest, of course, is the rhetorical invention of Cold War "idealists." What can the procedure outlined above reveal about their failure to supplant the vision, advanced by tough-minded "realists," of a barbarian foe bent upon destroying the United States? A case study of three Cold War "idealists," each at a different stage of the Soviet-American rivalry, provides at least a partial answer to this question, for the vehicles at work in their rhetoric reveal self-defeating metaphorical concepts.

HENRY A. WALLACE
AND THE "GAME OF POWER POLITICS"

The story of Harry Truman's underdog campaign and stunning victory over Thomas Dewey in 1948 is legendary. Yet few remember the name of the third-party candidate in that race who, under the banner of world peace, expected to draw as much as 10 percent of the total vote, mostly at the expense of an already hard-pressed incumbent. Henry A. Wallace risked his public career "to bring about understanding between Russia and the Western World before it was too late" (Wallace, 1952, p. 46) but managed as the Progressive Party candidate to attract only 1,157,140 votes, just over two percent of the total. Although he was the "most prominent critic of America's 'get-tough' posture toward the Soviet Union" (Walker, 1976, p. 3), Wallace was abandoned during the campaign by liberals and nearly everyone else except the communists (Hamby, 1968; Markowitz, 1973). Opponents branded the "prophet of peace" an "apologist for Russia" (Schapsmeier & Schapsmeier, p. 180), banishing him to the fringes of American politics and ending any chance of softening the administration's hard line on foreign policy. As Richard Walton (1976, p. 1) has observed: "The campaign [of 1948] was the last time that the basic assumptions of American foreign policy were questioned until the mid-1960s. Not until five Presidential elections later did American voters begin to re-examine the anti-communism that had been the motivating force of American foreign policy since the death of Franklin D. Roosevelt in April 1945." Wallace fought hard but failed even to dent the iron-curtain mentality of the early Cold War era.

Five texts furnish a good sample of Wallace's rhetoric on issues developed prior to and during the campaign of 1948: (1) his memorandum as Secretary of Commerce to President Harry S. Truman on the subject of foreign policy, dated July 23, 1946 (Wallace, 1973a); (2) his Madison Square Garden speech on September 12, 1946, which led a week later to his dismissal from the Cabinet (Wallace, 1973b); (3) his radio broadcast of December 29, 1947, declaring himself an independent candidate for the presidency (Wallace, 1948a); (4) his speech of July 24, 1948, accepting the Progressive Party's presidential nomination (Wallace, 1948b); and (5) his campaign book, *Toward World Peace* (Wallace, 1948c).

Analysis of these texts reveals seven clusters of vehicles that appear consistently throughout Wallace's speaking and writing on the Cold War. First is the GAME cluster comprising terms such as "game," "race," "cards," "competition," "play," "vie," "pawn," and "team." Wallace spoke of "the game of power politics" (1973a, p. 599) as a "competition [that] should be put on a friendly basis" (1973b, p. 666). Presently, he argued, the United States was relying on coercive tactics and violating the rules of fair play in its "card game" of atomic negotiations with the Russians:

> Realistically, Russia has two cards which she can use in negotiating with us: (1) our lack of information on the state of her scientific and technical progress on atomic energy and (2) our ignorance of her uranium and thorium resources. These cards are nothing like as powerful as our cards—a stockpile of bombs, manufacturing plants in actual production, B-29s and B-36s, and our bases covering half the globe. Yet we are in effect asking her to reveal her only two cards immediately—telling her that after we have seen her cards we will decide whether we want to continue to play the game.
>
> Insistence on our part that the game must be played our way will only lead to deadlock. . . . We may feel very self-righteous if we refuse to budge on our plan [the Baruch plan] and the Russians refuse to accept it, but that means only one thing—the atomic armament race is on in deadly earnest. (1973a, pp. 593–594)

The United States must make an effort "to head off the atomic bomb race," he insisted, because "Russia can play the present game as long as the United States" (1948c, pp. 3–4; 1973a, p. 594). We must stop "playing with matches," "conniving," and "scheming" and start "play[ing] ball with the Russians," for "our lives depend on it" (1948c, pp. 71, 114; 1973b, p. 666). In short, Wallace called for playing by the rules in a friendly game of power politics, letting "the results of the two [competing economic] systems speak for themselves" (1973b, p. 666); violating the rules, he insisted, would divide the world into "two armed camps" and lead ultimately to "the civilized world . . . go[ing] down in destruction" (1948a, p. 173; 1973a, p. 590).

The second cluster, featuring FORCE, contained many vehicles, including "tide," "drive," "pressure," "grind," "torrent," "flood," "conflagration," "upper hand," "bow," "ruthless," "tough," "outposts," "bully," "fight," "march," "Gideon's Army," "slam," "flexed muscles," "showdown," "steal," "clubs," "grip," "split," "rob," "hammer," "drag," "tug," "criminal," "stampede," "mob," "shout," "cry," "tantrums," and "force." Two kinds of force were emphasized: negative force and positive force. Negative force was that which violated rules and laws and consequently was destructive. Wallace complained, for instance, that "far too often hatred and fear, intolerance and deceit have had the upper hand over love and confidence, trust and joy. Far too often, the law of nations has been the law of the jungle; and the constructive spiritual forces of the Lord have bowed to the destructive forces of Satan" (1973b, p. 661).

Negative force, Wallace warned, included "ruthless economic warfare" that was "headed straight for boom, bust, and worldwide chaos" (1973b, p. 663), "criminal" talk about World War III by a "little handful of warmongers" who might "stampede" the "bulk of our people" (1948a, p. 173), Americans being used as "fire fighters armed with matches and gasoline," thus increasing the "danger of world conflagration" (1948c, p. 89), and "preach[ing] force and deceit" that leads to worldwide "faith in force as the ultimate arbiter" (1948c, pp. 117–118). Relying on negative force, such as the "get tough" policy, would only "spawn" a "get tougher" policy by the Russians (1948b, p. 620): "'Getting tough' never brought anything real and lasting—whether for schoolyard bullies or businessmen or world powers. The tougher we get, the tougher the Russians will get" (1973b, p. 664).

Negative force, the force of Satan, represented a mindless submission to trends, stampedes, drives, or tides of hate, fear, intolerance, deceit, and destruction. The "tide of American public opinion" was "again turning against Russia" (1973a, p. 596); power was "gravitat[ing] into the hands of a few people" (1948c, p. 83); the world had "ricocheted from crisis to crisis" (1948b, p. 620), and the "steady drive for heavy armament expenditure" was continuing "to push us toward war" (1948c, p. 33).

Positive force, on the other hand, was the constructive force of the Lord. It was active, renewing, and full of fight but blessed with love, joy, and hope. "In recent years," Wallace wrote, "there has been . . . a vast awakening, a stirring of new hope, new demands" (1948c, p. 90). Americans, liberals especially, could no longer afford to "turn over on their backs and wave their four paws in the air while the special interests tickle[d] their fears of communism"; they had to choose "either to sell their souls or stand up and fight" (1948c, p. 86). Wallace had assembled a "Gideon's Army, small in number, powerful in conviction, ready for action" that would lead the people on a "march" for "peace, progress and prosperity" and against "the powers of evil" (1948a, p. 174). His army would overcome "the suppression of the people's will" and "capture the imagination of all religious people" in order to "wake [the] world up to the fact that its quick profits on war prospects are suicidal" (1948c, pp. 33–34). His "crusade to rediscover the spirit of America" (1948c, p. 119) was designed to build public support for "establishing an atmosphere of mutual trust and confidence" between the United States and the Soviet Union (1948b, p. 620). He would "unleash [a] creative force beyond the power of man to imagine" (1948b, p. 622).

Thus, in Wallace's lexicon, playing the *game* of power politics properly—i.e., in a friendly manner and consistent with the rules of fair play—was a corollary of activating *positive force;* a spiritual awakening of love and trust among humankind would bring forth peaceful competition with the Russians. Conversely, unfair competition, coercion, and ultimately war were a function of succumbing passively to *negative force,* of submitting mindlessly to the forces of hatred and fear. This basic metaphorical concept, created by the interface of GAME and FORCE, was solidified by five reinforcing clusters: DARK-LIGHT, SICK, MONEY, BREED-PLANT, and PREACH.

Vehicles in the DARK-LIGHT cluster included "down," "dark," "fog," "blind," "shadow," "nightmare," "frozen," "distorted," "astigmatic," "thick," "smoke," "chaos," "abyss," "dawn," "light," "torchbearers," "x-ray," "vision," "dreams," "awakening," "stirring," "ray," and "wake." Images of darkness were associated with the negative force of coercion, distrust, fear, and death. Negative force, in short, was condemned as the dark force. Wallace complained "the atmosphere" between the U.S. and U.S.S.R. had become "so thick that a friendly word or a cry for peace [was] lost and stifled by the smoke of manufactured hate, of groundless fear" (1948c, p. 72). He argued that "when people are afraid, they are blinded to the good in each other" (1948c, p. 113), that "fearmongers" should not be allowed to "distort and becloud the issue by name calling" (1948c, p. 174), and that Americans "must understand the real Russia and not be guided by the distorted picture" presented daily "in our press" (1948c, p. 15). He warned that the threat of military domination was "stealing up on us" and insisted "negotiations on the establishment of active trade might well help to clear away the fog of political misunderstanding" (1973a, p. 599).

Images of light projected the sense of positive force onto Wallace's proposals for world peace. In his words, "The party of hope needs workers to bring light to the dark corners where the afflicted are oppressed by the parties of Hatred, Despair, Scarcity, Exploitation, Hunger, and War" (1948c, p. 121). An "atmosphere of mutual trust and confidence" would solve "many of the problems relating to the countries bordering on Russia" (1973a, p. 600). He spoke glowingly of Franklin Roosevelt who "looked beyond the horizon and gave us a vision of peace. . . . It was a dream that all of us had" (1948b, p. 620).

Wallace further denigrated negative force by associating it with vehicles in the SICK cluster, including "neurotic," "symptoms," "sick," "afflicted," "obsessed," "psychopathic," "fester," "infection," "rot," "suicide," and "graveyard." Wallace spoke derisively of candidates in "the graveyard parties," Democrats and Republicans, who "flexed their muscles" and "declared their intention to continue the cold war" (1948b, p. 622). He warned of a "neurotic, fear-ridden, itching-trigger psychology" in a world of several nations armed with atomic bombs (1973a, p. 592) and wrote that pursuing the Truman Doctrine was "the surest way of committing a long, slow, painful national suicide" (1948c, p. 115). Furthermore, trouble spots around the world were said to be "festering" to the point of being "shot through with social and economic infection that could lead to spreading conflict" (1948c, pp. 101–102). Quite simply, the world was "desperately sick," spiritually, economically, and politically (1948c, pp. 19–20).

Wallace also relied upon the negative connotations of MONEY terms to denigrate negative force. His favorite vehicles in this category included "price," "cost," "bought," "bankrupt," "cheap," "buy," "pay," "coin," "sold," "investments," "liquidate," "sell," and "money." He spoke of "cheap lies" (1948a, p. 173), "ruthless profiteering" (1948b, p. 623), "trying to buy the world . . . cheaply" (1948c, p. 39), and "social and moral bankruptcy" (1948c, p. 30). He referred to "the temples of the money changers and the clubs of the military" (1948b, p. 622). He warned that "those whom we buy politically with our food" would soon desert us; they would "pay us in the basic coin of temporary gratitude and then turn to hate us because our policies [were] destroying their freedom" (1948a, p. 174).

Vehicles in the BREED-PLANT cluster included "incubate," "stagnate," "breed," "cesspool," "cultivate," "circulate," "fertilize," "seed," "fruit," and "harvest." The BREED terms portrayed negative force as degenerative, spawning evil and its residue of war. Wallace warned that "hatred breeds hatred" (1973b, p. 662), that "stagnant pools of capital breed unemployment and degeneracy" (1948c, p. 41), that "money, like water, [could] be kept pure only by circulation" (1948c, p. 41), and that the Truman Doctrine had been "incubated in certain minds" (1948c, p. 10).

PLANT terms, on the other hand, reinforced Wallace's commitment to positive force by intensifying the image of renewal. The United Nations never would get off "dead center" until it developed "the courage to fertilize the thought of the world"; the time had come for "a modern Johnny Appleseed animated by the missionary spirit to go into all the world and preach the gospel to every creature. Broadcast the seeds of investment, science, technology, and productivity to all peoples" (1948c, p. 45).

Finally, Wallace advanced positive force as the key to world peace by drawing upon vehicles in the PREACH cluster, including "missionary," "spirit," "preach," and "crusade." He promised to lead "the forces of peace, progress and prosperity" in a "great fight" against "the powers of evil" by assembling a "Gideon's Army" (1948a, p. 174). In his view, "'Nationalism' [had] not given a sufficiently satisfying answer to the deep spiritual cry of man for a supreme allegiance"; therefore, he proclaimed "a crusade to rediscover the spirit of America" (1948c, pp. 20, 119). Wallace's crusade would bring positive force to bear on the resolution of the Cold War and its root causes. He would awaken, enlighten, and plant the world out of its suicidal submersion in the cesspool of shortsighted economic greed. His crusade would unleash the power of faith in humankind and commitment to human welfare that would allow America to play the game of power politics fairly, ultimately winning the competition with Russia without resorting to violence.

Overall, then, Wallace's critique of the Cold War was driven by an ideal image, or metaphorical concept, of a spiritually awakened America engaging the Soviet Union in peaceful competition to heal an economically sick world and eventually to win the allegiance of humankind. His metaphors placed the blame for the problem and the responsibility for its solution almost exclusively on the United States, which was associated with a sick, dark, and deceitful "get tough" policy designed to overpower the Russians and serve the evil interests of "reactionary capitalism" (1948c, p. 83). In his words, the "Wall Street–military control in Washington" was "so obsessed with fear and hatred of Russia" that it was "certain, sooner or later, to make war" (1948c, p. 68). Not surprisingly, the public simply was unwilling to accept any such analysis that focused the guilt on their nation alone. Thus Wallace was easily dismissed as Russia's naive apologist.

Not only was Wallace's ideal image rhetorically flawed by its preponderant criticism of the United States, blaming the American government and reactionary capitalists almost exclusively for the Cold War, but it also lacked a characterization of the Russians that was well suited to their designated role as responsible players in the friendly game of power politics. Wallace said hardly anything to assure the public of Russia's inherent goodwill and commitment to fair competition. Instead, he warned of "red hysteria" in the United States (1948c, p. 9) and allowed that communism itself had emerged in Russia only because of a "grinding poverty" caused by the exploitation of the Czars in cooperation with Western capitalists (1948c, p. 51). Just as hatred had bred hatred, he reasoned, friendly competition initiated by the United States would be reciprocated by the Soviets. America could make of its opponent whatever it chose: either an unbeatable rival in war or a cooperative opponent in peaceful competition. Faith in the inherent goodness of human nature and a willingness to act upon that faith was all that was required to bring about world peace and happiness. Yet the public's image of Soviet savagery, reinforced by the Cold War rhetoric of Wallace's critics, allowed for little faith in the inherent goodness of an atheistic and barbarian foe.

American voters were not the only ones to reject Wallace's vision of peace. Wallace himself recanted only a few years later in an article entitled, "Where I Was Wrong" (1952). He had failed to take into account, he now believed, "the ruthless nature of Russian-trained Communists." Russia was "still on the march," Wallace wrote, determined "to enslave the common man morally, mentally and physically for its own imperial purposes." He was now convinced by developments in Czechoslovakia, Korea, and elsewhere that "Russian Communism in its total disregard of truth, in its fanaticism, its intolerance and its resolute denial of God and religion is something utterly evil" (1952, pp. 7, 47).

Wallace ultimately fell victim to the inadequacies of his own rhetorical invention. His system of metaphorical concepts proved to be self-defeating because it did not enable him to explain Soviet initiatives without *either* continuing to blame the United States for creating the conditions that forced the Soviets to compete unfairly *or* deciding eventually that the Soviets were actually Satan's surrogates. As the vehicles of light and darkness, breeding and planting, sickness and greed, and ministering and crusading combined to reinforce Wallace's faith in peaceful competition, they undermined his ability to perceive the rhetorical limits of a vision that failed both to account for Soviet imperialism and to characterize the Russians as good sportsmen in the game of power politics. The only alternative, finally, was to adopt the opposing metaphor of Soviet savagery that (within Wallace's metaphorical system) made communism itself a dark, degenerative, negative force— the source of all evil. As we shall see, Cold War idealists who spoke out long after Wallace's defeat proved unable to avoid similar weaknesses in their own systems of rhetorical invention.

J. WILLIAM FULBRIGHT AND THE "PATHOLOGY OF POWER"

Ironically, the same senator who had concluded as early as 1946 that Soviet totalitarianism was an immoral, aggressive force, and who had criticized Henry Wallace in 1947 for delivering a speech that sounded "just as though it had been written in the Kremlin" (quoted in Tweraser, 1974, p. 29), was himself the author 30 years later of a powerful attack on U.S. Cold War doctrine (Fulbright, 1966). "Few modern books on foreign policy have been so influential," conceded one of his critics, "as Senator J. William Fulbright's classic lectures, *The Arrogance of Power.*

To find a work of comparable impact on American opinion one has to go back to Mahan" (Rostow, 1972, p. 179). Although signs of Fulbright's reassessment of Soviet-American relations were present in his *Old Myths and New Realities*, published in 1964, the transition was not complete until two years later. His "arrogance thesis" emerged in the midst of growing frustration over American involvement in Vietnam and was restated prior to American disengagement from the war in *The Crippled Giant* (Fulbright, 1972). Thus, my analysis of the senator's leading metaphorical concepts emphasizes vehicles displayed in his two principal works during the Vietnam era (Fulbright, 1966, 1972).

Unlike Wallace, Fulbright rejected the GAME metaphor which, in his assessment, led to a "conception of politics as warfare":

> Even the most dazzling success in the game of power politics does nothing to make life more meaningful or gratifying for anybody except the tiny handful of strategists and geopoliticians who have the exhilarating experience of manipulating whole societies like pawns on a chessboard. (1972, pp. 9, 12)

Fulbright believed the Johnson administration had made the mistake of fighting a "mindless game of power politics" in Indochina and the Nixon administration was repeating the error by "playing the spheres-of-influence game in a world of power politics" (1972, pp. 92, 96). In his view, power was not a game to be played correctly, but instead a "narcotic, a potent intoxicant" that had taken the nation on a "trip" (1972, p. 100). Power conceptualized as a game put too much emphasis on winning and losing, trivializing war "into a mindless contest to prove that we are 'Number One'" (1972, p. 87). Conceptualized as a narcotic, however, power was more easily recognized as an "addiction" that "nourished our vanity," drove us to acts of "arrogance," and created "a psychological need" to prove we are "bigger, better, or stronger than other nations" (1964, p. 5; 1972, pp. 99–100).

Also unlike Wallace, Fulbright rejected the CRUSADE metaphor. In the senator's view, "The crusading spirit" of great nations throughout history had "wrought havoc, bringing misery to their intended beneficiaries and destruction upon themselves" (1966, p. 138, see also p. 248). America's involvement in Vietnam, he believed, resulted from "the view of communism as an evil philosophy and the view of ourselves as God's avenging angels, whose sacred duty it is to combat evil philosophies" (1966, p. 107). Such misguided moralism had its roots in a "durable strand of intolerant puritanism" that "coexisted uneasily" in "our national character" with "a dominant strand of democratic humanism" (1966, p. 250). Warning the United States not to pursue the "anti-Communist crusade" (1972, p. 160), Fulbright relentlessly attacked vehicles associated with an arrogance of power (including "saints," "preaching," and "missionary"), denigrating them with the oxymoron "war prayer" and related vehicles such as "pontificating," "fanaticism," and "zealotry" (see 1966, pp. 138, 203, 245–251). Fulbright rejected the CRUSADE concept in order to condemn American missionary zeal, even though he had drawn upon the same language himself since 1946 to denounce "the crusading spirit of the Russians" (quoted in Tweraser, p. 29). By retaining, but also negating, the very terminology that had guided him between 1946 and 1963, Fulbright succeeded in freeing himself of an image that until then had defined the enemy as Soviet aggressive totalitarianism.

The senator's principal concept, however, was similar to the SICK cluster used by Wallace to denigrate negative force. Just as Wallace had emphasized "neurosis," "obsession," "suicide," and "psychopathology" among the various forms of physical and mental sickness, Fulbright primarily drew upon a cluster of PSYCHOLOGY vehicles, including essentially negative terms such as "psychotic," "delusions of grandeur," "projection," "pathology," "confuse," "arrogance," "irrational pressures," "drive," "instinct," "insane," "nervous breakdown," "paranoid fears," and "inferiority complex," as well as more positive terms such as "rehabilitation," "grow up," "empathy," "reconciliation," "mature," and "come of age."

In Fulbright's opinion, "The causes and consequences of war may have more to do with pathology than with politics, more to do with irrational pressures of pride and pain than with rational calculations of advantage and profit" (1966, p. 7). Americans viewing communism as an "evil philosophy" were looking through a "distorting prism," seeing "projections" of their "own minds rather than what is actually there" (1966, p. 107). The "unfathomable drives of human nature" created a "psychological need" for dominance, and "competitive instincts" led to "dehumanizing" antagonists (1966, pp. 5, 161, 165). Excessive pride was "born of power," undermining "judgment" and "planting delusions of grandeur in the minds of otherwise sensible people and otherwise sensible nations" (1966, p. 130). If war were to be avoided, America had to learn to control its competitive instincts, "confining them to their proper sphere, as the servant and not the master of civilization" (1966, p. 162).

Thus, according to Fulbright, "the reconciliation of East and West [was] primarily a psychological problem, having to do with the cultivation of cooperative attitudes and of a sense of having practical common objectives" (1966, p. 204). As he explained, "Perhaps the single word above all others that expresses America's need is 'empathy'" (1966, pp. 197–198). The nation must "mature," "come of age," and regard itself as a "friend, counselor, and example for those around the world who seek freedom" (1966, pp. 221–222, 257). The United States must learn to regard communist countries as "more or less normal states with whom [it] can have more or less normal relations," and it must "encourage communist imitation of [its] own more sensible attitudes" (1966, pp. 254, 257). Americans and Russians could "form the habit of working together as international civil servants" through "projects of direct cooperation" (1972, p. 168; 1966, p. 204).

Although Fulbright's system of metaphorical concepts differed significantly from Wallace's, it suffered from some of the same flaws. Most importantly, the senator's metaphorical system stressed the culpability of the United States almost exclusively, accusing it of an anti-communist obsession, an underlying lack of confidence in itself, an exaggerated fear of failure, an arrogance of power, and a crusading puritan spirit manifested as ideological warfare (1966, pp. 5, 250–251; 1972, pp. 18, 26–27). This American psychosis had driven the nation's policy makers to "irresponsible behavior" (1972, p. 27). The trouble between the United States and the Soviet Union was a function of misperception rooted principally in America's confusion of power with virtue. China's "paranoid fears" of American hostility were distorted and exaggerated but "not pure invention" (1966, p. 170). Russia's "paranoiac suspiciousness" and "inferiority complex" had been worsened by America's Cold War crusade: "by treating them as hostile, we have assured their hostility" (1966, p. 221; 1972, pp. 10, 20). It was up to the United States to heal itself of psychotic, destructive tendencies, to mature as a great power and seek reconciliation with the communists. Under no circumstances should America try to justify its own truculence as a response to communist intransigence, zealotry, subversion, intervention, and ideological warfare, for tolerance and accommodation are far better and more likely to resolve differences than "imitating the least attractive forms of communist behavior" (1966, p. 254).

Such idealism hardly took into account any better than Wallace's game metaphor the sources of Soviet behavior that could be expected to promote accommodation over confrontation, cooperation over subversion, or tolerance over totalitarianism. Fulbright depended on a psychological principle, grounded in a single research finding of Muzafer Sherif who had studied patterns of conflict and cooperation between two groups of eleven-year-old American boys in an experimental camp, to conclude that there "may be great promise for strengthening world peace in limited, practical projects of cooperation" between the U.S. and U.S.S.R. (1966, pp. 166–168). He advocated "practicing psychology in international relations" (1964, p. 168), but his dependence on PSYCHOLOGY as the dominant metaphorical concept was, at best, overdeveloped for the United States and underdeveloped for the Soviets.

Even though Fulbright was convinced "that Russia can now properly be regarded as a conservative power in international relations, as a nation whose stake in the status quo is a far more important determinant of her international behavior than her philosophical commitment to world revolution," there was little in the PSYCHOLOGY cluster to explain such a development. His conclusion was rooted in an allusion to revolutions passing through normal stages of development, as did the French Revolution, until a conservative reaction supplants extremism (1966, p. 80).

Although undeveloped, this "stages-of-revolution" vehicle could have been linked perhaps to certain of Fulbright's PSYCHOLOGY vehicles, such as "maturity," "growing up," and "coming of age," and to other seemingly related but infrequently used terms in his lexicon, terms such as "development," "gradual change," and "tide of change" (1966, pp. 202, 211). Certainly, the potential of such an extension was not explored by the senator, and no other concept in his metaphorical system could yield arguments that might pacify the fear of a barbarian foe. Again, Americans were expected to accept the full burden of guilt for the Cold War and to take on faith that the enemy would respond in kind to their leadership by example and acts of friendship.

HELEN CALDICOTT AND "NUCLEAR MADNESS"

About the same time as Senator Fulbright published *The Crippled Giant*, Helen Caldicott emerged as an anti-nuclear activist in Australia, arousing her countrymen to protest French atmospheric testing in the South Pacific and then organizing Australian labor unions against the mining and selling of their nation's uranium on the international market. A pediatrician, the founder of *Physicians for Social Responsibility,* and a former faculty member at Harvard Medical School, Caldicott earned recognition as the mother of the nuclear freeze movement.

Caldicott published her first book, *Nuclear Madness: What You Can Do!*, in 1978 (Caldicott, 1980), presented her standard anti-nuclear lecture in a controversial and award-winning film in 1983, *If You Love This Planet: Dr. Helen Caldicott on Nuclear War* (Caldicott, 1983), and published her second book, *Missile Envy: The Arms Race and Nuclear War,* in 1984 (Caldicott, 1985). Together, these materials advanced the message she had brought to countless audiences for over a decade, warning them of imminent danger and urging everyone to take action.

Caldicott's quest for a non-nuclear world, however, has been long on courage and energy but short on rhetorical invention. Her nearly total dependence on the MADNESS metaphor has left her unable to mollify America's fear of the enemy even when she has attempted to answer directly that haunting question:

> But what about the Russians? Every time the Pentagon needs more money, the Russian spectre is called up. The reality is that if both superpowers, together with the lesser powers, continue on this mad spiraling arms race, building more and more atomic bombs, sooner or later they will be used. We cannot trust in the sanity and stability of world leaders. (In fact, great power tends to attract disturbed individuals.) . . . Someone must make the first move away from death and toward life. . . . I believe that the Russian people are so frightened of nuclear war that they would heave a momentous sigh of relief and would want their own leaders to follow America's moral initiative toward nuclear disarmament (Caldicott, 1980, p. 78)

Thus, her answer has been to dismiss the question as a dangerous illusion and to pursue the pacifist's alternative in order to "save the human race."

MADNESS vehicles have pervaded Caldicott's rhetoric to a fault. Her favorite have been "crazy," "deranged," "madness," "insane," "pathogenesis," "pathological," "mad lust," "paranoia," "anxiety," "indignation," "anger," "frustration," "projection," "fantasy," "mental masturbation," "disease," "etiology," "psychic numbing," "missile envy," "suicide," "mental illness," "frantic desperation," "emotional cripple," "power-hungry," "egocentric," and "killing animus." As the list suggests, she has elaborated the concept well beyond Wallace's sick cluster and even pursued more vehicles than were featured in Fulbright's PSYCHOLOGY cluster. So complete a commitment has magnified the concept's limitations.

The first problem is that the metaphor has been used to circumvent the enemy-image rather than encompass it in a transcendent image. In answer to her own question—"Why are Russia and America such bitter enemies?"—Caldicott has pointed to "the passionate hatred and paranoia harbored by Americans," emphasized America's "seemingly implacable hatred and dislike of Russia," explained that "the nation's pathological reactions are rooted deep in the past," and charged that "the Russian menace has been dragged out of the closet to justify either personal or political ambitions or new weapons development." She has posed the question—"But what about the Russians?"—and then finessed it by suggesting "the question is a mechanism of psychic numbing, where the questioner refuses to emotionally integrate the facts . . . and a symptom of denial: 'If I can blame the Russians, I won't have to disintegrate emotionally if I contemplate the end of the earth'" (1985, pp. 44–45, 70). In short, the pattern has been to associate the United States with MADNESS, focusing attention on the sources of American culpability and dismissing fear of the Russians as a pathological condition, "the primitive mechanism of blaming the Russians" (1985, p. 348). The Soviet Union has been presented essentially as the victim of America's craziness. In Caldicott's view, "As America has led the arms race, so Russia has inevitably and inexorably copied and followed." Russian fears are justified; their leaders "have every cause to be realistically frightened and perhaps a little paranoid." The culprit is America who "has engineered her own suicide" through the mechanism of "paranoid projection" (1985, pp. 103, 308, 313).

The second problem with the MADNESS metaphor is that it has led to a healing image that assumes a loving, supportive environment. Just like the parents who show no sign of emotion when told their child has leukemia, America needs a psychiatrist so that it can become appropriately passionate about the world's survival (1983, p. 12). Just like the terminally ill patient brought into the emergency room, our terminally ill planet must be admitted to the intensive care unit and treated with loving care if it is to have a chance of surviving (1983, p. 14). Just as Caldicott resolves conflict with her husband by "capitulating" on her own wants, becoming "vulnerable," and making "the first move" to "give love," the United States must forget its "selfish needs" and "make the first move" to insure "a future life preserving relationship" with the Soviet Union, for "the superpowers are married to each other on this planet" (1985, p. 314). America must "reach out to," "make friends with," and "learn to love the Russians" (1985, pp. 363–365). If only the United States could bring itself to take this "simple, obvious, and easy" path by dropping its "ancient need for a tribal enemy," Russia "would cease to be an enemy and the weapons would become anachronistic" (1985, p. 364). Educating the American public and politicians, who have been so terribly ignorant of the nuclear threat, is the key to therapy, for the human being's strongest instinct is survival. Because the Russians are "people like ourselves," they will respond in kind to our informed initiatives for peace (1980, p. 69; 1985, pp. 350–353, 363).

Reduced to the level of the individual and the couple, the doctor and the patient, the parent and the child, such advice for healing the rift between ideological and nuclear rivals seems idealistic at best. Worse yet, from the perspective of "realists" Caldicott's solution could lead directly to war if taken seriously, for any sign of weakness would only incite the enemy's savage instinct to attack. It would be hard enough, probably impossible, for Americans to shoulder the full burden of guilt for their nuclear pathology, but the call to capitulate out of love for an enemy makes the analogy absurd.

Caldicott has offered Americans little reason to accept the Soviet Union as a supportive marital partner and has attempted even less to acknowledge Soviet ambitions. Thus, as George Moffett (1985, p. 16) recently reported, "forty years after the dawn of the cold war . . . the task of finding a balance between toughness and compromise remains as elusive as ever." Disagreement continues "among policymakers and public alike" over "the nature of the Soviet threat and how to deal with it." Polls consistently have shown that "the American people want arms control but don't trust the Soviets to honor the terms. The public is concerned about the rapid growth of nuclear arsenals, but also fears falling behind in the arms race." The image of Soviet savagery continues to haunt Americans even as they contemplate compromise and wish for arms control. As Lifton and Falk (1982, p. 210) have concluded, "The Soviet menace is generally perceived as real and must be addressed" if the peace movement is to avoid being dismissed as "naive, pacifist, or utopian."

TRANSCENDING THE IMAGE OF SAVAGERY

The metaphorical concepts guiding "idealist" rhetoric throughout the Cold War have been self-defeating largely because they have promoted a reversal, rather than transcendence, of the conventional image of a barbarian threat to civilization. Americans traditionally have exonerated themselves of any guilt for war, hot or cold, by decivilizing the image of their adversaries. This "victimage ritual," enacted with generic regularity, has sanctified the ideals of peace, freedom, and democracy. It has legitimized total victory over a foe caricatured as irrational, coercive, and aggressive, i.e., a foe who is totally uncivilized and therefore perfectly evil (Ivie, 1974, 1980; also see Corcoran, 1983; Hatzenbuehler & Ivie, 1984, pp. 114–126; and Ivie, 1979, 1984 for studies exemplifying the process).

Contrary to tradition, Cold War "idealists" have attempted to decivilize America's image rather than the enemy's. By relying upon metaphorical concepts such as MAD, PATHOLOGY, SICK, and FORCE, they have portrayed the United States as the irrational, coercive, and aggressive agent of extermination, urging Americans to follow instead the path of love, friendship, trust, and empathy. Thus, they have called for a redeeming act of self-mortification by a nation accustomed to condemning scapegoats, asking in effect that it purge itself of savagery without benefit of the principle of substitution (Burke, 1970). The victimage ritual has been turned inward upon a self-righteous nation, intensifying its guilt and ultimately increasing its need to sacrifice an external enemy "so powerful and cunning that his suffering and death will be a total purgation" (Duncan, 1968, p. 146; 1969, p. 259).

This error of turning savagery inward, instead of transcending it, has provoked "realists" to regress further into decivilizing imagery. One such realist was Walt Rostow, special assistant for national security affairs, whose memorandum to Lyndon Johnson on February 8, 1968, proposed a strategy for a speech to "slay the credibility-gap dragon with one blow." Feeling the pressure of "those who talk peace" and reeling from the Tet offensive, Rostow argued that it was time "to take on the peace issue squarely"—i.e., that it was "time for a war leader speech instead of peace-seeker speech"—and he attached a draft of a speech designed to accomplish that end. The most striking feature of Rostow's proposed speech was the predominance of explicit savagery symbols. The draft was laced with one reference after another to "the savage assault" on a defenseless civilian population "during the heart of the lunar New Year's celebration," to "a savage and vicious attack upon civilian populations with a callous and total lack of concern for the welfare of civilian lives," to attacks that were "savage in execution," to "the savagery of the past week," to "last week's savagery," to an "enemy who specialized in savagery," and to reminders that "we have known savagery before" (Rostow, 1968). Clearly, Rostow's inclination was to retreat to the basic symbol of national peril at a time when the administration's Vietnam policy was under siege and the public needed to be rallied to war.

Regardless of how compelling any metaphor may be, however, its limitations eventually are encountered in its application. Savagery, whether applied to the United States or its enemies, has been no exception. Thus, a cycle of adoption, extension, criticism, and reversal has been established and perpetuated throughout the Cold War.

American involvement in the Vietnam war, for instance, was largely a function of extending the early Cold-War image of Soviet and communist savagery to events in Southeast Asia (Berman, 1982, p. 130). The Johnson administration never reassessed the enemy image that led to Americanizing the war in 1965 and the emergence of a strong anti-war movement soon thereafter. The metaphor's compelling but essentially unstable opposition between the forces of civilization and savagery had been literalized by administration rhetoric from Truman through Eisenhower and Kennedy to Johnson (see Ivie, 1986, for a discussion of Truman's literalizing rhetoric). Such a long-term extension eventuated in an unpopular war and revealed flaws in the simple opposition between a savage enemy and a civilized savior. Peace advocates responded by portraying the enemy as the victim of American aggression. The administration's stubborn, uncompromising insistence on communist savagery and American innocence forced the issue to the point where an unstable opposition was partially reversed long enough for the United States to withdraw from the war and pursue détente with the communist world. This temporary modification of the savagery vs. civilization equation soon encountered its own opposition as détente proved illusive, Soviet "adventurism" became more difficult to ignore, and America's post-war malaise subsided (Hoffman[n], 1984). Reagan's election consummated a return to the original equation of America threatened by a barbarian and evil foe.

Huntington (1984) has advanced one suggestion for coping with this cycle, arguing that it should be conceptualized as a series of waves. In his view, "The détente wave slowly gathered force during the 1960s, became stronger, peaked in 1972, broke, reached its high point on the beach a year later, and then began to recede, as the renewed hostility wave began to move in and overlapped with the receding wave of détente" (p. 268). In Huntington's most "hopeful" extension of his wave metaphor, moderation in practice is seen as the child of extremism in rhetoric. That is, administrations that ride the wave of rhetorical hostility "are likely to come under significant pressures to moderate their stance and may be led to a middle-of-the-road, balanced policy in practice." The risk, of course, is that a wave of rhetorical hostility may thrust us onto the jagged rocks of nuclear war if political leaders lack "unusual insight and skill" (p. 289).

A better solution is to break the cycle by superseding the traditional opposition of savagery vs. civilization. At the point where reversal normally occurs, an opportunity exists for replacing savagery with a metaphor that encompasses the superpowers within the same system and identifies a common external enemy. The replacement metaphor must take into account the evidence that both parties are rational and irrational, aggressive and pacific, competitive and cooperative, independent and interdependent. It cannot ignore, for instance, established perceptions that the Soviets are obsessed with a paranoid desire for security, that they are secretive, xenophobic, and distrustful, that they suffer from an inferiority complex and are ruthless, imperialistic, authoritarian (even totalitarian), militaristic, and anti-capitalist. It cannot deflect attention, though, from other less threatening observations about the Soviets: that they possess a rich culture, suffer from limited resources and an inefficient economy, are basically conservative managers and technologists; that their revolutionary climate is localized (not a symptom of or inspiration for world revolution), that they are seeking to achieve limited objectives and to avoid war with the United States, that they endorse cooperative, communal, and altruistic ideals, that they are a patriotic people and a stable society, that they share with America a frontier heritage, and that they are officially atheistic but culturally religious (see Ground Zero, 1983 for an overview of established perceptions of the Soviets, both negative and positive). The replacement metaphor must serve the goal of co-existence by redefining the ideal of global freedom (or world communism) to one of mutual security and continued competition.

A replacement metaphor is needed to integrate mixed images of both superpowers in a manner that will promote arms reduction and manage conflict between them. The solution is not, as so many have suggested, a matter of eschewing abstraction and educating ourselves in the details and complexities of U.S.-Soviet relations (e.g. Caldicott, 1985, pp. 350–367). It requires more than recognizing our habit of demonizing the Soviets through an "endless series of distortions and oversimplifications" (Kennan, 1982, p. 197). Understanding is a function of conceptualization, not just information, and the best way to undermine a dysfunctional metaphorical concept "is to choose a new one" (Turba[y]ne, 1970, p. 65). As Lifton and Falk (1982, pp. 243, 245) have observed, "moving beyond nuclearism" and war requires "the displacement of Machiavellianism by a holistic world picture." The whole must be large enough to bind the United States and the Soviet Union together by mutual interests, a common threat, and continued co-rivalry.

Unfortunately, "we live in a period of transition, the old ways no longer work, but new ways have not yet become available" (Lifton & Falk, 1982, p. 242). Although the time for rhetorical transcendence has arrived, the mechanism of invention has yet to be discovered largely because attention has been fixed on extending a set of self-defeating metaphorical concepts without sufficient awareness of their operational significance.

"Spaceship earth," "hostages on a terminally ill planet," and "rowboat earth"—i.e., "recognizing that we are all in the same boat together" in "stormy seas" and that "we cannot make our end safer by making their end tippier"—are the vehicles to which some have tentatively turned (Barash & Lipton, 1982, pp. 9, 44). These vehicles, though, are limited in their application, undeveloped as a metaphorical concept for international relations, and inconsistent with some of the criteria for replacement metaphor mentioned above; viz., they emphasize interdependence and survival but ignore the motive of competition, and they encompass the U.S. and U.S.S.R. within the same holistic system but offer no basis, beyond the existence of a common threat, for trusting or tolerating each other. Détente failed in the 1970s partly because Nixon and Kissinger were determined through linkage to tame the Soviet monster rather than co-exist with a worthy competitor (Gaddis, 1982). Certainly, a sense of world stewardship and common interest in the survival of the species must be encouraged but not without also finding a metaphor that legitimizes collaboration between antagonists. Each must have something to lose from the other's demise and something to gain from the other's survival, and there must be recognized limits of competition beyond which neither can go without sacrificing their mutual self-interest. In short, some kind of a SYMBIOSIS metaphor must be identified and elaborated in order to move beyond the peril of pre-nuclear thinking in the nuclear age.

REFERENCES

Barash, D. P., & Lipton, J. E. (1982). *Stop nuclear war! A handbook.* New York: Grove Press.

Berman, L. (1982). *Planning a tragedy: The Americanization of the War in Vietnam.* New York: W. W. Norton.

Black, M. (1981). Metaphor. In M. Johnson (Ed.), *Philosophical perspectives on metaphor* (pp. 63–82). Minneapolis: University of Minnesota Press.

Burke, K. (1965). *Permanence and change: An anatomy of purpose.* Indianapolis: Bobbs-Merrill.

Burke, K. (1968). *Language as symbolic action: Essays on life, literature, and method.* Berkeley and Los Angeles: University of California Press.

Burke, K. (1970). *The rhetoric of religion: Studies in logology.* Berkeley and Los Angeles: University of California Press.

Caldicott, H. (1980). *Nuclear madness: What you can do!* (rev. ed.). New York: Bantam Books.

Caldicott, H. (1983). *If you love this planet: Dr. Helen Caldicott on nuclear war* [Film transcript]. Los Angeles Direct Cinema Limited.

Caldicott, H. (1985). *Missile envy: The arms race and nuclear war.* New York: Bantam Books. (Work originally published 1984)

Corcoran, F. (1983). The bear in the back yard: Myth, ideology, and victimage ritual in Soviet funerals. *Communication Monographs, 50,* 305–320.

Duncan, H. D. (1968). *Symbols in society.* New York: Oxford University Press.

Duncan, H. D. (1969). *Symbols and social theory.* New York: Oxford University Press.

Fulbright, J. W. (1964). *Old myths and new realities.* New York: Random House.

Fulbright, J. W. (1966). *The arrogance of power.* New York: Random House.

Fulbright, J. W. (1972). *The crippled giant: American foreign policy and its domestic consequences.* New York: Random House.

Gaddis, J. L. (1982). *Strategies of containment: A critical appraisal of postwar American national security policy.* New York: Oxford University Press.

Ground Zero. (1983). *What about the Russians—and nuclear war?* New York: Pocket Books.

Hamby, A. L. (1968). Henry A. Wallace, the liberals, and Soviet-American relations. *The Review of Politics, 30,* 153–169.

Hatzenbuehler, R. L., & Ivie, R. L. (1983). *Congress declares war: Rhetoric, leadership, and partisanship in the early republic.* Kent, OH: Kent State University Press.

Hoffmann, S. (1984). Detente. In J. S. Nye, Jr. (Ed.), *The making of America's Soviet policy* (pp. 231–263). New Haven, CT: Yale University Press.

Huntington, S. P. (1984). Renewed hostility. In J. S. Nye, Jr. (Ed.), *The making of America's Soviet policy* (pp. 265–289). New Haven, CT: Yale University Press.

Ivie, R. L. (1974). Presidential motives for war. *The Quarterly Journal of Speech, 60,* 337–345.

Ivie, R. L. (1980). Images of savagery in American justifications for war. *Communication Monographs, 47,* 279–294.

Ivie, R. L. (1982). The metaphor of force in prowar discourse: The case of 1812. *The Quarterly Journal of Speech, 68,* 240–253.

Ivie, R. L. (1984). Speaking "common sense" about the Soviet threat: Reagan's rhetorical stance. *Western Journal of Speech Communication, 48,* 39–50.

Ivie, R. L. (1986). Literalizing the metaphor of Soviet savagery: President Truman's plain style. *Southern Speech Communication Journal, 57,* 91–105.

Kennan, G. F. (1982). *The nuclear delusion: Soviet-American relations in the atomic age.* New York: Pantheon.

Lakoff, G., & Johnson, M. (1981). Conceptual metaphor in everyday language. In M. Johnson (Ed.), *Philosophic perspectives on metaphor* (pp. 286–325). Minneapolis: University of Minnesota Press.

Leff, M. (1983). Topical invention and metaphoric interaction. *The Southern Speech Communication Journal, 48,* 214–229.

Lifton, R. J., & Falk, R. (1982). *Indefensible weapons: The political case against nuclearism.* New York: Basic Books.

Markowitz, N. D. (1973). *The rise and fall of the people's century: Henry A. Wallace and American liberalism, 1941–1948.* New York: The Free Press.

Moffett, G. D. (1985, September 26). Keeping the Soviets in line: Consistent policy of "containment" eludes US. *The Christian Science Monitor,* pp. 16–17.

Richards, I. A. (1965). *The philosophy of rhetoric.* New York: Oxford University Press.

Rostow, E. V. (1972). *Peace in the balance: The future of American foreign policy.* New York: Simon and Schuster.

Rostow, W. W. (1968). W. W. Rostow to Lyndon B. Johnson, LBJ Library, NSC Country File: Vietnam.

Schapsmeier, E. L., & Schapsmeier, F. H. (1970). *Prophet in politics: Henry A. Wallace and the war years, 1940–1965.* Ames, IA: Iowa State University Press.

Schell, J. (1982). *The fate of the earth.* New York: Alfred A. Knopf.

Schell, J. (1984). *The abolition.* New York: Alfred A. Knopf.

Thompson, E. P. (1982). *Beyond the cold war: A new approach to the arms race and nuclear annihilation.* New York: Pantheon.

Turbayne, C. M. (1970). *The myth of metaphor* (rev. ed.). Columbia, SC: University of South Carolina Press.

Tweraser, K. (1974). *Changing patterns of political beliefs: The foreign policy operational codes of J. William Fulbright, 1943–1967.* Beverly Hills, CA: Sage.

Walker, J. S. (1976). Henry A. Wallace and American foreign policy. Westport, CT: Greenwood Press.

Wallace, H. A. (1948a, January 1). I shall run in 1948. *Vital Speeches of the Day,* pp. 172–174.

Wallace, H. A. (1948b, August 1). My commitments. *Vital Speeches of the Day,* pp. 620–623.

Wallace, H. A. (1948c). *Toward world peace.* New York: Reynal & Hitchcock.

Wallace, H. A. (1952, September 7). Where I was wrong. *New York Herald Tribune,* Sec. 7, pp. 7, 39, 46.

Wallace, H. A. (1973a). Henry A. Wallace to Harry S. Truman. In J. M. Blum (Ed.), *The price of vision: The diary of Henry A. Wallace, 1942–1946* (pp. 589–601). Boston: Houghton-Mifflin.

Wallace, H. A. (1973b). The way to peace. In J. M. Blum (Ed.), *The price of vision: The diary of Henry A. Wallace, 1942–1946* (pp. 661–669). Boston: Houghton-Mifflin.

Walton, J. W. (1976). *Henry Wallace, Harry Truman, and the cold war.* New York: Viking Press.

THE POLITICS OF THE PITCH: CLAIMING AND CONTESTING DEMOCRACY THROUGH THE IRAQI NATIONAL SOCCER TEAM

MICHAEL L. BUTTERWORTH

Sport is the human activity closest to war that isn't lethal.

Ronald Reagan[1]

It is not unusual for popular and political discourses to conflate sport and war. For decades, various sports have depended on the language of warfare to describe the games on the field. American football, in particular, is replete with references to "bombs," "trenches," and "territory." Ever popular is the use of sport terminology by military personnel. According to Sue Jansen and Don Sabo, the language of sport reached its most obvious salience during the first Gulf War. At that time, not only were military officials engaging in the sporting vernacular—General Norman Schwarzkopf's equation of a ground strategy with a "Hail Mary" pass, for example—but journalists also indulged in athletic metaphors to describe the events of war.[2] More troubling, perhaps, is the extension of this metaphor into the fantasy world of video games. As television images grow increasingly sophisticated, with multiple models and simulations standing in for flesh and blood and brick and mortar, the game metaphor serves as a "powerful form of cultural anaesthetic."[3] In the context of the "war on terrorism,"[4] this over-saturated, mass mediated sport/war culture constitutes a disturbing "confusion of war reality and sports fantasy."[5]

The rhetorical efficacy of this metaphor is enabled, in part at least, by the popular perception that sport and politics remain independent of one another. As sportswriter Ron Cook states, "sporting events should be about competition, not politics."[6] Yet it is precisely because sport is seen as disconnected from the world of politics that it is often "used for political purposes without the usual commensurate costs."[7] In using the term "politics," I am borrowing from the interpretation of Chantal Mouffe, who suggests that politics refers to the attempt [to] create order out of the antagonisms that constitute human life. Her concern, shared here, is that in the current state of neoliberal hegemony, politics is seen as a means of erasing difference and conflict, a purpose that is antithetical to democracy.[8] Democratic politics, defined by the condition of pluralism, must therefore come to terms with the "ineradicable character" of human antagonisms.[9] To enable democratic practice requires, among other things, a careful critique of rhetorical strategies that limit expression and construct an illusory unified polity. It is in this effort that I turn to the reciprocal metaphors of sport and war.

In 2004, President George W. Bush looked to sport as a rhetorical resource in the war on terrorism. Specifically, he turned to the largest of stages and the most spectacular of media events—the Summer Olympic Games in Athens—in a political ploy to take advantage of the success of the Iraqi national soccer team. As will become clear in this analysis, Bush's attempt to politicize the Olympics and claim the Iraqi's on-field victories as his own reveals the substantial "commensurate costs" that can result from the linkage between sport and politics. What is crucial, then, is to unmask the rhetorical work being done by sport, or at least by those who appropriate it, and to expose the consistency between this rhetoric and the rhetorics of politics and war. As articulated by the Bush administration, current American foreign policy dictates that freedom and democracy must be embraced, no matter the conditions under which they are imposed. Since sport has often been viewed as an ideal institution of democracy, only a critical reflection of sport's role in the "war on terrorism" may provide the possibility that sport can become a productive site of democratic culture.

My aim in this paper is to critique the relationship between Bush's broader rhetorical efforts and the 2004 Olympics, not only for what it reveals about politics, but for what it tells us about sport. The term "sport" is potentially broad, incorporating not only the mass-mediated, highly corporatized world of spectator sport, but also the various iterations of games and leisure that are a part of people's everyday lives. My argument here focuses on sport as an organized and institutionalized practice; i.e., professional and amateur sports that are regulated by leagues and international bodies. In the context of the discourses of "globalization" and the "war on terrorism," sport is a substantive site of analysis. As Alan Tomlinson notes, "Sports do not simply demonstrate the nature of globalization. They are generative of it."[10] For this reason, rhetorical and cultural critics must attend to the various deployments of sport in political culture.

In 2004, the Iraqi national soccer team became a metaphorical embodiment of the war in Iraq, a symbol used by the president on the one hand to trumpet freedom and democracy, and on the other hand to pursue a policy of preemptive war that altered the meanings of both. In this context, I want to demonstrate how the converging discourses about the war, the Olympics, and the US presidential election reveal the rhetorical machinations of the Bush administration. I argue that the president's rhetorical construction of democracy favors the symbolism of democratic institutions over the dynamic practice of democratic expression. The consequence of this construction is a political culture that reduces democracy to free elections and minimizes the role of rhetorical contestation and dissent. Bush himself has dismissed dissent as a quaint inconvenience of democracy. When confronted by the reality that record crowds had gathered *around the world* to oppose the imminent invasion of Iraq, Bush shrugged them off. "[D]emocracy is a beautiful thing . . . people are allowed to express their opinion," he said in a press conference. However, he continued, "you know, size of protest, it's like deciding, well, I'm going to decide policy based upon a focus group."[11]

At stake in this critique is the role of democracy, both in its potential in Iraq and in its unsettling limits in the United States. By "democracy," I wish to emphasize its *practice over institutions*. Following William Connolly, I suggest that a revitalized democratic culture requires that we see democracy as a process, a "politics of becoming."[12] For Connolly, this depends first upon an "agonistic respect," through which we acknowledge the inescapable contestability of claims to truth and reality. This suggests that no construct—democracy, science, religion, etc.—can be reduced to a single or universal element. In other words, holding elections is a *part*, not the *end*, of building a credible democracy. A second condition that must be met is that of "critical responsiveness." A politics of becoming, therefore, cultivates a reflexive humility as a component of democratic exchange. Rather than issuing demands and ultimatums, we must enliven democracy through a willingness to engage in "careful listening and presumptive generosity."[13]

Such an orientation is rare at the moment. All too often, politicians and media pundits listen selectively and reduce democracy to the act of voting. During the 2004 elections, for example, visitors to New York City's Rockefeller Center were invited to celebrate the "joy of voting" at a temporary exhibit named "Democracy Plaza."[14] From 20 October to 5 November, Democracy Plaza stood as a synecdoche of American citizenship, through which the essence of democratic practice is measured by casting a ballot. The act of voting, while certainly necessary, is not a sufficient condition for democracy. It reduces democracy to a single moment performed once every two or four years, and it favors the private act of selecting candidates over the public act of democratic deliberation. Most importantly, I contend, is that it limits our democratic imaginations, equating the mere presence of elections with the ideals of freedom and liberty.

In the case of President Bush, he has repeatedly declared that "freedom is on the march," while pointing to marginal successes in Afghanistan and Iraq. Despite the claims that Afghanistan and Iraq will become their own democracies, Bush has defaulted to a conception of democracy that privileges American values of liberalism and free-market capitalism.[15] Rather than accept this vision, we would be wise to heed the words of Benjamin Barber, who argues that "the objective for those seeking a democratic world ought not to be 'democracy' in the singular, or on the American model or any other, but 'democracies' in the plural."[16] So as the United States occupied Iraq and bombed much of it into ruins, President Bush declared victory for democracy and freedom. Although the 2004 Olympic Games represent a small element in the overall discourse about the war in Iraq, the appropriation of the Iraqi soccer team provides a suitable illustration of the extent to which this president rhetorically constituted the "war on terrorism" in terms that have constrained democratic citizenship at home and exploited its potential abroad.

THE GLOBAL GAME

The Olympic Games are the world's largest and most recognizable international sporting event. Historically, they have been as much a forum for fervent nationalism as they have been about peaceful competition. The global nature of the Olympics, in fact, makes them an ideal vehicle for political posturing. As Tomlinson notes, this kind of event represents the convergence of political, economic, and cultural dimensions like no other production. "An Olympic Games or a Grand Slam tennis tournament," he suggests, "articulate the history and culture of a time and place as well as the new formative alliances of a globalizing culture and economy."[17] The two most watched television occasions, in fact, are both international sporting events: the Olympics and the World Cup. Given this, politicians are eager to capitalize on the presence of their sports teams on the world stage. David Rowe argues that this political investment is teamed with sport and the media in a linkage he terms the "unruly trinity."[18] The result is that "international sporting competition functions so effortlessly as metaphor for the state of the nation at the popular political level."[19]

The metaphor of sport as nation constitutes an interpretive frame for understanding global politics, what Kenneth Burke terms a "way of seeing." Burke notes that metaphor allows humans not only to construct the world in which they live, but also to construct a purpose within that world.[20] At issue, then, is for what political purpose can sporting metaphors serve? It is quite common, on the one hand, for productions of American popular culture to promote a democratic metaphor through sport's presumed equality of opportunity.[21] This pervasive optimism is countered on the other hand by the reality of metaphor's potential to enable violence and injustice. In short, as George Lakoff reminds us, "Metaphors can kill."[22] In the case of the first Gulf War, and now during the "war on terrorism," Lakoff concludes that both Presidents Bush deployed metaphors that achieved the rhetorical feat of constituting the United States "as both victim and hero."[23] This conflation has contributed to the justification of a wide range of military actions, prompting critics to argue that American foreign policy increasingly endorses a politics of empire, in which sport plays a substantive rhetorical role.[24]

Accusations that the United States is engaged in a project of empire are far from new.[25] Especially since the collapse of Soviet communism, and the concomitant declaration by Francis Fukuyama that politics had reached the "end of history,"[26] many American leaders have been driven by a relentless affirmation of liberal democracy's moral superiority. Accordingly, the US "has become progressively more open and aggressive about its pursuit of a liberal world order which it would dominate."[27] That order is shaped by a fierce allegiance to the beneficence of the free market and the spread of global capitalism. American foreign policy has become therefore, "a convergence with neoliberalism, producing a novel hybrid of neoliberal empire, combining threat and profit, war and business."[28] Yet, while neoliberalism most clearly is characterized by the faith it literally grants to deregulation and open markets, Wendy Brown emphasizes that it is a philosophy that also metaphorically reduces all social institutions and actions to an economic rationality.[29] For this reason, popular culture generally, and sport specifically, are an integral part of the story of globalization.

Globalization, of course, cannot be seen as a static construct. Nor can it be easily defined. In its simplest terms, it "refers to the long-term historical trend of greater worldwide interconnectedness."[30] To this extent, globalization is not new to the twenty-first century, let alone the twentieth. What is new is the degree of control exercised by one political power, the United States. While it is safe to say that sport is a substantive component in the discourse of globalization, it is not at all clear what kind of global world is constituted by sport. As Rowe suggests, because international sport depends on the production of national cultural differences, it "may be constitutionally unsuited to carriage of the project of globalization in the fullest sense."[31] Rowe is using the term in its most optimistic sense, suggesting that utopian visions of a united global citizenry are far beyond the parameters of sport's reach. I agree. This does not mean, however, that there will not be those who attempt to use sport to achieve such ends. In fact, sport offers a compelling narrative for the proponents of globalization.

As Joseph Maguire argues, "Global sport involves . . . a form of patriot games in which images and stories are told and retold to ourselves, about ourselves, and about others."[32] In many cases, the stories we tell about ourselves and others are two sides of the same coin; we construct ourselves in opposition to an undesirable Other. Even in a democratic culture, any "us" is constituted by and constitutive of a "them."[33] The trick, Mouffe points out, is to "construct the 'them' in such a way that it is no longer perceived as an enemy to be destroyed, but as an 'adversary,' that is, somebody whose ideas we combat but whose right to defend those ideas we do not put into question."[34] Using the sport metaphor would seem to require favoring adversaries over enemies, for the destruction of an opponent prohibits future contests. In the "war on terrorism," however, George W. Bush has depended on a logic of good and evil that precludes such agonistic respect. This logic is articulated with a neoliberal worldview in order to legitimize and impose American policies around the world. Given this, the use of soccer becomes a powerful metaphor in the pursuit of this presidential agenda.

Co-Opting the "People's Game"

For the average American fan, the terrain of popular sport is dominated by the three major North American sports of baseball, football, and basketball.[35] When Major League Baseball ends its season with the *World* Series, or the Super Bowl winner is declared "*world* champion," the fact is largely ignored that a healthy portion of the world's sports fans view these champions with indifference. Instead, the majority of nations around the world favor soccer, [36] a game of only marginal interest to mainstream US fans. As Richard Giulianotti notes, "[soccer] is undeniably the world's premier sport."[37] To illustrate this point, while the World Series captures 185 million viewers around the world and the Super Bowl yields 133 million, the final match of the World Cup garners an audience somewhere between 1.5 and 2 *billion.*[38]

More than any other game, it would seem, soccer embodies a utopian interpretation of globalization. As Franklin Foer remarks:

> You could see globalization on the pitch: During the nineties, Basque teams, under the stewardship of Welsh coaches, stocked up on Dutch and Turkish players; Moldavian squads imported Nigerians. Everywhere you looked, it suddenly seemed, national borders and national identities had been swept into the dustbin of soccer history.[39]

Less euphorically, Giulianotti argues that the diversity found in soccer "is increasingly undermined by the interplay of economic and cultural forces which are transforming the game's cartography into a global marketplace."[40] So it is that soccer stands in metaphorically for the larger debate about globalization, one in which its proponents sell the virtues of a global neoliberalism while its opponents fear the dissolution of individual identities and cultures. Furthermore, Peter Donnelly adds that "if cultural globalization has occurred in sport, then it seems to be a very American form of sport culture that has been spread around the world during the second half of the 20th century."[41]

If global sport is primarily American in character, then it may seem surprising that soccer plays an important role in shaping this image. The "people's game," after all, occupies an ambivalent space in the American sporting landscape. On the one hand, many Americans regard the game as dull or incomprehensible.[42] As one defender of the game said in response to the typical American response to the World Cup, "It happens every four years, the jingoistic exclamations that our sports are better than theirs; that the United States is right and the rest of the world is wrong; that soccer is boorrrring."[43] In *Offside: Soccer & American Exceptionalism,* Andrei Markovits and Steven Hellerman detail the various ways in which the American media responds with arrogance, indifference, or outright hostility when forced to contend with the world's most popular game. Moreover, as their analysis reveals, while many journalists have written favorably about soccer, they have done so not in response to the game itself, but rather to the role of the United States in hosting an event like the World Cup in 1994.[44]

Accusations that the game is too slow or that it lacks sufficient scoring are among the most common complaints. But others object to soccer because the game's popularity in Europe and Latin America mark it as un-American. Former National League Football quarterback and US Senator Jack Kemp reflected this viewpoint when he declared that "[American] football is democratic, capitalism, whereas soccer is a European socialist [sport]."[45] Ironically, while Kemp conflates democracy with capitalism and restricts this union to American sports, he misses the extent to which soccer is equally a product of free markets and commercial expansion. Far from remaining the romanticized "province of the working class,"[46] the people's game is no more immune from the spread of neoliberalism than base-ball, football, or any other "American" sport.[47]

So if there are many in the United States who dismiss soccer,[48] the game's enormous presence in the global marketplace makes it a source of considerable capital for those interested in furthering the American global agenda. This is because on the other hand of the soccer landscape lies the participation of millions of suburban children in youth leagues across the United States. As David Andrews, et al. summarize, "In recent decades, soccer's culturally differentiating un-American identity has comfortably co-existed with the game's emergence as perhaps *the* sporting practice and symbol of fin-de-millennium suburban America."[49] Here, then, we have soccer standing in as a synecdoche for suburbia, co-articulated with subdivision housing developments, sport utility vehicles, and shopping malls, "as a standard signifier of the highly desirable bourgeois utopia that suburban America is supposed to be."[50]

If the suburb is the marker of US superiority, one would be hard pressed to find a more appropriate metaphor for neoliberal America than soccer. Conceived rhetorically, the un-American game of soccer is filtered through the lens of suburbia, then propelled back on an unsuspecting world. While this has yet to translate to US dominance on the international pitch, it provides a compelling metaphor for US leaders who trope the game as a reconstituted, uniquely American cultural form. In this form, the game is carefully constructed and protected against competing interpretations, thereby paradoxically offering soccer as a symbol of neoliberal capitalism while simultaneously constraining open competition around the world.[51] As such, it supports the notion that the quest for free markets is viable only insofar as it supports a US project of empire.

Meanwhile, as it is in most of the world, soccer is the most popular sport in Iraq. Before the cost of the Iran-Iraq war had over-burdened the Iraqi economy, and before UN sanctions crippled its infrastructure, Iraq was a regional soccer power as recently as 1986. After the invasion of Kuwait in 1990, Iraq had its membership in FIFA revoked at the behest of the UN. FIFA, or the Federation Internationale de Football Association, is the sport's international governing body, and with the exception of the UK, membership in it "remains dependent upon national recognition by the UN."[52] When the United States "liberated" Iraq in 2003, the UN recognized the nation again, allowing it to return to international play. The UN recognition of Iraq, of course, entailed the presumption of democratic governance and free-market capitalism. Thus, FIFA's decision to reinstate Iraq affirmed the neoliberal order promoted by American foreign policy. As Miller et al. note, FIFA is a civil association of cultural elites that has the power to dictate terms "to governments and businesses through a complex relationship of interdependency with nationalism and corporate funding."[53] In other words, the 2004 Iraqi national soccer team came into existence only because the conditions for global capitalism preceded its constitution.

By the time the Summer Olympic Games began in Athens, the Iraqi soccer team had already surprised nearly everyone by even qualifying for the tournament. When Saddam was in power, his son Uday was in charge of the Iraqi soccer federation. Although some now dismiss the allegations as rumor, most accounts agree that under Uday's control, players who under-performed were subjected to various forms of torture.[54] Despite an incapacitating lack of funds, and a lack of security at Iraqi stadiums that forced "home" games to be played in neighboring Jordan, the Iraqis managed to qualify for the Olympics by winning their preliminary group in South Asia. Their mere presence in Athens provided a compelling and inspiring story line; when they advanced to the semifinal round, opening the tournament with an upset of Euro 2004 runner-up Portugal, they arguably became *the* story of the Games. While the *New York Times* hailed the team as the top choice among their "warm and fuzzy Olympians," the *Athens News Agency* referred to them as a "miracle." The *Financial Times* called them "an immense and heartening surprise."[55]

As the Iraqi team celebrated its success, the US presidential election heated up, and the Bush campaign aired a commercial that valorized the liberation of Afghanistan and Iraq. According to the advertisement, "Freedom is spreading through the world like a sunrise."[56] The logical extension of this narrative was that a vote for Bush would enable this light to reach the rest of the world. Yet, as the Bush campaign declared its necessary function in promoting democracy, it simultaneously co-opted the athletes competing for Afghanistan and Iraq. Because the Iraqi national soccer team experienced unexpected success in Athens, they were especially alert to Bush's rhetoric. This is a rhetoric that not only took credit for the success of the Iraqi athletes, thereby annihilating the agency of the individual team members, but also reflected the president's conception of democracy both at home and around the world.

POLITICIZING THE PITCH

In a February 2004 interview with Tim Russert on *Meet the Press,* President Bush made clear that his democratic vision had been shaped by the terrorist attacks of 2001, and the subsequent "war on terrorism." "I'm a war president," he said, almost triumphantly. "And the American people need to know they got a president who sees the world the way it is."[57] This is a world that Bush has neatly and conveniently divided into good and evil. As Robert Ivie argues, a rhetoric of evil is precisely what Bush needed to compensate for a case for war that lacked evidentiary support.[58] The president has regularly defined war in religious terms, stating, for example, in the 2002 State of the Union address, "We've come to know truths that we will never question: evil is real, and it must be opposed. . . . Deep in the American character, there is honor, and it is stronger than cynicism. And many have discovered again that even in tragedy—especially in tragedy—God is near."[59] This religious construction of terrorism provided the president with the rhetorical grounds necessary for engaging in war. "The ritual demonizing of the enemy," writes Ivie, "symbolically transforms death into salvation, earthly battles into a cosmic struggle, and escalations of violence into the extermination of the evil Other."[60]

Underlying this justification was a politics of fear that consolidated Bush's leadership. After the 2004 presidential election, the American press focused on what appeared to be the president's new "mandate." Analysis was varied, but many attributed his success to his strength of leadership during the "war on terrorism." Yet, a turn to the British press suggests that rather than capitalizing on his own strengths, Bush instead exploited the considerable and multiple fears of the nation. The *Times London* reported, "Backed by the authority of office, the President mined a rich seam of suburban fear, fear of Muslim fundamentalism, fear of another 9/11 and fear of a Democratic moral collapse, led by abortion, embryo research, gay marriage and liberal Supreme Court judges."[61] The result is what Barber calls "fear's empire," through which the Bush administration has pursued "a reckless militancy aimed at establishing an American empire of fear more awesome than any the terrorists can conceive."[62]

Far from offering a reprieve from the discourses of globalization, empire, and war, sport articulates in compelling ways with American ideology and policy. Yet, Maguire notes that "very little attention has been paid to sport by those studying global cultural processes."[63] There can be little doubt that not only does sport influence the political, but sport is political. For many, "Sport is commonly characterized as the global cultural industry par excellence."[64] In particular, sport offers "critical sites and sources for the expression of forms of collective belonging, affiliation, and identity."[65] In light of this, George W. Bush turned to sport in multiple ways after the 9/11 attacks. For example, among his public appearances in the weeks after September 11 was Game Three of the World Series, where Bush visited Yankee Stadium to throw out the first pitch. Bob Woodward reports in his book, *Bush at War,* that the crowd's reaction to the president that night was so enthusiastic that it prompted political advisor Karl Rove to equate it to a Nazi rally.[66] Here, the president turned to the national pastime as a way to symbolically link himself, and his war, to the essence of American character; this was a theme he repeated at the 2004 Republican convention with a video presentation of his first pitch.

In another case, when the National Football League (NFL) opened its 2003 season, it was President Bush who introduced the game to the television audience by crediting football as an illustration of American character. Lest his message be seen merely as a coincidence, the NFL assured the audience that football and the war in Iraq were inseparable. Aside from scheduling the *New York* Jets to play the *Washington* Redskins, the league held its "Kickoff Live" festivities on the Washington, DC, mall, where among the 300,000 spectators were 25,000 military troops and family members. To further condense this hybrid of entertainment and politics, the NFL and the Pentagon agreed to encourage "service people to wear their short-sleeve, open-collar uniforms, to make a good impression on TV."[67] In addition, the president used the 2002 Salt Lake City Winter Olympics as a platform to legitimize the "war on terrorism," appealed to the cultural currency of NASCAR, and celebrated the heroism of former NFL player Pat Tillman, who was killed in Afghanistan in 2004 after giving up a lucrative football career.

Having appropriated sport as a metaphor for America on the home front, the president next turned to the international arena and the Athens Olympics. In the 2004 Summer Games, Iraq advanced to the medal round in soccer before losing to Paraguay and, in the bronze medal game, Italy. By reaching the penultimate game, the Iraqi team appeared, at first glance, to affirm the US mission of liberation. It was reasonable to assert that without the removal of Saddam Hussein by American troops, there would have been no Olympic Games for any Iraqi athlete. To a point, this is an accurate assessment. To be sure, President Bush sought to capitalize on this narrative. However, the story could be told differently, as many of the Iraqi players were resentful of the American occupation and the unending violence in their home country.

It is significant to note that the 2004 Summer Olympics were book-ended by the Democratic and Republican National Conventions in the United States. In the midst of a hotly contested presidential campaign, the Olympics served the political purpose of affirming American superiority in and through international athletic competition. This phenomenon, of course, is not new. In the clash of ideologies that sustained the Cold War, for example, the United States and Soviet Union regularly politicized international competitions, "using sporting victories as evidence of political superiority."[68] In 1936, Adolf Hitler attempted to showcase Aryan virtue at the Berlin Summer Games (though he was thwarted by African American runner, Jesse Owens). And few can dispute the political resonance of the Olympic platform. When John Carlos and Tommie Smith raised their gloved fists in a display of black power in Mexico City in 1968, it captured racial tensions to the point that some have claimed that "it is arguably the defining moment in raising black social consciousness in the 20th century."[69] Four years later, terrorists from the Palestinian Black September Organization killed 11 Israeli competitors in Munich, thereby permanently demonstrating the extent to which politics and sport are implicated in one another. In recent years, the Olympics have become an American-styled spectacle, in which the conflation of state, media, and corporatism have increasingly encroached on the territory of the games themselves.[70]

The above list is by no means exhaustive, but it does sufficiently direct our attention to the complexity of the political arena constituted by the Olympic Games. In particular, it is safe to conclude that the meanings of the Olympics have always been a contested matter, rhetorically as well as through the events themselves. Thus, to claim victory on behalf of one's own nation or form of government is itself a risky proposition, for political consequences often follow from athletic competitions. Taking credit for the triumphs of others, then, is an especially hazardous move on the Olympic stage. When President Bush did exactly this during the Athens Games, it came in the context of a global climate still coming to terms with the events of September 11 in 2001.

With the "war on terrorism" raging in August of 2004, many feared that attacks were possible or even likely in Greece. Some professional basketball players from the United States said they would not attend the Summer Games for fear of their safety. Indiana Pacers center Jermaine O'Neal, for example, was one of the few players to express publicly the safety concerns that many shared privately.[71] One columnist admitted, "in an even more complicated world, where US citizens no longer have to wonder how far a terrorist cell will go to attack our values and ways of life, or where American foreign policy has become fuel for intensifying hatred, the stakes are even higher."[72] Meanwhile, the International Olympic Committee (IOC) and local officials in Greece provided unprecedented resources to insure everyone's safety. However, while no violence marred the Games, the two weeks in Athens were not devoid of political disruptions. As the *Guardian* sharply noted, "After all the talk that cynical terrorists would use the platform of the 2004 Olympic Games to make a crass political statement, it turns out that a cynical president of the United States got in there before them."[73]

During the Olympics, President Bush extended his campaign rhetoric about the "war on terrorism" in order to absorb and re-deploy the success of the Iraqi national soccer team. He did this in three ways: a campaign commercial that took credit for the participation of Afghanistan and Iraq in the Olympics, a statement at a campaign stop in which he once again declared that the United States was responsible for allowing these nations to compete, and the suggestion that he would fly to Athens for the medal ceremonies if Iraq advanced to the gold-medal match.

The campaign advertisement represented the most obvious rhetorical effort from the administration to validate its policy of preemptive war. The *Washington Post* described the spot:

> The advertisement flashes the flags of Iraq and Afghanistan over a stadium and a swimming pool as an announcer says: "Freedom is spreading through the world like a sunrise. And this Olympics there will be two more free nations. And two fewer terrorist regimes."[74]

A spokesperson for the Bush campaign, Danny Diaz, justified the advertisement by stating, "It's not about politics. It's about the fact that our nation has been successful in helping spread freedom all around the world."[75] Perhaps Diaz would have been more credible were it not for Bush's comments at a *campaign rally* in Oregon. "The image of the Iraqi soccer team playing in this Olympics, it's fantastic isn't it," he remarked. "It wouldn't have been free if the United States had not acted."[76]

With these words, Diaz and Bush condensed the mission of the "war on terrorism" to the symbol of a soccer team competing in the name of a newly reconstituted Iraqi nation. The emphasis on "freedom" and "free" had the rhetorical effect of eliding the various ways in which Iraq remained battered country—military occupation by Western forces, outbreaks of violence from those resisting the invasion, damage to infrastructure, shortages of medical care, political and religious divisions, and so on. Deployed as a campaign slogan, the Iraqi national soccer team represented a typical Bush strategy of emphasizing the outward symbol of a democratic *institution*—in this case a state-sanctioned international sports team—while minimizing the staggering lack of democratic *practice* that "freedom" had failed to promote.

While the Bush administration looked to exploit the Olympic Games, there were several voices that rose in opposition to use of the commercial. From an official level, both the IOC and the United States Olympic Committee (USOC) objected to the conflation of the Olympics and politics. "The arrogance of the US administration is quite amazing," said one member of the IOC. "To hijack the Olympics name . . . it is difficult to put it into words." Difficulty aside, the choice of the word "hijack" was especially powerful in the context of terrorism and war. It spoke to a perceived duplicity of an administration that purported to favor freedom and liberty, yet delimited the use of symbols to strategically bolster its own position. Further opposition came from Gerhard Heiberg, the marketing head for the IOC, who responded, "This is not good. We do not want this to happen. We are politically neutral."[77] While no one can reasonably maintain that the IOC avoids politics (consider the process of selecting host cities for the Games, for example), it is safe to assume that Bush's chauvinism was unwelcome.

Meanwhile, the USOC directly asked the Bush campaign to stop running the ad because they had not been given permission to use the "Olympics" name in the United States. Spokesman Darryl Seibel explained, "It is the responsibility of the USOC to manage Olympic marks, terms and images in the US, and also to remain apolitical."[78] In the past, the USOC has aggressively protected the use of the "Olympics," for example going after the "Gay Games" for infringement.[79] Predictably, Bush's political team ignored the USOC. As Diaz replied, "We are on firm legal ground to mention the Olympics, to make a factual point in a political advertisement."[80] The "fact" that any legal resolution would likely have taken longer to reach than the two weeks of the Games notwithstanding, others contested the "factual point" in the first place.

Even as some Iraqi players claimed their first-round win as a "victory for freedom," others expressed concern about the occupation by American forces.[81] When they became unwitting players in the presidential campaign, many were outraged. One player stated, "You cannot speak about a team that represents freedom. We do not have freedom in Iraq, we have an occupying force." Another asked of Bush, "How will he meet his God, having slaughtered so many men and women? He has committed so many crimes." One more added, "I have a message for George Bush: Calm down a little bit. We want to live. Stop killing civilians. Help rebuild Iraq instead of destroying it."[82]

Other Iraqis echoed these sentiments. A former citizen living in Greece remarked, "Everyone here is mad at the US. They help us get rid of our government, but then they let other people destroy our country." An Iraqi businessman stated, "I don't know why the politicians must take advantage of sport. It's not because of Bush that the Iraqi team is here." Even one of the United States' premier Olympic heroes, Carl Lewis, decried the Bush administration. Of the campaign commercial, he said, "I felt it was disingenuous. . . . Of course, we've invaded Iraq and are in there and are using it for political gain. It bewilders me, and I understand why the Iraqi players are offended."[83]

More objections were raised when the rumor spread that President Bush would fly to Athens for the gold-medal match if Iraq advanced that far. "People here say, if Bush comes to our final game," said one fan, "they will use bad language on him."[84] Iraq failed to reach the final match. Yet, to the players who spoke out, even the suggestion that the president would attend suggested an arrogance from a man so consumed by righteousness that understanding any diversity of opinion on the "war on terrorism" was impossible. And criticism was not limited only to the president. Upon learning that Secretary of State Colin Powell was scheduled to attend the closing ceremonies, one protestor responded, "Colin Powell is coming here while the Americans are killing people in Iraq. He is a hawk, a war criminal and an arch murderer. . . . We do not want him here."[85] Out of security concerns, Powell cancelled the visit.

Eduardo Galeano writes, "Soccer and fatherland are always connected, and politicians and dictators frequently exploit those links of identity."[86] Throughout the US occupation of Iraq, the distinction between mere "politician" and "dictator" has been dangerously blurred in the person of President George W. Bush. Here is a man who has propped himself up as a righteous crusader of absolute Christian morality;[87] who has disregarded important civil liberties under the guise of pursuing terrorists;[88] and who has promised the spread of freedom and democracy in Iraq while simultaneously installing its leadership at his own discretion. As Peter McLaren and Nathalia Jaramillo state, under Bush, "When democracy announces itself, it arrives under the sign of its own negation."[89] Meanwhile, as the American mainstream press largely deferred to the president, international media continued to spotlight Bush's creeping totalitarianism.[90] The *Guardian* editorialized, "Bush and [British Prime Minister Tony] Blair are terrified of the Iraqi people voting for anti-occupation leaders. They will accept nothing short of the legitimisation, through sham elections supervised by the occupation authorities, of an Allawi-style puppet regime."[91] Elsewhere, it reported that in a meeting between Bush and chief US envoy Paul Bremer, "a revised plan was hatched: elections would be delayed for more than a year, and in the meantime, Iraq's first 'sovereign' government would be hand-picked by Washington. The plan would allow Mr. Bush to claim progress on the campaign trail, while keeping Iraq safely under US control."[92]

In early 2005, Iraq held elections under US supervision. Yet, despite the presence of this symbolically democratic institution, once again democratic practice remained a low priority. Within the US, not only did the president ignore voices of dissent, but in the aftermath of 9/11, legislation like the USA Patriot Act curtailed civil liberties. Senator Russ Feingold, the only voice of opposition to the bill, stated when it passed, "The new law goes into a lot of areas that have nothing to do with terrorism and a lot to do with the government and the FBI having a list of things they want to do."[93] It symbolized what, in Ivie's words, "may be the most invasive legislation passed or contemplated since World War I."[94] In Iraq, as the president championed the coming of democracy and freedom, many around the world recognized that "much of the uprising [in Iraq] can be traced directly to decisions made in Washington to stifle, repress, delay, manipulate and otherwise thwart the democratic aspirations of the Iraqi people."[95] In short, boasting of the "freedom" symbolized by the Iraqi national soccer team did little to legitimize democracy in Iraq or to enrich it in the United States.

DEMOCRACY'S HOPE

Once the Olympic Games passed and the election ended in triumph for the Bush administration, what became of the Iraqi national soccer team? As Allen Guttmann remarks, "International sports events are . . . opportunities for newly independent states to make known their presence to a world that customarily pays them little attention (except to report their natural or man-made disasters)."[96] With the close of the games, it would seem that the Iraqis were once again forgotten (except when the media reported their "insurgence" against US forces). When Bush celebrated Iraqi victories while on the campaign trail, did he give any consideration to the fact that Hussein Saeed, former confidant of none other than Uday Hussein, had been given the reins of the Iraqi Soccer Federation? How did Bush's proclamations of democracy sound to the players who vividly remembered the hardships of playing for Saeed and Hussein? More than taking credit for what success the Iraqi team had on the field, Bush's statement's also did damage by obscuring the very real limitations that still existed for these players.

Even if President Bush unfairly claimed the Iraqi national soccer team as his own democratic triumph, it does not mean that we cannot recover a more productive vision from the Olympic pitch. For if there was any kind of democratic practice that emerged in this case, it may ironically have been found in the voices of the players themselves. As the *Guardian* noted, "Rather than meekly accepting their designated role in Bush's re-election campaign—plucky foreigners saved by political colossus—members of the team reacted furiously when they were told their success had been appropriated by a man whom one player described as a mass-murderer."[97] From members of the team, then, we heard the voices of dissent and, to a degree, democracy. This is not to suggest that Iraqi soccer players were not guilty of their own mistakes and problematic worldviews. Reducing Bush to names or expressing a desire to kill Americans in their homeland is not a vision of democracy any more productive than that promoted by the US administration. However, there were other voices in the mix. The team's coach, Majeed Adnan Hamad, said, "All the people, the Americans too, are our brothers. . . . Even though our country is almost destroyed, we are loving all the people." Rather than characterize the US president in antagonistic terms, an Iraqi midfielder simply stated, "Iraq as a team does not want Mr. Bush to use us for the presidential campaign. He can find another way to advertise himself." Another coach focused on the newfound unity of his club. "We need the [Olympic] dream to put a smile on the face of Iraqis," he said. "America did not make this team. The team is Iraqi."[98]

These comments rejected the notion that the Iraqi people should be thankful for what the United States did for them. Yet they did not resort to demonizing or constructing Americans as evil enemies. In this respect, some members of the Iraqi national soccer team were more able to avoid constructing Americans as radical others, choosing instead to think more in terms of what Mouffe calls "agonistic pluralism," or what Ivie terms "consubstantial rivalry."[99] While Bush attempted to speak for the people of Iraq, these athletes refused to surrender their voice. Herein lies the essence of democracy—these Iraqi voices chose to exercise their democratic freedoms by speaking out, by constituting their own collective identity, and by refusing to allow American politicians ownership of their own triumph.

From those who spoke out against the US occupation and the administration's calculated attempt to capitalize on the team's Olympic success, we are reminded that the presence of the Iraqi team at the Olympics is diminished unless there is an ongoing contest over what their triumph means to Iraq and its relationship to democracy. In a limited and partial way, individual Iraqi players offered a lesson in democratic practice, not because they could be appropriated as symbols of freedom as defined by the president, but because they revealed the necessity of a dynamic and engaged polity. As Ivie argues, "An absence of dissenting voices in a democracy is the true sign of weakness and vulnerability."[100]

The absence of dissent, of course, is as relevant within the United States as it is in Iraq. Post–September 11 America and the Iraqi national soccer team share few traits in common; yet they are articulated in similar fashion by the Bush administration. Americans too often are citizens in name only. They should defer to the authority of the president. They must embrace the marriage of capitalism and democracy. In short, *they must speak of democracy, but they must dare not speak democratically*. In this way, the attempt to use Iraq's soccer success for political gain was less about Iraq than it was about the United States. As I have outlined in this argument, Bush's use of the Iraqi team accompanied overlapping discourses about war and the presidential election. In the post–9/11 moment of crisis, perhaps more than at any other time in the nation's history, US citizens needed to participate in an earnest debate about the future of American foreign policy. Instead, the president reduced the struggle to religious terms of good and evil, and the public largely fulfilled its patriotic duty by embracing consumer culture.[101] Dissent was minimal, and as Robert Jensen suggests, "it has never seemed clearer that free speech is fragile, and democracy is in danger in the United States."[102]

As seen through the case of the Iraqi national soccer team, the sport/war metaphor continues to have political currency in American culture. Rather than invoke the familiar "bombs" of American football, George W. Bush turned to international soccer to construct a metaphor of democratic triumph in the midst of his "war on terrorism." The accomplishments of the team offered the president a convenient symbol through which he could celebrate the "freedom" that his policies increasingly placed at risk. Moreover, Bush's claim that Iraq could not have fielded a team without US military intervention further justified the American occupation and deflected attention away from the failure to locate weapons of mass destruction.

While it may seem reasonable for an American president to celebrate the achievements of American athletes, it is highly questionable when those athletes compete for another nation. Celebrating the Iraqi victory as a triumph for the United States only served to validate the fears of those who have felt that Iraq will have its "democratic" government propped up merely to cast an American shadow over the Middle East. Moreover, while "freedom" and "democracy" eventually may become substantive components of Iraq's culture, it is clear that ownership of those concepts must be placed in the hands and heard through the voices of the Iraqi people themselves. In short, President Bush's claims about the Iraqi national soccer team may be many things; but they are surely not democratic.

The president's rhetorical strategy during the "war on terrorism" has largely depended on moral absolutes and universal claims to righteousness. Similarly, the Iraqi national soccer team was offered as a symbol of freedom that, accepted at face value, would have foreclosed additional democratic contestation. Critics of Bush, including members of the team itself, provide an important counter to this kind of delimited narrative. In the spirit of democratic pluralism, we must encourage continued deliberation and contestation over the values and policies that define our increasingly shared world. The use of sport as a political metaphor, therefore, is a complicated affair. This analysis privileges a reinvention of the metaphor in more democratic, agonistic terms, for the virtue of competitive sport is found in the fact that it requires the mutual survival and respect of both participants. It celebrates the triumph over an adversary, not the elimination of an enemy.

This essay is an effort to promote the social critique of sport as a part, albeit partial and limited, of the reinvigoration of democratic practice. International sporting events are particularly significant arenas for politics and conflict. I look to such moments as critical sites of contestation, as a reminder that democracy "is a process and not an end."[103] Moreover, I hope that this analysis serves as an invitation to communication scholars to engage more critically with the discourses of sport as they intersect with global culture and international politics. Miller et al[.] suggest that the point of the critique of sport and politics is "both to understand *and* to change them through democratic means."[104] As evidenced by George W. Bush's appropriation of the Iraqi national soccer team, this democratic contest is ongoing. And there is work to be done.

NOTES

[1]Quoted in Varda Burstyn, *The Rites of Men: Manhood, Politics, and the Culture of Sport* (Toronto: University of Toronto Press, 1999), 165.

[2]Sue Curry Jansen and Don Sabo, "The Sport/War Metaphor: Hegemonic Masculinity, the Persian Gulf War, and the New World Order," *Sociology of Sport Journal* 11 (1994): 3–4.

[3]Jeffrey Segrave, "The Sports Metaphor in American Cultural Discourse," *Culture, Sport, Society* 3 (2000): 50.

[4]Throughout this essay, I refer to the "war on terrorism," using quotation marks to indicate the invented and contestable nature of the term.

[5]Robert Lipsyte, "Sports Metaphors Trivialize War," *USA Today*, 7 April 2003, 15A.

[6]Ron Cook, "Protester Should Play Games, Not Politics," *Pittsburgh Post-Gazette*, 2 March 2003, http://web.lexisnexis.com/universe.

[7]Derrick Hulme, *The Political Olympics: Moscow, Afghanistan, and the 1980 US Boycott* (New York: Praeger, 1990), 9.

[8]This argument appears in much of her work, most recently in Chantal Mouffe, *On the Political* (London: Routledge, 2005).

[9]Chantal Mouffe, *The Democratic Paradox* (London: Verso, 2000), 22.

[10]Alan Tomlinson, *Sport and Leisure Cultures* (Minneapolis, MN: University of Minnesota Press, 2005), 14.

[11]George W. Bush, "New SEC Chairman Sworn In," White House News Conference, 18 February 2003, http://www.whitehouse.gov/news/releases/2003/02/20030218-1.html.

[12]William E. Connolly, *Pluralism* (Durham, NC: Duke University Press, 2005): 121–27.

[13]Connolly, 123, 126.

[14]"The Franchise: America's Elections," *MSNBC*, 21 October 2004, http://www.msnbc.msn.com/id/6073718/. Among the displays in Democracy Plaza were replicas of the Oval Office and Air Force One, a debate theatre that displayed highlights from presidential debates since 1960, interactive voter registration exhibits, and examples of voting booth technologies currently used in the United States.

[15]Jan Nederveen Pieterse, *Globalization or Empire?* (New York: Routledge, 2004), 42.

[16]Benjamin R. Barber, *Fear's Empire: War, Terrorism, and Democracy* (New York: W. W. Norton & Company, 2003), 176.

[17]Tomlinson, 229.

[18]David Rowe, *Sport, Culture, and the Media: The Unruly Trinity* (Buckingham, UK: Open University Press, 1999).

[19]David Rowe, "Sport and the Repudiation of the Global," *International Review for the Sociology of Sport* 38 (2003): 285.

[20]Kenneth Burke, *Permanence and Change: An Anatomy of Purpose*, 3rd ed. (Berkeley: University of California Press, 1984), 49, 194.

[21]For a recent example of this, see Michael Mandelbaum, *The Meaning of Sports: Why Americans Watch Baseball, Football, and Basketball and What They See When They Do* (New York: Public Affairs, 2004), 16–26.

[22]George Lakoff, "'Metaphor and War,' An Open Letter to the Internet from George Lakoff," 1991, http://philosophy.uoregon.edu/metaphor/lakoff-l.htm.

[23]George Lakoff, "Metaphor and War, Again," *AlterNet*, 18 March 2003, http://www.alternet.org/story/15414/.

[24]Here I wish to use the term "empire" in the sense that it characterizes a nation that seeks territorial or economic conquest and control. This is not, therefore, consistent with the use of "Empire" in which no specific nation-state, the United States included, can be seen as a central agent. For an engagement with Empire as a decentered phenomenon, see Michael Hardt and Antonio Negri, *Empire* (Cambridge, MA: Harvard University Press, 2000).

[25]For an historical account of this phenomenon, see Niall Ferguson, *Colossus: The Price of America's Empire* (New York: Penguin Press, 2004).

[26]Francis Fukuyama, "The End of History?" *The National Interest*, Summer 1989, 3–18.

[27]David Mosler and Bob Catley, *Global America: Imposing Liberalism on a Recalcitrant World* (Westport, CT: Praeger, 2000), xiii.

[28]Jan Nederveen Pieterse, "Can the United States Correct Itself?," *Cultural Studies Critical Methodologies* 4 (2004): 352.

[29]Wendy Brown, "Neo-liberalism and the End of Liberal Democracy," *Theory & Event* 7.1 (2003), http://muse.jhu.edu/journals/tae.

[30]Jan Nederveen Pieterse, *Globalization or Empire?* (New York: Routledge, 2004), v.

[31]Rowe, "Sport and the Repudiation of the Global," 281.

[32]Joseph Maguire, *Global Sport: Identities, Societies, Civilization* (Cambridge, UK: Polity Press, 1999), 90.

[33]The first theorist to clearly articulate this theme is Carl Schmitt, *The Crisis of Parliamentary Democracy,* trans. Ellen Kennedy (Cambridge, MA: MIT Press, 2001), 9–12.

[34]Chantal Mouffe, *Democratic Paradox,* 101–2.

[35]Traditionally, hockey would have been included as a fourth major sport, yet its popularity and influence have declined among American sports fans.

[36]Worldwide, soccer generally is known as "football," or "association football." However, because I am writing from an American standpoint about American attitudes toward sport, I will refer to the game as "soccer."

[37]Richard Giulianotti, *Football: A Sociology of the Global Game* (Cambridge, UK: Polity Press, 1999), xi.

[38]Rowe references 1.5 billion in "Sport and the Repudiation of the Global," 284; 2 billion is cited in Eduardo Galeano, *Soccer in Sun and Shadow,* trans. Mark Fried (London: Verso, 2003), 208.

[39]Franklin Foer, *How Soccer Explains the World: An Unlikely Theory of Globalization* (New York: HarperCollins, 2004), 3.

[40]Giulianotti, xii.

[41]Peter Donnelly, "The Local and the Global: Globalization in the Sociology of Sport," *Journal of Sport and Social Issues* 23 (1996): 249.

[42]This theme is regularly illustrated by columnists who write for American newspapers. For examples, see Norman Chad, "More Americans Watch Infomercials Than MLS," *Milwaukee Journal-Sentinel,* 18 November 2003, http://web.lexisnexis.com/universe, or Dan Shaughnessy, "Kicking Back With Soccer," *Boston Globe,* 4 August 1997, http://web.lexisnexis.com/universe.

[43]Steve Kelley, "Soccer Often Misunderstood, but Game is One of Beauty," *Seattle Times,* June 22, 1998, online at http://web.lexisnexis.com/universe.

[44]See Markovits and Hellerman, 286–93; Just prior to this section, the authors also detail the positive opinions that emerged during the 1994 World Cup, 282–85.

[45]Foer, 241.

[46]Foer, 238.

[47]For more on this, see Stephen Wagg, ed., *British Football and Social Exclusion* (London: Routledge, 2004).

[48]I do not want to argue here that soccer is not at all popular in the United States. It is beloved by millions, especially non-white and non-African American populations. This support, however, rarely translates into mainstream media coverage or political capital.

[49]David L. Andrews, Robert Pitter, Detlev Zwick, and Darren Ambrose, "Soccer, Race, and Suburban Space," in Ralph C. Wilcox, David L. Andrews, Robert Pitter, and Richard L. Irwin, ed., *Sporting Dystopias: The Making and Meaning of Urban Sport Cultures* (Albany, NY: SUNY Press, 2003), 198.

[50]Detlev Zwick and David L. Andrews, "The Suburban Soccer Field: Sport and America's Culture of Privilege," in Gary Armstrong and Richard Giulianotti, ed., *Football Cultures and Identities* (Houndmills, UK: Macmillan, 1999), 211–12.

[51]Toby Miller, David Rowe, Jim McKay, and Geoffrey Lawrence, "The Over-Production of US Sports and the New International Division of Cultural Labor," *International Review for the Sociology of Sport* 38 (2003): 427–40.

[52]Giulianotti, 27.

[53]Toby Miller, Geoffrey Lawrence, Jim McKay, and David Rowe, *Sport and Globalization: Playing the World* (London: Sage, 2001), 12.

[54]Adrian Wojnarowski, "Iraq Celebrates 'Victory for Freedom,'" *ESPN.com,* 12 August 2004, http://sports.espn.go.com/oly/summer04/soccer/news/story?id1858340.

[55]*The New York Times* piece appears as "Warm and Fuzzy Olympians," *International Herald Tribune,* 28 August 2004, http://web.lexisnexis.com/universe; "2004 Olympics: Miracle of the Iraqi Men's Olympic Soccer Team," *Athens News Agency,* 22 August 2004, http://web.lexisnexis.com/universe; James Drummond, James Harding, and David Owen, "Olympic Success Gives Iraqis Respite, and a Weapon for Bush's Campaign," *Financial Times,* 24 August 2004, http://web.lexisnexis.com/universe. It would be fair to point out here that soccer at the Olympics is met with a collective yawn by many devotees of the game. Yet while it is the World Cup that captures the respect and attention of soccer aficionados, the Olympic Games nevertheless receive massive coverage around the world. That the story was less about soccer itself, and more about how soccer enables the expression of freedom and democracy, illustrates its relevance during the "war on terrorism."

[56]Craig Whitlock, "Bush Campaign Won't Pull Ad Despite Complaint by USOC," *Washington Post,* 27 August 2004, http://web.lexisnexis.com/universe.

[57]George W. Bush, "Meet the Press with Tim Russert," *National Broadcasting Company,* 8 February 2004, http://www.msnbc.msn.com/id/4179618.

[58]Robert L. Ivie, "Evil Enemy Versus Agonistic Other: Rhetorical Constructions of Terrorism," *The Review of Education, Pedagogy, and Cultural Studies* 25 (2003): 181–200.

[59]George W. Bush, "President Delivers State of the Union Address," White House Press Release, 19 January 2002, http://www.whitehouse.gov/news/releases/2002/01/20020129-11.html.

[60]Ivie, "Evil Enemy," 184.

[61]Simon Jenkins, "The Inevitable Triumph of Guns, God, and a Large Slice of Apple Pie," *The Times London,* 4 November 2004, online at http://web.lexisnexis.com/universe.

[62]Barber, 15.

[63]Maguire, 7.

[64]Miller et al., 13.

[65]Tomlinson, 31.

[66]Bob Woodward, *Bush at War* (New York: Simon & Schuster, 2002), 277.

[67]Quoted in Samantha J. King, "Offensive Lines: Sport State Synergy in a Time of Perpetual War," unpublished manuscript, p. 17.

[68]Jim Riordan and Arnd Krüger, *The International Politics of Sport in the 20th Century* (E&FN SPON: London, 1999), x.

[69]Othello Harris, "The Rise of Black Athletes in the USA," In Riordan and Krüger, 150.

[70]See Tomlinson, "Magnificent Trivia: Olympic Spectacle, Opening Ceremonies, and Some Paradoxes of Globalization," 9–27.

[71]Marc Stein, "Olympics Won't Be in KG's Plans," *ESPN.com,* 29 April 2004, http://sports.espn.go.com/oly/columns/story?columniststein_marc&id1792114.

[72]Steve Woodward, "Athletes Asked to Behave," *ESPN.com,* 13 August 2004, http://sports.espn.go.com/oly/summer04/gen/columns/story?id1858597.

[73]Lawrence Donegan, "Bush's Games Hijack Leaves a Very Sour Taste," *The Guardian,* 24 August 2004, http://web.lexisnexis.com/universe.

[74]Whitlock.

[75]Bill Briggs, "Bush Camp Won't Pull Ad," *Denver Post,* 27 August 2004, http://web.lexisnexis.com/universe.

[76]Drummond, *et al.*

[77]Erskine McCullough, "Bush 'Hijacks' Games' Name," *Queensland Courier Mail,* 27 August 2004, http://web.lexisnexis.com/universe.

[78]Whitlock.

[79]Miller et al., 12.

[80]Briggs.

[81]Wojnarowski.

[82]Quoted in Briggs; Quoted in Art Thiel, "Soccer Team Gives Iraq Validation," *Pittsburgh Post-Gazette,* 26 August 2004, http://web.lexisnexis.com/universe; Quoted in Thanassis Cambanis, "Iraqis Have met Their Greater Goal of Pride," *Boston Globe,* 25 August 2004, http://web.lexisnexis.com/universe.

[83]Quoted in Bill Plaschke, "Defeat an All-Too-Familiar Reality for Iraqis," *Los Angeles Times,* 25 August 2004, http://web.lexisnexis.com/universe. Quoted in Cambanis. Quoted in Denis Campbell and Helena Smith, "Olympic Gold Hero Accuses Bush," *The Observer,* 29 August 2004, http://web.lexisnexis.com/universe.

[84]Plaschke.

[85]Whitlock.

[86]Galeano, 35.

[87]See Robert L. Ivie, "The Rhetoric of Bush's 'War' On Evil," *KB Journal* 1 (2004), http://www.kbjournal.org.

[88]This charge has been leveled at President Bush for many reasons. In the initial months following 9/11, critics worried that programs like the USA Patriot Act and Operation TIPS represented dangerous encroachments into the daily lives of average American citizens. These fears were seemingly confirmed by reports in 2006 that Bush has authorized secret surveillance of phone records. For more on the initial debate, see Nancy Chang, *Silencing Political Dissent: How Post-September 11 Anti-Terrorism Measures Threaten our Civil Liberties* (New York: Seven Stories Press, 2002; for more on domestic surveillance programs, see Bob Herbert, "Illegal and Inept," *New York Times,* 9 February 2006, A1, http://web.lexisnexis.com/universe.

[89]Peter McLaren and Nathalia E. Jaramillo, "A Moveable Fascism: Fear and Loathing in the Empire of Sand," *Cultural Studies Critical Methodologies* 4 (2004): 225.

[90]For a description of how mainstream American media have been surprisingly uncritical regarding George W. Bush, see Douglas Kellner, "The Media and the Crisis of Democracy in the Age of Bush-2," *Communication and Critical/Cultural Studies* 1 (2004): 29–58.

[91]Sami Ramadani, "Falluja's Defiance of a new Empire: It is Bush and Blair, not the Iraqi resistance, who Fear Free Elections," *The Guardian,* 10 November 2004, http://web.lexisnexis.com/universe.

[92]Naomi Klein, "Die, Then Vote," *The Guardian,* 13 November 2004, http://web.lexisnexis.com/universe.

[93]Quoted in Lewis H. Lapham, *Gag Rule: On the Suppression of Dissent and the Stifling of Democracy* (New York: Penguin Press, 2004), 7.

[94]Robert L. Ivie, "Prologue to Democratic Dissent," *The Public,* 11 (2004): 5.

[95]Klein.

[96]Allen Guttmann, *Games and Empires: Modern Sports and Cultural Imperialism* (New York: Columbia University Press, 1994), 184.

[97]Donegan.

[98]Quoted in Thiel. Quoted in Drummond, et al. Quoted in Cambanis.

[99]Mouffe, *Democratic Paradox;* Robert L. Ivie, *Democracy and America's War on Terror* (Tuscaloosa, AL: University of Alabama Press, 2005).

[100]Robert L. Ivie, "Rhetorical Deliberation and Democratic Politics in the Here and Now," *Rhetoric & Public Affairs* 5 (2002), 281.

[101]For more on this, see Greg Dickinson, "Selling Democracy: Consuming Culture and Citizenship in the Wake of September 11," *Southern Communication Journal* 70 (2006): 271–84.

[102]Robert Jensen, *Citizens of the Empire: The Struggle to Claim Our Humanity* (San Francisco: City Lights Books, 2004), 56.

[103]Barber, 180.

[104]Miller et al., 5.

Chapter VII

Social Movement Criticism

In its simplest form, social movement criticism is the analysis of rhetoric produced by members of social movements. This type of criticism uses a variety of perspectives, so there is no single "method." Indeed, an entire journal issue and several textbooks have been devoted to the diverse approaches and issues involved in social movement scholarship.[1] This chapter includes three essays that show different facets of social movement criticism and offer productive avenues for analysis.

Social movement criticism was launched in 1952, when Leland Griffin observed that the traditional study of the works produced by a single orator was not the only possible approach to rhetorical criticism. The critic could also evaluate a "multiplicity of speakers, speeches, audiences, and occasions." Griffin focused on the rhetoric produced by historical movements and proposed a method for evaluating such discourse. He observed that social movements existed in time with discernible beginnings, progressions, and terminations. The rhetoric produced by such movements, he maintained, fell into corresponding phases: "inception," "development," and "consummation." Moreover, Griffin theorized that social movements consisted of two general types: "pro" movements, which argued for "the creation or acceptance of an idea or institution," and "anti" movements, which attempted to "arouse public opinion to the destruction or rejection of an existing institution or idea." The main criterion for judging social movement discourse was its effectiveness. Thus, Griffin's standard for judgment remained essentially neo-classical, although he also claimed the discourse should be evaluated according to the theories of rhetoric available to the participants in the historical movements.[2]

Griffin's 1958 essay "The Rhetorical Structure of the Antimasonic Movement" recapitulates his method for analyzing social movements and illustrates it with a case study. Griffin traces the three stages of a nineteenth-century "anti" movement; analyzes the arguments, strategies, claims, and counter-claims; and delves into different types and media of rhetoric. Griffin concludes that the "defendant" rhetoricians, the Masons themselves, did not use effective rhetorical strategies in protecting themselves from Antimasonic Movement attacks.

A large number of movement studies were done in the 1960s and 1970s, when campuses erupted in protest rhetoric. The social movements of the sixties brought researchers into direct contact with discourse and symbolism that violated accepted standards for debate and discussion, and, as a result, seemed irrational or uncivilized to many people.[3] In order to account for these new rhetorical phenomena, the focus of study generally shifted from historical movements to contemporary movements.

Herbert W. Simons's 1970 essay, "Requirements, Problems, and Strategies: A Theory of Persuasion for Social Movements," reflects the social and intellectual ferment of the 1960s. Simons argues that social movement criticism should be based on theory. To accomplish this, he proposes a "leader-centered" model drawn from the field of sociology. He theorizes that, just like more formal entities such as governments or political parties, social movements must fulfill functional requirements. The functional needs of movements create "rhetorical requirements" for movement leaders. Further, inherent conflicts among these requirements result in "rhetorical problems" that must be resolved strategically. Simons advocates a serviceable theory of persuasion for social movements and establishes a series of benchmarks to evaluate the discourse of movement leaders.

Susan Zaeske's "Signatures of Citizenship: The Rhetoric of Women's Antislavery Petitions," published in 2002, departs from the "leader-centered" approach that Herbert Simons advocates. Zaeske analyzes the rhetorical efforts of ordinary participants in a social movement. Combining elements of feminist theory, critical rhetoric, and public sphere theory, among others, she undertakes "a multi-faceted reading of female antislavery petitions." Zaeske argues that handwritten signatures on a document "are rhetorical artifacts and can be read as texts." Through the act of signing petitions, the author says, women of a certain social class were able to "insinuate" themselves into the political discussion and make the transition from isolated individuals to political participants. Ironically, Zaeske points out, by portraying their "slave sisters" as voiceless victims, the white petitioners disregarded them as equals and potential allies.

NOTES

[1]See Charles J. Stewart, Craig Allen Smith, and Robert E. Denton, Jr., *Persuasion and Social Movements*, 4th ed. (Prospect Heights, Ill.: Waveland, 2001); Charles E. Morris III and Stephen H. Browne, *Readings on the Rhetoric of Social Protest* (State College, Pa.: Strata Publishing, 2001); [Special Issue on Social Movement Criticism], *Central States Speech Journal* 31 (1980): 225–315.

[2]Leland M. Griffin, "The Rhetoric of Historical Movements," *Quarterly Journal of Speech* 38 (1952), 184–188.

[3]See Robert L. Scott and Donald K. Smith, "The Rhetoric of Confrontation," *Quarterly Journal of Speech* 55 (1969): 1–8; James R. Andrews, "Confrontation at Columbia: A Case Study in Coercive Rhetoric," *Quarterly Journal of Speech* 55 (1969): 9–16; John Waite Bowers and Donovan J. Ochs, *The Rhetoric of Agitation and Control* (Reading, Mass.: Addison-Wesley, 1971).

THE RHETORICAL STRUCTURE OF THE ANTIMASONIC MOVEMENT

LELAND M. GRIFFIN

"I doubt if you have ever given the movement . . . an hour's thought. Yet I have seen your grandfather's eyes flash under his white knotted brows, and heard his voice tremble with emotion, as, even amid the excitement of our great Civil War, he told the story of that wonderful popular uprising."

Albion Tourgée, Letters to a King, *1888*

I

The conflict between secrecy and democracy would appear to be a recurrent phenomenon in our national history. Indeed, since the flowering of the modern secret society in the eighteenth century, antisecretism as a state of mind has been an enduring fiber in the pattern of Western culture. In countries where the totalitarian climate prevails, the spirit of antisecretism readily suppresses the secret order by the application of brute force. Where the question of suppression is left to the arbitrament of public opinion, however, the spirit of antisecretism relies on persuasion. Throughout the century following the Revolutionary War, sentiment against the secret society was strong in America. During this period three attempts to arouse public opinion to the destruction of secret societies—and the Masonic Society in particular—may be noted. The second of these movements, which flourished from 1826 to 1838, roughly spanning the Jacksonian period, was by far the most noteworthy of the three. The present essay will endeavor to trace, in broad outline, a few of the more significant aspects of the rhetorical structure of this movement.

In an earlier essay the writer has outlined a methodology for the study of the rhetorical structure of historical movements.[1] It will not be necessary to undertake a review of that methodology here; however, a brief summary of certain assumptions governing the analysis of the movement under discussion may prove helpful to the reader. Among these assumptions are the following: (1) that two broad classes of rhetorical movements may be said to exist: *pro* movements, in which the rhetorical attempt is to arouse public opinion to the creation or acceptance of an institution or idea, and *anti* movements, in which the rhetorical attempt is to arouse public opinion to the destruction or rejection of an existing institution or idea; (2) that within each movement two classes of rhetoricians may be distinguished: *aggressor* orators and journalists, who attempt in the *pro* movement to establish and in the *anti* movement to destroy, and *defendant* rhetoricians, who attempt in the *pro* movement to resist reform and in the *anti* movement to defend institutions;[2] and (3) that within each movement at least three phases of development may be noted: a period of *inception,* a period of *rhetorical crisis,* and a period of *consummation.* Within the frame of reference implied by these assumptions, certain generalizations concerning the rhetorical structure of the Antimasonic movement can be made.

II

The inception period of a movement may be described as that time when the roots of a pre-existing sentiment, nourished by interested rhetoricians, begin to flower into public notice or when some striking event occurs which immediately creates a host of aggressor rhetoricians and is itself sufficient to initiate the movement. Both pre-existing sentiment and a striking event were factors in the inception phase of the Antimasonic movement.

A discussion of the long history of opposition to secret orders antecedent to the Antimasonic movement cannot be undertaken here. It can be said, however, that the Society of Freemasons, as the earliest and most prominent of the esoteric orders, had borne the brunt of the antagonism. It can be said, also, that opposition to secret orders had, in general, been based on social, political, and religious (or moral) grounds. The suspicion that the secret rituals were sacrilegious, that the extrajudicial oaths, common to all secret societies, were in violation of Biblical injunction; the belief that secret orders encouraged vanity, frivolity, and intemperance and that they might serve to conceal crime, if they did not actually foster it; the fear that they were centers for political subversion—perhaps all of these elements of hostile sentiment were expressed by the Vermonter who, in the midst of the Illuminati Agitation of the 1790's, made the simple entry in his diary, "I hate Masonry."[3] At any rate, the existence of a precedent sentiment against secret societies must be borne in mind; for it does much to explain the rapid and vigorous development of the movement once the latent embers of social, political, and religious antagonism had been fired by the striking event.

That event, the immediate cause which precipitated the movement, may be readily identified. In the fall of 1826 rumor was circulated among Freemasons of western New York to the effect that a former member of the lodge at Batavia, a bricklayer named William Morgan, was planning to publish the secret signs, grips, passwords, and ritual of Ancient Craft Masonry. The anger of the Masons was soon translated into those actions which were to initiate the movement. Attacks were made on the person of the printer who had agreed to issue Morgan's book, and attempts were made to burn his press. Morgan himself was imprisoned on a false charge and shortly thereafter, abducted from his cell by a small band of Masons and driven in a closed carriage more than one hundred miles to Rochester; from there he was taken to the abandoned fort above Niagara Falls. The deserted Fort Niagara had been left in the charge of a retired army colonel and Mason, and with the consent of this official[,] Morgan was locked in the castle of the fort—where, from that moment, all historical trace of him vanishes.[4]

As news of the outrages against Morgan and his printer became known, excited citizens in the various towns of the Genesee country began to gather in a series of meetings. These so-called "indignation meetings" provided the first media for the expression of Antimasonic discourse.[5] The immediate result of the meetings in the various towns was the appointment of a number of citizens' investigating committees. The purpose of these Morgan Committees—the name soon given them—was expository: to discover the facts behind the Morgan affair and to communicate these facts to the public. In the spring of 1827 this purpose was realized—at least where the goal of communication was concerned—with the publication of a pamphlet entitled, *A Narrative of the Facts . . . Relating to the Kidnapping and Presumed Murder of William Morgan.* Thousands of copies of this document were distributed, not only in New York, but in neighboring states as well; and thus, in addition to providing the first significant venture in what was to become an Antimasonic program of exposition, the pamphlet proved an effective means for inaugurating the geographical spread of the movement.

While the Morgan Committees were in the midst of their investigations, legal inquiry into the affair began, and through the agency of the courtroom a further budget of exposition was developed. Over a five-year period more than forty so-called "Morgan trials" took place, and most of the forensic speaking of the movement, whether on the part of aggressor or defendant rhetoricians, was occasioned by these trials. At the first of the trials, held in January 1827, the presiding judge declared that the agitation to bring the abductors to justice was the manifestation of a "blessed spirit." Antimasonic speakers and writers adopted the phrase, and it became the first important catchword of the movement.

III

It was in connection with the investigations conducted by the Morgan Committees and in the courts that the defendant rhetoricians made their first tactical error, and it was an error which was perhaps implicit in the rhetorical theory of the day. In discussing means by which an unfavorable passion or disposition might be calmed, Campbell had recommended two courses: that speakers annihilate or diminish the object which raised the passion by proving the falsity of the narration on the supposed truth of which the passion was founded, or that speakers counter a passion by conjuring up some other passion or disposition which might overcome it.[6] The first course was virtually closed to the defendant rhetoricians, since certain of the convicted Masons had confessed their share of guilt in the abduction. Consequently, it was the second course which set the pattern of pro-Masonic discourse during the inception period. Thus, they attacked the character and motives of Antimasons, charged that they were merely trying to "raise an excitement," and declared that the "blessed spirit" was rather an inquisitorial spirit, a product of delusion as the Salem witchcraft trials had been. Had the defendant rhetoricians adopted, at the onset of the movement, a more conciliatory tone in their public discourse, had they not tacitly condoned the crime against Morgan, had they condemned the attempts made by certain members of the Order, as the trials progressed, to suborn judges and jurors, it is possible that the movement against them would have died in its inception phase. But the attitudes and actions of the defendant rhetoricians were fuel for the "blessed spirit" and, moreover, were directly responsible for the evolution of one fundamental in the Antimasonic rhetorical structure—the *extension of goals*. For from an intent to expose and bring to justice the individual Masons who had abducted Morgan the aggressor rhetoricians moved to an intent to destroy Freemasonry itself, and from this purpose it was a brief step, and one soon taken, that brought them to their ultimate purpose—the destruction of all secret orders then existing in the country. This primary fundamental in the rhetorical structure of the movement—the extension of goals, the focusing on ultimate purpose—had been realized by the time the inception period approached its termination in 1830.

A second fundamental realized during the inception period has been implied—the *laying of a groundwork of exposition*. As might be expected of men trained in the theory of Blair and Campbell, the Antimasonic rhetoricians were aware that conviction ought to precede persuasion, that the address to the understanding must come before the address to the will. The information developed by the Morgan Committees and through the Morgan trials comprised a significant body of the exposition that was an element in the address to the understanding. An additional corpora of expository matter, which developed gradually as the purpose of the Antimasons broadened in scope, derived from the attempt to inform the public concerning the nature of Freemasonry and such other esoteric groups as the Odd Fellows, Phi Beta Kappa, and the Orange Society. Morgan's own book was only the first in a long series of alleged "exposures" which purported to reveal the secrets of the orders under attack.[7] The efforts of the Masons to suppress Morgan's book, plus the fact that each of the later exposures was prepared by a "seceding" Mason, did much to convince the public that the Antimasonic revelations were true. In addition to satisfying the public thirst for information, the groundwork of exposition laid out by the aggressor rhetoricians was important, because it provided a foundation of common knowledge regarding secret societies on which a super-structure of argument could be built.

A third fundamental of the Antimasonic rhetorical pattern, also realized during the inception period, was the *development of avenues of propagation,* of media for the dissemination of oral and written discourse. The part played by the courtroom orator, as one type in the corps of aggressor speakers, has already been indicated. A second type, the pulpit orator, made significant contributions throughout the movement. *Masonry Proved to be a Work of Darkness, Repugnant to the Christian Religion, and Inimical to a Republican Government* was the title of a representative sermon, first preached by Lebbeus Armstrong at Northampton, New York, and later delivered from pulpits in Pennsylvania, New Jersey, Connecticut, and

Massachusetts.[8] Secrecy, as a principle, was frequently attacked from the pulpit. "If masonry contains anything good, why conceal it from mankind?" ran a typical argument of the Antimasonic ecclesiast; "The Scriptures are given to man 'without money and without price.' Is masonry more valuable?"[9] Nor did the pulpit orators neglect to post the testimony of such divines as John Wyclif ("men of sutel craft, as fre masons and othere, semen openly cursed")[10] and John Wesley ("What an amazing banter upon all mankind is Freemasonry! And what a secret is it which so many concur to keep! From what motive? Through fear—or shame to own it?")[11] Some clerical members of the Craft, like the fiery Lorenzo Dow, consistently declined to surrender their Freemasonry, their pulpits, or their scornful opinion of the "Antimasonic cattle." But as the movement progressed, the Antimasonic newspapers contained an increasing number of reports such as the one issued by a Methodist Episcopal church in Ohio, whose erstwhile Masonic membership voted never again "to attend a masonic procession, sit in a masonic lodge, or participate in a masonic festival."[12]

Still another type of speaker, the so-called "lecturer," proved an important ally of the pulpit orator in the work of spreading the "blessed spirit," particularly in remote areas and in communities not served by an Antimasonic newspaper. Generally a seceder from the Craft, the Antimasonic lecturer traveled from village to village, at times alone and at times accompanied by a small troupe of assistants, his coming heralded by handbills which proclaimed some such message as the following:

> *Freemasonry.* A practical demonstration of the first seven degrees of Freemasonry, viz. entered apprentice, fellow craft, master Mason, mark master, past master, most excellent master, and royal arch, will be given at the Town House in the town of Canandaigua, on Friday the 10th inst. . . . Doors opened at 6 o'clock P.M. Ceremonies to commence at 7 o'clock. Admittance 25 cts.[13]

As the text indicates, the function of the lecturer was largely expository. His demonstrations of Masonic degree work were generally preceded or followed by a denunciation of the Order, but the dramatic demonstration, the visual revelation of the secrets of the ritual, was always the staple of his program. Country audiences, consumed with curiosity, boredom, and a craving for dramatic entertainment, were always ready to fill a hall in order to witness the lecturer's exhibition; and, particularly during the first period of the movement, when exposition was the chief objective of the Antimasonic rhetoric, the lecturers served the cause to best effect.

In many ways, however, the most significant figure in the band of aggressor rhetoricians was the political orator. Early in the movement Antimasons became convinced that under its protective cloak of secrecy the Masonic Society might, at worst, be exploited for sinister ends by those interested in the subversion of the democracy and, at best, prove "an institution of dangerous tendency—liable to be used by the ambitious and designing as an engine for exalting unworthy men and erecting improper measures."[14] For confirmation of their fears, Antimasons pointed not only to the Morgan episode and its aftermath in the courts but also to the boast which had been voiced—in the year before Morgan's abduction—by the St. John's Day orator of the Union Lodge of Connecticut:

> What is Masonry now? It is powerful. It comprises men of rank, wealth, office, and talent, in power and out of power . . . active men, united together, and capable of being directed by the efforts of others, so as to have the force

of concert throughout the civilized world! They are distributed too, with the means of knowing one another, and the means of keeping secret, and the means of co-operating, in the desk—in the legislative hall—on the bench—in every gathering of business—in every party of pleasure—in every enterprise of Government. . . . So powerful, indeed, is it at this time, that it fears nothing from violence, either public or private, for it has every means to learn it in season, to counteract, defeat, and punish it.[15]

The conviction grew that secret societies could be fought most effectively through the agency of the polls,[16] and the development of a political party on the framework of the old Morgan Committees was a matter readily accomplished. In western New York, where political organization was first initiated, such men as Thurlow Weed, William Seward, and Millard Fillmore made their entry into politics as members of the Antimasonic Party. Political Antimasonry spread rapidly throughout the eastern states, taking root as far south as Georgia, as far west as Missouri; and soon, from the stump, the public platform, and the convention hall—and, as the party won victory at the polls, from the halls of the legislatures and the Congress—the voice of the Antimasonic orator was heard.

The Antimasonic journalist, like the orator, employed various channels in his approach to the public mind. Thus, early in the inception period, convinced that they could not secure a fair hearing in the majority of the existing newspapers, many of which were edited by Masons, Antimasons began to set up "free presses." Thurlow Weed, of Rochester, edited one of the first of these Antimasonic newspapers; Elijah P. Lovejoy performed a similar task before he moved on to Alton, Illinois; and William Lloyd Garrison, who served his first editorship on a "free press" in Vermont, reaffirmed his position in an early issue of *The Liberator:* "I go for the immediate, unconditional and total abolition of Freemasonry. Pillar after pillar is falling—the mighty Babel begins to shake—and, ere long, it will be broken into fragments by the American people, and scattered to the winds of heaven."[17] Editors of the "free presses" often sponsored the Antimasonic bookstores and reading rooms that began to appear in the towns and cities; and from their printing offices came not only newspapers but broadsides, tracts, pamphlets, periodicals, almanacs, and books as well. At the close of the inception period, in 1830, Antimasons claimed one-tenth of the newspapers of the country to be "free presses," founded "exclusively upon the principle of opposition to Freemasonry."[18]

A fourth fundamental in the developing rhetorical structure had to do with the geographical and social spread of the movement. The geographical boundaries of Antimasonry may be readily delineated: from New York, the movement spread into Pennsylvania, Ohio, Missouri, the Michigan Territory, and through all the New England states. Its hold in the South was always tenuous: "The free, the cold, clear, intelligent North," Seward wrote to Weed in 1831, "is the field for the growth of our cause." The social limits of the movement were less clear-cut, but, in general, Antimasonry was embraced by persons living in small towns and rural areas, by New Englanders and descendants of New England stock, and by persons reared in the climate of Protestant sectarianism.

A fifth fundamental in the rhetorical structure was concerned with the massing of basic charges against secret societies. Although the aggressor rhetoricians were primarily interested in exposition during the inception period, as has been remarked, a fund of argument was nevertheless advanced. By 1830, indeed, at the onset of the period of rhetorical crisis, the basic fund of argument which was to be utilized during the movement had been developed, and, as in former times, it was argument generally centered in objections based on social, political, and moral grounds.

IV

The period of rhetorical crisis may be defined as that time when one of the opposing groups of speakers and writers undertakes a decisive revision of its rhetorical strategy and so succeeds in irrevocably disturbing that balance (or relation) between the groups which had existed in the mind of the collective audience. The year 1830 may be taken to mark the period of rhetorical crisis both for the aggressor and for the defendant rhetoricians. It was during this year that the Masons, under the tacit leadership of President Jackson, and the open leadership of the Secretary of State, Edward Livingston, began to adhere to a new strategy of defense. At his installation in that year as General Grand High Priest of the General Grand Royal Arch Chapter of the United States, Livingston advised the Masons to adopt a policy of "dignified silence" in the face of the opposition's attack. After this address of Livingston's, the Masons became, in fact, virtually mute; and the discourse of the "Masons' Jacks"—those pro-Masonic defenders who were not themselves members of any of the beleaguered orders—began to diminish at an accelerating rate.

The year 1830 was one of rhetorical crisis for the aggressor rhetoricians in the sense that—having realized their ultimate purpose, having developed avenues of propagation, having massed a fund of basic charges, having inaugurated the spread of the movement, and having accomplished the task of exposition and conviction involved in their address to the understanding—they were now in position to concentrate on that address to the will, on the development of that persuasive flood of argument and appeal which would move the public to the destruction of secret societies.

The pattern of Antimasonic public address after 1830 is largely the reflection of an intensified use of available channels of discourse, with emphasis on greatly elaborated lines of argument rather than on exposition. Seceding Masons yielded to the "blessed spirit" in increasing numbers, and certain public figures—some no doubt sincere, and others seeing in the movement a device for striking at the Jackson administration—began to lend their dignity, as well as their persuasive powers, to the movement: men like Edward Everett, John Quincy Adams, Daniel Webster, Lyman Beecher, James Madison, the elder Charles Sumner, and John Marshall. The party grew rapidly. It became the first to hold a national political convention, the first to hold a national nominating convention; and in 1831—a year when ex-President Adams declared that "the dissolution of the Masonic institution [is] of more importance to us and our posterity than whether Mr. Clay or General Jackson shall be chosen President at the next election"—William Wirt received the nomination which made him the first Antimasonic candidate for the Presidency. In the ensuing election, Wirt carried only one state, Vermont, a fact which has led many historians to the conclusion that the movement was a "failure." This is a judgment which no one who examines the movement as a rhetorical operation can support. For from 1830 onward the labors of the aggressor speakers and writers began to bear fruit. States began to pass laws against extrajudicial oaths, legislation which was intended to emasculate the secret order; lodge charters were surrendered, sometimes under legal compulsion, but often voluntarily; Phi Beta

Kappa abandoned its oaths of secrecy; Masonic and Odd Fellows' lodges began to file bankruptcy petitions; and membership rolls in the various orders began to dwindle to the vanishing point.

V

The period of consummation, that time when the ranks of the aggressor rhetoricians begin to evaporate, varied somewhat as to locality: 1834 marked the virtual end of the movement in New York; 1836, in the New England states; and 1838 in Pennsylvania, where it was kept alive by Thaddeus Stevens (whose legislative committee was relentless with its question, "Are you, or have you ever been, a Freemason?") until given the deathblow by the Buckshot War—that historical fiasco known then, as now, as "the last kick of Antimasonry." Reasons for the withdrawal of the aggressor rhetoricians, again, were varied. Many abandoned the cause in the belief that the ultimate objective had been won; others, oddly enough, left the movement because they were convinced that victory—at least complete victory—was impossible; others resigned their labors out of sheer weariness or boredom or in disgust at excesses which the movement had shown; and still others, finally, turned their backs on Antimasonry to yield to the press of other causes, other movements—chiefly the absorbing new crusade which, as early as 1829, had wrung from Garrison the cry:

> All this fearful commotion has arisen from the abduction of *one man*. More than two millions of unhappy beings are groaning out their lives in bondage, and scarcely a pulse quickens, or a heart leaps, or a tongue pleads in their behalf. 'Tis a trifling affair, which concerns nobody. Oh for the spirit that now rages, to break every fetter of oppression![19]

VI

Certainly it must be said that the Antimasonic rhetoricians were effective in their efforts to generate a flood of argument and appeal. Many lines of argument, based generally on political, social, and religious reasons for objecting to secret societies, were developed. The rhetoricians were successful, evidently, in establishing the credibility of the seceding Masons and in building a fund of testimony by the technique of soliciting testimonials—a technique apparently used for the first time in a national political movement. While the pro-Masonic rhetoricians based their defense principally on the sanction of authority on the appeal of the "great names" of the Masonic fraternity, the aggressor rhetoricians evoked the sanctions of Justice and Equality; and they did so in an age when men, as rarely before, were scornful of authority and in search of equality and justice. It must be said, too, that the Antimasonic rhetoricians displayed remarkable facility in their employment of available channels of propagation. Their success in enlisting the aid of the clergy; their use of the lecture platform; their development of free presses; their organization for rhetorical purposes, for the first time in a movement, of a political party; their extensive use, again for the first time, of almanacs as a propaganda medium; their tireless broadcasting of pamphlets and tracts—all were important factors in bringing their persuasion to the people.

And yet the Antimasonic rhetoricians made errors, perhaps fatal ones, which resulted in the development of unfavorable opinion and were factors contributing to the dissolution of the movement before the rhetoricians had completely realized their objective. The conscious neglect of the citizens of the southern states as an audience for persuasion—with the consequence that Masonry continued to flourish in the South—was an unexplainable error. The policy of attacking the neutral elements of the public, the "Masons' Jacks," was undoubtedly an error. According to one contemporary, "The Jacks were as bitterly stigmatized as the Masons themselves, and even more so, by the Anties. This intolerant spirit sealed the fate of the Anti-Masonic party."[20] But most important, the rhetoricians erred in permitting the multiplicity of their argument and appeal, the sheer mass of their discourse, to reach a point of saturation with the public. Blair had warned "against extending arguments too far, and multiplying them too much. This serves rather to render a cause suspected, than to give weight. An unnecessary multiplicity of arguments . . . detracts from the weight of that conviction which a few well chosen arguments carry";[21] and again,

> Above all things, beware of straining passion too far, of attempting to raise it to unnatural heights. Preserve always a due regard for what the hearers will bear; and remember, that he who stops not at the proper point, who attempts to carry them farther in passion than they will follow him, destroys his whole design.[22]

In their eagerness to flood the public with a multiplicity of discourse, the aggressor rhetoricians did not stop at the proper point. On the one hand, through the use of arguments and appeals which grossly exaggerated any possible dangers inherent in Freemasonry, they offended just and reasonable men. Opponents of proscription in their beginning, they ended by becoming proscribers; and reaction developed and opinion set in against them. On the other hand, through the incessant din of their discourse, they became, in time, merely tiresome and repellent. As early as 1831, an exasperated citizen named Calvin Philleo was driven to the publication of a pamphlet entitled *Light on Masonry and Anti-Masonry and a Renunciation of Both*.[23] And Emerson, writing to his brother William in 1834, asked with a playful weariness that must have been typical of many Americans:

> And how have you decided these sad political questions? I am almost afraid to take up a newspaper, I am so sure of being pained by what I shall read. Is it not a good symptom for society this decided and growing taste for natural science which has appeared though yet in its first gropings? What a refreshment from Antimasonry and Jacksonism and Bankism is in the phenomena of the Polar Regions or in the habits of the Oak or the geographical problem of the Niger.[24]

What of the defendant rhetoricians? Their task, as must often be the case, was not easy. "To subdue the spirit of faction," Campbell had written, "and that monster, spiritual pride, with which it is invariably accompanied, to inspire equity, moderation, and charity into men's sentiments and conduct with regard to others, is the genuine test of eloquence."[25] After 1830, the defendant rhetoricians made no attempt to meet the test of eloquence, and for adhering to their policy of silence, no matter how dignified, they are probably to be condemned. It was through no effort of theirs that Antimasonry, in time, dwindled away, and Freemasonry was again permitted to flourish by an indifferent public. Silence, in a democracy, is likely to be poor policy. Truth, crushed to earth, may rise again—but the dictum does not furnish a trustworthy guide for rhetoricians or democratic citizens. More reliable is Lowell, in his discourse on democracy: "An appeal to the reason of the people has never been known to fail in the long run." With faith in this dictum, let rhetoricians raise a clamor, as Burke advised, whenever there is an abuse; and let those attacked raise the standard of truth and employ the arms of argument and persuasion. Truth and argument may be feeble means—"feeble, indeed, against prejudice and passion," as Fisher Ames observed—and yet "they are all we have, and we must try them."

NOTES

[1] Leland M. Griffin, "The Rhetoric of Historical Movements," *QJS*, XXXVIII (April 1952), 184–188.

[2] Thus, we are here concerned with an *anti* movement in which the ultimate purpose of the discourse was shaped by a desire to arouse opinion to the destruction of the secret orders then existing in American society. The class of *aggressor* rhetoricians was made up of those speakers and writers hostile to secret societies, the Antimasonic orators and journalists; and the class of *defendant* rhetoricians, of course, was composed of those speakers and writers who sought to defend secret orders, the pro-Masonic orators and journalists.

[3] Cited in D. M. Ludlum, *Social Ferment in Vermont* (New York, 1939), p. 91.

[4] While Morgan's ultimate fate remains a matter for speculation, the events detailed here may be taken as historically established. An important source for the study of the inception phase of the movement is the "Report of the Special Counsel on the Subject of the Abduction of William Morgan," *Legislative Documents of the Senate and Assembly of the State of New York, Fifty-Third Session* (Albany, 1830). See also C. T. McClenachan, *History of Freemasonry in the State of New York* (New York, 1892), II, 477ff.; and Charles McCarthy, "The Antimasonic Party: A Study of Political Antimasonry in the United States, 1827–1840," *Annual Report of the American Historical Society for the Year 1902* (Washington, 1903), pp. 367–574.

[5] As witness the item quoted from the *Rochester Telegraph* in the Penn Yan *Yates Republican,* March 20, 1827: "*Capt. Morgan.*—Nothing has yet transpired calculated to throw more light on this dark transaction. . . . Meetings continue to be held upon this subject in almost every town in the western part of the state. Reports of every description on both sides of the question, distorted and magnified, are flying in every direction. A letter from one of the editors of this paper, who is now at Albany, says, 'I have heard nothing talked of, in the stages and barrooms, but Morgan. The excitement is spreading far and wide. At a meeting held in Trumansburg, I was informed, some personal violence was inflicted upon a mason. The opinion which is now abroad, that Morgan was murdered at Fort Niagara, is alarming the whole country, and unless strong and efficient measures are taken to develop this awful transaction, it is impossible to predict where it will end.'"

[6] George Campbell, *The Philosophy of Rhetoric* (Boston, 1823), pp. 124–125.

[7] *Illustrations of Masonry* (New York, 1827), 99 pp. It may be noted that Morgan's book represented nothing new in the history of the Craft. Many such exposures had been printed in the eighteenth century, particularly in France and England. Probably the most widely circulated was *Jachin and Boaz; or An Authentic Key to the Door of Free Masonry* (London, 1762), a book well known in America and one which had gone through at least twenty-six editions by 1813. Perhaps the earliest exposure printed in America was one published by Franklin in his *Pennsylvania Gazette* in 1730; shortly after its appearance Franklin joined St. John's Lodge of Philadelphia. See *Pennsylvania Gazette,* No. 108 (Dec. 3 to Dec. 8, 1730). See also, S. N. Smith, "The So-Called 'Exposures' of Freemasonry in the mid-eighteenth Century," *Ars Quatuor Coronatorum* (Margate, 1946), LVI, 4–26.

[8] (New York, 1830), 24 pp.

[9]Daniel Dow, *Sermon on Secret Societies, delivered . . . September 11, 1829* (Norwich, Conn., 1829), 14 pp. See also *New England Anti-Masonic Almanac . . . for 1830* (Boston, 1829), p. 28.

[10]From "The Grete Sentens of Curs," *Works*, ed. T. Arnold (Oxford, 1871), III, 332.

[11]Journal, III (London, 1840), 473, See *Anti-Masonic Sun Almanac . . . for 1832* (Philadelphia, 1831), p. 32.

[12]*Anti-Masonic Almanac . . . for 1831* (Utica, 1830) p. 53.

[13]This was the advertisement of Colonel R. H. Witherill's troupe (*American Masonick Record* [Albany], January 22, 1831, p. 1).

[14]"Proceedings of the Anti-Masonic Convention of the Twelve Western Counties of N.Y.," in David Bernard, *Light on Masonry* (Utica, 1829), p. 424.

[15]W. F. Brainard, "Masonic Lecture Spoken before the Brethren of Union Lodge, New London, on the Nativity of St. John the Baptist, June 24, A.L., 5825," in C. T. McClenachan, II, 570–571.

[16]At the first national nominating convention of the Antimasonic Party, held in Baltimore in 1831, the following resolution was adopted: "RESOLVED, That discussion, persuasion and argument, in connection with the exercise of the right of suffrage, is a correct and speedy mode of diffusing information on the subject of freemasonry, and is the best method to ensure the entire destruction of the institution" (*Proceedings of the Second United States Antimasonic Convention, held at Baltimore, September, 1831* [Boston, 1832], pp. 61–62).

[17]*The Liberator* (Boston), Oct. 6, 1832, p. 158.

[18]Henry W. Taylor, "Report on the Public Press," *Proceedings of the United States Anti-Masonic Convention, Held at Philadelphia, September 11, 1830* (Philadelphia, 1830), p. 41. See also Milton W. Hamilton, "Anti-Masonic Newspapers, 1826–1834," *The Papers of the Bibliographically Society of America*, XXXII (1938), 71–97.

[19]*Journal of the Times* (Bennington, Vt.), Feb. 6, 1829, p. 1.

[20]Levi Beardsley, *Reminiscences* (New York, 1852), p. 226.

[21]Hugh Blair, *Lectures on Rhetoric and Belles-Lettres* (Philadelphia, 1784), p. 299.

[22]*Ibid.*, p. 303.

[23](Providence, R.I., 1831), 23 pp.

[24]Ralph L. Rusk, ed., *Letters of Ralph Waldo Emerson* (New York, 1939), I, 404.

[25]George Campbell, p. 144.

REQUIREMENTS, PROBLEMS, AND STRATEGIES: A THEORY OF PERSUASION FOR SOCIAL MOVEMENTS

HERBERT W. SIMONS

Given the usual problems of estimating the effects of a single speech, of assessing the factors that may have produced those effects, and of evaluating the speech in light of the speaker's intent,[1] it is not surprising that few rhetoricians have undertaken the much more difficult task of analyzing the role of persuasion in social movements.[2] When one advances to the movement as a unit of study, these problems are magnified and others are introduced. As any number of currently unemployed college presidents can attest, it is frequently impossible to separate detractors from supporters of a social movement, let alone to discern rhetorical intentions,[3] to distinguish between rhetorical acts and coercive acts,[4] or to estimate the effects of messages on the many audiences to which they must inevitably be addressed. Actions that may succeed with one audience (e.g., solidification of the membership) may alienate others (e.g., provocation of a backlash).[5] For similar reasons, actions that may seem productive over the short run may fail over the long run (the reverse is also true).[6]

Add to these problems of analysis the sheer magnitude of the unit of study: a time span that may extend through several stages[7] for a decade or longer; a host of varied and often unconventional symbols and media;[8] not one leader and one following but several of each (themselves frequently divided into competing factions).[9] Designed for microscopic analysis of particular speeches, the standard tools of rhetorical criticism are ill-suited for unravelling the complexity of discourse in social movements or for capturing its grand flow. Hence it is with good cause that the major contributor to the development of an appropriate methodology has himself cautioned the uninitiated against study of any but the most minute social movements, and then only in the light cast by historical perspective.[10]

Professor Griffin has prescribed a relativistic and essentially clinical process for identifying and evaluating "the pattern of public discussion, the configuration of discourse, the physiognomy of persuasion, peculiar to a movement."[11] Yet the analyst could probably fulfill and even go beyond Griffin's definition of his task if only he could draw more heavily on theory.[12] No theory of persuasion in social movements can as yet be applied predictively to particular cases or tested rigorously through an analysis of such cases. But theory can nevertheless be illuminative. In addition to suggesting categories for descriptive analysis (a skeletal typology of stages, leaders, media, audiences, etc. has already been provided by Griffin),[13] it can indicate—admittedly in general terms—the requirements that rhetoric must fulfill in social movements, the means available to accomplish these requirements, and the kinds of problems that impede accomplishment. By enumerating rhetorical requirements, theory identifies the ends in light of which rhetorical strategies and tactics may be evaluated. By suggesting parameters and directions to the rhetorical critic, theory places him in a better position to bring his own sensitivity and imagination to bear on analyses of particular movements.

This paper is aimed, in preliminary fashion, at providing a leader-centered conception of persuasion in social movements.[14] Rooted in sociological theory, it assumes that the rhetoric of a movement must *follow,* in a general way, from the very nature of social movements. Any movement, it is argued, must fulfill the same functional requirements as more formal collectivities. These imperatives constitute *rhetorical requirements* for the leadership of a movement. Conflicts among requirements create *rhetorical problems* which in turn affect decisions on *rhetorical strategy. The primary rhetorical test of the leader—and, indirectly, of the strategies he employs—is his capacity to fulfill the requirements of his movement by resolving or reducing rhetorical problems.*

A social movement may be defined, combining concepts offered by Smelser and by Turner and Killian, as an uninstitutionalized collectivity that mobilizes for action to implement a program for the reconstitution of social norms or values.[15] Movements should be distinguished, as such, from panics, crazes, booms, fads, and hostile outbursts, as well as from the actions of recognized labor unions, government agencies, business organizations, and other institutionalized decision-making bodies.

The focus of this paper is on reformist and revolutionary movements. Blumer distinguished these "specific" social movements from "general["] social movements (amorphous social trends) and from "expressive" social movements, of which religious cults are a prototype.[16] Although geared to specific social movements (and especially to contemporary cases), the theory is applicable with somewhat less consistency to general and expressive movements, perhaps neglected by Blumer's classification scheme, as secessionist movements and movements aimed at the restoration or protection of laws, rules, and/or agencies.[17]

In the pages that follow, examination is made of the necessary functions of reformist and revolutionary rhetoric and of the types of problems that arise from inherently conflicting demands. Presentation of the theory next proceeds to a consideration of alternative strategies of adaptation: the tactics and styles appropriate to each and their respective advantages and disadvantages.

RHETORICAL REQUIREMENTS

Sociological theorists have inferred the functional imperatives of formal organizations from an analysis of their structural characteristics.[18] A social movement is not a formal social structure, but it nevertheless is obligated to fulfill parallel functions.[19] Like the heads of private corporations or government agencies, the leaders of social movements must meet a number of rhetorical requirements, arranged below under three broad headings.

1. *They must attract, maintain, and mold workers (i.e., followers) into an efficiently organized unit.* The survival and effectiveness of any movement are dependent on adherence—to its program, loyalty to its leadership, a collective willingness and capacity to work, energy mobilization, and member satisfaction. A hierarchy of authority and division of labor must be established in which members are persuaded to take orders, to perform menial tasks, and to forego social pleasures. Funds must be raised, literature printed and distributed, local chapters organized, etc.[20]

2. *They must secure adoption of their product by the larger structure* (i.e., the external system, the established order). The product of any movement is its ideology, particularly its program for change.[21] Reformist and revolutionary rhetorics both seize on conditions of real deprivation or on sharp discrepancies between conditions and expectations—the reformist urging change or repair of particular laws, customs, or practices, the revolutionary insisting that a new order and a vast regeneration of values are necessary to smite the agents of the old and to provide happiness, harmony, and stability.[22]

3. *They must react to resistance generated by the larger structure.* The established order may be "too kind" to the movement or it may be too restrictive. It may steal the movement's thunder by anticipating its demands and acting on some of them, by appointing a commission to "study the problem," or by bribing or coopting personnel. On the other hand, it may threaten, harass, or socially ostracize the membership, refuse to recognize or negotiate with the movement, or deny it access to the mass media.[23] The leadership of a social movement must constantly adjust to backlash reactions and pseudosupportive reactions as well as to overreactions by officials on which it may capitalize.

Social movements are severely restricted from fulfilling these requirements by dint of their informal compositions and their positions in relation to the larger society. By comparison to the heads of most formal organizations, the leaders of social movements can expect minimal internal control and maximal external resistance. Whereas business corporations may induce productivity through tangible rewards and punishments, social movements, as voluntary collectivities, must rely on ideological and social commitments from their members. At best, the movement's leadership controls an organized core of the movement (frequently mistaken for the movement itself) but exerts relatively little influence over a relatively larger number of sympathizers on its periphery.[24] Existing outside the larger society's conceptions of justice and reality, moreover, movements threaten and are threatened by the society's sanctions and taboos: its laws, its maxims, its customs governing manners, decorum, and taste, its insignia of authority, etc.

Although organizational efficiency and adaptation to pressures from the external system are clearly prerequisite to promotion of a movement's ideology, in other respects the various internal and external requirements of a movement are incompatible. *Shorn of the controls that characterize formal organizations, yet required to perform the same internal functions, harassed from without, yet obligated to adapt to the external system, the leader of a social movement must constantly balance inherently conflicting demands on his position and on the movement he represents.*

RHETORICAL PROBLEMS

Unless it is understood that the leader is subjected to incompatible demands, a great many of his rhetorical acts must seem counterproductive. An agitator exhorts his following to revolutionary fervor and then propounds conservative solutions to the evils he has depicted.[25] Another leader deliberately disavows the very program he seeks to achieve.[26] A third leader encourages his supporters to carry Viet Cong flags or to "raze the Pentagon" or to heckle another spokesman for the movement, despite advance knowledge that these acts will fragment the movement and invite bitter reactions from outsiders.[27]

On the other hand, the disintegration of a movement may be traced to its failure to meet one or more of the demands incumbent upon it. To deal with pressures from the external system, a movement may lose sight of its ideological values and become preoccupied with power for its own sake.[28] Careful, by contrast, to remain consistent with its values, the movement may forsake those strategies and tactics that are necessary to implement its program.[29] To attract membership support from persons with dissimilar views, the movement may dilute its ideology, become bogged down with peripheral issues[,] or abandon all substantive concerns and exist solely to provide membership satisfactions.[30]

Short of causing disintegration, the existence of crosspressures enormously complicates the role of the leader, frequently posing difficult choices between ethical and expediential considerations. The following are illustrative of these dilemmas and of other rhetorical problems created by conflicting demands.

1. When George Wallace vowed, after losing a local election, that he would never again be "out-niggered," he was referring to a phenomenon that has its counterpart on the left as well. Turner and Killian have suggested that strong identification by members with the goals of a movement—however necessary to achieve *esprit de corps*—may foster the conviction that any means are justified and breed impatience with time-consuming tactics. The use of violence and other questionable means may be prompted further by restrictions on legitimate avenues of expression, imposed by the larger structure. Countering these pressures may require that the leader mask the movement's objectives, deny the use of tactics that are socially taboo, promise what he cannot deliver, exaggerate the strength of the movement, etc. A vicious cycle develops in which militant tactics invite further suppression, which spurs the movement on to more extreme methods. Lest the moderate leader object to extremist tactics, he may become a leader without a following.[31]

2. The leader may also need to distort, conceal, exaggerate, etc., in addressing his own supporters. To gain intellectual respectability within and/or outside the movement, ideological statements should be built on a logical framework and appear consistent with verifiable evidence.[32] Yet mass support is more apt to be secured when ideological statements are presented as "generalized beliefs," oversimplified conceptions of social problems, and magical, "if-only" beliefs about solutions.[33] Statements of ideology must provide definition of that which is ambiguous in the social situation, give structure to anxiety and a tangible target for hostility, foster in-group feelings, and articulate wish-fulfillment beliefs about the movement's power to succeed.[34] Hence the use of "god words" and "devil words"[35] as well as "stereotypes, smooth and graphic phrases and folk arguments."[36]

Among isolated individuals, those anxiety, hostility, and wish-fulfillment beliefs that are socially taboo are likely to be repressed or inhibited. They are expres[s]ed unconsciously[,] or if consciously, only to one's self, or if expressed to others, said more to expunge feelings than to share them.[37] What is largely expressive for the isolated individual is rhetorical for the movement's leadership. Particularly in militant movements, the leader wins and maintains adherents by saying to them what they cannot say to others or even to themselves. A major rhetorical process, then, consists of legitimizing privately-held feelings by providing social support and rationalizations for those feelings.

Apart from placing a strain on the ideological values of the movement and its leaders, the deliberate use of myths, deceptions, etc. creates practical problems. When outsiders discover that the size of the membership has been exaggerated or when followers learn that they are far from united, the leader must invent rationalizations for his deceptions through a new rhetoric of justification or apology. Worst of all, the leadership may come to believe its own falsehoods. As Kenneth Keniston has noted, "Movement groups . . . tend to develop strong barriers on their outside boundaries, which impede communication and movement outside the group; they frequently exhibit an 'anti-empirical' inability to use facts in order to counter emotion-based distortions and impressions; interaction within the group often has a quality of 'surreality.'"[38]

3. Pressures for organizational efficiency are incompatible with membership needs. An energized membership is the strength of any movement and its *esprit de corps* is essential to goal implementation. Yet morale cannot be secured through abdications of leadership. Members may feel the need to participate in decision-making, to undertake pet projects on their own initiatives, to "put down" leaders or other followers, to obstruct meetings by socializing, or to disobey directives. The leadership cannot ignore these needs; yet it cannot accede to all of them either. The problem is especially acute in movements that distrust authority and value participatory democracy. During the hectic days of Vietnam Summer, according to Keniston, the secretarial staff of the central office demanded and received equal status and responsibilities with a seasoned political staff. As a result, experienced organizers were forced to perform menial chores while the former clerical workers advised local projects.[39]

4. The leaders of social movements face discrepancies between role expectations and role definitions. The leader must appear to be what he cannot be. Expected to be consistent, for example, he must nevertheless be prepared to renounce previously championed positions. Expected to be sincere and spontaneous, he must handle dilemmas with consummate manipulative skill. When, in one year, Malcolm X broke with Elijah Muhammad, shifted positions on integration and participation

in civil rights demonstrations, and confessed his uncertainties on other issues, he inevitably alienated some followers and invited charges of weakness and inconsistency from his enemies.[40] When Allard Lowenstein politicked with student groups in behalf of Sen. Eugene McCarthy, he had to seem as unlike a "pol" as possible.[41]

5. The leader must adapt to several audiences simultaneously. In an age of mass media, rhetorical utterances addressed to one audience are likely to reach others. Outsiders include those who are sympathetic, indifferent, and opposed. As shall later be argued, another key variable is the extent to which those in the larger structure are susceptible to threats of force. Within the movement interfactional conflicts invariably develop over questions of value, strategy, tactics, or implementation. Purists and pragmatists clash over the merits of compromise. Academics and activists debate the necessity of long-range planning. Others enter the movement with personal grievances or vested interests. Pre-existing groups, known to have divergent ideological positions, are nevertheless invited to join or affiliate with the movement because of the power they can wield.[42]

6. Movements require a diversity of leadership types with whom any one leader must both compete and cooperate.[43] Theoreticians, agitators, and propagandists must launch the movement; political and bureaucratic types must carry it forward. Ideological differences among the leadership must also be expected insofar as the leadership reflects internal divisions among the following. Finally, there may well be cleavages among those vested with positions of legitimate authority, those charismatic figures who have personal followings, those who have special competencies, and those who have private sources of funds or influence outside the movement. Much of the leader's persuasive skill is exhibited in private interactions with other leaders.

RHETORICAL STRATEGIES

From the foregoing discussion it should be quite clear that the leader of a social movement must thread his way through an intricate web of conflicting demands. How he adapts strategies to demands constitutes a primary basis for evaluating his rhetorical output. Along a continuum from the sweet and reasonable to the violently revolutionary, one may identify *moderate, intermediate,* and *militant* types of strategies, each with its own appropriate tactics and styles.

Little needs to be said about the strategy of the moderate. His is the pattern of peaceful persuasion rhetoricians know best and characteristically prescribe, the embodiment of reason, civility, and decorum in human interaction. Dressed in the garb of respectability and exhibiting Ivy League earnestness and midwestern charm, the moderate gets angry but does not shout, issues pamphlets but never manifestos, inveighs against social mores but always in the value language of the social order. His "devil" is a condition or a set of behaviors or an outcast group; never the persons he is seeking to influence. They, rather, are part of his "we" group, united if only by lip-service adherence to his symbols. In textbook terms, the moderate adapts to the listener's needs, wants, and values; speaks his language, adjusts to his frame of reference; reduces the psychological distance between his movement and the larger structure. Roy Wilkins exemplified the approach when he argued that the "prime, continuing racial policy looking toward eradication of inequities must be one of winning friends and influencing people among the white majority."[44]

If moderates assume or pretend to assume an ultimate identity of interests between the movement and the larger structure, militants act on the assumption of a fundamental clash of interests. If moderates employ rhetoric as an alternative to force, militants use rhetoric as an expression, an instrument, and an act of force. So contradictory are the rhetorical conceptions of moderate and militant strategists that it strains the imagination to believe that both may work. Yet the decisive changes wrought by militant rhetorics in recent years gives credence to the view that the traditionally prescribed pattern is not the only viable alternative.

The core characteristic of militant strategists is that they seek to change the actions of their primary targets as a precondition for changes in attitudes.[45] By means of direct action techniques and verbal polemics, militants threaten, harass, cajole, disrupt, provoke, intimidate, coerce. Hostility is also expressed in dress, manners, dialect, gestures, in-group slogans, and ceremonies.[46] Although the aim of pressure tactics may be to punish directly (e.g., strikes, boycotts), more frequently they are forms of "body rhetoric," designed to dramatize issues, enlist additional sympathizers, and delegitimatize the established order.[47] The targets of sit-ins, sleep-ins, and other confrontational activities are invited to participate in a drama of self-exposure. Should they reject militant demands, they may be forced to unmask themselves through punitive countermeasures, thus helping to complete the rhetorical act.[48] Confrontation, according to Scott and Smith, "dissolves the line between marches, sit-ins, demonstrations, acts of physical violence, and aggressive discourse. In this way it informs us of the essential nature of discourse itself as human action."[49]

Militant and moderate strategies are antithetical, yet each has highly desirable characteristics. Decisions to employ "intermediate" strategies may be viewed as efforts to obtain the following advantages of each while still avoiding their respective disadvantages. Once again, the following dilemmas derive from conflicting rhetorical requirements.

1. Militant tactics confer visibility on a movement; moderate tactics gain entry into decision centers. Because of their ethos of respectability moderates are invited to participate in public deliberations (hearings, conferences, negotiating sessions, etc.), even after militants have occasioned those deliberations by prolonged and self-debilitating acts of protest. On the other hand, the militant has readier access to the masses. Robert C. Weaver has lamented that "today, a publicized spokesman may be the individual who can devise the most militant cry and the leader one who can articulate the most far-out position."[50]

2. For different reasons, militants and moderates must both be ambivalent about "successes" and "failures." Militants thrive on injustice and ineptitude by the larger structure. Should the enemy fail to implement the movement's demands, the militant is vindicated ideologically, yet frustrated programmatically. Should some of the demands be met, he is in the paradoxical position of having to condemn them as palliatives. The moderate, by contrast, requires tangible evidence that the larger structure is tractable in order to hold followers in line; yet "too much" success belies the movement's reason for being.

3. Militant supporters are easily energized; moderate supporters are more easily controlled. Having aroused their following the leaders of a militant movement frequently become victims of their own creation, Robespierres and Dantons who can no longer contain energies within prescribed limits or guarantee their own tenure.[51] On the other hand, moderate leaders frequently claim that their supporters are apathetic. As Turner and Killian have pointed out: "To the degree to which a movement incorporates only major sacred values its power will be diffused by a large body of conspicuous lip-service adherents who cannot be depended upon for the work of the movement."[52]

4. Militants are effective with "power-vulnerables"; moderates are effective with "power-invulnerables"; neither is effective with both.

As the writer has argued in an earlier article, a distinction needs to be made between two objects of influence.[53] Persons most vulnerable to pressure tactics are the leaders of public and quasi-public institutions: elected and appointed government officials who may be removed from office or given an unfavorable press; church and university leaders who are obliged to apply "high-minded" standards in dealing with protests; executives of large corporations whose businesses are susceptible to loss of income and who are publicly committed to an ethic of social responsibility.

"Power-invulnerables" are those who have little or nothing to lose by publicly voicing their prejudices and acting on their self-concerns. With respect to the movement for black equality:

> They are the mass of white Americans who are largely unaffected by rent strikes and boycotts and who have so far defended their neighborhood sanctuaries or have physically and psychologically withdrawn to the suburbs. The average American may fear riots but he can escape from them. He may or may not approve of boycotts and demonstrations but in either case he is largely unaffected by them. He is subject to legislation but in most cases until now he has been able to circumvent it. Only through communications aimed at a change in his attitudes or through carefully formulated and tightly enforced government policies can his actions be appreciably modified.[54]

By reducing the psychological distance between the movement and the external structure, the moderate is likely to win sympathizers, even among "power-vulnerables." But as those in positions of power allocate priorities (they, too, are subjected to conflicting demands), they are unlikely to translate sympathy into action unless pressured to do so. Should the leader of a movement strike militant postures, he is likely to actuate "power-vulnerables" but at the same time prompt backlash groups to apply their own pressure tactics.

Where the movement and the larger structure are already polarized, the dilemma is magnified. However much he may wish to plead reasonably, wresting changes from those in public positions requires that the leader build a sizable power base. And to secure massive internal support, the leader must at least *seem* militant.

So the leader of a social movement may attempt to avoid or resolve the aforementioned dilemmas by employing "intermediate" strategies, admittedly a catchall term for those efforts that combine militant and moderate patterns of influence. The leader may alternate between carrot and stick or speak softly in private and stridently at mass gatherings. He may form broadly based coalitions that submerge ideological differences or utilize spokesmen with similar values but contrasting styles. Truly the exemplar of oxymoronic postures, he may stand as a "conservative radical" or a "radical conservative," espousing militant demands in the value language of the established order or militant slogans in behalf of moderate proposals. In defense of militancy, he may portray himself as a brakeman, a finger in the dike holding back an angry tide. In defense of more moderate tactics, he may hold back an angry tide without loss of reputation, as Jerry Rubin and Abbie Hoffman did in urging nonviolence on their "yippie" following during the Democratic Convention in Chicago: "We are a revolutionary new community and we must protect our community. . . . We, not they, will decide when the battle begins. . . . We are not going into their jails and we aren't going to shed our blood. We're too important for that. We've got too much work to do."[55]

Intermediacy can be a dangerous game. Calculated to energize supporters, win over neutrals, pressure power-vulnerables, and mollify the opposition, it may end up antagonizing everyone. The well-turned phrase may easily appear as a devilish trick, the rationale as a rationalization, the tactful comment as an artless dodge. To the extent that strategies of intermediacy require studied ambiguity, insincerity, and even distortion, perhaps the leader's greatest danger is that others may find out what he really thinks.

Still, some strategists manage to reconcile differences between militant and moderate approaches and not simply to maneuver around them. They seem able to convince the established order that bad tasting medicine is good for it and seem capable, too, of mobilizing a diverse collectivity within the movement.

The key, it would appear, is the leader's capacity to embody a higher wisdom, a more profound sense of justice; to stand above inconsistencies by articulating overarching principles. Few will contest the claim that Martin Luther King, Jr. epitomized the approach. Attracting both militants and moderates to his movement, King could win respect, even from his enemies, by reconciling the seemingly irreconcilable. The heart of the case for intermediacy was succinctly stated by King himself in a speech which Professor Robert Scott has analyzed: "What is needed is a realization that power without love is reckless and abusive and love without power is sentimental and anemic. Power at its best is love implementing the demands of justice, and justice at its best is power correcting everything that stands against love."[56]

Viewed broadly, the great contemporary movements all seem to require combinations of militant and moderate strategies. Tom Hayden can be counted upon to dramatize the Vietnam issue; Arthur Schlesinger, to plead forcefully within inner circles. Threats of confrontation may prompt school boards to finance the building of new facilities in ghetto areas, but it may take reasonableness and civility to get experienced teachers to volunteer for work in those facilities. Demands by revolutionary student groups for total transformations of university structures may impel administrators to heed quasi-militant demands for a redistribution of university power. Support for the cause by moderate groups may confer respectability on the movement. Thus, however much they may war amongst themselves, militants and moderates each perform essential functions.

SUMMARY

This paper has attempted to provide a broad framework within which persuasion in social movements, particularly reformist and revolutionary movements, may be analyzed. Derived in large measure from sociological theory and from an examination of contemporary cases, it has examined rhetorical processes from the perspective of the leader of a movement: the requirements he must fulfill, the problems he faces, the strategies he may adopt to meet those requirements.

What emerges most sharply from the foregoing discussion are the extraordinary rhetorical dilemmas confronting those who would lead social movements. Movements are as susceptible to fragmentation from within as they are to suppression from without. Impelled to fulfill the same internal and external requirements as the heads of most formal organizations, their leaders can expect greater resistance to their efforts from both insiders and outsiders. The needs of individual members are frequently incompatible with organizational imperatives; appeals addressed to the intelligentsia of a movement incompatible with appeals addressed to the masses; the values for which the movement stands incompatible with tactical necessities. In the face of these and other problems, the leader may adopt the traditionally prescribed tactics and style of the moderate or those of his more militant counterpart. Yet the choice between moderate and militant strategies introduces still other dilemmas. The great leaders (and the great movements) seem capable of combining these seemingly antithetical strategies without inconsistency by justifying their use with appeals to higher principles.

NOTES

[1]See, for example, Lester Thonssen and A. Craig Baird, *Speech Criticism* (New York, 1948), ch. 17.

[2]For the decade prior to the writing of his text, Professor Edwin Black found only three such studies reported in *QJS* or *Speech Monographs*. See his *Rhetorical Criticism: A Study in Method* (New York, 1965), pp. 22–23.

[3]For a discussion of the problem of discerning intent, see Rudolf Heberle, *Social Movements* (New York, 1951), pp. 94–95. According to Lang and Lang, "the ideology presented to the mass of followers is a 'mask' for the real beliefs of the inner core. Its 'real' ideology is hidden from all but the initiated." See Kurt Lang and Gladys Engel Lang, *Collective Dynamics* (New York, 1961), p. 539.

[4]To understand the rhetoric of a militant movement requires an analysis of force as the backdrop against which communication frequently takes place and similarly requires an analysis of communication, not as an alternative to force, but as an instrument of force. Four recent articles in *QJS* have dealt with the problem and the questions of ethics raised by it. See Parke G. Burgess, "The Rhetoric of Black Power: A Moral Demand?" *QJS*, LIV (April 1968), 122–133; Franklyn S. Haiman, "The Rhetoric of the Streets: Some Legal and Ethical Considerations," *QJS*, LIII (April 1967), 99–114; James R. Andrews, "Confrontation at Columbia: A Case Study in Coercive Rhetoric," *QJS*, LV (February 1969), 9–16; and Robert L. Scott and Donald K. Smith, "The Rhetoric of Confrontation," *QJS*, LV (February 1969), 1–8.

[5]One variant of the problem is discussed by Wayne E. Brockriede and Robert L. Scott, "Stokely Carmichael: Two Speeches on Black Power," *Central States Speech Journal*, XIX (Spring 1968), 3–13.

[6]The problems of estimating long-range effects are nicely illustrated in Howard H. Martin's appraisal of the effects of the antiwar "teach-ins." See "Rhetoric of Academic Protest," *Central States Speech Journal*, XVII (Spring 1966), 244–250.

[7]For a classic typology of stages, see Carl A. Dawson and Warner E. Gettys, *An Introduction to Sociology,* rev. ed. (New York, 1935), ch. 19.

[8]For an intriguing analysis of nonobvious symbols, see Hugh D. Duncan, *Communication and Social Order* (New York, 1962).

[9]For example, during its hey-day, the civil rights movement encompassed SNCC, CORE and the NAACP, each of which was torn by internal fragmentation.

[10]Leland M. Griffin, "The Rhetoric of Historical Movements," *QJS*, XXXVIII (April 1952), 184–188.

[11]*Ibid.,* 185.

[12]Griffin has suggested that the development of theory must await further research. Yet there is reason to believe, here as elsewhere, that theory and research must develop apace of each other. As Black has argued (p. 22), the researcher can do little without a framework for analysis.

[13]Griffin, 185–187.

[14]Consistent with Scott and Smith's view of rhetoric as *managed* public discourse (p. 8), the paper focuses on the intentional symbolic acts of those who lead social movements.

Emphasis on more spontaneous acts of communication (rumor, milling, social contagion, etc. by non-leaders) has been provided by those who have stressed the primitive features of social movements. The "classic" is Gustave Le Bon, *The Crowd: A Study of the Popular Mind* (London, 1897).

[15]Neil J. Smelser, *Theory of Collective Behavior* (New York, 1962), pp. 110 and 129–130 and Ralph H. Turner and Lewis M. Killian, *Collective Behavior* (Englewood Cliffs, N.J., 1957), p. 308.

[16]Herbert Blumer, "Social Movements," in *New Outline of the Principles of Sociology*, ed. A. M. Lee (New York, 1946), pp. 200, 202, and 214.

[17]Any classification of social movements must have arbitrary features. For other categorizations, see Lang and Lang, pp. 497–505.

[18]See, for example, Chester I. Barnard, *The Functions of the Executive* (Cambridge, Mass., 1938) and Robert K. Merton, *Social Theory and Social Structure* (Glencoe, Ill., 1949).

[19]According to Lang and Lang (p. 493), it is the quasi-structural character of social movements that distinguishes them from formal organizations on the one hand and spontaneous mass behavior on the other. Although claiming to stress the nonstructural aspects of social movements, Lang and Lang have provided the most adequate account of their structural imperatives. See pp. 495–496 and 531–537. See also C. Wendell King, *Social Movements in the United States* (New York, 1956).

[20]See *From Max Weber: Essays in Sociology*, ed. H. H. Gerth and C. Wright Mills (New York, 1946); Barnard; Peter M. Blau, *The Dynamics of Bureaucracy* (Chicago, 1955); and Philip Selznick, *TVA and the Grass Roots* (Berkeley and Los Angeles, 1949).

[21]Blumer, pp. 210–211.

[22]See Smelser, pp. 109–110 and 121–122.

[23]*Ibid.*, pp. 282–286.

[24]Lang and Lang, p. 495.

[25]See Christopher Lasch on Stokely Carmichael, "The Trouble with Black Power," *New York Review of Books*, X (February 29, 1968), 4–14.

[26]According to Turner and Killian (p. 337) this is the usual case for revolutionary movements. They are forced to retain several identities. The same should also be true of retrogressive movements. See, for example, Henry Kraus, *The Many and the Few* (Los Angeles, 1947).

[27]See Norman Mailer, "The Steps of the Pentagon," *Harper's Magazine*, CCXXXVI (March 1968), 47–142. Mailer described the disruptive effects of Yippie leaders on "straights."

[28]The "iron law of oligarchy" may be overstated, but it is not without merit. See Turner and Killian, p. 372.

[29]Norman Mailer and others have ascribed just this failure to Eugene McCarthy. See "Miami Beach and the Siege of Chicago," *Harper's Magazine*, CCXXXVII (November 1968), 41–130. Cf. pp. 77 and 93.

[30]See, for example, Sheldon L. Messinger, "Organizational Transformation: A Case Study of a Declining Social Movement," *American Sociological Review*, XX (February 1955), 3–10.

[31]Turner and Killian, p. 373.

[32]Blumer, p. 210.

[33]Smelser, p. 82.

[34]The writer has inferred these rhetorical functions from Smelser's thorough analysis of the belief components common to all forms of collective behavior and to social movements in particular (pp. 79–130, 292–296, and 348–352). For comparable statements of these leadership requirements, see Eric Hoffer, *The True Believer* (New York, 1951).

[35]See Leland M. Griffin's use of the terms. "The Rhetorical Structure of the 'New Left' Movement: Part I," *QJS*, L (April 1964), 113–135. According to Eric Hoffer (p. 89), "mass movements can rise and spread without belief in a God, but never without belief in a devil."

[36]Blumer, p. 210.

[37]For a discussion of such nonrhetorical speech functions, see, for example, Jon Eisenson, J. Jeffery Auer and John V. Irwin, *The Psychology of Communication*, rev. ed. (New York 1963), pp. 20–29.

[38]*Young Radicals: Notes on Committed Youth* (New York, 1968), p. 159.

[39]*Ibid.*, pp. 160–161.

[40]See the *Autobiography of Malcolm X* (New York, 1965).

[41]See David Halberstam, "The Man Who Ran Against Lyndon Johnson," *Harper's Magazine*, CCXXXVII (December 1968), 47–66.

[42]For a discussion of other intramovement divisions, see Smelser, pp. 302–306 and 361–364.

[43]Like Margaret Sanger or Martin Luther King, Jr., the same leader may encompass all or almost all of the necessary roles. This is rare, however. See Turner and Killian, pp. 472–476.

[44]"What Now?—One Negro Leader's Answer," *New York Times Magazine*, August 16, 1964, p. 11.

[45]Considerable experimental evidence suggests that where actions and attitudes are discrepant, the latter are more likely to change. See Ralph L. Rosnow and Edward J. Robinson, *Experiments in Persuasion* (New York, 1967), pp. 297–308.

[46]In the "black power" movement, for example, what may actually be most frightening to whites are its nonprogrammatic symbols: faded levis, "hang loose" manners, clenched fist salutes, the "honkie" epithet, "soul" and "brother" identifications, the ritual handshake, etc. For an excellent analysis of nonverbal symbolism among black militants, see Ulf Hannerz, "The Rhetoric of Soul: Identification in Negro Society," *Race*, IX (April 1968), 453–465.

[47]See, for example, John R. Searle, "A Foolproof Scenario for Student Revolts," *New York Times Magazine*, December 29, 1968, pp. 4–5 and 12–15; Daniel Walker, *Rights in Conflict* (New York, 1968), chs. 2 and 3; and Herbert W. Simons, "Confrontation as a Pattern of Persuasion in University Settings," *Central States Speech Journal*, XX (Fall 1969), 163–169.

[48]See Scott and Smith, 8.

[49]*Ibid.*, 7.

[50]*Philadelphia Bulletin*, March 2, 1966, p. 3. See also Paul L. Fisher and Ralph L. Lowenstein, *Race and the News Media* (New York, 1967).

[51]Walker, pp. 49–51.

[52]Turner and Killian, p. 337.

[53]Herbert W. Simons, "Patterns of Persuasion in the Civil Rights Struggle," *Today's Speech*, XV (February, 1967), 25–27.

[54]*Ibid.*, 26.

[55]Quoted in Walker, pp. 136–137.

[56]Quoted in Robert L. Scott, "Black Power Bends Martin Luther King," *Speaker and Gavel*, V (March 1968), 84.

SIGNATURES OF CITIZENSHIP: THE RHETORIC OF WOMEN'S ANTISLAVERY PETITIONS

SUSAN ZAESKE

During the winter of 1835, Hannah H. Smith of Glastenbury, New York, obtained a petition requesting Congress to abolish slavery in the District of Columbia. After affixing her name, she convinced her relatives Julia E. and Nancy L. Smith to sign the plea. They did, and passed it along to Pamela and Sarah Hale, who conveyed it to Mrs. Joseph Wells and her circle of Lucy, Clarissa, Abigail, and

Maria. By the time the petition had progressed through town, clusters of women from various families such as the Collins, Hollisters, Hales, and Williams had added their signatures. Elsewhere in the state, the women of Marshfield—107 of them—signed the same statement. The petition that gained the assent of hundreds of women throughout New York designated signers as "ladies" and depicted them as "humbly" approaching congressmen. It stated that "scenes of party and political strife are not the field to which a kind and wise Providence [had] assigned" women, but when "the weak and innocent are denied the protection of law" and "all the sacred ties of domestic life are sundered for the gratification of avarice," then, the petition proclaimed, women "cannot but regard it as their duty to supplicate for the oppressed those common rights of humanity."[1]

The hundreds of signatures ascribed to this form of petition, significant though they were, constitute only a fraction of the millions of names women affixed to petitions over the course of their antislavery petitioning from 1831 to 1863.[2] The huge number of signatures provided a tangible indicator and constant reminder to congressmen that a growing northern public opinion deeply opposed the continuation of slavery, but the number of signatures alone does not tell the full story of the impact of women's antislavery petitioning. When in 1835 women began in earnest to join male abolitionists in submitting antislavery petitions to Congress, the increase of memorials so plagued the House of Representatives that it prompted passage of the "gag" rule, which immediately tabled petitions touching on the subject of slavery. Rather than quashing debate on this heated issue, the gag rule proved a "godsend" for the burgeoning abolitionist movement because it linked the popular right of petition with the unpopular cause of immediate abolitionism and was "a constant source of publicity for the antislavery crusade."[3] In addition to sparking discussion of slavery in Congress, women's signature-gathering efforts helped spread the abolition gospel door-to-door, especially in rural areas and to those unlikely to subscribe to antislavery newspapers or attend antislavery lectures. The petitions, in fact, probably were read by more people than any other form of antislavery rhetoric.[4]

Women's antislavery petitioning, it is clear, contributed significantly to the success of the abolitionist movement, especially in its earliest stages.[5] Yet rather than focusing on women's antislavery petitions as social movement discourse aimed at persuading others, this essay will examine the effects of these petitions on the reformulation of the political subjectivity of the rhetors themselves. For it was through antislavery petitioning that hundreds of thousands of northern, middle-class, predominantly white women bypassed the requirement of suffrage to participate publicly in the political debate over the heated national issue of slavery. Women's antislavery petitioning, moreover, figured centrally in the larger, ongoing, fluid struggle over defining and redefining different levels of citizenship in the antebellum United States.[6] Excluded from normative notions of the antebellum political subject, women who wished to influence the debate over slavery asserted political agency by inscribing on messages to Congress emblems of their existence, symbols of their opinions, marks of their identity—their "signatures," by which I mean both the actual marks they made on petitions and the discursive emblems of the formation of political subjectivity.

In order to understand how women's antislavery petitioning contributed to reformulations of free women's citizenship, it is useful to contemplate critical understandings of subjectivity—the process of forming political identities—especially in relation to the concept of signature. Subjectivity provides a lens through which to view the bounds of public political inclusion in the milieu of Jacksonian mass democracy, when the category of dominant political subject expanded to legitimize participation in the public sphere by a greater variety and number of white males, while it reinforced exclusion of women and people of color. Against this backdrop of exclusion we can witness antislavery women reconstructing female subjectivities through the signing of and "coming to signature" in the rhetoric of antislavery petitions. By affixing their signatures to abolition petitions, women defied prescriptions against female public activism and employed their literacy to express their opinions on a controversial national issue. Simultaneously, petition narratives reappropriated the discursive resources of the petition genre to overcome the barriers presented by antiabolitionists and gender traditionalists, which constituted what I shall call a "constraining audience," a discursive force that polices access to public deliberation. This subversion was achieved also by adopting, yet reconfiguring, a male-gendered antislavery republican subjectivity into "antislavery republican womanhood" to assert that northern middle-class women possessed qualifications necessary for participation in the public sphere. In order to demonstrate that free women retained the defining republican virtue of independence, the rhetoric of female petitions asserted that free women were the rightful representatives of slave women yet reappropriated the political hierarchy enfranchised males exerted over all women.[7]

This study of female antislavery petitioning offers historical insights into the discursive processes through which certain women during the antebellum period increased their participation in public debate and renegotiated their status as citizens. It seeks also to advance our understanding of social movement discourse by moving beyond leader-centered approaches, which tend to obscure the discursive actions of the majority of movement participants. Building on what Charles J. Stewart has termed a "functional approach" to the study of social movement discourse, it aims specifically to expand Richard B. Gregg's notion of the "ego-function" of protest rhetoric.[8] Rather than focusing on construction of a unified collective identity for a movement as a whole, this study directs our attention to differences in power and political status among movement sympathizers that require certain groups (often women) to invest discursive energy in formulating political subjectivities to legitimate their participation in the movement and, more generally, in political deliberation. The critical concept of "signature," I shall demonstrate, can be employed productively to excavate the discursive artifacts of the rhetorical process of reformulating political subjectivities. In addition to directing rhetorical scholars to the concepts of political subjectivity and signature, I hope to emphasize the usefulness of melding public sphere theory with methodologies for the study of social movement discourse. Likewise, I aspire to contribute to theorizing the public sphere by explicating a motivational relationship between constraining audiences and counterpublics.

READING SUBJECTS, READING SIGNATURES

By approaching the petitions with an eye to the reconstruction of female political subjectivity, I focus on processes through which individual women became political persons and, in turn, formed collectivities. The construction of political subjectivity is a cultural process, related to individuals' living experience and the ever-changing discursive resources available to them. This process involves discursive practices that facilitate not only development of an isolated individual identity but also "identity in relationship" or collective subjectivities. Yet although collective subjectivities function as categories of inclusion, they function also, Judith Butler reminds us, as rules of exclusion, particularly exclusion from political power along the lines of gender, race, class, and sexual preference. In other words, when requirements for inclusion in dominant subjectivities such as "citizen" differ from prevailing identities of certain groups such as "women" or "free blacks," members of these groups are delegitimated from participation in the public sphere and denied political power.[9]

The dual nature of political subjectivities as rules of both inclusion and exclusion is readily apparent in the history of the Jacksonian period. The growth of party organizing and political participation during the mid- to late-1820s are widely accepted as markers of a turning point in the nature of U.S. democracy and the character of the political subject. Andrew Jackson's ascendency coincided with the ongoing expansion of white manhood suffrage, mass literacy, proliferation of newspapers and magazines, and developments in transportation, all of which led to the politicization of the public. The "people" had come to exert greater power over their representatives not only through the vote, but also through the pressure of public opinion.[10] Yet although the rise of mass democracy enhanced the political power of white males, people of color and women continued to be excluded from the rights of citizenship.

As part of the popular politics of the Jacksonian era, men frequently made use of organized mass petitioning to agitate public opinion in order to achieve their political goals. But even as a greater number of white men made use of collective petitioning, as late as 1834 both white and black women's petitioning remained limited for the most part to individual prayers regarding personal issues. There were, however, important exceptions. As early as 1817 and 1818, Cherokee women collectively petitioned their nation's all-male council against ceding the tribe's land, and a decade later white women sent several petitions to the United States Congress opposing removal of the Cherokee.[11] The exclusion of women from voting, petitioning, and many other means of access to the public sphere was premised on antebellum conceptions of the idealized political subject, who was to be a rational actor capable of independent thought and action. Women, slaves of both sexes, Native Americans, and other peoples of color, by virtue of their status as dependents, fell outside the definition of the dominant political subject. Women in particular were believed to lack capacity for rational thought and to be ruled by passions. Characterization of the female subject as dependent and irrational marked women as different from the ideal republican actor, unfit for participation in the public sphere, and better suited for the role of nurturer to be played in the domestic sphere. These constructs of the dominant (white male) political subjectivity as juxtaposed to female subjectivity policed access to public debate and political power.[12]

They remained, nonetheless, normative conceptions and not descriptions of lived experience.[13] Despite principles of exclusion and lack of access to popular means of participation such as public speaking, publishing in newspapers, and pamphleteering, women and people of color found avenues to influence public debate.[14] Mary Ryan has described the "circuitous routes" women traveled to enter public discourse in the nineteenth-century United States such as "corrupted forms, like the cloying feminine symbols used in electoral campaigns" and deployment of "ladies" at political rallies as "badges of respectability."[15] I agree with Ryan that women were forced to seek alternative routes to the *polis,* but I think we need not travel so far afield to find women in public during the antebellum period. By petitioning Congress, middle-class northern women insinuated themselves into public discussion through use of a highly traditional form of political communication. Rather than operating at the margins of the bourgeois public sphere, petitioning women inserted their opinions into central sites of public debate such as the United States Congress and newspapers circulated throughout the nation.

Antislavery women accomplished this task through reformulation of female subjectivity in their petitions, and the critical concept of "signature" provides a useful tool for examining these reformulations. Feminist literary critics have used the term "signature" to denote discursive footprints of women writers' journeys from isolation to publication through development of authorial identity. Nancy K. Miller urges critics to read for "the signature of the gendered subject," by which she means icons or emblems in discourse that "obliquely figure the symbolic and material process entailed in becoming a (woman) writer." The concept of signature can be transferred from the realm of literature to the realm of political rhetoric[16] to read for signs of the process through which women were transformed from isolated individuals to political actors. We can read antislavery petitions to find the signature of the gendered subject, to excavate the process through which northern middle-class women reconstructed political subjectivities. The history of this process lies in the actual signatures on petitions as well as in the discursive practices employed in petitions to construct a subjectivity commensurate with the requirements for participation in the bourgeois public sphere.[17]

SIGNING THE SELF

At first glance, the most noticeable characteristic of women's antislavery petitions is the list of handwritten names, but each of these marks is more than a name—it is a signature, an individual's name written by herself.[18] The presence of female signatures indicates that by the mid-1830s a good many women possessed a level of literacy at least sufficient to write their names. This was no small matter, for among the first generation of Americans approximately half of white men and only a third of white women were able to sign their names, and although by the end of the colonial period about 80 percent of white men could write their names, only 40 to 45 percent of white women could do so. This percentage increased to about half during the Revolutionary period. A major spurt in white women's literacy occurred between 1790 and 1830, during which time nearly four hundred female academies were established in the United States and the female readership and sales of novels increased dramatically. By 1840 almost all white New England women could sign their names. In fact, feminist literary critics have observed that women frequently signed their names on the endpapers and covers of the novels they read, often doing so as many times as they read and reread a book, in a sense claiming "that the text was uniquely theirs." These marks of identity suggest that for antebellum women novels were a vehicle to achieving "a distinctive personality, a particular address to the world, a way of acting and thinking." Sometimes, writes Mary Kelley, "books confirmed an already familiar identity. Sometimes they became catalysts in the fashioning of alternative selves."[19]

Antebellum women also employed their signatures as marks of spiritual transformations and religious identities. Drawing upon the notion that God writes the names of the saved in "the lamb's book of life," Charles Finney and his disciples called forth sinners to the anxious bench during revivals urging them to repent.

Christian converts, the vast majority of them women, then signed their names to a church membership roll. Finneyite exhortations to "let your names be enrolled" were adopted by abolitionists, many of whom themselves had undergone conversion and several of whom, such as Theodore Weld, had worked with Finney. Women and men who joined antislavery societies signed the constitutions of the local organization, a practice also common among temperance activists whose signatures confirmed their identities as totally devoted to temperance—"Teetotalers."[20] All of these practices involved women employing their literacy to sign their names, an act that in one way or another marked transformations in their commitments and identities after being interpellated by discourse (novels, revivals, temperance rhetoric). Likewise, women's signatures on antislavery petitions signaled not only an abolitionist identity, but also the identity of a woman who had come to believe that religious conviction justified political action.

Female signatures on antislavery petitions also recorded women expressing their opinions independent of their husbands and fathers, an act that defied biblical and legal doctrine. As Elizabeth Cady Stanton wrote in *The Woman's Bible* (1895/98), for women, marriage "was to be a condition of bondage" and the wife was to remain "in silence and subjection." For all her material wants, she was to remain "dependent on man's bounty" and "for all the information she might desire on the vital questions of the hour, she was commanded to ask her husband at home."[21] Biblical teachings of the wife's submission in marriage were formalized in the legal doctrine of coverture. Originating in English common law, coverture was the legal assumption that when a woman married, her identity became submerged, or covered, by that of her husband. As Blackstone explained, "By marriage, the husband and wife are one person in law; that is, the very being or legal existence of the woman is suspended during marriage, or at least incorporated and consolidated into that of the husband, under whose wing, protection, and *cover,* she performs every thing." Unmarried daughters also were expected to submit to the control of their fathers or brothers.[22]

Based on accounts written by female signature-gatherers, these tenets of submission to male relatives influenced women's decisions about signing antislavery petitions. Upon gathering signatures in 1837, for example, a young antislavery woman and her friends were met at the door by "A certain Mr. ———." When they asked if there were any ladies within who would be interested in signing an antislavery petition, "he answered in a very decided, contemptuous manner, 'NO'—without even so much as asking them." Reflecting on this encounter, the young abolitionist wrote that "Mr. ——— apparently belonged to that class of men who claim the right to 'possess exclusive jurisdiction in all cases whatsoever' over their wives' consciences." Sarah Grimké, an experienced signature-gatherer, complained, "A woman who is asked to sign a petition for the abolition of slavery in the District of Columbia . . . not infrequently replies, 'My husband does not approve of it.'" The servility of women also bothered Hannah H. Smith, who lamented that "Women have been taught to depend on men for their opinions."[23]

When women affixed their signatures to petitions, making a mark that authorized petitions as statements of their opinions, they threw off the "cover" of their husbands or fathers and asserted their existence as political individuals. For some women, lending their signature to a petition may have involved rejecting the notion that the signature of a husband, father, or brother adequately represented their opinion—the doctrine of indirect representation. For other women, signing a petition was an act of defiance against the wishes of male protectors, who might have opposed abolitionism or opposed women petitioning, or both. It is worth noting, moreover, that throughout the campaign, the vast majority of women eschewed the use of marital titles, signing petitions as, for example, Chloe F. Metcalf, Lydia W. Fairbanks, and even Philomela Johnson Jr. rather than Mrs. Metcalf, Mrs. Fairbanks, and Mrs. Johnson.[24] Given that in 1890 Frances E. Willard was still urging women to write their names as individuals rather than as the wife of someone else, the petitioners' decision to drop "Mrs." during the 1830s appears to radically defy signature norms. Female signatures on antislavery petitions, then, constituted affirmations of women's right to express their opinions as individuals, as independent from male protectors, and provide evidence of women exerting political agency.[25]

The arrangement of women's signatures on antislavery petitions offers further insight into how women perceived and represented their political status in the republic. Throughout the 1830s antislavery petitioners took great pains to maintain strict separation between the signatures of male and female signers. Type-set forms often labeled the left column "MALES" and the right column "FEMALES." In 1837, when abolitionists embraced short forms, more and more women signed the same petitions as men, although they still kept their names in separate columns. On first thought, one might think this practice reflected a belief that women's signatures should not intermingle with men's because that would be a record of improper sexual mixing in the same way that audiences composed of both men and women were attacked as "promiscuous." Yet some petitions contained not two, but three columns of signatures. In such cases, the third column was reserved for "minors," where the names of boys and girls were mixed. It seems, then, that abolitionists separated the names of men from those of women and minors because they perceived that men's signatures—the marks of full, voting citizens—carried greater weight for congressmen who viewed petitions as a measure of public opinion. Indeed, on some petitions the columns were labeled "Legal Voters" and "Ladies."[26]

During the 1840s, there was a significant change in the manner in which women signed petitions. Rather than keeping their names separated in a column labeled "females," "ladies," "women," or "inhabitants," some women and men began to mix their signatures. This change is particularly evident in the 1842 Great Petition to Congress from the Citizens of Massachusetts, which asked representatives to separate the petitioners from all connections with slavery. Rather than placing all men's names in the left column and all women's in the right, men and women mixed their names in the same column, usually in family groups. This trend toward combining the names of men and women was not limited to residents of Massachusetts. When signing a petition for abolition in the District of Columbia in 1841, women of Ashtabula, Ohio, expended no effort to separate their signatures from those of men.[27] That certain abolitionists were signing petitions without categorizing their signatures by sex suggests that during the 1840s women had become increasingly comfortable with petitioning and perhaps were asserting that their opinions be given equal consideration as those of electors, and also that some men accepted this assertion of women's political power. Women continued to mix their names with men on antislavery petitions for the next two decades as well as on suffrage, anti-lynching, temperance, and polygamy petitions submitted through the end of the century.[28]

Changes in the patterns of women's signatures corresponded with the manner in which they identified themselves in the texts of petitions. Many of the forms circulated from 1834 to 1836 immediately indicated whether the petitions emanated from men or women. Those petitions printed for women's signatures represented subscribers as "Ladies," "Females," and "Women." In an 1835 petition, 800 women of New York approached congressmen as "ladies" rather than "citizens" or "voters," and rather than asserting heightened political status, described themselves in non-threatening terms as "wives and daughters of American citizens."[29] Those printed for men's signatures, by contrast, denoted the signers as "Citizens," "Electors," and "Voters." When women could not obtain a petition crafted specifically for their sex, they employed standard petitions that labeled the signers as "citizens." From 1834 to 1836, however, women appear to have understood that it would be controversial to describe themselves as citizens, so they commonly scratched out the label "citizen" and replaced it with "women," "ladies," and in some cases, "Female citizens." When women signed petitions with men, it could no longer be asserted confidently that the memorial came from "citizens." Faced with this situation, canvassers sought a term to represent the status of the signers. Because it was too awkward to write something like "citizens and their female relatives and neighbors," the petitioners settled for "inhabitants" or "residents" of such-and-such a town. By contrast, male abolition petitioners, most of them white and enfranchised, asserted their status as "voters," "electors," and "citizens." These labels encoded the perceived political status of potential signers, their authority to instruct elected representatives, and their expectations about how heavily their requests would be weighed by congressmen. During the early stages of the campaign, labels employed to refer to women signers remained within dominant notions of female subjectivity, avoiding the risk to potential signers of asserting political status equal to that of white men.

Changes in the rhetorical context of the petition campaign offered a new discursive resource through which antislavery women could alter the signing of their political identity. In June 1836, the House of Representatives passed the gag rule, which immediately tabled all petitions touching on the subject of slavery and prompted a change in abolitionists' petitioning strategy. After no small amount of contemplation, campaign coordinators realized that the gag did not prevent Adams and his cohorts in the House from announcing the title of a petition. In order to get their message across before cries of "Order!" rang out from all sides, abolitionists did away with the long petitions and composed short forms that in the same breath announced the title and the prayer of the petition.[30] Short forms afforded no space to offer elaborate justifications of women's petitioning, and these petitions often made no mention of the sex of the signer, resulting in an increase in the number of petitions signed by both men and women, although signers continued to separate their names by sex.

The switch to short forms not only affected presentation of the petitions in Congress, but also altered the manner in which female petitioners labeled their political identity. For example, a short form requesting repeal of the gag rule signed in 1838 by 228 women, including African American abolitionists Margaretta Forten, Sarah Forten, Sarah M. Douglass, and Grace Douglass, began, "To the House of Representatives of the United States: The memorial of the subscribers, citizens of Philadelphia respectfully represents. . . ."[31] As this petition illustrates, with the advent of the short form, more and more women were willing to affix their names to a petition that claimed to emanate from "citizens." This differed significantly from women's previous practice of crossing out the word "citizens" and replacing it with "inhabitants" or "residents." Use of the label of "citizen" suggests that free black and white women perceived themselves as occupying or at least were willing to assert that they occupied the status of citizen. As the political context shifted in the 1840s, so, too, did the way antislavery women labeled their political subjectivity. In the most popular female form of petition during the mid-1840s, signers portrayed themselves not as "ladies of Philadelphia" or "women of Putnam, Ohio," but as "women of America." This change may reflect a transformation from women seeing themselves only as members of local communities to viewing themselves as active members of a national community.[32]

Short forms also altered the appellations of petitions, which indicate the identity of the intended receiver and figure in the construction of the power relationship between petitioners and receivers. An especially vivid difference between the constructed identities of female petitioners and intended recipients is evident in the Fathers and Rulers of Our Country form, which was signed by women from almost every northern state and was the most popular of all petition forms employed by abolitionists before 1837.[33] Unlike petitions signed exclusively by men, which almost without exception were addressed "To the Honorable Senate and House," the popular women's form began "To the Fathers and Rulers of our Country," and signers were identified as "wives, as mothers, and as daughters." Such phrasing elevated the recipients from political representatives to powerful patriarchal/monarchical figures, and acknowledged that female petitioners were neither citizens, nor even constituents, but dependents of congressmen's constituents. Yet as women became more accustomed to petitioning and the short forms provided a new discursive resource, the depiction of women's status relative to that of congressmen changed. Women petitioners ceased to name recipients "fathers and rulers," and in addition to calling themselves "citizens," adopted the wording of men's forms, "To the Honorable Senate and House." This change in the labeling of recipients suggests that women were no longer willing to characterize themselves as subjects of rulers, or subjects of congressmen's male constituents, but had come to view congressmen as democratic representatives and themselves as constituents.

SUBVERTING THROUGH NARRATIVE REAPPROPRIATION

Inscribing their signatures and signing their identities were but a few of the multiple discursive practices employed by women to construct their political subjectivities in the course of antislavery petitioning. Even in their decision to employ the petition, women took hold of an available discursive resource and marked it as a means of expression particularly appropriate for females. Like other groups outside the domains of institutionalized government who in earlier times had employed the right of petition as an entering wedge into realms of political power, antislavery women availed themselves of the rhetorical tensions inherent in the speech act of petitioning. While on one hand the divine right of petition required use of supplicatory rhetoric due to its antecedents in monarchical England, on the other it was understood as carrying an incumbent obligation on the part of the receiver to read and respond to the grievance. Petitioning's ability to place demands on rulers or representatives, even while it obscured signers' motive of demand, gave the fundamental right of petition a deeply subversive potential. The radical potential of petitioning multiplied significantly when groups, rather than individuals (as in original practice), began to direct their grievances not only to governing bodies, but also to the public. By the early nineteenth century in the United States, petitioning had emerged as a potent instrument through which minority political causes and people denied the full rights of republican citizenship could exert considerable pressure on their representatives by appealing to the power of public opinion.

The supplicatory nature of petitioning rendered it particularly suitable for use by women, whom prevailing social norms directed to be pious and submissive. Indeed, during the first phases of the campaign, women's petitions emphasized the supplicatory nature of the signers' discursive action by linking the speech acts of petitioning and praying, in a sense "signing" the petition as a feminine form. The Fathers and Rulers form read like a public prayer and described signers as engaging in the speech act of praying. The petition began, "Suffer us, we pray you," and two sentences later stated that the "unnumbered wrongs of which the slaves of our sex are made the defenseless victims . . . constrain us . . . to pray for their deliverances." After listing numerous wrongs perpetrated against the slave, the Fathers and Rulers form restated that the petitioners were importuning "high Heaven with prayer, and our national legislatures with appeals."[34] By labeling their speech act as prayer, petition writers and the women who signed the forms reframed petitioning, which was public and political, by aligning it with praying, which was private, religious, and regarded as entirely appropriate for women. Prayer was not only considered acceptable behavior for women, but also the duty of women, who were idealized as inherently more religious than men.[35] By inscribing the very form of petition with a signature of feminine moral action (prayer), antislavery women took advantage of the popular view of petitioning as a pure expression of individual moral conscience. In the political context of mass democracy, petitioning was distinguished from voting, which was viewed as tainted with personal interest and party spirit.[36] Although petitioning was less direct than voting, in the 1830s it was not necessarily considered less powerful, and some male radical reformers, William Lloyd Garrison among them, eschewed voting in favor of petitioning to persuade the nation's people to create a moral republic.[37]

Unlike male reformers, however, female activists did not have the option of relinquishing the vote. As a category of people denied suffrage and whose political status in the republic underwent constant renegotiation, free white women—like slaves, free blacks, and Native Americans—stood somewhere between subject (in the sense of one who is subjected to the rule of another, as were the American colonists vis-à-vis England) and citizen. Given their questionable political status, petitioning held potential for women because it originated as a means through which subjects made requests of rulers. English constitutional law assumed that all subjects possessed the right of petition and that rulers were obliged to receive and respond to their prayers for redress. Although this expectation was restated in the First Amendment to the United States Constitution, in 1797 Congress denied slaves, whose political status remained unclear, the right of petition.[38] By employing the form of petition to voice their protests against slavery, abolition women asserted that despite their status as nonelectors, women did possess the right to petition Congress, and they held firm even when slaveholding congressmen questioned whether women in fact possessed that right.[39]

Antislavery women exploited not only the radical potential of the right of petition, but also the discursive resources of the petition genre. Two major elements of the form of petition, its narrative and its list of signatures, provided a means for women vividly to represent their presence in political space. Embedded in the petitions, as a remnant of their generic antecedents, were narratives of signers "appearing" before or "approaching" their rulers to make a request. An 1836 petition from the "females of Winthrop, Maine," for example, stated that the signers "approach your honorable body as humble supplicants," and the Fathers and Rulers petition urged legislators to "lend their ear to our appeals," as if representatives were listening to requests uttered by female petitioners appearing before them rather than reading women's petitions sent from afar.[40] In addition to petition narratives, the lists of signatures implied the presence of women not just individually but as a female collective, for they inscribed for all to see the existence of groups of women who coalesced discursively by signifying their agreement with the opinion printed on a petition. A written signature, as Jacques Derrida writes, "marks and retains [the signer's] having-been present in a past now, which will remain a future now, and therefore in a now in general, in the transcendental form of nowness (*maintenance*)." The narratives and signatures provided a discursive means not only to re-present women's opinions on slavery, but to assert women's presence individually and collectively in political space.[41]

As a genre of political communication, then, the petition held out radical possibilities for women to insinuate themselves into public discussion despite widespread beliefs that they were unsuited to participation in the republican political sphere. By casting petitioning as a form of prayer and by inserting themselves into familiar political narratives, female antislavery petitioners gained entry to political space, achieving what Luce Irigaray has called "subversiveness through reappropriation." By this she means that the women writer "plays with her cultural subordination in the symbolic order by replicating herself in the syntax of its familiar grammar, but always as a commentary on it. From within literature's commonplaces, she performs an operation of displacement."[42]

COMING TO SIGNATURE

In addition to signing their identities as individual political actors and appropriating the subversive potential of the petition genre, women exploited the text of the petition form to construct an ever-changing collective political subjectivity. Formulation of collective subjectivity was motivated primarily by a desire to expand women's participation in antislavery activism despite barriers posed by social prescriptions against their collective petitioning. An individual woman who contemplated signing antislavery petitions faced the threat of an onlooking audience composed of people who might indict her character after reading her signature on a petition, witnessing her signing it, or hearing that she had signed it. One such onlooker was Pastor Hubbard Winslow of Boston's Bowdoin Street Congregational Church. He rebuked women who sent "their names up to gentlemen holding official stations, gravely declaring their own judgment in regard to what they ought to do." Winslow branded female petitioners as bold, arrogant, rude, and indelicate. Another onlooker, Pastor Albert A. Folsom of the Universal Church in Hingham, Massachusetts, warned that a woman who made a habit of petitioning would soon neglect her domestic obligations, leave her children, and become a slave to her "appetites and passions" while she interested herself "with wonderful zeal in the cause of the Southern negro." "She, who is naturally amiable and modest, . . . is imperceptively transformed into a bigoted, rash, and morose being," Folsom cautioned. "Self-sufficiency, arrogance and masculating boldness follow naturally in the train."[43] Onlookers to the rhetorical act of women signing petitions such as Hubbard and Folsom as well as male relatives who denied women the opportunity to give their names functioned as a "constraining audience," one whose very presence and potential for discursive (or material) retribution wields the power to inhibit action.[44]

Given the ominous presence of this constraining audience, authors of female petitions were prompted to craft appeals that would reassure potential signers that by affixing their signatures they would not forfeit their reputation as respectable northern middle-class women. Petition texts provided a discursive resource for women to demonstrate that by signing antislavery petitions they were acting in accord with notions of acceptable class behavior. The rhetoric of female petitions constructed a collective political subjectivity based on an ideology they shared with men of their class. That rhetoric was informed by what Daniel J. McInerney has called an ideology of antislavery republicanism, which was embraced by abolitionists, who were for the most part members of the emerging northern middle class. Antislavery republicanism blamed slavery for creating the conditions of moral vice and concentrated power that had led to the demise of past republics. It decried slave labor, claiming that the health of the republic was based on the existence of independent landholders and free laborers. Of particular importance for women, antislavery republicanism embraced the myth that God had blessed Americans, choosing them to carry out the great experiment in republican government. By threatening this mission, antislavery republicans reasoned, slaveholders were sinning and provoking the wrath of God, who eventually would punish the nation. Because slavery was a sin that endangered the moral health of all those it touched, antislavery republicanism emphasized that true Christian Americans must sever all ties with and work to dismantle the institution of slavery.[45]

Antislavery republicanism perpetuated a concept of U.S. nationhood that protected northern middle-class interests and potentially appealed to women aspiring to membership in the middle class. Yet because a major tenet of antislavery republicanism was that the health of the republic rested on the ability of individuals to act independently, the implied subjectivity of antislavery republicanism excluded women. In order to authorize expanded female activism, the petitions appropriated major characteristics of the male-gendered antislavery republican in order to construct a collective political subjectivity that I call "antislavery republican womanhood." Although antislavery republican womanhood shared the majority of its traits with the category of antislavery republican, it stressed free, mostly white women's ability to operate independently in the *polis*. It did so by insisting on the dependence of slave women. The discursive renegotiation of the prevailing non-political female subjectivity into antislavery republican womanhood can be traced by examining how women's petitions replicated major traits of the antislavery republican—motivation to act based on Christian duty, concern for the health of the republic, belief in the superiority of free labor, and insistence that the *polis* be constituted of independent political actors. Founded upon republican principles, antislavery republican womanhood relates to Linda K. Kerber's concept of "republican motherhood," a political identity constructed during the Revolutionary period that valorized (white) mothers as custodians of civic morality charged with inculcating children, especially boys, with the virtues of republicanism.[46] Antislavery republican womanhood differed, however, in that it extended political responsibility to women in realms other than the raising of children to the work of moral reform, and beyond the home to the meeting hall and other spaces of public deliberation.

Reflecting a major tenet of antislavery republicanism, petitions written for and signed by women argued that slavery violated Christian principles. "As Christians," stated the women of Washington County, Vermont, "we mourn the toleration of this system, and deprecate the continuance of such flagrant violations of the pure and benignant precepts of our Holy Lawgiver, whose divine injunction is, 'Whatsoever ye would that men should do to you, do ye even so to them.'"[47] Like men's petitions and other immediate abolitionist rhetoric, women's petitions linked the judgment that slavery was a sin against God with principles of republicanism. For example, the popular women's petition attached to the 1836 Address of the Philadelphia Female Anti-Slavery Society said, "your memorialists, believing Slavery is a sin against God, and inconsistent with our declaration that 'equal liberty is the birth-right of all' urge abolition in the District."[48] Likewise, the Ladies of Dousa, New Hampshire, and those of Massachusetts argued that they "consider the toleration of slavery in the District of Columbia as a direct violation of the precepts of the Gospel, and shamefully inconsistent with the principles promulgated in the Declaration of Independence."[49]

Claims that women petitioners were motivated by Christian duty echoed the rhetoric of antislavery republicanism and indicated that women shared an important ideological trait with abolitionist men, whose right to participate in political dialogue was largely unquestioned (at least for white male abolitionists). Yet although expressions of Christian duty implied a similarity between antislavery women and men, these claims simultaneously exploited constructs of gender difference. Because middle-class women were thought of as morally superior to men, female petitions could claim convincingly that women were motivated to petition, not for political purposes, but out of religious duty. Time and again petitions designed to win female signatures called on women as Christians to overturn slavery and justified their petitioning by invoking the notion that women's Christian duty required them to lend their names to the cause. Hoping to appeal to potential signers, these arguments implied that should a woman refuse to sign, she was neither upholding her religious duty nor acting like a pious, true woman. The Christian duty argument, then, both asserted a shared characteristic with male abolitionists' political subjectivity and tempered that assertion by grounding the claim in essentialized notions of woman's morality. In this way, the petitions again performed "subversiveness through reappropriation" or, in particular, what Gayatri Chakravorty Spivak has called "strategic essentialism," by employing familiar notions about women often used to constrain their action in order to radically expand their role in the public. Indeed, the rhetoric of antislavery republicanism offered women a rhetorical resource precisely because it was grounded in the belief that upholding Christian duty entailed political action.[50]

A second antislavery republican trait employed in female petitions was the warning that slavery corroded the moral health of the republic, which would eventually provoke God to scourge the nation. A petition signed and sent by both men and women of Ohio in 1834 proclaimed: "We protest against permitting the District of Columbia to remain a mart of *human flesh,* to the disgrace of our national character, and to the cruel oppression of thousands of native Americans, who are loaded with chains, immured in jails, and sold under the hammer like brutes within the sight of the Capitol."[51] "As daughters of America, we blush for the tarnished fame of our beloved country," declared a petition signed by the Females of Washington County, Vermont. "We lament her waning glory, and we entreat that you, as patriots, will erase this stain from her dishonored character."[52] Likewise; the female inhabitants of South Reading, Massachusetts, warned that for the United States Congress, "the Representatives of a free, republican and Christian people," to declare "their consent to and approval of the extension of the evils of slavery in our land would be a blot on our national character that could never be effaced, and which would invoke the judgments of Heaven."[53] Expressions of concern for the health of the country implied that women met the republican requirement of being aware of the history of the republic and immediate challenges to its perpetuation. They implied, furthermore, that women's interest in preserving the national character extended beyond raising children to be good citizens to monitoring the morality of federal policy.

Women's petitions performed a third virtue of antislavery republicanism by insisting that slavery denigrated the dignity of labor and threatened the free laborer, whose independence was the very foundation of republican government. Slavery should be abolished in the District of Columbia, argued a popular petition signed by both women and men, because it was "oppressive to the honest free laborer, and tends to make labor disreputable as well as unprofitable." The same petition, which was circulated in Vermont, Ohio, and New York, claimed that immediate abolition was practicable because "It will not annihilate the laborers nor their labor, but will merely make it necessary for the employers to pay fair wages."[54] Men and women of Lockport, New York, inscribed their names to a petition for abolition in Washington, D.C., and the western territories by arguing that slavery was "detrimental to the interests and *subversive of the liberties of the labouring population of our republic.*"[55] Free labor arguments in petitions echoed other abolitionist discourse, which warned that the South's industrialism was expanding, and soon its products, made with slave labor, would undersell those of northern manufacturers, thereby forcing down wages or causing factories to close. Slaveholders conspired, abolitionists claimed, to enslave the entire working class of the United States.[56] That women signed antislavery petitions containing free labor arguments suggests their adherence to a reform ideology deeply committed to protecting northern middle-class interests. By reiterating commitments shared by men of their class, women helped establish their inclusion in the classed subjectivity of the antislavery republican.

Yet although women's petitions shared with men's several major arguments implying women's inclusion in the category of antislavery republican, they differed significantly on one claim. Women's petitions dwelled on the suffering of the female slave. The Fathers and Rulers petition, for instance, explained, "We should be less than women, if the nameless and unnumbered wrongs of which the slaves of our sex are made defenseless victims, did not fill us with horror and constrain us, in earnestness and agony of spirit to pray for their deliverances."[57] Descriptions of the horrors of slavery in women's petitions stressed the particular afflictions suffered by female slaves. Time and again they represented the slave woman as sexually and spiritually vulnerable, "degraded," "brutified," "the victims of insatiable avarice," "wronged," and "denied of male relatives to offer them protection." By condemning the harsh and indelicate treatment of slave women, women's antislavery rhetoric "redefined their suffering as feminine, and hence endowed them with all the moral value generally attributed to nineteenth-century American womanhood."[58] Attention to the particular sexual vulnerability and sexual violence perpetuated against slave women, in other words, accentuated the gendered nature of their victimage and imported ethical standards usually reserved for governing the treatment of white middle-class women to condemn slaveholders.

Although expressions of concern about the sexual vulnerability of slave women implied a shared gender identity based on shared experience, women's petitions enacted a significant power differential between free (mostly white) women and female slaves. As long as the female slave could not petition for herself, the petitions insisted, free women were obligated to petition for them. A petition circulated during the fall of 1835 in Massachusetts and New Hampshire emphasized that "Your petitioners believe it to be their duty to urge upon your serious consideration the perpetual wrongs of women and children, whose husbands and fathers are deprived of all legal power to protect them." The women explained that they could not remain silent "while thousands of their sex are condemned to helpless degradation, and even denied the privilege of making known their sufferings." "History would blush for American women," the petitioners predicted, "if, under such circumstances, they ever allowed their voice of expostulation and entreaty to cease throughout the land."[59] Similarly, a call to petition circulated among members of the Philadelphia Female Anti-Slavery Society stated, "It is noble to speak for the dumb."[60]

By insisting on the necessity of speaking for slave women, free women combined the rhetoric of female moral duty with a notion of stewardship to elevate themselves from dependents to representatives of those who lacked the autonomy to speak for themselves. In so doing, they accentuated the dependence of slave women and their contrasting independence, demonstrating that they met perhaps the most important requirement of the antislavery republican—the capacity for independent thought and action. Yet abolitionist women's shedding of the cloak of dependence by adopting the mantle of public representative of female slaves amounted to a reappropriation of the political power arrangements between white men and all women. Similar to the rationale that endowed white men with the political power to represent the interests of their dependents—wives, daughters, and sisters—the petitions asserted that free women were qualified to represent the interests of female slaves, who, they claimed, depended on them. In so doing, the petitions constructed identities for antislavery women and slave women that intersected along the line of gender but diverged along the line of race.[61] Ironically, the petitions' radical goal of expanding female abolitionists' access to public deliberation relied on the conservative rhetoric of woman's moral superiority. Even more ironic, perhaps, is that although petitions served an ultraist movement that professedly sought to overturn dominant social, economic, and political structures, the petitions invoked a deeply conservative political vision of indirect representation in an era of growing democracy that privileged a language of direct representation.

The petitions' preoccupation with the victimization of female slaves resembles the sentimental tactics of representation employed by Theodore Weld in *American Slavery As It Is* (1839), which compiled more than two hundred pages of excruciatingly detailed testimonies of the horrors of slavery. Like Weld and his narrators, the petitioners suffered from what Stephen Browne has identified as a common dilemma of reform discourse, especially that of abolitionists—in speaking for the oppressed, they spoke instead of the oppressed. These rhetors transposed from the voiceless the moral authority to represent slavery and, perhaps most important, the right to "translate its meaning, and proctor its reception." Noting that historians have been careful to avoid reducing reform motives to sheer altruism or to crude self-interest, Browne demonstrates that Weld used the slave's body as a site to resolve tensions between the simultaneous claims of humanitarian reform and class allegiance.[62] When we also consider gender as a force in the confluence of class, race, and morality that shaped abolitionist rhetoric, as I have here, we gain the further insight that women discursively appropriated the body of the slave woman as a site to negotiate not only tensions between moral commitments and class allegiance, but also the related issue of respectable gender behavior in the public sphere. This issue figured significantly in northern (mostly white) middle-class women's claims to political power. Although many female abolitionists no doubt were devoted to ending slavery, petitioning, and particularly insisting on the silence of slave women, simultaneously advanced their own political capacity.

CONCLUSION

By offering a multi-faceted reading of female antislavery petitions, I hope to have added to our knowledge of the ways and means through which northern middle-class women claimed expanded access to the public sphere and renegotiated their status as citizens. In a broader sense, I have endeavored to contribute to rhetorical scholarship of social movements by moving beyond leader-centered approaches and recognizing power differentials among movement participants. Social movements are more than their leaders, and we cannot fully understand the rhetoric of a given social movement and its consequences by examining only the discourse of its leaders. Indeed, if we are at all interested in recognizing the contributions of non-dominant groups within wider social movements, such as women in the abolitionist and civil rights movements or African American women in the woman suffrage and feminist movements, we need to ask not only how movements create and maintain in-group solidarity, but also to distill from constructions of a movement's collective identity notions of its ideal actor. We might then inquire whether constructions of the idealized actor exclude certain groups of sympathizers from full participation in the movement and how members of these groups formulate political subjectivities to legitimate their involvement in the cause and, to a wider extent, in political culture. Doing so, I believe, can set us on a path to discovering the broader impact of a given movement on social and political history.[63]

In addition, I have sought to extend feminist critiques of early work on the public sphere by illustrating the public's complex, fluid nature and by emphasizing the dynamics of exclusion and inclusion based on political subjectivities. Others such as Butler, Fraser, and Felski have noted that constructions of the bourgeois public imply dominant subjectivities that categorically exclude certain groups from political access along the lines of race, class, and gender. The concept of constraining audience contributes to our understanding of the exclusionary dynamic of publics by providing a means to denote certain forces that police access to publicity. Constraining audiences may be real onlookers to the performance of an action or may exist only in the minds of those contemplating taking action. These real or imagined onlookers possess the power to rebuke those who would act as unfit, inappropriate, or in some other way lacking in the qualifications of the legitimate public actor. Consequently, potential actors, such as antebellum women who considered signing petitions or speaking in public, faced political delegitimation and social denigration.

To overcome barriers posed by constraining audiences, subordinated individuals (such as women abolitionists) form what Fraser and others have called a "counterpublic." Fraser defines counterpublics as "parallel discursive arenas where members of subordinated social groups invent and circulate counterdiscourses to formulate oppositional interpretations of their identities, interests, and needs." Rather than appealing to the universality of the bourgeois public sphere, explain Robert Asen and Daniel C. Brouwer, counterpublics base their appeals on some axis of difference such as gender, race, or sexuality. The rhetoric of counterpublics, then, is directed inward, with an eye toward the discursive construction of oppositional identities. As Fraser notes, however, counterpublics also direct discourse outward; they both withdraw from and reengage with wider publics.[64] Owing to antislavery women's dislocation from the public sphere inflicted by gender traditionalists, including both pro-slavery advocates and abolitionists, they found it necessary to retreat to a counterpublic to develop distinct female political subjectivities to authorize their participation in the public debate over slavery. They founded female antislavery societies, held female antislavery conventions, and wrote and signed female anti-slavery petitions. Female antislavery petitions, then, are discursive productions of a counterpublic, which bear rhetorical marks of efforts to overcome the objections of the constraining audience through construction of a collective female political subjectivity of antislavery republican womanhood.

The process through which antislavery women constructed this collective subjec-tivity in social movement discourse was effectively excavated through use of the critical tool of "signature." Ruminating on the nature of signature as a mark of the identity of an individual made by herself or himself led to the insight that a signature and lists of signatures are rhetorical artifacts and can be read as texts. Signatures mark the existence of an individual, constitute an assertion of indi-vidual identity, and indicate at least a rudimentary level of literacy. In the case of antislavery petitions, signatures publicly decreed individual women's opinions and possessed the potential to persuade others to follow suit. The critical concept of signature, moreover, brought into relief the multiple steps involved in the process of developing subjectivity. In the signatures on antislavery petitions, we have arti-facts of a first step, the transformation from isolated individuals to individual polit-ical actors. Drawing upon the notion of "coming to signature," we can identify a second step in the discursive process, this one executed in the texts of petitions—construction of a collective subjectivity. As Patricia Waugh notes amid her discus-sion of coming to signature, the aim of women's discourse is "not an attempt to define an isolated individual ego, but to discover a collective concept of subjectivity which foregrounds the construction of identity *in relationship*."[65]

Reading for discursive signs of women "coming to signature" led to the iden-tification of multiple ways the petitions exploited available discursive resources to perform acts of subversion through reappropriation. Embracing the rhetoric of antislavery republicanism, for example, enabled abolition women to claim that, unlike slaveholders, they embodied the virtues of the American Revolution (albeit a distinctly northern middle-class interpretation of the Revolution). As true repub-licans under the cosmology of antislavery republicanism, the women who signed abolition petitions proved that they rightly belonged to a group that boasted a truer claim to U.S. Citizenship—in their minds, at least—than even the most powerful slaveholding senator. Retreat to a female antislavery counterpublic facilitated the construction of the political subjectivity of antislavery republican womanhood, which legitimized abolitionist women to re-engage with the wider public through petitioning.

Yet as analysis of the rhetoric of female antislavery petitions suggests, subordi-nate groups' retreat from and re-engagement with the dominant public may well replicate dynamics of public exclusion. The predominance in women's petitions of detailed (perhaps even prurient) descriptions of the horrors inflicted upon female slaves combined with repeated references to their silent suffering sought to authorize abolition women to speak for their "slave sisters." By insisting on the dependence of female slaves, abolition women parlayed white middle-class notions of woman's moral superiority into an assertion of political stewardship to complete their qualifications for membership in the category of antislavery republican.[66] Abolition women gained increased access to the wider public, then, by constructing a political subjectivity grounded on appropriation and exploitation of the subjectivity of the female slave. Although this appropriation was discursive, its effects were material because although abolition women tightened their grasp on the right of petition and redefined female citizenship, they benefited from the denial of political rights to slave women. Rather than demanding that female slaves be granted the right of petition, women's antislavery petitions and their rhetoric in general emphasized that slave women were unable to speak for themselves. The petitions reified abolitionist women into moral stewards driven purely by Christian duty to act as the saviors of their unprotected, morally degraded, sexually exploited "slave sisters." By emphasizing the silence of female slaves while dwelling on their sexual mistreatment by the morally corrupt slaveholder, female antislavery petitions reinforced the exclusion of slave women from the public as anything other than subjects acted upon, as anything other than speechless, victimized bodies.

NOTES

[1]Petition of the ladies of Glastenbury for abolition of slavery in the District of Columbia, 1836, HR24A–H1.3, National Archives Box 3 of Library of Congress Box 47; Petition of the ladies of Marshfield for abolition of slavery in the District of Columbia, December 18, 1835, to June 6, 1836, National Archives, HR24A–H1.3.

[2]Although missing documents make it impossible to know for certain how many antislavery memorials were sent to Congress by women, it is possible to estimate. Based on the figure that during the years from 1837 to 1863 women signed petitions at the conservative rate of 15,000 per year (the number sent in 1836 before the petition campaign was formally organized), the total number of female signatures gathered from 1831 to 1863 would amount to well over three quarters of a million. But this figure is assuredly too small, for women's petitioning increased dramatically after 1836. If even half as many women who signed petitions during 1837 did so from 1838 to 1863, the total number of female signatures gathered from 1836 to 1863 would amount to almost 3 million. And this total does not include the more than 65,000 female signatures gathered by the National Women's Loyal League in 1864 to secure passage of the Thirteenth Amendment.

[3]As Richard Sewell has noted, by leading many northerners to see that slavery threatened their own civil rights, the petition controversy "proved a godsend" to the abolitionists. Richard H. Sewell, *Ballots for Freedom: Antislavery Politics in the United States, 1837–1860* (New York: Oxford University Press, 1976), 7–8; Robert P. Ludlum, "The Antislavery 'Gag Rule': History and Argument," *Journal of Negro History* 26 (April 1941), 243, 228–229.

[4]Dwight L. Dumond, *Antislavery: The Crusade for Freedom in America* (New York: Norton, 1961), 144, 246.

[5]As Gerda Lerner writes, "Women, who played a crucial role in antislavery petitioning, had far more importance in transforming public opinion and thereby influencing political life than has hitherto been recognized." Lerner, "The Political Activities of Antislavery Women," in Lerner, ed., *The Majority Finds its Past: Placing Women in History* (New York: Oxford University Press, 1979), 113. Others who attest to the significance of women's antislavery petitioning include Gilbert H. Barnes, *The Antislavery Impulse, 1830–1844* (New York: Harcourt, Brace & World, 1933), 143. (Barnes spends a full

chapter discussing women's important contributions to the petition campaign.) Keith E. Melder, *Beginnings of Sisterhood: The American Woman's Rights Movement, 1800–1850* (New York: Schocken Books, 1977), 73; William Lee Miller, *Arguing About Slavery: The Great Battle in the United States Congress* (New York: Knopf, 1996), 311–323.

[6]I am building on and hope to add to an ongoing conversation about the role of women in U.S. political culture. Contributors to this dialogue include, among others, Linda Kerber, Karlyn Kohrs Campbell, Mary Ryan, Lori D. Ginzberg, Norma Basch, A. Cheree Carlson, and Jan Lewis, who have examined the ways in which women were denied full citizenship during the formation of the republic and the means through which they attempted to claim their rights throughout the nineteenth century and beyond. Karlyn Kohrs Campbell, "The Rhetoric of Women's Liberation: An Oxymoron," *Quarterly Journal of Speech* 59 (1973): 75–86; Linda K. Kerber, *Women of the Republic: Intellect and Ideology in Revolutionary America* (New York: W. W. Norton, 1980); Kerber, "Separate Spheres, Female Worlds, Woman's Place: The Rhetoric of Women's History," *Journal of American History* 75 (June 1988): 9–39; Kerber, *No Constitutional Right to be Ladies: Women and the Obligations of Citizenship* (New York: Hill and Wang, 1998); Norma Basch, "Equity vs. Equality: Emerging Concepts of Women's Political Status in the Age of Jackson," *Journal of the Early Republic* 3 (Fall 1983): 297–318; Paula Baker, "The Domestication of Politics: Women and American Political Society, 1780–1920," *The American Historical Review* 89 (June 1984): 620–647; Campbell, *Man Cannot Speak for Her: Key Texts of the Early Feminists*, 2 vols. (New York: Praeger, 1989); Mary P. Ryan, *Women in Public: Between Banners and Ballots, 1825–1880* (Baltimore: The Johns Hopkins University Press, 1990); Lori D. Ginzberg, *Women and the Work of Benevolence: Morality, Politics, and Class in the 19th-Century United States* (New Haven: Yale University Press, 1990); Ann M. Boylan, "Women and Politics in the Era Before Seneca Falls," *Journal of the Early Republic* 10 (Fall 1990): 363–382; A. Cheree Carlson, "Creative Casuistry and Feminist Consciousness: The Rhetoric of Moral Reform," *Quarterly Journal of Speech* 78 (1992): 16–32; Lisa M. Gring-Pemble, "Writing Themselves into Consciousness: Creating a Rhetorical Bridge Between the Public and Private Spheres," *Quarterly Journal of Speech* 84 (1998): 41–61; Jan Lewis, "'Of Every Age Sex & Condition': The Representation of Women in the Constitution," *Journal of the Early Republic* 15 (Fall 1995): 359–387; Elizabeth R. Varon, "Tippecanoe and the Ladies, Too: White Women and Party Politics in Antebellum Virginia," *Journal of American History* 82 (September 1995): 494–521; Mary Hershberger, "Mobilizing Women, Anticipating Abolition: The Struggle against Indian Removal in the 1830s," *Journal of American History* 86 (June 1999): 15–40.

    This study also aims specifically to contribute to our knowledge of women's antislavery petitioning, a subject that has been discussed by other scholars such as Gerda Lerner, Judith Wellman, and Deborah Bingham Van Broekhoven. Lerner, "Political Activities of Antislavery Women"; Judith Wellman, "Women and Radical Reform in Antebellum Upstate New York: A Profile of Grassroots Female Abolitionists," in *Clio Was a Woman: Studies in the History of American Women*, ed. Mabel E. Deutrich and Virginia C. Purdy (Washington, D.C.: Howard University Press, 1980), 113–127; Deborah Bingham Van Broekhoven, "'Let Your Names be Enrolled': Method and Ideology In Women's Antislavery Petitioning," in *The Abolitionist Sisterhood: Women's Political Culture in Antebellum America*, ed. Jean Fagan Yellin and John C. Van Home (Ithaca: Cornell University Press, 1994), 179–199.

[7]These claims are based on my study of thousands of antislavery petitions sent to Congress between the years 1831 to 1865, signed by both women and men, and representing every state and territory that submitted petitions during those years. The thousands of extant antislavery petitions are stored at the National Archives in Washington, D.C. Many of the petitions signed by women have been catalogued through the Our Mothers Before Us project, which gleaned the papers of Congress for documents submitted by and regarding women.

[8]Charles J. Stewart, "A Functional Approach to the Rhetoric of Social Movements," *Central States Speech Journal* 31 (Winter 1980): 298–305; Richard B. Gregg, "The Ego-Function of the Rhetoric of Protest," *Philosophy and Rhetoric* 4 (1971): 71–91.

[9]Nan Enstad, *Ladies of Labor, Girls of Adventure: Working Women, Popular Culture, and Labor Politics at the Turn of the Twentieth Century* (New York: Columbia University Press, 1999), 3, 121–122, 12, and Enstad, "Fashioning Political Identities: Cultural Studies and the Historical Construction of Political Subjects," *American Quarterly* 50 (December 1998): 745–782. Patricia Waugh discusses the link between collective feminist subjectivities and discursive practices in *Feminine Fictions: Revisiting the Postmodern* (London: Routledge, 1989), especially Chapter 1. Judith Butler, *Gender Trouble: Feminism and the Subversion of Identity* (New York: Routledge, 1990), 2, 145.

[10]Kenneth Cmiel, for instance, notes that public opinion had become so important that when in 1832 President Jackson exercised unprecedented authority by vetoing the charter for the Second Bank of the United States, he addressed his presidential message not to Congress, as was customary, but directly to the public. Kenneth Cmiel, *Democratic Eloquence: The Fight Over Popular Speech in Nineteenth-Century America* (New York: William Morrow, 1990), 64. See also John William Ward, *Andrew Jackson—Symbol for an Age* (New York: Oxford University Press, 1955), 49.

[11]Theda Perdue and Michael D. Green, eds., *The Cherokee Removal: A Brief History with Documents* (Boston: Bedford, 1995), 122–126; Hershberger, "Mobilizing Women, Anticipating Abolition."

[12]Ryan, for example, has linked the exclusion of women from the United States public developing circa 1825 to gendered constructions of political subjectivities. "The same stroke that inscribed gender differences on the public as a principle of exclusion placed a mark of selective social identity on citizenship in general," she writes. "Republican ideology held that the female sex embodied those uncurbed human passions that inevitably subverted the self-control and rationality required of citizens." Mary P. Ryan, "Gender and Public Access: Women's Politics in Nineteenth-Century America," in *Feminism, the Public and Private,* ed. Joan B. Landes (Oxford: Oxford University Press, 1998), 195–222, quotation from pages 201–202. Numerous feminist scholars have described the disciplining of women who, during the antebellum era and before, attempted to influence politics by publishing and speaking in public. See Susan Zaeske, "The 'Promiscuous Audience' Controversy and the Emergence of the Early Woman's Rights Movement," *Quarterly Journal of Speech* 81 (May 1995): 191–207; Campbell, "The Struggle for the Right to Speak," in *Man Cannot Speak for Her,* I, 17–36; Glenna Matthews, *The Rise of Public Woman: Women's Power and Woman's Place in the United States, 1630–1970* (New York: Oxford University Press, 1992).

[13]Enstad also emphasizes the distinction between the normative and descriptive, which, I believe, often is ignored and decontextualized in rhetorical scholarship, especially in discussions of republican motherhood, separate spheres, and the cult of domesticity. Enstad, *Ladies of Labor,* 86.

[14]Enstad succinctly describes the exclusion of women and people of color from the nineteenth-century middle-class public based on the incommensurability of the category of "woman" with the category of "citizen" in *Ladies of Labor,* 86, 227n2. See also Ryan, *Women in Public.*

[15]Ryan, "Gender and Public Access," 218, 206.

[16]I do not intend to imply that these are mutually exclusive categories, but rather to acknowledge that Miller demonstrates the concept with reference to the novel.

[17]Nancy K. Miller, *Subject to Change: Reading Feminist Writing* (New York: Columbia University Press, 1988), 129. I wish to thank Karlyn Kohrs Campbell for introducing me to literature on the critical concept of signature.

[18]Before the abolitionists made concerted efforts to ensure that all petitioners signed their own names, in some cases women copied the lists of signatures gathered to make the

petitions look neater. After congressmen questioned the authenticity of signatures, antislavery newspapers and petition circulars instructed name-gatherers that all petitioners must write their own names or make their own mark. An 1837 American Anti-Slavery Society petition circular, for example, directed, "Let everyone write their own name. Names should not be *copied on*—it might lead to a suspicion that they were forged." American Anti-Slavery Society Circular, 1837, Pennsylvania Abolitionist Society Collection, Philadelphia Female Anti-Slavery Society Papers, 1837 (formerly PAS Box 38).

[19]Nancy F. Cott, *Bonds of Womanhood: "Woman's Sphere" in New England, 1780–1835* (New Haven: Yale University Press,) 101, 103. Cott drew these statistics of signature rates from Kenneth A. Lockridge, *Literacy in Colonial New England* (New York: Norton, 1974), 38–42, 57–78. The female academies statistic comes from Mary Kelley, "Reading Women/Women Reading: The Making of Learned Women in Antebellum America," *The Journal of American History* 83 (September 1996), 407, 410, 403. The link between sign literacy and the reading of novels is made by Cathy N. Davidson, "Female Education, Literacy and the Politics of Sentimental Fiction," *Women's Studies International Forum* 9 (1986): 309–312. Another excellent discussion of the development of women's literacy can be found in Richard D. Brown, *Knowledge Is Power: The Diffusion of Information in Early America, 1700–1865* (New York: Oxford University Press, 1989), especially Chapter 7.

[20]Van Broekhoven, "'Let Your Names Be Enrolled,'" 182.

[21]Elizabeth Cady Stanton, *The Woman's Bible*, quoted in Aileen S. Kraditor, *Up From the Pedestal: Selected Writings in the History of American Feminism* (Chicago: Quadrangle, 1968), 114.

[22]Kerber, *Women of the Republic*, 9, 119–120.

[23]*Liberator*, August 4, 1837; Sarah Grimké, *Letters on the Equality of the Sexes* (1837), in *The Public Years of Sarah and Angelina Grimké: Selected Writings, 1835–1839*, ed. Larry Ceplair (New York: Columbia University Press, 1989), 239; Hanna H. Smith to Abby Kelley, July 25, 1839. Abby Kelley Foster Papers, American Antiquarian Society.

[24]Petition of the females of Winthrop, Maine, for abolition of slavery in the District of Columbia, March 21, 1836, HR 24–G22.4, National Archives Box 14 of Library of Congress Box 75.

[25]Frances E. Willard, "A White Life for Two," (1890) in Karlyn Kohrs Campbell, ed., *Man Cannot Speak for Her*, II, 335–336. I wish to thank Campbell for bringing Willard's appeal for name reform to my attention. I also wish to thank Campbell for lending her insight that signatures on petitions constituted affirmations of women's right to express themselves as individuals which she offered in Campbell, "The Drama of the Female Signature," paper presented at the Seventh Biennial Public Address Conference, Pennsylvania State University, October 2000, 3.

[26]See for example, Petition of the Inhabitants of Livingston County, New York, against the Admission of Florida and Texas, (n.d., circa 1843), HR27A–H1.1, TABLED, Admission of Florida and Texas to the Union folder.

[27]Great Petition to Congress from Citizens of Massachusetts, asking Congress to forever separate them from all connections with slavery, February 14, 1842–March 3, 1843, HR27 A–H1.7; Petition from the Inhabitants of the Town of Nantucket to end the Slave Trade in the District of Columbia, January 31, 1843, HR27A–H1.6; Petition from the citizens of Ashtabula, Ohio, for immediate abolition in the District of Columbia, HR26A–H1.2.

[28]See for example, Petition for Woman Suffrage from the Colored Citizens of the District of Columbia, 1877, HR45A–H11.7; Petition of 2,413 citizens of Massachusetts arguing for national legislation against the crime of lynching and mob violence, January 20, 1900, Judiciary, HR 56A–H13.3; *The Utah Bill. A Plea for Religious Liberty. Speech of Hon. W. H. Hooper, of Utah, Delivered in the House of Representatives, March 23, 1870,*

Together With the Remonstrance of the Citizens of Salt Lake City, in Mass Meeting, held March 31, 1870, to the Senate of the United States. (Washington, D.C.: Gibson Brothers, 1870).

[29]Petition of 800 Ladies of New York, *Emancipator,* February 24, 1835.

[30]Barnes, *Antislavery Impulse,* 262n15.

[31]Petition of the citizens of Philadelphia for repeal of the gag rule, February 14, 1838, National Archives Box 29 of Library of Congress, Box 110, folder 1 of 2.

[32]For an example of the "women of America" petition form, see Petition of Alma Lyman and 52 others, January 19, 1849, National Archives, HR30A–G9.2, folder 3 of 9.

[33]Gilbert H. Barnes and Dwight L. Dumond concluded that the Fathers and Rulers of Our Country form was "by far the most popular form for 'female petitions' until 1840. Tens of thousands are in the files of the House of Representatives (boxes 85–126) in the Library of Congress. Except for the short 'sentence forms' distributed by the American Anti-Slavery Society during the period 1837–1840, it was the commonest form in the campaign." Gilbert H. Barnes and Dwight L. Dumond, eds., *Letters of Theodore Dwight Weld, Angelina Grimké Weld, and Sarah Grimké, 1822–1844* (Gloucester, Mass.: Peter Smith, 1965), 175n1. Signed Fathers and Rulers petitions sent to Congress and yet extant include, for example, Petition of 600 Ladies of Utica, Oneida County, New York, for Abolition of Slavery and the Slave Trade in the District of Columbia, March 21, 1836, National Archives Box 3 of Library of Congress Box 47. A text of the Fathers and Rulers petition can be found in Barnes and Dumond, eds., *Weld-Grimké Letters,* I, 175–176.

[34]Fathers and Rulers Form, in Barnes and Dumond, eds., *Weld-Grimké Letters,* I, 175–176. The analogy between the act of petitioning and praying not only abounded in women's petitions, but also made its way into congressional debate over antislavery petitions. On February 6, 1837, John Quincy Adams rose to respond to a representative from Virginia who had argued that a certain petition should not be heard because it was from free "Negro" women who were allegedly prostitutes. The right of petition, Adams argued, was never predicated on the morality or virtue of the petitioner: "Petition is supplication—it is entreaty—it is prayer! And where is the degree of vice or immorality which shall deprive the citizen of the right to supplicate for a boon, or to pray for mercy?" *Gales and Seatons' Register of Debates in Congress,* February 6, 1837, 1596.

[35]During the nineteenth century there was a tendency to view religion as resting on the personal or domestic sphere, which was considered particularly feminine. Consequently, the general belief was that religion existed outside the secular realm, which was considered particularly masculine. This dichotomy was reinforced by prescriptive literature beginning in the late eighteenth century, which advised women to be devout and virtuous while men were excused from such standards because their "passions" were constantly "subject to be heated by the ferment of business." Statements that women should be more religious than men reflected that as a group women were indeed more religious than men because greater numbers of women than men belonged to churches. Whatever its origins, belief in women's natural inclination toward religion implied that piety was natural for women and somehow unnatural for men. For discussions of gender and religion during the nineteenth century, see Rosemary Radford Ruether and Rosemary Skinner Keller, *Women and Religion in America: Volume 1: The Nineteenth Century* (San Francisco: Harper and Row, 1981); Nancy Cott, "Young Women in the Second Great Awakening," *Feminist Studies* 3 (Fall 1975), and *The Bonds of Womanhood: "Woman's Sphere" in New England, 1780–1835* (New Haven: Yale University Press, 1977), Chapter 4; Barbara Welter, "The Feminization of American Religion, 1800–1860," in *Dimity Convictions,* ed. Barbara Welter (Athens: Ohio University Press, 1976).

[36]As Richard J. Carwardine observes, "For many, petitioning represented a means of operating in an era of mass politics without being compromised by the corruption of new partisanship." Carwardine, *Evangelicals and Politics in Antebellum America* (Knoxville: University of Tennessee Press, 1997), 32.

[37]Garrison, writes Henry Mayer, "audaciously believed that a citizen could be more influential by deciding not to vote and that a leader could be more faithful to his constituency by refusing to hold office." Henry Mayer, *All on Fire: William Lloyd Garrison and the Abolition of Slavery* (New York: St. Martin's Press, 1998), xiv.

[38]Stephen A. Higginson, "A Short History of the Right to Petition Government for the Redress of Grievances," *Yale Law Review Journal* 96 (1986): 142–166; Edmund S. Morgan, *Inventing the People: The Rise of Popular Sovereignty in England and America* (New York: W. W. Norton & Company, 1988), 222–230. David C. Frederick explains that the substantive meaning of the right of petition was shaped by the twin duties of reception and response. Further, it is possible to state with some certainty that by the eighteenth century "the right included the expectation that the government would receive the petition and issue a response whatever the subject matter of the plea. The development of the right to petition in practice, therefore, led to the expectation of a response, favorable or not." David C. Frederick, "John Quincy Adams, Slavery, and the Disappearance of the Right of Petition," *Law and History Review* 9 (Spring 1991), 115. Debate over slaves' right of petition and the vote to "not receive" a petition from slaves can be found in *Annals of Congress*, 4th Cong., 2nd Sess. (January 30, 1797), 2015–2024.

[39]Representative Henry A. Wise of Virginia, for example, directly called this right into question amid debate over reception of antislavery petitions. "Have women, too, the right of petition?" he asked rhetorically. "Are they citizens!" *Register of Debates*, 24th Cong., 1st Sess., (December 22, 1835), 2032–2033.

[40]Petition of the females of Winthrop, Maine, (1836); "Fathers and Rulers of Our Country Petition Form," in Barnes and Dumond, eds., *Weld-Grimké Letters*, I, 175–176.

[41]Jacques Derrida, "Signature Event Context," in *Margins of Philosophy*, trans. Alan Bass (Chicago: University of Chicago Press, 1982), 328.

[42]Irigaray's concept of subversiveness through reappropriation is discussed in Miller, *Subject to Change*, 133.

[43]Quoted in Boston Female Anti-Slavery Society, *Right and Wrong in Boston, Annual Report of the Boston Female Anti-Slavery Society . . . in 1837* (Boston: Isaac Knaap, 1837), 53; "A Lecture, Delivered Sunday Evening, by Albert A. Folsom, Pastor of the Universal Church, Hingham, Massachusetts," extracted in *Liberator*, September 22, 1837.

[44]Women who signed antislavery petitions risked repudiation not only from constraining audiences of those who desired to limit women's influence, but also from those who desired to arrest the growth of abolitionism. Antislavery petitioners were susceptible to criticism for the radical cause they espoused because immediate abolitionism was at the "ultraist" extreme of the spectrum of antebellum reform movements because it openly sought to effect a reconstruction of society. Throughout the 1830s to 1850s the vast majority of southerners and northerners regarded abolitionists, male and female alike, as a threat to the stability of the union. Abolitionists, they believed, needed to be halted through vociferous public denunciation and even violence. Ginzberg, *Benevolence*, 33. For a thorough discussion of the spectrum of nineteenth-century female reform movements and abolition's ultraism, see Nancy A. Hewitt, *Women's Activism and Social Change: Rochester, New York, 1822–1872* (Ithaca: Cornell University Press, 1984).

[45]Carwardine, *Evangelicals and Politics*, 134–135; Daniel J. McInerney, *The Fortunate Heirs of Freedom: Abolition and Republican Thought* (Lincoln: University of Nebraska Press, 1994).

[46]Kerber describes the construct of republican motherhood throughout *Women of the Republic*.

[47]Petition of the Females of Washington County, Vermont, for the Abolition of Slavery in the District of Columbia and Various States, 1836, HR24–G22.4, National Archives Box 14 of Library of Congress Box 75.

[48]*Address of the Female Anti-Slavery Society of Philadelphia to the Women of Pennsylvania with the Form of Petition to the Congress of the United States* (Philadelphia: Merrihew and Gunn, 1836), 8.

[49]Petition of the Ladies of Dousa, New Hampshire for Abolition of Slavery in the District of Columbia, 1836, HR 24–G22.4, National Archives Box 14 of Library of Congress Box 75; Petition of the Ladies of Massachusetts for Abolition of Slavery in the District of Columbia, December 18, 1835–June 6, 1836, HR24A–H1.3, TABLED.

[50]Gayatri Chakravorty Spivak, "Can the Subaltern Speak?" in *Colonial Discourse and Post-Colonial Theory: A Reader,* ed. Patrick Williams and Laura Chrisman (New York: Columbia University Press, 1994), 66–111. Spivak and others have argued that strategic essentialism "can be used as part of a 'good' strategy as well as a 'bad' strategy." Although the tactic can help subalterns or protest movements disrupt dominant discourses, as a form of essentialism it elides differences, can be appropriated by the dominant group, and, as I argue here, may inscribe new hierarchies of exclusion. For comments on the positive and negative potential of strategic essentialism, see Spivak, "Practical Politics of the Open End," in *The Post-Colonial Critic: Interviews, Strategies, Dialogues,* ed. Sarah Harasym (New York: Routledge, 1990), 108–109; and Lisa Lowe, "Heterogeneity, Hybridity, Multiplicity: Asian American Differences," *Diaspora* 1 (1991), 39.

[51]Petition of the Citizens of Ohio on Slavery in the District of Columbia, February 18, 1834, HR 23A–G4.3, DISTRICT OF COLUMBIA COMMITTEE, National Archives Box 3 of Library of Congress Box 48.

[52]Petition of the Females of Washington County, Vermont, 1836.

[53]Petition of the Female Inhabitants of South Reading, Massachusetts, Against the Admission of the Territory of Arkansas to the Union as a Slaveholding State, June 6, 1836, HR24A–H1.4, National Archives Box 3 of Library of Congress Box 46.

[54]Examples of this form are the Petition of the Citizens of the Town of Fayston, Vermont, for the Abolition of Slavery in the District of Columbia, February 29, 1836, HR24–G22.4, National Archives Box 14 of Library of Congress Box 75; Petition of the Ladies of Orange County, New York, for the Abolition of Slavery in the District of Columbia, 1836, HR24A–G22.4, National Archives Box 3 of Library of Congress Box 47; Petition of the Female Citizens of Ohio for the Abolition of Slavery in the District of Columbia, 1836, HR24A–G22.4, National Archives Box 12 of Library of Congress Box 71.

[55]Petition of the Citizens of Lockport, New York, for the Abolition of Slavery and the Slave Trade in the District of Columbia and the Territories, January 18–June 6, 1836, HR 24A–H1.3, TABLED, National Archives Box 3 of Library of Congress Box 47.

[56]Bernard Mandel, *Labor: Free and Slave* (New York: Associated Authors, 1955), 75–76.

[57]"Fathers and Rulers of Our Country Petition Form," in Barnes and Dumond, eds., *Weld-Grimké Letters,* I, 175–176.

[58]Karen Sanchez-Eppler, "Bodily Bonds: The Intersecting Rhetorics of Feminism and Abolition," *Representations* 24 (Fall 1988), 32.

[59]Examples of this form include Petition of the Ladies of Massachusetts for Abolition of Slavery in the District of Columbia, December 18, 1835, to June 6, 1836, HR24A–H1.3; Petition of the Ladies of Dousa, New Hampshire (1836).

[60]American Anti-Slavery Society Circular, 1837, Pennsylvania Abolitionist Society Collection, Philadelphia Female Anti-Slavery Society Papers, 1837 (formerly PAS Box 38).

[61]This observation builds on Jean Fagan Yellin's argument in her study of the "women & sister theme" in the rhetoric of women abolitionists. Yellin states that in emphasizing "the speechless agony of the female slave," white antislavery feminists were "identifying with the female slaves in terms of gender but articulating a feminist consciousness that was race-specific." Yellin, *Women & Sisters: The Antislavery Feminists In American Culture* (New Haven: Yale University Press, 1989), 25.

[62]Stephen Browne, "'Like Gory Spectres': Representing Evil in Theodore Weld's *American Slavery As It Is*," *Quarterly Journal of Speech* 80 (August 1994): 277–292.

[63]The approach I am describing draws from Gregg's orientation toward the ego-function of protest rhetoric, which ponders how rhetorical action may lead individuals to establish new identities for themselves and to aid others in doing the same. I hope to expand his method by directing the critic's attention to discursive formulation of identities by non-dominant groups within movements and to the ways that these formulations are directed at the bourgeois public in order to revise dominant political subjectivities. Gregg, "The Ego-Function of the Rhetoric of Protest."

[64]Nancy Fraser, "Rethinking the Public Sphere: A Contribution to the Critique of Actually Existing Democracy," in *Habermas and the Public Sphere*, ed. Craig Calhoun (Cambridge: Massachusetts Institute of Technology Press, 1992), 123–124, quoted in Robert Asen and Daniel C. Brouwer, *Counterpublics and the State* (Albany: SUNY Press, 2001), 7.

[65]Waugh, *Feminine Fictions*, 10.

[66]This claim builds on Nancy F. Cou's argument that during the nineteenth century, an ideology of woman's passionlessness strengthened women's claims to moral superiority, which enhanced their status and widened their opportunities for participation in evangelical reform. Given the argument I am making here, I would, of course, stress that the ideology of passionlessness endowed *white* women of the emerging middle class with moral superiority. Cott, "Passionless: An Interpretation of Victorian Sexual Ideology, 1790–1850," in *A Heritage of Her Own: Toward a New Social History of American Women*, ed. Nancy F. Cou and Elizabeth H. Pleck (New York: Simon and Schuster, 1979), 162–181.

Chapter VIII

Genre Criticism

Like social movement studies, genre criticism departs from the traditional emphasis on a single speaker or speech. Indeed, to be done properly, genre criticism must examine multiple speeches or other forms of discourse in order to draw conclusions about *categories* of rhetoric. Genre criticism has long been important in literary analysis but has only become a major critical focus in speech communication since the early 1970s.

Perhaps the single most concise, yet comprehensive, explanation of genre criticism is Karlyn Kohrs Campbell and Kathleen Hall Jamieson's introduction to *Form and Genre: Shaping Rhetorical Action,* published in 1978. The authors review how the literature of speech communication has treated the concept of genre since 1925. In addition, Campbell and Jamieson theorize about what constitutes a distinct genre. They conclude that a genre is a "fusion of elements, formed from a constellation of forms."

B. L. Ware and Wil A. Linkugel's 1973 publication, "They Spoke in Defense of Themselves: On the Generic Criticism of Apologia," analyzes the characteristics of self-defense speeches. The authors discover four major "factors" and four major "postures" that occur in apologia. These broad classifications give critics a means for pinpointing the specific persuasive tactics that speakers use to defend themselves against accusations. Ware and Linkugel note that classifying a genre is not criticism in itself, but does allow critics to discover strategies that recur in particular types of rhetoric. In other words, genre classification comes before the actual criticism.

James Darsey illustrates another approach to genre criticism in his 1995 essay "Joe McCarthy's Fantastic Moment." Rather than defining discourse in terms of a pre-existing class or proposing that a group of texts comprises an emerging genre, Darsey explains the power of McCarthy's rhetoric by comparing it to a critical touchstone, the literary genre of the fantastic, which is distinguished by "a celebration of ambiguity" with no established rules. Although McCarthy's rhetoric was, on the surface, a virulent quest to purge Communism from American society, Darsey maintains that it was actually designed to "sustain doubt," rather than seek "final judgment" for the people he accused of disloyalty. In other words, the author says, "The logical end of the fantastic is inaction," which is harmless enough in literature but "paralyzing" in the political realm.

FORM AND GENRE IN RHETORICAL CRITICISM: AN INTRODUCTION

KARLYN KOHRS CAMPBELL AND KATHLEEN HALL JAMIESON

On the night of July 12, 1976, Representative Barbara Jordan of Texas electrified the Democratic convention with a keynote address that began with these words:

> It was one hundred and forty-four years ago that members of the Democratic Party first met in convention to select a presidential candidate. Since that time, Democrats have continued to convene once every four years and draft a party platform and nominate a presidential candidate. And our meeting this week is a continuation of that tradition. But there is something different about tonight; there is something special about tonight. What is different? What is special? I, Barbara Jordan, am a keynote speaker.[1]

At that moment, for hundreds of black and female delegates and for millions of other listeners, she embodied the idea she expressed in the next paragraph: "And I feel that, notwithstanding the past, my presence here is one additional piece of evidence that the American dream need not forever be deferred." She herself *was* the proof of the argument she was making.

Many critics who watched and heard her speak will have recognized a recurrent rhetorical form, a reflexive form, a form called "enactment" in which the speaker incarnates the argument, *is* the proof of the truth of what is said. And if one recognized the form, one understood the force of her speech; one knew why her words were greeted with sustained applause.

Critics who have studied keynote addresses at national nominating conventions also recognized that this was a typical example of that kind of speech.[2] She set the "key note," established a basic theme intended to rejuvenate the faithful and attract all Americans. She contended that the Democratic party was the best available means through which the American dream could be realized. With the exception of the reflexive form used at the beginning and the end, and the self-conscious awareness of the rhetorical options available to a keynoter ("I could easily spend this time praising the accomplishments of this Party and attacking the record of the Republicans. I do not choose to do that. I could list the many problems which cause people to feel cynical, frustrated, and angry. . . . Having described these and other problems, I could sit down without offering any solutions. I do not choose to do that either."), this was a rather ordinary keynote that, like many others, returned to basic principles; in Jordan's case, the emphasis was on constitutional principles, a subtle echo of her opening speech in the House Judiciary Committee debate on articles of impeachment. In fact, the student of keynote addresses will be able to predict, we think accurately, that this speech will not be memorable except as a speech *given by* Barbara Jordan.

Why was Jordan's speech somewhat disappointing to those who were deeply moved by the opening statements? The explanation is most easily made if one compares her keynote address to a rhetorical act that fulfills the promise of the reflexive form more fully.[3]

Like Barbara Jordan, the narrative *persona* of Virginia Woolf's *A Room of One's Own* embodies the position she is arguing. More specifically, the author creates an imaginary woman, Shakespeare's sister Judith, who embodies all the dead women poets whose talents have been destroyed. Like Shakespeare, we are told, she was greatly gifted. To avoid early marriage to a neighboring wool-stapler, she ran away to London to seek her fortune in the theatre. Unlike Shakespeare, she could find no outlet for her talents ("a woman acting is like a dog dancing . . ."). Finally, the actor-manager Nick Green pities her and takes her in; she finds herself with child, kills herself, and is buried at an obscure crossroads. At the end of the book, the reflexive forms of the narrator and of Shakespeare's sister Judith come together.

> Now my belief is that this poet who never wrote a word and was buried at the crossroads still lives. She lives in you and in me, and in many other women who are not here tonight, for they are washing up the dishes and putting the children to bed. But she lives; for great poets do not die; they are continuing presences; they need only the opportunity to walk among us in the flesh. . . . For my belief is that if we live another century or so . . . and have five hundred a year each of us and rooms of our own; if we have the habit of freedom and the courage to write exactly what we think . . . then . . . the dead poet who was Shakespeare's sister will put on the body she has so often laid down.[4]

Barbara Jordan said, "A lot of years (have) passed since 1832, and during that time it would have been most unusual for any national political party to ask a Barbara Jordan to deliver a keynote address. But tonight, here I am." Imagine Congresswoman Jordan saying these words next:

> They did not make keynote addresses, nor indeed addresses of any sort, the Barbara Jordans of those days. They were not welcomed into this, or any other, political party. Surely some of them, some of those blacks, some of those women, were as able as I, and some undoubtedly were far more gifted. But they lived out their lives in obscurity, their talents unused and their abilities unexercised. And they died without knowing the joy of participation in the democratic system. They died, often in poverty and pain, and always without the fulfillment that America promised them.
>
> They were many in number, these women and blacks and minorities. They were scattered across this great nation. Yet on occasion, I somehow think of them as a single person, a single Barbara Jordan, alone, defeated in her fight to enter the arena of political life.
>
> And so tonight I ask your support for our Democratic Party and our democratic cause, not because of the principles I could enunciate, but simply because of Barbara Jordan. Simply because of Barbara Jordan. Not because of me; not for myself do I ask your aid. Such a plea is the beginning of tyranny and must always be rejected. No, it is not for *this* Barbara Jordan that I ask your help, but for *that other* Barbara Jordan that I have pictured struggling through the years, pleading to be allowed to contribute as I now do.
>
> Because you see, I do not think she died, that other Barbara Jordan. I hear her voice calling out tonight; I see her arms stretched out demanding access to the political life that I enjoy. And I lift my voice, and hold out my arms, and call, "Welcome."
>
> It is for that other Barbara Jordan, for all the blacks and women and minorities and poor people of yesterday and tomorrow, that I ask your support.

The form is now completed, fully realized. The imaginary speech (reflecting, we hope, the style of the real Barbara Jordan) enables the critic to compare the actual keynote with the model we have created in order to explain the limitations of the actual address. Critics may also compare Jordan's keynote with other keynote addresses to determine the essential characteristics of keynotes and to explain why, unlike the keynote delivered by John Glenn the same evening, Jordan's address evoked such intense response among the delegates.

This brief critique contains, in microcosm, the concepts and concerns of this volume. It discerns a recurrent form and uses the form to compare one rhetorical act to two other groups of rhetorical acts—keynote addresses (speeches given on similar occasions) and discourses based on the form of "enactment." It implies that the analysis of forms and the comparison of rhetorical acts are essential elements in critical interpretation and evaluation.

In this opening essay we shall 1) trace, briefly, the beginnings of formal and generic concerns in the modern history of rhetorical criticism; 2) discuss some selected criticisms that make generic claims; 3) examine the relationship between the concepts of "form" and "genre"; 4) suggest the role of a generic perspective in the total enterprise of criticism; 5) introduce this volume of essays.

RHETORICAL CRITICISM REVISITED

A survey of modern scholarship treating the nature of rhetorical criticism[5] reveals that an interest in formal analysis and in discovering affinities among discourses and traditions evident in the history of rhetoric is not a contemporary fad. From the inception of rhetorical criticism as a distinct scholarly enterprise, critics have attempted to specify what forms are of particular interest to rhetoricians. They have also recognized the need for a history of rhetoric that would highlight the relationships among rhetorical acts.

In 1925, Herbert Wichelns distinguished the criticism of rhetoric from the criticism of literature. The "felt difficulty" he expressed was an absence of serious criticism of oratory ("a permanent and important human activity") and a failure to take note of distinctively rhetorical dimensions of style, invention, organization, and adaptation to the experiences and expectations of an audience.[6] Although he emphasized that rhetorical criticism was concerned with immediate effects on a specific audience in a given situation, he criticized histories of oratory because they did not consider its evolution.[7] He recognized the relationships among rhetoric, politics, and literature, even literary forms: "Rhetorical criticism lies at the boundary of politics (in the broadest sense) and literature; its atmosphere is that of the public life; its tools are those of literature; its concern is with the ideas of the people as influenced by their leaders."[8] It is noteworthy that although scholars have used Wichelns to legitimate critical emphasis on the immediate effects of single speeches, he also called for an approach to oratory that recognized its evolution through history. Similarly, although he denied that the "permanence" and "beauty" of a discourse were of interest to rhetorical critics, he recognized the importance of literary tools in rhetorical criticism.

In 1948, building on the foundations laid by Wichelns and others, Lester Thonssen and A. Craig Baird produced, in *Speech Criticism,* a detailed statement of the methods, functions, and standards of judgment appropriate to rhetorical criticism. Their work surveyed the history of rhetorical theory to determine critical principles and presented a system for examining speeches and speakers that came to be called neo-Aristotelian[9]—analysis in terms of the canons and modes of proof, an emphasis on effects, and classification of speeches into deliberative, epideictic, and forensic genres. Because of the emphasis on individual speeches and speakers there is little room for a comparative or evolutionary approach. In one sense, however, this work recognizes the influence of prior rhetoric on subsequent rhetoric as it is based on a concept that criticism determines what is best in rhetorical practice and thus is the mechanism through which both theory and practice can be modified and improved.[10] The critical perspective of Thonssen and Baird is best illustrated by the criticisms found in the three volumes of *A History and Criticism of American Public Address*.[11]

Contemporaneously, Barnet Baskerville and Ernest Wrage recognized the need for a systematic approach to criticism[12] and for an historical approach to rhetoric.[13] Their collaboration produced two volumes of speeches with historical and biographical notes surveying American speechmaking from 1788 to the 1960's. The editors described the first volume in these terms: "This volume is not a garland of rhetorical flowers, a mere miscellany of eloquent passages. . . . Nor is its purpose that of catering to an antiquarian sentimental attachment to great speeches of the past. . . . Rather, we have selected and juxtaposed speeches in order to provide the substance and framework of an American forum as a venture in intellectual history through public address."[14] The preface to the second volume is more explicitly generic: "This issue-centered approach recommends itself because it establishes secure linkages between the function of speech in a free society and the historical processes which speech shapes and by which it is shaped."[15] The anthologies were arranged to compare and contrast statements of prevailing viewpoints on major issues and suggested a critical perspective that would chart conflicting attitudes toward central themes in American society. However, the volumes did not provide a developmental analysis to show how issues evolved through time or how earlier articulations influenced subsequent expressions of similar concepts.

In 1952, Leland Griffin wrote "The Rhetoric of Historical Movements." In his opening remarks he explained that the impulse toward the criticism of historical and social movements arose out of methodological constraints: "The recommendation has been made, for example, that we pay somewhat less attention to the single speaker and more to speakers—that we turn our attention from the individual 'great orator' and undertake research into such selected acts and atmospheres of public address as would permit the study of a multiplicity of speakers, speeches, audiences, and occasions."[16] Griffin's response was to propose the study of movements and to suggest methods by which this might be accomplished. Since that time, a plethora of movement studies, too numerous to cite, has examined political campaigns, the New Left, the Radical Right, old and new feminism, black protest, child labor reform, and many others.[17] The interest in movements and campaigns encouraged other critics to suggest ways to refine the study of movement rhetoric.[18] In our view, this activity attests to an intense interest in studying bodies of rhetoric that illustrate the development, fruition, and degeneration of rhetorical forms and strategies.

In 1965, a generic approach to rhetorical criticism received its first explicit sanction with the appearance of Edwin Black's *Rhetorical Criticism: A Study in Method*. Like Griffin and others, Black recognized a serious limitation in the dominant critical paradigm: "The neo-Aristotelians ignore the impact of the discourse on rhetorical conventions, its capacity for disposing an audience to expect certain kinds of justification in later discourses that they encounter, even on different subjects."[19] The traditional mode of criticism did not, and perhaps could not, trace traditions or recognize affinities and recurrent forms, the elements of a developmental rhetorical history. Black proposed an alternative, generic frame of reference.

For him, a generic perspective presumed that 1) "there is a limited number of situations in which a rhetor can find himself"; 2) "there is a limited number of ways in which a rhetor can and will respond rhetorically to any given situational type"; 3) "the recurrence of a given situational type through history will provide the critic with information on the rhetorical responses available in that situation"; and 4) "although we can expect congregations of rhetorical discourses to form at distinct points along the scale, these points will be more or less arbitrary."[20] Although the clusters described by Black were somewhat taxonomic, i.e., classifications based on the relative preeminence of rational or emotive elements in a discourse, the argumentative and exhortative genres he described were not discrete or sharply delineated. Rather, they represented modes of discourse characterized by certain strategies that seemed more likely to occur in certain kinds of situations. The scale of transactions he developed (a scale he argued would reflect situations, strategies, and effects to a relatively equal degree) serves to suggest affinities between discourses of different kinds as well as to suggest generic clusterings. However, the alternative frame of reference was only a beginning. It did not suggest how a generic approach to criticism might be used to write a developmental history of rhetoric nor did it provide a detailed introduction to a generic perspective. Whatever the limits of this beginning, Black's work was noteworthy on several counts: it argued for an organic critical method, one which emphasized form but was not formulary; it located clusters of discourses based on recurrent strategies, situations, and effects; and it revealed the weaknesses of the neo-Aristotelian perspective as a basis for writing a developmental history of rhetoric. For these reasons, among others, Black's book was a precursor of the explosion of unconventional critical essays that appeared in the late 1960's and 1970's.

In 1968, Lloyd Bitzer made a detailed analysis of the situational or scenic component of rhetorical action.[21] He argued that it was the situation which called the discourse into existence and provided a vocabulary through which to describe the variables in "rhetorical situations." The terminology permits critics to compare and contrast rhetorical situations and the discourses they engender. In addition to the provocative notions that both rhetorical acts and rhetorical criticism are grounded in rhetorical situations, the essay suggests the important influence of prior rhetorical action on subsequent discourse. According to Bitzer, comparable situations prompt comparable responses, "hence rhetorical forms are born and a special vocabulary, grammar and style are established. . . . because we experience situations and the rhetorical response to them, a form of discourse is not only established but comes to have a power of its own—the tradition itself tends to function as a constraint upon any new response in the form."[22]

Some of the controversies raised by Bitzer's positions have been examined elsewhere.[23] Other questions, more relevant to form and genre in criticism, remain. What, for example, would constitute a case disproving this theory of the relationship between the situation and the discourse? For instance, if Bitzer can claim that a presidential inaugural or a Fourth of July address, clearly inappropriate to the occasion on which it was given, was not a "fitting" response to the situation, then "appropriate" discourse confirms the theory but "inappropriate" rhetorical acts cannot disconfirm it. If so, how can the concept of the rhetorical situation be used as a basis for recognizing and defining recurrent forms? In addition, one may ask, do comparable situations ever exist? It is possible to accept Bitzer's formulation of the rhetorical situation while arguing that all situations are idiosyncratic and hence do not and cannot produce recurring forms. Finally, could an alternative theoretical model, a theory of commonplaces, for example, account for recurring forms more parsimoniously? While Bitzer's essay has made a significant contribution to a generic perspective, some questions persist.

In 1968, Lawrence Rosenfield published a critical essay based on a generic perspective in which he compared apologic speeches by Harry Truman and Richard Nixon.[24] In 1969, a second comparative criticism revealed the similarities between the rhetorical postures of Patrick Henry and George Wallace.[25] Neither essay seeks to discover a genre; each presumes a recognized genre already exists (the mass media apologia and the anti-aggressor rhetorician, respectively). Rosenfield's "analogs" serve to enumerate the factors of generic similarity and dissimilarity. The possibilities and limitations of comparative criticism that presumes a pre-existing genre are illustrated in essays by Chesebro and Hamsher,[26] Butler,[27] and by the essay on the historical jeremiad found in this volume.

In the late 1960's these critical interests and concerns culminated in an explosion of articles describing "genres," "rhetorics," or the salient formal attributes of certain groups of rhetorical acts. Retrospectively, it appears that, in most cases, the use of "genre" or "rhetoric of" was a matter of convenience rather than an assertion of the existence of a discrete type of symbolic act. For example, the phrase "the rhetoric of . . ." was used to describe bodies of discourse defined by purpose, as "the rhetoric of desecration"[28] or "the rhetoric of confrontation"[29] meaning, respectively, rhetorical acts intended to desecrate or confront. The phrase was also used to identify the source of the discourse, as for instance, "the rhetoric of the New Left"[30] or "the rhetoric of black power"[31] meaning, respectively, rhetorical acts emanating from groups identified as part of the New Left or from groups identifying themselves with the demands represented by the phrase "black power." While these phrases do touch on the strategic and substantive elements that ordinarily serve to define genres, they seem to have been used somewhat casually, in many cases, as the most succinct way in which to entitle the body of rhetorical acts the author wished to discuss without necessarily entailing a fully developed claim to generic particularity.

GENERIC CRITICISMS

However, in this same period, a small number of essays began to appear which made explicit claims that genres existed, genres as varied as the diatribe, the papal encyclical, doctrinal rhetoric, and contemporary women's rights rhetoric. Once these appeared, theoretical questions were inevitable: Just what is a genre? How does one justify a generic claim? Why do generic criticism? How does generic criticism differ from other kinds of rhetorical criticism? In Sections III and IV, we shall address these questions directly; here, we shall examine the answers given by critics in selected generic criticisms.

In 1950, Harold Zyskind, a scholar in the field of English, published a generic analysis of Lincoln's Gettysburg Address.[32] He presented his analysis as an example of generic criticism that would enable others to see its value as a method for treating texts in undergraduate courses. His approach to genres was deductive: the measurement of the text against a pre-existing model. After justifying his view of the Address as rhetoric (rather than as history or political philosophy), Zyskind attempted to determine whether the address was best viewed as epideictic or deliberative rhetoric. He justified this classical, even traditional, approach to genre on the grounds that it requires the student to scrutinize the text in a systematic manner. The value of generic classification should be tested by asking, "Are the meaning and purpose of the Address—in its uniqueness—in any way illuminated by an analysis of it as belonging to that genre?"[33] The bulk of his critique develops a case for concluding that the epideictic elements in the Address are subordinate to its deliberative purpose. This is done through an analysis of structure, imagery, diction, the role of the listener, and the relationship between the audience and the "we" of the Address. The criticism produces not only a generic placement but a statement of the unique qualities of this particular act:

> Thus the deliberative aim of the Address is not to persuade the listeners of the truth of the idea that the Union must be reborn. In a logical sense the truth of the general idea that future action is needed is largely taken for granted. The aim rather is to take this accepted general idea and sink it deeply into the feelings of the audience, fix it as an emotional experience so powerful that each listener will, at any crucial time, do what he can specifically for the future of the nation to which he is here dedicated.[34]

If Zyskind's essay is taken as the model he intends it to be, generic criticism is an orderly means of close textual analysis. It unifies the questions the critic asks about various formal and substantive elements. Generic analysis is justified if and only if the meaning and the purpose of the work are illuminated by struggling with the evidence to determine the work's best classification. Finally, Zyskind reminds us that each of the classical genres was an amalgam of elements drawn from the situation, the issue, the lines of argument, the audience, and the appropriate diction. As he notes in this case, an address may have some elements of one genre (epideictic) and still be an exemplar of another (deliberative).

Like Zyskind, Windt's method is deductive, at least in part.[35] He develops a model of the diatribe from the practices of the ancient Cynics, a model which is then applied to the practices of contemporary Yippies to establish a recurrent mode of symbolic action. Like Zyskind, Windt develops a genre which synthesizes situational, substantive, and stylistic elements, and he justifies his classification in terms of the illumination it provides of the behaviors of apparently self-defeating persuaders of both ancient and contemporary times.

Unlike Zyskind and Windt, Hart proceeds inductively to survey a variety of discourses to see if there are clusters of similar symbolic acts.[36] Out of these tests, he cautiously posits a genre of doctrinal rhetoric. Like Zyskind, this cluster of acts reflects not only substantive and stylistic features but the relationship between the speaker and the audience. Since this is the most systematically developed inductive genre, the points of similarity to Zyskind are of particular interest.

Jamieson also proceeds inductively but within a more limited body of discourses, papal encyclicals.[37] However, she does not presume a genre; she examines these discourses to determine if one exists. Like Zyskind, her motive is illumination—she wishes to understand the forces which constrain *Humanae Vitae* so that it cannot adapt to its times and its audience. Her work adds an additional insight for the generic critic: the power of conventions, traditions, prior rhetoric, to mold and constrain subsequent rhetorical action. She reminds us most strongly that rhetorical acts are born into a symbolic/rhetorical context as well as into an historical/political milieu. Once again, the genre which emerges is a complex of elements—a constellation of substantive, stylistic and situational characteristics.

Like Hart, Campbell's approach to contemporary women's rights rhetoric is inductive.[38] No prior model is assumed; a genre must emerge from or be discerned in the discourses themselves. Yet the concept of genre remains constant—it is formed out of substantive and stylistic elements and out of the unique situation of a female audience in 20th century America. And, like all the others, the justification for a generic claim is the understanding it produces rather than the ordered universe it creates.

These are only a few of the available generic criticisms. Since these first essays appeared, many have followed. But as a sample, they will do. Despite their variety, there are certain noteworthy constants: 1) Classification is justified only by the critical illumination it produces[,] not by the neatness of a classificatory schema; 2) Generic criticism is taken as a means toward systematic, close textual analysis; 3) A genre is a complex, an amalgam, a constellation of substantive, situational, and stylistic elements; 4) Generic analysis reveals both the conventions and affinities that a work shares with others; it uncovers the unique elements in the rhetorical act, the particular means by which a genre is individuated in a given case.

Ideally, theory develops out of and is tested by criticism. Whether or not that is true of generic concepts, these and other criticisms have raised the questions which have become so exigent in contemporary rhetorical criticism.

FORM AND GENRE

Northrop Frye, the most eminent critic to comment on generic criticism, wrote in his *Anatomy* that "The study of genres is based on analogies in form."[39] He called these forms "typical recurring images," "associative clusters," and "complex variables"; he compared them to the *topoi* or rhetorical commonplaces; and he described them as "communicable units," i.e., the forms through which experience and feeling can be made intelligible to others. In other words, formal similarities establish genres, and the forms relevant to genres are complex forms present in all discourse. If the forms from which genres are constituted have the characteristics indicated by Frye, they will be the kinds of forms that rhetoricians ordinarily call "strategies"—substantive and stylistic forms chosen to respond to situational requirements. For example, refutation may be described as a strategy in which one states an opposing position and responds to it by offering an alternative conclusion or by demonstrating the inadequacy of evidence or premises. As a strategy, refutation implies a situation in which there are competing positions and persuaders that must be taken into account. The power of such rhetorical forms is evident in this paragraph from John F. Kennedy's speech, *"Ich bin ein Berliner"*:

> There are many people in the world who really don't understand, or say they don't, what is the great issue between the free world and the Communist world. Let them come to Berlin. And there are some who say that communism is the wave of the future. Let them come to Berlin. And there are some who say in Europe and elsewhere we can work with the Communists. Let them come to Berlin. And there are even a few who say that it is true that communism is an evil system, but it permits us to make economic progress. *Lass' sie nach Berlin kommen.* Let them come to Berlin.[40]

The most evident form is *repetition,* a strategy implying a situation in which a key idea must be established and emphasized. In this case, the refrain not only repeats the theme, it also functions as *refutation.* The repeated sentence is a condensed, even *enthymematic,* answer to the four opposing positions. Sheer repetition produces yet another form. When the passage is read aloud, it is nearly impossible to repeat the refrain, "let them come to Berlin," with identical emphasis. Rather, each repetition tends to become more emphatic and intense, creating a *crescendo*. The situation is perceived and described by the speaker as a conflict, and the refrain becomes a climactic sequence dramatizing the conflict. There is still another form of critical interest. John Kennedy delivered this speech in the city of Berlin. The refrain is reflexive, a dramatic *enactment* which says, in effect, "do as I did—come to Berlin." This form is of particular importance because it is reinforced by the title and by the rest of the speech in which Kennedy says that not only is he, symbolically, a citizen of Berlin, but all of "us" (as opposed to "them") should become symbolic citizens of this beleagu[e]red city which stands for the struggle between the "free" and the "Communist" worlds.

As this analysis illustrates, rhetorical forms do not occur in isolation. In addition, it should be apparent that these forms are phenomena—syntheses of material that exists objectively in the rhetorical act and of perceptions in the mind of a critic, a member of the audience, or a future rhetor. The phenomenal character of forms is reflected in Kenneth Burke's reference to the "psychology of forms" and in his remark that "form is the creation of an appetite in the mind of the auditor, and the adequate satisfying of that appetite."[41] That forms are phenomena has persuasive and critical significance because, as a result, forms can induce participation by others. This is never more evident than in the quintessentially rhetorical form, the enthymeme, whose force is explained by the fact that auditors participate in the construction of the arguments by which they are persuaded.[42]

It should now be apparent that the rhetorical forms that establish genres are stylistic and substantive responses to perceived situational demands. In addition, forms are central to all types of criticism because they define the unique qualities of any rhetorical act, and because they are the means through which we come to understand how an act works to achieve its ends.[43]

From earliest antiquity, rhetoricians have been interested in forms. Analyses of recurrent lines of argument, such as those done by Measell and Carpenter in this volume, resemble the ancient study of the *topoi* or commonplaces.[44] The concept of *stasis* (or *status*) expressed a judgment that there were only a limited number of issues (being, quantity, quality, procedure) over which clash could occur.[45] Halloran's analysis of the issues in the public proceeding in this volume falls in this tradition. To Aristotle, the most important rhetorical form was the enthymeme, the form of deductive argument found in rhetoric. In this volume, Carpenter's interest in the interpretations of readers who filled in premises or drew inferences from relatively factual material reflects this tradition. As noted earlier, the canons and modes of proof can be used as a basis for formal analysis. Finally, from classical to contemporary times, the important role of literary forms has been acknowledged. As noted, Herbert Wichelns recognized the role of literary tools in rhetorical criticism; Hoyt Hudson refers to poetic expression as *"an indispensable means"* to instrumental ends;[46] and Northrop Frye assumes that "most of the features characteristic of literary form, such as rhyme, alliteration, metre, antithetical balance, the use of exempla, are also rhetorical schemata."[47]

If the recurrence of similar forms establishes a genre, then genres are groups of discourses which share substantive, stylistic, and situational characteristics. Or, put differently, in the discourses that form a genre, similar substantive and stylistic strategies are used to encompass situations perceived as similar by the responding rhetors. A genre is a group of acts unified by a constellation of forms that recurs in each of its members. These forms, *in isolation*, appear in other discourses. What is distinctive about the acts in a genre is the recurrence of the forms *together* in constellation.

The eulogy is illustrative. The eulogy responds to a situation in which a community is ruptured by death. In this situation, persons must alter their relationship with the deceased and also confront their own mortality. The very act of eulogizing acknowledges the death. In so doing, it necessitates a juxtaposition of past and present tense which recasts the relationship to the deceased to one of memory. The assurance that the deceased, hence the audience, survives, at least in memory, eases confrontation with mortality. Thus the assertion of persistent life is intrinsic to the eulogy. That conviction is expressed in claims that the deceased survives in memory—in deeds, family or history. Metaphors of rebirth articulate this eulogistic claim.

The act of eulogizing is, in another important respect, performative. By uniting the bereaved in a rhetorical act, the eulogy affirms that the community will survive the death. Typically, eulogies reknit the sundered community through rhetorical devices which appeal to the audience to carry on the works, to embody the virtues, or to live as the deceased would have wished. These are the situational requirements, strategic responses, and stylistic choices that, taken together, form the eulogy. These characteristics do not co-exist by chance. They exist in a reciprocal, dynamic relationship.

External factors, including human needs and exposure to antecedent rhetorical forms, create expectations which constrain rhetorical responses. But the internal dynamic of fused elements also creates expectations which testify to its constraining force. Generic exemplars have an internal consistency. For example, the papal encyclical presupposes truths of natural law known by God's vicar on earth who interprets and explicates the law. This premise dictates a deductively structured document which employs a formal and authoritative tone that is consistent with dogmatic statement. It also entails the use of absolutistic, categorical vocabulary. Encyclicals assume print form because the sort of doctrinal matters addressed require a careful, prepared, precise form of communicating God's will. (Clarification of truth and of doctrine are serious and exacting matters. An oral form is transitory in a way a print form is not.) Each of these elements implies the others. The rhetoric of dogma, for example, cannot be structured inductively without undermining the dogmatic tone and the sense of authority pivotal to the document. One might even argue that the concept of papal authority on certain doctrinal matters entails the form of address which is the encyclical.

In other words, a genre does not consist merely of a series of acts in which certain rhetorical forms recur; for example, it is conceivable that parallelism and antithesis might recur jointly without establishing a generic similarity. Instead, a genre is composed of a constellation of recognizable forms bound together by an internal dynamic.

When a generic claim is made, the critical situation alters significantly because the critic is now arguing that a group of discourses has a synthetic core in which certain significant rhetorical elements, e.g., a system of belief, lines of argument, stylistic choices, and the perception of the situation, are fused into an indivisible whole. The significance of this fusion of forms for the critic is that it provides an angle of vision, a window, that reveals the tension among these elements, the dynamic within the rhetorical acts of human beings, in different times and places, responding in similar ways as they attempt to encompass certain rhetorical problems—the death of a member of the community, an accusation to which no forensic defense is adequate, and the like.

Because a genre is a constellation of elements, the appearance of the same forms in different genres poses no critical problem; a genre is given its character by a fusion of forms not by its individual elements. Thus the argument that Aristotle's genres are not useful because epideictic elements are found in deliberative and forensic addresses, deliberative elements in epideictic and forensic works, etc., is irrelevant; Aristotle's schema is weak generically only if the constellation of elements forming epideictic works does not permit the critic to distinguish the epideictic clustering from the constellations which form the other Aristotelian genres.

The concept of an internal dynamic fusing substantive, stylistic, and situational characteristics permits the critic to determine the generic significance of recurring elements. For example, Rosenfield identifies the clustering of facts in one section of the mass media apologia as a generic characteristic.[48] To test whether the characteristic has generic significance, one must ask: Why would such an element occur in the apology? What is its necessary relationship to other elements in the apology? What substantive, stylistic or situational constraints might require the inclusion of this element and its particular positioning in the structure?

Generic claims are difficult to sustain because constellations of elements rarely fuse into unique and indivisible wholes of the sort described. In addition, generic claims are difficult because of the nature of the processes by which genres may be established.

Some genres, probably most, are established deductively from a model or touchstone. For instance, Socrates' *Apology* is taken as a paradigm and acts which resemble it in essential ways are said to form a genre; similar procedures are followed with the rhetoric of Jeremiah or the rhetoric of the Old Testament prophets, and so on. There are at least two major pitfalls in this method: 1) the critic may fail to delineate the essential characteristics of the model so that the basis for comparison is faulty, or 2) a generic "fit" is asserted although certain essential characteristics are absent or significant dissimilarities exist. The first problem can be eliminated if the critic analyzes the original and refuses to accept "received wisdom" about classic works. The second can be eliminated only if the critic makes the goal in analogic or comparative criticism that of delineating similarities *and differences* and proffers a generic claim only when the evidence *requires* such a claim.

Some genres are established inductively. One can look at a vast number of discourses delivered in response to the death of a member of the community and discover that, at least in Western cultures, they seem to evince essential similarities.[49] One can examine the papal encyclicals and establish a generic resemblance. One can examine all available samples of contemporary rhetoric demanding women's rights in the U.S. and make a case that they form a coherent whole which can be distinguished from the acts of other protest groups. Each of these is an enormous project and each claim is difficult to justify. In most cases, the results of inductive efforts will be disappointing, and a generic claim will not be warranted by the evidence. The problems with this approach are those inherent in any procedure that draws inductive generalizations. Until now, conscientious rhetorical critics have tested their claims about inductively derived genres by selecting specimens from dissimilar eras and/or rhetors to minimize the possibility that the characteristics of an age or a class of persons would be mistaken for generic qualities. Thus a student who generalized from a sample of 19th century eulogies to the conclusion that eulogies are stylistically florid would be told that a characteristic of 19th century rhetoric had been mistaken for a generic characteristic and would be urged to sample eulogies from different periods. This approach was based on the scientific notion that random sampling would minimize critical error. A deeper understanding of the nature of genres provides other rhetorical-critical tests: Why should a eulogy be characterized by a florid style? What is the necessary relationship between such a style and the substantive and situational elements which comprise the eulogy?

The confusion of deductive and inductive approaches to genres can also create difficulties. In a number of cases, critics have assumed, *a priori,* that a genre already exists and is known and defined—e.g., the sermon,[50] the presidential inaugural,[51] the apology,[52] among others—and an inductive procedure, content analysis in some cases, is applied to parse its elements. Such studies are suspect because the *a priori* definition of a genre and identification of its members generates a circular argument: an essential and preliminary procedure defining the generic characteristics has been omitted. Generic critics need to recognize explicitly the assumptions they are making and the procedures required to establish their claims.

An understanding of the genre as a fusion of elements, formed from a constellation of forms, permits one to distinguish between classification and generic analysis. There are some troublesome pieces of rhetoric, such as presidential inaugurals, in which a series of rhetorical elements recur. For example, the inaugurals establish the philosophy and tone of new administrations. Because they follow the divisive rhetoric of a campaign, they employ unifying appeals and articulate superordinate goals. In an attempt to overcome the fear that the incoming president is an incipient despot, each places the country in the hands of a higher power and acknowledges humility in the face of future tasks. The tone is dignified. Yet Lincoln's second inaugural and Washington's first are basically dissimilar. There are several possible explanations: 1) What have been isolated as inaugural elements are, in fact, elements inherent in a broader genre, rehearsal rhetoric; a hierarchical error, as Simons would call it, has been made; 2) A genre, the inaugural, does exist, but critics have failed to isolate the generic elements and the dynamic which binds them. Hence we cannot see the fundamental similarity between Lincoln's and Washington's addresses; 3) The evidence at hand would suggest that although it is possible that a genre properly termed "inaugural" does exist, it is not necessarily evoked in the situation created by the swearing-in of a President, as the inability to locate dynamic interrelationships among the elements of the inaugural and the inability to distinguish it from other rehearsal rhetoric testify.

The concept of a genre as a constellation of fused elements refines the notion that, in a genre, the significant rhetorical similarities outweigh the significant rhetorical differences. In its earlier form, generic "significance" resided in the mind of the critic, and any generic claim seemed vulnerable to a charge of subjectivism. Testing a generic claim on the grounds that "significant similarities will permit prediction of the form of an address not yet conceived or delivered" was problematic. The test does not assure that the critic is dealing with genre. For example, it is possible to predict certain characteristics of an inaugural address although there is general scholarly agreement that the claim that inaugurals form a genre has yet to be established. Unless the elements cohere in a necessary and significant relationship, in a dynamic fusion, the ability to predict that certain characteristics will appear in an act on a certain occasion does not assure that a genre has been located. If an element is generically significant, it is so fused to the other elements that its absence would alter the character of the address.

Critics have assumed that genres are bodies of discourses that, as distinctive symbolic acts, recur in different times and places. Conversely, Black has argued that a genre may have a single identifiable member and illustrated his view with Chapman's Coatesville Address, a piece of rhetoric that functions as a morality play.[53] The view of genre described here, as a dynamic constellation of forms, focuses not only on what has recurred but on what may recur. In this sense, a constellation of elements bound together dynamically need only exist in a single instance to establish a genre or a generic potential. Clearly, the dynamic of the constellation and the fusion of its forms are more easily recognized when their recurrence is observed, but it is now possible both to isolate the constellation and its dynamic without comparing multiple specimens of the genre.

Similarly, this definition helps to explain the perseveration of rhetorical forms which the critic judges to be inappropriate to the demands of the situation. Jamieson has argued that the papal encyclical, at least as a form illustrated by *Humanae Vitae*, is a perseverative rhetorical form. An internal dynamic combines the elements in an encyclical, and the internal dynamic accounts, at least in part, for its perseveration as a genre. One cannot abandon elements of a genre which are dynamically fused without undermining the genre itself. For example, classical Latin with its rigorous controlling verbs complements the deductive structure of the papal encyclical, and that structure itself is dictated by and consonant with the concept of papal authority on matters of dogma.

The definition emphasizes the interrelationships among generic elements. Genres often exist in dynamic responsiveness to situational demands—e.g., an encyclical appears in order to affirm papal authority. Those instances in which a dynamic is sustaining a genre in the absence of, or counter to, situational demands invite the label "degenerative." The critic labelling a form "degenerative" risks the charge that ideological bias has colored the critical act. In the context developed here, the "degenerative" nature of the diagnosed genre can be subjected to a test of evidence. Does an internal dynamic exist? Is it consonant with perceived demands of the situation? If not, the genre is rhetorically degenerate because the audience and other germane situational variables are being ignored—and also degenerative in a literal sense; that is, a genre which fails to achieve its purpose—e.g., reknit a community ruptured by death or affirm papal authority—is more likely to "degenerate" and ultimately to disappear than is a genre consonant with perceived situational demands.

The concept of genre may be illustrated by analogy. Biologists speak of the genetic code inherent in the germ plasm of each species. Although there will be variations, that code is the internal dynamic which determines the biological form of the individual member of the species. The internal dynamic of a genre is similar. It is the determinant of the generic form of the rhetorical utterance[,] although like individual members of species, individual rhetorical acts—although part of a common genre—will show some individual variation. What is significant about the concept of genre is the fusion of elements and the critical insight the fusion provides.

The term "constellation" suggests another metaphorical insight. The stars forming a constellation are individuals but they are influenced by each other and by external elements; consequently they move together and remain in a similar relation to each other despite their varying positions over time. Like genres, constellations are perceived patterns with significance and usefulness—they enable us to see the movements of a group of individual stars and they enable us to understand the interrelated forces in celestial space.

Both metaphors and the very concept of the internal dynamic suggest the difference between classification or creating a taxonomy on the one hand, and critical analysis on the other. A "genre" is a classification based on the fusion and interrelation of elements in such a way that a unique kind of rhetorical act is created. Approaching such acts generically gives the critic an unusual opportunity to penetrate their internal workings and to appreciate the interacting forces that create them.

GENRE AND CRITICISM

"Genre" is not the key term in a philosophy of rhetoric; it is an important concept in one kind of criticism. The theory underlying the concept of genre is critical theory, theory about the enterprise of criticism. It is no accident that Frye is a major source for material on genre as his *Anatomy* is a study of criticism as an autonomous enterprise. Frye argues strongly for a pluralistic approach to criticism, and he justifies his view by showing that all discourse is polysemous, i.e., that it has many levels of meaning or means in different ways. These different levels or kinds of meaning require different critical perspectives. Because all works are not only unique but also resemble other works, generic criticism is essential. Frye notes that part of the meaning of a work is derived from the tradition of which it is a part, from the conventions it observes. The conventions found in a discourse indicate the tradition to which it belongs and the works to which it has close affinities. Consequently, he says that

> When he [Milton] uses the convention of invocation, thus bringing the poem [*Paradise Lost*] into the genre of the spoken word, the significance of the convention is to indicate what tradition his work primarily belongs to and what its closest affinities are with. The purpose of criticism by genres is not so much to classify as to clarify such traditions and affinities, thereby bringing out a large number of literary relationships that would not be noticed as long as there were no context established for them.[54]

What Frye is describing is a *generic perspective* toward criticism[,] not a crusading search to find genres. The generic perspective recognizes that while there may be few clearly distinguishable genres, all rhetoric is influenced by prior rhetoric, all rhetorical acts resemble other rhetorical acts. Such a critical perspective emphasizes the symbolic and rhetorical contexts in which rhetorical acts are created.

Some elements of a generic perspective are intrinsic in all criticism because classification and comparison are integral parts of the critical process. As a critic, one is perpetually classifying and labelling—e.g., this is an introduction, this is an example, this is high style, this is satirical, this is a eulogy. Inherent in each classification are two comparative standards—the comparison of like to like, the comparison of like to unlike. The first comparison arises out of definition. To label some part of a discourse as an introduction is to have a definition that contains essential attributes and, implicitly, suggests an ideal or model. Such classifications are the basis of evaluative comparisons—this is better, this is more fully realized, and the like. The second, comparison or contrast, differentiates introductions and conclusions, one form of support from another, distinguishes styles, tones, and ultimately, between classifications by type or genre. These contrasts compel re-definitions and form the basis for strategic evaluations—e.g., this style was chosen, but an alternative style would have been preferable because of its ability to accomplish "x" objective. No one who recognizes the role of comparison and contrast in interpreting and evaluating rhetorical discourse is likely to ignore the traditions which have generated or shaped discourse and the relationships among discourses which extend the critic's capacity to make comparative judgments.

Because rhetoric is of the public life, because rhetorical acts are concerned with ideas and processes rooted in the here and now of social and political life, rhetoric develops in time and through time. Ironically, the traditional emphasis on individual speeches and speakers as rooted historically in a particular time and place is, in an important sense, anti-historical, because it fails to recognize the impact of rhetorical acts on other rhetorical acts, and it fails to recognize the powerful human forces which fuse recurrent forms into genres which, in an important sense, transcend a specific time and place. The critic who classifies a rhetorical artifact as generically akin to a class of similar artifacts has identified an undercurrent of history rather than comprehended an act isolated in time. Recurrence of a combination of forms into a generically identifiable form over time suggests that certain constants in human action are manifest rhetorically. One may argue that recurrence arises out of comparable rhetorical situations, out of the influence of conventions on the responses of rhetors, out of universal and cultural archetypes ingrained in human consciousness, out of fundamental human needs, or out of a finite number of rhetorical options or commonplaces. Whatever the explanation, the existence of the recurrent provides insight into the human condition.

A generic approach to rhetorical criticism would culminate in a developmental history of rhetoric that would permit the critic to generalize beyond the individual event which is constrained by time and place to affinities and traditions across time. It would move from the study of rhetors and acts in isolation to the study of recurrent rhetorical action. It would produce a critical history exploring the ways in which rhetorical acts influence each other. Such a "genealogy" would trace the imprint of form on form, style on style, genre on genre. It would, for example, trace imperial forms of address from the Roman emperor's decree to the papal encyclical in order to discern imperial tendencies in papal address, trace the form of the State of the Union address from the form of the King's speech to Parliament in order to account for monarchical qualities in early State of the Union speeches. It would trace the Congressional speeches in reply to State of the Union addresses back to the echoing speeches of Parliament in order to account for the curiously subservient tone of early Congressional responses. It would root the Presidential Inaugural in the theocratic addresses of Puritan leaders in order to explain the supplicative elements in early inaugurals.

It is now manifest that a concern with form and genre does not prescribe a critical methodology. Mohrmann and Leff have argued for a synthesis of neo-Aristotelian and generic perspectives.[55] Bitzer suggests a situational basis for generic study; Hart proceeds inductively using content analysis and other quantitative and non-quantitative methods; Campbell relies on dramatistic concepts.[56] In short, generic analysis is an available critical option regardless of the critical perspective that one cherishes.

However, a generic perspective does make some demands on the critic. It is a critical approach that requires careful textual analysis, for instance. It also heightens an awareness of the interrelationship between substantive and stylistic elements in discourse.

A generic perspective is intensely historical, but in a sense somewhat different from most prior efforts. It does not seek detailed recreation of the original encounter between author and audience; rather it seeks to recreate the symbolic context in which the act emerged so that criticism can teach us about the nature of human communicative response and about the ways in which rhetoric is shaped by prior rhetoric, by verbal conventions in a culture, and by past formulations of ideas and issues.

It can be argued that generic placement and comparison to an ideal type—touchstone criticism—are both familiar forms of rhetorical criticism. We have noted their classical origins and we note a contemporary, Walter Fisher, who writes that rhetorical criticism "says how and in what ways a rhetorical transaction fits, falls short of, or transcends other examples of its kind."[57] This essay amends that statement to emphasize the role of formal analysis in the process of generic placement. One's capacity to clarify and reveal a rhetorical act is based on one's ability to see it clearly, to understand its nature, to select the most apt characterization of it. It matters greatly, as Zyskind indicates, whether one calls Lincoln's Gettysburg Address an epideictic eulogy or labels it a deliberative act designed to urge the audience toward the actions it should follow if the Union is to be preserved. Similarly, Barnet Baskerville's critique of Nixon's "Checkers Speech" treats the address as forensic and demonstrates persuasively that it did not serve to answer the charges that had been made.[58] But if the speech is more properly classified as an apologia, such a "failure" is inevitable—the apologia is a speech in which one responds to forensic charges in a non-forensic way—by transcending them to present one's life and character to one's judges.

NOTES

[1] All cited material from the speech is transcribed from a tape of the address as delivered. Excerpts from the prepared text may be found in *The New York Times*, 15 July 1976, p. 26.

[2] An historical perspective on keynote addresses is provided by Edwin A. Miles, "The Keynote Speech at National Nominating Conventions," *Quarterly Journal of Speech*, 46 (February 1960), 26–31.

[3] Another example of reflexive form is found on pp. 18–19 below.

[4] Virginia Woolf, *A Room of One's Own* (Harbinger: Harcourt, Brace and World, 1929; rpt. 1957), 117–118. The earlier description of Judith is found on pp. 48–50.

[5] A detailed history of modern rhetorical criticism is found in Charles J. Stewart, "Historical Survey: Rhetorical Criticism in Twentieth Century America," in *Explorations in Rhetorical Criticism*, ed. Charles J. Stewart, Donovan J. Ochs, and Gerald Mohrmann (University Park: Pennsylvania State University Press, 1973), 1–31.

[6] Herbert A. Wichelns, "The Literary Criticism of Oratory," in *Speech Criticism: Methods and Materials*, ed. William A. Linsley (Dubuque, Ia.: Wm. C. Brown, 1968), 11–12. For another perceptive, early statement on the nature of rhetorical criticism, see Loren D. Reid, "The Perils of Rhetorical Criticism," *Quarterly Journal of Speech*, 30 (December 1944), 416–422.

[7] Wichelns, p. 28.

[8] Wichelns, p. 37.

[9]Edwin Black, *Rhetorical Criticism: A Study in Method* (New York: Macmillan, 1965), 27–35.

[10]Lester Thonssen and A. Craig Baird, *Speech Criticism: The Development of Standards of Rhetorical Appraisal* (New York: Ronald Press, 1948), 16. See also Marie Hochmuth Nichols[,] *Rhetoric and Criticism,* (Baton Rouge: Louisiana State University Press, 1963) for a later rationale for traditional rhetorical criticism with a strong emphasis on history. This work also serves as a bridge between traditional and modern perspectives as it includes critical perspectives drawn from Kenneth Burke and I. A. Richards.

[11]William Norwood Brigance, ed., vols. I & II (New York: McGraw-Hill, 1943); and Marie Kathryn Hochmuth, ed., vol. III, *A History and Criticism of American Public Address* (New York: Longmans, Green, 1955).

[12]Barnet Baskerville, "A Study of American Criticism of Public Address, 1850–1900" (Ph.D. dissertation, Northwestern University, 1948).

[13]Ernest Wrage, "Public Address: A Study in Social and Intellectual History," *Quarterly Journal of Speech,* 33 (December 1947), 451–457. See also Albert J. Croft, "The Functions of Rhetorical Criticism," *Quarterly Journal of Speech,* 42 (October 1956), 283–291.

[14]Ernest J. Wrage and Barnet Baskerville, eds. *American Forum: Speeches on Historic Issues, 1788–1900* (New York: Harper, 1960), viii.

[15]Ernest J. Wrage and Barnet Baskerville, eds. *Contemporary American Forum: Speeches on Twentieth Century Issues* (New York: Harper, 1962), v.

[16]Leland Griffin, "The Rhetoric of Historical Movements," *Quarterly Journal of Speech,* 38 (April 1952), 184. For an earlier illustration of movement analysis see J. Franklin Jameson's excellent work, *The American Revolution Considered as a Social Movement* (Princeton University Press, 1926).

[17]Griffin applied his critical approach in "The Rhetorical Structure of the 'New Left' Movement: Part I," *Quarterly Journal Of Speech,* 50 (April 1964), 113–135. See also "The Rhetorical Structure of the Antimasonic Movement" in *The Rhetorical Idiom,* ed. Donald Bryant (Ithaca, NY: Cornell University Press, 1958), 145–149.

[18]See Robert S. Cathcart, "New Approaches to the Study of Movements: Defining Movements Rhetorically," *Western Speech,* 36 (Spring 1972), 82–88; Herbert Simons, "Requirements, Problems, and Strategies: A Theory of Persuasion for Social Movements," *Quarterly Journal of Speech,* 56 (February 1970), 1–11; Leland Griffin, "A Dramatistic Theory of the Rhetoric of Movements," in *Critical Responses to Kenneth Burke*[,] ed. William H. Rueckert (Mpls.: University of Minnesota Press, 1969) 456–478, among others.

[19]Black, p. 35.

[20]Black, pp. 133–134.

[21]An earlier analysis of the situational element in symbolic action is found in Kenneth Burke, *A Grammar of Motives* and *A Rhetoric of Motives* (New York: World, 1945, 1950; rpt. 1962), 727–736.

[22]Lloyd Bitzer, "The Rhetorical Situation," *Philosophy & Rhetoric,* 1 (January 1968), 13.

[23]See Richard E. Vatz, "The Myth of the Rhetorical Situation," *Philosophy & Rhetoric,* 6 (Summer 1973), 154–161, and Scott Consigny, "Rhetoric and Its Situations," *Philosophy & Rhetoric,* 7 (Summer 1974), 175–184.

[24]Lawrence W. Rosenfield, "A Case Study in Speech Criticism: The Nixon-Truman Analog," *Speech Monographs,* 35 (November 1968), 435–450. An earlier essay, "The Anatomy of Critical Discourse," *Speech Monographs,* 25 (March 1968), 50–69, is an insightful statement on the nature of rhetorical criticism.

[25]Lawrence W. Rosenfield, "George Wallace Plays Rosemary's Baby," *Quarterly Journal of Speech,* 55 (February 1969), 36–44.

[26]James W. Chesebro and Caroline D. Hamsher, "The Concession Speech: The MacArthur-Agnew Analog," *Speaker and Gavel,* 11 (January 1974), 39–51.

[27]Sherry Devereaux Butler, "The Apologia, 1971 Genre," *Southern Speech Communication Journal*, 37 (Spring 1972), 281–289.

[28]Richard J. Goodman and William I. Gordon, "The Rhetoric of Desecration," *Quarterly Journal of Speech*, 57 (February 1971), 23–31.

[29]Robert L. Scott and Donald K. Smith, "The Rhetoric of Confrontation," *Quarterly Journal of Speech*, 55 (February 1969), 1–8.

[30]Griffin, "The Rhetorical Structure of the 'New Left' Movement"; James W. Chesebro, "Rhetorical Strategies of Radicals," *Today's Speech*, 21 (Winter 1972), 37–48.

[31]Parke Burgess, "The Rhetoric of Black Power: A Moral Demand," *Quarterly Journal of Speech*, 54 (April 1968), 122–133.

[32]Harold Zyskind, "A Rhetorical Analysis of the Gettysburg Address," *Journal of General Education*, 4 (April 1950), 202–212.

[33]Zyskind, p. 202.

[34]Zyskind, p. 212.

[35]Theodore Otto Windt, Jr., "The Diatribe: Last Resort for Protest," *Quarterly Journal of Speech*, 58 (February 1972), 1–14.

[36]Roderick P. Hart, "The Rhetoric of the True Believer," *Speech Monographs*, 38 (November 1971), 249.

[37]Kathleen M. Hall Jamieson, "Generic Constraints and the Rhetorical Situation," *Philosophy & Rhetoric*, 6 (Summer 1973), 162–170. See also "Interpretation of Natural Law in the Conflict over *Humanae Vitae*," *Quarterly Journal of Speech*, 60 (April 1974), 201–211.

[38]Karlyn Kohrs Campbell, "The Rhetoric of Women's Liberation[: An Oxymoron]," *Quarterly Journal of Speech*, 59 (February 1973), 74–86.

[39]Northrop Frye, *Anatomy of Criticism: Four Essays* (Princeton University Press, 1957), 99. See also pp. 95–115.

[40]*American Short Speeches*, eds. Bower Aly and Lucile Folse Aly (N.Y.: Macmillan, 1968), 132–133.

[41]Kenneth Burke, *Counter-Statement* (University of Chicago Press, 1931; rpt. 1957), 31.

[42]Lloyd F. Bitzer, "Aristotle's Enthymeme Revisited," *Quarterly Journal of Speech*, 45 (December 1959), 408.

[43]Kenneth Burke, *A Grammar of Motives* and *A Rhetoric of Motives*, 581–582.

[44]John F. Wilson and Carroll C. Arnold, *Public Speaking as a Liberal Art*, 3rd ed. (Boston: Allyn & Bacon, 1973).

[45]Otto Alvin Loeb Dieter, "Stasis," *Speech Monographs*, 17 (November 1950), 345–369.

[46]Hoyt H. Hudson, "Rhetoric and Poetry," *Quarterly Journal of Speech Education*, 10 (April 1924), 146.

[47]Northrop Frye, *Anatomy of Criticism*, 245.

[48]Rosenfield, "A Case Study . . [.] ," 441–442.

[49]See James O. Payne, "The American Eulogy: A Study in Generic Criticism," (M.A. Thesis, University of Kansas, 1975). We are indebted to Charley Conrad, a graduate student at the University of Kansas, for the concept of inductive and deductive approaches to the formation of genres.

[50]Thomas Clark, "An Analysis of Generic Aspects of Contemporary American Sermons." Paper presented at the Central States Speech Association Convention (April 1976).

[51]Donald Wolfarth, "John F. Kennedy in the Tradition of Inaugural Speeches," *Quarterly Journal of Speech*, 47 (April 1961), 124–132.

[52]B. L. Ware and Wil A. Linkugel, "They Spoke in Defense of Themselves: On the Generic Criticism of Apologia," *Quarterly Journal of Speech*, 59 (October 1973), 273–283.

[53]Black, 79–91.

[54]Frye, 247–248.

[55]G. P. Mohrmann and Michael C. Leff, "Lincoln at Cooper Union: A Rationale for Neo-Classical Criticism," *Quarterly Journal of Speech*, 60 (December 1974), 459–467.

[56]Karlyn Kohrs Campbell, "The Rhetoric of Radical Black Nationalism: A Case Study in Self-Conscious Criticism," *Central States Speech Journal,* 22 (Fall 1971), 151–160; "An Exercise in the Rhetoric of Poetic Injustice" in *Critiques of Contemporary Rhetoric,* (Belmont, California: Wadsworth, 1972), pp. 142–151; "The Rhetoric of Women's Liberation: An Oxymoron."

[57]Barnet Baskerville, "The Illusion of Proof," *Western Speech,* 25, (Fall 1961), 236–242.

[58]Walter R. Fisher, "Rhetorical Criticism as Criticism," *Western Speech,* 38 (Spring 1974), 76.

THEY SPOKE IN DEFENSE OF THEMSELVES: ON THE GENERIC CRITICISM OF APOLOGIA

B. L. WARE AND WIL A. LINKUGEL

Within the last three decades, Richard Nixon, Adlai Stevenson, Harry Truman, and Edward Kennedy stood trial before the bar of public opinion regarding the propriety of some public or private action; each chose to take his case to the people in the form of an apologia, the speech of self-defense. In so doing, they followed a custom of Occidental culture firmly established by Socrates, Martin Luther, Robert Emmet, and thousands of lesser men. These events, separated by time and differing in particulars, are alike in that in each case the accused chose to face his accusers and to speak in defense of himself. That there are rhetorical genres and that one such may be the family of apologetic discourse occurring in situations such as those mentioned above are hardly revelations in the study of public address.[1] Yet, although most critics assent to the existence of genres, few engage in anything which even resembles what might appropriately be called *generic* criticism. Edwin Black, whose own *Rhetorical Criticism: A Study in Method* is one of the few lengthy considerations of speech genres, contends that "critics can probably do their work better by seeing and disclosing the elements common to many discourses rather than the singularities of a few"; but he is quick to add that the history of speech criticism to date is primarily one of attempts to "gauge the effects of the single discourse on its immediate audience." In the end, however, Black is critical of his own study of a genre, the argumentative, and characterizes his work as being too "gross" in the sense that it does not discriminate "among the types of discourses within the genre."[2] His self-criticism is valid, as well as of considerable import to the topic of this study, in that he leaves open the question of whether the argumentative genre subsumes apologia, as Black implies,[3] or whether apologetics is a genre in its own right, as others insist.[4]

We believe that apologetical discourses constitute a distinct *form* of public address, a family of speeches with sufficient elements in common so as to warrant legitimately generic status. The recurrent theme of accusation followed by apology is so prevalent in our record of public address as to be, in the words of Kenneth Burke, one of those "situations typical and recurrent enough for men to feel the need of having a name for them."[5] In life, an attack upon a person's character, upon his worth as a human being, does seem to demand a direct response. The questioning of a man's *moral nature, motives,* or *reputation* is qualitatively different from the challenging of his policies. Witnesses to such a personal charge seem completely and most easily satisfied only by the most personal of responses by the accused.

In the case of men and women of position, this response is usually a public speech of self-defense, the apology.[6] Apologia appear to be as important in contemporary society as in years past, despite today's emphasis upon the legal representative and the public relations expert.

Our task in this paper is to examine a portion of the genre of speeches resulting from those occasions when men have spoken in self-defense. In the end, we hope to accomplish two goals. First, we attempt to discover those *factors* which characterize the apologetic form. Our choice of the term *factor* is problematic and requires some explanation. Factors are hypothetical variables which in various combinations account for or explain the variations in a particular kind of human behavior.[7] They are not found within the speech; they are merely classificatory instruments that the critic brings to the speech as a means of grouping like rhetorical strategies for ease in study. The use of the term factor as a means for classifying conglomerates of like strategies that are relatively invariant across apologia is not an attempt on our part to introduce scientific rigor into the critical act; it is likewise not intended to confuse, frighten, or threaten the speech critic of a traditional bent. Factor analytic theory as it is known in the social sciences serves merely as a source for a new departure in thought with regard to the criticism of public address.[8] For those who might find the use of the term objectionable on the grounds that it confuses "action," intended behavior on the part of sentient beings, with "motion," non-purposeful movement on the part of objects, we would remind them that no less of a humanist than Burke insists that "statistical" is another name for "symbolic," as "equations" is for "clusters" of terms, and that he speaks of the relationships among the terms of the dramatistic pentad as "ratios."[9]

Second, we hope to discover the sub-genres, the "types of discourses within the genre" of which Black speaks, by noting the *combinations* of factors found in speeches of self-defense. People speak in defense of themselves against diverse charges, in varied situations, and through the use of many different strategies. Each apology, therefore, is in some sense unique. The subgenres of the apologetic form, which we refer to as the *postures* of rhetorical self-defense, must not be viewed as a classification of speeches in the Aristotelian sense of *genus* and *differentia*.[10] Our determination of the apologetic postures is a mapping of the genre, a matter of detailed comparisons of differences and resemblances, which leaves open the possibility of finding intermediate cases.[11] Just as the genre itself is a rough grouping of speeches on the basis of occurrence in a situation of attack and defense of character, our divisions of the genre are merely working subcategorizations of apologetic discourses.

THE FACTORS OF VERBAL SELF-DEFENSE

The nature of the resolution process occurring when a rhetor attempts to reconcile a derogatory charge with a favorable view of his character is the subject of an extensive body of psychological literature.[12] We feel, however, that the theory developed by Robert P. Abelson pertaining to the resolution of belief dilemmas is the most fruitful source of factors pertinent to the body of apologetic rhetoric.[13] We note at the outset that we take Abelson's theory as a starting point only. We borrow certain concepts and terminology from his work, but we often adapt the meanings of those terms for better usage in speech criticism. Much of his theory is discarded, not because it does not adequately describe psychological processes or interpersonal interaction, but because it implies a degree of predictive power which is not yet available to the critic. Abelson identifies four "modes of resolution": (1) denial, (2) bolstering, (3) differentiation, and (4) transcendence. Each of these is hereafter considered a factor commonly found in speeches of self-defense, and each is illustrated from at least one of the apologetic speeches from which we shall draw our examples for this article.[14]

The first factor, that of denial, is easily imagined to be important to speeches of self-defense. One may deny alleged facts, sentiments, objects, or relationships. Strategies of denial are obviously useful to the speaker only to the extent that such negations do not constitute a known distortion of reality or to the point that they conflict with other beliefs held by the audience. Denial is *reformative* in the sense that such strategies do not attempt to change the audience's meaning or affect for whatever is in question.[15] Denial consists of the simple disavowal by the speaker of any participation in, relationship to, or positive sentiment toward whatever it is that repels the audience.[16] The use of such strategies has lent considerable psychological impact to a number of famous self-defense speeches.

Many apologia rely upon the denial of *intent* to achieve persuasiveness. Naive psychology dictates that people respond differently to the actions of others when they perceive those actions to be intended than when they perceive them to be merely "a part of the sequence of events."[17] The person who is charged with some despicable action often finds a disclaimer of *intent* as an attractive means of escaping stigma if the denial of the existence of the action itself is too great a reformation of reality to gain acceptance. Marcus Garvey's "Address to the Jury" in the 1923 trial concerning fraud in the activities of the Universal Negro Improvement Association is illustrative.[18] Garvey does not deny that people were defrauded of their investments in the Black Star Line. He does insist that he believed the steamship company to be a good investment and that, therefore, he had not intended to mislead investors.[19] However, the accused does not stop at this level of denial. Near the end of the speech, Garvey talks at some length concerning his race. Suddenly speaking of himself in the first instead of in the third person, as is his practice to this point, Garvey says: "I know there are certain people who do not like me because I am black; they don't like me because I am not born here, through no fault of my own."[20] Having established that neither his foreign birth nor his race is through his own intent, Garvey notes: "I didn't bring myself into this western world. You know the history of my race. I was brought here; I was sold to some slave master in the island of Jamaica."[21] Finally, he denies any purpose in working with the Black Star Line other than "to redeem Africa and build up a country" for the Negro.[22] Garvey cleverly uses stylistic strategies in his denials of intent to present himself as a *tragic* figure. Speaking of himself in the third person, he assumes the stance of one who is acted upon rather than one who acts with intent. Only at the end of the speech does he become an "I," but it proves to be to his own detriment when he does act, despite his good intent. The theme of the man who causes his own downfall in attempting great gain is common to tragedy, and by employing denial on several levels, Garvey manages to introduce an element of tragedy with all its implicit pathos into a speech of self-defense.[23]

We should conclude, therefore, that strategies of denial are not simplistic matters to be lightly passed over by the critic. To begin with, they compose an important element of many speeches of self-defense. Though only one lengthy illustration is presented here, many others would be equally suitable examples.

Clarence Darrow's "They Tried to Get Me" is noteworthy in part because of his excellent use of strategies of denial.[24] Richard Nixon's "Checkers" speech contains such strategies; Sam Houston's "Address to the House of Representatives" results in a tragic pose based upon denial in much the same way Garvey accomplishes this end.[25] Nor should we conclude that the examples here are exhaustive of all the possible uses of denial strategies, for such is certainly not the case. Due to considerations of space, however, we must now focus our attention upon the second reformative factor of apologia, that of bolstering.

The bolstering factor is best thought of as being the obverse of denial.[26] Bolstering refers to any rhetorical strategy which reinforces the existence of a fact, sentiment, object, or relationship. When he bolsters, a speaker attempts to identify himself with something viewed favorably by the audience. Bolstering, like denial, is reformative in the sense that the speaker does not totally invent the identification, nor does he try to change the audience's affect toward those things with which he can identify himself. In the case of bolstering strategies, the accused is limited to some extent by the reality the audience already perceives. Even so, this factor is an important component of the apologetic form.

Our examination of apologetic speeches disclosed a number of famous persons who have made effective use of bolstering strategies when speaking on their own behalf; few, however, proved as skillful as Senator Edward Kennedy in this respect. A careful reading of his "Chappaquiddick" address discloses the Senator's attempts to reinforce a "unit relationship," a feeling of belonging, between the public and the Kennedy family.[27] This is particularly true with regard to the people of Massachusetts, the group with which the Senator most closely identifies his family. This theme emerges early in the address. "In the weekend of July 18th," Kennedy observes, "I was on Martha's Vineyard Island participating with my nephew, Joe Kennedy, as for thirty years my family had participated, in the annual Edgartown sailing regatta." Referring to the party for Senator Robert Kennedy's campaign staff, special notice is taken of the efforts to make Mary Jo Kopechne "feel that she still had a home with the Kennedy family." The Senator refers to the weekend of her death as "an agonizing one for me, and for the members of my family"; it is the "most recent tragedy" in the family's history, a cause for speculation "whether some awful curse did actually hang over all the Kennedys." The death of Mary Jo Kopechne becomes identified with the tragedy of the Kennedy family. The Kennedy family, in turn, is inseparably linked with the people of Massachusetts. Speaking directly to those citizens, Kennedy recalls: "You and I share many memories, some of them glorious, some have been very sad." He then requests the "advice and opinion" of the people, much as one would ask a family member "to think this through with me," regarding whether he should keep his Senate seat or resign from Congress. The Senator through the use of bolstering strategies turns the entire affair into a family matter, a decision to be made by himself with the counsel of the many Americans who can identify with the tragedy of one of the first families of Massachusetts and of the United States.

Bolstering and denial, then, are factors vital to the apologetic form of public address. We should conclude that both subsume a number of diverse, lesser rhetorical forms which represent stylistic and strategic choices by speakers. They differ in the treatment they provide of the speaker's place in the audience's perception of reality. Denial is an instrument of negation; bolstering is a source of identification. Finally, strategies of bolstering and denial are reformative in the sense that they do not alter the audience's meaning for the cognitive elements involved. The two factors of apologetic discourse remaining to be discussed, differentiation and transcendence, are both, on the other hand, transformative.[28]

Differentiation subsumes those strategies which serve the purpose of separating some fact, sentiment, object, or relationship from some larger context within which the audience presently views that attribute. The division of the old context into two or more new constructions of reality is accompanied by a change in the audience's meanings. At least one of the new constructs takes on a meaning distinctively different from that it possessed when viewed as a part of the old, homogeneous context. In other words, any strategy which is cognitively *divisive* and concomitantly transformative is differentiation. The differentiation factor, therefore, consists of those strategies which represent a particularization of the charge at hand; the psychological movement on the part of the audience is toward the less abstract. Such strategies are useful in apologia only to the extent that the new meaning and the old lend themselves to radically different interpretations by the audience.[29] Quibbling over meanings of definitions is not likely to aid the accused, but strategies which place whatever it is about him that repels the audience into a new perspective can often benefit him in his self-defense. Indeed, this latter case has proven useful in numerous apologia.

The presence of differentiation as an important factor in apologia is often signaled by the accused's request for a suspension of judgment until his actions can be viewed from a different temporal perspective. Such is the case in Robert Emmet's speech from the dock delivered on September 19, 1803, prior to his sentencing to death for treason against Ireland. As a result of his secret dealings with the French, Emmet faces the charge of desiring to supplant British rule of Ireland with domination by Napoleon. Early in his speech, Emmet makes the observation that he sought "a guarantee to Ireland similar to that which Franklin obtained for America."[30] He then explains why "treason" is an inappropriate definition of his intrigues with the French. "Were the French to come *as invaders or enemies uninvited by the wishes of the people*," Emmet assures the court, "I should oppose them to the utmost of my strength."[31] He completes the differentiation in a phrase by suggesting that his actions are best termed "moral and patriotic,"[32] a conclusion that he is sure others will accept when his behavior is viewed from a future date as an attempt "to make Ireland totally independent of Great Britain, but not to let her become a dependent of France."[33] Hence, his strategies of differentiation permit him to make a final plea for the postponement of any judgment concerning his value as a human being:

> Let no man write my epitaph; for, as no man who knows my motives dares now vindicate them,—let not prejudice or ignorance asperse them. Let them rest in obscurity and peace; my memory be left in oblivion, and my tomb remain uninscribed, until other times and other men can do justice to my character. When my country takes her place among the nations of the earth, then and not 'till then, let my epitaph be written—I have done.[34]

In his "Chappaquiddick" speech, Edward Kennedy employs differential strategies for his own defense in a manner quite different from that of Emmet. The Senator notes that he "felt morally obligated to plead guilty to the charge of leaving the scene of an accident" and that he feels the need to "talk to the people of Massachusetts about the tragedy." With a plea of guilty already entered, he resorts to a lengthy differentiation of his normal self from the Edward Kennedy who barely escaped drowning that night at Chappaquiddick. After commenting upon his exhausted state following repeated efforts to rescue Miss Kopechne from the water, Kennedy discourses: "My conduct and conversation during the next several hours, to the extent that I can remember them, make no sense to me. My doctors informed me that I suffered a cerebral concussion as well as shock." He describes his thoughts during that period at some length as:

> All kinds of scrambled thought, all of them confused, some of them irrational, many of them which I cannot recall, and some of which I would not have seriously entertained under normal circumstances, went through my mind during this period.
>
> They were reflected in the various inexplicable, inconsistent and inconclusive things I said and did, including such question [sic] as whether the girl might still be alive somewhere out of that immediate area . . . whether there was some justifiable reason for me to doubt what had happened and to delay my report, whether somehow the awful weight of this incredible incident might in some way pass from my shoulders. I was overcome—I am frank to say, by a jumble of emotion—grief, fear, doubt, torture, panic, confusion, exhaustion, and shock.

Kennedy clearly does not expect to excuse his actions through this differentiation. "I do not seek," he says, "to escape responsibility for my actions by placing the blame either on the physical, emotional trauma brought on by the accident or on anybody else." However, he is careful to complete the differentiation by noting that he finally took the proper action the next morning when his mind became "somewhat more lucid."[35] We can now see the differentiation factor permits the Senator to assume a *palliative* pose in his explanation of his behavior. Seemingly introducing new information about the accident, he is actually emphasizing the extenuating circumstances that surrounded those events. In so doing, the stance of palliation enables him to mitigate successfully the blame he feels he must assume.[36]

The fourth and final major factor of self-defense, transcendence, is the obverse of differentiation. This factor takes in any strategy which cognitively joins some fact, sentiment, object, or relationship with some larger context within which the audience does not presently view that attribute. As is the case with differentiation, transcendence is transformative in the sense that any such strategy affects the meaning which the audience attaches to the manipulated attribute.[37] In sum, those strategies which involve a change in cognitive *identification* and in *meaning* factor together as transcendence. Transcendental strategies, therefore, psychologically move the audience away from the particulars of the charge at hand in a direction toward some more abstract, general view of his character. Such strategies are useful in apologetic discourse to the extent that the manipulated attribute(s) proves to be congruent with the new context in the minds of the audience. Several speeches of self-defense exemplify the transcendence factor as it results either from complex combinations of strategies or from relatively straightforward attempts by speakers to identify attributes with new contexts.

Speeches by Eugene V. Debs[38] and Clarence Darrow illustrate usage of transcendental strategies. Although charged with allegedly inciting "insubordination, mutiny, disloyalty and refusal of duty within the military,"[39] Debs claims that the important issue of the Cleveland trial is not his guilt or innocence. He readily admits responsibility for the inflammatory speech delivered at Canton, Ohio, on June 16, 1918, the address which led to his indictment for violation of the Espionage Law. He obviously wants to transcend the particulars of his own case when he links

World War I with the profit incentive of the capitalist class[40] and maintains: "I know that it is ruling classes that make war upon one another, and not the people. In all the history of this world the people have never yet declared a war. Not one."[41] Consequently, the Socialist leader is able to argue that his trial really does not concern his opposition to the war. He concludes:

> Gentlemen, I am the smallest part of this trial. I have lived long enough to appreciate my own personal insignificance in relations to a great issue, that involves the welfare of the whole people. What you may choose to do to me will be of small consequence after all. I am not on trial here. There is an infinitely greater issue that is being tried today in this court, though you may not be conscious of it. American institutions are on trial here before a court of American citizens.[42]

As Debs presents his case, the real issue becomes the First Amendment to the Constitution: freedom of speech, of the press, and of assembly.[43] He wisely attempts to justify his opposition to the war by identifying the attacks against himself with opposition to the people and to the people's Constitution. In such a manner, he places his actions into a context much more favorable to a public currently immersed in a patriotic fervor surrounding a massive war effort than would otherwise have been possible if he had dealt solely with the indictment and evidence presented in court. Transcendence strategies assist Debs in this speech by placing his reputation above the simple question concerning whether or not he opposes the war in Europe.

Clarence Darrow was apparently more assured than was Debs that his audience would see the broader context within which he cast his own trial. He began employing strategies of transcendence very early in his "They Tried to Get Me" speech.

> I am not on trial for having sought to bribe a man named Lockwood. . . . I am on trial because I have been a lover of the poor, a friend of the oppressed, because I have stood by labor for all these years, and have brought down upon my head the wrath of the criminal interests in this country. Whether guilty or innocent of the crime charged in the indictment, that is the reason I am here, and that is the reason that I have been pursued by as cruel a gang as ever followed a man.[44]

The exact nature of the new context into which the trial was to be placed did not, however, become apparent until Darrow began describing those who desired his conviction. In brief summary of the opposition, the Chicago attorney exclaimed: "Oh, you wild, insane members of the Steel Trust and Erectors' Association! Oh, you mad hounds of detectives who are willing to do your master's will! Oh, you district attorneys."[45] Having found such a diverse group of opponents, Darrow could then quite believably introduce a motive of conspiracy to his enemies, a theme which carried with it a certain sinister aura to Darrow's new perspective of the trial. "These men are interested," insisted Darrow, "in getting me. They have concocted all sorts of schemes for the sake of getting me out of the way."[46] Hence, the accused utilized one set of transcendental strategies to represent himself as a hero of the downtrodden and another set to shade his accusers as wicked plotters whose own evil deeds overshadowed any crimes charged against Darrow.[47] The persuasive impact of such an archetypal motive was made possible by the judicious use of transcendence strategies.

Transcendence and the other three major factors illustrated previously account for most of the strategies people find useful in speaking in their own defense. Two factors, denial and bolstering, are psychologically reformative and obversely related; the remaining two, differentiation and transcendence, are psychologically transformative and also represent an obverse relationship. Denial and differentiation are essentially divisive in that they result in a splitting apart, a particularization, of cognitive elements in the minds of the listeners. Bolstering and transcendence, on the other hand, end in a joining of cognitive elements, a newly realized identification on the part of the audience. Between the four, these factors subsume the many and varied strategies people invent in speaking in their own defense.

The critical value of the factor terminology, however, is not solely one of classification. The terms we employ as names for the various categories of strategies are dialectically related; each term, like the strategies they name, is a function of the others. A dialectic relationship among terms is a sign of ambiguity, and certainly, there are no objective means by which a critic can assign a given strategy to one factor as opposed to another. No two strategies are exactly alike. Therefore, the terms used to classify strategies are necessarily ambiguous, as ambiguous as the subject strategies are different. Such ambiguity in classificatory terminology meets the needs of the critic, for as Burke notes, the student needs *"not terms that avoid ambiguity, but terms that clearly reveal the strategic spots at which ambiguities necessarily arise."*[48] The factor terminology does exactly that; it focuses the attention of the critic upon what language does for the apologetic rhetor when he deals with the charge or his character attributes, the strategic points in any speech of self-defense. By employing the factor terminology, the student must necessarily determine whether the rhetor is denying, bolstering, differentiating, or transcending through the strategic use of language, for these are the only rhetorical choices available to him in the apologetic situation. As the examples indicate, a speaker may employ reformative strategies; he may choose either to deny the charge directly or to ignore the charge through bolstering his character. On the other hand, he may opt for transformative strategies and move the audience's attention away from the charge through transcendental abstraction or through differential particularization. The factor terminology forces the critic to discern which choices a given strategy represents. The total import of these factors of apologetic discourse, however, become apparent only after we consider the ways in which speakers usually combine them to produce that human behavior we term the speech of self-defense.

THE POSTURES OF VERBAL SELF-DEFENSE

Speakers usually assume one of four major rhetorical postures when speaking in defense of their characters: absolution, vindication, explanation, or justification. Each of these postures results from a heavy reliance upon two of the factors described above, and we consider each to constitute a subgenre of the apologetic form.[49] We are not surprised to find that each of the four stances involves the combination of a transformative with a reformative factor. In a rhetorical situation as complex as that of accusation and response, a speaker would be expected to attempt to change the meaning of some, but not all, cognitive elements in the minds of the audience. Nor are we surprised to learn that only four of the possible combinations of factors have found widespread usage. Each combination represents a locus within the form around which similar, not identical, apologia tend to cluster; the four subgenres represent those postures which Western culture, customs, and institutions seem to dictate as being *most* acceptable in dismissing charges against a rhetor's character. The assignment of speeches to the postures is problematic, for our terms naming the subgenres are dialectic and ambiguous for the same reasons we note in discussing the factor terminology.[50] Each of the postures is a recognizable category of addresses into which the critic may group speeches on the basis of dominant strategies found in the discourses; the postures, like the factors, are not completely distinct classifications void of intermediate cases.

An *absolutive* address, resulting from the union of primarily the differentiation and denial factors, is one in which the speaker seeks acquittal. This posture is in no way limited to legal proceedings; the accused may seek acquittal from an extra-judicial body or even by public opinion. The absolutive speech is one in which the accused denies any wrong and in which he differentiates any personal attribute in question from whatever it is that the audience finds reprehensible. In this self-defense stance, the speaker is primarily concerned with "clearing his name" through focusing audience attention upon the particulars or specifics of the charge, just as Robert Emmet considered the nature of treason in great depth in "My Country Was My Idol."[51] The absolutive speech differs from the vindicative address in that it is more specific than the latter. The *vindicative* address, due to the reliance upon transcendental strategies, permits the accused greater ease in going beyond the specifics of a given charge. Such an apology aims not only at the preservation of the accused's reputation, but also at the recognition of his greater worth as a human being relative to the worth of his accusers. A good example of the vindicative subgenre results from Clarence Darrow's use of transcendence strategies to formulate an implicit comparison between his own character and that of his prosecutors in his "They Tried to Get Me."[52]

A similar distinction is possible between the explanative and the justificative postures. The former, as a combination of bolstering and differentiation, is somewhat more defensive than is the latter, a category of discourse relying upon the use of bolstering and transcendence strategies. In the *explanative* address, the speaker assumes that if the audience understands his motives, actions, beliefs, or whatever, they will be unable to condemn him. This seems to have been the hope of Edward Kennedy in his "Chappaquiddick Address."[53] The *justificative* address, on the other hand, asks not only for understanding, but also for approval. Hence, Eugene V. Debs in his "Speech to the Jury" sought to establish the basis for his own actions in a concern with human dignity and fundamental rights such as freedom of speech.[54]

This conceptualization of the apologetic genre into subgenres should assist the critic in comparing the rhetorical uses of language occurring across somewhat different apologetic situations. The act is not, in and of itself, criticism, just as the categorizing of strategies into factors does not complete the critical act. Such classification taken alone lacks an evaluative dimension. However, the dialectic and ambiguous nature of the posture terminology focuses the critic's attention upon the strategic decision a speaker makes whenever he chooses a culturally acceptable stance from which to speak on his own behalf. Herein lies the critical advantage of mapping the apologetic genre, and as we argued in the beginning, the explication of the genre should precede the criticism proper of the apologetic form. We offer this conceptualization of the subgenres and the factor terminology as "experimental incursions into the field with which they deal; assays or examinations of specimen concepts drawn rather arbitrarily from a larger class; and finally *ballons d'essai,* trial balloons designed to draw the fire of others."[55]

NOTES

[1]Examples of criticism in the apologetic genre include James H. Jackson, "Plea in Defense of Himself," *Western Speech,* 20 (Fall 1956), 185–195; L. W. Rosenfield, "A Case Study in Speech Criticism: The Nixon-Truman Analog," *Speech Monographs,* 35 (Nov. 1968), 435–450; Wil A. Linkugel and Nancy Razak, "Sam Houston's Speech of Self-Defense in the House of Representatives," *Southern Speech Journal,* 43 (Sum. 1969), 263–275; Bower Aly, "The Gallows Speech: A Lost Genre," *Southern Speech Journal,* 34 (Spr. 1969), 204–213; David A. Ling, "A Pentadic Analysis of Senator Edward Kennedy's Address 'To the People of Massachusetts,' July 25, 1969," *Central States Speech Journal,* 21 (Sum. 1970), 81–86; and Sherry Devereaux Butler, "The Apologia, 1971 Genre," *Southern Speech Communication Journal,* 36 (Spr. 1972), 281–289.

[2](New York: Macmillan. 1965), pp. 176–177.

[3]*Ibid.,* pp. 150–161. Black considers John Henry Newman's *Apologia pro Vita sua* as a constituent of the argumentative genre.

[4]See Rosenfield, 435.

[5]*The Philosophy of Literary Form,* 2nd ed. (Baton Rouge: Louisiana State Univ. Press, 1967), p. 3.

[6]In recent years, only Senator Thomas Eagleton among men of national prominence has eschewed delivery of an apologia when one seemed advantageous.

[7]See Paul Horst, *Factor Analysis of Data Matrices* (New York: Holt, Rinehart, 1965), p. 3.

[8]Such a use of scientific literature is at least implied by Wayne Brockriede, "Trends in the Study of Rhetoric: Towards a Blending of Criticism and Science," *The Prospect of Rhetoric,* ed. Lloyd F. Bitzer and Edwin Black (Englewood Cliffs, N.J.: Prentice-Hall, 1971), pp. 123–139.

[9]*The Philosophy of Literary Form,* pp. 18–27; *A Grammar of Motives* (New York: Prentice-Hall, 1945), pp. 15–16.

[10]The possibility of such definition of linguistic contexts is even to be doubted given Ludwig Wittgenstein's denial of the general form of propositions. See *Philosophical Investigations,* trans. G. E. M. Anscombe, 3rd ed. (New York: Macmillan, 1971), No. 67.

[11]This discursive function of criticism is explained in detail in John Casey, *The Language of Criticism* (London: Methuen, 1966), pp. 16–17.

[12]For example, see T. M. Newcomb, "An Approach to the Study of Communicative Acts," *Psychological Review,* 60 (Nov. 1953), 393–404; C. E. Osgood and P. H. Tannenbaum, "The Principle of Congruity in the Prediction of Attitude Change," *Psychological Review,* 62 (Jan. 1955), 42–55; Leon Festinger, *A Theory of Cognitive Dissonance* (Stanford, Calif.: Stanford Univ. Press, 1957); R. P. Abelson and M. J. Rosenberg, "Symbolic Psycho-logic: A Model of Attitudinal Cognition," *Behavioral Science,* 3 (Jan. 1958), 1–13; and Bernard Kaplan and Walter H. Crockett, "Developmental Analysis of Modes of Resolution," in *Theories of Cognitive Consistency: A Sourcebook,* ed. Robert P. Abelson *et al.* (Chicago: Rand McNally, 1968), pp. 661–669.

[13]"Modes of Resolution of Belief Dilemmas," *Journal of Conflict Resolution,* 3 (Dec. 1959), 343–352.

[14]Speeches examined but not used as examples for this article include: Socrates' "Apology"; Isocrates' "On the Antidoses"; Demosthenes' "On the Crown"; Sir Thomas More's "Remarks at His Trial"; Martin Luther's "Speech at the Diet of Worms"; Thomas Cranmer's "Speech at the Stake"; Thomas Harrison's "Speech from the Scaffold"; The Earl of Strafford's (Thomas Wentworth) "Speech When Impeached for High Treason"; Sir Robert Walpole's "Address to the King for His Removal"; Edmund Burke's "Bristol Election Speech Upon Certain Charges Regarding His Parliamentary Conduct"; Mirabeau's "Against the Charge of Treason"; Marat's "Defense Against the Charges";

Robespierre's "Facing the Guillotine"; John Brown's "Courtroom Speech"; Susan B. Anthony's "Is It a Crime for a United States Citizen to Vote?"; Bartolomeo Vanzetti's "I Would Live Again"; Douglas MacArthur's "Address to Congress"; Harry S. Truman's "Television Address on Harry Dexter White"; Adlai Stevenson's "The Hiss Case"; and Thomas Dodd's "Address to the Senate Concerning Charges of Irregular Financial Dealings, June 14, 1967."

[15]The classification of strategies as "reformative" does not involve an ethical judgment on the part of the critic of the speaker's choices. Reformative strategies are those which simply revise or amend the cognitions of the audience.

[16]See Abelson, *Theories of Cognitive Consistency,* pp. 344–345.

[17]See Fritz Heider, *The Psychology of Interpersonal Relations* (New York: Wiley, 1958), p. 100. In the naive analysis of action, "intent" merely implies the perception of "trying."

[18]Text taken from *Philosophy and Opinion of Marcus Garvey,* ed. Amy Jacques-Garvey, 2nd ed. (London: Cass, 1967), pp. 184–216. Though not a lawyer, Garvey represented himself during the trial.

[19]*Ibid.,* p. 186. In 1919, Garvey had started the Black Star Line to provide employment opportunities for the Black community. Stock in the company was sold through the mails. See Edmund David Cronon, *Black Moses* (Madison: Univ. of Wisconsin Press, 1955), pp. 112–118.

[20]"Address to the Jury," p. 213.

[21]*Ibid.* Here, Garvey uses "I" to refer to his race; he was never personally a slave. He was, in fact, possibly a descendant of the Jamaican Maroons, runaway slaves who won their freedom and independence from England in 1739. See Cronon, p. 5.

[22]"Address to the Jury," pp. 213–214.

[23]For a discussion of the psychological aspects of tragedy, see Heider, p. 100.

[24]See *Attorney for the Damned,* ed. Arthur Weinberg (New York: Simon and Schuster 1957), pp. 494–531.

[25]See "My Side of the Story," *Vital Speeches of the Day,* 19 (15 Oct. 1952), 11–15. The text for Houston's speech is in *Gales and Seaton's Register of Debates in Congress,* Vol. 8, part 2, 1st session, 22nd Congress, pp. 2810–2822.

[26]See Abelson, p. 345.

[27]We take the text from "Kennedy Asks Voter Advice," *Kansas City Times,* 26 July 1969, p. 8A. For a discussion of the psychological processes involved in a sense of belonging, see Heider, p. 200ff.

[28]See Abelson, pp. 345–346.

[29]*Ibid.,* p. 351.

[30]We take the text from Thomas Addis Emmet, *The Emmet Family* (New York: Privately printed, 1898), pp. 161–164. For this citation, see p. 161.

[31]*Ibid.*

[32]*Ibid.,* p. 164.

[33]*Ibid.,* p. 162.

[34]*Ibid.,* p. 164. Marcus Garvey employs differentiation in much the same manner as does Emmet when he urged the jury to judge his actions with regards to the Black Star Line from an imagined perspective a hundred years in the future when there would be a "terrible race problem in America." See Garvey's "Address to the Jury," pp. 213–214.

[35]All quotations taken from "Kennedy Asks People's Advice," p. 8A.

[36]An easily identifiable use of differentiation occurs when a speaker employs *regenerative* strategies in an apology. Regeneration is the assertion that one is now somehow fundamentally different and worthy of increased valuation than at some previous time. Typically, therefore, a speaker employing these strategies will differentiate his present self from the old, a self guilty of wrongdoing. An excellent example of regeneration in a gallows speech is that of one John Whittington before his execution at Fort Smith, Arkansas, on September 3, 1875. See Fred Harvey Harrington, *Hanging Judge* (Caldwell, Idaho: Caxton, 1951), p. 35. Whittington claimed that "good instruction" in prison had led him to realize that liquor was the cause of his ruin and to wish that he could go free with his new lesson to live as a "good and happy man." Also, see Aly, 212.

[37]See Abelson, p. 346.

[38]The text is taken from "Debs' Speech to the Jury," *The Debs White Book* (Girard, Kansas: Appeal to Reason, n.d.), pp. 37–57.

[39]*Ibid.*, p. 38. These are only the most important charges against Debs.

[40]*Ibid.*, p. 53.

[41]*Ibid.*, p. 42.

[42]*Ibid.*, p. 57.

[43]*Ibid.*, pp. 48–49.

[44]Darrow, p. 495.

[45]*Ibid.*, p. 497.

[46]*Ibid.*, p. 496.

[47]The conspiracy theme is one common to many speeches of self-defense. For another example of the use of transcendental strategies to introduce the conspiratorial motif, see Garvey, p. 210.

[48]*A Grammar of Motives*, p. xviii.

[49]Any speech of self-defense is likely to contain all four of the factors of self-defense. We do not mean to imply that each of the apologetic postures contains only two of the factors. Rather, we contend that speeches of self-defense usually rely most heavily for their persuasive impact upon two of the factors. The determination of which two are most important in a given speech is, in this study at least, a subjective decision based only partly upon frequency of appearance of a given factor.

[50]See Burke, *A Grammar of Motives*, p. xix.

[51]Other examples of absolutive addresses would include Sam Houston's "Address to the House of Representatives"; Marcus Garvey's "Address to the Jury"; and Richard Nixon's "My Side of the Story."

[52]Two further examples of vindicative discourses are Socrates' "Apology" and Harry S. Truman's "Television Address on Harry Dexter White."

[53]Other famous explanative addresses are Martin Luther's "Speech at the Diet of Worms" and Adlai Stevenson's "The Hiss Case."

[54]Susan B. Anthony's "Is It a Crime for a United States Citizen to Vote?" and Douglas MacArthur's "Address to Congress" are also well known examples of justificative addresses.

[55]*The Uses of Argument* (Cambridge, England: Cambridge Univ. Press, 1957), p. 1.

JOE McCARTHY'S FANTASTIC MOMENT

JAMES DARSEY

I believe it because it is unbelievable.

Tertullian

Why, sometimes I've believed as many as six impossible things before breakfast.

White Queen to Alice, Through the Looking Glass

Joe McCarthy has been dead for almost 40 years. It seems wise to remind ourselves of this fact given the astonishing vitality of his presence in contemporary politics, national and international. The name of the great smear campaigner has, in recent years, been hurled at those whom we wished to discredit and used by the discredited to suggest the injustice of their trial.[1] Jeremiah Denton was compared to "that ultimate American witch-hunter, the late Joe McCarthy," and Kurt Waldheim, after charges were raised regarding his Nazi activities during the Second World War, claimed that he was a victim of McCarthyism. The Reagan administration's liberal application of the McCarren-Walter Act revived what playwright Arthur Miller (1984, July) referred to as "one of the pieces of garbage left behind by the sinking of the great scow of McCarthyism"[2] (p. 11). McCarthy's presence was felt in the 1988 presidential campaign when Democratic candidate Michael Dukakis, in response to aspersions cast on his patriotism, compared the tactics of his opponents to the slander of the late senator from Wisconsin. In one speech, Dukakis expressed his confidence that his Texas audience could "smell the garbage" (Turner, 1988; see also "Reagan Backs Bush," 1988; "Transcript of First TV Debate," 1988). In 1992, McCarthy made a return visit to presidential politics as the Clinton campaign accused George Bush of McCarthyism for his attacks on Clinton's patriotism. Most recently, "PC," or political correctness, has been denounced by its detractors as "McCarthyism of the Left" and the war on drugs as "chemical McCarthyism."

In his time, Joe McCarthy was hailed at the most gifted demagogue ever produced in America (Rovere, 1959/1960, p. 3). Nearly 40 years after his censure by his colleagues in the United States Senate, the man and the phenomenon still cast a pall over political discussion.[3] Nearly 40 years after his death, an unabated scholarly interest betrays, in its continued debates over the basic questions, how far we are from any satisfactory understanding of Joe McCarthy.[4] It is as if in not understanding him, we have not really buried him. McCarthy, by some power we even now fail to comprehend, made himself one of the most prominent symbols of the decade of the Fifties. The residual fear of that unidentified power still haunts the cloakrooms of American politics. There is something both elusive and perdurable about this incubus. We have failed to find the key that would exorcise it and consign it to memory.

As a rhetorical phenomenon, McCarthyism has received surprisingly slight attention, and our moralistic revelations of his lapses of logic, his shameless unoriginality, his torturing of evidence, his half-truths, his ugly barbarisms, and his unforgivable uncouthness have been more dyslogic than critical and have revealed more about our own good intentions and our ideal rhetoric than they have about the mystery that is Joe McCarthy. Indeed, perhaps it is in seeking to discredit the substance of McCarthyism that we have missed the larger question. Perhaps it is the metaphor of the spectre that is appropriate for discussing, not only McCarthy's continuing influence, but the source of that influence even while he was alive. Perhaps the substance of McCarthyism has remained so elusive and so invulnerable to exposure because there was no substance there at all. As Walt Kelly's Jayhawk, in a cartoon strip of the McCarthy era, responds when asked to prove the existence of the invisible Indians whom he claims raised him: "Bein' invisible they natural don't leave no traces an' to this day, no sign of 'em is ever been found. Sheer proof." "Sheer," affirms Pogo (Kelly, 1954/1955, p. 28).

McCarthy, I would argue, was a sublime fantasist in an age particularly susceptible to the fantastic. The notion of the fantastic used here, stemming from literary theory, should not be confounded with conceptions of fantasy most popular among students of rhetoric and speech communication.[5] The genre of the fantastic is a celebration of ambiguity, something indefinite, a moment of hesitation and indecision. Todorov (1975) finds the fantastic suspended between the uncanny— the bizarre and ultimately untrue—on the one hand and the marvelous—the extraordinary but ultimately credible—on the other. When we encounter an extraordinary event, for the moment that we cannot decide whether we are hallucinating or witnessing a miracle, we are participants in the fantastic. It is a moment of epistemological uncertainty. The literary fantastic, while it raises emotions and exploits attitudes, stubbornly refuses to render final judgments that would allow us to direct them. As Rabkin (1976) puts it: "The wonderful, exhilarating, therapeutic value of Fantasy [for Rabkin, the genre most characterized by the fantastic] is that it makes one recognize that beliefs, even beliefs about Reality, are arbitrary" (p. 218).[6]

Consistent with this tentative attitude, McCarthy never insisted on a final judgment regarding those he accused. Indeed, his most common pattern was to make the accusation, then, when the evidence to sustain it failed to materialize, to drop the charge and move on to the next, leaving neither hero nor villain, only the horrible and often destructive stigmata of doubts raised and left unresolved. The fantastic is a genre of escape; immediate realities are less relevant than potentialities, which may be tried on without the burden of commitment or the guilt of consequences (Rabkin, 1976, esp. chap. 2). In addition to the devastation his unfulfilled charges wreaked on his victims, McCarthy's failure of judgment also left his audience without a coherent and stable vision, understandings too fleeting and fragile to dispel the confusion of the time, epistemological straws grasped in desperation. To apply this notion to the 1950s in America requires a kind of understanding. We must be willing to hazard such ostensibly self-contradictory statements as "The 1950s in America was a time defined by chaos," or "It was an age united chiefly by its superficial placidity and underlying confusion."

Simons and Aghazarian (1986), in a statement reminiscent of Wrage's (1947) characterization of the study of public address as a specie of social and intellectual history, argue that genre criticism ought to be "a vehicle for cultural and historical insights" (p. ix). With respect to McCarthyism and the Fifties, the insight still most needed after four decades is "How could it have happened? How could the presumption of innocence have been abandoned wholesale? How did large and powerful institutions acquiesce as congressional investigators ran roughshod over civil liberties—all in the name of the war on communists" (Rabinowitz, 1990, p. 63)? Considering the fantastic nature of the rhetoric of McCarthyism reveals an important clue. What is most remarkable, in this as in other instances of large-scale social injustices, is the passivity, the acquiescence to use Rabinowitz's term, of those who should have known better. If, as Miller (1984) argues, "a rhetorically sound definition of genre must be centered not on the substance or the form of discourse but on the action it is used to accomplish" (p. 151), we can begin to discern that the logical end of the fantastic is inaction. A genre that "contradicts perspectives," that doggedly refuses a stable set of ground rules, that simultaneously insists on the regular operation of laws even as it denies them (Rabkin, 1976), thwarts the commitment necessary to action. In literature, the effect may be innocuous; in politics, it is paralyzing.[7]

In order to make this argument, it is necessary, first, to look at the Fifties to understand what made the rhetoric of the fantastic so fitting, at what made Americans so susceptible, at the exigence that, in Miller's (1984) view, favors a particular generic response; second, to analyze the ways in which McCarthy intuitively exploited the anxieties of his audience, maintaining a delicate suspension, characteristic of the fantastic, between threat and reassurance; and third, and finally, to evaluate this stubborn ethos that, I will argue, was finally overwhelmed and consumed by its own rhetorical creation.

Using the idea of the fantastic to explain McCarthyism and the man behind it, we can make consistent some of our reactions to him: our continued entertainment of his charges despite his failure to successfully expose a single conspirator and our failure to cry for punishment even when the hoax was finally admitted. We also learn something of that nexus where poetics meets politics that Bryant (1937, 1953, 1965, 1966, 1978) used to claim was rhetoric, particularly as regards the transposition of literary genres into the political world and, more particularly still, the social (in)action of the fantastic.

A GREAT CLOUD OVER THE 50S: A SETTING FOR McCARTHYISM

Contemporary historians and social critics have labored in recent years to rescue from Broadway and television the decade of the 1950s as it has been sanitized, idealized, and popularly associated with *I Love Lucy,* hula hoops, enormous gaudy automobiles, gauche fashions, and a congenial prosperity. The "Fabulous Fifties," in fact, were no more fabulous than the 1890s were gay; and the apparently frivolous entertainments reveal, just beneath the surface, the same desperate seriousness that fueled the Roaring Twenties. The celebration of material well-being as the ultimate good reflected, as had been the case at the turn of the last century, the desuetude of any other form of value, and it concealed gross inequalities in the distribution of wealth. The frenetic pace of spending and the enlargement of the credit culture suggest an interior voice murmuring "Eat, drink, and be merry, for tomorrow we die." Even our current nostalgia for the family of the Fifties, a family that seems, in shows like *Leave it to Beaver, Father Knows Best,* and *Ozzie and Harriet,* to have reached a state of beatitude, overlooks the degree to which these shows themselves reflected the nostalgic yearning of an anxious time for a presumably simpler and perhaps saner past. The Fifties simply cannot be adequately understood without recognizing World War II as their immediate predecessor and the "Great Fear" as much of their present.[8]

The horror of the Second World War, the second in as many generations, was certainly unsettling to Americans. Everything was on a scale that made a profanity of human beings—Hitler, the scope of the war, the new technologies of war, the bomb. Weaver (1976), in his noteworthy post-war polemic, called it "a marvelous confusion of values" (p. 179). If the war itself was unsettling, the aftermath was even more so. There was no return to "normalcy" as there had been after the First World War. For all our victory parades and celebrations of the end of the war to end war, there was an inconclusiveness about World War II; we could not simply disarm and return to a peace-time economy when it was over. America had new responsibilities in a world that had gotten smaller since the First World War. We had to help rebuild Europe and to maintain a cold war with our World War II ally the Soviet Union (Boyer, 1985, esp. pp. 7–14; Goldman, 1960; Jorstad, 1970, p. 45).

The 1949 announcement that the Soviet Union had exploded an atomic bomb exacerbated tensions. In 1947, Americans ranked the "A bomb" second behind electric lights and appliances as the greatest invention in history. In 1949, following Truman's announcement of evidence that the Soviet Union had exploded a nuclear weapon, 45% of Americans thought war was more likely as a result (Gallup, 1972, vol. 1, p. 625; vol. 2, p. 869). Between 1947 and 1954, Americans consistently reported, by large majorities, that they believed it was the intention of the Soviet Union to achieve dominance over the world (Gallup, 1972, vol. 1, p. 682; vol. 2, p. 925; see also Goldman, 1960, p. 262). The prevention of war was ranked as the most important problem facing the candidates in the 1950 elections, and a

1951 poll revealed that 50% of Americans would not feel safe in their cities or communities in the event of an atomic attack (Gallup, 1972, vol. 2, pp. 922, 967).[9] In two other 1951 polls, Americans ranked war as their biggest worry after "money, the high cost of living, prices, and paying bills," and ranked "war and foreign policy, Russia, threats to peace, cold war" as the most important problem facing the country as a whole (Gallup, 1972, vol. 2, pp. 1010, 1018). Churchy La Femme, in Walt Kelly's (1954/1955) comic strip "Pogo," complained of "these modern day disasters what consists of ten years of worry an' ten seconds of boom an' wango," and lamented days spent "scannin' the sky—not knowin' when—wonderin' whether to wear pajamas that night so's to be found decent—wonderin' whether to take a bath—whether to pack a light lunch" (p. 103). For a country that had grown up in the faith that they were God's chosen people, destined to work His will on this earth, such power in the hands of an enemy nation could only mean that America's select status had been decisively annulled, either by an angry God or by a rival one; there seemed to be little difference.[10]

W. H. Auden's (1969) 1947 poem "The Age of Anxiety," provided a convenient label for the time and gave eloquent expression to much that we could not or would not articulate. Auden wrote of "Lies and Lethargies" policing the world, and went on to develop a nightmare scenario around "The fears that we fear [when] We fall asleep . . . Nocturnal trivia, torts and dramas . . . Moulds and monsters on memories stuffed With dead men's doodles, dossiers written In lost lingos," and he recognized that, even in wakefulness, "athwart our thinking the threat looms, Huge and awful as the hump of Saturn Over modest Mimas, of more deaths And worse wars, a winter of distaste To last a lifetime." Our age, he mourned, was one "Infatuated with her former self Whose dear dreams though they dominate still Are formal facts which refresh no more" (pp. 268–270).

An autopsy on America's "dear dreams" of "her former self," the "formal facts" for which we now longed, revealed that they had been dead for some time. In the period following the Second World War, America finally faced an epistemological crisis that had its roots in the nineteenth century, the product of such diverse thinkers as Comte, Freud, Einstein, Nietzsche, Kierkegaard, Pierce, and James. The works of the existentialists, in particular, ignored for half a century by professional philosophers, suddenly became the concern of "even the weekly news magazines" (Aiken, 1956, p. 225; see also Marcuse, 1960, esp. pp. 267–268). Nineteen forty-eight saw the publication of the English translation of Albert Camus's *The Plague*, wherein Father Paneloux assured his congregation that God, after looking on the people of Oran with compassion for a long while, had grown weary of waiting, "His eternal hope was too long deferred, and now He has turned His face away from us. And so, God's light withdrawn, we walk in darkness, in the thick darkness of the plague" (1972, pp. 90–91).

Camus's was not an American voice, but he and Sartre and other existentialists spoke to our anxieties. Oakley (1986), in a recent history of the Fifties, notes that "much of the fiction of the day was concerned with individual alienation that led to despair, suicide, murder, rape, and other desperate acts of lonely individuals in mass society" (pp. 318–319). Like Father Paneloux's congregation, Americans faced with crisis returned to the church in increasing numbers. The reason most commonly provided as an explanation for this religious revival, given by almost one third of the respondents in a 1954 Gallup poll, was "fear, unrest, uncertainty of future" (Gallup, 1972, vol. 2, p. 1293). Richard Niebuhr called it part "of a rather frantic effort of the naturally optimistic American soul to preserve its optimism in an age of anxiety" (cited in Oakley, p. 324). In 1949, Schlesinger wrote:

> Western man in the middle of the twentieth century is tense, uncertain, adrift. We look upon our epoch as a time of troubles, an age of anxiety. The grounds of our civilization, of our certitude, are breaking up under our feet, and familiar ideas and institutions vanish as we reach for them, like shadows in the falling dusk.[11] (p. 1)

Behind much of the angst of the Fifties and providing it with a kind of coherence was modern science. There was the obvious fact of the bomb, but the more important questions were the subtle ones about what it meant. There is a certain irony in the fact that Hiroshima and Nagasaki were the products of a theory that both taught us the limits of our knowledge and laid the foundation for harnessing the greatest power known to human kind. The limited, philosophically speaking, pragmatic success of the atomic bomb granted the theory that made possible considerable credibility in its claim that we could not know in any transcendent sense (see Johnson, 1985, pp. 1–5 on the impact of Einstein's theory). It also suggested that such knowledge was superfluous. Weaver (1976, p. 58) termed it an exchange of truth for facts. Daniel Boorstin (1970) phrased our quandary this way:

> Man's power to make his own laws was, despite everything, the most burdensome of his new responsibilities for himself and the universe. His new powers to make things and his powers over nature would not have worried him much less if somehow he had felt confident that his laws were rooted outside his society. But in acquiring his mastery over nature he had acquired the guilty secret that his laws might be rooted only in his version of the needs of his time and place. (p. 75)

The explosion of the atomic bomb, then, was the zenith of industrialization, a process that had steadily decayed the half-life of God; it was, in the words of social historian Boyer (1985), an event of such magnitude that it seems to have become "one of those categories of Being, like Space and Time, that, according to Kant, are built into the very structure of our minds, giving shape and meaning to all our perceptions" (p. xvii). By 1950, left with a God who was no longer immanent in the world, who was both unknowable and unnecessary, history became at best inscrutable, at worst meaningless. The foundation of the common sense philosophy that had sustained earlier generations of Americans had been thoroughly eroded. It was in this era, the era in which Bell (1962, p. 400) saw "the end of ideology," the end of "secular religion[,]" that Joe McCarthy claimed a place in the spotlight of American politics; and it is in what Rabkin (1976) refers to as "the precarious world of the bomb [that] Fantasy . . . moved out of the Victorian nursery and into the adult library" (p. 181). And into politics.

PHOTOSTATS AND CHIMERAS: THE RHETORIC OF JOE McCARTHY

Joe McCarthy understood the feeling of moral arrest in his audience. He called it "an emotional hang-over . . . a temporary moral lapse which follows every war" (McCarthy, n.d., p. 14; all subsequent references will be McC, p. x):

> It is the apathy to evil which people who have been subjected to the tremendous evils of war feel. As the people of the world see mass murder, the

destruction of defenseless and innocent people, and all of the crime and lack of morals which go with war, they become numb and apathetic. It has always been thus after war. (McC, p. 14)

It was not, of course, "a temporary moral lapse which follows every war," not if the sketch of the Fifties just provided has any credibility. The crisis of the post-WWII period was significant enough to be thought to have ended the historical era of modernism, and it posed unprecedented problems for political leadership. The traditional response of great leaders in times of crisis is to judge. The leader provides a moral compass by which the people can find their way out of the spiritual wilderness. Joe McCarthy's response to chaos was not certitude, but incredulity. He looked upon the post-modern world and found it perplexing and preposterous. "Strangely, however, after the arrest of six suspects in that case of treason, there was an unusual sequence of events, resulting in a most fantastic finale," said McCarthy (p. 66), referring to the government's fumbled case against *Amerasia* magazine. Concerning the same case, McCarthy produced a letter from T. A. Bisson, an employee of the State Department and a member of the *Amerasia* board. Bisson's letter was "a fantastic document if ever there was one" (p. 92). In a second reference, the letter from Bisson was called "a rather fantastic document coming from the man whom Mr. Jessup used to initiate the smear campaign—a rather fantastic document coming from a man high up in the State Department, but not too fantastic, however, when coming from a man who worked under Frederick Vanderbilt Field on *Amerasia*" (p. 109). According to McCarthy, Owen Lattimore was able to beguile audiences with "fantasies and untruths," (p. 98) attempting to sell the American people "a rather fantastic bill of goods" (p. 102). The failure of the Tydings Committee to call a witness suggested by McCarthy was "the most fantastic situation conceivable, something unheard of in any Senate or House Committee; unheard of even in a kangaroo court" (p. 144). The alleged raping of State Department personnel files before committee members were allowed access to them was "the most fantastic project I have ever heard of" (p. 147). And orders concerning the mission of the seventh fleet during the Korean war were termed "the most fantastic order that has ever existed in war or peace" (p. 203) and a "fantastically incredible" position (p. 217).[12]

McCarthy's use of the term "fantastic" is coincidental to my argument that he exploits the genre of the fantastic. McCarthy does not mean by "fantastic" the moment of hesitation between accrediting and rejecting that is the essence of the genre. When McCarthy describes activities and events as "fantastic," he is in fact talking about what Todorov (1975) calls the uncanny; he emphasizes the extraordinary nature of what he has unveiled as an indication of its discreditability, its incredible nature, its untruth. McCarthy's language suggests that these incidents are so far removed from normal experience as not to deserve credence.

Rather than righteous indignation or avenging anger, McCarthy's (1952) reaction to his charges of malfeasance and deception was amazement and incredulity, and he invited his audiences to share in his mystification. Our foreign policy was an "amazing failure" (p. vii); the "picture of treason which I carried in my briefcase to that Caucus room was to shock the nation" (p. 1). A State Department document revealed the "astounding position of the Secretary of State," and McCarthy had no doubt that Senator Knowland of California would find much in it that would "shock him also" (McC, p. 121). "Even in normal times," McCarthy said, his evidence would be "shocking." "Today, however, it is doubly shocking" (p. 153). Dean Acheson's failure to read some Communist documents regarding

China was "disturbing in the extreme. . . . Incredible. Incredible" (p. 190). And the failure of the Truman administration to expedite the delivery of economic and military aid to Chiang Kai-shek was "one of the most shocking subversions of the will of the Congress by an administration that our history will show" (p. 298).[13] Owen Lattimore's discussion of the China problem in the *Sunday Compass* of New York, July 17, 1949, was "astounding" (p. 299), and the testimony of Secretary of State George Marshall "and his palace men" in their testimony before the Russell committee was one of "self-satisfied shocking revelations" (p. 303). Any attempt to understand one of Secretary of State Marshall's statements on China was certain to leave McCarthy's colleagues "dumbfounded" (p. 284). McCarthy's (1953, Nov. 25) picture of Communist infiltration in America was "amazing . . . disturbing . . . incredibly unbelievable" (p. 5).

Already the first contradiction in McCarthy's rhetoric begins to emerge, for if he were consistent in his refusal to grant these claims plausibility, it would be unnecessary for him to be calling the attention of the Senate to them. It is in his reaction to the chicanery he discovered that McCarthy begins to create the tension necessary to the fantastic, the infection of disbelief by conviction, the reversal of the ground rules, first of everyday life, then of his own narrative. McCarthy's characterization of elements in his world as "fantastic" and his incredulous reaction to them while simultaneously insisting on their seriousness combine to suggest that the usages are not insignificant or incidental. His astonishment that the rules have been broken even as he continues to believe in their binding force, his confrontation with the "anti-expected," signals the presence of the genre of the fantastic (Rabkin, 1976, pp. 10, *passim*). Jackson (1981), building on Todorov's (1975) work, writes: "A characteristic most frequently associated with literary fantasy has been its obdurate refusal of prevailing definitions of the 'real' or 'possible,' a refusal amounting at times to violent opposition" (p. 14). McCarthy created this opposition by announcing his skepticism at what he discovered while at the same time insisting on its veracity.

Consistent with the nature of the fantastic, McCarthy does not develop this opposition so much as he insinuates it, a rhetorical hit-and-run exercise. Rather than focus his audience's attention on contradictions that might explode under scrutiny, McCarthy adumbrates the tension through something like what Black (1970) referred to as "stylistic tokens" (p. 112). Black's "sometimes modest tokens" act as cues for auditors, "cues that tell them how they are to view the world, even beyond the expressed concerns, the overt propositional sense, of the discourse" (p. 113). Unlike Black's tokens, but completely congruous with the interpretation of McCarthy presented here, McCarthy's tokens are remarkably non-ideological, in part because they lack consistency among themselves. They act to tell the auditor how he/she is to view the word, the message itself, and the instructions are contradictory: we are to believe despite the incredibility of the evidence.

Against the incredible, McCarthy pitted the completely secular epistemology of his time, the objective, the verifiable, the political equivalent of scientific facts: "I have in my hand" (McC, p. 12), "The file shows" (p. 18), "I have here several documents" (p. 66), "I have a copy of it in my hand" (p. 86), "I have a photostat of the letter" (p. 104), "I have before me an affidavit" (p. 105), "I now hold in my hand two photostats" (p. 111), "I have before me a copy" (p. 155), "Mr. President, I have a file which I desire to insert in the Record today, containing photostats" (p. 175), "Here are photostats of official letterheads" (p. 324), "I have complete unchallengeable documentation" (McCarthy, 1952, Oct. 28, p. 26), "I hold in my hand the official record" (McCarthy, 1952, Oct. 28, p. 26); these are the phrases McCarthy used throughout his speeches to create a reality credible enough to balance his claims on the marvelous.

Baskerville (1954) termed McCarthy a "brief-case demagogue." The ever-present, overstuffed briefcase was a repository of the objective, the facts, photostatic reproductions, the record. Richard Rovere (1959/1960) saw in it McCarthy's desire to have "the dust of the archives clinging to him" (p. 168). The briefcase was external to McCarthy; it was not subjective. McCarthy only produced the evidence and invited the audience to share in his incredulity. McCarthy's speeches in the Senate are an endless request for unanimous consent to have articles, letters, memoranda, and other materials printed in the Congressional Record. *McCarthyism: The Fight for America* is similarly filled with photographs, photostatic copies of documents, letters, and articles, and appeals to published testimony by other sources, in other words, the public record. In the Army-McCarthy hearings, two of the most dramatic confrontations occur over a cropped photograph and a document, purportedly a carbon copy of a letter from J. Edgar Hoover, that Army counsel Joseph Welch derided as "a copy of precisely nothing,"[14] thus exacerbating the sense of unreality.

McCarthy's heavy dependence on documentation was, in a sense, crippling; it betrayed his own doubts about the colorability of the picture he presented to his audiences and made judgment impossible. There is no affirmation in McCarthy's discourse, only hesitation. As Jackson (1981) has put it:

> By foregrounding its own signifying practice, the fantastic begins to betray its version of the 'real' as a relative one, which can only deform and transform experience, so the 'real' is exposed as a category, as something articulated by and constructed through the literary or artistic text. (p. 84)

In a similar vein, Rabkin (1976) notes: "In the transcendent reality of the fiction, the fictional becomes real; and then we are reminded that the real is itself fictional. This self-reflection is fantastic" (p. 166). The effect is circular and inescapable. A dialectic is created in which each element undermines the other[,] making the synthesis absurd. Every time he presented evidence, McCarthy, with equal vigor, discredited it, making it impossible for his audience to decide which part of the claim to accept. In placing so much weight on evidence that he had termed questionable, McCarthy called into question, not just the particulars of his case, but the integrity of evidence itself. Like a magician exposing the pedestrian mechanics of his tricks, McCarthy suggested the illusory nature of all demonstration. McCarthy could not lead, for he had no direction, and he could not judge, for he had no standard. Joe McCarthy was not part of the sacred; he was not a transcendent being who bore supernal truths; he was just Joe, a skunk hunter from a small farm community in the Midwest, and he was just as amazed as the rest of us.

By creating, but not resolving, a tension between the uncanny and the marvelous, the real and the incredible, McCarthy subverted his own efforts at persuasion, but his Faustian exchange also broached untold possibilities. By implicitly denying the compelling power of his evidence, he called into question its theoretical basis. "Presenting that which cannot be, but is, fantasy exposes a culture's definitions of that which can be: it traces the limits of its epistemological and ontological frame," writes Jackson (1981, p. 23). This is the significance of McCarthy's posture— "Inconceivable? Yes. But it is true" (McC, p. 316). Unhampered by the laws of the everyday world, McCarthy was free to take his audience into a world in which unpleasant judgment could be withheld indefinitely (see Jackson, 1981, p. 34;

Todorov, 1975, p. 25). As Rabkin (1976) puts it: "This function of the fantastic is educational in the root sense: . . . it creates in the mind a diametric reversal and opens up new and fantastic worlds" (p. 25). Americans were not looking for a Father Paneloux to tell them that their sinfulness was responsible for the sorry state of the world, but a Father Paneloux who could hold marvelous evil forces in a balance with our culpability, commanding our assent to neither; this Father Paneloux had promise for America in the Fifties.

The world McCarthy fashioned was a dark world where things were not always what they seemed to be, a world where evil forces worked behind a veil of secrecy:

> How can we account for our present situation unless we believe that men high in this Government are concerting to deliver us to disaster? This must be the product of a great conspiracy, a conspiracy on a scale so immense as to dwarf any previous such venture in the history of man. A conspiracy of infamy so black that, when it is finally exposed, its principals shall be forever deserving of the maledictions of all honest men. (McC, p. 305, cf. p. 215)

Reflecting the hyperbolic tendencies of the fantastic, the conspiracy McCarthy described was of superhuman, supernatural proportions (on the hyperbolic in fantasy, see Todorov, 1975, pp. 77–82, 93). Populated with evil geniuses and sinister cabalists in unholy alliance, parading as newspapermen, honored Generals, Secretaries of State, and Presidents, all meeting in richly paneled but outwardly innocent looking barns, pouring over secret documents, engaged in secret plots involving spies, espionage, and infiltration, with the ultimate aim of destroying Western civilization, McCarthy's world had a nightmarish quality. McCarthy talked of "hidden and undisclosed forces," "dark forces," "chicanery," the "mysterious" disappearance of incriminating documents; secret contracts, and secret trials, and secret parleys; "treachery," and "lies."[15]

Metaphorically, McCarthy introduced octopi, snakes, and spiders into his dream: the hoax being perpetrated was "monstrous" (McC, p. 290); "the Communist party—a relatively small group of deadly conspirators—has now extended its tentacles to that most respected of American bodies, the United States Senate" (p. 297); a "world-wide web" of conspiracy has been spun from Moscow (p. 307); Drew Pearson and fellow travelers were "venomous" (p. 288); "the Truman Democratic Administration was crawling with Communists" (p. 218); Dean Acheson was "elegant" and "alien" (McCarthy, 1953, Nov. 25, p. 5; 1954, Nov. 10, p. 18). Homosexuals, too, figured prominently in this fantastic world, yet another threatening sign of the perversion of the rules of everyday life.[16]

Even more threatening than the ability of the enemy to assume malevolent forms was its ability to assume no form at all, to become invisible: "One knows that traitors are at work. One sees the political fingerprints of the Communists on every document drafted. One can see the footprints of Communist betrayals down every path they travel" (McC, p. 189; cf. Edelman, 1977, p. 34). In a metaphor that might have recalled the contemporaneous film *The Invisible Man,* McCarthy claims to see the signs of Communist presence, but not the Communists themselves.

McCarthy dwells on the unseen, on darkness, on things that are done in the night. In a discussion of rhetorical uses of archetypal metaphor, Osborn (1972, pp. 240–241) finds that darkness brings

> fear of the unknown, discouraging sight, making one ignorant of his environment—vulnerable to its dangers and blind to its rewards. One is

reduced to a helpless state, no long able to control the world about him. Finally, darkness is cold, suggesting stagnation and thoughts of the grave.[17]

What Osborn describes is remarkably similar to our description of the sense of chaos in the Fifties and is an apt characterization of the darkness metaphor as it is used by McCarthy: Sleep is no personal indulgence, but something induced by evil forces so that they might do their work undetected. McCarthy suggested that the American people had been given sleeping tablets by the President and the State Department in order to lull them into a false sense of security (McCarthy, 1952, p. 59; see also McC, pp. 204, 302) and that Truman was persuaded to fire MacArthur "in the dead, vast, and middle of the night" (McC, p. 216). "I awake each morning in the fear that overnight, in some secret chamber of the United Nations, the enemies of the United States, with Britain and India at their head, have made a secret deal—a new Yalta" (McC, p. 303).

As nocturnal creatures, McCarthy's enemies have an implicit association with witches, vampires, bats, rats, and wolves. "The enemies of our civilization, whether alien or native, whether of high or low degree, work in the dark," he warned. "They are that way more effective" (McC, p. 307). "The pattern of Communist conquest has been the same in every country over which the stygian blackness of Communist night has descended" (McCarthy, 1953, Nov. 25, p. 5). It is McCarthy's expressed intention to expose the Communists, to subject them to the searching light of truth, but they are powerful and his success is not guaranteed:

> If, after all is said and done, this unholy alliance should have its way, then I propose the premise that holds it together—that vigorous anti-communism is more dangerous than communism—as a fitting epitaph on the grave of American civilization. (McCarthy, 1954, Sept. 1, p. 14; see also McCarthy, 1952, pp. vii, 101; 1953, Dec. 4, p. 2:6; 1954, Nov. 10, p. 18)

In allowing for the possible death of our civilization, McCarthy reflects a theology of apocalyptic that was given a sophisticated treatment during this era in works like Reinhold Niebuhr's *Children of Light, Children of Darkness*. McCarthy reduces the Manichean tendency expressed in Niebuhr's title to its logical extreme. In his famous speech at Wheeling, West Virginia, he drew the lines of battle: "Today we are engaged in a final, all-out battle between communistic atheism and Christianity. The modern champions of communism have selected this as the time. And, ladies and gentlemen, the chips are down—they are truly down" (McC, p. 8). Two years later in another famous speech wherein he accused Adlai Stevenson of aiding the Communist cause, McCarthy said:

> We are at war tonight—a war which started decades ago, a war which we did not start, a war which we cannot stop except by either victory or death. The Korean war is only one phase of this war between international atheistic communism and our free civilization. (McCarthy, 1952, Oct. 28, p. 26)

The earthly war in Korea was insignificant; it was merely a symptom of the all-consuming cosmic war that would determine our fate. Human history is inadequate to contain forces of this magnitude. In 1954, just before his censure by the Senate, McCarthy (1954, Dec. 8) sang the same refrain: "At the risk of boring you with some repetition, I repeat, the world is in an ideological struggle, and we are on one side and the Iron Curtain countries are on the other" (p. 10). From the time he took up the anti-Communist cause until the virtual end of his career, McCarthy consistently warned of the imminence of the Armageddon.

The scale of McCarthy's war is matched by the power of his warriors. The world of the fantastic is a completely determined world; happenstance is abolished; the regnant powers control events to the most minute detail. Todorov (1975) calls it "pan-determinism": "everything," he writes, "down to the encounter of various causal series (or 'chance') must have its cause, in the full sense of the word, even if this cause can only be of a supernatural order" (p. 110). The obvious language for the expression of such power is the language of conspiracy. Conspiracies are not accidental; they are, literally, "a breathing together;" they are contrived. As McCarthy expressed it:

> The people, Mr. President, recognize the weakness with which the administration has replaced what was so recently our great strength. They are troubled by it. And they do not think it accidental. They do not believe that the decline in our strength from 1945 to 1951 just happened. They are coming to believe that it was brought about, step by step, by will and intention. They are beginning to believe that the surrender of China to Russia, the administration's indecently hasty desire to turn Formosa over to the enemy and arrive at a ceasefire in Korea instead of following the manly, American course prescribed by MacArthur, point to something more than ineptitude and folly. (McC, p. 305; see also McCarthy, 1954, Dec. 8, p. 10; 1954, Nov. 10, p. 18; 1953, Nov. 25, p. 5.)[18]

Accidents have no meaning. This is the source of the futility in every mother's "Why did you do that?" applied to a glass of spilled milk. It was an accident, a product, not of "will and intention" but of precisely the opposite, thoughtlessness and gravity; it was innocent. In this brief quotation, McCarthy attempts to remove certain events from the realm of the accidental (or incidental) and to place them in the context of a series of events progressing "step by step" to form a plot. There is an implication of motive and pattern behind what seeks to pass as "ineptitude and folly."

A tandem concept to pan-determinism in the fantastic is "pan-signification" (Todorov, 1975, p. 112). The world of the fantastic is a highly structured drama; every event contributes to the advancement of the plot. Pan-signification allows for (in McCarthy's case, calls for) the identification of causal agents and elements. The knowledge that all events are significant calls for constant watchfulness in the hope that the future may be foreseen and perhaps altered. In apocalyptic versions of the fantastic, all events are filled with foreshadowings of the end, all of which must be attended to and interpreted. McCarthy's world exhibits just such a logic; it is a world groaning with meaning. The idea of the innocuous and inconsequential is recognized only as camouflage: "At first blush the policy as set forth in the above document would appear disorganized and without clear point. It was not pointless, however. Those who drafted it understood very clearly the over-all plan being advanced" (McC, p. 260). "You need not seek far to find the real reason lurking behind this avowed one" (McC, p. 295). Pan-signification is the continuing testimony to the awesome powers at work in the world of the fantastic. To exercise such control that every action infallibly works toward a predetermined end with no extraneous or superfluous activity is precision on a terrifying scale:

> To fit this incident into the global picture, let me remind you, these prisoners have been held by the Chinese for two years, so their selection of a

time of announcement was, of course, a deliberate act. In fact, we have—we find little evidence in all of the actions of the Communist states that indicates any haphazard actions on their part. Everything they do is deliberate and well-thought out. (McCarthy, 1954, Dec. 8, p. 10)[19]

Only a superhuman intelligence could achieve the levels of determinism and signification evident in the fantastic, thus the "evil genius" theme so prominent in McCarthy's rhetoric.[20] Evil genius—"twisted-thinking intellectuals" (McC, p. 36)—has the power not only to execute its designs, its "blueprint for disaster," (McC, p. 159) but also the power to conceal its design by corrupting the judgment of the American people, tricking them into believing false interpretations of traitorous objectives (for examples of this theme, see McC, pp. 204, 208, 253, 254, 267, 292, 293, 302, 305, 333). The power of evil is often portrayed as that of the seductress exercising hypnosis or enchantment, casting spells that cause us to act, not in accordance with our own will, but not in accordance with the good either. Evil has both the power to conceal its influence and to parade as the good. It is this powerful evil that McCarthy presented to his audiences. McCarthy talks of Alger Hiss exercising a "Svengali-like influence over Secretary of State Stettinius" at Yalta (McC, p. 190) and of Marshall and Acheson having a "hypnotic influence over Truman" (McC, p. 285). "I regard as the most disturbing phenomenon in America today the fact that so many Americans still refuse to acknowledge the ability of Communists to persuade loyal Americans to do their work for them" (McCarthy, 1954, Nov. 10, p. 18). The American people must be alerted to the fact "that this vast conspiracy possesses the power to turn their most trusted servants into its attorneys-in-fact" (McCarthy, 1954, Nov. 10, p. 18). "It is," said McCarthy, "the clandestine enemy which taxes our ingenuity" (McC, 307).

McCarthy presented America with Tamino's choice and no clear criteria by which to make it. Sometimes he appeared to offer the lifeline of "just good, everyday American horse sense" (McC, p. 113; see also p. 153). For example, when identifying Communists, he simply looked for people and policies that reflected the Communist party line "right down to the dotting of every 'i' and the crossing of every 't'" (McC, 112; see also, p. 134): "As one of my farmer friends once said, if a fowl looks like a duck and quacks like a duck and eats like a duck we can assume it is a duck." (McC, p. 46) Such confidence in appearances, however, was undermined by those like ex-Communist and professional government witness Louis Budenz in his testimony on Owen Lattimore. In a performance that would have made Lewis Carroll proud, Budenz refused to assent to any stable criteria:

> Wasn't it true, asked Morgan, that Lattimore's Solution in Asia had been condemned by the *Daily Worker*? Yes, Budenz replied, but the Party often protected its members by criticizing them, 'that is to say, that is, to damn them with faint praise—rather, to praise them with faint damns, is the way I want to put it.' And hadn't Lattimore publicly opposed the Soviet invasion of Finland? True enough, said Budenz, but Party members were sometimes given 'exemptions' in order to disguise their real purpose.[21] (Oshinsky, 1983, p. 151)

In another case, a math teacher from the Bronx High School of Science, a native of Czechoslovakia, was called before McCarthy's committee for his part in a Voice of America broadcast given in his native tongue. Toward the end of the hearing, McCarthy admitted that the committee knew that there was no Communist propaganda in the broadcast, and the question was raised as to why Dr. Hlavaty had been called before the committee at all. It was McCarthy's special assistant, Roy Cohn, who attempted to provide reason for the proceedings by asking Hlavaty whether there had been anything anti-Communist in the broadcast. Hlavaty was left to confess to a sin of omission (Stone, 1963, p. 37). Cohn's question turned what appeared to be a praiseworthy act of patriotic voluntarism into a subject of suspicion.

In the world of the fantastic, it is not obvious what things mean; the rules have been subverted and cannot be depended on, and the problem is not innocent lack of clarity, but, as pan-signification would suggest, systematic distortion, the insidious parading of the significant as insignificant. McCarthy, his appeals to common sense not withstanding, understood this. He understood that he could not merely show, he had to interpret: "Do Senators follow me?" "Do Senators follow this?" "Do Senators get the picture?" he queried again and again (McC, pp. 18, 50, 74). "I wonder whether Senators get the awfulness of that picture" (p. 236). "Now what does this mean, my good friends, what does this mean to the 150,000,000 American people?" he asked his television audience (McCarthy, 1952, Oct. 25, p. 26). "I digress to explain the significance of that utterance" (McC, p. 259). "In order to recognize the significance of these two documents, it might be well for me to digress for a minute" (p. 111). "In other words . . . ." (p. 251). In other words, the documents that he held in his hand were not enough; they did not carry their own self-evident meaning. Sometimes they required translation; their veil of innocence had to be stripped away. After presenting a quotation that indicated that General Stilwell, Secretary of State Marshall's choice to command the U.S. Army in China, did not like Chinese officialdom but had a great regard for the Chinese people, McCarthy offered the following interpretation:

> As we all know, "people" in Communist parlance has a special meaning. It does not mean all the people in our sense. It is a catchword, an occult word, clear to the initiates, meaning Communists. They use it in a special sense to designate all their political organs. We all recall the various people's fronts organized to promote the Communist cause throughout the world. More specifically the Chinese Communist army was referred to in Communist parlance as the people's army. (McC, p. 253; see also McCarthy, 1952, p. 86, where McCarthy translates the phrase "progressive persons.")

"People" is one of the most generic and colorless terms available to denote an aggregate of human beings. McCarthy recognizes this when he contrasts the Communist "special meaning" of the term with "our sense," innocent and inclusive. The Communist "people," according to McCarthy, who freights the usage in this context with sinister implications, is only a ruse, an attempt to escape notice. The achievement of discerning a particular signification is secondary to the achievement of recognizing that there is significance to be discerned.

McCarthy's struggle to separate the significant from the insignificant is unremitting; figure-ground discriminations are not clearing the dark world of the fantastic: "Note those words, Mr. President." "Mr. President, listen to this." "I call the Senate's attention to this statement—" "Listen to this if you will" (McC, pp. 92, 144, 151, 176). In a complex, relativistic world, all events require interpretation; nothing is unworthy of our attention.

We have concentrated on how McCarthy used his evidence to create tensions between belief and doubt in his audiences, but all of McCarthy's evidence would never have been given a forum had it not been for the power of his office. There is no doubting that much of the credence given McCarthy's claims resulted from his status as a United States senator. As Oshinsky (1983, p. 112) has phrased the question that had to be raised by McCarthy's charges: "Would a United States senator go this far out on a limb without hard evidence?" Millard Tydings knew very well that, as a senator, McCarthy was more likely to be believed than someone standing "on the corner of 9th and G streets who is carrying on a casual conversation" (quoted in Oshinsky, 1983, p. 170), and Walter Lippman recognized the power of the office when he argued that McCarthy's charges, because he was a senator, were news and had to be treated as such, however reluctantly. McCarthy could not be suppressed by the media (Oshinsky, 1983, p. 187).[22]

Though the institutions of the media could not, without the benison of the Senate, themselves author McCarthy's undoing, the representational power of the media, especially television, did serve a critical enabling function when the Senate finally decided that McCarthy had overstepped the bounds of allowable conduct. And it is consistent with the thesis argued here that, in the instances where the media authored its own scripts, some of the most influential among them employed an ironic mode (Rosteck, 1989). Irony forgoes the head-on attack and unsettles its object indirectly. There is a sense in which, just as the fantastic simultaneously demands our assent and dismisses such a demand, irony also mounts its criticism and is able to retreat to a posture of "all in fun" or of having been misread. About satire, the close relative of irony, Rabkin (1976) writes:

> Satire is inherently fantastic. Not only does it depend on narrative worlds that reverse the perspectives of the world outside the narrative, but the style usually depends on irony, "stating the reverse of the truth as though it were clear truth." (p. 146 quoting Highet, 1962, p. 61.)

Even television, though, had to await a certain revocation of sanctuary before it could exercise its power against Wisconsin's junior Senator. As a Senator, McCarthy spoke from the temple and was provided, not only the protection of Congressional immunity, but even a certain amount of support in the reluctance of the Senate to disavow one of its own. Republicans, in fact, were eager to use McCarthy in the pursuit of their own political ends, so McCarthy received the blessing of the Tafts, the Lodges, and the McCarrans.[23]

Nowhere is McCarthy's dependence on the positive sanction of the Senate clearer than in the course of his career after his censure in 1954. The censure, although it did not materially affect McCarthy's standing in the Senate, did serve notice that he no longer participated in the collective ethos of that body. It had been admitted that McCarthy had said discreditable things, and in doing so, the spell of the fantastic was broken. Alice awoke from the dream, dismissing the court as nothing but a pack of cards, and was left with only reflections on the uncanny. Because McCarthy had built his case on the collective ethos of the Senate, he had tacitly ceded to it the effective power to discredit him as a part of itself. The effect of the censure on the press and the public was immediate and unmistakable; it was no longer necessary to pay attention to Senator McCarthy (Oshinsky, 1983, pp. 495*ff.*, Reeves, 1982, pp. 665*ff.*, Rovere, 1959/1960, pp. 232*ff.*).[24]

Joe McCarthy had an unfailing sense of the epistemological crisis of the Fifties with its "key terms": "irony, paradox, ambiguity, and complexity" (Bell, 1962, p. 300), and he exploited that understanding ruthlessly. McCarthy experienced the crisis as a participant; he did not comprehend it. His discourse does not indicate that he ever transcended it; his audience was not the prophetic "you" but the inclusive "we." Within that crisis, McCarthy struck a delicate balance that avoided judgment. As frightening as chaos was, it seems that it may have been preferable to the terrible truths that threatened America after the Second World War. By offering a discourse that did not command assent, McCarthy allowed America to contemplate some of its most dreadful monsters at a distance. The delicate equilibrium that McCarthy maintained for almost four years was wrecked when the hierarchical power bestowed on him by his seat in the Senate was symbolically revoked; the scale fell abruptly on the side of the uncanny, and we were left to wonder at how bizarre it all had been.

EVALUATING THE DREAM: JOE McCARTHY'S LINGERING SHADOW

McCarthyism has been termed a national nightmare. By taking the metaphor literally, we are in a position to understand some of the contradictions that still occupy the attentions of McCarthy's biographers, students of McCarthyism, and historians of the period. The underlying debate in all of the biographical works on McCarthy devolves on the question of sincerity, and it calls for ethical criticism in the most fundamental sense of the word, criticism of an ethos, a criticism that the rhetorical critic is particularly suited to provide.[25]

Beginning with Rovere's (1959/1960) biography at the end of the McCarthy decade, and continuing through Oshinsky's biography published in 1983, everyone who has focused on the man has felt compelled to look at the sources of McCarthy's anti-Communism: a series of conflicting impressions regarding the sometimes playful attitude he took toward his crusade in private, his apparent lack of passionate involvement with the topic, an obvious childish delight in playing spy games, and his nonchalant attitude toward particular cases; his documented fondness for lying; his statement to Jack Anderson that this was the real thing; and his willingness to endure censure rather than back down.[26] Much of the evidence divides along lines of a Jekyll-and-Hyde public presentation versus private behavior; McCarthy's willingness to excoriate a political opponent or a member of the press for the crowd and then to turn and throw a friendly arm around his victim is a source of constant perplexity to his chroniclers (see Griffith, 1970, p. 14; Oshinsky, 1983, pp. 14–15; Rovere, 1959/1960, pp. 54–55).

To find conflict in these apparent oppositions is to assume a stable set of rules. The fantastic has no such rules; it is, writes Jackson (1981), "founded on contradictions" (p. 21). And not just a single set of contradictions, but "the continuing diametric reversal of the ground rules within a narrative world" (Rabkin, 1976, p. 73). The fantastic embraces both fear of the demonic and a sense of play. The fantastic cannot find stable reference points or the moment of hesitation is lost, and it is no longer fantastic. McCarthy's failure to display a commitment to his individual cases may not have been an effective method of exposing Communists, but it was sublimely effective in prolonging the moment of hesitation. Finally, having sundered all other unities, all other sources of stability, the fantastic shatters the unity of the individual (Jackson, 1981, pp. 83–84). In a reversal of the apocalyptist's pseudonymity, McCarthy went beyond the bounds of ghostwriting to appropriate materials that were never intended for his use. "America's Retreat from Victory" (see note 13), a long speech presented to the Senate by McCarthy and generally devoted to discrediting Gen. George Marshall, is the most prominent example. Only its general themes are McCarthy's; the substantive language, the argumentative structure, and the examples are clearly the invention of someone else. McCarthy did not digest the materials provided by others and make them his own; he simply gave them voice. "McCarthyism" absorbed the identity of Joe McCarthy into the much larger phenomenon he represented.

The fantastic often signals the dissolution of identity with a narrative voice confused between first and third person singular (Jackson, 1981, pp. 30–31). McCarthy reveals the same split persona in his speeches and writings. McCarthy tells his audience: "The smear attacks on *McCarthy* are no longer being made with the hope that they can thereby force *me* to give up this fight to expose and get Communists out of government." "On that day the President of the Newspaper Guild, Harry Martin, attacked *McCarthy* and made it clear to the membership that any favorable coverage of *my* fight against Communists was taboo" (McCarthy, 1952, pp. 86, 90, emphasis added). "Even *my* bitterest enemy will admit, if he is honest, that these matters would not have been given a second thought if someone other than *McCarthy* were involved" (McCarthy, 1954, Nov. 10, p. 18, emphasis added).[27]

Does this leave us with anything to say about the McCarthy ethos, fragmented and disjointed as it is? Certainly we can say that McCarthy was no prophet: He was guided by no self-evident truths, no sacred canon, he did not offer judgment in time of crisis; all his cries of "smear" notwithstanding, the evidence overwhelmingly indicates that McCarthy did not suffer the burden of his commitments (at least not until after censure) but reaped the personal rewards of his message—notoriety, money, and political power. Nor did McCarthy confront his society with a radical position, for the fantastic cannot posit; it can only hold us in breathless hesitation. What was mistaken for radicalism by some of McCarthy's contemporaries was really just the hyperbolic, irrational discourse of the fantastic parading as politics. We can go further and suggest that, to the extent McCarthy made certain claims to prophecy, his opening statement before the Watkins Committee being perhaps the premier example,[28] he was a false prophet. Rovere (1959/1960) has written:

> McCarthy, though a demon himself, was not a man possessed by demons. His talents as a demagogue were great, but he lacked the most necessary and awesome of demagogic gifts—a belief in the sacredness of his own mission. A man may go a long way in politics—particularly in democratic politics— without much in the way of convictions, but to overcome adversity he needs the strength that can be drawn either from belief in an idea or from a sense of his own righteousness. If he has no convictions, he can scarcely draw courage from them. (p. 253)

Nor, we would add, was McCarthy possessed of gods. McCarthy the man, we must probably conclude, was a tragic figure. He participated in the epistemological chaos of his time to the point of psychosis.[29] The swaggering, loutish Marine hero was a cripple, and we watched him toss away his crutches in an evangelical fever and fall on his face—pitiable and for that reason all the more despicable. McCarthy never assumed a radical heroic stand against the overwhelming uncertainties of his day; his faith lacked the necessary substance. The notable absence of historical references in his speeches reveals the shallowness of McCarthy's response to the world. He had nothing to draw upon but the resources of his own profane experience. McCarthy could worship nothing larger than himself, only fear it.

McCarthy's fantastic world was his poor response to fear, and it is only when we recognize the fantastic as a form of spiritual impoverishment that we can properly evaluate what McCarthy wrought. Building her case on the work of Sartre, Foucault, and Jameson, Jackson finds in the fantastic human compensation for a failure of the transcendent. She quotes Levy's assertion that "the fantastic is a compensation that man provides for himself, at the level of imagination, for what he has lost at the level of faith" (Jackson, 1981, p. 18). The compensation that man can provide for himself, however, is insufficient to replace what has been lost, for as we have seen, the fantastic is hollow at its core:

> Unlike marvelous secondary worlds, which construct alternative realities, the shady worlds of the fantastic construct nothing. They are empty, emptying, dissolving. Their emptiness vitiates a full, rounded, three-dimensional visible world, by tracing in absences, shadows without objects. Far from fulfilling desire, these spaces perpetuate desire by insisting upon absence, lack, the non-seen, the unseeable. (Jackson, 1981, p. 45)

What McCarthy presented America in the Fifties was just such a world. In emphasizing the darkness of the post-war world, McCarthy concentrated on what was unseeable and thereby unknowable. His promises notwithstanding, he never turned on the light; rather he insinuated the lurking presence of "things that go bump in the night." There is no salvation here, only the articulation of anxiety.

Had McCarthy been alone in his disquiet and alienation, his case would be uninteresting, an example of personal psychopathology. But behind McCarthy's rhetoric is what Miller (1984) calls a "social motive," an exigence, "a set of particular social patterns and expectations that provides a socially objectified motive for addressing danger, ignorance, separateness. It is an understanding of social need in which I know how to take an interest, in which one can intend to participate" (p. 158). The problem with the patterns and expectations that constitute the fantastic, however, is that the participation is given no direction. The moments of insight are so fleeting and subject to contradiction as to not be insights at all. To an age increasingly suspicious of the bases of belief, McCarthy provided sustained doubt. The genre of the fantastic provides the sound and fury of political activity while, in fact, signifying nothing.

For a time in the Fifties, America played Joseph K. at Joe McCarthy's court. Like the man in the enigmatic parable at the end of Kafka's *The Trial*, we sat outside and waited for the law. We wanted McCarthy to execute judgment, to banish our demons, to provide us with a vision, a standard under which to march, and an enemy to march against; but McCarthy did not slay Ra'hab, the dragon of chaos, he only goaded it. We were left without gods or devils, heroes or villains, only the haunting suspicion that both existed. No clear, stable dramatic structure emerged, and the rules for judgment were systematically subverted. As soon as the show was over, the audience, as an audience, largely disintegrated, the residuum remaking itself on the edges of the politics of the 1960s as the John Birch Society. Only the McCarthy persona survives, precisely because of its insubstantiality, a ghost lurking about the dark places of American politics.

ENDNOTES

[1]Our most recent and visible example was when candidate for Secretary of Defense, Bobby Inman, removing himself from consideration for the position, accused members of the media of waging a McCarthyite campaign to discredit him. Several years ago, when Marxist scholar Barbara C. Foley was denied tenure at Northwestern University for her

role in interrupting the speech of a Nicaraguan rebel leader and other political activities, she accused the university of "McCarthyism" ("Teacher Accuses Northwestern U.," 1986).

[2]On Denton, see Henry, 1981, p. 20. Henry notes: "Some critics have begun to compare Denton to that ultimate American witch-hunter, the late Joe McCarthy." On the Reagan administration's liberal use of the McCarran-Walter act in denying visas to writers and scholars applying to visit and speak in the United States, see in particular the excerpt from Arthur Miller's speech "The Interrogation of Angel Rama" (Miller, 1984, July). Miller's speech was delivered at a program on "Forbidden Writers" sponsored by PEN American Center and Fund for Free Expression, April 30, 1984. See also Woodstock's (1984) account of how he was ruled "inadmissible to the United States of America" in December of 1983 because of activities in which he was engaged in the Thirties and Forties.

[3]In addition to the examples cited above, see Arthur L. Linman's protest of a characterization of his role as special counsel to the U.S. Senate select committee on the Iran-contra affair. (Linman, 1988, p. 7). Said (1983), refuting a charge in the *New Republic* that he was "an intellectual in the thrall of Soviet totalitarianism" calls it "a claim that is as disgustingly McCarthyite as it is intellectually fraudulent" (p. 26).

[4]In the past 15 years, two new biographies (Oshinsky, 1983; Reeves, 1982), one book-length study of McCarthy's relationship with the press (Bayley, 1981), one history of the "McCarthy era" (Fried, 1990), and a book-length study of McCarthy's impact on the academic community have been published (Schrecker, 1986). An underlying argument in all of the book-length studies (except Fried's and Schrecker's where McCarthy the man becomes eclipsed by the-ism) centers on the question of McCarthy's sincerity.

[5]Fantasy theme analysts (Bormann, 1972) and followers of Nimmo and Combs (1983) have in common the idea of fantasy as something constitutive, something capable of defining a group or a public. Such a conception stands in stark contrast to the epistemological recalcitrance of literary notions of those fantastic. Nimmo and Combs further confuse fantasy with melodrama, which is, in fact, a political and constitutive moral genre.

[6]Rabkin (1976), though he claims to be in "serious disagreement" with Todorov (1975) "in many regards" nonetheless notes how Todorov's work complements his own, especially in viewing the epistemological status of what is presented in the fantastic as liberating because unstable. For Rabkin, the essence of the fantastic is "the continuing diametric reversal of the ground within a narrative world" (pp. 118, 73; see also pp. 4, 8,12, [1]4, 28, 41, 120, 213).

[7]The move here may be seen to have some kinship with Browne's study of the implications for action when the literary genre of the pastoral is applied to politics (Browne, 1990, pp. 46–57).

[8]I. F. Stone has titled the volume of his "nonconformist history of our times" devoted to the Fifties *The Haunted Fifties: 1953–1963*. Recent less partisan academic works tend to corroborate Stone's assessment. Among them are Miller and Nowak (1977), Carter (1983), Coontz (1992), and Oakley (1986).

[9]In 1950, 73% expressed the opinion that, in the event of another world war, U.S. cities would be bombed. (Gallup, 1972, vol. 2, p. 916).

[10]Bell (1962, p. 120) mentions the tendency of Americans to view foreign policy in moral terms and some of the implications of this tendency in the Fifties.

[11]Schlesinger (1949) explains the "vogue of existentialism" in terms of our anxieties (p. 52) and finds in Durkheim's "anomie" "a state of social purgatory" (p. 243). Goldman (1960) paints a vivid picture of the anxieties of the age.

[12]For other examples of McCarthy's confrontation with the "fantastic," see McC, pp. 255, 257, 258, 273, 284, 316; "The Great Betrayal," delivered to the Republican National Convention, Chicago, IL, July 9, 1952, reprinted in Wrage and Baskerville (1962, p. 297).

[13]This speech, "America's Retreat from Victory," is an important one in McCarthy's career. It is agreed that McCarthy was not the principal author, yet the speech reflects his point of view and is embellished with enough pure McCarthy as to become his own. In addition to reprinting this speech in the volume *Major Speeches* (n.d.), McCarthy also had a version printed as a separate volume published by Devin-Adair, the publishers of *McCarthyism: The Fight for America* (McCarthy, 1952). The Devin-Adair version of the speech went through at least five printings and was in print from 1951 to 1962. According to Robert Welch, the John Birch Society was also responsible for publishing an edition of this speech (see McCarthy 1951). Sometime after 1979, the Senator Joseph R. McCarthy Educational Foundation, Inc. of Milwaukee, WI, published another reprint edition. Except for Foundation President Thomas J. Bergen's "Updated Memoranda," which serves as preface to this edition, there are no publication data.

[14]Both of these incidents are included in Emile de Antonio's (1964) film of selections from the Army-McCarthy hearings, *Point of Order.*

[15]For a sampling of these themes, see: McCarthy, 1952, pp. vii, 2, 3, 5, 7, 8, 31, 39, 46, 47, 48, 54, 61, 75, 81, 82, 85, 91, 92, 99; McC, pp. 8, 50, 121, 125, 142, 159, 160, 175, 189, 192, 204, 216, 217, 231, 242, 264, 277, 285, 333. See also: McCarthy, 1954, Sept. 1, p. 14; McCarthy, 1954, Nov. 10, p. 18; McCarthy, 1952, Oct. 28, p. 26.

[16]For McCarthy on "perverts," see, for example: McC, p. 22; McC, 1952, pp. 14–15. For the relationship of homosexual themes and the fantastic, see Todorov, 1975, pp. 131–132. For the fear of homosexuality in the Fifties and McCarthy's association of them with those in the State Department who practice diplomacy with perfumed handkerchiefs, see Riesman and Glazer (1964), "The Intellectuals and the Discontented Classes (1955)," p. 119.

[17]On the importance of the vision and darkness metaphors to fantasy, see Todorov (1975, esp. 120–123); Jackson (1981) writes: Uncertainty and impossibility are inscribed on a structural level through hesitation and equivocation, and on a thematic level through images of formlessness, emptiness and invisibility. That which is not seen, that which is not said, is not 'known' and it remains as a threat, as a dark area from which any object or figure can enter at any time. The relation of the individual subject to the world, to others, to objects, ceases to be known or safe, and problems of apprehension (in the double sense of perceiving and of fearing) become central to the modern fantastic. (p. 49)

[18]To dismiss accident, folly, or naivete as a cause of action in favor of malign deliberation and plotting is a favorite McCarthy refrain (see McC, pp. 216, 219, 251, 290, 307). A repeated McCarthy argument is that if incompetence or accident were responsible for our dire state, probability would dictate that some of the errors would have been to our advantage, while in fact their alarming consistency reveals a sinister design. "If Marshall were merely stupid, the laws of probability would dictate that part of his decisions would serve this country's interest" (McC, p. 307; see also pp. 194f, 203; McCarthy, 1952, p. 47).

[19]In the text of McCarthy's (1954, Nov. 10) speech for delivery in the censure debate as it was published by the *New York Times,* there is a long section built around anaphora and antithesis that follows this general pattern: "It is not significant that the Communists . . . . But it is frighteningly significant that they have succeeded . . . ." (p. 18).

[20]For example, see the chapter "The Evil Genius," in McCarthy, 1952, pp. 99–100. Owen Lattimore and others are dangerous precisely because they are brilliant. See, for example, McC, pp. 85–86, 235, 264.

[21]For a similar statement by McCarthy, see McCarthy, 1952, p. 89. Referring to the Madison, Wisconsin *Capital Times,* a paper "consistently paralleling the editorial line of the Communist *Daily Worker,*" McCarthy says: "They, of course, criticize Communism generally to obtain a false reputation of being anti-Communist. They then go all-out to assassinate the character and destroy the reputation of anyone who tries to dig out the really dangerous undercover Communists."

[22]The prerogative of office is the great unspoken assumption in Bayley's (1981) study of McCarthy and the press. For a general summary of findings on the tendency of the mass media to represent officialdom, see Denton and Woodward, 1985, esp. p. 154.

[23]These themes are developed in all of the major sources on McCarthy. The most systematic development is in Griffith (1970).

[24]The televised Army-McCarthy hearings are widely credited with being the event which made censure possible, and even here, McCarthy's failing was a failing of credibility rather than any conclusive judgment against him, for the hearings did not provide the latter. See Hitchcock's contribution to Haberman et al., 1955, p. 14.

[25]See Black (1980, pp. 76–77) for some pertinent comments about sincerity and rhetoric. The linking of sincerity, Freud, and Sade is particularly revealing in the present context. Walter Fisher's (1984, 1985) work in narrative is interesting here for the hints it contains of a return to a classical emphasis on ethos in rhetoric. For examples of the rhetorical criticism of ethos, see Bormann, 1954; Darsey, 1988.

[26]Rovere, in an admittedly partisan but still insightful biography, was first to define the territory, and it is his work that every biographical treatment since has taken as its foil (see Bayley, 1981, esp. 36, 44, 70, 73, 74, 103, 107, 136, 137, 150, 156, 217; Griffith, 1970, esp. 16, 140, 146, 215; Oshinsky, 1983, esp. 15, 16, 18, 23, 30, 31–3, 34–5, 51, 54, 62, 65, 71, 76, 113, 138, 189, 199, 205, 506; Reeves, 1982, esp. xi, 12, 15, 17, 22, 27, 29, 31, 39, 43, 47, 51, 67, 79, 80, 103, 134, 137, 167, 196ff, 229, 235, 242, 287f, 320, 321, 327, 401, 460, 474, 478, 656, 675; Rovere, 1959/1960, esp. 71–3, 248; see also Glazer, 1973). A detailed study of the tangled web of falsification surrounding McCarthy's "Tailgunner Joe" image is O'Brien (1973).

[27]These are obvious cases where McCarthy within a sentence mixes first- and third-person self-references. In larger discourses where the narrator is "I," he will often refer to himself in the third person. For example, see McCarthy, 1952, pp. 88, 94, 95; McC, pp. 316, 317, 318. See also the Devin-Adair edition of McCarthy's (1951) *America's Retreat from Victory*. In his introduction to this volume, McCarthy refers to himself in the third person.

[28]The statement begins: "Several years ago, Mr. Chairman, I became convinced that this country and its institutions were in imminent peril of destruction by international communism." This section of the statement concludes: "Once the weakness of our security system had been brought home to me, I conceived it my duty to expend every effort of mind and body to fight subversion, to help clean traitors out of the Government. I conceived this to be my first duty to my constituents, and to my country. I still do, Mr. Chairman." (McCarthy, 1954, Sept. 1, p. 14)

[29]For evidence of McCarthy's decline even before the censure and his extreme paranoia in his last years, see both Reeves (1982) and Oshinsky (1983), especially the incident reported in Reeves, p. 586, and Oshinsky, p. 412.

REFERENCES

Aiken, H. D. (Ed.) (1956). *The age of ideology*[.] New York: New American Library.

Auden, W. H. (1969). *Collected longer poems*. New York: Random House.

Baskerville, B. (1954). Joe McCarthy, brief-case demagogue. *Today's Speech*, 2, 8–15.

Bayley, E. R. (1981). *Joe McCarthy and the press*. Madison: University of Wisconsin Press.

Bell, D. (1962). *The end of ideology: On the exhaustion of political ideas in the Fifties* (rev. ed.). New York: Free Press.

Black, E. (1970). The second persona. *Quarterly Journal of Speech*, 56, 109–119.

Black, E. (1980). The mutability of rhetoric. In E. E. White (Ed.), *Rhetoric in transition* (pp. 71–85). University Park: Penn State University Press.

Boorstin, D. J. (1970). *The decline of radicalism: Reflections on America today*. New York: Vintage.

Bormann, E. G. (1954). Huey Long: Analysis of a demagogue. *Today's Speech*, 2, 16–20.

Bormann, E. G. (1972). Fantasy and rhetorical vision: The rhetorical criticism of social reality. *Quarterly Journal of Speech, 58,* 396–407.

Boyer, P. (1985). *By the bomb's early light: American thought and culture at the dawn of the atomic age.* New York: Pantheon.

Browne, S. H. (1990). The pastoral voice in John Dickinson's first letter from a farmer in Pennsylvania. *Quarterly Journal of Speech, 76,* 46–57.

Bryant, D. C. (1937). Some problems of scope and method in rhetorical scholarship. *Quarterly Journal of Speech, 23,* 182–189.

Bryant, D. C. (1953). Rhetoric: Its functions and its scope. *Quarterly Journal of Speech, 39,* 401–424.

Bryant, D. C. (1965). Uses of rhetoric in criticism. In D. C. Bryant (Ed.), *Papers in rhetoric and poetic* (pp. 1–14). Iowa City: University of Iowa Press.

Bryant, D. C. (1966). Edmund Burke: The new images, 1966. *Quarterly Journal of Speech, 52,* 329–336.

Bryant, D. C. (1978). Literature and politics. In D. M. Burks (Ed.), *Rhetoric, philosophy, and literature: An exploration* (pp. 95–107). W. Lafayette, IN: Purdue University Press.

Camus, A. (1972). *The Plague* (S. Gilbert, Trans.). New York: Vintage.

Carter, P. A. (1983). *Another part of the Fifties.* New York: Columbia University Press.

Coontz, S. (1992). *The way we never were: American families and the nostalgia trap.* New York: Basic Books.

Darsey, J. (1988). The legend of Eugene Debs: Prophetic *ethos* as radical argument. *Quarterly Journal of Speech, 74,* 434–452.

deAntonio, E., & Talbot, D. (Producers). deAntonio, E. (Director). (1964). *Point of Order* [film]. New York: Sterling Productions, USA.

Denton, R. E., Jr., & Woodward, G. C. (1985). *Political communication in America.* New York: Praeger.

Edelman, M. (1977). *Political language: Words that succeed and policies that fail.* New York: Academic Press.

Fisher, W. R. (1984). Narration as a human communication paradigm: The case of public moral argument. *Communication Monographs, 51,* 1–22.

Fisher, W. R. (1985). The narrative paradigm: An elaboration. *Communication Monographs, 52,* 347–367.

Fried, R. M. (1990). *Nightmare in red: The McCarthy era in perspective.* New York: Oxford University Press.

Gallup, G. H. (1972). *The Gallup poll: Public opinion, 1935–1971* (Vols. 1–3). New York: Random House.

Glazer, N. (1973). The methods of Senator McCarthy. In T. C. Reeves (Ed.), *McCarthyism* (pp. 25–36). Hinsdale, IL: Dryden Press.

Goldman, E. F. (1960). *The crucial decade—and after.* New York: Vintage Books.

Griffith, R. (1970). *The politics of fear: Joseph R. McCarthy and the Senate.* Lexington: University Press of Kentucky.

Haberman, F. W., with the assistance of Curvin, J. W., Wham, B., Ness, O. G., Hitchcock, O. A., & Park, B. (1955). Views on the Army-McCarthy hearings. *Quarterly Journal of Speech, 41,* 1–18.

Henry, W. A., III. (1981, June 8). An admiral from Alabama. *Time,* p. 20.

Highet, G. (1962). *The anatomy of satire.* Princeton, NJ: Princeton University Press.

Jackson, R. (1981). *Fantasy: The literature of subversion.* London: Methuen.

Johnson, P. (1985). *Modern times: The world from the Twenties to the Eighties.* New York: Harper & Row.

Jorstad, E. (1970). *The politics of doomsday: Fundamentalists of the Far Right.* Nashville: Abingdon Press.

Kelly, W. (1954/1955). *Potluck Pogo.* New York: Simon & Schuster.

Linman, A. (1988, March). *Harper's,* p. 7.

Marcuse, H. (1960). *Reason and revolution: Hegel and the rise of social theory.* Boston: Beacon Press.

McCarthy, J. R. (n.d.) *Major speeches and debates of Senator Joe McCarthy delivered in the United States Senate, 1950–1951.* Reprint from the Congressional Record[.] Washington, DC: United States Government Printing Office.

McCarthy, J. R. (1951). *America's retreat from victory: The story of George Catlett Marshall.* New York: Devin-Adair.

McCarthy, J. (1952). *McCarthyism: The fight for America.* New York: Devin-Adair.

[McCarthy, J. R.] (1952, October 28). Text of address by McCarthy accusing Governor Stevenson of aid to communist cause. *New York Times,* pp. 26–27.

[McCarthy, J. R.] (1953, November 25). Text of Senator McCarthy's speech accusing Truman of aiding suspected red agents. *New York Times,* p. 5.

[McCarthy, J. R.] (1953, December 4). McCarthy insists on red trade ban. *New York Times,* sec. 2, p. 6.

[McCarthy, J. R.] (1954, September 1). Excerpts from transcript of first day of Senate hearings on censure of McCarthy: Senator McCarthy's statement. *New York Times,* p. 14.

[McCarthy, J. R.] (1954, November 10). Text of McCarthy speech for delivery today in censure debate. *New York Times,* p. 18.

[McCarthy, J. R.] (1954, December 8). Texts of statement by McCarthy and some replies. *New York Times,* p. 10.

Miller, A. (1984, July). The interrogation of Angel Rama. *Harper's,* pp. 11–12.

Miller, C. R. (1984). Genre as social action. *Quarterly Journal of Speech, 70,* 151–167.

Miller, D. T., & Nowak, M. (1977). *The Fifties: The way we really were.* Garden City, NY: Doubleday.

Nimmo, D., & Combs, J. E. (1983). *Mediated political realities.* New York: Longman.

Oakley, J. R. (1986). *God's country: America in the Fifties.* New York: Dembner Books.

O'Brien, M. (1973). Robert Fleming, Senator McCarthy and the myth of the Marine hero. *Journalism Quarterly, 50,* 48–53.

Osborn, M. (1972). Archetypal metaphor in rhetoric: The light-dark family. In D. Ehninger (Ed.), *Contemporary rhetoric* (pp. 239–250). Glenview, IL: Scott Foresman. (Reprinted from *Quarterly Journal of Speech,* 1967, *53,* 115–126).

Oshinsky, D. M. (1983). *A conspiracy so immense: The world of Joe McCarthy.* New York: Free Press.

Rabinowitz, D. (1990, May). From the mouths of babes to a jail cell. *Harper's,* 52–63.

Rabkin, E. S. (1976). *The fantastic in literature.* Princeton, NJ: Princeton University Press.

Reagan backs Bush in assailing Dukakis over issue of pledge. (1988, September 21). *New York Times,* p. A30.

Reeves, T. C. (1982). *The life and times of Joe McCarthy: A biography.* New York: Stein & Day.

Riesman, D., & Glazer, N. (1964). The intellectuals and the discontented classes (1955). In D. Bell (Ed.), *The radical right.* (pp. 105–135). Garden City, NY: Anchor Doubleday.

Rosteck, T. (1989). Irony, argument, and reportage in television documentary: *See It Now* versus Senator McCarthy. *Quarterly Journal of Speech, 75,* 277–298.

Rovere, R. H. (1959/1960). *Senator Joe McCarthy.* Cleveland: World Publishing.

Said, E. W. (1983). Opponents, audiences, constituencies, and community. In W. J. T. Mitchell (Ed.), *The politics of interpretation* (pp. 7–32). Chicago: University of Chicago Press.

Schlesinger, A. M., Jr. (1949). *The vital center: The politics of freedom.* Boston: Houghton Mifflin.

Schrecker, E. W. (1986). *No ivory tower: McCarthyism and the universities.* New York: Oxford University Press.

Simons, H. W., & Aghazarian, A. A. (1986). Preface. In H. W. Simons & A. A. Aghazarian (Eds.), *Form, genre, and the study of political discourse* (pp. ix–x). Columbia: University of South Carolina Press.

Stone, I. F. (1963). *The haunted Fifties: 1953–1963*. Boston: Little, Brown.

Teacher accuses Northwestern U. of McCarthyism in tenure-denial controversy. (1986, June 4). *Chronicle of Higher Education*, p. 23.

Todorov, T. (1975). *The fantastic: A structural approach to a literary genre*. (R. Howard, Trans.). Ithaca: Cornell University Press.

Transcript of first TV debate between Bush and Dukakis. (1988, September 26). *New York Times*, pp. A16–A19.

Turner, R. (1988, September 10). Dukakis likens G.O.P. attacks to McCarthy's. *New York Times*, p. 8.

Weaver, R. (1976). *Ideas have consequences*. Chicago: University of Chicago Press.

Woodstock, G. (1984, September 27). On being 'inadmissible.' *New York Review of Books*, pp. 42–44.

Wrage, E. J. (1947). Public address: A study in social and intellectual history. *Quarterly Journal of Speech, 33*, 451–457.

Wrage, E. J., & Baskerville, B. (Eds.). (1962). *Contemporary forum: American speeches on twentieth-century issues*. Seattle: University of Washington Press.

Chapter IX

Ideographic Criticism

Ideographic criticism, as the name implies, analyzes rhetoric from an ideological perspective. Rhetorical critics, of course, have long recognized the centrality of ideology to persuasive discourse. In 1947, for example, Ernest J. Wrage urged scholars to investigate the ways in which ideology is embedded in public address.[1] Ernest G. Bormann claimed in 1972 that fantasy theme analysis could help critics discover the ideology symbolized in rhetorical visions.[2] In 1983 Philip Wander maintained that, instead of analyzing the effectiveness of discourse regardless of its political ends, communication scholars should openly use ideology as a basis for condemning corrupt rhetoric.[3] Today, many critics seek to explore the relationships between language, power, physical conditions, and the fundamental attitudes, values, and beliefs of a culture.

Michael Calvin McGee's 1980 article "The 'Ideograph': A Link between Rhetoric and Ideology" theorizes that condensed forms of ideology, known as "ideographs," operate in public communication as instruments of "political consciousness." Examples of ideographs are concepts such as "liberty," "equality," "property," and "religion." McGee argues that ideographs are the "building blocks" of ideology; they are specific to cultures and evolve gradually. In examining political discourse, critics can identify ideographs, trace their development over time, and analyze ways in which they clash with each other. McGee is particularly interested in understanding the connection between the material and symbolic. Ideographs, in his view, exist at the juncture between the objective reality of the human environment and the social reality projected in rhetorical discourse.

John Louis Lucaites and Celeste Michelle Condit illustrate how McGee's concept can be applied to the rhetorical criticism of language in their 1990 essay, "Reconstructing <Equality>: Culturetypal and Counter-Cultural Rhetorics in the Martyred Black Vision." They argue that Martin Luther King, Jr., and Malcolm X began with quite different notions of the ideograph "equality." King's rhetoric was "culturetypal," while Malcolm X's was "counter-cultural." The public vocabulary of "equality" was created by the interplay between these two voices.

In her 2005 article "The Male Madonna and the Feminine Uncle Sam: Visual Argument, Icons, and Ideographs in 1909 Anti–Woman Suffrage Postcards," Catherine H. Palczewski combines social movement and gender perspectives with ideographic criticism. Palczewski explains that postcards were used as political propaganda during the early twentieth-century debate that preceded women obtaining the right to vote in the United States. She explores connections between "verbal ideographs" of 1909 and "visual icons" that appeared in twelve anti-suffrage postcards published that year. The author maintains that analysis of these persuasive postcards provides a better understanding of the role of "visual argument" in influencing public views of "sex and citizenship." Palczewski concludes that visual icons can reinforce the authority of verbal ideographs to maintain social control of subordinate groups, in this case women.

NOTES

[1]Ernest J. Wrage's "Public Address: A Study in Social and Intellectual History" is reprinted in Chapter 1 of this volume.

[2]Ernest G. Bormann, "Fantasy and Rhetorical Vision: The Rhetorical Criticism of Social Reality," *Quarterly Journal of Speech*, 58 (1972), 396–407.

[3]Philip Wander's "The Ideological Turn in Modern Criticism" is reproduced in Chapter 1 of this anthology.

THE "IDEOGRAPH": A LINK BETWEEN RHETORIC AND IDEOLOGY

MICHAEL CALVIN McGEE

In 1950, Kenneth Burke, apparently following Dewey, Mead, and Lippmann, announced his preference for the notion "philosophy of myth" to explain the phenomenon of "public" or "mass consciousness" rather than the then-prevalent concept "ideology."[1] As contemporary writers have pushed on toward developing this "symbolic" or "dramatistic" alternative, the concept "ideology" has atrophied. Many use the term innocently, almost as a synonym for "doctrine" or "dogma" in political organizations;[2] and others use the word in a hypostatized sense that obscures or flatly denies the fundamental connection between the concept and descriptions of mass consciousness.[3] The concept seems to have gone the way of the dodo and of the neo-Aristotelian critic: As Bormann has suggested, the very word is widely perceived as being encrusted with the "intellectual baggage" of orthodox Marxism.[4]

Objecting to the use or abuse of any technical term would, ordinarily, be a sign of excessive crabbiness. But in this instance conceptualizations of "philosophy of myth," "fantasy visions," and "political scenarios," coupled with continued eccentric and/or narrow usages of "ideology," cosmetically camouflage significant and unresolved problems. We are presented with a brute, undeniable phenomenon: Human beings in collectivity behave and think differently than human beings in isolation. The collectivity is said to "have a mind of its own" distinct from the individual qua individual. Writers in the tradition of Marx and Mannheim explain this difference by observing that the only possibility of "mind" lies in the individual qua individual, in the human organism itself. When one appears to "think" and "behave" collectively, therefore, one has been tricked, self-deluded, or manipulated into accepting the brute existence of such fantasies as "public mind" or "public opinion" or "public philosophy." Symbolists generally want to say that this trick is a "transcendence," a voluntary agreement to believe in and to participate in a "myth." Materialists maintain that the trick is an insidious reified form of "lie," a self-perpetuating system of beliefs and interpretations foisted on all members of the community by the ruling class. Burke, with his emphasis on the individuals who are tricked, concerns himself more with the structure of "motive" than with the objective conditions that impinge on and restrict the individual's freedom to develop a political consciousness. Neo-Marxians, with focus on tricksters and the machinery of trickery, say that the essential question posed by the fact of society is one of locating precise descriptions of the dialectical tension between a "true" and a "false" consciousness, between reality and ideology.[5]

Though some on both sides of the controversy would have it otherwise, there is no *error* in either position. Both "myth" and "ideology" presuppose fundamental falsity in the common metaphor which alleges the existence of a "social organism." "Ideology," however, assumes that the exposure of falsity is a moral act: Though we have never experienced a "true consciousness," it is nonetheless theoretically accessible to us, and, because of such accessibility, we are morally remiss if we do not discard the false and approach the true. The falsity presupposed by "myth," on the other hand, is amoral because it is a purely poetic phenomenon, legitimized by rule of the poet's license, a "suspension of disbelief." A symbolist who speaks of "myth" is typically at great pains to argue for a value-free approach to the object of study, an approach in which one denies that "myth" is a synonym for "lie" and treats it as a falsehood of a peculiarly redemptive nature. Materialists, on the other hand, seem to use the concept "ideology" expressly to warrant normative claims regarding the exploitation of the "proletarian class" by self-serving plunderers. No error is involved in the apparently contradictory conceptions because, fundamentally, materialists and symbolists pursue two different studies: The Marxian asks how the "givens" of a human environment impinge on the development of political consciousness; the symbolist asks how the human symbol-using, reality-creating potential impinges on material reality, ordering it normatively, "mythically."

Errors arise when one conceives "myth" and "ideology" to be contraries, alternative and incompatible theoretical descriptions of the same phenomenon. The materialists' neglect of language studies and the consequent inability of Marxian theory to explain socially constructed realities is well-publicized.[6] Less well-described is the symbolists' neglect of the non-symbolic environment and the consequent inability of symbolist theory to account for the impact of material phenomena on the construction of social reality.[7] I do not mean to denigrate in any way the research of scholars attempting to develop Burke's philosophy of myth; indeed, I have on occasion joined that endeavor. I do believe, however, that each of us has erred to the extent that we have conceived the rubrics of symbolism as an *alternative* rather than *supplemental* description of political consciousness. The assertion that "philosophy of myth" is an alternative to "ideology" begs the question Marx intended to pose. Marx was concerned with "power," with the capacity of an elite class to control the state's political, economic, and military establishment, to dominate the state's information systems and determine even the consciousness of large masses of people. He was politically committed to the cause of the proletariat: If a norm was preached by the upper classes, it was by virtue of that fact a baneful seduction; and if a member of the proletarian class was persuaded by such an argument, that person was possessed of an "ideology," victimized and exploited. Not surprisingly, symbolists criticize Marx for his politics, suggesting that his is a wonderfully convenient formula which mistakes commitment for "historically scientific truth." By conceiving poetic falsity, we rid ourselves of the delusion that interpretation is scientific, but we also bury the probability that the myths we study as an alternative are thrust upon us by the brute force of "power." While Marx overestimated "power" as a variable in describing political consciousness, Burke, Cassirer, Polanyi, and others do not want to discuss the capacity even of a "free" state to determine political consciousness.[8]

If we are to describe the trick-of-the-mind which deludes us into believing that we "think" with/through/for a "society" to which we "belong," we need a theoretical model which accounts for both "ideology" and "myth," a model which neither denies human capacity to control "power" through the manipulation of symbols nor begs Marx's essential questions regarding the influence of "power" on creating and maintaining political consciousness. I will argue here that such a model must begin with the concept "ideology" and proceed to link that notion directly with the interests of symbolism.

I will elaborate the following commitments and hypotheses: If a mass consciousness exists at all, it must be empirically "present," itself a thing obvious to those who participate in it, or, at least, empirically manifested in the language which communicates it. I agree with Marx that the problem of consciousness is fundamentally practical and normative, that it is concerned essentially with describing and evaluating the legitimacy of public motives. Such consciousness, I believe, is always false, not because we are programmed automatons and not because we have a propensity to structure political perceptions in poetically false "dramas" or "scenarios," but because "truth" in politics, no matter how firmly we believe, is always an illusion. The falsity of an ideology is specifically rhetorical, for the illusion of truth and falsity with regard to normative commitments is the product of persuasion.[9] Since the clearest access to persuasion (and hence to ideology) is through the discourse used to produce it, I will suggest that ideology in practice is a political language, preserved in rhetorical documents, with the capacity to dictate decision and control public belief and behavior. Further, the political language which manifests ideology seems characterized by slogans, a vocabulary of "ideographs" easily mistaken for the technical terminology of political philosophy. An analysis of ideographic usages in political rhetoric, I believe, reveals interpenetrating systems or "structures" of public motives. Such structures appear to be "diachronic" and "synchronic" patterns of political consciousness which have the capacity both to control "power" and to influence (if not determine) the shape and texture of each individual's "reality."

HYPOTHETICAL CHARACTERISTICS OF IDEOGRAPHS

Marx's thesis suggests that an ideology determines mass belief and thus restricts the free emergence of political opinion. By this logic, the "freest" members of a community are those who belong to the "power" elite; yet the image of hooded puppeteers twisting and turning the masses at will is unconvincing if only because the elite seems itself imprisoned by the same false consciousness communicated to the polity at large. When we consider the impact of ideology on freedom, and of power on consciousness, we must be clear that ideology is transcendent, as much an influence on the belief and behavior of the ruler as on the ruled. Nothing *necessarily* restricts persons who wield the might of the state. Roosevelts and Carters are as free to indulge personal vanity with capricious uses of power as was Idi Amin, regardless of formal "checks and balances." The polity can punish tyrants and maniacs after the fact of their lunacy or tyranny (if the polity survives it), but, in practical terms, the only way to shape or soften power at the moment of its exercise is prior persuasion. Similarly, no matter what punishment we might imagine "power" visiting upon an ordinary citizen, nothing *necessarily* determines individual behavior and belief. A citizen may be punished for eccentricity or disobedience after the fact of a crime, but, at the moment when defiance is contemplated, the only way to combat the impulse to criminal behavior is prior persuasion. I am suggesting, in other words, that social control in its essence is control over consciousness, the a priori influence that learned predispositions hold over human agents who play the roles of "power" and "people" in a given transaction.[10]

Because there is a lack of necessity in social control, it seems inappropriate to characterize agencies of control as "socializing" or "conditioning" media. No individual (least of all the elite who control the power of the state) is *forced* to submit in the same way that a conditioned dog is obliged to salivate or socialized children are required to speak English. Human beings are "conditioned," not directly to belief and behavior, but to a vocabulary of concepts that function as guides, warrants, reasons, or excuses for behavior and belief. When a claim is warranted by such terms as "law," "liberty," "tyranny," or "trial by jury," in other words, it is presumed that human beings will react predictably and autonomically. So it was that a majority of Americans were surprised, not when allegedly sane young men agreed to go halfway around the world to kill for God, country, apple pie, and no other particularly good reason, but, rather, when other young men displayed good common sense by moving to Montreal instead, thereby refusing to be conspicuous in a civil war which was none of their business. The end product of the state's insistence on some degree of conformity in behavior and belief, I suggest, is a *rhetoric* of control, a system of persuasion presumed to be effective on the whole community. We make a rhetoric of war to persuade us of war's necessity, but then forget that it is a rhetoric—and regard negative popular judgments of it as unpatriotic cowardice.

It is not remarkable to conceive social control as fundamentally rhetorical. In the past, however, rhetorical scholarship has regarded the rhetoric of control as a species of argumentation and thereby assumed that the fundamental unit of analysis in such rhetoric is an integrated set-series of propositions. This is, I believe, a mistake, an unwarranted abstraction: To argue is to test an affirmation or denial of claims; argument is the means of proving the truth of grammatical units, declarative sentences, that purport to be reliable signal representations of reality. Within the vocabulary of argumentation, the term "rule of law" makes no sense until it is made the subject or predicable of a proposition. If I say "The rule of law is a primary cultural value in the United States" or "Charles I was a cruel and capricious tyrant," I have asserted a testable claim that may be criticized with logically coordinated observations. When I say simply "the rule of law," however, my utterance cannot qualify logically as a claim. Yet I am conditioned to believe that "liberty" and "property" have an obvious meaning, a behaviorally directive self-evidence. Because I am taught to set such terms apart from my usual vocabulary, words used as agencies of social control may have an intrinsic force—and, if so, I may very well distort the key terms of social conflict, commitment, and control if I think of them as parts of a proposition rather than as basic units of analysis.

Though words only (and not claims), such terms as "property," "religion," "right of privacy," "freedom of speech," "rule of law," and "liberty" are more pregnant than propositions ever could be. They are the basic structural elements, the building blocks, of ideology. Thus they may be thought of as "ideographs," for, like Chinese symbols, they signify and "contain" a unique ideological commitment; further, they presumptuously suggest that each member of a community will see as a gestalt every complex nuance in them. What "rule of law" means is the series of propositions, all of them, that could be manufactured to justify a Whig/Liberal order. Ideographs are one-term sums of an orientation, the species of "God" or "Ultimate" term that will be used to symbolize the line of argument the meanest sort of individual *would* pursue, if that individual had the dialectical skills of philosophers, as a defense of a personal stake in and commitment to the society. Nor is one permitted to question the fundamental logic of ideographs: Everyone is conditioned to think of "the rule of law" as a *logical* commitment just as one is taught to think that "186,000 miles per second" is an accurate empirical description of the speed of light even though few can work the experiments or do the mathematics to prove it.[11]

The important fact about ideographs is that they exist in real discourse, functioning clearly and evidently as agents of political consciousness. They are not invented by observers; they come to be as a part of the real lives of the people whose motives they articulate. So, for example, "rule of law" is a more precise, objective motive than such observer-invented terms as "neurotic" or "paranoid style" or *"petit bourgeois."*

Ideographs pose a methodological problem *because* of their very specificity: How do we generalize from a "rule of law" to a description of consciousness that comprehends not only "rule of law" but all other like motives as well? What do we describe with the concept "ideograph," and how do we actually go about doing the specific cultural analysis promised by conceptually linking rhetoric and ideology?

Though both come to virtually the same conclusion, the essential argument seems more careful and useful in Ortega's notion of "the etymological man" than in Burke's poetically hidden concept of "the symbol-using animal" and "logology":

> Man, when he sets himself to speak, does so *because* he believes that he will be able to say what he thinks. Now, this is an illusion. Language is not up to that. It says, more or less, a part of what we think, and raises an impenetrable obstacle to the transmission of the rest. It serves quite well for mathematical statements and proofs. . . . But in proportion as conversation treats of more important, more human, more "real" subjects than these, its vagueness, clumsiness, and confusion steadily increase. Obedient to the inveterate prejudice that "talking leads to understanding," we speak and listen in such good faith that we end by misunderstanding one another far more than we would if we remained mute and set ourselves to divine each other. Nay, more: since our thought is in large measure dependent upon our language . . . it follows that thinking is talking with oneself and hence misunderstanding oneself at the imminent risk of getting oneself into a complete quandary.[12]

All this "talk" generates a series of "usages" which unite us, since we speak the same language, but, more significantly, such "talk" *separates* us from other human beings who do not accept our meanings, our intentions.[13] So, Ortega claims, the essential demarcation of whole nations is language usage: "This gigantic architecture of usages is, precisely, society."[14] And it is through usages that a particular citizen's sociality exists:

> A language, *speech,* is "what people say," it is the vast system of verbal usages established in a collectivity. The individual, the person, is from his birth submitted to the linguistic coercion that these usages represent. Hence the mother tongue is perhaps the most typical and clearest social phenomenon. With it "people" enter us, set up residence in us, making each an example of "people." Our mother tongue socializes our inmost being, and because of this fact every individual belongs, in the strongest sense of the word, to a society. He can flee from the society in which he was born and brought up,

but in his flight the society inexorably accompanies him because he carries it within him. This is the true meaning that the statement "man is a social animal" can have.[15]

Ortega's reference, of course, is to language generally and not to a particular vocabulary within language. So he worked with the vocabulary of greeting to demonstrate the definitive quality of linguistic usages when conceiving "society."[16] His reasoning, however, invites specification, attention to the components of the "architecture" supposedly created by usages.

Insofar as usages both unite and separate human beings, it seems reasonable to suggest that the functions of uniting and separating would be represented by specific vocabularies, actual words or terms. With regard to political union and separation, such vocabularies would consist of ideographs. Such usages as "liberty" define a collectivity, i.e., the outer parameters of a society, because such terms either do not exist in other societies or do not have precisely similar meanings. So, in the United States, we claim a common belief in "equality," as do citizens of the Union of Soviet Socialist Republics; but "equality" is not the same word in its meaning or its usage. One can therefore precisely define the difference between the two communities, in part, by comparing the usage of definitive ideographs. We are, of course, still able to interact with the Soviets despite barriers of language and usage. The interaction is possible because of higher-order ideographs—"world peace," "detente," "spheres of influence," etc.—that permit temporary union.[17] And, in the other direction, it is also true that there are special interests within the United States separated one from the other precisely by disagreements regarding the identity, legitimacy, or definition of ideographs. So we are divided by usages into subgroups: Business and labor, Democrats and Republicans, Yankees and Southerners are *united* by the ideographs that represent the political entity "United States" and *separated* by a disagreement as to the practical meaning of such ideographs.

The concept "ideograph" is meant to be purely descriptive of an essentially social human condition. Unlike more general conceptions of "Ultimate" or "God" terms, attention is called to the social, rather than rational or ethical, functions of a particular vocabulary. This vocabulary is precisely a group of *words* and not a series of symbols representing ideas. Ortega clearly, methodically, distinguishes a usage (what we might call "social" or "material" thought) from an *idea* (what Ortega would call "pure thought"). He suggests, properly, that *language gets in the way of thinking,* separates us from "ideas" we may have which cannot be surely expressed, even to ourselves, in the usages which imprison us. So my "pure thought" about liberty, religion, and property is clouded, hindered, made irrelevant by the existence in history of the ideographs "Liberty, Religion, and Property."[18] Because these terms are definitive of the society we have inherited, they are *conditions* of the society into which each of us is born, material ideas which we must accept to "belong." They penalize us, in a sense, as much as they protect us, for they prohibit our appreciation of an alternative pattern of meaning in, for example, the Soviet Union or Brazil.

In effect, ideographs—language imperatives which hinder and perhaps make impossible "pure thought"—are bound within the culture which they define. We can *characterize* an ideograph, say what it has meant and does mean as a usage, and some of us may be able to achieve an imaginary state of withdrawal from community long enough to speculate as to what ideographs *ought* to mean in the best of possible worlds; but the very nature of language forces us to keep the two operations separate: So, for example, the "idea" of "liberty" may be the subject of philosophical speculation, but philosophers can never be *certain* that they themselves or their readers understand a "pure" meaning unpolluted by historical, ideographic usages.[19] Should we look strictly at material notions of "liberty," on the other hand, we distort our thinking by believing that a rationalization of a particular historical meaning is "pure," the truth of the matter.[20] Ideographs can *not* be used to establish or test truth, and vice versa, the truth, in ideal metaphysical senses, is a consideration irrelevant to accurate characterizations of such ideographs as "liberty." Indeed, if examples from recent history are a guide, the attempts to infuse usages with metaphysical meanings, or to confuse ideographs with the "pure" thought of philosophy, have resulted in the "nightmares" which Polanyi, for one, deplores.[21] The significance of ideographs is in their concrete history as usages, not in their alleged idea-content.

THE ANALYSIS OF IDEOGRAPHS

No one has ever seen an "equality" strutting up the driveway, so, if "equality" exists at all, it has meaning through its specific applications. In other words, we establish a meaning for "equality" by using the word as a description of a certain phenomenon; it has meaning only insofar as our description is acceptable, believable. If asked to make a case for "equality," that is to define the term, we are forced to make reference to its history by detailing the situations for which the word has been an appropriate description. Then, by comparisons over time, we establish an analog for the proposed present usage of the term. Earlier usages become precedent, touchstones for judging the propriety of the ideograph in a current circumstance. The meaning of "equality" does not rigidify because situations seeming to require its usage are never perfectly similar: As the situations vary, so the meaning of "equality" expands and contracts. The variations in meaning of "equality" are much less important, however, than the fundamental, categorical meaning, the "common denominator" of all situations for which "equality" has been the best and most descriptive term. The dynamism of "equality" is thus paramorphic, for even when the term changes its signification in particular circumstances, it retains a formal, categorical meaning, a constant reference to its history as an ideograph.

These earlier usages are vertically structured, related each to the other in a formal way, every time the society is called upon to judge whether a particular circumstance should be defined ideographically. So, for example, to protect ourselves from abuses of power, we have built into our political system an ideograph that is said to justify "impeaching" an errant leader: If the president has engaged in behaviors which can be described as "high crimes and misdemeanors," even that highest officer must be removed.

But what is meant by "high crimes and misdemeanors"? If Peter Rodino wishes to justify impeachment procedures against Richard Nixon in the Committee on the Judiciary of the House of Representatives, he must mine history for touchstones, precedents which give substance and an aura of precision to the ideograph "high crimes and misdemeanors." His search of the past concentrates on situations analogous to that which he is facing, situations involving actual or proposed "impeachment." The "rule of law" emerged as a contrary ideograph, and Rodino developed from the tension between "law" and "high crimes" an argument indicting Nixon. His proofs were historical, ranging from Magna Carta to Edmund Burke's impeachment of Warren Hastings. He was able to make the argument, therefore, only because he could organize a series of events, situationally similar, with an ideograph as the structuring principle. The structuring is "vertical" because of the element of *time;* that is, the deep meanings of "law" and "high crime" derive from knowledge of the way in which meanings have evolved over a period of time—awareness of the way an ideograph can be meaningful *now* is controlled in large part by what it meant *then*.[22]

All communities take pains to record and preserve the vertical structure of their ideographs. Formally, the body of nonstatutory "law" is little more than literature recording ideographic usages in the "common law" and "case law."[23] So, too, historical dictionaries, such as the *O.E.D.*, detail etymologies for most of the Anglo-American ideographs. And any so-called "professional" history provides a record in detail of the events surrounding earlier usages of ideographs—indeed, the historian's eye is most usually attracted precisely to those situations involving ideographic applications.[24] The more significant record of vertical structures, however, lies in what might be called "popular" history. Such history consists in part of novels, films, plays, even songs; but the truly influential manifestation is grammar school history, the very first contact most have with their existence and experience as a part of a community.

To learn the meanings of the ideographs "freedom" and "patriotism," for example, most of us swallowed the tale of Patrick Henry's defiant speech to the Virginia House of Burgesses: "I know not what course others may take, but as for me, give me liberty or give me death!" These specific words, of course, were concocted by the historian William Wirt and not by Governor Henry. Wirt's intention was to provide a model for "the young men of Virginia," asking them to copy Henry's virtues and avoid his vices.[25] Fabricated events and words meant little, not because Wirt was uninterested in the truth of what really happened to Henry, but rather because what he wrote about was the definition of essential ideographs. His was a task of socialization, an exercise in epideictic rhetoric, providing the youth of his age (and of our own) with general knowledge of ideographic touchstones so that they might be able to make, or comprehend, judgments of public motives and of their own civic duty.

Though such labor tires the mind simply in imagining it, there is no trick in gleaning from public documents the entire vocabulary of ideographs that define a particular collectivity. The terms do not hide in discourse, nor is their "meaning" or function within an argument obscure: We might disagree metaphysically about "equality," and we might use the term differently in practical discourse, but I believe we can nearly always discover the functional meaning of the term by measure of its grammatic and pragmatic context.[26] Yet even a complete description of vertical ideographic structures leaves little but an exhaustive lexicon understood etymologically and diachronically—and no ideally precise explanation of how ideographs function *presently*.

If we find forty rhetorical situations in which "rule of law" has been an organizing term, we are left with little but the simple chronology of the situations as a device to structure the lot: Case One is distinct from Case Forty, and the meaning of the ideograph thus has contracted or expanded in the intervening time. But time is an irrelevant matter *in practice*. Chronological sequences are provided by analysts, and they properly reflect the concerns of theorists who try to describe what "rule of law" *may* mean, potentially, by laying out the history of what the term *has* meant. Such advocates as Rodino are not so scrupulous in research; they choose eight or nine of those forty cases to use as evidence in argument, ignore the rest, and impose a pattern of organization on the cases recommended (or forced) by the demands of a current situation. As Ortega argues with reference to language generally, key usages considered historically and diachronically are purely formal; yet in real discourse, and in public consciousness, they are *forces:*

> [A]ll that diachronism accomplishes is to reconstruct other comparative "presents" of the language as they existed in the past. All that it shows us, then, is changes; it enables us to witness one present being replaced by another, the succession of the static figures of the language, as the "film," with its motionless images, engenders the visual fiction of a movement. At best, it offers us a cinematic view of language, but not a *dynamic* understanding of how the changes were, and came to be, *made.* The changes are merely results of the making and unmaking process, they are the externality of language and there is need for an internal conception of it in which we discover not resultant *forms* but the operating *forces* themselves.[27]

In Burke's terminology, describing a vertical ideographic structure yields a culture-specific and relatively precise "grammar" of one public motive. That motive is not captured, however, without attention to its "rhetoric."

Considered rhetorically, as *forces,* ideographs seem structured horizontally, for when people actually make use of them presently, such terms as "rule of law" clash with other ideographs ("principle of confidentiality" or "national security," for example), and in the conflict come to mean with reference to synchronic confrontations. So, for example, one would not ordinarily think of an inconsistency between "rule of law" and "principle of confidentiality." Vertical analysis of the two ideographs would probably reveal a consonant relationship based on genus and species: "Confidentiality" of certain conversations is a control on the behavior of government, a control that functions to maintain a "rule of law" and prevents "tyranny" by preserving a realm of privacy for the individual.

The "Watergate" conflict between Nixon and Congress, however, illustrates how that consonant relationship can be restructured, perhaps broken, in the context of a particular controversy: Congress asked, formally and legally, for certain of Nixon's documents. He refused, thereby creating the appearance of frustrating the imperative value "rule of law." He attempted to excuse himself by matching a second ideograph, "principle of confidentiality," against normal and usual meanings of "rule of law." Before a mass television audience Nixon argued that a President's conversations with advisers were entitled to the same privilege constitutionally accorded exchanges between priest and penitent, husband and wife, lawyer and client. No direct vertical precedent was available to support Nixon's usage. The argument asked public (and later jurisprudential) permission to expand the meaning of "confidentiality" and thereby to alter its relationship with the "rule of law," making what appeared to be an illegal act acceptable. Nixon's claims were epideictic and not deliberative or forensic; he magnified "confidentiality" by praising the ideograph as if it were a person, attempting to alter its "standing" among other ideographs, even as an individual's "standing" in the community changes through praise and blame.[28]

Synchronic structural changes in the relative standing of an ideograph are "horizontal" because of the presumed consonance of an ideology; that is, ideographs such as "rule of law" are meant to be taken together, as a working unit, with "public trust," "freedom of speech," "trial by jury," and any other slogan characteristic of the collective life. If all the ideographs used to justify a Whig/Liberal government were placed on a chart, they would form groups or clusters of words radiating from the slogans originally used to rationalize "popular sovereignty"—"religion," "liberty," and "property." Each term would be a connector, modifier, specifier, or contrary for those fundamental historical commitments, giving them a meaning and a unity easily mistaken for logic. Some terms would be enshrined in the Constitution, some in law, some merely in conventional usage; but all would be constitutive of "the people." Though new usages can enter the equation, the ideographs remain essential[l]y unchanged. But when we engage ideological argument, when we cause ideographs to *do work* in explaining, justifying, or guiding policy in specific situations, the relationship of ideographs changes. A "rule of law," for example, is taken for granted, a simple connector between "property" and "liberty," until a constitutional crisis inclines us to make it "come first." In Burke's vocabulary, it becomes the "title" or "god-term" of all ideographs, the center-sun about which every ideograph orbits. Sometimes circumstance forces us to sense that the structure is not consonant, as when awareness of racism exposes contradiction between "property" and "right to life" in the context of "open-housing" legislation. Sometimes officers of state, in the process of justifying particular uses of power, manufacture seeming inconsistency, as when Nixon pitted "confidentiality" against "rule of law." And sometimes an alien force frontally assaults the structure, as when Hitler campaigned against "decadent democracies." Such instances have the potential to change the structure of ideographs and hence the "present" ideology—in this sense, an ideology is dynamic and a *force,* always resilient, always keeping itself in some consonance and unity, but not always the *same* consonance and unity.[29]

In appearance, of course, characterizing ideological conflicts as synchronic *structural* dislocations is an unwarranted abstraction: An ideological argument could result simply from multiple usages of an ideograph. Superficially, for example, one might be inclined to describe the "bussing" controversy as a disagreement over the "best" meaning for "equality," one side opting for "equality" defined with reference to "access" to education and the other with reference to the goal, "being educated." An ideograph, however, is always understood in its relation to another; it is defined tautologically by using other terms in its cluster. If we accept that there are three or four or however many possible meanings for "equality," each with a currency and legitimacy, we distort the nature of the ideological dispute by ignoring the fact that "equality" is made meaningful, not within the clash of multiple usages, but rather in its relationship with "freedom." That is, "equality" defined by "access" alters the nature of "liberty" from the relationship of "equality" and "liberty" thought to exist when "equality" is defined as "being educated." One would not want to rule out the possibility that ideological disagreements, however rarely, could be simply semantic; but we are more likely to err if we assume the dispute to be semantic than if we look for the deeper structural dislocation which likely produced multiple usages as a disease produces symptoms. When an ideograph is at the center of a semantic dispute, I would suggest, the multiple usages will be either metaphysical or diachronic, purely speculative or historical, and in either event devoid of the force and currency of a synchronic ideological conflict.[30]

In the terms of this argument, two recognizable "ideologies" exist in any specific culture at one "moment." One "ideology" is a "grammar," a historically-defined diachronic structure of ideograph-meanings expanding and contracting from the birth of the society to its "present." Another "ideology" is a "rhetoric," a situationally-defined synchronic structure of ideograph clusters constantly reorganizing itself to accommodate specific circumstances while maintaining its fundamental consonance and unity. A division of this sort, of course, is but an analytic convenience for talking about two *dimensions* (vertical and horizontal) of a single phenomenon: No present ideology can be divorced from past commitments if only because the very words used to express present dislocations have a history that establishes the category of their meaning. And no diachronic ideology can be divorced from the "here-and-now" if only because its entire *raison d'etre* consists in justifying the form and direction of collective behavior. Both of these structures must be understood and described before one can claim to have constructed a theoretically precise explanation of a society's ideology, of its repertoire of public motives.

CONCLUSION

One of the casualties of the current "pluralist" fad in social and political theory has been the old Marxian thesis that governing elites control the masses by creating, maintaining, and manipulating a mass consciousness suited to perpetuation of the existing order.[31] Though I agree that Marx probably overestimated the influence of an elite, it is difficult *not* to see a "dominant ideology" which seems to exercise decisive influence in political life. The question, of course, turns on finding a way accurately to define and to describe a dominant ideology. Theorists writing in the tradition of Dewey, Burke, and Cassirer have, in my judgment, come close to the mark; but because they are bothered by poetic metaphors, these symbolists never conceive their work as description of a mass consciousness. Even these writers, therefore, beg Marx's inescapable question regarding the impact of "power" on the way we think. I have argued here that the concepts "rhetoric" and "ideology" may be linked without poetic metaphors, and that the linkage should produce a description and an explanation of dominant ideology, of the relationship between the "power" of a state and the consciousness of its people.

The importance of symbolist constructs is their focus on *media* of consciousness, on the discourse that articulates and propagates common beliefs. "Rhetoric," "sociodrama," "myth," "fantasy vision," and "political scenario" are not important because of their *fiction*, their connection to poetic, but because of their *truth*, their links with the trick-of-the-mind that deludes individuals into believing that they "think" with/for/through a social organism. The truth of symbolist constructs, I have suggested, appears to lie in our claim to see a legitimate social reality in a vocabulary of complex, high-order abstractions that refer to and invoke a sense of "the people." By learning the meaning of ideographs, I have argued, everyone in society, even the "freest" of us, those who control the state, seem predisposed to structured mass responses. Such terms as "liberty," in other words, constitute by our very use of them in political discourse an ideology that governs or "dominates" our consciousness. In practice, therefore, ideology is a political language composed of slogan-like terms signifying collective commitment.

Such terms I have called "ideographs." A formal definition of "ideograph," derived from arguments made throughout this essay, would list the following characteristics: An ideograph is an ordinary-language term found in political discourse. It is a high-order abstraction representing collective commitment to a particular but equivocal and ill-defined normative goal. It warrants the use of power, excuses behavior and belief which might otherwise be perceived as eccentric or antisocial, and guides behavior and belief into channels easily recognized by a community as acceptable and laudable. Ideographs such as "slavery" and "tyranny," however, may guide behavior and belief negatively by branding unacceptable behavior. And many ideographs ("liberty," for example) have a non-ideographic usage, as in the sentence, "Since I resigned my position, I am at liberty to accept your offer." Ideographs are culture-bound, though some terms are used in different signification across cultures. Each member of the community is socialized, conditioned, to the vocabulary of ideographs as a prerequisite for "belonging" to the society. A degree of tolerance is usual, but people are expected to understand ideographs within a range of usage thought to be acceptable: The society will inflict penalties on those who use ideographs in heretical ways and on those who refuse to respond appropriately to claims on their behavior warranted through the agency of ideographs.

Though ideographs such as "liberty," "religion," and "property" often appear as technical terms in social philosophy, I have argued here that the ideology of a community is established by the usage of such terms in specifically rhetorical discourse, for such usages constitute excuses for specific beliefs and behaviors made by those who executed the history of which they were a part. The ideographs used in rhetorical discourse seem structured in two ways: In isolation, each ideograph has a history, an etymology, such that current meanings of the term are linked to past usages of it diachronically. The diachronic structure of an ideograph establishes the parameters, the category, of its meaning. All ideographs taken together, I suggest, are thought at any specific "moment" to be consonant, related one to another in such a way as to produce unity of commitment in a particular historical context. Each ideograph is thus connected to all others as brain cells are linked by synapses, synchronically in one context at one specific moment.

A complete description of an ideology, I have suggested, will consist of (1) the isolation of a society's ideographs, (2) the exposure and analysis of the diachronic structure of every ideograph, and (3) characterization of synchronic relationships among all the ideographs in a particular context. Such a description, I believe, would yield a theoretical framework with which to describe interpenetrating material and symbolic environments: Insofar as we can explain the diachronic and synchronic tensions among ideographs, I suggest, we can also explain the tension between *any* "given" human environment ("objective reality") and any "projected" environments ("symbolic" or "social reality") latent in rhetorical discourse.

NOTES

[1]Kenneth Burke, *A Rhetoric of Motives* (New York: Prentice Hall, 1950), pp. 197–203; John Dewey, *The Public and Its Problems* (New York: Henry Holt, 1927); George H. Mead, *Mind Self, and Society* (Chicago: Univ. of Chicago Press, 1934); and Walter Lippmann, *Public Opinion* (1922; rpt. New York: Free Press, 1965).

Duncan groups the American symbolists by observing that European social theorists using "ideology" were concerned with "consciousness" (questions about the *apprehension* of society) while symbolists using poetic metaphors were concerned with a "philosophy of action" (questions about the way we do or ought to *behave* in society). In rejecting the concept and theory of "ideology," Burke refused to consider the relationship between consciousness and action except as that relationship can be characterized with the agency of an a priori poetic metaphor, "dramatism." His thought and writing, like that of a poet, is therefore freed from truth criteria: Supposing his *form,* no "motive" outside the dramatistic terminology need be recognized or accounted for *in its particularity.* Though Burkeans are more guilty than Burke, I think even he tends to redefine motives rather than account for them, to cast self-confessions in "scenarios" rather than deal with them in specific. One might say of "dramatism" what Bacon alleged regarding the Aristotelian syllogism, that it is but a form which chases its tail, presuming in its metaphoric conception the truth of its descriptions. See Hugh Dalziel Duncan, *Symbols in Society* (New York: Oxford Univ. Press, 1968), pp. 12–14; Richard Dewey, "The Theatrical Analogy Reconsidered," *The American Sociologist,* 4 (1969), 307–11; and R. S. Perinbanayagam, "The Definition of the Situation: an Analysis of the Ethnomethodological and Dramaturgical View," *Sociological Quarterly,* 15 (1974), 521–41.

[2]See, e.g., Arthur M. Schlesinger, Jr., "Ideology and Foreign Policy: The American Experience," in George Schwab, ed., *Ideology and Foreign Policy* (New York: Cyrco, 1978), pp. 124–32; and Randall L. Bytwerk, "Rhetorical Aspects of the Nazi Meeting: 1926–1933," *Quarterly Journal of Speech,* 61 (1975), 307–18.

[3]See, e.g., William R. Brown, "Ideology as Communication Process," *Quarterly Journal of Speech,* 64 (1978), 123–40; and Jürgen Habermas, "Technology and Science as 'Ideology,'" in *Toward a Rational Society,* trans. Jeremy J. Shapiro (1968; Boston: Beacon, 1970), pp. 81–122.

[4]Bormann's distrust of "ideology" was expressed in the context of an evaluation of his "fantasy theme" technique at the 1978 convention of the Speech Communication Association. See "Fantasy Theme Analysis: An Exploration and Assessment," S.C.A. 1978 Seminar Series, Audio-Tape Cassettes. For authoritative accounts of the various "encrustations," see George Lichtheim, "The Concept of Ideology," *History and Theory,* 4 (1964–65), 164–95; and Hans Barth, *Truth and Ideology,* trans. Frederic Lilge, 2nd ed. 1961 (Berkeley: Univ. of California Press, 1976).

[5]See Kenneth Burke, *Permanence & Change* 2nd ed. rev. (1954; rpt. Indianapolis: Bobbs-Merrill, 1965), pp. 19–36, 216–36; Karl Marx and Frederick Engels, *The German Ideology* (1847), trans. and ed. Clemens Dutt, W. Lough, and C. P. Magill, in *The Collected Works of Karl Marx and Frederick Engels,* 9+ vols. (Moscow: Progress Publishers, 1975–77+), 5:3–5, 23–93; Karl Mannheim, *Ideology and Utopia,* trans. Louis Wirth and Edward Shils (1929; rpt. New York: Harvest Books, 1952); and Martin Seliger, *The Marxist Conception of Ideology: A Critical Essay* (Cambridge: Cambridge Univ. Press, 1977).

My purpose here is to expose the issue between symbolists (generally) and materialists (particularly Marxians). This of course results in some oversimplification: With regard to the brute problem of describing "consciousness," at least two schools of thought are not here accounted for, Freudian psychiatry and American empirical psychology. Freudians are generally connected with the symbolist position I describe here, while most of the operational conceptions of American empirical psychology (especially social psychology) may fairly be associated with Marxian or neo-Marxian description. Moreover, I treat the terms "ideology" and "myth" as less ambiguous than their history as concepts would suggest. My usage of the terms, and the technical usefulness I portray, reflects my own conviction more than the sure and noncontroversial meaning of either "myth" or "ideology."

[6]See, e.g., Willard A. Mullins, "Truth and Ideology: Reflections on Mannheim's Paradox," *History and Theory,* 18 (1979), 142–54; William H. Shaw, "'The Handmill Gives You the Feudal Lord': Marx's Technological Determinism," *History and Theory,* 18 (1979), 155–76; Jean-Paul Sartre, *Critique of Dialectical Reason,* trans. Alan Sheridan-Smith (1960; Eng. trans. London: NLB, 1976), pp. 95–121; and Jean-Paul Sartre, *Search for a Method,* trans. Hazel E. Barnes (1958; Eng. trans. New York: Vintage, 1968), pp. 35–84.

[7]See W. G. Runciman, "Describing," *Mind,* 81 (1972), 372–88; Perinbanayagam; and Herbert W. Simons, Elizabeth Mechling, and Howard N. Schreier, "Mobilizing for Collective Action From the Bottom Up: The Rhetoric of Social Movements," unpub. MS., Temple Univ., pp. 48–59, forthcoming in Carroll C. Arnold and John Waite Bowers, eds., *Handbook of Rhetorical and Communication Theory.*

[8]Adolph Hitler, this century's archetype of absolute power—as well as absolute immorality—rose to dominance and maintained himself by putting into practice symbolist theories of social process. Hitler's mere existence forces one to question symbolist theories, asking whether "sociodramas" and "rhetorics" and "myths" are things to be studied scientifically or wild imaginings conjured up from the ether, devil-tools playing upon human weakness and superstition, and therefore things to be politically eradicated. In the face of Hitler, most symbolists adopted a high moral stance of righteous wrath, concentrating on the evil of the man while underplaying the tools he used to gain and keep power. But subtly they modified their logics: Burke is most sensitive to the problem, but in the end he does little more than demonstrate the moral polemical power of dramatistic methods of criticism, becoming the "critic" of his early and later years rather than the "historian" and "theorist" of his middle years. Cassirer's reaction is more extreme, backing away from the logical implications of the symbolist epistemology he argued for before Hitler, begging the problem of power by characterizing the state itself as nothing but a "myth" to be transcended. Hitler was an inspiration to Polanyi, causing him to take up epistemology as a vehicle to discredit social philosophy generally. In the process Polanyi became an unabashed ideological chauvinist of his adopted culture. See, resp., Kenneth Burke, "The Rhetoric of Hitler's 'Battle,'" in *The Philosophy of Literary Form*, 3rd ed. (Berkeley: Univ. of California Press, 1973), pp. 191–220, and cf. Kenneth Burke, *Attitudes toward History* (1937; 2nd ed. rev. rpt. Boston: Beacon, 1961), pp. 92–107; Ernst Cassirer, *The Philosophy of Symbolic Forms*, trans. Ralph Manheim (1923–29; Eng. trans. New Haven: Yale Univ. Press, 1953), 1:105–14; Ernst Cassirer, *The Myth of the State* (New Haven: Yale Univ. Press, 1946); Michael Polanyi, *The Logic of Liberty* (Chicago: Univ. of Chicago Press, 1951), pp. 93–110, 138–53; and Michael Polanyi, *Personal Knowledge: Towards a Post-Critical Philosophy* (1958; rpt. Chicago: Univ. of Chicago Press, 1962), pp. 69–131, 203–48, 299–324.

[9]I am suggesting that the topic of "falsity" is necessary whenever one's conception of consciousness transcends the mind of a single individual. This is so because the transcendent consciousness, by its very conception, is a legitimizing agency, a means to warrant moral judgments (as in Perelman) or a means to create the fiction of verification when verification is logically impossible (as in Ziman and Brown). To fail to acknowledge the undeniable falsity of *any* description of mass or group consciousness is to create the illusion that one or another series of normative claims have an independent "facticity" about them. In my view Brown and Ziman are reckless with hypostatized "descriptions" of the consciousness of an intellectual elite, a "scientific community," which itself is in fact a creature of convention, in the specific terms of "description" a fiction of Ziman's and Brown's mind and a rhetorical vision for their readers. See Brown; Ch. Perelman and L. Olbrechts-Tyteca, *The New Rhetoric: A Treatise on Argumentation*, trans. John Wilkinson and Purcell Weaver (1958; Eng. trans. Notre Dame: Univ. of Notre Dame Press, 1969), pp. 31–35, 61–74; J. M. Ziman, *Public Knowledge: An Essay Concerning the Social Dimension of Science* (Cambridge: Cambridge Univ. Press, 1968), pp. 102–42; and contrast George Edward Moore, *Principia Ethica* (1903; rpt. Cambridge: Cambridge Univ. Press, 1965), esp. pp. 142–80; and Bruce E. Gronbeck, "From 'Is' to 'Ought': Alternative Strategies," *Central States Speech Journal*, 19 (1968), 31–39.

[10]See Kenneth Burke, "A Dramatistic View of the Origins of Language and Postscripts on the Negative" in *Language as Symbolic Action* (Berkeley: Univ. of California Press, 1966), pp. 418–79, esp. pp. 453–63; Hannah Arendt, "What Is Authority?" in *Between Past and Future* (New York: Viking, 1968), pp. 91–141; Hannah Arendt, "Lying in Politics: Reflections on the Pentagon Papers," in *Crises of the Republic* (New York: Harcourt Brace Jovanovich, 1972), pp. 1–47; Jürgen Habermas, "Hannah Arendt's Communications Concept of Power," *Social Research*, 44 (1977), 3–24; J. G. A. Pocock,

Politics, Language and Time (New York: Atheneum, 1973), pp. 17–25, 202–32; and Robert E. Goodwin, "Laying Linguistic Traps," *Political Theory,* 5 (1977), 491–504.

[11]See Kenneth Burke, *A Grammar of Motives* (New York: Prentice Hall, 1945), pp. 43–46, 415–18; Burke, *Rhetoric,* pp. 275–76, 298–301; Ernst Cassirer, *Language and Myth,* trans. Susanne K. Langer (1946; Eng. trans. 1946; rpt. New York: Dover, 1953), pp. 62–83; Richard M. Weaver, *The Ethics of Rhetoric* (1953; rpt. Chicago: Gateway, 1970), pp. 211–32; and Rosalind Coward and John Ellis, *Language and Materialism* (London: Routledge & Kegan Paul 1977), pp. 61–152.

[12]José Ortega y Gasset, *Man and People,* trans. Willard R. Trask (New York: Norton 1957), p. 245.

[13]*Ibid.,* pp. 192–221, 258–72.

[14]*Ibid.,* p. 221.

[15]*Ibid.,* p. 251.

[16]*Ibid.,* pp. 176–91.

[17]See Murray Edelman, *Political Language* (New York: Academic Press, 1977), pp. 43–49, 141–55; Schwab, pp. 143–57; and Thomas M. Franck and Edward Weisband, *Word Politics: Verbal Strategy Among the Superpowers* (New York: Oxford Univ. Press, 1972), pp. 3–10, 96–113, 137–69.

[18]Ortega y Gasset, *Man and People,* pp. 243–52. Further, contrast Ortega and Marx on the nature of "idea"; José Ortega y Gasset, *The Modern Theme,* trans. James Cleugh (1931; rpt. New York: Harper, 1961), pp. 11–27; and Marx and Engels, pp. 27–37. See, also, Coward and Ellis, pp. 84–92, 122–35.

[19]Ortega y Gasset, *Man and People,* pp. 57–71, 94–111, 139–91. Husserl's recognition of *praxis* and contradiction in his doctrine of "self-evidence" confirms Ortega's critique: Edmund Husserl, *Ideas: General Introduction to Pure Phenomenology,* trans. W. R. Boyce Gibson (1913; Eng. trans. 1931; rpt. London: Collier Macmillan, 1962), pp. 353–67. See, also, Schutz's and Luckmann's elaboration of the bases of Carneadean skepticism: Alfred Schutz and Thomas Luckmann, *The Structures of the Life-World,* trans. Richard M. Zaner and H. Tristram Engelhardt, Jr. (Evanston: Northwestern Univ. Press, 1973), pp. 182–229.

[20]Michel Foucault, *The Archaeology of Knowledge,* trans. A. M. Sheridan Smith (1969; Eng. trans. New York: Pantheon, 1972), pp. 178–95; H. T. Wilson, *The American Ideology: Science, Technology and Organization as Modes of Rationality in Advanced Industrial Societies* (London: Routledge & Kegan Paul, 1977), pp. 231–53; and Roger Poole, *Towards Deep Subjectivity* (New York: Harper & Row, 1972), pp. 78–112.

[21]Michael Polanyi and Harry Prosch, *Meaning* (Chicago: Univ. of Chicago Press, 1975), pp. 9, 22: "We have all learned to trace the collapse of freedom in the twentieth century to the writings of certain philosophers, particularly Marx, Nietzsche, and their common ancestors, Fichte and Hegel. But the story has yet to be told how we came to welcome as liberators the philosophies that were to destroy liberty. . . . We in the Anglo-American sphere have so far escaped the totalitarian nightmares of the right and left. But we are far from home safe. For we have done little, in our free intellectual endeavors to uphold thought as an independent, self-governing force." Contrast this "personal knowledge" explanation with Max Horkheimer and Theodor W. Adorno, *Dialectic of Enlightenment,* trans. John Cumming (1944; Eng. trans. New York: Herder and Herder, 1972), pp. 255–56; and Jacques Ellul, *Propaganda: The Formation of Men's Attitudes,* trans. Konrad Kellen and Jean Lerner (1962; Eng. trans. New York: Vintage, 1973), pp. 52–61, 232–57.

[22]See Peter Rodino's opening remarks in "Debate on Articles of Impeachment," U.S., Congress, House of Representatives, Committee on the Judiciary, 93rd Cong., 2nd sess., 24 July 1974, pp. 1–4.

    The "vertical/horizontal" metaphor used here to describe the evident structure of ideographs should not be confused with Ellul's idea (pp. 79–84) of the structural effects of "Propaganda." Lasky's analysis of "the English ideology" represents the "vertical" description I have in mind: Melvin J. Lasky, *Utopia and Revolution* (Chicago: Univ. of Chicago Press, 1976), pp. 496–575.

[23]See Edward H. Levi, *An Introduction to Legal Reasoning* (Chicago: Univ. of Chicago Press, 1948), esp. pp. 6–19, 41–74; Perelman and Tyteca, pp. 70–74, 101–02, 350–57; and Duncan, pp. 110–23, 130–40.

[24]Collingwood suggests that the content or ultimate subject matter of history should consist of explaining such recurrent usages ("ideographs") as "freedom" and "progress": R. G. Collingwood, *The Idea of History* (1946; rpt. London: Oxford Univ. Press, 1972), pp. 302–34. See, also, Herbert J. Muller, *The Uses of the Past* (New York: Oxford Univ. Press, 1952) pp. 37–38.

[25]See William Wirt, *Sketches of the Life and Character of Patrick Henry,* 9th ed. (Philadelphia: Thomas Cowperthwait, 1839) dedication and pp. 417–43; Judy Hample, "The Textual and Cultural Authenticity of Patrick Henry's 'Liberty or Death' Speech," *Quarterly Journal of Speech,* 63 (1977), 298–310; and Robert D. Meade, *Patrick Henry: Portrait in the Making* (New York: Lippincott, 1957), pp. 49–58.

[26]At least two strategies (that is, two theoretical mechanisms) have the capacity to yield fairly precise descriptions of functional "meaning" within situational and textual contexts: See Hans-Georg Gadamer, *Philosophical Hermeneutics,* trans. David E. Linge (Berkeley: Univ. of California Press, 1976), pp. 59–94, and Umberto Eco, *A Theory of Semiotics* (Bloomington: Indiana Univ. Press, 1976), pp. 48–150, 276–313.

[27]Ortega y Gasset, *Man and People,* p. 247. Cf. Ferdinand de Saussure, *Course in General Linguistics,* trans. Wade Baskin, ed. Charles Bally and Albert Sechehaye in collaboration with Albert Riedlinger (1915 Eng. trans. 1959; rpt. New York: McGraw-Hill, 1966), pp. 140–90, 218–21.

[28]See Richard M. Nixon, "Address to the Nation on the Watergate Investigation," *Public Papers of the Presidents of the United States* (Washington, D.C.: U.S. Government Printing Office, 1975), Richard Nixon, 1973, pp. 691–98, 710–25. Lucas' analysis of "rhetoric and revolution" (though it is more "idea" than "terministically" conscious) represents the "horizontal" description I have in mind: Stephen E. Lucas, *Portents of Rebellion: Rhetoric and Revolution in Philadelphia, 1765–76* (Philadelphia: Temple Univ. Press, 1976).

[29]See Jürgen Habermas, *Communication and the Evolution of Society,* trans. Thomas McCarthy (1976; Eng. trans. Boston: Beacon, 1979), pp. 1–68, 130–205.

[30]See Foucault, pp. 149–65.

[31]See Nicholas Abercrombie and Bryan S. Turner, "The Dominant Ideology Thesis," *British Journal of Sociology,* 29 (1978), 149–70.

RECONSTRUCTING <EQUALITY>: CULTURETYPAL AND COUNTER-CULTURAL RHETORICS IN THE MARTYRED BLACK VISION

JOHN LOUIS LUCAITES AND CELESTE MICHELLE CONDIT

"The bitterly cold winter of 1962 lingered throughout the opening months of 1963, touching the land with chill and frost, and then was replaced by a placid spring. Americans awaited a quiet summer." This is how Dr. Martin Luther King, Jr. (1964, p. 15) recalled the national climate of expectations leading up to the fateful summer of 1963. By the time that summer had ended, those expectations had been cheated, and King himself had been a primary catalyst of the ferment that was released. Thus, he continued:

> Summer came, and the weather was beautiful. But the climate, the social climate of American life erupted into lightning flashes, trembled with thunder and vibrated to the relentless, growing rain of protest come to life through the land. Explosively, America's third revolution—the Negro Revolution—had begun.

King was not, of course, the cause of this revolution, but rather its most thunderous and publicly acclaimed voice, his rhetoric giving a direction to the social forces that had been gathering for decades (Marable, 1984, pp. 42–94; Branch, 1988). Nevertheless, as important as his speaking was, King articulated only one of the two major strands that have long been central to the martyred vision of black Americans.[1] The other strand of that vision, articulated by a chorus of voices that achieved somewhat less public acclaim, including Stokely Carmichael, Angela Davis, Huey P. Newton, and H. Rap Brown, is perhaps best represented by the revolution's other martyr of the 1960s, Malcolm X.

It is virtually a commonplace, although not a uniformly accepted one, that King preached a position of social and political reform, while Malcolm X shouted a virulent and revolutionary creed (Meier & Rudwick, 1968, pp. 295–296; Edmund, 1976, pp. 176–181, 233; White, 1985, pp. 164–165). King's testimony above, as well as his increasingly radical endorsement of the "Negro revolution," indicate that this categorization is oversimplified.[2] Both Malcolm X and King argued for continued commitments to values enshrined in the American creed, and both sought changes in the day-to-day practices of American society that could easily be identified as revolutionary. Their differences are not accurately characterized by socio-political labels portraying the relative degrees of radicality of their respective principles and ideals, but by the types of rhetorical structures each employed in his public discourse. Rather than being reformist or revolutionary[,] then, a careful analysis of the rhetorical structures eloquently employed by each to shape and articulate an effective vision of equality reveals King's rhetoric to be "culturetypal" and Malcolm X's rhetoric to be "counter-cultural."

This formulation rests on a view that portrays significant rhetors as those able to realign material life experiences and cultural symbols through the artful use of the available means of persuasion.[3] In what follows we will demonstrate this perspective by first identifying <equality> as one of the central ideographic commitments in the public discourse of both Malcolm X and Dr. Martin Luther King, Jr., and then by analyzing the symbolic, cultural resources each used to give meaning to that commitment.[4] Finally, we will argue that in the American experience, <equality> functions as a rhetoric of control, and the only way to transcend the restrictions structured by such an ideology is through a dualistic discourse which acts independently on both sides of a discursive paradox: One voice, generally lacking legitimacy and maintaining a shadowy profile, reworks the public vocabulary by transforming life-experiences into characterizations and narratives that reshape existing ideographs; another voice, legitimate and even popular, revivifies those ideographs central to the process of social change. In the end, the "audience" may affirm one speaker and castigate another, but the public vocabulary that is created (and articulated by subsequent rhetors) is a synthesis of both. It is in this context, we will conclude, that the tension created by King's culturetypal rhetoric and Malcolm X's counter-cultural rhetoric functioned to produce a revised and emancipatory conception of cultural equality.

VISIONS OF <EQUALITY>

Although a number of scholars have attended to the rhetoric of King and Malcolm X, none have focused on the centrality of the term <equality> in their discourses.[5] Perhaps this omission occurs because it has seemed so natural that <equality> would occupy a central position in their public utterances. After all, the terms of the debate over racial equality had been established long before Malcolm X or King entered the scene (Jordan, 1969; Woodward, 1974), and it is unlikely that either could have made a compelling case for racial justice in America in the absence of an articulated commitment to <equality>.

In employing the term <equality>, however, King and Malcolm X urged different meanings and practices. For Malcolm X, <equality> represented a commitment to a relationship of equivalence between two or more clearly separate entities, each of which possessed its own identity, but was similarly powerful, as one might say that the United States of America and the Union of Soviet Socialist Republics are equally strong nations (see e.g., Malcolm X & Haley, 1966, p. 272; 1966f, p. 139). This perspective was at direct odds with King's signification of <equality> as a formal and identical sameness between two entities, such that each was ultimately indistinguishable from and interchangeable with the other. Thus, whereas Malcolm X saw <equality> as an empowerment of the self, present only in the condition of opposition, King had a Christian concept of moral power or justice which could be achieved only through consolidation with a transcendental unity that eschewed separation (e.g., King, 1986b, pp. 293–294).

These differences are often summed up by labelling King an "integrationist" and Malcolm X a "separationist," and so they were, but to understand how rhetorics of assimilation and separation can gain cultural legitimacy in the face of a potent rhetoric of control, such as the Anglo-American commitment to <equality>, requires an understanding of their rhetorical structures. These differences are also often accounted for by the claim that King spoke to America's dominant white culture and to the growing black middle- and working-classes, whereas Malcolm spoke to the inmates of America's black ghettoes (Lomax, 1968, pp. 38, 83, 141; Goldman, 1973, p. 23; White, 1985, p. 164; and Edmund, 1976, pp. iv, 234–355). While such observations thus link the material conditions of one's social existence to rhetorical output, they seldom provide an explanation of *how* such material experiences are *transformed* by skillful rhetors into different, parallel, and compelling arguments based on a *shared public vocabulary*. We suggest the desirability of replacing such materialistic determinism (as well as its most frequent opponent, discursive idealism) with a theory accounting for the interplay of the material conditions of social existence and rhetoric.

NARRATIVES AND CHARACTERIZATIONS AS CULTURAL RESOURCES

A "bounded network" theory of language (see Railsback, 1983) assumes that ideographs exist as cultural ideals, but gain their meaning-in-use from collective interpretations of the recursive relationship between the objectively material and symbolic environments in which they operate. To explain the differences in the rhetorics of Malcolm X and Martin Luther King, Jr. from such a perspective thus requires an exploration of the specific ways in [which] they forged links between cultural values and their life conditions. Such rhetorical linkages are constructed of two different types of discourse units, characterizations and narratives (e.g., see Condit, 1987).

Characterizations are the labels attached to agents, acts, scenes, agencies, or purposes in the public vocabulary, and integrate cultural connotations and denotations while ascribing a typical and pervasive nature to the entity described (Burke, 1969). So, for example, the characterization "Northeastern liberal" has become a label which essentializes the politically active members of New England and surrounding states as elitist, radical, and out of touch with America's heartland. Characterizations such as this provide the first step in the move from the material experience of daily life to collective valuation through the simple process of providing concrete but motivationally loaded names to politically salient entities.

Narratives are the storied forms of public discourse that extend the network of a community's public vocabulary by structuring the particular relationships between and among various characterizations. They thus provide an understanding for how material reality holds together and functions. In doing so the narratives charge the characterizations with rhetorical puissance and resonance. This structuring and vivification provides the second step from material experience to collective valuation. Narratives also provide the bridge to the final step by incorporating the ideal cultural values or ideographs that constitute a community. Indeed, ideographs typically serve as the primary purpose term in most social narratives, such as <liberty> functions in the story we tell of Patrick Henry's public defiance of England at the time of our revolution for independence.

In any community there are always a number of culturally established and sanctioned narratives, characterizations, and ideographs. Taken together, they constitute what we call a social group's ideology or "public vocabulary." Everyday, ordinary individuals, as well as social and political advocates, draw upon this repertoire in their own public discourse, referring to particular narratives, characterizations, and ideographs with the same taken-for-granted propensity with which one typically refers to his or her family members. However, when conditions arise that invite or require social change, especially when a displaced group seeks to have its interests granted some kind of public legitimacy, the public vocabulary needs to be managed and reconstituted in ways that require two entirely different kinds of rhetorical skills. Rhetors who successfully rearrange and revivify the culturally established public vocabulary to produce social change are masters of culturetypal rhetoric.[6] Those rhetors who introduce new—and thus culturally unauthorized—characterizations and narratives to the public vocabulary and who challenge existing characterizations and narratives are masters of counter-cultural rhetoric. As the case of King and Malcolm X will indicate, when the different rhetorical means of culturetypal and counter-cultural rhetorics work together toward shared ends, they can produce radical changes in the public vocabulary, thus altering both a community's discursive and material practices. We will argue, therefore, that the disparate proposals for <equality> promoted during the 1960s by Martin Luther King, Jr. and Malcolm X can best be understood by examining their genesis as culturetypal and counter-cultural rhetorics.

MALCOLM X

We begin with Malcolm X. Born Malcolm Little, Malcolm X grew up in and around Lansing, Michigan, where two of his earliest remembered experiences were tinged with violence and white racist attitudes: the murder of his father, a vocal Garveyite, by the Black Legion, a KKK-like organization; and the certification of his mother's insanity by the state welfare agency for refusing to violate her religious commitments by feeding her family a butchered hog donated by a neighboring farmer (Malcolm X & Haley, 1966, pp. 9–21; Wolfenstein, 1981, pp. 42–44). Consequently, at the age of ten, Malcolm X landed in a white foster home and was enrolled in the white school system where he excelled, achieving high grades and the popular respect of his classmates.

It should not be hard to recognize how growing up with a white family and attending white schools socialized Malcolm X to the dominant American commitment to <equality> as an abstract term definitive of the conditions of community. But it was also in these early years that he was confronted with the fact that equality was in no sense absolute—even when qualified "in the eyes of the law"—and that it varied with the color of one's skin. So, for example, he makes a point in his *Autobiography* (Malcolm X & Haley, 1966, pp. 36–37, emphasis added) of telling the story of a white high school teacher who rejected his ambition to become a lawyer:

> [He] looked surprised, I remember, and leaned back in his chair and clasped his hands behind his head. He kind of half-smiled and said, 'Malcolm, one of life's first needs is for us to be realistic. Don't misunderstand me, now. We all here like you, you know that. But you've got to be realistic about being a nigger. A lawyer—that's no realistic goal for a nigger. You need to think about something that you *can* be. You're good with your hands—making things. Everybody admires your carpentry shop work. Why don't you plan on carpentry? People like you as a person—you'd get all kinds of work.' The more I thought afterwards about what he said, the more uneasy it made me. It just kept treading around in my mind. What made it really begin to disturb me was [his] advice to others in my class—all of them white. . . . They all reported that [he] had encouraged what they wanted. Yet nearly none of them had earned marks *equal* to mine. It was a surprising thing that I had never thought of it that way before, but I realized that whatever I wasn't, I *was* smarter than nearly all of those white kids. But apparently I was still not intelligent enough, in their eyes, to become whatever *I* wanted to be. It was then that I began to change—inside.

We see this narrative as pivotal, for it indicates the initial tension Malcolm X felt between the linguistic commitment to <equality> and its material instantiation in his life experiences.

Malcolm X had three alternative courses of action open to him: (1) he could capitulate to the tension between the idealistic commitment to <equality> and its limited practical application for one of his race, i.e., "to become something that he could be"; (2) he could completely reject the commitment to <equality> and thus become a social and political outcast; or (3) he could attempt to redefine <equality>, to recuperate it as a more useful and acceptable commitment. His initial response was an anger and frustration that led him to abandon his studies and to move to the ghettoes of Boston and Harlem. Here, he capitulated to the dominant definition of <equality>, accepting as natural and practical the limited range of options open to him. At the same time, however, he strove to appear as "white" as possible in the hope of eventually expanding his range of possible successes (Malcolm X & Haley 1966, pp. 56–150; see also Wolfenstein, 1981, p. 157; Goldman, 1982, p. 307). So, for example, he underwent the painful process of straightening his hair in order to look more like a white man, he openly flaunted his violation of rigid social codes regarding interracial dating, and, perhaps most revealing, he took great pride in his capitalistic success at being the "best possible" con-man, pimp, drug-dealer, and burglar that he could be. His first move, then, both violated and lived up to the dominant ideological arrangement of <equality>.

His ghetto life-style eventually landed him in prison, where the intervention of his original, black family led him to explore the vastly different ideological code of the Black Muslims. Though he originally embraced the black Islamic code of ideals as a con game designed to achieve him an early parole date, he claims to have been gradually intoxicated by the Black Muslim conception of "self" that allowed blacks to exceed the limited <equality> to which they had become accustomed in the United States (Malcolm X & Haley, 1966, pp. 151–190; see also Condit & Lucaites, 1989). In the end, the narratives of the Black Muslim religion led Malcolm X to embrace his "blackness" as a blessing by helping him to separate himself from what the Islamic code considered to be an inferior white race that had coded <equality> to mean identity and sameness in order to undermine black superiority. It is precisely at this point that Malcolm X abandoned the dominant American version of <equality>, and embraced the notion of <equality> as "power" dependent upon the separation of races into socially and politically autonomous communities.

Of course, for blacks socialized to the dominant conception of <equality> that promoted a dream of identity and eventual assimilation, Malcolm X's claims of black superiority and the necessity for separation seemed somehow wrong. To white audiences it was downright blasphemy, a culturally inappropriate usage of a sacred term of the community. Each of these responses arose from the difficulty of defining an ideograph in isolation. Ideographs are not free-floating terms. They are bound for their meaning and significance to other ideographs, to the community's dominant characterizations, and to existing and pervasive cultural narratives. To redefine a key term such as an ideograph thus requires the rhetorical reconstruction of substantial portions of the community's ideological substructure (McGee, 1980a, pp. 10–14; for specific examples, see Lucaites, 1984, pp. 121–235; Railsback, 1984). Consequently, Malcolm X's discourse was dominated by strategies of recharacterization through which he worked out the tension between his life experiences and the central ideographic issue of <equality> by forging new descriptions of the key agents and agencies faced by black Americans, and linking them with a cluster of reformulated ideographs through a narrative framework.

One of the dominant tasks of all black rhetors, extending back through Frederick Douglass, has been to describe their blackness in positive terms. Malcolm X's commitment to a separatist <equality> depended precisely on this positive characterization of blacks. He strengthened and extended the sense of black pride and selfhood in two ways. First, he cited the achievements of black Americans, as well as the specific contributions that they had made to American society in all of their various roles, ranging from being slaves to soldiers. In discussing the role of slavery he explained (Malcolm X, 1966c, p. 32):

> Our mothers and fathers invested sweat and blood. Three hundred and ten years we worked in this country without a dime in return—I mean without a *dime* in return. You let the white man walk around here talking about how rich this country is, but you never stop to think how it got so rich so quick. It got rich because you made it rich.

Such recharacterizations led his listeners to recognize their own abilities by developing a sense of worth through accomplishment that led to entitlement. But they also provided a sense of worth through identification with a larger community. Many of his efforts at recharacterization were directed at linking African-Americans with Africans. The strategy was sound. If a deficit of "power" is a major roadblock to being granted <equality>—as Malcolm X's experiences taught him it was—then to be a minority is always dangerous. By linking American blacks with black people around the world, he turned his people into a majority race. Repeatedly, he told his black audiences (Malcolm X, 1966c, p. 36):

African-Americans, that's what we are—Africans who are in America. You're nothing but Africans. In fact, you'd get farther calling yourself African instead of Negro. Africans don't catch hell. They don't have to pass civil rights legislation for Africans. An African can go anywhere he wants now.

This move created the possibility for black Americans to be *equal* (in power) to white Americans, and thus simultaneously made possible and salient his revision of <equality> as a commitment of community.

Malcolm X also "equalized" the races by viciously poking fun at white America and its pretension to values based in anything but power. Relying on the skills that he developed as a ghetto hustler, he slyly unraveled the white man's "con" in much the same manner as the slave trickster (Levine, 1977, pp. 102–135) of an earlier time. He constantly recharacterized the existing political institutions as a form of brute force aligned against black interests, refusing to allow the dominant white conception of them as necessary, neutral, or benign to persist. On one occasion, he insisted (Malcolm X, 1966e, p. 66), "Harlem is a police state; the police in Harlem, their presence is like occupation forces, like an occupying army. They're not in Harlem to protect us; they're in Harlem to protect the interests of the businessmen who don't even live there." A bit later in the same speech (p. 67) he continued, "Nowadays, our people don't care who the oppressor is: whether he has a sheet or whether he has on a uniform, he's in the same category." He similarly dismissed whites who pretended to support black liberation as "old, tricky, blue-eyed liberals" (p. 34), who belied any real support of blacks by refusing to deliver up those he referred to as the "snake heads" (Malcolm X, 1966b, p. 136), the Klansmen and Southern sheriffs who murdered blacks and civil rights workers.

This characterization strategy vividly aligned power and <equality>. By recharacterizing white Americans as self-interested hypocrites, he not only created a feeling of black empowerment by "evening the score" between the races, but he also made eminent his definition of <equality> as a reciprocity between two self-interested groups. The Americans depicted by Malcolm were therefore two powerful and separate groups who might meet as equals only by a balancing of power.

Through bitter wit, and fired by his street-hustler's insights, Malcolm X redrew the American scene to accommodate both his experiences of that world and the only version of <equality> that could fit the world he saw. Such characterizations, however, did not automatically align themselves with specific ideographs. Because Malcolm X was operating from outside the dominant ideological tradition of white America, there were no readily available stories to indicate how these separate and self-interested agents should act towards each other in the name of his newly defined <equality>. To provide such a linking account, he resorted to a black tradition of basic survival stories that frequently featured animals as protagonists and/or antagonists (Malcolm X, 1985, pp. 43–5). The black American folk tradition that emerged out of the pre-Bellum days of slavery consisted largely of fables, such as the tales of Uncle Remus, that functioned as guidelines of moral action for individuals otherwise cut off from their historical roots (see Harris, 1880; Levine, 1977, pp. 90–121). In Malcolm X's repertoire, the stark depiction of animals as dehumanized agents engaged in a dialectic of power and domination helped to emphasize the nature of the relationship between blacks and whites, as well as to point out contradictions implicit in the dominant white ideology. So, for example, in justi-fying immediate vengeance as a means of self[-]defense against a group of Klan members who had lynched three blacks in Mississippi, he analogized the Klan, and by extension the white race, to a "snake" (Malcolm X, 1966b, pp. 135–136):

> If I were to go home and find some blood on the leg of one of my little girls, and my wife told me that a snake bit the child, I'd go looking for the snake. And if I found the snake, I wouldn't necessarily take time to see if it had blood on its jaws. As far as I am concerned the snake is a snake. So if snakes don't want someone hunting snakes indiscriminately, I say that snakes should get together and clean out their snakey house . . . I think you well understand what I'm saying. Now those were twenty-one snakes that killed those three brothers down there. Twenty-one—those are snakes. And there is no law in any society on earth that would hold it against anyone for taking the heads of those snakes.

This tale is compelling, not only because it contextualizes the relationship between blacks and whites as one of raw power and domination, denuded of human rationalization, but also because it underscores the potential inadequacy of a system of justice that allows vigilantes to hide behind the guise of the <due process of law>. One cannot talk to or reason with a snake. The only law that effectively defines the relationship between man and snake is thus the law of survival. In such a relation-ship, <equality> is an immediate and direct function of maintaining a balance of power between opposing forces "by any means necessary." Such stories not only instructed blacks in new ways to deal with existing inequalities, but also threat-ened whites if they refused to realign their behaviors in light of this new vision of <equality>.

Fables such as this were only a subsidiary thread tying together Malcolm X's rhetorical recharacterization of blacks and whites. The more important narrative in his discourse was his retelling of the story of American slavery. This story would generally begin by reminding his black listeners of their specific heritage as white America's slaves. To this end he would frequently mock those among his audience who might have forgotten this fact and fallen into the more comforting belief that they shared the dominant white American heritage: "You think you came over here on the Mayflower? No, you came in chains on slave ships. You are nothing but an ex-slave" (Malcolm X, 1966f, p. 4). From here, the narrative history that he recre-ated took many guises, but it generally revolved around the relationship between the "house Negro" and the "field Negro." Prior to the Civil War, he would suggest, house Negroes expressed their love and loyalty for their master, and were well dressed and fed. "If the master got sick," he would note with bitter irony, "the house Negro would say, 'What's the matter, boss, *we* sick?' *We* sick!" By contrast, he would describe the field Negro who "slaved" from sunup to sundown, lived in tar paper shacks, and ate poorly. If you asked the field Negro to run away, he would point out, "he didn't say 'Where are we going?' He'd say, 'Any place is better than here'" (Malcolm X, 1966f, p. 11).

Malcolm X's story of a race still enslaved in the twentieth century by social, polit-ical, and economic chains vividly demonstrated the need for change by narrativizing black-white relations as a failure to enact <equality>. Blacks constituted a morally equivalent or superior race (depending on the era of Malcolm's speech), but whites were enslaving blacks. The answer was for blacks to gain the power necessary to break the shackles so that they could live in their own place and style ("anywhere's better than here"), and thereby achieve Malcolm X's version of <equality>. To be free *from* white oppression was not only to retain one's identity as a black man, but to share an <equality> of power in all social, economic, and political relationships. This narrative further entailed its own agencies for bringing about the appropriate changes.

In contrast to King's insistence on nonviolent massive resistance as the sole legitimate means of protest, Malcolm X advocated the use of "any means necessary," ranging from the "ballot" to the "bullet," to produce the power essential to the creation of <equality> (1970a, p. 56; see also 1966c, pp. 23–44; and 1966h, p. 140):

> This is the only way you end oppression—with power. Power never takes a back step—only in the face of more power. Power doesn't back up in the face of a smile, or in the face of a threat, or in the face of some kind of nonviolent loving action. It's not the nature of power to back up in the face of anything but some more power.

In line with this perspective, Malcolm X repeatedly scoffed at the civil rights movement represented by King. He nagged that all King and his people wanted was to be able to share a cup of coffee with a "cracker" (Malcolm X, 1966d, p. 56; 1966e pp. 124, 128). He argued that "all this crawling and sitting-in and crying-in and praying-in and begging-in hasn't gotten any meaningful results" (Malcolm X, 1966c, 35–38; 1966d, p. 50; 1966e, p. 70). Most crucially, he felt that nonviolence was an enslaving agency because it applied a double standard to blacks and whites, a standard that made it impossible for blacks to achieve his version of <equality> as power. He noted that Patrick Henry had not run a non-violent revolution, and that the U.S. Government is "violent when their interests are at stake. But for all that violence they display at the international level, when you and I want just a little bit of freedom, we are supposed to be nonviolent" (Malcolm X, 1966a, pp. 163–164).

Consequently, Malcolm X was particularly strident about the black person's right to self[-]defense. He warned (Malcolm X, 1966a, p.165):

> This is how they psycho you. They make you think that if you try to stop the Klan from lynching you you're practicing violence in reverse . . . [.] Well, if a criminal comes around your house with his gun, brother, just because he's got a gun and he's robbing your house, and he's a robber, it doesn't make you a robber because you grab your gun and run him out. No, the man is using some tricky logic on you. I say it is time for black people to pull the sheet off of them so they won't be frightening black people any longer. That's all.

In spite of this insistence on the right to resort to violent means of self-defense when necessary, and despite popular media characterizations of his violent intentions, Malcolm X did not advocate violence as the central or preferred means of achieving his goals (Malcolm X, 1970b, pp. 3–4). The agency he pursued most fully was in keeping both with his positive recharacterization of blacks and his focus on power: He argued (1966a, p. 157; 1966c, p. 35; 1966g, p. 143) that the oppression of American blacks should be adjudicated by the United Nations. As a ghetto hustler Malcolm X had learned not only of the importance of power, but also of its limitations. When he saw that the activist black minority did not have sufficient power to force the dominant white culture to judge itself guilty of its crimes against morality, he was inspired to seek a higher court. This appeal not only emphasized the problem of the criminal being one's own judge and jury, it also offered the force of the African nations as international allies.

Malcolm X's negotiation of the dominant American commitment to <equality> was thus accomplished through a chain of rhetorical moves developed outside of the common cultural storehouse of characterizations and narratives. From the perspective of white America, and to a lesser extent for the blacks who had grown up partially submersed in that culture, Malcolm X's rhetoric was counter-cultural. He provided vivid recharacterizations of the black and white worlds that elevated the accomplishments of blacks and stripped the white world of much of its pretension. He reconstituted the tale of American slavery as a narrative core which linked up and explained the current relationship between these worlds. In so doing, he enhanced the persuasiveness and effectiveness of his radicalized vision of <equality> in two ways simultaneously: first, by motivating his black audiences to social, political, and economic action; and second, by threatening his white audience's sense of security. Much of this "black power" rhetoric had come before and was to be repeated after, but it is Malcolm X who is generally remembered as "the greatest evangelist of black unity" (Smith, 1969, p. 60), in part because of the vividness of his characterizations, the unifying strength of his narratives, and the potency with which he infused the ideographs he demanded.

MARTIN LUTHER KING, JR.

Dr. Martin Luther King[,] Jr. was raised in social and economic circumstances that were significantly different from those encountered by Malcolm X. King was born in Atlanta, a Southern metropolis which sported a "large and varied professional class" of blacks (Lewis, 1978, p. 8). Like Malcolm X, King's family was strongly religious and had a history of black activism. Unlike Malcolm X, however, King's family had achieved "material success," and as an adolescent King was "insulated against the most brutal aspects of Southern bigotry" (Lewis, 1978, pp. 7, 11; Miller, 1968; Bishop, 1971; Oates, 1982, pp. 3–31). He never went hungry, and he never saw his family brutally attacked. In many ways, he had tremendous advantages for a black growing up in the American South in the 1940s. For example, he entered college at the age of fifteen, and went on to pursue a doctorate in theology as a relatively young man. At the age of twenty-five he accepted his first pastorate at the Dexter Avenue Baptist Church in Montgomery, Alabama.

In spite of these advantages, King did not escape the experience of bigotry and racism altogether; he was refused service in stores and restaurants, forced to stand on busses while whites sat, and made to sit behind a curtain on a train, all of which, he later claimed, seriously affected his "selfhood" (King, 1986d, pp. 342–344, see also Bennett, 1976, p. 25). These experiences motivated King to seek change. Nonetheless, in general, King's life experiences reinforced the virtues of the dominant American commitment to <equality> and the hope that it held out to black Americans who kept a Christian faith in the "American dream." This experience was so strong in King's life that it led him to view the social and political practices that promoted racial inequality as simple deviations from the constituted ideals of the nation (King, 1986b, pp. 301–302). King's rhetorical task, therefore, was to revivify the commitments of the culture in order to give them force in political and social life. To do so he masterfully engaged the tactics of culturetypal rhetoric.

The resources of culturetypal rhetoric are quite different from those of counter-cultural rhetoric. The culturetypal rhetor already has culturally authorized characterizations and narratives in place which link and support the community's key values. Hence, King's rhetoric was far more compact than that of Malcolm X. To characterize whites and blacks as essentially similar, King had only to refer to a concept of "generic man" as created by God. He did so tersely and most effectively in "I Have a Dream" (King, 1966a, pp. 218–219) simply by noting his dream that "one day right there in Alabama little black boys and black girls will be able to join hands with little white boys and white girls as sisters and brothers." He easily characterized the essential similarity of all human beings in his speech on "Love, Law and Disobedience" (King, 1986c, p. 45) in defining "love" in this manner: "When one rises to love on this level [*agape*], he loves men not because he likes them, not because their ways appeal to him, but he loves every man because God loves him."

King similarly drew on strong pre-existing narrative structures. His oratory was thus, essentially, an attempt to *enact* the dominant American commitment to <equality> by contextualizing it within the two culturally authorized narrative structures that emphasized and integrated the moral and ideological imperatives of identity, unity, and sameness: the "American dream" and the "Christian faith." However, King did not generally need to tell the full stories of Christianity or American faith to the audiences who already knew them. Instead, he subtly and tellingly wove them into his discourse through structure and trope.

The mechanics of King's "I Have A Dream," delivered at the 1963 March on Washington, highlight this point well.[7] Notice, first, that the speech was predicated on the commonly accepted, capitalistic commitment to contracts ("promises" and "performances"), as captured by the "check" metaphor in the opening paragraphs (King, 1966a, p. 217):

In a sense we have come to our nation's capital to cash a check. When the architects of our republic wrote the magnificent words of the Constitution and the Declaration of Independence, they were signing a promissory note to which every American was to fall heir. . . . It is obvious today that America has defaulted on this promissory note insofar as her citizens of color are concerned. Instead of honoring this sacred obligation, America has given the Negro people a bad check, which has come back marked 'insufficient funds.' But we refuse to believe that the bank of justice is bankrupt. We refuse to believe that there are insufficient funds in the great vaults of opportunity of this nation. So we have come to cash this check—a check that will give us upon demand the riches of freedom and the security of justice.

In terms that were easily accessible to the experiences of the common listener, King portrayed a political economy out of synchronization with its prescribed ideals.

The salvation of <equality> was further guaranteed by linking it with the audience's predisposition to Christianity via archetypal metaphors that universalized and legitimated the commitment (see Osborn, 1976, pp. 16–18). The significance of <equality> thus transcended political interpretation:

We have come to this hallowed spot to remind America of the fierce urgency of now. This is no time to engage in the luxury of cooling off or to take the tranquilizing drug of gradualism. Now is the time to make real the promises of democracy. Now is the time to rise from the dark and desolate valley of segregation to the sunlit path of racial justice. Now is the time to lift our nation from the quicksand of racial injustice to the solid rock of brotherhood. Now is the time to make justice a reality of all of God's children (King, 1966a, pp. 217–218).

The symbolic transformations in this passage, linking ideological "promises" with a transcendental Christian "justice," are obvious. The same general transformations take place under a variety of different guises throughout the speech. Consider, for example, the usage of the words "hope," "dream," and "faith." In the first third of the speech, where King is concerned about America's failure to perform her promise, he displays and portrays his fervent "hope" that this problem can be resolved. By the second third of the speech, that "hope" disappears as we are introduced to the "dream," a dream which King himself points out is linked clearly with the "American dream." But notice, that the "American dream" is specifically *not* a dream in the sense of a hope or wish for a better world, but rather a vision of the guarantee of every American's birthright to the commitment to <equality>. By the last third of the speech, the hope of the first section transcends even the ideological guarantees of the "American dream," and becomes precisely a transcendental "faith" in a Christian/American future, which is implicitly a faith in the ideologically dominant conception of <equality> that privileges the significance of sameness and identity.

The ready availability of a public vocabulary of narratives and characterizations served King well, but it also carried its own problems. The liveliness of Malcolm X's speeches was guaranteed by the freshness and ferocity of his ideas. His style was often rough, and his delivery casual, both tending towards understatement. In contrast, King's ideas were old, comfortable friends that had long slumbered quietly alongside inequality. King's task was to revivify these ideas, to force them to do work in modifying existing social conditions. To do so, he turned to the canons of style and delivery with consummate skill.

King's orations strengthened the audiences' commitments, in part, through the aural force they carried. His uses of the simple devices of repetition, broad vowel sounds, and subtle alliteration, as well as his baritone voice, were adept. Once again we turn to the "Dream" speech for our example, this time as he responds to those who criticized the members of the civil rights movement for demanding too much (King, 1966a, pp. 218–219):

> There are those who are asking the devotees of civil rights "When will you be satisfied?" We can never be satisfied as long as the Negro is the victim of unspeakable horrors of police brutality. We can never be satisfied so long as our bodies, heavy with the fatigue of travel, cannot gain lodging in the motels of the highways and the hotels of the cities. We cannot be satisfied as long as the Negro's basic mobility is from a smaller ghetto to a larger one. We can never be satisfied as long as our children are stripped of the selfhood and robbed of their dignity by signs stating "for whites only." We cannot be satisfied as long as a Negro in Mississippi cannot vote and a Negro in New York believes he has nothing for which to vote. No, we are not satisfied, and we will not be satisfied until justice rolls down like waters and righteousness like a mighty stream.

In this instance, as throughout his oratory, King masterfully secularized the sonoric strength of the black preacher to construct a resonance which empowered the audience's prior commitments.

The content of his discourse was likewise forcefully constituted by his choice and usage of figurative language. Having contextualized <equality>, freedom, and the dignity of the individual in the narrative structures of the Christian hope for salvation and the American dream, he simultaneously authorized and vitalized these commitments with archetypal and culturetypal metaphors. A particularly important source of such metaphors for King was the *Bible*. Using biblical imagery, as he so often used biblical narratives, he brought his audience to *feel* the "solid rock of human dignity." Relying on the light/dark archetypal metaphor pair, for example, he assured them of the inevitable "daybreak of freedom and justice" and guaranteed an emergence from "the bleak and desolate midnight of man's inhumanity to man into the bright and glittering daybreak of freedom and justice" (King, 1986c, p. 45; see Osborn, 1966, pp. 115–126). Alternately, he begged them to move vertically toward the archetypically "majestic heights of understanding and brotherhood." His simple, strong, and vivid imagery, grounded in the audience's transcendental, Christian beliefs, gave a special presence and legitimacy to the American commitment to <equality>, and thus empowered the audience to overcome the resistance to black justice momentarily subverted by history and economics.

Biblical imagery also played a significant role in King's efforts to characterize those who opposed him. With white racists, he turned to the Christian practice of "conversion" as a means of "redemption," insisting that "even the worst segregationist can become an integrationist" (King, 1986c, p. 48). In like manner, when disappointed with "white moderates," he "chastised," "begged," and "confessed" to his "Christian and Jewish brothers" (King, 1968b, p. 294–296).

Finally, King's characterization of the agency necessary to enact these metaphors, this powerful myth, this "integration" of an empowering Christian/American unity, was likewise expressed in biblical terms: the means of "non-violent massive resistance" was in one sense simply the enactment of Christian "love." King repeated the term "love" incessantly. He defined it in great detail on several occasions, always portraying it as an outgrowth of Christian conscience, its authority and force evident in his suggestion that "Jesus says love them, and love is greater than like. Love is understanding, redemptive, creative, good will for all men" (King, 1966c, p. 47). As King explicitly admitted, one could not bring about "unity" by a means that required or allowed division, violence, or separation. Only the broad sense of a Christian love, enacted through non-violence and the willingness to suffer for the other ("unearned suffering," he chanted, "is redemptive") was an appropriate agency for this form of <equality> (King, 1966a, p. 219; 1966c, p. 47).

In contrast to Malcolm X, Martin Luther King, Jr. embraced the dominant commitment to <equality> which emphasized the assimilable interchangeability of all humans. Rather than to redefine this commitment for his audience, as was Malcolm X's task, King attempted to empower it by motivating his audiences to enact its meaning. He intertextualized the narratives implicit in their knowledge and understanding of the life of Christ and the American dream. He revitalized these stories through overwhelming delivery and rousing style. In the end, the Christian commitment to assimilation and the American commitment to individual interchangeability were virtually indistinguishable from one another. In such a world, the differences between black and white would be "equally" indistinguishable.

MALCOLM AND MARTIN IN DIALOGUE

Malcolm X and Martin Luther King, Jr., contemporaries, equally martyred for speaking the black word, expressed their respective commitments to <equality> in strikingly different ways. Responding to the tension between the practice of racial discrimination in America and the dominant, liberal-democratic commitment to <equality> as a cultural ideal, King employed the resources of the culturetypal rhetor. Through the tactical application of archetypal and culturetypal tropes he vivified the key ideographs and narratives of American society so that they might gain the power to "overcome" opposition and fulfill the promise of cultural assimilation implicit in the dominant ideological commitment to <equality> as a cultural ideal. Responding to the tension between the material life conditions in the black ghetto and the promise of social and political <equality> implicit in the dominant white American ideology, Malcolm X employed the resources of the counter-cultural rhetor. Through the rhetorical tactics of recharacterization and narrative reconstruction he redefined the cultural ideal of <equality> as a relationship of equivalence between two different but similarly powerful groups.

Because of their different life experiences, King and Malcolm X had different visions of what <equality> could best mean. Each therefore employed different rhetorical means to achieve their respective ends. To assess either rhetor by standards appropriate to the other would be an error. To fault King for a lack of ideological innovation (as political theorists on the "left" have tended to do), or to slight Malcolm X for lack of a polished style (as we fear rhetoricians have tended to do indirectly by their silence), would be to ignore the character of rhetoric as a culturally and historically situated discourse designed specifically to "adjusting ideas to people and people to ideas" (Bryant, 1952, p. 413; see Cruse, 1967, pp. 201, 393, 546; Marable, 1984, pp. 71–89, 114–115).

Whatever the formal excellence of their oratory, the specific achievement of King and Malcolm X was to employ their skills as rhetors to revise the American conception of <equality>. However, this revision was *not* achieved by either man in the absence of the other, but was rather precisely a result of the efforts of both men together. We have treated their rhetorics together because we believe that the rhetorical character of social change requires that their opposition be read as *two voices in dialogue, simultaneously separated and connected by the similarities and differences which they shared.* To understand this mutual functioning, it is necessary to consider the paradox of discursive change that they faced.

As McGee (1980a) has argued, ideographs constitute a vocabulary of public motives, which authorize and warrant public actions. Whether individual audience members assent directly to these vocabularies and their meanings or not, changes in law and governmental policy must be justified in the terms of this public warranting vocabulary (Condit, 1989). To argue for change therefore requires a rhetor to speak *against* the dominant ideology, but from *within* its own vocabulary. The dilemma is acute: To accommodate this vocabulary in the explanation and justification of public beliefs and action is to accede to the meaning embedded within its structure; to fail to accommodate it is to risk losing public approbation.

Traditional scholarship on the issue of racial equality has tended to recommend assaulting one side of this paradox to the exclusion of the other. Materialist analyses have tended to favor Malcolm X's approach, advocating a "revolutionary" rhetoric that is grounded in material experiences and overthrows dominant values. Materialists generally concede, however, that according to material standards, neither King nor Malcolm X were successful because their rhetorical campaigns failed to eliminate significant economic and political discrepancies between blacks and whites (e.g. Cross, 1984, pp. 3–16, 189–378; Wilson, 1980, pp. 166–172). Materialist accounts of racial equality thus leave us as paralyzed agents of action hoping for a more perfect, a more "ideal" materialist rhetor.

Idealist analyses of racial equality have tended to favor King's approach, supporting the powerful "reformist" rhetoric that revivified existing commitments. Such analyses, however, typically focus attention on the implicit power of <equality> as the symbol of a timeless, cultural ideal whose dormant meaning finally comes to life (e.g., as in the linguistic idealism of Myrdal, 1972; see also Fisher, 1970, p. xi; McWilliams, 1986, p. 282). They can account neither for King's failure to change economic inequities, nor for the unique role he and his audiences had to play in creatively crafting and articulating persuasive and compelling interpretations of <equality>. Idealist accounts thus leave us as passive agents of action hoping for a more perfect, more "material" ideal.

Although our characterization of these two perspectives might suggest otherwise, they are not contrary opposites. Idealists are correct to suggest that <equality> exists in the popular consciousness as a cultural ideal, and materialists are correct to suggest that it functions to promote the material interests of the dominant culture. To treat the ideological revision of <equality> from a rhetorical perspective requires that we acknowledge the apparently competing insights of materialist and idealist perspectives as a tension requiring management, rather than as a contradiction demanding resolution or elimination. Thus, it is only if we look at <equality> as cultural ideal that gained its meaning-in-use from individual and collective interpretations of the recursive relationship between the objectively material and symbolic environments in which it operated that we can recognize the character of the social change wrought by Martin Luther King, Jr. and Malcolm X (see Condit, 1987, pp. 361–363; Giddens, 1986, pp. 165–233).

Accordingly, we maintain that King would not have achieved the position of cultural hero if the likely alternative to his Christianized, integrationist vision of the "American dream" had been the familiar status quo of the first half of the twentieth century, rather than the threatening vision of the future depicted by Malcolm X. By the same token, Malcolm X's rhetoric was initially too hostile to achieve any serious consideration as a viable avenue of change for most audiences, and it only received careful inspection and consideration in the wake of growing discontent with the perceived ineffectiveness of King's rhetoric. More important than these situational factors, however, we maintain that the counter-positioning of King and Malcolm X was necessitated by their rhetorical position on the broader canvas of history, for it was thus, as two voices in dialogue, that they contributed "equally" to the revised concept of <equality> which emerged from the 1960s.

<EQUALITY> RECONSTRUCTED

From the time of its institutionalization as one of the primary commitments of American democracy through *Brown v. the Board of Education,* the ideograph <equality> had been publicly modified at one time or another by the terms "political," "social," "economic," "religious," and "sexual," each in its turn restricting or expanding the domain of its application somewhere between the often inconsistent commitments to the equality of "opportunities" and the equality of "outcomes" (See Bell, 1976, pp. 260–274; Eastland & Bennett, 1979, pp. 3–22; Huntington,

1981; Redenius, 1981; Ryan, 1981; Verba & Orren, 1985, pp. 5–6; Kluegel & Smith, 1986, pp. 11–36). The result was a presumably pluralistic, cultural ideal, but the structure of its usage in practice modified that pluralism by requiring a condition of similitude between two equal parties: Two or more individuals or groups could be equal only in direct proportion to the degree to which they shared a common and "interchangeable" identity (see Pole, 1978, pp. 214–252, 325–358). Such a criterion implied the potentially noxious requirement that those who would achieve <equality> must sacrifice or repress their social, political, or cultural differences from those of the dominant ideology.

King and Malcolm X were each confronted with this vocabulary in the context of a variety of concrete historical situations shared by a black community. Trends intensified by World War II came to a peak when black lawyers eventually forced the Supreme Court to declare an end to the "separate but equal" doctrine in 1954. Two groups of blacks agitated to give force to the Court's declaration: the emergent black middle class exemplified in King's Atlanta, and the growing, black, urban "under class," intensified by northern migration following the war, exemplified in Malcolm X's experiences in the ghettoes of Boston and Harlem. To the extent that the culturetypal and counter-cultural rhetorics of King and Malcolm X were heard by blacks, it was the historical confluence of their personal experiences with those of their listeners which led their audiences to promote them to positions of leadership.

The rhetorical task King and Malcolm X both faced, therefore, was the same faced by all other black civil rights workers: (1) Because they were operating in a pluralistic society, the primary goal of most civil rights workers was to achieve social and political legitimacy by having their special interests expressed as a component of the dominant ideology of the community. (2) Given the terms of American liberal democracy, this desire was most readily expressed as an interest in being treated as equal. Because of the history of its authorized public meaning-in-use, such a condition of equality was understood to mean that individuals should be treated as if they were essentially identical.[8] (3) However, by promoting "identity" as the egalitarian ideal, the dominant ideology marginalized, and indeed, perhaps effectively eliminated the possibility of social, political, and cultural "differences." It thus functioned as a potentially tyrannizing rhetoric of control, compelling those who would achieve <equality> to repress or sublimate their differences, or to risk being labelled deviant. Thus, in a society in which the dominant ideology reflected a lily[-]white community, blacks were required to find some way to give up their "blackness"—if not physically, at least by sacrificing their cultural heritage and publicly embracing the ideologically sanctioned heritage of the dominant group—or to risk charges of being un-American (See Asante, 1987, pp. 3–18, 164–167; Anderson, 1978, pp. 42–65; Greene, 1981, p. 165–210; Karst, 1983, p. 266).

King's rhetoric prevented black and white Americans from giving up the "dream" of equality. Malcolm X's rhetoric provided a new cast to that dream. Today, the most advanced rhetorics of social equality borrow from both visions to create a new, more powerful option than that held by either of these early heroes. Following the rhetorics of King *and* Malcolm X, the specific ideographic commitment to <equality> could be publicly understood and applied in ways which transcended the fundamentally restrictive commitment to interchangeability. So, for example, in the political realm Barbara Jordan (1976) could enact the commitment to <equality>, while still calling attention to her race and sex as primary points of difference from the dominant white, male power structure, just as Jesse Jackson (1984) could speak of a "rainbow coalition" that sought to provide both equal opportunities and outcomes for its members, without "white-washing" the cultural identity of its various constituencies.[9]

Through their simultaneous but separate assaults on the dominant American vocabulary of the early sixties, Martin Luther King, Jr. and Malcolm X gave presence to a "black vision," a uniquely black American rhetoric which vividly portrayed the tension that has beleaguered black leaders since the time of Frederick Douglass: a commitment to the dominant American ideology of <equality>, and the need to mold that ideology to the unique, native experiences of the black American masses with which it was consistently perceived as being in some sort of material contradiction. Only in accommodating this tension by praising <equality> as a sacred purpose term in dominant cultural narratives, while simultaneously manifesting the contradictions and inconsistencies implicit in the social and political practices associated with it through rhetorically compelling narratives and characterizations, were King and Malcolm X able to achieve the attention that ultimately provided them with a national audience. Malcolm X and King, articulating together separate black visions, thereby produced the components of the "African-American" vision which was to follow, a vision that offers cultural uniqueness and political amalgamation, perhaps, indeed, replacing America's "melting pot" with "a brightly patterned quilt."

In attempting to understand how <equality> was situated differently in the discourses of Malcolm X and Martin Luther King, Jr., we have focused attention on the interaction of the material and symbolic environments central to the life experiences of each. Our analysis indicates, at least in this instance, that rhetorical style, the material conditions of existence, and the symbolic environment interact with each other *and* are perceived in relationship to each other by virtue of the skills and practices of individual rhetors. Accordingly, we are compelled to the conclusion that the particular ideographs, narratives, and characterizations employed by rhetors bear specific and necessary relationships to each other, and to their tactical enactments in public discourse, as well as to the material conditions from which a rhetor speaks. There exists, therefore, a dynamic tension, characterized by the essential recursivity of linguistic and social-material environments, which needs to be managed by active and responsible agents in the context of rhetorical practices. From this perspective, rhetoric is essentially and primarily a theory of social and political power that may help us to unite our understanding of social actors and material forces, and to undermine the potentially oppressive contradictions implicit in our ideological commitments. By following this lead we may gain the basis for a critical understanding of the creative capacity for change.

ENDNOTES

[1]One of the most useful historical overviews of the two major alignments of American black spokespersons is provided in White (1985). See also Cruse (1967, pp. 174–176), who additionally notes the limited existence of a tripartite division in the era of DuBois, Washington, and Garvey (p. 334). Parsis (1978) parses these two strands of black rhetoric into four positions, and they are further parsed in Edmund (1976, p. 8).

[2]This is evident in a comparison of King's early speeches with later ones and is described in Lomax (1968, 159). See also White (1985, p. 165).

[3]We offer this as a corrective to the definitions provided by Aristotle (1932, 1355b)—"the faculty power of discovering in the particular case what are the available means of

persuasion"—and Bryant (1952, p. 413)—"the function of adjusting ideas to people and people to ideas." The boldness to suggest revisions to their work arises from the pressing need for rhetoricians to take more directly into account the widely acknowledged importance of systems of social conditions and their impact on public discourse. See, e.g., Giddens's (1979, esp. pp. 49–130) call for a theory of structuration.

[4]We follow the convention (Lucaites, 1984, p. 48, Note 71; Condit, 1987) of identifying ideographic usages of terms and phrasing by setting them off in angle brackets (< >).

[5]For studies on King, see Smith (1964a, 1964b), Black (1969), Keele (1972), Bosmajian (1979), Fulkerson (1979), Snow (1985), Osborn (1989), Cox (1989); on Malcolm X, see Illo (1964), Epps (1968, pp. 47–99), Scott (1968), Campbell (1970), Smith & Robb (1971, p. 3), Benson (1974), Flick (1977).

[6]The term "culturetypal" is drawn from the work of Osborn (1976), where it refers to the sacred words of a particular culture which function to preserve and reform social and political traditions. We extend its meaning here beyond simply the "sacred words" of a society to include sacred narratives and characterizations as well. Additionally, because we believe that the resources of *public culture* are not tied inherently to particular types of political ends, we separate culturetypes from the presumption of a non-radical, reformist function, and focus attention instead on the structures of such terms, narratives, and characterizations in usage.

[7]To talk about King's rhetoric as a monolithic entity is an obvious oversimplification. His rhetoric was adapted to the many situations which he faced over a span of twenty years. Moreover, his rhetoric became less hopeful and indeed more militant as he grew older. To encompass these changes in any generalization is not entirely possible. To make what generalizations seem reasonable, we have focused our attention on a sample of King's rhetoric that seems to be representative of his life's work, including speeches and writings from each of the periods of his life presented to predominantly black audiences, predominantly white audiences, and mixed audiences, at the local, national, and international levels. In the end we have come to the conclusion that "I Have A Dream" is truly representative of King's rhetoric, and it is for that reason that we focus on it here. A partial list of the speeches that we examined are contained in Washington (1986, pp. 5–289). See also King (1964, 1965, p. 20, 25).

[8]We would note in this regard, for example, that in overturning the "separate but equal" doctrine in *Brown v. The Board of Education* (1954) the court argued specifically by definition that separate *cannot* be equal ("identical"), and ruled that the only way that equality in education could be achieved would be to reverse racial segregation by demanding the implementation of its contradictory opposite condition (i.e., "desegregation" or "integration").

[9]The point is emphasized, in a slightly different vein, in the realm of academic philosophy where Walzer (1983) has accommodated the rhetorics of both Malcolm X and King in his call for a revised commitment to political egalitarianism:

> The aim of political egalitarianism is a society free from domination. *This is the lively hope named by the word equality: no more bowing and scraping, fawning and toadying; no more fearful trembling; no more high-and[-]mightiness; no more masters, no more slaves.* It is not a hope for the elimination of differences; we don't all have to be the same or have the same amounts of the same things. Men and women are one another's equals (for all important moral and political purposes) when no one possesses or controls the means of domination. . . . Domination is always mediated by some set of social goods. Though the experience is personal, nothing in the persons themselves determines its character. *Hence, again, equality as we have dreamed of it does not require the repression of persons.* We have to understand and control social good; we do not have to stretch or shrink human beings (emphasis added).

REFERENCES

Anderson, J. D. (1978). Black cultural equality in American education. In W. Feinberg (Ed.), *Equality and social policy* (pp. 42–65). Urbana, IL: University of Illinois Press.

Aristotle. (1932). *The rhetoric of Aristotle* (L. Cooper, Trans.). Englewood Cliffs, NJ: Prentice Hall.

Asante, M. K. (1987). *The Afrocentric view.* Philadelphia: Temple University Press.

Bell, D. (1976). *The cultural contradictions of capitalism.* New York: Basic Books.

Bennett, L. D. Jr. (1976). *What manner of man: A biography of Martin Luther King, Jr.,* 4th ed. Chicago: Johnson.

Benson, T. W. (1974). Rhetoric and autobiography: The case of Malcolm X. *Quarterly Journal of Speech, 60,* 1–13.

Bishop, J. (1971). *The last days of Martin Luther King, Jr.* New York: Putnam's Sons.

Black, E. (1969). The "vision" of Martin Luther King. In *Literature as revolt and revolt as literature: Three studies in the rhetoric of non-oratorical forms: Proceedings of the Fourth Annual University of Minnesota Spring Symposium in Speech Communication,* May 3, 1969 (pp. 7–16). Minneapolis, MN: University of Minnesota Press.

Bosmajian, H. (1979). The rhetoric of Martin Luther King's "Letter from Birmingham jail." *Midwest Quarterly, 21,* 46–62.

Branch, T. (1988). *Parting the waters: America in the King years 1954–63.* New York: Simon and Schuster.

Brown v. Board of Education of Topeka, Kansas, 347 U.S. 483 (1954).

Bryant, D. C. (1952). Rhetoric: Its functions and its scope. *Quarterly Journal of Speech, 39,* 401–424.

Burke, K. (1969). *A grammar of motives.* Berkeley: University of California Press. (Original work published 1945).

Campbell, F. C. (1970). Voices of thunder, voices of rage: A symbolic analysis of Malcolm X's speech, "Message to the grass roots." *Communication Education, 19,* 101–110.

Condit, C. M. (1990). *Decoding abortion rhetoric: Communicating social change.* Urbana, IL: University of Illinois Press.

Condit, C. M. (1987). Democracy and civil rights: The universalizing influence of public argumentation. *Communication Monographs, 54,* 1–18.

Condit, C. M., & Lucaites, J. L. (1989, November). *Malcolm X: The limits of the rhetor of revolutionary dissent.* Paper presented at the annual meeting of the Speech Communication Association, San Francisco.

Cox, J. R. (1989). The fulfillment of time: King's "I have a dream" speech (August 28, 1963). In M. C. Leff & F. J. Kauffeld (Eds.), *Texts in context: Critical dialogues on significant episodes in American political rhetoric* (pp. 181–204). Davis, CA: Hermagoras.

Cross, T. (1984). *The black power imperative: Racial equality and the politics of nonviolence.* New York: Faulkner.

Cruse, H. (1967). *The crisis of the Negro intellectual.* New York: William Morrow.

Eastland, T., & Bennett, W. J. (1979). *Counting by race: Equality from the founding fathers to Bakke and Weber.* New York: Basic Books.

Edmund, T. (1976). *Martin Luther King and the black American's protest movement in the USA.* India: New Heights.

Epps, A. (Ed.). (1968). *Malcolm X and the American Negro revolution: The speeches of Malcolm X.* London: Peter Owen.

Fisher, S. (1970). *Power in the black community: A reader in racial subordination in the United States.* New York: Random House.

Flick, H. (1977). An historical perspective on Malcolm X. *North Carolina Journal of Speech and Drama, 11,* 1–12.

Fulkerson, R. P. (1979). The public letter as a rhetorical form: Structure, logic, and style in King's "Letter from Birmingham jail." *Quarterly Journal of Speech, 65,* 121–136.

Giddens, A. (1979). *Central problems in social theory: Action, structure and contradiction in social analysis.* Berkeley: University of California Press.

Green, P. (1981). *The pursuit of inequality.* New York: Pantheon Books.

Goldman, P. (1973). *The death and life of Malcolm X.* New York: Harper and Row.

Goldman, P. (1982). Malcolm X: Witness for the prosecution. In J. H. Franklin & A. M. Meier (Eds.), *Black leaders of the twentieth century* (pp. 305–330). Urbana, IL: University of Illinois Press.

Harris, J. C. (1880). *Uncle Remus: His songs and his sayings.* Boston: n.p.

Huntington, S. P. (1981). *American politics: The promise of disharmony.* Cambridge: Harvard University Press.

Illo, J. (1964). The rhetoric of Malcolm X. *Columbia University Forum,* pp. 5–12.

Jackson, J. (1984, November 15). The rainbow coalition. *Vital Speeches of The Day,* 77–81.

Jordan, B. (1976, August 15). Who then will speak for the common good. *Vital Speeches of the Day,* 645–646.

Jordan, W. (1969). *White over black: American attitudes toward the Negro, 1550–1812.* Baltimore: Penguin.

Karst, K. (1983). Why equality matters. *Georgia Law Review,* 17, 245–289.

Keele, L. A. M. (1972). *A Burkeian analysis of the rhetorical strategies of Dr. Martin Luther King, Jr.* Unpublished doctoral dissertation, University of Oregon.

King, M. L., Jr. (1964). *Why we can't wait.* New York: Harper and Row.

King, M. L., Jr. (1965). The civil rights struggle in the United States today, delivered 21 April 1965. In Supplement to *The Record of the Association of the Bar of the City of New York,* pp. 20, 25.

King, M. L., Jr. (1986a). I have a dream. In J. M. Washington (Ed.), *A testament of hope: The essential writings of Martin Luther King, Jr.* (pp. 217–20). New York: Harper and Row. (Originally presented 28 August 1963).

King, M. L., Jr. (1986b). Letter from Birmingham jail. In J. M. Washington (Ed.), *A testament of hope: The essential writings of Martin Luther King, Jr.* (289–302). New York: Harper and Row. (Originally published 16 April 1963).

King, M. L., Jr. (1986c). Love, law, and civil disobedience. In J. M. Washington (Ed.), *A testament of hope: The essential writings of Martin Luther King, Jr.* (pp. 43–53). New York: Harper and Row. (Originally presented 16 November, 1961).

King, M. L., Jr. (1986d). *Playboy* interview, Martin Luther King, Jr. In J. M. Washington (Ed.), *A testament of hope: The essential writings of Martin Luther King, Jr.* (pp. 340–77). New York: Harper and Row. (Originally published 1 January 1965).

Kluegel, J. R. & Smith, R. E. (1986). *Beliefs about inequality: Americans' views of what is and what ought to be.* New York: Aldine De Gruyter.

Levine, L. W. (1977). *Black culture and black consciousness: Afro-American folk thought from slavery to freedom.* New York: Oxford University Press.

Lewis, D. A. (1978). *King: A biography* (2nd ed.). Urbana, IL: University of Illinois Press.

Lomax, L. E. (1968). *To kill a black man.* Los Angeles: Holloway House.

Lucaites, J. L. (1984). *Flexibility and consistency in eighteenth-century Anglo-Whiggism: A case study of the rhetorical dimensions of Anglo-Whiggism.* Unpublished doctoral dissertation, University of Iowa.

Malcolm X. (1966a). After the bombing. In G. Breitman (Ed.), *Malcolm X speaks* (pp. 157–177). New York: Grove Press. (Originally presented 13 February 1965).

Malcolm X. (1966b). At the Audubon. In G. Breitman (Ed.), *Malcolm X speaks* (pp. 115–136). New York: Grove Press. (Originally presented 13 December 1964).

Malcolm X. (1966c). The ballot or the bullet. In G. Breitman (Ed.), *Malcolm X speaks* (pp. 23–44). New York: Grove Press. (Originally presented 3 April 1964).

Malcolm X. (1966d). The Black revolution. In G. Breitman (Ed.), *Malcolm X speaks* (pp. 45–57). New York: Grove Press. (Originally presented 8 April 1964).

Malcolm X. (1966e). The Harlem 'hate-gang' scare. In G. Breitman (Ed.), *Malcolm X speaks* (pp. 64–71). New York: Grove Press. (Originally presented 29 May 1964).

Malcolm X. (1966f). Message to the grass roots. In G. Breitman (Ed.), *Malcolm X speaks* (pp. 3–22). New York: Grove Press. (Originally presented 9–10 November 1963).

Malcolm X. (1966g). To Mississippi youth. In G. Breitman (Ed.), *Malcolm X speaks* (pp. 137–146). New York: Grove Press. (Originally presented 31 December 1964).

Malcolm X. (1966h). Prospects for freedom in 1965. In G. Breitman (Ed.), *Malcolm X speaks* (pp. 147–156). New York: Grove Press. (Originally presented 7 January 1965).

Malcolm X. (1970a). The founding rally of the OAAU, June 28, 1964. In G. Breitman (Ed.), *By any means necessary* (pp. 33–68). New York: Pathfinder Press.

Malcolm X. (1970b). An interview by A. B. Spellman, 28 June 1964. In G. Breitman (Ed.), *By any means necessary* (pp. 1–13). New York: Pathfinder Press.

Malcolm X. (1985). A televised interview by K. B. Clark, June 1963. In K. B. Clark (Ed.), *King, Malcolm, Baldwin* (pp. 31–48). Middleton, CT: Wesleyan University Press.

Malcolm X & Haley, A. (1966). *The autobiography of Malcolm X.* New York: Grove Press.

Marable, M. (1984). *Race, reform and rebellion: The second reconstruction in black America, 1945–1982.* Jackson: University of Mississippi Press.

McGee, M. C. (1980a). The "ideograph": A link between rhetoric and ideology. *Quarterly Journal of Speech, 66,* 1–16.

McGee, M. C. (1980b). The origins of "liberty": A feminization of power. *Communication Monographs, 47,* 23–45.

McWilliams, W. C. (1986). On equality as the moral foundation of community. In R. I. Horowitz (Ed.), *The moral foundations of the American republic* (pp. 282–312). Charlottesville: University of Virginia Press.

Meier, A., & Rudwick, E. (1978). *From plantation to ghetto.* New York: Hill and Wang.

Miller, W. R. (1968). *Martin Luther King, Jr.* New York: Weybright.

Myrdall, G. (1972). *An American dilemma: The Negro problem and modern democracy.* 2 vols. New York: Pantheon Books. (Originally published 1944).

Oates, S. B. (1982). *Let the trumpet sound: The life of Martin Luther King, Jr.* New York: New American Library.

Osborn, M. (1966). Archetypal metaphor in rhetoric: The light-dark family. *Quarterly Journal of Speech, 53,* 115–126.

Osborn, M. (1976). *On rhetorical style.* Chicago: Science Research Associates.

Osborn, M. (1989). "I've been to the mountaintop": The critic as participant. In M. C. Leff & F. J. Kauffeld (Eds.), *Texts in context: Critical dialogues on significant episodes in American political rhetoric* (pp. 149–66). Davis, CA: Hermagoras Press.

Parsis, P. (1978). *Black leaders in conflict: Joseph H. Jackson, Martin Luther King, Jr., Malcolm X, Adam Clayton Powell, Jr.* New York: Pilgrim Press.

Pole, J. R. (1978). *The pursuit of equality in American history.* Berkeley: University of California Press.

Railsback, C. C. (1983). Beyond rhetorical relativism: A structural-material model of truth and objective reality. *Quarterly Journal of Speech, 69,* 351–363.

Railsback, C. C. (1984). The contemporary American abortion controversy: Stages in the argument. *Quarterly Journal of Speech, 70,* 410–424.

Redenius, C. (1981). *The American ideal of equality: From Jefferson's Declaration to the Burger court.* Port Washington, NY: Kennikat Press.

Ryan, W. (1981). *Equality.* New York: Pantheon Books.

Scott, R. L. (1968). Justifying violence: The rhetoric of black power. *Central States Speech Journal, 19,* 96–104.

Smith, A. L. (1969). *Rhetoric of black revolution.* Boston: Allyn and Bacon.

Smith, A. L., & Robb, S. (1971). *The voice of black rhetoric.* Boston: Allyn and Bacon.

Smith, D. H. (1964). *Martin Luther King, Jr., rhetorician of revolt.* Unpublished doctoral dissertation, University of Wisconsin–Madison.

Smith, D. H. (1968). Martin Luther King, Jr.: In the beginning in Montgomery. *Southern Speech Communication Journal, 34,* 8–17.

Snow, M. (1985). Martin Luther King's "Letter from Birmingham jail" as Pauline epistle. *Quarterly Journal of Speech, 71,* 318–324.

Verba, S., & Orren, G. R. (1985). *Equality in America: The view from the top.* Cambridge: Harvard University Press.

Walzer, M. (1983). Spheres of justice: A defense of pluralism and equality. New York: Basic Books.

Washington, J. M. (Ed.). (1986). *A testament of hope: The essential writings of Martin Luther King, Jr.* New York: Harper and Row.

White, J. (1985). *Black leadership in America, 1895–1968.* New York: Longman.

Wilson, W. J. (1980). *The declining significance of race: Blacks and changing America* (2nd ed.). Chicago: University of Chicago Press.

Wolfenstein, E. V. (1981). *The victims of democracy: Malcolm X and the black revolution.* Berkeley: University of California Press.

Woodward, C. V. (1974). *The strange career of Jim Crow* (3rd ed.). New York: Oxford University Press.

THE MALE MADONNA
AND THE FEMININE UNCLE SAM:
VISUAL ARGUMENT, ICONS, AND IDEOGRAPHS
IN 1909 ANTI–WOMAN SUFFRAGE POSTCARDS

CATHERINE H. PALCZEWSKI

Although we now think of postcards as mass-produced slips of paper (festively decorated with generic images or off-color jokes) to be sent to family and friends from vacation destinations, the social import of postcards during their "Golden Age" (1893–1918)[1] rivals the power of the Internet in contemporary times. The postcard industry was technologically and artistically prepared to play a part in the 1908 presidential election,[2] with postcards reaching the height of their popularity during that campaign.[3] Although it would be impossible to quantify their direct effect on the election, postcards "offer a vivid chronicle of American political values and tastes."[4]

Postcards, and their chronicling of American political values, were not confined to electoral politics. Postcard historian Frank W. Staff remarks, "The detail and unusual items of domestic and social history which [postcards] show are of inestimable value to the historian"[5] and, I would add, to those who study the rhetoric of historical movements. In her comprehensive study of British women's suffrage[6] campaign imagery, Lisa Tickner cites John Fraser's research on the postcard, suggesting "that the pictorial postcard was 'possibly the great vehicle for messages of the new urban proletariat between 1900 and 1914' (it was cheap to buy and to post, simple to use, and quick to arrive in an age of frequent postal deliveries)."[7] In Britain, middle-class collectors formed and joined postcard clubs, subscribed to postcard journals, and attended shows where they would place their collections in competition for medals and awards.[8] During postcards' heyday in the United States, "no 'drawing room table' was complete without one of the special albums in which picture postcards could be preserved"[9] and "one's social standing could be determined by the style and quality of the picture postcards in the album."[10] Thus, it is no surprise that postcards both supporting and opposing woman suffrage in the U.S. were common during the movement's legislative doldrums from 1890–1915 and its developing organizational and philosophical renaissance from 1896 to 1910.[11] Accordingly, a fascinating intersection occurred between advocacy for and against woman suffrage, images of women (and men), and postcards.

Woman suffrage advocates recognized the utility of the postcard as a propaganda device. In the United States, the majority of the postcards supporting woman suffrage contained real-photo images of the suffrage parades,[12] verbal messages identifying the states that had approved suffrage, or quotations in support of extending the vote to women.[13] However, the most visually evocative images in the United States, as in Great Britain, came not from postcards officially commissioned by woman suffrage groups, but from ones produced by commercial postcard publishers.[14] Simply by tapping into prevailing ideology, postcard producers assisted anti-suffrage forces "almost incidentally" by creating "a public imagery of the female form" that used suffragists as "topical or humorous types."[15]

The intersection of postcards, images of women and men, and the U.S. woman suffrage battle is best represented by a twelve-card set of full-color lithographic cartoon postcards lampooning, satirizing, and opposing woman suffrage produced in 1909 by the Dunston-Weiler Lithograph Company of New York.[16] Although many companies produced series of woman suffrage related postcards,[17] the Dunston-Weiler set is noteworthy for its graphic appeal. Two postcards show fashionably dressed white women, one declaring that her love for the vote was more than her love for her husband (Suffragette Series No. 12) and the other a cigarette-smoking *Queen of the Poll* (Suffragette Series No. 9). Two other images depict white women fraudulently electioneering, either by bribing older women with money (Suffragette Series No. 2) or men with kisses (Suffragette Series No. 4). Gender-bending images are provided by a white high-heeled *Suffragette Coppette* in a police uniform (Suffragette Series No. 5), a white *Pantalette Suffragette* in overalls (Suffragette Series No. 3), and a white beardless *Uncle Sam, Suffragee* wearing a skirt (Suffragette Series No. 6). The remaining five images show white men at home, caring for infants and toddlers, while women left the home to vote, were away at suffrage rallies, or simply absent. In particular, the *Suffragette Madonna* (Suffragette Series No. 1) shows a white man with a halo behind his head bottle-feeding a small child.[18] This last image's deployment of a Catholic icon also makes clear that not only are the citizens depicted in the other images presumed white, but they also are presumed Protestant.

Accessing images of women and men, images that speak to the many intersecting and countervailing pressures at the turn of the century, warrants a turn to the images depicted in popular culture forms such as postcards. Michael Calvin McGee encourages scholars to look to "popular" history, such as "novels, films, plays, even songs" when tracking the vertical structures of ideographs,[19] ideographs being the "vocabulary of concepts that function as guides, warrants, reasons, or excuses for behavior and belief."[20] Although McGee believed "the political language which manifests ideology seems characterized by slogans,"[21] Janis L. Edwards and Carol K. Winkler persuasively argue that scholars should attend not only to verbal slogans, but also to visual ones.[22]

Edwards and Winkler distinguish the *"representative form"*[23] of the visual ideograph from the icon, citing Lester Olson's definition of icons as "a type of image that is palpable in manifest form and denotative in function."[24] Icons operate referentially, in this case denoting specific people (the Madonna and Uncle Sam) with identifiable characteristics. Particularly with the Madonna icon, the referential element is central; in many ways, the Madonna icon came not only to depict the person Virgin Mary, but was believed to be, at least in the pious conception, "a transparent avenue to and from the divine."[25] Extending work on the visual ideograph and its relation to icons, Dana L. Cloud has explored how visual ideographs, as more than recurring iconic images, can index and make concrete verbal ideographs.[26] This essay advances another way to read the interaction between visual icons and verbal ideographs, particularly as they relate to our understandings of sex/gender.

The images in these anti-suffrage postcards offer an interesting location in which to explore how the (necessarily visual) icons of the Madonna and Uncle Sam, as well as non-iconic images of women, were deployed to reiterate the disciplinary norms of the verbal ideographs of <woman> and <man>. This project embraces E. Michele Ramsey's call for a positionalist critical perspective when studying representations of women, a perspective that enables scholars to understand better the broader social context to which historical women rhetors reacted.[27] While it initially may seem strange to present <woman> and <man> as ideographs, as McGee notes,

·SUFFRAGETTE MADONNA·

COPYRIGHT 1909 BY DUNSTON-WEILER LITHOGRAPH CO.

COPYRIGHTED

ELECTIONEERING

COPYRIGHTED

NO. 1   NO. 2

"many ideographs . . . have a non-ideographic usage."[28] Pointing to my department head, and saying "John is the brunette man" is a non-ideographic usage; however, telling my department head to "be a man" is, insofar as I use the word as an agency of social control, imbuing the word with an intrinsic force.[29] Thus, the images in the postcards present one location in which to assess the "public vocabulary" defining <woman> *as well as* the public vocabulary defining <man>.[30]

This essay contributes to a happily expanding body of communication studies literature on woman suffrage in general,[31] and on images of <woman> emerging from the suffrage era in particular.[32] This essay adds to the insights of these studies by focusing on the images found in *anti-suffrage* items, and by attending to the way in which <man>, as well as <woman>, was ideographically deployed through images and icons.

In addition to exposing the intersection of icons and ideographs, the postcards analyzed here are fascinating both for how they reflect, and for how they depart from, verbal arguments concerning woman suffrage prevalent during this time period. Accordingly, this essay moves through the following arguments. First, I recognize that the postcards offer visual forms of the arguments against suffrage that highlight the coarsening effect the vote would have on women; the postcards offer visual indexes to measure the departure from the verbal ideograph of

PANTALETTE SUFFRAGETTE
IN THE SWEET BYE AND BYE.

NO. 3

SUFFRAGETTE VOTE-GETTING
THE EASIEST WAY.

NO. 4

<woman> caused by suffrage. The postcards show women forsaking their motherly duties and acting masculine by smoking, wearing masculine clothing, and engaging in the debauchery of the polls.

Second, I explore how the postcards present an argument that was absent in the verbal discourse surrounding suffrage: just as women would become de-feminized by the public activity of voting so, too, would men become feminized by the private activity of caring for infants, an activity forced on them by women's public activities. To detail the feminization of man argument, I specifically analyze *Uncle Sam, Suffragee* and the *Suffragette Madonna* postcards. In particular, the *Suffragette Madonna* postcard negotiated the anti-Catholic bias that was present in both suffrage and anti-suffrage arguments. In many ways, this postcard encapsulated the complex arguments concerning gender, sexuality, religion, nationality, and citizenship that circulated throughout the suffrage controversy.

REFLECTING THE VERBAL ARGUMENTS: WOMAN SUFFRAGE TAINTS AND DE-FEMINIZES WOMAN

During the Victorian era (1837–1901), clearly defined roles for men and women emerged, roles that persisted into the Edwardian era (1901–circa 1918). Women were to be the "angel in the house," while men were to face the vagaries of the

NO. 5   NO. 6

public world of politics and commerce. Of course, these separate spheres were not impermeable. Woman suffrage advocates challenged the notion that women and the vote were unfit for each other, whether it be that women were unfit to vote, or that the vote would make women unfit to be women. These challenges to the prevailing conception of womanhood did not go unanswered.

At the turn of the century, the "cult of domesticity," and its attendant images of man and woman, was a prevalent theme in "Victorian literature, art, and social commentary."[33] Women who violated the separation of spheres became the "Fallen Woman,"[34] modified in the case of suffrage to also include the "nagging wife" or the "embittered spinster."[35] Particularly in relation to suffrage, "the assumption that the 'public' woman was an unsexed harridan ran deep in contemporary thought."[36] Thus, women were disciplined to remain in the private sphere or risk losing their femininity. However, even those opposed to woman suffrage did not eschew the public realm as a locus of action for women.

The complexity and development of anti-suffrage (antis)[37] arguments should not be ignored or underestimated. As Manuela Thurner argues, "a case can be made for studying the losing side of a protracted historical struggle, such as the contest over woman suffrage" because "a fuller picture of the period's cultural and political climate emerges when both, or more, sides of the debate are taken into consideration."[38] Thus, even though woman suffrage may have been won,

NO. 7   NO. 8

anti-suffrage postcards offer valuable insights into how sex and citizenship were negotiated through visual argument. But, to recognize the distinctiveness of anti-suffrage images, like those contained in the Dunston-Weiler series, an understanding of the antis' verbal arguments is necessary.

Many male political leaders condemned the idea of a woman voting on the grounds that women were not biologically suited to such an endeavor, and male-run liquor interests played a significant role in combating suffrage. However, men were not the only opponents. Well-organized groups of women, known as remonstrants, also opposed suffrage, claiming as their motto "Home, Heaven, and Mother."[39] Remonstrants believed woman suffrage was a misguided and unnecessary reform.[40] For them, women of good character would be better able to influence public policy by means other than the vote; concomitantly, granting to all women the right to vote might enable those women with less than savory character to overwhelm their more upstanding sisters, as implied by the *Suffragette Vote-Getting* and *Queen of the Poll*.[41]

Typical verbal arguments against suffrage, made by men and used extensively in remonstrant literature, emphasized the effect of the vote on women. Daniel Webster (lawyer, congressperson, and statesperson) decried, "The rough contests of the political world are not suited to the dignity and the delicacy of your sex." Cardinal

NO. 9   NO. 10

James Gibbons (Catholic archbishop and the youngest prelate at the First Vatican Council) worried, "If woman enters politics, she will be sure to carry away on her some of the mud and dirt of political contact." Dr. S. Weir Mitchell (celebrated clinician and neurologist) exhorted, "woman accepts the irrevocable decree which made her woman and not man. Something in between she cannot be." And antis noted that not only would women be coarsened, but that suffrage would be "an appeal to the coarser strength of men."[42] Those opposed to suffrage were worried *more* about how women would be tainted and de-feminized, than about whether men would be feminized.

In many ways, one can read the visual arguments in pro– and anti–woman suffrage literature as responding to each other. E. Michele Ramsey argues that *The Woman Citizen*'s World War I era cartoons reconfigured citizenship's relationship to sex and gender by presenting woman as a "competent citizen" and redefining the meaning of "loyal citizen."[43] Functioning as a response to this argument, the Dunston-Weiler postcard series depicted the verbal anti–woman suffrage arguments that highlighted women's unsuitability for citizenship duties. Two themes in particular reinforce the verbal arguments opposing woman suffrage and supporting masculine conceptions of citizenship: (1) women lacked the physical power necessary to enforce their vote, and (2) the public realm was unsuited to proper women.

NO. 11   NO. 12

Suffragette Coppette

The *Suffragette Coppette* (No. 5) postcard reflected the antis' verbal arguments concerning women's inability to enforce the effect of their votes. Aileen S. Kraditor, in her germinal history of the movement, outlines the argument linking physical power to voting rights:

> If women were to vote, the thesis continued, half the electorate would be incapable of enforcing its mandate and vicious elements would be encouraged to resort to violence. A vote was not simply the registering of an opinion; it was a demand and consequently would be meaningless unless exercised only by the muscular portion of the community.[44]

The New York Association Opposed to Woman Suffrage, in a circa 1910 statement presented to both houses of the U.S. Congress, noted: "To extend the suffrage to women would be to introduce into the electorate a vast non-combatant party, incapable of enforcing its own rule."[45] Goldwin Smith (British-born historian and journalist), in his commentary on the question of woman suffrage, explained: "Political power has hitherto been exercised by the male sex . . . because man alone could uphold government and enforce the law."[46] In other words, physical power was needed in order for a vote to carry any force.

The *Suffragette Coppette* postcard,[47] one of six that focused on women in public, presented the idea of a woman being a law enforcement officer as laughable. Armed with a rolling pin instead of a truncheon, and accompanied by a demure puppy instead of a vicious police dog, her high-heeled stance makes clear her lack of power. In fact, the subtitle of the postcard makes clear where the real threat of force lies: "Beware of the dog."

Public Woman

The remainder of the postcards depicting women in public reflected the antis' verbal arguments concerning the coarsening effect the vote would have on women and their fear that improper women would populate the polls. Jane Jerome Camhi analyzes how the antis visualized "womanhood of consisting of set types," consisting of "the better class, the indifferent, and the degenerate."[48] Of particular worry to antis were the prostitutes, whom they feared would overwhelm their more upstanding sisters at the polls because "the best of women would shun political life and the most unprincipled would have the field to themselves."[49] Such worries were reflected in the smoking *Queen of the Poll* (No. 9), the bribery of *Electioneering* (No. 2), and the aggressive kissing of *Suffragette Vote-Getting, the Easiest Way* (No. 4).

Interestingly, and in contrast to the oft-seen renderings of suffragists as masculine, the Dunston-Weiler postcards depict women acting in public as still feminine in appearance, wearing attractive dresses and having beautiful faces. However, it would be a mistake to read these postcards as unqualifiedly liberatory. Instead, these images represent a moment in which "sex is both produced and destabilized in the course of this reiteration,"[50] where sex norms are both maintained and challenged. In these images, a public woman may not be a masculine woman, but that did not make her a good woman.

As Judith Butler notes, as sex is reiterated "gaps and fissures"[51] emerge and present opportune moments for resistance. Yet it would be incorrect to read the postcard images of women as subversively progressive because they contradicted the representations of suffragists as unsexed harridans.[52] These images are not an example of the widening of a fissure in our understanding of woman as citizen just because, in these images, woman maintained her femininity even as she voted. Why?

The type of femininity the voting woman was allowed to maintain is one that is sexualized. The connection between sexuality and publicity is not accidental. At this time, a prostitute was considered a "public woman"; thus, being a public woman meant one was a publicly accessible woman.[53] As Lisa Maria Hogeland points out in her discussion of public sex scandals and Victoria Woodhull, "'public women' are sexual(ized) women."[54] Thus, even as the postcards presented a public woman as still a feminine woman, she was not a good woman. Instead of using the loss of femininity as a disciplinary mechanism, the postcards instead deployed the loss of virtue. Either only bad women would vote, or if a woman voted she would be presumed bad.

Evidence of how the voting (public) woman was presented as the sexualized (public) woman is contained in the repeated theme of the exposed ankle, appearing in Suffragette Series Nos. 2, 3, 4, and 12. The repeatedly exposed ankle is not accidental. My argument here is not that actual 1909 women never exposed their ankles. Rather, my argument is that the exposed ankle functions as code, indicating that the woman who voted was to be read as a bad woman.

The sexual significance of the ankle was one that began long before the turn of the nineteenth into the twentieth century. For example, "The provocative effect of the exposed ankle or leg was a source of both moral outrage and ribald jests throughout the [eighteenth] century."[55] Although the story of Victorian piano legs prudishly being skirted in order to avoid exciting the erotic sentiments may be apocryphal,[56] one can still argue that the ankle was coded sexually. In 1850s United States, one of the primary objections to the dress reform represented by the Bloomer outfit was that it exposed the ankle, thus lending the outfit an erotic quality.[57] For a middle-class woman, showing an ankle was shocking, even up until 1909.[58] A cursory review of the *Sears Catalogue*, "the arbiter of fashion to small-town America,"[59] makes clear that women's dresses skirted to the floor were the norm in 1909, with barely a toe peeking out from underneath. Not until 1912 would ankles appear consistently as an acceptable fashion statement. Thus, the repeatedly exposed ankle (and even the, gasp!, calf in No. 4) appearing in these postcards is noteworthy.

Even as these postcards allowed women to maintain their attractiveness as they ventured into the public, the postcard images were not really progressive nor did they rearticulate an understanding of <woman>. Instead of women being disciplined by the loss of their looks, they were disciplined with the loss of their purity. The publicity of the voting woman was the publicity of a "public woman." In fact, the only images in which the woman's ankles were not exposed were still coded as sexual. *Queen of the Poll* (Suffragette Series No. 9) stands with a lit cigarette, and the woman in *Election-Day* (Suffragette Series No. 7) sports a low cut bodice as she bids farewell to her husband.

Half of the postcards in the Dunston-Weiler series reflected the verbal arguments concerning the effect of suffrage on women and <woman>. Should women venture into the public world of electoral politics, they risked losing their purity and good standing as women or, conversely, only those who had already lost their good standing would venture to the polls. However, the de-feminization/sexualization of women is not the only argument the postcards depict. In fact, the remaining images advance an argument that was not present in the verbal discourse, an argument appealing to the ideograph of <man> via the icons of Uncle Sam and the Madonna.

DEPARTING FROM THE VERBAL ARGUMENTS: WOMAN SUFFRAGE FEMINIZES MAN

E. Michele Ramsey and Cheryl Jorgensen-Earp both provide examples of how diffuse images of women found in the expansive cultural contexts of the dominant discourse structure the ideograph of <woman>.[60] Katherine Meyer, John Seidler, Timothy Curry, and Adrian Aveni, in their analysis of images of women in Fourth of July cartoons, demonstrate how cartoons are one of the expansive cultural mediums which structure the meaning of <woman>, even when that is not the intentional purpose of the cartoon.[61] Supplementing these scholars' work, this essay explores one location in which the dominant discourse and cultural images gave structure to the concept of <man> as well as <woman>, in part by presenting what is not manly and by presenting men in locations typically populated by women. The corollary to the woman unsexed (or oversexed) by the masculine vote was the man unsexed by the voting woman.

Popular culture images of men in the home appear to be the only traces of a potentially inarticulable fear of the emasculated man, a man made suitable for the private world of childrearing. Most often at this time, dominant cultural images showed men as incompetent in the nursery, the location perhaps most identified with "women's work."[62] Quite simply, by virtue of being a man, men were incapable of pursuits in the domestic realm. A number of British and U.S. postcards show men trying to do laundry, as the cat gets into the milk and the children sit squawking.[63] Consistent with this theme as presented in mass media and other postcard images, every time a man appears in the Dunston-Weiler series (which is in six of the twelve images), they are shown feminized. However, the specter of the feminized man was absent in the verbal discourse opposing suffrage.

The Dunston-Weiler series also presents a variation on the home-bound man theme, with its images of men competently caring for infants, as in the *Suffragette Madonna* (No. 1) and Suffragette Series Nos. 8 and 11. Yet even the competent male caregiver appealed to anti-suffrage sentiments, for then the image was of "the poor, tired husband home from his day's labor only to find that he must mind the baby or do the dishes so that his wife may prepare a speech or attend a public meeting."[64] He was the martyr to the suffrage cause.

As woman suffrage advocates attempted to stretch the meaning of <woman> to incorporate the public act of voting into their role as citizens, those opposed (or indifferent) to woman suffrage formulated images depicting the effect of women's vote on men. This demonstrates that the conflict over gender roles is always simultaneously about femininity and masculinity. In the dominant discursive structure, one cannot expand the meaning of <woman> without necessarily shrinking the understanding of <man>. Writing twenty years after the appearance of the Dunston-Weiler postcards, Virginia Woolf plays out why a gain by women is always simultaneously read as a loss on the part of men:

> Women have served all these centuries as looking-glasses possessing the magic and delicious power of reflecting the figure of man at twice its natural size. . . . That is why Napoleon and Mussolini both insist so emphatically upon the inferiority of women, for if they were not inferior, they would cease

to enlarge. That serves to explain in part the necessity that women so often are to men. . . . How is he to go on giving judgement, civilising natives, making laws, writing books, dressing up and speechifying at banquets, unless he can see himself at breakfast and at dinner at least twice the size he really is?[65]

More recently, Judith Butler has spoken to the theme of how the masculine/feminine binary constitutes what it means to be man or a woman.[66] Gender and sex are something we do, not something we are[67] and thus "'persons' only become intelligible through becoming gendered in conformity with recognizable standards of gender intelligibility."[68] The unintelligibility of a male Madonna and a feminine Uncle Sam speak to this move, as do the images of male caregivers.

The series contains five images of men in the home (Suffragette Series Nos. 1, 7, 8, 10, and 11), all of them caring for children. Perhaps best reflecting the idea that a zero-sum tradeoff exists between men and women's rights, *I Want to Vote But My Wife Won't Let Me* (No. 11) pictures a man washing clothes while also watching over an infant and cat. In this image, a woman's exercise of voting rights has stripped a man of those rights. However, the most interesting male caregiver image is represented by the *Suffragette Madonna,* which completes the transformation of a man (bottle-feeding an infant) into the mother of all mothers. Not only are fathers feminized in the Dunston-Weiler series, but so too are uncles, in the form of Uncle Sam. The remainder of this essay focuses on these two postcard images, primarily because of the way they represent intersections of icons and ideographs. I discuss the intersections of religion, gender, and the vote presented by the *Suffrage Madonna* later, but for now turn to a discussion of *Uncle Sam, Suffragee.*

Uncle Sam, Suffragee

The name Uncle Sam was first used to criticize the United States during the War of 1812,[69] and the first images of Uncle Sam appeared in 1832.[70] Although Brother Jonathan was the more popular image leading up to the Civil War, by the war's end, Uncle Sam became the dominant image, being used both as a positive icon and as a way to challenge the government. Uncle Sam was not depicted with facial hair until 1856, and the facial hair persisted most likely because the figure of Abraham Lincoln so influenced the depictions that after the Civil War, the bewhiskered Uncle Sam was the universally used and recognized likeness.[71] In fact, Uncle Sam would become known in slang as "Mr. Whiskers."[72] In the 1870s, Thomas Nast's cartoons solidified Uncle Sam's characteristics. As a result of Nast's illustrations, the adult Uncle Sam was always depicted with a beard, as he is in the most widely distributed and recognizable image: the 1917 James Montgomery Flagg recruiting poster "I Want You for the U.S. Army." In a collection of Uncle Sam images, all show him with a beard when he is not depicted as a child, except for the image of *Uncle Sam, Suffragee.*[73] In his comprehensive history of Uncle Sam, Alton Ketchum notes that one of the "last appearances of a beardless Uncle Sam" was in 1865.[74] As this postcard series demonstrates, however, Mr. Ketchum was off by 44 years.

Although not possessing the religious power of the Madonna icon, Uncle Sam still functions more like an icon than an ideograph. Although the form of Uncle Sam has changed across time, what he denotes has remained relatively constant.[75] According to the government official responsible for asking Herbert Noxon, at the behest of the State Department, to create the official version of Uncle Sam in 1950, "He is the United States. . . . He is our composite American personality—the symbolic projection of what our country means to us and to other nations."[76] Uncle Sam denotes the United States. Although typically shown as "benign, friendly, yet firm,"[77] manipulating the image enables one to play with the image of the United States. Thus, a cross-dressing Uncle Sam (or United States) warrants analysis. *Uncle Sam, Suffragee* depicts Uncle Sam clean-shaven, in star-spangled skirt, with hand on hip, and jaunty bonnet atop his head, giving a whole new meaning to "I want you."

The feminization of Uncle Sam is achieved through the change in clothes, the stripping of his secondary sex characteristic of facial hair, minimizing his height, and making him the object of the act of suffrage—the suffragee. Instead of wearing his traditional trousers, top hat, and tails, Uncle Sam is shown in a long skirt, red and white striped duster coat, heels, and oversized bonnet. Whereas many other postcards depicted women in masculine dress (as in *Pantalette Suffragette* and *Suffragette Coppette*), this one turned the tables, putting Uncle Sam in drag. The transformation is completed with the clean-shaven face. In this moment, Uncle Sam was stripped of his masculinity and lost a characteristic that had come to be part of his identity as the representative of the United States. Coupled with his posture, with hands on hip, his stature completes the transformation of the larger than life representative of U.S. power to a figure who is acted upon and passive.

Thomas H. Bivins, in his analysis of the changing shape of Uncle Sam across the decades, posits that part of his heroic nature is embodied in his stature. With the average man standing six and a half heads tall, comic characters are made to appear heroic by having smaller heads and larger bodies, so that they are eight or more heads tall. When Nast finally stabilized the image of Uncle Sam, he was "tall and Lincolnesque, about 7 1/2 heads, and would probably fall somewhere between thin (ectomorphic) and muscular (mesomorphic)."[78] This image persisted well into the 1900s, where his mesomorphic body depicted him as "paternal, protective and the epitome of strength."[79] In contrast, the *Suffragee* image shows him not as muscular, but as curvy with a suspicious bulge at his chest. He also stands only about six heads tall, including his high heels but excluding his patriotic bonnet.

Finally, as "suffragee," Uncle Sam as representative of the United States is on the receiving end of suffrage, not as a right but as something wielded against him. He is the one to whom suffrage is done, and the result of having suffrage done to him is the loss of his masculine power. But Uncle Sam is not the only one feminized by the vote.

The Suffragette Madonna

While the series as a whole negotiated the conflict between de-feminized women and feminized men, the *Suffragette Madonna* postcard in particular also negotiated the anti-Catholic bias that was present in both pro– and anti–woman suffrage arguments. In many ways, this postcard encapsulated the complex arguments concerning gender, sexuality, religion, nationality, and citizenship that circulated throughout the suffrage controversy. The image operated on multiple levels: it appealed to the anti–woman suffrage Catholic population by highlighting how the vote would violate the religious admonition that woman's place was in the home, it appealed to anti-Catholic sentiments fed by the fear that Catholics as a voting block would overtake Protestants, and it deployed the stereotype of Catholicism as effeminate to intensify the feminizing effect of the vote.

Anti-Catholicism was neither new to the time period, nor unique to either suffragists or remonstrants, as both responded to the influx of immigrants from a nativist perspective. During the early decades of the nineteenth century, immigration from Europe to the United States fueled the rapid growth in the Catholic Church until Catholicism represented the country's largest religious denomination by mid-century.[80] For the Irish and Germans who had arrived during this first wave of immigration, a unique period of Catholic religious vitality and political and economic stability occurred from 1870 to 1896. During the second half of the nineteenth century, however, new waves of Italian and Polish immigrants, with their "alternative expressions of Catholicism," arrived, presenting a challenge to this stability.[81] This second wave of growth in Catholicism, with its "massive waves of Catholic immigration to industrial and mining centers of the Northeast and Great Lakes states,"[82] combined with "a pre-existing distrust of Catholicism to precipitate an anti-Catholic, nativist reaction."[83] In these regions, most Protestants "banded together in the Republican party as a means for preserving the quasi-official . . . Protestant quality of American life."[84] These reactions made clear the way in which conceptions of American-ness, and citizenship, were bound up with issues of ethnicity and religion.

Given the depth of anti-Catholicism, it was unavoidable that both anti– and pro–woman suffrage groups would appeal to the bias. Anti-immigrant prejudice was evident within the suffrage movement, whose members bemoaned the fact that well-educated native women did not have the vote while expanded suffrage enabled illiterate immigrant men to overwhelm the polls. In order to limit the power of ethnic, often Catholic, political machines, suffragists argued that women should be given the vote. Such arguments were persuasive enough that in the 1890s the American Protective Association endorsed woman suffrage as a way of combating the rising political power of Irish Catholics.[85]

Immigrant communities were well aware of the implications of the suffragists' arguments. Immigrant organizations feared how the native-born population would use woman suffrage against them and, thus, stubbornly opposed any change in voting laws. Not only did immigrants fear the political effect of women's voting, but they also feared its social effect. Immigrant men saw suffragists as "dangerous radicals who sought to destroy the harmony of their traditional family unit by introducing the issue of 'women's' rights into the household. . . . [M]ale immigrants refused to see the 'Votes for Women' campaign as anything less than the destruction of their solitary refuge amid a life of turbulence and danger: the home."[86] These political and social fears explain why, even though the Catholic Church never took an official position, it functionally was the most unified national religious body to oppose woman suffrage.[87]

Remonstrants appealed to this anti–woman suffrage bias of recent Catholic immigrants, even as they also appealed to their Protestant audiences, by highlighting the threat of illiterate immigrant women overwhelming the polls. Even though antis made cursory appeals to the Catholic anti–woman suffrage vote, with the Massachusetts remonstrants publishing a brochure in Polish prior to a 1915 referendum campaign, generally "antis treated the immigrant community and the Catholic Church with disdain"[88] for the "root of anti-immigrant bigotry among remonstrants was anti-Catholic."[89] Thomas Jablonsky vividly explains antis' fear of how woman suffrage would supplement the immigrant vote:

Of special concern was the alleged nightmarish march of a female Catholic army descending upon the polls under orders of their priests and bishops. "Cathedrals and ignorance" awaited the future of America. Alarmed by the rise of urban political machines, which, in turn, were fueled by the votes of Irish, Polish, and Italian men, antis feared that the country would suffer greater harm at the hands of "Bridget," "Natasha," or "Maria."[90]

Into this anti-Catholic and highly sex-segregated society, the image of the *Suffragette Madonna* was introduced.

The *Suffragette Madonna* postcard advances the idea that when woman gains (masculine) political power, man becomes feminized, relegated to caring for infants, a duty typically delegated to women and to the domestic sphere. No longer the public citizen, the man becomes the private caregiver, a martyr to the suffrage cause. With its play on the Madonna image, this postcard also reflected a bias against Catholics (even as it appealed to Catholic males' fear that the vote would undermine the sanctity of the home) as it hinted that an expanded franchise might benefit the growing Catholic immigrant community to the detriment of Protestant groups.

It would be impossible to understand the significance of the Madonna image without understanding the concept of "visual piety."[91] For many, the act of looking upon a religious image is deeply spiritual; Catholics in medieval times believed that simply "looking upon relics afforded forgiveness of sin."[92] This led Middle Age European art and architecture to focus on the presentation of the relic and the host, converting the sacred into a visual experience, much as the icon had done in the East. Because the most powerful Catholic female role model is the Virgin Mary,[93] appropriation of the icon is fraught; it is likely to be extremely distasteful, if not outright sacrilegious, to Catholics unless the image, itself, were attempting to stabilize the meaning behind the icon.

However, if the Madonna icon functions so powerfully for Catholics, what enabled it to resonate at all with Protestants? During the nineteenth century, many homes would have displayed Murillo's *Immaculate Conception,* such that the Catholic Madonna and Child "were reinterpreted to be any mother and her child. The Mary was emblematic of all mothers and not merely the mother of Jesus."[94]

During the Victorian era, the standard up to which women had to live was the "angel in the house," with the "preeminent Angel in the House" being the Virgin Mary.[95] The angel ideology was premised on the notion that women's domestic duties were essentially a spiritual calling. In fact, the postcard's use of a child highlights the effeminate nature of care-giving, since the child was of an age where it most likely still required breast-feeding, substituted in this case by the bottle held by the man. The man is not left caring for a young adult, or even a toddler, but an infant—that creature most dependent on parental care. This image employs the representative form of the Madonna icons that show Mother Mary and infant Jesus, but it also highlights the hyper-feminized role of caregiving for infants.

The image appealed to the universally shared belief that woman's place was in the home, particularly with small children. But, even as the image spoke to Catholic men's fears of the loss of their (idealized) home, it also tapped into Protestant men's biases against Catholic immigrants. Although the "angel in the house" ideal transcended religious denominations, Protestants distrusted what they perceived to be Catholics' penchant for idol-worship, most typified by the new immigrant love of mass-produced Mary images.[96] Because the Madonna icon is identified with the Catholic love of religious images, the postcard was a subtle reminder that the type of woman voting would be a Catholic woman, with her Catholic husband caring for their (precipitously expanding number of) children while she was at the polls.[97]

Even as the image of a male caregiver appealed to Protestant and Catholic men's fear of emasculation (caused by the loss of their monopoly on the vote), and as the postcard appealed to Protestants' fear of an ever-burgeoning Catholic vote, it also played on Protestant men's fear of the emasculating effect of Catholicism. Religion scholars have recently focused on how gender and religion intersect, and it is now commonly accepted that "there were distinctive patterns of men's spiritual experience."[98] In contrast to the effeminacy of Catholicism (as perceived by non-Catholics given Catholic priests' celibacy and clothing), Protestants touted the ideal of "muscular Christianity."[99] In other words, not only were men in general emasculated by the vote, but when Catholics overwhelmed the polls and imposed their religion on everyone, Protestant men in particular would be emasculated by Catholicism.

The *Suffragette Madonna* potentially appealed to both Catholic men and to those with an anti-Catholic bias. For Catholic men, the image represented their greatest fear: loss of the sanctity of their home life, which for many was the only stable location in their tumultuous immigrant world. Given that Catholics tended to see women's calling in the home as even more scripturally determined than their non-Catholic counterparts, the appeal made clear that supporting woman suffrage would constitute sacrilege. For Protestants who feared the influx of Catholic immigrants, the image appealed to their fear that Catholic women would overwhelm the polls. However, even as the image spoke in a split voice to the two groups, it also appealed to both on the same level. The image tapped into men's fear, regardless of religion, that the vote would feminize them.

A POSTCARD POSTSCRIPT

For anyone interested in the study of sex/gender, <man> and <woman> should be a central focus of study. As Judith Butler consistently reminds us, "[s]exual difference, however, is never simply a function of material differences which are not in some way both marked and formed by discursive practices."[100] Construction of what it means to be a man or a woman is "a temporal process which operates through the reiteration of norms."[101] As this study and the existing literature examining the function of images in the suffrage controversy make clear, discursive and *non*discursive practices produced by suffragists, anti-suffragists, and institutions of popular culture mark and form understandings of sexual difference.

As Ramsey notes in her call to study the images of woman appearing in "nontraditional texts,"[102] norms are reiterated even when not produced by any entity officially allied with a movement. Supplementing Ramsey's call to study nontraditional texts such as advertisements, this study establishes the need to look beyond news media outlets when studying political and suffrage images, at least when examining controversies that occurred during the golden age of postcards. Interestingly, most rhetorical studies of political cartoons analyze ones that appeared in newspapers and magazines.[103] Although critical studies of postcards do exist,[104] none examine the intersection of political cartoons and postcards, even though postcards were cheap, easily accessible, and did not present the demands of literacy that newspapers did.[105]

Postcards were circulated more widely than magazines, were not dependent on literacy, and did not allow audience self-selection (one could not control what postcards one would receive). Studying the images of political controversies from the turn of the century, but ignoring the role of postcards, would be equivalent to studying a contemporary political campaign and ignoring the use of televised commercials and the Internet. Postcards were ubiquitous, cheap, easily accessible, and clearly participated in the suffrage controversy in a way that developed and extended the argument beyond what can be found in the verbal arguments contained in broadsides and print media. The postcards analyzed here represent one location of reiteration of what it means to be a <man> and to be a <woman>.

However, as critical race scholars note, identity is intersectional. One is never *only* a woman or *only* a man. We also are composed of races, genders, sexualities, classes, religions, ethnicities, etc. One cannot study sex/gender distinct from other identity ingredients, for no scholarly alchemic process exists by which to extract a description of sex pure of race, gender, sexuality, class, religion, ethnicity, etc.[106] How we do woman is informed by how we do race, how we do man is informed by how we do gender, and how we do citizenship is informed by how we do religion. Accordingly, I foregrounded the whiteness of the bodies depicted in the postcards when I described them earlier. I intentionally made clear that the images of <man> and <woman> are images of *white* men and *white* women.

In fact, it may be that the very ideograph of <woman> is raced white in the United States. For example, Barbara Welter, in her extremely influential book *Dimity Convictions,* notes how womanhood was defined as pure, pious, domestic, and submissive.[107] Yet, as Chandra Talpede Mohanty makes clear, such an idealized conception of womanhood was confined to white women of the middle and upper classes.[108] Women of color and poor women could never attain the ideal because of their race and class. This, of course, does not mean that the ideograph held no power over them; it was still able to discipline them, to declare each of them a bad <woman> as Sojourner Truth's query of "Aren't I a woman?" made clear. Ultimately, all the postcards in this series, and the *Uncle Sam, Suffragee* image in particular, offer a way to assess the means by which the nation and citizenship are presumed masculine and white.

Even as the postcards do not trouble the normativity of whiteness, the *Suffragette Madonna* postcard's deployment of religion allows recognition of the way in which nationality, ethnicity, religion, and citizenship are intertwined. Whiteness was not nearly as undifferentiated a race category at the turn of the century as it is now. Distinctions were made between native citizens and recent immigrants. Between immigrants, distinctions were made between Western and Eastern European, between Irish and German, Polish and Italian, etc. Thus, the Madonna image offers one way to explore the visualization of the ideograph of white <woman> and white <man> as informed by different strands of Christianity, particularly those strands embraced by immigrants.

In addition to exploring how white <woman> and white <man> was indexed through visual depictions, this essay also demonstrates how visual arguments function as part of a larger public controversy, in this case the controversy over woman suffrage which also necessarily implicated the controversies over sex, gender, citizenship, and religion. Studies of visual rhetoric populate our journals. However, when it comes to recognizing visuals' role in the rhetorical sub-species of argument, some continue to insist that visuals cannot argue,[109] despite a growing body of literature that recognizes visuals can function as argument, both in its propositional and in its process form.[110] This essay should resolve that dispute insofar as it demonstrates that a complete, and significant, argument in the suffrage controversy (that suffrage would feminize men) cannot be discerned and traced without recognizing the possibility of visual argument. Recognizing the role of visual argument, in this case represented by the postcard images although certainly contained in other visual forms, enables critics to read the clash of argument across symbolic forms. Argumentative engagement, thus, is not confined to discursive clash, but can be manifested by occupation of alternate cultural forms. The "answers" to woman suffrage arguments are to be found not only in the discursive creations of organized opposition, but also in the visual products of diffuse popular culture forms.[111]

Accordingly, this study also takes exception to one of the basic assumptions found in the study of political cartoons: that visual arguments merely reflect or intensify existing discursive arguments. Michael A. DeSousa and Martin J. Medhurst "believe the real significance of the political cartoon lies *not* in its character as propositional argument or as persuasion but in its ability to tap the collective consciousness of readers in a manner similar to religious rituals, civic ceremonies, and communal observances."[112] Although I agree with their assessment that cartoons tap into collective consciousness, I disagree that cartoons lack a significant propositional character. The postcards analyzed here demonstrate that political cartoons' propositional function is of real significance insofar as they present an argument in visual form that was absent in discursive form. As the icons of Uncle Sam and the Madonna evoke the ideographs of <man> and <woman>, the postcards make visible the argument that men will be feminized, sacrificing their masculinity and full citizenship to woman's sullied citizenship of equal suffrage.

As Robert Hariman and John Louis Lucaites' work on iconic photographs[113] makes clear, images can embody notions of civic and public identity as they form public culture. They believe the images they studied "become iconic because they coordinate a number of different patterns of identification."[114] This study provides an explanation not of how publicity is formed via the emergence of icons, but of how preexisting icons are deployed to contain emerging expansive definitions of citizenship. Once we accept the "constitutive function of public discourse,"[115] not only must we search for places where publicity is reconstituted and expanded, where a gap and fissure is exploited, but also those locations where it is reiterated through the re-inscription of binary sex/gender norms that are tied to race, religion, and class.

The postcard images studied here offer compelling visual arguments about the effect of the vote on white men's and white women's citizenship. Recognizing this is important, given that even contemporary studies of anti-suffrage arguments focus on how the vote would affect women, not men. Jean H. Baker's introduction to *Votes for Women: The Struggle for Suffrage Revisited* does note that men feared the vote because "political equality with women cut into their households, endangering domestic arrangements"; however, her description of the explanations offered as to why the arrangements existed was that "women were ill-suited to participate in public life because of their domesticity . . ."[116] The fact that men might be ill-suited to tend the home because of their publicity is not noted. Thomas Jablonsky, in his study of the antis, also focuses on the effect on women as represented in the antis' arguments: "The world of women . . . was blending too quickly with the world of men."[117] The point was not that the world of men was blending too quickly into the world of women. Although contemporary scholars note, and advocates from the period decried, the erosion of the distinction between who populated the public and private (home) spheres, almost all mention the detrimental effect women crossing spheres would have on the public and women's ability to care for the home, while none mention the possible effect women's crossing spheres would have on men's location in the spheres.

What might account for this theme appearing in postcards when it is absent in the verbal discourse? Cartoons are a particularly apt way in which to explore some of the enthymematic arguments present in anti-suffrage discourse. If it is true that "[c]artoons often seem to project unconscious desires and fears,"[118] then it seems plausible that while no suffrage opponent (especially a male one) would want to speak of man's (his) possible emasculation, such a fear could be explored in cartoon images where a clothes-washing man is not allowed to vote. Cartoons enabled deep-seated culturally grounded beliefs to be expressed visually, re-entrenching cultural ideals, even while those beliefs were verbally proclaimed to be biologically determined and, thus, not in need of reinforcement.

The recognition of the distinctiveness of the visual arguments against suffrage carries implications for the theory of visual ideographs and where we should search for them. Two forms of visual ideographs have been identified thus far. Edwards and Winkler argue that visual ideographs are representative forms in which depictive rhetoric functions ideographically.[119] Cloud has identified the way in which visual ideographs can "index verbal ideographic slogans, making abstractions . . . concrete."[120] This study presents a third version of the play between icons and ideographs: iconic images can be used to maintain the social control power of verbal ideographs, in this case the ideographs of <man> and <woman>. Instead of the Madonna carrying multiple connotations across multiple images (something Edwards and Winkler note is typical of a visual ideograph), or the Madonna meaning shifting depending on context (as Cloud notes), I believe the Madonna's connotation remains stable here and across her images in other postcards. The referential fixity of the iconic image assists in the proof of the unintelligibility of the feminine man. In fact, instead of multiple connotations appearing across multiple images, multiple connotations resonate within this one postcard depending on whether one is Catholic or not.

Although the Madonna image, as well as Uncle Sam, were appropriated and recontextualized, what Edwards and Winkler identify as the "central features of the transformation of visual images into representative forms,"[121] I do not believe this means the Madonna and Uncle Sam function as *representative forms* of the Madonna and Uncle Sam. Instead, the representative form was <man> and <woman>, of which Uncle Sam and the Madonna are examples. *Uncle Sam, Suffragee* and the *Suffrage Madonna* are not parodies, the form Edwards and Winkler argue often is used in visual ideographs. Instead, they are cautionary tales. They warn that the very meaning of core religious and secular icons would be altered should woman suffrage come to pass. These two postcards depict anti-icons and thus do not function as representative forms. They are referential forms, as icons always are. They are appeals to fix and stabilize the iconic form of Uncle Sam and the Madonna in the face of social pressures of destabilization. Taken together, the visual arguments of the Dunston-Weiler postcard series fix and stabilize the ideographs of <woman> and of <man>.

NOTES

[1]Susan Brown Nicholson, *The Encyclopedia of Antique Postcards* (Radnor, PA: Wallaca-Homestead Book Co., 1994), 196.

[2]Valerie Monahan, *An American Postcard Collector's Guide* (Poole: Blandford Press, 1981), 84.

[3]Roger A. Fischer, *Tippecanoe and Trinkets Too: The Material Culture of American Presidential Campaigns, 1828–1984* (Urbana: University of Illinois Press, 1988), 148.

[4]George Miller, foreword to *Political Postcards 1900–1980, A Price Guide,* by Bernard L. Greenhouse (Syracuse: Postcard Press, 1984).

[5]Frank Staff, *The Picture Postcard and Its Origins* (London: Lutterworth Press, 1966), 8.

[6]British suffragists referred to "women's suffrage" while U.S. suffragists spoke of "woman suffrage." Accordingly, when referring to British suffrage activities, I use the phrase "women's suffrage" and when referring to U.S. suffrage activities, I use the phrase "woman suffrage."

[7]Lisa Tickner, *The Spectacle of Women: Imagery of the Suffrage Campaign 1907–1914* (Chicago: University of Chicago Press, 1988), 50.

[8]Tickner, 50–1.

[9]James Laver, foreword to *The Picture Postcard and Its Origins* by Frank Staff, 7.

[10]Staff, 64.

[11]Eleanor Flexner, *Century of Struggle: The Woman's Rights Movement in the United States* (New York: Atheneum, 1973), 248; and Sara Hunter Graham, "The Suffrage Renaissance: A New Image for a New Century, 1896–1910," in *One Woman, One Vote: Rediscovering the Woman Suffrage Movement,* ed. Marjorie Spruill Wheeler (Troutdale, OR: NewSage Press, 1995), 159.

[12]The visual power of the suffrage parade is best explained in Linda J. Lumsden, "Beauty and the Beasts: Significance of Press Coverage of the 1913 National Suffrage Parade," *Journalism and Mass Communication Quarterly* 77, no. 3 (Autumn 2000): 593–611. She argues: "The parade marked a milestone in the incorporation of American women into Society. Part of that incorporation involved the portrayal of women in media" (602).

[13]This summary of postcard types comes from the author's personal collection, a review of postcards available on-line, examination of collections put up for auction, and consultations with suffrage postcard collectors. The differences between pro- and anti-suffrage postcards are not limited to their style and content. Their uses also differed: "Though most cards were heavily anti-suffrage, some were pro-suffrage. When the pro-suffrage cards are found today, they usually have not been postally used. Perhaps the social climate was such that these cards were hand exchanged or merely kept by the purchaser" (Nicholson, 196).

[14]Tickner, 51–2.

[15]Tickner, 162.

[16]Although I have not yet found exact production numbers for the series, it does appear to be the most widely circulated set of suffrage images in the United States. At least, if survival rates are any indication, it was the most widely produced since postcards from this series are the most commonly available to contemporary postcard collectors.

[17]The National American Woman Suffrage Association produced a series of motto and state postcards. I & M Ottenheimer of Baltimore, MD, and the Leet Bros. of Washington, DC, produced a number of real-photo images from suffrage parades. "Just by Way of a Change" was a series produced in Saxony but mailed in the United States. Walter Wellman produced the cartoonish "The Suffragette" series.

[18]This is not the only instance of the *Suffragette Madonna.* In 1910, another postcard by that name was circulated, showing a man with halo feeding a girl doll a bottle (available at http://winningthevote.org/anti4-big.html). The Nash postcard company also circulated a similar image.

[19]Michael C. McGee, "The 'Ideograph': A Link Between Rhetoric and Ideology," *Quarterly Journal of Speech* 66, no. 1 (February 1980): 11.

[20]McGee, 6.

[21]McGee, 5.

[22]Janis L. Edwards and Carol K. Winkler, "Representative Form and the Visual Ideograph: The Iwo Jima Image in Editorial Cartoons," *Quarterly Journal of Speech* 83, no. 3 (August 1997): 289–310.

[23]Edwards and Winkler, 289–90.

[24]Lester C. Olson, "Benjamin Franklin's Representations of the British Colonies in America: A Study in Rhetorical Iconology," *Quarterly Journal of Speech* 73, no.1 (February 1987): 38, note 1.

[25]David Morgan, *Visual Piety: A History and Theory of Popular Religious Images* (Berkeley: University of California Press, 1998), 124.

[26]Dana L. Cloud, "'To Veil the Threat of Terror': Afghan Women and the <Clash of Civilizations> in the Imagery of the U.S. War on Terrorism," *Quarterly Journal of Speech* 90, no. 3 (August 2004): 285–306.

[27]E. Michele Ramsey, "Addressing Issues of Context in Historical Women's Public Address," *Women's Studies in Communication* 27, no. 3 (Fall 2004): 352–76. Ramsey uses "woman" to refer to "discursively constructed representations" and "women" to denote the literal human beings (see Ramsey, 373, fn 3). Following other studies of ideographs, I use < > to designate when I am using the ideographic form of a word.

[28]McGee, 15.

[29]McGee, 6.

[30]Ramsey, "Addressing," 353. See also Celeste Michelle Condit, *Decoding Abortion Rhetoric* (Urbana-Champaign: University of Illinois Press, 1994); Celeste Michelle Condit and John Louis Lucaites, *Crafting Equality* (Chicago: University of Chicago Press, 1993).

[31]For examples of scholarship analyzing advocacy of woman suffrage, see Karlyn Kohrs Campbell, *Man Cannot Speak for Her* (New York: Praeger, 1989); Bonnie J. Dow, "Historical Narratives, Rhetorical Narratives, and Woman Suffrage Scholarship," *Rhetoric and Public Affairs* 2, no. 2 (Summer 1999): 321–40; Bonnie J. Dow, "The 'Womanhood' Rationale in the Woman Suffrage Rhetoric of Frances E. Willard," *Southern Communication Journal* 56, no. 4 (Summer 1991): 298–307; Susan Schultz Huxman, "Perfecting the Rhetorical Vision of Woman's Rights: Elizabeth Cady Stanton, Anna Howard Shaw, and Carrie Chapman Catt," *Women's Studies in Communication* 23, no. 3 (Fall 2000): 307–36; Sara Hayden, "Negotiating Femininity and Power in the Early Twentieth Century West: Domestic Ideology and Feminine Style in Jeannette Rankin's Suffrage Rhetoric," *Communication Studies* 50, no. 2 (Summer 1999): 83–102; Donna M. Kowal, "One Cause, Two Paths: Militant vs. Adjustive Strategies in the British and American Women's Suffrage Movements," *Communication Quarterly* 48, no. 3 (Summer 2000): 240–55; Wil A. Linkugel, "The Woman Suffrage Argument of Anna Howard Shaw," *Quarterly Journal of Speech* 49 (April 1963): 165–74; and Amy R. Slagell, "The Rhetorical Structure of Frances E. Willard's Campaign for Woman Suffrage, 1876–1896," *Rhetoric and Public Affairs* 4, no. 1 (Spring 2001): 1–23. For scholarship analyzing opposition to woman suffrage, see Elizabeth V. Burt, "The Ideology, Rhetoric, and Organizational Structure of a Countermovement Publication: 'The Remonstrance', 1890–1920," *Journalism and Mass Communication Quarterly* 75, no. 1 (Spring 1998): 69–83; Martha Hagan, "The Antisuffragists' Rhetorical Dilemma: Reconciling the Private and Public Spheres," *Communication Reports* 5, no. 2 (Summer 1992): 73–81; and Kristy Maddux, "When Patriots Protest: The Anti-Suffrage Discursive Transformation of 1917," *Rhetoric and Public Affairs* 7, no. 3 (Fall 2004): 283–310.

[32]For scholarship analyzing images of woman and women's rights, see Jennifer L. Borda, "The Woman Suffrage Parades of 1910–1913: Possibilities and Limitations of an Early Feminist Rhetorical Strategy," *Western Journal of Communication* 66, no. 1 (Winter 2002): 25–52; Katherine Meyer, John Seidler, Timothy Curry, and Adrian Aveni, "Women in July Fourth Cartoons: A 100-Year Look," *Journal of Communication* 30, no. 1 (Winter 1980); and E. Michele Ramsey, "Inventing Citizens During World War I: Suffrage Cartoons in *The Woman Citizen*," *Western Journal of Communication* 64, no. 2 (Spring 2000): 113–47; and Ramsey, "Addressing." For other disciplines' studies of images, see Brian Harrison, *Separate Spheres: The Opposition to Women's Suffrage in Britain* (London: Croon Helm, 1978); Ian McDonald, *Vindication! A Postcard History of the Women's Movement* (London: Bellew Publishing, 1989); Alice Sheppard, *Cartooning for Suffrage* (Albuquerque, NM: University of New Mexico Press, 1994); and Tickner.

[33]Cheryl Jorgensen-Earp, "The Lady, the Whore, and the Spinster: The Rhetorical Use of Victorian Images of Women," *Western Journal of Speech Communication* 54, no. 1 (1990): 83.

[34]Jorgensen-Earp, 84.

[35]Tickner, 164.

[36]Tickner, 151.

[37]The label "antis" generally refers to any person opposed to suffrage. Remonstrants, however, were exclusively women opposed to woman suffrage.

[38]Manuela Thurner, "'Better Citizens Without the Ballot': American Anti-suffrage Women and Their Rationale During the Progressive Era," *Journal of Women's History* 5, no. 1 (Spring 1993): 33.

[39]Thomas Jablonsky, "Female Opposition: The Anti-suffrage Campaign," in *Votes for Women: The Struggle for Suffrage Revisited,* ed. Jean H. Baker (New York: Oxford University Press, 2002), 123.

[40]Maddux, 287.

[41]Jane Jerome Camhi, *Women Against Women: American Anti-suffragism, 1880–1920* (Brooklyn, NY: Carlson Publishing, 1994); J. Howard, "Our Own Worst Enemies: Women Opposed to Woman Suffrage," *Journal of Sociology and Social Welfare* 9 (1982): 463–74; Billie Barnes Jensen, "'In the Weird and Wooly West': Anti-suffrage Women, Gender Issues, and Woman Suffrage in the West," *Journal of the West* 32 (1993): 41–51; Mrs. A. T. Leatherbee, *Why Should any Woman be an Anti-Suffragist?*, pamphlet issued by the Massachusetts Association Opposed to the Further Extension of Suffrage to Women, Room 615, Kensington Building, Boston, MA, n.d.; and Susan E. Marshall, *Splintered Sisterhood: Gender and Class in the Campaign Against Woman Suffrage* (Madison, WI: The University of Wisconsin Press, 1997).

[42]*Opinions of Eminent Persons Against Woman Suffrage*, pamphlet issued by the Massachusetts Association Opposed to the Further Extension of Suffrage to Women, Room 615, Kensington Building, Boston, MA, October 1912.

[43]Ramsey, "Inventing," 118, 140.

[44]Aileen Kraditor, *The Ideas of the Woman Suffrage Movement, 1890–1920* (New York: W. W. Norton, 1965), 28.

[45]Quoted in Mrs. B. Hazard, "New York State Association Opposed to Woman Suffrage," *The Chautauquan* (June 1910): 88.

[46]*Opinions of Eminent Persons,* 6.

[47]A similar postcard appeared in 1912. Produced by the C. Wolf company of New York, it is a black and white drawing of an attractive woman in a dress patterned after a police uniform. The caption of the postcard (sarcastically) reads, "Safely the males may walk on the street while such cops are patrolling the beat."

[48]Camhi, 53.

[49]Camhi, 55.

[50]Judith Butler, *Bodies That Matter: On the Discursive Limits of "Sex"* (New York: Routledge, 1993), 10.

[51]Butler, *Bodies,* 10.

[52]For a discussion of the dialectical function of "conflicting representations of woman," see Ramsey, "Addressing," 361.

[53]Glenna Matthews, *The Rise of Public Woman: Woman's Power and Woman's Place in the United States, 1630–1970* (New York: Oxford University Press, 1992), 3. Matthews opens her book with the story of the 1895 arrest of Lizzie Schauer, a young working class woman arrested when she asked for directions from two men. Because she was out at night, and unescorted, she was assumed to be a "public woman" or prostitute.

[54]Lisa Maria Hogeland, "Feminism, Sex Scandals, and Historical Lessons," *Critical Studies in Mass Communication* 16 (March 1999): 98.

[55]Kimberly Chrisman, "Unhoop the Fair Sex: The Campaign Against the Hoop Petticoat in Eighteenth-Century England," *Eighteenth-Century Studies* 30, no. 1 (1996): 18.

[56]Matthew Sweet, *Inventing the Victorians* (New York: St. Martin's Press, 2001).

[57]Shelly Foote, "Challenging Gender Symbols," in *Men and Women: Dressing the Part*, ed. Claudia Brush Kidwell and Valerie Steele (Washington: Smithsonian Institution Press, 1989), 148; see also Carol Mattingly, *Appropriate[ing] Dress: Women's Rhetorical Style in Nineteenth-Century America* (Carbondale: SIU Press, 2002).

[58]Sarah A. Gordon, "'Any Desired Length': Negotiating Gender through Sports Clothing, 1870–1925," in *Beauty and Business: Commerce, Gender, and Culture in Modern America*, ed. Philip Scranton (New York: Routledge, 2001), 27.

[59]JoAnne Olian, ed., *Everyday Fashions 1909–1920: As Pictured in Sears Catalogues* (New York: Dover Publications, 1995), i.

[60]Jorgensen-Earp, 93; and Ramsey, "Addressing," 353.

[61]Meyer, Seidler, Curry, and Aveni, 21.

[62]Jorgensen-Earp, 88.

[63]A plethora of postcards, other than those in the Dunston-Weiler set, employed the image of the home-bound and/or care-giving male. However, unlike the Dunston-Weiler set, the vast majority of these other images depicted men as incompetent caregivers. A circa 1910 American Colorgravure postcard (Series 138, Subject 2773) shows a man wheeling a baby buggy with a squalling infant inside, two circa 1910 Bamforth and Co. Publishers postcards (Nos. 1240 and 1048) show a man cleaning house (while caring for crying infants) proclaiming "my wife's joined the suffrage movement, (I've suffered ever since!)", a circa 1911 postcard (698/24) shows the "results of the Suffrage victory" to be a man taking care of a crying infant while the woman leaves, and a 1910 C. Hobson postcard also shows a man caring for children (and a hissing cat) as his wife leaves. English postcards also carried a similar sentiment (see B. B. London series A17).

[64]Jorgensen-Earp, 89.

[65]Virginia Woolf, *A Room of One's Own* (New York: Harvest /HBJ, 1929, 1957), 35–36.

[66]Judith Butler, *Gender Trouble: Feminism and the Subversion of Identity* (New York: Routledge, 1990).

[67]John M. Sloop, *Disciplining Gender: Rhetorics of Sex Identity in Contemporary U.S. Culture* (Amherst: University of Massachusetts Press, 2004), 6.

[68]Butler, *Gender*, 16.

[69]Maymie R. Krythe, *What So Proudly We Hail* (New York: Harper and Row Publishers, 1968), 49.

[70]Alton Ketchum, *Uncle Sam: The Man and the Legend* (New York: Hill and Wang, 1959), 61.

[71]Ketchum, 74, 80.

[72]Ketchum, 79.

[73]Gerald E. Czulewicz, Sr., *The Foremost Guide to Uncle Sam Collectibles* (Paducah, KY: Collector's Books, 1995), 35.

[74]Ketchum, 86.

[75]Thomas H. Bivins, "The Body Politic: The Changing Shape of Uncle Sam," *Journalism Quarterly* 64, no. 1 (Spring 1987): 13–20.

[76]Ketchum, 9.

[77]Ketchum, vii.

[78]Bivins, 15.

[79]Bivins, 15.

[80]Harvey Hill, "American Catholicism?: John England and 'The Republic in Danger,'" *Catholic Historical Review* 89, no. 2 (April 2003): 240.

[81]Colleen McDannell, *Material Christianity: Religion and Popular Culture in America* (New Haven: Yale University Press, 1995), 133.

[82]A. James Reichley, "Faith in Politics," *Journal of Policy History* 13, no. 1 (2001): 158, 240.

[83]Harvey Hill, 240.

[84]Reichley, 158.

[85]Thomas J. Jablonsky, *The Home, Heaven, and Mother Party: Female Anti-suffragists in the United States, 1868–1920* (Brooklyn, NY: Carlson Publishing, 1994), 66–7.

[86]Jablonsky, *The Home*, 66.

[87]Jablonsky, *The Home*, 67.

[88]Jablonsky, *The Home*, 69.

[89]Jablonsky, *The Home*, 45.

[90]Jablonsky, *The Home*, 45.

[91]David Morgan, *Visual Piety: A History and Theory of Popular Religious Images* (Berkeley: University of California Press, 1998).

[92]Morgan, 60.

[93]Eleanor Heartney, "Thinking Through the Body: Women Artists and the Catholic Imagination," *Hypatia* 18, no. 4 (2003): 3–22.

[94]McDannell, 61.

[95]Christine L. Krueger, review of *Women of Faith in Victorian Culture and Women's Theology in Nineteenth-Century Britain*, *Victorian Studies* 43, no. 1 (2000): 179.

[96]Protestants questioned the significance of Mary: "Mariology—the veneration of the Virgin Mary—is one of the points of doctrine that most clearly separates Protestants and Catholics. While Protestants tend to downplay Mary's role, seeing her simply as an exemplary woman, for Catholics she performs multiple functions. She is the embodiment of perfect motherhood . . ." (Heartney, 5). The differences over the role of Mary were not simply ones of degree. In fact, within Victorian England, the Virgin Mary was an extremely controversial figure, "a powerful presence who embodied what many Victorians considered to be the errors of the Roman Catholic Church. These included pagan idolatry, superstition and willful ignorance of the Bible, all of which were summed up in a single word: Mariolotry" (Carole Marie Engelhardt, "Victorian Masculinity and the Virgin Mary," in *Masculinity and Spirituality in Victorian Culture*, ed. Andrew Bradstock, Susan Gill, Anne Hogan, and Sue Morgan New York: St. Martin's Press, 2000, 44).

[97]The history of the icon within Catholicism also resonates with some of the anti-suffrage arguments concerning illiteracy overtaking the polls. The visual itself was not without controversy within Catholicism. Ultimately, iconoclasts supported the utility of images in "decorative arts and devotional devices to stimulate piety" because the "uneducated, women, and children were particularly responsive to sacred images" and "illiterate Christians needed them to understand and express their faith" (McDannell, 9). Protestant reformers in the sixteenth century, however, tended to limit the use of images only to instruction, and prohibited their presence in the church, lest worshipers confuse sign and referent, as "art and objects tempted a weak humanity that fell too easily into idolatry" (McDannell, 10).

[98]Andrew Bradstock, Sean Gill, Anne Hogan, and Sue Morgan, eds., *Masculinity and Spirituality in Victorian Culture* (New York: St. Martin's Press, 2000), 2.

[99]For discussions of muscular Christianity, see Donald E. Hall, ed., *Muscular Christianity: Embodying the Victorian Age* (Cambridge: Cambridge University Press, 1994); Tony Ladd and James A. Mathisen, *Muscular Christianity: Evangelical Protestants and the Development of American Sport* (Grand Rapids, MI: Baker Books, 1999); and Clifford Putney, *Muscular Christianity: Manhood and Sports in Protestant America, 1880–1920* (Cambridge: Harvard University Press, 2003).

[100]Butler, *Bodies*, 1.

[101]Butler, *Bodies*, 10.

[102]Ramsey, "Addressing," 353.

[103]For example, Michael A. DeSousa, "Symbolic Action and Pretended Insight: The Ayatollah Khomeini in U.S. Editorial Cartoons," in *Rhetorical Dimensions in Media: A Critical Casebook*, ed. M. J. Medhurst and T. W. Benson (Dubuque, IA: Kendall/Hunt, 1984, revised printing), 204–30; Michael A. DeSousa and Martin J. Medhurst, "The

Editorial Cartoon as Visual Rhetoric: Rethinking Boss Tweed," *Journal of Visual Verbal Languaging* 2 (Fall 1982): 43–52; Michael A. DeSousa and Martin J. Medhurst, "Political Cartoons and American Culture: Significant Symbols of Campaign 1980," *Studies in Visual Communication* 8, no. 1 (1982): 84–97; Janis L. Edwards, *Political Cartoons in the 1988 Presidential Campaign: Image, Metaphor, and Narrative* (New York: Garland Publishing, 1997); Janis L. Edwards and H. R. Chen, "The First Lady/ First Wife in Editorial Cartoons: Rhetorical Visions Through Gendered Lens," *Women's Studies in Communication* 23, no. 3 (Fall 2000): 367–91; Alette Hill, "The Carter Campaign in Retrospect: Decoding* the Cartoons," *Semiotica* 23, nos. 3 and 4 (1978): 307032; Martin J. Medhurst and Michael A. DeSousa, "Political Cartoons as Rhetorical Form: A Taxonomy of Graphic Discourse," *Communication Monographs* 48, no. 3 (September 1981): 197–236; Matthew C. Morrison, "The Role of the Political Cartoonist in Image Making," *Central States Speech Journal* (Winter 1969): 252–60; John F. Sena, "A Picture is Worth a Thousand Votes: Geraldine Ferraro and the Editorial Cartoonists," *Journal of American Culture* 8 (1985): 2–12; and James D. Steakley, "Iconography of a Scandal: Political Cartoons and the Eulenberg Affair," *Studies in Visual Communication* 9 (1983): 20–51.

[104]Lisa Z. Sigel, "Filth in the Wrong People's Hands: Postcards and the Expansion of Pornography in Britain and the Atlantic World, 1880–1914," *Journal of Social History* 33, no. 4 (2000): 859–85, available from Project Muse; and Yoke-Sum Wong, "Beyond (and Below) Incommensurability: The Aesthetics of the Postcard," *Common Knowledge* 8, no. 2 (2002): 333–56.

[105]Sigel, 860.

[106]Kimberlé Crenshaw, "Demarginalizing the Intersection of Race and Sex: A Black Feminist Critique of Antidiscrimination Doctrine, Feminist Theory and Antiracist Politics," *University of Chicago Legal Forum* (1989): 139–67; and Adrien Katherine Wing, ed., *Critical Race Feminism: A Reader* (New York: New York University Press, 1997).

[107]Barbara Welter, *Dimity Convictions: The American Woman in the Nineteenth Century* (Athens, OH: Ohio University Press, 1976).

[108]Chandra Talpede Mohanty, *Feminism Without Borders* (Durham: Duke University Press, 2003), 55.

[109]David Fleming, "Can Pictures be Arguments?" *Argumentation and Advocacy* 33, no.1 (Summer 1996): 11–22.

[110]David S. Birdsell and Leo Groarke, eds., "Toward a Theory of Visual Argument," Special Issues on Visual Argument, *Argumentation and Advocacy* 33, nos. 1–2 (Summer and Fall 1996): 1–10; Randall A. Lake and Barbara A. Pickering, "Argumentation, the Visual, and the Possibility of Refutation: An Exploration," *Argumentation* 12 (February 1998): 79–93; and Catherine H. Palczewski, "Keynote Address: Argument in an Off Key," in *Communicative Reason and Communication Communities,* ed. G. Thomas Goodnight et al. (Washington, DC: NCA, 2002), 1–23.

[111]The insights of this paragraph owe much to conversations with G. Thomas Goodnight and his work with Kathryn M. Olson on the function of nondiscursive oppositional argument in controversy. See Kathryn M. Olson and G. Thomas Goodnight, "Entanglements of Consumption, Cruelty, Privacy, and Fashion: The Social Controversy over Fur," *Quarterly Journal of Speech* 80, no. 3 (August 1994): 249–76.

[112]DeSousa and Medhurst, "Political Cartoons," 84. Emphasis mine.

[113]Robert Hariman and John Louis Lucaites, "Dissent and Emotional Management in a Liberal-Democratic Society: The Kent State Iconic Photograph," *Rhetoric Society Quarterly* 31, no. 3 (Summer 2001): 5–31; "Performing Civic Identity: The Iconic Photograph of the Flag Raising on Iwo Jima," *Quarterly Journal of Speech* 88, no. 4 (November 2002): 363–92; and "Public Identity and Collective Memory in U.S. Iconic Photography: The Image of 'Accidental Napalm,'" *Critical Studies in Media Communication* 20, no. 1 (March 2003): 35–66.

[114]Hariman and Lucaites, "Dissent," 8.

[115]Hariman and Lucaites, "Performing," 364.

[116]Jean H. Baker, ed., *Votes for Women: The Struggle for Suffrage Revisited* (New York: Oxford University Press, 2002), 6.

[117]Jablonsky, "Female Opposition," 129.

[118]Alette Hill, 308.

[119]Edwards and Winkler, 290.

[120]Cloud, 287.

[121]Edwards and Winkler, 305.

Chapter X

Gender Criticism

Gender criticism analyzes how the symbolic interactions of particular cultures define, inculcate, and impose performances of femininity and/or masculinity. A major element of gender criticism is the "feminist" perspective. Since the early 1970s, feminist rhetorical criticism has pursued diverse goals. Some feminist scholars focus on how language itself oppresses or marginalizes women. Others argue that women have distinctive methods and channels of communication that are no less sophisticated or meaningful than those recognized in conventional, male-dominated political rhetoric. Still others use the critical act to construct and advance feminist theory.

Karlyn Kohrs Campbell's 1973 essay "The Rhetoric of Women's Liberation: An Oxymoron" is an important milestone in the evolution of feminist criticism. Although this work can be profitably studied as an example of social-movement or genre criticism, it also meets the definition of feminist criticism because it analyzes gender definitions and advances feminist rhetorical theory. Campbell claims the rhetoric of women's liberation comprises a separate genre that has distinctive, interdependent characteristics in its style and substance that stem from the status of women in society. Campbell proposes that the central metaphor of this genre is the oxymoron and says traditional methods for explaining persuasion cannot account for the paradoxical nature of women's liberation discourse.

In her 2003 essay, "Feminism, Miss America, and Media Mythology," Bonnie J. Dow investigates how the mainstream mass media constructs feminism. She analyzes the feminist protest at the 1968 Miss America Pageant and contrasts feminist arguments about this event with media portrayals of Miss America Pageants over the next thirty years. As Dow demonstrates, the most notorious incident of the 1968 protest, public "bra-burning," never actually took place, but the media fixated on it as a way of "sexualizing, and thus trivializing, the women's concerns." They also depicted the protestors as obstinate, doctrinaire and "anti-woman." Dow argues that, over time, the dominant media promoted a view of liberal feminism that emphasized individual competitiveness within mainstream society. Media accounts of "contemporary feminism," she says, purport to celebrate the choices women can make, including the choice to become a beauty pageant participant. Ultimately, the author says, the media's rhetorical construction of feminism undermines those who challenge the unfairness of male-dominated society.

Charles E. Morris III takes another approach to gender criticism in his 2002 essay, "Pink Herring & The Fourth Persona: J. Edgar Hoover's Sex Crime Panic," which explores the complex connections between sexual identity and rhetoric. Morris contends that J. Edgar Hoover attempted to quell public uneasiness about his sexuality in 1937 by creating a diversion, or "pink herring." Hoover, in his public discourse, characterized himself as a relentless pursuer of "sex deviates" who preyed on innocent children. By adapting the "male rhetorical behavior" of "passing," the author argues, Hoover tried to portray himself as a "normal," masculine heterosexual. In addition, Morris says, by fostering a national sex-crime panic, Hoover's rhetoric acted to silence the "fourth persona"—those who recognized his "dangerous difference."

John M. Sloop's 2005 essay "Riding in Cars between Men" considers ways in which society reinforces "gender norms." For example, the automobile is often regarded from a "gender/sexual" perspective as an extension of the human body. Sloop examines media reporting of Deborah Renshaw, a rising star in the world of race car driving. When she was blamed for a controversial accident that killed fellow driver Eric Martin, the dominant media narrative concluded that, in car racing, the female body "is found in a place . . . in which it does not 'naturally' belong." In the news stories, Sloop maintains, we see evidence of how the issue of gender is used to maintain traditional definitions of the "proper" roles for men and women.

THE RHETORIC OF WOMEN'S LIBERATION: AN OXYMORON

KARLYN KOHRS CAMPBELL

Whatever the phrase "women's liberation" means, it cannot, as yet, be used to refer to a cohesive historical-political movement. No clearly defined program or set of policies unifies the small, frequently transitory groups that compose it, nor is there much evidence of organizational unity and cooperation.[1] At this point in time, it has produced only minor changes in American Society,[2] although it has made the issues with which it is associated major topics of concern and controversy. As some liberation advocates admit, it is a "state of mind" rather than a movement. Its major manifestation has been rhetorical, and as such, it merits rhetorical analysis.

Because any attempt to define a rhetorical movement or genre is beset by difficulties, and because of the unusual status of women's liberation I have briefly described, I wish to state explicitly two presuppositions informing what follows. First, I reject historical and socio-psychological definitions of movements as the basis for rhetorical criticism on the grounds that they do not, in fact, isolate a genre of rhetoric or a distinctive body of rhetorical acts.[3] The criteria defining a rhetorical movement must be rhetorical; in Aristotelian terminology, such criteria might arise from the relatively distinctive use or interpretation of the canons and modes of proof. However, rather than employing any codified critical scheme, I propose to treat two general categories—substance and style. In my judgment, the rhetoric of women's liberation (or any other body of discourses) merits separate critical treatment if, and only if, the symbolic acts of which it is composed can be shown to be distinctive on both substantive and stylistic grounds. Second, I presume that the style and substance of a genre of rhetoric are interdependent.[4] Stylistic choices are deeply influenced by subject-matter and context,[5] and issues are formulated and shaped by stylistic strategies.[6] The central argument of this essay is that the rhetoric of women's liberation is a distinctive genre because it evinces unique rhetorical qualities that are a fusion of substantive and stylistic features.

DISTINCTIVE SUBSTANTIVE FEATURES

At first glance, demands for legal, economic, and social equality for women would seem to be a reiteration, in a slightly modified form, of arguments already familiar from the protest rhetoric of students and blacks. However, on closer examination, the fact that equality is being demanded for women alters the rhetorical picture drastically. Feminist advocacy unearths tensions woven deep into the fabric of our society and provokes an unusually intense and profound "rhetoric of moral conflict."[7] The sex role requirements for women contradict the dominant values of American culture—self-reliance, achievement, and independence.[8] Unlike most other groups, the social status of women is defined primarily by birth, and their social position is at odds with fundamental democratic values.[9] In fact, insofar as the role of rhetor entails qualities of self-reliance, self-confidence, and independence, *its very assumption is a violation of the female role.* Consequently, feminist rhetoric is substantively unique by definition, because no matter how traditional its argumentation, how justificatory its form, how discursive its method, or how scholarly its style, it attacks the entire psychosocial reality, the most fundamental values, of the cultural context in which it occurs. As illustration, consider the apparently moderate, reformist demands by feminists for legal, economic, and social equality—demands ostensibly based on the shared value of equality. (As presented here, each of these demands is a condensed version of arguments from highly traditional discourses by contemporary liberationists.)

The demand for legal equality arises out of a conflict in values. Women are not equal to men in the sight of the law. In 1874, the Supreme Court ruled that "some citizens could be denied rights which others had," specifically, that "the 'equal protection' clause of the Fourteenth Amendment did not give women equal rights with men," and reaffirmed this decision in 1961, stating that "the Fourteenth Amendment prohibits any arbitrary class legislation, except that based on sex."[10] The legal inferiority of women is most apparent in marriage laws. The core of these laws is that spouses have reciprocal—not equal—rights and duties. The husband must maintain the wife and children, but the amount of support beyond subsistence is at his discretion. In return, the wife is legally required to do the domestic chores, provide marital companionship, and sexual consortium but has no claim for direct compensation for any of the services rendered. Fundamentally, marriage is a property relationship. In the nine community property states, the husband is considered the head of the "community," and so long as he is capable of managing it, the wife, acting alone, cannot contract debts chargeable to it. In Texas and Nevada, the husband can even dispose of the property without his wife's consent, property that includes the income of a working wife. The forty-one common law states do not recognize the economic contribution of a wife who works only in the home. She has no right to an allowance, wages, or income of any sort, nor can she claim joint ownership upon divorce. In addition, every married woman's surname is legally that of her husband, and no court will uphold her right to go by another name.[11]

It seems to me that any audience of such argumentation confronts a moral dilemma. The listener must either admit that this is not a society based on the value of equality or make the overt assertion that women are special or inferior beings who merit discriminatory treatment.[12]

The argument for economic equality follows a similar pattern. Based on median income, it is a greater economic disadvantage to be female than to be black or poorly educated (of course, any combination of these spells economic disaster).

Although half of the states have equal pay laws, dual pay scales are the rule. These cannot be justified economically because, married or single, the majority of women who work do so out of economic necessity, and some forty percent of families with incomes below the poverty level are headed by women. Occupationally, women are proportionately more disadvantaged today than they were in 1940, and the gap between male and female income steadily increases.[13] It might seem that these data merely indicate a discrepancy between law and practice—at least the value is embodied in some laws—although separating values and behavior is somewhat problematic. However, both law and practice have made women economically unequal. For example, so long as the law, as well as common practice, gives the husband a right to the domestic services of his wife, a woman must perform the equivalent of two jobs in order to hold one outside the home.[14] Once again, the audience of such argumentation confronts a moral dilemma.

The most overt challenge to cultural values appears in the demand for social or sexual equality, that we dispense forever with the notion that "men are male *humans* whereas women are human *females*,"[15] a notion enshrined in the familiar phrase, "I now pronounce you man and wife." An obvious reason for abolishing such distinctions is that they lead to cultural values for men as men and women as wives. Success for men is defined as instrumental, productive labor in the outside world whereas "wives" are confined to "woman's place"—child care and domestic labor in the home.[16] As long as these concepts determine "masculinity" and "femininity," the woman who strives for the kind of success defined as the exclusive domain of the male is inhibited by norms prescribing her "role" and must pay a heavy price for her deviance. Those who have done research on achievement motivation in women conclude that: "Even when legal and educational barriers to achievement are removed, the motive to avoid success will continue to inhibit women from doing 'too well'—thereby risking the possibility of being socially rejected as 'unfeminine' or 'castrating.'"[17] and "The girl who maintains qualities of independence and active striving (achievement-orientation) necessary for intellectual mastery defies the conventions of sex appropriate behavior and must pay a price, *a price in anxiety*."[18] As long as education and socialization cause women to be "unsexed" by success whereas men are "unsexed" by failure, women cannot compete on equal terms or develop their individual potentials. No values, however, are more deeply engrained than those defining "masculinity and femininity." The fundamental conflict in values is evident. Once their consequences and implications are understood, these apparently moderate, reformist demands are rightly seen as revolutionary and radical in the extreme. They threaten the institutions of marriage and the family and norms governing child-rearing and male-female roles. To meet them would require major, even revolutionary, social change.[19] It should be emphasized, however, that these arguments are drawn from discourses that could not be termed confrontative, alienating, or radical in any ordinary sense. In form, style, structure, and supporting materials, they would meet the demands of the strictest Aristotelian critic. Yet they are substantively unique, inevitably radical, because they attack the fundamental values underlying this culture. The option to be moderate and reformist is simply not available to women's liberation advocates.

DISTINCTIVE STYLISTIC FEATURES

As a rhetoric of intense moral conflict, it would be surprising indeed if distinctive stylistic features did not appear as strategic adaptations to a difficult rhetorical situation.[20] I propose to treat "stylistic features" rather broadly, electing to view women's liberation as a persuasive campaign. In addition to the linguistic features usually considered, the stylistic features of a persuasive campaign include, in my view, characteristic modes of rhetorical interaction, typical ways of structuring the relationships among participants in a rhetorical transaction, and emphasis on particular forms of argument, proof, and evidence. The rhetoric of women's liberation is distinctive stylistically in rejecting certain traditional concepts of the rhetorical process—as persuasion of the many by an expert or leader, as adjustment or adaptation to audience norms, and as directed toward inducing acceptance of a specific program or a commitment to group action. This rather "anti-rhetorical" style is chosen on substantive grounds because rhetorical transactions with these features encourage submissiveness and passivity in the audience[21]—qualities at odds with a fundamental goal of feminist advocacy—self-determination. The paradigm that highlights the distinctive stylistic features of women's liberation is "consciousness raising," a mode of interaction or a type of rhetorical transaction uniquely adapted to the rhetorical problem of feminist advocacy.

The rhetorical problem may be summarized as follows: women are divided from one another by almost all the usual sources of identification—age, education, income, ethnic origin, even geography. In addition, counter-persuasive forces are pervasive and potent—nearly all spend their lives in close proximity to and under the control of males—fathers, husbands, employers, etc. Women also have very negative self-concepts, so negative, in fact, that it is difficult to view them as an audience, i.e., persons who see themselves as potential agents of change. When asked to select adjectives to describe themselves, they select such terms as "uncertain, anxious, nervous, hasty, careless, fearful, dull, childish, helpless, sorry, timid, clumsy, stupid, silly, and domestic . . . understanding, tender, sympathetic, pure, generous, affectionate, loving, moral, kind, grateful, and patient."[22] If a persuasive campaign directed to this audience is to be effective, it must transcend alienation to create "sisterhood," modify self-concepts to create a sense of autonomy, and speak to women in terms of private, concrete, individual experience, because women have little, if any, publicly shared experience. The substantive problem of the absence of shared values remains: when women become part of an audience for liberation rhetoric, they violate the norms governing sex appropriate behavior.

In its paradigmatic form, "consciousness raising" involves meetings of small, leaderless groups in which each person is encouraged to express her personal feelings and experiences. There is no leader, rhetor, or expert. All participate and lead; all are considered expert. The goal is to make the personal political: to create awareness (through shared experiences) that what were thought to be personal deficiencies and individual problems are common and shared, a result of their position as women. The participants seek to understand and interpret their lives as women, but there is no "message," no "party line." Individuals are encouraged to dissent, to find their own truths. If action is suggested, no group commitment is made; each must decide whether, and if so which, action is suitable for her.[23] The stylistic features heightened in this kind of transaction are characteristic of the rhetoric as a whole: affirmation of the affective, of the validity of personal experience, of the necessity for self-exposure and self-criticism, of the value of dialogue, and of the goal of autonomous, individual decision making. These stylistic features are very similar to those Maurice Natanson has described as characteristic of genuine argumentation:

> What is at issue, really, in the risking of the self in genuine argument is the immediacy of the self's world of feeling, attitude, and the total subtle range of its affective and conative sensibility. . . . I open myself to the viable possibility

that the consequence of an argument may be to make me *see* something of the structure of my immediate world . . . the personal and immediate domain of individual experience. . . .

. . . feeling is a way of meaning as much as thinking is a way of formulating. Privacy is a means of establishing a world, and what genuine argument to persuade does is to publicize that privacy. The metaphor leads us to suggest that risking the self in argument is inviting a stranger to the interior familiarity of our home. . . .[24]

Even a cursory reading of the numerous anthologies of women's liberation rhetoric will serve to confirm that the stylistic features I have indicated are characteristic. Particularly salient examples include Elizabeth Janeway's *Man's World: Woman's Place,* "The Demise of the Dancing Dog,"[25] "The Politics of Housework,"[26] *A Room of One's Own,*[27] and "Cutting Loose."[28] The conclusion of the last essay cited will serve as a model:

The true dramatic conclusion of this narrative should be the dissolution of my marriage; there is a part of me which believes that you cannot fight a sexist system while acknowledging your need for the love of a man. . . . But in the end my husband and I did not divorce. . . . Instead I raged against him for many months and joined the Woman's Liberation Movement, and thought a great deal about myself, and about whether my problems were truly all women's problems, and decided that some of them were and that some of them were not. My sexual rage was the most powerful single emotion of my life, and the feminist analysis has become for me, as I think it will for most women of my generation, as significant an intellectual tool as Marxism was for generations of radicals. But it does not answer every question. . . . I would be lying if I said that my anger had taught me how to live. But my life has changed because of it. I think I am becoming in many small ways a woman who takes no shit. I am no longer submissive, no longer seductive. . . .

My husband and I have to some degree worked out our differences. . . . But my hatred lies within me and between us, not wholly a personal hatred, but not entirely political either. And I wonder always whether it is possible to define myself as a feminist revolutionary and still remain in any sense a wife. There are moments when I still worry that he will leave me, that he will come to need a woman less preoccupied with her own rights, and when I worry about that I also fear that no man will ever love me again, that no man could ever love a woman who is angry. And that fear is a great source of trouble to me, for it means that in certain fundamental ways I have not changed at all.

I would like to be cold and clear and selfish, to demand satisfaction for my needs, to compel respect rather than affection. And yet there are moments, and perhaps there always will be, when I fall back upon the old cop-outs. . . . Why should I work when my husband can support me, why should I be a human being when I can get away with being a child?

Women's liberation is finally only personal. It is hard to fight an enemy who has outposts in your head.[29]

This essay, the other works I have cited here, and the bulk of women's liberation rhetoric stand at the farthest remove from traditional models of rhetorical discourse, judged by the stylistic features I have discussed. This author, Sally Kempton, invites us into the interiority of her self, disclosing the inner dynamics of her feelings and the specific form that the problem of liberation takes in her life. In a rhetorically atypical fashion, she honors her feelings of fear, anger, hatred, and need for love and admits both her own ambivalence and the limits of her own experience as a norm for others. She is self-conscious and self-critical, cognizant of the inconsistencies in her life and of the temptation to "cop out," aware of both the psychic security and the psychic destruction inherent in the female role. She is tentatively describing and affirming the beginnings of a new identity and, in so doing, sets up a dialogue with other women in a similar position that permits the essay to perform the ego functions that Richard Gregg has described.[30] The essay asks for the participation of the reader, not only in sharing the author's life as an example of the problems of growing up female in this society, but in a general process of self-scrutiny in which each person looks at the dynamics of the problems of liberation in her own life. The goal of the work is a process, not a particular belief or policy; she explicitly states that her problems are not those of all women and that a feminist analysis is not a blueprint for living. Most importantly, however, the essay exemplifies "risking the self" in its most poignant sense. The Sally Kempton we meet in the essay has been masochistic, manipulative, an exploiter of the female role and of men, weak, murderous, vengeful and castrating, lazy and selfish. The risk involved in such brutal honesty is that she will be rejected as neurotic, bitchy, crazy, in short, as not being a "good" woman, and more importantly, as *not like us*. The risk may lead to alienation or to sisterhood. By example, she asks other women to confront themselves, recognize their own ambivalence, and face their own participation and collaboration in the roles and processes that have such devastating effects on both men and women. Although an essay, this work has all the distinctive stylistic features of the "consciousness raising" paradigm.

Although the distinctive stylistic features of women's liberation are most apparent in the small group processes of consciousness raising, they are not confined to small group interactions. The features I have listed are equally present in essays, speeches, and other discourses completely divorced from the small group setting. In addition, I would argue that although these stylistic features show certain affinities for qualities associated with psychotherapeutic interaction, they are rhetorical rather than expressive and public and political rather than private and personal. The presumption of most psychotherapy is that the origins of and solutions to one's problems are personal;[31] the feminist analysis presumes that it is the social structure and the definition of the female role that generate the problems that individual women experience in their personal lives. As a consequence, solutions must be structural, not merely personal, and analysis must move from personal experience and feeling to illuminate a common condition that all women experience and share.

Finally, women's liberation rhetoric is characterized by the use of confrontative, non-adjustive strategies designed to "violate the reality structure."[32] These strategies not only attack the psycho-social reality of the culture, but violate the norms of decorum, morality, and "femininity" of the women addressed. Essays on frigidity and orgasm,[33] essays by prostitutes and lesbians,[34] personal accounts of promiscuity and masochism,[35] and essays attacking romantic love and urging man-hating as a necessary stage in liberation[36] "violate the reality structure" by close analysis of tabooed subjects, by treating "social outcasts" as "sisters" and credible sources, and by attacking areas of belief with great mythic power. Two specific linguistic techniques, "attack metaphors" and symbolic reversals, also seem to be characteristic. "Attack metaphors" mix matrices in order to reveal the "nonconscious ideology"[37] of sexism in language and belief, or they attempt to shock through a kind of "perspective by incongruity."[38] Some examples are: "Was Lurleen Wallace *Governess* of Alabama?" A drawing of Rodin's "Thinker" as a female. "Trust in God; She will provide."[39] "Prostitutes are the only honest women because they charge for their services, rather than submitting to a marriage contract which forces them to work for life without pay."[40] "If you think you are emancipated, you might consider the idea of tasting your menstrual blood—if it makes you sick, you've got a long way to go, baby."[41] Or this analogy:

> Suppose that a white male college student decided to room or set up a bachelor apartment with a black male friend. Surely the typical white student would not blithely assume that his black roommate was to handle all the domestic chores. Nor would his conscience allow him to do so even in the unlikely event that his roommate would say: "No, that's okay. I like doing housework. I'd be happy to do it. . . ." But change this hypothetical black roommate to a female marriage partner, and somehow the student's conscience goes to sleep.[42]

Symbolic reversals transform devil terms society has applied to women into god terms and always exploit the power and fear lurking in these terms as potential sources of strength. "The Bitch Manifesto" argues that liberated women are bitches—aggressive, confident, strong.[43] W.I.T.C.H., the Women's International Terrorist Conspiracy from Hell, says, in effect, "You think we're dangerous, creatures of the devil, witches? You're right! And we're going to hex you!"[44] Some feminists have argued that the lesbian is the paradigm of the liberated female;[45] others have described an androgynous role.[46] This type of reversal has, of course, appeared in other protest rhetorics, particularly in the affirmation that "black is beautiful." But systematic reversals of traditional female roles, given the mystique associated with concepts of wife, mother, and loving sex partner, make these reversals especially disturbing and poignant. Quite evidently, they are attempts at the radical affirmation of new identities for women.[47]

The distinctive stylistic features of women's liberation rhetoric are a result of strategic adaptation to an acute rhetorical problem. Women's liberation is characterized by rhetorical interactions that emphasize affective proofs and personal testimony, participation and dialogue, self-revelation and self-criticism, the goal of autonomous decision making through self-persuasion, and the strategic use of techniques for "violating the reality structure." I conclude that, on stylistic grounds, women's liberation is a separate genre of rhetoric.

THE INTERDEPENDENCE
OF SUBSTANTIVE AND STYLISTIC FEATURES

The rhetorical acts I have treated in the preceding section, particularly as illustrated by the excerpt from an essay by Sally Kempton, may seem to be a far cry from the works cited earlier demanding legal, economic, and social equality. However, I believe that all of these rhetorical acts are integral parts of a single genre, a conclusion I shall defend by examining the interdependent character of the substantive and stylistic features of the various discourses already discussed.

Essays such as that of Sally Kempton are the necessary counterparts of works articulating demands for equality. In fact, such discourses spell out the meaning and consequences of present conditions of inequity and the implications of equality in concrete, personal, affective terms. They complete the genre and are essential to its success as a persuasive campaign. In the first section, I argued that demands for equality for women "attack the entire psycho-social reality." That phrase may conceal the fact that such an attack is an attack on the *self* and on the roles and relationships in which women, and men too, have found their identities traditionally. The effect of such an argument is described by Natanson, "When an argument hurts me, cuts me, or cleanses and liberates me it is not because a particular stratum or segment of my world view is shaken up or jarred free but because *I* am wounded or enlivened—*I* in my particularity, and that means in my existential immediacy—feelings, pride, love, and sullenness, the world of my actuality as I live it."[48] The only effective response to the sensation of being threatened existentially is a rhetorical act that treats the personal, emotional, and concrete directly and explicitly, that is dialogic and participatory, that speaks from personal experience to personal experience. Consequently, the rhetoric of women's liberation includes numerous essays discussing the personal experiences of women in many differing circumstances—black women, welfare mothers, older women, factory workers, high school girls, journalists, unwed mothers, lawyers, secretaries, and so forth. Each attempts to describe concretely the personal experience of inequality in a particular situation and/or what liberation might mean in a particular case. Rhetorically, these essays function to translate public demands into personal experience and to treat threats and fears in concrete, affective terms.

Conversely, more traditional discourses arguing for equality are an essential counterpart to these more personal statements. As a process, consciousness raising requires that the personal be transcended by moving toward the structural, that the individual be transcended by moving toward the political. The works treating legal, economic, and social inequality provide the structural analyses and empirical data that permit women to generalize from their individual experiences to the conditions of women in this society. Unless such transcendence occurs, there is no persuasive campaign, no rhetoric in any public sense, only the very limited realm of therapeutic, small group interaction.

The interrelationship between the personal and the political is central to a conception of women's liberation as a genre of rhetoric. All of the issues of women's liberation are simultaneously personal and political. Ultimately, this interrelationship rests on the caste status of women, the basis of the moral conflict this rhetoric generates and intensifies. Feminists believe that sharing personal experience is liberating, i.e., raises consciousness, because all women, whatever their differences in age, education, income, etc., share a common condition, a radical form of "consubstantiality" that is the genesis of the peculiar kind of identification they call "sisterhood." Some unusual rhetorical transactions seem to confirm this analysis. "Speakouts" on rape, abortion, and orgasm are mass meetings in which women share extremely personal and very negatively valued experiences. These events are difficult to explain without postulating a radical form of identification that permits such painful self-revelation. Similarly, "self-help clinics" in which women learn how to examine their cervixes and look at the cervixes of other women for purposes of comparison seem to require extreme identification and trust. Feminists would argue that "sisterhood is powerful" because it grows out of the recognition of pervasive, common experience of special caste status, the most radical and profound basis for cooperation and identification.

This feminist analysis also serves to explain the persuasive intent in "violating the reality structure." From this point of view, women in American society are always in a vortex of contradiction and paradox. On the one hand, they have been, for the most part, effectively socialized into traditional roles and values, as research into their achievement motivation and self-images confirms. On the other hand, "femininity" is in direct conflict with the most fundamental values of this society—a fact which makes women extremely vulnerable to attacks on the "reality structure." Hence, they argue, violations of norms may shock initially, but ultimately they will be recognized as articulating the contradictions inherent in "the female role." The violation of these norms is obvious in discourses such as that of Sally Kempton; it is merely less obvious in seemingly traditional and moderate works.

CONCLUSION

I conclude, then, that women's liberation is a unified, separate genre of rhetoric with distinctive substantive-stylistic features. Perhaps it is the only genuinely *radical* rhetoric on the contemporary American scene. Only the oxymoron, the figure of paradox and contradiction, can be its metaphor. Never is the paradoxical character of women's liberation more apparent than when it is compared to conventional or familiar definitions of rhetoric, analyses of rhetorical situations, and descriptions of rhetorical movements.

Traditional or familiar definitions of persuasion do not satisfactorily account for the rhetoric of women's liberation. In relation to such definitions, feminist advocacy wavers between the rhetorical and the non-rhetorical, the persuasive and the non-persuasive. Rhetoric is usually defined as dealing with public issues, structural analyses, and social action, yet women's liberation emphasizes acts concerned with personal exigences and private, concrete experience, and its goal is frequently limited to particular, autonomous action by individuals. The view that persuasion is an enthymematic adaptation to audience norms and values is confounded by rhetoric which seeks to persuade by "violating the reality structure" of those toward whom it is directed.

Nor are available analyses of rhetorical situations satisfactory when applied to the rhetoric of women's liberation. Parke Burgess' valuable and provocative discussion of certain rhetorical situations as consisting of two or more sets of conflicting moral demands[49] and Thomas Olbricht's insightful distinction between rhetorical acts occurring in the context of a shared value and those occurring in its absence[50] do not adequately explicate the situation in which feminists find themselves. And the reason is simply that the rhetoric of women's liberation appeals to *what are said to be* shared moral values, but forces recognition that those values are *not* shared, thereby creating the most intense of moral conflicts. Lloyd Bitzer's more specific analysis of the rhetorical situation as consisting of "one controlling exigence which functions as the organizing principle" (an exigence being "an imperfection marked by urgency" that "is capable of positive modification"), an audience made up "only of those persons who are capable of being influenced by discourse and of being mediators of change," and of constraints that can limit "decision and action needed to modify the exigence"[51]—this more specific analysis is also unsatisfactory. In women's liberation there are dual and conflicting exigences not solely of the public sort, and thus women's liberation rhetoric is a dialectic between discourses that deal with public, structural problems and the particularly significant statements of personal experience and feeling which extend beyond the traditional boundaries of rhetorical acts. A public exigence is, of course, present, but what is unavoidable and characteristic of this rhetoric is the accompanying and conflicting personal exigence. The concept of the audience does not account for a situation in which the audience must be *created under the special conditions* surrounding women's liberation. Lastly, the notion of constraints seems inadequate to a genre in which to act as a mediator of change, either as rhetor or audience member, is itself the most significant constraint inhibiting decision or action—a constraint that requires the violation of cultural norms and risks alienation no matter how traditional or reformist the rhetorical appeal may be.

And, similarly, nearly all descriptions of rhetorical movements prove unsatisfactory. Leland Griffin's early essay on the rhetoric of historical movements creates three important problems: he defines movements as occurring "at some time in the past"; he says members of movements "make efforts to alter their environment"; and he advises the student of rhetoric to focus on "the pattern of public discussion."[52] The first problem is that the critic is prevented from examining a contemporary movement and is forced to make sharp chronological distinctions between earlier efforts for liberation and contemporary feminist advocacy; the second problem is that once again the critic's attention is diverted from efforts to change the self, highly significant in the liberation movement, and shifted toward efforts to change the environment; and the third is a related deflection of critical concern from personal, consciousness-raising processes to public discussion. Herbert Simons' view of "a leader-centered conception of persuasion in social movements" defines a movement "as an uninstitutionalized collectivity that mobilizes for action to implement a program for the reconstitution of social norms or values."[53] As I have pointed out, leader-centered theories cannot be applied profitably to the feminist movement. Further, women's liberation is not characterized by a *program* that mobilizes feminist advocates to reconstitute social norms and values. Dan Hahn and Ruth Gonchar's idea of a movement as "socially shared activities and beliefs directed toward the demand for change in some aspect of the social order"[54] is unsuitable because it overlooks the extremely important elements of the personal exigence that require change in the self. There are, however, two recent statements describing rhetorical movements that are appropriate for women's liberation. Griffin's later essay describing a dramatistic framework for the development of movements has been applied insightfully to the inception period of contemporary women's liberations.[55] What makes this description applicable is that it recognizes a variety of symbolic acts, the role of drama and conflict, and the essentially moral or value-related character of rhetorical movements.[56] Also, Robert Cathcart's formulation, again a dramatistic one, is appropriate because it emphasizes *"dialectical enjoinment in the moral arena"* and the *"dialectical tension growing out of moral conflict."*[57]

And so I choose the oxymoron as a label, a metaphor, for the rhetoric of women's liberation. It is a genre without a rhetor, a rhetoric in search of an audience, that transforms traditional argumentation into confrontation, that "persuades" by "violating the reality structure" but that presumes a consubstantiality so radical that it permits the most intimate of identifications. It is a "movement" that eschews leadership, organizational cohesion, and the transactions typical of mass persuasion. Finally, of course, women's liberation is baffling because it has no program, because there is no clear answer to the recurring question, "What do women want?" On one level, the answer is simple; they want what every person wants—dignity, respect, the right to self-determination, to develop their potentials as individuals. But on another level, there is no answer—not even in feminist rhetoric. While there are legal and legislative changes on which most feminists agree (although the hierarchy of priorities differs), whatever liberation is, it will be something different for each woman as liberty is something different for each person. What each woman shares, however, is the paradox of having "to fight an enemy who has outposts in your head."

NOTES

[1] A partial list of the numerous groups involved in women's liberation and an analysis of them is available in Julie Ellis, *Revolt of the Second Sex* (New York: Lancer Books, 1970), pp. 21–81. A similar list and an analysis emphasizing disunity, leadership problems, and policy conflicts is found in Edythe Cudlipp, *Understanding Women's Liberation* (New York: Paperback Library, 1971), pp. 129–170, 214–220. As she indicates, more radical groups have expelled members for the tendency to attract personal media attention, used "counters" to prevent domination of meetings by more articulate members, and rejected programs, specific policies, and coherent group action (pp. 146–147, 166, 214–215). The most optimistic estimate of the size of the movement is made by Charlotte Bunch-Weeks[,] who says there are "perhaps 100,000 women in over 400 cities." ("A Broom of One's Own: Notes on the Women's Liberation Program," *The New Women,* ed. Joanne Cooke, Charlotte Bunch-Weeks and Robin Morgan [1970; rpt. Greenwich, Conn.: Fawcett Publications, 1971], p. 186.) Even if true, this compares unfavorably with the conservative League of Women Voters with 160,000 members (Cudlipp, p. 42) and the National Council of Women representing organizations with some 23 million members whose leadership has taken an extremely anti-liberationist stance. (See Lacey Fesburgh, "Traditional Groups Prefer to Ignore Women's Lib," *New York Times,* 26 Aug. 1970, p. 44.)

[2] Ti-Grace Atkinson said: "There is no movement. Movement means going some place, and the movement is not going anywhere. It hasn't accomplished anything." Gloria Steinem concurred: "In terms of real power—economic and political—we are still just beginning. But the consciousness, the awareness—that will never be the same." ("Women's Liberation Revisited," *Time,* 20 Mar. 1972, pp. 30, 31.) Polls do not seem to indicate marked attitude changes among American women. (See, for example, *Good Housekeeping,* Mar. 1971, pp. 34–38, and Carol Tavris, "Woman and Man," *Psychology Today,* Mar. 1972, pp. 57–64, 82–85.)

[3] An excellent critique of both historical and socio-psychological definition of movements as the basis for rhetorical criticism has been made by Robert S. Cathcart in "New Approaches to the Study of Movements: Defining Movements Rhetorically," *Western Speech,* 36 (Spr. 1972), 82–88.

[4] A particularly apt illustration of this point of view is Richard Hofstadter's "The Paranoid Style in American Politics," *The Paranoid Style in American Politics and Other Essays* (New York: Knopf, 1965), pp. 3–40. Similarly, the exhortative and argumentative genres developed by Edwin Black are defined on both substantive and stylistic grounds in *Rhetorical Criticism: A Study in Method* (New York: Macmillan, 1965), pp. 132–177.

[5] The interrelationship of moral demands and strategic choices is argued by Parke G. Burgess in "The Rhetoric of Moral Conflict: Two Critical Dimensions," *QJS,* 56 (Apr. 1970), 120–130.

[6] The notion that style is a token of ideology is the central concept in Edwin Black's "The Second *Persona" QJS,* 56 (Apr. 1970), 109–119.

[7] See Burgess, *op. cit.* and "The Rhetoric of Black Power: A Moral Demand?" *QJS,* 54 (Apr. 1968), 122–133.

[8] See Matina S. Horner, "Femininity and Successful Achievement: A Basic Inconsistency," *Roles Women Play: Readings Toward Women's Liberation,* ed. Michele Hoffnung Garskof (Belmont, Calif.: Brooks/Cole, 1971), pp. 105–108.

[9]"Woman's role, looked at from this point of view, is archaic. This is not necessarily a bad thing, but it does make woman's position rather peculiar: it is a survival. In the old world, where one was born into a class and a region and often into an occupation, the fact that one was also sex-typed simply added one more attribute to those which every child learned he or she possessed. Now to be told, in Erik Erikson's words, that one is 'never not-a-woman' comes as rather more of a shock. This is especially true for American women because of the way in which the American ethos has honored the ideas of liberty and individual choice . . . woman's traditional role in *itself* is opposed to a significant aspect of our culture. It is more than restricting, because it involves women in the kind of conflict with their surroundings that no decision and no action open to them can be trusted to resolve." (Elizabeth Janeway, *Man's World: Woman's Place: A Study in Social Mythology* [New York: William Morrow, 1971], p. 99.)

[10]Jo Freeman, "The Building of the Gilded Cage," *The Second Wave,* 1 (Spr. 1971), 33.

[11]*Ibid.,* 8–9.

[12]Judicial opinions upholding discriminatory legislation make this quite evident. "That woman's physical structure and the performance of maternal functions place her at a disadvantage in the struggle for subsistence is obvious . . . the physical well-being of woman becomes an object of public interest and care in order to preserve the strength and vigor of the race . . . looking at it from the viewpoint of the effort to maintain an independent position in life, she is not upon an equality . . . she is properly placed in a class by herself. . . . The reason . . . rests in the inherent difference between the two sexes, and in the different functions in life which they perform." (Muller v. Oregon, 208 U.S. 412 [1908], at 421–423.) This and similar judicial opinions are cited by Diane B. Schulder, "Does the Law Oppress Women?" *Sisterhood is Powerful,* ed. Robin Morgan (New York: Vintage Books, 1970), pp. 139–157.

[13]Ellis, pp. 103–111. See also Caroline Bird, with Sara Welles Briller, *Born Female: The High Cost of Keeping Women Down* (1968; rpt. New York: Pocket Books, 1971), particularly pp. 61–83.

[14]"The Chase Manhattan Bank estimated a U.S. woman's hours spent at housework at 99.6 per week." (Juliet Mitchell, "Women: The Longest Revolution [excerpt]," *Liberation Now!* ed. Deborah Babcox and Madeline Belkin [New York: Dell, 1971], p. 250.) See also Ann Crittenden Scott, "The Value of Housework," *Ms.,* July 1972, pp. 56–59.

[15]Aileen S. Kraditor, *Up From the Pedestal: Selected Writings in the History of American Feminism* (Chicago: Quadrangle Books, 1968), p. 24.

[16]The concepts underlying "woman's place" serve to explain the position that women hold outside the home in the economic sphere: "Are there any principles that explain the meanderings of the sex boundaries? One is the idea that women should work inside and men outside. Another earmarks service work for women and profit-making for men. Other rules reserve work with machinery, work carrying prestige, and the top job to men. Most sex boundaries can be explained on the basis of one or another of these three rules." (Bird, p. 72.)

[17]Horner, p. 121.

[18]From E. E. Maccoby, "Woman's Intellect," *The Potential of Woman,* ed. S. M. Farber and R. H. L. Wilson (New York: McGraw-Hill, 1963), pp. 24–39; cited in Horner, p. 106.

[19]In the economic sphere alone, such changes would be far-reaching. "Equal access to jobs outside the home, while one of the pre-conditions for women's liberation, will not in itself be sufficient to give equality for women. . . . Society must begin to take responsibility for children; the economic dependence of women and children on the husband-father must be ended. The other work that goes on in the home must also be changed—communal eating places and laundries for example. When such work is moved into the public sector, then the material basis for discrimination against women will be gone." (Margaret Benston, "The Political Economy of Women's Liberation," *Roles Women Play,* pp. 200–201.)

[20]The individual elements described here did not originate with women's liberation. Consciousness raising has its roots in the "witnessing" of American revivalism and was an important persuasive strategy in the revolution on mainland China. Both the ancient Cynics and the modern Yippies have used violations of the reality structure as persuasive techniques (see Theodore Otto Windt, Jr., "The Diatribe: Last Resort for Protest," *QJS*, 58 [Feb. 1972], 1–14). and this notion is central to the purposes of agit-prop theatre, demonstrations, and acts of civil disobedience. Concept of leaderless persuasion appear in Yippie documents and in the unstructured character of sensitivity groups. Finally, the idea that contradiction and alienation lead to altered consciousness and revolution has its origins in Marxian theory. It is the combination of these elements in women's liberation that is distinctive stylistically. As in a metaphor, the separate elements may be familiar; it is the fusion that is original.

[21]The most explicit statement of the notion that audiences are "feminine" and rhetors or orators are "masculine" appears in the rhetorical theory of Adolf Hitler and the National Socialist Party in Germany. See Kenneth Burke, "The Rhetoric of Hitler's 'Battle,'" *The Philosophy of Literary Form* (1941; rpt. New York: Vintage Books, 1957), p. 167.

[22]Jo Freeman, "The Social Construction of the Second Sex," *Roles Women Play*, p. 124.

[23]The nature of consciousness raising is described in Susan Brownmiller, "Sisterhood is Powerful" and June Arnold, "Consciousness-Raising," *Women's Liberation: Blueprint for the Future,* ed. Stookie Stambler (New York: Ace Books, 1970), pp. 141–161; Charlotte Bunch-Weeks, pp. 185–197; Carole Hanisch, "The Personal is Political," Kathie Sarachild, "A Program for Feminist 'Consciousness Raising,'" Irene Peslikis, "Resistances to Consciousness," Jennifer Gardner, "False Consciousness," and Pamela Keaton, "Man-Hating," in *Notes from the Second Year: Women's Liberation, Major Writings of the Radical Feminists,* ed. Shulamith Firestone and Anne Koedt (New York: By the Editors, 1970), pp. 76–86.

[24]Maurice Natanson, "The Claims of Immediacy," *Philosophy, Rhetoric and Argumentation,* ed. Maurice Natanson and Henry W. Johnstone, Jr. (University Park: Pennsylvania State Univ. Press, 1965), pp. 15, 16.

[25]Cynthia Ozick, "The Demise of the Dancing Dog," *The New Women*, pp. 23–42.

[26]Redstockings, "The Politics of Housework," *Liberation Now?,* pp. 110–115. Note that in this, as in other cases, authorship is assigned to a group rather than an individual.

[27]Virginia Woolf, *A Room of One's Own* (New York: Harbinger, 1929).

[28]Sally Kempton, "Cutting Loose," *Liberation Now!,* pp. 39–55. This essay was originally published in *Esquire,* July 1970, pp. 53–57.

[29]*Ibid.,* pp. 54–55.

[30]Richard B. Gregg, "The Ego-Function of the Rhetoric of Protest," *Philosophy & Rhetoric,* 4 (Spr. 1971), 71–91. The essay is discussed specifically on pp. 80–81.

[31]Granted, there are humanistic or existential psychological theorists who argue that social or outer reality must be changed fully as often as psychic or inner reality. See, for example, Thomas S. Szasz, *The Myth of Mental Illness* (1961; rpt. New York: Dell, 1961), R. D. Laing and A. Esterson, *Sanity, Madness, and the Family* (1964; rpt. New York; Basic Books, 1971), and William H. Grier and Price M. Cobbs, *Black Rage* (New York: Basic Books 1968). However, the vast majority of psychological approaches assumes that the social order is, at least relatively, unalterable and that it is the personal realm that must be changed. See, for example, Sigmund Freud, *A General Introduction to Psychoanalysis,* trans. Joan Riviere (1924; rpt. New York: Washington Square Press, 1960), Wilhelm Stekel, *Technique of Analytical Psychotherapy,* trans. Eden and Cedar Paul (London: William Brown, 1950), Carl A. Whitaker and Thomas P. Malone, *The Roots of Psychotherapy* (New York: Blakiscon, 1953), and Carl R. Rogers, *Client-Centered Therapy* (Boston: Houghton Mifflin, 1951).

[32]This phrase originates with the loose coalition of radical groups called the Female Liberation Movement (Ellis, p. 55). See also Pamela Keaton, "Power as a Function of the Group," *Notes from the Second Year,* pp. 108–110.

[33]See, for example, Anne Koedt, "The Myth of the Vaginal Orgasm," *Liberation Now!,* pp. 311–320, Susan Lydon, "The Politics of Orgasm," and Mary Jane Sherfey, M.D., "A Theory on Female Sexuality," *Sisterhood is Powerful,* pp. 197–205, 220–230.

[34]See, for example, Radicalesbians, "The Woman-Identified Woman," *Liberation Now!,* pp. 287–293; Ellen Strong, "The Hooker," Gene Damon, "The Least of These: The Minority Whose Screams Haven't Yet Been Heard," and Martha Shelley, "Notes of a Radical Lesbian," *Sisterhood is Powerful,* pp. 289–311; Del Martin and Phyllis Lyon, "The Realities of Lesbianism," *The New Women,* pp. 99–109.

[35]Sally Kempton's essay is perhaps the most vivid example of this type. See also Judith Ann, "The Secretarial Proletariat," and Zoe Moss, "It Hurts to be Alive and Obsolete: The Ageing Woman," *Sisterhood is Powerful,* pp. 86–100, 170–175.

[36]See Shulamith Firestone, "Love," and Pamela Keaton, "Man-Hating," *Notes from the Second Year,* pp. 16–27, 83–86.

[37]This term originates with Sandra L. Bem and Daryl J. Bem, "Training the Woman to Know Her Place: The Power of a Nonconscious Ideology," *Roles Women Play,* pp. 84–96.

[38]This phrase originates with Kenneth Burke and is the title of Part II of *Permanence and Change,* 2nd rev. ed. (Indianapolis: Bobbs-Merrill, 1965).

[39]Emmeline G. Pankhurst, cited by Ellis, p. 19.

[40]Ti-Grace Atkinson, cited by Charles Winick and Paul M. Kinsie, "Prostitutes," *Psychology Today,* Feb. 1972, p. 57.

[41]Germaine Greer, *The Female Eunuch* (New York: McGraw-Hill, 1970), p. 42.

[42]Bem and Bem, pp. 94–95.

[43]Joreen, "The Bitch Manifesto," *Notes from the Second Year,* pp. 5–9.

[44]"WITCH Documents," *Sisterhood is Powerful,* pp. 538–553.

[45]See, for example, Martha Shelley, "Notes of a Radical Lesbian," *Sisterhood is Powerful,* pp. 306–311. Paralleling this are the negative views of some radical groups toward heterosexual love and marriage. See "The Feminists: A Political Organization to Annihilate Sex Roles," *Notes from the Second Year,* pp. 114–118.

[46]See, for example, Caroline Bird, "On Being Born Female," *Vital Speeches of the Day,* 15 Nov. 1968, pp. 88–91. This argument is also made negatively by denying that there is any satisfactory basis for determining what differences, if any, there are between males and females. See, for example, Naomi Weisstein, "Psychology Constructs the Female, or the Fantasy Life of the Male Psychologist," *Roles Women Play,* pp. 68–83.

[47]Elizabeth Janeway makes a very telling critique of many of these attempts. She argues that the roles of shrew, witch, and bitch are simple reversals of the positively valued and socially accepted roles of women. The shrew is the negative counterpart of the public role of the wife whose function is to charm and to evince honor and respect for her husband before others; the witch is the negative role of the good mother—capricious, unresponsive, and threatening; the bitch is the reversal of the private role of wife— instead of being comforting, loving, and serious, she is selfish, teasing, emasculating. The point she is making is that these are not new, creative roles, merely reversals of existing, socially defined roles. (Pp. 119–123, 126–127, 199–201.)

[48]Natanson, pp. 15–16.

[49]Parke G. Burgess, "The Rhetoric of Moral Conflict: Two Critical Dimensions."

[50]Thomas R. Olbricht, "The Self as a Philosophical Ground of Rhetoric," *Pennsylvania Speech Annual,* 21 (Sept. 1964), 28–36.

[51]Lloyd F. Bitzer, "The Rhetorical Situation," *Philosophy & Rhetoric,* 1 (Jan. 1968), 6–8.

[52]Leland M. Griffin, "The Rhetoric of Historical Movements," *QJS,* 38 (Apr. 1952), 184–185.

[53]Herbert W. Simons, "Requirements, Problems, and Strategies: A Theory of Persuasion for Social Movements," *QJS,* 56 (Feb. 1970), 3.

[54]Dan F. Hahn and Ruth M. Gonchar, "Studying Social Movements: A Rhetorical Methodology," *Speech Teacher,* 20 (Jan. 1971), 44, cited from Joseph R. Gusfield, ed.,

Protest, Reform, and Revolt: A Reader in Social Movements (New York: Wiley, 1970), p. 2.

[55]Brenda Robinson Hancock, "Affirmation by Negation in the Women's Liberation Movement" *QJS*, 58 (Oct. 1972), 264–271.

[56]Leland M. Griffin, "A Dramatistic Theory of the Rhetoric of Movements," *Critical Responses to Kenneth Burke*, ed. William E. Rueckert (Minneapolis: Univ. of Minnesota Press, 1969), p. 456.

[57]Robert S. Cathcart, p. 87.

FEMINISM, MISS AMERICA, AND MEDIA MYTHOLOGY

BONNIE J. DOW

"I'm not contemplating any Maidenform bonfires, but they could certainly use something around here"

Joanna (Katharine Ross) in The Stepford Wives (1975)

When Joanna, the central protagonist in *The Stepford Wives*, utters these words in a conversation with her best friend, she is discussing the formation of a feminist consciousness-raising group. Both women feel stifled by the atmosphere in Stepford, Connecticut, the New York suburb to which they recently have moved with their families. In Stepford, as anyone familiar with the film remembers, formerly strong-willed, dynamic women are mysteriously transformed into perfectly groomed, robotic beings obsessed with housekeeping and the sexual satisfaction of their husbands, a fate that Joanna and her friend are desperate to avoid. *The Stepford Wives* was released in 1975, at the end of what historian Alice Echols has called the peak period of radical feminist activity in the United States,[1] and the second wave of feminism is, in many ways, the subtext required for making complete sense of the film. Seen in its original historical context, *The Stepford Wives* is a feminist horror film. It argues that American men, given the opportunity, would erase their wives' individuality by literally killing them and replacing them with identical automatons dedicated to domestic chores and sexual service. Despite their invocation of feminism, Joanna and her friend are no match for the forces of evil, and both become Stepford wives by the end of the film. Indeed, after the film's release, *Stepford wife* entered the American lexicon as a term referring to submissive, plastic-seeming women who were satisfied with the traditional domestic and sexual roles that second-wave feminism sought to challenge.

As a film, *The Stepford Wives* both contributed to and drew from popular notions of the purpose and meaning of second-wave feminist ideology and practices, and I invoke it here as a useful example of the ways that certain understandings of the second wave had solidified in public discourse by the mid-1970s. For example, Joanna's casual reference to "Maidenform bonfires" in the epigraph above is, of course, an allusion to the association of bra-burning with second-wave feminism, an association begun by media coverage of the 1968 protest by radical feminists at the Miss America pageant in Atlantic City.

This essay is an exploration of the legacy of that protest in media discourse about the Miss America pageant, and my highlighting of *The Stepford Wives* as part of that process is perhaps the perfect place to begin, as many of the issues raised by the film are similar, if not identical, to those raised by feminist protests against the pageant. Just as feminists charged that Miss America promoted an ideal of women as plastic, doll-like, submissive sex objects who paraded in swimsuits for the pleasure of men, *The Stepford Wives* took that vision to its nightmarish extreme by depicting a community in which women literally died so that their husbands could possess that ideal. Eerily, news discourse about the Miss America pageant in the 1990s has referred to "Stepford-Wife contestants," and a male pageant producer's comment in 1993 that he "didn't want these women looking like 45-year-old Stepford Wives marching like robots across the stage" was noted in reports on pageant reforms that were designed to "bring [the pageant] into the 90s."[2]

The legacy of second-wave feminism, and its echoes in popular culture, haunt public discourse about Miss America. In histories and memoirs of the second wave, the 1968 Miss America action is a source of both pride and regret: pride for the early visibility and membership it gained for the movement, regret for the unshakeable association of feminism with bra-burning that it fostered. This essay juxtaposes feminist discourse about the 1968 protest with mainstream public discourse about the Miss America pageant in the 30 years that followed, and I argue that these two groups of texts offer a useful case study of a key rhetorical strategy in mediated public discourse about contemporary feminism: the construction of female agency as an implicit repudiation of the feminist critique of patriarchy.

If the second-wave feminist mantra was the "personal is political," implying that women's individual problems were the outgrowth of their political status as an oppressed class, then the corresponding media mantra was precisely the reverse: the "political is personal," implying that the validity of feminist objections to a patriarchal system was easily discredited by the articulation of individual women's disavowal of that oppression. The implicit argument that sexism must not exist if even one woman denies that it does is hardly original; it has been used against feminist claims since the beginnings of the first wave in the nineteenth century. However, the discourse surrounding the Miss America pageant is a compelling example of the reemergence of this strategy in the late twentieth century, and it illustrates the continuing difficulty presented by dominant media's personalization of claims by and about feminism and its implications.

Indeed, as I argue below, the evolution of media discourse surrounding the intersection of feminism and the Miss America pageant shows the functioning of the personalization problem in a variety of ways, the most obvious of which is the longevity of the bra-burning trope itself, which quickly became a synecdoche used to trivialize feminists' critique of beauty politics. Bra-burning, it was implied, was the desperate bid for attention by neurotic, unattractive women who could not garner it through more acceptable routes. Yet, once the feminist critique of Miss America became a ritualistic invocation in media discourse about the pageant, the personalization strategy took another turn, focusing on the contestants themselves. By the mid-1970s, media discourse exhibits an increasing emphasis on the personal agency of beauty contestants, an emphasis that works to refute feminist objections by implying that if women claim that they freely choose to participate in the pageant and refuse to claim that they are being exploited, we should believe them.

By the 1990s, most media discourse about the pageant adopts a bemused, ironic tone toward Miss America, a tone that acknowledges the pageant as an anachronism at the same time that it validates it as an empowering vocation for the women who continue to compete in it. That is, at the same time that media discourse shows clear agreement with aspects of the feminist critique of the pageant, it also insists on a kind of liberal, evolutionary narrative in which the pageant has, in some senses, *become* feminism for its contestants. Hence the irony. Yet this version of mass-mediated feminism is devoid of the wide-ranging critique of class, race, and gender oppression that motivated the original feminist protest against Miss America; indeed, it is devoid of any ideological substance save the notion that women who exercise agency on their own behalf are practicing feminism. As I discuss in the conclusion, the transformation of feminism from a systemic critique of patriarchy to the practice of individualism by women is not a unique strategy in media discourse since the second wave. However, the evolution of media narratives about the intersections of feminism and Miss America since 1968 allows useful discussion of the continuing problem that the mythology of individualism presents for feminism at the turn of the century.

MISS AMERICA AND THE BRA-BURNING MYTH

As the first major public protest staged by radical feminists of the second wave, the events in Atlantic City in 1968 provide an origins story for historical and biographical accounts of contemporary feminism. The protest was mounted by the New York Radical Women (NYRW), an early radical feminist group that was formed in 1968 by several women who wished to extend the critique of other radical movements (civil rights, antiwar, and the New Left) to include an analysis of women's oppression. Robin Morgan, a member of NYRW and one of the key organizers of the protest, calls it "the first major action of the current wave of feminism in the United States." In her recent memoir of the movement, Susan Brownmiller writes that "the boardwalk hijinks and civil disobedience of the Miss America protest had global ripples as both national and foreign journalists seized on the story," and historian Flora Davis calls the protest the moment that "feminism suddenly burst into the headlines."[3]

Even Frank Deford, author of the laudatory history of the pageant, *There She Is: The Life and Times of Miss America,* wrote that, for Women's Liberation, "the skirmish at [Atlantic City's] Convention Hall is roughly analogous to the Boston Tea Party." In Alice Echol's germinal history of radical feminism, she notes that the protest "marked the end of the movement's obscurity"; similarly, in *The Sisterhood,* Marcia Cohen claims that the events in September 1968 were "a moment that changed the world's view of this rebellion—and therefore perhaps the rebellion itself—forever." Including a description of the protest in the chapter of her memoirs titled "The Origins of the Second Wave of Feminism," Sheila Tobias perhaps puts it most succinctly when she notes that the protest "both helped publicize and would later haunt the women's movement."[4]

As most of these accounts acknowledge, what "haunted" the women's movement was the image of bra-burning. Those knowledgeable about the history of second-wave feminism are well aware that no bras were burned at the 1968 protest; indeed, feminist historians, as well as participants and observers of the protest, have made considerable efforts to dispel the myth.[5] Regardless, bra-burning became what historian Ruth Rosen has called "the most tenacious media myth about the women's movement," and she maintains that, "in a breast-obsessed society, 'bra-burning' became a symbolic way of sexualizing—and thereby trivializing—women's struggle for emancipation."[6] Certainly, trivialization is a crucial implication of the "sexy trope" of bra-burning;[7] when Senator Jennings Randolph characterized feminists as "braless bubbleheads" two years after the protest in his widely reported response to the Women's Strike for Equality in 1970, he surely meant to trivialize them.[8] As Rosen points out, part of the issue is media conflation of the so-called "sexual revolution" with women's liberation, as if the women at the protest were fighting primarily for the right to go braless so that they could be more sexually available.[9] Susan Douglas agrees, arguing that "women who threw their bras away may have said they were challenging sexism, but the media, with a wink, hinted that these women's motives were not at all political but rather personal: to be trendy, and to attract men."[10]

Bras were only one of many items that were tossed into a "freedom trash can" on the boardwalk in Atlantic City on September 7, 1968: also included were girdles, high heels, cosmetics, eyelash curlers, wigs, issues of *Cosmopolitan, Playboy*, and *Ladies Home Journal*—what feminists termed "instruments of torture" to women.[11] The trash can was never lit on fire, but the rumor that it would be—and the later assumption that it had been—was begun by protest organizer Robin Morgan's discussion with a *New York Post* reporter a few days earlier. In that conversation with *Post* reporter Lindsy Van Gelder (who later became an active feminist), Morgan identified herself as a member of the Yippies (Youth International Party) and drew connections between the Miss America action and other New Left protests. Seizing on these links, Van Gelder wrote a lead to her story that read as follows: "'Lighting a match to a draft card or a flag has been a standard gambit of protest groups in recent years, but something new is due to go up in flames on Saturday. Would you believe a bra-burning?'" Further heightening the effect, the *Post* gave the story a headline that read: "Bra Burners and Miss America."[12]

As the Miss America protest occurred less than two weeks after the tumultuous 1968 Democratic National Convention in Chicago, and given that the majority of the members of NYRW were or had been aligned with civil rights, antiwar, and New Left movement groups, Van Gelder's analogy to the burnings of draft cards and flags was not out of place. But that context disappeared in later allusions to bra-burning, when it became less a symbolic act of political defiance—as other burnings had been—and was used more to symbolize feminists' personal disdain for conventional femininity. This is a crucial difference: it is the difference between a critique of an established system that oppresses women—much as the burning of draft cards was a critique of the military industrial complex—and a trivial gesture that dominant media used as evidence that feminists had so little of substance to complain about that they were concerned with undergarments.

Before, during, and after the protest, feminists did take pains to make their systemic critique. The memoir of Carol Hanisch, one of the members of NYRW and a participant in the protest, notes that NYRW held a consciousness-raising session about the Miss America pageant, concluding that the protest would be an ideal way "to unite women by taking on those issues that spoke to the oppression we all experienced in our daily lives." Robin Morgan's description of the protest, written in 1968 and published in various New Left outlets, defended the pageant as a fitting target because of its "perfect combination of American values—racism, militarism, capitalism—all packaged in one 'ideal' symbol: a woman." As she pointed out, in addition to the pageant's propagation of the "Mindless Sex-Object Image," a black woman had never been a finalist, the winner would entertain the troops in Vietnam, and "the whole gimmick of the million-dollar pageant corporation is one commercial shill game to sell the sponsor's products."[13]

Morgan's analysis, reflecting perspectives developed in other radical movements, indicates the kind of systemic critique the feminists meant to offer through the protest. The account of the protest included in the October 1968 issue of *Voice of the Women's Liberation Movement,* one of the first of the more than 500 feminist publications that would spring up over the next two years, was even more direct about this intent. The account noted specifically that "Our purpose was *not* to put down Miss America but to attack the male chauvinism, commercialization of beauty, racism and oppression of women symbolized by the pageant." The press release distributed in advance of the protest also outlined the critique of racism, militarism, and capitalism; in addition, it argued that the contest promoted the "'win-or-you're-worthless' competitive disease," the ideal of women as "young, juicy, and malleable," and the "Madonna-Whore combination" within which women must be both "sexy and wholesome." Moreover, the release charged that the pageant encouraged women to be "inoffensive, bland and apolitical" because conformity was "the key to the crown," and it made clear that "real power to control our own lives is restricted to men, while women get patronizing pseudo-power, an ermine cloak and a bunch of flowers." Finally, the feminists charged that the pageant "exercises thought control . . . to enslave us all the more in high-heeled, low-status roles; to inculcate false values in young girls; to use women as beasts of buying; to seduce us to prostitute ourselves before our own oppression."[14]

Not surprisingly, on the day after the pageant, the crowning of the new Miss America was a bigger story for the *New York Times* than was the protest. The crowning of Miss Illinois as the new Miss America was covered on page 54 of the paper, and there was no mention of the protest in an article that proclaimed that the key triumph for the winner was that she was the first blonde to win the title in 11 years. The account of the protest appeared on page 81, and it contained a small sidebar in which Miss America was asked for her reaction. She replied that "It was just too bad. I'm sorry it happened."[15]

Charlotte Curtis, the society reporter from the *New York Times,* had been dispatched by her paper to cover the crowning of the new Miss America, but she was forced to cover the protest as well, because the feminists had made it clear that they would not talk to male reporters. Susan Brownmiller later described Curtis's coverage as "colorful and sympathetic"; indeed, the first three paragraphs of the *Times* story managed to convey the activities at the protest as well as to include the protesters' critique of beauty politics, the racism of the pageant, and their intent to boycott pageant sponsors. Curtis's lead included a description of the "freedom trash can" and its contents as well as noted that the women were "armed with a giant bathing beauty puppet." She later described the chains encircling the puppet and included the feminists' claim that they represented "the chains that tie us to these beauty standards against our will." The entire first half of the news story provides a vivid picture of the protest, describing the live sheep (which Curtis called a ram, but was actually a ewe) that the protesters crowned "Miss America," noting that the women were peaceful and stayed behind police barricades, and detailing the generational and geographical diversity of the participants. The story also included Robin Morgan's assurance that the day's activities were designed as peaceful protest, as they "didn't want another Chicago," and there had been no intent to go beyond a "symbolic bra-burning," as the mayor of Atlantic City was concerned about the highly flammable boardwalk.[16]

Curtis's account was written before the day's events ended; during the pageant itself, several feminists entered the auditorium, unfurled a banner reading "Women's Liberation" over the balcony, began chanting "No More Miss America" and "Freedom for Women," and released stink bombs, supposedly containing Toni

Home Permanent Solution (Toni was a pageant sponsor) before they were ejected by police and at least one of them was arrested. The network television cameras never wavered from the stage.[17]

In typical journalistic style, Curtis included a depiction of the public reaction to the protest in the latter half of her story. She described the spectators as "generally unsympathetic," and quoted one that called the protesters "vulgar" because of their signs that read "Miss America Sells It," and "Up Against the Wall, Miss America." Another man was quoted as telling the feminists to "throw yourselves" into the freedom trash can because "it would be a lot more useful." Perhaps most interesting was the description of three counter-picketers, including a 1967 Miss America runner-up, who wore a sign reading "There's Only One Thing Wrong with Miss America. She's Beautiful." Curtis dutifully noted that the sign was pinned to the woman's dress with a "Nixon for President" button.[18]

The implication that feminists were motivated primarily by envy, and that their critique of Miss America was directed at contestants themselves rather than at the patriarchal system that had created the pageant, was buttressed by some of the tactics of the protesters described elsewhere in the article. These included the representation of Miss America as a sheep, the signs mentioned earlier, and a protester's claim that the only "'free' woman is 'the woman who is no longer enslaved by ludicrous beauty standards.'"[19] The protesters also sang songs with such lyrics as "Ain't she sweet/makin' profit off her meat/Beauty sells she's told, so she's out pluggin' it/Ain't she sweet."[20] Indeed, two months later, one of the protest participants, Carol Hanisch, penned a critique of the events in Atlantic City in which her primary objection was that "a definite strain of anti-womanism was presented to the public to the detriment of the action" because "Miss America and all beautiful women came off as our enemy instead of as our sisters who suffer with us." For example, according to Hanisch, "crowning a live sheep Miss America sort of said that beautiful women *are* sheep," and such signs as "'Miss America Is a Big Falsie' hardly raised any woman's consciousness and really harmed the cause of sisterhood."[21] Moreover, lines from the "No More Miss America" press release, such as "the Pageant contestants epitomize the roles we are all forced to play as women" and "Miss America is a walking commercial for the Pageant's sponsors. Wind her up and she plugs your product on promotion tours and TV" could be used to support Hanisch's analysis that contestants were depicted as both brainless and brainwashed.[22]

However, Hanisch perhaps laid too much blame for such misapprehensions at the protesters' feet. The cultural beliefs that women are inherently competitive with other women and that any critique of beauty politics was motivated by envy was hardly invented by feminists. Indeed, spectator reactions to the protest that were reported in the women's liberation press, such as hecklers who shouted "'You're just jealous—you couldn't be Miss America if you were the last man [?] on earth'" and "'Get back on your broom,'" as well as the suggestion that the protesters must be lesbians, are evidence that it took little encouragement for onlookers to resort to the "envy" explanation.[23] A few days after the protest, a column by the *New York Post*'s Harriet Van Horne offered further elaboration on this perspective. Calling the protesters "sturdy lasses in . . . sensible shoes," Van Horne wrote that she discarded her invitation to attend the protest because "this lady of the press usually has something nicer to do on Saturday night than burn her undergarments on the boardwalk in Atlantic City. And I suspect the deep-down aching trouble with these lassies is that they haven't." She thus neatly forwards the bra-burning myth as well as the notion that the protesters were driven less by ideology than by their failure in heterosexual romance, concluding that "my feeling about the liberation ladies is that they've been scarred and wounded by consorting with the wrong men."[24]

If it were the case, as one of the protesters later remarked on the David Susskind show, that "'[e]very day in a woman's life is a walking Miss America contest,'"[25] then one of the unfortunate perceptions created by the events in Atlantic City was that feminists were disgruntled because they could never win such a contest. That many feminists refused to participate in beauty politics was a clear message of the protest; at issue was their motivation. Two years later, the incoming president of the National Council of Women was asked her opinion about feminism and remarked that not only did she not believe that women faced discrimination, but that "so many of them [the feminists] are just so unattractive . . . I wonder if they're completely well." The implication, of course, is that protesting had become a way of getting the attention that ugly women were otherwise denied; as Susan Douglas astutely notes, "feminists were cast as unfeminine, unappealing women who were denouncing the importance of the male gaze, yet who secretly coveted that gaze for themselves by protesting in public. These poor girls, it was suggested, sought to get through political flamboyance what they were unable to get through physical attractiveness." Within this logic, bra-burning was simply a desperate bid for attention rather than a symbolic act of political defiance, and the feminists were little different from the women parading down the runway: they were simply less attractive.[26]

MISS AMERICA'S MEDIA MAKE-OVER

The 1969 cover stories in *Life* and the *New York Times Magazine* on the emerging women's liberation movement would both begin by recounting the events in Atlantic City in September 1968.[27] No one could doubt that the Miss America protest had put women's lib on the map, and feminists even predicted that it might not be long before the pageant was closed down entirely.[28] In 1969, a group labeled the "Women's Liberation Front" received a brief *New York Times* mention for its picketing of the pageant, and, in 1974, the National Organization for Women held its annual conference in Atlantic City in September and invited the Miss America contestants to attend their meetings and workshops. The *New York Times* article on the NOW conference noted that "the Miss America's swimsuit competition has been one of the targets for attack by women's liberation groups," and included a remark by the producer of the pageant that the swimsuit competition was not the "favorite operation" of the pageant, although he defended it as "a great test of poise."[29]

Although the prediction that feminists would shut down the pageant has not been realized, it is easy to link feminist pressure—and the general influence of feminism on American culture—with changes in the Miss America pageant since 1968. Despite media dismissal of the political significance of feminists' critique of beauty politics, the Miss America organization clearly felt pressure to update its image. In the last 20 years, the pageant has decreased the importance of the swimsuit score in the overall competition; banned professional hairdressers and makeup artists from the pageant; stopped announcing contestants' breast, waist, and hip measurements; started requiring that contestants choose a social issue for their "personal platform"; and even ceased requiring that they wear high heels during the swimsuit segment.[30] Most important for this analysis, however, is the fact that media coverage of Miss America began implicitly—and sometimes explicitly—making feminism a consistent subtext in discussion of the pageant. Equally as consistent, however, is the persistence of the personalization strategy: rather than engaging with feminists' charges about the hegemony of beauty standards, media discourse instead began to emphasize the personal agency of the Miss America contestants, putting to use the well-learned lesson that the most efficient way of refuting feminism was to feature individual women's disavowal of its claims.

In such a way, media professionals were able to congratulate themselves for taking Miss America to task on feminism's behalf while simultaneously eliding the larger implications of the feminist critique. This shift is clearly signaled by a 1974 story in the *New York Times* headlined "For Miss America '75, the Questions Get Tougher." Part of that curious genre of reportage in which a journalist attempts to describe the tactics of other members of her tribe, this story focuses on the strange situation at the 1974 pageant created by the fact that the National Organization for Women was holding its annual conference in Atlantic City at the same time. The lead for the story introduces this theme: "Miss America of 1975, clutching her chaperone's hand, walked nervously through the lobby of a hotel that was also housing 2,000 feminists," and the story went on to maintain that "what perhaps makes her more newsworthy [than past Miss Americas] is that she was crowned in a year when 2,000 feminists staged a 'Wonder Woman' parade down the boardwalk" as part of their conference titled "Wonder Woman Conference: No Myth, America." These few fragments from the story establish a narrative in which the newly crowned Miss America herself, not what the pageant symbolizes, becomes the "nervous" target of feminist wrath.[31]

Observing that reporters "seem to have grown more aggressive in their questioning of Miss Americas" and were leaving behind the "slightly worshipful quality" of questions in years past, the story notes that Miss America was asked for her opinion on the ERA, Watergate, amnesty for draft dodgers, and, of course, the feminist presence at the pageant. With regard to the latter, Miss America is quoted as expressly denying that pageant officials forbade her from attending events at the NOW conference (to which all contestants had been invited); rather, she "'simply didn't have any time—there were so many rehearsals'" for the pageant. Asked specifically about the women's movement, she replied that "'that is their thing . . . and this is my thing. I respect what they're doing and I hope they can respect me for what I'm doing.'" Her responses to later questions, however, imply a somewhat stronger negative reaction to feminism, as she announced that she did not believe in living together before marriage, that she would take her husband's name after marriage, and that she preferred "Miss" to "Ms." The story concludes with a description of events at the NOW conference, including an incident in which several feminists attempted to enter the guarded room where the Miss America contestants were having their farewell brunch, so that, as the reporter put it, they could get "a glimpse of 'Them,' as they called the beauty queens." Further reinforcing the impression that the feminists, in contrast to Miss America, were hardly respectful of women's individual differences, one of the NOW members was quoted as saying that, though she would "'like to try to rap'" with the contestants, that they were "'impenetrable. They're surrounded by plastic.'"[32]

Two months before the intersection of the pageant and the NOW convention in Atlantic City, the *New York Times* ran another story on Miss America, titled "Miss America: She's Always on the Road," a sort of "day-in-the-life" chronicle of the reigning queen's activities. The topic of the women's movement loomed large in this story as well, indicating that the physical presence of feminists protesting was not a necessary prerequisite to interrogating Miss America about her opinion on the movement. In this story, Miss America emerges as a sort of proto-feminist who eschews radicalism while displaying no shyness about her own ambitions. What becomes clear in this story is that, for the *New York Times,* personal ambition counts as feminism. The section of the story treating the women's movement begins as follows: "As for the women's movement, Miss King said she regards herself as 'middle of the road,' even though she is one of the few Miss Americas ever to talk constantly about wanting a career." Positing support for careerism even more firmly as an indicator of feminism, Miss King is further quoted as saying that "'if a woman wants to stay at home, fine, and if a woman wants to be a lawyer, fine.'" As her successor in Atlantic City would, this Miss America takes the position that women's different choices should be respected; interestingly, however, she goes on to assert that her role as a beauty queen is an effective feminist platform: "'Maybe I'm not as radical as some, but I do feel I'm in a position to do some good for women. Every day I speak with business people and community leaders—people in a position of power to help women. I feel I can do more this way than by carrying a picket sign.'"[33]

The genius of this story is that it suggests that, given the right young woman, being Miss America can be the equivalent of feminist activism. Indeed, it might even improve on feminism, as it avoids disruptive tactics like picketing and has the advantage of attractive packaging in a "blonde, 5-foot 9-inch, 125-pound queen." In this article, even the swimsuit segment becomes simply a means to an end. Asked if she felt that the Miss America contestants were treated as sex objects, Miss King replied that "'I'm not sure I even understand what that is. . . . I'm very proud of being a woman. I don't feel I'm exploited.'" Perhaps backtracking a bit from the implication that displaying one's body in a swimsuit is a sign of pride in womanhood, she goes on to insist that she "'got involved for the scholarship money,'" which she would use toward a law degree, and that "'after Atlantic City, you never again have to appear in a swimsuit.'" The article's discussion of feminism concludes with Miss America's opinions on marriage, in which she notes that, while she expects she will marry someday, "'I certainly want to fulfill myself and be my own being at the same time.'"[34]

This article is perhaps the exemplar of its type, as it defines the contours of what would become the dominant approach to the continuing problem that feminism presented for Miss America. First, in such stories, patriarchy was not the target of feminists; rather, it was Miss America herself, as embodied by the young women who vied for the crown. Those young women's defense of their own self-determination became the ritualistic response to feminist charges. Second, and related, these stories thus framed feminism as a battle between different *types* of women, rather than a struggle on behalf of *all* women against an oppressive system that maintained that it was somehow appropriate to judge women's qualifications for scholarship money through their appearance in swimsuits and evening gowns. This narrative was briefly ruptured in 1984, when Vanessa Williams, the reigning Miss America and the first African American woman to wear the crown, was forced to resign after nude photographs of her engaging in lesbian sex were published in *Penthouse*. Feminists defended Williams against what they labeled the hypocritically puritanical pageant promoters who had forced her out, arguing that the Miss America pageant itself was simply a softer version of pornography.

Indeed, 16 years earlier, the 1968 "No More Miss America" press release had made the point that "Miss America and *Playboy*'s centerfold are sisters over the skin," and Robin Morgan herself made the case again in 1984 in a column in *Ms.* magazine on the Williams scandal:

> For almost two decades, the Women's Movement has been exposing *connections* in the exploitation of women: how the pornographer and the puritan need each other to thrive. Pornography requires an atmosphere of sexual repression so that it can market sex as forbidden fruit; the puritanical sensibility needs to view sex as wicked so that it can measure its own Moral Majority fake wholesomeness in contrast. Both dehumanize women, whether through the applehood and mother-pie "good girl" image, or the plastic sex-doll centerfold fetish. Neither reflects real female human beings—our concerns, our bodies, our sexuality, our lives.[35]

Much as she had 16 years earlier, Morgan delivered a structural analysis of the pageant's sexism, racism, homophobia, and economic exploitation of women, making clear that feminists opposed the institution, not the women who participated in it. As she argued, "women who enter beauty contests and women who work in the pornography industry do so from simple economic necessity. Until we all have genuine equal access to education, who dare blame a woman for seeking the scholarship money such pageants proffer? Or blame a woman posing nude when her alternative still is earning only 60 cents to the dollar a man earns at 'legitimate' jobs?"[36]

Severely truncated versions of this analysis appeared in mainstream media outlets such as *Newsweek* and *U.S. News,* but feminists' support for Williams was easy to dismiss as a version of "the enemy of my enemy is my friend."[37] A perfect symbol of the pageant's hypocrisy, the treatment of Williams was a magnet for feminist outrage, but the media visibility it provided for the feminists' case was short-lived. By the end of September 1984, the pageant appeared to have triumphed over the scandal, when *Newsweek* ran a feature story titled "A Controversial 'Spectator Sport,'" for which the subtitle read: "Despite Vanessa Williams and attacks by feminists, the love affair with beauty pageants is going strong." The suggestion that pageants are "sport" runs throughout the article, which carries the theme that contestants train for pageants like ambitious athletes, honing their skills in lesser pageants and working with professional coaches. "Physical perfection is no longer enough," the article notes. "These days they must also be career-oriented and academically distinguished." As one state pageant chairman insisted, "'The girls who were winning pageants 10 years ago couldn't make the top 10 now. . . . They're better trained, they're better physically, they're smarter, they're more sophisticated.'" And they know just what they are getting into. Apparently asked the by now predictable question about exploitation, Miss America 1983 just as predictably replied: "'If this is being exploited, I hope every woman can be exploited like this.'" The story ends on an ironic note: "With this Saturday's passing of the tiara, one more Miss America will have that chance."[38]

By this point in the 1980s, media's tendency toward personalization has elided the feminist critique of beauty pageants. The discourse implies that, while pageants are still "going strong," they are hardly cause for concern; rather, they are just another example of free enterprise at work. As the *Newsweek* feature points out, pageants are a multimillion-dollar business in which the rules for success are increasingly obvious, and the women who participate in them have learned those rules well. The danger that feminists identified is past, this discourse suggests, because the women who chase the crowns are no longer in the grip of some romantic illusion about being chosen the "most beautiful girl in the world"; they are clear-headed, ambitious contenders who have chosen to play this game and are intent on playing it to win. Miss America 1988, Kaye Lani Rae Rafko, succinctly summarized this perspective in an article in the *Washington Post:* "'I've been working toward this moment for six years—well, more. I won my first local when I was 17 and I'm 24 now. I participated in Miss Ohio in '83, and the Michigan pageant three times. I've already earned about $11,000 toward my nursing career. . . . This money [a $30,000 scholarship] will really come in handy.'" The logic of this kind of discourse is that these women are hardly being exploited; indeed, it is almost the reverse. As another *Washington Post* story concluded, they have learned the logic of the pageant system, and "instead of blaming the rules for their misery, they have decided not only to play by them but to win."[39]

Thus, the potential for exploitation is soundly trumped by their belief in their individual agency and the worthiness of their goals, a perspective well expressed by Mary Ann Mobley, a former Miss America as well as a former host of the pageant. In 1988, in an impassioned defense of the swimsuit segment, which she called "'morally right and honorable,'" she added that "'I firmly believe you can't exploit me unless I allow you to,'" going on to imply that wearing a swimsuit is a small price to pay for the possibility of winning scholarship money.[40] Bolstering this theme, a spectator at the 1988 pageant, an aspiring Miss America herself, described her ambitions and her past pageant experience in terms of a blue-collar work ethic, concluding that "'it's a business, just like a business.'"[41] By 1995, within this emerging ethic of free enterprise and free choice, the pageant directors decided to submit the question of whether to eliminate the swimsuit segment to the viewing public's wisdom. The underlying rationale for this decision was somewhat paradoxical. On the one hand, by the 1990s, the pageant organizers were forced to admit that the pageant needed to become "more hip, more relevant," and that the swimsuit competition was a "'major Achilles' heel.'"[42]

On the other hand, pageant producers have long believed that the swimsuit segment was a key reason that the pageant attracted television viewers; as Leonard Horn, president of the Miss America organization put it, "'A lot of people who watch this program want to see a swimsuit competition. . . . So I don't think it's wise to eliminate it. Not as long as having lots of people watch the show is important.'"[43] The implication here is that, left to their own devices, pageant directors would prefer to focus on the less pulchritudinous aspects of the competition, but they were forced to be accountable to their public. Thus, the reasoning goes, if the viewers are the ones who want it, let them decide. Not surprisingly, the swimsuit referendum conducted during the 1995 pageant (in which viewers were encouraged to call in their opinion by telephone, at a cost of 50 cents per vote) revealed that 79 percent of the million Americans who responded approved of the swimsuit competition.[44] The deck was stacked in two key ways. First, the sample was biased in that only viewers voted, making it hardly representative of national sentiment. Second, the week before the pageant, the Miss America organization released the results of a poll of the pageant contestants themselves on the swimsuit issue. Of the 50 contestants, 42 voted to retain the segment. In a quotation from a contestant who had abstained from the vote, the *New York Times* highlighted the pragmatic attitude that had become commonplace in media depictions of Miss America hopefuls: "'I'm comfortable either way. . . . If they want me to do it [wear a swimsuit], I'm going to do it. It is a means to an end.'"[45]

In 1997, a change in pageant rules allowed contestants to wear two-piece swimsuits, rather than the modest one-pieces that had been de rigueur for over 75 years. This move was defended by the pageant president as another effort to recognize the contestants' individuality and to allow them to exercise personal choice. As he claimed, "'I just thought the girls would feel better if they could wear what they'd normally wear when they went to the beach or the swimming pool.'" The subtext here, of course, is that the "girls" need to "feel better" because they are still being forced to parade their bodies in a "scholarship" pageant; as always, the solution is to emphasize the illusion of agency that choosing their own swimsuit can provide. Certainly, there was no downside for the pageant; the appearance of bikinis in the 1998 pageant was a sure boost for the ratings.[46]

Generally, by the late 1990s, an ironic tone suffuses media discourse about Miss America. The pageant still receives ritualistic coverage in major media, but the aim of that coverage is to de-romanticize the pageant, to strip off its veneer of wholesomeness and reveal the contradictions underneath. The harshest coverage the pageant receives treats it as a shameful anachronism, a ritual unworthy of a culture that supposedly has accepted the basic logic of feminism. As one journalist argued,

> After more than 30 years of feminism, Americans have been trained to say that we value the same attributes in women as we do in men. But we're like a family trying to convince everyone we've moved beyond our hillbilly roots. We've got the Chippendale tables, the Lexus in the garage, the European kitchen fixtures. But somebody forgot to take the pink flamingos off the lawn. Miss America is like a pink flamingo on America's lawn, exposing us for what we still are.[47]

The lion's share of reflective media discourse about the pageant in the 1990s is hardly as judgmental, however. With irony as its controlling trope, it is more likely to suggest the ways that Miss America, while perhaps a symbol of patriarchy, is also its antidote. Likewise, while acknowledging the long-running feminist critique of the pageant, media discourse also suggests that Miss America contestants have become living instantiations of the progress of women. For example, relying on the analogy to sports that has appeared in various stories about the pageant, the author of a book about the pageant critiqued the disdain for beauty contests in the *New York Times*:

> Reporters from the East and West Coasts can't understand what it is to be an ambitious young lady from Middle America who doesn't have a lot of options. . . . Let's face it: the opportunities for boys and for girls in Middle America are not the same. The girls aren't going to have the football scholarships, the hockey scholarships. Maybe the father is more interested in sending the son to Harvard than the daughter. Miss America is a way out. It's a way of achieving the American Dream.[48]

Frank Deford, a former Miss America judge and the author of another book about the pageant, echoes this analysis in a *New York Times* feature in which he described the pageant as a "kind of" contest: "you're kind of good looking, . . . you're kind of talented, you're kind of smart. If you were superior at any of these things, you wouldn't need to bother with this." Frank Rich put it a bit more bluntly in his *New York Times* column defending the swimsuit segment. Acknowledging the argument that "Miss America is, after all, a competition for a scholarship, and that surely the contestants should be judged on their talent and intelligence, not their behinds," he countered with the claim that "Miss America wannabes know what they're getting into—the pageant is held on a burlesque ramp before hundreds of leering high-rollers in Atlantic City, after all—and that if the contestants were all so brilliant or talented they'd either be earning grants from bona fide academic institutions, if not the Citadel, or starring in a road company of 'Cats.'"[49]

All three of these commentaries coalesce around the notion that the Miss America pageant provides an opportunity for the kind of ordinary girl with a pretty face and nice body who gets left behind in a culture in which prospects for such women are limited. In a 1998 story on the pageant, this perspective is granted academic credibility when a professor of popular culture is quoted as commenting that the pageant is "'a legitimate, structured entry into society that gives women the visibility and potential for big bucks that professional sports does for men.'" The peculiar logic to this strain of argument is thus clear: the pageant, while it relies on patriarchal values vis-à-vis the importance of women's appearance, is actually a vehicle for women's empowerment in a culture in which the playing field between men and women is not yet even. What gets lost here, obviously, is the possibility that continued feminist activism dedicated to expanding women's opportunities might be a better solution to this problem than the perpetuation of the pageant system. Yet, the transmutation of Miss America into a sort of antidote to the unfairness of patriarchy gains added weight when the longtime director of the pageant, Leonard Horn, claims that it is "'no longer about a silly beauty contest,'" but, rather, that Miss America is "'a relevant, socially responsible activist whose message to women all over the world is that, in the American society, a woman can do anything and be anything she wants.'"[50]

That Horn describes the pageant as "no longer" a beauty contest, is an indicator of the evolutionary narrative that emerges in recent discussion of Miss America. As the *Washington Post* claimed, "the Miss America Organization has changed over the last decade, transforming itself into a financial savior and empowering vehicle for hundreds of girls." The consistent emphasis on the contestant's professional ambitions, and on scholarships as their motivation for entering the competition, supports this interpretation. Indeed, one journalist implied that feminist opposition to the pageant was somehow anti-education, because, as he argued, those who claim that the contest "exploits women," "seldom note that it is the biggest font of scholarships in the world." And he goes on to insist that every contestant he has talked to claims that she got involved "'for the scholarships.'"[51]

Yet another journalist suggests that Miss America contestants are more liberated than most women in that, "like every over achieving woman, Miss America is full of ambition—but, unlike many over achieving women, isn't afraid to admit it." For this journalist, Miss America is ultimately "a reflection" of the modern, ambitious woman; "ridicule her, and we ridicule every American woman who's ever tried to be a simultaneous genius, prom queen, and saint; every woman who has tried to have—no, to *be*—it all."[52] The implication here that pageant contestants represent the legacy of feminism is expressed even more strongly in a 1995 story which claimed that "although feminists have been unable to wipe out pageants and their destructive messages, their one secret weapon is the contestants themselves.

The increasingly ambitious, educated and independent competitors may play the game to win scholarships or fame, but many are unwilling to buy in wholesale" to the pageant's image.[53]

MISS AMERICA AND MEDIA MYTHOLOGY

So the Miss America pageant soldiers on, transformed over 30 years from the target of feminist protesters to a symbol of the success of feminism. This media-constructed narrative is partially a product of the pageant organization's own publicity machine, which always sought attention for the regular "updating" of its image. The shift from a "beauty contest" to a "scholarship pageant," and the concomitant requirements that contestants be enrolled in college, that they demonstrate social awareness, and that the majority of their pageant scores be determined by the talent and interview competitions, as well as the submission of the swimsuit segment to public judgment, indicate that the pageant organization took the feminist critique as seriously as it could without sacrificing ratings or risking extinction. Indeed, in 2001, an employee of the Miss America organization, discussing yet another round of pageant "updates," remarked that "[f]or the longest time, the Miss America Organization has been misunderstood, and we really couldn't understand why people didn't realize that she's not just a bathing beauty."[54] Yet the evolution into a feminist success story took more than the pageant organization's own flexibility; it also required an increasingly flexible media discourse, in which what counted as feminism was as subject to reinvention as the pageant itself. To be fair, media discourse about the pageant contributed to public literacy about some aspects of the feminist critique, which was usually distilled down to the basic notions that such contests objectified women, created unrealistic expectations for young girls who watched them, and perhaps contributed to rising rates of plastic surgery and eating disorders.[55]

It is hardly remarkable that dominant media oversimplifies feminism; in the case of Miss America, however, the version of feminism that media accounts emphasized created the conditions for its own refutation. That is, if the crucial problem was that pageants objectified and exploited their contestants, that they emphasized beauty over brains, and that they promoted the false belief that beauty could compensate for a lack of other, more substantive qualities, then it made perfect sense to have the contestants themselves defend the pageants. Who, this strategy implies, would know better than the women themselves if they were being exploited? Surely not feminists, who still suffer under the stereotype begun in 1968 that they oppose beauty contests because they cannot compete successfully in them. When contestants become the best judge of the worthiness of the pageant system, the feminist argument that the mere existence of pageants is de facto evidence of inequality, that however much good they do for individual participants is largely beside the point, and that it is their *symbolic* function as a condensation of ideologies about race, sex, and commodification that is at issue, gets trumped by media's pervasive and persuasive arguments for individual agency.

Thus, as is too often the case, feminists are portrayed as the ones who don't take women seriously and who wish to make contestants into victims against their will by never wavering from the opinion that pageants are exploitative. In 1995, one columnist made the argument that the Miss America organization's continued attempts to please "pageant-hating feminists" had damaged the pageant because it leaves contestants "with no clue how to prepare." Such changes are pointless, he argues, because "the folks at Miss America could eliminate the swimsuit competition, even institute a requirement that all contestants have crooked teeth and be 30 pounds overweight, and the people who detest the pageant would still detest it. . . . These people deplore the very idea of pageants; fine-tuning the competition, even eliminating the elements that they consider most blatantly sexist, will not appease them." In essence, this is an accurate description, but its point is to depict feminists as intractable, as dogmatic, and, as the conclusion to the column makes clear, as anti-woman: "Whoever becomes Miss America on Saturday, this much is certain. She will be smart, talented and articulate. She'll probably be beautiful. She might even look terrific in a swimsuit. One other thing: The pageant-bashers will have no use for her."[56]

Ultimately, public discourse about the Miss America pageant throws into relief several key issues related to the construction of feminism by dominant media. First, and particularly clear in this case, is the difficulty of maintaining a systemic critique in the face of general media norms toward personalization, a problem made even more acute when the topic at hand lends itself so easily to a focus on the personal. In the case of beauty pageants, the cultural beliefs that women compete over appearance and that they envy and dislike those more beautiful than they become a key frame for interpretation, as early reactions to the '68 protest indicate. As time passed, for journalists seeking a personal angle for their stories about Miss America, the contestants themselves provided an alluring prospect. Despite feminist insistence that the target is the pageant and what it symbolizes and not the contestants themselves, the easiest narrative for journalists to construct is one in which feminists are pitted against specific women and in which those specific women are eager to defend themselves.[57]

Second, and related, is the difficulty for feminists of being cast as unwilling to recognize women's right to make their own choices and to judge their own oppression. It has never been difficult to find women who see no need for feminism, who either claim that they do not experience sexism or that they have triumphed over it without the aid of feminism. The resulting implication in media discourse is that feminists think they know better than ordinary women, whom they must believe to be suffering from false consciousness, or, who, in the worst-case scenario, are just too stupid to realize what's going on. This interpretation relies on a tendency toward dualistic thinking characteristic of media discourse; that is, not only are there are two sides to every story, but there are usually *only* two.

Once the contestants' personal agency and disbelief in their exploitation has been established in media discourse, the two sides emerge: either these bright, articulate, ambitious women are fooling themselves, or feminists are out of touch with the average woman, are clinging to an out-of-date, extreme position, and are stubbornly unwilling to modify it in the face of progress. Indeed, the role of agency within feminist theory is complicated. On the one hand, if patriarchy were as powerful as is sometimes implied, women's agency (and, by extension, feminism) could not exist. On the other hand, if women's agency were as powerful as is sometimes implied, there would be no need for feminism. The truth lies somewhere between the two: patriarchy is powerful, but not so much so that resistance is impossible, and women do exercise agency, but often within a limited field (limited not just by patriarchy, but by race, class, and sexuality as well). Such subtleties do not work well within media's evolutionary narrative about Miss America, in which evidence of women's agency is used to put the lie to the notion that structural sexism still exists; indeed, it is used as evidence of the success of feminism. Is this not what feminists have fought for, media discourse implies: women's right to make their own choices, to pursue their ambitions, to use their talents however they choose? If the Miss America pageant were still so oppressive, would it attract such women in the first place? The answer, supplied by a slightly different media narrative, is that of course it would, because we live in a culture in which women's opportunities are more limited than men's. Yet even in this narrative, the Miss America pageant is hardly the problem; rather, it is part of the solution, and the implication is that feminists who want to eliminate it do not realize that they would be eliminating a vehicle for women's empowerment. Certainly, feminism is about agency in many ways, and women's right to make choices to better their lives is central to feminist ideology of all stripes. But feminism is also a collective politics, and it recognizes that the exercise of agency by individual women does not substitute for nor even necessarily contribute to the subversion of patriarchy or the expansion of choices for women as a group.

Third, and also related, the linkages between feminism and Miss America in mass media discourse point to dominant media's tendency to promote a particular version of liberal feminism—one that emphasizes individualism, self-actualization, and achievement within existing social hierarchies—as the *only* feminism. Thus, even if it is the case, as Sarah Banet-Weiser argues in her ethnography of pageant contestants, that "beauty pageant contestants . . . perform liberal narratives about women's rights, individual achievement, pluralism, self-determination, and voluntarism in a similar way and on similar grounds as liberal feminists articulate these very same narratives," such a realization does little to answer radical feminist claims that the pageant system as a whole is deeply complicit in upholding patriarchal notions of gender identity. Banet-Weiser enjoins that "the ways in which beauty pageant contestants imagine agency should not be dismissed as either 'false consciousness,' or, worse, a bit of commercialized fluff," and, indeed, I do not mean to dismiss them, but, rather, to interrogate them and to recognize their limitations. I posit that pageant contestants in the 1990s would not so easily produce "a liberal feminist rhetoric that relies on particular fantasies of agency, voice, and citizenship," had the ground for such articulations not been laid by more than two decades of mass media appropriation and interpretation of second-wave feminist rhetoric.[58]

Ultimately, only in a media culture in which the concept of sisterhood is always treated with skepticism, in which feminism is always about *women,* not *patriarchy,* and in which the romantic mythology of individualism controls our narratives about everything from welfare reform to comparable worth, could Miss America contestants become poster children for feminism. The feminist protest at the Miss America pageant in 1968 was, in many ways, the public beginning of the second wave of feminism, and its importance for our understanding of dominant media's relationship to women's liberation goes beyond the specificity of the bra-burning myth. Rather, it is the exemplar of a brand of media logic that has come to dominate treatment of feminism in the last 30-plus years, a logic within which the political must always be personalized, in which "divide and conquer" is a reliable strategy, and in which the articulated quest for self-actualization is the same as liberation, packaged as a rhinestone crown.

NOTES

[1]Alice Echols, *Daring To Be Bad: Radical Feminism in America, 1967–1975* (Minneapolis: University of Minnesota Press, 1989).

[2]Joan Ryan, "Be All That You Can Be (And Never Forget to Smile): Sorry, Folks, But They've Put the Bikinis Back," *San Francisco Chronicle,* September 21, 1997, 10/Z1;

Rick Marin, "Ms. America: Making Over an Icon Very, Very Carefully," *New York Times,* September 13, 1993, B1; see also Nathan Cobb, "Next They'll Call Her Ms. America," *Boston Globe,* August 4, 1993, 65.

[3] Robin Morgan, *The Word of a Woman: Feminist Dispatches, 1968–1992* (New York: W. W. Norton, 1992), 21; Susan Brownmiller, *In Our Time: Memoir of a Revolution* (New York: Dial, 1999), 41; Flora Davis, *Moving the Mountain: The Women's Movement in America Since 1960* (New York: Touchstone, 1991), 107. See also Jo Freeman, *The Politics of Women's Liberation* (New York: Longman, 1975), 112.

[4] Frank Deford, *There She Is: The Life and Times of Miss America* (New York: Viking, 1971), 256; Echols, *Daring To Be Bad,* 93; Marcia Cohen, *The Sisterhood: The True Story of the Women Who Changed the World* (New York: Simon and Schuster, 1988), 149; Sheila Tobias, *Faces of Feminism: An Activist's Reflections on the Women's Movement* (Boulder, Colo.: Westview, 1997), 86.

[5] See, for example, Brownmiller, *In Our Time;* Echols, *Daring To Be Bad;* Joanna Foley Martin, "Confessions of a Non-Bra-Burner," *Chicago Journalism Review* 4 (July 1971): 11, 15; Robin Morgan, *The Word of a Woman;* Ruth Rosen, *The World Split Open: How the Modern Women's Movement Changed America* (New York: Viking, 2000); Lindsey Van Gelder, "The Truth About Bra-Burners," *Ms.,* September/October 1992, 80–81; Suzanne Braun Levine, "The Truth Was Burned," *Media Studies Journal* 12 (1998): 110.

[6] Rosen, *The World Split Open,* 160–61. The tenacity of the bra-burning trope is made clear by a September 2000 item in *Newsweek* noting the recent marriage of prominent feminist Gloria Steinem. The item described the ceremony as follows: "The sunrise ceremony, held in Oklahoma, was part Cherokee, with 'a lot of burning stuff,' said bud-of the-bride actress Kathy Najimy. Like those old bras, huh?" See Alisha Davis, "A Surprise Hitch," *Newsweek,* September 18, 2000, 92.

[7] Rosen, *The World Split Open,* 160.

[8] See Bonnie J. Dow, "Spectacle, Spectatorship, and Gender Anxiety in Television News Coverage of the 1970 Women's Strike for Equality," *Communication Studies* 50 (1999): 143–57.

[9] Rosen, *The World Split Open,* 160.

[10] Susan Douglas, *Where the Girls Are: Growing Up Female with the Mass Media* (New York: Random House, 1994), 160.

[11] Judith Duffett, "WLM vs. Miss America," *Voice of the Women's Liberation Movement,* October 1968, 4.

[12] Van Gelder, "The Truth About Bra-Burners," 81.

[13] Carol Hanisch, "Two Letters from the Women's Liberation Movement," in *The Feminist Memoir Project: Voices from Women's Liberation,* ed. Rachel Blau DuPlessis and Ann Snitow (New York: Three Rivers Press, 1998), 198; Morgan, *Word of a Woman,* 25–26. Ironically, 1968 was the first year of the Miss Black America pageant, which was held four blocks up the boardwalk in Atlantic City on the same night as the Miss America pageant. The newly crowned Miss Black America, Saundra Williams, seemed to agree with the feminists' critique of the racism of the Miss America pageant in her comment in the *New York Times* that "'Miss America does not represent us because there has never been a black girl in the pageant. With my title, I can show black women that they too are beautiful even though they do have large noses and thick lips.'" However, the *New York Times* article goes on to note that Williams looked "bored when asked about the 100 women demonstrators, mostly white, who had picketed the Miss America Pageant," and her only comment was that "'They're expressing freedom, I guess . . . To each his own.'" See Judy Klemesrud, "There's Now Miss Black America," *New York Times,* September 8, 1968, 54.

[14] Duffett, "WLM vs. Miss America," 4; "No More Miss America," in *Sisterhood Is Powerful: An Anthology of Writings from the Women's Liberation Movement,* ed. Robin Morgan (New York: Vintage, 1970), 586–88.

[15]Charlotte Curtis, "Along with Miss America, There's Now Miss Black America," *New York Times*, September 8, 1968, 54; "Illinois Girl Named Miss America," *New York Times*, September 8, 1968, 81.

[16]Brownmiller, *In Our Time*, 40; Charlotte Curtis, "Miss America Is Picketed by 100 Women," *New York Times*, September 8, 1968, 81.

[17]Brownmiller, *In Our Time*, 40; Hanisch, "Two Letters from the Women's Liberation Movement," 199.

[18]Curtis, "Miss America is Picketed by 100 Women," 81.

[19]Curtis, "Miss America is Picketed by 100 Women," 81.

[20]Duffett, "WLM vs. Miss America," 5.

[21]Carol Hanisch, "What Can Be Learned: A Critique of the Miss America Protest," in *Voices from Women's Liberation*, ed. Leslie Tanner (New York: Signet, 1970), 133–34.

[22]"No More Miss America," 586.

[23]Duffett, "WLM vs. Miss America," 4.

[24]Harriet Van Horne, "Female Firebrands," *New York Post*, September 9, 1968, 38.

[25]Hanisch, "Two Letters from the Women's Liberation Movement," 198.

[26]Lacey Fosburgh, "Traditional Groups Prefer to Ignore Women's Lib," *New York Times*, August 26, 1970, 44; Douglas, *Where the Girls Are*, 156.

[27]Sara Davidson, "An 'Oppressed Majority' Demands its Rights," *Life*, December 12, 1969, 66–78; Peter Babcox, "Meet the Women of the Revolution, 1969," *New York Times Magazine*, February 9, 1969, 34ff.

[28]Duffett, "WLM vs. Miss America," 7.

[29]"Michigan Girl Chosen Miss America," *New York Times*, September 7, 1969, 68; Carlo M. Sardella, "Miss America Faces Ms.," *New York Times*, September 1, 1974, 54.

[30]In August 2001, pageant officials announced another round of changes designed to update the pageant. Among them were the renaming of the swimsuit, evening gown, and talent segments, which would henceforth be called "Lifestyle and Fitness," "Presence and Poise," and "Artistic Expression," respectively. Even more interesting, however, was the announcement that the pageant would adopt some of the conventions of "reality television," made familiar by programs like *Survivor* and *The Weakest Link*, including a quiz on historical and current events trivia (called the "Knowledge and Understanding" segment) and the creation of the "so-called Eighth Judge, a segment that will gather votes from non-finalists, making up 10 percent of the final tally. The cameras will periodically check into a 'jury room' and follow the runners-up as they watch the proceedings on a monitor." Interestingly, given the Miss America organization's commitment to its reputation as a scholarship pageant, the response of the executive director of the *Miss Illinois* program to the "Knowledge and Understanding" segment was that "I know it makes for good TV, but I don't know what it has to do with the skills one needs to be a good Miss America." See Andrew Jacobs, "Here She Comes, Miss America, Hoping Not to Be the Weakest Link," *New York Times*, August 15, 2001, 15.

[31]Judy Klemesrud, "For Miss America '75, the Questions Get Tougher," *New York Times*, September 9, 1974, 40.

[32]Klemesrud, "For Miss America '75, The Questions Get Tougher," 40.

[33]Klemesrud, "Miss America: She's Always on the Road," *New York Times*, July 4, 1974, 9.

[34]Klemesrud, "Miss America: She's Always on the Road," 9.

[35]Robin Morgan, "The Vanessa Williams Controversy: What's a Feminist to Think?" *Ms.*, October 1974, 154.

[36]Morgan, "The Vanessa Williams Controversy," 154.

[37]See Melinda Beck, "For Want of a Bathing Suit," *Newsweek*, August 6, 1984, 23, and "Beauty Contests—The Stakes Are Big," *U.S. News and World Report*, August 6, 1984, 14.

[38]Melinda Beck, "A Controversial 'Spectator Sport,'" *Newsweek*, September 17, 1984, 56, 59, 60.

[39] Eve Zibart, "Just What the Judges Ordered: Miss America 1988: The New Ideal," *Washington Post,* September 21, 1987, B1; Henry Allen, "They're Back on the Runway! In Atlantic City, It's Miss America's Class of '88," *Washington Post,* September 21, 1987, C1.

[40] Ann Trebbe, "Miss America: Substance vs. Swimsuits," *Toronto Star,* September 9, 1988, C1.

[41] Allen, "They're Back on The Runway!" C1.

[42] Marin, "Ms. America: Making Over an Icon Very, Very Carefully," B1; see also Cobb, "Next They'll Call Her Ms. America," 65.

[43] Cobb, "Next They'll Call Her Ms. America," 65.

[44] Frank Rich, "There She Is," *New York Times,* September 20, 1995, A21.

[45] Frank Bruni, "Here She Is, Miss America, Whose Ideal?" *New York Times,* September 16, 1995, A1.

[46] Bill Kent, "Mr. Miss America," *New York Times,* September 13, 1998, 14NJ: 1.

[47] Ryan, "Be All That You Can Be (And Never Forget to Smile)," 10/Z1.

[48] Marin, "Ms. America: Making Over an Icon Very, Very Carefully," B1.

[49] Bruni, "Here She Is, Miss America, Whose Ideal?" A1; Rich, "There She Is," A21.

[50] Kent, "Mr. Miss America," 14NJ: 1.

[51] Michael Colton, "The Cookie-Cutter Contestants: At Miss America Pageant, It's the Same-Mold Story," *Washington Post,* September 19, 1998, B01; Bob Curran, "They're in It for the Scholarships," *Buffalo News,* September 12, 1995, 2D.

[52] Tish Durkin, "There She Is—Again," *Mademoiselle,* September 12, 1995, 44.

[53] Rachel Giese, "Here She Comes, Miss Identity Crisis," *Toronto Star,* October 27, 1997, A17.

[54] "Miss America Pageant Changing?" August 14, 2001, <http://www.cnn.com/2001/SHOWBIZ/News/08/14/miss.america.changes.ap/index.html>. Retrieved August 15, 2001.

[55] See, for example, Dan Vergano, "There's Less of Miss America to Love," *USA Today,* March 22, 2000, 6D.

[56] Bill Thompson, "No Change Will Ever Suit Miss America's Critics," *Tampa Tribune,* September 16, 1995, 11.

[57] A recent example occurred on an episode of CNN's *Crossfire* the week after the 2002 Miss America pageant, when the exchange below took place between Margot Magowan (a cofounder of the Woodhull Institute, a think-tank for women leaders) and Erika Schwarz Wright (1996's Miss Louisiana and a 1997 Miss America runner-up). It demonstrates the continuing durability of the journalistic strategy of pitting feminist critics of the pageant against specific contestants, as well as the difficulty feminists have in mounting systemic critiques of the pageants when faced with the disavowal of exploitation by contestants:

> *Magowan:* Women learn to objectify themselves just like men learn to objectify women. And Miss America teaches us that. It teaches us that no matter what, we are going to be rated by how we look. If we want to be successful, we better do what Erika Schwarz did and dress right and look right because that's how we're . . .
> *Schwarz Wright:* But the question is, Margot, what is right? I mean, I didn't dress like everyone else. I dressed like an individual and how I wanted to dress. No one told me what to wear. No one told me what to do.

Earlier in the segment, *Crossfire* host Tucker Carlson encouraged this conflict, issuing the following challenge to Margot Magowan after Erika Schwarz Wright praised the pageant for providing the scholarship that allowed her to attend law school:

> Now Margot Magowan, I can't imagine how, as a committed feminist, you could in any way criticize what Erika Schwarz just said. I mean, this gave her an opportunity to go to law school, which she finished. And in return she did nothing

embarrassing. She wore a bathing suit much more modest than most people wear on South Beach in Miami. I mean, what in the world is wrong with this?

See "Miss America: Is She Out of Step?" September 23, 2002, <http://www.cnn.com/2002/ALLPOLITICS/09/23/cf.opinion.miss.america/index/html>. Retrieved September 23, 2002.

[58]Sarah Banet-Weiser, *The Most Beautiful Girl in the World: Beauty Pageants and National Identity* (Berkeley: University of California Press, 1999), 208, 210.

PINK HERRING & THE FOURTH PERSONA: J. EDGAR HOOVER'S SEX CRIME PANIC

CHARLES E. MORRIS III

Secrecy, J. Edgar Hoover discovered prior to the Cold War, could be measured in feet. "[H]e . . . walks with a mincing step, dresses fastidiously, with Eleanor blue as the favorite color for matched shades of tie, handkerchief and socks," a *Collier's* reporter revealed.[1] For Hoover, as for many Americans sobering from Prohibition's embrace of the pansy, this mischievous comment reinforced a vexing realization: the contours of masculinity had begun to blur at the same time that gender norms tightened. Presumptive silences were becoming audible, as audible as the sound of expensive shoes on a city sidewalk. To keep step with the passing crowd, one must not be caught mincing.

At the time his mincing was exposed in 1933, Hoover had for five years been in a relationship with fellow bachelor and Associate Director of the FBI Clyde Tolson. Until then, Hoover and Tolson had been spared speculation about their sexuality by the prominent cultural presence of the pansy, whose dramatic features offered a code that relieved those who fell somewhere else on the rather fluid spectrum of male homosocial desire.[2] Whatever other males might do sexually, their identity remained largely unquestioned because, given the pansy, most Americans "knew" a homosexual when they encountered one.

Prohibition's demise in the 1930s claimed with it the pansy's public sphere. As it controlled the burgeoning deviant subculture, the anti-crime movement successfully forced the pansy to the periphery of a visible social world. In chasing the most licit expression of male[3] homosexual desire into the shadows, regulators briefly unhinged homosexual meaning at a time when masculinity already suffered the debilitating effects of the Depression. What counted as homosexual and as homosocial (and heterosexual), therefore, had become unclear.

This tumultuous period, I contend, was marked by a "homosexual panic"[4] that transformed the homosexual from pansy into "menace."[5] The ensuing contest over sexual meaning entailed increased scrutiny and, correlatively, rhetorical performance. A wide range of male rhetorical behavior occurred that I interpret as "passing," the self-fashioning that constructs and preserves an ethos of gender and sexual "normalcy." Hoover's own rhetorical agency is implied by Richard Gid Power's conclusion that "Of all Hoover's secrets, the most tightly guarded were his own."[6]

In what follows I do not hazard conclusions about Hoover's secrets. Proof of Hoover's sexuality is not required to establish his public response to the homosexual panic that gripped straight and gay men alike. The question of what constituted the (homo)sexual on the homosocial continuum at the time would have been a dangerously open one for Hoover and other men. That he exhibited a style and enjoyed a relationship vulnerable to speculation tells us much about his felt exigence but nothing about his love life. The *question* of his sexuality, however, remains of central importance to the particular rhetoric I explore in this essay.

This question has proved rather troublesome and currently prohibits meaningful engagement of the relationship between Hoover's policy and sexual identity. Until recently, sexuality constituted the chief domain into which scholars feared to tread. The burden of proof too high, they acknowledged rumors of Hoover's relationship with Tolson only to omit, discredit, or diminish those scant scraps of circumstantial evidence too paltry to interpret. Because the governing assumption was that Hoover's private life, although intriguing, had no significant bearing on his federal responsibilities, such timidity seemed judicious.[7]

Anthony Summers raised the historiographical stakes with his 1993 expose that sensationalized Hoover's alleged sex life under the auspices of credible research.[8] Its allure hinged on titillating those wondering about Hoover's boudoir and satisfying longings to see him convicted of hypocrisy. Summers legitimated rumors of crossdressing and little boys, rubber gloves, and photographs depicting the Director on his knees, despite an appalling lack of substantive evidence. His homophobic fun-house projection has been dangerously consequential in raising doubts about the historical relevance of Hoover's sexuality, inviting a wide range of reactionary apologia.

The most vocal of these apologists is Athan Theoharis, who meticulously refuted Summers's "shoddy journalism."[9] Unfortunately, Theoharis's passionate corrective also inadvertently paralyzed the issue of Hoover's sexuality. Whereas in his earlier biography Theoharis considered the possibility that Hoover was closeted, he argued here that

> Whether or not Hoover was a homosexual—and I doubt that he was—the wily and cautious FBI director would never have put himself in a position that publicly compromised his sexuality. . . . If he was a practicing homosexual, he would also have taken whatever safeguards were needed to ensure that such a dark secret would go with him to the grave.[10]

Consequently, any meaningful discussion appears foreclosed, because, as Theoharis concluded, "Hoover's leadership of the FBI can best be understood not in terms of Summers's morality play of compromised homosexuality but as a by-product of the politics of Cold War America. . . . This story of institutional politics remains to be told."[11]

My critical effort resists such foreclosures in order to argue that sexual identity was significant to FBI policy in the years prior to Hoover's Cold War dominance. Toward that end, I explore Hoover's *pink herring,* which utilized moral panic about sex crime to alleviate his homosexual panic, thus diverting attention from his sexuality and silencing those who might question it. I interpret this as a tactic in his passing, and a peculiar response to an invisible audience I term the *fourth persona.* Having examined Hoover's pink herring in text and context. I conclude by drawing some relevant implications regarding passing as an object of rhetorical study.

THE PASSING CROWD

Secrecy is a necessarily rhetorical phenomenon. As Sissela Bok argues, "The word 'secrecy'. . . . denotes the methods used to conceal, such as codes or disguises or camouflage, and the practices of concealment. . . . Accordingly I shall take concealment, or hiding, to be the defining trait of secrecy."[12] A secret of dangerous difference motivates some to develop and sustain a double-consciousness in order to survive amid and sometimes to resist dominant, oppressive cultural practices. Especially when the markers of one's difference—skin, behavior, dress—can be camouflaged, "double-lives" manifest themselves publicly in skilled performances evincing the rhetorical forms of secrecy and disclosure.[13] To succeed in veiling one's identity, i.e., convincing certain audiences of an "acceptable" persona, these rhetors-with-secrets employ tactics of impersonation, deflection, and silence in the public sphere. Collectively, these elements constitute a species of secrecy and a mode of rhetorical action that I call "passing."[14]

Peter Rabinowitz offers a useful distinction between "social passing," by which one misleads others into believing he is something that he is not, and "rhetorical passing," which "is not simply a disguise, but a virtuoso tightrope performance." The rhetorical passer engages in "unnameable [sic] speech acts" that unfold before two audiences: "one audience that's ignorant and another that knows the truth *and remains silent about it*."[15] Similarly, Amy Robinson highlights two audiences in discussing the "triangular theater of the pass": "In such an economy of readable identity, the successful passer only disappears from view insofar as she appears (to her reader) to be the category into which she has passed. Adopting the presumptive mechanisms that read a racially and/or sexually indeterminate subject as an over-determined legible social identity, it is the spectator who manufactures the symptoms of a successful pass." Passing requires the dupe, one to be fooled, but also the "in-group clairvoyant" who, because "it takes one to know one," collaborates by recognition and silence.[16]

Often we attend to what appears to be an exclusive audience of dupes as the centerpiece of passing's rhetorical action. Indeed, there is no gainsaying the significance of the dominant audience, whose face must be mirrored in order for dangerous difference to be successfully camouflaged. The "overdetermined legible social identity" depends on dupe participation invited by a *subversive enthymeme:* an appeal that manipulates the assumptions of heteronormativity to achieve the telos of sexual secrecy; dupes facilitate the masking performance that deceives them.

I want to emphasize, however, the paramount significance of an invisible audience for whom the pass is legible; who in turn collaborates in preserving by silence the perilous secret kept from unsuspecting dupes. Every act of passing is enacted, in other words, by means of the *fourth persona:* a collusive audience constituted by the textual wink.[17] Similar to its counterpart, the second persona,[18] the fourth persona is an implied auditor of a particular ideological bent, presumably one who is sexually marginalized, understands the dangers of homophobia, acknowledges the rationale for the closet, and possesses an intuition that renders a pass transparent. A central distinction between these two personae, however, is that passing rhetoric must imply two ideological positions simultaneously, one that mirrors the dupes and another that implies, via the wink, an ideology of difference. The fourth persona also resembles its other counterpart, the third persona, in its partial constitution by silence.[19] Instead of a silence that negates and excludes, as with the third persona, here silence functions constructively as the medium of collusive exchange. What is not said is nonetheless performative, a speech act that can be read by certain audiences, and calls those audience members into being as abettors.[20]

Most passing rhetors embrace the fourth persona as a welcome beacon of safety, solidarity, and success. The motive of others, however, may be what Rabinowitz has labeled "social passing," emanating from a desire to blend with the normative without detection *by anyone*. I have argued elsewhere,[21] however, that the closet always functions rhetorically to disclose, in some fashion, the very secrets we would at all cost keep to ourselves. As a prospective social passer comes to realize this, that clairvoyants lurk everywhere among the dupes, a rather different rhetorical situation presents itself.[22] Like one who is the only person in a room seeing an apparition, the social passer's fear of being recognized manifests itself in the paranoid style.[23] One gay man quoted in George Henry's 1955 study *All the Sexes* captures well a feeling that, while affirming for most passers, would terrify the social passer: "The eyes of the homo usually stare right through you. He looks a second or two longer than the average, and as you gaze into his eyes, if you are a homo, there is a lightening like [sic] magnetic response, and a thrill passes through the very heart of you."[24] In response, the social passer might resist by rendering those clairvoyants transparent so as to eliminate them and fortify an enthymematic relation with his dupes.

In Hoover's case, the homosexual panic of the 1930s rendered him vulnerable to the shifting public signifiers of gender and sexuality. Men would have felt pressure to pass the muster of heteronormativity, an exigence more pressing and frustrating because normative standards were in flux. For many gays passing during this panic, the fourth persona would have afforded a means of community in the teeth of intensified homophobia. For some others, passing probably was accompanied by a homophobic paranoia regarding the fourth persona, which, to varying degrees, contributed to the pernicious construction of the panic's bogey, the homosexual menace. Fearing clairvoyants in his midst, Hoover's pink herring can be read as a subversive enthymeme forged on the hides of those most likely to read him for dangerous difference and, thus, most in need of silencing.

A TALE OF TWO PANICS

When Hoover met Tolson in 1928, he probably felt little anxiety about his marital status. Among his other attractions, Tolson provided the homosocial companionship Hoover cherished most when not working long hours at the FBI. Their preference for bachelorhood, far from anomalous, would have seemed normative during a decade experiencing a "cult of singleness."[25] *The New York Times Magazine*, for instance, proudly proclaimed, "For the nation's bachelors, this city is the Mecca."[26] Even if one were a *particular* sort of bachelor, his status as an unmarried man would not by itself have signified homosexuality.

During the 1930s, however, the rich bachelor subculture began to erode: "As American society struggled to emerge from the hard times . . . the bachelor life that had been so prominent in the previous half century faded beneath emphases on family solidarity and the communal effort to battle economic and foreign demons."[27] Those demons found their surest victim in masculinity. Michael Kimmel observes, "For most men the Depression was emasculating both at work and at home. Unemployed men . . . saw themselves as impotent patriarchs. And the consequences . . . were significant."[28] The disturbance of male homosociality was one significant consequence, resulting, I argue, in a homosexual panic. Although blame for the paralyzing assault on masculinity was dispersed as well among women, African Americans, and immigrants, homosexuals occupied a distinctive role in this crisis as men braced themselves against the pervasive threat of effeminacy and degeneracy.

The irony of this emerging panic is that it was intensified by the efforts employed to eradicate it. Homosocial bonds and, correlatively, dominant cultural meanings of homosexuality and heterosexuality, had been anchored in part by the pansy, an openly and flamboyantly gay fixture of the Prohibition era. The Pansy Craze, lasting roughly from 1920 until 1933, focused the cultural imagination squarely on a conception of homosexuality that had less to do with what men did sexually than how one performed one's gender and sexuality. "Today there is scarcely a school boy who doesn't know what a 'pansy' is," wrote La Forest Potter in 1933.[29] The primary marker of that knowledge, Potter asserted, was "the feminine gait of the effeminate homosexual . . . [which] is one of the most constant differences that exist between the homosexual and the heterosexual man."[30]

The pansy emerged as middle-class dominance of sociability crumbled during the 1920s, a product of working class and immigrant defiance of moral policing. Prohibition culture offered the pansy both the comforts and safety of sanctioned visibility. Although largely an urban phenomenon, the pansy's proliferation in mass media provided limited tolerance that was national in scope.[31] In return, the pansy provided succor to those who wished to control the meaning of sexuality by naming it, in keeping with Sedgwick's notion that "The importance . . . of the category 'homosexual,' . . . [is] its potential for giving whoever wields it a structuring definitional leverage over the whole range of male bonds that shape the social constitution."[32] Men engaging in homosocial behavior, but who did not behave like pansies, would not be considered homosexual: "At a time when the culture . . . might have undermined conventional sources of masculine identity, the spectacle of the pansy allowed men to confirm their manliness and solidarity with other men by distinguishing themselves from pansies."[33]

The onslaught of the Depression ended the pansy's reign. Motivated by cultural instability, authorities sought to restore moral order by mobilizing against "degenerates." By 1933, the visibility of pansies was resisted with the force of law, including the Volstead Act, which legalized alcohol precisely so that social spaces could be regulated.[34] The Motion Picture Production Code, strengthened in 1934, as well as other widespread measures against "obscenity," represented similar systemic efforts to extinguish the pansy's cultural presence.[35]

Historians have argued that this period of repressive moral backlash accounts for a shift to a new definition of homosexuality. I want to explain more clearly the dynamics of that symbolic shift as sexual and gender norms tightened en route to stability. The pansy's sudden invisibility produced ambiguity and uncertainty in sexual meaning, proliferating connotation even as "the coding of a wide range of behavior as homosexual and its definition as disorderly served to establish and enforce the boundaries of the normative gender order."[36] Implied here is a cultural struggle animated by homophobic fear; in other words, a homosexual panic.

As Sedgwick explains, homosexual panic constitutes a "secularized and psychologized homophobia" that structures male gender generally, and male homosocial bonds specifically, through the threat of guilt by homosexual identification. Insofar as homosexuality's definition is "arbitrary and self-contradictory" in nature, men are left wondering and worrying whether they will be labeled as such.[37] This panic functions as a "kind of ideological pincers-movement": "no man must be able to ascertain that he is not (that his bonds are not) homosexual. In this way, a relatively small exertion of physical or legal compulsion potentially rules great reaches of behavior and filiation."[38]

During historical periods when a clear locus of homosexual meaning is lacking, or gender norms are unsettled, homosexual panic erupts, precisely because of the indeterminacy of cultural identity. In the absence of homosexual denotation, according to D. A. Miller, one witnesses a proliferation of connotation, which, while readily deniable, also tends toward an "effluvium of rumination" and "limitless mobility."[39] Miller explains, "Yet if connotation has the advantage of constructing an essentially insubstantial homosexuality, it has the corresponding inconvenience of tending to raise this ghost all over the place."[40] Accompanied as it is by paranoia, such connotation sparks a struggle for denomination that Sedgwick describes accordingly: "the ability to set proscriptive and descriptive limits to the forms of male homosocial desire—[becomes] the object of competition among those who [wish] to wield it, as well as an implement of oppression against those whose practices it at a given time proscribed."[41]

During the post-pansy panic, that competition took a variety of homophobic forms, two of which warrant elaboration. Beginning in 1935, the Committee for the Study of Sex Variants convened with the express purpose of gathering multidisciplinary perspectives on the sex variant, its term for the homosexual, in order to offer counsel to a culture dealing with this expanding "problem."[42] The Committee's charge was to distinguish the sex variant from the "normal population," a charge forged by an assumption that "heterosexuality seemed to be imperiled as a result of inordinate modern pressures and cultural taboos that gave rise to 'substitute activities,' the most common of which seemed to be homosexuality."[43] The timing, scope, and theoretical bases of the study seem in keeping with the context of homosexual panic I have described, as Jennifer Terry's account makes clear:

> The paradigm of the CSSV researchers caused them to go to great lengths to tether homosexual orientation to gender and sex inversion. This tendency revealed that the Committee was as interested in demarcating norms of masculinity and femininity as it was in comprehending the distinct qualities that pertained to sexual attractions between women or between men. By focusing on the former, researchers generally believed they were accounting for the latter. In the end, the CSSV's conclusions indicate that remedying the problem of sex role inversion was part and parcel of a larger effort to place heterosexuality (i.e., sexual adjustment) back on stronger footing. . . . The Sex Variant Study was thus as much an effort to construct and maintain hygienic heterosexuality as it was to investigate homosexuality.[44]

Despite the CSSV's benevolent posture, its findings reified the assumption that homosexuality was a pathology in need of psychological adjustment, thus fueling rather than undermining trenchant homophobia.

At the same time, a sex crime panic gripped the nation, animating its quest to distinguish, and extinguish, the sexual deviant. This panic, which dates from the Lindbergh kidnapping case in 1932, solidified between 1935 and 1937 as the press prominently featured the cases of Albert Fish, Salvatore Ossido, Lawrence Marks, Thomas Smith, and many others.[45] *The Literary Digest* sounded an alarm commonplace throughout the nation: "At large . . . thousands of potential sex slayers, many of them well known to the authorities . . . walked the streets, human rattlesnakes coiled in the path of unsuspecting women and children."[46]

By the end of 1937 the panic had reached its zenith, constituted in the public discourse as a crime "wave" linked to sexual perversion.[47] *Time* magazine reported: "With these appalling examples of pedophilia, the lust of mature men for pre-pubescent children, spreading daily in the Press, it looked to laymen as if a national wave of sex crimes against children was in full surge."[48] Skeptical of the hysteria, Bertram Pollens, in his 1938 book *The Sex Criminal,* nonetheless concluded, "It almost seems as though sex, the 'evil urge', had suddenly broken loose from its long confinement and was on its devastating path to strike wherever it could."[49]

Pressure on law enforcement and politicians as a result of what Fredric Wertham called "almost a mass hysteria" culminated in crackdowns on any deemed to be sexually degenerate.[50] During this period, sexual psychopath laws were passed in California, Ohio, Minnesota, Michigan, and Illinois; citizens were urged to join the police in identifying potential suspects. Austin H. MacCormick, NYC Commissioner of Correction, advised: "The police . . . would make many more arrests if people were intelligent enough to report to them things that are very often common neighborhood knowledge." He concluded that the panic's solution required a clear conception of the problem: "[W]e must face the fact that the roots of the problem lie deep in some of the least known elements of human behavior. It is sex with which you are dealing—sex in its abnormalities rather than in its normal expression and in its aberrations rather than in its natural course."[51]

Chief among those aberrations was homosexuality.[52] Pollens emphasized that the problem "reaches down to the home of our best friend and next door neighbor, and . . . we may even find it lurking in a corner very close and proximate to our own hearth—the unknown skeleton in the closet."[53] The pervasive sense that those skeletons were homosexual derived from several assumptions. Terry explains:

> Much of the popular reporting about sex crimes reinforced an existing notion that homosexuals were, by definition, child molesters. This idea was abetted by the assumption that homosexuals were trapped at an arrested age in development which led them to prey upon innocent children to satisfy their perverse desires. . . . Since all homosexual acts were against the law and most were classified as "sex offenses," homosexual men were lumped together in the public imagination with violent offenders, rapists, and child molesters.[54]

For example, Potter argued, "homosexuals and abnormals are perhaps the only class of neurotics . . . who derive satisfaction in converting heterosexuals to their practices."[55] Utilizing the same assumptions, M[a]cCormick offered homosexuals as a prime example of sex criminals: "The number of people convicted of such offenses is comparatively small, but the number who commit them is very large. We have in our institutions . . . less than forty men known to be homosexuals. Anyone who knows anything about the subject knows that there are thousands of homosexuals in New York City."[56]

The cultural embodiment of homosexuality had begun to shift perceptibly from an innocuous pansy to a dangerous "menace." That the panic marked a struggle not merely to end sex crimes but also to eradicate gender and sexual ambiguity can be discerned in the hysterical tone and awkward link between homosexuality and assaults on women and children. Herein lies the answer to Henry Gerber's tortured question, found in his 1932 gay manifesto: "And why harp on the very few homosexuals who find satisfaction for their pathological craving to deal with the young boys, when the papers are at present full of details of atrocious killings of little girls by mentally deranged heterosexual men?"[57]

HUNTING THE FOURTH PERSONA:
HOOVER'S PINK HERRING

In response to the post-pansy homosexual panic, J. Edgar Hoover engaged in a skillful and insidious passing performance, the centerpiece of which was his *pink herring*. By defining the "sex deviate" as the chief moral threat to the nation's children, and in positioning himself as a hunter of those deviates, Hoover's pink herring helped to fix again the meaning of homosexuality and sought to vanquish debilitating speculation regarding his sexuality. In other words, a moral panic provided the rhetorical resources that would relieve Hoover's homosexual panic.

Given his long reign and nearly impenetrable persona, Hoover's vulnerability is scarcely imaginable. During the 1930s, thanks to Courtney Ryley Cooper, Hoover achieved iconic status as the nation's "master detective," a new hero who "represented the full power of American Justice, in 'getting his man.'"[58] Keenly aware of the potential afforded by this media blitz, Hoover learned to manage the FBI's rapidly growing public image. As Richard Powers argues, "While Hoover was not responsible for the country's fascination with celebrity criminals during the depression, and while he had not played the leading role in turning the anticrime movement into a ritual of national unity, he was imaginative enough to realize that Hollywood had given him a once-in-a-lifetime chance to turn his obscure agency into a major cultural force."[59]

These were formative years, however, even if Hoover was a quick study of the art of publicity. Prior to 1933, the FBI barely registered culturally, and invested almost no energy or resources in developing its public persona. Moreover, at that time Hoover's institutional power did not include unrestricted domestic surveillance. To make matters more precarious, FDR's original choice as Attorney General, Thomas Walsh, intended to fire Hoover; Hoover was spared only by Walsh's untimely death on Inauguration Day. Even as the friendlier replacement, Homer Cummings, launched the New Deal anticrime movement, Hoover's position in the hierarchy of leadership remained uncertain. Despite his position as FBI Director, Hoover was not nearly as invincible in the mid-1930s as he would be by the end of the decade.[60]

This brief period of vulnerability coincided with the homosexual panic undermining the nation's manhood. Like other men, Hoover could not escape the homophobic fear that accompanied turbulence in gender and sexual norms. Indeed, given his own position on the continuum of homosocial bonds, and as a newly minted celebrity, he was a likely target for cultural scrutiny. Although the public never gained access to Hoover's private world, dangerous signifiers abounded: he was a bachelor who lived with his mother; he did not date; his closest friend was Clyde Tolson, another bachelor with whom he rode to and from work, ate meals, socialized, traveled on business, and vacationed.[61] *Time*, which featured Hoover on its cover in August 1935, offered the once benign but now ominous description:

> Like all leaders of enterprises which require great morale, Director Hoover can always be counted on for an effective theatrical gesture where one seems needed. Like all men of action, he has a strong streak of sentimentality. . . . He is a bachelor, living with his semi-invalid mother. . . . His job gives him little time for friends, who are few and include no women.[62]

Hoover's demeanor and dress also drew attention. Ray Tucker's mischievous account in *Collier's* of his "mincing step" and preference for "Eleanor blue as the favorite color for the matched shades of tie, handkerchief and socks"[63] was not atypical. Jack Alexander, in his three-part profile in the *New Yorker*, observed, "From the day he entered the Department, certain things marked Hoover apart from scores of other young law clerks. He dressed better than most, a bit on the dandyish side."[64]

These markers are significant for the *questions* raised and the exigence those questions created for Hoover. Various factors may have contributed to increased gossip, his growing celebrity or accumulation of political enemies, to name two obvious examples; however, the context of homosexual panic goes far to explain why the subject of his sexuality and the suspicious reading of his signifiers heightened during these years. A decade earlier rumors about what these characteristics meant, which now circulated in the Bureau, nightclubs, and popular press, did not surface.[65] One agent's purported conclusion, "If he isn't queer, then he's weird," reveals a typical cultural judgment about bachelorhood, male companionship, and dress that made sense during a homosexual panic.[66] The dynamism of the panic expressed itself in the use of masculinity as a litmus test for cultural legitimacy and a weapon for character assassination. During a 1936 budget hearing, Kenneth McKellar, Chairman of the Senate Appropriations Committee and longtime critic of Hoover, attacked the Director's heroism and leadership by questioning his lack of prowess in arresting criminals.[67] A fuming Hoover surmised correctly "that his manhood had been impugned."[68]

Hoover seems to have been keenly aware for some time that his manhood was regularly evaluated and discussed. In the wake of *Collier's* insinuation, to cite the earliest instance, watchful eyes recognized public adjustments in Hoover's carriage. A *Washington Herald* gossip columnist asked if "anybody [had] noted that the Hoover stride has grown noticeably stronger and more vigorous since Tucker charged him with 'walking with mincing steps.'"[69] Moreover, Senator McKellar's assault may have inspired his high-profile participation in Alvin Karpis's arrest a month later. Curt Gentry writes, "There are those who suspected that Hoover's newly adopted 'tough cop' image was, at least in part, an attempt to counteract the rumors of his homosexuality. The publicist Lou Nichols . . . implied as much when, many years later, he told the author 'That [Karpis's capture] pretty much ended the "queer" talk.'"[70] Equally telling is the press coverage that Hoover helped shape, which often exaggerated his manliness. In *Liberty Magazine*, Frederick L. Collins, who collaborated with Hoover, observed that his "compact body, with shoulders of a light-heavyweight boxer, carries no ounce of extra weight—just a hundred and seventy pounds of live, virile masculinity."[71]

John Loughery has suggested that such efforts at bolstering the appearance of one's masculinity would have been sufficient to stave off speculation. "Many gay men who were of marrying age in the 1930s knew the terms of the social contract and counted on the timidity and willful ignorance of their peers and elders to shield them. . . . allow[ing] people to give men such as Hoover . . . the benefit of the doubt."[72] For an audience of dupes, which included most dominant audience members, the passing implied here might well have been successful.

Lurking, even haunting, however, is the fourth persona. Far from timid or willfully ignorant, the "in-group clairvoyant," one deeply intuitive regarding the tactics of passing because "it takes one to know one," looms as the ubiquitous source of anxiety for this hopeful social passer who, attempting to thwart the imagined inquisition, has already given himself away. Hoover's behavior suggests that, amid an "effluvium of rumination," garden-variety passing would not suffice; menacing clairvoyants needed to be exorcised, not ignored. Thus we witness

Hoover's investment in the sex crime panic that so occupied the nation. By hunting the (homosexual) "sex deviate," Hoover might appear the model of heteronormativity, stabilizing sexual norms and his reputation while silencing his fourth persona. This was Hoover's pink herring, a vicious deflection that throws dupes off the scent of lavender by snuffing out those who nose best.

I turn now to two textual manifestations of Hoover's pink herring. Despite the public hysteria, it must have seemed odd that Hoover would declare "War on the Sex Criminal" in the September 26, 1937, issue of the *New York Herald Tribune*.[73] Prior to this moment, he had scarcely uttered a word on the sex crime wave that had surged for the better part of two years. Strangely, the sex criminal had not been among Hoover's *Thousand Public Enemies* (1935) or *Persons in Hiding* (1938), those celebrity bank robbers, forgers, and murderers that had given him national celebrity. Yet in this most recent war declaration, he pronounced the sex fiend the "most loathsome of the vast army of crime." One senses here a discrepancy between the novelty of this criminal and his unparalleled notoriety. Every public enemy in the 1930s served Hoover's ethos; this new face on the most-wanted poster could be no different.

Whereas the continuous *presence* of Dillingers, Barkers, and Barrows had been required for the G-Man persona to burn brilliantly in the public eye, *absence* would provide the only sure measure that the taint of sex (and thus sexuality) had been eliminated. To achieve this absence, Hoover needed to distinguish the sex criminal from those public enemies craved by dominant audiences. In his opening salvo Hoover sounded an alarm that hyperbolized contemporary discourse regarding the sex crime wave: "The sex fiend, most loathsome of all the vast army of crime, has become a sinister threat to the safety of American childhood and womanhood."

Playing on the audience's familiarity with his criminal knowledge, Hoover labeled the sex fiend "the most loathsome" of that ignominious group so as to polarize and isolate him while fanning mass hysteria. "From one end of the United States to the other, women and little girls have been murdered by this beast. No parent can feel secure that his children are safe from attack. The sex fiend may strike anywhere, at any time. In one large eastern city alone, an arrest for sex crime is made every six hours, on the average, night and day." The severe dissonance Hoover invited here derives from the ubiquity and magnitude of the threat. There is no haven beyond the grasp of the beast, no hour of restful slumber while the sex fiend lurks. An apt portrayal too, I surmise, of the threat Hoover imagined his fourth persona to pose.

Lest the sex criminal become a caricature, which might preserve him, Hoover revealed the true "human beast": "He isn't some fabled monster; he isn't some demon, born full-blown, that suddenly descends upon women and little girls; he isn't a 'product of our modern age,' he is a definite and serious result of the apathy and indifference in the handling of out-of-the-ordinary offenders." Hoover had identified a rather innocuous category of offenders rapidly gaining national notoriety, that he constituted as more dangerous for their lack of monstrous proportion. He implies that the "beast" had long been in the midst of his victims, allowed to fester by a public's "apathy and indifference." This account sounds remarkably like the post-Repeal pansy. As Potter warned of homosexuality: "For the very foundations of our social structure, and its sane and normal relations may be threatened by our ignorance, our neglect and our bat-blind indifference to what may, before long, become a menace to every family in the land."[74]

Further indication that Hoover targeted homosexuals without explicitly naming them is found in his proclamation that the sex criminal is an "ordinary offender [turned] into a dangerous, predatory animal, preying upon society because he has been taught he can get away with it. . . . sex fiends. . . . [who] have been repeatedly dealt with as petty offenders when, in truth, their every action was a blazing signpost to a future of torture, rape, mutilation and murder." The timing here is central to understanding his implication because 1937 was the high-water mark of the sex crime panic that had rendered this "petty offender" presumptively homosexual. Terry explains, "increased arrests for homosexual-related activities, generally classified as sex crimes, fueled the dual perceptions that homosexuality was actually increasing and that it represented something as horrific as rape, lust, murder, and sexual assaults on children."[75]

In this appeal, Hoover crafted a subversive enthymeme by fashioning himself and the sex-fiend (i.e., homosexual) in mutually exclusive terms. Already reputed as an expert criminal hunter, Hoover's dramatic account of the sex fiend implicitly bolstered his ethos of sexual normalcy; a man so dedicated to this scourge of degenerates certainly could not be one. To insure that they invested in this portrayal, Hoover challenged his dupes (by scolding them) to look for and recognize the "blazing signpost(s)" that marked the slippery slope to tragedy. Here reading is fundamental, and the FBI, embodied in Hoover, provided the model: "The Federal Bureau of Investigation inquires into every phase of an offender's past history, and, as a result, we have learned volumes as to what part parental indifference, parole abuses, political protection, and other factors have played" in the creation of the sex fiend.

Hoover's passion, however, also alerts us to the question that clairvoyants, but not dupes, would likely have asked: why are *you* so adept at reading the "blazing signpost"? Is it because it takes one to know one? They, unlike the dupes, could decode the "Jekyll and Hyde lives" described by NYC Police Commissioner Lewis Valentine: "Some of them appear to be and are most of the time normal, reasonable citizens, some holding highly responsible positions . . . you would be surprised to know what positions some of them hold."[76] If his pass were to succeed, therefore, it required both deflection (by defining the homosexual in contrast to his masculine, crime-hunting persona) and exposure (the fiend, i.e., fourth persona, must *actually* be eliminated).

In order to rout clairvoyants from the shadows, Hoover enlisted common citizens and professionals in the hunt. "The present apathy of the public toward known perverts, generally regarded as 'harmless,' should be changed to one of suspicious scrutiny." Psychiatrists were urged to dedicate themselves to the "pathological and psychological study of perversion," and, if necessary, "the surgeon must play his part in removing the sex criminal as a distinct menace." Law enforcement must do its "utmost to bring about a public confidence where by citizens will be more prone to make complaints and follow these by prosecution." Hoover echoed a growing popular consensus that "Until such a method of conducting a civilization by having the members take in each other's moral washing can be made feasible, the sexual offender will remain in our midst, as a continually terrifying problem."[77]

One might think it counterintuitive for a man avoiding suspicion to insist on a high-profile hunt of would-be deviants; however, recall Sedgwick's notion that "the ability to set proscriptive and descriptive limits to the forms of male homosocial desire [becomes] . . . an implement of oppression against those whose practices it at a given time proscribed."[78] Hoover's effort to make the sex criminal and, thus, the homosexual visible was the means by which to control him and stabilize sexual norms. In doing so, Hoover's passing performance placed him in the spotlight but, ironically and strategically, beyond the pale of speculation.

In December 1937, Hoover reiterated his war declaration in a speech delivered before the Association of Life Insurance Presidents.[79] The speech is not significant for its innovations but for the train of Hoover's thought, the repetition that solidified his pink herring. "To those who pay you premiums on their life insurance, there is a personal realization of risk which causes them to be much more receptive to your educational programs. . . . Our efforts in education, however, while as thoroughly vital and while directed to the very same persons, who have an equally personal investment in the matter, all too often meet with apathy." Again Hoover stressed the twin themes of apathy and education, vital elements in reducing the nation's risk. That risk, Hoover emphasized, loomed larger for the apathy that abetted it. "Were it not for this widespread public indifference toward crime conditions, for a too general attitude of 'let the other fellow do it,' we should not be faced with the fact that the criminal army of America is composed of over 4,300,000 persons."

Hoover's words resembled his earlier claim that chief among that vast army was the degenerate treading an inevitable path to homicide: "there are roaming at large today some 200,000 potential murderers who during their lifetime will account for the deaths by violence of more than 300,000 persons, unless the present murder rate is reduced." Hoover's hyperbole, designed to fan panic, is familiar. So, too, is his enthymematic gesture toward that which popular discourse made plain. "It should interest you also to realize that many of these crimes are those of degeneracy, often committed by persons afflicted with diseases which only recently have been discussed in public." As I have described above, such degeneracy was naturally linked to homosexuality.

To complete the subversive enthymeme, Hoover rather deftly praised his audience for their skilled recognition of the problem: "[W]ithin the last few years you have been courageous path-finders in the distribution of information concerning the viciousness of our so-called social diseases. To my mind, crime is as malignant as any cancer, and it is as distinct a subject of health as tuberculosis." This ingratiation had everything to do with motivating his charges to join him in a particular understanding of that which was both legion and contagion, alien and yet communicable, but preventable if only they were vigilant.

Having achieved deflection, Hoover aimed to expose and eradicate his fourth persona. "The surprising increase of sex crimes within the last few years revealed an urgent necessity for corrective action by every public-minded body. . . . There should be given to the cure of degeneracy the same thought, the same eager perseverance, the same persistent investigation, that has resulted in the lessening of many other dangerous diseases." In the urgency of this anaphoric request, Hoover betrayed his need to search, find, name, and thus "cure" this "dangerous disease," a disease that was understood in gender/sexual and criminal terms, and included his menacing clairvoyants.

Before leaving my reading, I offer an epilogue which functions as *corroborative context*. Although historians are convinced that Hoover's 1937 war declaration rendered him the cultural ballast against sex crime,[80] and I am sure of his inspiration, there is little textual evidence to establish these claims. These texts lend compelling credence to such conclusions, but plausible deniability—endemic to this rhetorical mode—haunts and sabotages them, a legacy of the closet and the homophobic forces that forge it.

As corroborative context, therefore, it is significant that 1937 was the year that Hoover, having been granted greater latitude in Federal surveillance, launched a Sex Deviate Index Card File that "provided a centralized aid for identifying and retrieving all reports of alleged homosexuality."[81] Striking is the absence of evidence in this file of *heterosexual* men who molested children or assaulted women. Its obsession (over 300,000 documents by 1977, when the file was destroyed) began with what must have seemed central for eradicating sex crime: the homosexual. I would posit a further concern, namely the clairvoyants plaguing one gripped by homosexual panic.

Virtually his own institution of power by the 1940s, Hoover aggressively extended his policing of homosexuality, particularly rumors alleging his predilection for men. Any speculative comment was to be reported immediately, and in turn addressed by local agents.[82] To cite a typical example; a woman visiting her nephew (and FBI agent) in New Orleans related a second-hand story told at her bridge party in Cleveland, for which the offending gossip was severely chastised. According to her sworn statement of apology:

> [Name Withheld] claimed that she never said anything about this [the story of Hoover being queer that she overheard in a Baltimore restaurant] nor had she thought anything about it until the day of this bridge party. She said during the course of the bridge party . . . some mention was made of the Director. One of the girls pointed out that the Director was a bachelor and she wondered why. To this [Name Withheld] . . . replied she understood Mr. Hoover was queer. She said . . . she thought it should not have been made and. . . . she was going to point out to each of those present [each named, with her address, in the report] that her statement was not founded on fact and that she was deeply sorry that she made it and that it should not have been made at all.[83]

Coercive measures had replaced the pink herring as the means of insuring the Director's normalcy, but his motivating impulse seems unchanged. In response to a prominent New Yorker's comment (gleaned in an FBI interrogation) that he had heard the queer rumors, Hoover ranted, "I never heard of this obvious degenerate. Only one with a depraved mind could have such thoughts."[84] His persistent fear expressed here can be crystallized in the motto of the fourth persona: it takes one to know one.

At his most pernicious, Hoover matured after World War II into an avowed and champion homophobe. He manipulated a second sex crime wave in the late 1940s to lubricate the ascendancy of McCarthyism,[85] and by 1951 had unilaterally transformed his Sex Deviate Index Card File into a full-fledged program that provided information regarding the alleged homosexuality of present and past Federal employees (and later university and law enforcement employees) for the express purpose of purging them. Curt Gentry observed: "It was axiomatic, at the time, that the main reason homosexuals should be denied government employment was their susceptibility to blackmail. FBI Director J. Edgar Hoover proved that this was true, by blackmailing them himself."[86]

Whether or not Hoover was homosexual, there is no question that he was preoccupied with those bogeys that threatened his gendered/sexual public persona. His response to this threat began as a rhetorical exercise in passing, only to evolve into a highly sophisticated system of coercion, blackmail, and persecution. One constant seems to have been Hoover's intuition regarding the two passing audiences, dupes whose complicity depended on a performance that simultaneously played to, or attempted to annihilate, clairvoyants. Early on, Hoover's passing domesticated one panic by fanning another, producing the semblance of a man thought to be unimpeachable. As Courtney Ryley Cooper described him, "he has become the voice of honesty against the crime world; for the first time, someone in high office of law enforcement has risen who is able to picture crime in such a way that the average man can understand it and do something about it—because he knows the thing which he is facing."[87] Honest and the archenemy of crime—sex crime, in this context, meaning anti-homosexual—Hoover's passing achieved the perfect deflection. Except, of course, for the fourth persona, those menaces who understood *why* "he knows the thing which he is facing."

THE PERILS OF PASSING

Passing implies peril. Its inventional impulse reverberates in one who feels jeopardized by difference, or perceived difference. It entails a precarious combination of secrecy and disclosure. Its goal, an ethos transparently normative, constitutes less an achievement than a risky venture continuously engaged. As a critical object, it always threatens to elude and ensnare its pursuer. In charting the promise of passing as an object of rhetorical study, let me briefly reflect on these perils.

As rhetorical action, passing is distinguishable from familiar rhetorical situations. Exigence is always dramatically urgent and perpetual; audience is bifurcated between the visible and invisible; trope and argument create parallel and contradictory dimensions of meaning; constraints propel instead of prohibit the unsayable; and consensus is forged largely on deceit. Passing should entice us to explore the closet's rhetoric, a sophisticated persuasive praxis manifested daily by our marginalized predecessors as they "made do" in a broader homophobic culture. To say that the closet is rhetorically significant is to make a historically situated case for the existence of a subversive art of self-fashioning in the public sphere, an art "on the make," as it were, in the presence of specific, and perilous, audiences under palpable and shifting situational constraints.

In this essay I have highlighted features of passing that call to mind Foucault's notion that:

> Silence itself—the things one declines to say, or is forbidden to name, the discretion that is required between different speakers—is less the absolute limit of discourse, the other side from which it is separated by a strict boundary, than an element that functions alongside the things said, with them and in relation to them within over-all strategies. . . . There is not one but many silences, and they are an integral part of the strategies that underlie and permeate discourses.[88]

Pink herring, of course, is a queer version of the familiar tactic of deflection that protects a silent subject avoiding exposure. The stakes in this game of hide and seek, it must be remembered, are high. Unlike its conventional counterpart, pink herring must always deflect and signify at the same time. Obfuscation and intimation are the twin acts of every pass. Paradoxically, passing's silence must prove at once to be utterly mute while speaking incessantly.

This paradox is mandated by the presence of the *fourth persona,* a silent, savvy but discreet audience constituted as collaborator in making duplicitous utterances appear legitimate before an audience of dupes. "It is the double audience," Peter Rabinowitz writes, "and the kind of flaunting that makes it possible, that structurally distinguishes rhetorically passing texts from other complex texts that happen to have hidden meanings beneath the surface."[89] A delicate triangulation is required to invite complicity from a dupe who ultimately aids in constructing the passer's *subversive enthymeme* (and his own deception), all the while evoking the fourth persona as a stealth partner who quietly affirms and colludes by acknowledging the pass. For Hoover, the fourth persona proved menacing instead of comforting, confounding the dynamics of his passing, and inspiring rhetorical innovation with grave consequences for the clairvoyants in his midst.

J. Edgar Hoover was certainly no queer hero or, unfortunately, a passing phase. Simple justice, if not retribution, for his violence against gays and lesbians can be found in the irony that, for all his efforts, he could never escape the "effluvium of rumination" regarding his sexuality. The issue of his relationship with Clyde Tolson persisted throughout his life, fascinating politicians and hairdressers alike. As further penance, we here exact from Hoover lessons on passing he would never willingly have taught. We expose to critical scrutiny a decade in which he suffered the terror of homosexual panic, so as to witness him deflecting suspicion by entrapping homosexuals in a menacing denotation of his own making. He could protect his love story, if there was one, only by passing as the chief hunter of those dangerous bachelors he most resembled.

NOTES

[1]Ray Tucker, "Hist! Who's That," *Colliers* (August 19, 1933), 49.

[2]Male homosociality designates a continuum of non-sexual and sexual relations among men that shape broadly economic, social, and cultural dynamics. The male homosocial continuum is forged by homophobia and therefore distinguishes explicitly (disruptively) between homosexual and homosocial. It is historically contingent, and desire should be understood as an "affective or social force," or the "glue" in these powerful relations. See Eve Kosofsky Sedgwick, *Between Men: English Literature and Male Homosocial Desire* (New York: Columbia University Press, 1985).

[3]Although the panic I describe likely affected lesbians as well, the effects that directly shaped exigence for Hoover specifically related to homosexual males and, therefore, constitute my explicit focus.

[4]"Homosexual panic" refers to one's fear that he might be homosexual, harbor homosexual longings, or be thought homosexual by others. See Edward J. Kempf, *Psychopathology* (St. Louis: Mosby, 1920), 477–515; Sedgwick, *Between Men,* 83–96; Eve Kosofsky Sedgwick, *Epistemology of the Closet* (Berkeley: University of California Press, 1990).

[5]See George Chauncey, *Gay New York: Gender, Urban Culture, and the Making of the Gay Male World, 1890–1940* (New York: Basic Books, 1994); John Loughery, *The Other Side of Silence: Men's Lives and Gay Identities: A Twentieth-Century History* (New York: Henry Holt and Company, 1998); Estelle B. Freedman, "'Uncontrolled Desires': The Response to the Sexual Psychopath, 1920–1960," in *Passion and Power: Sexuality in History,* ed. Kathy Peiss and Christina Simmons (Philadelphia: Temple University Press, 1989).

[6]Richard Gid Powers, *Secrecy and Power: The Life of J. Edgar Hoover* (New York: The Free Press, 1987), 2.

[7]See Richard Gid Powers, *Secrecy and Power,* 172–73; Athan G. Theoharis and John Stuart Cox, *The Boss: J. Edgar Hoover and the Great American Inquisition* (Philadelphia: Temple University Press, 1988), 108; Curt Gentry, *J. Edgar Hoover: The Man and His Secrets* (New York: W. W. Norton, 1991), 190–91.

[8]Anthony Summers, *Official and Confidential: The Secret Life of J. Edgar Hoover* (New York: G. P. Putnam's Sons, 1993).

[9]Athan Theoharis, *J. Edgar Hoover, Sex, and Crime: An Historical Anecdote* (Chicago: Ivan R. Dee, 1995).

[10]Theoharis, *J. Edgar Hoover, Sex, and Crime*, 55.

[11]Theoharis, *J. Edgar Hoover, Sex, and Crime*, 80.

[12]Sissela Bok, *Secrets: On the Ethics of Concealment and Revelation* (New York: Pantheon, 1982), 6.

[13]See Edwin Black, "Secrecy and Disclosure as Rhetorical Forms," *Rhetorical Questions: Studies of Public Discourse* (Chicago: University of Chicago Press, 1992), 51–78.

[14]For discussions of gender/sexual passing, see Sedgwick, *The Epistemology of the Closet;* Judith Butler, *Bodies That Matter: On the Discursive Limits of 'Sex'* (New York: Routledge, 1993); Elaine K. Ginsberg, ed., *Passing and the Fictions of Identity* (Durham: Duke University Press, 1996); George Chauncey, *Gay New York;* Charles E. Morris III, "'The Responsibilities of the Critic': F. O. Matthiessen's Homosexual Palimpsest," *Quarterly Journal of Speech* 84 (August 1998): 261–82.

[15]Peter J. Rabinowitz, "'Betraying the Sender': The Rhetoric and Ethics of Fragile Texts," *Narrative* 2 (October 1994), 202–205.

[16]Amy Robinson, "It Takes One to Know One: Passing and Communities of Common Interest," *Critical Inquiry* 20 (Summer 1994), 715–724.

[17]For an excellent discussion of the "homosexual wink," see James Creech, *Closet Writing/ Gay Reading: The Case of Melville's Pierre* (Chicago: University of Chicago Press, 1993).

[18]Edwin Black, "The Second Persona," *Quarterly Journal of Speech* 56 (1970): 109–119.

[19]Philip Wander, "The Third Persona: An Ideological Turn in Rhetorical Theory," *Central States Speech Journal* 35 (1984): 197–216.

[20]On silence in passing, see Rabinowitz, "'Betraying the Sender,'" 204–205; Sedgwick, *Epist[e]mology of the Closet*, 3–4 and chapter 1.

[21]Charles E. Morris III, "Contextual Twilight/Critical Liminality: J. M. Barrie's *Courage* at St. Andrews, 1922," *Quarterly Journal of Speech* 82 (August 1996): 207–227.

[22]Erving Goffman observes: "The presence of fellow-sufferers (or the wise) introduces a special set of contingencies in regard to passing, since the very techniques used to conceal stigmas may give the show away to someone who is familiar with the tricks of the trade, the assumption being that it takes one (or those close to him) to know one." Goffman, *Stigma: Notes on the Management of Spoiled Identity* (New York: Simon & Schuster, 1963), 85.

[23]Richard Hofstadter, *The Paranoid Style in American Politics and Other Essays* (New York: Alfred A. Knopf, 1965), 3–40. Like Hofstadter, I see the paranoid style as a feeling of persecution systematized in grandiose theories of conspiracy. He distinguishes the political from the "clinical" paranoid by stressing that the latter does not see the conspiracy as directed against him. For the paranoid passer the opposite is true. I find it telling that researchers in the 1930s found an "intimate relationship between paranoidism and homoeroticism," specifically paranoia as a "defense reaction against a repressed homoerotic wish phantasy." James Page and John Warkentin, "Masculinity and Paranoia," *Journal of Abnormal and Social Psychology* 33 (1938): 527–31.

[24]George W. Henry, *All the Sexes: A Study of Masculinity and Femininity* (New York: Rinehart, 1955), 292.

[25]Kevin White, *The First Sexual Revolution: The Emergence of Male Heterosexuality in Modern America* (New York: New York University Press, 1993), 169–71; Howard P. Chudacoff, *The Age of the Bachelor: Creating an American Subculture* (Princeton, New Jersey: Princeton University Press, 1999), 247–50.

[26]"The Bachelors of New York," *New York Times Magazine*, September 9, 1928.

[27]Chudacoff, *The Age of the Bachelor*, 253.

[28]Michael Kimmel, *Manhood in America: A Cultural History* (New York: Free Press, 1996), 199.

[29]La Forest Potter, *Strange Loves: A Study in Sexual Abnormalities* (New York: The Robert Dodsley Company, 1933), 4.

[30]Potter, *Strange Loves,* 101. Chauncey more thoroughly describes the signifiers that bespoke one's status as a pansy, including "unconventional styles in personal grooming," but also carriage, demeanor, dress, and speech, all of which signaled the gender inversion or effeminacy thought to be constitutive of homosexuality. Chauncey, *Gay New York,* 54–56.

[31]See James Levin, *The Gay Novel in America* (New York: Garland, 1991); Vito Russo, *The Celluloid Closet: Homosexuality in the Movies,* Revised Edition (New York: Harper and Row, 1987). On the geographic scope of the craze, see Chauncey, *Gay New York,* 320; David K. Johnson, "The Kids of Fairytown: Gay Male Culture on Chicago's Near North Side in the 1930s," in Brett Beemyn, ed., *Creating a Place for Ourselves: Lesbian, Gay, and Bisexual Community Histories* (New York: Routledge, 1997), 97–118.

[32]Sedgwick, *Between Men,* 86. See also Jonathan Ned Katz, *The Invention of Heterosexuality* (New York: Dutton, 1995).

[33]Chauncey, *Gay New York,* 328.

[34]See Chauncey, *Gay New York,* chapter 12.

[35]See Russo, *The Celluloid Closet;* Felice Flanery Lewis, *Literature, Obscenity, and Law* (Carbondale: Southern Illinois University Press, 1976).

[36]Chauncey, *Gay New York,* 346.

[37]Sedgwick, *Epistemology of the Closet,* 185.

[38]Sedgwick, *Epistemology of the Closet,* 185; *Between Men,* 86–7.

[39]D. A. Miller, "Anal Rope," in *Inside/Out: Lesbian Theories, Gay Theories,* ed. Diana Fuss (New York: Routledge, 1991), 123–29.

[40]D. A. Miller, "Anal Rope," 125.

[41]Sedgwick, *Between Men,* 87.

[42]See Jennifer Terry, *An American Obsession: Science, Medicine, and Homosexuality in Modern Society* (Chicago: University of Chicago Press, 1999), especially chapters 6–8; and George W. Henry, *Sex Variants: A Study in Homosexual Patterns,* 2 vols. (New York: Paul B. Hoeber, 1941).

[43]Terry, *An American Obsession,* 179.

[44]Terry, *An American Obsession,* 214.

[45]Philip Jenkins, *Moral Panic: Changing Concepts of the Child Molester in Modern America* (New Haven: Yale University Press, 1998), chapters 2–4.

[46]"Sex Crime Wave Alarms U.S.," *The Literary Digest* 123 (April 10, 1937), 5.

[47]See "To Counsel Hurley on Sex Crime Laws," and "Views of Conferees," *New York Times* (September 5, 1937), 7; Sheldon Glueck, "Sex Crimes and the Law," *The Nation* 145 (September 25, 1937), 318–20; Charles J. Dutton, "Can We End Sex Crimes?" *The Christian Century* 51 (December 22, 1937), 1594.

[48]"Pedophilia," *Time* 30 (August 23, 1937), 42–44.

[49]Bertram Pollens, *The Sex Criminal* (New York: The Macaulay Company, 1938), 17.

[50]Fredric Wertham, "Psychiatry and the Prevention of Sex Crime," *JAICLC* 28 (1938), 847.

[51]Honorable Austin H. MacCormack, "New York's Present Problem," *Mental Hygiene* 22 (January 1938), 9–10.

[52]See George W. Henry, "Psychogenic Factors in Overt Homosexuality," *The American Journal of Psychiatry* 93 (January 1937), 889–908; Special Issue, "The Challenge of Sex Offenders," *Mental Hygiene* 22 (January 1938), 1–24; George W. Henry, "Social Factors in the Case Histories of One Hundred Under-privileged Homosexuals," *Mental Hygiene* 22 (1938), 591–611; Jack Frosch, "The Sex Offender—A Psychiatric Study," *American Journal of Orthopsychiatry* 9 (October 1939), 761–69.

[53]Pollens, *The Sex Criminal,* 22–23. He notes further, "The problem of homosexuality deserves our attention not only because of the number who commit sexual crimes, but also because of the untold misery which many of them bring to their families in their feeble attempts to cast this shadow from them." Pollens, *The Sex Criminal,* 132–33.

[54]Terry, *An American Obsession,* 272. Katz concurs: "Although all the reported sex crimes concerned adult males and little girls. . . . [t]he use of the same language to refer to

coercive adult-child relations and homosexual relations between consenting adults confounded these behaviors in the public mind." Jonathan Ned Katz, *Gay/Lesbian Almanac: A New Documentary* (New York: Carroll & Graf, 1983), 531.

[55] Potter, *Strange Loves,* 62.

[56] "Crimes against Children," *The Literary Digest* 124 (October 2, 1937), 16.

[57] Parisex [Henry Gerber), "In Defense of Homosexuality." In *A Homosexual Emancipation Miscellany, c. 1835–1952* (New York: Arno Press, 1975), 296.

[58] Courtney Ryley Cooper, "Getting the Jump on Crime," *American Magazine* 116 (August 1933), 100. Cooper wrote several books and twenty-three articles on the FBI in *American Magazine* between 1933 and 1940, ushering Hoover into the cultural spotlight. See Richard Gid Powers, *G-Men: Hoover's FBI in American Popular Culture* (Carbondale: Southern Illinois University Press, 1983).

[59] Powers, *G-Men,* 113.

[60] Theoharis and Cox, *The Boss,* 111–16; Gentry, *J. Edgar Hoover,* 153; Powers, *G-Men,* 33–34; *Secrecy and Power,* 180–85.

[61] See Powers, *Secrecy and Power,* 169–73; Theoharis and Cox, *The Boss,* 107–08, 133–34; Gentry, *J. Edgar Hoover,* 159, 190–192; William W. Turner, *Hoover's F.B.I.* (1970; New York: Thunder's Mouth Press, 1993), 80–82.

[62] "Sleuth School," *Time* 26 (August 5, 1935), 12.

[63] Tucker, "Hist! Who's That," 49.

[64] Jack Alexander, "Profiles: The Director-II," *The New Yorker* 13 (October 2, 1937), 21.

[65] See Ralph Blumenthal, *Stork Club: America's Most Famous Nightspot and the Lost World of Café Society* (Boston: Little, Brown, and Company, 2000), 38–39; Gentry, *J. Edgar Hoover,* 159, 192; Turner, *Hoover's F.B.I.,* 80–81.

[66] Theoharis and Cox, *The Boss,* 108.

[67] See Alexander, "Profiles: The Director-II," 26; Alexander, "Profiles: The Director-III," *The New Yorker* 13 (October 9, 1937), 22. See also Gentry, *J. Edgar Hoover,* 182–188; Theoharis and Cox, *The Boss,* 136–37.

[68] Ralph de Toledano, *J. Edgar Hoover: The Man and His Time* (New Rochelle, New York: Arlington House, 1973), 132.

[69] *Washington Herald,* August 28, 1933.

[70] Gentry, *J. Edgar Hoover,* 179–80.

[71] Frederick L. Collins, "The Private Life of J. Edgar Hoover," *Liberty Magazine* 17 (March 16, 1940), 10. Collins argued that Hoover certainly could have married but seldom went to parties, had incredibly high standards, and cared more for the job than "domesticity." Agents in the 1950s similarly declared, "He *is* married, to the FBI." *New York Times,* October 8, 1959.

[72] Loughery, *The Other Side of Silence,* 101.

[73] Edgar Hoover, "War on the Sex Criminal," *New York Herald Tribune,* September 26, 1937. All subsequent quotations are from the text.

[74] Poller, *Strange Loves,* 10–11.

[75] Terry, *An American Obsession,* 189; 275–281.

[76] Quoted in "Sex Crime Wave Alarms U.S.," 7.

[77] "Crimes Against Children," 16. See also Special Issue, "The Challenge of Sex Offenders," *Mental Hygiene* 22 (January 1938), 1–24.

[78] Sedgwick, *Between Men,* 87.

[79] John Edgar Hoover, "Combatting Lawlessness: America's Most Destructive Disease," *Vital Speeches of the Day* 4 (February 5, 1938), 269–72. All subsequent quotations are from the text.

[80] Historians typically cite Freedman, "'Uncontrolled Desires,'" 206. See also Jack Frosch and Walter Bromberg, "The Sex Offender—A Psychiatric Study," *American Journal of Orthopsychiatry* 9 (October 1939), 761; Sheldon S. Levy, "Interaction of Institutions and Policy Groups: The Origin of Sex Crime Legislation," *The Lawyer and Law Notes* 5 (Spring 1951), 7; Terry, *American Obsession,* 271–72, 323–24; Jenkins, *Moral Panic,* 55–56.

[81] Athan Theoharis, *From the Secret Files of J. Edgar Hoover* (Chicago: Ivan R. Dee, 1993), 292, 357–58.

[82] Name Withheld #75 and #113 folders and John Monroe folder, Official and Confidential File of FBI Director J. Edgar Hoover; The Director folder, Official and Confidential File of FBI Assistant Director Louis Nichols.

[83] Memo, June 30, 1943, Name Withheld #75 folder, Hoover O & C File.

[84] Memo, June 27, 1944, Name Withheld #75 folder, Hoover O & C File.

[85] For the second sex crime panic, see George Chauncey, Jr., "The Postwar Sex Crime Panic," in *True Stories from the American Past*, ed. William Graebner (New York: McGraw-Hill, 1993), 160–178.

[86] Gentry, *J. Edgar Hoover*, 413.

[87] Courtney Ryley Cooper, "Foreword," in J. Edgar Hoover, *Persons in Hiding* (Boston: Little, Brown, 1938), xviii.

[88] Michel Foucault, *The History of Sexuality*, vol. I, *An Introduction* (New York: Pantheon, 1978), 27.

[89] Rabinowitz, "'Betraying the Sender,'" 203.

RIDING IN CARS BETWEEN MEN

JOHN M. SLOOP

The car has become an article of dress without which we feel uncertain, unclad, and incomplete in the urban compound. . . . Cars have become the real population of our cities, with a resulting loss of human scale. . . .

Marshall McLuhan[1]

What happens when women drive cars, instead of adorning men's cars, instead of sitting, fixed and still, draped across them? What happens when women wear cars instead of clothes?

Sharon Willis[2]

The highs and lows of NASCAR and ARCA driver Deborah Renshaw's 2002 racing season were extreme to say the least.[3] During this one year, Renshaw first saw her star rise rapidly as the dual effect of her skill as a driver and of her role as a "victim" in a well-publicized "conspiracy" at the Nashville Speedway. By season's end, however, Renshaw's fortunes reversed as she was involved in a near career-ending disaster when the car she was driving during a practice session broadsided another car, instantly killing driver Eric Martin. While a number of lessons have been drawn from this case by race officials, it is also useful as one route by which cultural critics might draw lessons about the intersections of popular understandings of the proper performance of gender and the relationship between body media (i.e., prosthetics broadly defined) and the gendered body. As I will illustrate, first, the constraints of gender performativity—at least as described by Judith Butler[4]—are thrown into relief not only in the *reported* actions and statements of those involved in this case *but also* in the discourse reporters use to describe those actions and statements.[5] Second, while some contemporary discussions of the posthuman body (i.e., the changing meaning of the body as it merges with a wide variety of prosthetics and technologies) suggest possibilities for the blurring of gender norms, this case highlights the cultural constraints on such transitions.

The story, *as conveyed primarily through print news reports*, unfolds as follows.[6] In early 2002, one who followed the lower divisions of NASCAR would likely have begun to notice the name "Deborah Renshaw" appearing repeatedly. Not only was Renshaw racing on a weekly basis, but she was also placing well in many of those races, for a short time leading the point standings for the weekly series at the Nashville Fairgrounds Speedway. Moreover, and perhaps more pointedly, Renshaw was being held forth as the "prototype" of female drivers by those in NASCAR circles who thought female drivers would be a way to expand the demographic of NASCAR's fan base. In short, she was positioned as a marketable female, combining driving skills with "ladylike" attractiveness.

In mid-July, however, events on the racing circuit moved Renshaw from the pages of local (regional and sport) press coverage to a broader realm of sports and news interest, garnering interview opportunities with Connie Chung, Bryant Gumble, and *The Regis and Kelly Show,* and news coverage in large market dailies as well as *USA Today.*[7] Here is what is reported to have happened. On 14 July, competing driver Mark Day pooled money from almost all of the other (male) drivers racing that night, entered a car which pitted early in the race, and posted the $3,600 fee required to have another driver's engine inspected.[8] Understanding that the protest was a plot by most, if not all, of the male drivers, Nashville Fairgrounds Speedway President Dennis Grau received permission from NASCAR officials to void the protest. Renshaw's team, confident that the engine met regulations, insisted that Grau have it broken down and inspected. By the time the inspection was over, Renshaw had been disqualified. The inspectors found a cylinder hold less than one centimeter too large—a violation that Grau claimed would not by itself have given Renshaw's car any advantage. Nonetheless, rules dictated that Renshaw's sixth place finish, and the season points that would be accrued with that finish, be forfeited. In effect, the points she forfeited in this one race also ended her quest for the season title at the track.

The day following the protest and forfeiture, Renshaw declared publicly that she would never race in Nashville again, feeling humiliated and at risk because she was surrounded by male drivers who had chosen to gang up on her. However, public outcry against the group of male drivers—accompanied by dual assurances by high-level NASCAR officials that Renshaw would not face such behavior again and that she (and her family) would be protected—encouraged her enough that she agreed to return to the track. When she did return, it was not only to the track but also to a media environment in which she was now in the role of the "star female driver" who had been ganged up on by a large number of boys—boys whose masculinity had been threatened by her driving skills.[9] Moreover, precisely because of the attention that was given to the plot, NASCAR team owner Rick Goodwin also became aware of Renshaw. While acknowledging that he had never heard of Renshaw before the controversy, he hired her to be the driver of his Busch Series car for the 2003 season.[10] Ultimately, the plot against Renshaw worked rhetorically in her favor, enabling her to garner a larger fan base, more sponsorship, a "promotion" for the 2003 season, and the opportunity to race faster cars on the ARCA circuit in 2002.[11]

With trouble seemingly behind her, Renshaw drove in a number of races at both small tracks and on the ARCA circuit with longer tracks and faster cars. In early October, while practicing at Lowe's Motor Speedway in Concorde, NC, for the EasyCare 150, Renshaw's car broadsided the car driven by racer Eric Martin, who was killed instantly by the impact. While Renshaw underwent surgery for multiple fractures in her left foot and ankle, drivers and sports reporters began to question her skills, her level of responsibility for Martin's death, and, finally, ARCA safety regulations. As the year came to a close, not only did ARCA institute new policies as a result of this incident, but Renshaw lost her sponsorship deal with Goodwin and was implicitly and explicitly blamed for Martin's death.

When the discursive field that surrounded Renshaw during these events—a discourse that helped produce and resignify her "femininity" in this "masculine" domain—is understood as partially the product of the gendered history of the automobile, we have an interesting location from which to investigate the ways in which the "common sense" ideology of mass culture *encourages* the reiteration of particular gender norms.[12] Thus, I focus specifically on the public discussion of Renshaw's story both as a way of bringing the sedimented discourses of gender's cultural "common sense" into relief and as a way of troubling those norms and expectations.[13] I begin by outlining some of my assumptions about the automobile as a technology or (prosthetic) medium with implications for gender, gender's performative qualities, and, finally, the historical articulations made between and among gender, automobiles and stock car racing. Second, I provide a critical reading of the discourse concerning the plot against Renshaw early in the season and reporting about Renshaw after the death of driver Eric Martin. Ultimately, I see this case, like all cases of public controversy with gender as a primary focus, as a location or opportunity to problematize the particular configuration of gender performance and gender expectations loosely shared in contemporary US culture, as well as a route to further conversations about the body's relationship to technology.[14]

THE AUTOMOBILE AS PROSTHETIC AND CULTURAL OBJECT

To begin to think about a relationship between cars and gender is to think of the automobile both as a *medium or prosthetic* for the body and as a *discursive object* that enters a culture with preexisting gender/sexual meanings. That is, we must think about the car both as an "extension of the self" and as an object of ideological meanings. Ultimately, there is a rhetorical tension between the ways in which the "automobile as medium/prosthetic" encourages an erasure of the importance of gender (via McLuhan's "loss of human scale") and sedimented cultural understandings of gender and of the automobile (Sharon Willis is concerned, after all, with women wearing cars rather than clothes).

In the first epigraph of this essay, Marshall McLuhan asks that the car—like all technologies—be understood as a prosthetic, yet another "extension of man" [sic]. From this perspective, one interested in gender would ask, "Regardless of the cultural context in which the automobile emerged, what are its influences on cultural understandings of gender or sexuality?" That is, what are the ways in which the existence of the automobile as a dominant technology changed or transformed cultural understandings of gender because of the ways the car altered our relationship with geographic space and time?[15] As cars become readily available, obviously enough, space and distance are changed; we can cover more ground and move more efficiently with the car than without, and this efficiency alters social relations and the meaning of particular locations. For example, as John Howard illustrates in his history of male homosexuality in the southern United States, as more and more people began to own cars, gay spaces—and a sense of a gay community—could develop more easily: "The automobile provided not only the means of transport, but also a place of intersection. The quasi-public space of the interior became the site for communication."[16] Transportation allowed the creation of a larger sense of communication and confirmation of marginal sexualities, and, as a result, it helped blur stable definitions and essential qualities.[17] Further, Scharff suggests that the very existence of cars helped problematize gender because it began to blur public and "private" or domestic spaces, encouraging a slow devolution of the assignment of males to the public and females to the private.[18]

More directly, drawing upon the well-known work of Donna Haraway, Gilles Deleuze, Claudia Springer, and others, Rosi Braidotti has recently addressed the potential of contemporary "prosthetic"/cyborg technologies to aid a cultural rethinking of the meaning of the (post)-human body.[19] Braidotti notes that one common characteristic of many early theories of the post-human body is a slightly utopian tendency to underscore the ways in which the human/technology merge aids a blurring or rethinking of gender subject positions. In such an equation, the automobile becomes one of many technological "prosthetics" which function as a supposedly gender-troubling/gender-blurring extension of the body. Hence, if we think of the car as body covering or as an extension of the body, it is a costume or prosthetic that is equally open to all drivers regardless of gender/sexuality and that functions "equally" for all, making each person equally fast, similarly shaped.

Only a moment's reflection, however, would tell us that the equation between technology and culture is not quite that smooth. Indeed, as John Jordan recently observed in drawing upon contemporary scholarship on the cyborg imaginary, notions of smooth cyberbodies are being challenged as undelivered and perhaps undeliverable.[20] For example, in the case of automobiles, not only do most of us have some vague idea of what colloquially constitutes a "male" and a "female" car, but we know that cars, like all new technologies, enter a culture with gendered meanings that in turn shape its meaning. For example, as both Scharff and Sean O'Connell respectively discuss in their histories of gender and automobiles in the United States and in British society, the automobile was gendered since its inception, since marketing concerns drove our cultural understanding of the car almost as soon as it became a "product." As Scharff observes, the automobile was "born in a masculine manger and when women sought to claim its power, they invaded a male domain."[21] Indeed, in underscoring this point, Scharff points out that when the car first appeared as a commodity, the word "traffic" was most commonly used as a disparaging word to refer to notions like "trafficking in drugs" or the ways in which women of low character were said to "traffic in charms."[22] A female driver was the cause of gender trouble, as no *proper woman,* a woman who fittingly "reiterated the expectations of gender behavior," could drive the car by definition.[23] Moreover, Scharff argues that designers such as Henry Ford always tended to see the automobile—precisely because it was loud, dirty, and mechanical— as articulated strictly along gendered lines as a masculine machine.[24]

While the automobile's representation has certainly altered over time, Scharff's analysis illustrates that "while the auto transformed the particular places men and women went and the things they did, people remained, at the general level, embedded in their gendered identities, just as gender remained a critical category of American culture."[25] Similarly, Judy Wajcman, acknowledging technology as a social construct and "femininity" and "masculinity" as malleable concepts, argues that technology in general is represented as "male" and, hence, to enter the world of the car, "to learn its language, women have first to forsake their femininity."[26] Finally, while O'Connell, like Scharff, sees "women motorists" as "symbolic of shifting gender relations," his overall story is one in which the car is understood through the normative regulation of femininity and masculinity.[27] Hence, for example, even when changes in the car were recommended and desired by both men and women (e.g., the ignition switch, the enclosed roof), such changes were represented as a feminization of the car in that they made the car less "manly." Even though women were driving and such changes became ubiquitous, these changes were also ones which reinforced, rearticulated, resignified cultural meanings of men and women.[28] This "founding" ideology of the car haunts our present, continuing to factor into how we understand cars, how we market cars, and how we interact with other forms of transportation.[29] In short, this ideological configuration writes gender onto the meaning of the prosthetics functions.

On the one hand, then, the automobile is a technology or medium that potentially encourages at least a situational erasure of gender—anyone can *wear* a car, and, because cars in some *senses* replace our bodies, they erase gender difference in particular ways. On the other, cultural historians have illustrated that the car was born within a culture of bi-gendered norms and has been consistently marketed and understood through the lens of those norms. As Braidotti notes of other media, the "alleged triumph of high-technologies is not matched by a leap of the human imagination to create new images and representations. Quite on the contrary, what I notice is the repetition of very old themes."[30] While gender may indeed have been altered by the automobile, the circulation of common-sense ideology tends toward stability (i.e., people interpret events through the lens of their previous understandings of the world). The gendered body may move inside the structure of the automobile, but that body's gender still *matters*. Drawing on Fiske and Hartley, we might say that public arguments tend to "claw" meanings back to the familiar rather than to the new or transitional.[31] Because of a desire for stable definitions, and because of a market system that rewards the popular or familiar over the strange and indeterminate, gender norms are difficult—although clearly not impossible—to displace.

Together, then, these two different impulses in the relationship of the automobile and the body emerge in the discourse surrounding the Renshaw case. On the one hand, because anybody can assumedly drive a car with equal skill regardless of gender, those involved in competitive racing must deny gender's significance in a way that is not true of most other sports. On the other hand, because automobiles and all body technologies have traditionally been articulated on hetero-normative, bi-gendered lines, it is never possible that just any-*body* is driving a car; rather, it is always a particular type of body—and the meanings articulated with that body—in the driver's seat. As a result, the Deborah Renshaw case, a case in which a woman finds herself in trouble (gender and otherwise) in a "male" sport, is perhaps the ideal location for understanding some of the contours of our shared gender ideology. Further, in laying bare the articulations that hold together cars and normative gender assumptions, such an analysis hopefully also helps dismantle such assumptions.

THE TROUBLE WITH DEBORAH RENSHAW, A "FIRST WOMAN" RACER

Homosocial Desire between Cars

In her classic analysis of homosocial desire, *Between Men*, Eve Sedgwick argues that homosocial (rather than homoerotic or homosexual) desire functions in part to mark the differences between men and women. More strongly, Sedgwick suggests that historically different shades of male and female homosociality may be taken as "articulations and mechanisms of the enduring inequality of power between women and men."[32] More often than not, Sedgwick observes, male homosocial relations exclude women from political formations generally held by men: "We can go even further . . . to say that in any male-dominated society, there is a special relationship between male homosocial desire and the structures for maintaining and transmitting patriarchal power."[33] Sedgwick is not constructing a facile model that configures women as overtly disciplined and excluded by men in a heavy-handed manner. Rather, Sedgwick argues that men and women as a whole act in what could be considered a "common sense" fashion, assuming and naturalizing gender binarisms as the basis for much human behavior.

In the context of this case, when Renshaw began *outperforming* many of the men on the Nashville circuit, homosocial bonding can be seen as at work in the drivers' attempt to have Renshaw disqualified, excluding her from a traditionally masculine space. If we read Renshaw's success as a disruption of the male driver's "oval jerk," their conspiracy can be read as a protection of a homosocial space.[34] Moreover, and perhaps more importantly, public denunciations of this "male" conspiracy—denunciations which were seemingly meant to critique exclusion on the basis of gender—inadvertently reinforced the very gender binarisms the male drivers were protecting.

I wish to suggest that this hetero-normative assumption is rearticulated publicly in the following ways. First, despite repeated claims that gender is irrelevant in racing because the technology equalizes competition, Renshaw is repeatedly described in terms that emphasize her traditional female appearance and "highly cultured" feminine interests that are seemingly at odds with the aesthetic and cultural position of stock-car racing. Second, the male-female binarism is maintained through public discussions that describe the disqualification plot as a "soap opera" and as a "gang bang" and represent Renshaw as a traditional female victim. Third, Renshaw's driving ability is described through the cultural frame of the "bad female driver," with her success said to emerge solely as the result of public fascination with her gender.

The repeated claims made by Renshaw and others concerning the irrelevance of gender in racing emerges as the product of both the requirement that a competitive playing field be level for all and as a result of her featured role in what Ruth Rosen has called the "first woman" story—a mediated narrative of the "first" woman to enter any traditional male domains.[35] Focusing on mass mediated stories that arose around "first women" in the 1960s and early 1970s, Rosen observes several common themes: the reports discuss the "first woman's" appearance and social status (i.e., married, children) and consistently deny gender's role in the lives of these women. More specifically, "first women" overtly claim that "being a woman had never harmed them, nor had it helped them," that men do not express hostility toward them, and that they feel just like "one of the guys."[36] Finally, "first women" repeatedly stress that success comes from merit and from making the right choices.[37] While Renshaw is clearly not the "first woman race car driver," such racers remain rare enough on any given circuit that much of the coverage of Renshaw puts her in a "sole woman" narrative that, despite its appearance 30 years after the stories Rosen reports, repeats much of their logic.

For example, in press coverage of Renshaw appearing before the "plot" at the Nashville Speedway, gender is repeatedly invoked in order to deny its significance. In an article in the *Atlanta Journal-Constitution*, Renshaw makes the following claim, inadvertently offering a summary of what Sarah Projansky refers to as "equality and choice postfeminism":[38] "It's not gender that helps you win. It's the *choices* you make. . . . A woman is just as capable behind the wheel as any man."[39] Moreover, an Associated Press story quotes competing driver David Binkley as observing of Renshaw: "When she puts that helmet on and climbs into her race car you can't tell if she's a man or a woman—she's *just* a race driver" (emphasis mine).[40] In an almost identical statement made after he hired Renshaw, team owner Goodwin claims that "When you sit in that seat, you're not a man or a woman. You're a driver."[41] What I want to emphasize is that such denials of gender relevance are always built with a caveat that is impossible to bring to fruition. The claim—overt or implied—is that one is neither male nor female "*when* you sit in that seat," but it is impossible to sit in that seat removed from cultural understandings when doing so. Bodies *matter,* Butler might remind us here, as they are interpreted through cultural meanings and discourses. Hence, one never sits in a driver's seat as an unmarked body; the body always signifies, always matters. In this case, Renshaw's body—a woman's body—is found in a place (not only a car but a race car) in which it does not "naturally" belong. Moreover, because Renshaw was so successful, because she was "passing" so convincingly, her gender became even more of an issue. The outcome of the races she participated in contradicted the cultural understandings of the meaning of *that* body in *that* seat. According to cultural gender logic, she was not supposed to win.

Renshaw, then, finds herself in a problematic situation. On the one hand, in order to fit fairly within the ideology of technology and "fair competition," she and others must continually emphasize that, in racing, gender is unmarked. On the other hand, cultural articulations of her body in a race car are ones that trouble gender expectations. As a result, as Butler notes, when gender expectations are troubled, the disciplinary constraints of culture (which work through representations, through public discussion, through the ways in which individuals discipline one another in everyday behavior) operate to encourage the gender-troubling parties to rearticulate their behavior to fit the expectations of proper gender behavior (or to explain how the improper behavior—here, racing—is only one aberration in an otherwise proper performance).

Day, the leader of the disqualification plot, may make the crassest male-female gender distinctions when he muses, "Maybe we're all a bunch of redneck racers. Maybe most drivers won't say it, but if they look at a woman, they'll think, 'What's she doing' here?' Hey, it's a man's sport. That's just the way it is," but he is certainly not alone in rearticulating those differences.[42] For example, Renshaw's own reported voice and those of others describing her consistently work to emphasize her "feminine" and refined qualities. Renshaw's official website suggests that she "is not exactly the picture of your typical stock car driver. She is an educated, 26-year-old with a Bachelor's Degree."[43] Reporter Jack Wilkinson describes her in the *Atlanta Journal-Constitution* as different than male drivers, in effect, as feminine: "She is an attractive, pony tailed, personable, 25-year-old college graduate, the well-heeled daughter of a wealthy car dealer."[44] Charleston's *Post and Courier* describes Renshaw as a "daddy's girl" with dark brown hair.[45] Similarly, a *Roanoke Times and World News* reporter first observes Renshaw walking "into the Darlington Raceway media center wearing low-rider jeans with a wide black belt and a tight black knit shirt that exposed her midriff," then notes that "Renshaw has good looks, a college degree and acting school experience."[46] Finally, Renshaw's appearance on a local (Nashville) sports talk show also provides an example of her representation as a "proper" woman, different than we expect from women involved in racing. During a commercial break on the show, host Hope Hines informs Renshaw that the first three questions will be coming from women. He then pauses and adds that while the "first three callers are women, we don't know if they're ladies." Turning back and referring to Renshaw as "Ms. Deborah," he ultimately articulates Renshaw as a proper lady, as opposed to what we expect from women involved in racing.[47] Indeed, Day might say, what is *she* doing here?

Reporting about the disqualification plot and Renshaw's behavior as a result of the plot also functions to stress Renshaw's proper performance of femininity (indeed, her *difference* from male drivers). The overall arch of the story as covered in multiple newspaper accounts would run something like this: Renshaw is the star of a soap opera in which a group of boys attempted to chase her away from their playground. While Renshaw at first tears up and runs away, she ultimately decides to stand up to the bullies. For example, an *Atlanta Journal-Constitution* article is headlined "A Stock Car Soap Opera."[48] The body of the article, after emphasizing Renshaw's good looks and personality, describes the events as "a juicy little stock car soap opera" in which the male racers ganged up on Renshaw in a fit of jealousy. In line with the representation of the event as soap opera, several reporters make note of Renshaw's emotional response to the disqualification, once again emphasizing and naturalizing gender difference despite the simultaneous attempts at gender erasure. For example, Teresa Walker of the Associated Press writes that while Renshaw was aware that some of the men at the track resented her, "their collusion to get her car disqualified got the best of her. . . . Renshaw sat in the stands and cried. 'I'm a woman and women tend to have more emotions than men do, and they show it in different ways'."[49]

This narrative furthermore lends itself repeatedly to emphasizing that the "plot" pitted "boys" against "girls." Renshaw claims in the *Commercial Appeal* (Memphis), for example, that she had decided to return to racing because she "didn't want to leave the perception that the boys ran the girl off."[50] Elsewhere, Renshaw is "some hot-shot girl,"[51] a "girl playing a *man*'s game" (emphasis mine),[52] a "girl role model."[53] In each case, we have a clear articulation that the differences between Renshaw and the male drivers is a vast one, marking Renshaw as different than her opponents and similar to other women.

Descriptions of the plot itself, and the ways the male drivers and Renshaw are configured in this plot, hauntingly recreate the dynamics of homosocial/homosexual triangulation and exclusion. Indeed, the single most common metaphor to describe the "conspiracy" is that it was a case of a group of boys "ganging up on a girl." This is a metaphor that invokes violent exclusion through physical and sexual (i.e., gang bang) terror. The language of such stories creates a scenario in which men gather together as one to attempt to eliminate or exclude Renshaw; that is, they create bonds *between men* in order to exclude the "so-called feminine in men" and the masculine in women.[54]

Throughout the coverage of the disqualification plot, one finds persistent references to a gang of men who pick on an innocent "girl." On several occasions when interviewed about her initial decision to quit racing in Nashville, Renshaw herself employs the metaphor: "When 12 or 13 men gang up . . . [t]he good ol' boys can have their track back."[55] Reporter John Romano of the *St. Petersburg Times* more bluntly observes, "If you have not heard the story, a bunch of male drivers ganged up on the track's only female competitor in a shameful display of piston envy."[56] Similarly, reporter Jack Wilkinson summarizes the story as one of "A bunch of good ol' boy drivers ganging up on . . . this poor *innocent little girl*" (emphasis mine).[57]

As Sedgwick points out, the discourse of the "gang bang" always implies a strong homosocial (sometimes homosexual) desire between the male aggressors. Hence, the understanding of the "plot" as a group of men attempting to exclude Renshaw also works to reconfigure the "proper performance" of masculinity of the men involved in the plot, especially the leaders. For example, the crowds at the Nashville race track the following weeks reportedly not only began to openly support Renshaw more enthusiastically than they had before, but also began to openly question the masculinity of the male drivers. Reporter Jack Wilkinson provides the following illustration of one fan's reaction at seeing Day the week following the disqualification: "'Crybaby!' cried [racing fan] Joe Ryman . . . over a cascading chorus of boos. 'You've always been a little *sissy crybaby*!'" (emphasis mine).[58] Moreover, racing fan Harold Bryan reportedly began to shout that all of the conspirators were a "bunch of wimp rednecks."[59] Such terms—"wimp," "sissy" and "crybaby"— coupled with the narrative in which the men ganged up on an innocent girl works in a cultural logic which questions the men's ability to properly perform *as* men.

The male-female binary is similarly upheld by the employment of the historically grounded representation of women as unskilled drivers. In *Taking the Wheel*, Scharff observes that although cars as a technology were represented early in their history as dangerous machines, when they became seemingly essential or necessary for culture, the blame for deaths by automobiles had to shift from the technology itself to particular users of the technology. (If the technology itself was at fault, the solution is to get rid of the technology. If, however, particular users are at fault, the solution is to keep them from using the technology.) While blame was initially placed on pedestrians for accidents, blame slowly moved to female drivers. Scharff observes, "Early critics of women drivers, much like their contemporaries who opposed women's entry into higher education and woman suffrage, cited three presumed sources of women's inferiority at the wheel: emotional instability, physical weakness, and intellectual deficiencies."[60] Such charges are clearly linked to almost all transportation technology. As Constance Penley and Projansky have illustrated, "lack of skill" charges were made against both Christa McAuliffe and child airplane pilot Jessica Dubroff in narratives and news reports published after the Challenger disaster and the Dubroff tragedy, respectively.[61]

Given the historical roots of this trope and our awareness of its functioning in contemporary culture, when one claims that Renshaw is a "bad driver," one is once again illustrating that Renshaw can never be "just" a driver. Rather, claims about her relative lack of skills once again discipline her back into the proper iteration of cultural understandings of "femininity" and therefore once again reiterate the gender norms themselves. Hence, when Day tells an Associated Press reporter that he questions "the ability of women to compete," finding most of them to be bad drivers, he reiterates this norm.[62] More directly, when Day tells reporter Teresa Walker, "I'm not upset at Deborah because she's a woman. I'm upset at her because she's a bad driver,"[63] he simultaneously denies the importance of gender and reinvokes its proper performative iteration.

In sum, in the discourse surrounding the disqualification plot, we see the ways in which—again, despite the insistence that gender is invisible in the racing arena— gender consistently raises its head to generally reinforce traditional and "proper" cultural understandings of gender and sexuality. Combining our cultural understandings of "male" and "female" behaviors with the articulations of gender/ sexuality which have historically emerged around cars, we find a discursive field that is *fraught with a tendency toward stability*. That is, while meanings change, and while the "proper iterations" of gender/sexuality are indeed historical, the intersections of gender, occupation, and automobiles create a discourse that partially re-stabilizes when faced with transgression (although never completely).

Moreover, given the economic costs of racing, which require that drivers be both skilled and attractive in order to gain sponsorship, Renshaw finds both ideological and economic incentives for proper gender behavior. Renshaw, like all "first women," is represented as highly cultured and educated, hard working, and able to conclude that gender is irrelevant, while she simultaneously is faced with a culture that not only consistently tests her proper femininity but also provides her with economic incentives for proper performance. In the end, despite the discourse of gender blindness articulated with prosthetic technologies, gender largely overdetermines, rearticulating and re-signifying the gender of the body in that car.

Judging and Regulating Renshaw

O'Connell observes that by 1993, over half a million deaths had occurred on British highways alone as a result of automobile accidents.[64] As I noted above, in public arguments, this high number of deaths must be balanced against the benefits the technology brings to a society. Again, rather than place the blame on the technology itself, public discourse could justify the use of the car more effectively if the blame were put on individual types of drivers, or other factors external to the technology itself (e.g., poorly designed roads, insufficient laws). Early on, and despite "factual evidence" to the contrary, female drivers became an effective and convincing scapegoat in the public imaginary.[65] One of the implications of this configuration of women as dangerous drivers is that new laws and regulations concerning "automotive safety" often were created and/or enforced only after highly publicized accidents involving women.[66] As I will argue below, in the death of driver Eric Martin, this familiar pattern emerges, one clearly articulated along the lines of gender. Not only are Renshaw's general driving skills called into question as a result of the accident, but new track rules and regulations that would have been useful previous to the accident are only called for and enacted afterwards.

To recall, in early October 2002, while Renshaw was practicing at Lowe's Motor Speedway in Concord, NC, for the Easy Care 150 ARCA RE/MAX race, peer driver Eric Martin lost control of his car in the fourth turn of the 1.5 mile track, evidently as the result of a blown tire. Renshaw, a half track behind Martin, came around turn four—reportedly 15 seconds after his blow out—at 160 mph, broadsiding Martin's car and killing him instantly.[67] The press coverage that followed the accident, in addition to persistently retelling the story of the "plot" against Renshaw in Nashville, implicates Renshaw as the cause.[68]

For instance, on the day following the accident, reporter Lindsey Young helps us wonder: "At question is why Renshaw, who according to eye witnesses hit Martin several seconds . . . after three other cars had avoided Martin's car, was not informed of Martin's spin or did not see the car."[69] Given a narrative setting in which we are reminded repeatedly that female drivers are very rare, we are invited to presume that the three cars which avoided the accident were all driven by men. Further, Tony Fabrizio of the *Tampa Tribune* observes that "something terrible had to go wrong for her to have hit Martin at nearly full speed. Witnesses estimate that the collision took place as much as 15 seconds after Martin's initial wreck."[70] If others had avoided Martin's car, we are asked to wonder, why did Renshaw, with 15 seconds' warning, have the accident?

In the days that followed, two arguments crystallized. First, Renshaw was unprepared as a driver to race in this league. Second, new regulations were needed to force racing teams to be more careful in the future. An example of the first argument appears in the *Chattanooga Times* when Track President H. A. "Humpy" Wheeler and driver Bobby Labonte are said to have "expressed surprise that Renshaw didn't know what was ahead of her," and both wondered "if she was qualified to be racing on Lowe's 1.5 mile oval."[71] Chris Jenkins of *USA Today* investigates on-line discussion sites and notes that Renshaw's lack of skill became the primary focus almost immediately: "Big-Time drivers were questioning her right to race such powerful cars. . . . The implication: She was in over her head and now somebody was dead."[72] Further, after reporting that Winston Cup drivers had declared Renshaw "guilty" in kangaroo courts up and down the garage area the day after the accident, Jenkins quotes Wayne Hixon, the owner of Martin's car, as saying that he did not "think Renshaw belonged on the track. 'It is racing, some of it is,' he says, 'but some of it is stupidity.'"[73]

In a second line of argument, calls for new regulations meant to protect drivers against incompetence are raised as a result of the accident. Although Lowe's speedway had witnessed eight driver's deaths since opening, many presumably from a similar "cause" (i.e., the fact that the driver's spotters—those who warn drivers about accidents on the track—were not required to sit in the grandstand during practice sessions),[74] calls for new regulations did not emerge or were not effective until after (and seemingly as a result of) the Renshaw-Martin accident.

Paralleling the ways in which Renshaw is blamed for the accident, calls for regulation emerge almost immediately in news reports. For example, Jerry Gappens, the spokesman for the Speedway, noted the day after the accident that "this is something ARCA officials need to look at."[75] Similarly, the *New York Times* reported that ARCA series president Ron Drager wanted to see a change in rules as a result of the accident.[76] Tying the two lines of argument together, Tony Fabrizio of the *Tampa Tribune* argues that the accident should not only force ARCA to change rules about spotters, but also investigate rule changes that might keep inexperienced drivers like Renshaw off the track.[77] A mere three days after the accident, ARCA indeed did pass new regulations that required spotters to be in the grandstand whenever team drivers were on the track.[78] Hopefully, it is obvious that I am not suggesting that these new regulations were a "bad idea"—clearly, this is an easily implemented precaution. Rather, what I want to point out is the fact that the regulation became an exigency only after this particular accident.

A comparison of the Renshaw case to discourse and actions following the death of Dale Earnhardt at NASCAR's Daytona 500 indicates some gendered differences. In February 2001, *USA Today*'s Jenkins notes that "Three drivers died of similar severe head injuries last year. Justifiably, the cry goes out: What can be done to make racing safer?"[79] In this case, however, reports make it clear that any pressures for change in safety regulations are emerging from outside the sport rather than inside and that the accident was inherent to racing itself rather than the fault of any individual, including driver Sterlin Marlin, who was involved in the accident. For example, Gwen Knapp of the *San Francisco Chronicle* observes that while safety changes will probably be implemented, it will be at the insistence of fans rather than as the desire of NASCAR itself: "The changes will come now. The outsiders will insist."[80] While changes did come, most notably in the use of head and neck restraint systems by NASCAR drivers, these changes took a full year compared to the immediate reaction in the Renshaw case. At several points during public discussion of the accident, NASCAR President Mike Helton noted, "We're simply not going to react for the sake of reacting,"[81] and CART medical advisor Steve Olvey noted that "The key thing at a time like this is to make sure we don't get a knee-jerk reaction."[82]

In addition, while Renshaw was posited as at fault in her accident, the Earnhardt accident ultimately gets positioned as inherent to the sport, after initial attempts were made to place the blame on individuals. For example, immediately after the accident, Nick Harvey, team manager of the PPI Motorsports Winston Cup Team says of racing: "It's kind of like boxing. You can try to make it as safe as you want, but a guy still has to hit another guy."[83] More pointedly and directly, Dale Earnhardt Jr., son of the Winston Cup champion, openly rebuked those attempting to place blame on individuals for the accident: "Any notion or any idea of placing blame on anyone—whether it be Sterlin Marlin or anybody else, for that matter—is ridiculous and will not be tolerated."[84] Hence, compared to the Renshaw accident, Earnhardt's death is posed as inherent to racing and the fault of equipment rather than individuals. Rather than attempt to rush to provide regulations, "studies" are conducted to make sure that there were no "knee-jerk" reactions to the accident.

If common-sense ideology still largely operates with a configuration in which male drivers are largely evaluated as individuals while female performance is more closely tied to the "natural compulsions of sex," it should be no surprise that the exigency is to create a regulation that protects individual men from *all* female drivers.[85] Again, while Renshaw and others may consistently repeat that racing is not about gender, that it is about the "choices" one makes, gender concerns largely overdetermine the understanding of Renshaw's skills, of the "cause" of an accident, and of the need for regulations. The cultural logic again pulls in many different directions. While Renshaw as "first woman" must make it clear that she will work hard to achieve success on her own and that others have mostly given her a "fair shake," she is simultaneously configured as part of "women" as a whole and carries their inefficiencies onto the track.

Renshaw as "Media Hoax"

As noted above, despite the fact that other women have raced in both local and national circuits before Renshaw, her story was treated in news media very clearly along the patterns of the "first women" stories outlined by Ruth Rosen. Again, one of the patterns Rosen observed is that the "first woman" story provides great attention to the "woman" while telling a story in which her skills and efforts, rather than her gender, led to her success or failure. While the Renshaw case clearly follows this pattern early in the year, one of the more interesting aspects of the case later in the year, after the death of Eric Martin, is the way in which media coverage of the "first woman" story itself becomes an area of blame in Martin's death. That is, while the "first woman" story itself works to erase gender, when tragedy arises, "the media" is blamed—and blames itself—for paying too much attention to a woman and thereby placing her in a position to cause damage to herself and/or to others.

While not using the language of "first women" stories, Projansky argues that in the case of "first women pilots" of any sort (i.e., first balloonist, first female in space, etc.), news reporters and media representatives have had similar responses when these "firsts" have resulted in tragedy. For example, Projansky notes, in the cases of balloonist Pearl White, pilot Amelia Earhart, and "child pilot" Jessica Dubroff, media coverage ultimately "admonished 'the media' itself for paying attention to a 'media hoax,' a story about a woman who was 'not really a pilot' or who was 'not really a good pilot.[']"[86] That is, media outlets, through editorials or through publishing the views of those close to the tragedy, ultimately chastised "the media" itself for providing so much attention to a "first woman" that the woman oversteps her abilities, resulting in injury and death of the pilot and others.[87] In effect, such reports offer an apologia for the fact that their own spectacle encouraged a poorly qualified woman, even though that early coverage attempted to erase gender from the equation. Ultimately, the news coverage acts as an admission that gender *matters* after all.

In Renshaw's case, the critique of her popularity as unearned and as potentially dangerous is made early on by some of her competitors (especially those involved in the disqualification plot), even though it is initially discounted by reporters who are aligned with the "first woman" erasure of gender. For example, Day suggested that Renshaw is a dangerous driver because she is "so star-struck that she can't focus on racing."[88] Moreover, when Goodwin hired Renshaw to be his Busch Series driver, the *Tampa Tribune* notes as an aside that while Goodwin knew little about Renshaw's "driving ability, he thought she could be a marketing gem—a 'female' Jeff Gordon."[89] More recently, a letter to the *Tennessean* makes the following argument after suggesting that Renshaw was getting opportunities above her skill level: "I'm not a sexist, but I am for fairness. In racing, you have to earn your right to be there. How many men racers who are more qualified don't get opportunities because they are not women? A lot. I'm sure."[90] In each case, news outlets report that others think Renshaw is receiving too much attention based on gender rather than skill, even though the news reports themselves highlight Renshaw's skills as a driver rather than as a woman.

Paralleling Projansky's claims about coverage of women in flight, media reports later self-reflexively concede that perhaps their coverage was in fact part of the problem. For instance, John Romano of the *St. Petersburg Times* offers the following concession to Renshaw's competition: "In a small way, their complaints had merit. Renshaw's growing popularity owed more to her gender than her skills."[91] After the Martin accident, reporter Jenna Fryer suggests that "Renshaw's racing career was on a fast track" due to the media attention she was receiving, and that this perhaps encouraged Renshaw to enter upper-division racing circuits before she was prepared.[92] Similarly, the *Tampa Tribune* observes after the accident that while Renshaw was "unknown outside Tennessee until this year, she gained attention in July when fellow drivers at Nashville's Fairgrounds Speedway pooled their money to file a protest. . . . [T]he resulting news coverage caught the eye of Busch Series team owner Goodwin" and hence moved Renshaw quickly up the racing ladder.[93] Again, I am not suggesting that self-reflection by individual reporters and/or media outlets is a bad idea; rather, I would like to suggest that such arguments ultimately work within a logic that implies that Renshaw was unqualified precisely because she is a woman. Moreover, given this configuration and the fact that it is a theme oft-repeated in narrative accounts of female firsts, the cultural logic becomes one which must muse, if Renshaw is in "over her head" because of gendered publicity, that perhaps this is true of all female drivers.

CONCLUSION

As cultural histories of the automobile have illustrated, the entry of automobiles into mass culture as a technology—as a prosthetic or "extension of man"—functioned to trouble a number of different existing cultural logics (e.g., demarcations of public and private, the boundaries of geographic space) and opened up new social possibilities (e.g., improved zones for homosexual encounters, altered notions of gender, changing patterns of dating). That is, the automobile as a technology (i.e., as a medium) altered relationships among people—the automobile as medium carried its own message.[94] However, and as the oft-repeated critique of media determinism would have it, this is not the entirety of the story. While cars may have become the "real population of our cities,"[95] they did not enter a vacuum but rather entered a cultural landscape that already contained distinctions of class, race, gender, sexuality, and occupation—a culture with a performative language that encouraged its own reiteration, that encourages its own resignification even when, for instance, "women drive cars, instead of adorning men's cars."[96] With Braidotti, we see here that the technological imaginary cannot wipe out gender (or class) distinctions as they are ultimately protected by other means.[97]

While I am not denying that ongoing changes have occurred in the logics of gender and sexuality and am not denying that there are ways in which consumers can actively rethink cultural logics, I am using this case to note ways in which contemporary ideological "common sense" remains powerful, reiterating and resignifying. The case of Deborah Renshaw provides a "first woman" narrative that ends in tragedy, a first woman narrative that simultaneously denies the importance of gender while ultimately reemphasizing it in its own logic. It is a story in which "choice" and "skill" are at first highlighted over gender, ultimately only to be found subsumed once again under gender expectations.

In short, the Renshaw case reminds us that gender is never, and perhaps can never be, invisible. Moreover, when one intersects the logic of gender with its articulation around automobiles generally and racing specifically, one finds the expectations of gender more rigidly binding, more difficult to ignore. As I have illustrated, in the discourse surrounding both of the stories about Renshaw's 2002 season, gender is resignified in multiple ways—in Renshaw's own *reported* words, in other people's discussion about Renshaw and in the logic of the news reports themselves. For example, Renshaw is reported as suggesting that women naturally react emotionally in ways different than men; Renshaw's appearance and clothing are emphasized in particularly gendered ways and in ways absent from descriptions of most male drivers; her male peer group "gangs up" to discipline her for, in effect, receiving too much of the attention that they deserve. Moreover, after the death of fellow racer Eric Martin, Renshaw receives blame in a context that questions her abilities as a driver, and—given Renshaw's connection to future female drivers via the "first woman" narrative and male-female differences that are reiterated in reports about her—in a context that questions the ability of all female drivers and *all* potential female racers.

In *The Car in British Society*, O'Connell goes to some pains on several occasions to make his reader aware that the "ideological" intersections of gender and automobiles generally operate "automatically," as common sense, that bi-gendered logic was *assumed* historically by most men and women in their relationships with automobiles.[98] As O'Connell puts it, the history of the automobile is "not a story of brutish men denying women their freedom. . . . What has been explained is the role played by gender ideology in the normative regulation of femininity and masculinity within the context of motoring."[99] Whether behaving to gender expectations automatically or thinking about the consequences of not doing so, we largely reinforce the logic of those expectations, perhaps especially so when those expectations are troubled.

Hence, when Renshaw finds herself riding in cars "between men," men who bond socially and professionally through her exclusion and the preservation of male space, Renshaw initially decides to "let the old boys" have their game back. On those grounds, gender performative expectations are protected. However, those expectations are perhaps more importantly—or rather, more insidiously—protected by the common sense with which people operate when Renshaw decides to continue racing. When NASCAR's "diversity council," for example, posits Renshaw as the prototype of women drivers who could attract a larger female audience (she is attractive and well spoken), they are implicitly acknowledging that she is the "proper" type of female driver.[100] Or, when a reporter notes, after Renshaw was hired by Goodwin, that "[r]acing insiders don't know much about her driving ability, but they say she could be a marketing gem" because she has "good looks, a college degree and acting school experience," that reporter is acknowledging—and simultaneously reiterating—the power of capital on proper gender performance.[101] Or, when Goodwin is quoted in the same news report as saying that "[w]hen you sit in that seat, you're not a man or a woman" *and* observes that he was interested in hiring Renshaw because "as an attractive woman, she's attractive to sponsors," we understand that one is never just a driver, never *just* sitting in that seat.[102] When a television host consistently refers to Renshaw as "the lovely Deborah Renshaw" and contrasts "the lovely Deborah Renshaw" with "unladylike" callers, we know that he understands the proper performance of gender and assumes that his audience shares that understanding.[103]

Ultimately, then, this essay should be read as an attempt to underline the discursive weight of gender ideology and its intersection with the cultural logic of automobiles and of automobile racing. Moreover, this is an attempt not only to trace out some contemporary links between gender and the automobile, between gender and a particular occupation, but to make an argument about those links that will help us all remember to problematize them. Revolutions are slow, as Raymond Williams continues to whisper, because meanings often change at a snail's pace. In bringing "common sense" into relief, I mean to encourage each of us to trouble this case in particular and to continue to remain vigilant in problematizing the constraints of gender ideology in all other domains.[104]

NOTES

[1]Marshall McLuhan, *Understanding Media: The Extensions of Man* (New York: McGraw-Hill, 1965), 217–18.

[2]Sharon Willis, *High Contrast: Race and Gender in Contemporary Hollywood Film* (Durham, NC: Duke University Press, 1997), 108.

[3]I will try to clarify the different racing circuits in which Renshaw competed. To parallel loosely with professional baseball, Renshaw raced in what could be seen as unaffiliated minor leagues (local small tracks, ARCA series) as well as NASCAR minor leagues, and was headed for NASCAR's Busch series. In short, she competed during that year in the equivalent of Single and Double A baseball and was preparing through Rick Goodwin to move to Triple A.

[4]I am assuming that Butler's theses have become widespread enough that I do not need to rehearse her arguments thoroughly in the body of the essay. For Butler, to say that gender is 'performative' is to suggest that regardless of the physicality of gender, it is something that is understood, or has meaning, through discourse or culturally accepted practices, including appearance, manners of speaking, occupational roles, choices of sexual partners, and so forth. See Judith Butler, *Gender Trouble: Feminism and the Sub[v]ersion of Identity* (New York: Routledge, 1990), 139. Moreover, given how heavily policed gender norms are in popular culture, Butler observed, bi-gendered heterosexual norms become materialized, naturalized as if they were essential rather than contingent. As a result, individuals "perform" gender to a great deal without reflection, simply behaving in ways that "make sense" given their own gender identification. Further, they inspect other people's gender performances without a great deal of regard or thought given to the

way in which we "police" one another's gender behaviors. Performativity, then, "cannot be understood outside of a process of iterability, a regularized and constrained repetition of norms. . . . This repetition is what enables a subject and constitutes the temporal condition for the subject. This iterability implies that 'performance' is not a singular 'act' or event, but a ritualized production, a ritual reiterated under and through constraint, under and through the force of prohibition and taboo, with the threat of ostracism and even death controlling and compelling the shape of production, but not, I will insist, determining it fully in advance," Judith Butler, *Bodies that Matter: On the Discursive Limits of "Sex"* (New York: Routledge, 1993), 95.

[5]I, of course, assume that the discourse is far more complex than I posit it in these opening sentences, and I trace out the subtleties of the discourse later in the essay. Indeed, this "gender discipline" occurs precisely because the events described in this paper were ones that at first opened up possibilities for stretching public understandings of proper gender performance. It might be more correct to note that the discourse analyzed here only partially reiterates traditional bi-gendered heteronormativity.

[6]To clarify, I am not claiming that this telling of the story is "authentic" or true. Rather, the story I tell here is one I have drawn together out of over 50 different newspaper articles gathered through Lexis-Nexis searches. While I will be referring to individual articles in detail later in my analysis, this version is more simply my general "reading" or "gathering of fragments" of those newspaper articles. For a discussion of this methodology, see Raymie E. McKerrow, "Critical Rhetoric: Theory and Praxis," *Communication Monographs* 56 (1989): 91–111 or, more recently, Kent A. Ono and John M. Sloop, *Shifting Borders: Rhetoric, Immigration, and California's Proposition 187* (Philadelphia, PA: Temple University Press, 2002), 1–25. I take mine to be a reading that would be familiar and fair to most other people who read these reports. In addition, I also refer to a small number of radio broadcasts as well as Renshaw's appearance in late 2002 on a local talk show.

[7]Renshaw consistently makes the point that she turned down most of these interviews as she thought it would be bad for NASCAR as a whole to have a "gender fight" and would have worked against her career as the news would focus on her gender. See, for example, John Romano, "Chauvinism Rears Its Ugly Gearhead," *St. Petersburg Times,* 26 July 2002, 1C, and Tony Fabrizio, "Controversy Opens Way for Renshaw," *Tampa Tribune,* 31 August 2002, Sports 12.

[8]NASCAR rules for this series require that a driver can only protest the cars that finish ahead of them. The driver of the pitted car, Scottie Smothers, was making his first race at the track for the sole purpose of quitting early so that he would be able to protest Renshaw's engine.

[9]Again, I am not making "truth" statements here; rather, I am reiterating press claims about these events. Claims about threats to the other driver's masculinity are both implicit and explicit in a variety of reports.

[10]Busch Series is one step below Winston, NASCAR's "major league." Goodwin had recently moved his 2002 Busch Series drivers into his Winston (now Nextel) Cup car.

[11]ARCA (the Automobile Racing Club of America), not affiliated with NASCAR, uses Winston (Nextel) Cup style stock cars, which travel 60–80 mph faster than Renshaw drove in the late Model Series at Nashville. See Jenna Fryer "Renshaw's Career Now in Question," *Chattanooga Times/Free Press,* 11 October 2002, D1. ARCA is generally a step taken by drivers who want to move from small tracks to Busch and Winston (Nextel) series racing.

[12]I was tempted to discuss both gender and sexuality throughout the paper as the two are certainly tied together culturally; however, because the case most overtly discusses gender and most often only alludes to sexuality, I will generally frame the paper in terms of gender. As I will illustrate (but not highlight), the case also relies on class and racial norms in the resignification of what it means to be a "proper" NASCAR driver.

[13]That is, my goal is to help trouble gender norms and expectations precisely by illustrating how efficiently and powerfully "dominant mass mediated" discussions of gender work

toward closing down gender trouble. Such closure and reiterations of gender norms are never complete, however, and it is my hope that my illustration of disciplinary discourses will work to help individual readers loosen their own gender expectations.

[14]I realize, of course, that "U.S. culture" is not a particularly meaningful term given the wide variety of audiences, media outlets, and cultural groups that exist. What I mean to signify is: (a) I am not making claims for a world wide configuration of gender expectations; (b) I understand the gender expectations are historical, although history does have material influence on the present; and (c) "dominant" media outlets provide, and work with, loosely shared understandings of gender expectations. My assumption is that these expectations are also shared by audiences because, in order to gain and maintain an audience to sell to advertisers, mass media outlets must be loosely within the parameters of their audience's expectations.

[15]When one employs or encounters McLuhan, one must always be aware of the always available (always necessary) critique of McLuhan as a "media determinist." Regardless of whether or not McLuhan's writings warrant the criticism that has cohered around his thesis, it is certainly true that his emphasis on media as "extension of the self" emphasized technological changes over cultural changes rather than allowing insights from both technological and cultural criticism. For a good summary of McLuhan, criticisms of McLuhan and reworkings of McLuhan's theses, see Ronald J. Deibert, *Parchment, Printing, and Hypermedia: Communication in World Order Transformation* (New York: Columbia University Press, 1997).

[16]John Howard, *Men Like That: A Southern Queer History* (Chicago: University of Chicago Press, 1999), 4.

[17]I should point out that Howard's book also discusses issues of class and "gender" in minor ways.

[18]Virginia Scharff, *Taking the Wheel: Women and the Coming of the Motor Age* (Albuquerque: University of New Mexico Press, 1991), 1–50.

[19]Rosi Braidotti, *Metamorphoses: Towards a Materialist Theory of Becoming* (Cambridge, UK: Polity Press, 2002), 244–63. Obviously, I am over-generalizing Braidotti's claims in summarizing an entire chapter. Nonetheless, what I hope to point to here are the ways in which contemporary cultural discourses problematize alterations in our common understandings of gender.

[20]John W. Jordan, "(Ad)Dressing the Body in Online Shopping Sites," *Critical Studies in Media Communication* 20 (2003): 253. Indeed, almost all recent scholarship in this area would make this claim. The last decade has witnessed article after article which draws back on the earlier utopian visions of technology.

[21]Scharff, 13. Similarly, Sean O'Connell, *The Car and British Society: Class, Gender, and Motoring, 1896–1939* (New York: Manchester University Press, 1998) begins his chapter on gender and the car by observing that "the agency that gender came to have in shaping ideas about car use has ultimately prevented millions of women from taking to the driving seat" (43).

[22]Scharff, 3–4.

[23]Moreover, both Scharff and O'Connell argue that women who *raced* cars were seen as being especially "gender troubling" because their behavior worked as a double contradiction against the "rules of gender performativity" (i.e., they were not only enthusiastic about driving cars but also competitive) (Scharff, 68–79; O'Connell, 96). In addition to marketing plans, this understanding of the female racer as "unfeminine" woman was rearticulated and reemphasized in news reports as women like Catherine McCulloch of the Illinois Equal Suffrage Association sponsored women-only automobile trips to publicize suffrage but also in literature as multiple links were produced between female drivers and lesbianism. See Scharff, 79 and O'Donnell, 211. O'Donnell makes this link through a reading of Radclyffe Hall's *The Well of Loneliness* and other novels. However, both Scharff, 107 and O'Connell, 49–50 also suggest that representations of woman drivers' corps members during World War II—women such as Gertrude Stein and Alice Toklas—also carried the underlying suggestion of lesbianism.

[24]Scharff, 15–16, 54–55.

[25]Scharff, 166.

[26]Judy Wajcman, *Feminism Confronts Technology* (Cambridge, UK: Polity Press, 1991), 45.

[27]O'Connell, 220.

[28]Scharff, 57–58, 222; O'Connell, 64–69. The electric starter and a variety of colors are two other innovations that all people seemed to want but were attributed to "feminizing" the car, making it less brutal. Scharff, 132, reports that the "color and paint" division at General Motors in the 1920s was referred to derisively as "the beauty parlor" and was one of the few divisions that employed a large number of women.

[29]While I do not mean to belabor the point, I want to stress the ways in which gender differences—bi-gendered normativity—remain an underlying assumption (no longer as overt as it was in O'Connell and Scharff's analyses) in all "public discussions" of transportation technologies. For example, in her analysis of female car sales staff, Helene M. Lawson, *Ladies on the Lot: Women, Car Sales, and the Pursuit of the American Dream* (Lanham, MD: Rowman & Littlefield, 2000) argues that the gendered behavior expectations of men and women on sales lots are strongly bi-gendered and heteronormative, and hence, many of the characteristics associated with normal male behavior are also those aspects of personality said to create successful car sales staff (e.g., the push for the hard sale, ability to work rather than raise children, and ability to take full credit for sales that are not their own (Lawson, 34, 43, 64, 75, 90). Or, to turn to discourse concerning space shuttle technology, Constance Penley, "Spaced Out: Remembering Christa McAuliffe," *Camera Obscura* 29 (1992): 179–213, has argued that the public discourse concerning Christa McAuliffe illustrates the ways in which gendered discourse and gender expectations continue to function and continue to work against the success of women in NASA programs. Similarly, Sarah Projansky, "Girls Who Act like Women Who Fly: Jessica Dubroff as Cultural Troublemaker," *Signs* 23 (1998): 771–807, in an analysis of the Jessica Dubroff flight, suggests that similar gendered discourses operate in the ways in which we, as a public culture, configure air transport.

[30]Braidotti, 250.

[31]John Fiske and John Hartley, *Reading Television* (New York: Methuen, 1978), 85–91.

[32]Eve Sedgwick, *Between Men: English Literature and Male Homosocial Desire* (New York: Columbia University Press, 1985), 5.

[33]Sedgwick, 25.

[34]I am indebted to Charles Morris for suggesting this phrase.

[35]Ruth Rosen, *The World Split Open: How the Modern Women's Movement Changed America* (New York: Penguin, 2000), 302–8.

[36]Rosen, 303.

[37]Rosen, 306.

[38]Sarah Projansky, *Watching Rape: Film and Television in Postfeminist Culture* (New York: New York University Press, 2001), 72–79.

[39]Stephania H. Davis, "Auto-Racing Group is Crossing Barriers," *Atlanta Journal and Constitution,* 7 March 2002, 1JD, emphasis mine.

[40]"Renshaw Returns to Track Where Plot Got Her Disqualified," Associated Press State and Local Wire, 4 August 2002.

[41]Gene Sapakoff, "Busch Series' Renshaw Just the Driver NASCAR Needs," *Post and Courier,* 31 August 2002, 7C.

[42]Jack Wilkinson, "A Stock Car Soap Opera," *Atlanta Journal-Constitution,* 3 August 2002, 1E. When coupled with comments about Renshaw's "sophistication" and education, Day's reference to "redneck racers" clearly illustrates that issues of class are at work here as well. While I do not want to deny that there are articulations that connect gender and class, for the purposes of this essay, I remain focused on gender. Clearly, other analyses of this case could draw the distinctions somewhat differently.

[43]http://www.deborahrenshaw.com/about.cfm (accessed 11 March 2003).

[44]Wilkinson, 1E.

[45]Sapakoff, 7C.

[46]Tony Fabrizio, "Controversy Opens Way for Renshaw," *Tampa Tribune*, 31 August 2002, Sports 12. See also Dustin Long, "NASCAR Rolling in Right Direction," *Roanoke Times and World News*, 31 August 2002, C5 and Sapakoff 7C.

[47]"Sportsline with Hope Hines."

[48]Wilkinson, 1E.

[49]Teresa M. Walker, "Renshaw: Plot by Fellow Drivers Devastating, but Won't Stop Her," Associated Press, 19 July 2002, Sports News.

[50]Steve Smith, "Female Driver Vows to Race Despite Plot," *Commercial Appeal*, 24 July 2002, D2.

[51]Romano, 1C.

[52]Wilkinson, 1E.

[53]"Sportsline."

[54]Sedgwick, 25.

[55]Walker, "Renshaw." See also Walker, "Kentucky," C11, "Male Drivers Plot to Get Woman Disqualified, Drive Her from Track," Associated Press, 15 July 2002, Sports News, and "Some Unsporting Behavior," *Commercial Appeal*, 16 July 2002, D1.

[56]Romano, 1C.

[57]Wilkinson, 1E.

[58]Wilkinson, 1E.

[59]Wilkinson, 1E.

[60]Scharff, 26. Similarly, in line with Scharff's observations, Sean O'Connell argues that traditional arguments against female drivers in England were based in genetics, evolution, and, surprisingly, women's lack of sexual satisfaction (leading some publications to recommend that men satisfy their wives' sexual needs in order to help them be safer drivers). While any observer of popular culture could vouch for the continuation of this articulation in a variety of forms today, Helene Lawson's ethnography of women who work at car dealerships (and their employers) illustrates that many dealers overtly refuse to hire women because they perceive them to know so little about driving or about the technology of automobiles (34).

[61]Projansky, 790; Penley, 179–80.

[62]"Male Drivers," Sports News.

[63]Walker, "Renshaw," Sports News.

[64]O'Connell, 114.

[65]O'Connell, 120. It would be easy to suggest that "the elderly" have become another scapegoat to deaths caused by automobiles.

[66]O'Connell, 120–23.

[67]See "ARCA Driver Martin Killed When Disabled Car is Struck," *Newsday*, 10 October 2002, A84 and Lindsey Young, "Hixson's Martin Killed in Crash," *Chattanooga Times*, 10 October 2002, D1 for detailed reports about the accident.

[68]I want to make clear at the outset of this analysis that I am not making an argument about "blame." That is, I am neither defending nor criticizing Renshaw. I am more interested in the ways that—given the multiple narratives that could have been created—one particular narrative about the accident becomes dominant.

[69]Young, D1.

[70]Tony Fabrizio, "ARCA Oversight Can Be Corrected," *Tampa Tribune*, 12 October 2002, Sports 12. For other examples of this same logic, see "Crash Kills ARCA Rookie," *Atlanta Journal-Constitution*, 10 October 2002, 3D; Viv Bernstein, "Stock-Car Series Mulls Rule Change," *New York Times*, 11 October 2002, D7; Fryer, D1; "Drivers Work Hard to Forget Tragedy," *News & Record*, 12 October 2002, C1.

[71]Fryer, D1.

[72]Chris Jenkins, "Haunted—But Undaunted," *USA Today*, 6 February 2003, 1C.

[73]Jenkins, 1C. See also Fryer, D1.

[74]Technically, the spotters only had to stand on the team's trailer during practice sessions, which made it difficult for the spotter to see the full track. See "Crash Kills" for a discussion of this difficulty. While the regulation would ultimately affect everyone, the

discourse makes it clear that it is an attempt to protect drivers from incompetent peer drivers and teams.

[75]Young, D1.

[76]Bernstein, D7. See also Fryer, D1.

[77]Fabrizio, "ARCA," Sports 12. See also "NASCAR Considers Changes After Crash," *New York Times,* 12 October 2002, D7.

[78]Reports of this change are widespread. See Rick Minter, "Fatality Brings Spotter Requirement," *Atlanta Journal-Constitution,* 13 October 2002, 6E; David Caraviello, "All Too Often, Racing Learns Its Lesson Too Late," *Post and Courier,* 13 October 2002, 7C; Dustin Long, "Rule Change Sets Spotter Placement," *News & Record,* 13 October 2002, C13; Dave Kallman, "Something Stinks at Road America," *Milwaukee Journal Sentinel,* 18 October 2002, 8C; "No Blame Assigned in Fatal ARCA Crash," *St. Petersburg Times,* 20 October 2002, 5C; Tony Fabrizio, "In Memory," *Tampa Tribune,* 20 November 2002, Sports 5.

[79]Chris Jenkins, "Curbing the Risks," *USA TODAY,* 20 February 2001, 1C. I analyzed 50 articles following the Earnhardt case for this example.

[80]Gwen Knapp, "Another Call for Reason," *San Francisco Chronicle,* 20 February 2001, E1.

[81]H. A. Branham, "Death Reopens Car Racing Questions," *Tampa Tribune,* 20 February 2001, 1.

[82]"He Said It," *The Gazette,* 20 February 2001, E1. For a reiteration of this claim a full six months later, see Joanne Korth, "How Earnhardt Died," *St. Petersburg Times,* 1A.

[83]H. A. Branham, "Death Reopens Car Racing Questions," *Tampa Tribune,* 20 February 2001, 1.

[84]Liz Clarke, *Washington Post,* "Probe: Seat Belt Failed," 24 February 2001, D1.

[85]Scharff, 28.

[86]Projansky, 790.

[87]Projansky, 790.

[88]Walker, "Renshaw," Sports News.

[89]Fabrizio, "Controversy," Sports 12; see also Long, "NASCAR," C5.

[90]Tim Oliphant, "Driver Renshaw Hasn't Paid Racing Dues Yet," *Tennessean,* 8 July 2003, 7A.

[91]Romano, 1C.

[92]Fryer, D1.

[93]Fabrizio, "ARCA," Sports 12.

[94]As a rhetorician, I am not suggesting that we can discuss technologies outside the realm of discourse. I am simply suggesting that different technologies do have different influences on meaning, given the particular culture in which they emerge.

[95]McLuhan, 217–18.

[96]Willis, 108.

[97]Braidotti, 245.

[98]Again, this is not to say that people do not actively resist such articulations. It is, rather, to suggest that this cultural logic—like all ideology—works because *most* people assume its logic *most* of the time.

[99]O'Connell, 220.

[100]Walker, "Kentucky," C11.

[101]Fabrizio, "Controversy," Sports 12.

[102]Sapakoff, 7C.

[103]"Sports Line."

[104]As a critic influenced heavily by both Foucault and Butler, I am not assuming that we can be "free" of ideology or that there is a space for the "pure expression" of gender. Rather, I hope that in "shaking up common sense," we are simultaneously encouraged to think of multiple possibilities.

Chapter XI

Critical Rhetoric

Since the late 1980s, rhetorical criticism has been increasingly influenced by what Raymie E. McKerrow defines as "critical rhetoric."[1] Indeed, most recent rhetorical critiques have been at least flavored by critical rhetoric, sometimes called critical/cultural studies. Critical rhetoric identifies multiple, competing realities, rather than absolute truths or "metanarratives." It addresses the construction of identity and how power is assigned and exercised in society.

By design, critical rhetoric does not conform to a standard paradigm, but it does tend to reflect a set of overlapping perspectives, philosophies, and ideological commitments. Among these are an expansive view of what constitutes a text, or valid critical object. Critical rhetoric analyzes cultural fragments or artifacts such as monuments, museums, commercial spaces, visual images, popular culture, and everyday life practices.[2] It usually focuses on issues of race, ethnicity, class, gender, sexuality, and material conditions, viewing scholarship as a means to bring about social change, correct inequalities, and promote democracy.

Thomas K. Nakayama and Robert L. Krizek's 1995 essay, "Whiteness: A Strategic Rhetoric," investigates how groups construct identity, control power, and find meaning in everyday life. The authors maintain that the language, behavior, and perceptions of white people are taken as the "norm" against which "Others" are measured. They argue that "whiteness" has no meaning in itself, and is best understood as a rhetorical construction. Through the analysis of ethnographic interviews, discourse from popular culture, and survey results, the authors expose six rhetorical strategies that "mark the space" of whiteness. By doing so, Nakayama and Krizek aim to reveal the "invisible position" of whiteness and, ultimately, "displace its centrality" in society.

Dana L. Cloud's 1996 essay, "Hegemony or Concordance? The Rhetoric of Tokenism in 'Oprah' Winfrey's Rags-to-Riches Biography," combines rhetorical analysis of race, class, gender, narrative, and genre. Cloud examines how Oprah Winfrey's biographies have been "appropriated" by the popular culture. She argues that the "Oprah" narratives, framed by "liberal individualism and an oppressively gendered meaning system," "represent a rhetoric of tokenism." Winfrey's success as an African-American woman, however atypical, Cloud concludes, is taken as affirmation that the American Dream is available equally to everyone, regardless of race, class, or gender.

In their 2000 essay, "Imaging Nature: Watkins, Yosemite, and the Birth of Environmentalism," Kevin Michael DeLuca and Anne Teresa Demo explore the persuasive power of Carleton Watkins's nature photographs. In considering these 1860s landscape photographs as visual rhetoric, the authors ask, "what vision of nature do the photographs authorize, warrant, and legitimate?" They contend that, in the 1860s, the depiction of Yosemite as a "pristine paradise" was taken as proof of national superiority and "divine favor." These visual images played a significant role in the preservation of the Yosemite Valley as a wilderness area; however, they also concealed the forced expulsion of Native Americans and ignored the presence of workers. As a consequence, the authors argue, for a century the environmental movement put undue emphasis on preserving pristine places at the expense of the inhabited environment.

NOTES

[1] See Raymie E. McKerrow's essay "Critical Rhetoric: Theory and Praxis," reproduced in Chapter 1, for a more detailed discussion of the theoretical foundations for critical rhetoric.

[2] See, for example, Carole Blair, Marsha S. Jeppeson, and Enrico Pucci, Jr.'s essay, "Public Memorializing in Postmodernity: The Vietnam Veterans Memorial as Prototype," reproduced in Chapter 1 of this anthology.

WHITENESS: A STRATEGIC RHETORIC

THOMAS K. NAKAYAMA AND ROBERT L. KRIZEK

Consider, for example, how age, gender, being an outsider, and association with a neocolonial regime influence what the ethnographer learns. The notion of position refers to how life experiences both enable and inhibit particular kinds of insight. (Rosaldo 19)

[A]lthough all people exist within what we might call the "strata" of subjectivity, they are also located at particular positions within the strata, each of which enables and constrains the possibilities of experience, but even more, of representing and legitimating those representations. (Grossberg 13)

We open with discourses grounded in two diverse, yet related universes, ethnography and cultural studies. Each addresses the possibilities of human experience as both barriers and bridges that influence knowledge and its expression. In addition, each invokes the metaphor of space by naming those possibilities as "positions."

The emergence of the spatial metaphor in academic work has encouraged scholars in cultural studies and ethnography alike to rethink the ways in which individuals and groups construct identity, administer power, and make sense of their everyday lives. Our dialogues are now replete with spatial tropes of boundaries, centers, margins, and borderlands. More recently, in addition to the uncomplicated binary reality of centers and margins, we find an expanding discussion of discursive spaces, fields of interaction, trajectories, and territories, each contributing a somewhat distinct and theoretically challenging lens. These "new" metaphors invite the disarrangement of modern thought by promoting a complex spatial view of postmodern life which honors the legitimacy of multiple realities. At the same time, these spatial metaphors consider the milieu present at the intersection of differing "realities" while recognizing the variance within each of the "realities."

In this essay we are interested in a specific position—the discursive space of "white." "White" is a relatively uncharted territory that has remained invisible as it continues to influence the identity of those both within and without its domain. It affects the everyday fabric of our lives but resists, sometimes violently, any extensive characterization that would allow for the mapping of its contours. It wields power yet endures as a largely unarticulated position.[1]

The place from which power is exercised is often a hidden place. When we try to pin it down, the center always seems to be somewhere else. Yet we know that this phantom center, elusive as it is, exerts a real, undeniable power over the entire framework of our culture, and over the ways we think about it. (Ferguson 19)

We come to this project with highly personal, yet similar expectations. For reasons rooted in accidents of our remote biographies, we both seek to expose the meanings of "white." One of us knows what it is to be a Japanese American from the South, a position often diminished by the two primary racial realities—white and black. "I've always been aware of terms or words others use and that I use to describe myself. For a long time I was very sensitive. I wanted people to call me a Japanese American, not a Japanese. But my position as an American was not the defining position. White was." The other of us grew up in a well-positioned suburb of Chicago, a suburb with a single racial reality. "It was the opposite for me. I've gone through life never consciously thinking about labels. I suppose we defined ourselves as one of those people we didn't label, although nobody ever said that. We were just white, not black or brown, and I don't really know what that means. No one ever questioned it."

Although we have experienced the influence of "white" from different positions, one inside the territory of white and one outside (or at least not on the inside), we both come to this project in search of the "hidden place." One of us pursues rhetorical urges, the other ethnographic, both critical. And though we both "read" texts for the purpose of rendering an informed interpretation, our motivations for reading the text of white differ.

"For me it's clarifying some of the ways that white has exerted its force on everybody else, on me. The ways that they have been able to maintain that position through invisibility, that everything-ness, that normalizing potential or whatever you want to call it. I want to disrupt the power that resides in white's discursive space."

"There is another side to being culturally invisible. When I started realizing that other people were able to articulate and appreciate aspects of their cultural heritage, I began to feel uncomfortable about being transparent. Although I understand that mapping the territory of white will be disruptive, I encourage the disruption. I don't believe that my identity is continuous with white's invisible power, and I'm searching for those discontinuities as meaningful cultural experiences."

Despite our different motives, biographical details, and research agendas, we both recognized our own experiences in Ferguson's words presented above. We both caught a glimpse of our own reflections. As such, we believe that the time has come to deterritorialize the territory of "white," to expose, examine, and disrupt. In this essay we begin that process by surveying (exposing and examining) the territory of "white" so that it, like other positions, may be placed under critical analysis. In order to accomplish this end, we investigate the strategies that mark the space of whiteness. Our critical move is attained through a nominalist rhetoric; that is, by naming whiteness, we displace its centrality and reveal its invisible position. We undertake this examination of whiteness through a mixture of textual data revealed in popular discourse, open-ended surveys,[2] and interviews.[3] Our goal is to develop some initial insights into how whites have constructed their own social locations of whiteness. In this essay, then, we examine whiteness as a rhetorical construction and discuss some of the ways it resecures its central position. Ultimately, the goal of this project is to extend our understanding of positionality and its relation to research through this exploration of whiteness.

MAKING THE CENTER INVISIBLE

Historically, the development of the study of communication has followed a focus on the center. Plato and Aristotle, from a privileged class, were not interested in theorizing or empowering ways that women, slaves, or other culturally marginalized people might speak. The rhetor was always already assumed to be a member of the center. Spelman argues that "both Plato and Aristotle have a normative notion of humanness that is inseparable from a notion of masculinity (which is of course normative)" (54). Spelman's analysis demonstrates the ways that "race" and gender get conflated in order to center male citizens. While the configuration of the racial/ethnic territory has shifted from the place of ancient Greece to contemporary North America, the assumption of centeredness has remained intact and unquestioned.

As a consequence of this historical framework, in U.S. culture, whiteness has assumed the position of an uninterrogated space. In sum, we do not know what "whiteness" means. An earlier attempt to get at this problem, by a citizen of the center, underscores an important paradox and risk:

> When we examine ourselves as whites and all that we stand for in the world today, we find a paradox. We are not what we suppose ourselves to be. We have fancied ourselves the good guys who make a few mistakes. But that is not what we find. (Dutcher 97)

The risk for critical researchers who choose to interrogate whiteness, including those in ethnography and cultural studies, is the risk of essentialism. Whatever "whiteness" really means is constituted only through the rhetoric of whiteness. There is no "true essence" to "whiteness"; there are only historically contingent constructions of that social location.

Foucault's principle of "exteriority" explains the rhetorical sensibility, rather than essential nature, of discursive events:

> [W]e are not to burrow into the hidden core of discourse, to the heart of thought or meaning manifested in it; instead, taking the discourse itself, its appearance and its regularity, that we should look for its external conditions of existence, for that which gives rise to the chance series of these events and fixes its limits. ("Discourse on Language" 229)

Yet, the social location of "whiteness" is perceived as if it had a normative essence. It is important that we acknowledge that "the radicality or conservatism of essentialism depends, to a significant degree, on *who* is utilizing it, *how* it is deployed, and *where* its effects are concentrated" (Fuss 20). By viewing whiteness as a rhetorical construction, we avoid searching for any essential nature to whiteness. Instead, we seek an understanding of the ways that this rhetorical construction makes itself visible and invisible, eluding analysis yet exerting influence over everyday life.

The invisibility of whiteness has been manifested through its universality. The universality of whiteness resides in its already defined position as everything. Richard Dyer makes an important point:

> In the realm of categories, black is always marked as a colour (as the term "coloured" egregiously acknowledges), and is always particularizing; whereas

white is not anything really, not an identity, not a particularizing quality, because it is everything—white is no colour because it is all colours. (45)

Thus, the experiences and communication patterns of whites are taken as the norm from which Others are marked. If we take a critical perspective to whiteness, however, we can begin the process of particularizing white experience. This move displaces whites from a universal stance which has tended to normalize and to naturalize their positionality to a more specific social location in which they confront the kinds of questions and challenges facing any particular social location. As Frye underscores, "What this can mean to white people is that we are not white by nature but by political classification" (118).

In light of the influential political position of whiteness, it is surprising that critical scholars have not yet scrutinized the center in the ways that they have been probing the margins. Despite the historical domination of the center and the myriad of ways it exerts its influence on the margins, our discipline has not been critical of this dominance over communication studies. In this paper we push the territory of the center in new directions, much as critical scholars have pushed the margins. By critically examining this space, it gains particularity, while losing universality. We see this conceptual move as one that is counterhegemonic, as it challenges the normalizing position of the center, whiteness.

MAKING THE CENTER VISIBLE

In *Marxism and the Philosophy of Language,* Volosinov comments on the multiaccentuality of the ideological sign: "various different classes will use one and the same language. As a result, differently oriented accents intersect in every ideological sign. Sign becomes an arena of the class struggle" (23). His emphasis on the sign as a site of class struggle opens up the sign, "white," to a range of interpretations, contradictions, and meanings as it unfolds within existing social relations, but not necessarily limited to class. In order to expose the complex, and often contradictory, functionings of "white," we explore what de Certeau might identify as a strategic rhetoric by combining Foucault's concepts of discursive formations and power with Deleuze and Guattari's notion of assemblage to uncover the ways in which whiteness exerts its influence throughout the social fabric.

Although the writings of Deleuze and Guattari "have been given little attention in the field of critical communication studies" (Chen 44), we believe that the importance of their work is easily recognized in its compatibility with contemporary critical work, as well as its offering of a new approach to viewing critique. First, like critical rhetoric (McKerrow, "Theory and Praxis"), Deleuze and Guattari do not prescribe methodology. Instead, they offer the concept of the nomadic scholar who is not constrained by methodology, but by perspective. Second, they offer a spatial view of power relations that upends traditional, linear histories. Thus, it is important that we understand the assemblages that produce and reproduce power relations in particular ways. This is compatible with Grossberg's call that "cultural studies explore the concrete ways in which different machines—or, in Foucault's terms, apparatuses—produce the specific spaces, configurations, and circulations of power" (8). Finally, Deleuze and Guattari offer a new way of critique, i.e., deterritorialization. Once we view power spatially, a rearticulation of the space of the assemblage is a counterhegemonic move. Prior to rewriting this space, however, we must first identify the assemblage and see how it functions mechanically. We believe that some of the importance of Deleuze and

Guattari can be seen in how this spatial politics can function as critique, rather than theory. Hence, we identify and critique the assemblage of whiteness.

TACTICAL RHETORICS

In *The Practice of Everyday Life,* Michel de Certeau makes an interesting distinction between strategies and tactics. We find this frame useful for exploring the larger discursive framework that guides white identity:

> A distinction between *strategies* and *tactics* appears to provide a more adequate initial schema. I call a *strategy* the calculation (or manipulation) of power relationships that becomes possible as soon as a subject with will and power (a business, an army, a city, a scientific institution) can be isolated. It postulates a *place* that can be delimited as its *own* and serve as the base from which relations with an *exteriority* composed of targets or threats (customers or competitors, enemies, the country surrounding the city, objectives and objects of research, etc.) can be managed. . . . By contrast with a strategy . . . a *tactic* is a calculated action determined by the absence of a proper locus. No delimitation of an exteriority, then, provides it with the condition necessary for autonomy. The space of a tactic is the space of the other. Thus it must play on and with a terrain imposed on it and organized by the law of a foreign power. It does not have the means to *keep to itself,* at a distance, in a position of withdrawal, foresight, and self-collection. (35–37)

We conclude from this that the discursive frame that negotiates and reinforces white dominance in U.S. society operates strategically. It is this strategic rhetoric that we wish to explore. This strategic rhetoric is not itself a place, but it functions to resecure the center, the place, for whites.

Before we examine this strategic rhetoric, we turn to a discussion of the tactical rhetorics that have emerged in response to this center. Racial and ethnic identity is certainly not a new topic of discussion, particularly by those in the margins. In the face of social, economic and political changes, these discourses have shifted over time. While these places are now marked as marginalized, "Others" have long been reflexive on their positionalities vis-à-vis the center. African Americans (Asante, Bobo, Bogle, Christian, Collins, Combahee River Collective, Henry Louis Gates, Jr., Gray, hooks, Houston Stanback, Lorde, Nesteby, Smith, Cornel West), Arab Americans (Said, Sheehan), Asian Americans (Asian Women United of California, Leong, Nakagawa, Nakayama, Omi, San Juan, Tachiki et al., Takaki, Trinh), Latino/as (Anzaldúa, Fregoso and Chabram, Moraga, Noriega, Tanno), and Native Americans (Churchill, Friar and Friar, Valaskakis) have all interrogated the complex relations (social, historical, cultural, political, economic) various groups have to the center. Those who are not a part of the domestic U.S. social sphere have also interrogated their relationships to whiteness from a variety of perspectives as well (Centre for Contemporary Cultural Studies, Fanon, Gilroy, Hall, Memmi, Spivak, Uchida).

Our intent is not to diminish the importance of these researchers attempting to inscribe their social locations (gender and sexual orientation as well as racial/ethnic positions)[4] into their work. Nor is it our intent to discourage ongoing discussions about whiteness by writers of color. These studies have made significant contributions toward understanding the ways that people of color have interrogated and examined their complex relationships with whiteness. They have also opened up the territory of whiteness to critique. The interests of these writers, however, are geared toward exposing and questioning the spaces that exist between various groups and whiteness. For example, in *Black Looks,* bell hooks observes that "the oppositional black culture that emerged in the context of apartheid and segregation has been one of the few locations that has provided a space for the kind of decolonization that makes loving blackness possible" (10). She warns, correctly we believe, that attempts to treat whiteness as victimizing to whites as well "in the hopes that this will act as an intervention is a misguided strategy" (13). In contrast, our concerns are focused on the ways that the territory of whiteness is able to mask and resecure its space through a movement between universality and invisibility. To treat whiteness as marginalized, or marginalizing, seems wrongheaded as it levels the power differentials between that which is strategic and that which is tactical.

STRATEGIC RHETORIC

Foucault, like Deleuze and Guattari, is particularly useful in analyzing the strategic rhetoric of whiteness because he does not see power as exercised in a naked manner. For him, power operates in much more complex, relationally-situated ways. In Deleuze's reading of Foucault, power-relations "are not 'localized' at any given moment. They constitute a strategy, an exercise of the non-stratified, and these 'anonymous strategies' are almost mute and blind, since they evade all stable forms of the visible and the articulable" (73). The anonymity of power is a significant cornerstone of Foucault's conceptualization of discursive formations. We are not looking for a major figure to impose his/her definition of "white" from above; instead, we are seeking the ways it is constituted in everyday discourse and reinscribes its position on the social landscape. In "What Is An Author?" Foucault rejects the construction of the autonomous individual as a source of power; in this study, we did not look for significant rhetors on whom to pin our analysis of "white."

Instead, we take the lens of everyday life in order to survey this territory. Maurice Blanchot underscores the significance of everyday life:

> Whatever its other aspects, the everyday has this essential trait: it allows no hold. It escapes. It belongs to insignificance, and the insignificant is without truth, without reality, without secret, but perhaps also the site of all possible signification. The everyday escapes. (14)

The everydayness of whiteness makes it a difficult territory to map. It is not constituted in ways that traditional methodologies can explore as Lefebvre observes: "The everyday, established and consolidated, remains a sole surviving common sense referent and point of reference. 'Intellectuals', on the other hand, seek their systems of reference elsewhere" (9). In order to survey critically the territory of whiteness, we turn toward Deleuze and Guattari's nomad science, in contrast to State science, to explore the everydayness of whiteness. A nomad science, in our reading, is not driven by methodology, but by perspective. Deleuze and Guattari explain that nomad science "*follows* the connections between singularities of matter and traits of expression, and lodges on the level of these connections, whether they be natural or forced. This is another organization of work and of the social field through work" (369). We are not driven by a desire to reproduce the invisibility and universality of the center; instead, we take everyday discourse as a starting point in the process of marking the territory of whiteness and the power relations it generates.

While power relations are non-stratified and not fixed, the discursive formation does have an element of the strata, but is not contained by it. In this case, the territory is defined by what constitutes and does not constitute "white." Deleuze and Guattari's assemblage is useful in extending Foucault's discursive formation in this situation as "the assemblage no longer presents an expression distinct from content, only unformed matters, destratified forces, and functions" (505). The discourses that constitute "white" are material, whereas their social functions remain hidden from analysis.

In his work on discursive formations, Foucault argues that these are not logically organized frameworks that function in non-contradictory ways. The construction of "white" as a category is replete with contradictions in the ways it expresses itself. The recognition of contradictions within discursive formations is underscored by Foucault:

> A discursive formation is not, therefore, an ideal, continuous, smooth text that runs beneath the multiplicity of contradictions, and resolves them in the calm unity of coherent thought; nor is it the surface in which, in a thousand different aspects, a contradiction is reflected that is always in retreat, but everywhere dominant. It is rather a space of multiple dissensions; a set of different oppositions whose levels and roles must be described. Archaeological analysis, then, erects the primacy of a contradiction that has its model in the simultaneous affirmation and negation of a single preposition. (*Archaeology of Knowledge* 155)

The central contradiction at work within the "white" discursive formation is its functional invisibility, yet importance: "If whiteness is everything and nothing, if whiteness as a racial category does not exist except in conflict with others, how can we understand racial politics in a social structure that centers whites, yet has no center?" (Nakayama and Penaloza 54)

In order to approach this contradiction, we need to expose whiteness as a cultural construction as well as the strategies that embed its centrality. We must deconstruct it as the locus from which Other differences are calculated and organized. The purpose of such an inquiry is certainly not to recenter whiteness, but to expose its rhetoric. It is only upon critically examining this strategic rhetoric that we can begin to understand the influences it has on our everyday lives and, by extension, our research.

Traditional approaches to rhetorical study have tended to privilege public speeches as focal points of analysis. In the late 20th century, however, white public figures tend to avoid addressing the topic of whiteness with rare exception. To feature speeches in our analysis would lead to the examination of the distorting rhetoric of individuals such as David Duke or Evan Mecham, two of the few whites to address publicly the issue of whiteness. Instead, we found it necessary to address more popular or everyday rhetoric.

The discourses we examine are drawn from popular culture literature, survey data, and ethnographic interviewing. Our initial impulse was to focus on popular culture and everyday interactions through the method of participant-observation. We turned to survey data and ethnographic interviewing because discussions of whiteness are not often accessible through non-confrontational aspects of participant observation. We reached this conclusion based in part on a number of ethnographic encounters similar to the following. In response to the question posed by a white ethnographer ("What does it mean to be white?"), a white individual stated: "I don't know exactly know what it means to be white, but we all know don't we? I mean I never talk about it, but I know that we understand each other at some level. Like when a black guy gets on an elevator or when you have a choice to sit or stand next to a white person or a black person. You pick the white person and you look at each other, the whites, and just know that we've got it better. You don't say anything but you know. It's in the look." We believe that this kind of communication about whiteness by whites makes it difficult to study, but vital that we do so. This phenomenon may be what one scholar has identified and named as "white bonding." Sleeter explains what this interaction means:

> I began to pay attention to what I will call "White racial bonding" processes White people engage in everyday. . . . These communication patterns take forms such as inserts into conversations, race-related "asides" in conversations, strategic eye-contact, and jokes. Often they are so short and subtle that they may seem relatively harmless. I used to regard such utterances as annoying expressions of prejudice or ignorance, but that seems to underestimate their power to demarcate racial lines and communicate solidarity. (8)

These discourses on whiteness are relatively hidden in everyday interaction, but when whites are confronted, when they are asked directly about whiteness, a multiplicity of discourses become visible. It is this multiplicity that drives the dynamic nature of its power relations or forces, always resecuring the hegemonic position of whiteness.

In order to map a strategic rhetoric of whiteness, we have assembled a multiplicity of discourses into a discursive formation. These strategies mark out and constitute the space of whiteness. By marking this territory, we are making the critical move of not allowing white subjectivity to assume the position of the universal subject—with its unmarked territory. Our discussion of these discourses, however, is not to be read hierarchically; to do so would be to build a strata [*sic*] rather than an assemblage.

WHITENESS AS A STRATEGIC RHETORIC

We have uncovered six strategies of the discourse of whiteness. One discursive strategy uncovered in our marking of this territory ties "white" closely to power in a rather crude, naked manner. Responding to an open-ended survey question, one student simply defined "white" as "majority" while another wrote "status." The slippage between these two social positions is rather slight; both emphasize a privileged social position grounded in their racial identity. Another student explained that white "means that I am part of the majority of people living in American [*sic*] and that I have been brought up a White American." The specific histories and consciousness that construct the majority position remain hidden from analysis. In this space, the majority ("white") position is not universal, rather it is particular to whites. And the power embedded in this particular position is hidden from analysis. As a commentator in a local newspaper observed:

> White males are everywhere. They control money and finance; they control the flow of information; they control corporate boards and union leadership. They predominate in police departments; they outnumber everyone in the officer ranks of the military. They are the majority of doctors and lawyers in the country. They dominate political offices at all levels of

government. . . . White males are simply not happy unless they have monopoly over everything they do. (Contreras 13)

Despite the statistical evidence demonstrating their secure position on power, the recognition of this power is often masked. As *Newsweek* observed: "This is a weird moment to be a white man. True, one of them just became president—but one of them *always* becomes president" (David Gates 48). Yet, this naturalized dominance is not entirely hidden from view, which is critical if it is to function as powerful.

A second strategy surfaces in negative definitions of white as opposed to a positive definition. People engaging in this discourse see white as meaning that they lacked any other racial or ethnic features; hence, they must be white by default. Thus, individuals described white as "not being black, hispanic, or the like." Presumably "the like" refers to the people given more specificity by other respondents who said: "I'm a white person w/o any black/asia/color [sic] in my background," or "It means I am White. Not Black, Brown, Yellow or Red." In his opening tale, one of the authors of this essay employed this strategy: "we were just white, not black or brown."

This strategy coincides with Kenneth Burke's conception of humans as being defined by the negative, which suggests that in every affirmation there is a negation. The strategy uncovered here reverses those poles and intimates that with every negation there is an affirmation. In the case of whites, that affirmation remains an invisible entity.

The use of colors here is important in understanding the workings of the assemblage. White is seen as a non-color, so that when a respondent notes that white means "not a colored person," the subtext may be the same as the respondent who notes that "the person is white with no other blood lines such as black, hispanic, asian, etc." As we read these answers, the unstated, silenced implication given its meaning and power from historical usage, is that white means not having any other "blood lines" to make it impure. Unlike other categories, one can only be white by not being anything else. This negative definition may be related to the invisibility of whiteness as a category or a position from which one speaks. A columnist for *The Arizona Republic* observed that, to him, "oddly, 'white' seems neutral and appropriate when the only other ethnic group mentioned is black" (Cook D1). White, as a subject position, is otherwise unmarked, which feels more appropriate and occupies a more universal discursive space. A writer for *The Village Voice* observes that "the little qualifier *non* [in 'White-non-Hispanic'] contains multitudes. It demonstrates how white people only appear after subtraction. The cultural markings of everyone else are spun out, separated, and identified in the statistical centrifuge, leaving only . . . pure whites" (Ball 26). Whiteness is only marked in reverse. This is a characteristic of domination. Deleuze and Guattari note that "the race-tribe exists only at the level of an oppressed race, and in the name of the oppression it suffers: there is no race but inferior, minoritarian; there is no dominant race; a race is defined not by its purity but rather by the impurity conferred upon it by a system of domination" (379). Within a discursive system of naming oppression, but never the oppressive class, white can only be a negative, an invisible entity. This characteristic of whiteness is unique to its discursive construction and must be understood as a part of its power and force. Its invisibility guarantees its unstratified nature.

In an analysis of clothing catalogues, *The Village Voice* critiqued J. Crew's racial representation: "'We don't do race-oriented marketing,' said Adrienne Perkov,

J. Crew's director of new market development, 'we try to make the product available to everyone.' That's an old standby: We don't market to a particular ethnic group, we sell a lifestyle. As if whites are 'everyone', because it's assumed they have no race" (Jones 52). Or as Gary Indiana reflects in *The Village Voice*, "We were only white when somebody wasn't" (28). The rhetoric of invisibility and universality, then, is reflected in popular press discourse. This rhetoric extends white space to the universal.

A third strategy emerged which "natural"izes "white" with a scientific definition. As a scientific classification, it holds little meaning other than reference to what people perceive to be superficial racial characteristics: "It just classifies people scientifically and not judgementally." Within this discourse, "white" means "nothing, except that is what color I am." We see here that whiteness is drained of its history and its social status; once again it becomes invisible. Jacques Derrida sees this invisibility as one that undergirds Western thinking: "White mythology—metaphysics has erased within itself the fabulous scene that has produced it, the scene that nevertheless remains active and stirring, inscribed in white ink, an invisible design covered over in the palimpsest" (213). The history that constructed and centered whiteness becomes invisible and its functions hidden.

Perhaps part of what is at work in this strategy is another invisible discursive power imbedded in Western metaphysics, one that privileges the Mind in the Mind/Body hierarchy of knowing. By referencing whiteness through science, the historical and experiential knowledge of whiteness is hidden beneath a scientific category. Conquergood reminds us that in this tradition "mental abstractions and rational thought are taken as both epistemologically and morally superior to sensual experience; bodily sensations, and the passions" (180). The invocation of science serves to privilege reason, objectivity, and masculinity, concepts that have long been viewed in the Western tradition as stable, and therefore more trustworthy, poles in the dialectic relationships that exist as reason/emotion, objectivity/subjectivity, masculinity/femininity. Gergen traces the lofty status accorded reason to the writings of Descartes, Spinoza, Hobbes, and Newton and then onto the "thinkers of the so-called Enlightenment in the eighteenth century—Locke, Hume, and Voltaire, among others" who placed an emphasis on the rationality of science (20). Conflating the discourse of whiteness with the label of science serves to mask irrationality and contradictions with a rational image possessing cultural currency.

By conceptualizing "white" as natural, rather than cultural, this view of whiteness eludes any recognition of power relations embedded in this category. This naturalization process is a crucial function of culture, according to Roland Barthes, and an expression of a conservative ideology. This third discourse appears to function in contradiction with the first discourse in which whiteness is related to a position of power.

A fourth strategy confuses whiteness with nationality (a legal status conferred by social institutions). In this depiction of whiteness, the vision of whiteness is bounded by national borders and recenters whiteness. Such a rhetorical move toward territorialization is a characteristic of an assemblage. Whiteness means "that I'm of American descent," or "white" means "white American." One white respondent explicitly stated, "A lot of times when people think of American, I bet you they probably think of white. They probably think it's redundant." Clearly, all Americans are not white, nor are all whites necessarily Americans. Yet, this confusion has appeared in other cultural discourses, such as confusion between "race" and nationality in Britain. Paul Gilroy notes "some of the strange conflicts that have emerged in circumstances where blackness and Englishness appear as mutually exclusive attributes and where the conspicuous antagonism between them proceeds on cultural terrain" ("Cultural Studies and Ethnic Absolutism" 190). To conflate nationality and "race" is an expression of power since it relegates those of other racial groups to an marginal role in national life.

Indeed, the history and tradition of the United States is replete with relentless efforts to retain and guard the boundaries of nationality with whiteness. After all, "the first Congress convened under that Constitution voted in 1790 to require that a person be 'white' in order to become a naturalized citizen of the US. Predictably enough, the hopeless imprecision of the term left the courts with impossible problems of interpretation that stretched well into the twentieth century" (Roediger 181). This historical legacy has staked out the bounds of citizenship that have been contested ever since. As a discursive strategy, the conflation of whiteness and U.S. citizenship challenges the very notion of a nation of immigrants; yet the persistence of this discourse reflects territorial claims to vital political terrain.

A fifth strategy can be recognized in the discourse of those individuals who refused to label themselves: "I don't agree with using ethnic terms. I'm an American & that's all. My ethnic heritage does not matter to me because that doesn't say who I am." In the same survey, when asked to provide an ethnic label for him/herself, this respondent noted: "I prefer not to be labeled. I don't like the terms black, white, brown, etc. I don't see the point in labels that say nothing more about a person than the color of their skin. 'Grouping' people by color has been done for too long. I think it's time we stopped. Character is the issue (should be). Not color." The assumption here is that ethnicity is racially defined. Another responded: "American—I think all other terms separate people & build barriers between ethnic groups. I want to break down walls & no longer call attention to color, but the person as a human." But this same individual also wrote: "I like my ethnic heritage. I'm part German, Irish, Swedish, English & some other countries. I love my heritage b/c it says where you came from." Thus, while ethnicity communicates heritage, it is something that is not to be named. For these people, two tensions became evident. On the one hand, those who felt that their ethnic heritage was irrelevant to their social location clearly rejected any claims of history. On the other hand, some respondents felt proud of their heritage, but did not want to use their ethnicity as an anchoring point for their identity. In either case, the emphasis on the ideology of individualism over subjectivity, the social construction of identity, is quite clear. Also, we observed within this discursive strategy the re-emergence of whiteness as invisible, as a non-label. As one white respondent noted: "Labels have negative meanings a lot of the time. Any label—Black, African American, nigger, honkey—any of them so I don't like to use labels. I'm just me—white." White in this case, is not seen as a label, but the other discursive markers are labels. The contradiction here is significant in the way it masks whiteness.

In addition to an overt resistance to labels and particular groups or categories of labels, there is a second less obvious form of resistance at work[,] which is the process of labeling itself. With only one or two exceptions, the individuals employing this aspect of the fifth strategy were male. In our reading of these instances, a reading based on our ethnographic involvements that allowed us to observe and record bodily reactions as well as verbal responses, we concluded that these white males reacted negatively when asked to provide an ethnic label for themselves.[5]

White males, by occupying a more strategic position than white females, have been accorded essentially a label-free existence. White females, although spared the double-indemnity of non-white females, still have been involved in on-going battles over identity and labels. Women struggle with multiple labels and meanings of all of the gender-biased terms that frequent the vernacular of the day. In addition, women today often consider a variety of surname options following the exchange of marriage vows. Men usually do not. Our point here is that white women may be more accepting of the labeling process than white males because of their more tactical position as women. We see this distinction as an element of that which is strategic and that which is tactical. Contemporary debates over homosexual vs. gay vs. queer, Black vs. African American, Hispanic vs. Latino vs. Chicano, and others reflect tactical rhetorics. Here we see a struggle over *who* gets to label *whom* in the social construction of identity.

Finally, a small group of the whites interviewed and surveyed saw their whiteness in relation to European ancestry. This historical foundation for their ethnic identity reflects an interest in what Gans has earlier identified as "symbolic ethnicity." These individuals recognize their European heritage and give a specificity to whiteness: "It means I am descended from European white people." While this discourse recognizes a part of its historical constitution, "White, of European descent," this reflexivity does not necessarily mean that there has been a recognition of the power relations embedded in that history. In fact, we did not find this extended reflexivity in the responses, except perhaps in a rather vague, coded way, "My ethnicity determines many factors in my life."

In a more recent study of symbolic ethnicity, Mary Waters found that many whites selected their ethnicity, much as one might try to accessorize a wardrobe. Ethnicity for them is not a substantial part of their everyday lives. Waters notes that "symbolic ethnicity persists because it meets a need Americans have for community without individual cost and that a potential societal cost of this symbolic ethnicity is in its subtle reinforcement of racism" (164).

Whether or not one discursively positions oneself as "white," there is little room for maneuvering out of the power relations imbedded in whiteness. Whiteness, stated or unstated, in any of its various forms, leaves one invoking the historically constituted and systematically exercised power relations. This creates an enormous problem for those in the center who do not want to reinforce the hegemonic position of the center and for those elsewhere who would challenge this assemblage and its influence on their lives.

As Foucault observed, discursive formations are replete with contradictions. In the assemblage of whiteness, we find that these contradictions are an important element in the construction of whiteness, as it is by these contradictions that whiteness is able to maneuver through and around challenges to its space. The dynamic element of whiteness is a crucial aspect of the persuasive power of this strategic rhetoric. It garners its representational power through its ability to be many things at once, to be universal and particular, to be a source of identity and difference. The discourses of nationality, for example, run counter to those of scientific classification; yet the emergence of a racialized nation has been marked out time and again in the U.S. and elsewhere. The discourses that define whiteness through its historical relationships to Europe further problematize these discursive movements. Whiteness eludes essentialism through this multiplicity and dynamism, while at the same moment containing within it the discourses of essentialism that classify it scientifically or define it negatively.

Our point here is not that there are contradictions within this discursive assemblage. Rather our principal thesis is that these contradictions are central to the dynamic lines of power that resecure the strategic, not tactical, space of whiteness, making it all the more necessary to map whiteness. Whiteness is complex and problematic; yet in communication interactions we are expected to understand what it means when someone says "white" or "American" or even "All-American." It is perhaps when whites use whiteness in communicating with other whites that the lines of power are particularly occluded, yet resilient as ever. This also has significant implications for communication researchers.

CONCLUSION AND AN INVITATION

In her analysis of how race influences the lives of white women, Ruth Frankenberg concludes that "whiteness changes over time and space and is in no way a transhistorical essence" (236). Indeed, this assumption has guided our inquiry into the terrain of whiteness. We have not sought any essentialized category in which borders and markers are fixed in any biological or "natural" sense. Whiteness, in our inquiry, is rhetorically constituted through discursive strategies that map the field of whiteness. Our survey is limited to the discourses of the late twentieth century in the U.S.; maps of whiteness in other nations at other times may reveal maps constituted within differing lines of power. Rather than offer any definitive conclusions, we offer instead an invitation to further consideration and dialogue about whiteness. We prescribe no framework for this discussion but see the concept of reflexivity as an important direction for further inquiry.

Hilary Lawson suggests that reflexivity is the central guiding term for life in the late 20th century, particularly for those interested in discourse: "all of our claims in general . . . are reflexive in a manner which cannot be avoided" (9). We see this reflexivity occurring in a number of disciplines, including communication studies. What follows are three aspects of reflexivity that may be helpful in further examining the space of whiteness.

First, reflexivity encourages consideration of that which has been silenced or invisible in academic discussions. Thus, the "white" social practice of not discussing whiteness is especially disturbing. Sleeter explains: "I suspect that our privileges and silences [about whiteness] are invisible to us [whites] partly because numerically we constitute the majority of this nation and collectively control a large portion of the nation's resources and media, which enable us to surround ourselves with our own varied experiences and to buffer ourselves from the experiences, and the pain and rage[,] of people of color" (6). Within the context of academic writing that silences whiteness, what kinds of power relations are reproduced within our own discipline? McKerrow, in one of his principles of critical rhetoric, notes that "*absence* is as important as *presence* in understanding and evaluating symbolic action" ("Theory and Praxis" 107). In what ways and under what conditions does the silencing of whiteness, its presumed understanding, reproduce communication interactions between and among whites? Do our academic practices and publications reinforce these white communication practices by not interrogating whiteness? As we have shown above, whiteness is a complex, dynamic, and power-laden assemblage that remains elusive. And, as Volosinov has noted, the ideological sign is always already multi-accentual. To assume that readers of communication scholarship already understand the multi-accentuality of whiteness is a mistake, for it presumes a white audience. "White" here is ideological, as one must play the white game; it does not require that one be "white"—discursively or scientifically.

Second, reflexivity encourages consideration of the presentation of research and the articulation of the researcher's position vis-à-vis social and academic structures. In his response to Raymie McKerrow's essay on critical rhetoric, Robert Hariman critiques McKerrow's presentation (read: performance) as a modernist, rather than postmodernist, subject. Hariman writes "that the writer of critical rhetoric appears as a thoroughly modern self: a disembodied thinker having no identifiable social location, writing in an impersonal style, and managing the disturbing powers of social life through the application of reason" (68). While both Hariman and Charland, as respondents to McKerrow, are concerned with the modernist discourse adopted by McKerrow, neither makes the critical move toward reflexivity, particularly around their relations to whiteness. At issue is not whether critical rhetoricians or those who critique critical rhetoric have social positions from which they write, but rather how they might articulate those social positions.

Following from the first and second points, reflexivity encourages an examination of the institutions and politics that produce "knowledge." Spearheaded by Conquergood, Wander and others, the postmodernist influence in communication studies supports an ideological reflexivity in scholarly endeavors that rests upon the recognition that the actions and the narratives (including reports of social research) that describe and interpret communication interactions, are "politically created" within constitutive sociohierarchical power relations (Deetz and Mumby 19).

James West claims, in addressing ethnographic research practices, the modernist faction of communication studies remains "anchored in modernist social science . . . that allows them to view their work and Others as apolitical" (210). Furthermore he states that those adhering to the dialogic/reflexive perspective advanced by the postmodernists examine the political nature and discursive strategies of our institutions and institutionalized practices. West notes that, "although many discourses do not focus on power as an overt central topic, ALL discourses are enacted within relations of power" (213). In his essay West challenges the power located in the discursive fields of institutional arrangements such as academia. He asserts that the power of academic discourse is maintained in part by journals that "discipline" and "silence" through "rules of exclusion." He does not interrogate, however, the privileged status that is reproduced in the discourses of whiteness which, in the sociohierarchical arrangement of U.S. culture, prefigures the power bases of academic institutions. West leaves that territory unmapped and unnamed. We contend that, by not naming and interrogating whiteness, authors such as West unwittingly conspire to secure its invisibility. While we applaud West for his project, we urge him and other communication scholars to move beyond a focus limited to the politics of academia that overlooks the strategic rhetoric of whiteness. As Michele Wallace underscores, "Much more insidious to me than the problem of white intellectuals theorizing nativist 'data' is the problem of 'whiteness' itself as an unmarked term" (7).

As a facet of this mapping process, we urge a consideration of whiteness in the context of other social relations, such as gender, sexual orientation, class, religion. This is an important next step in the development of this type of study. As Wood and Cox argue:

> Explicating one's self positioning, however, does not free one from responsibility for what is said and its consequences. Nor does it excuse the absences in one's knowledge. For instance, when a person says "I am a white, middle class, woman, so that is the only perspective I know and it performs what I say about women" and then proceeds to speak about and for women as a group, she has abused her position. (286n)

And, if she speaks for whites as a group, she has similarly abused her position. This demonstrates how whiteness (and class) becomes invisible again in Wood and Cox's observation.

We see a particularly glaring imbalance in the reflexivity accorded the terms "white" and "women"—an imbalance that has evolved through years of dialogue and inquiry about feminism and its relation to communication studies. As Lana Rakow correctly observes in the preface to her edited collection, "The terms 'women' and 'feminist' cannot be taken for granted; indeed, as several authors discuss in their chapters, the terms are themselves the site for significant epistemological, cultural, and political disagreements among those of us engaged in work on gender and race" (vii–viii). While these inquiries have investigated gender concerns and their complex relations to ideological issues, there has not been an equivalent interrogation of whiteness and its relation to ideological concerns. One step in that direction is to examine whiteness as the position from which scholars perform their studies. For example, Bette Kauffman states, "This narrative is about white women; it excludes women of color and the research from which it is drawn excluded women of color, albeit unwittingly, by virtue of its very design" (200). Kauffman begins to map the discursive territory of whiteness when she tells us that "white women have capitalized upon the margin of privilege so maintained, the attendant economic, educational, and cultural perquisites, in setting the agenda and claiming the benefits of the contemporary women's movement" (200). What is required is an ongoing discussion of the effects of whiteness on our research and on our personal and academic pursuits. The imbalance between discussions on gender and discussions on whiteness stems from a power differential between that which is tactical and that which is strategic. What is required are more sophisticated maps of the discursive field of whiteness.

The construction of discursive space of whiteness has material effects on the entire social structure and our places in relation to it. Grossberg notes that, "A territorializing machine attempts to map the sorts of places people can occupy and how they can occupy them. It maps how much room people have to move, and where and how they can move" (15). The power relations inherent in these spatial relations are embedded in our identities vis-à-vis whites or *qua* whites. They influence communication research and our everyday lives. This is why it is important for us to map these spaces. Our essay is an invitation for communication scholars to begin to mark and incorporate whiteness into their analyses and claims—an invitation to become reflexive.

NOTES

[1] In this essay, we are interested in exploring the constructed space of whiteness, not the ways that it influences the margins. Thus, we do not address racism or racist ideology, although these are closely aligned to many of the ways that whiteness is constructed.

[2] The answers to the open-ended survey questions we examined in this essay are part of a broader nationwide survey project. The goal of this project is to identify the preferences and comfortability of self-identifying ethnic labels for white students. To this date, we have received over 350 completed surveys from white students at twelve public and private universities in the United States. The number of responses are relatively balanced from the four areas of the United States, roughly defined as the North, South, Midwest, and West. The open-ended questions we included for our purposes for this essay asked white students to provide us with their meaning(s) of ethnic/racial labels.

In our analyses of their answers, we followed standard content analytic techniques as prescribed by Holsti and Krippendorf and followed procedures described in previous studies investigating ethnic labeling by Hecht, Collier, and Ribeau and by Larkey, Hecht, and Martin.

[3]The interviews are being conducted as part of an ongoing ethnographic project examining the ethnic/racial self-labeling practices of whites. The ethnographer is gathering these interviews at various non-academic and informal settings as a member of a primarily white bowling league, as a frequent visitor to an almost exclusively white gun club, and as an event-goer at various sporting events which are attended primarily by whites.

[4]While our focus in this essay is on the territory of white, we also recognize that the territory is composed of various sectors reflecting distinct characteristics and, in some cases, combinations of characteristics. We also recognize that the most invisible sector of the center is not only white but also male, heterosexual, Christian, and from privileged classes. So while we speak of white as a centered territory, we are sensitive to the marginal positions of females, alternative sexual orientations, non-traditional religious beliefs, and disadvantaged socio-economic groups within the broader territory. We must leave those issues, however, for future surveyors who will include more detail in the maps they produce.

[5]Further evidence for this interpretation stems from the significant number of white males who refused to complete the surveys. Included in this number were a group of white males who expressed hostility toward being asked questions about their racial/ethnic identity.

WORKS CITED

Anzaldúa, Gloria. *Borderlands/La frontera: The New Mestiza.* San Francisco: Spinsters/ Aunt Lute, 1987.

Asante, Molefi K. *The Afrocentric Idea.* Philadelphia: Temple UP, 1987.

———. "Television and Black Consciousness." *Journal of Communication* 26/4 (Autumn 1976): 137–141.

Asian Women United of California, eds. *Making Waves: An Anthology of Writings By and About Asian American Women.* Boston: Beacon, 1989.

Ball, Edward. "The White Issue." *The Village Voice,* 18 May 1993, pp. 24–27.

Barthes, Roland. *Mythologies.* Trans. Annette Lavers. New York: Hill and Wang, 1972.

Blanchot, Maurice. "Everyday Speech." Trans. Susan Hanson. *Yale French Studies,* 73 (1987): 12–20.

Bobo, Jacqueline. "The Color Purple: Black Women as Cultural Readers." In E. D. Pribram, ed., *Female Spectators.* New York: Verso, 1988.

Bogle, Donald. *Toms, Coons, Mulattoes, Mammies and Bucks: An Interpretive History of Blacks in American Films.* New York: Continuum, 1973/1989.

Burke, Kenneth. *Language as Symbolic Action: Essays on Life, Literature, and Method.* Berkeley: U of California P, 1966.

Centre for Contemporary Cultural Studies. *The Empire Strikes Back: Race and Racism in 70s Britain.* London: Hutchison in association with the Centre for Contemporary Cultural Studies, University of Birmingham, 1982.

Certeau, Michel. *The Practice of Everyday Life.* Trans. Steven Rendell. Berkeley: U of California P, 1988.

Charland, Maurice. "Finding a Horizon and Telos: The Challenge to Critical Rhetoric." *Quarterly Journal of Speech,* 77 (1991): 71–74.

Chen, Kuan-Hsing. "Deterritorializing 'Critical' Studies in 'Mass' Communication: Towards a Theory of 'Minor' Discourses." *Journal of Communication Inquiry,* 13/2 (1989): 43–61.

Christian, Barbara. "The Race for Theory." *Cultural Critique,* 6 (1987): 51–64.

Churchill, Ward. *Fantasies of the Master Race: Literature, Cinema and the Colonization of American Indians.* Ed. M. Annette Jaimes. Monroe, ME: Common Courage, 1992.

Collins, Patricia Hill. *Black Feminist Thought: Knowledge, Consciousness, and the Politics of Empowerment.* Boston: Unwin Hyman, 1990.

Combahee River Collective. "A Black Feminist Statement." In A. M. Jaeger and P. S. Rothenberg, eds., *Feminist Frameworks,* 2nd ed. New York: McGraw-Hill, 1984.

Conquergood, Dwight. "Rethinking Ethnography: Towards a Critical Cultural Politics." *Communication Monographs,* 58 (1991): 179–194.

Contreras, Raoul Lowery. "White males are bad sports about having to share power." *Tempe Daily News Tribune,* 4 April 1993, p. 13.

Cook, James E. "Watch Your Language!" *The Arizona Republic,* 7 November 1991, pp. D1–D2.

Deetz, Stanley and Dennis Mumby. "Power, Discourse, and the Workplace: Reclaiming the Critical Tradition." *Communication Yearbook,* 13 (1990): 18–47.

Deleuze, Gilles. *Foucault.* Trans. & ed. Seán Hand. Minneapolis: U of Minnesota P, 1988.

Deleuze, Gilles and Félix Guattari. *A Thousand Plateaus: Capitalism & Schizophrenia.* Trans. Brian Massumi. Minneapolis: U of Minnesota P, 1987.

Derrida, Jacques. *Margins of Philosophy.* Trans. Alan Bass. Chicago: U of Chicago P, 1982.

Dutcher, Patricia N. "The Meaning of Whiteness." In *Straight/White/Male.* Ed. Glenn R. Bucher. Philadelphia: Fortress Press, 1976, pp. 85–98.

Dyer, Richard. "White." *Screen* 29 (Autumn 1988): 44–65.

Fanon, Frantz. *Black Skins, White Masks.* Trans. C. L. Markmann. New York: Grove Press, 1967.

Ferguson, Russell. "Introduction: Invisible Center." In *Out There: Marginalization and Contemporary Cultures.* Ed. Russell Ferguson et al. New York and Cambridge: New Museum of Contemporary Art and MIT Press, 1990, pp. 9–14.

Foucault, Michel. *The Archaeology of Knowledge.* Trans. A. M. Sheridan Smith. New York: Pantheon, 1972.

———. "The Discourse on Language." In *The Archaeology of Knowledge,* pp. 215–237.

———. "What Is An Author?" In *Textual Strategies: Perspectives in Post-Structuralist Criticism.* Trans. & ed. Josué V. Harari. Ithaca: Cornell UP, 1979, pp. 141–160.

Frankenberg, Ruth. *White Women, Race Matters: The Social Construction of Whiteness.* Minneapolis: U of Minnesota P, 1993.

Fregoso, Rosa Linda and Angie Chabram, eds. "Chicano/a Cultural Representations." Special issue, *Cultural Studies,* 4/3 (October 1990).

Friar, Ralph E. and Natasha A. Friar. *The Only Good Indian . . . : The Hollywood Gospel.* New York: Drama Book Specialists, 1972.

Frye, Marilyn. "On Being White: Toward A Feminist Understanding of Race and Race Supremacy." In *The Politics of Reality: Essays in Feminist Theory.* Trumansburg, NY: The Crossing Press, 1983.

Fuss, Diana. *Essentially Speaking; Feminism, Nature & Difference.* New York: Routledge, 1989.

Gans, Herbert. "Symbolic Ethnicity: The Future of Ethnic Groups and Cultures in America." *Ethnic and Racial Studies,* 2 January 1979): 1–20.

Gates, David. "White Male Paranoia." *Newsweek,* 29 March 1993, pp. 48–53.

Gates, Henry Louis, Jr. *"Race," Writing, and Difference.* Chicago: U of Chicago P, 1986.

Gergen, Kenneth. *The Saturated Self: Dilemma of Identity in Contemporary Life.* New York: Basic Books, 1991.

Gilroy, Paul. "Cultural Studies and Ethnic Absolutism." *Cultural Studies.* Ed. Lawrence Grossberg, Cary Nelson, and Paula A. Treichler. New York: Routledge, 1992, pp. 187–198.

———. *The Black Atlantic: Modernity and Double Consciousness.* Cambridge, MA: Harvard UP, 1993.

———. *There Ain't No Black in the Union Jack: The Cultural Politics of Race and Nation.* London: Hutchinson, 1987.

Gray, Herman. "Television, Black Americans, and the American Dream." *Critical Studies in Mass Communication,* 6/4 (December 1989): 376–386.

Grossberg, Lawrence. "Cultural Studies an[d]/in New Worlds." *Critical Studies in Mass Communication,* 19 (1993): 1–22.

Hall, Stuart. "Gramsci's Relevance for the Study of Race and Ethnicity." *Journal of Communication Inquiry,* 10/2 (Summer 1986): 5–27.

———. "Signification, Representation, Ideology: Althusser and the Post-Structuralist Debates." *Critical Studies in Mass Communication,* 2 (June 1985): 91–114.

———. "The Whites of Their Eyes: Racist Ideologies and the Media." In *Silver Linings: Some Strategies for the Eighties.* Ed. George Bridges and Rosalind Brunt. London: Lawrence and Wishart, 1981, pp. 28–52.

Hariman, Robert. "Critical Rhetoric and Postmodern Theory." *Quarterly Journal of Speech,* 77 (1991): 67–70.

Hecht, Michael L., Mary Jane Collier, and Sidney Ribeau. *African American Communication.* Newbury Park, CA: Sage, 1993.

Holsti, O. R. *Content Analysis for the Social Sciences and Humanities.* Reading, MA: Addison Wesley, 1969.

hooks, bell. *Ain't I a Woman? Black Women and Feminism.* Boston: South End, 1981.

———. *Black Looks: Race and Representation.* Boston: South End, 1992.

———. *Feminist Theory: From Margin to Center.* Boston: South End, 1984.

———. *Yearning: Race, Gender, and Cultural Politics.* Boston: South End, 1990.

Houston Stanback, Marsha. "What Makes Scholarship About Black Women and Communication Feminist Communication Scholarship?" *Women's Studies in Communication,* 11 (Spring 1988): 28–31.

Indiana, Gary. "Memoirs of a Xenophobic Boyhood." *The Village Voice,* 18 May 1993, pp. 27–28.

Jones, Lisa. "1-800-WASP." *The Village Voice,* 10 September 1991, p. 52.

Kauffman, Bette J. "Feminist Facts: Interview Strategies and Political Subjects in Ethnography." *Communication Theory,* 2, 187–206.

Krippendorf, Klaus. *Content Analysis.* Beverly Hills, CA: Sage, 1980.

Larkey, Linda K., Michael L. Hecht, and Judith N. Martin. "What's in a Name: African American Ethnic Identity Terms and Self-Determination." *Journal of Language and Social Psychology,* 12/4 (1993): 302–317.

Lawson, Hilary. *Reflexivity: The Post-Modern Predicament.* La Salle, IL: Open Court, 1985.

Lefebvre, Henri. "The Everyday and Everydayness." Trans. Christine Levich with Alice Kaplan and Kristin Ross. *Yale French Studies,* 73 (1987): 7–11.

Leong, Russell, ed. *Moving the Image: Independent Asian Pacific American Media Arts.* Los Angeles: UCLA Asian American Studies Center and Visual Communications, Southern California Asian American Studies Central, Inc., 1991.

Lorde, Audre. *Sister Outsider.* Freedom, CA: Crossing Press, 1984.

McKerrow, Raymie, E. "Critical Rhetoric: Theory and Praxis." *Communication Monographs,* 56 (June 1989): 91–111.

———. "Critical Rhetoric in a Postmodern World." *Quarterly Journal of Speech,* 77 (1991): 75–78.

Memmi, Albert. *The Colonizer and the Colonized.* Trans. H. Greenfield. Boston: Beacon, 1965.

Moraga, Cherrie. "From a Long Line of Bendidas: Chicanas and Feminism." In T. de Lauretis, ed., *Feminist Studies/Critical Studies.* Bloomington: Indiana UP, 1986.

Nakagawa, Gordon. "'No Japs Allowed': Negation and Naming as Subject-Constituting Strategies Reflected in Contemporary Stories of Japanese American Internment." *Communication Reports,* 3/1 (Winter 1990): 22–27.

Nakayama, Thomas K. "Dis/orienting Identities: Asian Americans, History and Intercultural Communication." In *Our Voices: Essays in Communication, Culture, and Ethnicity*. Ed. Alberto Gonzalez, Marsha Houston, and Victoria Chen. Los Angeles: Roxbury, 1994, 12–17.

———. "'Model Minority' and the Media: Discourse on Asian America." *Journal of Communication Inquiry*, 12/1 (1988): 65–73.

Nakayama, Thomas K. and Lisa N. Penaloza. "Madonna T/Races: Music Videos Through the Prism of Color." In *The Madonna Connection: Representational Politics, Subcultural Identities, and Cultural Theory*. Ed. Cathy Schwichtenberg. Boulder, CO: Westview, 1993, pp. 39–55.

Nesteby, James R. *Black Images in American Film, 1896–1954*. Washington, DC: University Press of America, 1982.

Noriega, Chon A., ed. *Chicanos and Film: Representation and Resistance*. Minneapolis: U of Minnesota P, 1992.

Omi, Michael. "In Living Color: Race and American Culture." In *Cultural Politics in Contemporary America*. Ed. Ian Angus and Sut Jhally. New York: Routledge, 1989, pp. 111–122.

Rakow, Lana F., ed. *Women Making Meaning: New Feminist Directions in Communication*. New York: Routledge, 1992.

Roediger, David R. *Towards the Abolition of Whiteness: Essays on Race, Politics, and Working Class History*. New York: Verso, 1994.

Rosaldo, Renato. *Culture and Truth: The Remaking of Social Analysis*. Boston: Beacon, 1989.

Said, Edward W. *Orientalism*. New York: Vintage, 1979.

———. *The Question of Palestine*. New York: Vintage, 1980.

———. *Covering Islam: How the Media and the Experts Determine How We See the Rest of the World*. New York: Pantheon, 1981.

———. *After the Last Sky: Palestinian Lives*. New York: Pantheon, 1986.

———. *Racial Formations/Critical Transformations: Articulations of Power in Ethnic and Racial Studies in the United States*. Atlantic Highlands, NJ: Humanities Press International, 1992.

San Juan, Jr., E. "Symbolizing the Asian Diaspora in the United States: A Return to the Primal Scene of Deracination." *Border/Lines* 24/25 (1992): 23–29.

Sheehan, Jack G. *The TV Arab*. Bowling Green: Bowling Green State University Popular Press, 1984.

Sleeter, Christine. "White Racism." *Multicultural Education*, Spring 1994, pp. 5–8, 39.

Smith, Barbara, ed. *Home Girls: A Black Feminist Anthology*. New York: Kitchen Table, 1983.

Spelman, Elizabeth B. *Inessential Woman: Problems of Exclusion in Feminist Thought*. Boston: Beacon, 1988.

Spivak, Gayatri Chakravorty. "Can the Subaltern Speak?" In Cary Nelson and Lawrence Grossberg, eds., *Marxism and the Interpretation of Culture*. Urbana: U of Illinois P, 1988, pp. 271–313.

———. *In Other Worlds: Essays in Cultural Politics*. New York: Methuen, 1987.

Tachiki, Amy, et al., eds. *Roots: An Asian American Reader*. Los Angeles: UCLA Asian American Studies Center, 1971.

Takaki, Ronald. *Iron Cages: Race and Culture in 19th-Century America*. Seattle: U of Washington P, 1979.

———. *Strangers from a Different Shore: A History of Asian Americans*. Boston: Little, Brown, 1989.

Tanno, Dolores V. "Names, Narratives, and the Evolution of Ethnic Identity." In *Our Voices: Essays in Communication, Culture, and Ethnicity*. Ed. Alberto Gonzalez, Marsha Houston, and Victoria Chen. Los Angeles: Roxbury, 1994, pp. 30–33.

Trinh T. Minh-ha. *Woman, Native, Other: Writing Postcoloniality and Feminism.* Bloomington: Indiana UP, 1989.

———. *When the Moon Waxes Red: Representation, Gender and Politics.* New York: Routledge, 1991.

Uchida, Aki. "'We are named by others and we are named by ourselves': On the other- and self-labeling of non-white women." Paper presented at the 78th Annual Meeting of the Speech Communication Association, 29 October–1 November 1992, Chicago.

Valaskakis, Gail G. "The Chippewa and the Other: Living the Heritage of Lac du Flambeau." *Cultural Studies,* 2 (1988): 267–293.

Volosinov, V. N. *Marxism and the Philosophy of Language.* Trans. Ladislav Matejka and I. R. Titunik. New York: Seminar Press. 1973.

Wallace, Michèle. "Multiculturalism and Oppositionality." *Afterimage,* 19/3 (October 1991): 6–9.

Wander, Philip. "The Ideological Turn in Modern Criticism." *Central States Speech Journal,* 34 (Spring 1983): 1–18.

———. "The Third Persona: The Ideological Turn in Rhetorical Theory." *Central States Speech Journal,* 35 (Winter 1984): 197–216.

Waters, Mary C. *Ethnic Options: Choosing Identities in America.* Berkeley: U of California P, 1990.

West, Cornel. *Race Matters.* Boston: Beacon, 1993.

West, James T. "Ethnography and Ideology: The Politics of Cultural Representation." *Western Journal of Communication,* 57 (Spring 1993): 209–220.

Wood, Julia T. and Robert Cox. "Rethinking Critical Voice: Materiality and Situated Knowledges." *Western Journal of Communication,* 57 (Spring 1993): 278–287.

HEGEMONY OR CONCORDANCE? THE RHETORIC OF TOKENISM IN "OPRAH" WINFREY'S RAGS-TO-RICHES BIOGRAPHY

DANA L. CLOUD

A black person has to ask herself, 'If Oprah Winfrey can make it, what does it say about me?' They no longer have any excuse.

—Oprah Winfrey, quoted in Mair (1994, p. 183)

The journey of Oprah Gail Winfrey from Hattie Mae's pig farm in Mississippi to the pinnacle of wealth, power, and success in American television is a journey we must all admire. . . . She is the ultimate American success story. That a tiny, illegitimate black girl from dirt-poor Mississippi can transform herself into the richest and most powerful black woman in the world is a triumph of the human spirit and the American dream.

(Mair 1994, p. 349)

The story of individual triumph over humble beginnings is a staple of a culture steeped in Horatio Alger mythology, in the service of an inegalitarian economic order buttressed by an ideology of individual achievement and responsibility. As Weiss (1969) summarizes in his book on the Horatio Alger myth,

The idea that ours is an open society, where birth, family, and class do not significantly circumscribe individual possibilities, has a strong hold on the

> popular imagination. The belief that all men, in accordance with certain rules, but exclusively by their own efforts, can make of their lives what they will has been widely popularized for well over a century. (p. 3)

Rooted in the Protestant ethic and popularized in novels and self-help literature, the success myth is continually belied by the realities of class, race, and gender stratification in capitalist society.

Recent communication scholarship on Bill Cosby and the *Cosby Show* has suggested that popular discourse about black family life often deploys assumptions of liberalism that interpret poverty and hardship as individual or family failures, and success exclusively as individual triumph (Gray, 1989; Jhally and Lewis, 1992). This work argues that *Cosby* perpetuates self-blame among African-Americans for failure and complacency in the dominant culture regarding the fight against racism. Even when black people produce their own images, as Cosby and Oprah Winfrey do, secondary texts, including the news, star discourse, and biographical profiles work to frame those images and build the personae of black stars in hegemonic ways that escape the stars' control.

McMullen and Solomon (1994) make a similar argument about Steven Spielberg's appropriation and adaptation of Alice Walker's novel *The Color Purple*. They argue that the film turned the book, which was a powerful account of racism, sexism, and poverty from the vantage of its protagonist Celie, into

> the *melodramatic* narrative of an individual who successfully triumphs over interpersonal and economic adversity. Like other melodramas, the heroine's success results not only in personal glory, but also in the restoration and reaffirmation of the social order. (p. 163)

This strategy of appropriation and adaptation marks the proliferation of popular biographies of Oprah Winfrey. This article examines these narratives in order to understand how they construct an "Oprah" persona whose life story as it is appropriated in popular biographies resonates with and reinforces the ideology of the American Dream, implying the accessibility of this dream to black Americans despite the structural economic and political obstacles to achievement and survival posed in a racist society. I do not mean to indict Oprah Winfrey herself, but rather challenge her persona as it is constructed and performed both with and without her direct participation. In referring to "Oprah," a first name bracketed by quotation marks, rather than to Oprah Winfrey the "real" person, I mean to aim my criticisms at the way in which popular culture appropriates and uses the images and stories of black Americans. Popular biographers of Winfrey almost exclusively use only her first name, in the rhetorical construction of a persona who is not necessarily coterminous with the person. McMullen and Solomon (1994) write that popularizations function as "terministic screens" or filters that foreground some features of reality and obscure others, and that produce conventional, ideological narratives out of complex experience.

This article argues that the content, pervasiveness, and popularity of the "Oprah" narratives warrant the recognition of a "terministic screen" or genre of discourse called tokenist biography, defined as biographical narratives that authorize a person from a marginalized or oppressed group to speak as a culture hero *on the condition* that the person's life story be framed in liberal capitalist terms. Like Clarence Thomas during his Supreme Court confirmation hearings (see Morrison, 1992), "Oprah" is constructed in the biographical narratives that frame her rise to stardom in the late 1980s as a black person who, refusing identification with the politics of black liberation, "proves" that the American Dream is possible for all black Americans.

The article theorizes the concepts of hegemony, tokenism, star personae, and biographical narrative, arguing against Condit's (1994) reframing of hegemony as an acceptable cultural negotiation or compromise. Then I summarize the generic Oprah Winfrey biography, drawing out its constituent elements, and describe how this narrative represents a rhetoric of tokenism. Third, the essay analyzes specific instances of biographical tribute to Oprah Winfrey, focusing on a televised video biography of Oprah aired in 1990. Finally, I challenge the assumption of identity politics that representatives of oppressed groups automatically speak in an authentic oppositional voice.

Although texts like the television tribute to Oprah Winfrey invoke histories of race- and gender-based oppression, they recuperate and neutralize these histories in the liberal discourse of individual success. This bootstraps philosophy obscures the collective nature of oppression and the need for collective social action, exemplified in the sit-ins, marches, demonstrations, strikes, and other collective challenges of the civil rights movement, to remedy social injustice. Often, such discourse takes the form of biographical narratives glorifying a person for overcoming hardship. My examination of television and magazine biographies of "Oprah" reveals the hegemonic effect of elements of these narratives. This essay explores how the rags-to-riches narrative of much popular biography serves the hegemony of liberal individualism in U.S. popular and political culture.

LIBERAL HEGEMONY: CONCORDANCE OR CONTAINMENT?

By hegemony, I refer to the process by which a social order remains stable by generating consent to its parameters through the production and distribution of ideological texts that define social reality for the majority of the people. Condit (1994) has challenged this notion of hegemony, arguing that critics should take "hegemony" to mean "concordance," or the emergence of tenable compromise out of multicultural conflict, "the best that can be negotiated under the given conditions" (p. 210). Condit accuses feminist and Marxist critics of over-estimating the forces of domination and oversimplifying the process of cultural negotiation. Even so, I maintain that an understanding of hegemony as concordance is an appropriate critical model only if one is satisfied with the compromises allowed within and by the "given conditions." Indeed, an analysis of "Oprah" biographies as an example of a kind of cultural compromise will test Condit's assumptions.

Condit's reworking of Gramsci's (1971/1936) theory depends upon her argument that economic relations of contemporary Western society are no longer based on prominent class divisions; rather, she suggests, contemporary U.S. society runs on a "mixed economy" that provides an adequate safety net for the poor and a large measure of material equality. For this reason, her purpose is to give the term "hegemony"—previously associated with a negative critique of a dominant and dominating culture—a more positive valence with the term "concordance." However, Condit's assumption that domination and division are no longer primary features of contemporary Western society is fundamentally mistaken. While affluent nations, in times of economic growth, do provide jobs and some measure of security to wage laborers (the majority of the population), that security by no means negates the fundamental class relations of the society. In other words, the relative prosperity of some sectors of the working class does not mean that those workers are "amalgamated with capitalists" (Condit, 1994, p. 208) in their long-term interests. The erosion of prosperity during the protracted periods of economic recession in the world economy over the last two decades makes class divisions easier to see.

While Condit points out that the United States is a society of relative affluence, she fails to note that fully one-third of black Americans (and nearly half of all black children; see Edmonds & U[s]dansky, 1994) live in poverty. Further, real wages overall in the United States have declined twenty percent in the past two decades. An October, 1994, census report showed that from 1989 to 1993, the typical American household lost $2,344 in annual income, a decline of seven percent. Further, the number of Americans living in poverty was up sharply in 1994 from 1989. The *New York Times* reported,

> While average per capita income was up, by 1.8 percent, most of the benefits flowed to the wealthiest Americans. The Census report showed record levels of inequality, with the top fifth of American households earning 48.2 percent of the nation's income, while the bottom fifth earned just 3.6 percent. (DeParle, 1994, p. A16)

This report confirmed what Bartlett and Steele (1992) and Phillips (1990) have noted, namely that class divisions in the United States have become more, not less, pronounced in recent decades, as CEO incomes average more than 150 times the average worker's salary, and the minimum wage is, in real terms, worth less than it was in the 1930s. And because of ongoing racism and sexism, black Americans and women are overrepresented among the working poor. Clearly, the United States (indeed, the world) is still a society divided not only by class but also by race and gender.

In this context, classical hegemony theory usefully calls attention to the limits of compromises within the available conditions. It is crucial to understand how a rhetorically crafted concordance presents the facade of democratic compromise while obscuring the conservative effects of such a compromise. Gramsci (1971/1936) and later writers on hegemony (see Gitlin, 1980; Hall, 1986a; Lears, 1985; Murphy, 1992; Williams, 1973) understood that capitalist societies produce relations of power not only in structures of commodity production and exchange, but also through structures of ideas, or ideologies, that become the taken-for-granted common sense of the society. Cultural texts win the adherence of the mass audience to "the values, norms, perceptions, beliefs, sentiments, and prejudices that support and define the existing distribution of goods, the institutions that decide how this distribution occurs, and the permissible range of disagreement about those processes" (Lears, 1985, p. 569).

However, because social systems and their prevailing ideological justifications (capitalism and liberalism in the United States) are always contested, social stability depends on the ability of the ideology to absorb and re-frame challenges (see also Hall, 1986a). For this reason, contradiction, rupture, and multivocality are taken by the hegemony theorist not as signs that a democratic compromise has been achieved, but that a few token voices are allowed to speak within the "permissible range of disagreement." This critical emphasis is important if we are to guard against overplaying small moments of contradiction, rupture, or textual play in a social system and ideological frame that has been relatively effective at containing the impact of those moments. The rhetoric of tokenism, as it will be defined below, participates in the hegemony of liberal capitalism in so far as it acknowledges black voices, but redefines oppression as personal suffering and success as individual accomplishment.

This individualism is central to liberalism, the ideological counterpart to modern capitalist economics. As Hall (1986b) explains, liberalism varies between conservative, "laissez-faire" libertarianism (Reaganism, Thatcherism) and a social-democratic liberalism that favors state moderation of the effects of capitalism and tempers radical individualism with notions of social justice, as in the New Deal. Regardless of its variations, however, liberalism's core is its notion of the autonomous individual who is ostensibly free from structural or economic barriers to fortune. In his essay "A Liberal Legacy: Blacks Blaming Themselves for Economic Failures," Wayne Parent defines liberalism as the belief in America as a land of abundant opportunity and resources for everyone, and "a common belief in the propriety of individual labors producing individual rewards" (1985, pp. 3–4). Parent adds, "Blacks have been the most glaring exception to the uniquely American experience" (p. 5). An analysis of the Oprah Winfrey biography reveals how liberal individualism requires the "rags-to-riches" story as "proof" that the dream of individual achievement against all odds is real. This dream, in turn, justifies continuing inattention to structural factors, like race, gender, and class, that pose barriers to the dream for some Americans.

BIOGRAPHY, AUTOBIOGRAPHY, AND STAR DISCOURSE

One way in which biographical and autobiographical narratives encode the American Dream is through the invention of the classical liberal self who is the hero of the story, which is presented as "true." For example, Mair (1994) gives his biography of "Oprah" the title *Oprah Winfrey: The Real Story,* as if editing, selection of narratives, framing, chapter organization, and so forth were not rhetorical choices on the part of the biographer. As a realist form of narrative, biography naturalizes its rhetorical strategies and ideological motives (Nadel, 1984, p. 6). Recent scholarship on autobiographical writing and performance has suggested that even (self-authored) autobiographies construct selves and narrate lives as "critical fictions" (Smith, 1987, p. 6) rather than as expositions of "authentic" life experience. Smith (1987) writes that in autobiography, "the narrative 'I' becomes a fictive persona" (p. 46). Oprah Winfrey's autobiography, originally due out from Knopf in 1993, has been put on hold. However, it follows that what is true of self-constructs in autobiography—that they *are* constructs—is even more evident in the practice of biography, which reveals more about cultural ideologies than about its purported objects, the personalities of popular heroes.

Although "Oprah" herself participates in the construction of her persona (in interviews and so forth), the invention of "Oprah" has assumed dimensions beyond "Oprah"'s—or any single agent's—direct control. Because race, gender, and other dimensions of identity are products of cultural definition rather than essential characteristics of a person, popular culture heroes, more than most people, "speak the culture" and are not the sole agents in the creation of their selves and social roles. Hall (1981) writes, "We have to 'speak through' the ideologies which are active in our society and which provide us a means of 'making sense' of social relations and our place in them" (p. 32). So even when "Oprah" is speaking on her show or to reporters, her persona has a cultural life of its own.

More to the point is how biographers appropriate the lives of celebrities to create a public persona that works within "the permissible range of disagreement" of liberal society. Richard Dyer's (1986) study of how "stars function as media texts" (p. ix) notes that "stars are involved in making themselves into commodities. . . . They do not produce themselves alone" (p. 5). Dyer goes on to describe how "the star him/herself as well as make-up artists, hairdressers, . . . body-building coaches, . . . publicists" and others perform the labor of transforming the raw material of a person into a star—a publicly held icon of fame and fortune (p. 6). Dyer argues that because individualism is at the heart of both the liberal ideology and the making of a star, "protest about the lack of control over the outcome of one's labor can remain within the logic of individualism" (p. 7). "Oprah" herself provides an example of this containment mechanism. In a recent *People* profile (Dale, Fisher, & McFarland, 1994), "Oprah" expresses frustration with and resistance to audience expectations regarding her weight, her engagement to Stedman Graham, or her show's topics and style. It is clear from her statements that she, like the stars in Dyer's study, resents her lack of control over her image and her lack of privacy: "You reach the point where you're not willing to accept the bull that you used to. . . . I don't feel the pressure now to make sure people like me" (quoted in Dale, Fisher, & McFarland, 1994, p. 87). Most recent profiles of "Oprah" emphasize her new "to-hell-with-what-the-world-thinks attitude" (Kanner, 1994). The cancellation of her autobiography, a last-minute decision, is hailed as a demonstration of "Oprah"'s independent will (see Randolph, 1993). Dyer (1986) explains that the tension between the sometimes incongruent private and public "selves" of a celebrity can generate moments of reflexivity about the production of a public persona. In other words, "Oprah"'s self-authorizing in an autobiography may have been at odds with public expectations about her persona and role. But resistance to expectations in the form of the assertion of individual autonomy (rather than criticizing the ideological uses to which one's life has been put) is acceptable within the frame of a larger, entrepreneurial ethos.

The Oprah Biography

Dyer's point that stars do not make themselves alone provides insight into the production of discourses about Oprah Winfrey. Biographical profiles framing "Oprah" as liberal hero have proliferated and continue to appear in a wide range of popular outlets, from *Reader's Digest* (Culhane, 1989) and *People* (Dale, Fisher & McFarland, 1994; Levitt, Fisher & Mills, 1993; Rosen & Fisher, 1994; Richman, 1987) to *Ebony* (Randolph, 1993; Whitaker, 1987), *Essence* (Edwards, 1986; Noel, 1985; Taylor, 1987), *Redbook* (Rogers, 1993), *Cosmopolitan* (Cameron, 1989), *Ladies Home Journal* (Brashler, 1991; Gerosa, 1994; Grass, 1988; Kanner, 1994), *Good Housekeeping* (Anderson, 1986; Ebert, 1991), *Time* (Zoglin, 1986 & 1988), *Ms.* (Angelou, 1989; Barthel, 1986; Gillespie, 1988), and *Working Woman* (Goodman, 1991; Noglows, 1994).[1] In addition, there have been at least four popular book-length "Oprah" biographies (Bly, 1993; King, 1987; Mair, 1994; Waldron, 1987) and a television tribute (*America's All Star Tribute,* 1990) to Oprah Winfrey. The book-length biographies, all "unauthorized" by Winfrey, routinely appear on national bestseller lists. Bly (1993), for example, sold more than one million copies in its first year, and was one of only six mass-marketed non-fiction books to become a best-seller in that year, according to *Publisher's Weekly* (McEvoy, 1994, p. 36). Bly's "Oprah" biography also made the mass market best-seller lists in 1994 (Simson, 1994 & 1995).

Despite the cultural and political range of the periodicals represented (*Reader's Digest* to *Ms.*), the "Oprah" biography is generic. Without exception, these narratives, reaching audiences of millions in major popular periodicals, deal exhaustively with "Oprah"'s struggle to control her eating and her weight, her shopping sprees and exotic vacations, her on-and-off engagement to Stedman Graham, her ongoing confrontation with memories of childhood sexual abuse, and her subsequent campaign to educate her audiences about child sexual abuse.

But most consistently (with the exception of Harrison, 1989, discussed below), the narratives of "Oprah"'s life begin with stories of her humble and difficult childhood, which included episodes of physical and sexual abuse as well as poverty and racism, trace her life through her college years during which she rejected the claims and politics of the civil rights movement, and celebrate her rise to fame and her philanthropic spirit during her film and television career. In *Redbook*, Rogers (1993) proclaims,

> Oprah Winfrey's life is a modern-day Horatio Alger story of a poor, illegitimate black girl who went from rags to incredible riches while challenging all the rules. (p. 94)

Similarly, the flyleaf to Robert Waldron's best-selling biography of "Oprah" (1987) reads,

> Here's the COMPLETE story of the life of the incredible Oprah Winfrey . . . a woman who beat the traumas of a downtrodden childhood and the racial barriers put up by society—a woman who has gone on to become a gifted and acclaimed actress, and a TV personality whose bonds of trust and warmth with her guests and her audience have made her one of the nation's most beloved personalities.

In addition to narrating Oprah Winfrey's life as an incredible individual triumph over adversity, another generic convention of "Oprah" biographies is an emphasis on "Oprah"'s refusal to participate in the civil rights movement. Waldron quotes "Oprah" on her college years:

> "Everybody was angry for four years. . . . Whenever there was any conversation on race, I was on the other side, maybe because I never felt the kind of repression other black people are exposed to." (quoted in Waldron, 1987, p. 63)

Likewise, Mair (1994) notes that

> When she was in college, she worked in broadcasting during the burgeoning civil rights movement and didn't have either time or sympathy for black militants on campus. To Oprah this was an enormous waste of time and it still is. *She thinks you have to make it on your own and be answerable for your own success or failure* (p. 174, emphasis added).

The mythos of the self-made person, in concert with the rejection of structural critique of racism and sexism, resonates throughout all of the biographies. "Oprah"'s refusal of civil rights agitation and repeated assertion that she was not oppressed contradict other stories she has told countless reporters about growing up with cockroaches for pets, living with the shame of a mother who cleaned the houses of her white schoolmates, and so on. Paradoxically, Winfrey's sister, Patricia Lee, denies "Oprah"'s tales of hardship, claiming a difficult but not desperately poor childhood. Why might "Oprah" invent herself—and be invented by her biographers—in terms of a childhood of oppression and suffering? Perhaps a starker contrast between past and present makes for a compelling narrative documentation of the rise from penury to profit.

The contrast between past and present, and the contradiction between oppression and triumph, is a central tension of tokenist biography, which must pry into and recognize oppression while at the same time disclaiming its salience with regard to an individual's success or failure. The motion in the narratives is always from a linguistic emphasis on "Oprah"'s difference and her collective group identification, to individualistic themes of self-determination and success: Oprah goes from being a self-described "little nappy-haired colored girl" (quoted in Bly, 1994, p. 376) to "the world's highest paid entertainer" (Bly, p. 376) unmarked by race or gender difference in the generic narrative.

Tokenism and Liberal Hegemony

The rhetoric of tokenism is one strategy by which texts authorize people whose difference (along the axes of race, class, gender, sexual orientation, or other category) if politicized and collectively articulated might pose a threat to a dominant order in which some groups are kept subordinate to others. A token is the cultural construction of a successful persona who metonymically represents a larger cultural grouping. Tokens, as the word implies, are a medium of exchange, through which group identity, politics, and resistance are traded for economic and cultural capital within popular cultural spaces. Tokenism glorifies the exception in order to obscure the rules of the game of success in capitalist society.

But tokenism is not one-sided. For someone to be constructed as a token, she or he must by definition have overcome the oppression resulting from membership in a subordinate group. For this reason, texts that make tokens out of figures like Bill Cosby or Oprah Winfrey always acknowledge the dire straits from which they rose. In the sociological literature on organizations, tokens are women and/or racial minorities, recruited in small numbers, who are "hired, admitted, or appointed to a group *because* of their differences from other members, perhaps to serve as 'proof' that the group does not discriminate against such members" (Zimmer, 1988, p. 65) when in fact discrimination remains ongoing and systematic (see Pettigrew & Martin, 1987; Yoder, 1991 & 1994). Laws (1975) provides a definition of tokenism with particular bearing on my argument:

> Tokenism is likely to be found wherever a dominant group is under pressure to share privilege, power, or other desirable commodities with a group which is excluded. Tokenism is the means by which the dominant group advertises a promise of mobility between the dominant and excluded classes. By definition, however, tokenism involves mobility which is severely restricted in quantity, and the quality of mobility is severely restricted as well. . . . The Token is a member of an underrepresented group, who is operating on the turf of the dominant group, under license from it. The institution of tokenism has advantages both for the dominant group and for the individual who is chosen to serve as Token. These advantages obtain, however, only when the defining constraints are respected: the flow of outsiders into the dominant group must be restricted numerically, and they must not change the system they enter. (pp. 51–52)

This passage highlights the rhetorical processes by which tokenism operates. According to Laws, tokenism "advertises a promise of mobility" that pays lip service to multiculturalism and difference, and to opportunity for previously excluded groups. But that promise, a concordance between the token and the group licensing or authorizing the token, serves to obscure the limits of mobility. Laws also notes that one condition regulating the participation of tokens in an organization or culture is that they be exceptional, and that their exceptionalism "bolsters the premises of meritocracy and individualism" (p. 57).

Of course, to describe tokenism as a rhetorical and ideological process is not by any means to underestimate the real talent and effort required on the part of women and minorities in racist, sexist society in order to attain positions of relative power and prominence. Nor do I mean that persons filling token positions are present only by virtue of their race or gender; indeed, in my experience representatives of oppressed groups often must be more qualified and hardworking than members of dominant groups in the same positions. My point is simply that once someone has struggled through the barriers of discrimination to achieve power or prominence, her persona is appropriated by the dominant ideology of liberalism and inscribed in public texts in such a way as to perpetuate individualist myths and lessons necessary to liberalism and capitalism.

Laws' analysis also suggests a connection between tokenism and hegemony: Tokenism is the calculated, negotiated response of a "dominant group under pressure to share privilege," just as hegemony refers to the attempts of the dominant culture to incorporate challenges without having to change substantially itself. Laws' essay, like most of the research on tokenism, refers to this process as it occurs in corporate organizations. But this literature sheds some light on how a culture hero can become a token not in an organization but in the culture at large. In popular culture, therefore, a token can be defined as a persona who is constructed from the character and life of a member of a subordinated group, and then celebrated, authorized to speak as proof that the society at large does not discriminate against members of that group. Narratives about the culture token "advertise a promise of mobility" by emphasizing the exceptional qualities of the token in a rhetorical justification of liberal meritocracy. In this way, a cultural persona is created and authorized to testify on behalf of the dominant culture.

TRIBUTE AND BIOGRAPHY AS TOKEN MACHINES

Biographical narratives of token personae acknowledge the subordinate positions of the oppressed, giving members of a subordinate group opportunities to identify with the hero of the story. The narratives dramatize extreme suffering and dejection, situations with which oppressed audiences can easily identify. For example, Waldron (1987) describes the "terrible obstacles" (p. 30) facing "Oprah"'s mother, a single black parent on welfare. But the texts always re-frame suffering in individualist terms, chronicling individual faith, work, and determination to make it through hard times to wild success. Again, Waldron (1986) writes, "Oprah believes a more positive approach is to accept the responsibility not for what happened but for *overcoming* what happened" (p. 36). Ironically the texts work by affirming oppression, then neutralizing that affirmation in an individualistic rhetoric. For example, Nellie Bly (1993) includes the following among the "six keys to Oprah's success" (p. 310): persistence, self-discipline, and "faith in yourself."

The motion from awareness of structural barriers, on the one hand, to exhortation toward individual transcendence of those obstacles, on the other, is a key strategy of the texts constituting "Oprah" Winfrey as a liberal hero. In 1990, Oprah Winfrey was the third recipient (after Bob Hope and Elizabeth Taylor) of the "America's Hope" award, honoring "outstanding individuals who exemplify the spirit of America" (*TV Guide,* 1990, p. 216). The video of the *America's All Star Tribute* ceremony (1990) is one example that reveals several aspects of the rhetoric of tokenism: unquestioned faith in the American Dream and its accessibility to all people, the belief in a universal human nature, celebration of philanthropy as an appropriate means of social change (in contradistinction to political activism), and above all the exhortation to transcend racial or cultural conflict. The tribute spectacle is divided into segments of "Oprah" biography, speeches applauding "Oprah"'s success and contributions to American society, and comic and musical performances. On the face of it, these segments are performed by an odd assortment of public figures: Sinbad and Lily Tomlin, Bob Hope and Whoopi Goldberg, Roseanne Barr and the Voices of Calvary Choir, among others.

On this night, "Oprah" provides a shining example of someone who made it. Her gown, of black satin and sequins, glitters like a thousand points of light as she mugs for the camera and takes her seat. This image of "Oprah" in the frame of her box seat is a significant one, because she is the object of these proceedings, framed by an all-star gala that defines her and her role in popular culture as it celebrates her. She is a cultural persona constructed by this text, a self-conscious curtsey to the camera indicating that she does not feel quite "herself" here. As Dyer (1986) notes, the tension between public image and private self is a site of constant negotiation for the star, regardless of the extent to which the star has participated in the construction of her public image. In the tribute, "Oprah" must witness with (real or feigned) pleasure the appropriations of her life story, as it is told by personages ranging the gamut from M. C. Hammer to then–First Lady Barbara Bush.

Here she is defined as an American hero, someone in charge of her life and her discourse. But even as these definitions take shape, "Oprah" becomes (as she does in all of the discourse surrounding her in the popular media) part of the larger story of liberal individualism in capitalist society. The authorization of "Oprah" also occurs through the gendering of her persona with regard to children, represented by the child stars featured in the tribute, Fred Savage and Neil Patrick Harris. The tribute program explores the theme "Help Our Children" in a song by this title performed by M. C. Hammer, and in its continual emphasis on "Oprah"'s philanthropic projects such as literacy campaigns and big-sister programs. Here "Oprah" is constituted as mother-figure to the children of the world, and more specifically as the mammy, benevolent black guardian of white children everywhere (and on her talk show, of the women in her audience).

This racist stereotype has its roots in slavery, when demeaning images of slaves happy to serve white people served to justify the practice of slavery (see Riggs, 1986; 1991). In popular culture, Hattie McDaniel performed the role of mammy in films of the 1930s. Film scholar Donald Bogle describes the mammy as "big, fat, and cantankerous," and "firmly wedged into the dominant white culture" (Bogle, 1989, p. 9). Bogle explains that the mammy image "of the jolly black cook was completely manufactured and presented for mass consumption" (p. 63). The function of the mammy, like all of the "servant-figures" popular in racist culture since slavery, is to provide an unthreatening, subservient fantasy role for blacks to fill in American popular culture (see Cloud, 1992; Hall, 1981). So "Oprah" is authorized to speak only if first, her life story is told as an allegory of the American Dream, and second, she is sufficiently feminine in the mammy mold, giving to society in traditionally feminine ways to children and adults regardless of race.

"Oprah"'s battle with her weight and the obsessive reporting in the tabloid press of her eating habits, exercise regimens, and clothes size are related to the mammy image, which is traditionally fat; Louise Beavers had to struggle to *gain* weight to play the mammy in the 1934 film *Imitation of Life*. In this light, "Oprah"'s weight loss regimens might be read as a partial, though atomized and limited, refusal of the mammy role. The slimmer "Oprah" body better fits the needs of the liberal entrepreneurial ideology. As Susan Bordo (1993) argues, the "hard bodies" sought by men and women in 1980s American culture represent mastery and control in the economic and political realm. "The ability of the (working-class) heroine and hero to pare, prune, tighten, and master the body operates as a clear symbol of successful upward aspiration, of the penetrability of class boundaries to those who have 'the right stuff'" (Bordo, 1993, p. 195). In this light it is possible to read "Oprah"'s current grueling daily workout as an attempt to emulate and embody entrepreneurial success: "She says she is in the process of becoming an all-new Oprah" (Reynolds, 1993, p. 86), with a lean political show to match her remade body (see also Gerosa, 1994; Rosen & Fisher, 1994).

The structure of the video tribute to Oprah Winfrey portrays "Oprah" as the success-object of white adoration. The program features white stars, both child and adult, whose performances frame the black performers as if to embrace them, claiming the token successes for the dominant culture and the ideology of liberalism. But first the program, like the print biographies, must acknowledge oppression based on race and gender. This acknowledgment happens in the segment narrated by film and television actress Whoopi Goldberg. In a series of racial jokes, Goldberg articulates her awareness that she and "Oprah" share in common an experience that excludes the majority of the audience. Explaining that the Palm Springs auditorium was difficult to find, she jokes, "I'm not the first black Jew to wander in the desert. Moses made it, and here I am." Later she refers to "Oprah" as a "sister," mocking the white audience for paying $500 a head to participate in the glorification of a black woman. But the politically charged language of difference and mutual empowerment is immediately recovered in her introduction to the generic "Oprah" biography. Goldberg says, "You can win the race no matter how far behind you start out." With the emphasis placed on "Oprah"'s individual ability to come from behind (and implicitly, Goldberg's own ability to do the same), the possibility of a structural critique of American racism is undermined.

Goldberg's remarks introduce a video version of the same narrative of "Oprah"'s life that one finds everywhere: the hard childhood under her grandmother's iron rule, the early and repeated sexual abuse at the hands of various male relatives, abject poverty and adolescent rebellion, and her miraculous turn-around under the tutelage of her father (in a gesture toward the ideological significance of black fatherhood in the popular imagination). Finally we see images of "Oprah"'s current success, the history of her broadcast career, her ratings triumph over Phil Donahue during the 1986 fall television season, and her assertion that it can only get better. The segment ends on an interesting reflexive note. Looking up at "Oprah"'s box, Whoopi Goldberg says, "If we didn't have an Oprah Winfrey, we'd have to invent one." Is Goldberg calling our attention to the process of invention at hand? For the popular culture *has* invented an "Oprah" persona whose biography undermines a critique of racism, sexism, and class exploitation. In the words of a *New York*

Times Magazine article, "Her audiences are co-creators of the self and the persona she crafts. . . . Here she is, an icon, speaking" (Harrison, 1989, p. 28).

"Oprah"'s iconic status allows both Whoopi Goldberg and Barbara Bush, at extremes or any cultural or political spectrum, to claim "Oprah" as a friend in this text. On a theory of hegemony as concordance, one might applaud the construction of an "Oprah" who can bring together liberal and conservative, black and white, in liberal harmony. However, attending to what is obscured or dismissed in Bush's narrative reveals a darker side to the concordance that is established. In his introduction to Barbara Bush's speech, Fred Savage emphasizes "Oprah"'s triumph over an "unhappy" (notably, not an "oppressed") childhood and her contributions to generic "children," unmarked by race or gender. Bush reinforces Savage's emphases, writing "Oprah" into the Bush administration's "thousand points of light" rhetoric, a political philosophy that places the burden of change and the blame for failure squarely on the shoulders of individuals. Bush says,

> Tonight we honor the third recipient of America's Hope Award, given each year to an individual who exemplifies the spirit of America through their words, actions, and deeds. You've made a superb choice in Oprah Winfrey. She overcame her own personal adversity through education, inner strength, and faith. Today she shares that success in so many ways, giving millions of dollars and hundreds of hours to the cause of literacy, to historically black colleges, to help abused and battered women. The list goes on and on. Tonight, Oprah my dear friend, we salute you as an educator, entrepreneur, actress, humanitarian, philanthropist, and all around wonderful woman. Thank you for helping make America a kinder and gentler place.

Again, the stress is on individual accomplishment. Bush redefines "Oprah"'s oppression, arguably a product of racist and sexist power structures shared by women and blacks, as "her own personal adversity" that requires only individual efforts toward education, inner strength, and faith in the entrepreneurial dream. Bush also applauds "Oprah"'s contributions to charity. Philanthropy, as part of the rhetoric of tokenism, shares in its contradictions. One is supposed to acknowledge that in this country, many people are hungry, homeless, abused, and illiterate. Yet one is required to overlook the collective nature and structural sources of this suffering and call for individual giving as the solution.

This text's emphases on philanthropy as the agency of social change, the narrative of "Oprah"'s exceptional triumph over collective adversity, and the stress on the importance of individual responsibility firmly place "Oprah" (as a product of this text) within the realm of the liberal ideology. In absorbing "Oprah"'s experience into the "thousand points of light" theme, Bush makes a political argument to replace social programs with the voluntarism of individuals.

Predictably, the structure of this televisual tribute to "Oprah" appears over and over again in the mass of material on "Oprah" in the popular press. Yet these narratives are not seamless. In particular, two sites in the print texts expose interesting contradictions in the narrative of tokenism. The ways in which the biographies foreground issues of race and gender briefly acknowledge the reality of oppression, only to elide and naturalize the structural origins of racism, sexism, and poverty.

RACE AND GENDER IN THE RHETORIC OF TOKENISM

Many writers and interviewers call attention to "Oprah"'s blackness. In *Cosmopolitan*, Markey (1986) writes, "No ma'am, there is nothing blonde, white bread, or benign about Oprah Winfrey. There she sits, 175 pounds of brass, sass, and candor . . . , something of a cross between a puppy and Pearl Bailey, nuzzling her audiences one minute and then knocking them breathless the next." The article's definition of black womanhood as brash and aggressive, animal-like, and extravagant reinforces questionable racial stereotypes. And, the article shifts its focus from racial difference to mainstream success and to "Oprah"'s distance from the black political struggle during her college years. Similarly, Norman King (1987) in his book-length biography of "Oprah" describes her as "brassy," "soulful," "taunting," and "sassy" (1987, p. 10). In these ways, Oprah's race is highlighted as a salient feature of her identity.

In a 1987 interview with *Essence* (Taylor, 1987), "Oprah" explicitly identifies herself with the black community: "As black people we all share the same kind of emotional roots," she says. She also tells a story of feeling oppressed because she was bused to a white, upper-middle class school while her own mother worked [as] a maid in the homes of the other students. Later in the same interview she says, "I know and understand that I am where I am because of the bridges that I crossed over to get here. Sojourner Truth was a bridge. Harriet Tubman was a bridge. . . . I feel very strongly about black womanhood." Although her experience of hardship is so rooted in her identity as a black woman, she also comments, "But I am where I am because I believed in my possibilities. Everything in your world is created by what you think." Or, in *People Weekly* (Richman, 1987), "I never felt the kind of repression other black people are exposed to . . . Blackness is something I just am. I'm black. I'm a woman. I wear a size ten shoe. It's all the same to me." It is her willingness to deny the importance of her difference that endears her to biographers, who make choices in deciding which quotations and details to foreground. Because a key point here is that biographers work as filters or screens, producing life stories that are ideological fictions, it is interesting to note that both Waldron (1987) and King (1987) write glowingly about "Oprah"'s willingness to leave racial antagonism behind.

"Oprah" simultaneously identifies herself with black culture and the legacy of oppression faced by many black Americans, as she does in some of her show topics and in the film projects she chooses, and she distances herself from that history. Of course, "Oprah" does move, if minutely, toward critique before backtracking. Although one can hardly fault Winfrey as an individual for hedging (her refusal of collective identification has earned her millions of dollars), those small moments should not be read as emancipatory. For "Oprah"'s ambivalence is replicated in the culture at large, which features simultaneous acknowledgment and denial of race-and gender-based oppression. The discourse of tokenism must acknowledge difference, because it is difference that allows for exploitation. One cannot exploit a group unless one dehumanizes its members and distinguishes them from oneself. But the discourse must also mask that process of dehumanization and distancing in order to prevent serious resistance. In a 1989 speech to an American Woman's Economic Development Corporation conference, Winfrey herself mixed acknowledgment of oppression with denial of it, saying both that the "notion that you can do and be anything you want to be" is "a very false notion we are fed in this country," *and* that "The life I lead is good. All things are possible" (quoted in Harrison, 1989, p. 46). This contradiction, between the critique of individual success as a "false notion" and the faith that "all things are possible," is the foundation of the rhetoric of racial tokenism.

However, tokenism does not work in exactly this way with regard to gender difference. "Oprah"'s biographical trajectory as it is chronicled in popular texts takes her from a racially marked position to an e-raced position, but emphasizes rather than negates her femininity. The construction of a feminine persona is nowhere more evident than in the contrasts noted in the popular press between "Oprah" and Donahue. "They have different styles, of course," writes Richman (1987), "Donahue coming at you hard and smart and Winfrey sidling up soft and accessible . . . 'He'd do nuclear disarmament much better than I would,' she says." Here and elsewhere, "Oprah" is characterized as soft, empathic, emotional, instinctive, mystical, and sensuous rather than smart, in contrast to a hard, smart, and politically astute masculine position. Carbaugh (1988; see also Zoglin, 1986) describes Donahue as the quintessential liberal individual, committed to a discourse of political rights, "talking American." Reviewers note that "Oprah," by contrast, touches her audiences, loves them, caring for and reaching out to them in a traditionally feminine mode (Zoglin, 1988). As King (1987, p. 9) puts it, "You are aware of a sense of . . . pervasive human warmth, an enveloping hug of empathy." Or, "She'll hug anyone who happens by. She'll sing to herself. She'll fling her arms out exuberantly . . . or she'll break out into a hip-swinging, arms-extended shimmy" (Reynolds, 1993). Haag (1992/93) argues that on her program and in interviews, "Oprah" is constructed as "every viewer's favorite girlfriend" (Kanner, 1994, p. 96), approachable, warm, and empathetic. It is her culturally feminine qualities of warmth, empathy, and connection that give "Oprah"—to a greater degree than Phil Donahue—authority to talk with people about their emotional lives.

On her show "Oprah" is expected to appeal to and empathize with women, to talk about women's concerns, their abusive relationships and their self-esteem problems. Often she does deal with problems that have as their cause systemic, gender-based oppression (divorce, battering, incest, relationships). "She is a giggling best friend, inspiring older sister, and stern mother" (Rogers, 1993, p. 130). In this way, "Oprah" is caught in the double-bind of having to continue to stress empathy, emotion, and identification with women on her show while endorsing a therapeutic discourse that blames individuals, extracted from their social context, for their problems. She can never admit the need for systematic structural change and collective political activity. Thus the contradictory statement: "The message is, you're responsible for your life. People watch our show and realize they're not alone" (Taylor, 1987).

The apparent contradiction between collective consciousness ("they're not alone") and individual responsibility ("you're responsible for your life") is resolved through narrative emphasis on "Oprah"'s substantial philanthropic giving and individual hard work. Through philanthropy, individuals, especially women, are allowed the expression of their caring for transformations that make great hero stories but oversimplify the process of overcoming hardship.

TOKENISM, CLASS POLITICS, AND CULTURAL CRITICISM

Oprah Winfrey has taken some criticism in the popular press, most notably in a *New York Times Magazine* article that accuses her candor and goodwill of being "more apparent than real" (Harrison, 1989, p. 54). The author lambastes Winfrey as an individual for contriving her own Horatio Alger story, embracing wealth as a God-ordained reward, and rejecting any political civil rights discourse in order to become popular and successful. "In a racist society," Harrison writes,

> the majority needs, and seeks, from time to time, proof that they are loved by the minority whom they have so long been accustomed to oppress, to fear, or to treat with real or assumed disdain. . . . Oprah Winfrey—a one-person demilitarized zone—serves that purpose. (p. 46)

In particular, Oprah has been criticized for giving white supremacists air time (in a 1987 episode featuring a town in Forsyth County, Georgia). I have been interested less in this article in accusing Oprah Winfrey herself of bad faith or false consciousness than in why and how popular culture iconizes characters whose stories enact liberal success myths and provide the society at large with easy tokens of good faith toward black Americans. As the title of one biography suggests, "Everybody Loves Oprah!" (King, 1987). But should "everybody"—including critics of popular culture—love "Oprah"?

There is a tendency among critics of racism, sexism, and capitalism to muffle criticism of popular figures who represent socially marginalized groups simply because they are women, or black women, or black lesbian women, and so on. This tendency is often labeled a politics of difference or identity. Its representatives maintain that a person's voice is automatically distinctive and politically charged if that person comes from the ranks of the oppressed (and, conversely, that someone from outside those ranks has a less legitimate critical voice). An analysis from this perspective would seek some authentic aspect of the "Oprah" phenomenon, some word or gesture that is not mired in the dominant ideology and its contradictions. Although the oppressed have had sometimes to adopt the mannerisms of the dominant culture in order to survive, Lorde (1984) argues, black women retain a distinctive and liberating voice (p. 114). Henry Louis Gates' (1988) theory of Signifyin(g) suggests that black people create their own vernacular structures in relation to the dominant white culture, producing a double-voiced set of texts that mimic and participate in the canonical, dominant culture but always with meaningful differences signifying resistance and transgressive appropriation. Lorde and Gates might hail the contradictory sides of "Oprah"'s persona as evidence of such double-voiced vernacular structures.

One can question the extent to which *The Oprah Winfrey Show* or any of the texts constructing "Oprah"'s persona constitutes a "vernacular" discourse, if one defines "vernacular" as "discourse that resonates in and from historically oppressed communities" (Ono & Sloop, 1995, p. 20). Ono and Sloop suggest that black vernacular discourse "constitutes African American communities, constructs social relations, and protests representations of African Americans circulating in dominant culture" (p. 22). Although Oprah Winfrey is a black woman whose voice and experience clearly resonate not only with blacks and women but with men and women of all races, the texts surrounding her and constructing her as a star are located firmly in the dominant culture, in the ways I have described. Ono and Sloop suggest that critical scholars turn our attention away from the discourses of the dominant culture and toward the "subaltern" expressions and self-constitutions of marginalized and subordinated groups. Yet at the very least an examination of "Oprah" texts troubles the distinction between "dominant" and "vernacular" in so far as it is difficult to locate these texts squarely in one or the other category.

Further, the popularity and pervasiveness of the "Oprah" biography, as with other mainstream mediated texts, is what makes it a necessary target of critique. Contrary to Ono and Sloop, I wish to suggest that critics continue to attend carefully to the most persuasive, most popular, and most widely-available dominant culture narratives and icons in order to understand and critique—not to reify, as Ono and Sloop fear—the continuing force of racism, sexism, and class-based exploitation in our society.

Some media critics have emphasized the complexity, ambivalence and potential oppositional nature of the relationship of even dominant-culture television representations of racial difference to black viewers (Gray, 1993; hooks, 1992). Analyses of stereotypes often point out that stereotypes occur in binary oppositions that have their roots in slavery: happy slave *vs.* wild and dangerous savage (Dates and Barlow, 1990; Cloud, 1992; Morrison, 1992). Herman Gray (1993, 1995) argues that while television is primarily a medium of normalization, commodification, and absorption of difference, the process of incorporation of difference is "not always uniform or effective" (1993, p. 191; 1995, p. 3). Gray warns critics against excessive, pessimistic structuralism with regard to televisual constructions of "blackness," but also against "uncritical celebrations of the practices of collective and individual subjects . . . as resistance" (1995, p. 3).

An example of celebratory criticism is Masciarotte's (1991) argument that Oprah Winfrey's show is a complex, empowering site of consciousness-raising that has been wrongly attacked by ideology critics. Masciarotte attempts to dispel what she sees as "wholesale disregard" of the talk show genre, arguing that Winfrey "begins to articulate a significantly different politics of the subject which re-inscribe the 'making of a self'" (p. 83). In pointing out how the *Oprah Winfrey Show* gives voice to difference, Masciarotte credits the show with oppositional potential. However, this kind of rehabilitation of a demonstrably conventional set of texts risks overlooking the role popular appropriations and constructions of racial difference play in reinforcing hegemonic assumptions about social reality.

On the other hand, critics of hegemony have noted the limitations of talking about social problems in the therapeutic frame of the talk show, which locates responsibility for problems with the individual and mitigates against political awareness or action (Peck, 1992; Banks and Tankel, 1992). Peck (1992) details the ways in which the *Oprah Winfrey Show* itself deploys "liberal, therapeutic, and religious frames of meaning" (p. 91) in order to blunt a critique of racism. Peck describes how the definition of racism as an individual psychological problem and a religious discourse of love work against the efforts of some guests on the show to call attention to the appropriateness of anger and collective action in the face of structural racism. Given the ideological limits of "Oprah"'s discourse in her own program, Peck argues against a valorization of difference that "vacates space from which arguments for intercollective struggle, identification, and empathy might be formulated" (p. 118).

Dates and Barlow (1990, p. 296) argue that representations of African Americans in the mass media are schizoid or split, between those created by and for white culture and those produced by blacks themselves. With regard to Oprah Winfrey, who owns her own production company, chooses her own projects, and has some autonomy and control over her representations of race, the matter is not so simple. For no matter whether "Oprah" or her biographers or publicists are the agents of persona construction, "Oprah"'s identity is articulated within a liberal frame that guarantees continued high ratings and profits. It is not enough that in the *Oprah Winfrey Show* and in the biographies under consideration here, constructions of black identity, language, and culture proliferate—so long as articulation of difference remains at the level of identity and does not imply political opposition or activity against the system that produces racism and sexism. No doubt Oprah Winfrey, the person, transgresses a "social and cultural order that has historically stereotyped, excluded, objectified, and silenced black subjects" (Gray, 1993, p. 191). She is neither silent nor excluded, although she is often stereotyped and objectified. In her film and television projects, she has celebrated black women, and for this reason Angelou (1989) hails her as a "roadmaker" for black women.

Yet, to hail the simple presence of a black woman on television risks ignoring the conditions imposed on that presence and the political inflections of those voices chosen to speak. Indeed, it is necessary to set aside the problematic of "difference" if we are to understand how popular culture texts and personae participate in the maintenance of economic and political power in racist, capitalist society. More crucial than representations of "difference" are the ideological uses to which difference is put in popular texts.

Framing biographies like the America's Hope award ceremony and the other profiles are significant cultural texts at work in this process of cultural authorization. Although "Oprah" is a member of an oppressed group, her life story is appropriated by the dominant culture for the construction of meanings that recover any threatening implications of "Oprah"'s racial difference. We cannot "discover" "Oprah" as an authentic black woman. To take such a position is to risk falling into unhelpful identity politics, emphasizing issues of identity and textual play at the expense of attention to material (economic and physical) aspects of oppression and the possibility of collective political resistance to systemic injustice (see Adams, 1989; Bordo, 1990; Briskin, 1990; Clarke, 1991; Escoffier; 1991; Kauffman, 1990; Smith, 1994).

"Oprah"'s identity and her politics are securely located by framing narratives within liberal individualism and an oppressively gendered meaning system. My analysis of biographical narratives about Oprah Winfrey reveals that a patterned, generic narrative constituting a rhetoric of tokenism pervades popular discourse about "Oprah." These biographical narratives inflate the persona of "Oprah" so that she becomes a larger-than-life cultural icon of racial harmony and opportunity. Further work might examine biographical narratives of other popular black Americans, women, and other minorities. For example, the dust jacket to Howard Means' *Colin Powell* (1992), a biography of the prominent black U.S. military leader, claims, "General Powell emerges as *the embodiment of the American Dream*: the son of Jamaican immigrants, he rose from the hard life of the South Bronx to become the most talked about military leader since World War II" (emphasis added). This example once again suggests that in general, the rhetoric of tokenism, while internally contradictory regarding the existence of inequality, serves to interpret success and failure as a matter of individual responsibility regardless of one's structural location in systems of power and privilege; it provides the dominant culture a defense against charges of racism while continuing to naturalize and justify racism; it makes heroes out of blacks willing to abnegate political resistance in favor of speaking on behalf of the system.

This conclusion challenges Condit's (1994) (re)definition of hegemony as acceptable compromise. The concordance established in the rhetoric of tokenism obviously benefits a class based, racist social order dependent upon the ideals of meritocracy. Further, in the context of bipartisan attacks on the American social safety net, narratives of "Oprah"'s heroic life story lend persuasive weight to those who wish to accelerate the erosion of social services like welfare and indigent health care. Biographies like the ones of "Oprah" acknowledge difference, giving the appearance of negotiation and compromise. But the implication of those narratives is that because there are no structural barriers to individual advancement, blacks (and other oppressed groups) must blame themselves for failure to thrive.

Of course, many African Americans do make it through the persistent barriers of racism and injustice. This does not mean that those barriers have dissolved. According to census data, the proportion of black households earning at least $50,000 a year rose between 1967 and 1991 from 5.2 to 12.1 percent (reported in Cose, 1993, pp. 36–37). On the other hand, The Milton S. Eisenhower Foundation (1993) recently reported on a study showing that the number of blacks living in poverty and the degree of *de facto* racial segregation in the U.S. have changed little or grown worse since the 1960s. Despite a continuing legacy of racism felt by black Americans of all economic classes, Cose (1993) writes,

> America likes success stories. We also prefer to believe that our country—give or take a David Duke or two—is well on the road to being color-blind. And since the predicament of the black underclass seems so hopeless, many find it comforting to concentrate on those who are doing well. (pp. 37–38)

Cose goes on to argue that while success stories may be comforting, they have a double edge: They hold up "paragons of middle-class virtue" (p. 37) as ideological lessons to blacks who are still struggling in a society that is still far from color-blind or racially just. Ideological constructions of race and power in texts like biographies of Oprah Winfrey correspond to and legitimate ongoing oppression by holding up representatives of the black elite as "proof" that the system is just and that racism is a thing of the past.

White respondents to a Los Angeles survey in the wake of the videotaped police beating of black motorist Rodney King expressed beliefs in a ratio of two to one that joblessness and poverty were the result of moral failures of individual black and Latino people (Mydans, 1993). The respondents could not see the structures of racism and exploitation as contexts of individual hardship. Such attitudes are the product of persuasion, of rhetorics that systematically obscure structure and system in favor of individualistic explanations of poverty and despair. The rhetoric of tokenism, exemplified in the Oprah Winfrey profiles, is one such rhetoric. Although it is contradictory, tokenist biography serves to blame the oppressed for their failures and to uphold a meritocratic vision of the American Dream that justifies and sustains a more troubling American reality.

NOTES

[1]The patterns I describe are replicated in the tabloid press. In order to make this project manageable, I have limited my analysis to glossy trade magazine and book-length writings that feature Oprah Winfrey's life story (as opposed to her riches, her chef, or her weight).

REFERENCES

Adams, M. L. (1989). There's no place like home: On the place of identity in feminist politics. *Feminist Review, 31,* 22–33.

America's all-star tribute to Oprah Winfrey (1990, September 18). [Television program]. ABC.

Anderson, C. (1986, August). Meet Oprah Winfrey. *Good Housekeeping.*

Angelou, M. (1989, January/February). Women of the year: Oprah Winfrey. *Ms.,* p. 88.

Banks, J. and J. D. Tankel (1992). Constructions of sexuality on television talk shows. Paper presented to the 42nd Annual conference of the International Communication Association, Miami, FL.

Barthel, J. (1986, August). Here Comes Oprah. *Ms.*

Bartlett, D. L. and J. B. Steele (1992). *America: What went wrong?* Kansas City: Andrews and McMeel.

Bly, N. (1993). *Oprah! Up close and down home.* Zebra Books.

Bogle, D. (1989). *Toms, coons, mulattos, mammies, and bucks: An interpretive history of blacks in American films.* New York: Continuum.

Bordo, S. (1990). Feminism, postmodernism, and gender-skepticism. In L. J. Nicholson (Ed.), *Feminism/Postmodernism* (pp. 133–156). New York and London: Routledge.

Bordo, S. (1993). *Unbearable weight: Feminism, Western culture, and the body.* Berkeley: University of California Press.

Brashler, B. (1991, August). Next on Oprah . . . *Ladies Home Journal,* no page given (Lexis/Nexis).

Briskin, L. (1990). Identity politics and the hierarchy of oppression. *Feminist Review, 35,* 102–108.

Cameron, J. (1989, February). Simply . . . Oprah! *Cosmopolitan,* no page given.

Carbaugh, D. (1988). *Talking American: Cultural discourses on Donahue.* Norwood, NJ: Ablex.

Clarke, S. A. (1991). Fear of a black planet. *Socialist Review, 21* (3), 38–59.

Cloud, D. (1992). The limits of interpretation: Ambivalence and the stereotype in *Spenser: For Hire. Critical Studies in Mass Communication, 9,* 311–324.

Condit, C. M. (1994). Hegemony in a mass-mediated society: Concordance about reproductive technologies. *Critical Studies in Mass Communication, 11,* 205–230.

Cose, E. (1993). *Rage of a privileged class.* New York: Harper Collins.

Culhane, J. (1989, February). Oprah Winfrey: How truth changed her life. *Reader's Digest,* pp. 101–105.

Dale, S., L. Fisher, and S. McFarland (1994, Sept. 12). In full stride. *People Weekly,* pp. 84–90.

Dates, J. L. and W. Barlow, Eds. (1990). *Split image: African Americans in the mass media.* Washington, D.C.: Howard University Press.

DeParle, J. (1994, October 7) Census sees falling income and more poor. *New York Times,* p. A16.

Dyer, R. (1986). *Heavenly bodies: Film stars and society.* New York: St. Martin's.

Ebert, A. (1991, September). Oprah Winfrey talks openly about Oprah. *Good Housekeeping.* No page given (Lexis/Nexis).

Edmonds, P. and M. L. Usdansky (1994, November 14). Children get poorer, nation gets richer. *USA Today,* p. 1A.

Edwards, A. (1986, October). Oprah Winfrey Stealing the Show. *Essence.*

Escoffier, J. (1991). The limits of multiculturalism. *Socialist Review, 27* (3), 61–73.

Gates, H. L. (1988). *The signifyin(g) monkey: A theory of Afro-American literary criticism.* New York, Oxford: Oxford University Press.

Gillespie, M. A. (1988, November). Winfrey takes all. *Ms.,* pp. 50–54.

Gitlin, T. (1980). *The whole world is watching: Mass media in the making and unmaking of the new left.* Berkeley, Los Angeles: University of California Press.

Gerosa, M. (1994, November). What makes Oprah run? *Ladies Home Journal,* p. 200ff.

Goodman, F. (1991, December). The companies they keep [on Oprah Winfrey and Madonna]. *Working Woman,* pp. 52ff.

Gramsci, A. (1971). *Selections from the prison notebooks.* (Q. Hoare and G. N. Smith, Trans.). New York: International Publishers. (Work originally written in 1936–37).

Gray, H. (1989). Television, black Americans, and the American dream. *Critical Studies in Mass Communication, 6,* 376–386.

Gray, H. (1993). The endless slide of difference. Critical television studies, television and the question of race. *Critical Studies in Mass Communication, 10,* 190–197.

Gray, H. (1995). *Watching race: Television and the struggle for "blackness."* Minneapolis: University of Minnesota Press.

Gross, L. (1988, December). Oprah Winfrey, Wonder Woman. *Ladies Home Journal.*

Haag, L. (1992/93). Oprah Winfrey: The construction of intimacy in the talk show setting. *Journal of Popular Culture, 26,* 115–121.

Hall, S. (1981). The whites of their eyes: Racist ideologies and the media. In G. Bridges & R. Brunt (Eds.), *Silver linings* (pp. 28–52). London: Lawrence and Wishart.

Hall, S. (1986a). Gramsci's relevance for the study of race and ethnicity. *Journal of Communication Inquiry, 10,* 5–27.

Hall, S. (1986b). Variants of liberalism. In J. Donald and S. Hall (Eds.), *Politics and Ideology* (pp. 34–69). Philadelphia: Open University Press.

Harrison, B. G. (1989, June 11). The importance of being Oprah. *New York Times Magazine,* pp. 28–29ff.

hooks, b. (1992). *Black looks.* Boston: South End Press.

Jhally, S., & J. Lewis (1992). *Enlightened racism: The Cosby Show, racism, and the myth of the American dream.* Boulder, CO: Westview Press.

Kauffman, L. A. (1990). The anti-politics of identity. *Socialist Review, 20 (1),* 67–80.

Kanner, M. (1994, February). Oprah at 40. *Ladies Home Journal,* pp. 96ff.

King, N. (1987). *Everybody loves Oprah.* New York: William Morrow and Co.

Laws, J. L. (1975). The psychology of tokenism. *Sex Roles, 1,* 51–67.

Lears, T. J. J. (1985). The concept of cultural hegemony: Problems and possibilities. *American Historical Review, 90,* 567–593.

Levitt, S., L. Fisher, & B. K. Mills (1993, November 29). Oprah's mission. *People,* p. 106.

Lorde, A. (1984). *Sister outsider: Essays and speeches.* Trumansburg, NY: Crossing Press.

Mair, G. (1994). *Oprah Winfrey: The real story.* Secaucus, NJ: Carol Publishing.

Mann, B. (1986, September 8). Oprah Winfrey: A refreshingly different TV host. Oakland, CA *Tribune* [Newsbank microfiche].

Means, H. (1992). *Colin Powell.* New York: Donald I. Fine.

Markey, J. (1986, September). Brassy, sassy Oprah Winfrey. *Cosmopolitan,* pp. 94–100.

Masciarotte, G. (1991, Fall). C'mon girl: Oprah Winfrey and the discourse of feminine talk. *Genders, 11,* 81–110.

McEvoy, D. K. (1994, Sept. 25). Fighting for mass market space. *Publishers' Weekly,* p. 36.

McMullen, W. J., & Solomon, M. (1994). The politics of adaptation: Steven Spielberg's appropriation of *The Color Purple. Text and Performance Quarterly, 14,* 158–174.

Milton S. Eisenhower Foundation. (1993). *Investing in children and youth, reconstructing our cities: Doing what works to reverse the betrayal of American democracy.* Washington, D.C.

Morrison, T., Ed. (1992). *Race-ing justice, En-gendering power: Essays on Anita Hill, Clarence Thomas, and the Construction of Social Reality.* New York: Pantheon.

Murphy, J. M. (1992). Domesticating dissent: The Kennedys and the Freedom Rides. *Communication Monographs, 59,* 61–78.

Mydans, S. (1993, June 10). Los Angeles elects a conservative as mayor and turns to a new era. *New York Times* [National Edition], p. A1ff.

Nadel, I. B. (1984). *Biography: Fiction, fact, and form.* New York: St. Martin's Press.

Noel, P. (1985, April). Lights, Camera, Oprah! *Ebony.*

Noglows, P. (1994, May). Oprah: the year of living dangerously. *Working Woman,* pp. 52ff.

Ono, K. & J. M. Sloop (1995). The critique of vernacular discourse. *Communication Monographs, 62,* 19–46.

Parent, W. (1985). A Liberal legacy: Blacks blaming themselves for economic failures. *Journal of Black Studies, 16,* 3–20.

Peck, J. (1994, Spring). Talk about racism: Framing a popular discourse of race on *Oprah Winfrey*. *Cultural Critique,* pp. 89–125.

Pettigrew, T. F. and J. Martin (1987). Shaping the organizational context for Black American inclusion. *Journal of Social Issues, 43,* 41–78.

Phillips, K. (1990). *Politics of rich and poor.* New York: Random House.

Randolph, L. B. (1993, October). Oprah opens up about her weight, her wedding and why she withheld the book. *Ebony,* pp. 130–132.

Reynolds, G. (1993, November). Oprah unbound. *Chicago Magazine,* pp. 86ff.

Richman, A. (1987, January 12). Oprah. *People Weekly,* pp. 48ff.

Riggs, M. (1986). *Ethnic notions* [documentary film]. San Francisco: California Newsreel.

Riggs, M. (1991). *Color adjustment* [documentary film]. San Francisco: California Newsreel.

Rogers, J. (1993, September). Understanding Oprah. *Redbook,* pp. 94ff.

Rosen, M. & L. Fisher (1994, January 10). Oprah overcomes. *People,* p. 42ff.

Rubenstein, L. (1987, August). Oprah! Thriving on Faith! *McCall's.*

Simson, M. (1994, March 7). The red and the black: Tallying the books '93. *Publishers' Weekly,* p. S21.

Simson, M. (1995, March 20). The red and the black: Paperback bestsellers. *Publishers' Weekly,* p. S24.

Smith, S. (1987). *A poetics of women's autobiography.* Bloomington, IN: Indiana University Press.

Smith, S. (1994). Mistaken identity. *International Socialism, 62,* 1–49.

Taylor, S. (1987, August). An intimate talk with Oprah. *Essence,* pp. 57–59ff.

TV Guide (1990, September 14–21) [Television schedule listings].

Waldron, R. (1987). *Oprah!* New York: St. Martin's.

Weiss, R. (1969). *The American myth of success: From Horatio Alger to Norman Vincent Peale.* New York: Basic Books.

Whitaker, C. (1987, March). Oprah Winfrey: The most talked about TV talk show host. *Ebony.*

Williams, R. (1973). Base and superstructure in Marxist cultural theory. *New Left Review, 82,* 3–16.

Yoder, J. D. (1991). Rethinking tokenism: Looking beyond numbers. *Gender and Society, 5,* 178–192.

Yoder, J. D. (1994). Looking beyond numbers: The effects of gender status, job prestige, and occupational gender-typing on tokenism processes. *Social Psychology Quarterly, 57,* 150–159.

Zimmer, L. (1988). Tokenism and women in the workplace. *Social Problems, 35* (1), 64–77.

Zoglin, R. (1986, September 15). "People sense the realness." *Time,* p. 99.

Zoglin, R. (1988, August 8). Lady with a calling. *Time,* pp. 62–64.

IMAGING NATURE: WATKINS, YOSEMITE, AND THE BIRTH OF ENVIRONMENTALISM

KEVIN MICHAEL DeLUCA AND ANNE TERESA DEMO

Carleton Watkins clicked, Abraham Lincoln signed, Yosemite was "saved" and environmentalism born. It was not that simple, but almost. The initial proposal to preserve Yosemite Valley originated (perhaps surprisingly) with a captain of industry, Israel Ward Raymond, the California agent of the Central American Steamship Transit Company. Raymond forwarded a draft of the Yosemite bill and Watkins' 1861 photographs of Yosemite to California Senator John Conness in a February 20, 1864, letter that advised Congress to "prevent occupation and especially to preserve the trees in the valley from destruction" (as cited in Huths, 1948, pp. 47–48). Conness routed Raymond's proposal to the General Land Office and then introduced the bill to Congress in March of 1864. The legislation passed and was signed into law by Abraham Lincoln on June 30, 1864, thereby deeding Yosemite Valley and Mariposa Big Tree Grove to the state of California "for public use, resort and recreation" (as cited in Cahn & Ketchum, 1981, p. 125). In the few months between Raymond's drafting and Lincoln's signing, the pristine image of Yosemite Valley quickly became iconic of an American vision of nature itself—"the one adequate symbol for all that California promised," wrote Kevin Starr (as cited in Trachtenberg, 1989, p. 135). The legislative protection of this national "natural" landscape placed preservation policy as the cornerstone of American environmental politics.

The fundamental role of landscape photography in the creation of Yosemite as the world's first wilderness area created "for the benefit of the people, for their resort and recreation, to hold them inalienable for all time" points to the crucial role of images in politics and confirms that image politics did not start with the advent of television (as cited in Schama, 1995, p. 191). Focusing on a period during the infancy of photography, this essay traces the ur-history of image politics as linked to the birth of environmentalism. Disciplines avowedly concerned with political discourse, such as political science and, to some degree, rhetoric and movement studies, have tended to give insufficient attention to the historically integral role of images in politics. This essay engages the political dimensions of images, a line of analysis explored most directly in art history. Specifically, with respect to landscape photography and art, art historians have explored the role of pictures in the rhetorics of nationalism, expansionism, racial and religious supremacism, capitalism, and scientific exploration (Truettner, 1995; Novak, 1995; Kinsey, 1992; Hales, 1988). This essay contributes to this scholarship in three ways.

First, in addition to reading Watkins' pictures as high art, this study considers them as political rhetoric and popular culture. In taking this position, this work is cognizant that Watkins' landscape photographs are enmeshed in a turbulent stream of multiple and conflictual discourses that shape what these images mean in particular contexts. This essay is contesting, however, that these images are in any simple way determined or limited by verbal frames. More significantly, it is contended that these pictures are not merely evidence in a conventional political argument. They are not simply representing reality or making an argument about reality. Instead, this article makes the stronger claim that the pictures are constituting the context within which a politics takes place—they are creating a reality.

Second, the role of pictures in the origins of environmentalism is illuminated. Chroniclers of the history of environmentalism in America invariably trace its roots to Thoreau and Muir (Nash, 1967; Oelschlaeger, 1991). Although not wanting to downplay the significance of their writings, this study of Watkins' pictures suggests that landscape photography and paintings are founding texts in the construction of a wilderness vision that has shaped the contours and trajectory of environmental politics. Finally, this essay unearths an episode in the construction of pristine wilderness as the sublime object of nascent environmentalism. The analysis counters mainstream environmental discourse that pays homage to the wilderness icon without paying heed to the political and cultural costs of such devotion.

In what follows, the relevant literatures regarding visual criticism are surveyed and specify this approach to reading images. After situating Watkins in context, this essay then offers close readings of three of his Yosemite photographs. It closes with an extended consideration of the cultural reception and multiple effects of Watkins' visual rhetoric.

VISUAL CRITICISM: HABITS OF SEEING

A cursory review of scholarly literature both in and outside communication studies reveals that the "visual" is not a new phenomenon for the study of rhetoric. Indeed, one might look to the 1970 Wingspread Conference as the starting point of the visual turn in rhetorical studies. "Perhaps it is enough for now," Wayne Booth argued thirty years ago, "to note that the rhetoric of the image, reinforcing or producing basic attitudes towards life that are frequently not consciously faced by the rhetor, constitutes an enormous part of our daily diet of rhetoric" (1971, p. 101). The relationship between rhetoric and images, as critics such as Charles Altman (1980) have revealed, extends back to Carolingian times. Attending to Booth's call, critics such as Thomas Benson, Carole Blair, Sonja Foss, Bruce Gronbeck, and Kathleen Hall Jamieson have addressed questions elemental to visual rhetoric in their respective work on film, public monuments, the visual arts, and politics (Benson, 1980, 1986; Blair, 1999; Foss, 1994; Gronbeck, 1995; Jamieson, 1988). In cultural studies, work by scholars such as Paula Treichler and Douglas Crimp reveal how instrumental representational vocabularies have been to AIDS activism (Treichler, 1988; Crimp, 1988/1990). Although contemporary criticism reflects an agility with a variety of different visual sites, including film, political/activist imagery and public monuments, systematic rhetorical accounts of images remain at the disciplinary periphery of communication studies.

A number of disciplines do offer formalized rules and practices for reading images. Indeed, rhetorical accounts of images often rely on the grammar of art and film criticism to reveal the process and effect of visual meaning making (Harrington, 1973). Filmic techniques such as mobile framing and reframing, which use a pan, tilt, or tracking shot to create the illusion of movement, have been used to explain how the imaging of archival photographs in Ken Burns' civil war documentary constitutes a visual rhetoric that dramatizes the contingent nature of history (Lancioni, 1996). The study of images in semiotics, most notably by Roland Barthes, demonstrated that photographic discourse could be systematically examined by isolating and tracing the signification of codes (1964). Although Susan Sontag laments that the "language in which photographs are generally evaluated is extremely meager," she too emphasizes composition, light, an innovativeness with regard to formal schemes, and the quality of presence (1973). In addition to isolating particular compositional elements governing visual images, a recurrent theme evident across disciplinary fields is a concern with how images offer a way of seeing. It is this trajectory of analysis that serves as the point of departure for our examination of Watkins' Yosemite photographs.

Alternately conceptualized as photographic seeing or regimes of visibility, the position that all images embody a way of seeing often functions as a first principle for the study of images (Berger, 1972). In *On Photography*, Sontag introduces the notion of photographic seeing to stress how photographs function not only as evidence but also as evaluation. That is, photographic seeing not only records events and experiences, but also establishes a habit of viewing that transforms the very experience or event into a way of seeing. For Sontag, the visual criticism of photographs seeks to determine "what dependencies they [photographic images] create, what antagonisms they pacify—that is, what institutions they buttress, whose needs they really serve" (1973, p. 178). Despite beginning with patterns of convention and codes formed through the composition of formal qualities such as light, balance, and framing, an analysis of photographic seeing stresses how the "horizon of the taken-for-granted" is formed visually (Hall, 1988, p. 44). Echoing Sontag's discussion, Victor Burgin characterizes photography as a signifying system that acts as "a structured and structuring space within which the reader deploys, and is deployed by, what codes he or she is familiar with in order to *make sense*." From this perspective, images produce "the ideological subject in the same movement in which they 'communicate' their ostensible 'contents'" (1982, p. 153). Therefore, the question that motivates our examination of Watkins' Yosemite survey photographs is not "what do we see?" but "what do the images want?" (Mitchell, 1996, pp. 540–544). Most specifically, what vision of nature do the photographs authorize, warrant, and legitimate?

In answering this question, a cue is taken from John Hartley's analysis in *The Politics of Pictures*. Hartley suggests that there is no real public, but rather that the public is the product of publicity, of pictures. The public's fictional status, however, should not be "taken as a disqualification from but as a demonstration of the social power (even truth) of fictions" (Hartley, 1992, p. 84). Pictures then are important not because they represent reality, but create it: "They are the place where collective social action, individual identity and symbolic imagination meet— the nexus between culture and politics" (Hartley, p. 3). By offering this perspective of Watkins' images, it is understood that his photos are not to be representing nature, but creating it. Watkins' pictures do not represent the reality of Yosemite. Instead, in conjunction with the discourses of tourism, nationalism, romanticism, expansionism, and religion, they construct Yosemite. Yes, Half Dome exists, but its meaning as icon of pristine wilderness is the result of the work and confluence of multiple discourses, especially a photographic discourse of which Watkins' images are paradigmatic. Watkins' photographs established both an iconic vocabulary for environmentalist claims to public preservation and a way of viewing landscape that endures in contemporary renderings of the American West.

SUBLIME PHOTOGRAPHS: CAPTURING/CREATING NATURE

As a focus for artists and industrial engineers throughout much of the nineteenth century, the national landscape served as a key site of artistic, industrial, and commercial energy. Following westward expansion and often working for the U.S. Geological Survey and Army Corp[s] of Engineers, photographers such as Watkins, Charles Weed, William Henry Jackson, Eadweard Muybridge, and Timothy O'Sullivan documented sites like Yosemite Valley and Mariposa Big Tree Grove, Yellowstone, the Colorado Rockies, and the Grand Canyon. Survey photography increasingly realized commercial profits as prints and stereographs by photographers like Watkins were widely distributed. Works like Josiah Whitney's 1861 *Yosemite Book,* which included 24 of Carleton Watkins' photographs, not only popularized the site within the American rhetorical imagination, but also played a role in Yosemite's preservation. According to Robert Cahn, "the publication of photographs in the survey reports, and their availability to the media were factors in building public support for preserving the areas" (Cahn & Ketchum, p. 129). The invitation by landscape photographs to "see firsthand," the inducement to trust the image, belies how the very images used to depict nature are themselves an expression of state power. The geological survey photos of the 1860s and 70s are telling examples. In his analysis of the relationship between photographic records and the growth of the state, cultural critic John Tagg aptly deconstructs the false promise of photography's self evidence:

> Like the state, the camera is never neutral. The representations it produces are highly coded, and the power it wields is never its own. As a means of record, it arrives on the scene vested with a particular authority to arrest, picture and transform daily life; a power to see and record. . . . This is not the power of the camera but the power of the apparatuses of the local state which deploy it and guarantee the authority of images it constructs to stand as evidence or register a truth. (1999, p. 246)

Even if Tagg too completely dismisses the power of technology qua technology, his point remains significant. It is particularly true for state-sponsored survey images because in this complex social and political process survey photography made "real" unknown and unseen regions of the United States, thus sanctioning and sanctifying an *interested* version of "reality."

Perhaps the preeminent survey photographer, Watkins was in many ways a product of his times, a nodal point for multiple discourses—romantic and artistic, to be sure, but also commercial, industrial, and technological. This is reflected in the breadth of his subjects, from the wilderness landscapes of Yosemite to the industrial mining at Mariposa. It is also manifested in the effects of his images, which constitute the nascent beginnings of environmentalism and foment the extractive frenzy of industrialism. Watkins established dual legacies as both founder of landscape photography and chronicler of industrial progress, celebrator of sublime nature and creator of the technological sublime.[1]

Watkins' early photos of Yosemite highlight, more than anything else, the sublime. Although this may have been an artistic imperative (and Watkins' naming of his studio the Yosemite Art Gallery speaks of his artistic aspirations for photography), it was also a commercial exigence as Watkins left the financial security and comforts of portrait work for the uncertainties and hardships of landscape photography. As Stanford Demars explains in *The Tourist In Yosemite*, for the leisure class that made Yosemite a tourist stop, the appeal of Yosemite consisted in its potential cultural capital as a sublime spot that could trump the picturesque places of Europe (1991, pp. 12–13). Watkins gave these seekers of the sublime what they were looking for.

The sublime is a longstanding concept in Western thought with roots in Ancient Greece (Longinus, trans. 1984). We are more interested in it as a rhetorical force than a philosophical idea. So, instead of documenting the idea and fixating on Immanuel Kant's theory of the sublime, the essay works from Edmund Burke's formulation and traces how the term is developed and used in public discourse, especially artistic and touristic.

For Burke, the sublime is an intense passion rooted in horror, fear, or terror in the face of objects that suggest vastness, infinity, power, massiveness, mystery, and death (Burke, 1757; Nicolson, 1973; Gould, 1995). In addition, objects linked to privation are a source of the sublime: "All *general* privations are great because they are all terrible; *Vacuity, Darkness, Solitude,* and *Silence*" (as cited in Nicolson, p. 337; also see Lyotard, 1991, pp. 98–101). The most sublime object is God, though many objects of nature are often seen as traces of God. Sublime nature as a manifestation of God is evident in the words of Starr King, minister and publicizer of the California landscape: "God's purpose in creating such glories was not to receive our poor appreciation, it is to express the fullness of his thought, the overflow of his art, the depth of his goodness" (as cited in Palmquist, 1983, p. 15).[2] Although there is a sense in Burke (that is even more developed in Kant) that the sublime is unrepresentable, 19th Century landscape painters and, later, photographers, spent much effort representing the sublime. Eventually, under their influence

> "sublime" was used increasingly to refer to the "wild" in nature, and rather than focus on some work of man that gave meaning to the scene, romanticists tended to perceive a sublime landscape as a nondirect expression of God Himself. Again, the matter of scale was important, as well as the greater element of mystery, of supernatural manifestation that engendered a more reverential perception of the natural scene. Well recognized features of a wild, romantic landscape included references to amplitude or greatness of extent, vast and boundless prospects, great power and force exerted. (Demars, 1991, pp. 12–13)

The current interest is not only in how public discourse puts in play the sublime, but also how the discourse of the sublime directs and constrains how nature is perceived, pictured, and discussed.

Burke writes of Astonishment as the "passion caused by the great and sublime in *nature,* when those causes operate most powerfully" (Burke, 1757, p. 130). Watkins' Yosemite Valley #1 (Figure 1) is astonishing. We have a god's eye view of the valley stretching out before us in all its vastness. Cliffs jut out from the valley floor, intimidating in their sheer verticality. The stubble of trees atop the cliffs and the "toy trees" on the valley floor highlight the massiveness of the rocks. The

FIGURE 1

cliffs also dwarf the trees and us in terms of time, for their craggy faces tell of geological ages. Those cliffs, silent and immutable, have always been and always will be. They bear witness to eternity and deign not note humanity's ephemeral moment. The sedimented composition of the valley's chasm suggests an edenic space-time continuum that transcends even geological time. The human scale, both in terms of time and size, has no place here and, indeed, the view is devoid of human marks. In approaching the vastness of infinity and the timelessness of eternity, Yosemite Valley appears before us inhuman, a power that mocks human claims to significance.

The transcendence of the view, however, is accompanied by the terror of vertigo, for we seem to be perched on a precipice. One step further and we would tumble into the chasm separating us from the neighboring rock formation. The astonishment tinged with horror and fear that is the sublime is provoked, then, by the confrontation with both the immortal valley and our own mortality, perched precariously on the edge of this vastness (Burke, 1757, p. 130).

The vision of sublime nature is tempered to a certain extent because it is a picture, the product of a technological process. The sublime experience has been captured by technology, reproducing a vicarious domesticated sublime. The vastness of the valley and massiveness of the cliffs has been captured by a mammoth-plate camera, reproducing and reducing the view on 16" X 21" prints. We are not really tottering on a precipice, a gust of wind cannot blow us into the abyss. Watkins' photography transforms the spectacular sublime into the domestic spectacle, the private possession of tourists, East Coast urban dwellers, armchair adventurers. The comments of a contemporary admirer illustrate this transformation of the spectacular sublime into the domestic spectacle and point to the public significance of the dissemination of Watkins' photographs. The Reverend H. J. Morton writes in the 1866 *Philadelphia Photographer:*

> [His] photographic views, which open before us the wonderful valley whose features far surpass the fancies of the most imaginative poet and eager romancer . . . without crossing the continent by the overland route in dread of scalping Indians and waterless plains; without braving the dangers of the sea by the Chagres and Panama [sea] route; nay, without even the trouble of the brief land trip from San Francisco, we are able to step, as it were, from our study into the wonders of the wondrous valley, and gaze at our leisure on its amazing features. (Morton, 1886, p. 337)

The process of producing the domesticated sublime, however, also produces a technological sublime. Watkins' stereoscopic pictures "portray the valley as seen with superhuman eyes: They take in vast areas with every wrinkle and crevice on the rock faces in the distance as sharp as the foliage in the foreground" (Solnit, 1994, p. 235). The camera gives us a god's eye view, presenting an image more real than real, rendering with equal clarity the near and far, giving us a better view of the Valley than being there. Moreover, the photograph freezes Yosemite Valley, turning a moment into the eternal. This technological capturing of the view cloaks Yosemite in an immense and unfathomable stillness, provoking the twin terrors of silence and solitude. The viewer is confronted by the mute and immutable. Still, it is a capturing. The Valley is at the mercy of the viewer, and the viewer can contemplate the image at their leisure, put it away, return to it later, compare it to other collected images, and, indeed, own it, so that sublime nature is now commodified nature, a private possession, nature as cultural capital.

In other Yosemite photographs, Watkins creates the future icons of pristine American wilderness in a similar sublime style, with the notable difference that many of the images depict the union of the sublime and the beautiful (or picturesque). While the sublime is infinite, vast, massive, solid, rugged, vertical, and obscure mystery, the beautiful is comparatively small, smooth, delicate, clear, and pleasingly variable in shape (Burke, 1757, pp. 191–207). In practice, the beautiful has often meant pastoral and picturesque serves as a mediating term to describe landscapes that are rougher and less cultivated but on a human scale, not the grand scale of the sublime. Watkins' pictures often presents bifurcated landscapes, with beautiful foregrounds that both point to and are overshadowed by sublime backgrounds. In an 1865–1866 photo of Half Dome (Figure 2), a placid river, with only the faintest suggestion of ripples, occupies the immediate foreground before meandering into an open forest.[3] The rest of the foreground space is filled by the bushes and trees bordering the river. Trees fill in the left and right borders to the top of the frame, but the center upper half of the image is reserved for the background. In this spot looms Half Dome. The massive granite formation towers over the human scale trees and bushes. Complete with dead trees, the intricate foreground tangles of bushes, trees, and water suggests the fecundity and ephemerality of life. In stark contrast, Half Dome and the neighboring cliff are largely devoid of vegetation. Their rugged granite faces suggest ages, eternity.

Two compositional elements sharpen the sublimity of Watkins' Half Dome. First, the foregrounded scene draws viewers to the summit. The water's stillness, breached only by a fallen trunk and wavelets of reflected light, position the monolith as the image's vanishing point. Second, contrastive lighting further dramatizes the scene's

FIGURE 2

stillness. While the foreground is shot in a familiar black and white, the background is a distinctly brighter shade giving Half Dome a decidedly celestial hue. In the union of the sublime and the beautiful is born the tourist gaze. The beautiful foreground gives the tourist a pleasing place from which to view the spectacular spectacle of the sublime. Positioned at the water's edge, viewers experience the scene at ground level. Apprehending the scene from this plane envelops viewers within nature rather than positioning them at the precipice. By constructing a pleasurable place from which to view the sublime, Watkins anticipates and constructs a sublime experience in which comfort displaces risk as the spectator replaces the participant. The distanced position of the spectator obviates the emotional experience of the sublime. The sublime experience depends on the feeling of terror or fear in the face of the sublime object. As Burke differentiates, the sublime and the beautiful, "are indeed ideas of a very different nature, one being founded on pain, the other on pleasure" (1757, p. 206). In a sense, Watkins' images blaze a trail for the tourist at the expense of the adventurer and hollow out the sublime, leaving only spectacle. Indeed, by the late 1860s, "spectacular viewing already threatened to become a leading recreation at the site," so that the famous geologist Clarence King, with whom Watkins worked in a survey party, remarked, "I always go by this famous point of view now [Inspirational Point], feeling somehow that I don't belong to that army of literary travelers who have planted themselves and burst into rhetoric" (as cited in Trachtenberg, 1989, pp. 139–140).

The photo of El Capitan (1861) (Figure 3) also suggests the sublime, only more so. A closer shot heightens the sheer verticality of El Capitan. The foreground of river, trees, and bushes is foreshortened, and El Capitan looms ominously, the background threatening to swallow up the foreground. The immense size of the El Capitan monolith nearly overpowers Watkins' attempt to capture it, even within a mammoth plate panorama. Unable to contain it within his view, Watkins must position us at a distance. Peering at El Capitan from the corner of the photographic frame prompts viewers to crane necks even while taking in the scale of the photographic representation. This distancing effect created by foreshortened perspective underscores the almost immeasurable interval between nature and human existence. Dwarfed by the size of El Capitan, we are also dwarfed by its vast perpetuity.

This notion of an undefined, even perpetual, past, works in tandem with religious appropriations of the site to render the landscape in sacred terms. "El Capitan," according to one travel account, "was the title given by the old padres to God. What was done, therefore, sometime in the undefined past, was the splendidly daring thing of naming this stupendous cliff with the very name of the Almighty! How true the poetry of it! How fitting the suggestion!" (Jump, 1916, pp. 63–64). Cut away from the rest of the valley, the barren rock of El Capitan stands in dramatic relief to the trees and vegetation that surround the rock's base and the other cliff framed in the image. Its monumentality may, as the Reverend Morton warns, suggest that "Thus far shalt you go and no farther" (Burke, 1757, p. 377). As a visual admonishment of preservation, the image of El Capitan induces a reverence of nature's massiveness as a sign of sublime sacredness.

What is it about Carlton Watkins' photographs that make them such compelling statements for preservation? Watkins' formal composition of the Yosemite landscape dramatized preservationist arguments in his time as well as our own. His ability to orchestrate the "experience of nature" sedimented the nation's commitment to public preservation. By mediating nature as he effaced his own construction of it, Watkins captured the structure of feeling embodied in

FIGURE 3

preservation ideals. His images rely on perspectival framing to immerse viewers within nature. The expansive scenes he crafted almost overpower the photographic frame. Facing such an overwhelming scenic panorama induces a profound reverence for nature. Moreover, by effacing his orchestration of the image, Watkins rendered "living natural scenes" onto an edenic referential frame. Finally, Watkins fashions Yosemite's topography so as to inscribe nature within a perpetual geological past that dwarfs the present. These formal qualities work aesthetically and ideologically as Watkins' images not only resonate with, but also comment on, larger cultural narratives regarding national identity, scientific and industrial progress, and even race and class privilege.

CULTURAL RECEPTION:
PRESERVING AND PORTRAYING NATURE

Watkins' photographs of Yosemite Valley provided an important backdrop to the 1864 Act designating Yosemite Valley the nation's first federally protected wilderness area. The lore surrounding Yosemite suggests that California Senator John Conness passed Watkins' photographs around the halls of Congress (Palmquist,

1983, pp. 19–20; Fels, 1983, p. 34; Sanborn, 1981, p. 99). The photographer's role in preserving Yosemite, however, extended well beyond the Congressional floor. Thousands of people on the East Coast saw Watkins' photos, either in art galleries or as reprints in their homes. His images garnered such popular support for preservation that it led Edward Wilson, editor of the *Philadelphia Photographer,* to comment, "It has been said that 'the pen is mightier than the sword,' but who shall not say that in *this* instance, at least, *the camera is mightier than the pen?*" (as cited in Palmquist, 1983, p. 20). In particular, Watkins' influence on Frederick Law Olmsted, the First Commissioner for the Yosemite Commission, placed his photographs as a common referent for public debate regarding the preservation of Yosemite. In an 1865 letter to Watkins and two other artists, Olmsted solicited two queries concerning how the valley could be modeled into more pleasurable scenery:

> 1st Are there any conditions affecting the scenery of the Yo Semite unfavorably which it would be in the power of the State to remove, or the further and increased effect of which might be prevented? 2nd What can be done by the State to enhance the enjoyment now afforded by the scenery of the Yo Semite? (1865/1985, p. 433)

Although no official record exists documenting Watkins' response to Olmsted's August 1865 letter, the photographer's influence surfaces throughout Olmsted's treatise on preservation—his 1865 Yosemite Commission Report on Yosemite Valley and Mariposa Grove. Early in the report Olmsted points to the role that images played in making the American public aware of the need to protect and preserve Yosemite:

> It was during one of the darkest hours, before Sherman had begun the march upon Atlanta or Grant his terrible movement through the Wilderness, when the paintings of Bierstadt and the photographs of Watkins, both productions of the War time, had given to the people on the Atlantic some idea of the sublimity of the Yo Semite, and of the stateliness of the neighboring Sequoia grove, that consideration was first given to the danger that such scenes might become private property and through the false taste, the caprice or the requirement of some industrial speculation of their holders; their value to posterity be injured. To secure them against this danger Congress passed an act providing that the premises should be segregated from the general domain of the public lands, and devoted forever to popular resort and reaction, under the administration of a Board of Commissioners, to serve without pecuniary compensation, to be appointed by the Executive of the State of California. (1865/1985, p. 489)

Widely recognized as providing the philosophical grounding for the preservation and protection of state and national parks, Olmsted's 1865 report established a public vocabulary for debates over scenic preservation. Watkins' views of Yosemite function within this public narrative as more than a visual referent to Olmsted's philosophical defense of the nation's commitment to environmental preservation. Indeed, the pristine views rendered in Watkins' photographs provide a visual lexicon for the meaning of preservation in nineteenth century America.

Although Olmsted remarks on the monetary advantage of preserving Yosemite for tourists, the body of the commission report outlined the association between scenic contemplation and civic cultivation. "The power of scenery to affect men is," according to Olmsted, "in a large way, proportionate to the degree of their civilization and to the degree in which their taste has been cultivated" (1865/1985, p. 503). He situates the argument for scenic preservation in relation to the English pastoral tradition yet critiques the English for withholding the curative properties of such scenery from those who need it most:

> The enjoyment of the choicest natural scenes in the country and the means of recreation connected with them is thus a monopoly, in a very peculiar manner, of a very few, very rich people. The great mass of society, including those to whom it would be of the greatest benefit, is excluded from it. (1865/1985, p. 505)

Olmsted not only extends the curative properties of wilderness areas like Yosemite to all, but also constructs the establishment of public grounds as the political duty of a sovereign state. It is important to note that Olmsted's democratic impulse is accompanied by the impulse of the social reformer to improve the masses, as evident in his references to "degree of civilization" and "taste." Through the latter impulse nature becomes "a tool of prescriptive improvement aimed down the social scale at class and racial others" (Davis, 1997, p. 32).

Even as Olmsted used the power of Watkins' images to represent Yosemite, he also attempted to complicate the iconic relationship between Watkins' view of Yosemite Valley and the experience of being immersed within the scenery. For Olmsted,

> No photographs or series of photographs, no paintings ever prepare a visitor so that he is not taken by surprise, for could the scenes be faithfully represented the visitor is affected not only by that upon which his eye is at any moment fixed, but by all that with which on every side it is associated, and of which it is seen only as an inherent part. (1865/1985, p. 500)

Olmsted's ambivalence over the images is suggested by his certainty that "There was no single element or view that constituted the glory of Yosemite" (1865/1985, p. 465). Yet, Olmsted's criticisms of the shortcomings of photographs actually reinforces Watkins' theme of the sublimity of Yosemite. As sublime, Yosemite is in part beyond representation, even by Watkins' stunning photos.

IMPLICATIONS AND CONSEQUENCES OF WATKINS' VISUAL RHETORIC

If rhetoric is defined as the mobilization of signs for the articulation of identities, ideologies, consciousnesses, communities, publics, and cultures, it is clear that Watkins' images operate on many registers, including the short-term, long-term, political, cultural, commercial, and scientific. Watkins' 1860s photographs had numerous intentional and unintentional effects. As among the first of the landscape photographers, Watkins sought to establish landscape photography as an art, secure his own preeminence, achieve commercial success, arouse national and international interest in Yosemite, and provide scientifically accurate information for geological survey teams. As the premier pioneer of the art of landscape photography, Watkins succeeded. Watkins' pictures eclipsed the work of his only earlier competitor, Charles Weed, and set the standard for his successors, from Eadweard Muybridge to Ansel Adams. Ralph Waldo Emerson and Oliver Wendell Holmes remarked favorably on Watkins' work. Holmes described Watkins' photos as "a perfection of art which compares with the finest European work" (1863, p. 8). His photographs were displayed in the prestigious New York City Goupil's Art Gallery, won prizes in competitions in the United States and Europe, including the 1867 Paris Exposition, and were held in generally high regard by his photographer and artist peers. Indeed, the landscape painter Albert Bierstadt considered him the "Prince of Photographers" and used his photos when painting (Palmquist, 1983). It has been suggested that Bierstadt's visit to Watkins exhibition at Goupil's Gallery inspired him to make his first trip to Yosemite. Bierstadt's subsequent Yosemite paintings further popularized the park.

Commercially, Watkins' prints and albums sold fairly well, and he was able to open his own Yosemite Art Gallery. Although Watkins' artistic and commercial success helped spark interest in Yosemite and spur tourism, it did not translate into personal financial security. The combination of Watkins' lack of business acumen, the 1870s recession, and copyright problems conspired to put Watkins in a perpetually precarious financial position throughout his career.

In scientific circles, Watkins was considered a photographer without peer. His photos were used by the Harvard botanist Asa Gray and Watkins' presence was prized by geological survey teams (Palmquist, 1983). As the eminent geologist and surveyor King remarked in 1863 to a colleague, "How kind it was of the Indians to shoot the other Watkins [no relation to Carleton] and let the immortal one go free . . . providence will take care of him I am sure till he has 'taken' Mt. Shasta and the Mono Lake region" (as cited in Palmquist, 1983, p. 25). The surveyors' gratitude was such that they named a prominent peak in Yosemite overlooking Mirror Lake "Mt. Watkins."

The most important unintentional short-term effect of Watkins' photographs was political. As previously noted, Watkins' images of Yosemite influenced the Congress to create the world's first wilderness park. As cultural historian Solnit succinctly summarizes the effects of Watkins' photographs, "And so a man who had never seen the place [Senator John Conness] induced more who had never been near the state [Congressional members and Lincoln] to preserve it for a public which had hardly reached it" (p. 243). Watkins' photos also had long-term unintentional political and cultural effects. Although Watkins had no known environmental or political intentions, arguably his most important legacy is how his imagistic construction of nature has influenced environmentalism. Watkins' pictures mark the beginning of environmental preservationism and ecotourism, for in his work Watkins both perpetuates and constructs an image of nature that sets the parameters for what is nature and what counts as environmental politics even today.

As discussed earlier, Watkins' photos cultivate and propagate an image of a sublime nature, but, to be precise, a spectacularly sublime nature reduced to a domestic spectacle, a nature both sublime and a source of sustenance for the civilized tourist. The consequences of such a nature are multiple and especially significant along the axes of race and class.[4]

Watkins imaged a Yosemite devoid of human markings, a pristine wilderness where one could glimpse the sublime face of God. In picturing a nature apart from culture, Watkins was obeying the dictates of the nature/culture dichotomy central to Western civilization, wherein a nature out there ontologically divided from culture serves as a source of resources, artistic inspiration, spiritual awe, emotional succor, and so on. Viewing nature as pristine wilderness apart from humanity becomes cultural convention and environmental policy, evident in pictures of other natural areas, from the Grand Canyon to Yellowstone, and inscribed in the Wilderness Act of 1964: "A wilderness in contrast with those areas where man and his works dominate the landscape, is hereby recognized as an area where the earth and its community of life are untrammeled by man, where man himself is a visitor who does not remain" (Frome, 1974, p. 29).

Yosemite as pristine paradise was read in terms of nationalism and divine favour. Nationalist skirmishes over the virtue of the American landscape led English cultural critic John Ruskin to counter American claims to the pastoral in his 1856 letter to Charles Eliot Norton. Ruskin contests, "I have just been seeing a number of landscapes by an American painter of some repute; and the ugliness of them is wonderful" (Ruskin, 1904, p. 29). As more and more Europeans encountered images and actual fragments of the American West, however, arguments like those advanced by Ruskin waned. Ruskin himself eventually recanted and became an admirer of the landscape painter Thomas "Yellowstone" Moran:

> Nor are there any descriptions of the Valley of Diamonds, or the Lake of the Black Islands, in the "Arabian Nights," anything like so wonderful as the scenes of California and the Rocky Mountains which you may . . . see represented with most sincere and passionate enthusiasm by the American landscape painter, Mr. Thomas Moran. (as cited in Kinsey, 1992, p. 14)

"The opening of the Far West," Demars argues, "with its astonishing array of natural wonders, provided Americans, at last[,] with claims to scenic superiority that were difficult to dispute. Everything 'western' seemed to exist on a monumental scale" (1991, p. 21). For example, almost nothing in the European imagination could exceed the magnitude of the Yosemite Valley Giant Sequoias. The awe engendered by their immense size and life span led visitors to discount the authenticity of a tree bark from the Calaveras Grove (315 feet in height and 61 feet in circumference) exhibited at the 1854 Crystal Palace exhibition: "Owing to the immensity of the circumference, nobody would believe that the bark had come from one tree, and finally, being branded a humbug, the exhibit had to be ended" (Huth, 1948, p. 63). In 1864 Senator Conness used this incident to put before the Senate a patriotic argument for the preservation of Yosemite:

> From the Calaveras grove some sections of a fallen tree were cut during and pending the great World's Fair that was held in London some years since. The English who saw it declared it to be a Yankee invention, made from beginning to end; that it was an utter untruth that such trees grew in the country; that it could not be . . . we were not able to convince them that it was a specimen of American growth. . . . They would not believe us. (as cited in Runte, 1990, p. 20)

By 1867, however, the Paris International Exhibition recognized Watkins' images of the "grand mountains and gigantic vegetation of America" (Vogel, 1867, p. 77). These included Watkins' portraits of the Grizzly Giant, the oldest living Sequoia (having sprouted circa 1500 BC). Olmsted had suggested in his *Preliminary Report upon the Yosemite and Big Tree Grove* that the Grizzly Giant may be the "noblest tree in the world" (1865/1985, p. 491). Images documenting the monumental scale of Yosemite's mountains and trees dramatized the nation's magnitude by constituting America as a sacred space:

> These vast trees, bearing upon their charred rind the marks of scorching fires which might have been coeval with the siege of Jerusalem, were felt to unite our frail beings with the past, and to present to the imagination the procession of the ages, as a chain of which we were among the latest links. (Pfeiffer, 1995, p. 83)

The Giant Sequoia served as an iconic representation of the divine providence of the American West. They created a sense of being at the center of the world—thus designating the nation as an axis mundi. Horace Greeley noted that the Big Trees "were of very substantial size when David danced before the Ark, when Solomon laid the foundations of the Temple, when Theseus ruled in Athens, when Aeneas fled from the burning wreck of vanquished Troy, when Sesostris led his victorious Egyptians into the heart of Asia" (as cited in Runte, 1990, p. 15). At a time when the ongoing Civil War was read as a sign of God's disfavor, Americans, through Watkins' pictorial evidence, embraced Yosemite as a manifestation of God's continuing favor. Yosemite, then, served not merely as an environmental park but as a redemptive site. Representing Yosemite as Edenic, however, constitutes a form of imagistic genocide. Yosemite was not pristine, but cleansed.

Just ten years prior to Watkins' discovery of Yosemite, the Mariposa Battalion had entered the valley with the intent of relocating or exterminating the Ahwahneechee. The ability of whites to rhapsodize about Yosemite as paradise, the original Garden of Eden, depended on the forced removal and forgetting of the indigenous inhabitants of the area for the past 3,500 years, people whose practices of habitation, including planned burnings of the meadows, had created the pristine wilderness whites were celebrating. As Solnit notes, "The West wasn't empty, it was emptied—literally by expeditions like the Mariposa Battalion, and figuratively by the sublime images of a virgin paradise created by so many painters, poets, and photographers" (1992, p. 56). In not taking photos of Native Americans and their traces, Watkins contributed to the larger cultural project of effacing Native Americans both literally and figuratively in service to the national myth of pristine nature a myth made material in the "pristine paradise" of Yosemite.

Workers, also, were effaced from the images of Yosemite. Although Watkins took photos of industrial activity at other sites, due to numerous reasons signs of shepherds, miners, and loggers are absent in his images of Yosemite. Artistically, workers and the scars of industrialism do not figure in representations of Romantic, sublime wilderness. Additionally, the elite urban tourists of the industrial East that constitute a large part of Watkins' audience are turning to Yosemite in search of the restorative properties of wilderness, not in search of signs of the omnipresence of industrialism. In fact, the development of artistic and cultural practices for the appreciation of an anesthetized nature mark the upper classes as distinct from the working class and function to naturalize hierarchical social relations (see Williams, 1980, pp. 67–85; Davis, 1997, pp. 31–32). The camera is a stunningly effective means to naturalize reality, to create a world without history and a people without memory. As critics Barthes, Sontag, and John Berger note, photography transforms the world into a series of unrelated, free-standing traces of reality, events without contexts, moments outside of history and memory (1981; 1973; 1980).

This essay is pointing to some of the racial and class consequences of the concept of sublime nature not in order to cast moral recriminations at Watkins and his time, but to highlight the practical effects that this particular construction of nature, materialized in Watkins' iconic images, had on American culture and environmental politics. In placing Watkins' timeless Yosemite in a complex and charged context, the attempt is to imagine a critical practice that enacts Berger's alternative photography: "The task of an alternative photography is to incorporate photography into social and political memory, instead of using it as a substitute which encourages the atrophy of any such memory" (1980, p. 62). In placing Watkins' photographs in a larger social and political landscape, the attempt is to *remember* the origins of Yosemite and the roots of environmentalism in a way that enables the emergence of alternative environmental practices. To remember is to hope and to act: "Memory implies a certain act of redemption. What is remembered has been saved from nothingness. What is forgotten has been abandoned" (Berger, 1980, p. 58).

The construction of pristine wilderness as nature, largely the product of an urban, upper-class, white, industrialized cultural formation, marginalized other cultures' visions of nature and human-nature relations, most obviously those of Native Americans. The rhetoric of nature as pristine and separate from human culture set in motion the trajectory of environmental politics for its first one hundred years. As evident in their pictures, writings, and actions, environmental groups have been consumed with preserving "pristine" places. This narrow focus has had the major effect of reproducing the nature-culture dichotomy and circumscribing environmentalism in two complementary ways. In taking as their charge the preservation of wilderness, environmental groups relieved themselves of the responsibility of protecting non-pristine areas and of critiquing the practices of industrialism that degraded the general environment. In exchange for pockets of wilderness, environmental groups ignored industrialism's progressive plundering of the planet. Similarly, if the places people live are by definition not nature, environmental groups need not concern themselves with inhabited environments. So, for example, while the Sierra Club was sparing no efforts in saving the desolate Dinosaur National Monument, the nation's major waterways were dying (Hudson, Potomac, Mississippi) and, in some cases, even catching fire (Boston's Charles River and Cleveland's Cuyahoga River). The conceptual blinder of nature as pristine wilderness prevented these groups from focusing on pollution as a major environmental issue.

Of course, since the 1960s Rachel Carson and others have alerted environmentalists and everyone else to the dangers of pollution, deep ecologists have challenged the separation of nature and culture, and environmental justice groups have made a clean environment a social justice and human rights issue. Environmental justice groups have also pointed out how understanding nature as pristine wilderness had race and class dimensions since it led to an environmental movement composed of those who have the time and the money to travel to and play in these pristine places and thus are concerned about wilderness while ignoring degraded prosaic places and those who must live there.

In response to these criticisms mainstream environmental groups have expanded their range of issues beyond just wilderness issues, have started to think of humans as embedded in nature, and have forged links across racial and class lines through alliances with environmental justice, civil rights, and labor groups. With these moves, environmental groups are finally constructing a vision of nature that transcends the sublime wilderness created in no small part by the visual rhetoric of Carleton Watkins and his successors.

NOTES

[1]For a thorough and compelling account of the rise of the technological sublime in the United States, see David Nye's *American Technological Sublime* (1994).

[2]We do not correct or add to the sexist language used by some of those quoted in this work for the reason that such sexist language is not merely a matter of terminology, but is often of theoretical or historical significance. For example, when theorists write on "man" as a universal category, often their analyses are only of men and pay little attention to the experience of women, though they proceed to universalize their findings.

[3]We use this photo instead of an essentially identical 1861 photo because of better production quality. Thematically, the photos are identical.

[4]Although not explored in this essay, it is important to note that there are also gender consequences, for the sublime and beautiful are gendered concepts.

REFERENCES

Altman, C. (1980). The medieval marquee: Church portal sculpture as publicity. *Journal of Popular Culture, 74,* 37–46.

Barthes, R. (1964/1977). Rhetoric of the image. In S. Health (Ed.), *Image, music, text.* New York: Hill and Wang.

Barthes, R. (1981). *Camera lucida: Reflections on photography.* New York: The Noonday Press.

Benson, T. (1986). Respecting the reader. *Quarterly Journal of Speech, 72,* 197–204.

Benson, T. (1980). The rhetorical structure of Frederick Wiseman's *High School. Communication Monograph[s], 47,* 233–261.

Berger, J. (1980). *About looking.* New York: Vintage International.

Blair, C., & Michel, N. (1999). Commemorating in the theme park zone: reading the astronauts memorial. In T. Rosteck (Ed.), *At the intersection: Cultural studies and rhetorical studies* (pp. 29–83). New York: Guilford Press.

Booth, W. (1971). The scope of rhetoric today: a polemical excursion. In L. F. Bitzer & E. Black (Eds.), *The prospect of rhetoric* (pp. 93–114). Englewood Cliffs, NJ.: Prentice-Hall.

Burgin, V. (1982). Looking at photographs. In Victor Burgin (Ed.) *Thinking photography* (pp. 142–153). London: Macmillan Press.

Burke, E. (1757). *The works of the right honorable Edmund Burke* (9th ed., Vol. 1). Cambridge: University Press.

Cahn, R., & Ketchum, R. (1981). *American photographers and the national parks.* New York: Viking Press.

Crimp, D. (1988). *AIDS: Cultural analysis and cultural activism.* Cambridge: MIT Press.

Davis, S. (1997). *Spectacular nature: Corporate culture and the Sea World experience.* Berkeley: University of California Press.

Demars, S. (1991). *The Tourist in Yosemite: 1855–1985.* Salt Lake City: University of Utah Press.

Fels, T. (1983). *Carleton Watkins: Photographer.* Williamstown, MA: Sterling and Francine Clark Art Institute.

Foss, S. (1994). A rhetorical schema for the evaluation of visual imagery. *Communication Studies, 45,* 213–224.

Frome, M. (1974). *Battle for the Wilderness.* New York: Praeger.

Gould, S. J. (1995). *Dinosaur in a haystack: Reflections in natural history.* New York: Harmony Books.

Gronbeck, B. E. (1995). Rhetoric, ethics, and telespectacles in the post-everything age. In R. H. Brown (Ed.), *Postmodern representations: Truth, power, and mimesis in the human sciences and public culture* (pp. 217–238). Urbana: University of Illinois Press.

Hales, P. B. (1988). *William Henry Jackson and the transformation of the American landscape.* Philadelphia: Temple University Press.

Hall, S. (1988). The toad in the garden: Thatcherism among the theorists. In C. Nelson & L. Grossberg (Eds.), *Marxism and the interpretation of culture* (pp. 35–57). Urbana, IL: University of Illinois Press.

Harrington, J. (1973). *The rhetoric of film.* [Holt,] Rinehart and Winston.

Hartley, J. (1992). *The politics of pictures.* New York: Routledge.

Holmes, O. W. (1863). Doings of the sunbeam, *Atlantic Monthly, 72:* 1–16.

Huths, H. (1948). Yosemite: The story of an idea. *Sierra Club Bulletin, 33,* 47–48.

Jamieson, K. H. (1988). *Eloquence in an electronic age.* New York: Oxford University Press.

Jump, H. A. (1916). *The Yosemite: A spiritual interpretation.* Boston: The Pilgrim Press.

Kinsey, J. (1992). *Thomas Moran and the surveying of the American West.* Washington: Smithsonian Institution Press.

Lancioni, J. (1996). The rhetoric of the frame revisioning archival photographs in the civil war. *Western Journal of Communication, 60,* 397–414.

Longinus. (1984). *On the sublime* (J. A. Arieti, Trans.). New York, E. Mellon Press. (Original work published in the 1st century).

Lyotard, J. F. (1991). *The inhuman: Reflections on time.* Stanford: Stanford University Press.

Mitchell, W. J. T. (1996). Interdisciplinarity and visual vulture. *The Art Bulletin, 77,* 540–544.

Morton, H. J. (1886). *Philadelphia Photographer, 3,* 377.

Nash, R. (1967). *Wilderness and the American mind* (rev. ed.). Binghamton: Vail-Ballou.

Nicolson, M. H. (1973). Sublime in external nature. In P. Wiener (Ed.), *Dictionary of the history of ideas* (pp. 336–337). New York: Scribner.

Novak, B. (1995). *Nature and culture: American landscape and painting, 1825–1875.* New York: Oxford University Press.

Nye, D. E. (1994). *American technological sublime.* Cambridge: MIT Press.

Oelschlaeger, M. (1991). *The idea of wilderness.* New Haven: Yale University.

Olmsted, F. L. (1865/1985). Letter to Carleton Watkins. In P. R. Ranney (Ed.), *The Papers of Frederick Law Olmsted: The California Frontier 1863–1865* (Vol. 5) (pp. 433–435) Baltimore: Johns Hopkins University Press.

Olmsted, F. L. (1865/1985). Preliminary report upon the Yosemite and Big Tree Grove. In P. R. Ranney (Ed.), *The Papers of Frederick Law Olmsted: The California Frontier 1863–1865* (Vol. 5) (pp. 488–517). Baltimore: Johns Hopkins University Press.

Palmquist, P. (1983). *Carleton E. Watkins: Photographer of the American West.* Albuquerque: University of New Mexico Press.

Pfeiffer, E. (1885). *Flying leaves from the east to west.* London: Field and Tuer.

Runte, A. (1990). *Yosemite: the embattled wilderness.* Lincoln: University of Nebraska Press.

Ruskin, J. (1904). *Letters of John Ruskin to Charles Eliot Norton.* New York: Houghton, Mifflin and Company.

Sanborn, M. (1981). *Yosemite: Its discovery, its wonders, and its people.* New York: Random House.

Schama, S. (1995). *Landscape and memory.* New York: A. A. Knopf.

Solnit, R. (1994). *Savage dreams: A journey into the hidden wars of the American West.* San Francisco: Sierra Club Books.

Solnit, R. (1992). Up the river of mercy. *Sierra, 77,* 50, 53–58, 78, 81, 83–84.

Sontag, S. (1973). *On photography* (7th printing). New York: Farrar, Straus, and Giroux.

Sontag, S. (1966/1978). *Against interpretation: And other essays.* New York: Octagon Books.

Tagg, J. (1999). Evidence, Truth and Order: A Means of Surveillance. In Jessica Evans & Stuart Hall (Eds.), *Visual culture: A reader.* London: Sage Publication[s].

Trachtenberg, A. (1989). *Reading American photographs: Images as history[,] Mathew Brady to Walker Evans.* New York: Hill and Wang.

Treichler, P. (1988). An epidemic of signification. In D. Crimp (Eds.), *AIDS: cultural analysis and cultural activism* (pp. 17–31). Cambridge: MIT Press.

Truettner, W. (1991). *The west as America: Reinterpreting images of the frontier, 1820–1920.* Washington: Smithsonian Institution Press.

Vogel, H. (1867). Paris Correspondence; Paris International Exhibition. *Philadelphia Photographer, 4,* 77.

Williams, R. (1980). *Problems in materialism and culture.* London: NLB.

Additional Readings

Chapter 1. Purposes of Rhetorical Criticism

Baskerville, Barnet. "Must We All Be 'Rhetorical Critics'?" *Quarterly Journal of Speech* 63 (1977): 107–16.

Benson, Thomas W. "The Senses of Rhetoric: A Topical System for Critics." *Central States Speech Journal* 29 (1978): 237–50.

Brockriede, Wayne. "Rhetorical Criticism as Argument." *Quarterly Journal of Speech* 60 (1974): 165–74.

Campbell, Karlyn Kohrs. "An Exercise in the Rhetoric of Mythical America." In *Critiques of Contemporary Rhetoric*, 50–57. Belmont, Calif.: Wadsworth, 1972.

Croft, Albert J. "The Functions of Rhetorical Criticism." *Quarterly Journal of Speech* 42 (1956): 283–91.

Foss, Sonja K. "Rhetorical Criticism as the Asking of Questions." *Communication Education* 38 (1989): 191–96.

Gregg, Richard B. "A Phenomenologically Oriented Approach to Rhetorical Criticism." *Central States Speech Journal* 17 (1966): 83–90.

Grossberg, Lawrence. "Marxist Dialectics and Rhetorical Criticism." *Quarterly Journal of Speech* 65 (1979): 235–49.

Hart, Roderick P. "Contemporary Scholarship in Public Address: A Research Editorial." *Western Journal of Speech Communication* 50 (1986): 283–95.

Hillbruner, Anthony. *Critical Dimensions: The Art of Public Address Criticism.* New York: Random House, 1966.

Reid, Loren D. "The Perils of Rhetorical Criticism." *Quarterly Journal of Speech* 30 (1944): 416–22.

Rosenfield, Lawrence W. "The Anatomy of Critical Discourse." *Speech Monographs* 35 (1968): 50–69.

Rosteck, Thomas. "Form and Cultural Context in Rhetorical Criticism: Re-Reading Wrage." *Quarterly Journal of Speech* 84 (1998): 471–90.

Wander, Philip, and Steven Jenkins. "Rhetoric, Society, and the Critical Response." *Quarterly Journal of Speech* 58 (1972): 441–50.

Chapter 2. Neo-Classical Criticism

Andrews, James R. *The Practice of Rhetorical Criticism.* 2d ed. New York: Longman, 1990.

Arnold, Carroll C. *Criticism of Oral Rhetoric.* Columbus, Ohio: Merrill, 1974.

Arnold, Carroll C. "George William Curtis." In *A History and Criticism of American Public Address,* Vol. 3, edited by Marie Hochmuth, 133–74. New York: Longmans, Green, 1955.

Arnold, Carroll C. "Lord Thomas Erskine: Modern Advocate." *Quarterly Journal of Speech* 44 (1958): 17–30.

Gross, Alan G. "Renewing Aristotelian Theory: The Cold Fusion Controversy as a Test Case." *Quarterly Journal of Speech* 81 (1995): 48–62.

Hansen, Andrew C. "Rhetorical Indiscretions: Charles Dickens as Abolitionist." *Western Journal of Communication* 65 (2001): 26–44.

Houck, Davis W., and Miheaela Nocasian, "FDR's First Inaugural Address: Text, Context, and Reception." *Rhetoric & Public Affairs* 5 (2002): 649–78.

Medhurst, Martin J. "Eisenhower's 'Atoms for Peace' Speech: A Case Study in the Strategic Use of Language." *Communication Monographs* 54 (1987): 204–20.

Mohrmann, Gerald P. "Elegy in a Critical Grave-Yard." *Western Journal of Speech Communication* 44 (1980): 265–74.

Mohrmann, G. P., and Michael C. Leff. "Lincoln at Cooper Union: A Rationale for Neo-Classical Criticism." *Quarterly Journal of Speech* 60 (1974): 459–67.

[Nichols], Marie Hochmuth. "The Criticism of Rhetoric." In *A History and Criticism of American Public Address*, Vol. 3, edited by Marie Hochmuth, 1–23. New York: Longmans, Green, 1955.

[Nichols], Marie Hochmuth. "Lincoln's First Inaugural." In *American Speeches*, edited by Wayland Maxfield Parrish and Marie Hochmuth, 21–71. New York: Longmans, Green, 1954.

O'Rourke, Sean Patrick. "Cultivating the 'Higher Law' in American Jurisprudence: John Quincy Adams, Neo-Classical Rhetoric, and the *Amistad* Case." *Southern Communication Journal* 60 (1994): 33–43.

Patton, John H. "A Transforming Response: Martin Luther King Jr.'s 'Letter from a Birmingham Jail.'" *Rhetoric & Public Affairs* 7 (2004): 53–66.

Reid, Ronald F. "Edward Everett: Rhetorician of Nationalism, 1824–1855." *Quarterly Journal of Speech* 42 (1956): 273–82.

Ryan, Halford Ross. "Roosevelt's First Inaugural: A Study of Technique." *Quarterly Journal of Speech* 65 (1979): 137–49.

Thonssen, Lester, A. Craig Baird, and Waldo W. Braden. *Speech Criticism*. 2d ed. 1970. Reprint. Malabar, Fla.: Krieger, 1981.

Zarefsky, David. "Henry Clay and the Election of 1844: The Limits of a Rhetoric of Compromise." *Rhetoric & Public Affairs* 6 (2003): 79–96.

Zarefsky, David. "Making the Case for War: Colin Powell at the United Nations." *Rhetoric & Public Affairs* 10 (2007): 275–302.

Chapter 3. Close Textual Analysis

Browne, Stephen H. "Edmund Burke's *Letter to a Noble Lord*: A Textual Study in Political Philosophy and Rhetorical Action." *Communication Monographs* 55 (1988): 215–29.

Browne, Stephen H. "Encountering Angelina Grimké: Violence, Identity, and the Creation of Radical Community." *Quarterly Journal of Speech* 82 (1996): 55–73.

Ehrenhaus, Peter. "Why We Fought: Holocaust Memory in Spielberg's *Saving Private Ryan*." *Critical Studies in Media Communication* 18 (2001): 321–37.

Frank, David A. "The Mutability of Rhetoric: Haydar 'Abd al-Shafi's Madrid Speech and Vision of Palestinian-Israeli Rapprochement." *Quarterly Journal of Speech* 86 (2000): 334–353.

Hansen, Andrew C. "Dimensions of Agency in Lincoln's Second Inaugural." *Philosophy and Rhetoric* 37 (2004): 223–54.

Hariman, Robert, and John Louis Lucaites. "Public Identity and Collective Memory in U.S. Iconic Photography: The Image of 'Accidental Napalm.'" *Critical Studies in Media Communication* 20 (2003): 35–66.

Hostettler, Michael J. "Washington's Farewell Address: Distance as Bane and Blessing." *Rhetoric & Public Affairs* 5 (2002): 393–407.

Leff, Michael. "Textual Criticism: The Legacy of G. P. Mohrmann." *Quarterly Journal of Speech* 72 (1986): 377–89.

Leff, Michael C. "Things Made by Words: Reflections on Textual Criticism." *Quarterly Journal of Speech* 78 (1992): 223–31.

Leff, Michael, and Andrew Sachs. "Words the Most Like Things: Iconicity and the Rhetorical Text." *Western Journal of Speech Communication* 54 (1990): 252–73.

McClure, Kevin R. "Frederick Douglass' Use of Comparison in His Fourth of July Oration: A Textual Criticism." *Western Journal of Communication* 64 (2000): 425–44.

Medhurst, Martin J. "Reconceptualizing Rhetorical History: Eisenhower's Farewell Address." *Quarterly Journal of Speech* 80 (1994): 195–218.

Owen, A. Susan. "Memory, War and American Identity: *Saving Private Ryan* as Cinematic Jeremiad." *Critical Studies in Media Communication* 19 (2002): 249–82.

Pfau, Michael William. "Time, Tropes, and Textuality: Reading Republicanism in Charles Sumner's 'Crime against Kansas.'" *Rhetoric & Public Affairs* 6 (2003): 385–414.

Slagell, Amy R. "Anatomy of a Masterpiece: A Close Textual Analysis of Abraham Lincoln's Second Inaugural Address." *Communication Studies* 42 (1991): 155–71.

Stelzner, Hermann G. "'War Message,' December 8, 1941: An Approach to Language." *Communication Monographs* 33 (1966): 419–37.

Chapter 4. Dramatistic Criticism

Birdsell, David S. "Ronald Reagan on Lebanon and Grenada: Flexibility and Interpretation in the Application of Kenneth Burke's Pentad." *Quarterly Journal of Speech* 73 (1987): 267–79.

Blankenship, Jane, Marlene G. Fine, and Leslie K. Davis. "The 1980 Republican Primary Debates: The Transformation of Actor to Scene." *Quarterly Journal of Speech* 69 (1983): 25–36.

Brummett, Barry. "Burkean Comedy and Tragedy, Illustrated in Reactions to the Arrest of John Delorean." *Central States Speech Journal* 35 (1984): 217–27.

Brummett, Barry. "Burkean Scapegoating, Mortification, and Transcendence in Presidential Campaign Rhetoric." *Central States Speech Journal* 32 (1981): 254–64.

Brummett, Barry. "A Pentadic Analysis of Ideologies in Two Gay Rights Controversies." *Central States Speech Journal* 30 (1979): 250–61.

Burke, Kenneth. "Mind, Body and the Unconscious." In *Language as Symbolic Action,* 63–80. Berkeley: University of California Press, 1966.

Conrad, Charles. "Phases, Pentads, and Dramatistic Critical Process." *Central States Speech Journal* 35 (1984): 94–104.

Darr, Christopher R. "Civility as Rhetorical Enactment: The John Ashcroft 'Debates' and Burke's Theory of Form." *Southern Communication Journal* 70 (2005): 316–28.

Goldzwig, Steven R. "LBJ, the Rhetoric of Transcendence, and the Civil Rights Act of 1968." *Rhetoric & Public Affairs* 6 (2003): 25–54.

Hahn, Dan F., and Anne Morlando. "A Burkean Analysis of Lincoln's Second Inaugural Address." *Presidential Studies Quarterly* 9 (1979): 376–79.

Kelley, Colleen E. "The 1984 Campaign Rhetoric of Representative George Hansen: A Pentadic Analysis." *Western Journal of Speech Communication* 51 (1987): 204–17.

Kimble, James J. "My Enemy, My Brother: The Paradox of Peace and War in Abraham Lincoln's Rhetoric of Conciliation." *Southern Communication Journal* 72 (2007): 55–70.

Kuseski, Brenda. "Kenneth Burke's 'Five Dogs' and Mother Teresa's Love." *Quarterly Journal of Speech* 74 (1988): 323–33.

Ling, David A. "A Pentadic Analysis of Senator Edward Kennedy's Address to the People of Massachusetts, July 25, 1969." *Central States Speech Journal* 21 (1970): 81–86.

O'Leary, Stephen D., and Mark H. Wright. "Psychoanalysis and Burkeian Rhetorical Criticism." *Southern Communication Journal* 61 (1995): 104–21.

Rountree, Clarke. "Instantiating 'the Law' and its Dissents in *Korematsu v. United States:* A Dramatistic Analysis of Judicial Discourse." *Quarterly Journal of Speech* 87 (2001): 1–24.

Stuckey, Mary E. "'The Domain of Public Conscience': Woodrow Wilson and the Establishment of a Transcendent Political Order." *Rhetoric & Public Affairs* 6 (2003): 1–24.

Tonn, Mari Boor, and Valerie A. Endress. "Looking under the Hood and Tinkering with Voter Cynicism: Ross Perot and 'Perspective by Incongruity.'" *Rhetoric & Public Affairs* 4 (2001): 281–308.

Whedbee, Karen. "Perspective by Incongruity in Norman Thomas's 'Some Wrong Roads to Peace.'" *Western Journal of Communication* 65 (2001): 45–64.

Chapter 5. Narrative Criticism

Bass, Jeff D. "The Appeal to Efficiency as Narrative Closure: Lyndon Johnson and the Dominican Crisis, 1965." *Southern Speech Communication Journal* 50 (1985): 103–20.

Bormann, Ernest G. "The Eagleton Affair: A Fantasy Theme Analysis." *Quarterly Journal of Speech* 59 (1973): 143–59.

Bormann, Ernest G. "Fantasy and Rhetorical Vision: The Rhetorical Criticism of Social Reality." *Quarterly Journal of Speech* 58 (1972): 396–401.

Bormann, Ernest G. "A Fantasy Theme Analysis of the Television Coverage of the Hostage Release and the Reagan Inaugural." *Quarterly Journal of Speech* 68 (1982): 133–45.

Bormann, Ernest G. "Fetching Good out of Evil: A Rhetorical Use of Calamity." *Quarterly Journal of Speech* 63 (1977): 130–39.

Bormann, Ernest G. *The Force of Fantasy: Restoring the American Dream.* Carbondale: Southern Illinois University Press, 1985.

Bormann, Ernest G., John F. Cragan, and Donald C. Shields. "An Expansion of the Rhetorical Vision Component of the Symbolic Convergence Theory: The Cold War Paradigm Case." *Communication Monographs* 63 (1996): 1–28.

Burgchardt, Carl R. "Discovering Rhetorical Imprints: La Follette, 'Iago,' and the Melodramatic Scenario." *Quarterly Journal of Speech* 71 (1985): 441–56.

Carcasson, Martin. "Unveiling the Oslo Narrative: The Rhetorical Transformation of Israeli-Palestinian Diplomacy." *Rhetoric & Public Affairs* 3 (2000): 211–45.

Carpenter, Ronald H. "Admiral Mahan, 'Narrative Fidelity,' and the Japanese Attack on Pearl Harbor." *Quarterly Journal of Speech* 72 (1986): 290–305.

DeLuca, Kevin Michael. "Trains in the Wilderness: The Corporate Roots of Environmentalism." *Rhetoric & Public Affairs* 4 (2001): 633–52.

Dorsey, Leroy G. "Sailing into the 'Wondrous Now': The Myth of the American Navy's World Cruise." *Quarterly Journal of Speech* 83 (1997): 447–65.

Dorsey, Leroy G., and Rachel Harlow. "'We Want Americans Pure and Simple': Theodore Roosevelt and the Myth of Americanism." *Rhetoric & Public Affairs* 6 (2003): 55–78.

Fisher, Walter R. *Human Communication as Narration: Toward a Philosophy of Reason, Value, and Action.* Columbia, S.C.: University of South Carolina Press, 1987.

Goldzwig, Steven R., and Patricia A. Sullivan. "Narrative and Counternarrative in Print-Mediated Coverage of Milwaukee Alderman Michael McGee." *Quarterly Journal of Speech* 86 (2000): 215–31.

Gring-Pemble, Lisa M. "'Are We Going to Now Govern By Anecdote?': Rhetorical Constructions of Welfare Recipients in Congressional Hearings, Debates, and Legislation, 1992–1996." *Quarterly Journal of Speech* 87 (2001): 341–65.

Hensley, Carl Wayne. "Rhetorical Vision and the Persuasion of a Historical Movement: The Disciples of Christ in Nineteenth Century American Culture." *Quarterly Journal of Speech* 61 (1975): 250–64.

Jorgensen-Earp, Cheryl R., and Darwin D. Jorgensen. "'Miracle from Mouldy Cheese': Chronological versus Thematic Self-Narratives in the Discovery of Penicillin." *Quarterly Journal of Speech* 88 (2002): 69–90.

Kraig, Robert Alexander. "The Narration of Essence: Salmon P. Chase's Senate Oration against the Kansas-Nebraska Act." *Communication Studies* 48 (1997): 234–53.

Kraig, Robert Alexander. "The Tragic Science: The Uses of Jimmy Carter in Foreign Policy Realism." *Rhetoric & Public Affairs* 5 (2002): 1–30.

Kuypers, Jim A., Marilyn J. Young, and Michael K. Launer. "Composite Narrative, Authoritarian Discourse, and the Soviet Response to the Destruction of Iran Air Flight 655." *Quarterly Journal of Speech* 87 (2001): 305–20.

Mohrmann, G. P. "An Essay on Fantasy Theme Criticism." *Quarterly Journal of Speech* 68 (1982): 109–32.

Rowland, Robert C. "Narrative: Mode of Discourse or Paradigm?" *Communication Monographs* 54 (1987): 264–75.

Rowland, Robert C. "On Limiting the Narrative Paradigm: Three Case Studies." *Communication Monographs* 56 (1989): 39–54.

Roy, Abhik, and Robert C. Rowland. "The Rhetoric of Hindu Nationalism: A Narrative of Mythic Redefinition." *Western Journal of Communication* 67 (2003): 225–48.

Stroud, Scott R. "Multivalent Narratives: Extending the Narrative Paradigm with Insights from Ancient Indian Philosophical Texts." *Western Journal of Communication* 66 (2002): 369–93.

Warnick, Barbara. "The Narrative Paradigm: Another Story." *Quarterly Journal of Speech* 73 (1987): 172–82.

Chapter 6. Metaphoric Criticism

Adams, John Charles. "Linguistic Values and Religious Experiences: An Analysis of Clothing Metaphors in Alexander Richardson's Ramist-Puritan Lectures on Speech, 'Speech is a garment to cloath our reason.'" *Quarterly Journal of Speech* 76 (1990): 58–68.

Ausmus, William A. "Pragmatic Uses of Metaphor: Models and Metaphor in the Nuclear Winter Scenario." *Communication Monographs* 65 (1998): 67–82.

Baym, Geoffrey. "Strategies of Illumination: U.S. Network News, Watergate, and the Clinton Affair." *Rhetoric & Public Affairs* 6 (2003): 633–56.

Benoit, William L. "Framing through Temporal Metaphor: The 'Bridges' of Bob Dole and Bill Clinton in Their 1996 Acceptance Addresses." *Communication Studies* 52 (2001): 70–84.

Blankenship, Jane. "The Search for the 1972 Democratic Nomination: A Metaphorical Perspective." In *Methods of Rhetorical Criticism: A Twentieth-Century Perspective*, 2d ed., rev., edited by Bernard L. Brock and Robert L. Scott, 321–45. Detroit, Mich.: Wayne State University Press, 1980.

Carpenter, Ronald H. "America's Tragic Metaphor: Our Twentieth-Century Combatants as Frontiersmen." *Quarterly Journal of Speech* 76 (1990): 1–22.

Darsey, James. "Barack Obama and America's Journey." *Southern Communication Journal* 74 (2009): 88–103.

Daughton, Suzanne M. "Metaphorical Transcendence: Images of the Holy War in Franklin Roosevelt's First Inaugural." *Quarterly Journal of Speech* 79 (1993): 427–46.

Farrell, Thomas B., and Thomas Goodnight. "Accidental Rhetoric: The Root Metaphors of Three Mile Island." *Communication Monographs* 48 (1981): 271–300.

Hayden, Sara. "Family Metaphors and the Nation: Promoting a Politics of Care through the Million Mom March."*Quarterly Journal of Speech* 89 (2003): 196–215.

Ivie, Robert L. "Literalizing the Metaphor of Soviet Savagery: President Truman's Plain Style." *Southern Speech Communication Journal* 51 (1986): 91–105.

Ivie, Robert L. "The Metaphor of Force in Prowar Discourse: The Case of 1812." *Quarterly Journal of Speech* 68 (1982): 240–53.

Jamieson, Kathleen Hall. "The Metaphoric Cluster in the Rhetoric of Pope Paul VI and Edmund G. Brown, Jr." *Quarterly Journal of Speech* 66 (1980): 51–72.

Kuusisto, Riikka. "Heroic Tale, Game, and Business Deal? Western Metaphors in Action in Kosovo." *Quarterly Journal of Speech* 88 (2002): 50–68.

Leeman, Richard W. "Spatial Metaphors in African-American Discourse." *Southern Communication Journal* 60 (1995): 165–80.

Osborn, Michael. "The Evolution of the Archetypal Sea in Rhetoric and Poetic." *Quarterly Journal of Speech* 63 (1977): 347–63.

Osborn, Michael, and Douglas Ehninger. "The Metaphor in Public Address." *Speech Monographs* 29 (1962): 223–34.

Perry, Steven. "Rhetorical Functions of the Infestation Metaphor in Hitler's Rhetoric." *Central States Speech Journal* 34 (1983): 229–35.

Stelzner, Hermann G. "Ford's War on Inflation: A Metaphor That Did Not Cross." *Communication Monographs* 24 (1977): 284–97.

Chapter 7. Social Movement Criticism

Andrews, James R. "The Passionate Negation: The Chartist Movement in Rhetorical Perspective." *Quarterly Journal of Speech* 59 (1973): 196–208.

Bowers, John W., Donovan J. Ochs, and Richard J. Jensen. *The Rhetoric of Agitation and Control.* Prospect Heights, Ill.: Waveland, 1993.

Burgchardt, Carl R. "Two Faces of American Communism: Pamphlet Rhetoric of the Third Period and the Popular Front." *Quarterly Journal of Speech* 66 (1980): 375–91.

Cathcart, Robert S. "New Approaches to the Study of Movements: Defining Movements Rhetorically." *Western Journal of Speech Communication* 36 (1972): 82–88.

Central States Speech Journal 31 (1980): 225–315 [Special Issue on Social Movement Criticism].

Cox, J. Robert. "Perspectives on Rhetorical Criticism of Movements: Anti-War Dissent, 1964–1972." *Western Journal of Speech Communication* 38 (1974): 254–68.

Darsey, James. *The Prophetic Tradition and Radical Rhetoric in America.* New York: New York University Press, 1997.

DeLuca, Kevin Michael. "Unruly Arguments: The Body Rhetoric of Earth First!, Act Up, and Queer Nation." *Argumentation and Advocacy* 36 (1999): 9–21.

Gregg, Richard B. "The Ego-Function of the Rhetoric of Protest." *Philosophy and Rhetoric* 4 (1971): 71–91.

Griffin, Charles J. G. "'Movement as Motive': Self-Definition and Social Advocacy in Social Movement Autobiographies." *Western Journal of Communication* 64 (2000): 148–64.

Griffin, Leland M. "A Dramatistic Theory of the Rhetoric of Movements." In *Critical Responses to Kenneth Burke,* edited by William H. Rueckert, 456–78. Minneapolis: University of Minnesota Press, 1969.

Griffin, Leland M. "The Rhetoric of Historical Movements." *Quarterly Journal of Speech* 38 (1952): 184–88.

Jensen, Richard J. "Interdisciplinary Perspectives on Rhetorical Criticism: Analyzing Social Movement Rhetoric." *Rhetoric Review* 25 (2006): 372–75.

Lake, Randall A. "Enacting Red Power: The Consummatory Function in Native American Protest Rhetoric." *Quarterly Journal of Speech* 69 (1983): 127–42.

Lucas, Stephen E. *Portents of Rebellion: Rhetoric and Revolution in Philadelphia, 1765–1776.* Philadelphia: Temple University Press, 1976.

Mercieca, Jennifer Rose. "The Culture of Honor: How Slaveholders Responded to the Abolitionist Mail Crisis of 1835." *Rhetoric & Public Affairs* 10 (2007): 51–76.

Railsback, Celeste Condit. "The Contemporary American Abortion Controversy: Stages in the Argument." *Quarterly Journal of Speech* 70 (1984): 410–24.

Scott, Robert L., and Donald K. Smith. "The Rhetoric of Confrontation." *Quarterly Journal of Speech* 55 (1969): 1–8.

Stewart, Charles J. "Championing the Rights of Others and Challenging Evil: The Ego Function in the Rhetoric of Other-Directed Social Movements." *Southern Communication Journal* 64 (1999): 91–105.

Stewart, Charles J. "The Evolution of a Revolution: Stokely Carmichael and the Rhetoric of Black Power." *Quarterly Journal of Speech* 83 (1997): 429–46.

Stewart, Charles J., Craig Allen Smith, and Robert E. Denton, Jr. *Persuasion and Social Movements,* 4th ed. Prospect Heights, Ill.: Waveland, 2001.

Theodore, Alisse. "'A Right to Speak on the Subject': The U.S. Women's Antiremoval Petition Campaign, 1829–1831." *Rhetoric & Public Affairs* 5 (2002): 601–24.

Voss, Cary R. W., and Robert C. Rowland. "Pre-Inception Rhetoric in the Creation of a Social Movement: The Case of Frances Wright." *Communication Studies* 51 (2000): 1–14.

Chapter 8. Genre Criticism

Benoit, William L. "Beyond Genre Theory: The Genesis of Rhetorical Action." *Communication Monographs* 67 (2000): 178–92.

Campbell, Karlyn Kohrs, and Kathleen Hall Jamieson, eds. *Form and Genre: Shaping Rhetorical Action.* Falls Church, Va.: Speech Communication Association, [1978].

Campbell, Karlyn Kohrs, and Kathleen Hall Jamieson. "Inaugurating the Presidency." In *Form, Genre, and the Study of Political Discourse*, edited by Herbert W. Simons and Aram A. Aghazarian, 203–25. Columbia, S.C.: University of South Carolina Press, 1986.

Fisher, Walter R. "Genre: Concepts and Applications in Rhetorical Criticism." *Western Journal of Speech Communication* 44 (1980): 288–99.

Goldzwig, Steven R., and Patricia A. Sullivan. "Post-Assassination Newspaper Editorial Eulogies: Analysis and Assessment." *Western Journal of Communication* 59 (1995): 126–50.

Hansen, Andrew C. "Rhetorical Indiscretions: Charles Dickens as Abolitionist." *Western Journal of Communication* 65 (2001): 26–44.

Harrell, Jackson, and Wil A. Linkugel. "On Rhetorical Genre: An Organizing Principle." *Philosophy and Rhetoric* 11 (1978): 262–81.

Jamieson, Kathleen M. "Antecedent Genre as Rhetorical Constraint." *Quarterly Journal of Speech* 61 (1975): 406–15.

Jamieson, Kathleen M. "Generic Constraints and the Rhetorical Situation." *Philosophy and Rhetoric* 6 (1973): 162–70.

Jamieson, Kathleen Hall, and Karlyn Kohrs Campbell. "Rhetorical Hybrids: Fusions of Generic Elements." *Quarterly Journal of Speech* 68 (1982): 146–57.

Kelley-Romano, Stephanie. "Trust No One: The Conspiracy Genre on American Television." *Southern Communication Journal* 73 (2008): 105–21.

Kennedy, Kimberly A., and William L. Benoit. "The Newt Gingrich Book Deal Controversy: Self-Defense Rhetoric." *Southern Communication Journal* 62 (1997): 197–216.

Lucas, Stephen E. "Genre Criticism and Historical Context: The Case of George Washington's First Inaugural Address." *Southern Speech Communication Journal* 51 (1986): 354–70.

Miller, Carolyn R. "Genre as Social Action." *Quarterly Journal of Speech* 70 (1984): 151–67.

Mueller, Alfred G., II, "Affirming Denial through Preemptive Apologia: The Case of the Armenian Genocide Resolution." *Western Journal of Communication* 68 (2004): 24–44.

Murphy, John M. "'Our Mission and Our Moment': George W. Bush and September 11th." *Rhetoric & Public Affairs* 6 (2003): 607–32.

Pearce, Kimber Charles. "The Radical Feminist Manifesto as Generic Appropriation: Gender, Genre, and Second Wave Resistance." *Southern Communication Journal* 64 (1999): 307–15.

Ritter, Kurt W. "American Political Rhetoric and the Jeremiad Tradition: Presidential Nomination Acceptance Addresses, 1960–1976." *Central States Speech Journal* 31 (1980): 153–71.

Rosenfield, Lawrence W. "A Case Study in Speech Criticism: The Nixon-Truman Analog." *Communication Monographs* 35 (1968): 435–50.

Ryan, Halford Ross, ed. *Oratorical Encounters: Selected Studies and Sources of Twentieth-Century Political Accusations and Apologies.* Westport, Conn.: Greenwood, 1988.

Simons, Herbert W., and Aram A. Aghazarian, eds. *Form, Genre, and the Study of Political Discourse.* Columbia, S.C.: University of South Carolina Press, 1986.

Stoda, Mark, and George N. Dionisopoulos. "Jeremiad at Harvard: Solzhenitsyn and 'The World Split Apart.'" *Western Journal of Communication* 64 (2000): 28–52.

Chapter 9. Ideographic Criticism

Charland, Maurice. "Constitutive Rhetoric: The Case of the *Peuple Québécois.*" *Quarterly Journal of Speech* 73 (1987): 133–50.

Cloud, Dana L. "The Rhetoric of <Family Values>: Scapegoating, Utopia, and the Privatization of Social Responsibility." *Western Journal of Communication* 62 (1998): 387–419.

Condit, Celeste Michelle. "Democracy and Civil Rights: The Universalizing Influence of Public Argumentation." *Communication Monographs* 54 (1987): 1–18.

Condit, Celeste Michelle. "Rhetorical Criticism and Audiences: The Extremes of McGee and Leff." *Western Journal of Speech Communication* 54 (1990): 330–45.

Condit, Celeste Michelle, and John Louis Lucaites. *Crafting Equality: America's Anglo-African Word.* Chicago: University of Chicago Press, 1993.

Delgado, Fernando Pedro. "Chicano Movement Rhetoric: An Ideographic Interpretation." *Communication Quarterly* 43 (1995): 446–54.

Delgado, Fernando. "The Rhetoric of Fidel Castro: Ideographs in the Service of Revolutionaries." *Howard Journal of Communications* 10 (1999): 1–14.

Depoe, Stephen P. "'Qualitative Liberalism': Arthur Schlesinger, Jr., and the Persuasive Uses of Definition and History." *Communication Studies* 40 (1989): 81–96.

Edwards, Janis L. and Carol K. Winkler. "Representative Form and the Visual Ideograph: The Iwo Jima Image in Editorial Cartoons." *Quarterly Journal of Speech* 83 (1997): 289–310.

Gaonkar, Dilip Parameshwar. "Object and Method in Rhetorical Criticism: From Wichelns to Leff and McGee." *Western Journal of Speech Communication* 54 (1990): 290–316.

Hasian, Marouf, Jr. "The 'Hysterical' Emily Hobhouse and Boer War Concentration Camp Controversy." *Western Journal of Communication* 67 (2003): 138–63.

Hasian, Marouf, Jr. "Legal Argumentation in the Godwin-Malthus Debates." *Argumentation and Advocacy* 37 (2001): 184–97.

Johnson, Davi. "Mapping the Meme: A Geographical Approach to Materialist Rhetorical Criticism." *Communication and Critical/Cultural Studies* 4 (2007): 27–50.

Martin, Martha Anna. "Ideologues, Ideographs, and 'the Best Men': From Carter to Reagan." *Southern Speech Communication Journal* 49 (1983): 12–25.

McCann, Bryan J. "Therapeutic and Material <Victim>hood: Ideology and the Struggle for Meaning in the Illinois Death Penalty Controversy." *Communication and Critical/Cultural Studies* 4 (2007): 382–401.

McGee, Michael Calvin. "In Search of 'The People': A Rhetorical Alternative." *Quarterly Journal of Speech* 61 (1975): 235–49.

McGee, Michael Calvin. "'Not Men, but Measures': The Origins and Import of an Ideological Principle." *Quarterly Journal of Speech* 64 (1978): 141–54.

McGee, Michael Calvin. "The Origins of 'Liberty': A Feminization of Power." *Communication Monographs* 47 (1980): 23–45.

McGee, Michael Calvin. "Text, Context, and the Fragmentation of Contemporary Culture." *Western Journal of Speech Communication* 54 (1990): 274–89.

Moore, Mark P. "The Cigarette as Representational Ideograph in the Debate over Environmental Tobacco Smoke." *Communication Monographs* 64 (1997): 47–64.

Moore, Mark P. "Constructing Irreconcilable Conflict: The Function of Synecdoche in the Spotted Owl Controversy." *Communication Monographs* 60 (1993): 258–74.

Parry-Giles, Trevor. "Ideology and Poetics in Public Issue Construction: Thatcherism, Civil Liberties, and 'Terrorism' in Northern Ireland." *Communication Quarterly* 43 (1995): 182–96.

Short, Brant. "'Reconstructed but Unregenerate': *I'll Take My Stand*'s Rhetorical Vision of Progress." *Southern Communication Journal* 59 (1994): 112–24.

Chapter 10. Gender Criticism

Anderson, Karrin Vasby. "From Spouses to Candidates: Hillary Rodham Clinton, Elizabeth Dole, and the Gendered Office of U.S. President." *Rhetoric & Public Affairs* 5 (2002): 105–32.

Anderson, Karrin Vasby. "'Rhymes with Rich': 'Bitch' as a Tool of Containment in Contemporary American Politics." *Rhetoric & Public Affairs* 2 (1999): 599–623.

Campbell, Karlyn Kohrs. "The Discursive Performance of Femininity: Hating Hillary." *Rhetoric & Public Affairs* 1 (1998): 1–19.

Carlson, A. Cheree. "Creative Casuistry and Feminist Consciousness: A Rhetoric of Moral Reform." *Quarterly Journal of Speech* 78 (1992): 16–32.

DeLaure, Marilyn Bordwell. "Planting Seeds of Change: Ella Baker's Radical Rhetoric." *Women's Studies in Communication* 31 (2008): 1–28.

Dow, Bonnie J. "Spectacle, Spectatorship, and Gender Anxiety in Television Coverage of the 1970 Women's Strike for Equality." *Communication Studies* 50 (1999): 143–57.

Dow, Bonnie J., and Mari Boor Tonn. "'Feminine Style' and Political Judgment in the Rhetoric of Ann Richards." *Quarterly Journal of Speech* 79 (1993): 286–302.

Flores, Lisa A. "Creating Discursive Space through a Rhetoric of Difference: Chicana Feminists Craft a Homeland." *Quarterly Journal of Speech* 82 (1996): 142–56.

Foss, Karen A., and Sonja K. Foss. *Women Speak: The Eloquence of Women's Lives*. Prospect Heights, Ill.: Waveland, 1991.

Foss, Sonja K., and Karen A. Foss. "The Construction of Feminine Spectatorship in Garrison Keillor's Radio Monologues." *Quarterly Journal of Speech* 80 (1994): 410–26.

Gibson, Katie. "*United States v. Virginia:* A Rhetorical Battle between Progress and Preservation." *Women's Studies in Communication* 29 (2006): 133–64.

Golombisky, Kim. "Mothers, Daughters, and Female Identity Therapy in *How to Make an American Quilt.*" *Western Journal of Communication* 65 (2001): 65–88.

Griffin, Cindy L. "Rhetoricizing Alienation: Mary Wollstonecraft and the Rhetorical Construction of Women's Oppression." *Quarterly Journal of Speech* 80 (1994): 293–312.

Griffin, Cindy L. "Women as Communicators: Mary Daly's Hagiography as Rhetoric." *Communication Monographs* 60 (1993): 158–77.

Hurt, Nicole E. "Disciplining through Depression: An Analysis of Contemporary Discourse on Women and Depression." *Women's Studies in Communication* 30 (2007): 284–309.

Japp, Phyllis M. "Esther or Isaiah?: The Abolitionist-Feminist Rhetoric of Angelina Grimké." *Quarterly Journal of Speech* 71 (1985): 335–48.

Johnson, Ann. "The Subtleties of Blatant Sexism." *Communication and Critical/Cultural Studies* 4 (2007): 166–83.

Kaplan, Michael. "Rebel Citizenship and the Cunning of the Liberal Imaginary in *Thelma & Louise.*" *Communication and Critical/Cultural Studies* 5 (2008): 1–23.

Parry-Giles, Shawn J., and Diane M. Blair, "The Rise of the Rhetorical First Lady: Politics, Gender Ideology, and Women's Voice, 1789–2002." *Rhetoric & Public Affairs* 5 (2002): 565–600.

Rushing, Janice Hocker. "Evolution of 'The New Frontier' in *Alien* and *Aliens:* Patriarchal Co-Optation of the Feminine Archetype." *Quarterly Journal of Speech* 75 (1989), 1–25.

Solomon, Martha. "The 'Positive Woman's' Journey: A Mythic Analysis of the Rhetoric of STOP ERA." *Quarterly Journal of Speech* 65 (1979): 262–74.

Spitzack, Carole, and Kathryn Carter. "Women in Communication Studies: A Typology for Revision." *Quarterly Journal of Speech* 73 (1987): 401–23.

Tonn, Mari Boor. "Militant Motherhood: Labor's Mary Harris 'Mother' Jones." *Quarterly Journal of Speech* 82 (1996): 1–21.

Zaeske, Susan. "The 'Promiscuous Audience' Controversy and the Emergence of the Early Woman's Rights Movement." *Quarterly Journal of Speech* 81 (1995): 191–207.

Chapter 11. Critical Rhetoric

Blair, Carole. "The Statement: Foundation of Foucault's Historical Criticism." *Western States Communication Journal* 51 (1987): 364–83.

Buescher, Derek, and Kent Ono. "Civilized Colonialism: 'Pocahontas' as Neocolonial Rhetoric." *Women's Studies in Communication* 19 (1996): 127–54.

Calafell, Bernadette Marie, and Fernando P. Delgado. "Reading Latina/o Images: Interrogating *Americanos.*" *Critical Studies in Media Communication* 21 (2004): 1–21.

Crenshaw, Carrie. "Resisting Whiteness' Rhetorical Silence." *Western Journal of Communication* 61 (1997): 253–78.

Flores, Lisa A., and Dreama G. Moon. "Rethinking Race, Revealing Dilemmas: Imagining a New Racial Subject in *Race Traitor.*" *Western Journal of Communication* 66 (2002): 181–207.

Flores, Lisa A., Dreama G. Moon, and Thomas K. Nakayama. "Dynamic Rhetorics of Race: California's Racial Privacy Initiative and the Shifting Grounds of Racial Politics." *Communication and Critical/Cultural Studies* 3 (2006): 181–201.

Foss, Sonja K., and Ann Gill. "Michel Foucault's Theory of Rhetoric as Epistemic." *Western Journal of Speech Communication* 51 (1987): 384–401.

Hasian, Marouf, Jr. "Nostalgic Longings and Imaginary Indias: Postcolonial Analysis, Collective Memories, and the Impeachment Trial of Warren Hastings." *Western Journal of Communication* 66 (2002): 229–55.

Holling, Michelle A. "Forming Oppositional Social Concord to California's Proposition 187 and Squelching Social Discord in the Vernacular Space of CHICLE." *Communication and Critical/Cultural Studies* 3 (2006): 202–22.

Jasinski, James. "The Feminization of Liberty, Domesticated Virtue, and the Reconstitution of Power and Authority in Early American Political Discourse." *Quarterly Journal of Speech* 79 (1993): 146–64.

Lay, Mary M., Billie J. Wahlstrom, and Carol Brown. "The Rhetoric of Midwifery: Conflicts and Conversations in the Minnesota Home Birth Community in the 1990s." *Quarterly Journal of Speech* 82 (1996): 383–401.

McDorman, Todd F. "Controlling Death: Bio-Power and the Right-to-Die Controversy." *Communication and Critical/Cultural Studies* 2 (2005): 257–79.

Nakayama, Thomas K. "Show/Down Time: 'Race,' Gender, Sexuality, and Popular Culture." *Critical Studies in Mass Communication* 11 (1994): 162–79.

Ono, Kent A., and Derek T. Buescher. "Deciphering Pocahontas: Unpackaging the Commodification of a Native American Woman." *Critical Studies in Media Communication* 18 (2001): 23–43.

Shome, Raka. "Race and Popular Cinema: The Rhetorical Strategies of Whiteness in 'City of Joy.'" *Communication Quarterly* 44 (1996): 502–18.

Solomon, Martha. "'With firmness in the right': The Creation of Moral Hegemony in Lincoln's Second Inaugural." *Communication Reports* 1 (1988): 32–37.

Terrill, Robert E. "Protest, Prophecy, and Prudence in the Rhetoric of Malcolm X." *Rhetoric & Public Affairs* 4 (2001): 25–53.

Index

About the Editor

Carl R. Burgchardt teaches methods of rhetorical criticism, analysis and history of United States oratory, and film criticism at Colorado State University. He received his bachelor's degree from Penn State. His master's and doctorate degrees are from the University of Wisconsin–Madison. He has published essays and book reviews in the *Quarterly Journal of Speech*. His previous book, *Robert M. La Follette, Sr.: The Voice of Conscience,* won the Outstanding Scholarship Award from the Colorado Speech Communication Association.